West Bromwich Albion

The Complete Record

Acknowledgements

I would like to thank Colin Mackenze, an Albion fanatic and great friend of mine for many years, for confirming, checking and adding to certain players' statistics, updating the international section and contributing quite a bit more, as he always does. Also I say a big thank you to the following for loaning several of the photographs: Lawrie Rampling ('Lensman'), Barry Marsh, Dave Bowler, Terry Price, David Morris, Neil Reynolds, Carol Salmon, Marc Soulsby, Jeff Berry, Kevin Grice, Charlie Poultney and Dean Walton. And I can't forget the splendid co-operation afforded to me by Steve Caron, Michelle Grainger and the rest of the staff at Breedon Books (Derby), plus, of course, the encouragement given to me, once again, by my lovely wife Margaret. And, oh, I mustn't forget my fellow Albion 'nut' Adrian Childs!

Tony Matthews

West Bromwich Albion

The Complete Record

Every game, every scorer, every player and every attendance.
FA Cup finals, complete history, pen pictures, manager profiles, appearance records

Tony Matthews

breedon books
PUBLISHING

First published in Great Britain in 2007 by
The Breedon Books Publishing Company Limited
Breedon House, 3 The Parker Centre,
Derby, DE21 4SZ.

ISBN 978-1-85983-565-4

Printed and bound by Cromwell Press, Trowbridge, Wiltshire.

Contents

West Bromwich Albion Old Boys

The West Bromwich Albion Former Players' Association was founded in 2003 following a conversation between two former players, Brendon Batson MBE, then managing director of West Bromwich Albion, and Graham Williams, captain of the 1968 Cup-winning team. The association was formed to bring together former players under an official banner as they all had one thing in common: West Bromwich Albion. The criteria for being a member is that they should have played in the first team at least once during their careeer.

The association raises funds by working closely with the football club, which includes match-day hospitality and attending official club functions. We also work closely with the supporters' clubs, who support the Former Players' Association very generously. Funds are raised by organising dinners and golf days on an annual basis and many former players attend these popular and well-supported functions.

The association has over 100 members and has helped those members or their relatives less fortunate than others with financial, personal and moral support when required.

Brendon Batson

Tony Brown

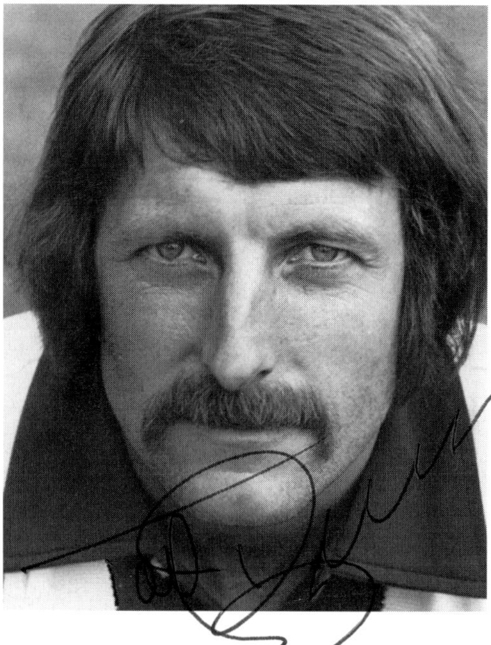

Bobby Hope

Cyrille Regis

Alistair Robertson

Bob Taylor

Graham Williams

Foreword

By Adrian Childs

BBC television presenter and a West Bromwich Albion fanatic... who always will be!

A few months ago I was watching footage of a match at The Hawthorns from some time in the 50s. I'm always interested to see such films, although it never really feels like my team. It's in black and white, obviously, and the ground looks different, and the film never seems to be running at the right speed.

But then, listening to the crowd noise, a thought struck me: my grandad's in there. I know the crowd noise is probably dubbed on afterwards, and the voices are from yet another time and place, but the principle holds true: my grandad is in there. I felt connected with the club's past more than I ever have done before.

It should be clear to us all when we see footage like that, or read books like this – a real beauty compiled by Albion statistician and a good friend of mine for many years, Tony Matthews, what an enormous thing we are part of when we support a club.

Every fan is, in a sense, related to or descended from all those fans who've suffered before us. Similarly every player should realise what he's becoming part of when he pulls on the shirt. And no chairman or director could read this book and think that he owns the club. No one owns the club... we just look after it for another generation.

Read and enjoy – and up the Baggies!

Introduction

West Bromwich Albion was one of the first big names in Association Football.

Founded as far back as 1878, the Baggies (the name every ardent supporter calls the team) were one of the original 12 members of the Football League in 1888-89 and between then and 1895, from 1910 to 1913, from 1919 to 1925, between 1930 and 1935, from 1952 to 1954, from 1966 to 1970, in seasons 1978-82 and occasionally thereafter, they were regarded as one of the strongest sides in the country, blessed with some outstanding players.

Albion have won the League Championship once, the FA Cup five times, the League Cup once, played in Europe (reaching the quarter-finals of the Cup-winners' Cup), graced the Premiership, and in 1930-31 completed the unique double by winning the FA Cup and gaining promotion from the Second Division in the same season, a feat never achieved before or since. They have toured and won in far away places as Russia and China, and over the years some of the game's greatest players have donned the famous navy blue and white striped shirt, among them Billy Bassett, Jesse Pennington, Fred Morris, Joe Carter, Tommy Glidden, Teddy Sandford, Ronnie Allen, Ray Barlow, Jeff Astle, Tony Brown, Cyrille Regis, John Wile and Bob Taylor.

This book – *West Bromwich Albion: The Complete Record 1878–2007* – is the most comprehensive work I, or anyone else, has ever done on the famous Black Country club. It covers all of Albion's achievements and more; it is packed full of statistics, gives you all the personal details of every player who has appeared in Albion's first team at competitive level; there are sections on those who have gained international honours with the club, information on the managers; a brief history of every ground used by Albion; attendance facts; sendings-off; the team's playing record against every other League club; the transfer trail; results of matches played in other major competitions, including test matches, Play-off games; details of performances in the Fairs Cup, European Cup-winners' Cup, Anglo-Italian and Anglo-Scottish tournaments and also in the FA Charity Shield; and there is also a summary of each season of League football from 1888 to date.

Since my last 'Complete Record', which was published in 1993, much more research has been undertaken regarding Albion's history (not only by me but by other enthusiasts as well) and quite a few discrepancies from the past have now been cleared up, especially attendance figures. A lot have been changed from my previous listings in as much that the figures now printed in this book have come directly from official sources, either from the club itself or from the Football League and/or the FA. In the past many were taken from newspapers.

Some of the players' personal details have also changed, although most of the corrections were printed in the recent *Who's Who of West Bromwich Albion* also published by Breedon Books (2005).

Should any new information relating to Albion and its players come to light in the future, I would be more than pleased to receive it in writing via the publishers, Breedon Books.

The views in this book are not necessarily those of West Bromwich Albion football club or anyone directly associated with the club.

Tony Matthews

West Bromwich Albion History

The Beginnings

The history of West Bromwich Albion is almost unrivalled so far as interest goes. The club was not formed in an hour by those who had wealth at their disposal and the willingness to acquire and equip a suitable ground and assemble a formidable team...far from it.

Albion came into being courtesy of a group of enthusiastic sportsmen who played an honest game of cricket in the summer and kicked a ball around for fun on wasteland in the winter. In fact, it is now believed that the first steps to form a football team were made by these energetic sportsmen on 23 November 1878, when a 12-a-side friendly was arranged between them (West Bromwich Strollers) and a team from Hudson's, the local soap factory.

The 0–0 draw was immaterial. The Strollers were up and running, and these players had started the ball rolling: Bob Roberts (goal); Harry Bell, James Stanton; Jack Forrester, Harry Evans, Tom Waterfield; Jack Siddons, John Stokes, Sid Evans, Ted Evans, Billy Jones and Sid Jones.

Most of these players worked at the George Salter spring factory in West Bromwich and, with their colleagues, proved to be good footballers – so much so that a year later they started competing in earnest against stronger opposition.

Going from strength to strength, the Strollers probably changed their name to Albion in March 1879, and these men, all born within a three-mile radius of each other, were registered as players: George Bell, Robert Biddulph, Billy Bisseker, Joey Law, Denny Smith, Tom Smith, Luther Walker and John While, whose career ended prematurely after he broke his leg against Nottingham Forest in the Wednesbury Charity Cup Final of 1883. All were desirous of having an incentive to remain as a unit, and it was agreed that each should subscribe 6p (3p) to help buy kit, a ball and also a set of goal posts!

A seven-man committee (all players) was formed, comprising Stanton, Harry and George Bell, new signing Timmins, Stokes, Bisseker and While. The club was up and running, and it is only right that these pioneers should go down in posterity as those who were wholly responsible for forming West Bromwich Albion football club.

Having purchased a football from a Wednesbury shop, a strip of land – Cooper's Hill near Dartmouth Park – became the club's first home ground, although another pitch inside the park was occasionally used.

There are references to suggest that Albion played at least 20 games in 1879–80, recording some fine victories, including 7–0 and 13–0 against West Bromwich White Hart, 5–0 against Bullock's Foundry and 6–0 against Wednesbury Robin Hood. The team also suffered their first defeat, losing 2–1 to West Bromwich St Magdalene.

New faces were introduced, among them Harry Aston, Sam Biddlestone, Joe Johnstone and Harry Twist, and all bedded in well.

At the club's first annual general meeting in the summer of 1880, it was announced that George Bell would succeed Stanton as captain, Bisseker was named vice-captain and a new enclosed ground, Bunn's Field, Walsall Street, was acquired on a 12–month lease. Players, officials and supporters rolled the pitch flat, and it was agreed, for the first time, to charge an entry fee to watch matches. The ground (renamed the Birches) was opened on 10 September 1881 when a crowd of 500 (paying 15s 2d – 76p) saw Albion beat Oldbury 5–1.

1883 Staffordshire Cup winners.

The money taken at the gate was wealth indeed to the youthful Albion club, and they immediately entered the Birmingham Senior Cup, reaching the semi-final stage before losing 3–2 to Wednesbury Old Athletic.

Unfortunately Albion could not negotiate a new deal on Bunn's Field but were lucky when the Dartmouth cricket club offered them their Four Acres ground as a replacement, but with a clause in the contract whereby Albion could play only two matches there in any one week, on a Saturday and Monday. Season tickets were issued at 2s 6d (13p) each and the opening fixture, played on 7 October 1882, saw Stourbridge Standard thumped 10–0, Bisseker scoring six goals. Albion spent three seasons at the Four Acres before switching to Stoney Lane in 1885.

Now a force to be reckoned with, Albion appointed local businessman George Salter as president, and in 1882–83 the team entered the Birmingham, Wednesbury and Staffordshire Cup competitions, beating Stoke 3–2 in the Final of the latter to clinch their first major trophy. George Bell scored the winning goal.

In the second round Albion drew 3–3 at Aston Villa, before winning the replay 1–0 with a Timmins goal in front of a record crowd of almost 10,500. This was the club's first victory over Villa, who had been formed four years earlier. The clubs were to become keen rivals through the years.

On 11 November 1882 Albion gained their biggest-ever win, thrashing Coseley 26–0 in a Birmingham Cup tie – and every outfield player figured on the score sheet.

In 1883–84 Albion, strong, confident, with a good squad of players, entered four Cup competitions but won only one, the Birmingham Cup, beating Wolves in the Final. Their first FA (English) Cup tie ended in a 2–0 home defeat at the hands of Wednesbury Town …but things were to be somewhat different over the next decade or so in this prestige tournament. Albion reached the quarter-finals of the FA Cup in 1885, losing to Blackburn Rovers in front of a record crowd of 16,393 at the Four Acres, while in a Birmingham Cup tie they hammered Bloxwich 15–0.

With Tom Smith now secretary and Joey Law senior trainer, Albion began 1885–86 at Stoney Lane and secured a long-term lease until May 1899 at £25 per annum. £150 was spent on improving the popular enclosure and erecting a grandstand.

New Ground – Three Cup Finals

Albion opened at Stoney Lane with a 4–1 friendly win over Third Lanark Rifle Volunteers, and after that the season went superbly well as Albion became the first Midland team to reach the FA Cup Final. Luck smiled on the team as they played each round at home up to the semi-final. Small Heath were then clipped 4–0 at Aston to set up a final showdown with the holders Blackburn Rovers at the Oval. A record crowd of 15,156 (receipts £650) witnessed a 0–0 draw and almost 1,000 extra spectators attended the replay at Derby, which Rovers won 2–0. Albion did, however, gain some consolation, winning both the Birmingham and Staffordshire Cup Finals. Twelve months on Albion reached their second FA Cup Final. This time they faced Aston Villa, who proved too strong on the day, winning 2–0.

Obviously disappointed, Albion buckled down to business, and in 1888 it was third time lucky as they won the trophy, beating the Invincibles, Preston North End, 2–1 with an all-English XI before another record Oval crowd of 18,904. Prior to the Final, Preston's captain Nick Ross asked referee Major Marindin if his team could be photographed with the trophy. 'Had you not better win it first?' was the laconic reply of the military official. Soon after that Final, Albion lined up against the Scottish Cup winners Renton for the 'Championship of the World', which Albion lost 4–1 in Glasgow.

Albion's side now contained some brilliant footballers, among them Albert Aldridge, Billy Bassett, 'Jem' Bayliss, Charlie Perry, goalkeeper Roberts, George 'Spry' Woodhall, Ezra Horton, Tom Pearson

The 1888 FA Cup winners.

and Joe Wilson. The first six were also England internationals. Billy Bassett's wing play against Preston in the Cup Final had created such a furore that he was chosen to play for England against Scotland that same evening.

Following a brainwave by William McGregor, the Football League was introduced in 1888–89. Albion were one of 12 founder members, and they won their first match, beating Stoke 2–0 to head the table on goal average. They eventually finished sixth and reached the FA Cup semi-final, but they were beaten by double winners Preston 1–0.

Albion's League form during 1889–90 and 1890–91 was moderate – and for the second time running they lost in the semi-final of the FA Cup, beaten 3–2 by Blackburn Rovers at Stoke.

Although the team had been strengthened with the introduction of quality players like John 'Baldy' Reynolds, Tom Perry (brother of Charlie), Sam Nicholls and Scotsmen Willie Groves and Roddy McLeod, Albion's form was below par during the first half of 1891–92, but after Christmas it improved greatly, and with another new face, Jasper Geddes, sparkling on the left wing, Albion reached their fourth FA Cup Final. Their opponents in the Final were their foes from Aston, the Villa – but this time, in front of 32,710 fans, Albion came out on top, winning 3–0 in hollow style.

Jubilant and in form, a fortnight after that victory Albion thrashed Darwen 12–0 – the biggest League win ever recorded, and it still holds good today, although Nottingham Forest equalled it in 1909 when beating Leicester.

Secretary-manager Louis Ford was now directing Albion's fortunes, and his net was cast far and wide as he engaged English, Irish and Scots in his team. One of these players – John Reynolds – deserves a special mention as he represented two countries. He won five caps for Ireland before Albion found out he had been born in Blackburn, and after re-registering him with the FA he went on to play eight times for England. Reynolds later played for Aston Villa and, with another ex-Albion man Willie Groves, gained a second FA Cup-winners' medal when Albion were defeated 1–0 in the 1895 Final before a record crowd of 42,652 at Crystal Palace, the only goal coming inside the first minute. Albion should never have lost the game. They were far better than Villa but failed to take their chances. After the game, Albion's centre-half Tom Higgins was presented with a five pound note by Colonel North for his brave display, despite having his head swathed in bandages.

Albion's League form in the mid-1890s was very disappointing, and in 1894–95 they had to win their last game, at home to Sheffield Wednesday, by five clear goals to retain their First Division place. They won 6–0 to make sure! And the following season it took Test Match victories over Liverpool and Manchester City to keep them in the top flight.

During the period 1895–1900 it is fair to say that Albion didn't play at all well in League or Cup competitions. Plenty of new blood was introduced (27 players were used overall), but the blend was simply not right. Joe Reader was now first-choice goalkeeper. Billy Williams, Tom Perry, Jack Banks, Billy Richards, Ben Garfield and Albert Flewitt were also blooded, and as the 20th century approached George Cave, Abe Jones, Harry Hadley, Amos Adams and Amos Dunn, 'Chippy' Simmons, Billy Walker, Dick Roberts and Jack Paddock were all called into action. Reader, Williams, Perry, Banks, Hadley and Garfield all played for England, and Simmons went on to score over 80 goals for the Albion in two separate spells.

In the summer of 1899 Albion had taken out an extra year's lease on their Stoney Lane ground, which was one of the poorest in the First Division. They played their last League game there on 16 April 1900 and celebrated with an 8–0 win over Nottingham Forest, Walker scoring a hat-trick. The club had been searching for a new ground since early 1899 and had spotted a piece of land close to the

West Bromwich/Handsworth border that suited their requirements. On 5 December that year, a letter, written by Benjamin Karliese, secretary of the Sandwell Park Colliery, to Albion sparked off the move to The Hawthorns!

The letter read 'My board direct me to offer you a lease of the piece of land forming the corner of Halford's Lane and the Birmingham Road about 10 acres (less sufficient land next to the Oaklands to make a road across, 40 to 50 feet wide) for 14 years at a rental of £750 per annum for the first seven years and £80 per annum for the second seven years. The West Bromwich Albion Football Club Company to have option of terminating the lease at the end of the first seven years on giving such notice as may be mutually agreed. The Football Club Company to pay to the Company one-third of the revenue that may be derived from any hoarding that may be erected by the Club on the land in question during the existence of the lease, the Club retaining two-thirds of the revenue for the cost of the erecting and maintaining the hoarding and collecting the revenue arising therefrom. My board will reserve full powers for working the mines under and adjacent to the land, without being liable for damage to surface or erections thereon, and would require the covenants usual in their leases to be embodied in this. It is understood that this offer is left open for your acceptance till 1 February 1900, but if practicable my Board would be glad of a decision earlier.'

Two days before the deadline, the Albion board agreed to the deal, and the appropriate paperwork was signed, sealed and delivered on 14 May 1900. It took workmen just under four months to complete the ground, which was ready for use on 3 September 1900.

A new era at The Hawthorns

Derby County were the first visitors to Albion's new ground, and a crowd of 20,104 witnessed the 1–1 draw. Steve Bloomer put the Rams ahead in the first half, but Simmons's goal ensured Albion a point. After that the team's performances were very inconsistent, and unfortunately the first season at The Hawthorns ended in bitter disappointment, Albion suffering relegation for the first time in their history. They gained only seven victories, 7–2 over Bolton Wanderers being the best, and finished bottom of the table after suffering 19 defeats.

Some of the more established players, including England internationals Joe Reader, Tom Perry and Freddie Wheldon (ex-Aston Villa), were nearing the end of their careers, while another England star, Billy Williams, was forced to retire through injury. However, Fred Buck made the first of his 319 appearances for the club.

Despite their dismal League form, Albion had a good run in the FA Cup, reaching the semi-finals before losing 4–0 to Tottenham Hotspur at Villa Park. Albion also lost in the Final of the Birmingham Charity Cup to Aston Villa.

During the 1901 summer break several new players were recruited to reinforce the squad. Pick of the bunch were right-half Dan Nurse, who became captain, and inside-left Tom Worton, both from Wolves. Goalkeeper Ike Webb arrived from Small Heath (now Birmingham City) and Jack Kifford (from Portsmouth) replaced the unfortunate Williams. Scot Jimmy Stevenson took over from Abe Jones at centre-half, Jimmy McLean was introduced on the right wing and soon after the start of the season centre-forward Billy Lee came in to partner Chippy Simmons.

After an opening day defeat by Glossop, Albion quickly got into their stride and, playing some scintillating football, they registered some superb wins. The key to all this was a settled side, and a

West Bromich Albion at the opening ofThe Hawthorns, 3 September 1900.

record 17 games unbeaten, from 7 December to 22 March, took them deservedly to the Championship and rapid promotion back to the First Division. Even a shock 5–1 defeat at Bury in the FA Cup didn't upset Albion's romp towards the title, which they took in fine style with 55 points, four ahead of Middlesbrough. They also won the Staffordshire Cup but lost to Aston Villa in the Final of the Birmingham Charity Cup. The second XI also won some silverware, as champions of the Birmingham & District League.

In the summer of 1902, secretary-manager Frank Heaven resigned. In his place stepped Fred Everiss, who had been with the club since 1896. Some years later, Fred's son, Alan, became Albion's secretary, director and life member, meaning that the Everiss family had links with the club for over 100 years.

Fred Everiss's early days were fraught with difficulties. There were internal quarrels about policy and half the board gave up their positions. The club's bank balance was looking sick, despite promotion, and it was plain to see that there was an overall lowering of standards. But out on the field the team battled well and at one point topped the First Division table after some handsome wins – 6–1 against Newcastle, 3–0 at Villa Park and 5–3 against Blackburn. The crowds were good as well (the seasonal average was 15,657) and new signing George Dorsett was a star performer on the left wing. But all of a sudden things went horribly wrong, and after losing to Spurs in the FA Cup Albion's form slumped dramatically. They won only one of their last 12 games, lost eight on the bounce and eventually finished seventh, six points behind champions Sheffield Wednesday. Albion also lost to Aston Villa in the Final of the Birmingham Cup and to Wolves in the Final of the Birmingham Charity Cup, but they did lift the Staffordshire Cup. It was all so frustrating – not the greatest of starts for Mr Everiss.

Things didn't get any better, 1903–04 proving to be another disastrous season as Albion suffered relegation for the second time in three years, finishing bottom of the pile yet again. The defence took most of the blame, conceding 60 goals.

One player who appeared on the scene in 1903 was Jesse Pennington. He would become one of the greatest full-backs in the game and appeared in almost 500 games for Albion, also winning 25 caps for England. Two other newcomers to emerge during this sad season were right-half Arthur Randle and Harry Brown, who accompanied Simmons in attack but found it hard going.

Fred Everiss and his directors knew there was a lot of work to be done if Albion were to climb back into the top flight – and at the club's AGM in the summer positive moves were forthcoming in this respect – although it must be said there wasn't a great deal of money around to spend on new players!

Back in the Second Division, with problems mounting all the time, Albion began 1904–05 with Jack Manners at centre-half and three new faces in the forward line – Laurie Bell, Walter Jack and Albert Lewis. In fact, Lewis got off to a flying start, scoring all the goals in Albion's 4–1 victory at Burnley on the opening Saturday.

After that Albion's on-field performances were rather mixed, despite the introduction of more new players, among them Llewellyn Davies (a future Welsh international), Jack Dawes, Freddie Haycock and goalkeeper Jimmy Stringer (ex-Wolves). For long periods the team played sub-standard football, only occasionally clicking into gear, especially when beating Doncaster 6–1 and Burton United 4–0. And to make matters worse, the old stand ('Noah's Ark'), which had been transferred from Stoney Lane, burned down on Bonfire Night, the cause being put down to an errant sky rocket!

Ted Pheasant, a defender from Molineux, arrived at the club, but his presence made little difference, and as 1904 gave way to 1905 Albion found themselves hovering mid-table. They were quickly dumped out of the FA Cup by Leicester Fosse, who won a preliminary round tie at The Hawthorns by 5–2, and in the end Albion finished 10th, 28 points behind champions Liverpool, yet only three away from having to apply for re-election!

Upheaval in the Boardroom

Albion's creditors were now hammering on the door hard and long. Consequently, in the summer of 1905, the entire board resigned, including chairman and ex-player 'Jem' Bayliss. Harry Keys returned to take the 'chair' (he had previously held office from 1899–1903) and former player Billy Bassett and several local businessmen became directors. Some sort of security was obtained from the bank, and Albion carried on!

On the playing side, Fred Shinton, signed towards the end of the previous campaign from Hednesford, and Adam Haywood (ex-Wolves) joined Simmons in attack. And what an impact they had – Shinton netted 18 goals and Haywood 21.

Albion's form improved considerably in 1905–06. They finished in fourth place and embarked on a 16-match unbeaten run on 14 October. Unfortunately they failed in the FA Cup and lost in the Birmingham Charity Cup Final to Aston Villa by 4–3. Several new players were introduced during the second half of the season, among them former Everton wingers Ben Rankin and Tom Dilly, who, in fact, was the last Scotsman to play for Albion for 30 years, and Dudley-born wing-half Eli Bradley, while Buck returned after a spell with Liverpool.

Albion began 1906–07 with a new right-back, Dick Betteley, secured from Wolves, and within three months they were leading the Second Division. The team had a settled look about it, with Tommy Broad playing well on the right wing.

Albion's League form slumped early in the New Year, but progress was made in the FA Cup.

However, following an injury to Shinton (who was replaced by England amateur international Bill Jordan, who had earlier scored six goals for his country in a 15–0 win over France), Albion's League challenge floundered, although they remained on course to reach the FA Cup Final. But it all ended in bitter disappointment when Everton won the semi-final at Bolton by 2–1. Albion eventually finished fourth in the League – 13 points behind the champions Nottingham Forest.

Albion began the 1907–08 campaign with a morale-boosting 2–1 win over rivals Wolves at Molineux, and as the weeks ticked by the team's overall play became fluent and purposeful and there was a solid look about the defence, which included former Aston Villa full-back Albert Evans, who broke his leg four times during a lengthy career.

Handily placed at the turn of the year, things looked very rosy indeed, and, despite losing to Southampton in the FA Cup, Albion continued to push Bradford City, Leicester and Oldham all the way at the top of the table. However, two home defeats and a crucial reverse at Leicester upset the promotion challenge, and in the end Albion had to settle for fifth place, seven points adrift of champions Bradford City. It was obviously disappointing, but there was a feeling within the camp that the good times were just around the corner.

In January 1908 Hubert Pearson made the first of 377 appearances in Albion's goal. He was to remain at the club until 1926, by which time he had been joined by his son, Harold, also a goalkeeper. At the club's AGM Harry Keys was replaced as chairman by former player Billy Bassett, who would remain in office until his death in 1937.

Albion missed promotion to the First Division by just 0.0056 of a goal in 1908–09 – and claimed that they were robbed of that extra goal by a referee's decision at Blackpool. The match at Bloomfield Road on 28 November resulted in a 2–0 win, but it should have been 3–0 as Charlie Hewitt's effort struck the crossbar and bounced down behind the line. The referee and his linesman thought otherwise and disallowed the goal. An irate Billy Garraty, who could have put the ball back into the net, was severely reprimanded by the official for his over zealous actions! Bolton won the title that season.

New blood at The Hawthorns included the ageing George Baddeley from Stoke, who went on to serve the club until he was almost 40; half-backs Sammy Timmins and Jack Manners and forwards Willie Thompson (ex-Sunderland), former Liverpool star Charlie Hewitt and Leicester Fosse's England international Billy Garraty, who had helped Aston Villa win both the Division One title and the FA Cup.

In May 1909 Albion went on their first-ever overseas tour, playing seven games in Scandinavia, including friendlies against two English clubs, Hull City and Newcastle United. They recorded four victories, 10–0 being the best versus Gefle 10–0.

Albion finished 11th in Division Two in 1909–10 – their lowest position in the Football League up to that time. And they didn't do much better in the FA Cup, losing to Bradford City in the third round. Pearson was now in goal; former Sheffield Wednesday defender Harry Burton was partnering Pennington at full-back and Sid Bowser, George Simpson (also from Wednesday) and Bob Pailor all figured in the front line.

Promotion and Cup Final agony

Half-backs Frank Waterhouse from Langley Green and Bobby McNeal, a future England international, from County Durham both came to the fore in 1910–11, as did wingers Billy Wollaston and Amos Lloyd, while Pennington acquired a new full-back partner in Black Country-born Joe

Second Division Champions 1910–11.

Smith, who became a quality player, winning England honours and making 471 appearances for Albion in 16 years. Another newcomer who was to figure prominently over the next few years was inside-forward Harry Wright.

These fresh faces certainly contributed greatly as Albion at last regained their First Division status by winning eight of their last 10 matches, clinching promotion on the final day with a 1–0 victory over Huddersfield Town, Fred Buck's 30th-minute penalty doing the trick in front of a 30,135 best-of-season crowd at The Hawthorns.

Albion played well as a unit, losing only eight matches, one of them in the FA Cup at Derby. They had their bad times, albeit only a few, and realistically speaking looked like promotion material from the word go.

Back in the First Division after a seven-year sojourn, Albion finished ninth in 1911–12, 10 points behind champions Sunderland, but only five short of third-placed Newcastle. In fact, it was an excellent run in the FA Cup competition which probably cost the team a much higher placing – even the Championship – for they had to play no fewer than nine League games during the month of April, five of them in eight days with the two Cup matches in between!

They battled through to the FA Cup Final with some splendid performances, only to lose to Second Division Barnsley in a replay at Sheffield, Harry Tufnell scoring the only goal in the last minute of extra-time after Pennington had refused to 'foul' the Barnsley forward as he broke clear of the Baggies defence.

Secretary-manager Fred Everiss started the season with Stan Allan (ex-Newcastle) at centre-forward in place of the injured Pailor and Ben Shearman from Bristol City on the left wing, and halfway through the campaign he introduced the speedy Claude Jephcott to the right flank. His career was to end prematurely with a broken leg, but he served the club as a director for many years after retiring. There were also debuts from two players who would become vital members of the team after World War One – goalscorer Fred Morris from Tipton and left-winger Howard Gregory from Aston Manor.

Albion's performances were professional rather than dashing. Pailor top scored while goalkeeper Hubert Pearson found the net with two penalties. The average League attendance of over 18,000 at The Hawthorns was the highest in the club's history, and again Albion succumbed to Aston Villa in the Final of the Birmingham Charity Cup.

The last three pre-World War One seasons all turned out to be rather moderate for Albion, who finished 10th, fifth and 10th again in the First Division. They also failed to make progress in the FA Cup, unable to venture beyond the third round. Centre-forward Alf 'Snobby' Bentley was signed from Bolton Wanderers, and he made a terrific start to his Albion career, scoring all his side's goals in a 4–1 home win over Burnley in September 1913.

England amateur international and Cambridge University graduate Harold Bache, who scored on his debut in that Cup encounter at Villa Park, also arrived at The Hawthorns, while Alonzo Poulton, Irishman Louis Bookman, craggy centre-half Fred Reed and striker Arthur Swift all made their first appearances for the club.

Albion did not play competitive football between April 1915 and March 1919. A handful of friendly matches were arranged, but these were few and far between and sadly, on 15 February 1916, it was announced that Harold Bache, a Lieutenant in the army, had been tragically killed on a Flanders battlefield.

Although they lost one star player, Albion gained another when Tommy Magee was signed after being recommended to the club by an army colleague, Tom Brewer. Magee joined the club in January 1919 and would go on to make 400 appearances for the Baggies, helping them win the League Championship and FA Cup as well as gaining England recognition.

After peace had been declared, Albion participated in the Midland Victory League during March and April 1919. They won the title by beating Aston Villa twice, Derby County once and drawing with Wolves. This competitive tournament certainly reunited the players and the following were all ready, willing and eager to get back into First Division action: goalkeeper Pearson, full-backs Smith, Pennington and Arthur Cook, half-backs Sammy Richardson (Black Country born), Bowser, Reed, McNeal and Waterhouse and forwards Claude Jephcott, Jack Crisp, Magee, Andy Smith, Bentley, Morris and Gregory.

League Champions

The 1919–20 season turned out to be Albion's finest as they romped away with the League title for the first, and so far only, time in the club's history. In doing so, they set three new records – most points (60), most wins (28) and most goals scored (104), clinching the title on 10 April 1920 with a 3–1 home win over Bradford.

Albion won nine of their first 11 matches, which included an 8–0 home victory over Notts County, when Morris netted five times, and a 4–1 win over Bradford City, when Bowser cracked in a hat-trick (including two penalties) to become the first defender ever to score three goals in a competitive game for the club.

Even an early exit from the FA Cup (beaten by Barnsley) didn't affect Albion's confidence as they

League Champions 1919–20.

powered on with some terrific performances. They lost only two of their last 15 matches and finished up deserved champions, finishing nine points clear of Burnley. The team collected some more silverware by beating Tottenham 2–0 to lift the FA Charity Shield. Morris created a new club scoring record with 37 goals in the season, while the best-ever average home League attendance of 30,532 was registered at The Hawthorns.

The not so roaring twenties

Albion began the defence of their League crown in unconvincing fashion, drawing their first four games and losing the fifth. In fact, they won only two of their opening 11 fixtures, dropped off the pace and never recovered, finishing 14th.

Fielding practically the same set of players who had done the club proud in 1919–20, Albion never matched the performances of the previous season and won only eight home matches. They had several poor spells and suffered four successive defeats over Easter. They didn't last long in the FA Cup either, losing 3–0 at Notts County.

A handful of new signings were made, including centre-forward Bobby Blood from Port Vale for £4,000. He scored on his debut versus Spurs and went on to net 26 goals in 53 games for the Baggies before leaving in 1924. And right at the end of the campaign a star of the future, Joe Carter, arrived. He became an England international, as did goalkeeper George Ashmore, who conceded five goals on his debut at Blackburn.

In November 1921 Albion's squad was boosted by the signing of the versatile Welsh international Stan Davies, and towards the end of the season his fellow countryman Ivor Jones arrived from

Swansea. Inside-forward Charlie Wilson also burst onto the scene, playing in his first senior game at the age of 16 years and 63 days at Oldham in October to become Albion's youngest League debutant. However, as this trio moved in, one great player moved out as Jesse Pennington announced his retirement after 19 years and almost 500 appearances for the club.

Unfortunately 1921–22 was another disappointing season for Albion, who finished 13th in the table, eight points clear of relegation. The team had a poor pre-Christmas record, winning only six games. Performances improved slightly in the New Year but faded quickly.

Changes were made frequently and 29 players were used, consistent right-back Joe Smith being the only ever present. Towards the end of the season Albion recruited Tommy Glidden from Sunderland West End, and he later skippered the team in two Wembley Cup Finals.

Albion's overall performances improved considerably in 1922–23 as they rose to seventh in the table. Ashmore was now in goal, Billy Adams had replaced Pennington and wingers Jimmy Spencer and Glidden and inside-right Carter all came into the side.

At times Albion produced some sparkling football, whipping Arsenal 7–0 and Tottenham 5–1 at The Hawthorns and Nottingham Forest 4–0 at The City Ground. Davies and Morris teamed up well in attack, netting 37 goals between them, and in mid-March just 5,520 fans saw the home game with Newcastle – the lowest at The Hawthorns since April 1915.

Albion began 1923–24 with a 2–0 home win over the reigning champions Liverpool, and the team, as a unit, looked strong and purposeful, but performances deteriorated slowly, and when Everton visited The Hawthorns in late November the Baggies were on the edge of the relegation zone.

A 5–0 annihilation of the Merseysiders, aided by Blood's hat-trick, was quickly followed by a 4–1 victory over Spurs, all the goals coming from Carter. These results boosted confidence, but Albion couldn't keep it up, and although they made progress in the FA Cup, reaching the fourth round, their League form left a lot to be desired, and only two late wins over Sunderland and Sheffield United effectively kept the Baggies in the top flight. It was certainly a frustrating season for the diehard supporters, and the average League crowd dropped to 17,381, the lowest since World War One.

In the summer of 1924 two star players departed. Bowser joined Walsall and Morris signed for Coventry, the latter having hit 118 goals in 287 appearances for the club.

Making their names now were forwards Charlie Wilson and George James, winger Jack Byers, signed from Blackburn, and full-back Arthur Perry, a relative of former players Charlie, Tom and Walter Perry from the late 1800s.

Albion came mighty close to winning the League title for the second time in five years in 1924–25, finishing runners-up to Huddersfield, who edged home by two points: 58–56. Albion lost the race for the top prize right at the death, picking up just four points from their last four games.

The side mainly comprised: Ashmore; Smith, Perry (Dickie Baugh late on); Magee, Reed, McNeal (Richardson from Boxing Day); Spencer (Glidden from November), Carter, James, Wilson and Byers.

In December 1924 James scored the fastest goal ever recorded at The Hawthorns, netting five seconds into the home game with Nottingham Forest. He went on to score four times in a 5–1 win and also hit a hat-trick in a 4–1 victory over Aston Villa and topped Albion's scoring charts with 30 goals.

Having signed Harold Pearson, son of Hubert Pearson, from Tamworth Castle, Albion were among the favourites to win the title in 1925–26. But they never got going and ended up a poor 13th. They won only three of their first 10 matches, lost two of the next 10 and from Boxing Day onwards were totally inconsistent.

Most of the players who had performed so well the previous season were still at The Hawthorns, although Magee, James, Byers and Adams struggled with injury. Prior to Christmas, the team looked very efficient when beating West Ham 7–1, Bury 4–0, Burnley 5–2, Newcastle 4–0 and Manchester United 5–1. Forwards Glidden, Carter, Davies and Wilson were on song, but after the New Year celebrations it all fell apart. Jones was one of two internationals who left The Hawthorns that season, rejoining his former club Swansea. The other was Joe Smith, who switched to Birmingham. Bob Finch made his League debut at full-back against Leicester – the first of 234 outings for Albion – and Harry Dutton established himself in the side at left-half.

In the summer of 1926 Albion recruited left-half Nelson Howarth from Bolton. He made his debut in the opening day 3–0 home win over Sunderland, but after that things went horribly wrong for both the player and for Albion! Only five wins were gained from 26 starts as the team slipped into the relegation zone. They never recovered, and, although the players battled hard and long during the latter stages of the campaign, the Baggies went down with Leeds United. Home wins over Tottenham 5–0, Aston Villa 6–2 and Newcastle 4–2 were Albion's best, but they suffered 16 defeats, the worst being 7–3 at Bury. Albion also failed in the FA Cup, losing in the third round to Hull. One consolation was that the second XI won the Central League title for the third time in five years.

Two new full-backs were introduced halfway through the season – England international Bill Ashurst from Notts County and George Shaw from Huddersfield, signed for a record £4,100. Teddy Rooke held down the centre-half berth from December and Sammy Short came into the side at inside-left.

Playing in the Second Division for the first time since 1911, Albion's forward line was boosted by the arrival of Jimmy Cookson from Chesterfield. He was to become a truly magnificent marksman who scored 92 goals in his first three seasons at The Hawthorns. He eventually amassed 110 in 131 appearances before leaving for Plymouth in 1933.

Having already notched 83 League goals for Chesterfield, Cookson made a great start to his Baggies career, scoring in each of his first two games against Oldham and Stoke. He continued to find the net on a regular basis, setting two new club scoring records by bagging a double hat-trick (six goals) in a 6–3 win over Blackpool in September (which still stands today) and claiming a seasonal tally of 38.

Albion's form, however, was mixed, and after winning six of their opening 11 League matches they won only two of their next 12 and slid down the table from what was once a promising position. Changes were made frequently and new faces brought in, one being the former England international Harry Chambers from Liverpool. His presence certainly injected some life into Albion's performances, and after losing to Arsenal in the third round of the FA Cup they regained some form and eventually settled for eighth place.

Albion transferred Stan Davies to Birmingham in November 1927 after he had scored 83 goals in 159 games, and in April 1928 left-winger Stan Wood was signed from Winsford. He was to become one of the stars of the 1930s.

Albion began the 1928–29 campaign disappointingly, losing three of their opening four matches. After a slight improvement, they fell away again and found themselves hovering near the relegation area, rather than challenging for a top-six place. After an unbeaten run during the Christmas period, and a decent FA Cup run, they bounced back and collected 18 points out of a possible 24 to finish with a flourish in seventh position.

Two local finds, inside-left Jimmy Edwards and centre-half Bill Richardson, were now firmly established in side along with Wood, Shaw, Magee, Glidden and Carter. They were to become key members of the side over the next three seasons.

Of those who moved on, Chambers became player-manager of Oakengates, Howarth retired through injury and James signed for Reading after scoring 57 goals in 116 games for the Baggies.

June 1929 saw the arrival at The Hawthorns of one of the finest strikers ever to play for Albion, 'W.G.' Richardson, who signed from Hartlepool. A former bus driver, he was given his debut against Millwall on Boxing Day, when he scored the first of 328 goals in a 6–1 win.

Albion had started the season well. The forward line looked sharp and decisive and the goals flowed thick and fast, 20 coming in the first seven League matches, Cookson bagging 12 of them. The goals continued – another 28 being scored up to Christmas, by which time Albion were well placed for promotion, particularly after Wolves had been whipped 7–3.

Unfortunately, a poor March saw them fall off the pace, and despite a late flourish, which revealed seven straight wins, they had to settle for sixth spot, having scored a record 105 goals. Only 1,495 fans bothered to turn up for the mid-week game with Nottingham Forest – the lowest to this day for a senior match at The Hawthorns.

Harold Pearson was now first-choice goalkeeper. Full-back Trentham made his senior debut that season and soon became a first-team regular, partnering Shaw. Frank Cresswell played at inside-left for the majority of this season but was soon to move to Chester, and Jimmy Edwards was ready to be switched to left-half.

The unique double

Everything was now becoming clear as to what secretary-manager Fred Everiss wanted, and soon everyone associated with Albion would be rejoicing in more ways than one as they team created football history in 1930–31 by gaining promotion from the Second Division and winning the FA Cup in the same season – a feat never achieved before or since.

Albion made a cracking start to the campaign, winning five of their first six matches and losing two of the first 12. Joining Everton, Tottenham Hotspur and Wolves at the head of the table, they kept up the momentum and at the halfway stage had gained 28 points out of a possible 42, but, surprisingly to some people, Cookson had lost his place in the side to 'W.G.' Richardson, while a young local lad, Teddy Sandford, was introduced at inside-left.

Albion's jigsaw was complete, and they looked a very good side, which comprised: Pearson; Shaw, Trentham; Magee, W. Richardson, Edwards; Glidden, Carter, 'W.G.' Richardson Sandford and Wood.

The Baggies, who ended the year with a thumping 6–1 home win over Nottingham Forest (their biggest of the season), then battled through a tedious FA Cup tie with Charlton Athletic to reach the fourth round, while vital League points were steadily chalked up, although rivals for promotion Everton took the honours at Goodison Park.

Making progress in the Cup at the expense of Spurs, Portsmouth and Wolves (after a replay), Albion approached Easter on a high – going for glory on both fronts. A tough Cup semi-final win over Everton at Old Trafford in front of a record 69,241 crowd took them through to Wembley for the first time, but before taking on Birmingham in the Final there were still some important League games to play. From these, Albion collected 11 points to keep them on course for promotion, but it was now getting mighty close at the top.

Jimmy Edwards shaking hands at the start of the 1931 FA Cup Final.

A hard-fought but deserved 2–1 victory over Blues in the Cup Final ('W.G.' Richardson scoring both goals) earned Albion the first half of the double, but they still had some work to do. They required maximum points from their remaining two League games to gain promotion with Everton – and they did it by beating Stoke City 1–0 at the Victoria Ground ('W.G.' on target again) and then narrowly defeating Charlton Athletic 3–2 in a nail-biting encounter in front of a record Hawthorns League crowd of 52,415, 'W.G.' heading home the deciding goal at the packed Birmingham Road End. It was a great moment for the players and management and, indeed, the supporters.

Albion fulfilled 52 games that season (42 in the League) and netted 99 goals, with 'W.G.' Richardson top scoring with 24, and three players, Pearson, Shaw and Bill Richardson, were ever present. The average League attendance at The Hawthorns rose by 7,700 to a healthy 21,722.

Back in the top flight after a four-year absence, Albion began in style, beating the reigning champions Arsenal 1–0 at Highbury, Stan Wood scoring in front of a 55,380 crowd.

The team played very well during the first half of the season, and, despite losing 1–0 to Arsenal in the FA Charity Shield game at Villa Park, they ran in some impressive victories, among them three 4–0 scorelines at home to Blackpool, Chelsea and Derby County and those of 5–2 at Manchester City and 5–1 at West Ham in November, when 'W.G.' Richardson made history by scoring four goals in a five-minute spell at the start of the game.

As holders of the FA Cup, Albion were expected to do well again, but this time round they fell at the first hurdle, beaten 2–1 by Aston Villa. Back in the League, points were picked up gradually and there was still an outside chance that Albion could actually win the title, even take second spot, but during a cold, miserable four-week period in March, three defeats were suffered and this meant a final placing of sixth, 10 points behind champions Everton. And, for the record, Harold Pearson and George Shaw played for England against Scotland at Wembley.

Two Welshmen, Jimmy Murphy and Walter Robbins, who became full internationals, along with schoolteacher Arthur Gale signed from Chester, were among a handful of players seeking to establish themselves in Albion's first XI when the 1932–33 campaign kicked off. However, secretary-manager Fred Everiss and his aides, including trainer and former player Fred Reed, confidently stuck with the team which was now regarded as one of the best in the top flight. And what a fine start Albion made, winning their first four matches and drawing the next two. They were in excellent form, scoring goals, and reports in the national press suggested that this could be Albion's season – again!

The Baggies continued to perform well and, despite the occasional glitch, maintained a reasonably high level of consistency, which enabled them to keep in touch with the League leaders Arsenal, Aston Villa and Sheffield Wednesday.

Albion looked superb around the turn of the year, stringing together a run of seven games without defeat (four wins), and although they were dumped out of the FA Cup by West Ham the Baggies still looked capable of challenging for the title. But sadly, and no one really could explain the change in fortunes, Albion ended the season rather disappointingly, registering only two wins and three draws from their last eight matches to finish fourth, just nine points behind champions Arsenal.

One bright spot saw Albion's reserves win their fourth Central League title, scoring 106 goals in the process.

Albion had another good season in 1933–34, taking seventh place. Fielding a relatively settled side during the first half of the campaign, they were forced to make changes after Christmas, and among those who showed a lot of promise were wing-half Jack Sankey, Wally Boyes and versatile forward Gale. However, the team never really got into a position to challenge for honours. They had some good spells and some indifferent ones, and their best sequence of results came between the end of September and the end of December when they won seven and drew six of their 16 matches.

They started 1934 off in style, beating Manchester City 7–2 at Maine Road, with the great Frank Swift in the home goal. But after losing to Chelsea in the FA Cup, Albion's League form was bit of a mish-mash from thereon in, although they did draw 4–4 at Villa Park. The reserves, however, had another excellent season, retaining the Central League crown by gaining 28 wins and scoring 101 goals – and a record second XI crowd of 22,372 saw the home game against Aston Villa in March.

By now goal ace Cookson had left The Hawthorns (for Plymouth) and Magee had also departed to Crystal Palace after 15 years and 434 appearances for the Baggies.

Cup Final defeat, then relegation!

For the second time in four seasons, Albion played at Wembley Stadium – but on this occasion they ended up second best, losing 4–2 to Sheffield Wednesday in the 1935 FA Cup Final after conceding two late goals. Equalising twice through Boyes and Sandford, Albion looked the stronger team during the latter stages, despite carrying two 'injured' players – Glidden and Carter – but some slack defending allowed Owls winger Ellis Rimmer to strike two killer blows right at the end. Albion's 'keeper Pearson and full-back Shaw were the ones at fault, but 'W.G.' Richardson had an off day and admitted afterwards that he should have scored to give Albion a 3–2 lead with quarter of an hour remaining.

En-route to Wembley, Albion ousted Port Vale, Sheffield United (7–1), Stockport County (5–0 away), Preston North End and Bolton Wanderers (after a replay). Gale, deputising for Glidden, scored in each round up to the semi-final but was dropped for the Final in favour of his captain, along with ex-Preston North End striker Harry 'Popeye' Jones, who had stood in for Carter since early March. It was a big mistake to rely on the fitness of Glidden and Carter, and one feels that if Jones (or even Sankey) had accompanied Gale on the right wing then Albion would have won the game.

In the First Division the team stuttered along to finish in ninth position, 14 points behind the champions Arsenal. They had some bright and breezy spells, and none moreso than in November and December when they claimed four successive victories. From 23 March to 4 May they lost only once in nine League outings – at a time when the Cup Final was firmly on their mind!

The team throughout the campaign was fairly settled, but, with injuries creeping in after Christmas, reserves Gale, Sankey, and Jones, along with winger Sid Rawlings and Bob Finch, all pulled their weight, while 'W.G.' Richardson, who was top scorer with 33 goals, was finally capped by England against Holland in Amsterdam.

Albion's reserves made it a hat-trick of Central League successes, scoring a record 121 goals in the process.

In-form Richardson set a new scoring record for Albion in 1935–36 with 40 goals, 39 in the First Division. He was in terrific form from October onwards and netted four times in a crushing 7–0 win at Villa Park, doing likewise in a 5–2 Boxing Day home triumph over Middlesbrough, while striking hat-tricks in successive wins over Blackburn (8–1) and Liverpool (6–1) and scoring five separate braces. However, his goals failed to inspire Albion, who finished the season in 18th position – just three points clear of relegation. The reason, perhaps, was an abysmal away record – 14 defeats. They also went out of the FA Cup in the fourth round, beaten at Bradford Park Avenue.

Secretary-manager Fred Everiss relied on the experience of his senior professionals for most of the season, but injuries and loss of form certainly upset his plans, and, in fact, he used 27 players, including new signing Jack Mahon from Leeds – the most at first-team level since 1921–22.

The splendid right-wing duo of Glidden and Carter both ended their Albion careers that season. Glidden retired to become coach after scoring 140 goals in 479 games, while Carter joined Tranmere after scoring 155 goals in 451 games. He made a quick return, however, after failing a medical and later signed for Walsall.

Season 1936–37 was not a good one for Albion. They finished 16th in the First Division, avoiding relegation by six points, and suffered the heaviest League defeat in their history, losing 10–3 at Stoke. They also went down 4–1 to Preston North End in the FA Cup semi-final at Highbury, a few days after the death of one of the club's greatest servants, chairman and former player Billy Bassett.

After winning only two of their opening eight League games, Albion failed to get any sort of rhythm into their game, and, in truth, had a very moderate campaign. They were poor away from home, losing 15 times and conceding 66 goals. They played slightly better at home and a thrilling 10-goal encounter with FA Cup finalists Sunderland finished 6–4 in their favour.

In the Cup itself, Albion looked powerful when they beat Spennymoor United 7–1 in the third round. But they made hard work of knocking out Darlington 3–2 (winning the game thanks to 'W.G.' Richardson's hat-trick) and Coventry City by the same score at Highfield Road, when new signing from Wolves Cecil Shaw missed the first penalty of his career. A never-to-be-beaten record crowd of

64,815 packed into a snow-bound Hawthorns to see Albion beat Arsenal 3–1 in the quarter-final, but at Highbury against Preston the death of chairman Bassett seemed to get to the players and they never performed, losing 4–1.

Three goalkeepers were used during the campaign – Billy Light, signed from Southampton in March, Jimmy Adams and Harold Pearson, who moved to Millwall at the end of the season after 303 appearances for Albion. There were also debuts for centre-half Bill Brockhurst, forward Sammy Heaselgrave and wingers Jimmy Prew and Lol Coen. Also, at the club's AGM it was announced that Mr Lou Nurse would take over as chairman.

The 1937–38 season was a disaster for Albion, who were relegated after conceding a record 91 goals. They also crashed out of the FA Cup to Third Division North opponents York City. Albion could, and should, have stayed up despite their awful form as there were so many other teams battling against relegation when the season drew to its close, and it transpired that three more points would have saved them from the drop. They lost their last three fixtures and finished up with 36 points, the same as Manchester City (also relegated) but two fewer than Stoke City, Birmingham, Portsmouth and Grimsby Town.

In an attempt to stave off relegation, Albion signed two experienced players, Scottish international wing-half Sandy McNab from Sunderland and England left-winger Joe Johnson from Stoke City. Defenders Harry Lowery, Idris Bassett and Cyril Davies plus goalkeeper Harry Baldwin were also introduced, and the up-and-coming Ike Clarke from Tipton scored six times. Two players who departed were Boyes to Everton, after 165 games for Albion, and George Shaw to Stalybridge Celtic, after 425 appearances.

Back in the Second Division for the first time since 1931, Albion were favourites to win promotion in what was to be the last full League season before the outbreak of World War Two. But they never really got in a challenge and finished a disappointing 10th, slipping out of the FA Cup in the fourth round to the eventual winners Portsmouth, having beaten Manchester United 5–1 in an Old Trafford replay. 'Popeye' Jones took over the mantle as leading scorer that season, while 'W.G.' Richardson, struggling with injury, netted just five times.

Among those who left The Hawthorns around this time were Sandford (to Sheffield United, after scoring 75 goals in 317 games), Robbins (to Newport), Murphy (to Swindon) and Mahon (to Huddersfield). Those introduced to first-team action included winger Billy Elliott, a Wolves reject, full-back Harold White, centre-halves Billy Gripton and Bill Tudor and forward Meynell Burgin.

League football was suspended from September 1939 to August 1946 due to World War Two, and during this enforced lay-off Albion completed almost 300 first-class matches, 266 in regional competitions.

They played in the Midland Regional League in 1939–40, the Football League South Midland Group in 1940–41, the Football League South in 1941–42 and the Football League North in 1942–43, 1943–44 and 1944–45. In the transitional season of 1945–46, when teams were slowly getting back into some sort of order after the hostilities, Albion participated in the Football League South.

They won the Midland War Cup in 1944, beating Nottingham Forest in the two-leg Final. After a 2–2 home draw, they edged home 4–3 after extra-time in the second leg, which is the longest match any Albion team has ever played in, lasting 145 minutes, from 3pm until 5.25pm.

Albion's winning team for the second leg was: Norman Heath; Jim Southam, Jack Smith; Len Millard, Gripton, McNab; Heaselgrave, Clarke, Jack Acquaroff, Charlie Evans and Frank Hodgetts. Acquaroff (2), Hodgetts and Clarke scored the goals.

West Bromwich Albion on a tour of Belguim in 1946.

Normal service resumed

In the summer of 1946 Albion signed centre-forward Dave Walsh from Linfield to replace the departed 'W.G.' Richardson (who was transferred to Shrewsbury). And what a great start the Irishman made to his career in England, scoring in each of his first six League games to set a new club and competition record. A superb marksman, he went on to net 100 goals for Albion and starred in 23 internationals. Fellow countryman Jack Vernon was also recruited from Belfast Celtic in February 1947, and he, too, gave Albion great service for five years.

However, despite the efforts of Vernon and Walsh, Albion finished seventh in the Second Division, never looking like promotion candidates. Their biggest win was 7–2 at Newport when Ike Clarke scored four times. Among the other wartime players who made their League debuts that season were goalkeeper Jimmy Sanders (bought from Charlton), Jim Pemberton, George Tranter, Len Millard, who later became captain, Jimmy Duggan, Cliff Edwards, Glyn Hood, Ray Barlow, who became an all-time great, Reg Ryan and Billy Lunn. At the end of the season, Vernon represented Great Britain against the Rest of Europe at Hampden Park in front of 134,000 fans. And at the club's AGM, Major H. Wilson Keys, a director since 1930, took over as chairman from Lou Nurse.

Fielding a settled side, Albion began 1947–48 very well, winning nine of their opening 13 League matches, but after a poor winter and an FA Cup defeat by Spurs, they once again finished in seventh place.

Changes were made in the team, Arthur Rowley being introduced to the attack. He scored five goals, but after leaving The Hawthorns (for Fulham in 1948) he became the most prolific marksman of all-time, amassing 434 League goals before retiring in 1965. Jackie Haines, signed from Leicester in a part-exchange deal with Peter McKennan, scored a hat-trick in Albion's best win of the season, 6–0 against Bradford Park Avenue, and 'Biff' Taylor from Dudley netted five times in four games at the end of the campaign.

The season was also notable for the home League game with Doncaster in April, in which Alun Evans tradgically suffered a blow to the head which resulted in early retirement, and he eventually lost his sight in one eye, and the average home League attendance that season was Albion's best so far – 30,856.

The end of an era, promotion and Ronnie Allen

In the summer of 1948 Fred Everiss, after 46 years in office, resigned as secretary-manager and became a director of the club. He was replaced as secretary by Ephraim Smith, while Jack Smith became Albion's first full-time team manager.

Smith, a former player with Wolves and Chelsea, who had been coaching at Molineux and had served as a guest with Albion during the war, guided the Baggies back to the First Division after an 11-year absence, and there is no doubt that his experience as a player had a lot to do with that success.

After registering just two wins in their opening nine games, Albion hit top form and from late September to Christmas produced some exciting football, winning 12 matches out of 14. Three defeats in four either side of the New Year disrupted the team slightly, but, aided by three FA Cup wins over Lincoln, Gateshead and Chelsea, they picked up the momentum again, and as Easter approached they were chasing the runaway leaders Southampton and second-placed Fulham. Knocked out of the Cup by Wolves, they didn't let that defeat disturb their routine, and they played exceedingly well during April, registering five important wins. As Southampton's challenge faded and with Fulham looking strong, Albion moved into second place, clinching promotion with a 3–0 win over FA Cup finalists Leicester with one game remaining. And if they had won (and not lost) at Grimsby on the final Saturday then the Baggies would have gone up as champions.

Walsh was brilliant, top-scoring with 28 goals (League and Cup). Cyril Williams, recruited from Bristol City, Vernon, Elliott and Haines (who scored twice for England in a 6–0 win over Switzerland) also played well, as did Jimmy Sanders, who saved nine penalties, while Barlow and Joe Kennedy (signed from Altrincham for £750) made important contributions. As a result, Albion's average home League attendance rose to a club record of 33,379 in the season.

Albion, fielding the following team, began their first season back in the top flight with a 1–0 home win over Charlton: Sanders; Pemberton, Millard; Kennedy, Vernon, Barlow; Elliott, Williams, Walsh, Haines and George Lee, the latter having been signed from Nottingham Forest. But the Baggies found it difficult to maintain any sort of consistency and scoring goals became a problem – they managed only 20 in their opening 14 fixtures. But successive home victories over Portsmouth (3–0), Everton (4–0) and Fulham (4–1) boosted confidence as the season progressed.

Dumped out of the FA Cup by Cardiff, Albion's form dipped again, and, after a run of eight games without a win, in March 1950 manager Smith paid £20,000 for Ronnie Allen, a 21-year-old winger from Port Vale. One of the finest footballers ever to don an Albion shirt, he remained at The Hawthorns for 11 years, scoring a then record 234 goals in 458 games and winning five England caps. He later had two spells as manager.

Almost 61,000 fans turned up to see Allen make a scoring debut in the 1–1 home draw with Wolves, and he netted another four goals before the season ended, helping Albion edge up to 14th position. Boosted by that huge Black Country derby crowd, Albion's average home League attendance of 38,819 set another club record.

Following an injury to Pemberton, which ended his career after 172 games for Albion, Stan Rickaby, signed from Middlesbrough towards the end of the previous season, came in at right-back during 1950–51, while forwards Andy McCall (from Blackpool) and Fred Richardson (from Barnsley) also made their mark, the latter replacing Walsh who was surprisingly sold to Aston Villa.

Shooting pratice for Reg Ryan with Arthur Filton (trainer) and Norman Heath (goalkeeper) watched by Ronnie Allen and Johnny Nicholls, 1953.

Taking the season as a whole, it was a disappointing one for Albion, who finished 16th, just five points clear of relegation. There were very few high spots – a 5–0 thumping of reigning champions Portsmouth and a 2–0 victory over the FA Cup holders Arsenal among the best. The team also suffered some heavy defeats, including a 5–0 hiding at Tottenham. There was no joy either in the FA Cup as the Baggies went out in the third-round replay to Derby.

Allen, in his first full season, top scored with 10 goals, and Barlow was the only ever present. Norman Heath, a wartime signing, was now making his name in the Albion goal, and star of the future right-winger Frank Griffin, signed from Shrewsbury in April 1951, made his debut at Sunderland. On the international front, Vernon, besides representing his country, played for the United Kingdom against Wales at Cardiff.

Albion did not make the greatest of starts to their 1951–52 campaign, winning only one of the opening 10 matches, and by the time New Year arrived they were in a spot of bother at the wrong end of the table. Thankfully, performances improved, and after six wins from their last eight matches they edged up to 13th position. Again, their best win was against Portsmouth (5–0), and they also defeated Wolves 4–1 at Molineux courtesy of an Allen hat-trick. Liverpool were also thumped 5–2 at Anfield.

Albion's FA Cup exploits ended in round five, beaten by a late Bill Eckersley penalty at Blackburn. Star of the future Johnny Nicholls made his debut in this game in place of Allen, who by now had been switched to centre-forward. He top scored with 35 goals – the first time an Albion player had netted this many since 1936. And for his efforts Allen was rewarded with his first England cap versus Switzerland. This was also Vernon's last season with the club. He left with a firm handshake and loads of wonderful memories, having made exactly 200 appearances for the Baggies. Other players who left included Richardson to Chester, McCall to Leeds and Arthur Smith to Plymouth.

In April 1952 Smith quit as manager, handing over his duties to the former Newcastle and Blackburn defender Jesse Carver, who was employed basically as a coach, having been very successful in Holland and Italy. Under Carver's shrewd coaching methods, Albion got off to a flying start in 1952–53, winning seven of their opening nine matches, three away from home, including a 4–3 triumph at Tottenham in sweltering heat.

After a poor spell over the autumn period, Albion gathered pace again and hit top form with a magnificent 5–4 victory at Hillsborough before commencing 1953 with a cracking 5–3 win at Newcastle. They made progress in the FA Cup, but after heavy defeats at Burnley and Stoke it came as a shock to the players when, completely out of the blue, Carver left the club. Into his place came Vic Buckingham, the former Spurs right-back, who moved down from Bradford Park Avenue. Albion were kicked out of the Cup (at the fourth attempt) by Chelsea in his first game in charge, yet quickly realised that he had inherited a fine squad of players. He took his time with regard to making changes to the team and slowly but surely worked things out for the better, seeing Albion end the season on a high by claiming fourth place, their highest finish since 1933. Allen, with 21 goals, top scored again, and the fans also saw centre-half Jimmy Dugdale keep England's centre-forward Nat Lofthouse firmly under control when making his debut against Bolton.

In July 1953 Buckingham went back to his former club Bradford to make his first signing, paying a modest £3,000 for centre-forward Derek Kevan. What a bargain he turned out to be!

So close to the double

Albion came agonisingly close to becoming the first team since 1897 to achieve the double in the 1953–54 season. They beat Preston North End 3–2 in the FA Cup Final and only injuries and international calls prevented them from winning the League Championship, finishing a cruel second to Wolves after a titanic battle. From the word go it was a two-horse race for the First Division title between the Black Country rivals – and, in truth, it was Albion who looked the better equipped and more forceful and enterprising side for most of the time – that is until they collapsed late on, allowing their near neighbours to go on and lift the star prize by a margin of four points (57–53).

Albion lost just one of their first 15 League games (at home to Charlton). But then they managed just four victories in their next 10, yet after embarking on that terrific Cup run they still managed to keep in touch with Wolves with some important wins. However, injuries to key players, namely goalkeeper Heath at Sunderland (he never played again) and right-back Rickaby in the Cup semi-final at Villa Park, plus England call-ups for strikers Allen and Nicholls, took their toll, and from their last 10 matches Albion conjured up a mere six points out of a possible 20 and waved goodbye to the title in the process! Perhaps the crucial game was the four-pointer against Wolves at The Hawthorns in early April. Both teams lost players to international duty, but Albion suffered the most and, to make matters worse, Barlow was injured early on as Wolves nicked it 1–0.

Albion's away form in 1953–54 was superb, especially early on, the highlight being a magnificent 7–3 win at Newcastle when Nicholls struck his first hat-trick for the club. Burnley were also defeated 4–1 at Turf Moor, and, in fact, Albion won their first six away games.

At The Hawthorns they were equally as impressive, and among their triumphs were those of 4–0 against Huddersfield, 5–2 versus Chelsea and 6–1 against Cardiff, with Allen scoring a hat-trick in each game.

Albion were unbeaten over Christmas when they ran up successive home wins over Liverpool (5–2) and Preston (3–2), and they started off on that road to Wembley by ousting Chelsea 1–0, before demolishing Rotherham 4–0 on an ice rink.

As they progressed in the Cup, so their League form began to suffer, but after defeating Newcastle 3–2 with another Allen treble in a cracking fifth-round tie in front of more than 61,000 fans at The Hawthorns, and knocking out Spurs 3–0 in the quarter-final, the double was definitely on. But then it all went wrong!

Albion beat Third Division North Champions-elect Port Vale 2–1 in the semi-final at the cost of Rickaby, and soon afterwards Heath was carried off at Roker Park. So, manager Buckingham brought in his reserves – Kennedy, Wilf Carter, Freddie Cox (his old Spurs teammate) and ex-Wrexham right-back Stuart Williams – but the results went against Albion and after losing their last two matches – 6–1 at Villa Park and 3–0 at Portsmouth – they watched as the League trophy annoyingly found its way to Molineux.

Albion, however, celebrated at Wembley and won the Cup for the fourth time with two goals from Allen (one a penalty) and one from Griffin, who fired in the winner in the 87th minute to beat Tom Finney's Preston in front of almost 100,000 fans. So it was a 'double' in the end for the West Midlands – but not as Albion had hoped it would be!

Allen top scored once more with 34 League and Cup goals, while his strike partner Nicholls netted 32. Albion's average home League attendance went up to 38,279 – the second best in the club's history, while over 134,000 fans saw both Allen and Nicholls score in England's 4–2 international win over Scotland at Hampden Park (on the afternoon when Wolves won at The Hawthorns).

The moderate fifties

Albion started their League programme in 1954–55 like they ended the previous one, losing two matches in a row – at Sunderland 4–2 and Newcastle 3–0. But they responded quickly and won seven of their next eight matches to fly to the top of the table. At this juncture, the team was playing exceptionally well – and scoring goals. They defeated Arsenal 3–1, gained revenge over Newcastle with a 4–2 home victory and beat Leicester 6–4 in a thrill-a-minute encounter at The Hawthorns, with Nicholls hitting his first home hat-trick. They even shared eight goals in the FA Charity Shield game with Wolves at Molineux, where Allen slotted in another treble in front of 45,000 fans.

However, after an exciting 3–3 draw at Chelsea, where Millard scored a late equaliser in front of a 67,440 crowd (which was to remain the biggest for a League game involving Albion for more than 50 years), and a 5–3 defeat at the hands of the crack Hungarian side Honved in a prestige friendly in Brussels, performances began to falter as Albion plummeted down towards the relegation zone. And to make matters worse, in November manager Buckingham was seriously injured in a car crash while returning home from a testimonial match at Hereford (a game Albion lost 10–5 incidentally). Cox, who was also involved in the accident, ran the team for the remainder of the season.

Albion's loss of form was quite alarming – and, to add salt to the wound, they went out of the FA Cup to Charlton, beaten 4–2 at home in the fourth round. Cox (with some advice from his manager) was pulling his hair out in an effort to halt Albion's decline, and as a desperate measure Barlow was switched to attack. Billy Brookes came into the side at left-half, Williams was introduced at right-back and Carter at inside-right. These changes worked, and the Baggies hauled themselves to safety with victories over Wolves, Charlton, Bolton, Portsmouth, Manchester City and Huddersfield. They eventually finished 17th – a drop of 15 places from the previous season – and avoided the drop by five points after conceding 96 goals! Allen managed to bag another 30 goals this term.

Players who made their debuts included forwards Alec Jackson and Allan Crowshaw (both at Charlton) and goalkeeper Geoff Barnsley (at Preston). Rickaby and Ryan both moved on – the former became player-manager of Poole Town after making 205 appearances for Albion – and Ryan joined Derby for £3,000 after more than 270 outings for the club. On the international scene, Barlow gained his long-awaited England cap against Northern Ireland, and he also represented the Football League.

For the second season running Albion made an uneasy start to their 1955–56 League programme, but the manager did introduce two future England internationals, Kevan, who scored twice on his debut against Everton, and right-back Don Howe. They became key men in the Baggies first team for the next eight years.

With Allen still finding the net on a regular basis, Albion's form improved slightly, but it all went wrong in the winter months as the team slithered towards the bottom end of the table. Changes were made, Buckingham bringing in wing-half Gerry Summers, Maurice Setters (signed from Exeter) and former Rhyl left-winger and future Welsh international Graham Williams, who would later captain two Cup-winning teams.

Soon after Christmas the tide turned again as Albion regained their composure and started winning matches. However, after losing to Birmingham City on a snowbound Hawthorns pitch in the fifth round of the FA Cup, their League form took a turn for the worse with six defeats coming in the next eight outings. Inside-right Bobby Robson was signed from Fulham for £25,000 in March, but he didn't have the greatest of baptisms, Albion suffering successive 4–0 defeats in his first two outings. Thankfully the season was all but over by now, and when the final curtain came down Albion found themselves in 13th place, six points clear of relegation!

For the third season running, Albion failed to get off to a good start in 1956–57, winning only three of their opening 12 League games. Manager Buckingham was seriously concerned and made frequent changes, bringing in Kevan at centre-forward, switching Allen to the left wing, re-introducing Nicholls (in place of Brian Whitehouse), inserting Setters for Dudley and recalling the experienced Millard for Williams at left-back.

There was some improvement as Albion stuttered through to January, managing only one League win – 1–0 at home to Newcastle, which was the last Christmas Day game at The Hawthorns. They squeezed through the opening rounds of the FA Cup, beating Doncaster, Sunderland, Blackpool and Arsenal, but the players simply couldn't get to grips with the League situation. Only two more matches (out of the last 10) were won, and they also lost to Aston Villa in the Cup semi-final, going down 1–0 in a replay at St Andrew's after allowing their arch rivals to snatch a late equaliser (at 2–2) in the initial encounter at Molineux.

Albion's final League position was a safe but disappointing 11th. Kevan took over the mantle of leading scorer this term with 20 goals, Allen netted 15 and Robson 13, and the 6,397 crowd for the mid-week game with Blackpool was Albion's smallest since April 1939. International honours that season went to Derek Kevan, who scored on his England debut against Scotland at Wembley, and, on the transfer front, Nicholls joined Cardiff after scoring 64 goals in 145 games for the Baggies, Carter moved to Plymouth Argyle and Summers to Sheffield United.

In the summer of 1957 Albion travelled behind the Iron Curtain and played three prestigious friendly games in Russia, winning two, 3–0 versus Dynamo Tbilisi and 4–2 against CSKA Red Army, and drawing 1–1 with FC Zenit – thus becoming the first British professional team to record a victory in the USSR.

West Bromwich Albion 1958–59 team.

Albion scored 112 League and Cup goals and netted six in a floodlit friendly against the CSKA Army side from Moscow during 1957–58. Using five attacking forwards, they certainly gave their fans value for money, although at times the defence wasn't all that secure, conceding 70 in the League!

Albion lost only one of their first 21 matches and were on course for the title, having recorded some splendid victories, including a 9–2 hammering of Manchester City, their best ever League win at The Hawthorns. Griffin netted a hat-trick in this game as all five front men scored to destroy City's 'M' plan.

Either side of the New Year, Albion went nap in three successive games, winning 5–3 at Birmingham, 5–1 versus Burnley and 5–1 against Manchester City in the FA Cup. They then drew 3–3 with Nottingham Forest in the fourth round of the Cup before winning the replay 5–1 with only 10 men after Setters had been carried off injured.

At this stage of the season Albion were playing brilliantly, and there was every chance that they could go on and complete the League and Cup double, which had eluded them four years earlier. Sadly though, as Sheffield United were ousted in the fifth round of the Cup, Albion's in-form Griffin fractured his leg. It was a body blow, but the team battled on and in the quarter-final faced Manchester United only a few weeks after the Munich Air disaster. The game at The Hawthorns ended 2–2, but in the cauldron of Old Trafford the Baggies were beaten in the very last minute in front of an emotional 60,523 crowd.

Amazingly, three days later, Albion returned to the same ground for a League game and whipped United 4–0 in front of 3,000 more spectators! After that Cup exit, Albion's League form deteriorated. They fell badly to finish fourth, 14 points behind the champions Wolves. Between them, three players scored 78 of Albion's 92 League goals: Allen 28, Robson 27 and Kevan 23. Also, Kevan and Robson, along with Howe, represented England in the World Cup Finals in Sweden, while Stuart Williams was also on World Cup duty with Wales.

At the end of this campaign three 1954 Cup winners left the club: Jimmy Sanders, after 391 appearances, signed for Coventry; Millard joined Stafford Rangers, after 21 years and 625 appearances, and Lee moved to Lockheed Leamington, having scored 65 goals in 295 games.

Season 1958–59 was another good one for Albion, who finished fifth in the First Division and reached the fifth round of the FA Cup. A 6–0 win at Birmingham in pouring rain was one of many fine away performances, others coming at Portsmouth (won 6–2) and Villa Park (won 4–1). The best home win was 4–0 against Chelsea, while on the down side Albion lost 5–2 at Wolves, 5–0 at Tottenham and, despite Kevan's hat-trick, 4–3 at Arsenal.

Clive Jackman, who was signed the previous season from Aldershot, started in goal but was badly injured at Villa Park in October and never played for Albion again. His place went to Ray Potter, bought from Crystal Palace. Chuck Drury, a local lad who made his debut at Bolton in February 1958, had some useful games at half-back, as did wingers Jimmy Campbell (replacing Griffin who subsequently joined Northampton) and Derek Hogg, who was signed from Leicester.

In the summer of 1959 Albion toured Canada and North America, winning seven of their nine games, including 6–1 against Ontario All Stars, 15–0 against Alberta All Stars (when Robson scored six times), 7–1 against the Scottish club Dundee in Calgary, 10–1 against Manitoba All Stars and 9–0 against Ottowa All Stars.

However, on returning home, manager Buckingham departed company with the club, replaced in July 1959 by the former Manchester City full-back and ex-Peterborough boss Gordon Clark, who had been with Albion since 1955 as a scout and assistant manager.

In March 1959 one of Albion's greatest-ever goalscorers, 'W.G.' Richardson, collapsed and died while playing in a Charity Match in Birmingham.

Six years of disappointment: 1959–65

In 1959–60, for the third season running, Albion finished in the top five of the First Division, this time taking fourth spot, six points behind the champions, Burnley. Had they not gone through a sticky patch during September and October, when they collected just seven points out of 20, then it could well have been a completely different story!

The team played enough and registered some excellent wins, including a 6–2 victory over Everton at The Hawthorns, when Kevan became the first Albion player to score five goals in a game since 1927, and a win against Birmingham 7–1 at St Andrew's, when Allen and Kevan both netted hat-tricks.

Albion's FA Cup journey ended in the fifth round at Leicester, where they lost 2–1 despite a rare Kennedy goal. Sadly the match is also notable for the death of referee Jack Husband in the dressing room at half-time.

Goalkeeper Jock Wallace was signed in October from Airdrieonians to replace Potter. Graham Williams established himself at left-back, and Jackson, after recovering from a broken leg, took over on the right wing, while 16-year-old Bobby Hope made his debut on the last day of the season against Arsenal. In the January Setters joined Manchester United for £30,000, and in June 1960 Barlow joined Birmingham after 16 years and 482 appearances for Albion. At the AGM that season assistant-secretary Alan Everiss took over as secretary from Ephraim Smith.

After a series of disappointing results, Albion slipped down to 10th in the First Division in 1960–61. Their home form let them down badly (eight defeats), and with 11 losses on the road they were never able to challenge for honours. Their best wins were 6–0 against Newcastle, when Jackson hit a hat-trick, and 6–3 versus Manchester City, when Allen – in his last season with the club – also grabbed a treble. On the debit side, Jimmy Greaves hit five goals in a 7–1 defeat at Chelsea.

Albion's best spell – 11 games unbeaten – came right at the end of the season following the signing of left-winger Clive Clark from QPR for £20,000 and the introduction of centre-forward Jack Lovatt.

Albion's interest in the FA Cup ended at the first hurdle when they were beaten 3–1 at Lincoln, and Kevan again headed the scoring charts that season with 18 goals. Howe was the only ever present, and manager Clark used 25 players in total, including two ex-Walsall stars, Peter Billingham and Stan Jones.

At the end of the season Albion gave free transfers to two great players – Allen and Kennedy – who had both starred in the 1954 FA Cup win. Allen joined Crystal Palace after scoring 234 goals in 415 games for the Baggies, while Kennedy signed for Chester, having amassed 397 appearances. Stan Steele, recruited from Port Vale in March, played one game for Albion at Blackburn before returning to the Valiants in August.

In October 1961 Archie Macaulay, the former Arsenal and Scottish international, took over from Clark as Albion's manager. However, he had a very disappointing first season, finishing ninth. The team registered only six wins in 23 matches before Christmas, and at one stage relegation was a possibility, but battling performances late on, including a terrific 5–1 win at Molineux and a 7–1 home victory over Blackpool when Kevan scored four times, saw them survive.

The holders Spurs dumped Albion out of the FA Cup in the fifth round in front of the last 50,000 plus crowd at The Hawthorns. Kevan top scored with 34 goals, and Smith netted 19 in his first full season. Goalkeeper Tony Millington, later to play for Wales, made his debut, and Robson, on his return from England's World Cup exploits in Chile, rejoined Fulham after scoring 61 goals in 257 appearances in six years at The Hawthorns.

The 1962–63 season turned out to be Albion's worst since 1954–55. Starting off reasonably well, with a 6–1 hammering of Fulham, when Kevan scored four times, and a 5–4 victory over Bolton 5–4 with another Kevan hat-trick, their overall form dipped alarmingly from late September, and only two wins were gained before the Arctic winter set in. In fact, from Albion's point of view, things got worse on the pitch before they got better, and with the weather playing havoc with the fixture list (very few games were played between 15 December and 2 March) it was certainly looking grim around The Hawthorns.

Defeat in the fourth round of the FA Cup at Nottingham Forest did little to boost morale, and when Kevan was sensationally transferred to Tommy Docherty's Chelsea for £50,000 in March – having said farewell to the fans with another blistering hat-trick in a 6–1 home win over Ipswich – Albion's season was all but over.

Manager Macaulay departed, replaced in April 1963 by the former England international Jimmy Hagan, and surprisingly results improved towards the end of the campaign, Albion winning four and drawing two of their last eight matches. But it was, in truth, a very disappointing season all round.

New faces this term included winger Kenny Foggo, Max Murray from Glasgow Rangers, who went to Third Lanark in double-quick time, Ronnie Fenton from Burnley for £15,000 and full-back Ray Fairfax, whose first outing was in front of 44,000 fans at Anfield. Stuart Williams, who made 246 appearances in 12 years and gained a club record 33 caps for Wales, left for Southampton (with Davey Burnside), while Smith moved to Peterborough after netting goals in 70 outings for the Baggies. Also that season the average League crowd nosedived to 18,637 – the lowest since 1938–39.

Goalkeeper Millington, who had the misfortune to concede 15 goals at Molineux that season, when Albion lost 7–0 to Wolves in a re-arranged First Division game and 8–0 in a reserve fixture, made his international debut for Wales, and at the club's AGM Major H. Wilson Keys was replaced as Albion chairman by 'Jim' W. Gaunt.

Albion began 1963–64 with two more new players in their line-up – left-half Terry Simpson from Peterborough and centre-forward John Kaye from Scunthorpe. They settled in well, and a month or so into the League programme two more new faces had been introduced – craggy Scotsman Doug Fraser from Aberdeen and teenager Tony Brown, who scored on his debut at Ipswich. Albion's pre-November performances were generally good. Playing confidently, they ran up some impressive victories, including those of 4–0 over Arsenal, 4–3 versus Aston Villa and 3–1 against Birmingham – all at home. In fact, they lost only three of their opening 13 matches, but they then had a run of six without a win before a much-publicised transfer rebellion early in December, which was quickly followed by the infamous tracksuit saga when manager Hagan refused to allow his players to wear tracksuit bottoms in freezing temperatures. This was thankfully resolved and Albion quickly put together an unbeaten sequence of seven matches in the League either side of Christmas, which included a thrilling 4–4 home draw with Tottenham. Exit from the FA Cup, beaten in a fourth-round replay at Arsenal after a 3–3 draw at The Hawthorns, triggered off an indifferent stretch which lasted from February onwards, only two more victories being recorded in the last eight League fixtures.

Albion finished the season in 10th position, 14 points behind the champions Liverpool but well clear of the relegation zone.Winger Clark had a fine season, top-scoring with 17 goals, while a young Micky Fudge weighed in with four, including a hat-trick in a 4–0 win over Everton. Also that season, in April 1964, Howe was transferred to Arsenal for £40,000 after making 379 appearances for Albion, and

West Bromwich Albion, 1964–65.

the first 'Throstle Club' (for Baggies supporters) opened next to the Woodman pub on the Handsworth side of the ground, Graham Williams and former player Jesse Pennington supping the first pints.

Albion commenced the 1964–65 season with a 2–2 draw in front of 52,000 fans at Old Trafford, and four days later Brown scored his first hat-trick for the club in a 4–1 home win over Sunderland, who fielded 15-year-old goalkeeper Derek Forster. But results didn't materialize as one would have liked, and in September manager Hagan paid £25,000 for the Notts County striker Jeff Astle – and what a terrific buy he turned out to be! The 'King', as he would become known, made his Albion bow in a 4–2 defeat at Leicester before scoring twice on his home debut in a 5–1 win over Wolves.

Astle immediately gelled with Kaye, and with Clark (now at outside-right) and Hope both in good form Albion's forward line looked strong and penetrative. However, sadly the results didn't come, and Albion failed to register a single win from 10 starts between 7 November and 16 January, and they lost interest in the FA Cup, beaten 2–1 at home by Liverpool. A 2–0 victory over Tottenham ended that dismal run, and from February onwards Albion played positive football, winning seven and drawing three of their final 15 matches, thrashing Leicester 6–0, Everton 4–0 and West Ham 4–2 at The Hawthorns, and the latter three days after suffering a 6–1 defeat at Upton Park when Brian Dear netted five times. Albion eventually finished in 14th position in the table that season, which saw debuts for several players, including youngsters Graham Lovatt, Ian Collard and Dick Krzywicki, and Ray Crawford, the former England international centre-forward, signed from Wolves.

Four Cup Finals in five years

Albion entered the Football League Cup for the first time in 1965–66, and they won it, beating West Ham 5–3 in the last of the two-leg Finals. Playing terrific attacking football, Albion ousted Walsall (3–1 at home in front of a then record crowd for the competition of over 41,000), Leeds (4–2 away), Coventry (6–1 in a Hawthorns replay, Fraser netting a hat-trick), Aston Villa (3–1, also at home) and manager Hagan's former club Peterborough in the semi-final (winning 2–1 at home and 4–2 at London Road when Brown hit a treble). They then lost 2–1 at Upton Park in the first leg of the Final but turned things round at The Hawthorns, crushing the Hammers 4–1 thanks mainly to a magnificent first-half performance in front of a 32,000-plus crowd. This victory booked Albion a place in the Fairs Cup for 1966–67 – their first ever taste of competitive European football.

In the League Albion did very well, claiming sixth position – their highest finish for six years. It was due to an excellent run of nine games without defeat from early April to when the last ball was kicked in May. Prior to that, Albion's form had been hit and miss, and they were dumped out of the FA Cup 3–0 at Bolton. Their best wins were 6–2 against Stoke (when Kaye scored a hat-trick), 6–2 against Fulham and 5–1 at Sunderland on New Year's Day. Tony Brown was the top scorer with 28 goals (League and Cup), Astle netted 25 and John Kaye 23, with the aggregate total being 122.

The following season, in March 1967, Albion returned to Wembley for the first time in 13 years when they met Third Division Queen's Park Rangers in the Final of the League Cup. But after leading 2–0 at half-time, thanks to a brace from Clark, Albion's defence collapsed, and Rangers, inspired by Rodney Marsh, stormed back to win 3–2, Mark Lazarus netting a disputed winning goal.

On their way to Wembley Albion knocked out Aston Villa 6–1 (with a Hope hat-trick), Manchester City 4–2, Swindon 2–0, Northampton 3–1 and West Ham 6–2 on aggregate in the semi-final (4–0 at home, with an Astle hat-trick, and 2–2 away).

1966 League Cup winners.

However, in League football Albion put in far too many indifferent performances and finished 13th. They were in relegation trouble when March arrived, but eight wins and two draws from their last 11 matches edged them to safety. They ended the season with a 6–1 home win over Newcastle with another hat-trick for 'Bomber' Brown, who had netted a treble in a 3–0 home win victory against Tottenham earlier in the season. A nine-goal thriller at Goodison Park finished 5–4 in Everton's favour, while League champions Manchester United won 4–3 at The Hawthorns in mid-December.

Albion's first taste of European football ended in the second round, beaten 6–1 over two legs by Bologna. They began well with a 6–3 aggregate victory over DOS Utrecht, Brown registering another hat-trick in a 5–2 win at home, after Hope had become the first Albion player to score in Europe by netting in the 1–1 draw in Holland. It was also a poor run for Albion in the FA Cup, beaten in the fourth round at Leeds by 5–0, their worst ever defeat in this competition.

On Boxing Day (versus Spurs) Albion handed club debuts to Dennis Clarke and centre-half John Talbut, a £30,000 signing from Burnley. A month later John Osborne was bought from Chesterfield for £10,000 and in February 1967 defender Eddie Colquhoun arrived from Bury. Clark – who was the only ever present that season – was Albion's leading marksman with 29 goals, the first Albion winger ever to pass the 25-goal mark, and he also scored in every game of the League Cup.

In May 1967 Hagan quit as Albion's manager and soon afterwards the club sold Potter to Portsmouth, Simpson to Walsall and Campbell-Crawford to Exeter. Jones had earlier returned to Fellows Park after missing the League Cup Final. Alan Ashman, a former Cumbrian chicken-farmer and Nottingham Forest centre-forward, left Carlisle to take over as manager of Albion in May 1967 – and what a terrific first season he had at The Hawthorns!

Albion, after a difficult third-round FA Cup tie at Colchester, settled down, defended resolutely and scored telling goals to reach Wembley for the second successive season – and this time they won, beating Everton 1–0 after extra-time to lift the FA Cup for the fifth time. It was a great occasion, especially for Astle, who scored the winning goal in the 92nd minute, giving him the honour of netting in every round.

En route to Wembley, Albion eventually overcame Colchester 4–0 (after a 1–1 draw), beat Southampton 3–2 when Williams had to take over in goal (also after a 1–1 draw), Portsmouth 2–1 at Fratton Park, Liverpool (winning 2–1 at the third attempt, at Maine Road) and Birmingham 2–0 in the semi-final at Villa Park.

Everton were favourites to win the Cup, but Albion, full of Black Country grit and determination, battled through to victory with the following team: Osborne; Fraser, Williams; Brown, Talbut, Kaye (who had been converted to a defender when Colquhoun was badly injured in a League game at Newcastle); Lovett, Collard, Astle, Hope and Clark. Clarke came on for Kaye at the start of extra-time to become the first substitute to be used in an FA Cup Final. Two months before the Cup Final Everton had beaten Albion 6–2 in a League match at The Hawthorns, Alan Ball scoring four times. But the World Cup winner never got a look in at Wembley!

These players also did themselves justice in the First Division, finishing a creditable eighth after an unconvincing start. They were 12 points behind the champions Manchester City, whom they defeated twice, 3–2 at home and 2–0 at Maine Road. Albion also walloped Burnley 8–1 to record their best home League win since September 1957, and the European Cup winners-to-be Manchester United were thumped 6–3 and West Ham 3–1 in the space of three days, Astle netting a hat-trick in both games. In the League Cup Albion lost to Reading in the opening round – but that was insignificant compared with what was to follow later.

Astle was leading scorer with 26 goals, including three hat-tricks – and he was also voted 'Midland Footballer of the Year.' Centre-half Talbut, as reliable as ever, appeared in all 53 League and Cup games and Welsh international winger Ronnie Rees (signed from Coventry in March) and Asa Hartford both made their first-team debuts that season.

After an eventual and somewhat controversial end-of-season tour to East Africa, where they played five friendlies, it was so near yet so far for Albion in 1968–69 when they almost made it to Wembley for the third successive season. However, this time they failed in the semi-final of the FA Cup, losing 1–0 to Leicester City at Hillsborough, Allan Clarke scoring in the last minute! Having knocked out Norwich, Fulham, Arsenal and Chelsea, Albion were confident of beating Leicester, but a local-born player had the last laugh in Yorkshire.

Earlier, on a freezing cold evening at The Hawthorns, Dunfermline knocked Albion out of the European Cup-winners' Cup in the quarter-final, winning 1–0 after a goalless draw in Scotland. In the First Division, Albion finished 10th and went out of the League Cup to lowly Peterborough at London Road in the third round. They also lost 6–1 to Manchester City in the FA Charity Shield game at Maine Road prior to the start of the League campaign.

Manager Alan Ashman, for most of the time, stuck with the players who did the club proud in 1967–68. Rees, Hartford and Clark shared the left-wing position, with the former also appearing on the right with Krzywicki. Ray Wilson established himself at left-back, teenager Len Cantello made his debut in midfield, while Dennis Martin (signed from Carlisle) and youngsters Lyndon Hughes and Alan Merrick all played their first senior game.

Astle, with 25 goals, and Brown, with 20, were the leading marksmen, and Astle won the first of his five England caps, while Fraser and Hope played for Scotland. Colquhoun was transferred to Sheffield

United in October, Clarke joined Huddersfield in January, Rees left for Nottingham Forest the following month, 'keeper Sheppard moved to Bristol Rovers in June and soon afterwards Clark, after scoring 98 goals in 351 outings for the Baggies, was sold to Preston.

Albion recruited their first-ever £100,000 player in June 1969, bringing in Colin Suggett from Sunderland. Goalkeeper Jim Cumbes was another new face – signed from Tranmere for £30,000 – and so too was inside-forward Danny Hegan, recruited from Ipswich in an exchange deal that took Collard to Portman Road.

Suggett made a great start to his Baggies career, scoring twice in an opening day 2–0 League victory at Southampton. But it was not to last for 'Suggo' or Albion, and only two more wins were recorded in the next 15 First Division matches as the team slipped deep into relegation trouble. Osborne, a young Gordon Nisbet, later to become an England Under-23 international right-back, and Cumbes all played in goal during the first month, but it was 'Ossie' who retained his position despite some poor League results.

In the League Cup, though, Albion made good progress at the expense of Aston Villa, Ipswich, Bradford City and Leicester, and as they awaited a semi-final clash with Carlisle, so their First Division form improved considerably with five wins coming in the space of six weeks. Carlisle were duly eliminated from the League Cup 4–2 on aggregate, as Albion reached their fourth Cup Final in five years, but they went out of the FA Cup to Sheffield Wednesday despite a brilliant goal from Brown.

Albion met Manchester City in the League Cup Final on a soggy Wembley pitch, ruined by the recent horse show, and they took an early lead through Astle's looping header. But City, inspired by Francis Lee, slowly got on top and went on to steal the prize, winning 2–1 with an extra-time goal

1968 FA Cup winners.

John Osborne collects the ball for West Bromwich Albion from a right-sided Everton corner, 1968 FA Cup Final.

from Glyn Pardoe... after Suggett had missed an open goal in the second half. After that disappointment the season fizzled out and Albion eventually finished 16th – their lowest position in the top flight since 1954–55. Astle, with 30 goals, was top marksman, Suggett scored 15 and Brown 13. Defender Alistair Robertson made an impressive start to his professional career and played for England in two World Cup matches in Mexico.

At the end of this season – after Albion had contested four uneasy matches in the Anglo-Italian tournament – Williams retired as a player after 16 years with the club. He made 360 appearances, scored 11 goals and skippered the Baggies to victory in the 1966 League Cup and 1968 FA Cup Finals. Joining Albion's coaching staff, he remained at The Hawthorns for a further two seasons before taking over as player-manager of Weymouth.

Relegation, promotion and Johnny Giles

Despite producing some useful performances, especially at home, Albion had a poor 1970–71 season, taking 17th position in the table. They gained only 35 points – eight clear of relegation – and at one stage were among the clubs fighting to avoid the drop.

The Baggies held their own up to Christmas, beating the reigning champions Everton 3–0 and Tottenham 3–1 with a Brown hat-trick, but they crashed 6–2 at double-chasing Arsenal and 4–1 at Manchester City, while in the League Cup they suffered their heaviest defeat in the competition, losing 5–0 at Spurs.

John Wile, who would appear in 500 League games for Albion, arrived in December from Peterborough to replace Talbut, while winger George McVitie was secured from Carlisle and Hartford was engaged on the left wing and Cumbes in goal.

The on-field results disappointed the fans, the only highlight being a 4–3 win over Manchester United, Brown netting another treble. There was no joy in the FA Cup either, Albion losing to Ipswich in the fourth round, and for the second year running the team failed to make an impact in the ill-fated Anglo-Italian Cup. Brown, with 30 goals, was top scorer and his form that season as the only ever present earned him his solitary England cap against Wales at Wembley.

Unfortunately the season turned out to be Alan Ashman's last as Albion's manager, and he was replaced by ex-player Howe in July 1971. Defender Talbut also left the club, signing for KV Mechelen of Belgium after 193 games for the Baggies. With the experienced Howe at the helm, Albion had hoped for far better things out on the pitch, but instead of challenging for honours they were involved in a relegation battle.

After losing in the Final of the Watney Cup on penalties to Colchester, Albion triumphed in their opening two League games but then everything went pear-shaped. Attendances dropped below the 20,000 mark and the goals completely dried up.

At the back Albion looked reasonably sound, with Wile and Robertson starting their long association together following Kaye's move to Hull after 361 games for the club. Hartford, Hope and Cantello were in midfield and Graham Smith (ex-Colchester) was now challenging Osborne for the goalkeeping berth after Cumbes's transfer to Villa Park. Bobby Gould arrived from Molineux to join Astle, Suggett and Brown in attack, but he was never the answer as Howe struggled to get his players motivated.

There were early exits from the two knockout competitions, Albion losing to Spurs in the League Cup and Coventry in the FA Cup, and back in the League important points were won with victories over Liverpool, Ipswich, Manchester United, Leicester and Southampton, but there were some crucial defeats as well. Thankfully, Nottingham Forest and Huddersfield got cut off at the bottom and went down as Albion edged clear to claim 16th position, but it was a close call and the fans weren't too impressed. Brown again top scored with 18 goals and Gould netted 12 – the only two players in double figures. Wile was the only ever present, and in March another Brown, Ally, was signed from Crystal Palace.

In the summer of 1972 Hope was sold to Birmingham after 13 years and 403 appearances for Albion. Another FA Cup winner, Lovett, also departed, joining Worcester City. Everyone at The Hawthorns anticipated a far better season in 1972–73, and nobody expected Albion to be relegated, but down they went, into the Second Division for the first time in 24 years, and in truth they didn't deserve to stay up.

They began miserably and slipped into the bottom group early, and to add to their worries Albion also went out of the League Cup to Liverpool. From early December through to mid-February, despite the introduction of record signing Willie Johnston from Glasgow Rangers for £138,000, they were poor and looked relegation certainties after going out of the FA Cup to Leeds. A Houdini escape act was now required if relegation was to be averted.

Frequent changes were made to the side – David Shaw was signed from Huddersfield, Astle was recalled after being out for 10 months and Allan Glover and Roger Minton were also called into action. It was now a case of 'any two from four' to go down – Albion and Crystal Palace were favourites to miss out, but Norwich and Coventry were also in danger. They produced their worst football at a time when results were imperative and collected only seven points out of a possible 24, and in the end they needed to win at least two of their last four games to have any chance of staying up. They lost them all and finished rock bottom, going down with Palace.

Albion's tally of 28 points was their lowest since the 42-match League programme was introduced in 1919–20, and the 38 goals scored was the lowest total since 1900–01, when they were also demoted.

Playing in the Second Division for the first time since 1949, Albion got off to a sound start, winning their opening two matches – 3–2 at Blackpool and 1–0 at home to Crystal Palace. However, after that they failed to win any of their next 10 League games, slipped out of the League Cup at the hands of Exeter and saw attendances at The Hawthorns drop to under 12,000.

Peter Latchford was now in goal, former 'keeper Nisbet was at right-back with Merrick as his partner (Wilson being out through injury). Wile and Robertson were the two centre-halves, Tony Brown, Cantello, Hartford and Glover were manning midfield between them, while Ally Brown, Shaw and Johnston occupied the forward positions.

Results gradually improved and a 2–0 Boxing Day win over Aston Villa in front of 43,119 fans at The Hawthorns certainly boosted morale. In fact, this was the first time the clubs had ever met each other in the Second Division. But moving into 1974 Albion's form slumped again, although they did knock First Division Everton out of the FA Cup, winning 1–0 in a fourth-round replay after a goalless Sunday afternoon draw at Goodison Park in front of 53,000 fans. Albion, though, went out to Newcastle in the next round.

Back in the League, Albion were hesitant and lacked confidence, and they were perched in eighth position when the curtain came down. It had been a disappointing season, and manager Howe admitted that the players weren't good enough to win promotion. Tony Brown top scored once more with 23 goals, including seven in successive matches against the Nottingham clubs – a hat-trick against County in the FA Cup and four in the League match at Forest. The average League attendance at The Hawthorns was 16,001 – the lowest since 1929–30.

In July 1974 – after 10 glorious years with Albion and a well-deserved testimonial match – Astle bid farewell to the team, joining South African side Hellenic. He scored 174 goals in 361 appearances for Albion. At the club's AGM outgoing chairman 'Jim' Gaunt praised the efforts of the 'King' as he handed over to 'Bert' Millichip, Gaunt becoming Albion's president.

In August 1974 Hartford left Albion for Manchester City for a record fee of £225,000, three years after a proposed move to Leeds had fallen through because the Scottish international was diagnosed with a heart problem. He scored 26 goals in 275 games for the Baggies, and his performances in midfield were sorely missed. Results were poor, and Howe immediately started to ring the changes.

Dave Rushbury replaced Robertson in defence and Osborne was brought back in goal. Things perked up for a while as Albion edged slowly towards the top six, but their inconsistency remained, and after another mediocre spell they finished with a late flourish to claim sixth place – eight points shy of promotion. Albion also suffered early exits from the League Cup (beaten by Norwich) and from the FA Cup (ousted by Carlisle) that season. It was all too much for the hardy supporters, who let their feelings be known – home attendances dropping to 7,812, the lowest for a League match at The Hawthorns since 1957, while the seasonal average of 12,679 was the lowest for 60 years.

Albion's best League win was 4–0 against Sheffield Wednesday, when Ian Edwards scored on his debut. Tony Brown was again leading scorer with 13 goals, and towards the end of the season Bryan Robson was introduced to first-team action at York, six days before manager Howe lost his job. Howe was replaced in June 1975 by the club's first ever player-manager, Johnny Giles. The Republic of Ireland international, formerly of Manchester United, moved to The Hawthorns from Leeds for £45,000, and what an impact he had, both on the players and the supporters.

After a wobbly start, with Giles dominating in midfield, where he was partnered by Mick Martin (signed from Manchester United) and Cantello, Albion's form improved dramatically, and after being next to bottom in October they slowly but surely climbed the ladder.

Giles's international teammate Paddy Mulligan arrived from Crystal Palace to take over at right-back. Former Walsall striker Joe Mayo replaced England's 1966 World Cup hero Geoff Hurst, who had been brought in as a stop-gap from Stoke. With the two Browns, Ally and Tony, Johnston, Robson, centre-backs Wile and Robertson and goalkeeper Osborne also all pulling their weight and playing out of their skin, Albion went on to win promotion after a terrific second half to the season.

In fact, it all went down the last day. Albion HAD to win their final League game at Oldham to regain their First Division status – and, backed by over 15,000 fans, a goal, his 12th of the season, by Tony Brown early in the second half did the trick. That 1–0 victory took the Baggies up with Sunderland (the champions) and Bristol City.

Osborne and Robertson were both ever present, and Osborne set a new club record by keeping 22 clean-sheets in the League, conceding only 33 goals. Albion entered but failed to perform in the Anglo-Scottish Cup that season, but the youngsters did well and won the FA Youth Cup, beating Wolves 5–0 on aggregate in the Final with a team that included Derek Statham, Wayne Hughes, Steve Lynex and Kevin Summerfield.

Enter Atkinson, Cunningham and Regis

During the scorching hot summer of 1976 Giles dropped a bombshell and quit as manager – but after some serious talking he was persuaded to stay on for another season. Albion's first match back in the top flight took them to Giles's old hunting ground at Elland Road, and in front of a 40,248 crowd the Baggies earned a 2–2 draw, Leeds equalising in the last minute.

Albion were determined to make an impression in Division One, and although they lost a League Cup tie to Brighton, when Johnston was sent off for aiming a kick at the referee, they produced some splendid football, especially in October when, inspired by Johnston, they came back from 2–0 down to beat Spurs 4–2, thrashed Manchester United 4–0 and clipped West Ham 3–0, all at home.

Shrugging off a nightmare performance at Ipswich, where they lost 7–0, Albion bounced back and continued to play some delightful football, comfortably holding their own. Giles brought Ray Treacy back to The Hawthorns to replace Ally Brown in attack and signed David Cross from West Ham to take over from Mayo. With a new team plan, coupled with new faces, the results improved even more, and from mid-February to early April only one defeat was suffered in 11 League outings – this despite going out of the FA Cup to Manchester City. Albion also gained revenge over Ipswich, winning 4–1 with a Bryan Robson hat-trick. Leicester were slammed 5–0 at Filbert Street and Everton were defeated 3–0 as Albion went on to finish a respectable seventh, 12 points behind the champions Liverpool.

Tony Godden took over in goal after Osborne had been injured at Highbury, and a dynamic new forward arrived on the scene – Laurie Cunningham – signed from Leyton Orient for £110,000. He and Godden made impressive debuts together in a 2–0 win at Tottenham, but Albion's season ended disappointingly with a 4–0 defeat at Villa Park – Giles's last game in charge. Cross top scored with 12 goals, rock solid centre-backs Robertson and Wile were both ever present, and 41,867 fans saw the 1–1 draw with Aston Villa, the first game between the clubs in the top flight since November 1966.

In June 1977 former Baggies favourite Ronnie Allen returned to The Hawthorns as Albion's manager in place of Giles, and within a month or so he watched his new charges beat Glasgow Rangers in the Final of the Tennent-Caledonian Cup at Ibrox Park. Soon after, the League programme got underway, and Allen signed Cyrille Regis from non-League Hayes, paying £5,000 from his own bank account to bring the strapping centre-forward to The Hawthorns. And it wasn't long before the 19-year-old from French Guyana was hitting the headlines after scoring on his senior debut in a 4–0 League Cup win over Rotherham and then following up with a cracking goal on his League bow against Middlesbrough.

Although they lost to Bury at a foggy Gigg Lane in the League Cup, Albion produced some exciting League form and ran up some impressive wins – 3–0 at Newcastle, 3–1 against Birmingham and 4–0 over Manchester United (again). With Regis, Cunningham, Tony Brown, Robson, Cantello and Johnston all attack-minded, Albion were a potent force, but as 1977 ended, so too did Ronnie Allen's reign as manager; he accepted a lucrative offer to coach in Saudi Arabia. Into his place stepped the former Oxford player Ron Atkinson from Cambridge United – and immediately Albion were on TV receiving worldwide coverage and the team was going places.

Regis scored in the FA Cup tie versus Blackpool, and, after seeing off Manchester United 3–2 in a splendid Hawthorns replay and winning at Derby, Albion then ended Nottingham Forest's long unbeaten run with a 2–0 quarter-final victory at home. The crowds were now flocking to The Hawthorns – almost 37,800 fans saw that Manchester United Cup replay and 36,500 witnessed the Forest tie. Also that season, right-back Brendon Batson arrived from the boss's old club to partner Statham and Ally Brown was brought back in place of Cross.

Wembley's twin towers were beckoning – but, alas, it was not to be. Albion failed to rise to the occasion at Highbury and were beaten 3–1 by Ipswich in the semi-final. And besides losing the match, they also lost skipper Wile, who went off with a nasty head wound suffered when future Albion star Brian Talbot put Town in front, and Martin was sent off. It was disappointment all round, but Albion battled on in the League and finished sixth to qualify for the UEFA Cup, capping a very good season overall. And the future was certainly looking rosy!

Cantello left the club at the end of the campaign, transferring to Bolton for £400,000 having appeared in 369 games for Albion. Goalkeeper Osborne also departed after 11 years and 312 appearances.

In May 1978 Albion made an historic trip to China and Hong Kong, winning all five matches, each attracting capacity crowds, with 89,400 watching the 2–0 victory over the Chinese national team 2–0 in Peking. Also that year, Argentina staged the World Cup Finals, and Albion's Johnston was in the Scottish party, but he was sent home in disgrace after using drugs.

Manager Atkinson, the players, the chairman (Bert Millichip) and scores of supporters believed that 1978–79 would be Albion's season. The team produced some cracking performances, especially in the League, FA Cup and UEFA Cup, but at the end of the day there was sadly no silverware on display in the trophy room.

Fielding mostly an unchanged line-up from August through to mid-January, Albion were as good as, if not better, than any team in the Division and produced some terrific wins, including those of 4–0 vesus Bolton, 3–1 at Chelsea, 3–1 at Leeds (when Tony Brown broke Allen's club scoring record), 7–1 against Coventry, 3–0 at Wolves, a magnificent 5–3 victory over Manchester United at Old Trafford (when both Cantello and Regis scored stunning goals) and a 3–1 New Year's Day win over Bristol City on a snow-covered Hawthorns pitch.

After that, however, the bad weather set in, severely disrupting Albion's rhythm. At the time the Baggies were challenging for the title with Liverpool and Nottingham Forest. But only one more game was played in January – a 1–1 draw at Norwich, which took Albion to the top of the table – and when play resumed again two vital matches were lost in succession – at Liverpool (where David Mills, a record £516,000 signing from Middlesbrough, made his debut) and at home to Leeds. After that Albion never got in another worthwhile challenge, and although they still registered some fine wins – 4–0 against Manchester City and 2–0 at Everton among them – it was Liverpool who took the title ahead of Forest, with Albion third – their best League placing since 1954.

In the three major knockout competitions, Albion went out of the League Cup to Leeds early on, lost in the fifth round of the FA Cup in a replay at Southampton and their first taste of UEFA Cup football saw them reach the last eight before losing to Red Star Belgrade 2–1 on aggregate, after Galatasaray (Turkey), Sporting Braga (Portugal) and Valencia (Spain) had been ousted in the earlier rounds.

Ally Brown took over as leading scorer this term with 24 goals and a young defender, Martyn Bennett, was introduced to League action against Everton. Transfer activity at the end of the season and before the start of 1979–80 saw Albion sign midfielder Gary Owen and winger Peter Barnes from Manchester City for fees of £465,000 and £748,000 respectively. They arrived after Cunningham had joined Real Madrid for a record fee of £995,000 and Johnson, after seven years at The Hawthorns, switched to Vancouver Whitecaps for £100,000. Striker John Deehan was added to the squad, bought from Aston Villa for £424,000 – the first player to move from Villa Park to The Hawthorns for 70 years – George Harris being the last in 1909 – and experienced defender Garry Pendrey arrived from St Andrew's soon after playing against Albion in his testimonial match. Mulligan teamed up with his former boss Johnny Giles at Shamrock Rovers.

Albion began 1979–80, which was billed as their 'Centenary Season', disappointingly but recovered well to finish 10th. They drew 19 of their 42 matches, eight in the last 10, five goalless. In fact, if half of those draws had been converted into victories then the Baggies would have probably won the title. They failed to make progress in any of the Cup competitions, losing to Norwich in the League Cup,

Albion's centenary match versus Ajax in 1979.

West Ham in the FA Cup, when Tony Brown scored his last goal for the club, and to East German side Carl Zeiss Jena in the UEFA Cup.

New signing Barnes was top marksman with 15 goals, including a hat-trick in a 4–4 draw with Bolton.

After 20 years as club secretary, long-serving employee Alan Everiss JP was replaced by Tony Rance. As a shareholder, he remained in contact with the club and in 1981 became a director.

The good, the bad and the ugly 80s!

After an uneasy start, Albion had a far better 1980–81 than expected, finishing fourth, although they didn't do at all well in Cup competitions. In the summer of 1981 manager Atkinson stunned the club, and the fans, by quitting to takeover as boss of Manchester United. He was replaced by Ronnie Allen, who returned for a second spell in the hot seat. Players Barnes and Trewick also departed, joining Leeds for £930,000 and Newcastle for £244,000 respectively.

From Albion's point of view, 1981–82 was a very frustrating and certainly disappointing season. They were defeated in two Cup semi-finals – 1–0 by Spurs over two legs in the League Cup and 1–0 by QPR in the FA Cup – and they had to fight for their lives to avoid relegation. They also slipped out of the UEFA Cup in the first round to Zurich Grasshoppers and two of the club's finest post-war players, Robson and Brown, departed. Robson joined Atkinson at Old Trafford for a record £1.5m (Moses, valued at £500,000, followed him to Old Trafford), while Brown signed for Torquay after scoring 279 goals in 720 appearances in 20 years at The Hawthorns.

Manager Allen made numerous signings and team changes as he strove to get the balance of the side right – and not all were to the fans' liking. Midfielder Steve Mackenzie arrived from Manchester City for £650,000, Andy King was recruited from Everton, Dutchmen Maarten Jol and Romeo Zondervan transferred from Twente Enschede, Clive Whitehead was bought from Bristol City and a handful of former youth stars also made their first-team debuts. Their League form was mediocre, and they finished 17th, only escaping relegation with a last match home win over demoted Leeds. This game was marred by crowd trouble as visiting fans smashed through the retaining wall behind the Smethwick End goal and threatened to disrupt the game – even cause it to be abandoned.

In July 1982 Albion moved manager Allen 'upstairs' and replaced him with Ron Wylie, the former Aston Villa and Birmingham player. And one of his first signings was Peter Eastoe from Everton (in exchange for King), and the ex-Wolves striker scored on his home debut against Brighton (won 5–0).

Initially things went along smoothly for Wylie, and despite a heavy League Cup defeat by Nottingham Forest Albion slipped smartly into the top three. However, it all went wrong after Batson was injured in a 6–1 thumping at Ipswich.

Only two more victories were gained in the next 12 matches, and despite the signings of Crystal Palace goalkeeper Paul Barton and Coventry's striker Garry Thompson, plus a heavy FA Cup defeat at Tottenham, their League form deteriorated and 11th place was the final outcome...but it should have been better.

In 1983 Ally Brown moved to Crystal Palace after scoring 85 goals in 359 appearances, Mills joined Sheffield Wednesday for a cut-down price, Grew signed for Leicester and centre-half Wile – after almost 13 years with Albion – returned to Peterborough as player-manager. He made 715 first-team appearances for the Baggies (500 in the League), skippered the team in three Cup semi-finals and was a superb ambassador when Albion toured China in 1978. He later returned to the club as chief executive. At the club's AGM Bert Millichip handed over the position of Albion chairman to Sid Lucas, Millichip assuming the role of president.

Prior to the start of 1983–84, manager Wylie went back to his old club Aston Villa to sign centre-half Ken McNaught, who made his debut, ironically, at Villa Park in a 4–3 defeat. A six-match unbeaten run pushed Albion up the table, but they failed to maintain their form, and after a League Cup defeat by Aston Villa Wylie lost his job in mid-December, replaced by ex-boss Giles, who brought with him coaches 'Nobby' Stiles and Norman Hunter.

Unfortunately Giles found it tough as Albion continued to lose matches, and after losing to Third Division Plymouth in the FA Cup midfielders Steve Hunt (Coventry) and Tony Grealish (Brighton) were signed in an effort to improve performances. With the former Aston Villa and England winger Tony Morley in good form, they clawed their way clear of trouble and finished 17th, but it had been a tough season all round, not helped by chronic injury problems.

In the summer of 1984 commercial manager Gordon Dimbleby stepped up to replace Tony Rance as Albion's secretary, while four players departed: Romeo Zondervan to Ipswich, Maarten Jol to Coventry and Alan Webb and Derek Monaghan to Port Vale.

The 1984–85 season turned out to be another poor one for Albion, who managed 12th position in the First Division after a horrible second half to their League programme, having lost to Watford in the League Cup and Third Division Orient in the FA Cup. And, to top it all, in October Regis moved to Coventry for £300,000 after scoring 141 goals in 371 appearances. The only bright spot of the

West Bromwich Albion, 1985–86.

campaign was a 5–1 win over West Ham in early May, and the fans certainly vented their annoyance by staying away – Albion's average home League crowd of 13,958 was their lowest in the top flight for 70 years.

Regulars in the side now were Godden; Whitehead, Statham; Hunt, Bennett, Robertson; Grealish, Thompson, Nicky Cross, Mackenzie and Morley, and they were joined by David Cross (back for a second spell), winger Carl Valentine from Vancouver Whitecaps, the former Manchester United, Sunderland, Rangers and Northern Ireland full-back Jimmy Nicholl from Toronto Blizzard and ex-Wolves goalkeeper Paul Bradshaw, also from Vancouver. Ken McNaught (Sheffield United), Mickey Lewis (Derby), Wayne Ebanks (Port Vale), Tony Morley (Seiko, Hong Kong), David Cross (Bolton) and Paul Barron (QPR) all found new clubs during the course of the season.

Without any doubt, 1985–86 was a horror season for Albion – especially at The Hawthorns. Some supporters never even saw them win a match, while thousands more were so disgruntled after the first two months of the campaign that they either threw away their season tickets or decided to stay at home instead, resulting in the average attendance falling to just 12,194, with only 6,021 hardy souls watching the game against Sheffield Wednesday in April – the lowest since April 1939. Giles resigned as manager in September, replaced in the hot seat by Stiles, who then handed over the reins to ex-Aston Villa and Blues boss Ron Saunders in February when relegation was already a certainty. And in the end Albion went down with a terrible record and many club records to go with it:

- Fewest wins (four)
- Record number of defeats (26)
- Fewest away wins (one)
- Fewest home wins (3)
- Most home defeats (10 from 21 games played), equalling the 1950–51 record
- Lowest number of home points gained (17)
- Fewest number of home goals scored (21)
- Lowest number of points gained (24 – from 42 games)
- Nine consecutive League games lost (20 August–28 September 1985)
- Most players used in a season (34)
- Most home goals conceded in the First Division (36)
- Most away goals conceded in the First Division (53), equalled by Oxford United
- Lowest home League crowd since World War Two (6,021)
- Five goalkeepers used in a season
- Nine teenage players given their club debuts
- Albion were bottom of the League from the third match until the last
- Albion had three managers during the season
- And, to cap it all, Albion's second XI suffered relegation as well

Throughout the season players shuffled in and out of The Hawthorns. At the start Garth Crooks (ex-Stoke and Tottenham) and Imre Varadi (formerly of Sheffield Wednesday, Newcastle and Everton) started up front following the departure of Thompson to Sheffield Wednesday. Lanky George Reilly arrived from Newcastle and late on Craig Madden was signed from Bury. Steve Bull was also called up, along with Gerry Armstrong, ex-Spurs, Watford and Real Mallorca, and Robbie Dennison from Glenavon. In midfield Welsh international Mickey Thomas arrived from Chelsea, Martin Dickinson

Goalmouth action at The Hawthorns, 1988.

from Leeds and Darren Bradley from Aston Villa, while Paul Dyson (ex-Stoke) partnered long-serving Ally Robertson in defence. Colin Anderson, once of Torquay, had a few games at left-back, Stuart Naylor, a £100,000 buy from Lincoln City, took over in goal and four youngsters, David Burrows, Carlton Palmer, Mark Robinson and Andy Thompson, were all handed senior debuts.

Playing in the Second Division for the first time in 11 years, and with two new strikers in the side – Stewart Evans (from Wimbledon) and Bobby Williamson (from Rangers) – Albion started 1986–87 moderately, losing in the League Cup 5–1 on aggregate to Derby. To boost his squad, Saunders swapped Imre Varadi for Manchester City's Robert Hopkins, and as Christmas approached Albion were in mid-table, not too far off the leading group, but a disastrous run either side of the New Year, including a humiliating 3–2 FA Cup defeat at Swansea, knocked them back considerably.

The double-signing of former Albion youngster Steve Lynex from Leicester and striker Don Goodman from Bradford City boosted the team and relegation was averted, Albion claiming 15th position, just three points clear of the drop zone. Also, as a result of poor performances, for the first time since 1905–06 the average League attendance at The Hawthorns dropped below 10,000 to 9,280.

Several players left The Hawthorns in 1986–87, among them Bull, Dennison, Robertson, after making 729 appearances for Albion, and Andy Thompson, all to Wolves; Madden to Blackpool; Whitehead to Portsmouth; Grealish to Manchester City; Crooks and Mackenzie to Charlton and Evans to Plymouth.

Another disastrous season for Albion followed in 1987–88. The team finished in their lowest ever League position – 20th in Division Two – just one point clear of relegation. Saunders was in charge for the first month of the campaign but was then replaced by Atkinson, who became the third manager to return for a second spell at The Hawthorns. With coach Colin Addison, he set about refloating a sinking ship with confidence, but the players simply weren't good enough and the results were awful.

There was another swift influx of players with Scottish international Andy Gray from Aston Villa; Stewart Phillips from Hereford; Tony Morley, for a second time, from Den Haag; Tony Kelly and Brian Talbot from Stoke; Simeon Hodson from Newport; Graeme Hogg and Kenny Swain on loan from Manchester United and Portsmouth respectively; Stacey North from Luton and goalkeeper Peter Hucker on loan from Oxford all coming in. Bennett and Dyson were long-term injury casualties and, having to contend with suspensions, Atkinson was never able to field a settled side. However, The Hawthorns faithful stood by their team (the poorest for years) and the average gate rose by 800 as Albion struggled to get back on track. One consolation was that the reserves gained promotion from the Central League Division Two and won the Birmingham Senior Cup for the first time since 1895.

In August 1988 Sid Lucas was replaced as chairman by John Silk, while Gordon Bennett was made secretary. Three newcomers to the playing squad – left-back Arthur Albiston (from Manchester United), centre-half Chris Whyte (ex-Crystal Palace and Arsenal) and South African striker John Paskin – all figured in Albion's first team during the early stages of 1988–89, and after an excellent first half to their League programme Albion topped the table on 2 January after a 4–0 home win over Shrewsbury.

Under the managership of Talbot, following Atkinson's departure to Spain, Albion looked like promotion material, but it all went wrong after an FA Cup exit at Everton and injuries to Anderson and Goodman. Sheffield Wednesday's Colin West was brought in to replace the latter (exchanged for Palmer), Tony Ford was recruited from Stoke, Kevin Bartlett from Cardiff and Ian Banks from Bradford City, while Doncaster's Paul Raven arrived after David Burrows had joined Liverpool for £500,000.

The second half of the season realised just 28 points as Albion settled in ninth position, three places short of the Play-offs. They drew far too many matches (a club record 18), and they didn't score enough goals, only 55 in the League.

Just before the season ended, Dr John Evans, a keen supporter, was appointed secretary in succession to Gordon Bennett, and among the season's departures on the playing side were Albiston to Dundee, Banks to Barnsley, Paskin to Wolves, Robinson to Rotherham, Gray to Rangers, Phillips to Swansea, Morley to Tampa Bay Rowdies, Hopkins to Birmingham, Kelly to Shrewsbury and Dyson to Darlington.

The 1989–90 season turned out to be yet another poor one for Albion, who finished 20th in Division Two, equalling their lowest ever League position, and for the second time in three years they just squeezed out of relegation trouble. A disastrous home record was perhaps responsible for their poor campaign, Albion winning only six times at The Hawthorns, and over 30 players were used in senior competitions that season, including four goalkeepers, five different right-backs, five central-defenders and left-wingers! No fewer than 20 players received treatment, three suffering broken legs. But in truth it was inconsistency that was the key to Albion's failure out on the pitch, and in the end 12 points taken off Bradford City, Watford, Hull and Brighton late in the season lifted the Baggies to safety – but it was mighty close.

The best win was 7–0 over Barnsley – Bennett's last game for Albion, for whom he made over 200 outings. Manager Talbot also quit as a player after more than 21 years in the game. Newcomers in the Baggies camp included John Thomas from Bolton; Gary Hackett and Steve Parkin, both from Stoke; Bernard McNally from Shrewsbury; Mark Barham from Middlesbrough; Craig Shakespeare from

Sheffield Wednesday; Graham Harbey from Ipswich and Gary Bannister from Coventry, and from the youngsters emerged Daryl Burgess and Adrian Foster. Among those who left were Chris Whyte, who went to Leeds, Kevin Bartlett to Notts County and Paul Bradshaw to Peterborough.

Third Division football, Ossie Ardiles, Play-off glory

At 4.44pm on Saturday 11 May 1991 Albion were relegated to the Third Division for the first time in the club's history after what was their worst ever season of League football, even surpassing that dreadful 1985–86 campaign. A dejected chairman, John Silk, admitted 'It is a "black day" for all Albion supporters,' but vowed 'We'll be back.'

Albion ended their League programme with a nine-match unbeaten run (seven draws) and still went down. One extra win would have kept them up. They were awful at times and crashed out of the FA Cup to non-League side Woking 4–2 at The Hawthorns – a humiliation that led to the immediate departure of manager Talbot, coach Stuart Pearson taking charge for six games before ex-player Bobby Gould moved into the hot seat. Almost immediately, Gould – not a popular choice with the fans – came under pressure as Albion suffered six straight defeats, which plunged them into trouble.

On transfer deadline, in an effort to avoid the drop, Gould splashed out £250,000 on striker Paul Williams from Stockport, £35,000 on Winston White from Burnley and took Kwame Ampadu on loan from Arsenal. Nothing changed. Albion collected only 13 points out of the last 27 and in the end equalled the club record of 18 draws. They even missed two penalties in the home draw with Port Vale.

Albion travelled to Twerton Park for the last game of the season knowing that they had to beat Bristol Rovers to stay up. Disappointingly, they could only manage a 1–1 draw after playing against 10 men from as early as the third minute…and so, after 3,634 First and Second Division matches, Albion descended ignominiously into the Third Division. Conceding late goals proved costly and at the end of the day Albion got what they deserved. There was some consolation when the second XI won the Pontins League Division Two title and also the Birmingham Cup.

Three new players were recruited in 1990–91: Graham Roberts (£200,000 from Chelsea), goalkeeper Mel Rees (from Watford) and Gary Strodder (£190,000 from West Ham). Out went North (to Fulham), Anderson (to Walsall) and Dobbins (to Torquay).

At the end of the season Sid Lucas resigned from the Board to be replaced by Clive Stapleton, and President Bert Millichip was knighted for services to football.

Playing in the Third Division, season 1991–92 for Albion was one of the most turbulent in the club's history, and it ended in sheer frustration and total disappointment as the team missed out on the Play-offs, finishing seventh in the table, their lowest-ever League position. Eliminated early from the League Cup by Swindon, not only did Albion's League form suffer, but they also went out of the FA Cup to Leyton Orient and were beaten at home by Exeter in the Autoglass Trophy. Manager Gould had hoped to win promotion by using the same squad of players who had been relegated the year before. Domineering his staff, he introduced maverick ideas which worked initially, Albion going top of the table in February after an emphatic 3–0 win at Birmingham, but there followed a shattering demise which left the fans calling for the heads of the manager and the entire board.

A total of 34 players were used by Gould. The defence looked solid enough but the midfield struggled to a certain extent, certainly over the last three months, and scoring goals was difficult. The selling of Goodman to Sunderland for £1m (eventually replacing him with Bob Taylor, a £350,000 buy from Bristol City in February) was a body blow, and the team simply disintegrated under the pressure, results were disastrous, and when Gould sacked his coach Pearson there was uproar among the fans. Things went from bad to worse after that, and soon after the season ended Gould was dismissed, chairman Silk resigned (replaced by Trevor Summers) and the Argentinian World Cup winner Ossie Ardiles moved in as Albion's new manager.

Newcomers included Wayne Fereday from Bournemouth, loan signings Alan Miller from Arsenal, Frank Sinclair from Chelsea, Andy Dibble from Manchester City and youngsters Carl Heggs and Roy Hunter. Rees (to Sheffield United), West (Swansea), Ford (Grimsby), Harbey (Stoke), Bannister (Nottingham Forest), Foster (Torquay), Roberts (Enfield) and Parkin (Mansfield) were among the departures.

Season 1992–93 turned out to be a memorable one for Albion, who won at Wembley on their first visit to the Stadium in 23 years. The players responded magnificently to the guidance of Ardiles and his assistant Keith Burkinshaw. There was an air of anticipation and optimism right from the outset, and despite an early exit from the League Cup Albion prospered in the League and hit the top spot after beating Huddersfield in the second match. They held pole position until mid-October, but a couple of indifferent results saw them slip down to third before they regained the top slot again at the end of that month.

At this juncture, Taylor was scoring at will, being ably assisted by Kevin Donovan (bought from Huddersfield) and Simon Garner, ex-Blackburn. Goalkeeper Naylor, left-back Steve Lilwall (who a few months earlier had been playing for Kidderminster Harriers), centre-halves Raven and Strodder and midfielders Bradley, McNally and Hamilton (ex-Scunthorpe) were all doing the business in a workmanlike side as Albion powered on.

Aylesbury (8–0) and Wycombe Wanderers were beaten in the FA Cup, and when 1993 arrived Albion were in with a great chance of winning automatic promotion, but a poor spell, which included defeat in the FA Cup against West Ham, saw the team slip down to fourth place in the table. Enter striker Andy Hunt, signed from Newcastle to partner Taylor in attack. He struck a hat-trick on his home debut in a 5–0 win over Brighton and claimed nine goals in the last 10 League games as the Baggies finished fourth in the table, missing automatic promotion by just five points.

Paired with Swansea in the two-leg Play-off semi-final, Albion lost 2–1 at Vetch Field, but goals by Hunt and Hamilton in a tension-packed second leg took Albion through to Wembley, where they met and beat Port Vale 3–0 to the delight of more than 42,000 travelling supporters. Admittedly, Vale had Peter Swan sent off when the game was goalless, but Albion always looked the more likely winners, and so it proved. Hunt, man of the match, former Manchester City and Blackburn star Nicky Reid (with his first and only goal for Albion) and Donovan were the goalscorers. It was celebrations all round for Ardiles and co. Taylor ended the season with 37 goals, only four short of breaking 'W.G.' Richardson's club record of 40 in 1935–36. Tony Lange (from Wolves) and Micky Mellon (ex-Bristol City) also helped Albion gain promotion, along with Gary Robson, who moved to Bradford City in the summer. Also on the move were Williams (to Stockport County), Hodson (Doncaster) and Shakespeare (Grimsby).

Albion began 1993–94 without Ardiles. He quit The Hawthorns, to the disappointment of the board, players and, indeed, the fans, to take charge of his former club Tottenham. Keith Burkinshaw was promoted to the manager's chair and had a difficult and, at times, very tense first season as Albion, attempting to consolidate themselves in the First Division, scrambled to safety on the very last day of the campaign thanks to a nail-biting 1–0 victory at Portsmouth, Lee Ashcroft's header doing the trick, much to the relief of the 10,000 travelling Baggies supporters. Anything other than a win would have sent the Baggies straight back down from where they had just escaped.

Albion played well for the first 10 weeks, rising to fourth in the table, but by mid-October they were in among the strugglers, and although they picked up around Christmas, moving up to 16th, thereafter it was a real battle for survival. Injuries and suspensions were frequent and only occasionally was the manager able to field an unchanged side. Nevertheless, certain players performed well below par for far too long, and although Taylor and Hunt netted 30 League goals between them Albion's overall scoring record let them down badly, especially away from home. They made an inglorious exit from the FA Cup, losing 2–1 at non-League Halifax, a truly dreadful result.

Thirty players were called into action, including newcomers Neil Parsley and Kieran O'Regan from Huddersfield; Ashcroft from Preston, for £225,000; Paul Mardon and David Smith from Birmingham and left-back Paul Edwards from Wolves. Two loan players, Graham Fenton (Aston Villa) and Paul Williams (Coventry), added some impetus to the side, but despite pleas from the fans Albion failed to secure the transfer of the former on a permanent basis. Five players who left The Hawthorns in 1993–94 were Fereday to Cardiff, Hackett to Peterborough, Garner and Reid to Wycombe and Ampadu to Swansea. Trevor Summers relinquished his position as chairman, handing over to Tony Hale.

Albion were involved in a battle to stave off relegation in 1994–95 yet again, and once more they just managed to retain their First Division status, avoiding the drop with two games remaining. Due to massive redevelopment work at The Hawthorns, Albion played their first five League matches away, drawing two and losing three, and quickly found themselves at the foot of the table. They slowly improved but were always lingering too near the trapdoor for comfort. Inconsistency was their main

West Bromwich Albion, 1994–95.

problem, and if it hadn't been for their reasonable home form – 13 wins gained – they would have gone down.

In late October – after Albion had suffered the humiliation of losing to Third Division Hereford in the League Cup – Burkinshaw was replaced as manager by Alan Buckley, who came down from Grimsby where he had been an outstanding success. He was accompanied by his assistant Arthur Mann, who played for Manchester City against Albion in the 1970 League Cup Final. From a position of 23rd in the table, he quickly turned things round, and within three months Albion had risen to 16th, but after losing to Coventry in the FA Cup Albion's League form began to wane, and they slipped back down to 19th in early March, before edging clear of danger after winning six and drawing two of their last 12 matches.

Again, injuries and suspensions played their part in a difficult season. Thankfully, Albion were well covered in defence and attack, but it was in midfield where they struggled. Mike Phelan, a much heralded close-season signing from Manchester United, rarely lived up to his large signing-on fee, and the left-back position was also a problem until Buckley signed Paul Agnew from his old club Grimsby. He also brought in Tony Rees as an extra attacker. Several players of first-team pedigree left The Hawthorns during and at the end of the season: Lange to Fulham, Hunter to Northampton, McNally to Hednesford, Bradley to Walsall, Parsley to Exeter, Lilwall to Rushden & Diamonds, Darton and Mellon to Blackpool, Heggs to Swansea and Strodder to Notts County.

The following season, 1995–96, turned out to be quite an extraordinary one for Albion. Not many clubs can say they held second and 23rd places in the same Division in the same campaign and were also one step from a Wembley Final....but that's precisely what happened this term.

Albion started off brightly with new signing Dave Gilbert from Grimsby and strikers Taylor and Hunt and defenders Mardon and Raven in fine form, and come the end of October, with 13 games played but out of the League Cup, they travelled to Millwall knowing that victory would take them to the top. They lost 2–1, and this reverse set the Baggies on an astonishing run of 11 successive League defeats, with only one win coming in 15 games overall as they slipped to second from bottom.

Manager Buckley refused to panic, and despite an FA Cup defeat at Crewe, Albion slowly but surely got themselves back on track, although they did miss out on a trip to Wembley by losing to Port Vale in the area Final of the Anglo-Italian Cup. Into the camp came veteran goalkeeper Nigel Spink (from Aston Villa), full-backs Paul Holmes (from Everton) and Shane Nicholson (from Derby), on-loan midfielder Peter Butler (from Notts County) and Dutchman Richard Sneekes (who cost £400,000 from Bolton). With Sneekes in excellent goalscoring form (he netted 10 times in the last 13 matches), Albion eased themselves up to a creditable 11th spot in the table, gaining 24 points from a possible 39 during the last third of the campaign.

Taylor, who skippered the side during the second half of the season, netted his first Albion hat-trick in a 4–4 draw with Watford, and he also netted his 100th goal for the club in the final League game against Derby. Naylor left The Hawthorns for Bristol City after more than 400 appearances in goal, Rees went to Merthyr Tydfil, Edwards joined Hednesford and Phelan signed for Norwich.

Unfortunately 1996–97 was yet another very ordinary season for Albion, who finished a moderate 16th in the First Division and went out of both knockout competitions early on, losing to Third Division minnows Colchester in the League Cup and to Chelsea in the FA Cup. Expectations had been high when the League programme kicked off, especially after that splendid late surge of goals from Sneekes at the end of the previous campaign. But, alas, Albion started off disappointingly and never recovered – and the fans soon started to show their disgust, moreso after rivals Wolves won 4–2 at The Hawthorns. Appearances by Paul Peschisolido (a £600,000 buy from Birmingham City) were restricted because of international calls from Canada; fellow striker Taylor was never fully fit; defender Mardon was sidelined through injury; ex-Grimsby 'keeper Paul Crichton never endeared himself to the fans, while midfielder Peter Butler missed the first four months of the season after injuring his knee in a pre-season friendly against Coventry.

Manager Buckley switched his team around as best he could in an effort to find a winning formula, but generally Albion were unimpressive, failing to maintain any sort of consistency, except for a brief unbeaten period approaching Christmas. So, Buckley lost his job early in the New Year, replaced by the former Blackburn boss Ray Harford, who brought with him ex-Baggies favourite Cyrille Regis as coach, accompanied by John Trewick. At this juncture (February) Albion were in trouble, but, thanks to the poor form of the teams below them, they survived and finished 13 points clear of the trapdoor.

Other new faces at The Hawthorns that season were Aussie right-back Andy McDermott (secured from QPR for £400,000), midfielders Paul Groves (from Grimsby for £600,000) and Graham Potter (from Southampton), goalkeeper Alan Miller (£400,000 from Middlesbrough, who had been on loan at Albion in 1991) and Shaun Murphy (from Notts County). Those who left included Ashcroft (to Preston) along with Agnew, Cunnington, Donovan, Darby, Groves and Joseph.

Shortly before Christmas 1996, plans to float Albion shares on the Alternative Investment Market were passed by an overwhelming vote of shareholders, and when the shares were launched the following month Albion was valued at £7.5m.

In March 1997 former captain John Wile was appointed Albion's first-ever chief executive, and he subsequently joined the board of directors. Two months later Albion announced a new sponsorship deal with the West Bromwich Building Society worth more than £800,000 over a three-year period.

For Albion the 1997–98 season was one of two completely different halves. From August to December, under manager Harford, they were up with the leaders, but following Harford's sudden 'transfer' to QPR and the arrival of new boss Denis Smith from Oxford, their fortunes dipped and the team slipped agonisingly down the table and out of the promotion race, eventually finishing a moderate 10th.

Albion topped the table early in September and were hardly out of the top four until Christmas. They reached the third round of the League Cup before Christmas, but once into the New Year their form went pear-shaped. Confidence drained away, and although they managed to keep in touch with the promotion contenders until mid-February they never looked Play-off material. And so it proved. Albion scrambled a series of home wins to keep them in the top bracket, but their away form was very poor – crashing out of the FA Cup 4–0 to Aston Villa and losing 5–0 at Charlton in the League. One consolation was that they won at Molineux and so completed the double over Wolves, both games finishing 1–0. Injuries didn't help matters either, and during the season 34 players were called into action by the two managers.

On the bright side, a £250,000 signing from Kidderminster Harriers, Lee Hughes, did exceedingly well in his first season of League football, finishing joint top scorer with Hunt on 14 goals. Matt Carbon and Sean Flynn, both signed from Derby County, battled long and hard in defence and midfield; Northern Ireland international James Quinn, a £500,000 buy from Blackpool, did well as an attacking midfielder and record signing Kevin Kilbane, who cost £1.25m from Preston, played in 50 of Albion's 53 first-team matches. Others who tasted first-team football were Mickey Evans, who arrived from Southampton, and loanees James Thomas (Blackburn), Paul Beesley (Manchester City) and ex-Liverpool star Steve Nicol (Sheffield Wednesday), winger Franz Carr and Australian international Jason van Blerk (Manchester City).

Unfortunately, this was to be the last time strikers Hunt and Taylor played together for Albion. Hunt moved to Charlton, while Taylor signed for Bolton, where he had been on loan since January. Between them they netted almost 200 goals for Albion in just over 520 appearances (Taylor scoring 113 times). Other players who left the club were Hamilton to Sheffield United, Peschisolido to Fulham for £1 million, Spink to Millwall and Coldicott and Smith to Grimsby. Gilbert, Nicholson and Butler also moved on, Nicholson later teaming up with Chesterfield.

One has to say that Albion began the 1998–99 season with promotion ambitions – the bookies, pricing them at 16–1 to finish in the top six. Manager Smith strengthened his squad by signing Mark Angel (from Sunderland) and the Italian midfield duo of Mario Bortolazzi (from Genoa) and teenager Enzo Maresca (from Cagliari), and he also upgraded talented youngster Adam Oliver.

Despite an early League Cup exit, Albion moved into third place in the table, and with Hughes in good form, having struck a hat-trick against Port Vale, they looked to be a useful side. However, Evans got injured and was replaced by former Bolton star Fabien DeFreitas, signed from Osasuna. As a result, Albion lost their way and slipped down to 11th, becoming something of a hit and miss team, although they did beat Wolves 2–0 in their home local derby, which was goalkeeper Miller's last appearance of the season before being replaced by £250,000 signing from Oxford Phil Whitehead.

After an embarrassing FA Cup defeat by Second Division Bournemouth, Albion were in ninth place, yet with Hughes still scoring well and heading towards the 30-goal mark, a place in the Play-offs was still in their sights. Sadly though the roof fell in during February and March, and Albion hit rock bottom on Easter Monday when they crashed 5–1 at home to bottom-of-the-table Crewe – their fifth League defeat on the trot. There were some ugly scenes after the final whistle of this encounter as irate and disgruntled fans demanded that both the manager and the board should resign. But Smith stuck in there, as did the chairman and directors, to see the season through.

Into the 21st century and Premiership football

The last season of the 20th century (1999–2000) was another that involved a relegation battle – and thanks to a draw and a win in the last two matches Albion escaped the drop by three points. But apart from the on-field activities, behind the scenes the club was hit by a spate of in-fighting, back-stabbing and utter incompetence, and they saw three different managers in office as well.

At the summer's AGM there was a failed bid to oust chairman Tony Hale who, soon afterwards, appointed three new directors, who were soon to depart. After being guaranteed his job and promised £2.6m to spend on new players, manager Smith was sacked just before the League programme got underway, replaced by the former England forward Brian Little, who had walked out as boss of his three clubs, Leicester, Aston Villa and Stoke. In fact, Albion had to pay Stoke £50,000 in compensation to get him three weeks earlier.

Little remained in office for eight months, the first part of which saw Albion play some excellent football, being unbeaten for the opening 13 games from the start of the season. They then followed up with some mediocre performances, and in the end they were playing very badly. Little lost his job in March after a 6–0 drubbing at Sheffield United and a 3–0 hiding by Birmingham. Little had brought in Larus Sigurdsson and Andy Townsend but was 'told' to sell Kilbane to Sunderland for £2.5m instead of the valuation price of £4m. Many people were outraged at this decision and chairman Hale quickly departed, succeeded on Christmas Eve by Paul Thompson.

Up stepped the former Sheffield Wednesday, Nottingham Forest and Norwich midfielder Gary Megson as the new manager, and it was he, to a certain degree, who instigated the team's escape act. A run of 14 games without a win plummeted Albion into the relegation zone. Two more key players were sold – Miller and Maresca, the latter for a club record £4.3m to Juventus – and the relegation trapdoor was now opening up, but Megson moved in and began with a 1–0 win at Stockport, but at a cost: defender Sigurdsson suffering an injury that would keep him out for a year. Late goals, however, cost Albion dearly in vital games, and although they weren't playing badly, they simply couldn't win and games were fast running out. Fresh faces were introduced: giant goalkeeper Brian Jensen, Des Lyttle, George Santos, Neil Clement and Tony Butler, and, to put the icing on the cake, and in a brave bid to escape the drop, he brought back Bob Taylor. 'Super Bob' scored five important goals and with Jensen in form Albion survived – just.

Boosting his squad even further by bringing in goalkeeper Russell Hoult from Portsmouth, Bristol Rovers striker Jason Roberts, midfielder Derek McInnes from Glasgow Rangers, Jordao from Sporting Braga, former Norwich City and Newcastle star Ruel Fox from Spurs and Igor Balis from Slovan Bratislava, Megson formulated a very workmanlike and well-organised side, and his efforts were rewarded as Albion qualified for the Play-offs, but they were denied a place in the Premiership by Bolton, who won the semi-final 5–2 on aggregate after Albion had held a 2–0 first-leg lead.

Without Burgess, Carbon, Hughes and Sneekes, Megson brought in strikers Danny Dichio from Sunderland and Scott Dobie from Carlisle for the 2001–02 season, quickly adding to his squad defender Darren Moore from Portsmouth and Andy Johnson from Nottingham Forest. However, Albion lost their opening two games, but after that they always looked like promotion material and, despite the odd hiccup here and there, kept themselves within striking distance of automatic promotion, which they achieved as runners-up behind Manchester City.

Albion, having leap-frogged over faltering Wolves, were denied victory against Rotherham United in their 44th match when Jordao's effort was clearly over the line but no goal was given. Around 6,500 Baggies supporters made the trip to Bradford for the penultimate game, knowing a win was imperative and would put more pressure on Wolves. It was a tense contest, decided right at the death by the ice-cool Balis, who stroked home a 94th-minute penalty to earn a 1–0 victory. Amazingly, five Albion players had missed eight spot kicks between them that season, but on this occasion, when it mattered most, Balis held his nerve. That left a home encounter against Crystal Palace, and a win would send Albion up.

In an interview prior to the game, Palace striker Clinton Morrison stirred things up by saying none of his teammates liked Albion. Megson printed out his words, stuck the sheet of paper on the dressing room notice board, asked the players to take note and said 'Go out and win!' The boss asked all the players to bring their wives, partners and relatives to meet him before kick-off as he got everyone in the right frame of mind for the 'big one', and how well the team responded, winning 2–0. Darren Moore struck first on 17 minutes to settle the nerves, and then Taylor's early strike in the second half sealed the points to trigger off a Hawthorns carnival like no one had ever seen before.

The key to their success was a stable and hard-working, even water-tight, defence, with Hoult playing magnificently behind a superb back four. In fact, Hoult set a new club record by keeping 27 clean sheets (24 in the League), and he also helped Albion register a record 17 1–0 wins (15 in the League).

Before a ball was kicked in the Premiership, the bookies made Albion favourites to go straight back down – and halfway through the season they knew they were right! Albion eventually went down in 19th place, having been in the bottom three since Boxing Day. They amassed only 26 points – 19 from safety. Despite the acquisition of Jason Koumas from Tranmere, Ronnie Wallwork from Manchester United, Lee Marshall from Leicester (who had the pleasure of scoring Albion's first Premiership goal against Leeds), Sean Gregan from Preston and the return of Hughes from Coventry, the Baggies struggled week after week, only occasionally achieving a favourable result. But it must be said that they only received two heavy defeats, losing 6–0 at home to Liverpool and 5–2 at Arsenal. Skipper McInnes had the misfortune to be sent off in Albion's first Premiership game at Old Trafford, and Moore's goal against Fulham clinched the first Premiership win that season.

Back in the First Division, manager Megson boosted his options by signing Swiss right-back Bernt Haas from Sunderland, Thomas Gaardsoe from Ipswich, Joost Volmer from Fortuna Sittard, Rob Hulse from Crewe, James O'Conner from Stoke and the Macedonian midfielder Artim Sakiri from CSKA Sofia, later adding Watford's left-back Paul Robinson to his squad, and they all played their part, along with Hoult, Clement, Gregan, Johnson, Koumas, Dobie, Hughes and Moore, as Albion established themselves in an automatic-promotion slot.

Halfway through the season former Blues striker Geoff Horsfield was signed from Wigan, and soon afterwards Mark Kinsella arrived from Villa Park, while Lloyd Dyer and Delroy Facey also entered the fray as the Baggies drove on towards promotion, which they achieved with three games remaining, beating Bradford 2–0 at The Hawthorns on 24 April to clinch second spot behind Norwich.

Could Albion retain their top-flight status this time round? That was the question a lot of people were asking, and manager Megson was optimistic when he said 'We've learnt a lot over the last two years, and I will stick my neck out and say yes.'

Into The Hawthorns camp for 2004–05 came Riccy Scimeca from Leicester, Darren Purse from Birmingham, Jonathan Greening from Middlesbrough and Nigerian international Kanu from Arsenal, and they all made their Albion debuts on the opening day of the 2004–05 season at Blackburn. Soon afterwards the Hungarian midfielder Zoltan Gera, signed from Ferencvaros, stepped out for his first Baggies game against Aston Villa.

After a bright start, results started to deteriorate and news of trouble in the dressing room and also on the team coach didn't help matters. Striker Rob Earnshaw was eventually signed from Cardiff, and after manager Megson fielded an under-strength team against League Two side Colchester in the League Cup, which Albion lost, it triggered off a 'situation' between the manager and chairman. Matters came to a head after a 3–0 League defeat at Crystal Palace when another new recruit, Japanese international Junichi Inamoto, sat on the bench. At this point Albion were lying in 16th position, and when Megson informed his chairman that he would not be signing a new contract at the end of the season he was 'put out to grass – on gardening leave', while the search began for his replacement, with Frank Burrows taking charge of the team on a caretaker basis.

Tomasz Kuszcak, Curtis Davis and Martin Albrechtsen guard Albion's goal against Fulham, Craven Cottage, 2005–06.

Glenn Hoddle, Sir Bobby Robson and Bryan Robson were all in the frame to become Albion's next boss, and in the end the latter was given the job, taking office after a 2–2 draw at Southampton. Robson's first game in charge was against his former club Middlesbrough, which Albion lost 2–1 after an outrageous miss by Kanu. This defeat plunged the Baggies into the relegation zone, where they remained for 21 weeks.

At Christmas Albion were struggling at the foot of the table, knowing that never before had a team escaped relegation after being in such a position halfway through the season. Made to utilise Megson's players until the transfer window opened in January, Robson was still optimistic that he could turn things round. Experienced striker Kevin Campbell was engaged from Everton, Kieran Richardson was secured on loan from Manchester United, right-back Scimeca made way for Danish star Martin Albrechtsen (formerly of FC Copenhagen), Wallwork was called into midfield and Clement was switched to the centre of the defence in place of Purse. But there was no place for the unsettled Jason Koumas.

Performances improved, but defensive lapses cost the team dearly, especially against Crystal Palace (2–2) and at Norwich (lost 3–2). Then things started to go Albion's way, and after wins over Birmingham (2–0), Charlton (4–1, courtesy of a hat-trick by Earnshaw to ensure their first win away from home) and Everton (1–0), there was a distinct chance that survival could be achieved.

Showing plenty of determination and playing some pretty good football, Albion battled on and picked up vital points against Aston Villa, Tottenham and Blackburn but lost heavily at Middlesbrough, and they also went down at home to Arsenal as the tension mounted. A 1–1 draw at Old Trafford was a tremendous result, leaving only one game left at home to Portsmouth.

Albion had to win and nobody else in the bottom four could if they were to remain in the

Premiership. It was a big ask – but amazingly that's what happened. Pompey were beaten 2–0 (Horsfield and Richardson the scorers), none of the other struggling teams recorded a victory and once again it was carnival day at The Hawthorns…manager Robson and the players had achieved the impossible, a great escape had been completed, and the music from that film blazed out around the ground as the fans celebrated in style.

Season 2005–06, however, was something completely different. It proved to be yet another struggle for survival, and this time round Albion simply couldn't cope, being relegated for the ninth time in their history. The signings of Curtis Davies from Luton, Steve Watson from Everton, Diomansy Kamara from Portsmouth, Nathan Ellington from Wigan and Darren Carter from Birmingham bolstered up the squad, but it was a pity that Koumas (on loan at Cardiff) and Earnshaw (sold to Norwich) couldn't settle their differences with the club. Polish goalkeeper Tomasz Kuszczak (signed from Hertha Berlin the previous July) was outstanding for most of the season, pulling off the save of the century in a 1–0 win at Wigan, when Darren Moore was sent off before half-time, but overall a lack of goals cost Albion dear. They won only seven and lost 22 of their 38 Premiership matches and netted only 31 goals, finishing in 19th position, nine points away from safety. Only Greening appeared in every game and in total Robson used 31 players, giving club debuts to 12 of them, including midfielders Nigel Quashie (signed from Southampton) and Richard Chaplow (ex-Burnley).

Unfortunately, after a decent start, Albion's form under Mowbray began to wane and they slipped from third to 10th in the table before getting back on track during December and slowly edging upwards over the next few weeks.

When the transfer window opened in January, Mowbray boosted his squad by bringing in experienced goalkeeper Dean Kiely from Portsmouth (to replace the departing Russell Hoult after he had committed a serious misdemeanour), midfielder Robert Koren from Lillestrøm and the Dutch striker McDonald on loan from AGOVV Apeldoorn.

In the FA Cup, Albion beat Leeds United 3–1 at home and arch rivals Wolves 3–0 at Molineux before earning a 2–2 draw in the fifth round at Premiership side Middlesbrough. Unfortunately, after a battling performance, the replay went to a penalty shoot-out which the visitors won and left Albion bitterly disappointed.

Having leapt to the top of the table on 24 February (after a 1–1 draw at Leicester), this tough encounter with Middlesbrough took its toll on several players, and Albion went four games without a win before claiming a crucial victory at Queen's Park Rangers. However, three more defeats followed in quick succession and, with two games remaining, a Play-off place was not guaranteed. In fact, Albion needed to win at Coventry and beat Barnsley on the final day of the season to be sure of a top-six finish. They did just that, pipping the Sky Blues 1–0 and thumping Barnsley 7–0, with Kevin Phillips grabbing his second hat-trick for the club. This was a repeat of the scoreline from the League game against the Tykes some 18 years earlier.

Albion were paired with Wolves in the two-leg Play-off semi-final, and in front of two full houses they did the business in style, winning the contest 4–2 on aggregate, with a 3–2 victory at Molineux and 1-0 triumph at The Hawthorns, to reach the new Wembley where they would take on Derby County for a place in the Premiership and with it a prize of around £60 million.

Phillips scored three of those four goals against Wolves, and, along with his strike partner Diomansy Kamara who netted the other, was bang in form and ready for the big occasion. But sadly, in front of almost 74,000 fans (over 33,000 of them supporting the Baggies), luck was against Albion as the Rams squeezed out a 1–0 win to regain their top-flight status after five years.

Phillips, who struck the top of the bar, Kamara, Koumas, by far the game's most outstanding player,

Captains, mascots and officials meet at the start of the Play-off Final at the new Wembley.

and Gera all came close, but in the end it was a huge disappointment for everyone associated with the club. Stand-in skipper Paul Robinson was devastated, and he said 'You can be the best team and play the best football, which we did, and still not get the result. I'm gutted, seriously gutted, especially for the supporters who were magnificent. But we will stick together, like we have always done, and go again next year.'

Manager Mowbray, vastly experienced, knows what he has to do and with the backing of the board he will certainly recruit some new players and get his squad up and running for another crack at gaining promotion in 2007–08.

During the 2007 close season there was a lot of transfer talk within the club. Diomansy Kamara, Curtis Davies, Jason Koumas, Paul McShane and Paul Robinson all being pursued by Premiership clubs.

West Bromwich Albion's Grounds

Cooper's Hill and Dartmouth Park
Bunn's Field (The Birches)
The Four Acres
Stoney Lane
The Hawthorns

Dartmouth Park

During the few years before Albion moved to their first enclosed ground (Bunn's Field), they utilised both Cooper's Hill and Dartmouth Park, playing in the latter regularly during season 1880–81 under skipper Jimmy Stanton. The pitch they used was situated near to the main entrance to the park (at the end of New Street), although occasionally (owing to bad weather) they occupied a 'stretch of grass' at the Herbert Street end, changing in the nearby Globe Inn in Reform Street.

Even after Albion had made the move to Bunn's Field, and while playing at The Four Acres, an occasional pre-season friendly took place at Dartmouth Park, usually against Wednesbury Old Athletic, to officially open the annual West Bromwich Flower Show. In September 1979 a crowd of around 10,000 saw a mixed team of current and former Albion players take on and beat a Celebrity Press XI at Dartmouth Park to celebrate the club's centenary, albeit a year late!

Bunn's Field (The Birches)

Bunn's Field was Albion's first enclosed ground, situated in Walsall Street (now Alfred Street), West Bromwich, where they played for one season (from August 1881 to May 1882) after agreeing on a nine-month lease. The players equipped the ground themselves, levelling and rolling flat the pitch, erecting two sets of goalposts with a tape acting as the crossbar at each end and putting up a rather filmsy perimeter rail.

The main (official) entrance was opposite Christ Church School, attended by several early Albion players, while the changing rooms were at first based inside the White Hart public house, at the junction of Herbert Street, Bull Street and Walsall Street, and later in the Roebuck Inn, which was situated on the corner of New Street and Walsall Street.

Having an enclosed ground, the club was now able to charge admission prices for the first time, and the opening game at The Birches (the name the locals called it) saw Albion beat Oldbury 5–1 on 10 September 1881 before 600 spectators. Albion, wearing yellow and white quartered jerseys at first and then chocolate and blue halves with the Staffordshire knot embroidered on the front, were practically unbeatable at Bunn's Field, and among their many victories were those of 12–0 versus Milton, 10–0 versus St Luke's, 9–1 versus Nechells, 6–1 versus West Bromwich Rangers and 5–0 versus Fallings Heath Rovers. Albion also reached the semi-final of the Birmingham Cup while at Bunn's Field before taking a new ground, the Four Acres – home of West Bromwich Dartmouth Cricket Club.

Four Acres

In September 1882 Albion moved from their primitive ground in Walsall Street to more comfortable accommodation at The Four Acres, home of West Bromwich Dartmouth Cricket Club, who had been playing there since 1834. The Four Acres – taken initially on a one-year agreement – was a well-known local centre, where athletics meetings were staged at festivals and on public holidays. It was originally dedicated by William, The Fourth Earl of Dartmouth, to the recreation of local inhabitants.

There was a clause in the agreement, however, whereby Albion could only play football matches there two days a week – on a Saturday and Monday.

Season tickets were issued at a cost of 2s 6d (13p), and the opening fixture saw Albion beat Stourbridge Standard 10–0 in a friendly on 7 October 1882, Billy Bisseker scoring six goals.

Improvements were made to the ground gradually, and by the summer of 1883 the playing area had been enclosed by a form of tubing instead of ropes, and wooden racks were laid on the ground around the reserve portion for the comfort of the spectators.

At Albion's AGM in July 1883 it was disclosed that the cricket club had agreed to let The Four Acres for a further two years at a rental of £15 per annum, and that Albion would have to cover the costs of building a new ticket office and pavilion.

Facts

- The biggest match ever staged at The Four Acres was an FA Cup tie between Albion and Blackburn in February 1885, when a record crowd of 16,393 saw Rovers win 2–0.
- Albion played 61 first-team games at The Four Acres. They won 48 and lost only seven, scoring 268 goals and conceding just 56. Only five were in the FA Cup (see below).
- Albion's best win on the ground was 26–0 versus Coseley in a Birmingham Cup tie on 11 November 1882, and their heaviest defeat was 5–1 by Stoke in a friendly in October 1882.
- The last game at The Four Acres (now Park Crescent, Seager Street) was played on 6 April 1885, when Albion beat Wednesbury Old Athletic 3–2 in a friendly wearing cardinal and blue halved shirts and white shorts.

Albion's FA Cup record at The Four Acres was:

				Goals	
Played	Won	Drawn	Lost	For	Against
5	3	0	2	8	6

Stoney Lane

Stoney Lane, situated behind the Sandwell Brewery, was Albion's home for 15 years, from 1885 to 1900, yet the club's administration was dealt with at the nearby Plough & Harrow public house and afterwards at offices on High Street, West Bromwich.

Albion moved to Stoney Lane from Four Acres because they wanted a more spacious ground, and the club's committee members were authorised to secure the tenancy of the field which belonged to the local undertaker, Mr H. Webb, on 27 February 1885.

The lease was drawn up for an initial seven-year term at an annual rent of £28, and work started almost immediately to convert the field into a suitable pitch for Albion to play on. The field was levelled and returfed, and ashes were spread around the perimeter of the ground, which was 120 yards long by 82 yards wide. The playing area measured 110 yards by 78 – one of the largest in the area.

A wooden grandstand, with planking serving as seats, was erected. Known affectionately as 'Noah's Ark', this was on the Sandwell Road side of the ground (the brewery side). The centre of the stand had covering for 600 spectators while the two uncovered portions at each end could house 1,500 fans. The opposite side of the ground was covered in ash, and this was gradually raised towards the back so that everyone could get a clear view of the pitch. There was no covered accommodation of any sort there.

Fencing and a boundary wall were also put in place and two simply-furnished brick 'dressing tents' sporting corrugated-iron roofs were also constructed, along with three refreshment stalls. Wagonettes and vehicles were permitted to drive into the ground and were stationed behind the bank at the Stoney Lane end, where there were also five 'pay boxes'. These were found to be inefficient, so supporters gained admission by purchasing ground tickets through openings in the walls! Ground tickets could also be bought from the Plough & Harrow pub, and for big matches neighbouring houses were also utilised to sell tickets.

The pitch had a pronounced slope towards the Stoney Lane end, and the cost of equipping the entire ground cost Albion £370.

To help cover the cost, a series of home friendly matches were arranged, starting with a fixture against a strong Scottish side, Third Rifle Volunteers, on 5 September 1885, which Albion won 4–1, Tommy Green scoring a hat-trick in front of 2,122 spectators.

As the years rolled by, so the standards at Stoney Lane slumped – simply because the Albion directors refused to spend money on the ground, which became one of the poorest in the First Division in the early 1890s, and in the end Albion simply had to leave.

Facts

- The first season tickets at Stoney Lane cost 5s (25p) each, and the gate receipts from Albion's first campaign there amounted to just £1,190.
- The first groundsman, Mr R. Russell, was paid 5s (25p) a week.
- The usual entrance fee for games at Stoney Lane was 6d (3p).
- The first League fixture at Stoney Lane ended Albion 4 Burnley 3, on 29 September 1888.
- Stoney Lane's biggest crowd – 20,977 – attended the third round FA Cup tie versus Wolves in March 1895. Albion won 1–0.
- Albion's last game at Stoney Lane was played on 16 April 1900, when Nottingham Forest were defeated 8–0 before a crowd of 5,187, Billy Walker scoring a hat-trick.
- Preston North End were the most successful opposing team at Stoney Lane, winning five times.
- Of the 27 FA Cup games staged at the ground, none were drawn, and between 1885 and 1893 Albion were undefeated in 14 consecutive home ties.

Albion's senior playing record at Stoney Lane was:

Competition	P	W	D	L	F	A
League	170	88	33	49	343	230
FA Cup	27	23	0	4	84	26
Test Matches	2	2	0	0	8	1
Totals	199	113	33	53	435	257

The Hawthorns Smethwick End.

The Hawthorns

The Hawthorns was the last Football League ground to be built in the 20th century. Work commenced on a large site near the Handsworth/Smethwick/West Bromwich border in mid-May 1900, having been initiated the previous year, and it was completed inside four months in readiness for the official 'opening' on 3 September 1900.

The lease on Albion's previous ground, Stoney Lane, expired in 1899, and at the time it was one of the worst grounds in the Football League. However, being unable to finalise details on a new ground, the lease was renewed for a further 12 months, thus allowing enough time for the ground committee, with Harry Keys a key member, to search for a suitable site to build Albion's new stadium.

On 14 May 1900 the club's seal was affixed to a 14-year lease of the field that was to become known as The Hawthorns.

Why The Hawthorns? On the surveyor's map, the area surrounding the 'ground' was referred to as 'Hawthorns Estate', and hawthorn bushes had flourished there at one time. Therefore, it seemed an apt and obvious choice of name.

The land itself had a marshy look about it when building work commenced, and there was a brook flowing nearby which formed the boundary between Smethwick, Handsworth and West Bromwich. However, this did not deter work, and in no time at all the ground was ready for use.

Initially, the field of play sloped dramatically from the Halfords Lane/Birmingham Road corner, across and down towards the Smethwick End/now East Stand corner.

Over the years, though, the playing area itself has been built up and now there is a gradual slope of just 2ft 4in. Bearing this in mind, there haven't been too many waterlogged pitches over the years, with only three League games being abandoned (once they had started) owing to the state of the pitch – those against Bury in 1925, Luton in 1958 and Aston Villa in 1965 (all in the old First Division). There have been other matches called off through fog, poor light and falling snow.

Hawthorns Calendar 1900–2007

1900 – The ground was officially opened on Monday 3 September 1900 for the First Division game between Albion and Derby County. At the time, The Hawthorns could house 35,500 fans and there were 20,104 present on the opening day to see Steve Bloomer (County) score the first goal, with 'Chippy' Simmons equalising for Albion.

1904 – The 'Noah's Ark' stand, which had been transferred from Stoney Lane, burned down on Guy Fawkes' Night!

1905 – A half-time scoreboard installed for the first time.

1906 – A new stand was constructed at the Smethwick End of the ground.

1911 – The main Halfords Lane stand was overhauled and banking increased on the Handsworth side.

1912 – Following a mini subsidence, The Hawthorns pitch was completely returfed.

1913 – Albion purchased the freehold of The Hawthorns for just £5,350.

1914 – The Halfords Lane stand was extended.

1920 – Concrete terracing was installed and a concrete wall constructed to replace the wooden fencing around the playing area.

1923 – The Handsworth side embankment (opposite the Halfords Lane stand) was extended back and the roof made higher.

1924 – The ground capacity was officially put at 65,000.

1931 – Terracing all round the ground was finally completed with tip-up seats installed in the wing stands, and the nearby Hawthorns Halt railway station on the Great Western Line was officially opened on Christmas Day.

1934 – A new stand, with 750 extra seats, was completed at the Smethwick/Halfords Lane corner, upping the capacity of The Hawthorns to almost 66,000.

1935 – A new oak-panelled tea room was constructed in the Halfords Lane stand.

1939 – The wooden roof over the Halfords Lane stand was dismantled and replaced by asbestos sheeting, which rested on five giant steel stanchions. The roof was also extended outwards to the front of the terraces.

1940–45 – Owing to World War Two, very little work was carried out on the ground.

1947 – A new block of turnstiles was erected on the Handsworth side, behind the Woodman Corner.

1949 – The wooden terraces at the front of the main Halfords Lane stand were replaced by concrete and 750 extra seats were installed in the stand itself. The first electronic turnstile aggregator to be installed on a Football League ground in Britain was housed at The Hawthorns.

1950 – A new directors' box was provided and the club's offices and dressing rooms were re-modernised.

1951 – Eight new turnstiles were introduced at the Smethwick End.

1957 – Floodlights were installed at the ground for the first time at a cost of £18,000.

1958 – A wing stand (at the West Bromwich/Birmingham Road End) was added to the main Halfords Lane stand.

1961 – A new car park for some 600 vehicles was opened off Middlemore Road (behind the Handsworth Road stand).

1964 – There were now four car parks within 800 yards of the ground and the Rainbow Stand, costing £40,000, was erected on the Handsworth side. It contained some 4,000 tip-up seats and was paid for with funds from the Development Association. The 'old' Handsworth stand roof was transferred across to cover the terracing behind the Birmingham Road goal.

1965 – The first Throstle Club (for Baggies supporters) was opened next to The Hawthorns. It was officially opened by Graham Williams and ex-skipper Jesse Pennington.

1967 – Buffet bars inside the ground were renovated at a cost of £20,000.

1968 – The Hawthorns Halt railway station was closed down.

1969 – The first-ever 'Open Day' for supporters was held at The Hawthorns with over 6,000 fans attending.

1970 – Floodlighting renovated four-fold to fall in line with colour TV transmissions.

1976 – Fourteen executive boxes were installed in front of the Rainbow Stand and an extra 750 paddock seats were also put in.

1977 – Executive box complex completed. Terracing reconstructed at the Smethwick and Birmingham Road Ends and new crush barriers erected.

1979 – Work started on the new £2.5 million stand to accommodate 4,500 spectators on the Halfords Lane side of the ground. This was built in two phases, between 1979–82, and included 26 executive boxes.

1983 – The Hawthorns Throstle Club (next to ground) was closed down. A large electronic scoreboard was erected on the front of the stand at the Smethwick End (this was removed in 1985).

1985 – Smethwick End stand was re-roofed. New safety measures were installed at the ground.

1986 – A crowd control video system was installed at the ground.

1988–92 – Major safety work was carried out at the ground following the tragedies at Valley Parade and Hillsborough.

1989 – The Sponsors' Lounge opened in the corner of the Halfords Lane stand next to the Birmingham Road terraces.

1990 – The Hawthorns pitch was completely returfed for only the second time in 90 years. Sods of turf were then sold to supporters as souvenirs.

1991 – In February a major pipe burst caused thousands of pounds' worth of damage in the Halfords Lane complex. In December, television pictures of Albion's away FA Cup tie with Leyton Orient were beamed back to The Hawthorns on two giant screens, which were erected in front of the main stand.

1992 – The roof was removed from above the Smethwick End terracing as plans were put into motion to redevelop the ground and make it into an all-seater stadium.

1994 – Birmingham Road terracing was dug up as work continued on redeveloping The Hawthorns, and Albion kicked off the 1994–95 season with five away League games as the ground redevelopment came to a conclusion.

1995 – Work was completed on Albion's all-seater stadium (including a new set of floodlights priced at £88,000) at a combined cost of £4.15 million, of which the club received

£2,097,000 from the Football Trust. The 'new' modernised Hawthorns was officially opened for the First Division League visit of Bristol City on Boxing Day (Albion won 1–0 courtesy of a bizzare own-goal).

1995 – The Hawthorns Museum was officially opened by manager Alan Buckley and The Hawthorns railway station was re-opened after 27 years. The capacity of the ground was cut to around 27,000.

1997 – The Hawthorns was now an all-seater stadium with a capacity of 25,296.

1998 – The Hawthorns pitch was completely dug up and returfed for only the third time in 98 years (following similar excercises in 1912 and 1990).

2000 – Plans were drawn up and work commenced on the re-development of the new East Stand (to replace the Rainbow Stand).

2001 – The new East Stand, with almost 8,800 seats, was completed at a cost of around £8 million, and for the first time in 101 years the whole ground was enclosed, as the respective corners at the Birmingham Road End and Smethwick End adjoining the East Stand were universally linked together to increase the capacity to just under 27,700.

2002 – Albion's first-ever Premiership game against Manchester United at Old Trafford on 17 August was beamed back to The Hawthorns, where 7,636 fans saw the 1–0 defeat on two giant screens. A 'second' Hawthorns museum was opened in the New East Stand at the Hawthorns and Albion played their first home game in the Premiership, beaten 3–1 by Leeds United on Saturday evening (k.o 5.30pm) on 24 August 2002 in front of more than 26,600 spectators.

2003 – Over 16,000 fans attended Bob Taylor's testimonial match – the biggest for a non-competitive game since 1957.

2005 – Albion retained their Premiership status with a last match win over Portsmouth at The Hawthorns.

2006 – With extra seating, the capacity of The Hawthorns rose to 28,003.

2007 – Albion qualified for the Championship Play-off Final by beating Wolves 1–0 (4–2 on aggregate) in the semi-final.

Non-Albion games at The Hawthorns

Senior International & Representative Matches

7 October 1914	Football League 2 Irish League 1	Att. 9,250
9 February 1920	England 2 The South 1	Att. 14,427
	England 2 Ireland 0	Att. 20,173
	England 4 Belgium 0	Att. 15,405
23 January 1928	England 6 The Rest 3	Att. 9,345
27 February 1935	England 2 The Rest 2	Att. 12,845
20 October 1945	England 0 Wales 1	Att. 54,611

B International

10 February 1998	England 1 Chile 2	Att. 13,970

Junior Internationals

4 April 1908	England 4 Scotland 0	Att. 3,000
18 April 1925	England 4 Scotland 1	Att. 5,000
13 April 1935	England 3 Scotland 1	Att. 4,000

Youth Internationals

9 January 1974	England 1 Wales 0	Att. 1,800
13 February 1974	England 1 Holland 1	Att. 2,000
9 March 1977	England 1 Wales 0	Att. 1,400
10 November 1986	England 3 Sweden 3	Att. 1,000

Other Youth Matches

18 November 1969	Albion Youth 0 England 1	Att. 1,100
14 December 1976	Albion Youth 0 England 0	Att. 1,500

Women's International

21 April 1998	England 1 Italy 2	Att. 2,520

InterToto Cup

22 July 2000	Aston Villa 3 Marila Pribram 1	Att. 8,200
2 August 2000	Aston Villa 1 Celta Vigo 2	Att. 11,909

Intermediate Final Replays

12 May 1987	Burton A 1 Kidderminster Harriers 2 (FACT)	Att. 15,524
12 May 1988	Telford United 2 Enfield 3 (FACT)	Att. 6,916

Cup semi-finals (not involving Albion)

15 March 1902	Derby County 1 Sheffield United 1 (FAC)	Att. 33,603
26 March 1960	Aston Villa 0 Wolves 1 (FAC)	Att. 55,596
5 April 1967	Hendon 1 Skelmersdale 3 (FAAC)	Att. 5,034
18 December 1968	Burnley 2 Swindon Town 3 (FLC)	Att. 20,084
3 April 1971	Telford United 3 Yeovil 1 (FACT)	Att. 9,012

Schoolboy Internationals

15 March 1972	England 1 Northern Ireland 1	Att. 4,500
1 May 1978	England 6 Wales 0	Att. 2,000
21 March 1986	England 4 Scotland 2	Att. 2000

Football League

29 November 1919	Wolves 2 Barnsley 4 (Div 2)	Att. 8,000
6 December 1919	Wolves 2 Stockport County 2 (Div 2)	Att. 6,000
25 February 1970	Walsall 0 Brighton & Hove Albion 3 (Div 3)	Att. 7,535

Cup Replays

19 February 1955	Aston Villa 1 Doncaster Rovers 3 (FAC)	Att. 17,155
1 March 1965	Aston Villa 1 Wolves 3 (FAC)	Att. 37,534
31 August 1971	Aston Villa 4 Wrexham 3 (FLC)	Att. 20,697
20 December 1971	Hereford Town 2 Northampton 1 (FAC)	Att. 8,331
20 September 1972	Southampton 2 Chester 0 (FLC)	Att. 2,417
12 February 1973	Bolton Wanderers 1 Cardiff City 0 (FAC)	Att. 6,609
13 January 1975	Bury 2 Millwall 0 (FAC)	Att. 3,041
12 January 1981	Fulham 1 Bury 0 (FAC)	Att. 2,468
11 January 1986	Telford United 1 Leeds United 2 (FAC)	Att. 6,460

Cricket matches

29 July 1977	India versus Pakistan	Att. 2,641
15 October 1980	Warwicks XI versus Ian Botham's XI*	Att. 2,020

* Played under floodlights

Baseball

7 August 1944	US Army versus Canadian Army	Att. 5.125

Athletics meeting

9 May 1908	Inc 100, 220, 880 yds and 1 mile races	Att. 9,000*

* Estimated attendance over two days (9–10 May)

Other Events:

There have been Finals of several local Cup competitions staged at The Hawthorns over the years, including those for the Birmingham Charity Cup, the Birmingham Senior Challenge Cup, the Staffordshire Cup and the FA Sunday Cup.

On Saturday 9 May 1908 a Spring Athletics Sports meeting took place at The Hawthorns. The attendance was over 10,000.

In 1913 a well-organised two-day boxing tournament featuring Jimmy Wilde, among others, was staged at The Hawthorns and attracted enormous crowds overall.

Facts and Figures

- The Hawthorns is the highest League ground above sea level in the UK at 551ft. Non-League Tow Law's ground in the north east of England is said to be 998ft above sea level.
- A never-to-be-beaten attendance record of 64,815 was set at The Hawthorns on 6 March 1937, when Arsenal were the visitors for a sixth-round FA Cup tie. Albion beat the favourites 3–1.
- The Hawthorns pitch size (in 2007) was 115 yards long by 74 yards wide.
- Tony 'Bomber' Brown played in a record 282 Football League games for Albion at The Hawthorns. He made 361 first-team appearances on the ground and scored 173 goals (132 in the League).
- 'W.G.' Richardson scored more goals at The Hawthorns than any other player – 216 in all first-team matches.

- Well over 4,400 matches (at various levels) have now been staged at The Hawthorns over a period of 107 years (from September 1900).
- Albion's arch-rivals Wolves played two Second Division League games at The Hawthorns in 1919 versus Barnsley and Stockport County, after their Molineux home had been closed following crowd disturbances.
- Walsall played Brighton & Hove Albion in a Third Division game at The Hawthorns in 1970 because their Fellows Park ground was waterlogged.
- On 11 May 1931 HRH the Prince of Wales (later King Edward VIII) visited The Hawthorns to offer his congratulations to Albion on their unique 'double' achievement.
- The limited overs cricket match staged at The Hawthorns between the Indian and Paskistan Test XI in 1977 resulted in a win for the Indians by four wickets. All proceeds went towards a children's charity and Imran Khan's benefit.
- In 1980 the first floodlit cricket match took place at The Hawthorns when Ian Botham's XI, including David Gower, lost to Warwickshire in a 30-overs match. The proceeds from this event went towards Ally Robertson's testimonial fund.

Albion's senior playing record at The Hawthorns (1900-2007)

Competition	P	W	D	L	F	A
Premiership	57	14	15	28	55	82
League	1,946	1,009	478	459	3,678	2,221
FA Cup	137	78	33	26	275	130
League Cup	72	39	19	14	133	77
European	11	6	1	4	21	13
Play-offs	3	2	1	0	5	2
Others	26	11	7*	8	49	37
Totals	2,252	1,159	554	539	4,206	2,562

Others include all first-team competitions besides those named above.

* Two of these seven draws ended in penalty shoot-out defeats.

Matches to Remember

24 April 1883 – Stoke 2 Albion 3
Staffordshire Cup Final

This was Albion's first trophy success, and it came in their first Cup Final appearance of any kind, the victory over Stoke doing much to put the team on the football map and make the likes of Aston Villa and Wolves sit up and take notice!

There was a great deal of excitement in the Black Country as Albion prepared to take on the Potters, who had scored 42 goals in their previous four rounds, including a 19–0 win over Stoke Priory.

A cheap railway excursion took 1,500 fans from West Bromwich station to the Potteries, and it turned out to be a great occasion for all concerned, as Albion, fielding their strongest side, won 3–2, George Bell scoring the winning goal 15 minutes from time.

Albion, regarded as the underdogs, went behind just before the 15-minute mark when Teddy Johnson scored from 20 yards. But three minutes later George Timmins powered through to equalise with a 'capital' shot.

Play was fast and furious, with Albion just about on top, and their efforts were rewarded on 31 minutes when Abel 'Bunny' Bunn, 5ft 3ins tall and one of the smallest defenders ever to play for the club, scored a superb goal from Ezra Horton's right-wing corner.

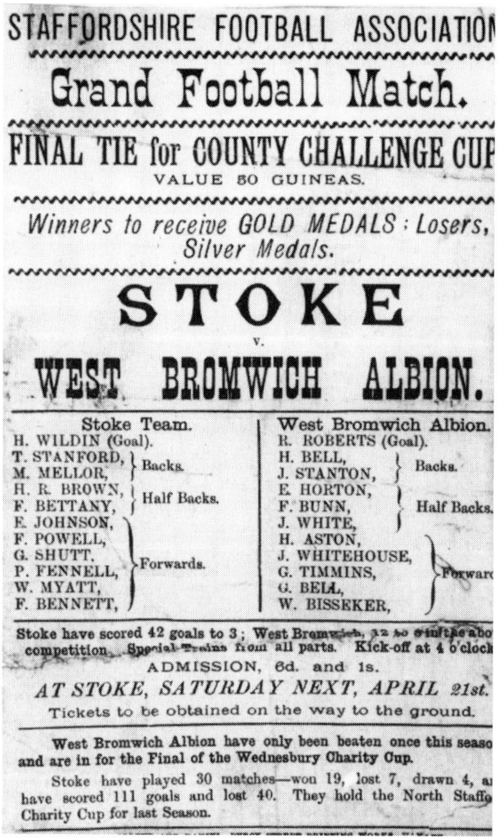

STAFFORDSHIRE FOOTBALL ASSOCIATION

Grand Football Match.

FINAL TIE for COUNTY CHALLENGE CUP

VALUE 50 GUINEAS.

Winners to receive GOLD MEDALS: Losers, Silver Medals.

STOKE

v.

WEST BROMWICH ALBION.

Stoke Team.		West Bromwich Albion.	
H. WILDIN (Goal).		R. ROBERTS (Goal).	
T. STANFORD,	Backs.	H. BELL,	Backs.
M. MELLOR,		J. STANTON,	
H. R. BROWN,	Half Backs.	E. HORTON,	Half Backs.
F. BETTANY,		F. BUNN,	
E. JOHNSON,	Forwards.	J. WHITE,	
F. POWELL,		H. ASTON,	Forwards.
G. SHUTT,		J. WHITEHOUSE,	
P. FENNELL,		G. TIMMINS,	
W. MYATT,		G. BELL,	
F. BENNETT,		W. BISSEKER,	

Stoke have scored 42 goals to 3; West Bromwich, [illegible] in the above competition. Special Trains from all parts. Kick-off at 4 o'clock

ADMISSION, 6d. and 1s.

AT STOKE, SATURDAY NEXT, APRIL 21st.

Tickets to be obtained on the way to the ground.

West Bromwich Albion have only been beaten once this season and are in for the Final of the Wednesbury Charity Cup.

Stoke have played 30 matches—won 19, lost 7, drawn 4, and have scored 111 goals and lost 40. They hold the North Staffs Charity Cup for last Season.

However, hesitancy between centre-half John While, the Albion skipper, and Jim Stanton, let in Johnson for his second goal and Stoke's equaliser five minutes before the interval.

Albion started after the break with an aggressive attitude and twice came close to scoring, while at the other end goalkeeper Bob Roberts saved with his legs from George Shutt.

With time running out, Albion began to press more men forward, and on 75 minutes Harry Aston attempted a shot from fully 35 yards. The Stoke 'keeper Jack Wildin stopped the ball but only succeeded in sending it high into the air, allowing Bell to race in and head it between the posts.

Stoke were stunned, but they battled on and won two late corners as Albion's defence held firm. From that second flag-kick the ball was kicked downfield to Billy Bisseker, who raced clear and was all set to score Albion's fourth goal, only for the referee to halt play because fans had encroached on to the pitch.

That effectively was the last action of the game, and at the final whistle the Albion players and their fans celebrated before While stepped forward to collect the silver trophy from Stoke's Alderman Arthur Minton.

Albion: Roberts; H. Bell, Stanton; E. Horton, Bunn, While; Aston, Whitehouse, Timmins, Bisseker, G. Bell.

Stoke: Windin; Stanford, Mellor; H. Brown, Bettany, Johnson; S. Brown, Shutt, Fennell, Myatt, Bennett.

Attendance: 6,150

---

24 March 1888 – Albion 2 Preston North End 1 FA Cup Final

Before the start of this Cup Final – Albion's third in succession – Preston, with a seasonal goal average of 154 for and 38 against, asked the referee, Major Marindin, if they could be photographed with the trophy – so confident were they of beating Albion, having demolished hapless Hyde 26–0 in an earlier round! 'Had you not better win it first', was the official's abrupt reply.

Albion were quietly confident themselves, but never let it be known – until they took to the field in front of a record Oval crowd of almost 19,000, the gates being closed way before kick-off – a first in the history of the game.

Albion, fielding an all-English team – every player being born within a four or five mile radius of West Bromwich, whose weekly wage bill was no more than £10 – began well, getting their long passing game up and running straightaway.

This frustrated Preston, whose artistry was swept aside by a series of wing attacks, spearheaded down the right by George Woodhall and Billy Bassett, the latter being in sparkling form, so much so that shortly after the game had ended he was chosen to play for England.

After some sustained pressure, Albion took the lead on 20 minutes. The lively Bassett intercepted a poor throw out by the Preston 'keeper Mills-Roberts, darted clear down the right before centring perfectly for 'Jem' Bayliss to score with a crisp low shot.

Preston slowly clawed themselves back into the game, and John Goodall fired high over the bar. Albion, though, always looked likely to score. Bayliss hit a post from another shrewd Bassett pass, and both Tom Pearson and Joe Wilson went close in quick succession.

Then, out of the blue, Preston equalised on 52 minutes. Fred Dewhurst fired in a low hard shot, which was partly stopped by Roberts, who, with the help of Perry, scrambled the ball clear – only for the goal to be awarded by referee Marindin. Several Albion defenders complained that it never crossed the line, and Ezra Horton got a severe ticking off from the official.

Undeterred and full of Black Country determination, Albion went on the offensive again. A splendid effort by Woodhall was saved; Bassett was only inches away from converting Woodhall's reverse pass and Bayliss headed against a post, while at the other end Jim Ross had a shot deflected onto the Albion woodwork.

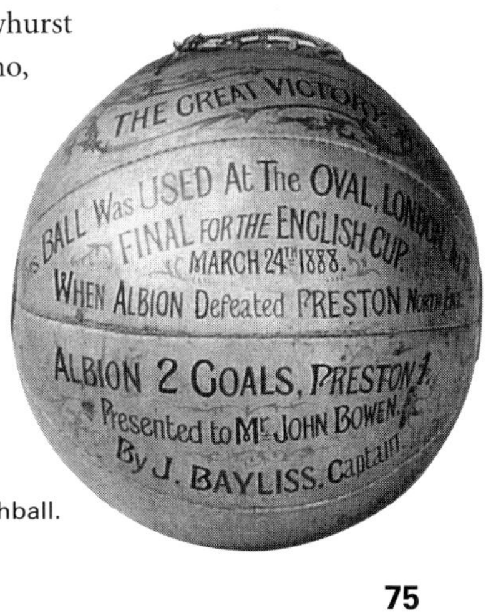

1888 FA Cup matchball.

With 13 minutes remaining, Albion deservedly took the lead, Woodhall firing the ball past Mills-Roberts after some fine work by Bassett and Tom Pearson. Although Preston went in search of a second equaliser, Albion's defence stood firm, and in the end it proved to be third time lucky. As he presented the trophy, Major Marindin praised the 'Indomitable pluck and perseverance of the Albion'.

Albion: Roberts; Green, Aldridge; Horton, Perry, Timmins; Woodhall, Bassett, Bayliss, Pearson, Wilson.

Preston: Mills-Roberts; Howarth, N. Ross; Holmes, Russell, Graham; Gordon, J. Ross, Goodall, Dewhurst, Drummond.

Attendance: 18,904

---

8 September 1888 – Stoke 0 Albion 2
League

This was Albion's and, indeed, Stoke's first-ever game in the newly-formed Football League, and it was the visitors who came out on top after a hard-fought encounter at The Victoria Ground, where, five years earlier, Albion had won their first ever prize – the Staffordshire Cup.

Going into the game brimming with confidence after pre-season friendly wins over Sheffield Wednesday and neighbours Wolves, Albion, backed by 1,000 travelling supporters, pushed the Potters back into their own half of the field from the outset and dominated the early exchanges, causing goalkeeper Billy Rowley some anxious moments.

Yet the goal which Albion had threatened never materialised, as first Tom Pearson then Willie Hendry and Pearson again were thwarted by last-ditch tackles or goalline clearances.

It was the same story in the second half, with Albion in control and Stoke defending stubbornly, although Bob Roberts had to be at his best to keep out a shot from home striker Jimmy Sayer. But at last the breakthrough arrived, 10 minutes from time.

Rowley came under pressure and threw the ball out far too quickly for his full-back (Tommy Clare) to react. Joe Wilson gained possession and fired it straight back past Rowley and between the posts, to register Albion's first goal in League football.

Hendry had a chance of doubling the advantage soon afterwards, but in the 83rd minute George Woodhall rose above George Shutt to head home Billy Bassett's centre to secure the points.

Stoke: Rowley; Clare, Underwood; Ramsey, Shutt, Smith; Sayer, McSkimming, Staton, Edge, Tunnicliffe.

Albion: Roberts; J. Horton, Green; E. Horton, C. Perry, Bayliss; Bassett, Woodhall, Hendry, Pearson, Wilson.

Attendance: 4,524

---

4 April 1892 – Albion 12 Darwen 0
League

A fortnight after winning the FA Cup, Albion went out and created a bit of footballing history by becoming the first team to score more than 10 goals in a League game. In fact, they bagged 12 without reply to set a new competition record which still stands today, although it was equalled in April 1909 by Nottingham Forest, who defeated Leicester Fosse by the same score.

Albion were quite magnificent against the Lancashire cotton town team of Darwen. They attacked from the first to the last whistle, and although Darwen occasionally threatened, especially in the first half, the Baggies could and should have claimed another half a dozen goals, at least!

Tom Pearson set the ball rolling as early as the second minute, firing wide of goalkeeper Billy McOwen's right hand from Jasper Geddes's low cross. Billy Bassett then struck the crossbar and Tom Pearson shot over; Groves had a goal disallowed before John Reynolds headed the second from Geddes's left-wing corner.

Bassett, finding loads of space, added a third after a mazy dribble, which took him past four defenders and Reynolds diverted Geddes's low free-kick past the unsighted 'keeper for number four.

Right on the stroke of half-time, Pearson, ably assisted by Bassett, made it 5–0. And as the players left the pitch, Albion's 'keeper Joe Reader reflected that he had not been called upon to make a single save during the first period.

Albion continued to attack immediately after the break, and in the space of five minutes (48th and 52nd) Bassett scored twice to complete his hat-trick – tapping home from close range after McOwen had spilled a Geddes cross and firing in a long-range free-kick following a foul on Pearson.

Surprisingly, for the next 20 minutes Albion were relatively quiet, although McLeod went close on two occasions. However, the floodgate reopened on 73 minutes when Pearson moved forward to head home goal number eight (from Bassett's astute pass). Darwen's right-back Ted Hunt, under pressure, nodded the ball into his own goal to make it 9–0 two minutes later, and virtually straight from the kick-off Pearson gained possession, raced past three defenders and took Albion into double-figures.

Geddes rose to head a brilliant 11th goal (from Bassett's high cross) on 84 minutes, and in the dying seconds Sammy Nicholls completed the scoring by putting both the ball and the unfortunate McOwen over the line to end a very one-sided game.

Albion: Reader; J. Horton, McCulloch; Reynolds, C. Perry, Groves; Bassett, McLeod, Nicholls, Pearson, Geddes.

Darwen: McOwen; Hunt, Aspin; Entwistle, Owen, McAvoy; Wad, Nightingale, Fish, Alexander, Craven.

Attendance: 1,109

---

27 December 1893 – Wolverhampton Wanderers 0 Albion 8 League

FA Cup holders Wolves were in pretty good form when they met Albion at Molineux 48 hours after Christmas. They had defeated Preston North End 3–1, Aston Villa 3–0 and Blackburn Rovers 5–1 in the space of 10 days and had only lost one home game all season. In contrast, Albion had lost two and drawn one of their previous four League games, and they hadn't been playing too well away, yet they were still looking to beat Wolves on their own patch.

Despite it being cold, there was a decent crowd present to see if unchanged Wolves could make it four wins on the bounce, but those inside the ground, and supporting the home side, suddenly got a rude awakening as Albion stormed into the lead inside the first minute, with Owen Williams, deputising for Tom Pearson, setting up Roddy McLeod for an easy tap in from eight yards.

A terrific block tackle by Jack Horton and a fine diving save by 'keeper Joe Reader from Harry Wood prevented a Wolves equaliser. Alf Griffin then had a goal disallowed for being offside and Albion's Jasper Geddes hit the outside of the post before Charlie Perry made it 2–0 from Bassett's right-wing corner on 16 minutes.

Eight minutes later Bassett cut inside George Swift and tucked away goal number three, and on the half-hour mark the impressive McLeod grabbed number four after a dreadful error by full-back Tommy Dunn. McLeod was then denied his hat-trick by the thickness of an upright but celebrated soon afterwards when Bassett latched onto Geddes's pass to make the score 5–0 at the break.

Wolves came out strongly at the start of the second half, and future Albion forward Joe Butcher struck the crossbar, while Wood and Griffin had shots saved by Reader.

Albion, though, had something more to offer and responded in style, McLeod deservedly completing his hat-trick on 62 minutes after taking a pass from Bassett, gliding past two defenders and slipping the ball past Crispin Rose. Williams added a seventh goal in the 70th minute, the ball squirting underneath Rose, and six minutes from time Bassett completed his hat-trick with a tremendous right-footed volley, struck on the turn from 15 yards.

This remains as Albion's best-ever away League win, while at the same time it is Wolves' heaviest home defeat in all competitions. And it would be another 60 years before two Albion players would each score a hat-trick in the same League game.

Wolves: Rose; Dunn, Swift; Griffiths, Owen, Kinsey; Wykes, Butcher, Griffin, Wood, Edge.

Albion: Reader; Nicholson, J. Horton; T. Perry, C. Perry, Taggart; Bassett, Norman, McLeod, Williams, Geddes.

Attendance: 8,000

---

22 April 1895 – Albion 6 Sheffield Wednesday 0
League

Albion simply HAD to win this game, their last of the season, to avoid competing in the dreaded Test Matches, which ultimately could result in relegation to the Second Division – and the margin of victory over mid-table Sheffield Wednesday had to be at least five goals!

The other struggling teams immediately above them were Stoke (24 points), Derby County (23) and Liverpool (22), and all had completed their fixtures. Albion (22 points), with a poor goal average, needed to win, and win well, to leapfrog over all three. And they did just that, to the tune of 6–0 – their biggest victory of the season.

Albion had re-signed the ageing but vastly-experienced outside-left Jasper Geddes, from Millwall Athletic, for their last three games, and what a terrific influence he had grabbing the winner in the penultimate home game versus Nottingham Forest (1–0) and adding two more in the win over Wednesday.

Albion began like a house on fire against the Owls, Geddes scoring with a smart header from Billy Bassett's wonderfully-flighted right-wing cross after just 50 seconds. Fifteen minutes later it was 2–0 when Tom Green, making only his fourth senior appearance, headed home from close range after Bassett's effort had been blocked.

As Albion continued to press, full-back Billy Williams had an effort ruled out after banging in an indirect free-kick, the ball failing to touch another player en-route, and both Roddy McLeod and then Green struck the woodwork.

It was all frantic stuff, and, after Geddes had missed an open goal, Bassett got clear down the right (again) and from his perfect cross Geddes made amends by heading home Albion's third goal. And then, shortly before half-time, Tom Hutchinson drove home goal number four after some delightful touch football by Geddes and Bassett.

Four-nil up and on a roll, Albion powered on after the break, and, although reduced temporarily to 10 men when Geddes left the field for treatment after being elbowed in the face, the vital fifth goal was scored by McLeod, who found the net with a low drive through a ruck of players after Jack Taggart had touched a free-kick in front of him 20 yards out.

In command and confident, Albion continued to push forward, knowing full well that if they conceded it could prove costly. But Reader and his co-defenders were in no mood to concede anything, not even a free-kick, and after Tom Higgins, McLeod and Bassett had all gone close to adding to the score, Albion claimed a sixth goal through Tom Perry with 15 minutes remaining, his high looping shot finding the net via the angle.

Albion safely held out and the two points gained lifted them into 13th position above Stoke, Derby and Liverpool, the Merseysiders being relegated after losing their Test Match against the Second Division champions Bury.

Albion: Reader; J. Horton, Williams; T. Perry, Higgins, Taggart; Bassett, McLeod, Green, Hutchinson, Geddes.

Wednesday: Allan; Sutherland, Langley; H. Brandon, Petrie, Jamieson; Webster, Fox, Davis, Brady, Spiksley.

Attendance: 8,217

3 September 1900 – Albion 1 Derby County 1
League

This was the first League game played at The Hawthorns, and despite it taking place on a Monday afternoon over 20,000 saw Albion held by a strong Derby County side, who had reached the FA Cup Final two years earlier and finished sixth in Division One the previous season.

Albion, fielding former England international Fred Wheldon, ex-Aston Villa and Small Heath, looked tentative early on as they attacked the Birmingham Road goal. They eventually settled down and created the first chance, Harry Hadley shooting wide from Dick Roberts's corner.

When Derby got forward, all eyes were focussed on England international and Cradley Heath-born striker Steve Bloomer, but it was centre-forward Dicky Wombwell who had the visitor's first shot, grazing the crossbar from 25 yards.

On the half-hour mark Derby got the breakthrough. Jimmy Crawford found space down Albion's right, and from his cross a scrimmage developed inside the six-yard area. Bloomer, getting in front of Abe Jones, reacted the quickest and headed the ball into the net from almost on the goalline.

John Chadburn had one effort brilliantly saved by Derby 'keeper Jack Fryer, who repeated the feat by saving from Roberts.

Early in the second half Chippy Simmons almost levelled things up for Albion but was thwarted once more by Fryer, who also did well to stop two goal-bound efforts from Chadburn.

After a lengthy period of pressure, Albion, at long last, gained an equaliser with 10 minutes remaining, Simmons firing home after Jones had set him up 10 yards from goal. Right at the death Roberts almost won it for Albion, but he snatched at his shot and the ball flew over the bar.

It was a fair result to an entreating match – but for Albion their first season at their new home was to end very disappointingly!

Albion: Reader; Adams, W. Williams; Dunn, Jones, Hadley; Chadburn, Pickering, Simmons, Wheldon, Roberts.

Derby: Fryer; Methven, Blackett; May, Goodall, Leckie; Crawford, Bloomer, Wombwell, Arkesden, McQueen.

Attendance: 20,104

---

14 October 1922 – Albion 7 Arsenal 0
League

Albion had been beaten 3–1 at Highbury seven days before this fixture and were determined to gain sweet revenge over their London opponents.

They started off slowly and may well have slipped behind, but after half an hour had passed there was only going to be one result – a win for the Baggies – and it was achieved with style and commitment, every player performing splendidly.

Ivor Jones headed Jack Crisp's centre wide in Albion's first worthwhile attack, but it was Arsenal who set the early pace, and Voysey and Young came close to breaking the deadlock. But it was Albion who went in front, against the run of play, with Fred Morris pouncing from close range to slot the ball home after goalkeeper Dunn had mishandled Stan Davies's ground shot. Two minutes later Howard Gregory and Morris broke clear down the left, and, from the winger's inside pass, Morris drove home his second goal.

After Arsenal 'keeper Dunn had saved from Crisp and Morris, and Albion's Pearson had done likewise from Young and Boreham, the visitors collapsed and conceded five goals in just 13 second-half minutes.

In the 71st minute, Gregory found Davies, who in turn whipped in a low cross for Crisp to nudge past Dunn. Five minutes later, Gregory's shot came, rebounded off an upright to Jones who touched the ball to Morris for him to gleefully complete his hat-trick.

Back came Albion, and within 50 seconds Crisp latched on to a loose ball to make it 5–0. That scoreline quickly changed to 6–0 when Gregory raced into the penalty area to bang home Morris's pass, and after Stan Davies had shaved a post Morris completed the scoring by walking the ball into an empty net with six minutes remaining.

To this day, this remains as Albion's biggest-ever League win over Arsenal.

Albion: Pearson; Smith, Adams; Magee, Bowser, McNeal; Crisp, Jones, Davies, Morris, Gregory.

Arsenal: Dunn; Bradshaw, Turnbull; Baker, Voysey, Graham; Rutherford, White, Young, Boreham, Paterson.

Attendance: 21,730

Fred Morris scored four in Albion's biggest defeat of Arsenal.

Pre-season training with Carter, Richardson, Sandford and Shaw, 1931.

24 April 1931 – Albion 2 Birmingham 1
FA Cup Final

This was the first all-Midland FA Cup Final at Wembley, and it was Second Division Albion who came out on top, thanks to two goals from their leading scorer 'W.G.' Richardson.

The Baggies didn't play all that well on a soggy pitch, but they showed tremendous team spirit, especially in defence, and had three quality forwards in Joe Carter, who pulled the strings in centre-field, skipper Tommy Glidden, who caused problems down the Blues left, and hot-shot Richardson through the middle.

In persistent rain, and after Blues' inside-left Bob Gregg had been denied an eighth-minute goal by a linesman's offside flag, Richardson gave Albion the lead on 21 minutes, squeezing his low shot under 'keeper Harry Hibbs after a smart move involving the influential Carter and a young Teddy Sandford.

But Birmingham always looked threatening and had at least three chances to equalise before half-time. They finally drew level just before the hour mark when Joe Bradford took a pass from Ernie Curtis and, unmarked inside the area, beat 'keeper Harold Pearson with a perfectly-placed shot from 15 yards.

But straight from the restart, three Albion players powered through the middle of the Blues defence, and 'W.G.' Richardson ran the ball over the line to make it 2–1.

Some inspired goalkeeping by Hibbs saved Birmingham from a much heavier defeat and victory set Albion up for their great and unique Cup and promotion double.

Albion: Pearson; Shaw, Trentham; Magee, W. Richardson, Edwards; Glidden, Carter, 'W.G.' Richardson, Sandford, Wood.

Birmingham: Hibbs; Liddell, Barkas; Cringan, Morrall, Leslie; Briggs, Crosbie, Bradford, Gregg, Curtis.

Attendance: 93,406

May 1931 – Albion 3 Charlton Athletic 2
League

Having beaten Birmingham 2–1 at Wembley the previous Saturday and accounted for Stoke City 1–0 in their penultimate League game at The Victoria Ground on the Thursday afternoon, Albion knew they had to defeat Charlton Athletic in their final match of the season to clinch promotion.

A record League crowd assembled at The Hawthorns to see if Albion could become the first team to complete the unique double – lift the FA Cup and gain promotion in the same season – but on a nervous afternoon, it was the visitors who took an early lead, Dai Astley heading firmly past Pearson after just eight minutes. Stunned, Albion almost went 2–0 down when Pugsley, completely unmarked, screwed his shot wide with an open goal in front of him. This was certainly a wake up call for the Baggies, who responded magnificently, and seven minutes before the interval Teddy Sandford equalised when he lobbed the ball home following a corner which the Charlton 'keeper had failed to collect.

Three minutes later, with the Albion fans still applauding, Charlton swept upfield and regained the lead, Astley nodding home Horton's right-wing cross – a replica of his first goal.

But Albion stuck to their task, and a minute before half-time Tommy Glidden grabbed a second equaliser, slotting the ball home at the far post after 'W.G.' Richardson had completely missed Stan Wood's precise low cross from the left.

The second half was nerve-wracking as both goals came under pressure, Astley shooting narrowly wide at one end and Wood likewise at the other. But then, on 68 minutes, Albion went in front for the first time.

Glidden found space on the right, got to the byeline and crossed high for 'W.G.' Richardson to dart forward and head the ball past Robertson amidst great excitement.

Albion's defence held firm after that, Charlton failing to create another chance, and at the final whistle thousands of supporters raced on to the pitch to congratulate their heroes on achieving the unique double.

Albion: Pearson; Shaw, Trentham; Magee, W. Richardson, Edwards; Glidden, Carter, 'W.G.' Richardson, Sandford, Wood.

Charlton Athletic: Robertson; Smith, Langford; Pitcairn, Pritchard, Pugsley; Whyper, McKay, Astley, McLeod, Horton.

Attendance: 52,415

---

19 October 1935 – Aston Villa 0 Albion 7
League

For Albion supporters, victory at Villa Park is always sweet, but in 1935 it was much more than that, as 'W.G.' Richardson and co. completely demolished the foe from Aston with a magnificent display of attacking football.

It must be said that Villa were a poor side at this time, having already conceded 23 goals in their first 10 League games, including seven at Middlesbrough. But they still had some decent players, including several internationals. However, Albion simply went out and produced some exhilarating football and tore Villa apart.

Harry 'Popeye' Jones, 'W.G.' Richardson and Jack Sankey in 1935.

The travelling Baggies fans had something to cheer about as early as the seventh minute, when Richardson darted forward to fire in Jack Mahon's right-wing cross.

Less than a minute later it was 2–0, Stan Wood shooting home unchallenged after good work by Richardson.

Playing with a strong wind at their backs, Albion powered forward and made it 3–0 in the 25th minute, Richardson skipping past Jimmy Allen to net a beauty from another terrific cross by Mahon.

Four minutes before the interval – after Wood had been denied a goal due to a dubious offside decision – Mahon got on the score sheet himself, steering Wood's pass beyond 'keeper Fred Biddlestone after Danny Blair had been robbed on the edge of the box.

It was much of the same after the break – Albion driving forward and Villa defending desperately. Yet it wasn't until the 75th minute that the lead was increased, Jack Sankey scoring from close range after Biddlestone had failed to hold Richardson's shot.

Joe Carter then supplied a great pass to set up Richardson for Albion's sixth goal on 77 minutes, and the same player bagged his fourth of the game 60 seconds later, scuffing Wood's low cross over the line from six yards.

In the dying seconds Richardson could well have equalled Jimmy Cookson's scoring record for most goals in a game, but he fluffed two rather simple chances as Villa gave up.

Villa: Biddlestone; Beeson, Blair; Gibson, Allen, McLuckie; Houghton, Brocklebank, Broome, Astley, Cunliffe.

Albion: Pearson; Shaw, Trentham; Murphy, W. Richardson, Sankey; Mahon, Carter, 'W.G.' Richardson, Sandford, Wood.

Attendance: 38,037

---

6 March 1937 – Albion 3 Arsenal 1
FA Cup

A record, never to be bettered, Hawthorns crowd witnessed this FA Cup quarter-final encounter on a snow-bound pitch. At the time Albion were in the bottom five of the First Division, whereas the Gunners were lying in second place, hoping to claim their fifth League title in six years.

But League form went out of the window as the Baggies rose to the occasion and pulled off a memorable victory. Fresh from a 6–4 home win over Sunderland and roared on by their fans, they took the lead on 10 minutes when 'W.G.' Richardson pounced on a mistake by 'keeper Frank Boulton. The centre-forward's shot was so hard that the ball rebounded 20 yards back into play after hitting the net – some spectators thinking it had struck a post.

Arsenal hit back strongly but found Albion's defence a hard nut to crack, and a minute before half-time Jack Mahon made it 2–0, firing home from 20 yards, the ball deflecting off Roberts's shoulder and over the stranded Boulton's head.

Arsenal lost winger Jimmy Milne (injured) at the start of the second half, but after Albion had missed two easy chances the visitors reduced the deficit on 76 minutes through Cliff Bastin, who looked marginally offside when he fired home following an Alex James free-kick. Albion's 'keeper Jimmy Adams then made three important saves before Mahon clinched the tie by heading a third goal from Richardson's right-wing cross in the 88th minute.

Albion's defensive strength, marshalled by Sandford who had switched to centre-half, was an important factor in a pulsating Cup tie.

Unfortunately Albion couldn't make it through to the Final, losing their semi-final showdown with Preston North End 4–1 shortly after the death of club chairman Billy Bassett.

Albion: Adams; Finch, C. Shaw; Murphy, Sandford, Sankey; Mahon, Jones, Richardson, Boyes, Coen.
Arsenal: Boulton; Male, Hapgood; Crayston, Roberts, Copping; Milne, Bowden, Kirchen, James, Bastin.
Attendance: 64,815

---

16 September 1953 – Newcastle United 3 Albion 7
League

In Coronation Year, Albion reached the crowning glory of football perfection with this magnificent win at St James' Park. Under the darkening Newcastle sky, the Baggies played some of the best attacking football ever seen on the ground and at the end of the game were applauded off the pitch by the appreciative home crowd.

Albion got off to a flying start, and in the opening quarter of an hour they had a goal disallowed, struck a post, had a clear penalty appeal turned down and saw two shots kicked off the line. They were forced to wait until the 33rd minute before taking a deserved lead, Ronnie Allen netting with a cracking drive from 30 yards after a quick break down the right by Frank Griffin.

Two minutes later Johnny Nicholls was on the spot to turn the ball into the net after another Allen shot had been saved by the diving Ronnie Simpson. And before half-time Allen scored again, his low shot taking a slight deflection off Frank Brennan.

Early in the second half, Vic Keeble pulled a goal back for United with a snap shot from just inside the area, and, with Albion back-pedalling, left-winger Bobby Mitchell found the net with a low drive on 60 minutes to cut the deficit to one.

But back came Albion, and after a smart build up involving Barlow and Allen, Nicholls stole in to make it 4–2 halfway through the half.

Newcastle, urged on by a big crowd, rallied again and Mitchell made it 4–3 with 15 minutes remaining. Albion, though, were strong and resilient, and they went into overdrive, scoring three more goals in nine minutes to clinch a brilliant win.

On 78 minutes, Nicholls completed his first-ever hat-trick when he raced through the middle to fire home Allen's measured pass. Reg Ryan smashed in number six shortly afterwards following another defence-splitting passing movement, and with five minutes remaining Griffin charged past Ron Batty and whipped the ball past Simpson to complete the scoring. And right at the end Allen got the ball stuck under his foot two yards from goal and allowed the 'keeper to snatch it away.

This was Albion's third successive win at St James' Park, following on from 4–1 and 5–3 triumphs, and Ray Barlow and Ronnie Allen were brilliant in all of them.

Newcastle: Simpson; Cowell, Batty; Scoular, Brennan, Crowe; Milburn, Davies, Keeble, Hannah, Mitchell.

Albion: Heath; Rickaby, Millard; Dudley, Dugdale, Barlow; Griffin, Ryan, Allen, Nicholls, Lee.

Attendance: 58,075

---

1 May 1954 – Albion 3 Preston North End 2
FA Cup Final

Back at Wembley for the first time in 19 years, Albion were confident of winning the FA Cup for the fourth time, having already beaten Preston twice in the League – 2–0 at Deepdale and 3–2 at The Hawthorns.

On a bright afternoon, in front of a near-capacity crowd, Albion, who had Joe Kennedy in the unfamiliar right-back position in place of the injured Stan Rickaby and Jimmy Sanders deputising for Norman Heath in goal, started the better team, but Preston had the first chance, Bobby Foster firing wide from 10 yards. Then Ronnie Allen received lengthy treatment after a clash with Joe Marston but was on his feet in time to steer Albion ahead on 21 minutes following a dash and cross from George Lee.

However, Preston equalised immediately, Angus Morrison jumping highest to head home Tom Finney's right-wing cross.

After that Finney hardly got a look in, marshalled superbly by Albion's skipper Len Millard. But despite Albion playing the more fluent football, it was Preston who stole the lead on 51 minutes when

Albion's first goal, scored by Ronnie Allen, in the 1954 FA Cup Final.

Charlie Wayman, looking a few yards offside, collected Foster's pass, rounded Sanders and found the net with ease.

Albion hit back, and after two near misses Barlow burst into the 18-yard area on 64 minutes, only to be blocked and brought down by Tommy Docherty. 'Penalty' said referee Leon Luty, and up stepped Allen, who had cracked home a spot-kick in the semi-final against Port Vale, to drive his shot to the 'keeper's right. George Thompson got his hand to the ball but couldn't prevent it from crossing the line.

Frank Griffin glides home the winner in the 1954 FA Cup Final.

With the scores level, it was now all Albion, and although Preston had two chances, Sanders saving brilliantly on both occasions, Allen had the opportunity to complete his hat-trick but missed the post by inches. Was that the last chance Albion would get? No it wasn't. Three minutes from time, Kennedy played the ball forward to Ryan who helped it on to Griffin. The winger nodded it down, raced past full-back Joe Walton and, with Allen shouting for a square pass, he ignored his teammate's call and somehow squeezed the ball under Thompson's body and into the net. Albion had won 3–2 and what joy there was in the Black Country that evening, especially after Wolves had pipped the Baggies for the League title.

Albion: Sanders; Kennedy, Millard; Dudley, Dugdale, Barlow; Griffin, Ryan, Allen, Nicholls, Lee.
Preston: Thompson; Cunningham, Walton; Docherty, Marston, Forbes; Finney, Foster, Wayman, Baxter, Morrison.
Attendance: 99,852

29 September 1954 – Wolverhampton Wanderers 4 Albion 4 FA Charity Shield

This game between the League champions Wolves and the FA Cup winners Albion turned out to be a real classic under the Molineux floodlights.

It was end to end action throughout, and perhaps in the end a draw was a fair result, although Albion were denied what looked like a clear-cut fifth goal.

An evenly-contested first half produced only one goal, scored in the 12th minute by Wolves centre-forward Roy Swinbourne, who chased Eddie Russell's long through ball and lifted it over the advancing Jimmy Sanders.

Straight after the interval, Wolves went 2–0 up when Norman Deeley headed home Peter Broadbent's flick-on from Johnny Hancocks's well-driven right-wing corner.

Ten minutes later Ronnie Allen belted home a 30-yard bullet that almost tore the net off the framework, and 90 seconds later the England striker equalised with another thunderous drive past the hapless Bert Williams.

With play hotting up, Wolves counter-attacked and Swinbourne nudged his side back in front after smart work by Deeley. Replacing the injured George Lee with Ken Hodgkisson, Albion then found themselves 4–2 down on 73 minutes when Hancocks thumped home a left-footer from 15 yards. But back came Albion, and after Reg Ryan had found the net with a full-blooded drive from 30 yards, and

Dudley had gone off injured, Allen brought the scores level with a tap-in five minutes from time. Soon afterwards, Stan Rickaby rattled a post but then came the decision that robbed Albion of victory. Awarded a free-kick 20 yards out, Ryan tapped the ball to Allen who thumped it past Williams into the net. 'No goal' said Manchester referee Frank Gibson, who stated that the ball had not travelled its full circumference before being struck by Allen.

Both clubs kept the shield for six months – but Albion should have had it for 12!

Wolves: Williams; Guttridge, Shorthouse; Flowers, Russell, Clamp; Hancocks, Broadbent, Swinbourne, Deeley, Wilshaw.

Albion: Sanders; Rickaby, Millard; Dudley (Dugdale), Kennedy, Brookes; Griffin, Ryan, Allen, Carter, Lee (Hodgkisson).

Attendance: 45,035

---

21 September 1957 – Albion 9 Manchester City 2
League

After some mixed early-season performances – three wins, four draws and a home defeat in their opening eight matches – Albion, without leading marksman Ronnie Allen, went goal crazy in this game and completely destroyed Manchester City's much vaunted 'M' plan, right-winger Frank Griffin leading the onslaught with his first hat-trick for the club.

Don Howe fired the Baggies ahead on 21 minutes, his 35-yard drive deflecting off the luckless Keith Marsden before trickling agonisingly beyond City's giant goalkeeper John Savage.

Fifteen minutes later it was 2–0. Griffin's measured pass found Ray Barlow, whose low shot flew into the net via the outstretched leg of Brian Whitehouse.

City pulled a goal back in the 39th minute when Roy Clarke fired home, but two minutes later Griffin, racing on to Barlow's astute through ball, cracked home a beauty from 12 yards to make it 3–1.

Ten minutes into the second half Fionan Fagan dragged City back to 3–2, sliding the ball home after Marsden's shot had been blocked, but 50 seconds later Griffin, cutting in from the right, saw his shot carried by Savage into the path of Bobby Robson, who stroked the ball home (4–2).

A minute later Ken Barnes (father of Peter, a future Albion winger) shot wide from the penalty spot after Barlow had fouled Fagan. And to rub salt into the wounds, Albion went straight to the other end of the field where Griffin dribbled past four defenders to score a terrific fifth goal.

Roy Horobin was next on target, netting with a fine left-footer (6–2) and in the 80th minute the winger was brought down by City's centre-half Dave Ewing, enabling Howe to make it 7–2 from the spot.

A minute later Griffin completed his hat-trick from Horobin's pass and in the 84th minute the unfortunate Ewing conceded a second penalty when he floored Kevan. The England striker picked himself up, placed the ball on the spot and promptly blasted it past Savage to complete the massacre to give Albion their biggest-ever League win at The Hawthorns. City's 'keeper Savage kicked the ball over the stand when this last Albion goal went in – to round off his day!

Albion: Sanders; Howe, S. Williams; Dudley, Kennedy, Barlow; Griffin, Whitehouse, Robson, Kevan, Horobin.

City: Savage; Brannagan, Little; Barnes, Ewing, McTavish; Fagan, Hayes, McAdams, Marsden, Clarke.

Attendance: 26,222

29 October 1957 – Albion 6 CDSA (Moscow) 5
Friendly

It was amazing that on such a wet and miserable night, approximately 53,000 fans should attend The Hawthorns to see the first-ever visit to West Bromwich of a Russian soccer team. And what a night it was…11 goals, several near misses and a ball juggling act of the highest quality by Baggies' youngster Davey Burnside during the half-time interval…and all this in front of the live TV cameras at The Hawthorns for the first time! The occasion was the official inauguration of Albion's first set of floodlights.

After the pre-match preliminaries had taken quarter of an hour to complete, the army side took the lead on 17 minutes through Vasiliy Busunov, only for Don Howe to level things up on 28 minutes with a sizzling 20-yard drive. Encouraged by this, Albion swarmed forward and seven minutes before half-time another vicious 20-yard strike, this time from Bobby Robson, put them 2–1 in front.

Albion's delight, however, was short-lived, as the army side equalised two minutes later when Vladimir Emishev crossed low for Valentin Babukin to fire past 'keeper Jimmy Sanders.

On 44 minutes, right-winger Frank Griffin made it 3–2 with a low shot that flicked off Derek Kevan before crossing the line – but Frank claimed the goal.

Immediately after the restart, a sharp movement, involving Robson and Howe, split open the Russian defence, allowing Kevan to dart into the box where he was brought down. Allen stepped up and fired home the resulting penalty.

Soon afterwards Kevan was again felled inside the 18-yard area, but this time Allen, changing from right foot to his left, sent his spot-kick a fraction wide of goalkeeper Yuriy Beljoev's right-hand post (a rare miss for the striker).

Ronnie allen scoring the penalty to make it 4–2 against CDSA (Soviet Army), The Hawthorns, 1957.

Busunov scored a third goal for the army side in the 62nd minute, and it looked as though Allen's penalty miss might prove crucial, but Kevan put the centre-forward's mind at rest with two fine goals in the 64th and 82nd minutes to push Albion into a seemingly commanding 6–3 lead. However, the resolute Russians had other ideas, and they netted twice more through Busunov on 83 minutes (his hat-trick goal) and Emishev (88), to make it 6–5 on the night. Wonderful stuff – and this was only a friendly!

Albion: Sanders; Howe, Setters; Dudley, Kennedy, Barlow; Griffin, Robson, Allen, Kevan, Horobin.

CDSA: Beljoev; Parchunov, Krutikov; Grichin, Linyaev, Petrov; Apuchtin, Babukin, Busunov, Voroshilov, Emishev.

Attendance: 52,805

18 April 1960 – Birmingham City 1 Albion 7
League

Over the course of three seasons Albion scored a total of 18 goals against Birmingham City in League games at St Andrew's, winning 5–3 in December 1957, 6–0 in September 1959 and 7–1 in April 1960.

The third victory was, in fact, Albion's best on the road in terms of goal difference and goals scored since 1936, and on reflection the final result could well have been 10–1, so well did the Baggies play against a poor Blues side battling against relegation.

Albion, with five wins under their belt from the previous seven games, looked confident but were stunned in the fourth minute when Johnny Gordon got in front of goalkeeper Jock Wallace to steer Gordon Astall's corner into the net from point-blank range.

But Blues' defence had been leaking goals all season, and six minutes later winger Derek Hogg raced down the left flank, past full-back Brian Farmer and crossed to the far post where Derek Kevan headed the ball down for Ronnie Allen to slam in the equaliser.

Albion dictated the play after that and peppered the Blues goal time and again, and only some fine acrobatic saves by Johnny Schofield kept the hosts in the game. Albion, though, deservedly went in front five minutes before the interval when, after seeing his low, angled shot blocked by Schofield, Allen reacted quickest to fire the rebound high into the net.

Two minutes later Albion's centre-half Joe Kennedy carried the ball unchallenged 50 yards downfield before laying it off to Alec Jackson, who, taking one touch, found the net with a cracking shot from fully 20 yards to make it 3–1.

As Allen had been brilliant in the first half, so Kevan (a five-goal hero against Everton a month earlier) was likewise in the second, and his rampaging runs into the penalty area caused loads of problems for Blues.

He scored Albion's fourth goal on 57 minutes with a powerful right-footed shot after making a strong run into the box to get on the end of Davy Burnside's pass, and six minutes later 'The Tank' netted with a bullet header from Hogg's precise free-kick. Then, in Albion's next attack, the England international almost cracked the crossbar with another pile-driver after being set up by Bobby Robson.

Five–one up and strolling with 20 minutes remaining, Albion continued to drive forward, and 90 seconds from time Kevan completed his hat-trick after robbing full-back George Allen and tapping the ball home from a yard!

In the 91st minute, the unfortunate and clumsy Allen then tripped his namesake inside the area in Albion's last attack of the game, allowing Ronnie to complete his hat-trick with one of his rasping penalty-kicks.

Not since January 1936, when Jack Mahon and 'W.G.' Richardson both netted trebles in an 8–1 home win over Blackburn Rovers, had two Albion players scored a hat-trick in the same League game – and, indeed, it was only the third time this had happened in the club's history.

Blues: Schofield; Farmer, Allen; Watts, Smith, Neal; Astall, Gordon, Weston, Murphy, Hooper.

Albion: Wallace; Howe, G. Williams; Drury, Kennedy, Robson; Jackson, Burnside, Allen, Kevan, Hogg.

Attendance: 28,865

---

23 February 1966 – Albion 4 West Ham United 1
League Cup Final second leg

The second leg of the 1966 League Cup Final saw Albion overturn a one goal deficit against a Hammers side that included Bobby Moore, Geoff Hurst and Martin Peters.

In front of more than 32,000 fans, Albion started off well, John Kaye smashing home Bobby Cram's cross after only 10 minutes. Nine minutes later Tony Brown made it 2–0 from close range, and in the 28th minute Albion were 3–1 up (4–3 on aggregate), when Clive Clark headed the ball practically out of goalkeeper Jim Standen's hands as the Worcestershire cricketer failed to gather a high cross.

Left-half and skipper Graham Williams drove forward from the halfway line to make it 4–0 in the 35th minute with a crisp drive from 30 yards, and at this point it was virtually game over as far as the Hammers were concerned.

Albion had been brilliant for 45 minutes, and they continued to run the show during the early stages of the second half. West Ham, to their credit, stuck in there and rallied late on, Peters reducing the arrears in the 75th minute. But it was Albion's night and Williams joyously climbed the steps leading to the directors' box to collect the club's first major trophy in 12 years...and with it came a place in the Fairs Cup for 1966–67.

Albion: Potter; Cram, Fairfax; Fraser, Campbell, Williams; T. Brown, Astle, Kaye, Hope, Clark.

West Ham: Standen; Burnett, Peters; Bovington, K. Brown, Moore; Brabrook, Boyce, Byrne, Hurst, Sissons.

Attendance: 32,013

---

14 September 1966 – Albion 6 Aston Villa 1
League Cup

Albion, the League Cup holders, annihilated Aston Villa in this second-round tie at The Hawthorns. Jimmy Hagan's team of attackers dealt out a sparkling six-goal hammering to their near-neighbours in an embarrassingly one-sided contest.

From the first seconds of the game, Albion outplayed, outran and outwitted a poor Villa side, who took a thrashing far greater than the score suggests.

Scottish midfielder was the genius behind a terrific Albion performance, netting a hat-trick (the first of his career) and having a hand in two of the other three goals.

Albion got off to an explosive start, scoring three times in the first 29 minutes, and it would have been six if it hadn't been for the heroics of Villa's 'keeper Colin Withers.

The opening goal came on 12 minutes from their seventh corner. Picking up the ball some 25 yards out after Clive Clark had hit a post, Doug Fraser moved forward to thump a beauty straight into the net.

Seven minutes later, non-stop Fraser did it again, chipping the ball smartly over Withers after collecting Jeff Astle's smart pass. And after John Kaye had seen his effort saved at the foot of a post, Kenny Foggo burst down the right and crossed to the opposite flank where Clark headed the ball back for Hope to thrash home. Lew Chatterley missed a sitter in a rare Villa attack before Hope struck the bar with another superb shot.

Albion's stampede continued after the break, and on 56 minutes Clark skipped past three defenders before slipping the ball past the bemused Withers to make it 4–0. Tony Hateley pulled one back on 59 minutes after a mistake by Stan Jones, but Albion still had a lot to offer as Hope raced in to make it 5–1 halfway through the second half, before completing his hat-trick and Villa's misery with a sixth on 80 minutes.

This was Albion's biggest win (in League and Cup) over Villa for 31 years.

Albion: Sheppard; Cram, Collard; Lovett, Jones, Fraser; Foggo, Astle, Kaye, Hope, Clark.
Villa: Withers: Bradley, Aitken; Tindall, Sleeuwenhoek, Deakin; MacLeod, Park, Hateley, Chatterley, Scott.
Attendance: 25,039

---

9 November 1966 – Albion 5 DOS Utrecht 2
Fairs Cup

A crowd of almost 20,000 witnessed Albion's first-ever European home game, but the Baggies made hard work of beating a rather weak Dutch side, who in the first leg had certainly given a good account of themselves when gaining a 1–1 draw.

Albion were the bookies' favourites to win the return game at The Hawthorns, but in the end they had fit-again hat-trick hero Tony Brown to thank for their 6–3 aggregate victory.

Brown's and Albion's first goal came from a 13th-minute penalty awarded after DOS defender Eddy Achterberg had foolishly handled Bobby Hope's inviting cross. After that, play was rather scrappy with few goalmouth incidents, Hope fluffing Albion's best chance shortly before half-time.

After a stern word from manager Jimmy Hagan, Albion began the second half with a surge, and in the 49th minute Jeff Astle headed on for Clive Clark to steer home goal number two. Utrecht pulled one back on 58 minutes when Leo de Vroet scored from a corner, but 11 minutes later Brown got on the end of Hope's measured cross to head Albion into a 3–1 lead.

That was increased to 4–1 in the 75th minute when John Kaye powered home Astle's downward header, but almost immediately Arie de Kuyper's shot was deflected into the net by Fraser to make it 4–2.

But thankfully Brown had the last laugh, and he completed his hat-trick with a smart finish, with two minutes remaining.

Albion: Potter; C. Campbell, Collard; Brown, Jones, Fraser; Williams, Astle, Kaye, Hope, Clark.
Utrecht: Hoogeveen; De Weerd, Veenstra; Plagemaan, Aarts, Achterberg; De Vroet, Van den Bogert, De Kuyper, Van der Linden, Wery.
Attendance: 19,962

18 May 1968 – Albion 1 Everton 0
FA Cup Final

This was Albion's 10th appearance in an FA Cup Final, and although this wasn't a classic encounter it was certainly absorbing and interesting, and in the end it took a piece of magic from the 'King' himself, Jeff Astle, to clinch victory for the Baggies.

Six weeks before the Final, Everton had whipped Albion 6–2 in a League game at The Hawthorns, Alan Ball scoring four times. But the England World Cup winner hardly got a look in at Wembley as Albion, for long periods, had the better of the midfield exchanges but lacked penetration up front. John Osborne pulled off several fine saves, and his heroics in tight situations earned great applause from the fans.

Clive Clark came closest to scoring for Albion in the first half, while Jimmy Husband (twice) and Joe Royle both missed chances for the Merseysiders.

The football in the second half was rather pedestrian, although there were a few goalmouth incidents, and Husband missed a real sitter when it looked easier to score. At the end of normal time, Albion boss Alan Ashman created history by taking off the injured John Kaye and replacing him with Dennis Clarke, who thus became the first substitute to play in an FA Cup Final.

John Osborne (WBA), collects the ball from a right-sided corner, 1968 FA Cup Final.

Then, just as the sun came out, in the 94th minute Graham Williams and Doug Fraser linked up on the left. The ball found its way up to Astle, who drove forward and tried a shot at goal. The ball came back to him off Brian Labone and with his weaker left foot he drilled it high into the net past 'keeper Gordon West's right hand. 'The King' had done it, scored in every round of the competition and this extra-special effort was worth its weight in gold. Albion had won the Cup and with it gained a place in the 1968–69 European Cup-winners' Cup competition.

Albion: Osborne; Fraser, Williams; T. Brown, Talbut, Kaye (Clarke); Lovett, Collard, Astle, Hope, Clark.

Everton: West; Wright, Wilson; Kendall, Labone, Harvey; Husband, Ball, Royle, Hurst, Morrissey. Sub (not used): Kenyon.

Attendance: 99,665

24 April 1976 – Oldham Athletic 0 Albion 1 League

Albion had to go out and win this game – their last of the season – to ensure a return to the First Division after an absence of three years.

An army of more than 15,000 Baggies fans travelled to Boundary Park to cheer on Johnny Giles's men, and although the game wasn't a classic it was certainly tense and nerve-wracking.

Albion had chances in the first half but nothing clear cut, and in the dressing room at the break the players learned that their nearest challengers Bolton Wanderers, who could over take them if they lost to Oldham, were winning at Charlton.

After Giles had given his pep talk, the team came out with all guns blazing at the start of the second period, and after 54 minutes Boundary Park erupted as Tony Brown volleyed Albion in front from his namesake Ally's downward header after some terrific work down the right involving Paddy Mulligan and Mick Martin.

Although Robins and ex-Albion man Dave Shaw came close to equalising, Tony Brown almost made it 2–0, but the Baggies held out, and it was certainly celebration time on the homeward journey down the M6 for players and supporters alike.

Oldham: Ogden; Wood, Whittle; Bell, Edwards, Hicks; Blair, Shaw, Robins, Chapman (Branagan), Groves.

Albion: Osborne; Mulligan, Cantello; T. Brown, Wile, Robertson; Martin, A. Brown, Mayo, Giles, Johnston. Sub (not used): Robson.

Attendance: 22,356

21 October 1978 – Albion 7 Coventry City 1 League

Coventry City – wearing a horrible chocolate-coloured strip – were well and truly licked by a highly-skilled, confident and very efficient Albion side in this First Division encounter at The Hawthorns.

Len Cantello scored the Baggies' opening goal in the 14th minute, finishing off Tony Brown's pin-point pass in style, the ball flying high into the net off the hands of diving 'keeper Les Sealey.

Albion's two black England internationals.

Laurie Cunningham made it 2–0 in the 28th minute, tucking home a fine cross from the overlapping Brendon Batson. And seven minutes later Cyrille Regis added number three with a powerful header after some excellent work by Cantello and Tony Brown.

The impressive Cunningham grabbed his second goal of the game and Albion's fourth in the 62nd minute, heading home skipper John Wile's flick-on from Brown's left-wing corner. And after Mick Ferguson had somehow pulled one back for Coventry on 70 minutes, heading in Tony Green's left-wing centre, Brown rammed in Albion's fifth goal on 76 minutes from Bryan Robson's pass.

Regis bagged number six in the 82nd minute, storming through the middle of a static Coventry defence to hammer his shot beyond Sealey, and left-back Derek Statham rounded things off with a seventh goal a minute from time, picking up the pieces after Terry Yorath had lost possession just outside the penalty area.

Albion: Godden; Batson, Statham; Cunningham, Wile, Robertson; Robson, A. Brown, Regis, Cantello (Johnston), T. Brown.

Coventry: Sealey; Coop, McDonald; Yorath, Holton (Green), Gillespie; Hutchinson, Wallace, Ferguson, Powell, Hunt.

Attendance: 27,409

30 May 1993 – Albion 3 Port Vale 0
Second Division Play-off Final

This was Albion's first visit to Wembley for 23 years and over 42,300 fans went with them – the biggest away following the club has ever had.

Ossie Ardiles's side had battled their way through to this Play-off Final with determination and no mean skill, and they were clear favourites to beat Port Vale, who had actually finished a place higher in the table than Albion and with four more points.

Fielding his strongest side, Ardiles saw his charges pepper the Vale goal throughout the first half without success, but after the Valiants centre-half Peter Swan was dismissed by referee Roger Milford for a professional foul on Bob Taylor in the 59th minute (becoming only the ninth player to take an early bath at Wembley in 70 years), the floodgates opened and Albion drove clean through.

The inevitable breakthrough came on 69 minutes. Kevin Donovan's right-wing corner was headed against the post by Gary Strodder, 'keeper Musslewhite flicked the ball up only for Andy Hunt to jump and send a form header into the net.

It was a case of 'Boing, Boing' around three parts of the stadium at this point, and when Donovan broke clear and laid the ball into the path of full-back Nicky Reid to crash home his first goal for the Baggies, it was game over and promotion won for Ardiles's men.

Later on, Donovan, who had missed three far-easier chances during the game, made it 3–0 with a close range finish after Bob Taylor had won a 50–50 ball with his namesake Ian.

A delighted skipper, Darren Bradley walked joyfully up the 39 steps to collect the Trophy and afterwards said 'That was the best feeling of my life.'

Albion: Lange; Reid, Lilwall; Bradley, Raven, Strodder; Hunt (Garner), Hamilton, R. Taylor, McNally, Donovan. Sub (not used): G. Robson.

Vale: Musselwhite; Aspin, Kent (Billing); Porter, Swan, Glover; Slaven, Van der Laan (Cross), Foyle, Kerr, I. Taylor.

Attendance: 53,471

8 May 1994 – Portsmouth 0 Albion 1 League

This was another must win game for Albion. If they failed to beat Pompey and neighbours Birmingham City won (or even drew) at Tranmere on the same afternoon, then they would stay in Division One and the Baggies would be relegated.

It was certainly a crucial, nail-biting climax to a disappointing season, but Albion, backed by around 10,000 travelling supporters, set about the task in an honest and forthright manner.

Gary Strodder headed wide, Bob Taylor hesitated in a one-on-one situation and Andy Hunt had a goal disallowed for Albion, while Stuart Doling, Mark Chamberlain and Bjorn Kristensen went close for Portsmouth. It was frantic stuff. Then, on 39 minutes, came the decisive goal – scored by Lee Ashcroft with a close-range header after a wonderful cross from the left by Ian Hamilton.

It took at least two minutes for stewards to clear the pitch as Baggies' supporters celebrated in their beachwear before the half-time whistle.

The second period was tense, mighty tense. Albion's substitute 'keeper Tony Lange made the save of the season to keep out a curling effort from Paul Hall, Donovan tried a shot from fully 70 yards, Taylor and Hunt both fired over, and Strodder and McNally both cleared shots off their own goalline. News filtered through that Birmingham had beaten Tranmere 2–1 courtesy of a last-minute winner and their game finished well before Albion's. The last few minutes were unbearable, but when referee David Elleray blew the final whistle it was celebration time yet again for the Baggies escapees!

Portsmouth: Knight; Dobson, Powell, Gittens, Pethick; Stimson (Butters), Chamberlain, Hall, Doling (Burton); Wood, Kristensen. Sub (not used): Flahaven.

Albion: Lange; Parsley, Raven, Strodder, Darton; Hamilton, McNally, Donovan, Ashcroft (Mellon); Hunt, Taylor. Subs (not used): Mardon, Cutler.

Attendance: 17,629

21 April 2002 – Albion 2 Crystal Palace 0 League

In front of an all-ticket crowd, Albion knew if they beat Crystal Palace by any score then they would win a place in the Premiership. A draw might be enough, but that would depend on the outcome of another crucial game at Hillsborough.

Manchester City had already been crowned First Division champions. The second automatic promotion spot was between just two teams: Albion and their Black Country neighbours Wolves, who were playing at Sheffield Wednesday.

A return ticket to the top flight for the first time since 1986 was there for the taking! Again it was tense, mighty tense, even tenser as news broke that Wolves had scored in the first minute at Hillsborough. But the Baggies' roar started to unfold. The players responded, although some tentative play produced a couple of close shaves around Hoult's goal. Then Neil Clement's free-kick from the left found the head of Darren 'Big Dave' Moore. Danny Dichio challenged in the air, the ball fell back to Moore who side-footed home: 1–0. Albion were in charge and they remained so, competently holding their opponents at bay. News filtered through that the Owls had levelled things up against Wolves. The noise got louder as the fans roared on their heroes. At half-time it was still 1–0 to the Albion and 1–1 at Hillsborough.

Then, in the 54th minute, just as Wednesday took the lead against Wolves, so Bob Taylor pounced to put Albion 2–0 up against Palace. What joy!

Clement's free-kick was fumbled by 'keeper Kolinko and as the ball squirted free, Super Bob reacted quickest of all to plant it into the net. Albion were on fire; the fans celebrated in glorious fashion, and although Wolves scraped a draw at Hillsborough the Baggies held on confidently and proudly to earn their place with the elite of English football.

The after-match scenes of joy and delight will remain in the memories of everyone who was present at The Hawthorns that afternoon.

Albion: Hoult; Balis, Moore, Gilchrist, Sigurdsson, Clement; McInnes, Johnson (Jordao), A. Chambers; Taylor (Dobie), Dichio (Fox). Subs (not used): Cummings, Petterson.
Palace: Kolinko; Austin, Popovic, Granville, Rodger (Rubins); Mullins, Riihilahti (Kirovski), Hopkin, Fleming; Morrison, Akinbiyi (Black). Subs (not used): Berhalter, Carasso.
Attendance: 26,712

---

15 May 2005 – Albion 2 Portsmouth 0
Premiership

Going into this final weekend of the season, any three of four teams could drop out of the Premiership. Norwich had 33 points, Southampton and Crystal Palace 32 and Albion 31.

Albion had to win – nothing else – and hope that Norwich slipped up at Fulham, and that Southampton and Palace drew or lost against Manchester United and Charlton respectively.

Eleven years earlier it was a similar situation – Albion had to beat Portsmouth on the last day of the campaign to avoid relegation. It was the same here in 2005 inside a packed Hawthorns. The 'Great Escape' was on, and if Albion could stay up they would create history by becoming the first team to avoid relegation after propping up the Premiership table at Christmas. Manager Bryan Robson got his players in the right frame of mind for the big occasion, and they responded to his call, and to the cheers of the supporters, by recording a famous victory.

Rob Earnshaw sent one effort wide and Kevin Campbell was off target with a header, while at the other end Tomasz Kuszczak was by far the more busy of the two goalkeepers as Portsmouth had the better of a scrappy first half.

Robson introduced Geoff Horsfield just before the hour mark and with his first touch he set The

Hawthorns alight with a cracking goal, volleying the ball under 'keeper Jamie Ashdown after Zoltan Gera's cross had dropped to him off the head of Dejan Stefanovic.

At this point, Norwich were 3–0 down at Craven Cottage, Saints were level at 1–1 with United and Palace had just equalised at Charlton. The tension was unbearable.

Then news came through that Palace had taken the lead and so too had Manchester United against Southampton. All of a sudden The Hawthorns went quiet, and it remained so even when Kieran Richardson, on loan from Manchester United, made it 2–0 with 15 minutes remaining.

There were headphones attached to virtually every other Albion supporter inside the ground as the minutes ticked by...Southampton still trailed, Norwich were by now dead and buried, and Palace were still in front at the Valley. 'Come on Charlton' was the cry, and then, with just eight minutes or so remaining, a terrific roar went up. Charlton had equalised and that meant that if the scores remained as they were at that juncture then Albion would escape. Those last few minutes seemed endless, but at the final whistle thousands of delirious supporters raced on to the pitch to congratulate the players, and of course Robson, as the theme tune from the famous film (*The Great Escape*) bellowed out through the loudspeakers. What a result, what drama, what a day – well it was Albion who were involved, who else!

Albion: Kuszczak; Albrechtsen, Gaardsoe, Clement, Robinson; Gera, Wallwork, Richardson, Greening (Horsfield); Campbell, Earnshaw (Kanu). Subs (not used): Inamoto, Murphy, Moore.

Portsmouth: Ashdown; Primus, Stefanovic, De Zueew, Taylor; Cisse, Kamara (Rodic), Hughes (Skopelitis), O'Neill; Fuller, Keene (Mezague). Subs (not used): Chalkis, Duffy.

Attendance: 27,751

Top 100 players

ALLEN Ronnie

Centre-forward/winger: 415 apps. 234 goals.

Born: Fenton, Stoke-on-Trent, 15 January 1929.

Died: Great Wyrley, Staffs, 9 June 2001.

Career: Hanley High School (football and rugby union), Bucknall Boy's Brigade, Wellington Scouts, Northwood Mission, Staffs County Youths, Port Vale, RAF (two years), ALBION (£20,050 March 1950–May 1961), Crystal Palace (£4,500, player-coach, retired 1965), Wolverhampton Wanderers (coach, then manager), Athletic Bilbao (manager), Sporting Lisbon (manager), Saudi Arabia (coach), Walsall (manager), ALBION (scouting advisor January–June 1977, manager June–December 1977), Saudi Arabia (national coach), Panathinaikos (manager), ALBION (manager July 1981–May 1982, general manager June 1982–May 1983). Director of Black Country oil-rig company and ALBION (coach May 1993–May 1996).

■ Initially a right-winger, Ronnie Allen was converted into a brilliant centre-forward by Albion after scoring on his debut for the club in the 1–1 home draw with Wolves in March 1950, when a record League crowd of almost 61,000 assembled at The Hawthorns. An ace marksman, superb volleyer of the ball and possessing a powerful right-foot shot, he netted 234 goals for Albion, of which 208 came in the Football League (all in Division One), a total bettered only by Tony Brown. Allen gained five full England caps (his first against Switzerland in 1952) as well as playing for his country's B team, representing the Football League and also starring for the FA XI. In 1954 he netted twice in a 3–2 FA Cup Final victory over Preston North End, including a dramatic equalising penalty, having clinched a place in the Final with a penalty winner against his former club Port Vale in the semis. In that same year he also scored a hat-trick in a 4–4 Charity Shield draw with Wolves at Molineux.

Allen went on to claim a total of 276 goals in 637 League matches in his career, and in all games his record was 354 goals in 812 outings. He scored in each season, from 1944–45 to 1964–65 inclusive, and was the First Division's top marksman in 1954–55 with 27 goals. He also netted 21 goals in 25 reserve games for the Baggies. After becoming an Albion shareholder, he was a part-time coach at the club and made a brief appearance as 'substitute' in a friendly at Cheltenham, aged 66. Allen, who was awarded a testimonial versus Aston Villa in August 1997, Albion through and through.

Allen was also an excellent golfer, twice winning the Professional Footballers' Golf title – 1959 and 1961 – and finishing runner-up in 1963 and 1964. His son, Russell, played briefly for Albion before becoming a prolific scorer for Tranmere.

ASTLE Jeff

Striker: 361 apps. 174 goals.

Born: Eastwood, Nottingham, 13 May 1942.

Died: Burton-on-Trent, 20 January 2002.

Career: Devonshire Drive Junior & Walker Street Secondary Schools, West Notts Juniors, Holy Trinity Youth Club, Notts County (trial), Coventry City (trial), John Player, Notts County, ALBION (£25,000 September 1964–May 1974), Hellenic, Dunstable, Weymouth, Atherstone, Hillingdon Borough (retired 1977). He ran his own industrial cleaning business near Burton-on-Trent, also appeared on TV's Fantasy Football *with Frank Skinner and David Baddiel and in 1996 entered variety performance with the* Jeff Astle Road Show.

■ Jeff Astle was a brilliant centre-forward with great heading ability and a strong right-foot shot. 'The King' to all Baggies supporters, he was groomed by the great Tommy Lawton at Meadow Lane and scored 41 goals for Notts County before serving Albion for 10 years. He made his debut at Leicester 24 hours after signing and netted twice at The Hawthorns shortly afterwards in a 5–1 win over

Wolves. Capped five times by England, he played in the 1970 World Cup Finals in Mexico, appeared against Young England in 1969, had three games for an England XI (scoring seven goals, four against Liga University in 1970) and twice represented the Football League (four goals). A member of Albion's League Cup and FA Cup-winning teams in 1966 and 1968 respectively, he netted in every round of the latter competition and was the first player to score goals in both the FA Cup and League Cup Finals at Wembley, doing so in 1968 versus Everton and in 1970 versus Manchester City. Midland Footballer of the Year in 1968, he scored 20 goals in 46 reserve matches for Albion. Astle's death was tragic and, on 21 November 2002, South Staffordshire coroner Andrew Haigh concluded that he died from brain injuries caused by repeatedly heading a ball (dementia: footballers' migraine).

ASHMORE George

Goalkeeper: 268 apps.

Born: Plymouth, Devon, 5 May 1898.
Died: Handsworth, Birmingham, 12 May 1973.
Career: South Devon & District Schools, Nineveh Wesley (Handsworth), ALBION (professional, November 1919). Chesterfield (October 1931); retired, May 1935; later worked for the MEB (Birmingham) for many years.

■ George 'Cap' Ashmore spent almost 12 years at The Hawthorns, during which time he accumulated a fine appearance record and in 1926 played for England against Belgium in Antwerp, his only international cap. A loyal and dedicated servant to the club, he played under the shadow of Hubert Pearson for a number of years and then understudied his son, Harold, after that. He made his League debut against Blackburn Rovers at Ewood Park in October 1920 when the Baggies lost 5–1, but undeterred he quickly put that result behind him and developed

into a fine, agile and courageous goalkeeper, a fine shot-stopper with a good right-foot kick. Besides his first-team exploits, Ashmore also made 114 appearances for Albion's second XI, collecting both Birmingham & District and Central League championship-winning medals in 1919–20 and 1922–23 respectively. After leaving The Hawthorns he played in 71 League matches for Chesterfield.

BARLOW Ray

Half-back, inside/centre-forward: 482 apps. 48 goals.

Born: Swindon, 17 August 1926.
Career: Sandford Street School, Swindon Town, Garrards FC, ALBION (amateur June 1944, professional November 1944–June 1960), Swindon Town, Birmingham City, Stourbridge (retired 1962), West Bromwich Albion Old Stars. Ran tobacconist and confectionery shop in West Bromwich, later managed a sub-post office/newsagents shop near Stourbridge and now living in Pedmore, Stourbridge.

■ One of the finest footballers ever to don an Albion shirt, Ray Barlow was mainly a left-half but could also play equally as well at centre-half, centre-forward and inside-left. He made his first-team debut for the club in a 2–0 home Wartime League Cup defeat by Walsall in February 1945, following up with his League debut against Newport County at Somerton Park in September 1946, when he scored in a resounding 7–2 win. A wonderfully gifted footballer, tall, elegant in style and long striding, he could pass a ball with pin-point accuracy and possessed a strong right-foot shot, which produced several superb

goals, including a real cracker in Albion's FA Cup quarter-final win over Tottenham Hotspur on their way to winning the trophy in 1954.

The driving force in Albion's midfield during the early part of the 1950s, he served the club for a total of 16 years, during which time he appeared in 403 League games. Surprisingly to a lot of people, especially Albion fans, Barlow gained just one England cap, deputising for Portsmouth's Jimmy Dickinson against Northern Ireland in Belfast when he starred in a 2–0 win. He also represented England B, the Football League on four occasions and the FA XI once, also netting 10 goals in 41 Central League games for Albion. Approaching the veteran stage of his career when he left The Hawthorns, Barlow made only seven appearances for Birmingham City. Besides his footballing ability, he was also a very useful cricketer who played quite a few games in the Birmingham League for West Bromwich Dartmouth.

BASSETT Billy JP

Outside-right: 311 apps. 77 goals.

Born: West Bromwich, 27 January 1869.

Died: West Bromwich, 9 April 1937.

Career: Christ Church School, Oak Villa, West Bromwich Strollers (not Albion), Old Church Club, ALBION (August 1886, retired April 1899), coach at The Hawthorns. West Bromwich publican, ALBION (shareholder, then director August 1905, chairman from 1908 until his death) and qualified as a Football League linesman.

■ One of the club's all-time greats, Billy Bassett was, for 13 years, the star of Albion's forward line, firstly at inside-right (he made his debut in that position against Wednesbury Old Athletic in an FA Cup tie in October 1887) and then more predominantly on the right wing. Quick, direct and highly effective, he possessed superb ball control and could score goals as well as make them. He averaged a goal every four

games for Albion, claiming a total of 135 in 560 first-team appearances with 77 coming in 311 first-class appearances. He gained two FA Cup-winners' medals, the first in 1888 when he was brilliant against Preston North End and the second four years later against arch-rivals Aston Villa, whom he played against in the losing Final of 1895.

Bassett also scored when Albion beat Great Bridge Unity 10–1 in the Final of the West Bromwich Charity Cup in 1888, and that same year he lined up against the Scottish Cup winners Renton in a game billed as the Championship of the World. He won a total of 16 full caps for England, eight coming in successive matches against Scotland between 1889 and 1896, scoring in his last. He also represented the Football League on three occasions between 1891 and 1897, played for an England XI, a Football League XI, represented the FA and appeared in several international trials. After retiring at the age of 30 – his last outing for Albion was in a 7–1 League defeat away to Aston Villa in April 1899 – Bassett coached the youngsters for a short while. He then bought some shares and subsequently became a director, later acting as chairman of the club for a period of 27 years, from 1905 to 1937. He rarely missed a board meeting and his influence at Albion was incalculable. At the club's Annual General Meeting in 1936, he was presented with a silver casket and quality 'illuminated' scroll/address to mark his 50 years' association with the club (in all categories). For seven years from August 1930 he was a member of the Football League management committee, sitting on the international selection panel in season 1936–37. Bassett, who was appointed Justice of the Peace at a ceremony in West Bromwich in 1935, died shortly before Albion's FA Cup semi-final against Preston North End at Highbury in 1937. The players were shocked by his demise and never performed on the day, losing the game 4–1. For his obituary produced in the Albion official programme, the editor described him as 'a guide, philosopher and friend' to the club, and the Football League secretary, Fred Howarth, declared him to be 'the most popular man in the game.'

Bassett's son, Norman Bassett, and his brother, Harry Bassett, were both associated with Albion. Norman was a director of the club for 15 years, from 1937 to 1952, following Billy into office, and Harry was a reserve inside-right who partnered Billy for the first time on the wing against the Birmingham & District representative side in April 1892.

BATSON Brendon MBE

Right-back: 220 apps. 2 goals.

Born: St George, Grenada, 6 February 1953.

Career: Arsenal, Cambridge United, ALBION (£30,000 February 1978, retired May 1984), joined PFA (became deputy chief executive), Witton Albion, WBA All Stars, ALBION (managing-director July 2002–June 2003); now a consultant for the FA.

■ Brendon Batson was a very efficient footballing right-back. Always keen to overlap, he accumulated well over 400 appearances at club level with over half for Albion, for whom he scored just two goals – in a 4–0 home FA Cup replay win over Coventry City in January 1979 and in a 3–1 League victory over Ipswich Town at The Hawthorns in April 1981. He helped Arsenal win the FA Youth Cup and Cambridge United win the Fourth Division title, starred for Albion as they reached two major Cup semi-finals (losing them both) and helped them qualify for and reach the quarter-finals of the UEFA Cup. He was manager Ron Atkinson's first signing for Albion, having made his League debut for his first club, Arsenal, against the Baggies in 1971. His initial outing for Albion came in the Midlands derby victory at Birmingham City a few days after joining when he replaced Paddy Mulligan. Batson also played in seven Central League games for the club and was capped three times by England B in 1980. Unfortunately his career came to an abrupt end at the age of 31 and, after a deserved testimonial match, he immediately joined the PFA. Returning to The Hawthorns in 2002, he was placed in charge of footballing matters, a position he held for just 12 months. He was awarded the MBE in 2001.

BAYLISS 'Jem'

Forward: 95 apps. 36 goals.

Born: Tipton, 14 January 1863.

Died: West Bromwich, 19 August 1933.

Career: Great Bridge & Horseley Heath Council Schools, Great Bridge Unity, Tipton Providence, Wednesbury Old Athletic (1880), ALBION (amateur August 1884, professional August 1885, retired March 1892), Walsall Town, ALBION (director August 1891–August 1905, life member of club August 1909).

■ Gentleman 'Jem' Bayliss ('Jem' was derived from the initials of three of his Christian names, James Edward Matthias) was still a registered player when he was appointed as a director, when the club became a limited company in August 1891. He remained on the board for 14 years, until replaced by his former playing colleague Billy Bassett. During his eight years as an Albion player, Bayliss – a quality footballer, fast and clever, with an eye for goal – played in almost 300 first-team matches for Albion (mainly friendlies and local Cup competitions) and averaged more than a goal every two games, claiming an overall tally of 158, including 121 in the space of three seasons – 1885–86, 1886–87 and 1887–88. He scored on his senior debut against Derby Street Junction (away) in the FA Cup in October 1884 and appeared in three successive FA Cup Finals, those of 1886, 1887 and 1888, gaining a winners' medal in the latter when he scored the opening goal in the 2–1 victory over Preston North End at The Oval. He also grabbed four goals in Albion's 10–1 West Bromwich Charity Cup Final win over Great Bridge Unity in 1888 and scored in three Staffordshire Cup Final victories – claiming a brace when Stoke were beaten 4–2 in 1886, two more in a 4–0 victory over Walsall Swifts in 1887 and another effort when Leek lost 2–1 in 1889. Initially an out-and-out centre-forward, Bayliss was successfully converted into a right-half by Albion and gained his only full England cap in that position against Ireland in March 1891, helping his country to an emphatic 6–1 win. Six years later, on his return from holiday in Gibralter, he actually read his own obituary in a local paper. It was rumoured that while abroad he had developed typhoid fever and died of the ailment at his Great Bridge home. Bayliss, despite being rather upset at what he had read, quickly reported himself fit and well and, in fact, lived for another 36 years!

BOWSER Sid

Inside-left/centre-half: 371 apps. 72 goals.

Born: Handsworth, Birmingham, 6 April 1891.

Died: Birmingham, 10 February 1961.

Career: Astbury Richmond, Willenhall Town, Birmingham, Willenhall Town, ALBION (July 1908–April 1913), Belfast Distillery, ALBION (February 1914–August 1924), Walsall (£250, retired May 1927); became a licensee in Dudley.

■ The tenacious, resilient and hard-working Sid Bowser had two excellent spells at The Hawthorns. He divided his immense talents between two completely different roles – those of inside-forward and centre-half – and he excelled in both. He was a goalscorer in his first period at the club, having learned his trade while playing locally in the Handsworth and Wolverhampton Leagues. He netted twice on his League debut as a 17-year-old in a resounding 7–2 home win over Grimsby in January 1909, thus becoming the club's youngest League marksman at that time. He actually held the record until Geoff Richards surpassed it against Luton in December 1946. Bowser helped the Baggies win the Second Division title in 1910–11

(appearing in all 38 League games) and a year later played in the FA Cup Final when Albion lost 1–0 in a replay to Barnsley. When he returned to the club after spending eight months in Ireland (moving there after a wage dispute), he was converted into a redoubtable, no-nonsense centre-half and became a key figure at the heart of the defence as Albion won the First Division title in 1919–20. He missed only one game and netted 10 goals, his total including a hat-trick (two penalties) in a 4–1 home victory over Bradford City, being the first defender to achieve this feat for the club. Bowser gained just one full England cap, competing in the 1–1 draw against Ireland in October 1919, having earlier represented the Irish League as a Distillery player. He left Albion, for the second time round, for Walsall and retired at the end of the 1926–27 season, having played 28 times for the Saddlers along with winger Lewis Bedford, who had been with Albion during seasons 1920–22. Bowser was born just a stone's throw from The Hawthorns and, as a lad, he stood on the Handsworth side of the ground. He attended his first match in 1900, having previously watched a few games at Villa Park with his father. He still followed the fortunes of Albion right up until his death at the age of 70.

BOYES Wally

Inside and outside-left/left-half: 165 apps. 38 goals.

Born: Killamarsh, Sheffield, 5 January 1913.

Died: Sheffield, 12 September 1960.

Career: Sheffield Boys, Woodhouse Mills United, ALBION (February 1931–February 1938), Everton (£6,000); World War Two guest for

Aldershot, Brentford, Clapton Orient, Leeds United, Manchester United, Middlesbrough, Millwall, Newcastle United, Preston North End and Sunderland; Notts County (player-coach), Scunthorpe United (player-trainer), Retford Town (player-manager), Hyde United (player-manager, retired 1959), Swansea Town (trainer); sports master at Oakwood Collegiate School and later coach at schools in the Sheffield area.

■ Standing a fraction under 5ft 4in tall, Wally 'Titty' Boyes was a diminutive but well-built footballer, who occupied three different positions for Albion and always gave 100 percent. He made his League debut in front of almost 60,000 fans in the local derby against Aston Villa nine months after signing, lining up at inside-left in a 3–0 victory. He gained a regular place in the side towards the end of that season, mainly occupying the left-half position (in place of Jimmy Edwards) before finally bedding down on the left-wing from January 1934 after taking over from Stan Wood. Just over a year later, Boyes scored in the 1935 FA Cup Final defeat by Sheffield Wednesday, the team he supported as a lad! He also scored 24 goals in almost 100 games for Albion's second string, gaining two Central League Championship medals – the first in 1932–33 and the second when the Baggies retained the title the following season. Moving to Everton, perhaps unwillingly, when still a regular in the Albion team, he collected a League Championship-winners' medal at the end of his first full season at Goodison Park. He then added two more full England caps to his tally, having gained his first as an Albion player in a 1–0 win over Holland in Amsterdam in May 1935, when he lined up with his Albion teammate 'W.G.' Richardson. He also played in the Jubilee international, England against Scotland, in 1938. As a youngster Boyes once scored 17 goals in one game, which his team won 31–2.

BROWN Ally

Striker: 331+28 apps. 85 goals.

Born: Musselburgh near Edinburgh, 12 April 1951.

Career: Edinburgh & District Schools, Leicester City, ALBION (£61,111 March 1972–March 1983), Portland Timbers, Crystal Palace, Walsall, Port Vale (retired, injured 1986); licensee in Great Barr and later steward of The Throstle Club near to The Hawthorns.

■ A key member of Albion's attack during the 1970s and early 1980s, Ally Brown played alongside some fine marksmen including Jeff Astle, his namesake Tony Brown and Cyrille Regis. He scored his fair share of goals, 85 in 11 years at The Hawthorns, and he also netted 38 times in 109 second XI games, but, surprisingly, and certainly annoyingly, he never received a testimonial for his efforts...although he was subsequently presented with the Mecca Loyalty Award by former Wimbledon tennis star and Baggies fan Ann Jones.

Brown, who top scored for Leicester in 1970–71 when the Foxes won the Second Division title, netted on his debut for the Baggies against Crystal Palace at home in March 1972 and played his part in helping Johnny Giles's team win promotion to the First

Division in 1976, having had a couple of lean seasons under Don Howe's management prior to that. He then proved to be a vital cog in Albion's mechanism under future bosses Ronnie Allen and Ron Atkinson. Voted Midland Footballer of the Year (jointly with Tony Brown) in 1978–79, Brown, along with two other ex-Albion players, helped Port Vale win promotion from the Third Division in 1986.

BROWN Tony

Striker/midfield: 704+16 apps. 279 goals.

Born: Oldham, 3 October 1945.

Career: St Columba's, St Peter's & St Clare's Schools, Manchester District & Lancashire Boys, ALBION (amateur April 1961, professional October 1963–October 1981), Jacksonville Tea Men (two spells), Torquay United, Stafford Rangers (retired 1984); worked as a sales representative for a local electrical company; ALBION (coach February 1984–May 1986), Birmingham City (coach), also played for WBA All Stars (1979–88); had two hip replacements, now a columnist for a local paper and Capital Radio match summariser.

■ One of the greatest footballers in the club's history, Tony 'Bomber' Brown appeared in more first-team games (826) and scored more goals (313) than any other Albion player during his 20 years at The Hawthorns (1961 to 1981). In fact, he played in more senior matches on Albion's home ground than any other footballer – 361 – including 282 in the Football League alone. His League record for the club was outstanding: 218 goals in 574 appearances – 459 of them coming in the First Division and 115 in the Second. And you can also include another 51 goals in 66 outings for the reserves, plus a further 51 goals at intermediate level. Brown, a penalty expert who was successful with 51 out of 61 spot kicks in all matches, had two excellent years as an apprentice before joining the professional ranks at The Hawthorns on his 18th birthday – signing in manager Jimmy Hagan's office shortly after making a scoring League debut in a 2–1 win over Ipswich Town, at Portman Road, in September 1963. He quickly established himself in the first team and was a regular for 15 years, from 1964 to 1979, helping Albion win both the League Cup (at the first attempt) in 1966 and the FA Cup two years later. He also appeared in two losing League Cup Finals, the first against Queen's Park Rangers in 1967 and the second against Manchester City in 1970. He played his last League game for Albion in the Midlands derby against Coventry in December 1979 and his farewell appearance for the club followed soon afterwards, in the 2–1 FA Cup defeat at West Ham in January 1980, when he celebrated the occasion with his final goal. Honoured by England at Youth-team level, he gained just one full cap (it should have been more), playing for 74 minutes in the goalless draw with Wales in front of 85,000 fans at Wembley in May 1971. He was twice a Football League representative: against the Irish League at Norwich in September 1970 when he and his teammate Jeff Astle both scored in a resounding 5–0 win, and in the 1–0 victory over the Scottish League at Hampden Park in March 1971. Brown was also named an England reserve on several occasions. Voted Midlands Footballer of the Year on three separate occasions – in 1969, 1971 and 1979, the latter jointly with Ally Brown – he had the pleasure, and indeed the honour, of topping the First Division scoring charts in season 1970–71 with a total of 28 goals. Besides his Albion exploits, he also netted 17 goals in 69 games in the NASL, scored 11 times in 50 outings for Torquay United (having his last game in the Football League in December 1982 away to Port Vale) and claimed another three goals in 11 outings for Stafford Rangers – and you can add to that an extra 40 more strikes while assisting the WBA All Stars in various charity matches. Brown was coach at The Hawthorns under managers Johnny Giles, then Nobby Stiles and finally Ron Saunders, and at St Andrew's under ex-Baggies defender Garry Pendrey. Oh yes, 'Bomber' Brown was one heck of a player, certainly one of the best I've ever seen in an Albion shirt. I know that hundreds more agree, including his former boss Ron Atkinson, who said that the club should erect a monument in his honour in the centre circle at The Hawthorns.

BUCK Fred

Inside-forward/centre-half: 319 apps. 94 goals.

Born: Newcastle-Under-Lyme, Staffs, 12 July 1880.
Died: Stafford, 12 June 1952.
Career: Stafford Wesleyans, Stafford Rangers, ALBION (November 1900–May 1903). Liverpool, Plymouth Argyle, ALBION (April 1906–May 1914), Swansea Town (retired 1917); served in the Army in France during World War One and later a Stafford licensee.

■ The smallest centre-half ever to don an Albion shirt and, indeed, to play in an FA Cup Final, Fred Buck, at 5ft 4in tall, was a real tough nut. He gave the Baggies tremendous service in the second of two spells with the club, during which time he took his club record to an impressive 319 appearances and 94 goals, mostly scored as an inside-forward, before he moved to centre-half from where he skippered the team. Buck represented the Football League in 1910–11, the same season that Albion won the Second Division title – his penalty winner on 30 minutes at home to Huddersfield on the last day of the League programme clinching the title. The following year he gained a runners'-up medal when Barnsley beat the Baggies 1–0 in the FA Cup Final replay at Bramall Lane, Sheffield. He also played in 22 second XI games for Albion, gaining a Birmingham & District League Championship medal in 1902, and he hit both goals when Albion defeated Stoke 2–0 in the Final of the Staffs Cup in 1903.

BURGESS Daryl

Defender: 359+18 apps. 13 goals.

Born: Birmingham, 24 January 1971.
Career: ALBION (apprentice April 1987, professional July 1989–July 2001), Northampton Town, Rochdale, Kidderminster Harriers.

■ Daryl Burgess was a regular in Albion's defence for a decade. He made his League debut at Port Vale in 1989 and was still an important member of the side a decade later. Starting out as an orthodox right-back, he subsequently starred in the middle of the back four and also as a sweeper. A strong-tackling defender, he always maintained a steady level of performance and

received a well-deserved testimonial match against Newcastle before becoming a Cobbler in 2001. He also played in 120 second XI games for Albion, including reserves and the Birmingham Cup, scoring six goals. In all, he made 377 first-class appearances for the club – 332 in the Football League – and served under 16 different managers. In October/November 2004, Burgess had the misfortune of being sent off twice in the space of four games playing for Rochdale, once against his former club Northampton when he also conceded an own-goal and gave away a penalty.

CANTELLO Len

Midfield: 365+4 apps. 21 goals.

Born: Newton Heath, Manchester, 11 September 1951.
Career: Albert Memorial School (Manchester), Manchester & District Boys & Newton Heath Schools, ALBION (apprentice July 1967, professional October 1968–June 1979), Dallas Tornados, Bolton Wanderers, Eastern Athletic, Burnley, Altrincham, Stafford Rangers, Hereford United, Bury, SC Cambuur (player-coach), Peterborough United, Northwich Victoria, Stockport County (assistant manager), Stafford Rangers, Radcliffe Borough (manager); later a scout for Blackpool, Coventry City, Peterborough United and Wigan Athletic and coach at Manchester City's School of Excellence.

■ Len Cantello donned 10 different shirts while playing first-team football for the Baggies. Playing with style, artistry and total commitment, he was predominantly a midfielder but could also do an excellent job at

left-back and occasionally as an extra forward. He won six Schoolboy, four Youth and eight Under-23 caps for England and played for Albion in the 1970 League Cup Final at the age of 18. Six years later he helped the Baggies win promotion from the Second Division, and in December 1978 he scored ITV's Goal of the Season in a superb 5–3 win over Manchester United at Old Trafford. Cantello, who also netted 10 times in 85 Central League games for Albion, left the club immediately after his testimonial match for a then record fee for an outgoing player.

CARTER Joe

Inside-forward: 451 apps. 155 goals.

Born: Aston, Birmingham, 27 July 1899.

Died: Handsworth, Birmingham, 7 January 1977.

Career: Farm Street Council & Hockley Hill Schools (Birmingham), Westbourne Celtic, ALBION (April 1921–February 1936), Sheffield Wednesday (£500). ALBION (February–May 1936), Tranmere Rovers (£450), Walsall, Vono Sports, (player-manager, retired 1942); later licensee of The Grove, Handsworth, Birmingham.

■ Joe Carter, a wonderfully-balanced, upright player with a fine dribbling technique, great body swerve and exceptional positional sense, gave Albion 15 years' loyal service as a quality inside-right, making more than 450 appearances and averaging a goal every three games. Partnering his captain Tommy Glidden, they played together in more than 350 first-team matches for Albion, starring in the unique FA Cup and promotion double-winning season of 1930–31 and also in the 1935 FA Cup Final defeat by Sheffield Wednesday when, realistically, neither should have taken to the field due to injury problems! In the late 1920s Carter won three England caps, scoring

four goals – two in a 4–3 defeat in Spain in May 1929 (the first time a foreign country had beaten England). Besides his first-team exploits, he also scored 34 goals in 57 Central League matches, gaining successive Championship medals in 1922–23 and 1923–24. He left Albion for Hillsborough in 1936 but returned to The Hawthorns after six days following a failed medical. Transferred to Tranmere Rovers three months later, he didn't settle down in Birkenhead and quickly joined Walsall.

CLARK Clive

Outside-left: 351+2 apps. 98 goals.

Born: Leeds, 19 December 1940.

Career: Huddersfield Town (trial), Leeds United, Queen's Park Rangers, ALBION (£20,000 January 1961–June 1969), Queen's Park Rangers, Preston North End. Southport, Telford United, Washington Diplomats, Dallas Tornados, Philadelphia Fury, Skegness Town (retired 1978); now in a Filey nursing home.

■ Dashing left-winger Clive Clark could score goals as well as make them. Nicknamed 'Chippy', he became an instant success at The Hawthorns following his

transfer from QPR, and over a period of eight and a half years he netted almost 100 goals in more than 350 appearances for the Baggies, figuring in both the 1966 League Cup and 1968 FA Cup-winning teams. He also played in the 1967 losing League Cup Final when he netted twice against his former club QPR, while at the same time becoming the first player to score in every game of that competition in a season. Clark was Albion's leading scorer three times: 1963–64 with 17 goals, 1964–65 when he and Astle both scored 11 and in 1966–67 with 29 goals – being the first direct winger to register over 25 goals in a season for the club. Capped by England at Under-23 level, Clark also scored three times in 10 reserve games for Albion. He won a Third Division Championship medal with Preston in 1971.

CLARKE Ike

Inside/centre-forward: 213 apps. 98 goals.

Born: Tipton, 9 January 1915.
Died: Canterbury, 2 April 2002.
Career: Princes End Boys School, Boys Brigade FC, Princes End Baptists, Coseley Juniors, Toll End Wesley, ALBION (amateur January 1937, professional April 1937–November 1947); World War Two guest for Nottingham Forest and Walsall; Portsmouth (£5,000), Yeovil Town (player-manager), Sittingbourne (manager), Canterbury City (manager), Ashford Town (manager, retired 1973); later worked as a fundraiser for Kent CCC.

■ Fearless with boundless energy, a solid frame and terrific goalscoring technique, Ike Clarke spent over 10 years at The

Hawthorns, helping Albion win the Midland Wartime Cup in 1944. He netted 55 of his 98 goals for the club in 96 World War Two games and also contributed eight more in 26 Central League matches. At senior level he bagged seven hat-tricks and two four-timers, finishing up as the team's leading marksman in 1945–46 (22 goals) and second in 1938–39 and 1946–47. After leaving The Hawthorns (unable to dislodge Dave Walsh from the centre-forward position), Clarke helped Pompey win the First Division Championship twice, in 1949 and 1950, scoring a total of 49 goals in 119 League games during his time at Fratton Park. He also represented the FA in five tour games against Australia in 1951. He served as a non-League manager for 20 years.

COOKSON Jimmy

Centre-forward: 131 apps. 110 goals.

Born: Manchester, 6 December 1904.
Died: Warminster, December 1970.
Career: South Salford Lads' Club, Clayton FC, Manchester North End, Manchester City, Southport, Chesterfield, ALBION (£2,500 August 1927–August 1933). Plymouth Argyle, Swindon Town (retired 1938); became a licensee and played in charity matches until 1952; ALBION (scout 1943–53).

■ Jimmy Cookson was a magnificent two-footed marksman and a goal poacher of the highest quality, whose scoring record for Albion was excellent. He had been a prolific marksman prior to arriving at The Hawthorns, netting 85 League goals in just three years for Chesterfield. Three months after joining Albion, for what was to prove a bargain fee, he struck a double hat-trick in a 6–3 home win over Blackpool in a Second Division match, and four years later he helped the Baggies win promotion to the First Division, having set a new club record of 38 goals in 1927–28 – which was later

beaten by his strike partner 'W.G.' Richardson in 1935–36. Cookson also netted 95 times in 92 second XI games for Albion, helping them win the Central League title in 1932–33 when he top scored with 29 goals. The previous season he had netted seven times in a 10–1 home win over Chesterfield's reserves. After leaving Albion he continued to find the net for both Plymouth Argyle and Swindon Town before announcing his retirement in 1938. In a 15-year professional career, Cookson hit 256 League goals in 392 games. Leading scorer in Division Three North in 1925–26 and Division Two in 1927–28, his 100th League goal came in only his 89th match when playing for Albion versus South Shields in December 1927 – a record that still stands for the quickest-ever century of goals. He toured Canada with the FA in the summer of 1931 – his only representative honour. As a scout, he spotted Ray Barlow in 1944. His elder brother, Sammy Cookson, played for Stalybridge Celtic, Macclesfield, Manchester City, Bradford Park Avenue and Barnsley (1915–35).

CUNNINGHAM Laurie

Winger: 106+8 apps. 30 goals.

Born: St Mary's Archway, London, 8 March 1956.

Died: near Madrid, Spain, 15 July 1989.

Career: Stroud Green School (Highgate), Highgate Wood Boys, Haringey Schools, South East Counties Schools, North London Boys, Leyton Orient, ALBION (£110,000 March 1977–June 1979), Real Madrid, Manchester United, Sporting Gijon, Olympique Marseille, Leicester City, Rayo Vallecano, Real Betis, RSC Charleroi (Belgium), Wimbledon, Rayo Vallecano (until his death).

■ Laurie Cunningham made his debut at Tottenham in March 1977 and went on to become one of the finest goalscoring wingers in English football. Making an immediate impact at The Hawthorns, he created a piece of footballing history when he teamed up with Brendon Batson and Cyrille Regis for the away game at Ipswich in March 1978 – this being the first time three black players had appeared together for the same team in a League game. By naming this trio, manager Ron Atkinson therefore challenged the established racism in English football, marking a watershed that allowed a generation of footballers to enter the game who would previously have been excluded for their ethnic background.

Cunningham's exciting footballing skills, plus his shooting power and charisma, genuinely lit up The Hawthorns, and he certainly put more than a smile or two on the faces of the Baggies supporters, and, as a result, Albion became one of the most attractive and exciting sides in the First Division (and Europe) in the late 1970s. They reached the FA Cup semi-final and UEFA Cup quarter-final, and Cunningham soon started to attract attention. At times his displays were brilliant. He loved to hug the touchline and gave some fine full-backs a real testing time. He was superb when Albion beat Manchester United 5–3 at Old Trafford in December 1978 and followed up with a brilliant display when Albion held Valencia to a 1–1 draw in a UEFA Cup game in Spain. This display set Real Madrid talking and it came as no surprise when he moved to Spain, for a record fee, in the summer of 1979.

Earlier, Cunningham had become the first black player to wear an England shirt at senior level when he appeared in the Under-21 international against Scotland at Bramall Lane in April 1977, scoring to celebrate the occasion. He went on to gain six full caps, winning his first versus Wales in May 1979. Although Viv Anderson had made his England bow in a friendly six months previously, Cunningham was the first black player to appear for the senior England team.

Though he never quite recaptured his early brilliance with Real Madrid, he was nevertheless adored by the fans who labelled him 'Black Beauty' and 'The Black Pearl'. He helped Real complete the League and Cup double in his first season in Spain and appeared in the 1981 European Cup Final defeat by Liverpool.

His later career saw him increasingly distracted by off-field interests and, after leaving Real in 1983, he had several loan spells before returning to England to win an FA Cup-winners' medal with Wimbledon in 1988. Tragically, aged 33, he was killed in a car crash on the outskirts of Madrid.

DUDLEY Jimmy

Wing-half/inside-forward: 320 apps. 11 goals.

Born: Gartosh, Glasgow, 24 August 1928.

Died: West Bromwich, 25 April 2006.

Career: Burnt Tree Mixed School (Dudley), Hill Top School (West Bromwich), Walsall Conduits, Albright Youth Club, ALBION (amateur August 1944, professional August 1945–December 1959), Walsall (£4,000), Stourbridge, Guest Motors (retired 1967).

■ Able to play at inside-forward or wing-half, Jimmy Dudley settled into the latter berth superbly for Albion and became a key player in the side during the 1950s. He actually started out as a goalkeeper, switched to inside-right in 1947 and established himself in Albion's second XI in 1949 before becoming the club's regular right-half two years later. He occupied that berth until 1959, during which time he appeared in over 30 matches, including 166 in succession between 1952 and 1956...a record that stood for over 20 years until beaten by Ally Robertson in 1979. His most important goal for the Baggies was a vital equaliser against Port Vale in the 1954 FA Cup semi-final at Villa Park. He made his Albion debut at Manchester City in December 1949 and was to become part of two splendid middle lines, first with Joe

Kennedy and Ray Barlow as his centre-half and left-half colleagues, and then with Jimmy Dugdale as pivot and Barlow alongside. Dudley also played in 115 reserve games for the Baggies, was capped by Scotland B and in 1954 gained a Cup-winners' medal. He helped Walsall win promotion from the Fourth and Third Divisions in successive seasons (1961 and 1962). His brother George and cousin Jimmy Edwards (below) also played for Albion.

EDWARDS Jimmy

Left-half/inside-left: 202 apps. 9 goals.

Born: Tipton, 11 December 1905.

Died: West Bromwich, 4 April 1982.

Career: Horseley Bridge & Tipton Schools, Tipton Park, Newport Foundry, Stourbridge (two spells), Great Bridge Celtic, ALBION (£350 May 1926–May 1937). Norwich City (£750), Bilston United, Kingswinford, Dudley Town (retired 1944).

■ Tough-tackling wing-half Jimmy 'Iron' Edwards gave Albion tremendous service at all levels for 11 years, during which time he

accumulated over 200 first-team appearances after making his League debut against Hull in March 1928. Initially an inside-forward, he was successfully switched to left-half and was a key figure during Albion's double-winning season of 1930–31 and again in 1934–35, when the Baggies reached the FA Cup Final. Edwards played in 184 second-team games for the club, scoring 63 goals and gaining a Central League Championship medal in 1926–27. He also represented the Football League. Albion's 1930s half-back line of Jack Sankey, Billy Richardson and Edwards was known as 'salt, pepper and mustard'.

ELLIOTT Billy

Outside-right: 303 apps. 157 goals.

Born: Harrington, Cumberland, 6 August 1919.
Died: Canary Islands, 12 July 1966.
Career: Harrington Junior & Carlisle Grammar Schools, Carlisle United, Dudley Town, Wolverhampton Wanderers, Bournemouth, ALBION (£4,000 December 1938–June 1951), Bilston United (player-manager, retired 1954); licensee of The Farcoft Hotel (Birmingham) and Red Lion (Smethwick) and started the first Albion Supporters Club (1951).

■ Billy Elliott was a brilliant outside-right, fast and clever with incredible close ball control and a powerful shot. He was rejected by Wolves manager Major Frank Buckley as a 16-year-old and went on to play for Albion for 13 years, appearing in more than 300 games and scoring over 150 goals in all competitions. He made his debut for the club in a Second Division game at Luton in December 1938 and also played in 13 Central League games. During the 1939–45 hostilities he was quite superb, netting 117 times in just 148 outings for the Baggies as well as starring for England against Wales and Scotland in Wartime and Victory internationals and in an England XI against the Combined Services. He also represented the Western Command, the army and the FA. If it hadn't been for Stanley Matthews then Elliot would have certainly gained full England honours. He helped Albion win promotion from the Second Division in 1948–49 and was in tip-top form until suffering an Achilles tendon injury against Manchester United which effectively ended his League career. He was a qualified FA coach and member of the Players' Union Committee.

FINCH Bob

Full-back: 234 apps.

Born: Hednesford, 31 August 1908.
Died: Hednesford, 13 December 2000.
Career: Hill Top & West Hill Council Schools, Hednesford Prims, Hednesford Town, ALBION (amateur April 1925, professional September 1925–May 1939). Swansea Town, Hednesford Town; World War Two guest for Tamworth and served in Staffs County Police Force (1942–56).

■ Bob Finch was a redoubtable full-back who spent 14 years at The Hawthorns; he appeared in more than 230 senior games but failed to score a single goal, although he did concede three past his own 'keeper. He netted twice in 231 appearances for the second XI, with whom he won four Central League Championship medals in 1926–27, 1932–33, 1933–34 and 1934–35, skippering the side in the last three. Quick-witted, zealous, alert and confident in his kicking, Finch had to compete for a first-team place with several other fine full-backs and missed out on Albion's two FA Cup Final appearances in 1931 and 1935. He did, however, star in a 3–1 FA Cup win over Arsenal before a record Hawthorns crowd of 64,815, but was a loser one step from Wembley as Preston won the semi-final at Highbury. Finch played in two England international trials and made his League debut versus Leicester in February 1926. He was also a fine golfer.

FRASER Doug

Wing-half/full-back: 325 apps. 12 goals.

Born: Busby, Lanarkshire, Scotland, 8 December 1941.

Career: Busby Junior & Senior Schools, Rolls Royce, Eaglesham Amateurs, Blantyre Celtic, Glasgow Celtic (trial), Leeds United (trial), Aberdeen, ALBION (£23,000 September 1963–January 1971), Nottingham Forest (£35,000), Walsall (later manager); he was then prison officer at Nottingham Gaol.

■ After making 70 appearances for Aberdeen, Doug Fraser immediately established himself at Albion. A strong-tackling wing-half, he made his debut in the local derby against Birmingham and helped Albion beat West Ham in the 1966 League Cup Final, lose in the Final of the same competition a year later to QPR and lift the FA Cup versus Everton in 1968 before switching to full-back. He skippered the side in the 1970 League Cup Final defeat by Manchester City and made over 300 senior and 12 second XI appearances for Albion, as well as gaining two caps for Scotland. He quit soccer in 1977 to join the prison service. In 1973, as a Walsall player, Fraser hit the headlines when he was sent off for fighting with his former Albion teammate Kenny Stephens, then of Bristol Rovers.

GERA Zoltan

Midfield: 78+28 apps. 15 goals.

Born: Pecs, Hungary, 22 April 1979.

Career: Pecs District XI, Pecs FC (Hungary), PMSC (Hungary), Ferencvaros, ALBION (£1.5m July 2004).

■ Zoltan Gera, Albion's first senior professional from Hungary, made his debut for the Baggies as a substitute in the Premiership game at Blackburn in August 2004 and scored within three minutes of starting his first Premiership game versus Spurs (at home) soon afterwards. An inspirational captain of Hungary's national team, he prefers to play on the right of midfield, displaying aggression, skill and commitment. He won his first full cap in 2001, having earlier represented his country at Under-21 level. Gera was voted Hungary's Footballer of the Year in 2004 and Baggies supporters' Player of the Year in 2005. He missed a huge chunk of the 2005–06 campaign through injury before returning to his best in 2006–07.

GILES Johnny

Midfield: 87+1 apps. 5 goals.

Born: Cabra, Dublin, 6 November 1940.

Career: Brunswick Street School (Dublin), St Colombus FC, Dublin Schools Select, Dublin City/Munster Victoria, Stella Maris Boys, Leprechauns, Home Farm, Manchester United, Leeds United, ALBION (£48,000 June 1975–June 1977). Shamrock Rovers, Philadelphia Fury, Vancouver Whitecaps (coach), ALBION (manager February 1984–September 1985); became a soccer writer for a national newspaper and a journalist, and a TV presenter in Ireland; also Republic of Ireland (player-manager), WBA All Stars and Worcester Ramblers (guest).

■ Johnny Giles was Albion's first player-manager, signed to replace Don Howe in 1975, shortly after appearing for Leeds against Bayern Munich in the European Cup Final. Making his debut against Chelsea (at home) in August 1975, he succeeded in getting Albion out of the Second Division in his first season in charge and then took them to the brink of European football before leaving The Hawthorns to become player-manager of Shamrock Rovers, much to the dismay of the supporters. In fact, Giles had threatened to quit after a year but was persuaded to stay longer after irate fans made their opinions heard in no uncertain terms.

Earlier, as a right-winger for Manchester United, he gained an FA Cup-winners' medal versus Leicester in 1963 before being

successfully converted into a world-class midfielder by Leeds United's manager Don Revie, under whom he collected medals galore. These included winners' prizes for both the First and Second Division Championships, the FA Cup, League Cup and Fairs Cup, as well as becoming an established member of the Republic of Ireland national team. Giles collected his first cap at the age of 18 and went on to add 59 more to his tally, scoring five goals. He played in 11 FA Cup semi-final matches and five FA Cup Finals (six counting the 1970 replay) – the latter equalling the inter-war record set by Joe Hulme of Huddersfield and Arsenal. Unfortunately, things didn't go too well for him during his second spell in charge of Albion, and after 18 months he quit competitive football. One of the finest midfielders ever to play for the Baggies, Giles's League career spanned 18 years, during which time he hit 99 goals in 554 games and notched 125 goals in 863 games (all levels). His son, Michael, was with him at The Hawthorns in 1984–85, and the 1970s rock group Thin Lizzy dedicated a track on their Johnny the Fox album to Giles.

GLIDDEN Tommy

Outside-right: 479 apps. 140 goals.

Born: Coxlodge, Newcastle-upon-Tyne, 20 July 1902.

Died: West Bromwich, 10 July 1974.

Career: Castletown School (Tyneside), Sunderland & District Boys, Durham Boys, Sunderland, Bristol City (trial), Colliery Old Boys (Newcastle), Bolden Villa, Sunderland West End, ALBION (professional April 1922, retired May 1936, became club coach); later ran a tobacconists shop in West Bromwich; ALBION (shareholder, then director 1951–74).

■ A terrific goalscoring winger, Tommy Glidden served Albion for over 50 years – as a player, coach, shareholder and director. Able to play in any forward position, but best as a right-winger, he made his League debut at Everton in November 1922. After a few games on the left flank, he settled down on the right from where he skippered the Baggies to the FA Cup and promotion double in 1930–31 and also the FA Cup Final of 1935. Taking over from Jack Crisp, he formed a superb 'wing' partnership with Joe Carter and was perhaps unfortunate not to gain a full cap after starring in an England trial in 1925–26. Besides his first-team record, Glidden also scored 17 goals in 91 reserve games for Albion, gaining successive Central League Championship medals in 1923 and 1924. His brother, Sid Glidden, was an Albion reserve in the 1920s and later played for Halifax, Doncaster, York, Peterborough, Newport and Wigan Athletic.

GODDEN Tony

Goalkeeper: 329 apps.

Born: Gillingham, Kent, 2 August 1955.

Career: Napier Secondary Modern School (Gillingham), Leonard Star FC, Eastcourt United, Gillingham & District Schools, Medway & Kent Schools (Gillingham), Ashford Town, Wolverhampton Wanderers (trial), ALBION (professional August 1975–March 1986), Preston North End, Happy Valley (guest), Luton Town, Chelsea, Birmingham City, Bury, Sheffield Wednesday, Peterborough United, Leicester City, Wivenhoe Town, Colchester United, Warboys Town, Torquay United, March Town (manager),

King's Lynn (manager), Bury Town (manager), Wisbech Town (manager), Northampton Town (coach); later goalkeeping coach at Rushden & Diamonds, Lincoln City, Peterborough United, Leicester City, Derby County (two spells) and Notts County.

■ In October 1981 Tony Godden set a new Albion record that will take some beating – he appeared in his 228th consecutive first-team match and, in doing so, eclipsed defender Ally Robertson's previous total of successive outings by a considerable margin. Some four and a half years earlier, Godden made his Albion debut (with Laurie Cunningham) in a 2–0 win at Tottenham and the media immediately described him as 'a goalkeeper with a big future'. How right they were, for he went from strength to strength and, over the next nine years, amassed a tremendous record for the Baggies, helping them reach the FA Cup semi-finals and qualify for the UEFA Cup in 1978. He was a safe handler of the ball and a terrific shot-stopper, although many supporters will never forget his howler against Liverpool in 1978 when he allowed Kenny Dalglish to come in behind him and walk the ball into an empty net! He was perhaps vulnerable at times when going for high crosses, but generally he was an excellent 'keeper, whose professional career realised more than 450 senior appearances. Goddon also played in 72 second XI games for Albion, helping them win the Central League Championship in 1982–83. Granted a testimonial to celebrate 10 years at The Hawthorns, he once scored a goal from 90 yards playing for Peterborough's reserves against Northampton in 1989–90.

GOODMAN Don

Striker: 163+18 apps. 63 goals.

Born: Leeds, 9 May 1966.

Career: Collingham FC, Leeds United (trial), Bradford City, ALBION (£50,000 March 1987–December 1991), Sunderland (£900,000), Wolverhampton Wanderers, San Frecce Antlers, Hiroshima (Japan), Barnsley, Motherwell, Walsall, Exeter City, Doncaster Rovers, Stafford Rangers (retired 2003); Kidderminster Harriers (fitness coach); now match summariser on local radio.

■ Fast and aggressive, with good ability and a strong right-foot shot, Don Goodman won a Third Division Championship medal with Bradford City in 1985 and joined Albion soon after the Valley Parade fire disaster, in which his girlfriend died. He became a firm favourite with the Baggies fans, averaging a goal every three games and producing some wonderful displays, including hat-trick-winning performances against Crystal Palace in November 1988 (won 5–3) and Barnsley 12 months later (won 7–0). He was the leading scorer in both of those seasons.

Leaving The Hawthorns for Sunderland, he netted over 40 goals in three years at Roker Park. Then, to the dismay of diehard Baggies fans, he teamed up with Steve Bull at Molineux, becoming Wolves' top scorer in 1995–96. After recovering from a serious head injury, he played in the Japanese J-League, only to return to England six months later. During an excellent career, Goodman scored almost 200 goals in some 675 appearances, including a League record (in England and Scotland) of 127 goals in 435 outings. He made his Albion League debut against Oldham in March 1987, and, besides his senior exploits, he scored six goals in 11 reserve games for the club. In later years Goodman helped Walsall gain promotion to the First Division via the Play-offs at Cardiff's Millennium Stadium in 2001 (scoring against Reading in the Final), and two years later he helped Doncaster regain their Football League status after winning the Conference Play-off Final.

GREGORY Howard

Outside-left: 181 apps. 45 goals.

Born: Aston Manor, Birmingham, 6 April 1893.
Died: Handsworth, Birmingham, 15 August 1954.
Career: Gower Street & Aston Hall Schools (Birmingham), Aston Manor, Birchfield Trinity, ALBION (professional May 1911, retired, injured, May 1926); later licensee of the Woodman Inn (next to The Hawthorns) and other pubs.

■ Known as the 'Express Man', ginger-haired left-winger Howard Gregory was quick-witted, fast and plucky, and teamed up superbly well in Albion's attack with Fred Morris immediately after World War One. Surprisingly, he made his League debut against Everton at Goodison Park in April 1912 in the inside-right position, and it wasn't until after World War One that he actually gained a regular place in the team, taking over the left-wing berth from Ben Shearman.

Over the next seven years or so, he did exceedingly well, scoring plenty of goals while competing in more than 150 first-team appearances for the Baggies and helping them win the League Championship in 1920 when he netted 12 times in 34 starts – two of his goals setting up a fine 4–2 win at Villa Park. He had earlier contributed greatly to Albion's Birmingham & District League side during the four campaigns leading up to World War One, making over 100 appearances and gaining a Championship medal in 1902. He followed up, after the hostilities, with 22 goals in 37 outings for the second team, having lost his place in the senior side to Jack Byers. Gregory was a guest at a reception to celebrate Albion's 1954 FA Cup win.

GRIFFIN Frank

Outside-right: 275 apps. 52 goals.

Born: Pendlebury, Manchester, 28 March 1928.
Died: Shrewsbury, 4 June 2007.
Career: Pendlebury Central School, St Augustine's Youth Club, Newton Heath, Hull City, Bolton Wanderers, Eccles Town, Shrewsbury Town, ALBION (£9,500 April 1951–June 1959), Northampton Town (£1,500), Wellington Town, GKN Sankey's (retired 1962), Worthen United (manager).

■ The scorer of Albion's 87th minute 1954 FA Cup-winning goal against Preston North End, Frank Griffin was, without doubt, an exceptionally fine outside-right, who took over the number-seven shirt from Billy Elliott and made his senior debut against Sunderland at Roker Park in April 1951. A player who enjoyed

hugging the touchline and keeping his full-back occupied, he possessed good pace, had excellent ball control and delivered precise crosses as well as packing a fair shot with his right foot. Griffin spent eight years at The Hawthorns, averaging a goal every five games and grabbing a hat-trick in a record 9–2 home League win over Manchester City in September 1957. He also netted twice when Liverpool were defeated 5–2 at The Hawthorns on Christmas Day 1953 and was quite brilliant when Albion hammered Newcastle 7–3 at St James' Park earlier in that 1953–54 season, when he was part of a wonderful forward line assembled by manager Vic Buckingham. Sadly, Griffin was in line for an England cap when he broke his right leg playing against Sheffield United in an FA Cup replay in February 1958. Although he regained his fitness, he was never the same player he was before the injury and subsequently left The Hawthorns for Northampton in 1959. He scored five goals in 42 Central League games for Albion.

GROVES Willie

Wing-half/forward: 69 apps. 110 goals.

Born: Leith, Scotland, 9 November 1869.

Died: Edinburgh, 13 February 1908.

Career: Thistle FC, Edinburgh (1884), Leith Harp (1885), Hibernian (professional, August 1886), Celtic (£25, August 1888), Everton (£40, January–February 1889), Celtic (£40, March 1889), ALBION (£50, October 1890), Aston Villa (£100, four payments of £25 each, September 1893),

Hibernian (£75, August 1895), Celtic (£100, November 1896), Rushden (August 1898, retired, May 1902); struck down with tuberculosis and died at the age of 38.

■ Swarthy and smart-looking with a broad grin, Willie Groves was an exciting footballer who, although having no claims to greatness in heading or goalscoring, was second to none in ball-winning and distribution. He could play anywhere (even in goal), was enthusiastic and thoroughly enjoyed his game. Albion converted him from a thrustful forward into a purposeful wing-half, and during a wonderful career he won three Scottish caps (1888–90, scoring a splendid hat-trick against Ireland in his second international), represented the Football League XI in 1891–92 and played for Edinburgh in an Inter-City match. In his first spell with Hibs, he gained a Scottish Cup-winners' medal (1887), receiving a runners'-up prize in the same competition in 1896. With Celtic, he was the recipient of a second Cup runners'-up medal in 1889 and three years later helped Albion lift the FA Cup in 1892, setting up two of the three goals against his future club Aston Villa in the final. As a Villa player, Groves won a First Division Championship medal in 1894 and all told (with Hibs, Celtic, Albion and Villa in the main) he claimed over 30 goals in almost 200 senior matches. He did not get a game with Everton and on joining Albion had to serve out a month's suspension after Everton had claimed he was still registered with them! When he signed for Villa in 1893 (after more objections from Everton) Groves became the first player in Football history to command a three-figure transfer fee (£100). He made his Albion debut in the home game against rivals Wolverhampton Wanderers in December 1890 and besides the League and Cup appearance for the club, he also played in over 75 'other' first-team games, mainly in local Cup competitions and friendlies.

HARTFORD Asa

Inside-forward: 266+9 apps. 26 goals.

Born: Clydebank, Scotland, 24 October 1950.

Career: Fairfley Primary & Clydebank High Schools, Dunbartonshire Boys, Drumchapel Amateurs, ALBION (apprentice April 1966, professional October 1967–November 1971), Leeds United (for 24 hours), ALBION (November 1971–August 1974), Manchester City (£225,000), Nottingham Forest, Everton, Manchester City, Fort Lauderdale Sun, Wolverhampton Wanderers, Norwich City; Norway (coach), Bolton Wanderers, Stockport County (player-manager), Oldham Athletic, Shrewsbury Town (coach then manager), Boston United (retired 1991), Blackburn Rovers (coach), Stoke City (coach/assistant manager), Manchester City (coach,

assistant manager & reserve-team manager); also played for WBA All Stars.

■ Asa Hartford made his League debut as a 17-year-old against Sheffield United at Bramall Lane in February 1968. He developed quickly and became an international midfield dynamo – a player who darted here, there and everywhere, covering acres of ground every game he played in as he endeavoured to create chances for his colleagues. Full of energy and always buzzing around in midfield, Hartford's career realised over 800 appearances, including 275 for Albion, for whom he also starred in 38 Central League games (eight goals). In 1971 he was rejected by Leeds (on medical advice) after doctors diagnosed a hole in the heart. Three years later, however, he was sold to Manchester City for almost a quarter of a million pounds. In 1979 he switched from Maine Road to Nottingham Forest for twice that amount, and Everton paid £500,000 for him later in that same year. A Scottish international at Youth, Under-21, Under-23 and full-team levels (50 caps won in the latter category), Hartford played for Albion in the 1970 League Cup Final defeat by his future club Manchester City, with whom he gained a winners' medal in the same competition in 1976, adding a second to his tally with Norwich in 1985 when his deflected 'goal' gave the Canaries a 1–0 victory over Sunderland. He also played in the Freight Rover Trophy Final for Bolton against Bristol City, collecting another runners'-up medal. He was christened Asa after the famous American singer Al Asa Jolson.

HEATH Norman

Goalkeeper: 169 apps.

Born: Wolverhampton, 31 January 1924.
Died: Great Barr, Birmingham, 12 November 1983.
Career: Bushbury Hill School, Wolverhampton Boys, Henry Meadows, ALBION (amateur May 1942, professional October 1943, retired, injured, June 1955); later Great Barr Gunners (manager).

■ Norman Heath was a fine and courageous goalkeeper, whose agility and brilliant reflexes were key features of his splendid displays as Albion's last line of defence. He came to The Hawthorns during World War Two and made his first-team debut against his home-town club Wolves (at home) in the Football League North in September 1943, and at the end of that season he celebrated with a Midland Wartime Cup-winners' prize after Nottingham Forest had been beaten 6–5 on aggregate in the two-leg Final. In November 1944 he joined the army and was based at Shrewsbury before linking up with the King's Shropshire Light

Infantry at Llandrindrod Wells. He was then transferred to India where, at Poona, he was posted to the 2nd Leicester Regiment. He represented his platoon, company and battalion and also the brigade team, playing for the Combined Services XI on several occasions. He also rose to the rank of CQMS.

On his return to The Hawthorns, Heath had to wait 18 months before making his Football League debut, replacing Jimmy Sanders at Sheffield Wednesday in a Second Division encounter in December 1947, when he saved a penalty in a 2–1 win. After that, he understudied Sanders for quite a long period before establishing himself in the first team in 1952.

Producing some superb displays, he kept his place on merit until suffering a career-ending injury during a vital League match at Sunderland in March 1954, when he was involved in a collision with the home centre-forward Ted Purdon. Heath suffered crippling neck and back injuries. He was hospitalised for quite some time and, on discharge, was confined to a wheelchair for the rest of his life. Disappointed at missing the FA Cup Final win over Preston, he was awarded a testimonial at the end of the 1955–56 season and over 55,000 attended a game against an international XI to say thank you to a fine goalkeeper. Besides his tally of senior appearances, he also had 138 reserve outings for the Baggies.

HOPE Bobby

Inside-forward: 398+5 apps. 42 goals.

Born: Bridge of Allan, Stirlingshire, 28 September 1943.

Career: Clydebank High & Dunbartonshire West Schools, Drumchapel Amateurs, Sunderland (trial), ALBION (amateur August 1959, professional September 1960–May 1972), Birmingham City (£66,666), Philadelphia Atoms, Dallas Tornados (three spells), Sheffield Wednesday, Bromsgrove Rovers (player-coach, retired 1982, then manager for two spells), Burton Albion (manager), ALBION (youth development officer July 1998, then chief scout from August 2001); also played for WBA All Stars (1979–88).

■ Bobby Hope turned down the team he had supported since he was six years of age, Glasgow Rangers, to join Albion in 1959 – immediately after appearing in a Schoolboy international against England. A player who developed into a master tactician in midfield, his splendid ball skills and telling passes were highlights of a wonderful association with Albion, with whom he collected a League Cup-winners' tankard in 1966, an FA Cup-winners' medal two years later and runners'-up prizes in the League Cup competitions of 1967 and 1970. Also honoured by his country at Under-23 level, Hope added two full caps to his tally versus

Holland in Amsterdam in May 1968 and Denmark in Copenhagen five months later. He appeared in over 400 games for Albion, plus another 100 for the second XI, scoring 17 goals. He had the pleasure of claiming the club's first ever goal in a European Cup competition against DOS Utrecht in Holland in November 1966, having scored the only hat-trick of his career in a 6–1 League Cup win over Aston Villa two months earlier. For Albion, the Blues and Wednesday, Hope made a total of 407 League appearances and netted 45 goals. In all matches, including his spell in the NASL, he played in over 525 first-class matches and scored 60 times. He was only 16 years and 219 days old when he made his League debut for Albion against Arsenal (at home) in April 1960, deputising for Davy Burnside in the 1–0 win.

HORTON Ezra

Right-half: 83 apps. 1 goal.

Born: West Bromwich, 20 August 1861.

Died: West Bromwich, 11 July 1939.

Career: Christ Church & Beeches Road Schools (West Bromwich), George Salter Works FC, West Bromwich FC, ALBION (amateur August 1882, professional August 1885, retired June 1891); also guest for Port Vale and Aston Villa; became a referee and later played for the West Bromwich hockey team, only the second Midlander to represent England at his sport.

■ Ezra Horton, nicknamed 'Ironsides', was a very sporting player – a largely defensive right-half who was good at heading, strong with his kicking and fearsome in the tackle, hence his nickname! He played in three

successive FA Cup Finals for Albion (1886–88), being a winner in the latter against Preston. He skippered Albion in 1884–85 and had the distinction of playing in each of the club's first 36 FA Cup ties. In fact, Horton played in Albion's first-ever FA Cup tie, his senior debut against Wednesbury Town (at home) in November 1883, and in the club's first-ever Football League match at Stoke in September 1888 – one of only two players to do so. He actually played his first game for the club against St George's (away) in September 1882. In all, he appeared in over 350 matches for Albion (all levels) in his nine years with the club. His brother, Jack Horton, also played for Albion.

HOULT Russell

Goalkeeper: 196 apps.

Born: Ashby-de-la-Zouch, 22 November 1972.

Career: Leicester City, Lincoln City (two spells), Blackpool, Bolton Wanderers, Derby County, Portsmouth, ALBION (£500,000 January 2001), Nottingham Forest.

■ Russell Hoult set two new Albion club records during 2001–02: 27 clean sheets in total and 24 in the League, blanking out his opponents in seven successive games in January and February. Cool, composed and a terrific shot-stopper, he certainly had a wonderful campaign as the Baggies leapt into the Premiership ahead of their arch-rivals Wolves. He was voted Albion's Player of the Season and was also included in the PFA's Division One side, being rated as the best 'custodian' outside the Premiership at the time. After failing to establish himself at Filbert Street, he had 138 outings for Derby and made his Albion debut in the League home game against his former club Portsmouth in February 2001, taking over from Brian Jensen. Midland Footballer of the Year in 2002, he was in line for an England call up during the season when David Seaman was injured, but Sven Goran Eriksson preferred David James instead. Hoult performed well again in 2003–04, despite a back injury, and conceded only 39 goals in 44 League games as the Baggies regained their Premiership status. He had a loan spell with Nottingham Forest in 2005–06. Hoult became only the second Albion goalkeeper to be sent off in a League game when he was dismissed during a game against Liverpool at Anfield in September 2002. England international Joe Reader was the first, banished at Bolton in April 1895.

HOWE Don

Right-back: 379 apps. 19 goals.

Born: Springfield, Wolverhampton, 12 October 1935.

Career: St Peter's School and Wolverhampton & District Boys, Wolverhampton Wanderers (trial), ALBION (December 1950, professional November 1952–April 1964). Arsenal (£40,000, retired, injured, 1967; became coach at Highbury, then assistant manager), ALBION (manager July 1971–April 1975), Galatasaray (coach), Leeds United (coach), Arsenal (coach then manager), England B (coach and assistant manager), England (chief coach), Saudi Arabia (coach), Bristol Rovers (coach), Wimbledon (assistant manager/coach), Queen's Park Rangers (assistant manager, then manager/coach), Wimbledon (coach), Barnet (coach), Coventry City (manager), Chelsea (coach then assistant manager); covered Serie A football in Italy for Channel 4; Arsenal (youth-team coach and technical advisor), also FA technical adviser on coaching.

■ Deft positioning, reliability and strength in kicking and acumen were generally the hallmarks of Don Howe's overall play at right-back for Albion and, indeed, for England. Although in later years he did occupy the number-four and eight shirts for the Throstles, it was as an attacking full-back that he became such a fine footballer, playing in 23 consecutive

internationals for England between October 1957 and November 1959. He replaced Stuart Williams in Albion's team in August 1955, making his debut (with Derek Kevan) against Everton (at home). Establishing himself in the side before the end of the year, he went on to amass over 370 appearances (plus 43 in the second XI) in a long association with the club. He was also honoured by his country at Under-23 level, represented England B and played for the Football League and the FA XI, touring New Zealand with the latter in 1961. When he broke his right leg in March 1966 with Arsenal (after being signed by Billy Wright), he was forced to retire and became coach at Highbury and saw Arsenal complete the double in 1971. He returned to The Hawthorns as manager in 1971, but two years later Albion slipped into the Second Division. Howe's best signing was Scottish international winger Willie Johnston from Rangers, for a record £138,000. When he returned to Arsenal, he coached the Gunners to three successive FA Cup Finals (1978, 1979 and 1980) and was coach when Wimbledon won the 1988 FA Cup Final. Howe was awarded an Honorary Fellowship at Wolverhampton University in 2001.

HUGHES Lee

Striker: 192+45 apps. 98 goals.

Born: Smethwick, 22 May 1976.

Career: Bustleholme Boys & Charlemont Boys (West Bromwich), Forest Falcons (Stourbridge), Fresher FC (Oldbury), ALBION (trial March 1991), Walsall (schoolboy), Oldbury United, Wolverhampton Wanderers (trial), Sheffield Wednesday (trial), Kidderminster Harriers, ALBION (£250,000 May 1997–August 2001), Coventry City (£5m + £1), ALBION (£2.5m August 2002, contract cancelled August 2004), Featherstone Prison (seasons 2004–07).

■ In his first spell at The Hawthorns Lee Hughes could do no wrong with the supporters, and when he rejoined Albion for a record fee in August 2002 it was thought that he would reproduce

the form he had shown in the late 1990s. Unfortunately he didn't produce the goods and his career came to a sad end when he was sent to prison in 2004. A former building site labourer and nicknamed 'Ginger Ninja' and the 'Balti-Kid', Hughes won four semi-professional caps for England with Kidderminster, and as soon as he entered The Hawthorns the Baggies fans quickly made him their hero too. After his League debut as a 'sub' against Tranmere Rovers (at home) on the opening day of the 1997–98 season, he scored twice in a 3–2 win at Crewe, and after that he was a pretty special player, ending his first season with 14 goals, adding 32 more in 1998–99 and 16 the following season. In all, he netted 85 times in 177 appearances in four seasons before transferring to Highfield Road, bitterly disappointed that Albion had lost their end-of-season Play-off semi-final to Bolton. Like scores of other footballers, he desperately wanted to play in the Premiership…and after returning to The Hawthorns he made his debut in the 'top flight' against Fulham. Hughes certainly knew where the net was, and, after his worst scoring season, he bounced back in style in 2003–04 by striking 12 goals as the Baggies regained their Premiership status. Hughes also played in 15 second XI games (four goals scored) before his career ended abruptly, when he was handed a six-year gaol sentence at Coventry Crown Court for causing death by dangerous driving. Stupidly, Hughes left the scene of the accident in Warwickshire on 22 November 2003 and did not contact the police for 34 hours, knowing that if he had remained with his car he would have been breathalysed. He was also banned from driving for 10 years, having also received an 18-month ban for drink-driving when he was an 18-year-old. He scored on his debut for his prison team but was later sent off and suspended for four months.

HUNT Andy

Striker: 228+12 apps. 85 goals.

Born: Thurrock, Essex, 9 June 1970.
Career: Ashill FC, Kings Lynn, Kettering Town, Newcastle United, ALBION (loan March 1993, signed for £100,000 May 1993–July 1998), Charlton Athletic; emigrated to Sanignacio, Belize; formed his own export business, The Green Dragon Company; played for Banana Bank FC (Belize two spells); Charlton Athletic (again) and Belmopan Bandits.

■ The final piece of Ossie Ardiles's 1993 promotion-winning jigsaw, Andy Hunt was a tall, lean but alert and competent striker, who scored on his debut at Bradford and then netted a hat-trick in his first game at The Hawthorns against Brighton shortly afterwards. He was terrific alongside Bob Taylor and netted the crucial opening goal in the Play-off Final at Wembley, when Albion beat Port Vale 3–0 to clinch a place in the First Division. He then top scored in 1994–95, his form at this time starting to attract the attention of Premiership clubs. A centre-half at the start of his career, Hunt developed into a competent front-runner who never gave up the ghost. He struck 13 goals in 51 games for Newcastle and proceeded to find the net regularly for Albion, claiming a goal every three games as well as netting 12 times in 14 second XI games before a 'Bosman' free transfer took him to Charlton – much to the annoyance of scores of Baggies supporters! He did well at The Valley before quitting top-class football through illness in 2000.

JEPHCOTT Claude

Outside-right: 190 apps. 16 goals.

Born: Smethwick, 30 October 1891.
Died: Penn near Wolverhampton, 5 October 1950.
Career: West Smethwick School. Olive Mount FC, Stourbridge, Brierley Hill Alliance (two spells), ALBION (£100 April 1911, retired, injured, May 1923); became a local businessman; ALBION (director January 1934 until his death).

■ Claude Jephcott was a brilliant winger, full of dash and vigour. He certainly had terrific pace and was wonderfully consistent, a player who rose to the big occasion. An England junior international in 1911, he suffered a broken leg in 1922 versus Aston Villa, which eventually ended his career when he was perhaps in peak form. He appeared in almost 200 competitive games for Albion (plus several more for the second team in the Birmingham & District League) but managed only 16 goals. Yet reports indicate, clearly, that he probably created another 65–70! Jephcott appeared in the 1912 FA Cup Final versus Barnsley, and in 1919–20 he helped Albion win the League Championship – when his form was quite superb. He played for the Football League and for an England Select XI and was unlucky not to win full international recognition. He made his League debut as a 20-year-old at Sunderland in December 1911.

JOHNSTON Willie

Outside-left: 254+7 apps. 28 goals.

Born: Maryhill, Glasgow, 19 December 1946.
Career: Fife County Schools, Fife District Schools Select, Bowhill Strollers, Manchester United (trial), Glasgow Rangers (amateur), Lochore Welfare, Glasgow Rangers, ALBION (£138,000 December 1972–March 1979), Vancouver Whitecaps (two spells), Birmingham City, Glasgow Rangers, Heart of Midlothian, South China, Heart of Midlothian (player-coach), East Fife (player-coach), Raith Rovers (coach); became a publican in Glasgow; Falkirk (coach); later licensee of the Port O'Brae pub, Kirkcaldy, Fife.

■ With his ability to beat the defence with either footwork or speed and cap a move with a fierce shot, Willie Johnston was a welcome acquisition to Albion in a defence-orientated game. On the downside, however, Johnston, as good as he undoubtedly was, had the tendency to hold on to the ball far too long and was often in trouble with referees (he was actually sent off 17 times during his professional career, which is perhaps a record). He had just finished 67 days' suspension when he joined Albion. But, nevertheless, he was a fine winger who played in 393 competitive games for Rangers (in two major spells at Ibrox Park), scoring 125 goals and winning medals galore in League, Cup and European competitions. In November 1971 he scored a hat-trick (two penalties and a follow up after a miss from the spot) in a League away game for Rangers at St Johnstone, and six months later he scored two vitally-important goals to help Rangers win the European Cup-winners' Cup (against Moscow Dynamo). For Albion, Johnston's appearance tally topped the 260 mark (plus 13 in the second XI), and after leaving The Hawthorns after six years he carried on adding to his personal record by appearing regularly for Birmingham, Hearts and East Fife, as well as helping the Whitecaps win the NASL title in 1979. When he retired to take on coaching, Johnston had amassed well over 700 competitive appearances in a 20-year professional career. He gained 22 Scottish caps (13 with Albion), had two games for the Scottish League side, two for the Under-23 XI and also represented his country at youth-team level. He gave thousands of fans in England, Scotland and perhaps in Canada many hours of high-quality entertainment as a dashing left-winger who could sprint 40 yards in approximately five seconds from a standing start! Johnston, one of Albion's greatest post-war wingers, made his Baggies debut against Liverpool (at home) in Division One in December 1972.

JONES Harry 'Popeye'

Inside-right/centre-forward: 169 apps. 104 goals.

Born: Haydock, Lancs, 26 October 1911.

Died: Preston, 22 February 1957.

Career: Haydock & Newton Le Willows Schools, Haydock Athletic, Preston North End, ALBION (£500 May 1933, retired, through injury and illness, August 1943); World War Two guest for Blackburn Rovers and Everton; ALBION (scout 1946–42); later worked in engineering.

■ Harry 'Popeye' Jones was a jovial, loquacious character, able to play equally well in any forward role, although he thoroughly enjoyed the centre-forward berth. He had an aggressive style, reminiscent of Trevor Ford in his heyday. Often, Jones would bundle both ball and 'keeper into the net as he tore in on the goal

from deep positions. He was a huge favourite with The Hawthorns faithful, he had an appetite for goals, and during his career with Albion he netted over 100 in less than 170 first-team matches. In 1939–40 he rattled in 50 goals in 40 outings (all games) and scored at least once in 11 consecutive matches – a club record later equalled by winger Billy Elliott, his forward colleague in so many wartime fixtures with Albion. Indeed, during World War Two, Jones – who served in the army and played for London Command and London District – scored 47 goals in just 40 regional games for Albion (1939–43). In February 1943, as a guest with Everton, he kept goal in a game against Burnley. Without doubt, Harry 'Popeye' Jones was a great player, a fine club man and a real prize guy when it came to goalscoring. Making his Albion debut at Sheffield Wednesday in January 1935, he also scored 39 goals in 69 Central League games for the club, including 18 in 26 starts when the title was won in 1934–35. In June 1932 he was awarded the Royal Humane Society Testimonial Medal after diving into a Haydock canal to save a child from drowning.

JONES Stan

Centre-half: 267 apps. 3 goals.

Born: Highley, Shropshire, 16 November 1938.
Career: Highley Council & Bridgnorth Grammar Schools, Staffordshire Youths, Kidderminster Harriers, Wolverhampton Wanderers (amateur), Walsall, ALBION (£7,000 May 1960–March 1968), Walsall, Burton Albion, Kidderminster Harriers (player-manager), Hednesford Town (retired 1976),

Coleshill Town (coach), Walsall (trainer), Burton Albion (trainer), WBA All Stars XI (1979–88); now runs sports equipment business in Walsall.

■ Stan Jones was a big, burly defender, inspiring, strong in the air, hard in the tackle and a player who rarely put a foot wrong, although in one five-match spell in the mid-1960s he had the dubious record of scoring three own-goals! In a long and steady career he served Walsall for 10 years in two spells, amassing 265 appearances in major competitions and gaining a Fourth Division Championship medal in 1959–60. Signed by Albion as a straight replacement for Joe Kennedy, he largely held on to the number-five shirt until Eddie Colquhoun arrived from Bury in 1967. Jones was injured and, sadly, missed the 1966 League Cup Final victory over West Ham and was dropped for the 1967 Final against QPR at Wembley. He played only once more for the Baggies, returning to Fellows Park in 1968. He made his Albion debut at Birmingham City in August 1960 and also appeared in 41 Central League games.

KAYE John

Inside-forward/wing-half: 358+3 apps. 54 goals.

Born: Goole, 3 March 1940.
Career: Goole & District Schools, Goole Town Boys, Goole United, Goole Dockers FC, Hull City, Goole Town, Scunthorpe United, ALBION (£44,750 May 1963–November 1971), Hull City (£28,000; retired 1974, appointed coach), Scunthorpe United (assistant manager/coach), Goole Town (manager), Brigg Town (manager); became a hotelier, later worked as an engineer on oil rigs.

■ John 'Yorky' Kaye was a goalscoring forward with Scunthorpe when he was snapped up by Albion manager Jimmy Hagan in 1963 for a club record fee. He spent three of his first four years at The Hawthorns playing alongside Jeff Astle, but during the team's FA Cup run in 1968 he was successfully converted into a dominant, highly efficient and resourceful left-half. He helped Albion win the trophy that year, having earlier received winners' and runners'-up prizes in the 1966 and 1967 League Cup Finals, and three years later he collected

another runners'-up medal when Albion lost to Manchester City in the 1970 League Cup Final. In 1965–66 Kaye, a battler to the last and a wholehearted player in every sense of the word, represented the Football League and twice, in 1966 and 1970, he was voted Midland Footballer of the Year. In all, he appeared in well over 350 games for Albion plus 12 in the Central League (three goals) and during his career amassed 433 League appearances, claiming 79 goals. Kaye made his debut for the Baggies against Leicester City (at home) in August 1963.

KENNEDY Joe

Centre-half: 397 apps. 4 goals.

Born: Cleator Moor, Whitehaven, 15 November 1925.
Died: West Bromwich, 17 September 1986.
Career: St Patrick's School, Whitehaven & District Boys, Cleator Moor Celtic, Workington Town, Brentford (trial), Millwall (trial), Gravesend, Freelands FC, Altrincham, ALBION (£750 December 1948–June 1961), Chester, Stourbridge (player-manager), Brockhouse Works FC (retired 1966); employed by Brockhouse (West Bromwich) until his death.

■ Joe Kennedy began his Albion career as an inside-right before having a decent spell as a right-half. He was then switched to centre-half where he performed brilliantly, being steady, totally reliable, consistent, superb in the air, and sure and sound on the ground. A wonderful player, he developed into one of the club's best post-war pivots, certainly since Jack Vernon left in 1952. He was desperately unlucky not to gain a full England cap. Raven haired, he seemed destined to play for his country after being a permanent reserve during the early '50s, but injury forced him out of the reckoning at crucial times and the only representative calls he received were to skipper England B on three occasions and play for the FA XI. After being injured and ultimately losing his place in the side to a young Jimmy Dugdale, Kennedy was drafted into the right-back position to replace Stan Rickaby in Albion's 1954 FA Cup-winning side. He played superbly well and started the build up that led to Frank Griffin's 87th match-winning goal. Five years earlier he had helped Albion gain promotion from the Second Division, having made his debut for the Baggies against Luton Town (away) in April 1949. The aforementioned Irishman, Jack Vernon, was commanding the centre-half position when Kennedy first arrived at The Hawthorns, but when Vernon returned 'home' Kennedy took over and went on to appear in almost 400 senior games for the Baggies, teaming up with Jimmy Dudley (4) and Ray Barlow (6) to form one of the club's famous half-back lines. He also made 68 Central League appearances for Albion.

KEVAN Derek

Centre-forward: 291 apps. 173 goals.

Born: Ripon, Yorkshire, 6 March 1935.
Career: Ripon Secondary Modern School, Harrogate & District Schools, Ripon YMCA, Ripon City, Sheffield United (trial), Bradford Park Avenue, ALBION (£3,000, July 1953–March 1963), Chelsea (£50,000), Manchester City, Crystal Palace, Peterborough United, Luton Town, Stockport County, Macclesfield Town, Stourbridge, Ansells FC (retired, 1975); WBA Old Stars (1972–85, later manager, 1985–93); ALBION (lottery office 1983–84); became a licensee and delivery driver.

■ Derek 'The Tank' Kevan was an Albion great. Standing 6ft tall and weighing almost 13st, he had power in every department, a big heart, heaps of stamina and a lust for goals. He could head a ball as hard as some players could kick one, and he packed a fierce shot in his right foot and a fair one in his left! A marvellous competitor in every sense, 'Kevvo' won 14 full caps for England (eight goals scored), played four times for the Under-23 XI and also had outings for the Football League side. He spent almost 10 years with Albion, scoring a goal every 151 minutes, including five against Everton at The Hawthorns in 1960. Five years earlier he had scored twice on his debut in a 2–0 League win over the Merseysiders. He also netted 35 goals in 45 appearances for Albion's second XI. Having fallen out with manager Archie Macaulay, he left the Baggies just a couple of days after bagging a hat-trick in a 6–1 win over Ipswich Town. Kevan created a new post-war scoring record for Manchester City (30 League goals in 1963–64), and in 1967 he gained a Fourth Division Championship medal with Stockport. His League career (1952–68) yielded 235 goals in 440 matches, topping the First Division charts in 1961–62 with 33 to his name. A shade clumsy at times, especially when he first joined Albion, Kevan developed into one of the greatest strikers the club has ever seen – his record proves that beyond all doubt.

LEE George

Outside-left: 295 apps. 65 goals.

Born: York, 4 June 1919.
Died: Norwich, 1 April 1991.
Career: Knavesmere School (York), York City Schools, Yorkshire County Boys, Acomb FC, Tottenham Hotspur (trial), Scarborough, York City; served in the army; guest for Bradford Park Avenue, Lincoln City and Chester during World War Two; Nottingham Forest, ALBION (£12,000 July 1949–June 1958), Lockheed Leamington, Vauxhall Motors (retired 1959); ALBION (trainer/coach June 1959–April 1963), Norwich City (trainer/coach).

■ George 'Ada' Lee was an industrious player who varied his game and style judiciously.

Strong, with powerful legs, a useful turn of speed and a cracking left-foot shot, he stepped in to fill the left-wing gap splendidly, being first choice for that position for seven seasons – having made his debut against Charlton (at home) in Division One in August 1949. Injuries cropped up occasionally, but generally he was always the guy lined up to wear that number-11 jersey and did so wonderfully well in almost 300 senior games for the Baggies, plus 36 more in the second XI (nine goals scored). He gained an FA Cup medal in 1954, setting up Ronnie Allen's opening goal, and after leaving The Hawthorns was Norwich's trainer when they won the Second Division title in 1972. Lee gave 25 years' service to the Canaries. At the end of World War Two he played for BAOR (British Army on the Rhine) in the European Championships. He was the first player to score 100 goals for York City.

McLEOD Roddy

Inside-forward: 185 apps. 65 goals.

Born: Kilsyth, Stirlingshire, 12 February 1872.
Died: Lambeth, London, 5 December 1931.
Career: Kilsyth & Kirkintillock Schools, Westburn FC, Partick Thistle, ALBION (£50 January 1891–August 1897), Leicester Fosse (£50), Brighton United, Southampton, Brentford (retired 1904); became a warehouseman; later worked in a brewery, as a tiller in a London bank and as a boiler mechanic.

■ Roddy McLeod was a grand little player, occupying the inside-right position most of the time. He possessed intricate footwork skills and his passing and shooting ability were outstanding. He was the perfect foil to Billy Bassett, with whom he performed wonderfully well in so many games for Albion during the 1890s. McLeod's own record with Albion was exceptional – a goal every three matches – and besides scoring regularly he also set up several more scoring chances for his colleagues. He made his Albion debut at Sheffield Wednesday in a third-round FA

Cup tie in February 1891 and appeared in two FA Cup Finals, gaining a winners' medal in 1892 versus Aston Villa and a runners'-up medal against the same opponents in 1895. Besides his first-team appearances for the club, McLeod also played in more than 125 'other' matches. A Southern League Division Two title winner with Brentford in 1911, after retiring he fell on hard times.

McNEAL Bobby

Left-half: 403 apps. 10 goals.

Born: Hobson Village, County Durham, 19 January 1891.
Died: West Bromwich, 12 May 1956.
Career: Hobson Day School (Durham), Hobson Wanderers, ALBION (professional June 1910; retired, injured, May 1925; club coach 1926–27); guest for Fulham, Middlesbrough, Notts County and Port Vale during World War One; became a West Bromwich licensee.

■ Bobby McNeal was a stylish left-half with a footballing brain. He distributed the ball accurately, and defended with commendable steadiness and reliability. Arriving at The Hawthorns as a raw-boned 19-year-old in the summer of 1910, he made his debut as an inside-left against Leeds City (at home) in October of that year, but he was later switched to left-half where he became an international-class player in a relatively short period of time. Once McNeal had bedded himself into Albion's first XI at left-half he was virtually immovable, and only injuries, suffered during the 1924–25 season, resulted in him losing his place. In the end, it was his left knee that finally ended his career at the age of 34. He gained two England caps (against Wales and Scotland in 1914) and also represented the Football League on five occasions (1912–14). He won four medals with Albion: as Division Two champions (1910–11), FA Cup runners-up (1912), League champions (1919–20) and FA Charity Shield victors (1920). A penalty expert, he also enjoyed firing in free-kicks from 25 yards, usually hitting the target. A magnificent club man, McNeal appeared in over 400 games for Albion (370 in the League) and during the first four seasons, after serving in the army during World War One, he missed only eight matches – such was his reliability and consistency. He also played in over 50 second-team matches. He helped Fulham beat Chelsea in the Victory Cup Final at Highbury in 1918.

MAGEE Tommy

Wing-half: 434 apps. 18 goals.

Born: Widnes, 6 May 1899.
Died: Widnes, May 1974.
Career: St Mary's School (Widnes), Appleton Hornets and St Helen's Recreation Club (Rugby League), Widnes Athletic, ALBION (professional January 1919–May 1934), Crystal Palace (player-coach), Runcorn (player-manager, later coach, retired 1947); later worked in engineering in Wigan.

■ Tommy Magee was a midget right-half, formerly an outside or inside-right, who played with evident enjoyment, tenacity, wonderful consistency and constructiveness. Nicknamed 'Pocket Hercules' and the 'Mighty Atom', Magee played well over 400 games for Albion over a period of 15 years. He was initially signed while serving in the trenches in France during World War One, sending the appropriate papers back to The Hawthorns by air. He won five caps for England (all at right-half), twice toured Canada with the FA party and is the only Albion player (so far) to have won both First Division and FA Cup-winners' medals. Magee also played in over 100 second XI games, helping the reserves win the Birmingham & District League in 1920 and the Central League in 1933 and 1934. Magee is reputed to be the smallest player ever to wear an England shirt at only 5ft 2½in tall, and he's certainly the smallest first-team player Albion have ever had. But what a footballer! He made his debut against Derby County (at

home) in the Midland Victory League in April 1919 – scoring in Albion's 3–1 win – and followed up with his first League outing at Oldham on the opening day of the Champ-ionship-winning season of 1919–20.

MILLARD Len

Defender: 627 apps. 18 goals.

Born: Coseley, 7 March 1919.
Died: Coseley, 15 March 1997.
Career: Christ Church School (Coseley), Wallbrook, Coseley Town, Bilston Town, Sunbeam FC, ALBION (amateur May 1937, professional September 1942–June 1958); guest for Bilston Borough and Sedgley Rangers during World War Two; Stafford Rangers (manager, retired 1961).

■ Len Millard was Albion's left-back for many years, skippering the side in the 1954 FA Cup Final. A defender who stuck to his task, he gave fine service to several wing-halves and left-wingers he played behind, always being fair in the challenge, strong and clean with his kicks, and honest in his keen and thoughtful approach to the professional game. Starting as a centre-forward – scoring two hat-tricks in wartime football – he successfully switched to wing-half before settling down at left-back in 1949, replacing Harry Kinsell. Nicknamed the 'Agitator', Millard appeared in almost 650 first-team matches for Albion, 625 at senior level including 436 in the Football League. He made his debut at Northampton Town in a League South fixture in August 1942 and, two years later, won a Midland Wartime Cup-winners' medal. He also played in 17 Central League games. Without doubt, he was a great servant to the club, assisting Albion through thick and thin for 21 years. He missed only 13 games in the immediate 10 post-war seasons, being an ever present twice. He had a leg amputated in 1989.

MORRIS Fred

Inside-left: 287 apps. 118 goals.

Born: Tipton, 27 August 1893.
Died: Tipton, 12 July 1962.
Career: Great Bridge Primary School, Bell Street Primitives, Tipton Victoria, Redditch, ALBION (professional May 1911–August 1924); guest for Fulham, Watford and Tipton Excelsior during World War One; Coventry City (£625), Oakengates Town (retired 1930); returned to work in Tipton.

■ Fred Morris was a strongly built and courageous forward, who displayed glorious talents, neat control, rapid acceleration, dynamic shooting powers and intelligent off-the-ball running. He was a great competitor and formed a wonderful left-wing partnership with Howard Gregory just after World War One. A junior international, capped in 1911, he slowly got into his stride with Albion's second XI during the 1911–12 season, scoring some superb goals. He finally made his League debut against Sunderland (at home) in April 1912, netting the winner (1–0). Then, in 1919–20, the dashing Morris hit a club record 37 goals, including a five-timer, in an 8–0 home win over Notts County as the Baggies won the League title for the first and, so far, only time. At the end of that season he gained two full caps for England, scoring against Scotland in a 5–4 win and also against Ireland (2–0). He also represented the Football League and the FA and, in 1921–22, became the first Baggies player to reach the milestone of 100 League goals. He was top scorer for the Baggies three seasons running either side of World War One and, before leaving The Hawthorns, he made three appearances in Albion's Central League side, having earlier (in 1913) helped the Baggies second string win the Birmingham & District League. He also scored in Albion's 1–0 win over Aston Villa in the Final of the Birmingham Charity Cup in 1914 and in their 2–0 victory over the Blues in the Final of the same competition eight years later. Morris served in the Ministry of Transport Base Depot in Ruislip (Middlesex), Bookham (Surrey) and France during World War One and hit 24 goals as a guest for Fulham.

MURPHY Jimmy

Right-half: 223 apps.

Born: Ton Pentre, South Wales, 27 October 1910.
Died: Manchester, 14 November 1989.
Career: Ton Pentre Village School, Ton Pentre Boys, Treorchy Thursday FC, Treorchy Juniors, Mid-Rhondda Boys, ALBION (professional February 1928–March 1939), Swindon Town (£140), Morris Commercial FC (retired 1940); Manchester United (as coach, assistant manager, caretaker-manager, scout and scouting advisor); also Welsh team manager.

■ 'Spud' Murphy was a vigorous and attacking wing-half, skilled in tackling and a glutton for hard work. Already a Welsh Schoolboy

international when he joined Albion, he developed fast and went on to win 15 full caps for his country as well as playing in over 220 games for Albion, including an appearance in the 1935 FA Cup Final defeat by Sheffield Wednesday. He made his League debut at Blackpool in March 1930 and replaced Tommy Magee in Albion's middle line, doing a splendid job for seven seasons (1931–38). He also scored 11 goals in 146 second XI games and during World War Two served overseas with the Eighth army, based in Bari, Italy. It was over there that he first met Matt Busby, who asked him to join Manchester United as his assistant manager.

NAYLOR Stuart

Goalkeeper: 419+1 apps.

Born: Wetherby, Yorkshire, 6 December 1962.
Career: Leeds United (trial), Yorkshire Amateurs, Lincoln City, Kettering Town, Peterborough United, Crewe Alexandra, ALBION (£110,000 February 1986–August 1996), Crewe Alexandra (again), Bristol City, Mansfield Town, Walsall, Exeter City, Rushden & Diamonds (retired 2001).

■ Tall, well built and with good reflexes, Stuart Naylor cost Albion a record fee for a goalkeeper. He conceded a Jesper Olsen hat-trick on his Baggies debut against Manchester United, but he quickly put that disappointment behind him and went on to set a new club record by appearing in more games for Albion than any other 'keeper – 468 in the first team alone (355 League, 13 FA Cup, 22 League Cup, 20 others and 58 friendlies). He also had 25 outings in the reserves. Capped by England at Youth and B team levels and known as 'Bruiser', he helped Albion gain promotion in 1993, although he missed the Play-off Final against Port Vale as he was replaced by Tony Lange. Granted a testimonial (versus Coventry), he was released by Albion on a free transfer in 1996 and later joined his ex-boss Brian Talbot at Rushden & Diamonds. Naylor played centre-forward for Lincoln against Newport in 1982. His father, Bill, and uncle, Tommy, both played for Oldham between 1948 and 1959.

NICHOLLS Johnny

Forward: 145 apps. 64 goals.

Born: Wolverhampton, 3 April 1931.
Died: West Bromwich, 1 April 1995.
Career: Prestwood Road, Holy Trinity & Springfield Road Schools (Wolverhampton), Heath Town FC, ALBION (trial July–September 1946), Heath Town Wesley, Heath Town United, Wolverhampton Wanderers (trial), ALBION (amateur August 1950, professional August 1951–May 1957), Cardiff City (£4,000), Exeter City, Worcester City, Wellington Town, Oswestry Town, GKN Sankey (retired 1963); Henry Meadows FC (technical advisor), Red Dragon FC (manager); also played for WBA All Stars (1969–73).

■ One of Albion's greatest post-war strikers, Johnny 'Poacher' Nicholls was a player who could dart into the right place at precisely the right moment and score a vital goal. He had an instructive knack of 'poaching' crucial goals, which he did regularly during his stay with Albion. He could also unleash a cracking shot and delicately flick the ball home with either foot or his head, back to goal or not. He made his senior debut at Blackburn in a fifth-round FA Cup tie in February 1952 and went on to form a magnificent 'twin-striking' partnership with Ronnie Allen. Indeed, he and Allen scored 105 goals between them in two seasons (1953–55). Nicholls also played alongside Allen in two full internationals for England, scoring on his debut against Scotland in front of 134,544 spectators at Hampden in April 1954. He also collected a B cap and one at Under-23 level. He was a key figure in Albion's attack in 1953–54 when the Baggies so very nearly carried off the coveted League and Cup double. Nicholls, in fact, was in Albion's Cup-winning team at Wembley in 1954, although he admits that he had one of his worst games in a striped shirt that afternoon. His overall record for Albion was an exceptionally good one, and he netted frequently for the reserves as well, grabbing 46 goals (in only 69 games), plus another 50 for the intermediates and 40 for the juniors. In his entire career (with Albion, Cardiff and Exeter), Nicholls, who was also nicknamed 'Johnny on the Spot', struck 95 goals in 225 outings – a first-class record. He suffered a stroke and a heart attack in the mid-70s and his sudden death occurred when driving home from Albion's home game with Middlesbrough in 1995.

OSBORNE John

Goalkeeper: 312 apps.

Born: Barlborough, Derbyshire, 1 December 1940.
Died: Worcester, 2 December 1998.
Career: Barlborough Junior & Staveley Netherthorpe Grammar Schools, Chesterfield Boys, North East Derbyshire & District Schools, Barlborough Colliery Miners' Welfare, Netherthorpe FC, Chesterfield, ALBION (£15,000 January 1967; retired 1972; returned within six months; stayed until July 1978), Walsall, Shamrock Rovers, Preston North End, Telford United, Coventry City, Birmingham Post and Mail Rangers, Walsall; also played for WBA All Stars (1982–87); Corinthians FC (manager); worked for the Sandwell Evening Mail, then Commercial Manager of Worcestershire CCC.

■ John Osborne became known as the 'Bionic' goalkeeper after having a strip of plastic inserted into his finger to act as an extra joint. A product of Chesterfield's famous goalkeeping academy, which produced Gordon Banks and Alan Stevenson, he served Albion splendidly for 10 years, often performing miracles between the posts. Certainly one of the finest post-war 'keepers the club has had, he had safe hands and was alert, courageous and dedicated – a great guy all round. Initially an outfield player, gaining two England Schoolboy caps as a left-half, 'Ossie' appeared in Albion's 1968 FA Cup-winning side, the 1970 League Cup runners-up and helped the club clinch promotion in 1976 by conceding only 33 goals – a club record. Signed to replace Ray Potter and Dick Sheppard, he was Albion's first-choice 'keeper before losing his place to Peter Latchford in 1970, regaining it a year later. Disillusioned with manager Don Howe's regime in 1972, he actually retired, only to return within six months. He eventually took his tally of senior appearances with Albion past the 300 mark, having made his debut against Nottingham Forest in January 1967. He also played in over 50 second XI games and in total, during his career, he played in 420 football matches. He loved ornithology, sports quizzes and cricket and once ran a sports outfitters business with fellow 'keeper Jimmy Cumbes. He was the first Albion goalkeeper to receive a testimonial (1978), the fund raised was £32,000 – a record for a Midland footballer at that time. Osborne gained a reputation as a quiz king when he appeared on BBC television's football-based programme *Quiz Ball*, which the Albion team won in 1968.

OWEN Gary

Midfield: 225+4 apps. 26 goals.

Born: St Helen's, Lancashire, 7 July 1958.

Career: St Aidan's Church of England School (St Helens), Eccleston Youth Club, Warrington & District Boys, Manchester City, ALBION (£465,000 May 1979–July 1986), Panionios (£25,000), Sheffield Wednesday, Apoel Nicosia, (retired, injured, 1990); became an art dealer (Gary Owen Fine Art); also employed by Radio Piccadilly and Century Radio (Manchester); coach at Manchester City's School of Excellence.

■ Gary Owen was a skilful midfielder and quality ball player, whose career with Albion was ruined late on by a series of niggling injuries including a fractured shin, gashed calf (which required a skin graft) and torn thigh muscle. Nevertheless, he had the ability to grace any football pitch, any match and any competition, if he put his mind to it. He certainly had the craft, the know-how and indeed the confidence to dictate the midfield arena, but he never really enforced his authority on the game in question. He had five excellent seasons with Albion (1979–84), but after breaking his shin bone at West Ham in January 1984 he was never the same player again, and when manager Ron Saunders arrived at The Hawthorns Owen's days were numbered. He eventually left the club in 1986, signing an initial two-year contract with Panionios. As a Manchester City player, he won England recognition at Youth and B levels and held the record for most Under-21 caps (22) while also representing the Football League. He made his Albion debut against Derby County (at home) in August 1979 and scored once in 31 Central League games for the club.

PEARSON Harold

Goalkeeper: 303 apps.

Born: Tamworth, 7 May 1908.
Died: West Bromwich, November 1994.
Career: Tamworth & Amington Schools, Glascote United, Glascote Methodists, Belgrave YMCA, Belgrave United, Two Gates FC, Nuneaton Borough, Tamworth Castle, ALBION (amateur April 1925, professional May 1925–August 1937), Millwall (£300, retired 1940); guest for West Ham United in World War Two; ALBION (coach 1948–52, scout 1953–55); later worked for W.J. and S. Lees, iron founders, West Bromwich.

■ For a big man, Harold 'Algy' Pearson made goalkeeping look so easy. Equally adept with high or low crosses, he had tremendous reach, kicked vast distances out of his hands and could throw the ball a fair way too. He was on Albion's books along with his father, Hubert (1925), and went on to make over 300 senior appearances for the club, including 281 in the League, his debut coming against South Shields (at home) in Division Two in December 1927. He won an FA Cup medal in 1931 and a runners'-up prize in the 1935 Final. Three years later he collected a Third Division South Championship medal with Millwall. Earlier in his career Pearson had gained a junior international cap for England (1927) and his only full cap was against Scotland at Wembley in 1932, when he played behind his teammate George Shaw. He also played for Tamworth Castle in the 1927 Bass Charity Vase Final triumph. Pearson replaced George Ashmore between the posts for Albion and was subsequently dislodged by Billy Light (briefly) and then Jimmy Adams in 1937. In three seasons (1930–33) with Albion, Pearson missed only one League game. He also appeared in almost 100 second XI games for the Baggies, helping them win the Central League title in 1934. A very consistent goalkeeper, he was one of Albion's best. His cousin, Harry Hibbs, played for Birmingham and another cousin, Horace Pearson, kept goal for Coventry City.

PEARSON Hubert

Goalkeeper: 377 apps. 2 goals.

Born: Kettlebrook, Tamworth, 15 May 1886.
Died: Tamworth, 12 October 1955.
Career: Kettlebrook & Wilnecote Schools, Kettlebrook Oakfield, Tamworth Castle, Tamworth Athletic, ALBION (amateur February 1906, professional March 1906, retired May 1926); guest for Oldbury Town when serving in the army during World War One.

■ Hubert Pearson replaced Jim Stringer in the Albion goal during 1909–10 and was subsequently ousted by George Ashmore, who then handed over to Hubert's son, Harold, in 1927. Well balanced, agile and with an abundance of confidence, Pearson made his debut at Birmingham in a first-round FA Cup replay in January 1908 and played his last senior game 17 years later at West Ham. He had the pleasure of scoring two goals for Albion, both from the penalty spot, against Bury on Boxing Day 1911 (won 2–0) and versus Middlesbrough in April 1912 (won 3–1). He also played over 100 second-team games for the Baggies, 88 in the Central League, gaining a Championship medal in 1924. Pearson served in the AA Reserve Brigade, stationed on the Isle of Wight during World War One.

Between them, the goalkeeping Pearsons won every honour in the game: First, Second and Third Division South Championship medals; runners'-up medals in the first two Divisions; FA Cup-winners' and runners'-up medals; FA Charity Shield winners' and runners'-up medals; junior and full England international caps and Football League and FA honours.

PEARSON Tom

Inside-left: 171 apps. 88 goals.

Born: West Bromwich, 20 May 1866.
Died: West Bromwich, 4 July 1918.
Career: Christ Church School, Oak Villa, West Bromwich Sandwell, ALBION (professional, April 1886, retired, injured, May 1894).

■ Tom Pearson was Albion's first great marksman who top scored in each of the first five Football League seasons: 1888–93. A brilliant inside-left, he had endurance, resolution, high quality shooting power (with both feet), alertness, presence of mind and a distinctive short gait. A natural marksman, he made his debut at Notts County in a sixth-round FA Cup tie in February 1887 and went on to score 150 goals in more than 400 first-team games (at all levels) for Albion. He played in the 1887, 1888 and 1892 FA Cup Finals, picking up winners' medals in the last two, and in his six seasons as a League player he missed only 14 matches, all through injury. He would surely have earned international honours for England had his playing days not ended prematurely in 1894 with a serious leg injury.

PENNINGTON Jesse

Left-back: 496 apps.

Born: West Bromwich, 23 August 1883.
Died: Kidderminster, 5 September 1970.
Career: Brasshouse Lane & Devonshire Road Day Schools (Smethwick), Summit Star, Smethwick Centaur, Langley Villa, Langley St Michael's, Dudley Town (two spells), Aston Villa (amateur), ALBION (professional March 1903, retired May 1922); guest for Oldbury Town and Notts County during World War One; ALBION (coach May 1922–August 1923), Kidderminster Harriers (coach and manager), Malvern College (coach), Rafman FC (coach), Wolverhampton Wanderers (scout), ALBION (scout 1950–61).

■ One of the greatest names in the annals of West Bromwich Albion, Jesse 'Peerless' Pennington was a superbly equipped left-back and scrupulously fair in his play. Notably quick in recovery and a defender with exquisite balance, a sharp eye and splendid kick down the line, he was a magnificent club captain, wonderful sportsman and indeed a grand club man of the highest calibre. Pennington played in a then record 455 League games for Albion, holding the record for 54 years until

beaten by Tony Brown in 1976. He also appeared in 39 FA Cup matches, including the Final of 1912 when Albion lost to Barnsley in a replay. A Cup-winners' medal was the only major honour that eluded Pennington during his career. He won 25 England caps (1907–20), represented the Football League on nine occasions, played for an England XI five times and also starred in five international trials. He skippered his country twice and the League XI once at the age of 36. He led Albion to the Second Division title in 1911 and nine years later won a League Championship-winners' medal. In his career, Pennington never scored a goal. He was only dropped once by Albion, and his displays were always edged with genius. Universally regarded as the nonpareil of Albion and England left-backs, he formed a terrific partnership with Bob Crompton of Blackburn – lining up together in 23 internationals. Pennington had the unique experience of playing his first and last League games against Liverpool, in September 1903 and April 1922 respectively. In 1910 he had a dispute with Albion regarding pay and actually signed for Kidderminster Harriers. That dispute, however, was soon sorted out and the appropriate forms cancelled before they found the post. Three years later, Pennington, forthright and honest, was the subject of a bribe scandal when he was approached with money to 'fix' a League game between Albion and Everton so that the Merseysiders would not lose. He immediately informed the police as well as the Albion directors. A trap was set and the culprit – Samuel Johnson, alias Frederick Pater – was arrested and later sentenced to six months' imprisonment at Stafford Assize Court. In 1969 Pennington was made a life member of Albion – a fitting tribute to a king-size footballer, one of Albion's greatest.

PERRY Charlie

Centre-half: 219 apps. 16 goals.

Born: West Bromwich, 3 January 1866.
Died: West Bromwich, 2 July 1927.
Career: Christ Church School (West Bromwich), West Bromwich Strollers (not Albion), ALBION (March 1884, professional August 1885, retired May 1896, became director 1896–1902); licensee of the Golden Cup, West Bromwich.

■ Charlie Perry was a superb player and a grand captain. He had a polished style, was determined in everything he did, cool under pressure and a man

who marshalled his defence magnificently from the centre-half position, which was undoubtedly his best. Brother of Tom and Walter, he won three England caps (1890–93), had two outings for the Football League and appeared in four international trials. He was Albion's pivot in the 1886, 1887, 1888 and 1892 FA Cup Finals, gaining winners' medals in the last two but missing the 1895 Final through injury, which eventually forced him to retire. Tall and strong, Perry was Albion's first 'great' centre-half, and besides his tally of first-team appearances he also played in 280 'other' games in local Cups and friendlies, being a regular in the side for seven years, from 1888 to 1895. He had the distinction of making his senior debut in the 1886 FA Cup Final against Blackburn at The Oval, almost two years after his first appearance for the second XI.

PERRY Tom

Half-back: 291 apps. 15 goals.

Born: West Bromwich, 5 August 1871.
Died: West Bromwich, 18 July 1927.
Career: Christ Church School (West Bromwich), Christ Church FC, West Bromwich Baptist, Stourbridge, ALBION (professional July 1890–October 1901), Aston Villa (£100, retired 1902); later worked in accountancy.

■ A stalwart for Albion during the 10 years leading up to the club's move to The Hawthorns, Tom Perry was a capable, efficient and extremely enthusiastic performer – wholehearted in every way – whose hard graft and dedicated approach to the game

made him such a key figure in the 1890s. He made his debut at Preston in September 1890 at outside-left but soon became respected for his splendid displays as a half-back, lining up alongside his elder brother Charlie. He gained one England cap, played three times for the Football League and starred for the League Select XI against Aston Villa in 1894. He was Albion's right-half in the 1895 FA Cup Final, losing to his future club Villa, and appeared in almost 300 competitive games for the Baggies, also starring in 170 'other' first-team matches. Another brother, Walter, also played for Albion, making 15 first-class appearances.

RAVEN Paul

Defender: 294+10 apps. 21 goals.

Born: Salisbury, 28 July 1970.
Career: Doncaster Rovers (two spells), ALBION (£150,000 March 1989–July 2000), Rotherham United, Grimsby Town, Carlisle United, Barrow (player-coach).

■ A capable defender, Paul Raven formed fine partnerships at The Hawthorns with Daryl Burgess, Gary Strodder and Paul Mardon. Strong in the tackle and commanding in the air, he showed good pace and ability on the ground and made over 300 senior appearances for Albion; he scored seven goals in 82 outings for the second team and gained a second XI Championship medal in 1991, before being released by the club at the end of 1999–2000. An England Schoolboy international (1985), he made his debut for the Baggies at right-back at Portsmouth in May 1989, played in the Play-off Final win over Port Vale four years later and was granted a testimonial before his departure in 2000, joining his former boss Alan Buckley and a cluster of ex-Baggies players at Grimsby.

READER Joe

Goalkeeper: 370 apps.

Born: West Bromwich, 27 February 1866.

Died: West Bromwich, 8 March 1954.

Career: Beeches Road & St Phillips Schools (West Bromwich), ALBION (amateur January 1885, professional August 1885, retired April 1901, became trainer-coach and later ground steward until 1950).

■ Joe Reader was a goalkeeper to rank with the finest the game has produced. Superb in handling and with marvellous reflexes, he used his feet, as much as anything else, to divert goal-bound shots or headers. He appeared in 315 League games, 39 FA Cup ties and 16 'other' games for Albion, as well as starring in more than 150 local Cup and friendly matches during his 16-year playing career. An ever present in five League campaigns during the 1890s, he participated in the 1892 and 1895 FA Cup Finals, gained one England cap, represented the Football League three times and played a League XI once. Dedicated to the last, his love for the club was clear when he turned out in one match with his arm in a sling. Nicknamed 'Kicker', he is the only player to have served Albion on three of their home grounds – Four Acres, Stoney Lane and The Hawthorns. He was forced to give up the game through illness, yet he still remained an active member of the club when employed as a coach. He saw his last game at The Hawthorns two weeks before he died, and it is said that Reader was the last goalkeeper to discard the customary long white trousers, doing so in the mid-1890s. He took over from the great Bob Roberts in Albion's goal and in 1901 handed over to Ike Webb. Reader made his League debut at Aston Villa in October 1889 and was associated with Albion for 65 years.

REGIS Cyrille

Centre-forward: 297+5 apps. 112 goals.

Born: Maripiasoula, French Guyana, 9 February 1958.

Career: Cardinal Hinsley School (Harlesden), Borough of Brent Boys, Ryder Brent Valley (two spells), Oxford & Kilburn Boys, Moseley, Hayes, ALBION (£5,000 May 1977–October 1984), Happy Valley (guest), Coventry City (£300,000), Aston Villa, Wolverhampton Wanderers, Wycombe Wanderers, Chester City (retired 1996), ALBION (coach February 1997–January 2000); now a football agent.

■ Cyrille Regis had seven wonderful years with Albion, during which time he scored 140 goals in 370 matches, including tour and friendly games. A huge favourite with the fans from his debut day, when he scored twice in a 4–0 home League Cup win over Rotherham in August 1977, he found the back of the net regularly and scored some quite spectacular and breathtaking goals on the way. Indeed, Regis created a club record – unique if you like – by netting on his debut for Albion in five different competitions: Football League, FA Cup, League Cup, Tennent-Caledonian Cup and Central League. He actually netted three times in his four second XI games. Strong, muscular and aggressive, with a terrific shot, his heading ability was A1, and he could leave opponents standing with his devastating speed over 25-30 yards. He would often collect the ball around the halfway line and head towards goal, brushing aside his markers with his powerful shoulders before unleashing a cannonball shot. TV cameras have several of his classic goals on film so that we can relive his explosive style in years to come. A snip of a signing by Ronnie Allen, he was capped by England at full, B and Under-21 levels, voted PFA Young

Footballer of the Year in 1979 and was runner-up to Footballer of the Year Steve Perryman in 1982. In 1987, four years after turning down a £750,000 move to the French club St Etienne, he was voted *Evening Mail* Footballer of the Year, Midland Soccer Writer's Player of the Year and Merit Man after helping Coventry win the FA Cup. His transfer to Highfield Road was a shock to every Albion fan, and Regis himself said it was a wrench to leave The Hawthorns. However, he soon settled down with the Sky Blues and in 1985 scored five goals against his future club, Chester, in a League Cup tie. He is only the second player to net from the penalty spot on his debut for Albion (the first was Bobby Blood in 1921), and in May 1996, at the age of 37 years and 86 days, Regis became the oldest player to appear in a League game for Wycombe. During his career he scored over 200 goals in more than 700 matches and is the first 'professional' to play for Albion, Villa, Wolves and Coventry. A born-again Christian, other members of the Regis family include Dave Regis, Jason Roberts and Olympic athlete John Regis.

REYNOLDS John 'Baldy'

Wing-half: 46 apps. 6 goals.

Born: Blackburn, 21 February 1869.
Died: Sheffield, 12 March 1917.
Career: Portglenone & Ballymena Schools, County Antrim, Park Road (Blackburn two spells), Witton (Blackburn), Blackburn Rovers, East Lancs Regiment, Distillery (guest), Ulster, ALBION (professional March 1891–April 1892), Droitwich Town, Aston Villa (£50), Celtic, Southampton, Bristol St George, Grafton FC (New Zealand, player and coach), Stockport County, Willesden Town (retired April 1905), Cardiff City (coach); later employed as a miner near Sheffield.

■ John 'Baldy' Reynolds, at 5ft 4in tall, was a stumpy wee man and yet a marvellous wing-half, who sometimes bewildered his own teammates as well as the opposition. He mastered every trick in the book, and, aided by some quite remarkable ball skills, his footwork was at times exceptionally brilliant. Although born in Blackburn, he spent his youth in Ireland, returning to his home town in 1884. He joined the forces at the age of 17 and after two years' service signed for Distillery. When based in Ireland, Reynolds was capped five times for that country (1890–91), but, after returning to England, he went on to gain another eight caps – this time for the country of his birth – thus making him one of only a handful of footballers to have represented two countries at international level. Reynolds also played for the Football League on four occasions, for the Professionals XI three times and he appeared in one England trial. He also gained an FA Cup-winners' medal in 1892 – scoring in a 3–0 win over Aston Villa – and in 1895 he was in Villa's Cup-winning side against Albion! The following year he won a second League Championship medal, and in 1897 he was a key member of Villa's 'double-winning' team, scoring 17 goals in 110 games for Villa in four seasons. Reynolds helped Celtic win the Scottish First Division title in 1898, having earlier, with Ulster, collected an Irish Cup-winners' medal (1891). He also had the pleasure of scoring Albion's first penalty-kick against Nottingham Forest in April 1893. He left the club under a cloud after falling out with the directors. Ironically, he scored on his debut for Villa against Albion in September 1893, having two years earlier made his Albion bow against his home-town club Blackburn (October 1891). Reynolds played in 40 'other' games for Albion.

RICHARDSON Billy

Centre-half: 352 apps. 1 goal

Born: Great Bridge, Tipton, 14 February 1908.
Died: West Bromwich, 19 August 1985.
Career: Greets Green Infants & Junior Schools, Whitehall Road Schools (Great Bridge), Greets Green Boys, Greets Green Prims, Great Bridge Celtic, ALBION (professional November 1926–May 1937), Swindon Town (£200), Dudley Town, Vono Sports FC (retired 1941), ALBION (scout 1950–53)

■ Bill Richardson, a shade casual at times, was nevertheless a splendid pivot, unflagging and good in the air. No relation to 'W.G.', but brother to Sammy, he gave Albion 11 years' service, making over 350 appearances. He first set foot inside The Hawthorns when the centre-half slot and wing-half positions were causing the management some concern. Richardson buckled down to the task ahead of him and settled into the team's style of play without much effort, after making his debut in December 1928. With Tommy Magee on his right and Len Darnell on his left, this trio formed a steady and reliable middle line. He also played in both wing-half positions but was at his best in the centre, where he played consistently well, apart from the odd hiccup here and there. A popular and reliable player, he appeared in two FA Cup Finals, holding together the defence during that double-winning season of 1930–31. He made his League debut at Middlesbrough in December 1928 and also appeared in 62 second XI games for Albion (three goals).

RICHARDSON 'W.G.' Bill

Centre-forward: 444 apps. 328 goals.

Born: Framwellgate Moor, County Durham, 29 May 1909.

Died: Perry Barr, Birmingham, 29 March 1959.

Career: Framwellgate Moor & Easington Colliery Schools, Durham Schools, Horden Wednesday, United Bus Company (Hartlepool), Hartlepools United, ALBION (£1,250 June 1929–November 1945); guest for Derby County and Walsall during World War Two, Shrewsbury Town (£250), ALBION (assistant trainer/coach until his death).

■ On his day, 'W.G.' Richardson had few equals and no superiors at snapping up half-chances, especially those that flew hard and low across the face of the goal from either wing, deflected or not. A truly dynamic centre-forward, who depended on his alertness rather than his weight, he was quick, assertive and pretty sharp inside the box. During the 1930s Richardson was seemingly always hitting the net and the headlines. He scored both goals when Albion beat Birmingham to win the 1931 FA Cup Final, and he secured the match-winning goal against Charlton, which ensured Albion would win promotion in that same 1930–31 season to bring them a unique double. He grabbed four goals in five minutes at West Ham in November 1931, hit three in six minutes against Derby in 1933, set an Albion record with 40 goals in season 1935–36 (which still stands today) and claimed 14 hat-tricks in major competitions, including four 'fours'. During World War Two, Richardson continued to score goals and twice netted six times against Luton and the RAF in 1941–42. He grabbed five-timers versus Swansea in 1941 and Aston Villa in 1943, and his wartime exploits revealed 123 goals in only 106 games – exactly 100 coming in 'competitive' matches – gaining a Midland Wartime Cup-winners' medal in 1944 as well. He also played and scored for the Metropolitan Police, the National Police and Civil Defence teams during the hostilities and netted 55 times for Shrewsbury before returning to The Hawthorns as trainer-coach. In a brilliant career, Richardson won just one full England cap against Holland in 1935, but he deserved a lot more. He netted 202 League goals for Albion, a record that stood for over 20 years, struck 26 in the FA Cup and another 83 in 79 second XI games (eight hat-tricks). He made his Baggies debut versus Millwall on Boxing Day in 1929, scoring in a 6–1 win.

The 'G' was added to Billy's name to help people distinguish him from the other Richardson who was also at The Hawthorns. The 'G' stood for ginger (hair).

RICKABY Stan

Right-back: 205 apps. 2 goals.

Born: Stockton-on-Tees, 12 March 1924.

Career: Stockton Grammar School, Stockton & District Schools, South Bank, Middlesbrough, ALBION (£7,500 February 1950–June 1955), Poole Town (player-manager), Weymouth, Newton Abbot Spurs (retired 1964); entered accountancy, moved to Australia 1969 and now lives in North Beach, Perth.

■ A strong, accomplished right-back, good in the tackle and with a powerful kick, Stan Rickaby was a player who was never flustered. He came to Albion as cover for Jimmy Pemberton, but in six months he had replaced the injury-stricken right-back and held his place in the side for quite a while afterwards. In contrast, Rickaby was lucky with injuries at Albion until the semi-final of the FA Cup against Port Vale in 1954, when he suffered a leg injury which forced him to miss the Final against Preston. However, along with 'keeper Norman Heath, he was awarded a winners' medal, having played in all the previous rounds. Capped by England against Ireland in 1953, Rickaby played in over 200 games for Albion, all at right-back. He left The Hawthorns in 1955, alleging that he had been made a 'soccer slave' and later became involved in a constant battle with the club regarding the way in which he was released. He made his Baggies debut against Manchester City in April 1950 and also played in six second-team matches. Rickaby's autobiography, *Upover and Downunder,* was published in 2003.

ROBERTS Bob

Goalkeeper: 84 apps.

Born: West Bromwich, 9 April 1859.

Died: Byker, Newcastle-upon-Tyne, 20 October 1929.

Career: Christ Church School (West Bromwich), George Salters Works, ALBION (Strollers September 1879, professional August 1885–May 1890), Sunderland Albion, ALBION (free May 1891–May 1892), Aston Villa (retired 1893).

■ Albion's first international, Bob Roberts was a giant of a man, just the right size for a goalkeeper of that time. He was so well built that he could deal comfortably with high crosses and with any robust forward that cared to barge into him! He had a tremendous reach, a big safe pair of hands, wore size 13 boots (which assisted him in kicking vast distances) and, above all, he had a wonderful temperament. Roberts started off his playing career as an outfield-player, occupying many different positions before finally settling down between the uprights. He won three England caps, his first against Scotland in 1887, played for the Football Alliance, in three international trials and in three

successive FA Cup Finals – 1886, 1887 and 1888 – gaining a winners' medal in the latter against Preston when he played superbly well. During his 12 years with the club he amassed over 400 appearances, 84 at senior level, the rest in other local Cup competitions and friendlies. A quite magnificent player, he was very popular and, without doubt, an Albion great. Roberts and Ezra Horton both featured in Albion's first FA Cup tie versus Wednesbury Town in 1883 and the first League game versus Stoke in 1888.

ROBERTSON Ally

Defender: 622+4 apps. 12 goals.

Born: Philipstoun, Lothian, Scotland, 9 September 1952.

Career: Bridgend Junior & East Lothian Schools, Linlithgow Academy, Uphall Saints, ALBION (apprentice July 1968, professional September 1969–September 1986), Wolverhampton Wanderers (retired 1990), Worcester City (manager). Cheltenham Town (manager); now a sales representative for a car company.

■ After 18 years' service and more than 700 games (626 at competitive level – second behind Tony Brown) Ally Robertson left Albion for rivals Wolves, sold by manager Ron Saunders who said he would not figure in his future plans. It was a sad occasion for Robertson, who had made his debut against Manchester United in October 1969 as a 17-year-old. He served Albion through thick and thin, as a steady, unobtrusive central-defender, producing solid challenges and crunching tackles (not all of them legal!). Forming a fine partnership with John Wile, they played together 573 times in Albion colours, helping the team gain promotion in 1976 and reach three major Cup semi-finals. In 1979 Robertson passed Jimmy Dudley's record of 166 consecutive League appearances for Albion and when he left for Molineux only two players – Tony Brown and Wile – had played in more League games for the club. In fact, Robertson's tally of 729 appearances for Albion (all games, including friendlies) places him second in the club's all-time appearance list behind 'Bomber' Brown. He also starred in 112 reserve matches. At the age of 18, Robertson broke a leg playing against Charlton in a League Cup tie at The Hawthorns, but he bounced back in style and went roaring on towards the top, becoming one of Albion's finest defenders. As a youngster he won four Scottish Schoolboy caps, later adding six Youth caps to his collection, but he failed to gain full international recognition – hard though he tried. In five seasons (1975–80) he missed only seven League games out of 210 as Albion established themselves in the First Division. He helped Wolves win the Fourth Division title and Sherpa Van Trophy in 1988 and the Third Division Championship a year later.

ROBSON Bryan OBE

Midfielder/defender: 242+7 apps. 46 goals.

Born: Witton Gilbert, Chester-le-Street, County Durham, 11 January 1957.

Career: Chester-le-Street Council & Birtley Comprehensive Schools, Washington & Chester-le-Street Schools, Chester-le-Street Cubs, Burnley (trial), Coventry City (trial), Newcastle United (trial), ALBION (apprentice April 1972, professional August 1974–October 1981), Happy Valley (Hong Kong, guest), Manchester United (£1.5m), Middlesbrough (player-manager, retired as a player 1997), Manchester United (coach), Bradford City (manager), ALBION (manager November 2004–October 2006), Sheffield United (manager June 2007).

■ Bryan Robson was the most costly footballer in Britain when he joined Manchester United in 1981. He went on to captain England over 60 times and gained 90 full caps, scoring 26 goals, including one inside the first 30 seconds in the 1982 World Cup clash against France in Spain. One of the finest midfield players in world football, he participated in three World Cups and won medals galore at Old Trafford,

including successive Premiership titles (1993 and 1994), three FA Cup Final victories (1983, 1985 and 1990) and European Cup-winners' Cup success (1991), also adding a League Cup runners'-up medal to his tally (1991)...all this after helping Albion gain promotion from the Second Division in 1976. He later took Middlesbrough into the Premiership twice and lost in three domestic Cup Finals. Robson occupied the left-back, centre-half, wing-half and inside-forward positions during a superb career. An aggressive competitor with an endless supply of dynamic stamina, he had awareness, was creative, possessed excellent passing skills and a powerful shot, was a superb header of the ball and had an appetite for hard work. He went on to appear in almost 250 first-team appearances for Albion, with caretaker manager and former player Brian Whitehouse handing him his League debut at York in April 1975. He also played in 58 second XI games and netted 15 goals. He starred in 465 first-team games for Manchester United (100 goals) and played in 27 games for Middlesbrough. Besides his quota of full England caps he also appeared in four Youth, two B and seven Under-21 internationals. He retired with 832 competitive appearances under his belt (for club and country) and 172 goals. In November 2004, following the sacking of Gary Megson, Robson returned to The Hawthorns to become Albion's 27th managerial change since World War Two. He brought in Nigel Pearson, the former Shrewsbury, Sheffield Wednesday and Middlesbrough defender, as his assistant. At the end of that season he did something no other boss had done before, he kept Albion in the Premiership after they had been bottom of the pile at Christmas. However, just over a year later, following relegation, he was sacked after a run of poor results.

ROBSON Sir Bobby CBE

Inside-right/right-half: 257 apps. 61 goals.

Born: Sacriston, County Durham, 18 February 1933.

Career: Waterhouse Secondary Modern School, Langley Park Juniors, Chester-le-Street, Middlesbrough, Southampton (trial). Fulham, ALBION (£25,000 March 1956–August 1962), Fulham (£20,000), Oxford University (trainer-coach), Vancouver Royals (player-manager, August 1967, retired 1968), Fulham (manager), Chelsea (scout), Ipswich Town (manager), England (B-team manager and senior team manager), PSV Eindhoven (manager, two spells), Sporting Lisbon (manager), FC Porto (manager), CF Barcelona (manager), Newcastle United (manager), Republic of Ireland (advisory coach).

■ During his early Fulham days Bobby Robson formed part of an excellent inside trio, with Bedford Jezzard and Johnny Haynes. Leaving Craven Cottage in March 1956, his first two games for the Baggies both ended in 4–0 defeats, but after that he gave Albion great service, playing alongside Ronnie Allen and Derek Kevan before being successfully converted from a goalscorer into a goal maker by manager Vic Buckingham. After gaining 20 England caps (netting twice on his debut versus France in 1957), he returned to Fulham where he ended his senior career with 673 appearances and 151 goals to his name. A model competitor who oozed confidence, Robson's temperament was a shining example to the rest of his teammates. Hard working and with great awareness, he inspired his teammates and was a tireless

performer wherever he played. Besides his England outings, Robson played five times for the Football League, once for the Under-23s, once for England B, toured South Africa with the FA in 1956, played for the FA XI in the 1962 Charity Shield game and went to the 1958 and 1962 World Cup Finals. He also scored six times in seven Central League games for Albion. As Ipswich manager he won the Texaco Cup (1973), the FA Cup (1978) and UEFA Cup (1981) – the same year he just missed out on the League title. He then took England to the 1986 World Cup Finals and was 71 when he lost his job. He played cricket for Sacriston, Worcester Park (London) and West Bromwich Dartmouth, was awarded the CBE in 1991, knighted in 2002 and later received The Freedom of Ipswich as well as being presented with a Special Lifetime Award by UEFA.

RYAN Reg

Wing-half/Inside-forward: 272 apps. 31 goals.

Born: Dublin, 30 October 1925.
Died: Sheldon, Birmingham, 10 February 1997.
Career: Marino School, Dublin (Gaelic Soccer), Claremont School (Blackpool), Blackpool Boys, Claremont Juniors, Sunbeam Cars (Coventry), Sheffield United (trial), Jaguar Cars (Coventry), Nuneaton Borough, Nottingham Forest (trial), Coventry City, ALBION (£750 April 1945–June 1955), Derby County (£3,000), Coventry City (retired 1960; pools organiser), ALBION (pools/lottery supervisor December 1961, chief scout September 1962–October 1976); later scout for Aston Villa, Derby County, Hereford United and Leeds United.

■ Paddy Ryan made his Albion debut at Millwall in a Football League South game in November 1945 and played his last match almost 10 years later against Aston Villa in March 1955. A stocky, mobile player, he took time to settle at The Hawthorns, but once bedded in he gave some impressive displays as a wing-half

and inside-forward. A very consistent performer, he helped the Baggies gain promotion from Division Two in 1949 and win the FA Cup in 1954, when he linked up superbly in centre field with Ray Barlow and Jimmy Dudley. Ryan also scored five goals in 107 Central League games for Albion, and after leaving he appeared in 139 games (31 goals) for Derby, collecting a Third Division North Championship medal in 1957, having represented that section against the 'South' in 1955. At international level, Ryan won 17 caps (16 for the Republic of Ireland and one for Northern Ireland) and, in a splendid career, he amassed 432 League appearances (234 with Albion) and struck 70 goals.

SANDERS Jimmy

Goalkeeper: 301 apps.

Born: Hackney, London, 5 July 1920.
Died: Tamworth, 11 August 2003.
Career: Hackney Grammar School, North London Boys, Longlands (London), Charlton Athletic; World War Two guest for Chelsea, Liverpool, Southampton, West Ham; ALBION (guest, then signed for £2,250, November 1945–June 1958), Kettering Town, Coventry City, Hinckley Athletic (retired 1960); later a licensee in Derby, Birmingham and Solihull.

■ Jimmy Sanders was a very consistent goalkeeper, never acrobatic but always steady and capable, and an expert at stopping penalties, saving 25 during his career. He was invalided out of the RAF during World War Two, having completed 120 operations as a gunner pilot against enemy forces before being shot down. His injuries yielded partly to

treatment, but he was in terrible pain and was told he would never play football again. 'Nonsense' said Sanders, and he proved everyone wrong by regaining full fitness inside 18 months. He joined Albion and made his debut at Millwall in the Football League South in November 1945 as a guest, signing permanently four days later. He went on to appear in almost 400 games for the Baggies, helping them gain promotion in 1949 and win the FA Cup in 1954. He also played in 101 reserve games and scored one goal – direct from a corner versus Derby reserves in 1946–47. He was at The Valley with Sam Bartram but left knowing that he'd never oust such a fine 'keeper. Sanders, such a jovial character, always wore a bow tie and displayed his 1954 Cup medal on a chain around his neck.

SANDFORD Teddy

Inside-forward: 317 apps. 75 goals.

Born: Handsworth, Birmingham, 22 October 1910.
Died: Great Barr, Birmingham, 20 May 1995.
Career: Wattville Road & Holyhead Road Schools (Handsworth), Tantany Athletic, Overend Wesley, Birmingham Carriage Works, Smethwick Highfield, ALBION (amateur October 1929, professional May 1930–March 1939), Sheffield United (£1,500), Morris Commercial (retired 1943); ALBION (coach 1950–57, scout 1961–67); later ran a café near The Hawthorns for many years.

■ Nephew of former Albion player 'Abe' Jones, Teddy Sandford spent 10 seasons with Albion. Arriving at the club in the midst of an abundance of inside-forward talent, he spent his first term playing with the reserves before making a scoring debut in a 3–2 win at Preston in November 1930. The season ended in triumph for both Albion and Sandford with that unique Cup and promotion double. A quiet player and never flashy, Sandford was an excellent goalscorer, quick to pounce and dispossess an opponent. He had an enviable physique, which held him in good stead later in his career when he switched to centre-half. He won an FA Cup runners'-up medal in 1935, despite scoring against Sheffield Wednesday in the Final, and in between times (1932) he was capped by England. He also netted four goals in 24 reserve games for Albion.

SHAW George

Full-back: 425 apps. 11 goals.

Born: Swinton, 13 October 1899.
Died: Doncaster, 10 March 1973.
Career: Swinton Schools, Bolton-on-Deane, Rossington Main Colliery, Doncaster Rovers (two spells), Gillingham, Huddersfield Town, ALBION (£4,100 November 1926–May 1938), Stalybridge Celtic (player-manager), Worcester City (player-manager), FC Floriana (Malta, player-manager/coach, retired 1951); later worked at Hamworth Colliery, Doncaster.

■ Nicknamed 'Teapot', 'Singer' and 'Cocky', ex-Navy man George Shaw gave Albion long and dedicated service. Admirably built for a full-back, he was dominant in the air, strong in the tackle and safe and sure with his kicking. A grand volleyer and useful dead-ball specialist, he was an occasional member of Huddersfield's League Championship-winning sides of 1924, 1925 and 1926, making 24 appearances in those three seasons. With Albion he won the FA Cup and promotion in 1931, a Cup runners'-up medal in 1935, an England cap in 1932, as well as playing for the Football League XI and going on two FA Tours (Belgium 1929, Canada 1931). He made his Albion debut at Sheffield United in December 1926 (48 hours after signing for a then record fee) and missed only five of the next 300 League games up to January 1934, eventually taking his appearance tally for the club past the 400 mark. He played in 32 Central League games (two goals).

SIMMONS CHARLIE 'CHIPPY'

Forward: 193 apps. 81 goals.

Born: West Bromwich, 9 September 1878.
Died: Wednesbury, 12 December 1937.
Career: Beeches Road School (West Bromwich), Trinity Victoria, Oldbury Town, Worcester Rovers, ALBION (professional April 1898–July 1904), West Ham United (£700), ALBION (£600 May 1905–March 1907), Chesterfield Town, Wellington Town, Royal Rovers (Canada, retired 1922); later a West Bromwich licensee.

■ 'Chippy' Simmons became a regular scorer for Albion after making his debut at Burnley in November 1898; he teamed up with Billy Bassett, Jimmy McLean and Fred Buck in his first spell and then partnered Fred Shinton in 1905–06. Possessing a lethal shot, Simmons was fast, crafty and often found space. The leading scorer with 24 goals when Albion won the Second Division in 1902, he was given a trial by England for his efforts and later represented the Professionals against the Amateurs (1905). The first Albion player to score at The Hawthorns – equalising against Derby County in the opening League game on 3 September 1900 – Simmons also played several times for the Baggies second XI in 1906–07 and scored in Albion's 5–0 Staffordshire Cup Final victory over Burslem Port Vale in 1900.

SMITH Joe

Right-back: 471 apps.

Born: Darby End, Dudley, 10 April 1890.
Died: Wolverhampton, 9 June 1956.
Career: Halesowen Road Council School (Netherton), Netherton St Andrews, Darby End Victoria, Cradley Heath St Luke's, ALBION (professional May 1910–May 1926); World War One guest for Everton and Notts County; Birmingham, Worcester City (player-manager, retired 1932); later mine host of the Red Lion (Darby End); then employee at Lloyds Proving House.

■ Joe Smith was a splendid right-back who served Albion for 16 years, making his League debut at Bolton in September 1910 and playing in his last game in

February 1926 versus Bury. He appeared in over 470 games for the Baggies, gained two England caps and starred in a Victory international after army service in Bootle. He helped Albion win the Second Division title in 1911 and the First Division crown in 1920, when he partnered Jesse Pennington. A marvellous positional player, clearing his lines with long and telling kicks, he was also a strong tackler who maintained a remarkable level of consistency, appearing in 247 out of 252 League games between 1919 and 1925. A junior international in 1909, this honour set him up for a fine career.

STATHAM Derek

Left-back: 377+1 apps. 10 goals.

Born: Whitmore Reans, Wolverhampton, 24 March 1959.
Career: St Mary's Primary & St Edmund's Junior Schools (Wolverhampton), ALBION (apprentice July 1975, professional April 1976–August 1987). Southampton (£100,000), Stoke City, Aston Villa (trial), Walsall, Telford United, King's Lynn (retired 1995), WBA All Stars (1995–2002); now runs a café/bar in Marbella, Spain.

■ Derek Statham won seven England Youth caps, six in the Under-21 side, and also represented England B before breaking into the full England team, under Bobby Robson's management, in 1982, playing in three full internationals. He was previously kept out of the team by Kenny Sansom, Albion boss Ron Atkinson saying that Statham was miles better than Sansom, England caps or not. A cheerful, buoyant character who tackled aggressively, with total commitment, and a player who loved to attack, Statham scored past Peter Shilton on his Albion debut at Stoke in December 1976, having gained an FA Youth Cup-winners' medal earlier that year. Voted the Midland Sportswriter's Young Player of the Year in 1978, Statham struggled at times with injuries during his last two seasons at The Hawthorns, and in 1987 a proposed £250,000 transfer to Liverpool was called off at the 11th hour due to medical reports on his fitness. He was transfer-listed at the end of that season and subsequently joined Southampton for a six-figure fee. He went on to appear in over 150 games after leaving Albion, making his last

appearance for Walsall against Albion in the AWS Shield at The Hawthorns in 1990. Statham also played almost 60 reserve games for Albion.

TAYLOR Bob

Striker: 299+78 apps. 131 goals.

Born: Littlethorpe, Easington, County Durham, 3 February 1967.
Career: Horden Comrades Welfare, Horden Colliery Welfare, Newcastle United (trial), Hartlepool United (trial), Horden Colliery, Leeds United, Bristol City, ALBION (£300,000 January 1992–January 1998), Bolton Wanderers, ALBION (£90,000 March 2000–August 2003), Cheltenham Town, Tamworth (retired 2006).

■ Bob Taylor was manager Bobby Gould's finest signing for Albion. A hero at The Hawthorns, he scored on his debut against Brentford and netted eight times in 19 games during the second half of the 1991–92 season. In his second term, 'Super Bob' top scored with 37 goals, helping Albion win promotion to the First Division via the Play-off Final against Port Vale. After Albion had turned down bids of £1.5m and then £1m from Coventry City and Sheffield United in double-quick time, it still came as a huge surprise to the supporters when Taylor left The Hawthorns for Bolton in 1998. However, after helping the Lancashire club reach the Premiership, Taylor returned to Albion and once again the fans took him into their hearts, as his goal versus Crystal Palace clinched promotion to the Premiership in April 2002. Strong and powerful both on the ground and in the air and a perpetual hard worker, Taylor averaged a goal every three games for Albion, who awarded him a testimonial in 2003. One of only nine players to have scored over 100 League goals for Albion, Taylor also bagged 17 in 48 reserve games. In October 2001 he was sent off in the League away game at Barnsley – the 100th dismissal in Albion's history at first-team level.

THOMPSON Garry

Striker: 105 apps. 45 goals.

Born: Kings Heath, Birmingham, 7 October 1959.

Career: Brandwood & Maypole Schools, Coventry City, ALBION (£225,000 February 1983–August 1985), Sheffield Wednesday (£450,000), Aston Villa, Watford, Crystal Palace, Queen's Park Rangers, Cardiff City, Northampton Town (retired 1997, appointed reserve-team manager/coach), Brentford (coach), Bristol Rovers (coach-assistant manager, caretaker manager), Brentford (assistant manager, caretaker coach).

■ A tall striker, powerful in the air, and sharp and decisive on the ground, Garry Thompson won six England Under-21 caps and scored as regular as clockwork throughout his career, ending up with 164 goals in 614 senior matches. By his own admission his form slumped at times, especially after leaving Albion, but it must be said that the fans were somewhat annoyed when he packed his bags and left The Hawthorns so soon after Cyrille Regis had departed. 'Thommo' made his debut versus Arsenal (at home) in February 1983 and netted a goal almost every two games for the Baggies. He helped Villa win promotion in 1988 and Watford reach the Play-offs in 1989.

TRENTHAM Bert

Full-back: 272 apps.

Born: Chirbury, Salop, 22 April 1908.

Died: Ward End, Birmingham, 23 June 1979.

Career: Chirbury St John's School, Knighton Town, Knighton Victoria, Knighton United, Hereford United, Aston Villa (trial), ALBION (£600 April 1929–May 1937), Hereford United, Darlaston (retired 1942); later ran an ironmonger's business in Birmingham.

■ Bert 'Corker' Trentham was a capable and reliable full-back, a model of consistency and sound rather than outstanding, who

always had a handkerchief wrapped round his withered right hand. He formed a fine partnership with George Shaw and together they played in over 230 games for Albion in the 1930s, lining up in both the 1931 and 1935 FA Cup Finals and being valuable members of the double-winning side. During a fine career Trentham won junior international honours in 1929 and represented the Football League in 1933. He never scored a goal for Albion but had the misfortune of conceding three own-goals! A League debutant at Blackpool in March 1930, he also appeared in 54 reserve games for the club.

VERNON Jack

Centre-half: 200 apps. 1 goal.

Born: Belfast, 26 September 1919.

Died: Belfast, 12 August 1981.

Career: St Paul's School (Belfast), Springfield Road Juniors, Dundela Juniors, Liverpool, Belfast Celtic, ALBION (£9,500 February 1947–July 1952), Crusaders (retired 1954); worked in family butchery business until his death.

■ Without doubt, Jack Vernon was one of Albion's greatest centre-halves, fine in defence, supreme in the air and masterful on the ground – a true sportsman of the highest calibre. Albion signed him for a record fee in 1947, but, owing to arctic weather conditions that winter, he was forced to wait five weeks before making his Baggies debut in a 3–2 defeat at West Ham, whose centre-forward Frank Neary scored a hat-trick. Vernon won 22 caps (two for the Republic of Ireland, 20 for Ireland) and skippered the latter on 17 occasions. He also captained the United Kingdom versus Wales in 1951 and starred for the Great Britain XI against The Rest of Europe at Hampden Park in 1947 – an honour that proved he was the game's top pivot at that time. Before he arrived at The Hawthorns, Vernon – nicknamed 'Twinkletoes' due to his size five feet – won Irish Cup medals in 1941, 1943 and 1944, Irish League Championship medals in 1939 and 1940, and represented the Irish FA Select on several occasions while also starring for the Irish Regional League 12 times between 1941–46. He led Albion to promotion in 1949 and made 200 appearances for the Baggies, scoring just once – the winner versus Sheffield Wednesday (at home) on Christmas Day 1948. He also played in four reserve games. As an agreement, Albion continued to pay Vernon's wages for two years after he left The Hawthorns.

WALSH Dave

Centre-forward: 174 apps. 100 goals.

Born: Waterford, Ireland, 28 April 1923.

Career: St Joseph's School (Waterford), The Corinthians, Shelbourne, Glen Rovers, Limerick, Shelbourne (Dublin), Linfield, ALBION (£3,500 May 1946–December 1950), Aston Villa (£25,000), Walsall, Worcester City (retired 1957); ran a sports outfitters at Droitwich before moving to Thurlestone, Devon, where he still lives.

■ Dave Walsh was the ideal build for a striker – a job he did superbly throughout his career. A player with speed and thrust, he gained 31 caps (11 for Ireland and 20 for Eire), represented the Irish League twice in 1946 and helped Albion gain promotion from

Division Two in 1949, netting 23 League goals. As keen as mustard in and around the 'box', Walsh struck 62 goals for Linfield in 1945–46 when they won the Irish League and netted twice in the Irish Cup Final win over Distillery that same season, having gained a winners' medal 12 months previous. Attracting the attention of Albion (having scored 122 goals in Irish football) he became the club's first signing after World War Two and set off like a house on fire when the English League season started in August 1946, creating a record by scoring in each of his first six games, including two on his debut at Swansea. His Hawthorns career yielded exactly 100 goals plus three more for the second XI. He later added 45 to his tally with Villa and Walsall before drifting into non-League football in 1956.

WATERHOUSE Frank 'Puffer'

Defender: 188 apps. 6 goals.

Born: Langley Green Oldbury, 23 July 1889.

Died: Smethwick, 5 June 1967.

Career: Langley Infants & Junior Schools, Langley St Michael's, Langley St Michael's Guild, Langley Green, Wednesbury Old Athletic, ALBION (February 1908–August 1913), Kidderminster Harriers, Derby County, Leeds United, Dudley Town (retired 1924); worked in engineering for 20 years either side of World War Two.

■ Frank 'Puffer' Waterhouse gained a junior international cap in 1909 and made his League debut against Leicester Fosse (at home) in November that same year. After that he never looked back, going from strength to strength with Albion and

appearing in almost 190 first and 50 second XI games, winning a Second Division Championship medal in 1911. A player of sound judgment and all round efficiency, he was a fine tackler and kicker, a stickler for hard work and one who gave opponents little or no room in which to use their ability. He took over the centre-half berth from Ted Pheasant, later switching to right-half in place of George Baddeley. He never really got a chance during his spells with Derby and Leeds.

WHELDON Fred

Inside-forward: 29 apps. 3 goals.

Born: Langley Green, Oldbury, 1 November 1869.
Died: Worcester, 13 January 1924.
Career: Chance's School (Oldbury),

Rood End White Star, Langley Green Victoria, ALBION (trial April–May 1890), Small Heath, Aston Villa, ALBION (£100 August 1900–December 1901), Queen's Park Rangers (£50), Portsmouth, Worcester City (retired 1907); played cricket for Worcestershire and Carmarthenshire.

■ Fred 'Diamond' Wheldon demoralised many a defence with his intricate dribbling and was brilliant at creating chances. He gained four England caps (1897–98), played four times for the Football League and won three League Championship medals with Aston Villa (1897, 1899 and 1900) as well as an FA Cup medal in 1897 when the double was achieved. Earlier, Wheldon helped Small Heath win the Second Division and a year later helped the Blues gain promotion. After appearing in 140 games for Villa and being the First Division's top scorer in 1897–98, with 21 goals, he became Albion's captain. He made his debut for Albion in the Black Country derby at Wolves in September 1900, but his efforts couldn't keep the Baggies in the top flight. As a Worcestershire cricketer (1899–1906), Wheldon hit 4,938 runs, including three centuries, and took 93 catches as a wicketkeeper.

WHITEHEAD Clive

Utility: 183+13 apps. 9 goals.

Born: Northfield, Birmingham, 24 November 1955.
Career: Alston Junior & Waverley Grammar Schools (Birmingham), Bordesley Green Boys, Northfield Juniors, Wolverhampton Wanderers (trial), Bristol City, ALBION (£100,000 November 1981–July 1987), Portsmouth, Wolverhampton Wanderers, Exeter

City, Yeovil Town (player-manager, retired 1991), Bristol City (academy coach-scout); now a football agent and referee's assessor.

■ Clive Whitehead, a former England Youth international (1973), was a gritty, unselfish professional who could perform equally well in any full-back position, as a central-defender or in midfield. Starting out as a skilful left-winger, he helped Bristol City win promotion to Division One in 1975–76 (with Albion) and played 256 games for the Ashton Gate club before moving to The Hawthorns. He made his Albion debut at Tottenham in November 1981 and during that season occupied six different positions for the Baggies, but always preferred the right-back slot. At the end of 1986–87, 'Scrumpy', as he was called, was released and subsequently joined Portsmouth. During his League career, Whitehead scored 26 goals in 544 games. He also played in 14 reserve games for Albion.

WHYTE Chris

Defender: 95+1 apps. 9 goals.

Born: Islington, London, 2 September 1961.
Career: Highbury & District Schools, Highbury Grove, Highbury Hill, Islington Boys & Inner London Schools, Arsenal, Crystal Palace, New York Express, Los Angeles Lazers, ALBION (free August 1988–June 1990), Leeds United (tribunal fee of £450,000), Birmingham City, Coventry City, Charlton Athletic, West Ham United, Detroit Neon (US Indoor League), Leyton Orient, Oxford United, Rushden and Diamonds, Harlow Town (retired 2001).

■ Strong in the air and good at intercepting passes, the tall, elegant Chris Whyte made his League bow for Arsenal in 1979 and gained four Under-21 caps for England before having a decent spell in America. He made almost 100 senior and two reserve appearances in his two seasons at The Hawthorns and was voted Baggies' Player of the Year in 1989, having made his debut at Peterborough in the League Cup in September 1988. He helped Leeds win the Premiership title in 1992 and the Blues win the Second Division Championship in 1995. Whyte reached the milestone of 500 appearances in 1997, made his debut for Oxford against Albion and was signed by ex-Albion boss Brian Talbot for Rushden & Diamonds in 1997.

WILE John

Centre-half: 618+1 apps. 19 goals.

Born: Sherburn, County Durham, 9 March 1947.
Career: Sherburn Secondary Modern School, Eppleton Juniors (Hetton), Hetton Juniors, Durham City, Peterborough United (trial), Sunderland, Peterborough United, ALBION (£32,000 December 1970–May 1983), Vancouver Whitecaps (loan), Rotherham United (non-contract), Peterborough United (player-manager, retired as a player 1986), WBA All Stars (1987–88); later manager of Solihull Indoor Cricket School and chief executive of Walsall and Cradley Heath Indoor Cricket Schools; Sutton United, ALBION (chief executive March 1997–2002).

■ John Wile's 500th and last League appearance for Albion was against his former club Sunderland in May 1983, and it crowned a magnificent 13-year association with the Baggies. An astute, reliable, commanding, powerful and forthright player, Wile goes down as being one of Albion's finest ever centre-halves. He had the will to win, gave everything he had in terms of effort and commitment, and fans still recall his tremendous display in the 1978 FA Cup semi-final defeat by Ipswich when he played on with his head swathed in heavy bandages after a clash of heads with scorer Brian Talbot. Blood filled his eyes, but he bravely battled on, sadly to no avail. That was the true essence of John Wile: a master defender, a born fighter, never a quitter and a 90-minute crusader. He retired as a player in 1986 with nearly 1,000 club appearances under his belt. Alan Ashman's last major signing as manager at The Hawthorns, Wile took over the number-five shirt from John Talbot, made his debut against Blackpool in December 1970 and was a pillar of strength over the next 13 years before being replaced by Ken McNaught in 1983. During his reign at The Hawthorns, Albion completed 525 League games and 'Big Wiley' missed only 25. In 1978–79 Albion fulfilled 76 first-team matches, and Wile lined up in all but one of them, the most appearances ever made by an Albion player in a single season. He also played more matches at centre-half than any other player in Albion's history – 613 plus one as substitute – and in the League alone he wore the number-five shirt on 497 occasions. The club's third highest appearance maker (behind Tony Brown with 818 and Ally Robertson with 729), unfortunately he never won a major honour in football. The nearest he came was to play in three Cup semi-finals for Albion and in the quarter-finals of the UEFA Cup, although he did help the team gain promotion in 1975–76. An ever present in seven seasons – an Albion record – there's never been a defensive partnership to equal that of Wile

and Robertson. 'Robbo' was, in fact, his skipper's centre-back colleague for most of the time he was at The Hawthorns. Ex-Albion chief Johnny Giles said of Wile 'If you could play football from nine in the morning till nine at night, seven days a week, 52 weeks a year, he still wouldn't be satisfied.' Wile became Albion's first-ever chief executive/director in 1997.

WILLIAMS Billy

Full-back: 208 apps. 12 goals.

Born: West Smethwick, 20 January 1876.
Died: West Bromwich, 11 January 1929.
Career: Oldbury Road School (Smethwick), West Bromwich Hawthorns, West Smethwick, Hawthorn Villa, Old Hill Wanderers, ALBION (£20 May 1894, retired, injured, June 1901, appointed trainer, later coach); became a licensee.

■ Billy Williams was a brilliant defender, stylish, dedicated and, above all, safe and sure under

pressure. He possessed a long, raking kick and scored quite a few goals from far distances, including one blinder from 55 yards in an FA Cup tie against Nottingham Forest in February 1898. He was also an expert with penalty-kicks. Williams won six England caps (1897–99), played for the Football League and also for the Professionals XI in various representative matches. He gained an FA Cup runners'-up medal in 1895, and besides his 208 senior appearances for Albion he also played in over 100 'other' games. His enforced retirement was a bitter blow to the club, who suffered relegation for the first time at the end of his 'farewell' season. He made his League debut at Sheffield United in September 1894.

WILLIAMS Graham

Full-back: 354 apps. 11 goals.

Born: Hellan near Rhyl, North Wales, 2 April 1938.
Career: Emmanuel Secondary School, Flintshire Boys, Burnley (trial), Rhyl Athletic, ALBION (amateur September 1954, professional April 1955–April 1972), Weymouth (player-manager), Sports Klub Kuwait, OFI, Greece (coach), Poole Town (manager), Cardiff City (coach, then manager), Newport County (scout), Leopards FC, Nigeria (coach). FC Rovaniemen, Finland (manager); coach in Far East, Kuwait and Dubai; Newcastle United (scout), Cheltenham Town (chief scout); Chairman of West Bromwich Albion ex-Players' Association (from 2003).

■ Graham Williams spent 18 years with Albion, starting out as an orthodox outside-left and finishing up as an international

left-back, powerful, determined and courageous. He also put in some terrific displays at left-half, but it was in the number-three shirt where he performed best, skippering Albion to victory in the 1966 League Cup and 1968 FA Cup Finals and also playing in the 1967 League Cup Final defeat by QPR. Capped 26 times by Wales, he made two appearances for the Under-23 side and played in over 400 matches for Albion, 314 in the First Division, making his League debut against Blackpool in November 1955. He also played in 229 Central League games, scoring 18 goals. It was not until 1962–63 that he became a firm fixture in Albion's defence – taking over from his namesake Stuart, whom he played alongside for both the club (Albion) and Wales. In 1981 Williams took Poole Town to the Final of the Anglo-Italian Tournament.

WILLIAMS Stuart

Full-back: 246 apps. 9 goals.

Born: Wrexham, North Wales, 9 July 1930.

Career: Acton Park Junior & Grove Park Grammar Schools, Wrexham Boys, Victoria Youth Club, Wrexham, Birmingham City (trial), ALBION (amateur November 1950, professional February 1951–September 1962), Southampton (£15,000), ALBION (trainer 1967–69), Aston Villa (trainer), Payhaan, Iran (manager), Morton (trainer-coach), Southampton (coach-assistant manager), Carlisle United (scout), Stavanger, Norway (manager), Southampton (trainer); later ran a guest house in Southampton.

■ One-time inside-right and the son of a Wrexham director, Stuart Williams was converted into an international full-back who gave Albion 12 years' yeoman service and won 33 caps for Wales, a club record. After leaving Albion, 'Stu' added a further 10 caps to his collection with Southampton. He made his debut for Albion at Huddersfield in February 1952, the first of 246 outings for the Baggies, for whom he also starred in 180 reserve games (11 goals). He followed up with 147 League appearances for Southampton. It seemed likely that he would replace the injured Stan Rickaby in Albion's 1954 FA Cup Final team, but at the last minute manager Vic Buckingham left him out in favour of the more experienced Joe Kennedy. He did get to Wembley with Albion later, as trainer of the 1968 FA Cup-winning side.

Williams was honoured by the Welsh FA in 2003 for services to the game.

WILSON Charlie 'Tug'

Inside-forward: 133 apps. 45 goals.

Born: Heeley, Sheffield, 20 July 1905.

Died: Kidderminster, 8 April 1985.

Career: Netherthorpe Schools (Sheffield), Sheffield Boys, Stonehouse FC, Chesterfield (trial), Sheffield United (trial), Hallam, ALBION (amateur December 1920, professional November 1922–February 1928), Sheffield Wednesday (£3,000), Grimsby Town, Aston Villa, Coventry City, Kidderminster Harriers, Worcester City, Kidderminster Harriers; guest for Charlton Athletic and Aldershot during World War Two; Kidderminster Police (retired 1947) and later a Kidderminster licensee.

■ Charlie Wilson was an opportunist striker with an unquenchable thirst for goals. He had film-star looks and was a constant threat to opposing defenders; he could shoot from any angle, seemingly from any distance, with either foot and usually found the target. Curiously, he had a habit of keeping himself clean on the muddiest of pitches yet was still a worker, who moved back to left-half later on in his career. He had the distinction of being the youngest ever player to appear in a League game for Albion, making his debut at Oldham at the age of 16 years and 63 days in October 1921. He gained three Central League Championship medals

with Albion in the 1920s, scoring 71 goals in 98 games, and he also assisted Sheffield Wednesday in their First Division Championship seasons of 1928–29 and 1929–30. With Albion, Wilson linked up splendidly with fellow front men Stan Davies, George James and Joe Carter, and also performed exceedingly well with his left-wing partners Arthur Fitton and Jack Byers. His best scoring season for Albion was in 1925–26, when he struck 17 goals in 30 League outings. He also scored when Albion beat the Blues in the Final of the Birmingham Charity Cup in 1922.

WILSON Joe

Outside-left: 53 apps. 20 goals.

Born: Handsworth, Birmingham, 8 January 1861
Died: Acocks Green, Birmingham, 20 October 1952.
Career: St Mary's Council School, Handsworth Grammar School, Hamstead Swifts, Aston Unity, Stoke, Walsall Town, Aston Villa, Walsall Town, ALBION (professional September 1887–May 1890), Kidderminster Harriers, Birmingham St George's (retired 1892); became a Football League referee and linesman; a goldsmith by profession, he worked in Birmingham's jewellery quarter for 25 years.

■ Albion's first-ever League goal was scored by Joe Wilson at Stoke on 8 September 1888. Six months earlier he had gained an FA Cup-winners' medal when Preston were beaten 2–1. He scored half a dozen goals in earlier rounds, including two in the quarter-final over Old Carthusians, having made his debut for Albion versus Wednesday Old Athletic in the first round in October 1887 when he also scored twice in a 7–1 win. A year later he claimed two goals in Albion's 10–1 West Bromwich Charity Cup Final win over Great Bridge Unity. A

smart, unobtrusive left-winger of dashing style and all-out aggression, Wilson kept defences on the alert with his cunning wing play. He formed an excellent partnership and understanding with Tom Pearson and was virtually an ever present in Albion's first two League campaigns. Besides his senior appearances for the club, Wilson also participated in close to 100 'other' games, and after his playing days were over he did a fine job for some 16 years as a referee and linesman, officiating in both First and Second Division matches, in various FA Cup ties and also at non-League level. He was once placed on standby to run the line in an England international match.

WILSON Ray

Outside-left/left-back: 282+3 goals.

Born: Grangemouth, Stirlingshire, 8 April 1947.
Career: Dundas Primary and Grangemouth High Schools, Stirlingshire Boys, Woodburn Athletic, ALBION (amateur July 1963, professional May 1964, retired, injured, March 1977); later a businessman in Birmingham.

■ Ray Wilson began his career as an outside-left before making his name as an efficient left-back, gaining Scottish Under-23 recognition in 1970 – the year he also played in the League Cup Final at Wembley, collecting a runners'-up medal. A stern tackler, quick to recover and confident on the overlap, he became Albion's regular left-back in the late 1960s, taking over from Graham Williams. His first League game was against Chelsea in October 1965 and his last at Luton during the 1975–76 promotion-

winning campaign. He suffered a shattered knee cap against the Hatters, which resulted in early retirement. Wilson appeared in 134 reserve games (36 goals) and was rewarded with a testimonial match (Albion versus Aston Villa) in 1975.

WOOD Stan

Outside-left: 281 apps. 66 goals.

Born: Winsford, Cheshire, 1 July 1905.

Died: Halifax, Yorkshire, 22 February 1967.

Career: Meadow Bank School (Winsford), Whitegate Victoria, Winsford United, ALBION (professional April 1928–May 1938), Halifax Town (retired 1946, became trainer); World War Two guest for Huddersfield Town.

■ Stan 'Splinter' Wood was a wiry, slippery outside-left, whose cleverness stood him in good stead for a decade with Albion, completing an impressive record in terms of games played and goals scored. A star in the double-winning season of 1930–31, he represented the Football League as reserve for England on two occasions. His best season with Albion came in 1930–31 when had had 50 outings and netted 17 goals. Wood made his debut versus Notts County in September 1928, taking over from Arthur Fitton, and held his place until Wally Boyes came along in 1934. After that he was in and out of the team but still managed his fair share of outings, especially in 1935–36 and 1936–37. Besides his first-team achievements, Wood also scored 37 goals in 92 reserve games, helping the 'stiffs' win three successive Central League titles in the mid-1930s.

WOODHALL George 'Spry'

Forward: 74 apps. 20 goals.

Born: West Bromwich, 5 September 1863.

Died: West Bromwich, 9 September 1924.

Career: Hateley Heath School, West Bromwich Saints, Wednesbury Town, Churchfield Foresters, ALBION (amateur May 1883, professional August 1885–July 1892), Wolverhampton Wanderers, Berwick Rangers (Birmingham League), Oldbury Town (retired 1898); later mine host of the Golden Cup, West Bromwich.

■ George 'Spry' Woodhall was certainly a sprightly footballer, figuring prominently for Albion in the late 1880s. Able to cross a ball with great accuracy, he combined well with his colleagues, especially Billy Bassett (after early disagreements when the players refused to pass to each other!) and was a regular in Albion's forward line for nine seasons. Making his senior debut against Junction Street School, Derby (away), in the first round of the FA Cup in October 1884, he won two England caps and was the first Black Country-born player to score for his country (against Scotland in 1888). That same year saw him grab Albion's winner in their 2–1 FA Cup Final victory over Preston. He was also on target in the 10–1 West Bromwich Charity Cup Final win over Great Bridge Unity, having earlier notched the deciding goal against Walsall Swifts in the Birmingham Cup Final replay of 1886. Woodhall, who had a delightful personality and was one of the most popular players of the 'Old Brigade' – a generous and wholehearted sportsman – played in the 1886 and 1887 Finals and appeared in over 275 first-team games for Albion. Richie Woodhall, Britain's Olympic gold medal-winning boxer, is a relation.

The Managers

(also caretaker managers and assistant managers)

1890–92	Louis Ford
1892–94	Henry Jackson
1894–95	Edward Stephenson
1895–96	Clemet Keys
1896–1902	Frank Heaven
1902–48	Fred Everiss
1948–52	Jack Smith
1952–53	Jesse Carver
1953–59	Vic Buckingham
1959–61	Gordon Clark
1961–63	Archie Macaulay
1963–67	Jimmy Hagan
1967–71	Alan Ashman
1971–75	Don Howe
1975–77	Johnny Giles
1977	Ronnie Allen
1978–81	Ron Atkinson
1981–82	Ronnie Allen
1982–84	Ron Wylie
1984–85	Johnny Giles
1985–86	Nobby Stiles, MBE
1986–87	Ron Saunders
1987–88	Ron Atkinson
1988–91	Brian Talbot
1991–92	Bobby Gould
1992–93	Ossie Ardiles
1993–94	Keith Burkinshaw
1994–97	Alan Buckley
1997	Ray Harford
1997–2000	Denis Smith
2000	Brian Little
2000–05	Gary Megson
2005–06	Bryan Robson, OBE
2006 to date	Tony Mowbray

* Prior to Jack Smith's appointment in 1948, the title of Albion's manager was secretary-manager

Albion's caretaker managers:

Brian Whitehouse*	April–June 1975
John Wile*	December 1977–January 1978

Brian Talbot*	October–November 1988
Stuart Pearson	January–February 1991
Arthur Mann	January–February 1997
Richie Barker	December 1997
John Trewick*	December 1997
Cyrille Regis*/Allan Evans	February–March 2000
Cyrille Regis*/John Gorman	March 2000
Nigel Pearson	September–October 2006

* Also played for Albion

Managers

Louis Ford was a local businessman who was an Albion director for four years: 1892–96. He became a committee member of the club in the late 1880s, was honorary financial secretary for three years from 1887 before his appointment as Albion's General Secretary (manager) on 5 June 1890, being involved deeply with team selection. He was, in fact, Albion's first official paid secretary, receiving a salary of £50 per annum. He was responsible for bringing on some exceptionally-fine footballers ,including Willie Groves, Roddy McLeod and John 'Baldy' Reynolds. He was an FA Councillor (1890–93), member of the Football League management committee and vice-president of the Football League from 1894 to 1897. In 1900 Ford became a League referee. Prior to that he worked as secretary of neighbouring Walsall (1896–1900) and before World War One served as secretary of Leicester Fosse (1914–15).

Henry 'Swin' Jackson was a member of Albion's first board of directors, elected on 1 September 1891. He remained a director for two years, taking over as the club's general secretary-manager after his first year and retaining that position for a further 18 months before he handed over his duties to Edward Stephenson. A more than useful Staffordshire and West Bromwich Dartmouth cricketer, Jackson later (like his predecessor Ford) became secretary of Leicester Fosse and after that held a similar position with Luton Town. He later emigrated to Canada where he worked as a parish registrar and postmaster until his death in 1930.

Ted Stephenson, a local man, was appointed Albion's general secretary-manager in November 1895 but was dismissed for incompetence in January 1895 after having been in office for barely eight weeks. He was an avid supporter and shareholder of the club.

Clement Keys, Albion's former Financial Secretary (1892–95), followed Stephenson as the club's secretary-manager in August 1895, and he remained in office for just the one season. A member of the famous Keys family, his firm later became the club's accountants, based in West Bromwich.

Frank Heaven (born 1873) held office as Albion's secretary-manager for six years, from 1896 to 1902. Another keen West Bromwich Dartmouth cricketer, Heaven gave the club unstinting service before he resigned over a disagreement with the board of directors in 1902. He kept out of football for a short time but returned to spend the first part of the 1904–05 season with the Scottish club Third Lanark, but on returning south he died tragically on Boxing Day 1905 when he was still only 32 years of age.

Fred Everiss (born in West Bromwich in 1882) was effectively Albion's first manager. Although assuming the title of club secretary-manager in 1902, it was he, in the main, who looked after the team's affairs right up until 1948, steering Albion to three FA Cup Finals (1912, 1931 and 1935), to Second and First Division Championship glory in 1911 and 1920 respectively, and to the double, also in 1931, as well as collecting a handful of runners'-up prizes as well. While he was 'in charge' of team affairs, Albion played well over 1,750 competitive matches (including both World Wars).

Jack Smith (born Aberaman, October 1911) was a 16-year-old trialist at The Hawthorns and played for Aberaman, Aberdare Athletic, Merthyr Town, Wolverhampton Wanderers (1930–34), Bristol Rovers (1934–35), Swindon Town (1935–37) and Chelsea (1938–44). He guested in over 70 games for Albion during World War Two and coached at Molineux (1946–48) before becoming Albion's first-ever official manager (appointed on 22 June 1948). He remained in office until 17 April 1952, when he left The Hawthorns to become boss at Reading, holding office until 1954. He guided Albion to promotion from Division Two in 1948–49 and signed some exceptionally fine footballers, including Ronnie Allen. A Welsh Wartime international versus England in 1940, Smith later became a Dorset hotelier. He died in 1975, aged 63. Albion completed 177 first-class matches under Smith's leadership; 70 were won, 45 drawn and 65 lost.

Jesse Carver (born Liverpool, July 1911) was an England Schoolboy international centre-half, who, between 1929 and 1940, played for Blackburn Rovers, Newcastle United and Bury. He was appointed assistant trainer of Huddersfield Town in 1946–47, and coached the Dutch FA, Xerves (Rotterdam) and Millwall prior to his appointment as Juventus coach in 1949. He then held similar positions in Italy with Marzotto, Inter Milan, Genoa, SCC Lazio and Juventus (again), before becoming Albion's manager-coach, appointed on 18 April 1952. He stayed at The Hawthorns for less than eight months,

Jesse Carver (coach), Harry Ashley (trainer), Fred Redley (physio) and Arthur Fitton (trainer coach) bowling.

leaving the club on 9 December to take up a coaching position with Valdagno, later serving in the same capacity with Torino and AS Roma before taking over as manager of Coventry City (June–December 1955). He had second spells as a coach with Lazio and Inter Milan, and coached Sweden in the 1958 World Cup Finals. After assisting Tottenham Hotspur as trainer-coach in 1958–59, he joined his former club Genoa (also as coach) and later coached in Portugal and the US. He guided Juventus to the Serie 'A' title in 1950. Albion played only 19 games under Carver, winning 10 and drawing four.

Vic Buckingham (born in Greenwich, London, in October 1915) played full-back for Bromley and Tottenham Hotspur, and gained two England Wartime caps. He was a coach for the Middlesex County FA, Oxford University and Pegasus, before taking over as manager of Bradford Park Avenue in 1951. He left the Yorkshire club for Albion on 2 February 1953 and held office at The Hawthorns until 18 June 1959. He later managed Ajax Amsterdam (two spells), Plymouth Argyle, Sheffield Wednesday, Fulham, Ethnikos (Greece), FC Barcelona and Sevilla (1972). He led Albion to the runners'-up spot in the First Division and to FA Cup glory over Preston in 1954, signing some brilliant footballers along the way, among them Maurice Setters, Graham Williams, Bobby Robson and Derek Kevan. He left the club soon after returning from a summer tour to Canada and the US. He died in Worthing in 1995 at the age of 79. Buckingham was in charge of Albion for 306 matches: 135 were won, 65 drawn and 96 lost.

Vic Buckingham checking the pitch at The Hawthorns.

Gordon Clark (born in Guisborough in April 1914) was a full-back with Goldthorpe United, Southend United, Manchester City, Waterford (player-manager) and Hyde United (player-manager), before retiring as a player to take over as boss of Belfast Distillery in 1949. He then managed Aldershot, became Albion's chief scout in 1955 and moved into the manager's chair at The Hawthorns on 9 July 1959, remaining in office until 11 October 1961. Thereafter he served with Sheffield Wednesday (assistant manager), Peterborough United (manager), Arsenal (chief scout), Fulham (assistant manager), Philadelphia Fury (senior coach) and Queen's Park Rangers (assistant manager), quitting football in 1980. He joined his former boss Vic Buckingham at Hillsborough and took Peterborough to the League Cup semi-final in 1966, where they lost to Albion over two legs. His best bit of business for Albion was to sign his namesake Clive Clark from QPR. Clark, who died on 18 October 1997, was in charge of Albion for exactly 100 senior matches; 42 were won, 19 drawn and 39 lost.

Archie Macaulay (born in Falkirk in July 1915) was a Scottish international wing-half (seven full and six wartime caps gained), who played for Camelon Juniors, Glasgow Rangers, West Ham United, Brentford, Arsenal, Fulham and Guildford City (as player-manager) before retiring in 1955. He then served Dundee as trainer-coach and managed Norwich City, before taking over at Albion on 19 October 1961, agreeing a £3,000-a-year salary. He held office until the 2 April 1963 and after that bossed Brighton & Hove Albion. Macaulay later became a traffic warden in Brighton. He represented a Great Britain XI, won a League Cup war medal with West Ham in 1940 and gained League Championship and Cup-winners' medals with Rangers as a player. As a manager, he took Brighton to the Fourth Division title in 1965. As Albion boss he made the mistake of selling Derek

Kevan to Chelsea and Bobby Robson to Fulham. He died in June 1993. Macaulay had a moderate record, Albion winning 27 and drawing 16 of the 65 games played under his charge.

Jimmy Hagan (born in Washington, Co. Durham, in January 1918) was an England Schoolboy and full international inside-forward (one senior cap and 16 wartime caps won). An Albion trialist in 1933, he played for Washington Colliery, Liverpool, Derby County and Sheffield United, pending 20 years at Bramall Lane, during which time he made 364 League appearances and scored 118 goals. He then managed Peterborough United (1958–62) before taking over the reins at Albion on 10 April 1963 and remaining in office until 3 May 1967. Later scout for Manchester City, he managed Benfica and coached in Kuwait, before taking the hot seat at four Portuguese clubs – Sporting Lisbon, FC Porto, Boavista and Vitória Setúbal. He guided Peterborough from the Midland League into the Football League and saw Albion twice reach the League Cup Final, winning in 1966 and losing in 1967. Among his better signings were Jeff Astle, John Kaye, John Osborneand and John Talbut. Hagan died in Sheffield on 26 February 1998. Hagan's record as Albion's manager read: played 201, won 90, drew 48 and lost 73.

Alan Ashman (born in Rotherham in May 1928), a former chicken farmer, played centre-forward for Sheffield United, Nottingham Forest and Carlisle United before retiring in 1959. He then coached Penrith FC and managed his former club Carlisle before taking charge of Albion on 23 May 1967, holding office until 2 July 1971. Thereafter he managed Olympiakos, Carlisle again, Workington and Walsall, as well as scouting for Manchester United, Derby County, Plymouth Argyle, Notts County, Mansfield Town, Telford United and Aston Villa, and acting as assistant boss at Hereford United. Ashman guided Albion to FA Cup glory in 1968 and to runners-up in the 1970 League Cup Final. He signed the club's first £100,000 footballer (Colin Suggett) and also secured the transfers of Ronnie Rees, Jim Cumbes and John Wile. Ashman had a level record as Albion boss, the team won 79 and lost 79 out of a total of 229 matches.

Don Howe (born in Wolverhampton in October 1935) was an amateur with Wolverhampton Wanderers before spending 14 years with Albion. After leaving The Hawthorns he served with Arsenal but a broken leg curtailed his career. He gained 23 caps for England and played in the World Cup. He later became a very successful coach and was Albion's manager from 9 July 1971 to 6 April 1975, before returning to coaching duties in Turkey and Saudi Arabia, at Leeds United, Arsenal (again), Chelsea and QPR. He also managed at Loftus Road and Coventry City, as well as being a key figure on the England staff. Unfortunately, Albion were relegated when he was at the helm, and although he signed strikers Ally Brown, Bobby Gould and Davis Shaw and winger Willie Johnston for a club record fee of £138,000 he sold Asa Hartford to Manchester City, goalkeeper Peter Latchford to Celtic and a certain Jeff Astle to Hellenic! Howe was in the hot seat for 196 matches, of which 62 were won, 55 drawn and 77 lost. (See Albion Stars)

Don Howe

Johnny Giles (born in Cabra, Dublin, in January 1940) was initially an outside-right and later a skilful midfielder, who played for the St Columbus School team, Dublin City (later Munster Victoria), Stella Maris, Leprechauns FC and Home Farm, before joining Manchester United in 1956. He moved to Leeds United in 1963 and became player-manager of Albion on 19 June 1975, retaining his position for almost two years until 27 May 1977. He was later player-manager of Shamrock Rovers, guested for Philadelphia Fury and coached Vancouver Whitecaps prior to having a second spell as Albion chief from 13 December 1983 to 29 September 1985. The recipient of 60 caps for the Republic of Ireland, he also managed that country (1973–80) and won League and Cup medals with Manchester United, Leeds and Shamrock Rovers and guided Albion to promotion from Division Two in 1975–76. In his first spell in charge he bought in some quality players, including Paddy Mulligan, Mick Martin, Laurie Cunningham and Tony Goddem, completely transforming the team. But in his second spell both he and the team struggled and Giles admitted later that it was 'The wrong thing to do' (to return to The Hawthorns). In his two spells as manager Albion played 187 games, won 56, drew 54 and lost 77. (See Albion Stars)

Ronnie Allen

Ronnie Allen (born in Fenton, Stoke-on-Trent, in January 1929) played for Port Vale, Albion and Crystal Palace before retiring in 1965. He later coached/managed Wolves, Athletico Bilbao, Sporting Lisbon and Walsall before returning to The Hawthorns as Albion's boss on 22 June 1977. He stayed for six months, up to 22 December, when he left to take over as coach of the Saudi Arabia National team. He went on to manage Panathinaikos, had a second spell as Albion's boss (from 26 July 1981 to 30 June 1982) and was then named as the club's general manager. Allen later returned to The Hawthorns as coach in the 1990s. He won five full England caps, led Bilbao to victory in the Spanish Cup Final and took Albion to two major Cup semi-finals (both lost in 1982). He died in June 2001, aged 72. Albion completed 77 matches with Allen at the helm. They won 30, drew 20 and lost 27. (See Albion Stars)

Ron Atkinson

Ron Atkinson (born in Liverpool in March 1939) was a tough-tackling wing-half (or defender) with BSA Tools FC, Wolves (as a junior), Aston Villa reserves and Headington United/Oxford United (1960–71). He then became player-manager of Kettering Town, managed Witney Town briefly and then took charge of Cambridge United (1974–78) before moving into the hot seat at The Hawthorns on 12 January 1978, remaining in charge until 9 June 1981. He then 'transferred' his duties to Manchester United, served Bolton Wanderers (as a coach) and returned as Albion's manager on 3 September 1987, staying this time until 12 October 1988. After that he coached Atletico Madrid and managed Sheffield Wednesday (twice), Aston Villa, Coventry City and Nottingham Forest. As a player Atkinson helped Oxford win two Southern League titles, gain Football League status and climb up from the Fourth to the Second Division in double-quick time. As a soccer boss he guided Cambridge to the Fourth Division Championship, assembled a superb Albion side which reached the FA Cup semi-final in 1978, finished third in the First Division and also qualified for the UEFA Cup quarter-finals. He won two Wembley FA Cup Finals with Manchester United, was successful with Sheffield Wednesday (first time), winning the League Cup and gaining promotion in the 1991, and guided Aston Villa to victory in the 1994 League Cup Final. Unfortunately, he didn't have a happy time in Spain...although on a contract, worth £500,000, he was dismissed after just 96 days in office, despite taking Bilbao to third spot in La Liga. Atkinson, however, did receive the princely sum of £100,000 in compensation following his dismissal by Manchester United in November 1986. He later worked for ITV Sport as a soccer analyst and summariser before losing his job in 2004. In his two spells as manager, Atkinson saw Albion compete in 232 first-class matches, winning 95, drawing 74 and losing 63.

Ron Wylie (born in Glasgow in August 1933) was an inside-forward with Clydesdale Juniors, Notts County, Aston Villa and Birmingham City before becoming a coach at Villa Park and then Coventry City, later taking over as assistant manager at Highfield Road. After that he worked as an adviser in Cyprus, managed Bulova (Hong Kong), Albion (from 27 July 1982 to 13 December 1983) and thereafter served as reserve-team coach, manager, scout and community officer at Villa Park. He won both the Second Division Championship (1960) and the League Cup (1961) with Villa, and was voted Midland Footballer of the Year in 1965. He failed to do the business with Albion, as his record shows: played 80 games, won 30, drew 16 and lost 34.

Nobby Stiles, MBE (born in Manchester in May 1942) was a terrific wing-half with first Manchester United and England, and later with Middlesbrough and Preston North End. He became manager at Deepdale and also assisted his brother-in-law Johnny Giles at Vancouver Whitecaps before becoming Albion's coach, then assistant manager and finally manager on 15 October 1985, remaining in office until 14 February 1986. He later returned to Old Trafford as coach (under Alex Ferguson). Stiles won 28 full caps, starred in the 1966 World Cup, gained a European Cup-winners' medal and helped United win the League Championship and FA Cup. He became an after-dinner speaker and charity committee member and suffered a mild heart-attack in 2002, but he made a good recovery, saying 'Don't panic...I'm okay!' Albion won only four games and drew eight out of 23 when Stiles was in charge.

Ron Saunders

Ron Saunders (born in Birkenhead in November 1932) was an England Youth international centre-forward, as hard as nails, who 'scored' for Birkenhead & Liverpool Schools, Everton, Tonbridge, Gillingham, Portsmouth, Watford and Charlton Athletic (up to 1967). He retired to become general manager of Yeovil Town and later took charge of Oxford United, Norwich City, Manchester City, Aston Villa and Birmingham City before holding office at The Hawthorns from 14 February 1986 to 1 September 1987. He took three clubs – Norwich, Manchester City and Villa – to Wembley League Cup Finals in successive seasons (1973, 1974 and 1975), but only Villa won the trophy (beating Norwich in 1975). He did, however, lead the Canaries to the Second Division title in 1972, Villa to the Football League Championship in 1981 and then set them on the road to European Cup glory before leaving for St Andrew's. He failed at Albion and the fans will certainly never forgive him for selling Steve Bull (and to a certain extent Andy Thompson). He scored 207 goals in 392 League appearances for his five major clubs. Saunders's record as Albion's manager saw the team play 67 games, of which only 14 were won, 19 drawn and 34 lost.

Brian Talbot

Brian Talbot (born in Ipswich in July 1953) played in midfield for Ipswich Town, Toronto Metros, Arsenal,Watford and Stoke City before joining Albion for £15,000 in January 1988. He was appointed caretaker manager at The Hawthorns on 13 October 1988 and was upgraded to manager on 2 November of that same year. Unfortunately, he lost his job on 8 January 1991, after the Baggies had been dumped out of the FA Cup by non-League Woking. Talbot was later with Fulham, Aldershot (as manager), Sudbury Town (1992) and Hibernians (Malta) before taking over as boss of Rushden & Diamonds, whom he guided into the Football League as Conference winners in 2001. A year later they reached the Third Division Play-off Final but lost to Cheltenham Town. He won six England caps, was an FA Cup winner with both Ipswich and Arsenal in successive seasons (1978 and 1979), and made 533 League appearances in a fine career. He netted six goals in his 83 first-team outings for Albion, and as the club's manager he took the team to the top of the Second Division table before a bad set of results led to his departure. Talbot managed Albion for 121 matches; 39 were won, 38 drawn and 44 lost.

Bobby Gould (born in Coventry in June 1946) was a tough-nut centre-forward who served with Coventry City, Arsenal and Wolves before joining Albion for £66,666 in September 1971. He remained at The Hawthorns until December 1972 when he switched to Bristol City. He later served with West Ham United, Wolves again, Bristol Rovers and Hereford United, and assisted FC Aalsund of Norway as player-coach. He was later employed by Charlton Athletic (coach), Chelsea (assistant manager), Wimbledon (non-contract player-coach), Aldershot (assistant manager), Bristol Rovers (two spells as manager), Coventry City (two spells as manager), Wimbledon (manager), QPR (coach) and Albion (manager from 26 February 1991 to 5 May 1992, during which time the Baggies slipped into the Third Division for the first time in their history). He later became Welsh national team manager (1995–98), appointing former Albion skipper Graham Williams as his assistant. An FA Cup winner with West Ham in 1975 and a Second Division Championship winner with both Coventry (1967) and Wolves (1977), as a manager he guided Wimbledon to FA Cup glory (against Liverpool) in 1988. He scored 19 goals in 60 senior appearances for Albion, but his record as the club's manager was moderate: 24 wins, 23 draws and 22 defeats from 69 matches.

Ossie Ardiles

Ossie Ardiles (born in Cordoba, Argentina, in August 1952) was a brilliant midfield player who starred for South American clubs Red Star (Cordoba), Instituto de Cordoba and FC Huracan before joining Tottenham Hotspur for £325,000 in 1978, shortly after helping his country clinch the World Cup. He made over 400 appearances in 10 years at White Hart Lane, gaining two FA Cup-winners' medals. He also assisted Paris St Germain, Blackburn Rovers, Queen's Park Rangers and Fort Lauderdale Strikers before managing Swindon Town, Newcastle United, Albion (from 8 May 1992 to 18 June 1993) and his former club, Tottenham. He went on to coach Deportiv Guadelajara (Mexico) and thereafter managed Shimizu S-Pulse (Japan), Croatia Zagreb, Yokohama F Marinos (Japan), Racing Club Buenos Aries and Beitar FC (Jerusalem). Capped 52 times by Argentina, he successfully guided Albion to promotion from Division Two via a Wembley Play-off Final in 1993, and he drew up a fine record as manager, winning 33 and drawing 11 of the 59 games completed. He is now a qualified lawyer.

Keith Burkinshaw (born in Higham in June 1935) played for Denaby United, Wolves (amateur), Liverpool and Workington before taking over as manager of the latter club in 1964. He then managed Scunthorpe United and coached in Zambia, at Newcastle United and Tottenham Hotspur before moving into the manager's office at White Hart Lane in 1976, retaining the position for eight years. After further coaching appointments in Bahrain and Portugal (Sporting Lisbon), and spells as manager of Gillingham and chief scout at Swindon Town, he became Albion's assistant manager (to Ardiles) in May 1992, taking over as team manager on 2 July 1993 (when Ardiles left) and retaining his post until 16 October 1994. In 1997 he joined Aberdeen as an advisor. Burkinshaw led Spurs to the Second Division title in 1978, to two FA Cup Final triumphs (1981 and 1982), to League Cup success (also in 1982) and to UEFA Cup glory in 1984. Albion played 71 games with 'Burky' in charge – winning 17, drawing 19 and losing 35.

Alan Buckley (born in Mansfield in April 1951) was a goalscorer with Nottingham Forest, Walsall (two spells) and Birmingham City in the Football League, and for Stourbridge and Tamworth at non-League level. He went on to manage the Saddlers, Kettering Town and Grimsby Town, the latter for six years from 1988. He became boss at Albion on 20 October 1994 and he left on 20 January 1997, later returning to Grimsby, who he guided to victory in the 1988 AWS Trophy Final versus Bournemouth, having earlier steered the Mariners from the old Fourth to the old First Division in successive seasons (1990–91). He went on to manage Lincoln City and Grimsby (again). Sacked by Albion after a dismal run of home results, his record as Baggies' chief was poor: of the 124 games played, 41 were won, 37 drawn and 46 lost.

Ray Harford (born in Halifax, Yorkshire, in June 1945) was a defender with Charlton Athletic, Exeter City, Lincoln City, Mansfield Town, Port Vale and Colchester United. He retired in May 1975 with over 400 senior appearances under his belt, 354 in the Football League. His managerial career began at Fulham (1984), and after that (as well as acting as coach and/or assistant manager at each club) he took charge of Luton Town, Wimbledon and Blackburn Rovers before moving into the hot seat at Albion on 6 February 1997 and remaining until 4 December 1997. After that he was boss at Queen's Park Rangers and Oxford United and held coaching positions at Millwall, Swindon Town and Reading. As manager of Luton, he guided the Hatters to League Cup Final glory in 1988, to League Cup runners-up in 1989 and to victory in the Simod Cup Final, also in 1988. As coach at Ewood Park, he saw Blackburn win promotion from the First Division and lift the Premiership title – having failed to gain any honours as a player. He did pretty well during his short time at The Hawthorns, pushing Albion into the top spot (albeit briefly) early on in the 1997–98 season, but then perhaps surprisingly he quit The Hawthorns after barely 10 months to take over at QPR. Albion won 20 and drew seven of the 44 games they played under Harford, who died in August 2003.

Denis Smith (born in Meir, Stoke-on-Trent, in November 1947) was one of the finest defenders ever to play for Stoke City, whom he served for 17 years (1965–82), amassing 493 appearances and scoring 41 goals. He won Football League honours and helped the Potters win the League Cup in 1972. He then managed York City for five years, Sunderland for four years, Bristol City and Oxford United, becoming Albion's boss on Christmas Eve 1997. His first win as the Baggies chief came in the FA Cup over his former club Stoke in January 1998, but unfortunately, after some poor results, Smith left The Hawthorns on 27 July 1999. He later returned as manager of hard-up Oxford United before taking over the reins of struggling Wrexham in 2001. Albion's playing record under Smith was played 74, won 22, drew 20 and lost 32.

Denis Smith

Brian Little (born in County Durham in November 1953), a former Hawthorns trialist, was a forward with Aston Villa, whom he served for 13 years (1969–82), scoring 82 goals in 301 appearances and helping them win the FA Youth Cup (1972), the League Cup (1977) and the Second Division (1975). He also played once for England as a late substitute versus Wales in 1975. On his retirement (through injury) Little became coach at Villa Park, later taking a similar position with Wolves where he also acted as carertaker manager prior to the arrival of Graham Turner in 1986. From Molineux he went to Middlesbrough as a coach, managed Darlington from 1989–91 and was in charge of Leicester City for three years before returning to Villa Park as boss in 1994. Little then managed Stoke City where, ironically, he was replaced by Gary Megson and was appointed as Albion's manager on 11 August 1999, but after a run of disappointing results he was sacked on 6 February 2000. He later managed Hull City and Tranmere Rovers. Little's record as Albion boss wasn't good: nine wins, 18 draws and 15 defeats from 42 matches.

Brian Little

Gary Megson (born in Manchester in May 1959), the son of Don Megson (the former Sheffield Wednesday left-back and 1966 FA Cup Final captain), was an aggressive midfielder who played, in turn, for Plymouth Argyle, Everton, Sheffield Wednesday, Nottingham Forest, Newcastle United, Sheffield Wednesday again, Manchester City, Norwich City, Lincoln City and Shrewsbury Town. He retired in 1995 with 588 club appearances under his belt (50 goals). After coaching at Bradford City he then managed at

Gary Megson

Carrow Road, Blackpool, Stockport County and Stoke City before taking charge at Albion on 9 March 2000. He did an excellent job at The Hawthorns, twice leading the Baggies into the Premiership while signing several quality players to boot. Unfortunately things started to go wrong a third of the way into season 2005–06, and as a result he lost his job on 26 October. He later took charge of Nottingham Forest. Megson's record as Albion's manager was decent enough: 222 games played, 96 wins, 70 draws and 66 defeats.

Bryan Robson, OBE (born in Chester-le-Street in January 1957) played for Albion from 1972 to 1981, making almost 250 senior appearances and scoring 46 goals. He then served with Manchester United until 1994 and skippered the Reds to Premiership, FA Cup and European Cup-winners' glory, as well as taking his tally of England caps to 90. He hit 100 goals in 465 games for United before transferring to Middlesbrough, whom he later managed. Robson was appointed manager of Albion on 9 November 2004, bringing with him his assistant Nigel Pearson. He helped the Baggies achieve the 'Great Escape' at the end of his first season but failed to keep the team in the Premiership and after a run of poor results was dismissed on 18 September 2006, leaving Pearson in charge until his former Middlesbrough colleague Tony Mowbray took over in October. Robson's record during his 23 months in charge was rather disappointing: only 20 wins, 24 draws and 38 defeats from 82 matches. (See Star Players.)

Bryan Robson

Tony Mowbray (born in Saltburn in November 1963) was a defender with Middlesbrough, Celtic and Ipswich Town between 1979 and 2001, making well over 670 senior appearances and scoring 47 goals. He also gained two England 'B' caps. He had a very successful spell as manager of Hibernian before taking over as boss at The Hawthorns on 12 October 2006 – shortly before Albion thrashed his former club Ipswich Town 5–1 at Portman Road when caretaker boss Nigel Pearson was looking after the team. Mowbray took the team to the Championship Play-off Final in his first season but, disappointingly, the day ended in a 1–0 defeat at the hands of Derby County at Wembley. To May 2007 Mowbray's record as Albion's manager was played 42, won 20, drawn seven and lost 15, including a penalty shoot-out defeat by Middlesbrough in the FA Cup.

Caretaker managers

Allan Evans, ex-Dunfermline Athletic, Aston Villa, Leicester City, Brisbane United (Australia), Darlington and Scotland defender who worked under Brian Little.

John Gorman, a full-back with Celtic, Carlisle United, Tottenham Hotspur and Tampa Bay Rowdies who was Glenn Hoddle's right-hand man when the former Spurs midfielder was boss of England.

Stuart Pearson, a centre-forward with Hull City, Manchester United and West Ham who was associated with Albion from 1988 to 1992. He won one Under-23 and 15 full caps for England.

Arthur Mann, a full-back with Hearts, Manchester City, Blackpool, Notts County,

Shrewsbury Town and Mansfield, he played against Albion in the 1970 League Cup Final. He worked under Alan Buckley at Grimsby Town and then The Hawthorns. He was tragically killed in a fork-lift truck accident in Birmingham in February 1999.

Richie Barker did not enter League football until he was 28. He played for Derby County, Notts County and Peterborough United and held non-playing positions at Shrewsbury, Wolves, Stoke City, Meadow Lane, in Greece and Egypt, and Sheffield Wednesday. He was Albion's chief scout and caretaker manager in 1997–98 and was later assistant manager at Halifax Town.

Nigel Pearson, born in Nottingham in 1963, played for Shrewsbury Town, Sheffield Wednesday and Middlesbrough between 1981 and 1998, amassing almost 550 club appearances. He returned as a coach at Wednesday before joining Albion as assistant manager-coach (to Bryan Robson) on 1 December 2004, leaving on 14 October 2006 to become Newcastle United's coach and assistant manager.

Assistant managers

Since the 1970s, Albion's managers have virtually always had an assistant, and they have included: Brian Whitehouse/George Wright (to Don Howe), Sam Allardyce (to Brian Talbot/Bobby Gould), Colin Addison and Mick Brown (to Ron Atkinson), Gerry Summers (to Ronnie Allen), Nobby Stiles (to Johnny Giles), Stuart Pearson (to Brian Talbot), Keith Burkinshaw (to Ossie Ardiles), Arthur Mann (to Alan Buckley), John Trewick (to Ray Harford/Denis Smith), Malcolm Crosby (to Denis Smith), Cyrille Regis (to Ray Harford), John Gorman (to Denis Smith), Allan Evans (to Brian Little), Frank Burrows (to Gary Megson), Nigel Pearson (to Bryan Robson) and Mark Venus (to Tony Mowbray).

Albion's League/Premiership Record Against Other Clubs

Up to end of 2006-07 season. Play-offs and Test Matches not included

Opponents	*Home*						*Away*					
	P	*W*	*D*	*L*	*F*	*A*	*P*	*W*	*D*	*L*	*F*	*A*
Accrington	5	4	1	0	18	5	5	0	1	4	7	12
Arsenal	55	22	12	21	80	69	55	9	14	32	67	121
Aston Villa	65	28	17	20	101	89	65	15	10	40	76	121
Barnsley	29	16	8	5	74	39	29	6	12	11	36	46
Birmingham City	57	25	18	14	78	59	57	22	15	20	73	70
Blackburn Rovers	53	27	15	11	101	61	53	11	9	33	57	111
Blackpool	37	21	6	10	86	46	37	12	6	19	43	60
Bolton Wanderers	64	27	22	15	119	92	64	15	18	31	66	115
Bournemouth	5	3	2	0	11	3	5	1	1	3	6	8
Bradford City	24	13	8	3	41	18	24	5	9	10	21	41
Bradford PA	13	8	2	3	30	9	13	4	3	6	27	30
Brentford	6	6	0	0	13	5	6	2	2	2	7	6
Brighton & Hove Albion	9	5	4	0	17	4	9	3	3	3	9	10
Bristol City	18	8	7	3	26	16	18	6	4	8	19	21
Bristol Rovers	3	2	1	0	8	3	3	0	2	1	3	4
Burnley	60	32	12	16	122	67	60	19	14	27	76	106
Burton Swifts/United	4	4	0	0	14	2	4	2	1	1	11	5
Bury	21	11	5	5	42	22	21	4	4	13	25	31
Cardiff City	21	13	3	5	43	24	21	7	6	8	34	34
Carlisle United	2	1	1	0	4	1	2	1	1	0	2	1
Charlton Athletic	23	10	6	7	32	24	23	6	7	10	32	42
Chelsea	53	21	13	19	91	64	53	14	14	25	72	105
Chester City	2	1	1	0	3	1	2	2	0	0	5	2
Chesterfield	10	7	2	1	23	8	10	3	4	3	14	10
Colchester United	1	1	0	0	2	1	1	1	0	0	2	1
Coventry City	23	13	7	3	50	18	23	9	4	10	27	31
Crewe Alexandra	6	2	2	2	10	11	6	3	2	1	8	7
Crystal Palace	20	11	4	5	32	26	20	7	6	7	22	23
Darlington	1	1	0	0	3	1	1	1	0	0	1	0
Darwen	2	1	1	0	14	2	2	0	1	1	2	3
Derby County	50	26	14	9	84	49	50	7	13	30	60	115
Doncaster Rovers	3	1	1	1	9	6	3	1	0	2	2	4
Everton	69	37	17	15	143	81	69	14	15	40	87	150
Exeter City	2	2	0	0	8	3	2	1	1	0	4	3

Opponents			*Home*						*Away*			
	P	*W*	*D*	*L*	*F*	*A*	*P*	*W*	*D*	*L*	*F*	*A*
Fulham	31	18	6	7	73	36	31	9	8	14	26	44
Gainsborough Trinity	8	7	0	1	29	5	8	2	2	4	12	16
Gillingham	3	3	0	0	5	1	3	2	0	1	5	3
Glossop	9	5	3	1	20	7	9	4	2	3	15	11
Grimsby Town	24	16	3	5	60	34	24	5	7	12	33	45
Hartlepool United	2	1	0	1	4	3	2	0	2	0	2	2
Huddersfield Town	33	16	8	9	57	43	33	8	8	17	36	56
Hull City	20	10	7	3	33	17	20	5	5	10	19	33
Ipswich Town	30	11	7	12	52	41	30	7	6	17	32	65
Leeds City	6	6	0	0	15	3	6	2	1	3	7	8
Leeds United	37	19	5	13	63	48	37	9	10	18	40	63
Leicester City	45	26	9	10	95	49	45	15	11	19	65	80
Leyton Orient	14	11	2	1	31	8	14	5	6	3	16	12
Lincoln City	8	6	2	0	23	6	8	6	0	2	15	5
Liverpool	57	19	16	22	79	76	57	9	17	31	48	100
Luton Town	19	14	2	3	40	14	19	6	6	7	20	27
Manchester City	62	32	16	14	115	65	62	16	10	36	91	141
Manchester United	53	26	11	16	100	80	53	11	14	28	64	107
Mansfield Town	1	1	0	0	2	0	1	1	0	0	3	0
Middlesbrough	41	22	9	10	65	41	41	5	10	26	30	73
Millwall	17	7	4	5	23	19	16	3	4	8	19	25
Newcastle United	52	24	17	11	102	65	52	14	12	27	73	110
Newport County	1	0	1	0	2	2	1	1	0	0	7	2
Northampton Town	1	0	1	0	1	1	1	1	0	0	4	3
Norwich City	21	10	6	5	29	18	21	6	7	8	28	30
Nottingham Forest	56	29	11	16	113	83	56	21	12	23	82	86
Notts County	30	17	9	4	74	41	30	6	7	17	29	54
Oldham Athletic	25	10	11	4	28	19	25	5	6	14	23	39
Oxford United	11	8	2	1	24	11	11	3	4	4	11	13
Peterborough United	2	2	0	0	7	0	2	0	1	1	0	2
Plymouth Argyle	13	5	3	5	20	23	13	1	5	7	15	25
Port Vale	16	6	7	3	27	16	16	6	1	9	23	33
Portsmouth	35	25	3	7	81	35	35	15	9	11	51	55
Preston North End	47	23	11	13	81	61	47	12	12	23	52	84
Queen's Park Rovers	14	6	5	3	22	14	14	5	2	7	15	15
Reading	13	10	1	2	26	8	13	5	4	4	24	20
Rotherham United	3	0	2	1	3	4	3	2	0	1	6	2
Sheffield United	50	25	9	16	85	57	50	13	14	22	49	78
Sheffield Wednesday	51	15	17	19	80	75	51	13	7	31	73	109
Shrewsbury Town	4	3	0	1	9	3	4	2	1	1	5	3
South Shields	1	1	0	0	3	0	1	1	0	0	3	2
Southampton	28	17	6	5	40	22	28	2	12	14	27	47

Opponents	*Home*						*Away*					
	P	*W*	*D*	*L*	*F*	*A*	*P*	*W*	*D*	*L*	*F*	*A*
Southend United	5	3	2	0	12	4	5	2	0	3	9	9
Stockport County	14	11	2	1	32	9	14	7	4	3	17	16
Stoke City	59	29	11	19	113	71	59	9	18	32	58	111
Sunderland	68	32	18	18	124	98	68	10	21	37	67	144
Swansea City	10	6	3	1	30	13	10	1	3	6	11	21
Swindon Town	10	3	3	4	14	15	10	3	3	4	11	12
Torquay United	1	1	0	0	1	0	1	0	0	1	0	1
Tottenham Hotspur	56	33	9	14	119	72	56	14	15	27	59	97
Tranmere Rovers	9	5	1	3	16	11	9	1	3	5	10	21
Walsall	4	2	1	1	3	1	4	0	1	3	3	8
Watford	14	8	3	3	30	16	14	6	3	5	17	20
West Ham United	36	20	6	10	67	39	36	12	4	20	50	75
Wigan Athletic	4	2	1	1	9	5	4	2	0	2	2	2
Wimbledon	3	1	0	2	4	3	3	2	1	0	2	0
Wolverhampton W	70	32	21	17	123	92	70	19	17	34	94	130
York City	2	1	1	0	4	2	2	2	0	0	4	0

Summary of Albion's League Seasons

		Home						Away						
Season	*Pos*	*P*	*W*	*D*	*L*	*F*	*A*	*P*	*W*	*D*	*L*	*F*	*A*	*Pts*
						FOOTBALL LEAGUE								
1888–89	6th	11	6	2	3	25	24	11	4	0	7	15	22	22
1889–90	5th	11	8	1	2	37	20	11	3	2	6	10	30	25
1890–91	12th	11	3	1	7	17	26	11	2	1	8	17	31	12
1891–92	12th	13	6	3	4	37	24	13	0	3	10	14	34	18
						DIVISION ONE								
1892–93	8th	15	9	2	4	35	17	15	3	3	9	23	52	29
1893–94	8th	15	8	4	3	35	23	15	6	0	9	31	36	32
1894–95	13th	15	9	2	4	38	21	15	1	2	12	13	45	24
1895–96	16th	15	5	4	6	18	22	15	1	3	11	12	37	19
1896–97	12th	15	7	2	6	18	16	15	3	4	8	15	40	26
1897–98	7th	15	8	5	2	25	16	15	3	5	7	19	29	32
1898–99	14th	17	11	1	5	28	9	17	1	5	11	14	48	30
1899–1900	13th	17	8	6	3	27	11	17	3	2	12	16	40	30
1900–01	18th	17	4	4	9	21	27	17	3	4	10	14	35	22
						DIVISION TWO								
1901–02	1st	17	14	2	1	52	13	17	11	3	3	30	16	55
						DIVISION ONE								
1902–03	7th	17	10	2	5	37	27	17	6	2	9	17	26	36
1903–04	18th	17	4	8	5	19	19	17	3	2	12	17	41	24
						DIVISION TWO								
1904–05	10th	17	8	2	7	28	20	17	5	2	10	28	28	30
1905–06	4th	19	13	4	2	53	16	19	9	4	6	26	20	52
1906–07	4th	19	15	2	2	62	15	19	6	3	10	21	30	47
1907–08	5th	19	13	3	3	38	13	19	6	6	7	23	26	47
1908–09	3rd	19	13	5	1	35	9	19	6	8	5	21	18	51
1909–10	11th	19	8	5	6	30	23	19	8	0	11	28	33	37
1910–11	1st	19	14	2	3	40	18	19	8	7	4	27	23	53
						DIVISION ONE								
1911–12	9th	19	10	6	3	23	15	19	5	3	11	20	32	39
1912–13	10th	19	8	7	4	30	20	19	5	5	9	27	30	38
1913–14	5th	19	11	7	1	30	16	19	4	6	9	16	26	43
1914–15	10th	19	11	5	3	31	9	19	4	5	10	18	34	40
1915–19			Competition suspended due to World War One											
1919–20	1st	21	17	1	3	65	21	21	11	3	7	39	26	60
1920–21	14th	21	8	7	6	31	23	21	5	7	9	23	35	40
1921–22	13th	21	8	6	7	26	23	21	7	4	10	25	40	40
1922–23	7th	21	12	7	2	38	10	21	5	4	12	20	39	45
1923–24	16th	21	10	6	5	43	30	21	2	8	11	8	32	38

		Home						Away						
Season	Pos	P	W	D	L	F	A	P	W	D	L	F	A	Pts
1924–25	2nd	21	13	6	2	40	17	21	10	4	7	18	17	56
1925–26	13th	21	13	5	3	59	29	21	3	3	15	29	49	40
1926–27	22nd	21	10	4	7	47	33	21	1	4	16	18	53	30
						DIVISION TWO								
1927–28	8th	21	10	7	4	50	28	21	7	5	9	40	42	46
1928–29	7th	21	13	4	4	50	25	21	6	4	11	30	54	46
1929–30	6th	21	16	1	4	73	31	21	5	4	12	32	42	47
1930–31	2nd	21	14	3	4	40	16	21	8	7	6	43	33	54
						DIVISION ONE								
1931–32	6th	21	12	4	5	46	21	21	8	2	11	31	34	46
1932–33	4th	21	16	1	4	50	23	21	4	8	9	33	47	49
1933–34	7th	21	12	4	5	49	28	21	5	6	10	29	42	44
1934–35	9th	21	10	8	3	55	33	21	7	2	12	28	50	44
1935–36	18th	21	12	3	6	54	31	21	4	3	14	35	57	38
1936–37	16th	21	13	3	5	45	32	21	3	3	15	32	66	38
1937–38	22nd	21	10	5	6	46	36	21	4	3	14	28	55	36
						DIVISION TWO								
1938–39	10th	21	15	3	3	54	22	21	3	6	12	35	50	45
1939–46						Competition suspended due to World War Two								
1946–47	7th	21	12	4	5	53	37	21	8	4	9	35	38	48
1947–48	7th	21	11	4	6	37	29	21	7	5	9	26	29	45
1948–49	2nd	21	16	3	2	47	16	21	8	5	8	22	23	56
						DIVISION ONE								
1949–50	14th	21	9	7	5	28	16	21	5	5	11	19	37	40
1950–51	16th	21	7	4	10	30	21	21	6	7	8	23	34	37
1951–52	13th	21	8	9	4	38	29	21	6	4	11	36	48	41
1952–53	4th	21	13	3	5	35	19	21	8	5	8	31	41	50
1953–54	2nd	21	13	5	3	51	24	21	9	4	8	35	39	53
1954–55	17th	21	11	5	5	44	33	21	5	3	13	32	63	40
1955–56	13th	21	13	3	5	37	25	21	5	2	14	21	45	41
1956–57	11th	21	8	8	5	31	25	21	6	6	9	28	36	42
1957–58	4th	21	14	4	3	59	29	21	4	10	7	33	51	50
1958–59	5th	21	8	7	6	41	33	21	10	6	5	47	35	49
1959–60	4th	21	12	4	5	48	25	21	7	7	7	35	32	49
1960–61	10th	21	10	3	8	43	32	21	8	2	11	24	39	41
1961–62	9th	21	10	7	4	50	23	21	5	6	10	33	44	43
1962–63	14th	21	11	1	9	40	37	21	5	6	10	31	42	39
1963–64	10th	21	9	6	6	43	35	21	7	5	9	27	26	43
1964–65	14th	21	10	5	6	45	25	21	3	8	10	25	40	39
1965–66	6th	21	11	6	4	58	34	21	8	6	7	33	35	50
1966–67	13th	21	11	1	9	40	28	21	5	6	10	37	45	39
1967–68	8th	21	12	4	5	45	25	21	5	8	8	30	37	46

		Home						Away						
Season	Pos	P	W	D	L	F	A	P	W	D	L	F	A	Pts
1968–69	10th	21	11	7	3	43	26	21	5	4	12	21	41	43
1969–70	16th	21	10	6	5	39	25	21	4	3	14	19	41	37
1970–71	17th	21	9	8	4	34	25	21	1	7	13	24	50	35
1971–72	16th	21	6	7	8	22	23	21	6	4	11	20	31	35
1972–73	22nd	21	8	7	6	25	24	21	1	3	17	13	38	28
DIVISION TWO														
1973–74	8th	21	8	9	4	28	24	21	6	7	8	20	21	44
1974–75	6th	21	13	4	4	33	15	21	5	5	11	21	27	45
1975–76	3rd	21	10	9	2	29	12	21	10	4	7	21	21	53
DIVISION ONE														
1976–77	7th	21	10	6	5	38	22	21	6	7	8	24	34	45
1977–78	6th	21	13	5	3	35	18	21	5	9	7	27	35	50
1978–79	3rd	21	13	5	3	38	15	21	11	6	4	34	20	59
1979–80	10th	21	9	8	4	37	23	21	2	11	8	17	27	41
1980–81	4th	21	15	4	2	40	15	21	5	8	8	20	27	52
1981–82	17th	21	6	6	9	24	25	21	5	5	11	22	32	44
1982–83	11th	21	11	5	5	35	20	21	4	7	10	16	29	57
1983–84	17th	21	10	4	7	30	25	21	4	5	12	18	37	51
1984–85	12th	21	11	4	6	36	23	21	5	3	13	22	39	55
1985–86	22nd	21	3	8	10	21	36	21	1	4	16	14	53	24
DIVISION TWO														
1986–87	15th	21	8	6	7	29	22	21	5	6	10	22	27	51
1987–88	21st	22	8	7	7	29	26	22	4	4	14	21	43	47
1988–89	9th	23	13	7	3	43	18	23	5	11	7	22	23	72
1989–90	20th	23	6	8	9	35	37	23	6	7	10	32	34	51
1990–91	23rd	23	7	11	5	26	21	23	3	7	13	26	40	48
DIVISION THREE														
1991–92	7th	23	12	6	5	45	25	23	7	8	8	19	24	71
1992–93	4th	23	17	3	3	56	22	23	8	7	8	32	32	85
DIVISION ONE														
1993–94	21st	23	9	7	7	38	31	23	4	5	14	22	38	51
1994–95	19th	23	13	3	7	33	24	23	3	7	13	18	33	58
1995–96	11th	23	11	5	7	34	29	23	5	7	11	26	39	60
1996–97	16th	23	7	7	9	37	33	23	7	8	8	31	39	57
1997–98	10th	23	9	8	6	27	26	23	7	5	11	23	30	61
1998–99	12th	23	12	4	7	43	33	23	4	7	12	26	43	59
1999–2000	21st	23	6	11	6	25	26	23	4	8	11	18	34	49
2000–01	6th	23	13	5	5	37	23	23	8	6	9	23	39	74
2001–02	2nd	23	15	4	4	36	11	23	12	4	7	25	18	89
PREMIERSHIP														
2002–03	19th	19	3	5	11	17	34	19	3	3	13	12	31	26

		Home						Away						
Season	Pos	P	W	D	L	F	A	P	W	D	L	F	A	Pts
						DIVISION ONE								
2003–04	2nd	23	14	5	4	34	16	23	11	6	6	30	26	86
						PREMIERSHIP								
2004–05	17th	19	5	8	6	17	24	19	1	8	10	19	37	34
2005–06	19th	19	6	2	11	21	24	19	1	7	11	10	34	30
						CHAMPIONSHIP								
2006–07	4th	23	14	4	5	51	24	23	8	6	9	30	31	76

* Three points for a win introduced for season 1981–82

Albion's 1939–46 wartime record (League and Cup):

Season	P	W	D	L	F	A
1939–40	37	23	5	9	107	67
1940–41	32	14	5	13	92	82
1941–42	31	18	4	9	115	69
1942–43	38	17	6	15	84	83
1943–44	39	14	11	14	90	93
1944–45	40	15	11	14	75	74
1945–46	46	23	9	14	110	74
Totals	263	124	51	88	673	542

Players used, leading scorers and attendance details

Home Attendances

Season	Players Used	Leading Scorer	Aggregate	Average
		FOOTBALL LEAGUE		
1888–89	20	Billy Bassett/Tom Pearson 11	50,409	4,582
1889–90	22	Tom Pearson 17	57,650	5,241
1890–91	23	Tom Pearson 13	48,605	4,418
1891–92	23	Tom Pearson 13	93,114	7,162
		DIVISION ONE		
1892–93	20	Billy Bassett/Tom Pearson 11	69,301	4,620
1893–94	21	Roddy McLeod 14	76,852	5,123
1894–95	24	Tom Hutchinson 15	103,818	6,921
1895–96	27	Roddy McLeod/Billy Richards 6	85,671	5,711
1896–97	22	Albert Flewitt 6	87,855	5,857
1897–98	21	Ben Garfield 12	105,102	7,006
1898–99	23	Billy Richards 10	82,955	4,879
1899–1900	19	Chippy Simmons 12	93,353	5,491
1900–01	24	Chippy Simmons/Dick Roberts 5	202,950	11,938
		DIVISION TWO		
1901–02	23	Chippy Simmons 23	132,974	7,822

Season	Players Used	Leading Scorer	Aggregate	Average
		DIVISION ONE		
1902–03	25	Billy Lee 10	266,176	15,657
1903–04	25	Chippy Simmons 8	215,057	12,651
		DIVISION TWO		
1904–05	33	Walter Jack 13	83,032	4,884
1905–06	25	Adam Haywood 23	164,093	8,637
1906–07	24	Fred Shinton 28	230,397	12,126
1907–08	30	Fred Buck 18	210,902	11,100
1908–09	26	Charlie Hewitt 15	339,061	17,845
1909–10	27	Fred Buck 16	222,398	11,705
1910–11	22	Sid Bowser 22	296,427	15,601
		DIVISION ONE		
1911–12	24	Bob Pailor 10	342,803	18,042
1912–13	21	Bob Pailor 16	323,908	17,047
1913–14	24	Alf Bentley 16	391,948	20,629
1914–15	26	Fred Morris 11	205,657	10,823
1915–19		Competition suspended due to World War One		
1919–20	18	Fred Morris 37	641,187	30,532
1920–21	25	Fred Morris 16	583,835	27,802
1921–22	29	Stan Davies 14	455,514	21,691
1922–23	24	Stan Davies 20	395,152	18,817
1923–24	25	Bobby Blood 9	365,010	17,381
1924–25	23	George James 25	432,522	20,596
1925–26	23	Stan Davies 19	390,507	18,595
1926–27	25	Joe Carter/Stan Davies 15	455,919	21,710
		DIVISION TWO		
1927–28	26	Jimmy Cookson 38	411,517	19,596
1928–29	25	Jimmy Cookson/Tommy Glidden 21	277,263	13,220
1929–30	26	Jimmy Cookson 33	294,501	14,023
1930–31	19	'W.G.' Richardson 18	456,179	21,722
		DIVISION ONE		
1931–32	21	'W.G.' Richardson 27	509,284	24,251
1932–33	18	'W.G.' Richardson 30	478,781	22,799
1933–34	23	'W.G.' Richardson 26	421,647	20,078
1934–35	23	'W.G.' Richardson 25	469,342	22,350
1935–36	25	'W.G.' Richardson 39	484,345	23,064
1936–37	28	Harry Jones 17	455,855	21,707
1937–38	25	'W.G.' Richardson 15	488,183	23,246
		DIVISION TWO		
1938–39	28	Harry Jones 18	387,828	18,467
1939–46		Competition suspended due to World War Two		
1946–47	28	Dave Walsh 28	517,498	24,642
1947–48	27	Dave Walsh 22	647,985	30,856

Season	*Players Used*	*Leading Scorer*	*Aggregate*	*Average*
1948–49	23	Dave Walsh 23	700,961	33,379
		DIVISION ONE		
1949–50	22	Dave Walsh 15	815,217	38,819
1950–51	24	Ronnie Allen 10	652,741	31,082
1951–52	22	Ronnie Allen 32	623,962	29,712
1952–53	20	Ronnie Allen 20	662,063	31,527
1953–54	21	Johnny Nicholls 28	803,852	38,279
1954–55	21	Ronnie Allen 27	656,201	31,247
1955–56	26	Ronnie Allen 17	565,361	26,922
1956–57	22	Derek Kevan 16	490,217	23,343
1957–58	23	Bobby Robson 24	683,717	32,558
1958–59	20	Derek Kevan 26	662,495	31,547
1959–60	25	Derek Kevan 26	577,595	27,504
1960–61	25	Derek Kevan 18	518,840	24,707
1961–62	19	Derek Kevan 33	440,953	20,998
1962–63	23	Alec Jackson/Derek Kevan 14	391,381	18,637
1963–64	22	Clive Clark 16	431,601	20,552
1964–65	22	Clive Clark 11	407,508	19,405
1965–66	21	Jeff Astle/John Kaye 18	414,414	19,781
1966–67	26	Clive Clark 19	490,393	23.352
1967–68	24	Jeff Astle 26	542,580	25,837
1968–69	24	Jeff Astle 21	526,924	25,091
1969–70	24	Jeff Astle 25	585,309	27,871
1970–71	21	Tony Brown 28	539,526	25,691
1971–72	23	Tony Brown 17	541,471	25,784
1972–73	22	Tony Brown 12	450,207	21,438
		DIVISION TWO		
1973–74	19	Tony Brown 19	336,023	16,001
1974–75	23	Tony Brown 12	266,260	12,679
1975–76	21	Ally Brown 10	361,900	17,233
		DIVISION ONE		
1976–77	22	David Cross 12	514,995	24,523
1977–78	17	Tony Brown 19	506,798	24,133
1978–79	17	Ally Brown 18	560,745	26,702
1979–80	20	Peter Barnes 15	477,442	22,735
1980–81	19	Cyrille Regis 14	428,038	20,382
1981–82	28	Cyrille Regis 17	353,874	16,851
1982–83	25	Cyrille Regis 9	320,460	15,260
1983–84	27	Garry Thompson 13	307,037	14,620
1984–85	21	Garry Thompson 19	293,132	13,958
1985–86	33	Imre Varadi 9	256,076	12,194
		DIVISION TWO		
1986–87	28	Garth Crooks 11	194,893	9,280

Season	*Players Used*	*Leading Scorer*	*Aggregate*	*Average*
1987–88	30	Andy Gray 10	222,780	10,126
1988–89	30	Don Goodman 15	293,618	12,766
1989–90	30	Don Goodman 21	260,199	11,313
1990–91	28	Gary Bannister 13	276,023	12,001
		DIVISION THREE		
1991–92	34	Gary Robson 9	292,263	12,707
1992–93	28	Bob Taylor 30	349,016	15,174
		DIVISION ONE		
1993–94	29	Bob Taylor 18	387,320	16,840
1994–95	27	Andy Hunt 13	349,623	15,201
1995–96	30	Bob Taylor 17	346,404	15,061
1996–97	29	Andy Hunt/Paul Peschisolido 15	346,472	15,064
1997–98	33	Lee Hughes 14	383,226	16,662
1998–99	25	Lee Hughes 31	335,455	14,585
1999–2000	30	Lee Hughes 12	335,432	14,584
2000–01	26	Lee Hughes 21	406,111	17,657
2001–02	25	Scott Dobie 10	475,893	20,691
		PREMIERSHIP		
2002–03	23	Danny Dichio/Scott Dobie 5	503,937	26,523
		DIVISION ONE		
2003–04	28	Lee Hughes 11	569,595	24,765
		PREMIERSHIP		
2004–05	27	Rob Earnshaw 11	493,753	25,987
2005–06	29	Nathan Ellington/Kana 5	482,676	25,404
		CHAMPIONSHIP		
2006–07	27	Diomansy Kamara 20	470,845	20,471

1888-89

Division One

	P	W	D	L	F	A	Pts
Preston North End	22	18	4	0	74	15	40
Aston Villa	22	12	5	5	61	43	29
Wolverhampton W	22	12	4	6	51	37	28
Blackburn Rovers	22	10	6	6	66	45	26
Bolton Wanderers	22	10	2	10	63	59	22
West Bromwich Albion	22	10	2	10	40	46	22
Accrington	22	6	8	8	48	48	20
Everton	22	9	2	11	35	47	20
Burnley	22	7	3	12	42	62	17
Derby County	22	7	2	13	41	61	16
Notts County	22	5	2	15	40	73	12
Stoke	22	4	4	14	26	51	12

Manager: Committee

- Albion were officially the first team to top the Football League – doing so after their 2–0 away win at Stoke on the opening day.
- The 10–1 victory at Chatham in the third round of the FA Cup remains to this day Albion's biggest in the competition, home or away.
- Albion's FA Cup semi-final encounter with the subsequent winners of the trophy, Preston North End, attracted a then record crowd of 22,688 to Bramall Lane, Sheffield.
- Joe Wilson and George Woodhall (versus Stoke on 8 September) and Fred Crabtree (against Everton on 23 February) all scored on their League debuts for Albion.
- Brothers Charlie and Walter Perry played together for the first time at competitive level against Burnley on 29 September – the day Albion registered their first home League win.
- Albion beat Studley & District 23–2 in a friendly – the club's second biggest win at that time (after their 26–0 Birmingham Cup victory over Coseley in 1882).
- Edward W. Heelis succeeded Henry Jackson as chairman of the club. He was to remain in office for two seasons.

Match No.	Date			Opponents	Result		Scorers	Attendance
1	Sep	8	A	Stoke	W	2-0	Wilson, Woodhall	4,524
2		15	A	Derby County	W	2-1	Bassett, Pearson	3,700
3		22	A	Blackburn Rovers	L	2-6	Pearson, Bayliss	8,000
4		29	H	Burnley	W	4-3	W. Perry, Bassett, Hendry, Shaw	2,100
5	Oct	6	H	Derby County	W	5-0	W. Perry, Pearson 2, Bassett, Hendry	5,500
6		13	A	Preston North End	L	0-3		10,200
7		20	H	Notts County	W	4-2	Pearson 2, Wilson, Woodhall	3,448
8	Nov	3	H	Accrington	D	2-2	Wilson, Bassett	3,000
9		5	H	Bolton Wanderers	L	1-5	Bassett	4,000
10		10	A	Burnley	L	0-2		5,000
11		17	A	Bolton Wanderers	W	2-1	Hendry, Pearson	4,230
12		24	A	Accrington	L	1-2	W. Perry	3,000
13	Dec	1	A	Everton	W	4-1	W. Perry, Bassett 2, Hendry	5,700
14		15	A	Wolverhampton Wanderers	L	1-2	Pearson	8,600
15		22	H	Blackburn Rovers	W	2-1	Bassett, Pearson	4,100
16		26	H	Preston North End	L	0-5		5,150
17		29	H	Stoke	W	2-0	Bassett, Wilson	4,896
18	Jan	5	H	Wolverhampton Wanderers	L	1-3	Woodhall	4,000
19		12	A	Notts County	L	1-2	Bassett	1,500
20		19	A	Aston Villa	L	0-2		10,000
21		26	H	Aston Villa	D	3-3	Bassett, Pearson 2	8,515
22	Feb	23	H	Everton	W	1-0	Crabtree	2,100

Appearances

Goals

FA Cup

R1	Feb	2	A	Small Heath	W	3-2	W Perry, Wilson, Pearson	3,034
R2		16	H	Burnley	W	5-1	Bayliss 2, Bassett, Wilson, W Perry	5,104
R3	Mar	2	A	Chatham	W	10-1	Bassett 2, W. Perry, Wilson 3, Bayliss 2, Timmins, Conquer (og)	17,000
SF		16	A	Preston North End	L	0-1		22,688

SF at Bramall Lane, Sheffield

Appearances

Goals

Roberts RJ	Horton JH	Green H	Horton E	Perry C	Bayliss AEJM	Bassett WI	Woodhall G	Hendry WH	Pearson T	Wilson JJ	Timmins G	Walker L	Perry W	Shaw RC	Millard AR	Oliver HSM	Haynes GH	Ramsey AR	Crabtree FW	Robinson B	
1	2	3	4	5	6	7	8	9	10	11											1
1	2	3		5	4	8	7	9	10	11	6										2
1	3	2	4	5	6	7		9	10	11	6										3
1	2			5	4	7		9	10		6	3	8	11							4
1	2	3		5	4	7		9	10	11	6		8								5
1	2	3		5	4	8	7	9	10	11	6										6
1	3	2			4	7	8	9	10	11	6				5						7
1	3		4	5	8	7		9	10	11	6	2									8
1	3		4	5	8	7		9	10	11	6	2									9
1			4	5	2	7		9	10	11	6		8			3					10
1	2			5	4	7		9	10	11	6	3	8								11
1	3			5	4	7		9	10		6	2	8				11				12
1	3			5	4	7		9	10	11	6	2	8								13
1	2			5	4	7	8		10	11	6	3	9								14
1	3			5	4	8	7		9	11	6	2					10				15
1	2			5	4	8	7		9	11	6	3					10				16
1				5	4	8	7		9	11	6	3					10	2			17
1	2			5	4	8	7	9	10	11	6	3									18
1	2		4	5	9	7		8	10	11	6	3									19
1	2	3	4		9	7	8	5	10	11	6										20
1		3	4	5	9	7		2	10	11	6		8								21
1		3	4	5	9			2	10	11	6		8						7		22
22	18	9	9	20	22	21	10	18	22	20	21	12	9	1	1	1	4	1	1		
				1	11	3	4	11	4			4	1					1			

1		3	4	5	9	7			10	11	6		8							2	R1
1		3	4	5	9	7			10	11	6		8							2	R2
1	2	3	4	5	9	7			10	11	6		8								R3
1		3	4	5	9	7			10	11	6		8							2	SF
4	1	4	4	4	4	4			4	4	4		4							3	
				4	3			1	5	1		3									

One own-goal

1889-90

Division One

	P	W	D	L	F	A	Pts
Preston North End	22	15	3	4	71	30	33
Everton	22	14	3	5	65	40	31
Blackburn Rovers	22	12	3	7	78	41	27
Wolverhampton W	22	10	5	7	51	38	25
West Bromwich Albion	22	11	3	8	47	50	25
Accrington	22	9	6	7	53	56	24
Derby County	22	9	3	10	43	55	21
Aston Villa	22	7	5	10	43	51	19
Bolton Wanderers	22	9	1	12	54	65	19
Notts County	22	6	5	11	43	51	17
Burnley	22	4	5	13	36	65	13
Stoke	22	3	4	15	27	69	10

Manager: Committee

- Inside-left Tom Pearson became the first Albion player to score a hat-trick in a League game when his four-timer helped destroy Bolton Wanderers 6–3 in November.
- Albion signed their first Welshman, international full-back Seth Powell, arriving from Oswestry Town. He went on to gain seven caps for his country, four as an Albion player.
- Goalkeeper Joe Reader made his League debut in the local derby against Aston Villa in October – the first of 370 senior appearances for the club.
- Other debutants this season were Charles Donnachie (ex-Dundee), George Evans (formerly of Derby County), Powell, Scotsman Bill Johnstone, Jim Nicholls (against Wolves), West Bromwich-born Sammy Nicholls and Jim Pittaway, who scored the winning goal against Burnley.
- Winger Joe Wilson, who hit Albion's first ever League goal against Stoke, joined Kidderminster Harriers after three seasons with the club.
- Surprisingly Albion transferred England international goalkeeper Bob Roberts to Sunderland Albion (May). He was the first Albion player to be capped by England (in a 3–2 defeat by Scotland in March 1887).
- Albion defeated Burton Wanderers 23–0 in a Staffordshire Cup tie – to register their second best win at competitive level.

Match No.	Date			Opponents	Result		Scorers	Attendance
1	Sep	14	A	Derby County	L	1-3	Bayliss	6,000
2		21	A	Notts County	W	2-1	Pearson, Bayliss	6,200
3		28	H	Aston Villa	W	3-0	Woodhall, Wilson, Bayliss	10,122
4	Oct	5	A	Preston North End	L	0-5		10,000
5		12	A	Burnley	W	2-1	Wilson, Pittaway	6,000
6		19	H	Wolverhampton Wanderers	L	1-4	Evans	1,550
7		26	A	Aston Villa	L	0-1		8,000
8	Nov	4	H	Bolton Wanderers	W	6-3	Pearson 4, Bassett, Woodhall	4,813
9		9	H	Derby County	L	2-3	Wilson, Bassett	5,100
10		16	A	Stoke	W	3-1	Pearson, Perry, Evans	3,900
11		23	H	Burnley	W	6-1	Bayliss 2, Haynes, Bassett, Evans, Pearson	7,100
12		30	A	Blackburn Rovers	L	0-5		6,600
13	Dec	7	A	Bolton Wanderers	L	0-7		3,500
14		21	H	Accrington	W	4-1	Pearson 3, Bayliss	3,500
15		26	H	Preston North End	D	2-2	Evans, Pearson	10,065
16		28	A	Wolverhampton Wanderers	D	1-1	Pearson	8,5000
17	Jan	4	H	Notts County	W	4-2	Bayliss, Pearson 3	4,700
18		11	H	Blackburn Rovers	W	3-2	Evans 2, Bayliss	5,100
19	Feb	8	A	Accrington	D	0-0		2,100
20	Mar	8	A	Everton	L	1-5	Pearson	8,400
21		15	H	Stoke	W	2-1	Woodhall, Bayliss	1,600
22		22	H	Everton	W	4-1	Evans 2, Pearson, Wilson	4,000
								Appearances
								Goals

FA Cup

R1	Jan	18	A	Accrington	X	1-3	Wilson	3,400
R1		25	A	Accrington	L	0-3		5,300
								Appearances

First game declared void after protest on the state of the pitch.

Goal and appearances not included in players' records.

	Roberts RJ	Horton JH	Green H	Horton E	Perry C	Timmins G	Bassett WI	Evans G	Bayliss AEJM	Pearson T	Wilson JJ	Woodhall G	Millard AR	Pittaway J	Walker L	Nicholls J	Reader J	Haynes GH	Johnstone WR	Donnachie C	Powell S	Nicholls S
1	1	2	3	4	5	6	7	8	9	10	11											
2	1	2	3	4	5	6	8		9	10	11	7										
3	1	2	3	4	5	6	8		9	10	11	7										
4	1	2	3	4	5	6	8		9	10	11	7										
5	1	2	3	4	5		8			10	11	7	6	9								
6	1		3	4	5			8	9	10	11	7			2	6						
7			3	4	5		8		9	10	11	7	6		2		1					
8			3	4	5	6	8	9		10	11	7			2		1					
9		2	3	4	5	6	8		9	10	11	7					1					
10	1	2		4	5	6	7	9	8	10	11				3							
11	1	2	3	4	5	6	7	9	8	10								11				
12	1	2	3	4	5	6	7	9	8	10	11											
13	1	3		4	5	6			8	10		7			2			11	9			
14	1	2	3	4	5		7		8	10	11								9	6		
15	1	2	3	4	5	6	7	9	8	10	11											
16	1	2		4	5	6	7	9	8	10	11										3	
17	1	2	6	4	5		7	9	8	10	11										3	
18	1	2	3	4	5		7	9	8	10	11					6						
19	1	2		4	5		7			10	11	8				6			9		3	
20	1		3	4	5		7	9	6	10	11				2							8
21		2	3	4				9	8	10	11	7				5	1			6		
22	1		3	4	5		7	9	6	10	11										2	8
	18	17	18	22	21	12	19	13	19	22	20	11	2	1	6	4	4	2	3	2	4	2
					1		3	8	9	17	4	3		1				1				
R1	1	2	3	4	5		7	9	8	10	11					6						
R1	1	2		4	5		7	9	8	10	11					6					3	
	1	1		1	1		1	1	1	1	1					1					1	

1890-91

Division One

	P	W	D	L	F	A	Pts
Everton	22	14	1	7	63	29	29
Preston North End	22	12	3	7	44	23	27
Notts County	22	11	4	7	52	35	26
Wolverhampton W	22	12	2	8	39	50	26
Bolton Wanderers	22	12	1	9	47	34	25
Blackburn Rovers	22	11	2	9	52	43	24
Sunderland	22	10	5	7	51	31	23
Burnley	22	9	3	10	52	63	21
Aston Villa	22	7	4	11	45	58	18
Accrington	22	6	4	12	28	50	16
Derby County	22	7	1	14	47	81	15
West Bromwich Albion	22	5	2	15	34	57	12

Manager: Committee

- Albion signed three Scotsmen in the space of six days in January 1891 – Willie Groves (from Celtic), Tom McCulloch (from Glasgow Rangers) and Roddy McLeod (from Partick Thistle). Also recruited were John 'Baldy' Reynolds from Ulster and Tom Perry. The first four players would later star in the 1892 FA Cup Final win over Aston Villa and Reynolds represented two countries, Ireland and England.
- George Timmins moved to Old Hill Wanderers and right-half Ezra Horton retired after nine years with the club. He appeared in Albion's first FA Cup tie against Wednesbury Town in 1883 and the club's first League game against Stoke in 1888.
- Albion and Sunderland met for the first time in a League game.

Match No.	Date			Opponents	Result		Scorers	Attendance
1	Sep	6	H	Everton	L	1-4	Pearson	5,600
2		13	A	Preston North End	L	0-3		8,500
3		20	H	Sunderland	L	0-4		8,537
4		27	A	Aston Villa	W	4-0	Dyer, Bayliss, Pearson, Burns	12,000
5	Oct	4	H	Burnley	W	3-1	Pearson, Burns 2	6,000
6		11	A	Notts County	L	2-3	T. Perry, Woodhall	4,900
7		18	H	Notts County	D	1-1	Pearson	7,367
8		25	A	Everton	W	3-2	Dyer, Nicholls, Burns	9,200
9	Nov	1	H	Aston Villa	L	0-3		8,000
10		3	H	Bolton Wanderers	L	2-4	Pearson 2	1,506
11		8	A	Sunderland	D	1-1	Woodhall	3,400
12		22	A	Derby County	L	1-3	Pearson	4,000
13		29	H	Derby County	L	3-4	Bayliss, Pearson, Nicholls	405
14	Dec	6	A	Burnley	L	4-5	C. Perry, Riley, Pearson 2	5,500
15		13	H	Wolverhampton Wanderers	L	0-1		3,400
16		20	A	Blackburn Rovers	L	1-2	Pearson	5,500
17	Jan	3	A	Wolverhampton Wanderers	L	0-4		9,300
18	Feb	7	H	Preston North End	L	1-3	Burns	4,300
19	Mar	7	H	Accrington	W	5-1	Nicholls 2, Pearson 2, Groves	800
20		9	H	Blackburn Rovers	W	1-0	McLeod	2,700
21		14	A	Bolton Wanderers	L	1-7	Gardiner (og)	5,200
22	Apr	18	A	Accrington	L	0-1		3,300

Appearances

Goals

FA Cup

R2	Jan	31	A	Birmingham St George's	W	3-0	Nicholls, Dyer, C. Perry	7,000
R3	Feb	14	A	Sheffield Wednesday	W	2-0	Groves, Pearson	16,871
SF		28	N	Blackburn Rovers	L	2-3	Groves, Pearson	21,774

SF at the Victoria Ground, Stoke

Walkover in R1 after Old Westminsters scratched.

Appearances

Goals

Reader J	Green H	Powell S	Horton E	Perry C	Bayliss AEJM	Bassett WI	Nicholls S	Dyer F	Pearson T	Roberts RHC	Woodhall G	Perry T	Burns JA	Horton JH	Roberts TF	Haynes GH	Riley JH	Groves W	Timmins G	McCulloch T	McCullum WD	McLeod R	Robinson B	
1	2	3	4	5	6	7	8	9	10	11														1
1	2	3	4	5		8	9	6	10		7	11												2
1	3	2		5	4		9	6	10		7	8	11											3
1		3	4	5	9	7		6	10			8	11	2										4
1		3	4	5	9	7		6	10			8	11	2										5
1		3	4	5		7		6	10		9	8	11	2										6
1		3	4	5	9	7		6	10		8		11	2										7
1		3	4	5		7	8	6	10		9		11	2										8
1		3	4	5		7	8	6	10		9		11	2										9
1	3		4			7	8	6	10		9		11	2	5									10
1		3	4	5		7	8	6	10		9			2		11								11
1		3	4	5		7		6	10		9	8	11	2										12
1		3	4	5	9		8	6	10		7		11	2										13
1	2	3	4	9			8	5	10		7		11				6							14
1		2		5		8		6	10		7		11	3			4	9						15
1	3		4	5		8		2	10		7		11					9	6					16
1			4	5		7		3	10		8		11	2				9	6					17
1				5	6		8	4	10		7		11					9		2	3			18
1							8	4	11		7			3			6	9		2	5	10		19
1				5		7	8	6	11					2				9		3	4	10		20
1		2	4	5		7	8	6	10									9		3		11		21
1		3		5	4	7	8	6	10					2		11		9						22
22	6	16	16	20	8	17	14	22	22	1	16	6	15	15	1	2	3	8	2	4	3	3		
				1	2		4	2	13		2	1	5				1	1				1		

One own-goal

Reader J	Green H	Powell S	Horton E	Perry C	Bayliss AEJM	Bassett WI	Nicholls S	Dyer F	Pearson T	Roberts RHC	Woodhall G	Perry T	Burns JA	Horton JH	Roberts TF	Haynes GH	Riley JH	Groves W	Timmins G	McCulloch T	McCullum WD	McLeod R	Robinson B	
1		3		5	4		8	6	10		7		11	2				9						R2
1		2		5	4	7	8	6	10									9		3		11		R3
1		3		5	4	7	8	6	10				11					9					2	SF
3		3		3	3	2	3	3	3		1		2	1				3		1		1	1	
				1			1	1	2									2						

1891-92

Division One

	P	W	D	L	F	A	Pts
Sunderland	26	21	0	5	93	36	42
Preston North End	26	18	1	7	61	31	37
Bolton Wanderers	26	17	2	7	51	37	36
Aston Villa	26	15	0	11	89	56	30
Everton	26	12	4	10	49	49	28
Wolverhampton W	26	11	4	11	59	46	26
Burnley	26	11	4	11	49	45	26
Notts County	26	11	4	11	55	51	26
Blackburn Rovers	26	10	6	10	58	65	26
Derby County	26	10	4	12	46	52	24
Accrington	26	8	4	14	40	78	20
West Bromwich Albion	26	6	6	14	51	58	18
Stoke	26	5	4	17	38	61	14
Darwen	26	4	3	19	38	112	11

Manager: Committee

- Albion's 12–0 home win over Darwen in April still remains a Football League record – shared by Nottingham Forest who beat Leicester Fosse by the same score in April 1909.
- England international George Woodhall joined Wolverhampton Wanderers, and Bob Roberts, who had rejoined Albion in May 1891, moved to nearby Aston Villa where he would remain for just one season, while Seth Powell switched to Burton Swifts.
- 'Jem' Bayliss, who had been appointed a director in 1891, retired as a player, having scored 36 goals in 95 competitive games for Albion, whom he joined in 1884.

Match No.	Date			Opponents	Result		Scorers	Attendance
1	Sep	5	H	Everton	W	4-0	Nicholls, Groves, McLeod 2	6,000
2		12	A	Aston Villa	L	1-5	Pearson	12,100
3		19	H	Wolverhampton Wanderers	W	4-3	Groves 2, Nicholls, C. Perry	10,000
4	Oct	3	H	Blackburn Rovers	D	2-2	Pearson, Nicholls	4,700
5		10	A	Notts County	L	0-4		4,000
6		17	H	Sunderland	L	2-5	McLeod, Bassett	5,500
7		24	A	Sunderland	L	0-4		6,000
8		31	H	Notts County	D	2-2	Pearson 2	5,200
9	Nov	2	H	Bolton Wanderers	L	0-2		6,700
10		7	A	Everton	L	3-4	Bassett 2, Pearson	8,100
11		14	H	Aston Villa	L	0-3		14,085
12		21	H	Preston North End	L	1-2	Geddes	13,000
13		28	A	Burnley	L	2-3	Bassett, Geddes	8,000
14	Dec	5	H	Accrington	W	3-1	Woodhall, Pearson, Geddes	6,000
15		12	H	Derby County	W	4-2	Woodhall, Pearson, Geddes 2	5,800
16		19	A	Bolton Wanderers	D	1-1	McLeod	7,000
17		26	H	Burnley	W	1-0	Pearson	5,000
18		28	A	Wolverhampton Wanderers	L	1-2	Ross (og)	7,200
19	Jan	9	A	Preston North End	L	0-1		6,400
20		23	A	Accrington	L	2-4	Nicholls, Pearson	4,200
21	Feb	6	A	Derby County	D	1-1	Nicholls	7,300
22	Mar	12	A	Blackburn Rovers	L	2-3	McLeod 2	6,000
23	Apr	4	H	Darwen	W	12-0	Pearson 4, Reynolds 2, Bassett 3, Hunt (og), Geddes, Nicholls	1,109
24		11	H	Stoke	D	2-2	T. Perry 2	10,000
25		16	A	Darwen	D	1-1	Nicholls	3,000
26		23	A	Stoke	L	0-1		5,400

Appearances

Goals

FA Cup

R1	Jan	16	A	Old Westminsters	W	3-2	McLeod, Pearson, Reynolds	10,000
R2		30	H	Blackburn Rovers	W	3-1	Pearson 2, Geddes	12,135
R3	Feb	13	H	Sheffield Wednesday	W	2-1	C. Perry, Nicholls	10,477
SF		27	N	Nottingham Forest	D	1-1	Geddes	21,076
rep	Mar	5	N	Nottingham Forest	D	1-1	Bassett	15,930
rep2		9	N	Nottingham Forest	W	6-2	Geddes 3, Bassett, Groves, C. Perry	8,024
F		19	N	Aston Villa	W	3-0	Geddes, Nicholls, Reynolds	32,710

SF and replay at Molineux, Wolverhampton. Replay 2 at the County Ground, Derby

Final at the Oval

Appearances

Goals

Roberts RJ	Nicholson MD	Powell S	Bayliss AEJM	Perry C	Dyer F	Bassett WI	Nicholls S	Groves W	McLeod R	Pearson T	McCulloch T	Reynolds J	Woodhall G	Reader J	Haynes GH	Geddes AJ	Charsley CC	Castle J	Horton JH	Millard AR	Wheldon S	Perry T	
1	2	3	4	5	6	7	8	9	10	11													1
1	2	3	4	5	6	7	8	9	10	11													2
1	2	3		5	6	7	8	9	10	11	4												3
1	2	3		5	6		8	9	10	11		4	7										4
	2	3	4		6	7		9	10	11		5	8	1									5
1	2	3	4	5	6	7	8	9	10	11													6
1	2	3		5	6	7	8	9	10	11	4												7
	2		4	5	6	7	8	9		10	3			1	11								8
	2		9	5	6	7	8	4		10	3			1	11								9
1	2	3		5	6	7	8	9		10	4					11							10
1	2		9	5		7	8	6		10	3	4				11							11
		3		5	6	7		8		10	2	9				11	1	4					12
				5		7		6	10	8	3	9		1		11		4	2				13
	2			5		7			8	10	3	6	9	1		11		4					14
	2			5		7			8	10	3	6	9	1		11		4					15
	2			5	6	7		9	8	10	3	4		1		11							16
	2			5	6	7			8	10	3	4	9	1	11								17
	2			5	6	7			8	10	3	4	9	1		11							18
				5	6	7		9	8	10	3	4		1		11			2				19
					6	7	9		8	10		5		1		11			3	4	2		20
		2		5		7	9	6	8	10	3	4		1		11							21
	2			5		7	9	6	8	10	3	4		1		11							22
				5		7	9	6	8	10	3	4		1		11			2				23
1				5	6		9		8		3		7			11			2	4		10	24
	2			5	6	7	9	10	8		3	4		1		11							25
	3			5	6	7	9	8		10		4		1					2			11	26
9	19	10	7	24	19	24	17	20	20	24	19	17	7	16	3	15	1	4	6	2	1	2	
				1		7	7	3	6	13		2	2			6						2	

Two own-goals

	2			5	6	7		9	8	10	3	4		1		11							R1
	2			5	6	7	9		8	10	3	4		1		11							R2
	2			5	6	7	9		8	10	3	4		1		11							R3
	2			5		7	9	6	8	10	3	4		1		11							SF
	2		9	5		7	8	6		10	3	4		1		11							rep
	2			5		7	9	6	8	10	3	4		1		11							rep2
	2			5		7	9	6	8	10	3	4		1		11							F
	7		1	7	3	7	6	5	6	7	7	7		7		7							
				2		2	2	1	1	3		2				6							

1892-93

Division One

	P	W	D	L	F	A	Pts
Sunderland	30	22	4	4	100	36	48
Preston North End	30	17	3	10	57	39	37
Everton	30	16	4	10	74	51	36
Aston Villa	30	16	3	11	73	62	35
Bolton Wanderers	30	13	6	11	56	55	32
Burnley	30	13	4	13	51	44	30
Stoke	30	12	5	13	58	48	29
West Bromwich Albion	30	12	5	13	58	69	29
Blackburn Rovers	30	8	13	9	47	56	29
Nottingham Forest	30	10	8	12	48	52	28
Wolverhampton W	30	12	4	14	47	68	28
Sheffield Wednesday	30	12	3	15	55	65	27
Derby County	30	9	9	12	52	64	27
Notts County	30	10	4	16	53	61	24
Accrington	30	6	11	13	57	81	23
Newton Heath	30	6	6	18	50	85	18

Manager: Committee

- Tom Pearson became the first Albion player to appear in 100 League games when he scored against Stoke in November. England's outside-right Billy Bassett reached the same milestone a month later against Wolves.
- On the transfer front, defenders Bob Crone and Jack Taggart were both signed from Middlesbrough, wing-half John Reynolds was transferred to Aston Villa, having scored Albion's first League penalty against Nottingham Forest (April) and George 'Spry' Woodhall joined Wolves.
- Giant goalkeeper Bob Roberts retired after two spells and more than 400 appearances for Albion.
- Albion met Manchester United (Newton Heath), Nottingham Forest and Sheffield Wednesday for the first time at League level.

Match No.	Date			Opponents	Result		Scorers	Attendance
1	Sep	10	A	Bolton Wanderers	L	1-3	Geddes	4,100
2		17	H	Wolverhampton Wanderers	W	2-1	Bassett, Bastock	4,000
3		19	H	Aston Villa	W	3-2	McLeod, Pearson 2	11,239
4		24	A	Derby County	D	1-1	Pearson	7,000
5	Oct	1	H	Newton Heath	D	0-0		4,000
6		8	A	Newton Heath	W	4-2	McLeod, Bassett, Bastock 2	4,600
7		15	H	Everton	W	3-0	Wood, Pearson 2	4,800
8		22	A	Sunderland	L	1-8	Bassett	8,000
9		29	H	Notts County	W	4-2	Geddes, Pearson, Bassett, Bastock	3,000
10	Nov	5	A	Aston Villa	L	2-5	Geddes 2	12,100
11		7	H	Bolton Wanderers	W	1-0	Geddes	4,000
12		12	H	Accrington	W	4-0	Groves 2, McLeod, Bostock	4,000
13		19	A	Notts County	L	1-8	McLeod	8,000
14		26	H	Stoke	L	1-2	Pearson	607
15	Dec	10	H	Preston North End	L	0-1		4,000
16		17	A	Accrington	L	4-5	McLeod, Pearson, Bastock 2	3,000
17		24	H	Sunderland	L	1-3	Bassett	8,000
18		26	H	Blackburn Rovers	L	1-2	Pearson	7,000
19		27	A	Wolverhampton Wanderers	D	1-1	McLeod	8,000
20		31	A	Burnley	L	0-5		3,500
21	Jan	2	A	Sheffield Wednesday	L	0-6		15,000
22		7	H	Burnley	W	7-1	McLeod 3, Bassett 2, Pearson, Geddes	1,000
23		14	A	Everton	L	0-1		10,000
24		28	A	Blackburn Rovers	L	1-2	Geddes	2,300
25	Feb	11	A	Stoke	W	2-1	Bassett 2	6,000
26	Mar	2	A	Nottingham Forest	W	4-3	Geddes, Bassett 2, Groves	4,100
27		18	H	Sheffield Wednesday	W	3-0	McLeod, Pearson, Boyd	5,000
28	Apr	1	H	Derby County	W	3-1	C. Perry 2, Geddes	3,655
29		3	H	Nottingham Forest	D	2-2	C. Perry, Reynolds (pen)	5,000
30		13	A	Preston North End	D	1-1	C. Perry	8,200

Appearances

Goals

FA Cup

R1	Jan	21	A	Everton	L	1-4	Pearson	23,867

Appearances

Goals

Reader J	Horton JH	McCulloch T	Reynolds J	Perry C	Groves W	Bassett WI	McLeod R	Bostock AME	Pearson T	Geddes AJ	Nicholson MD	Perry T	Wood HF	Hadley B	Fellows JE	Boyd H	Crone R	Neale W	Taggart J	
1	2	3	4	5	6	7	8	9	10	11										1
1		3	4	5	6	7	8	9	10	11	2									2
1	2	3	4	5	6	7	8	9	10	11										3
1	3		4	5	6	7	8	9	10	11	2									4
1	3		4	5	6	7	8	9	10		2	11								5
1		3	4	5	6	7	8	9	10	11	2									6
1		3	4	5	6	7	8	9	10		2		11							7
1		3	4	5	6	7	8	9	10	11	2									8
1		3	4	5	6	7	8	9	10	11	2									9
1		3	4	9	6	7	8	10		11	2	5								10
1	2	3	4	5	9	7	8	10		11		6								11
1	2	3	4	5	9	7	8	10		11		6								12
1	2	3	4	5	9	7	8	10		11		6								13
1	3			5	6	7	8	9	10	11	2	4								14
1	3			5	6	7	8	9	10	11	2	4								15
1	2	3		5	6	7	8	9	10	11				4						16
1	2	3	4	5	6	7	8	9	10	11										17
1	2	3	4	5	6	7	8	9	10	11										18
1	2	3	4	5	6	7	8		10	11					9					19
1	2	3		5	6	7	8		10	11		4			9					20
1	2	3		5	6	7	8		10	11		4			9					21
1	2	3		5	6	7	8		10	11		4				9				22
1	2	3		5	6	7	8		10	11		4				9				23
1	2	3		5	6	7	8			11		4			10	9				24
1	2	3	4	5	6	7	8		10	11						9				25
1		3	2	5	6	7	8		10	11		4				9				26
1			4	5	6	7	8		10	11	2					9	3			27
1				5	7		8		10	11	2	4					3	9	6	28
1			4	5	11	7	8		10		2	6					3	9		29
1		3		2	4	7	8		10	11		5				9			6	30
30	19	23	20	30	30	29	30	18	25	27	13	16	1	1	4	7	3	2	2	
			1	4	3	11	10	7	11	9			1			1				
1	3	2		5	6	7	8		10	11		4				9				R1
1	1	1		1	1	1	1		1	1		1				1				
									1											

1893-94

Division One

	P	W	D	L	F	A	Pts
Aston Villa	30	19	6	5	84	42	44
Sunderland	30	17	4	9	72	44	38
Derby County	30	16	4	10	73	62	36
Blackburn Rovers	30	16	2	12	69	53	34
Burnley	30	15	4	11	61	51	34
Everton	30	15	3	12	90	57	33
Nottingham Forest	30	14	4	12	57	48	32
West Bromwich Albion	30	14	4	12	66	59	32
Wolverhampton W	30	14	3	13	52	63	31
Sheffield United	30	13	5	12	47	61	31
Stoke	30	13	3	14	65	79	29
Sheffield Wednesday	30	9	8	13	48	57	26
Bolton Wanderers	30	10	4	16	38	52	24
Preston North End	30	10	3	17	44	56	23
Darwen	30	7	5	18	37	83	19
Newton Heath	30	6	2	22	36	72	14

Manager: Committee

- Albion's 8–0 victory at Molineux in December remains to this day Wolves' biggest ever home League defeat, while at the same time it is also Albion's biggest away win in the same competition. Roddy McLeod's hat-trick in this game was the first by an Albion player away from home.
- Future England wing-half Jack Banks was signed from Oldbury Town, while Scottish international Willie Groves was transferred to Aston Villa where he was re-united with his former colleague John Reynolds. Tom Nicholson signed for Stirling and Sam Richards retired.
- Albion opposed Sheffield United for the first time in the Football League.

Match No.	Date			Opponents	Result		Scorers	Attendance
1	Sep	2	A	Aston Villa	L	2-3	Geddes, Cowan (og)	15,100
2		9	H	Newton Heath	W	3-1	Pearson, McLeod, Nicholls	4,500
3		16	A	Derby County	W	3-2	McLeod 2, Nicholls	7,000
4		23	H	Burnley	D	1-1	McLeod	3,000
5		25	A	Sheffield Wednesday	W	4-2	Bassett 2, Geddes 2	6,000
6		30	A	Nottingham Forest	W	3-2	McLeod 2, Bassett	5,000
7	Oct	7	H	Wolverhampton Wanderers	D	0-0		10,000
8		14	A	Newton Heath	L	1-4	Norman	8,000
9		21	H	Aston Villa	L	3-6	C. Perry, Geddes, McLeod	14,000
10		28	A	Sheffield United	W	2-0	Bassett, Neale	6,000
11	Nov	4	H	Stoke	W	4-2	C. Perry 2, McLeod, Nicholls	3,000
12		6	H	Bolton Wanderers	W	5-2	Neale, Pearson 4	4,000
13		11	A	Darwen	L	1-2	Neale	2,000
14		25	A	Sunderland	L	1-2	Bassett	9,500
15		27	H	Sheffield Wednesday	D	2-2	Bastock, McLeod (pen)	4,828
16	Dec	4	H	Preston North End	W	2-0	Norman 2	2,000
17		9	A	Burnley	L	0-3		5,000
18		16	H	Darwen	D	2-2	McLeod, Bassett	2,000
19		23	H	Sunderland	L	2-3	Geddes 2	7,500
20		26	H	Sheffield United	W	3-1	Bassett, Pearson, Norman	7,000
21		27	A	Wolverhampton Wanderers	W	8-0	McLeod 3, Bassett 3, C. Perry, Williams	8,000
22		30	A	Everton	L	1-7	Williams	14,000
23	Jan	6	H	Blackburn Rovers	W	2-1	Williams, Hadley	2,024
24		13	A	Blackburn Rovers	L	0-3		6,000
25		20	A	Stoke	L	1-3	Bassett	3,000
26	Feb	3	H	Everton	W	3-1	Williams 2, Pearson	3,000
27	Mar	3	A	Preston North End	L	1-3	McLeod	5,000
28		24	H	Derby County	L	0-1		3,000
29		26	H	Nottingham Forest	W	3-0	Bastock, Williams 2	7,000
30	Apr	7	A	Bolton Wanderers	W	3-0	Geddes, Bastock 2	3,500

Appearances

Goals

FA Cup

R1	Jan	27	H	Blackburn Rovers	L	2-3	McLeod 2	10,243

Appearances

Goals

Reader J	Nicholson MD	Crone R	Perry T	Perry C	Taggart J	Norman AEO	McLeod R	Nicholls S	Pearson T	Geddes AJ	Bassett WI	Hadley B	Horton JH	Bostock AME	Burns J	Neale W	Roberts TF	Williams O	Banks J	Humpage WLF	
1	2	3	4	5	6	7	8	9	10	11											1
1	2	3	4	5	6		8	9	10	11	7										2
1	2	3	4	5	6		8	9	10	11	7										3
1	2	3	4	5	6		8	9	10	11	7										4
1		3	4	2	6		8	9	10	11	7	5									5
1		2	4	5	6		8		10	11	7		3	9							6
1	2		4	5	6	9	8		10	11	7		3								7
1	2		4	5	6	7			10	11			3	9	8						8
1	2		4	5	6		8		10	11	7		3	9							9
1	2	3	4	5	6		8		10	11	7					9					10
1	2	3	4	5	6		8	9	10	11	7										11
1	2	3	4	5	6		8		10	11	7					9					12
1	2	3	4	5	6		8		10	11	7					9					13
1	2	3	4	5	6		8	9	10	11	7										14
1		3	4	5	6		8		10	11	7		2	9							15
1		3	4	2	6	8	9		10	11	7	5									16
1	2	3	4	5		8	9		10	11	7						6				17
1	2	3	4	5	6		8		10	11	7							9			18
1	2	3	4	5	6	8	9		10	11	7										19
1	2	3	4	5	6	8	9		10	11	7										20
1	2		4	5	6	8	9			11	7		3					10			21
1	2	3	4	5	6	8	9		11		7							10			22
1	2	3			6	8	9			11	7	5						10	4		23
1	2	3	4	5		8	9			11	7							10	6		24
1	2	3		5			8		10		7	4				9		11	6		25
1	2	3	4	5	6		8		10	11	7							9			26
	2	3		5	6		8			11	7			9				10	4	1	27
1		3	4	2	6		8			11	7	5		9				10			28
1		3	4	5	6		8			11	7		2	9				10			29
1	2	3	4	5	6	7	8	9		11				10							30
29	24	26	27	29	27	12	29	8	23	28	27	5	7	8	1	4	1	10	4	1	
				4		4	14	3	7	7	11	1		4		3		7			

One own-goal

1	2	3	4	5	6		8			11	7					9		10			R1
1	1	1	1	1	1		1			1	1					1		1			
							2														

1894-95

Division One

	P	W	D	L	F	A	Pts
Sunderland	30	21	5	4	80	37	47
Everton	30	18	6	6	82	50	42
Aston Villa	30	17	5	8	82	43	39
Preston North End	30	15	5	10	62	46	35
Blackburn Rovers	30	11	10	9	59	49	32
Sheffield United	30	14	4	12	57	55	32
Nottingham Forest	30	13	5	12	50	56	31
Sheffield Wednesday	30	12	4	14	50	55	28
Burnley	30	11	4	15	44	56	26
Bolton Wanderers	30	9	7	14	61	62	25
Wolverhampton W	30	9	7	14	43	63	25
Small Heath	30	9	7	14	50	74	25
West Bromwich Albion	30	10	4	16	51	66	24
Stoke	30	9	6	15	50	67	24
Derby County	30	7	9	14	45	68	23
Liverpool	30	7	8	15	51	70	22

Manager: Committee

- Ex-Albion star John Reynolds played for Aston Villa in the FA Cup Final, which was decided inside the first minute, Bob Chatt scoring fortuitously from close range in front of a then record crowd of 42,562 at Crystal Palace.
- Albion had to beat Sheffield Wednesday by five goals on the last day of the season to retain their First Division status. They went one better and won 6–0, winger Jesper Geddes scoring his only hat-trick for the club.
- Albion played Everton at Goodison Park with only 10 men – Billy Richards having missed the morning train to Liverpool.
- Transfer activity saw Albion sign full-back Billy Williams from Old Hill Wanderers, while full-back Mark Nicholson moved to Luton Town and Geddes to Clapham Rovers.
- Inside-left Tom Pearson announced his retirement through injury, having scored 88 goals in 171 games for the club in eight years.
- Goalkeeper Joe Reader became the first Albion player to be sent off in a League game, dismissed at Bolton in April.
- Albion played both Birmingham City (Small Heath) and Liverpool for the first time at League level.
- For the first time Albion had a League game abandoned. They were 2–1 up when it was called off at Stoke in March due to heavy rain.

Match No.	Date			Opponents	Result		Scorers	Attendance
1	Sep	1	A	Sheffield United	L	1-2	McLeod	12,000
2		8	H	Wolverhampton Wanderers	W	5-1	McLeod, Richards, Bassett, Newall, Hutchinson	5,100
3		15	H	Liverpool	W	5-0	Bassett, W. Williams, Richards, McLeod, Hutchinson	6,951
4		22	A	Sunderland	L	0-3		7,150
5		29	A	Everton	L	1-4	Bassett	19,900
6	Oct	13	A	Aston Villa	L	1-3	McLeod	15,000
7		20	H	Derby County	D	2-2	Newall, Hutchinson	5,000
8		27	A	Derby County	D	1-1	Bassett	1,990
9	Nov	3	H	Sheffield United	W	1-0	Hutchinson	3,250
10		5	H	Bolton Wanderers	D	1-1	Hutchinson	3,500
11		10	H	Small Heath	W	4-1	Basett, Richards, Hutchinson, C. Perry	4,523
12		17	H	Aston Villa	W	3-2	Hutchinson, Richards 2	12,000
13		24	A	Burnley	L	0-2		6,000
14	Dec	1	H	Everton	L	1-4	Hutchinson	6,000
15		8	A	Nottingham Forest	L	3-5	T. Perry, McLeod, Bassett	5,800
16		15	H	Stoke	W	3-2	Hutchinson 2, Taggart	4,400
17		22	A	Blackburn Rovers	L	0-3		1,200
18		26	H	Sunderland	L	0-2		15,086
19		27	A	Wolverhampton Wanderers	L	1-3	Hutchinson	6,500
20		29	H	Burnley	L	0-1		2,535
21	Jan	1	A	Liverpool	L	0-4		19,720
22		5	H	Preston North End	L	4-5	Bassett, Hutchinson 2, Richards	19,700
23		26	H	Blackburn Rovers	W	2-0	Hutchinson, Banks	3,200
24	Feb	23	A	Small Heath	W	2-1	Taggart 2	8,100
25		26	A	Preston North End	L	0-5		6,400
26	Mar	25	A	Stoke	D	1-1	McLeod	5,100
27	Apr	1	A	Sheffield Wednesday	L	2-3	McLeod 2	14,150
28		13	A	Bolton Wanderers	L	0-5		10,200
29		15	H	Nottingham Forest	W	1-0	Geddes	4,355
30		22	H	Sheffield Wednesday	W	6-0	Geddes 2, Green, Hutchinson, McLeod, T. Perry	8,217

Game 5 played with 10 men.

Appearances

Goals

FA Cup

R1	Feb	2	A	Small Heath	W	2-1	McLeod, Banks	10,203
R2		16	A	Sheffield United	D	1-1	Bassett	14,559
rep		20	H	Sheffield United	W	2-1	Hutchinson, Foulke (og)	10,025
R3	Mar	2	H	Wolverhampton Wanderers	W	1-0	McLeod	20,977
SF		16	N	Sheffield Wednesday	W	2-0	Hutchinson, Williams (pen)	25,013
F	Apr	20	N	Aston Villa	L	0-1		42,652

SF at the County Ground, Derby

Final at Crystal Palace

Appearances

Goals

Match	Reader J	Williams W	Crone R	Perry T	Perry C	Taggart J	Bassett WI	McLeod R	Hutchinson T	Williams O	Newall WT	Richards W	Higgins JT	Fellows JE	Horton JH	Norman AEO	Banks J	Rea JC	Paddock JW	Perry W	Parry J	Green T	Roberts TF	Geddes AJ
1	1	2	3	4	5	6	7	8	9	10	11													
2	1	2	3	4	5	6	7	8	9		11	10												
3	1	2	3	4	5	6	7	8	9		11	10												
4	1	2	3	4	5	6	7	8	9		11	10												
5	1	2	3	4	5	6	7	8	9		11													
6	1	2	3	4	5	6	7	8	9		11		10											
7	1	2	3	4	5	6	7	8	9		11			10										
8	1	2		4	5	6	7		9		11				3	8	10							
9	1	2		4	5	6	7	8	9		11				3		10							
10	1	2	3	4	5	6	7		9		11					8	10							
11	1	2		4	5	6	7	8	9		11	10			3									
12	1	2		4	5	6	7	8	9		11	10			3									
13	1	2		4	5	6		8	9			10			3	7	11							
14	1	2		4	5	6	7	8	9		11	10			3									
15	1	2		4	5	6	7	8	9			10			3		11							
16	1	2	3	4	5	6	7	8	9			10						11						
17	1	2		4	5	6	7	8	9			10			3		11							
18	1	2	3	4	5	6	7	8	9		11			10										
19	1	2		4	5		7		8	9			6	10	3				11					
20	1	2		8		6	7		10			9	5		3		11			4				
21	1	2		4	5	6	7	8	10			9			3		11							
22	1	2		4	5	6	7	8	10			9			3						11			
23	1	2		4	3	6	7	8	9			10	5				11							
24	1			4	3	6			10			9	5		2	7	11					8		
25	1			4	2	6			10			9	5			7	11					8	3	
26	1	3		4		6	7	8	9	10			5		2		11							
27	1		2	4		6	7	8	10				5				11					9	3	
28	1	3		4		6	7	8	10			9	5		2									11
29	1	3		4		6	7	8	10			9	5		2									11
30	1	3		4		6	7	8	10				5		2							9		11
	30	27	11	30	24	29	27	24	30	3	14	18	11	3	17	5	13	1	1	1	1	4	2	3
		1		2	1	3	7	9	15		2	6					1					1		3

Round	Reader J	Williams W	Crone R	Perry T	Perry C	Taggart J	Bassett WI	McLeod R	Hutchinson T	Williams O	Newall WT	Richards W	Higgins JT	Fellows JE	Horton JH	Norman AEO	Banks J	Rea JC	Paddock JW	Perry W	Parry J	Green T	Roberts TF	Geddes AJ
R1	1	3		4	2	6	7	8	10			9	5				11							
R2	1	3		4	2	6	7	8	10			9	5				11							
rep	1	3		4	2	6	7	8	10			9	5				11							
R3	1	3		4	2	6	7	8	10			9	5				11							
SF	1	3		4	2	6	7	8	10			9	5				11							
F	1	3		4		6	7	8	10			9	5		2		11							
	6	6		6	5	6	6	6	6			6	6		1		6							
							1	2	2	1							1							

One own-goal

1895-96

Division One

	P	W	D	L	F	A	Pts
Aston Villa	30	20	5	5	78	45	45
Derby County	30	17	7	6	68	35	41
Everton	30	16	7	7	66	43	39
Bolton Wanderers	30	16	5	9	49	37	37
Sunderland	30	15	7	8	52	41	37
Stoke	30	15	0	15	56	47	30
Sheffield Wednesday	30	12	5	13	44	53	29
Blackburn Rovers	30	12	5	13	40	50	29
Preston North End	30	11	6	13	44	48	28
Burnley	30	10	7	13	48	44	27
Bury	30	12	3	15	50	54	27
Sheffield United	30	10	6	14	40	50	26
Nottingham Forest	30	11	3	16	42	57	25
Wolverhampton W	30	10	1	19	61	65	21
Small Heath	30	8	4	18	39	79	20
West Bromwich Albion	30	6	7	17	30	59	19

Manager: Committee

- Albion retained their First Division status after registering two wins and a draw in their four Test Matches.
- Forwards Albert Flewitt and Tom Hutchinson were recruited from Everton and Stockport County respectively, while Bob Crone was transferred to Burton Swifts and long-serving defender Charlie Perry retired after 219 appearances and 12 years with the club. Charlie's brother Walter ended his second spell with the club by joining Burton Swifts, and Jack Taggart signed for Walsall.
- Albion's home League game against Bury in December was abandoned after 15 minutes because of heavy snow.

Match No.	Date			Opponents	Result		Scorers	Attendance
1	Sep	2	A	Aston Villa	L	0-1		18,150
2		7	H	Burnley	L	0-2		5,000
3		14	H	Preston North End	L	1-2	Hutchinson	4,250
4		21	A	Stoke	L	1-3	Green	12,000
5		28	H	Nottingham Forest	W	3-1	Paddock 2, Bassett	3,000
6	Oct	5	A	Sheffield Wednesday	L	3-5	Hutchinson 2, W. Richards	8,000
7		12	H	Aston Villa	D	1-1	Paddock	17,570
8		19	A	Everton	D	1-1	McLeod	18,900
9		26	H	Sheffield Wednesday	L	2-3	Paddock, Banks	5,550
10	Nov	2	A	Bury	L	0-3		8,000
11		4	H	Bolton Wanderers	L	2-3	McLeod, Sutcliffe (og)	3,500
12		9	H	Stoke	W	1-0	McLeod	3,500
13		16	A	Nottingham Forest	L	0-2		6,000
14		23	H	Everton	L	0-3		3,950
15		30	H	Wolverhampton Wanderers	W	2-1	W. Richards, McLeod	3,000
16	Dec	14	A	Derby County	L	1-4	W. Richards	8,000
17		21	A	Small Heath	D	2-2	McLeod, Banks	6,000
18		26	H	Sunderland	D	1-1	Bassett	15,124
19	Jan	4	A	Sheffield United	L	0-2		5,000
20		11	A	Burnley	L	0-3		5,500
21		18	H	Derby County	D	0-0		8,877
22		25	A	Sunderland	L	1-7	McLeod	10,500
23	Feb	17	A	Blackburn Rovers	L	0-1		5,700
24		22	H	Sheffield United	W	1-0	W. Richards	3,900
25	Mar	7	A	Wolverhampton Wanderers	W	2-1	W. Richards, Flewitt	8,114
26		9	H	Bury	L	1-3	Flewitt	4,200
27	Apr	3	A	Preston North End	D	0-0		6,700
28		4	A	Bolton Wanderers	L	1-2	Banks	7,000
29		6	H	Small Heath	D	0-0		3,750
30		29	H	Blackburn Rovers	W	3-2	W. Richards, Hutchinson, Taggart	560

Appearances
Goals

FA Cup

R1	Feb	1	A	Blackburn Rovers	W	2-1	J. Richards, W. Richards	10,035
R2		15	A	Grimsby Town	D	1-1	McLeod	7,108
rep		20	H	Grimsby Town	W	3-0	McLeod, W. Richards 2	8,443
R3		29	A	Derby County	L	0-1		14,117

Appearances
Goals

Test Matches

	Apr	18	A	Manchester City	D	1-1	T. Perry	8,000
		20	H	Manchester City	W	6-1	Flewitt 2, Higgins, J. Richards, W. Williams, Johnson	8,000
		25	A	Liverpool	L	0-2		20,100
		27	H	Liverpool	W	2-0	W. Williams (pen), W. Richards	15,000

Albion stayed in Division One.

Appearances
Goals

	Reader J	Perry C	Williams W	Perry T	Higgins JT	Banks J	Bassett WI	McLeod R	Green T	Hutchinson T	Saunders S	Richards W	Horton JH	Williams O	Paddock JW	Norman AEO	Kelsey AG	Humpage WLF	Fellows JE	Spooner J	Richards J	Wright F	Hadley B	Haywood A	Taggart J	Cave GH	Flewitt AW	Johnson G
1	1	2	3	4	5	6	7	8	9	10	11																	
2	1	2	3	4	5	6	7	8	9	10		11																
3	1		3	4	5	6	7	8	9	10	11		2															
4	1		3	4	5	6	7	8	9				2	10	11													
5	1		3	4	5	6	7	11		8		9	2		10													
6	1		3	4	5	6		8		9		10	2		11	7												
7	1		3	4	5	6	7	8		9			2		11		10											
8	1		3	4	5	6	7	8		9			2		11		10											
9	1		3	4	5	6	7	8		9			2		11		10											
10	1		3	4	5	6	7	8		9			2		11		10											
11	1	2	3	4	5	6	7	8		9					11		10											
12			3	4	5	6	7	8		9			2				10	1	11									
13			3	4	5	6	7	8		9			2		11		10	1										
14			3	4	5	6	7	8				9	2				10	1	11									
15	1		3	4	5	6	7	8				10	2				11			9								
16	1		3	4	5		7	8				10	2		11		6			9								
17	1		3	4	5	11	7	8				10	2				6				9							
18	1		3	4	5	11	7	8				10	2								9	6						
19	1		3	4	5	11	7	8				10	2								9	6						
20	1		3	4	5		7	8				10	2								9		6	11				
21	1		3	4	5		7	8				10	2								9			11	6			
22	1		3	4	5		7	8				10	2								9			11	6			
23	1		3	4	5		7	9				10									11				6	2	8	
24	1		3	4	5		7	8				10	2								11				6		9	
25	1		3	4	5			7		8		10	2								11				6		9	
26	1		3	4	5		7	8				10	2								11				6		9	
27	1		3	4	5			7		8		10	2								11				6		9	
28	1		3	4	5	11		8				10	2								7				6		9	
29	1		3	4	5		7	8				10	2								11				6		9	
30	1		3	4	5	11		8		9		10									7				6	2		
	27	3	30	30	30	20	25	30	4	15	2	20	25	1	10	1	11	3	2	2	14	2	1	3	10	2	7	
						3	2	6	1	4		6			4										1		2	

One own-goal

	Reader J	Perry C	Williams W	Perry T	Higgins JT	Banks J	Bassett WI	McLeod R	Green T	Hutchinson T	Saunders S	Richards W	Horton JH	Williams O	Paddock JW	Norman AEO	Kelsey AG	Humpage WLF	Fellows JE	Spooner J	Richards J	Wright F	Hadley B	Haywood A	Taggart J	Cave GH	Flewitt AW	Johnson G
R1	1		3	4	5		7	8		9		10	2								11				6			
R2	1		3	4	5		7	8		9		10	2								11				6			
rep	1		3	4	5		7	8		9		10	2												6			11
R3	1		3	4	5	11	7	8		9		10	2												6			
	4		4	4	4	1	4	4		4		4	4								2				4			1
								2				3									1							

	Reader J	Perry C	Williams W	Perry T	Higgins JT	Banks J	Bassett WI	McLeod R	Green T	Hutchinson T	Saunders S	Richards W	Horton JH	Williams O	Paddock JW	Norman AEO	Kelsey AG	Humpage WLF	Fellows JE	Spooner J	Richards J	Wright F	Hadley B	Haywood A	Taggart J	Cave GH	Flewitt AW	Johnson G
	1		3	4	5			8		10		11	2								7				6		9	
	1		3	4	5			8				11	2								7				6		9	10
	1		3		5	4		8		11		10	2								7				6		9	
	1		3	4	5	11		8				10	2								7				6		9	
	4		4	3	4	2		4		2		4	4								4				4		4	1
			2	1	1							1									1						2	1

1896-97

Division One

	P	W	D	L	F	A	Pts
Aston Villa	30	21	5	4	73	38	47
Sheffield United	30	13	10	7	42	29	36
Derby County	30	16	4	10	70	50	36
Preston North End	30	11	12	7	55	40	34
Liverpool	30	12	9	9	46	38	33
Sheffield Wednesday	30	10	11	9	42	37	31
Everton	30	14	3	13	62	57	31
Bolton Wanderers	30	12	6	12	40	43	30
Bury	30	10	10	10	39	44	30
Wolverhampton W	30	11	6	13	45	41	28
Nottingham Forest	30	9	8	13	44	49	26
West Bromwich Albion	30	10	6	14	33	56	26
Stoke	30	11	3	16	48	59	25
Blackburn Rovers	30	11	3	16	35	62	25
Sunderland	30	7	9	14	34	47	23
Burnley	30	6	7	17	43	61	19

Secretary-manager: Frank Heaven

- Two players who left the club were Roddy McLeod, who joined Leicester Fosse after scoring 65 goals in 185 games, and Tom Hutchinson, who moved to Stockport County. Into the camp came Arthur Watson from Mansfield Town and winger Ben Garfield from Burton Wanderers.
- Billy Bassett, who celebrated 10 years with Albion, took over as team captain from Tom Higgins.
- Local businessman and West Bromwich Dartmouth cricketer Frank Heaven became the club's first ever secretary-manager, appointed at the age of 23 in the summer of 1896. He was to remain in office for six years.
- Brothers Harry 'John Bull' and William Hall Keys both joined the board of directors. The Keys family, thereafter, would remain associated with the club for 78 years. Harry served as chairman for seven years (1899–1903 and 1905–08) and his son, Major H. Wilson Keys, was in the chair from 1947–63. A second brother of Harry's, Clement, was Albion's secretary (1892–95 and 1896–97) and later his company acted as the club's auditors until 1974.

Match No.	Date			Opponents	Result		Scorers	Attendance
1	Sep	1	A	Blackburn Rovers	W	2-1	Richards, McLeod	3,000
2		5	H	Aston Villa	W	3-1	Garfield 2, Williams (pen)	10,000
3		12	A	Sheffield Wednesday	L	1-3	Ford	6,800
4		19	H	Preston North End	D	1-1	Watson	9,500
5		26	A	Liverpool	D	0-0		15,100
6	Oct	3	H	Sheffield Wednesday	L	0-2		10,291
7		10	A	Aston Villa	L	0-2		15,500
8		17	H	Wolverhampton Wanderers	W	1-0	McLeod	6,000
9		24	H	Bury	D	0-0		5,000
10		31	H	Liverpool	L	0-1		6,100
11	Nov	2	H	Bolton Wanderers	W	1-0	Bassett	5,200
12		14	H	Sheffield United	L	0-1		5,700
13		21	A	Stoke	D	2-2	Flewitt, Garfield	6,200
14		28	H	Sunderland	W	1-0	Cameron	4,000
15	Dec	5	A	Sheffield United	W	1-0	Bassett	6,000
16		12	H	Stoke	L	1-2	Garfield	1,105
17		19	A	Bolton Wanderers	D	2-2	Flewitt, Cameron	7,000
18		25	A	Derby County	L	1-8	Flewitt	8,000
19		26	H	Blackburn Rovers	W	1-0	Flewitt	9,909
20		28	A	Wolverhampton Wanderers	L	1-6	Bassett	11,561
21	Jan	2	A	Nottingham Forest	W	1-0	Dean	5,300
22		16	H	Everton	L	1-4	Perry	3,950
23		23	H	Nottingham Forest	W	4-0	Richards 3, Williams	2,000
24	Feb	6	H	Derby County	L	1-4	Garfield	6,000
25	Mar	6	A	Sunderland	L	1-2	Richards	4,600
26		13	A	Bury	L	0-3		8,000
27	Apr	3	H	Burnley	W	3-0	McLeod, Williams, Flewitt	3,100
28		10	A	Burnley	L	0-5		4,900
29		16	A	Preston North End	D	0-0		8,000
30		17	A	Everton	L	3-6	Perry, Flewitt, McLeod	9,700
								Appearances
								Goals

FA Cup

R1	Jan	30	A	Luton Town	W	1-0	Flewitt	6,898
R2	Feb	13	H	Liverpool	L	1-2	Watson	16,147
								Appearances
								Goals

Reader J	Evans TJ	Williams W	Perry T	Higgins JT	McManus P	Bassett WI	McLeod R	Ford WG	Richards W	Garfield BW	Banks J	Watson AEC	Flewitt AW	Vigrow S	Cameron JR	Horton JH	Cave GH	Dean A	Law A	Flavell AE	Fellows JE	
1	2	3	4	5	6	7	8	9	10	11												1
1	2	3	4	5		7	8	9	10	11	6											2
1	2	3	4	5		7	8	9	10	11	6											3
1	2	3	4	5		7	8	9		11	6	10										4
1	2	3	4	5	6	7		9		11		10	8									5
1	2	3	4	5	6	7	8	9	10	11												6
1	2	3	4	5		7	8	9		11	6	10										7
1	2	3	4	5	6	7	8		9	11			10									8
1	2	3	4	5		7		9	10	11	6		8									9
1		3	2	5		7		4	9	11	6		8	10								10
1	2	3	4	5		7		9		11	6	10	8									11
1	2	3	4	5		7		9		11	6	10	8									12
1	2	3	4	5		7		10		11	6		8		9							13
1	2	3	4	5	6	7				10		11	8		9							14
1	2		4	5	6	7				10		11	8		9	3						15
1	2	3	4	5	6	7				10		11	8		9							16
1	2	3	4	5	6	7			10			11	8		9							17
1	2	3	4	5	6	7			10			11	8		9							18
1		3	4	5	6	7			10			11	8		9	2						19
1		3	4	5	6	7			10			11	8		9	2						20
1		3	4	5	6		8		10			11			9		2	7				21
1	2	3	4	5			8		10		6	11	9					7				22
1	2	3	4	5		7			10		6	11	8		9							23
		3	4	5		7				10	6	11	8		9	2			1			24
	2	3	4	5	6				10	11		7	8		9					1		25
	2	3	4	5		7					6	8	10		9					1	11	26
1		3	4		5		9		10	11	6	7	8				2					27
1		3	4		5		9		10	11	6	7	8				2					28
1		3	4		5		9		10	11	6	7	8				2					29
1		3	4		5		9		10	11	6	7	8				2					30
26	21	28	29	26	16	23	12	12	18	21	16	21	22	1	13	4	4	2	1	2	1	
		3	2			3	4	1	5	5		1	6		2			1				

Reader J	Evans TJ	Williams W	Perry T	Higgins JT	McManus P	Bassett WI	McLeod R	Ford WG	Richards W	Garfield BW	Banks J	Watson AEC	Flewitt AW	Vigrow S	Cameron JR	Horton JH	Cave GH	Dean A	Law A	Flavell AE	Fellows JE	
1		3	4	5			7		10		6	11	8		9	2						R1
1	2	3	4	5					10		6	11	8		9			7				R2
2	1	2	2	2			1		2		2	2	2		2	1		1				
												1	1									

1897-98

Division One

	P	W	D	L	F	A	Pts
Sheffield United	30	17	8	5	56	31	42
Sunderland	30	16	5	9	43	30	37
Wolverhampton W	30	14	7	9	57	41	35
Everton	30	13	9	8	48	39	35
Sheffield Wednesday	30	15	3	12	51	42	33
Aston Villa	30	14	5	11	61	51	33
West Bromwich Albion	30	11	10	9	44	45	32
Nottingham Forest	30	11	9	10	47	49	31
Liverpool	30	11	6	13	48	45	28
Derby County	30	11	6	13	57	61	28
Bolton Wanderers	30	11	4	15	28	41	26
Preston North End	30	8	8	14	35	43	24
Notts County	30	8	8	14	36	46	24
Bury	30	8	8	14	39	51	24
Blackburn Rovers	30	7	10	13	39	54	24
Stoke	30	8	8	14	35	55	24

Secretary-manager: Frank Heaven

- Full-back Billy Williams scored a goal from fully 60 yards in the third-round FA Cup tie against Nottingham Forest in February. His effort was to no avail as Albion lost 3–2.
- Three Scotsmen, Joe Connor, Abe Jones, and Archie McKenzie, along with Harry Hadley, John Knowles, Josiah Nock and ex-Sheffield Wednesday forward George Reid all made their Albion debuts, McKenzie celebrating his first game by scoring against Aston Villa.
- Albion also signed brothers Ralph and Sammy Brett and the versatile Charlie 'Chippy' Simmons from Worcester Rovers in readiness for the 1898–99 season.

Match No.	Date			Opponents	Result		Scorers	Attendance
1	Sep	4	A	Aston Villa	L	3-4	McKenzie, Higgins, McManus	20,950
2		11	H	Nottingham Forest	W	2-0	Garfield 2	5,000
3		18	A	Derby County	L	2-3	Watson, Higgins	6,700
4		25	H	Stoke	W	2-0	Flewitt, Higgins	8,200
5	Oct	2	A	Bury	L	2-3	Bassett, Higgins	4,500
6		9	H	Aston Villa	D	1-1	Garfield	12,244
7		16	A	Sunderland	W	2-0	Bassett, McNeill (og)	6,500
8		23	H	Wolverhampton Wanderers	D	2-2	Flewitt, Garfield	11,750
9		30	A	Stoke	D	0-0		6,400
10	Nov	1	H	Bolton Wanderers	W	2-0	Dean, Jones	8,200
11		6	H	Everton	D	2-2	Garfield, Dean	5,750
12		13	H	Liverpool	W	2-1	Williams, Jones	8,200
13		20	H	Derby County	W	3-1	Garfield, Flewitt, Reid	10,500
14		27	A	Everton	L	1-6	Flewitt	15,700
15	Dec	11	A	Nottingham Forest	W	1-0	Perry	10,400
16		18	H	Bury	W	1-0	Garfield	6,303
17		27	H	Blackburn Rovers	D	1-1	Williams (pen)	5,300
18		28	A	Wolverhampton Wanderers	D	1-1	Reid	8,100
19	Jan	1	A	Liverpool	D	1-1	Flewitt	10,000
20		15	H	Preston North End	W	3-1	Garfield 2, Flewitt	7,000
21	Feb	5	A	Blackburn Rovers	W	3-1	Reid, Flewitt, Bassett	4,000
22		19	H	Sunderland	D	2-2	McKenzie 2	5,000
23	Mar	12	H	Sheffield Wednesday	L	0-2		3,455
24		19	A	Notts County	D	2-2	Garfield, Jones	3,600
25		26	H	Sheffield United	W	2-0	Garfield, Richards	4,200
26		31	A	Preston North End	D	1-1	Garfield	5,900
27	Apr	2	A	Bolton Wanderers	L	0-2		3,650
28		4	H	Notts County	L	0-3		4,000
29		9	A	Sheffield Wednesday	L	0-3		3,200
30		11	A	Sheffield United	L	0-2		2,800

Appearances

Goals

FA Cup

R1	Jan	29	H	New Brighton Tower	W	2-0	Garfield, Flewitt	15,897
R2	Feb	12	H	Sheffield Wednesday	W	1-0	Flewitt	16,012
R3		26	H	Nottingham Forest	L	2-3	Williams, Bassett	17,483

Appearances

Goals

Reader J	Cave GH	Williams W	Perry T	McManus P	Banks J	Watson AEC	Flewitt AW	Higgins JT	McKenzie AD	Garfield BW	Bassett WI	Richards W	Jones A	Dean A	Reid GA	Knowles JW	Nock JF	Hadley H	Connor MJJ	Horton JH	
1	2	3	4	5	6	7	8	9	10	11											1
1	2	3	4	5	6	7	8	9	10	11											2
1	2	3	4	5	6	7	8	9	10	11											3
1	2	3	4	5	6	7	8	9	10	11											4
1	2	3	4	5	6		8	9	10	11	7										5
1	2	3	4	5	6		8	9	10	11	7										6
1	2	3	4	5	6		8	9	10	11	7										7
1	2	3	4	5	6		8	9	10	11		7									8
1	2	3	4	5	6	7	8	9	10	11											9
1	2	3	4		6		8	9	10	11			5	7							10
1	2	3	4		6		8	9	10	11			5	7							11
1	2	3	4		6		8		10	11			5	7	9						12
1	2	3	4		6		8		10	11			5	7	9						13
1	2	3	4		6		8		10	11			5	7	9						14
1	2	3	4		6		8		10	11			5		9	7					15
1	2	3	4		6		8		10	11			5		9	7					16
1	2	3	4		6		8		10	11	7		5		9						17
1	2	3	4		6		8		10	11	7		5		9						18
1	2	3	4		6		8		10		7		5		9		11				19
1	2	3	4		6		8		10	11	7		5		9						20
1	2	3	4	6			8		10	11	7		5		9						21
1	2	3	4		6		8		10	11	7		5		9						22
1	2	3	4		6		8		10	11	7	9	5								23
1	2	3	4						10	11	7	9	5					6	8		24
1	2	3	4		6				10	11	7	9	5						8		25
1	2	3	4		6				10	11	7	9	5						8		26
1	2		4	5	6				10	11	7	9	3						8		27
1	2	3	4						10		7	9	5				11	6	8		28
1	2				4	11			10		7	9	5					6	8	3	29
1	2	3	4		6				10	11	7	9	5						8		30
30	30	28	29	11	27	6	23	11	30	27	17	9	21	5	11	2	2	3	7	1	
		2	1	1		1	7	4	3	12	3	1	3	2	3						

One own-goal

Reader J	Cave GH	Williams W	Perry T	McManus P	Banks J	Watson AEC	Flewitt AW	Higgins JT	McKenzie AD	Garfield BW	Bassett WI	Richards W	Jones A	Dean A	Reid GA	Knowles JW	Nock JF	Hadley H	Connor MJJ	Horton JH	
1	2	3	4		6		8		10	11	7	9	5								R1
1	2	3	4		6		8		10	11	7		5		9						R2
1	2	3	4		6		8		10	11	7		5		9						R3
3	3	3	3		3		3		3	3	3	1	3		2						
		1					2			1	1										

1898-99

Division One

	P	W	D	L	F	A	Pts
Aston Villa	34	19	7	8	76	40	45
Liverpool	34	19	5	10	49	33	43
Burnley	34	15	9	10	45	47	39
Everton	34	15	8	11	48	41	38
Notts County	34	12	13	9	47	51	37
Blackburn Rovers	34	14	8	12	60	52	36
Sunderland	34	15	6	13	41	41	36
Wolverhampton W	34	14	7	13	54	48	35
Derby County	34	12	11	11	62	57	35
Bury	34	14	7	13	48	49	35
Nottingham Forest	34	11	11	12	42	42	33
Stoke	34	13	7	14	47	52	33
Newcastle United	34	11	8	15	49	48	30
West Bromwich Albion	34	12	6	16	42	57	30
Preston North End	34	10	9	15	44	47	29
Sheffield United	34	9	11	14	45	51	29
Bolton Wanderers	34	9	7	18	37	51	25
Sheffield Wednesday	34	8	8	18	32	61	24

Secretary-manager: Frank Heaven

- Billy Bassett played in his 311th and final competitive game for Albion, lining up in the 7–1 League defeat at Villa Park on the last day of the season. He later became a shareholder, director and then chairman of the club, serving Albion for more than 50 years in total.
- Two other players who retired were both defenders, Tom Higgins and the long-serving Jack Horton; the latter joined the club in November 1882 and made over 150 appearances.
- Albion and Newcastle United met for the first time at League level.

Match No.	Date			Opponents	Result		Scorers	Attendance
1	Sep	3	A	Bolton Wanderers	D	3-3	Brett, Garfield 2	6,300
2		10	H	Derby County	D	1-1	Brett	7,026
3		17	H	Bury	W	2-0	Garfield, Flewitt	5,521
4		24	A	Blackburn Rovers	L	1-4	Garfield	4,600
5	Oct	1	H	Sheffield Wednesday	W	2-0	Perry, McKenzie	6,767
6		8	A	Sunderland	L	0-2		15,000
7		15	H	Wolverhampton Wanderers	L	1-2	Bassett	6,457
8		22	A	Everton	L	0-1		9,000
9		29	H	Notts County	W	2-0	McKenzie, Richards	4,286
10	Nov	5	A	Stoke	L	1-2	Richards	7,500
11		7	H	Everton	W	3-0	Richards 2, Brett	6,686
12		12	H	Aston Villa	L	0-1		15,896
13		19	A	Burnley	D	1-1	Williams (pen)	7,500
14		26	H	Sheffield United	W	3-0	Nock, Thickett (og), Richards	1,999
15	Dec	3	A	Newcastle United	L	0-3		16,200
16		10	H	Preston North End	W	2-0	Dunn, McKenzie	2,433
17		17	A	Liverpool	D	2-2	Nock 2	5,100
18		24	H	Nottingham Forest	W	2-0	Nock 2	2,578
19		26	H	Liverpool	L	0-1		8,483
20		27	A	Wolverhampton Wanderers	L	1-5	McKenzie	12,052
21		31	H	Bolton Wanderers	W	1-0	Nock	1,571
22	Jan	7	A	Derby County	L	1-4	Richards	3,200
23		14	A	Bury	D	1-1	Richards	1,500
24		21	H	Blackburn Rovers	W	6-2	Flewitt 2, McKenzie 2, Garfield, Bassett	1,957
25	Feb	4	H	Sunderland	W	1-0	Richards	4,947
26		14	A	Sheffield Wednesday	W	2-1	Richards 2	3,503
27	Mar	4	H	Stoke	L	0-1		1,714
28		9	A	Notts County	D	0-0		2,488
29		18	H	Burnley	L	0-1		2,330
30		25	A	Sheffield United	L	0-5		3,996
31	Apr	1	H	Newcastle United	W	2-0	Smith, Bassett	2,304
32		8	A	Preston North End	L	0-4		2,976
33		22	A	Nottingham Forest	L	0-3		3,015
34		24	A	Aston Villa	L	1-7	Perry	10,000

Appearances
Goals

FA Cup

R1	Jan	28	H	South Shore	W	8-0	Bassett 3, Jones 2, Richards, Garfield, Barrow (og)	5,870
R2	Feb	11	H	Bury	W	2-1	Richards 2	14,094
R3		25	H	Liverpool	L	0-2		17,124

Appearances
Goals

	Reader J	Cave GH	Williams W	Perry T	Jones A	Banks J	Bassett WI	Flewitt AW	Brett RS	Richards W	Garfield BW	Dunn A	Connor MJJ	McKenzie AD	Foster J	Turner I	Simmons C	Nock JF	Hadley H	Brett SS	Adams A	Smith A	Fellows JE
1	1	2	3	4	5	6	7	8	9	10	11												
2	1	2	3	4	5	6	7	8	9	10	11												
3	1	2	3	4	5	6	7	8	9	10	11												
4	1	2		4	5	6	7	8	9	10	11	3											
5	1	2		4	5			8	9	6	11	3	7	10									
6	1	2	3	4	5				9	6	11		8	10	7								
7		2	3	4	5	6	7		9		11		8	10		1							
8	1	2	3	4	5	6	7		9	10	11			8									
9	1	2	3	4	5	6	7		9	10	11			8									
10	1	2		4	5	6	7		9	10	11	3		8									
11	1	2	3	4	5	6	7		9	10	11			8									
12	1	2	3	4	5	6	7	9		10	11			8									
13	1	2	3	4		6	7			9		5		10			8	11					
14	1	2	3	4	5	6	7			10		9		8				11					
15	1	2	3	4	5	6	7			10		9		8				11					
16	1	2	3	4	5	6	7			10		9		8				11					
17	1	2	3	4	5	6	7			10		9		8				11					
18	1	2	3	4	5		7			10		9		8				11	6				
19	1	2	3	4	5		7			10		9		8				11	6				
20	1	2		4	3		7			10		5		8				11	6	9			
21	1	2	3	4	5		7	8		9		6		10				11					
22	1	2	3	4	5		7	8		9		6		10				11					
23	1	2	3	4	5		7			9		6		10			8	11					
24	1	2		4	3		7	9		5	11	6		10			8						
25	1	2	3	4	5	6	7	9		10	11						8						
26	1	2	3	4	5		7	9		10	11	6					8						
27	1	2	3	4	5		7	9		10	11	6					8						
28	1	2	3	4	5		7			10				11			8		6		9		
29	1	2	3	4	5		7		9	10	11	6					8						
30	1	2	3	4	5		7										8	11	6			9	10
31	1	2		8	5		7				11	4							6		3	9	10
32	1	2		8	5	6	7			10	11								4	9	3		
33	1	2		8	5		7			10	11	4							6		3	9	
34	1	2		9	5		7			10		4					8	11	6		3		
	33	34	25	34	33	17	32	12	12	31	20	21	3	21	1	1	10	13	9	2	5	3	2
			1	2			3	3	3	10	5	1		6				6				1	

One own-goal

	Reader J	Cave GH	Williams W	Perry T	Jones A	Banks J	Bassett WI	Flewitt AW	Brett RS	Richards W	Garfield BW	Dunn A	Connor MJJ	McKenzie AD	Foster J	Turner I	Simmons C	Nock JF	Hadley H	Brett SS	Adams A	Smith A	Fellows JE
R1	1	2	3	4	5		7	9		10	11	6					8						
R2	1	2	3	4	5		7	9		10	11	6					8						
R3	1	2	3	4	5		7			9	11	6		10			8						
	3	3	3	3	3		3	2		3	3	3		1			3						
					2		3			3	1												

One own-goal

1899-1900

Division One

	P	W	D	L	F	A	Pts
Aston Villa	34	22	6	6	77	35	50
Sheffield United	34	18	12	4	63	33	48
Sunderland	34	19	3	12	50	35	41
Wolverhampton W	34	15	9	10	48	37	39
Newcastle United	34	13	10	11	53	43	36
Derby County	34	14	8	12	45	43	36
Manchester City	34	13	8	13	50	44	34
Nottingham Forest	34	13	8	13	56	55	34
Stoke	34	13	8	13	37	45	34
Liverpool	34	14	5	15	49	45	33
Everton	34	13	7	14	47	49	33
Bury	34	13	6	15	40	44	32
West Bromwich Albion	34	11	8	15	43	51	30
Blackburn Rovers	34	13	4	17	49	61	30
Notts County	34	9	11	14	46	60	29
Preston North End	34	12	4	18	38	48	28
Burnley	34	11	5	18	34	54	27
Glossop	34	4	10	20	31	74	18

Secretary-manager: Frank Heaven

- Albion bid farewell to their Stoney Lane ground (their home since 1885) by beating Nottingham Forest 8–0.
- Albion played Manchester City in the League for the first time.

Match No.	Date			Opponents	Result		Scorers	Attendance
1	Sep	2	H	Newcastle United	D	1-1	Simmons	6,135
2		9	A	Aston Villa	W	2-0	Garfield, Simmons	17,482
3		16	H	Liverpool	W	2-0	Garfield 2	6,431
4		23	A	Burnley	L	0-2		10,027
5		30	H	Preston North End	W	1-0	Simmons	4,684
6	Oct	7	A	Nottingham Forest	L	1-6	Perry	17,106
7		14	H	Glossop	D	3-3	Williams, Richards 2	5,629
8		21	A	Stoke	L	0-1		3,603
9		28	H	Sunderland	W	1-0	Garfield	6,117
10	Nov	4	A	Wolverhampton Wanderers	L	0-2		10,089
11		6	H	Sheffield United	L	1-2	Perry	14,905
12		11	A	Everton	W	3-1	Paddock, Richards 2	8,996
13		25	A	Derby County	L	1-4	Richards	6,520
14	Dec	2	H	Bury	L	0-1		3,729
15		9	A	Notts County	W	2-1	Garfield 2	4,186
16		16	H	Manchester City	D	0-0		2,429
17		23	A	Sheffield United	D	1-1	Garfield	3,492
18		26	H	Everton	D	0-0		8,509
19		30	A	Newcastle United	L	2-4	Simmons 2	10,887
20	Jan	6	H	Aston Villa	L	0-2		6,575
21		13	A	Liverpool	L	0-2		10,531
22		20	H	Burnley	W	2-0	Hadley, Brett	3,427
23	Feb	3	A	Preston North End	L	2-5	Jones, Simmons	4,612
24	Mar	3	A	Sunderland	L	1-3	Perry	10,490
25		10	H	Wolverhampton Wanderers	W	3-2	Simmons 2, Richards	6,680
26		19	H	Stoke	W	4-0	Jones, Brett, Chadburn, Simmons	1,717
27		24	A	Blackburn Rovers	L	0-2		5,026
28		31	H	Derby County	D	0-0		4,063
29	Apr	2	H	Blackburn Rovers	W	1-0	Roberts	3,342
30		7	A	Bury	L	0-1		2,978
31		14	H	Notts County	D	0-0		3,254
32		16	H	Nottingham Forest	W	8-0	Walker 3, Roberts 2, Simmons 2, Chadburn	5,187
33		21	A	Manchester City	L	0-4		9,960
34		24	A	Glossop	D	1-1	Simmons	2,025
								Appearances
								Goals

FA Cup

R1	Jan	27	A	Walsall	D	1-1	Roberts	9,106
rep	Feb	1	H	Walsall	W	6-1	Jones 2, Brett, Roberts, Richards, Simmons	4,892
R2		17	A	Liverpool	D	1-1	Simmons	15,116
rep		21	H	Liverpool	W	2-1	Dunn, Chadburn	8,994
R3		24	A	Southampton	L	1-2	Simmons	10,067
								Appearances
								Goals

Reader J	Cave GH	Williams W	Dunn A	Jones A	Banks J	Paddock JW	Perry T	Simmons C	Richards W	Garfield BW	Adams A	Hadley H	Walker WW	Gollings P	Roberts RJ	Brett SS	Chadburn J	Smith A	
1	2	3	4	5	6	7	8	9	10	11									1
1	2	3	4	5	6	7	8	9	10	11									2
1	2	3	4	5	6	7	8	9	10	11									3
1	2	3	4	5	6	7	8	9	10	11									4
1		3	4	5		7	8	9	10	11	2	6							5
1		3	4	5		7	8	9		11	2	6	10						6
1		3	4	5		7	8	9	10	11	2	6							7
1		3		5		7	8	9		11	2	6	10	4					8
1		3	4	5	6	7	8	9		11	2		10						9
1		3	4	5	6	7	8	9		11	2		10						10
1		3	4	5	6	7	8	9		11	2		10						11
1			5	3	6	7	4	8	9	11	2		10						12
1		3	6	5		7	4	8	9	11	2		10						13
1		3	5	2	6		4	8	9	11			10		7				14
1		3	4	5	6	7	8		9	11	2		10						15
1		3	6	5		7	4	8	9	11	2		10						16
1		3	4	5	6	7	8	9	10	11	2								17
1		3	5			7	8	9		11	2	4	10	6					18
1		3	5			7	8	9	10		2	4		6	11				19
1		3	5		6	7	8	9	10		2	4			11				20
1		3	5		6	7		9	10		2	4	8			11			21
1		3	4	5				9	10		2	6			11	8	7		22
1		3	4	5			8	9	10		2	6			11	7			23
1		3	4	5			8	9	10		2	6			11	7			24
1		3	4	5			8	9	10		2	6			11		7		25
1		3		5			4	9	10		2	6			11	8	7		26
1		3		5			4	9	10		2	6			11	8	7		27
1		3	8	5			4	9	10		2	6			11		7		28
1		3		5			4	9	10		2	6	8		11		7		29
1		3	4	5				9	10		2	6	8		11		7		30
1		3	4	5				9	8		2	6	10		11		7		31
1		3	4	5				9			2	6	10		11		7	8	32
1		3	4	5				9			2	6	10		11		7	8	33
1		3	4	5				9			2	6	10		11		7	8	34
4	4	33	30	30	13	20	27	33	25	18	29	21	18	3	16	6	11	3	
	1		2		1	3	12	6	7		1	3		3	2	2			

1		3	4	5			8	9	10		2	6			11	7			R1
1		3	4	5			8	9	10		2	6			11	7			rep
1		3	4	5			8	9	10		2	6			11		7		R2
1		3	4	5			8	9	10		2	6			11		7		rep
1		3	4	5			8	9	10		2	6			11		7		R3
5		5	5	5			5	5	5		5	5			5	2	3		
		1	2				3	1						2	1	1			

1900-01

Division One

	P	W	D	L	F	A	Pts
Liverpool	34	19	7	8	59	35	45
Sunderland	34	15	13	6	57	26	43
Notts County	34	18	4	12	54	46	40
Nottingham Forest	34	16	7	11	53	36	39
Bury	34	16	7	11	53	37	39
Newcastle United	34	14	10	10	42	37	38
Everton	34	16	5	13	55	42	37
Sheffield Wednesday	34	13	10	11	52	42	36
Blackburn Rovers	34	12	9	13	39	47	33
Bolton Wanderers	34	13	7	14	39	55	33
Manchester City	34	13	6	15	48	58	32
Derby County	34	12	7	15	55	42	31
Wolverhampton W	34	9	13	12	39	55	31
Sheffield United	34	12	7	15	35	52	31
Aston Villa	34	10	10	14	45	51	30
Stoke	34	11	5	18	46	57	27
Preston North End	34	9	7	18	49	75	25
West Bromwich Albion	34	7	8	19	35	62	22

Secretary-manager: Frank Heaven

- On 3 September 'Chippy' Simmons scored Albion's first goal at The Hawthorns, equalising Steve Bloomer's opener for Derby County.
- Albion went on to have an awful season, being relegated to the Second Division for the first time in their history, their fate sealed after a then record 19 League defeats, nine at home.
- Dick Roberts scored the first Albion hat-trick at The Hawthorns, versus Bolton Wanderers, in December.
- The lowest ever League attendance at The Hawthorns – 1,050 – saw the game with Sheffield United in April.
- Fred Buck (from Stafford Rangers), England international inside-forward Fred Wheldon (from Aston Villa), Jimmy McLean (from Walsall), Jim Stevenson (from Preston North End) and Arthur Randle (from Darlaston) were Albion's major signings this season.
- Retirements included full-back Billy Williams (through injury, aged 26) and Joe Reader (after spending 16 years with the club); Jack Banks and Billy Richards moved to Newton Heath (Manchester United), Archie Dunn joined Bristol Rovers and Abe Jones signed for Middlesbrough.

Match No.	Date			Opponents	Result		Scorers	Attendance
1	Sep	1	A	Wolverhampton Wanderers	D	0-0		12,000
2		3	H	Derby County	D	1-1	Simmons	20,104
3		8	H	Aston Villa	L	0-1		35,417
4		15	A	Liverpool	L	0-5		15,000
5		22	H	Newcastle United	L	0-1		11,859
6		29	A	Sheffield United	D	1-1	Simmons	10,000
7	Oct	6	H	Manchester City	W	3-2	Jones, Richards, Garfield	11,183
8		13	A	Bury	L	1-6	Simmons	7,000
9		20	H	Nottingham Forest	L	1-6	Adams	9,535
10		27	A	Blackburn Rovers	D	1-1	Smith	9,000
11	Nov	3	H	Stoke	D	2-2	Dunn, Garfield	11,052
12		5	H	Notts County	W	1-0	Chadburn	10,492
13		10	H	Sheffield Wednesday	D	1-1	Stevenson	10,338
14		17	A	Everton	L	0-1		20,000
15		24	H	Sunderland	W	1-0	Stevenson	10,045
16	Dec	1	A	Derby County	L	0-4		11,700
17		8	H	Bolton Wanderers	W	7-2	Banks, Roberts 3, Wheldon, Garfield, Buck	8,157
18		15	A	Notts County	L	0-1		6,500
19		22	H	Preston North End	L	0-1		7,997
20		29	H	Wolverhampton Wanderers	L	1-2	Simmons	18,188
21	Jan	5	A	Aston Villa	W	1-0	Simmons	30,000
22		19	A	Newcastle United	D	1-1	Garfield	10,500
23	Feb	16	H	Bury	L	1-2	Wheldon	9,691
24	Mar	2	H	Blackburn Rovers	D	1-1	Wheldon	11,876
25		9	A	Stoke	L	0-2		12,000
26		13	A	Nottingham Forest	W	3-2	Walker, Stevenson, Roberts	3,500
27		16	A	Sheffield Wednesday	L	1-2	Roberts	9,000
28		30	A	Sunderland	L	0-3		10,500
29	Apr	5	A	Manchester City	L	0-1		11,400
30		13	A	Bolton Wanderers	L	2-3	Adams (pen), Smith	5,536
31		15	A	Preston North End	W	3-2	Walker, Pickering, Perry	7,500
32		22	H	Everton	L	1-2	Pickering	6,992
33		29	H	Liverpool	L	0-1		8,974
34		30	H	Sheffield United	L	0-2		1,050
								Appearances
								Goals

FA Cup

R1	Feb	9	H	Manchester City	W	1-0	Garfield	10,026
R2		23	A	Woolwich Arsenal	W	1-0	Garfield	11,024
R3	Mar	23	A	Middlesbrough	W	1-0	Buck	24,769
SF	Apr	8	N	Tottenham Hotspur	L	0-4		34,979
								Appearances
								Goals

Reader J	Adams A	Williams W	Dunn A	Jones A	Hadley H	Chadburn J	Pickering TG	Simmons C	Wheldon GF	Roberts RJ	Gollings P	Walker WW	Garfield BW	Richards W	Banks J	Knowles JW	Perry T	Smith AW	Stevenson J	Williams GO	Lowe JA	Cave GH	Buck FR	
1	2	3	4	5	6	7	8	9	10	11														1
1	2	3	4	5	6	7	8	9	10	11														2
1	2	3	4	5	6	7	8	9	10	11														3
1	2	3	4	5	6	7	8	9	10	11														4
1	2	3	4	5	6	7	8	9	10	11														5
1	2		3	5	6	7		9	10		4	8	11											6
1	2		3	5	6	7			10		4	8	11	9										7
1	2		3	5	6	7		9	10			8	11		4									8
1	2	3	4	5	6	7			9			8	11			10								9
1	2	3		5	6	7			10			8	11				4	9						10
1	2	3	5		6	7			10			8	11				4		9					11
1	2		3		6	7		8	10				11				4		9	5				12
1	2		3		6			8	10	7			11				4		9	5				13
1	2		3		6	7		8	10	11					4				9	5				14
1	2		3	5	6	7		8	10	11									9	4				15
	2		3		6	7		8	10	11					4				9	5	1			16
1	2				6				10	7			11		4				9	5		3	8	17
1	3				6				10	7			11		4				9	5		2	8	18
1	2				6			8	10	7			11		4		3		9	5				19
1	2				6			10		7			11		4		3		9	5			8	20
1	2				6	3		8	10	7			11		4		5		9					21
1	2				6	3		8	10	7			11				4		9	5				22
1	2				6	3		8	10	7			11				4		9	5				23
1	2				6	3		8	10	7			11				4		9	5				24
1	2			5	6	3		8	10	7		11					4		9					25
1	2		3	5	6					7		11					4	10	9				8	26
1	2		3	5	6					7		11					4	10	9				8	27
1	2		3	5	6					7		11						10	9	4			8	28
1	2		3	5	6					7		11						10	9	4			8	29
1	2		3		6		8			7		11					4	10	9	5				30
1	2			5	6	3	8			7		11					4	10	9					31
1	2			5	6	3	8			7		11					4	10	9					32
1	2			5	6	3	8		10	7			11				4		9					33
1	2			5	6	3	8	9	10	7			11						4					34
33	34	8	20	20	34	24	10	20	26	27	2	14	18	1	8	1	17	8	24	15	1	2	7	
	2		1	1		1	2	5	3	5		2	4	1	1		1	2	3				1	

Reader J	Adams A	Williams W	Dunn A	Jones A	Hadley H	Chadburn J	Pickering TG	Simmons C	Wheldon GF	Roberts RJ	Gollings P	Walker WW	Garfield BW	Richards W	Banks J	Knowles JW	Perry T	Smith AW	Stevenson J	Williams GO	Lowe JA	Cave GH	Buck FR	
1	2				6	3		8	10	7			11				4		9	5				R1
1	2				6	3		8	10	7			11				4		9	5				R2
1	2		3	5	6					7		11					4	10	9				8	R3
1	2		3	5	6				10	7		11					4	8	9					SF
4	4		2	2	4	2		2	3	4		2	2				4	2	4	2			1	
												2										1		

1901-02

Division Two

	P	W	D	L	F	A	Pts
West Bromwich Albion	34	25	5	4	82	29	55
Middlesbrough	34	23	5	6	90	24	51
Preston North End	34	18	6	10	71	32	42
Woolwich Arsenal	34	18	6	10	50	26	42
Lincoln City	34	14	13	7	45	35	41
Bristol City	34	17	6	11	52	35	40
Doncaster Rovers	34	13	8	13	49	58	34
Glossop	34	10	12	12	36	40	32
Burnley	34	10	10	14	41	45	30
Burton United	34	11	8	15	46	54	30
Barnsley	34	12	6	16	51	63	30
Burslem Port Vale	34	10	9	15	43	59	29
Blackpool	34	11	7	16	40	56	29
Leicester Fosse	34	12	5	17	38	56	29
Newton Heath	34	11	6	17	38	53	28
Chesterfield	34	11	6	17	47	68	28
Stockport County	34	8	7	19	36	72	23
Gainsborough Trinity	34	4	11	19	30	80	19

Secretary-manager: Frank Heaven

- Albion regained their Division One place at the first attempt, going up as champions when establishing several new records including most wins (25), most goals scored (82) and most points gained (55).
- 'Chippy' Simmons became the first Albion player to score 20 goals in a League season when he netted the first of his three goals in the 7–2 home win over Blackpool.
- Activity in the transfer market saw Albion sign Dan Nurse and Tom Worton from Wolves, goalkeeper Ike Webb from Small Heath (Birmingham), Jack Kifford from Portsmouth winger Jimmy McLean from Walsall, centre-forward Billy Lee from Bournville Athletic and George Dorsett from Brownhills Albion. Out of the camp went Tom Perry to Villa Park (after 291 appearances) and Fred Wheldon to Southern League side Queen's Park Rangers.
- Albion met Arsenal, Blackpool, Middlesbrough and Port Vale for the first time in the Football League.
- The FA Cup semi-final between Derby County and Sheffield United was staged at The Hawthorns. A crowd of 33,603 witnessed the 1–1 draw.

Match No.	Date			Opponents	Result		Scorers	Attendance
1	Sep	2	H	Glossop	L	0-1		5,064
2		7	H	Preston North End	W	3-1	McLean, Garfield, Simmons	8,132
3		9	H	Chesterfield	W	4-0	Simmons 2 (1 pen), Worton, A. Smith	10,845
4		14	A	Burnley	D	0-0		4,992
5		21	H	Burslem Port Vale	W	3-1	Worton 2, A. Smith	5,096
6		28	A	Chesterfield	W	3-0	Hadley, Worton, Thacker (og)	3,201
7	Oct	5	H	Gainsborough Trinity	W	7-0	Worton 2, Simmons 2, McLean, A. Smith, Lee	5,368
8		12	A	Middlesbrough	W	2-1	Lee, Simmons	15,117
9		19	H	Bristol City	D	2-2	Lee, McLean	7,829
10		26	A	Blackpool	D	2-2	Nurse, Simmons	3,626
11	Nov	9	A	Newton Heath	W	2-1	Simmons 2	13,029
12		23	A	Doncaster Rovers	L	0-2		8,370
13	Dec	7	A	Burton United	W	3-1	Worton, Lee, Simmons	2,955
14		9	H	Lincoln City	W	4-1	Simons 2, Lee, Harper	6,224
15		14	H	Middlesbrough	W	2-0	Simmons, Lee	6,868
16		21	H	Barnsley	W	3-1	Worton 2, Simmons	5,577
17		26	H	Stockport County	W	3-0	Simmons, Lee 2	23,697
18		28	A	Leicester Fosse	W	3-0	Simmons 2, McLean	2,034
19	Jan	4	A	Preston North End	W	2-1	McLean, Lee	11,397
20		6	H	Leicester Fosse	W	1-0	Nurse	6,483
21		11	H	Burnley	W	3-0	Lee 2, Dorsett	9,149
22		18	A	Burslem Port Vale	W	3-2	Simmons, Lee, Worton	2,861
23	Feb	1	A	Gainsborough Trinity	D	1-1	Worton	2,016
24		15	A	Bristol City	W	2-1	Worton, Simmons	14,175
25		22	H	Blackpool	W	7-2	Kilford, Worton 2, Stevenson, Simmons 3	6,249
26	Mar	1	A	Stockport County	W	2-0	Lee, A. Smith	5,049
27		8	H	Newton Heath	W	4-0	Worton 3, McLean	10,206
28		15	A	Glossop	W	2-1	A. Smith, E. Smith	1,658
29		22	H	Doncaster Rovers	D	2-2	A. Smith, Worton	6,103
30		29	A	Lincoln City	L	0-1		4,460
31		31	A	Woolwich Arsenal	L	1-2	Worton	15,752
32	Apr	5	H	Burton United	W	2-1	Poynton, Buck	1,206
33		12	H	Woolwich Arsenal	W	2-1	Simmons, Lee	8,879
34		19	A	Barnsley	W	2-0	Poynton, Stevenson	4,014
							Appearances	
							Goals	

FA Cup

R1	Jan	25	A	Bury	L	1-5	Simmons	5,622
							Appearances	
							Goals	

Webb I	Adams A	Kifford J	Nurse DG	Stevenson J	Hadley H	McLean JC	Buck FR	Appleby B	Worton T	Walker WW	Simmons C	Smith AW	Garfield BW	Taylor O	Lee W	Williams GO	Randle AJ	Harper WE	Chadburn J	Dorsett G	Smith E	Poynton W	
1	2	3	4	5	6	7	8	9	10	11													1
1	3	2	4	5	6	7			10		8	9	11										2
	3	2	4	5	6	7			10		8	9	11	1									3
1	3	2	4	5	6	7			10		8	9	11										4
1	3	2	4	5	6	7			10		8	9	11										5
1	3	2	4	5	6	7			10		8	11			9								6
1	3	2	4	5	6	7			10		8	11			9								7
1	3	2	4	5	6	7			10		8	11			9								8
1	3	2	4	5	6	7			10		8	11			9								9
1	3	2	4	5		7			10		8	11			9	6							10
1	3	2	4	5		7			10		8				9		6	11					11
1	2		4	5	6	7			10		8				9			11	3				12
1	3	2	4	5	6	7			10		8				9			11					13
1	3	2	4	5	6	7			10		8				9			11					14
1	3	2	4	5	6	7			10		8				9			11					15
1		2	4	5	6	7			10		8				9			11	3				16
1		2	4	5	6	7			10		8				9			11	3				17
1		2	4	5	6	7			10	11	8				9				3				18
1	3	2	4	5	6	7			10		8				9					11			19
1	2		4	5	6	7			10		8				9				3	11			20
1	3	2	4	5	6	7			10		8				9					11			21
1	3	2	4	5	6	7			10		8				9					11			22
1	3	2	4	5	6	7			10		8				9					11			23
1	3	2	4	5	6	7			10		8				9					11			24
1	3	2	4	5	6	7			10		8				9					11			25
1	3	2	4	5	6	7			10			8			9					11			26
1	3	2	4	5	6	7			10			8			9					11			27
1	3	2	4	5	6	7			10			9								11	8		28
1	3	2	4	5	6	7			10			8			9					11			29
1	3	2	4	5	6	7			10		8				9					11			30
1	3	2	4	5	6	7			10		8				9					11			31
1	3	2	4	5	6		8		10						9					11		7	32
1	3	2	4	5	6	7			10		8				9					11			33
1	3	2	4	5	6				10		8				9					11		7	34
33	31	32	34	34	32	32	2	1	34	2	28	13	4	1	28	1	1	7	5	16	1	2	
		1	2	2	1	6	1		19	1	23	6	1		14					1	1	2	

One own-goal

1	3	2	4	5	6	7			10		8				9					11			R1
1	1	1	1	1	1	1			1		1				1					1			
											1												

1902-03

Division One

	P	W	D	L	F	A	Pts
Sheffield Wednesday	34	19	4	11	54	36	42
Aston Villa	34	19	3	12	61	40	41
Sunderland	34	16	9	9	51	36	41
Sheffield United	34	17	5	12	58	44	39
Liverpool	34	17	4	13	68	49	38
Stoke	34	15	7	12	46	38	37
West Bromwich Albion	34	16	4	14	54	53	36
Bury	34	16	3	15	54	43	35
Derby County	34	16	3	15	50	47	35
Nottingham Forest	34	14	7	13	49	47	35
Wolverhampton W	34	14	5	15	48	57	33
Everton	34	13	6	15	45	47	32
Middlesbrough	34	14	4	16	41	50	32
Newcastle United	34	14	4	16	41	51	32
Notts County	34	12	7	15	41	49	31
Blackburn Rovers	34	12	5	17	44	63	29
Grimsby Town	34	8	9	17	43	62	25
Bolton Wanderers	34	8	3	23	37	73	19

Secretary-manager: Fred Everiss

- Fred Everiss, initially engaged by Albion as an office junior in 1896, took over from Frank Heaven as secretary-manager, a position he would retain, unchallenged, until 1948.
- Harry Hadley became the first Albion player to win a full England cap in the 20th century when he starred against Ireland at Molineux in February.
- Full-back Jesse Pennington was signed from Dudley Town. He was to serve Albion for 19 years, during which time he would make almost 500 senior appearances, captaining the team and also leading his country (England).
- Players who left the club included Fred Buck (to Liverpool) and wingers Ben Garfield (to Brighton & Hove Albion) and Jimmy McLean (to Preston North End).

Match No.	Date			Opponents	Result		Scorers	Attendance
1	Sep	1	H	Everton	W	2-1	McLean, Simmons	16,051
2		6	A	Notts County	L	1-3	Kifford (pen)	12,339
3		13	H	Bolton Wanderers	W	2-1	Simmons, Dorsett	12,263
4		20	A	Middlesbrough	D	1-1	Blackett (og)	20,157
5		27	H	Newcastle United	W	6-1	Lee, Buck 2, Simmons, Stevenson, McLean	22,160
6	Oct	4	A	Wolverhampton Wanderers	W	2-1	Dorsett, Simmons	14,072
7		11	H	Liverpool	L	1-2	McLean	20,210
8		18	A	Sheffield United	W	2-1	Simmons 2	11,863
9		25	H	Grimsby Town	W	1-0	Lee	18,047
10	Nov	1	A	Aston Villa	W	3-0	Kifford 2 (1 pen), Lee	35,128
11		8	H	Nottingham Forest	W	2-0	Kifford (pen), Dorsett	12,612
12		15	A	Bury	W	2-1	Lee, Dorsett	13,498
13		22	H	Blackburn Rovers	W	5-3	Lee, Simmons, Kifford (pen), Stevenson, Worton	12,134
14		29	A	Sunderland	D	0-0		10,452
15	Dec	6	H	Stoke	W	2-1	McLean, Smith	11,235
16		13	A	Everton	L	1-3	Lee	14,854
17		20	H	Sheffield Wednesday	L	2-3	Simmons, Dorsett	14,560
18		27	A	Derby County	L	0-1		21,909
19	Jan	1	A	Liverpool	W	2-0	Dorsett, Lee	35,731
20		3	H	Notts County	W	3-2	Lee 2, Worton	16,785
21		10	A	Bolton Wanderers	W	1-0	Lee	15,442
22		17	H	Middlesbrough	W	1-0	Worton	18,033
23		24	A	Newcastle United	L	0-1		20,156
24		31	H	Wolverhampton Wanderers	D	2-2	Kifford (pen), Cole	26,081
25	Feb	14	H	Sheffield United	D	3-3	Stevenson, Dorsett, Elmore	17,122
26		28	H	Aston Villa	L	1-2	Buck	28,536
27	Mar	7	A	Nottingham Forest	L	1-3	Buck	7,052
28		21	A	Blackburn Rovers	L	0-1		10,354
29		28	H	Sunderland	L	0-3		10,517
30	Apr	4	A	Stoke	L	0-3		5,540
31		10	A	Grimsby Town	L	0-4		10,514
32		18	A	Sheffield Wednesday	L	1-3	Smith	19,000
33		20	H	Bury	L	1-3	Kifford (pen)	5,682
34		25	H	Derby County	W	3-0	Smith, Simmons, Farrington	4,148

Appearances

Goals

FA Cup

R1	Feb	7	A	Tottenham Hotspur	D	0-0		26,125
rep		11	H	Tottenham Hotspur	L	0-2		32,097

Appearances

Webb I	Kifford J	Adams A	Nurse DG	Stevenson J	Hadley H	McLean JC	Simmons C	Lee W	Worton T	Dorsett G	Smith AW	Buck FR	Randle AJ	Hobson AF	Smith E	Harper WE	Taylor O	Chadburn J	Cole JS	Elmore GV	Lowe JA	Smith WA	Brittain JW	Farrington GS	
1	2	3	4	5	6	7	8	9	10	11															1
1	2	3	4	5	6	7	8	9	10	11															2
1	2	3	4	5	6	7	8		10	11	9														3
1	2	3	4	5	6	7	8	9	10	11															4
1	2	3	4	5	6	7	8	9		11		10													5
1	2	3	4	5	6	7	8	9		11		10													6
1	2	3		5	6	7	8	9		11		10	4												7
1	2	3	4	5	6	7	8	9	10	11															8
1	2	3	4	5	6	7	8	9		11		10													9
1	2	3	4	5	6		8	9	10	11		7													10
1	2	3	4	5	6		8	9	10	11		7													11
1	2	3	4	5	6		8	9	10	11		7													12
1	2	3	4	5	6	7	8	9	10		11														13
1	2	3	4	5	6	7		9	10	11				8											14
1	2	3	4	5	6	7		9	10						8	11									15
1	2	3	4	5	6	7		9	10	11		8													16
1	2	3	4	5	6	7	8	9	10	11															17
1	2	3	4	5	6	7	8	9	10	11															18
	2	3	4	5	6	7	8	9	10	11							1								19
		3	4	5	6	7	8	9	10	11							1	2							20
1	2	3	4	5	6	7		9	10	11									8						21
1	2	3	4	5	6	7		9	10	11									8						22
1	2	3	4	5	6	7		9	10	11									8						23
1	2	3	4	5	6	7		9	10	11									8						24
1	2	3	4	5		7		9	10	11			6							8					25
1	2	3	4	5	6	7	8	9		11		10													26
1	2	3	4	5			8	9	10	11		7	6												27
1	2	3	4	5	6	7		9	10	11										8					28
1	2	3	4	5	6	7		9	10	11		8													29
	2	3	4	5	6			9	10	11		8					1			7					30
	2	3	4	5	6		8	9	10	11		7					1								31
	2		4	5	6		8	9		11					10			3			1	7			32
	2		4	5	6		8	9		11					10			3			1	7			33
	2			5	6		8			11			4		10						1	7	3	9	34
27	33	31	32	34	32	25	23	32	26	32	2	13	4	1	4	1	4	3	4	3	3	3	1	1	
	7			3		4	9	10	3	7		4			3				1	1				1	

One own-goal

1	2	3	4	5	6	7		9	10	11		8													R1
1	2	3	4	5	6	7		9	10	11										8					rep
2	2	2	2	2	2	2		2	2	2		1								1					

1903-04

Division One

	P	W	D	L	F	A	Pts
Sheffield Wednesday	34	20	7	7	48	28	47
Manchester City	34	19	6	9	71	45	44
Everton	34	19	5	10	59	32	43
Newcastle United	34	18	6	10	58	45	42
Aston Villa	34	17	7	10	70	48	41
Sunderland	34	17	5	12	63	49	39
Sheffield United	34	15	8	11	62	57	38
Wolverhampton W	34	14	8	12	44	66	36
Nottingham Forest	34	11	9	14	57	57	31
Middlesbrough	34	9	12	13	46	47	30
Small Heath	34	11	8	15	39	52	30
Bury	34	7	15	12	40	53	29
Notts County	34	12	5	17	37	61	29
Derby County	34	9	10	15	58	60	28
Blackburn Rovers	34	11	6	17	48	60	28
Stoke	34	10	7	17	54	57	27
Liverpool	34	9	8	17	49	62	26
West Bromwich Albion	34	7	10	17	36	60	24

Secretary-manager: Fred Everiss

- Jesse Pennington made his League debut against Liverpool in September. Other players who had their first outings for the club were three Harrys, Aston, Brown, and Clements, goalkeeper Fred Cook and forwards Fred Fenton, amateur Billy Folks and Alf Owen.
- 'Chippy' Simmons was transferred to West Ham United but was to return to The Hawthorns within a year, and Jim Stevenson signed for Dumbarton after 129 appearances.

Match No.	Date			Opponents	Result		Scorers	Attendance
1	Sep	2	H	Sheffield Wednesday	L	0-1		8,995
2		5	H	Newcastle United	L	1-2	Nurse	10,352
3		12	A	Aston Villa	L	1-3	Simmons	38,920
4		19	H	Middlesbrough	D	0-0		14,130
5		26	A	Liverpool	W	3-1	Simmons, Hobson, Dorsett	15,578
6	Oct	3	H	Bury	W	3-2	Hobson 2, Cole	14,381
7		10	A	Blackburn Rovers	L	0-2		10,057
8		17	H	Nottingham Forest	D	1-1	Stevenson	14,276
9		24	A	Sheffield Wednesday	L	0-1		12,000
10		31	H	Sunderland	D	1-1	Worton	10,128
11	Nov	7	A	Wolverhampton Wanderers	L	0-1		12,431
12		14	A	Small Heath	W	1-0	Nurse	12,563
13		21	H	Everton	D	0-0		10,190
14		28	A	Stoke	L	0-5		3,724
15	Dec	12	A	Manchester City	L	3-6	Fenton, Simmons, Dorsett	14,471
16		14	H	Derby County	D	0-0		13,525
17		19	H	Notts County	D	0-0		8,188
18		26	A	Sheffield United	L	0-4		10,227
19		28	H	Blackburn Rovers	W	2-1	Brown, Simmons	19,554
20	Jan	2	A	Newcastle United	L	0-1		13,376
21		9	H	Aston Villa	L	1-3	Simmons	31,418
22		16	A	Middlesbrough	D	2-2	Hobson, Dorsett	18,021
23		23	H	Liverpool	D	2-2	Randle, A. Smith	10,740
24		30	A	Bury	L	1-2	Adams	7,193
25	Feb	20	A	Notts County	W	3-2	Brown, Lee, Dorsett	5,991
26		27	A	Sunderland	D	1-1	W.A. Smith	5,632
27	Mar	5	H	Wolverhampton Wanderers	L	1-2	Dorsett	6,338
28		12	H	Small Heath	L	0-1		22,760
29		26	H	Stoke	W	3-0	Simmons, Dorsett, Brown	8,107
30		30	A	Nottingham Forest	L	0-2		2,624
31	Apr	2	A	Derby County	L	2-4	Simmons 2	18,140
32		9	H	Manchester City	W	2-1	Aston, Owen	7,508
33		18	A	Everton	L	0-4		12,025
34		23	H	Sheffield United	D	2-2	Cole, Dorsett (pen)	4,467
								Appearances
								Goals

FA Cup

R1	Feb	10	H	Nottingham Forest	D	1-1	Simmons	10,367
rep		13	A	Nottingham Forest	L	1-3	A. Smith	15,084
								Appearances
								Goals

Webb I	Kifford J	Adams A	Nurse DG	Stevenson J	Hadley H	Smith WA	Simmons C	Lee W	Smith E	Dorsett G	Clements HW	Worton T	Pennington J	Hobson AF	Cole JS	Cook CFW	Fenton F	Brown H	Randle AJ	Smith A	Corfield S	Owen AG	Aston JH	Folks WT	
1	2	3	4	5	6	7	8	9	10	11															1
1	2	3	4	5	6	7	8	9	10	11															2
1	2	3	4	5	6		8	9		11	7	10													3
1	2	3	4	5	6		8	9		11	7	10													4
1		2	4	5	6		8			11	7	10	3	9											5
1		2	4	5	6					11	7	10	3	9	8										6
1		2	4	5	6					11	7	10	3	9	8										7
1		2	4	5	6		8			11	7	10	3	9											8
1		2	4	5	6		8			11	7	10	3	9											9
1		2	4	5	6		8			11	7	10	3	9											10
1		2	4	5	6		8			11	7	10	3	9											11
		2	4	5	6		8			11		10	3		9	1	7								12
		2	4	5	6		8			11		10	3			1	7	9							13
		2	4	5	6		8			11	7	10	3			1		9							14
		2	4	5	6		8		10	7			3			1	11	9							15
		2		5	6		8		10	7			3			1	11	9	4						16
		2	4	5	6		8		10	7			3			1	11	9							17
	2		4	5	6	9				7			3	10		1	11	8							18
	2			5	6		8			11			3	9		1		10	4	7					19
1	2			5	6		8			11			3	9				10	4	7					20
1	2			5	6		8			11			3	9				10	4	7					21
1	2	3			6		8			11				9				10	4	7	5				22
1		2		5	6		8	9		11			3					10	4	7					23
1		2		5	6			9		11			3		8			10	4	7					24
1	2	3			6	7	8	9		11								10	4		5				25
1	2	3			6	7	8	9		11								10	4		5				26
1	2	3	4			7		9		11								10	6	8	5				27
1	2		4			7	8	9		11			3					10	6		5				28
1	2	3		9	6		8			11								10	4		5	7			29
1	2	3		9	6		8	10		11									4	7	5				30
1	2	3		5	6		8			11								10	4			7	9		31
	2	3		5	6		8			11						1		10	4			7	9		32
	2	3		5	6		8			11						1		10	4			7	9		33
	2	3			6					11					8	1		10	4		5		9	7	34
23	19	29	19	28	32	7	28	11	5	34	10	12	20	12	5	11	6	21	17	8	8	4	4	1	
		1	2	1		1	8	1		7		1		4	2		1	3	1	1		1	1		

Webb I	Kifford J	Adams A	Nurse DG	Stevenson J	Hadley H	Smith WA	Simmons C	Lee W	Smith E	Dorsett G	Clements HW	Worton T	Pennington J	Hobson AF	Cole JS	Cook CFW	Fenton F	Brown H	Randle AJ	Smith A	Corfield S	Owen AG	Aston JH	Folks WT	
1		2		5	6		8	9		11			3	10					4	7					R1
1		2		5	6		8	9		11			3	10					4	7					rep
2		2		2	2		2	2		2			2	2					2	2					
							1													1					

1904-05

Division Two

	P	W	D	L	F	A	Pts
Liverpool	34	27	4	3	93	25	58
Bolton Wanderers	34	27	2	5	87	32	56
Manchester United	34	24	5	5	81	30	53
Bristol City	34	19	4	11	66	45	42
Chesterfield	34	14	11	9	44	35	39
Gainsborough Trinity	34	14	8	12	61	58	36
Barnsley	34	14	5	15	38	56	33
Bradford City	34	12	8	14	45	49	32
Lincoln City	34	12	7	15	42	40	31
West Bromwich Albion	34	13	4	17	56	48	30
Burnley	34	12	6	16	43	52	30
Glossop	34	10	10	14	37	46	30
Grimsby Town	34	11	8	15	33	46	30
Leicester Fosse	34	11	7	16	40	55	29
Blackpool	34	9	10	15	36	48	28
Burslem Port Vale	34	10	7	17	47	72	27
Burton United	34	8	4	22	30	84	20
Doncaster Rovers	34	3	2	29	23	81	8

Secretary-manager: Fred Everiss

- Albert Lewis, signed from Stafford Rangers, scored a hat-trick on his League debut against Burnley on the opening day of the season.
- Other debutants included two ex-Wolves players, goalkeeper Jim Stringer and centre-half Ted 'Cock' Pheasant, wing-half Jack Manners (formerly of Morpeth Harriers) and centre-forward Fred Shinton, signed from Hednesford Town.
- Among the players who left The Hawthorns were George Dorsett (to Manchester City), Harry Hadley (to Aston Villa), Jack Kifford (to Millwall), Billy Lee (to Portsmouth) and Ike Webb (to Sunderland). Tom Worton and Dan Nurse both retired through injury. The latter became a director of the club in 1910, retaining his position until 1927.

Match No.	Date			Opponents	Result		Scorers	Attendance
1	Sep	3	A	Burnley	W	4-1	Lewis 3, Dorsett	5,389
2		10	H	Grimsby Town	L	0-2		4,123
3		17	A	Blackpool	D	0-0		3,852
4		24	H	Doncaster Rovers	W	6-1	Dorsett 3, Lewis, Jack 2	5,261
5	Oct	1	A	Gainsborough Trinity	L	2-4	Jack, Aston	4,523
6		8	H	Burton United	W	4-0	Dorsett 3 (1 pen), Bell	4,873
7		15	A	Liverpool	L	2-3	Jack, Brown	16,147
8		29	A	Bristol City	L	1-2	Jack	10,795
9	Nov	5	H	Manchester United	L	0-2		5,578
10		7	H	Blackpool	W	4-2	Aston, Pheasant, Manners, Birkett (og)	4,951
11		19	H	Chesterfield	L	0-2		3,753
12		26	A	Bradford City	L	1-3	Aston	11,854
13	Dec	3	H	Lincoln City	W	2-0	Smith, Davies	3,124
14		15	A	Leicester Fosse	L	1-3	Aston	7,890
15		17	H	Barnsley	W	4-1	Aston, Smith, Brown, Pheasant (pen)	2,675
16		24	A	Bolton Wanderers	L	1-2	Bell	7,341
17		26	H	Burslem Port Vale	L	0-1		7,166
18		31	H	Burnley	D	1-1	Aston	7,374
19	Jan	7	A	Grimsby Town	W	3-1	Pheasant, Bell, Aston	6,105
20		21	A	Doncaster Rovers	W	1-0	Bell	4,761
21		28	H	Gainsborough Trinity	W	4-3	Jack, Bell 2, Aston	2,072
22	Feb	11	H	Liverpool	L	0-2		8,788
23		18	A	Burslem Port Vale	L	2-3	Jack 2	3,550
24		25	H	Bristol City	D	0-0		4,172
25	Mar	4	A	Manchester United	L	0-2		9,950
26		7	A	Glossop	L	1-2	Jack	2,765
27		11	H	Glossop	W	1-0	Lewis	3,547
28		18	A	Chesterfield	L	0-1		3,568
29		25	H	Bradford City	L	0-2		2,366
30	Apr	1	A	Lincoln City	W	2-0	Jack 2	4,138
31		8	H	Leicester Fosse	W	2-0	Pheasant 2	3,104
32		15	A	Barnsley	D	1-1	Haycock	5,661
33		21	A	Burton United	W	6-0	Williams, Jack 2, Lewis, Pheasant, Haycock	2,820
34		22	H	Bolton Wanderers	L	0-1		10,105

Appearances

Goals

FA Cup

IR	Jan	14	H	Leicester Fosse	L	2-5	Aston, Pheasant	5,230

Appearances

Goals

Webb I	Kifford J	Adams A	Randle AJ	Manners JA	Hadley H	Bell SLT	Jack WR	Brown H	Lewis AE	Dorsett G	Pennington J	Davies A	Bowden JW	Aston JH	Millar J	Edwards SH	Pheasant E	Davies LC	Smith WA	Cook CFW	Dawes J	Brittain JW	Turner SI	Owen AG	Haycock FJ	Bradley CH	Bamford JAE	Burton EC	Haywood T	Williams J	Stringer J	Shinton F	
1	2	3	4	5	6	7	8	9	10	11																							1
1	2	3	4	5	6	7	8	9	10	11																							2
1		2	4	5	6	9		8	10	11	3	7																					3
1	2	3	4	6			8		10	11		7	5	9																			4
1	2	3	4	6			8		10	11		7	5	9																			5
1		2	4	6		8			10	11	3	7	5		9																		6
1		2	4		6		8	9	10	11	3	7	5																				7
1		2	6				8	9	10	11	3	7	5			4																	8
1		2	4	6				8	10	11	3	7		9			5																9
1		2	4	6		8		10		11		7		9			5	3															10
1	2		4					10		11	3	7		9			5	6	8														11
1	2		4	6				10		11	3	7		9			5		8														12
1			4	6			2	10		11	3	7		9			5		8														13
			4	6		7	8	10	11		2			9			5	3		1													14
			4	6			2	10			3	7		9			5		8	1	11												15
			4	11		7		10			2		6	9			5		8	1		3											16
			4	11		7					2		6	9			5		8	1		3	10										17
			4	6			10		11		2			9			5			1		3		7	8								18
			4	6		7	9		11		2			10			5		8	1		3											19
	2	3	4	6		7		10	11				5	9					8	1													20
	2	3	4	6		7	10		11					9			5		8	1													21
	2	3	4	6		7	10		11					9			5		8	1													22
	2	3	4	6		7	10		11					9			5		8	1													23
	2	3	4	6		7	10		11					9			5			1						8							24
	2	3	4	6			10		11					9			5			1				7		8							25
		2	4	6			10		11		3			9			5			1				7		8							26
		2	4	6		7	8		10		3			9			5			1							11						27
		2	4	6		9	8		10		3						5			1							11	7					28
		2		6			9		10		3						5			1					8		11		4	7			29
		2	4	6			10		11		3						9			1					8				5	7			30
		2	4	6			10		11		3						9								8				5	7	1		31
		2	4	6			10		11		3						9								8				5	7	1		32
		2	4	6			10		11		3						9								8				5	7	1		33
		2	4	6			10		11		3														8				5	7	1	9	34
13	12	25	33	31	4	16	25	14	27	13	23	12	8	21	1	1	24	3	11	17	1	4	1	3	7	3	3	1	6	6	4	1	
				1		6	13	2	6	7		1		8			6		2						2					1			

One own-goal

			4	6		7	9	11			2			10			5		8	1		3											IR
			1	1		1	1	1			1			1			1		1	1		1											
														1			1																

1905-06

Division Two

	P	W	D	L	F	A	Pts
Bristol City	38	30	6	2	83	28	66
Manchester United	38	28	6	4	90	28	62
Chelsea	38	22	9	7	90	37	53
West Bromwich Albion	38	22	8	8	79	36	52
Hull City	38	19	6	13	67	54	44
Leeds City	38	17	9	12	59	47	43
Leicester Fosse	38	15	12	11	53	48	42
Grimsby Town	38	15	10	13	46	46	40
Burnley	38	15	8	15	42	53	38
Stockport County	38	13	9	16	44	56	35
Bradford City	38	13	8	17	46	60	34
Barnsley	38	12	9	17	60	62	33
Lincoln City	38	12	6	20	69	72	30
Blackpool	38	10	9	19	37	62	29
Gainsborough Trinity	38	12	4	22	44	57	28
Glossop	38	10	8	20	49	71	28
Burslem Port Vale	38	12	4	22	49	82	28
Chesterfield	38	10	8	20	40	72	28
Burton United	38	10	6	22	34	67	26
Clapton Orient	38	7	7	24	35	78	21

Secretary-manager: Fred Everiss

- Albion produced their first ever official matchday programme: *The Albion News*. Around 5,000 copies were printed for the home League game with Burnley at the start of the season.
- 'Chippy' Simmons was re-signed from West Ham, Fred Buck returned to the club via Liverpool and Plymouth Argyle and goalkeeper Hubert Pearson was recruited from Tamworth Athletic.
- Albion opposed Chelsea for the first time in the Football League.

Match No.	Date			Opponents	Result		Scorers	Attendance
1	Sep	2	H	Burnley	L	1-2	Shinton	7,223
2		9	A	Leeds City	W	2-0	Haycock 2	6,802
3		16	H	Burton United	W	3-0	Simmons, Shinton, Haycock	6,500
4		23	A	Chelsea	L	0-1		10,123
5		30	H	Gainsborough Trinity	W	4-0	Haycock, A. Haywood 2, Shinton	5,300
6	Oct	7	A	Bristol City	L	0-1		8,000
7		14	H	Manchester United	W	1-0	A. Haywood	7,024
8		21	A	Glossop	W	3-1	Shinton, A. Haywood 2	5,000
9		28	H	Stockport County	W	3-1	A. Haywood, Pheasant (pen), Shinton	8,200
10	Nov	4	A	Blackpool	W	3-0	Peters, Shinton, Simmons	5,000
11		11	H	Bradford City	W	6-1	Shinton 3, A. Haywood, Simmons 2	9,000
12		25	A	Leicester Fosse	D	0-0		6,500
13	Dec	2	H	Hull City	D	1-1	Pheasant (pen)	11,203
14		9	A	Lincoln City	W	2-1	Pheasant, A. Haywood	4,000
15		16	H	Chesterfield	W	3-0	A. Haywood, Simmons, Shinton	12,554
16		23	A	Burslem Port Vale	W	1-0	Simmons	3,500
17		25	H	Clapton Orient	D	1-1	Simmons	18,048
18		26	H	Barnsley	W	5-3	Simmons 3, Shinton 2	23,021
19		30	A	Burnley	W	2-0	Simmons, Shinton	6,500
20	Jan	6	H	Leeds City	W	2-1	A. Haywood, Pheasant (pen)	2,553
21		20	A	Burton United	D	2-2	Bradley, Shinton	4,000
22		27	H	Chelsea	D	1-1	Manners	5,000
23	Feb	3	A	Grimsby Town	L	2-3	A. Haywood, Simmons	5,100
24		10	H	Bristol City	L	1-3	Pheasant (pen)	6,400
25		17	A	Manchester United	D	0-0		8,000
26		24	H	Glossop	W	6-0	Rankin, Bradley, Simmons 2, Pheasant (pen), A. Haywood	7,200
27	Mar	3	A	Stockport County	D	2-2	Manners, Perkins	4,000
28		10	H	Blackpool	W	5-0	Simmons 2, A. Haywood 2, Bradley	6,500
29		17	A	Bradford City	W	1-0	A. Haywood	5,106
30		24	H	Grimsby Town	W	2-0	Rankin, Pheasant	7,500
31		31	H	Leicester Fosse	W	3-0	Shinton, Haycock 2	10,067
32	Apr	7	A	Hull City	L	0-4		9,033
33		13	A	Barnsley	L	0-3		3,120
34		14	H	Lincoln City	D	1-1	A. Haywood	6,000
35		16	A	Clapton Orient	W	2-0	Shinton, A. Haywood 2	3,517
36		18	A	Gainsborough Trinity	L	1-2	A. Haywood	4,223
37		21	A	Chesterfield	W	3-0	Manners, A. Haywood, Shinton	5,558
38		28	H	Burslem Port Vale	W	4-1	Pheasant (pen), Shinton, A. Haywood 2	4,800
								Appearances
								Goals

FA Cup

R1	Jan	13	A	Everton	L	1-3	A. Haywood	18,023
								Appearances
								Goals

Stringer J	Young G	Pennington J	Randle AJ	Pheasant E	Manners JA	Williams J	Simmons C	Shinton F	Haywood A	Perkins EE	Haycock FJ	Adams A	Haywood T	Peters S	Varney H	Brittain JW	Nicholls F	Law WD	Bradley EJ	Lewis AE	Rankin B	Dilly T	Picken T	Buck FR	
1	2	3	4	5	6	7	8	9	10	11															1
1	2	3	4	5	6		8	9	10	11	7														2
1	2	3	4	5	6		8	9	10	11	7														3
1	2	3	4	5	6		8	9	10	11	7														4
1		3		5	6		8	9	10	11	7	2	4												5
1	2	3	6	5			8	9	10	11	7		4												6
1	2	3	6	5			8	9	10	11				4	7										7
1	2	3	6	5			8	9	10	11				4	7										8
1	2	3	6	5			8	9	10	11				4	7										9
1	2	3	6	5			8	9	10	11				4	7										10
1	2	3	6	5			8	9	10	11				4	7										11
1			4	5	6		8	9	10	11		2				3	7								12
1			4	5	6		8	9	10			2				3	7	11							13
1	2		4	5	6		8	9	10			3					7	11							14
1		3	4	5	6		8	9	10			2					7	11							15
1	2	3	4	5	6		8	9	10								7	11							16
1	2	3	4	5	6		8	9	10								7	11							17
1	2	3	4	5	6		8	9	10								7	11							18
1		3	4	5	6	2	8	9	10									11	7						19
1		3	4	5	6	2	8	9	10									11	7						20
1		3	4	5	6	2	8	9										11	7	10					21
1		3	4	5	6	2	8	9	10									11	7						22
1		3	4	5	6	2	8	9	10	11									7						23
1		3	4	5	6	2	8		10	11									9		7				24
1		3	4	5	6	2	8		10	11									9		7				25
1		3	4	5	6	2	8		10	11									9		7				26
1		3	4	5	6	2	8		10	11									9		7				27
1		3	4	5	6		8		10	11		2							9		7				28
1		3	4	5	6		8		10	11		2							9		7				29
1		3	4	5	6		8		10	11		2							9		7				30
1		3	4	5	6			9	10		8	2									7	11			31
1		3	4	5	6			9	10		8	2									7	11			32
1	2		4	5	6			9	10		8	3									7	11			33
1	2		4	5	6			9	8			3								10	7	11			34
1			4	5	6			9	10			2				3			8		7	11			35
1				5	6			9	10			2		4		3			8		7	11			36
		3	4	5	6			9	10			2							8		7	11	1		37
		3	4	5	6			9	10			2									7	11	1	8	38
36	16	31	36	38	32	10	30	31	37	20	8	16	2	6	5	4	7	10	15	2	15	8	2	1	
				8	3		16	18	21	1	6			1					3		2				

1		3	4	5	6	2	8	9	10									11	7						R1
1		1	1	1	1	1	1	1	1									1	1						
									1																

1906-07

Division Two

	P	W	D	L	F	A	Pts
Nottingham Forest	38	28	4	6	74	36	60
Chelsea	38	26	5	7	80	34	57
Leicester Fosse	38	20	8	10	62	39	48
West Bromwich Albion	38	21	5	12	83	45	47
Bradford City	38	21	5	12	70	53	47
Wolverhampton W	38	17	7	14	66	53	41
Burnley	38	17	6	15	62	47	40
Barnsley	38	15	8	15	73	55	38
Hull City	38	15	7	16	65	57	37
Leeds City	38	13	10	15	55	63	36
Grimsby Town	38	16	3	19	57	62	35
Stockport County	38	12	11	15	42	52	35
Blackpool	38	11	11	16	33	51	33
Gainsborough Trinity	38	14	5	19	45	72	33
Glossop	38	13	6	19	53	79	32
Burslem Port Vale	38	12	7	19	60	83	31
Clapton Orient	38	11	8	19	45	67	30
Chesterfield	38	11	7	20	50	66	29
Lincoln City	38	12	4	22	46	73	28
Burton United	38	8	7	23	34	68	23

Secretary-manager: Fred Everiss

- Jesse Pennington won the first of 25 full caps for England, partnering Blackburn Rovers' Bob Crompton against Wales at Craven Cottage.
- Dick Betteley was signed from Wolves to partner Pennington in Albion's defence. And besides Betteley, seven other players made their Albion debuts: Dick Bourne, Tommy Broad (against Wolves), goalkeeper Harry Jones, amateur centre-forward Willie Jordan, who celebrated by becoming the first player to score a hat-trick in his first game at The Hawthorns against Gainsborough Trinity, Sammy Legge, who also netted a debut goal against Nottingham Forest, Harry Parkes and Sammy Timmins.
- Winger Bruce Rankin was transferred to Manchester City.
- 'Cock' Pheasant took over the captaincy from Amos Adams.

Match No.	Date		Venue	Opponents	Result		Scorers	Attendance
1	Sep	1	A	Burnley	W	1-0	Buck	7,500
2		8	H	Leeds City	W	5-0	Shinton 2, Buck 2, Pheasant	15,500
3		10	A	Burslem Port Vale	L	1-2	Shinton	5,500
4		15	A	Barnsley	W	1-0	Shinton	6,000
5		22	H	Chelsea	L	1-2	Haywood	25,562
6		29	A	Wolverhampton Wanderers	W	3-0	Shinton, Haywood, Buck	25,000
7	Oct	6	H	Clapton Orient	W	5-0	Shinton 4, Buck	10,482
8		13	A	Gainsborough Trinity	W	4-2	Shinton 3, Buck	3,500
9		20	H	Stockport County	D	1-1	Buck (pen)	12,300
10		27	A	Hull City	W	1-0	Buck	6,140
11	Nov	3	H	Glossop	W	5-1	Shinton 4, Buck	13,000
12		10	A	Blackpool	L	1-2	Pheasant	5,772
13		17	H	Bradford City	W	3-0	Buck 3	9,000
14		24	H	Chesterfield	W	5-2	Rankin, Dilly 3, Shinton	11,335
15	Dec	1	A	Leicester Fosse	L	0-3		19,820
16		8	H	Nottingham Forest	W	3-1	Rankin, Shinton, Legge	17,000
17		15	A	Lincoln City	L	1-2	Haywood	5,240
18		22	H	Burton United	W	5-1	Legge, Simmons 2, Shinton 2	5,300
19		25	H	Grimsby Town	W	6-1	Dilly, Haywood, Shinton 4	19,047
20		26	H	Burslem Port Vale	W	3-0	Rankin, Dilly, Shinton	17,000
21		29	H	Burnley	W	3-2	Dilly (pen), Shinton, Legge	12,000
22	Jan	5	A	Leeds City	L	2-3	Shinton 2	10,330
23		26	A	Chelsea	L	0-2		41,168
24	Feb	9	A	Clapton Orient	D	1-1	Dilly	3,700
25		16	H	Gainsborough Trinity	W	5-0	Buck 2, Jordan 3	8,112
26	Mar	2	H	Hull City	W	3-0	Jordon 2, Buck	10,130
27		16	H	Blackpool	W	3-0	Buck 2, Jordan	5,500
28		29	A	Grimsby Town	L	1-2	Jordan	8,202
29		30	A	Chesterfield	D	2-2	Bradley, Buck	8,000
30	Apr	1	H	Wolverhampton Wanderers	D	1-1	Buck	22,000
31		6	H	Leicester Fosse	L	0-1		5,034
32		8	A	Stockport County	W	1-0	Parkes	5,623
33		13	A	Nottingham Forest	L	1-3	Bradley	7,174
34		16	A	Glossop	D	0-0		3,121
35		20	H	Lincoln City	W	2-1	Parkes, Bourne	6,995
36		23	A	Bradford City	L	0-4		6,220
37		25	H	Barnsley	W	3-1	Parkes, Jordan, Buck	5,100
38		27	A	Burton United	L	0-2		3,580

Appearances

Goals

FA Cup

R1	Jan	12	H	Stoke	D	1-1	Broad	32,232
rep		17	A	Stoke	D	2-2*	Rankin, Randle	13,545
rep2		21	H	Stoke	W	2-0	Pheasant, Dilly (pen)	32,050
R2	Feb	2	H	Norwich City	W	1-0	Simmons	25,388
R3		23	H	Derby County	W	2-0	Jordan, Buck	35,529
R4	Mar	9	H	Notts County	W	3-1	Jordan 2, Buck	27,474
SF		23	N	Everton	L	1-2	A. Haywood	32,381

R1 replay 2 at Villa Park, Birmingham

SF at Burnden Park, Bolton

* after extra-time

Appearances

Goals

Match	Stringer J	Betteley RH	Pennington J	Randle AJ	Pheasant E	Manners JA	Rankin B	Buck FR	Shinton F	Haywood A	Dilly T	Perkins EE	Broad TH	Simmons C	Timmins S	Haywood T	Legge SG	Williams J	Jones H	Bradley EJ	Jordan WC	Bourne RA	Parkes HA	Adams A
1	1	2	3	4	5	6	7	8	9	10	11													
2	1	2	3	4	5	6	7	8	9	10	11													
3	1	2	3	4	5	6	7	8	9	10	11													
4	1	2	3	4	5	6	7	8	9	10		11												
5	1	2	3	4	5	6	7	8	9	10		11												
6	1	2	3	4	5	6		8	9	10		11	7											
7	1	2	3	4	5	6		8	9			11	7	10										
8	1	2	3	4	5	6		8	9		10	11	7											
9	1	2	3	4	5	6		8	9	10		11	7											
10	1	2	3	4	5	6		8	9	10		11	7											
11	1	2	3	4	5	6		8	9	10		11	7											
12	1	2	3	4	5			8	9	10		11	7		6									
13	1	2	3	4				8	9		10	11	7		6	5								
14	1	2	3	4			7	8	9		10	11			6	5								
15	1	2	3	4			7	8	9		10	11			6	5								
16	1	2	3	4	5		7	8	9	10					6		11							
17	1	2	3	4			7		9	10				8	6		11	5						
18	1	2	3	4	5		7		9	10				8	6		11							
19	1	2	3	4	5		7		9	8	10				6		11							
20		2	3	4	5		7		9	8	10				6		11		1					
21		2	3	4	5		7		9	8	10				6		11		1					
22	1	2	3	4	5			7	9	8	10				6		11							
23	1	2	3	4	5	6	11	8			10		7							9				
24	1	2	3	4	5	6			9		10	11	7	8										
25	1	2	3	4	5	6		8			10							7			9	11		
26	1	3		4	5	6		8		10	11		7					2			9			
27	1		3	4				8		10	11				6			2		5	9		7	
28	1		3	4	5	6		8	9									2			10	11	7	
29	1		3	4				8	9	10					6					5		11	7	2
30	1		3	4	5	6		8		10											9	11	7	2
31	1			4	5	6		8		10	11				3						9		7	2
32	1			4		6		8		10					3					5	9	11	7	2
33	1		3	4		6		8	9		11				2					5	10		7	
34	1		3	4		6		8	9		11				2	10				5			7	
35	1			4		6		8						10	3	5					9	11	7	2
36	1		3	4		6		8	9	10					2	5						11	7	
37	1		3	4		6		8	10		11					5					9		7	2
38	1			4		6		8	9		11			10	3					5			7	2
	36	26	33	38	25	25	14	32	30	24	21	13	11	6	20	7	7	5	2	7	10	7	12	7
					2		3	20	28	4	7			2			3			2	8	1	3	

Round	Stringer J	Betteley RH	Pennington J	Randle AJ	Pheasant E	Manners JA	Rankin B	Buck FR	Shinton F	Haywood A	Dilly T	Perkins EE	Broad TH	Simmons C	Timmins S	Haywood T	Legge SG	Williams J	Jones H	Bradley EJ	Jordan WC	Bourne RA	Parkes HA	Adams A
R1	1	2	3	4	5			8	9	10	11		7		6									
rep	1	2	3	4	5	6	11	8	9		10		7											
rep2	1		3	4	5	6	11	8			10		7							9				2
R2	1	2	3	4	5	6			9		10	11	7	8										
R3	1	2	3	4	5	6		8		10	11							7			9			
R4	1		3	4	5	6		8		10	11							2			9		7	
SF	1		3	4	5	6		8		10	11							2			9		7	
	7	4	7	7	7	6	2	6	3	4	7	1	4	1	1	0	0	3	0	1	3	0	2	1
				1			1	2		1	1	1	1	1							3			

1907-08

Division Two

	P	W	D	L	F	A	Pts
Bradford City	38	24	6	8	90	42	54
Leicester Fosse	38	21	10	7	72	47	52
Oldham Athletic	38	22	6	10	76	42	50
Fulham	38	22	5	11	82	49	49
West Bromwich Albion	38	19	9	10	61	39	47
Derby County	38	21	4	13	77	45	46
Burnley	38	20	6	12	67	50	46
Hull City	38	21	4	13	73	62	46
Wolverhampton W	38	15	7	16	50	45	37
Stoke	38	16	5	17	57	52	37
Gainsborough Trinity	38	14	7	17	47	71	35
Leeds City	38	12	8	18	53	65	32
Stockport County	38	12	8	18	48	67	32
Clapton Orient	38	11	10	17	40	65	32
Blackpool	38	11	9	18	51	58	31
Barnsley	38	12	6	20	54	68	30
Glossop	38	11	8	19	54	74	30
Grimsby Town	38	11	8	19	43	71	30
Chesterfield	38	6	11	21	46	92	23
Lincoln City	38	9	3	26	46	83	21

Secretary-manager: Fred Everiss

- A record crowd at The Hawthorns – 36,727 – witnessed Albion's first-round FA Cup tie against Birmingham in January. This beat the previous best of 35,529 versus Derby County in February 1907.
- On the transfer side, Albert Evans was recruited from Aston Villa and Charlie Hewitt arrived from Liverpool, while Arthur Randle and Fred Shinton both joined Leicester Fosse.
- The first representative match took place at The Hawthorns when England beat Scotland 4–0 in a Junior international.

Match No.	Date			Opponents	Result		Scorers	Attendance
1	Sep	2	A	Wolverhampton Wanderers	W	2-1	Buck (pen), Walker	24,000
2		7	H	Burnley	W	5-0	Buck 2, Pheasant, Garratt, Jordan	16,032
3		14	A	Oldham Athletic	L	1-2	Garratt	11,000
4		21	H	Clapton Orient	W	3-0	Jordan, Walker, Buck	12,336
5		28	A	Leeds City	L	0-1		19,058
6	Oct	5	H	Wolverhampton Wanderers	W	1-0	Brooks	30,026
7		12	A	Gainsborough Trinity	W	2-1	Dilly 2	4,900
8		19	H	Stockport County	W	2-0	Walker 2	14,000
9		26	A	Glossop	L	1-2	Buck (pen)	1,828
10	Nov	2	H	Leicester Fosse	D	1-1	Bradley	17,000
11		4	H	Oldham Athletic	L	1-2	Walker	10,500
12		9	A	Blackpool	W	1-0	Buck (pen)	9,145
13		16	H	Stoke	W	1-0	Young	10,000
14		23	A	Grimsby Town	D	2-2	Walker, Buck	4,552
15		30	A	Bradford City	D	0-0		18,025
16	Dec	7	H	Hull City	W	1-0	Buck	15,500
17		14	A	Derby County	L	0-2		8,000
18		21	H	Lincoln City	W	5-2	Buck (pen), Walker 2 (1 pen), Jordan, Wilcox	7,000
19		25	H	Chesterfield	W	4-0	Walker 2, Buck, Wilcox	12,478
20		26	A	Barnsley	W	3-1	Buck 3 (1 pen)	5,520
21		28	A	Fulham	D	1-1	Wilcox	20,063
22	Jan	4	A	Burnley	D	1-1	Walker	10,146
23		18	A	Clapton Orient	D	2-2	Buck, Evenson	15,252
24		25	H	Leeds City	W	1-0	Young	8,000
25	Feb	8	H	Gainsborough Trinity	L	0-1		7,500
26		15	A	Stockport County	W	2-1	Walker, Garratt	4,000
27		22	H	Glossop	D	1-1	Parkes	4,140
28		29	A	Leicester Fosse	L	0-3		6,337
29	Mar	7	H	Blackpool	W	3-0	Walker 2, Timmins	7,000
30		14	A	Stoke	D	1-1	Jordan	3,224
31		21	H	Grimsby Town	L	1-2	Pheasant	5,400
32		28	H	Bradford City	W	3-2	Wilcox, Buck, Walker	7,000
33	Apr	4	A	Hull City	L	2-4	Pheasant, Timmins	6,086
34		11	H	Derby County	W	1-0	Wilcox	10,000
35		17	A	Chesterfield	L	0-1		5,539
36		18	A	Lincoln City	W	2-0	Buck 2	6,850
37		20	H	Barnsley	D	1-1	Buck (pen)	10,000
38		25	H	Fulham	W	3-1	Jordan, Wright, Thompson	6,990

Appearances

Goals

FA Cup

R1	Jan	11	H	Birmingham	D	1-1	Wilcox	36,727
rep		15	A	Birmingham	W	2-1	Wilcox, Jordan	24,895
R2	Feb	1	A	Southampton	L	0-1		18,728

Appearances

Goals

Stringer J	Betteley RH	Pennington J	Timmins S	Pheasant E	Manners JA	Garratt GT	Buck FR	Jordan WC	Walker D	Brooks J	Williams J	Evenson I	Shinton F	Dilly T	Bowser W	Randle AJ	Haywood A	Adams A	Bradley EJ	Parkes HA	Bourne RA	Evans AJ	Young WC	Wright HF	Wilcox HM	Owers EH	Pearson HP	Thompson WT	Hewitt CW	
1	2	3	4	5	6	7	8	9	10	11																				1
1		3	4	5	6	7	8	9	10	11	2																			2
1		3	4	5		7	8	9	10	11	2	6																		3
1		3	4	5	6	7	8	9	10	11	2																			4
1		3	4	5	6	7	8	9	10	11	2																			5
1	2	3	4	5	6	7	8		10	11			9																	6
1	2	3	4	5	6	7	8		10	11				9																7
1	2	3	4	5	6	7	8		9	11					10															8
1		3	2	5	6	7	8		9	11						4	10													9
1		3	4	5	6	7	8		10	11								2	9											10
1		3	4	5	6		8		10									2	9	7	11									11
1		2	6	5			8		10	11			9							7		3	4							12
1		2	6	5		7	8		10	11												3	4	9						13
1		2	6	9		7	8		10	11		5										3	4							14
1		2	9	5		7	8		10	11		6										3	4							15
1		2	4	5		7	8		10	11		6										3			9					16
1	2	3	6	5		7	8		10	11													4			9				17
1	2	3	6			7	10	9	11			5											4		8					18
1	2	3	6	5		7	8		10	11						4									9					19
1		2	6	5		7	8		10	11						4						3			9					20
1	2	3	6	5		7	8		10	11													4		9					21
1	2			5	6	7	8		10	11												3	4		9					22
		2		5	6		11	9	10			8								7		3	4				1			23
	2	3			6		8		10			5								7	11		4	9			1			24
1		2		5	6		11		10											7		3	4		8	9				25
	2			5	6	7	8		10											11		3	4		9		1			26
		3		5	6	7	8		10		2									11			4		9		1			27
1		3		5	6	7	8		10	11	2												4		9					28
		2	8	5	6		11		10		7											3	4			9	1			29
		2	8	5	6		11	9			7											3	4		10		1			30
		2	8	5	6		11	9	10		7											3	4				1			31
1		2		5	6	7	11	9	10			4										3			8					32
	2		9	5	6	7	11		10													3	4		8		1			33
		2	4	5	6	7	11	9	10													3			8		1			34
		2	4	5	6	7	11		10													3			8	9	1			35
1		2	4	5	6	7	11	9	10													3			8					36
1		2	4		6	7	11	9	10										5			3			8					37
1		3	4	5	6		11	9			2													7				8	10	38
28	12	35	30	35	27	29	38	14	36	21	10	8	2	1	1	3	1	2	3	7	2	19	18	3	17	4	10	1	1	
			2	3		3	18	5	15	1		1		2					1	1			2	1	5		1			

Stringer J	Betteley RH	Pennington J	Timmins S	Pheasant E	Manners JA	Garratt GT	Buck FR	Jordan WC	Walker D	Brooks J	Williams J	Evenson I	Shinton F	Dilly T	Bowser W	Randle AJ	Haywood A	Adams A	Bradley EJ	Parkes HA	Bourne RA	Evans AJ	Young WC	Wright HF	Wilcox HM	Owers EH	Pearson HP	Thompson WT	Hewitt CW	
1		2	6	5		7	8		10	11												3	4		9					R1
		2		5	6		8	10	11											7		3	4		9		1			rep
		2		5	6		11		10											7		3	4	9	8		1			R2
1		3	1	3	2	1	3	1	3	1										2		3	3	1	3		2			
								1																	2					

1908-09

Division Two

	P	W	D	L	F	A	Pts
Bolton Wanderers	38	24	4	10	59	28	52
Tottenham Hotspur	38	20	11	7	67	32	51
West Bromwich Albion	38	19	13	6	56	27	51
Hull City	38	19	6	13	63	39	44
Derby County	38	16	11	11	55	41	43
Oldham Athletic	38	17	6	15	55	43	40
Wolverhampton W	38	14	11	13	56	48	39
Glossop	38	15	8	15	57	53	38
Gainsborough Trinity	38	15	8	15	49	70	38
Fulham	38	13	11	14	58	48	37
Birmingham	38	14	9	15	58	61	37
Leeds City	38	14	7	17	43	53	35
Grimsby Town	38	14	7	17	41	54	35
Burnley	38	13	7	18	51	58	33
Clapton Orient	38	12	9	17	37	49	33
Bradford Park Avenue	38	13	6	19	51	59	32
Barnsley	38	11	10	17	48	57	32
Stockport County	38	14	3	21	39	71	31
Chesterfield	38	11	8	19	37	67	30
Blackpool	38	9	11	18	46	68	29

Secretary-manager: Fred Everiss

- Albion met Tottenham Hotspur for the first time at League level.
- In May 1909 Albion went on their first overseas tour, playing seven games in Scandinavia, including friendlies against Hull City and Newcastle United.
- On the transfer front, Albion signed George Baddeley from Stoke, Sid Bowser from Willenhall, Billy Garraty from Leicester Fosse, Bob Pailor from West Hartlepool for £500 and both Harry Burton and George Simpson from Sheffield Wednesday.

Match No.	Date			Opponents	Result		Scorers	Attendance
1	Sep	5	A	Grimsby Town	D	1-1	Buck (pen)	6,000
2		7	H	Wolverhampton Wanderers	L	0-2		28,600
3		12	H	Fulham	D	1-1	Skene (og)	14,529
4		15	A	Bolton Wanderers	D	1-1	Buck (pen)	5,500
5		19	A	Burnley	W	2-0	Buck, Hewitt	11,340
6		26	H	Bradford Park Avenue	W	1-0	Hewitt	21,496
7	Oct	3	A	Wolverhampton Wanderers	W	1-0	Davies	20,000
8		10	H	Oldham Athletic	W	1-0	Hewitt	18,190
9		17	A	Clapton Orient	L	0-1		10,500
10		24	H	Leeds City	W	2-1	Thompson, Buck	13,554
11		31	A	Barnsley	W	2-0	Hewitt, Dorsett	7,000
12	Nov	2	H	Chesterfield	D	2-2	Garraty, Buck (pen)	9,540
13		7	H	Tottenham Hotspur	W	3-0	Hewitt 2, Garraty	27,224
14		14	A	Hull City	D	2-2	Garraty 2	10,000
15		21	H	Derby County	W	2-0	Buck, Thompson	13,241
16		28	A	Blackpool	W	2-0	Buck (pen), Timmins	5,500
17	Dec	12	A	Glossop	W	3-1	Buck 2, Hewitt	3,074
18		19	H	Stockport County	W	2-0	Hewitt, Garraty	6,240
19		25	H	Gainsborough Trinity	W	2-0	Thompson, Buck	18,250
20		26	H	Birmingham	D	1-1	Buck (pen)	38,049
21		28	A	Birmingham	D	0-0		30,035
22	Jan	2	H	Grimsby Town	W	7-0	Bowser 2, Garraty 2, Buck, Manners, Thompson	5,177
23		9	A	Fulham	L	0-2		25,000
24		23	H	Burnley	D	0-0		18,220
25		30	A	Bradford Park Avenue	D	0-0		17,600
26	Feb	13	A	Oldham Athletic	L	0-2		22,000
27		20	H	Clapton Orient	W	1-0	Davies	14,565
28		27	A	Leeds City	D	1-1	Garraty	12,140
29	Mar	13	A	Tottenham Hotspur	W	3-1	Garraty, Hewitt 2 (1 pen)	35,532
30		20	H	Hull City	W	1-0	Buck	17,602
31		24	H	Barnsley	D	1-1	Hewitt	4,982
32	Apr	3	H	Blackpool	W	5-1	Hewitt 2 (1 pen), Miller (og), Fielding, Garraty	17,426
33		9	A	Gainsborough Trinity	L	0-2		7,149
34		10	A	Chesterfield	D	2-2	Davies, Garraty	5,033
35		12	H	Bolton Wanderers	W	2-0	Jordon, Hewitt	34,012
36		17	H	Glossop	W	1-0	Hewitt	18,344
37		24	A	Stockport County	D	0-0		7,424
38		26	A	Derby County	L	1-2	Garraty	6,508

Appearances

Goals

FA Cup

R1	Jan	16	H	Bolton Wanderers	W	3-1	Garraty, Harris (pen), Buck	19,164
R2	Feb	6	H	Bradford City	L	1-2	Garraty	32,105

Appearances

Goals

Pearson HP	Pennington J	Evans AJ	Baddeley G	Pheasant E	Timmins S	Davies WC	Thompson WT	Jordan WC	Legge SG	Buck FR	Manners JA	Hewitt CW	Stringer J	Brown JF	Fielding AR	Wright HF	Betteley RH	Dorsett JAH	Garraty W	Bowser S	Harris GA	Pailor R	Hancock H	Burton HA	Simpson G	
1	2	3	4	5	6	7	8	9	10	11																1
1	2	3		5	4	7	8	9	10	11	6															2
	2	3		5	4	7	8			11	6	10	1	9												3
	2	3	4	5	6	11	7			10		8	1	9												4
	2	3	4	5	6	11				10		8	1	9	7											5
	2	3	4	5	6	11				10		8	1	9	7											6
	2	3	4	5		11				10	6	8	1	9		7										7
	2	3	4		5	11	7			10	6	8	1	9												8
	2	3		5	4	11	7			10	6	8	1	9												9
	3		4	5			9			10	6	8	1			7	2	11								10
	2	3	4		5		7			10	6	8	1					11	9							11
	2	3	4		5		7			10	6	8	1					11	9							12
	2	3	4		5		7			10	6	8	1					11	9							13
	2	3	4		5		7			10	6	8	1					11	9							14
	2	3	4		5	11	7			10	6	8	1						9							15
	2	3	4		5	11	7			10	6	8	1						9							16
	2	3	4		5	11	7			10	6	8	1						9							17
	2	3	4		5	11	7			10	6	8	1						9							18
	2	3	4		5	11	7			10	6	8	1						9							19
	3		4		5	11	7			10	6	8	1				2		9							20
	3		4		5	11	7	10		8	6		1				2		9							21
	3		4		5	11	7			8	6		1				2		9	10						22
			4		5	11	7			8	6		1				2		9	10	3					23
	2		4		5	11	7			8	6		1						9	10	3					24
	2		4		5	11	7			8	6		1							10	3	9				25
	3		4		5	11	7			10			1				2		8		6	9				26
			4		5	11				8	6		1		7		2		9		3		10			27
	3		4		5	11				8	6		1		7		2		9				10			28
	3		4		5	11				10		8	1		7		2		9		6					29
	3		4		5	11	7			10		8	1				2		9		6					30
	3		4		5	11	7			10		8	1				2		9		6					31
			4		5	11				10		8	1		7		2		9		6			3		32
	3		4		5	7				10		8	1						9		6			2	11	33
	3		4			11				10	6	8	1		7		2		9		5					34
	3		4			11		9		10	6	8	1		7		2		5							35
	3		4			11	7	9		10		8	1						5		6			2		36
	3		4			11		9		10	6	8	1		7						5			2		37
	3		4		5	11	7	9		10	6		1						8					2		38
2	35	18	35	9	32	33	27	7	2	38	27	27	36	7	9	2	14	5	26	4	13	2	2	5	1	
		1		1	3	4		1	13	1	15		1				1	11	2							

Two own-goals

2		4		5	11	7			8	6		1						9	10	3	R1
2		4		5	11	7			8	6		1						9	10	3	R2
2		2		2	2	2			2	2		2						2	2	2	
									1									2		1	

1909-10

Division Two

	P	W	D	L	F	A	Pts
Manchester City	38	23	8	7	81	40	54
Oldham Athletic	38	23	7	8	79	39	53
Hull City	38	23	7	8	80	46	53
Derby County	38	22	9	7	72	47	53
Leicester Fosse	38	20	4	14	79	58	44
Glossop	38	18	7	13	64	57	43
Fulham	38	14	13	11	51	43	41
Wolverhampton W	38	17	6	15	64	63	40
Barnsley	38	16	7	15	62	59	39
Bradford Park Avenue	38	17	4	17	64	59	38
West Bromwich Albion	38	16	5	17	58	56	37
Blackpool	38	14	8	16	50	52	36
Stockport County	38	13	8	17	50	47	34
Burnley	38	14	6	18	62	61	34
Lincoln City	38	10	11	17	42	69	31
Clapton Orient	38	12	6	20	37	60	30
Leeds City	38	10	7	21	46	80	27
Gainsborough Trinity	38	10	6	22	33	75	26
Grimsby Town	38	9	6	23	50	77	24
Birmingham	38	8	7	23	42	78	23

Secretary-manager: Fred Everiss

- Full-back Joe Smith joined Albion from Cradley Heath St Luke's. He would stay at The Hawthorns until 1926.
- Albion transferred Joe Dorsett (brother of George) to Manchester City, Ted Pheasant to Leicester Fosse (after 152 appearances) and Charlie Hewitt to Spennymoor United.

Match No.	Date			Opponents	Result		Scorers	Attendance
1	Sep	1	A	Stockport County	W	2-0	Rouse, Hewitt	6,000
2		4	H	Bradford Park Avenue	W	1-0	Rouse	18,990
3		6	H	Stockport County	L	0-1		14,883
4		11	A	Oldham Athletic	W	2-1	Manners, Garraty	12,000
5		18	H	Barnsley	W	4-3	Garraty, Hewitt 2, Buck	10,520
6		25	A	Fulham	W	2-0	Thompson, Buck	18,100
7		29	A	Lincoln City	W	3-0	Pheasant, Buck, Garraty	6,500
8	Oct	2	H	Burnley	L	1-2	Garraty	15,175
9		9	A	Leeds City	W	1-0	Buck (pen)	17,500
10		16	A	Wolverhampton Wanderers	L	1-3	Buck	24,000
11		23	A	Gainsborough Trinity	L	1-3	Buck (pen)	3,500
12		30	H	Grimsby Town	W	4-3	Hewitt 2, Buck 2 (1 pen)	7,225
13	Nov	6	A	Manchester City	L	2-3	Hewitt, Dorsett	29,800
14		13	H	Leicester Fosse	L	1-2	Hewitt	9,040
15		27	H	Clapton Orient	W	3-0	Davies, Buck, Hewitt	12,167
16	Dec	4	A	Blackpool	L	1-2	Hewitt	7,700
17		11	H	Hull City	L	0-2		8,208
18		18	A	Derby County	L	1-2	Bowser	10,400
19		25	H	Wolverhampton Wanderers	L	0-1		24,899
20		27	H	Birmingham	W	3-1	Simpson, Bowser, Manners	12,104
21	Jan	1	A	Birmingham	W	1-0	Simpson	15,500
22		8	A	Bradford Park Avenue	L	0-1		7,980
23		22	H	Oldham Athletic	D	1-1	Pailor	7,901
24	Feb	12	A	Burnley	W	3-2	Garraty 3	6,000
25	Mar	5	H	Gainsborough Trinity	W	5-0	Bowser, Simpson 2, Buck, Garraty	10,155
26		7	H	Leeds City	W	3-1	Buck 2, Bowser	6,664
27		12	A	Grimsby Town	L	0-3		5,800
28		19	H	Manchester City	D	0-0		13,042
29		26	A	Leicester Fosse	L	1-2	Bowser	7,000
30		28	H	Glossop	D	0-0		12,360
31		29	H	Fulham	W	3-2	Waterhouse, Buck, Hewitt	11,714
32	Apr	2	H	Lincoln City	D	1-1	Garraty	12,150
33		9	A	Clapton Orient	W	3-1	Dorsett, Buck, Hewitt	15,000
34		14	A	Barnsley	L	1-2	Buck (pen)	16,105
35		16	H	Blackpool	L	0-3		6,103
36		23	A	Hull City	L	1-5	Simpson	18,744
37		26	A	Glossop	L	2-3	Bowser, Buck (pen)	5,225
38		30	H	Derby County	D	0-0		9,098
								Appearances
								Goals

FA Cup

R1	Jan	15	H	Clapton Orient	W	2-0	Pailor 2	7,339
R2	Feb	5	A	Bristol City	D	1-1	Pailor	16,885
rep		9	H	Bristol City	W	4-2	Hewitt 2, Pailor, Simpson	14,870
R3		19	A	Barnsley	L	0-1		19,121
								Appearances
								Goals

Pearson HP	Burton HA	Pennington J	Baddeley G	Garraty W	Harris GA	Dorsett JAH	Hewitt CW	Rouse FW	Buck FR	Simpson G	Thompson WT	Stringer J	Betteley RH	Timmins S	Manners JA	Davies WC	Pheasant E	Dicken HJ	Young WC	Bowser S	Waterhouse F	Pailor R	Corbett R	Crump A	Price GW	Brown JF	
1	2	3	4	5	6	7	8	9	10	11																	1
1	2	3	4	5	6		8	9	10	11	7																2
1	2	3	4	5	6		8	9	10	11	7																3
	3		4	9			8		10		7	1	2	5	6	11											4
	3		4	9			8		10		7	1	2	5	6	11											5
	3		4	9			8		10		7	1	2		6	11	5										6
	3		4	9			8		10		7	1	2		6	11	5										7
	3		4	9			8		10		7	1	2		6	11	5										8
	3		4	9			8		10		7	1	2		6	11		5									9
	3		4	9	5		8		10		7	1	2		6	11											10
	3		5	9		11		8	10		7	1	2		6				4								11
	3		4	8		11	9		10		7	1	2	5	6												12
	3		4			11	9		8		7	1	2	6			5			10							13
	3		4			11	9		8		7	1	2				5			10	6						14
	3		4	8			9		10		7	1	2		6	11	5										15
	3		4	8			9		10		7	1	2		6	11	5										16
	2	3	4	8			9		10		7	1			6	11	5										17
	2	3	4				8		10	11	7	1		5	6					9							18
	2	3	4				8		10	11	7	1		5	6					9							19
	2	3				10	8			11		1		4	6	7	5			9							20
	2	3		4		8			10	11		1		5	6	7				9							21
	2	3		4					10	11		1		5	6	7				8		9					22
		3		4					10	11		1	2	5	6	7				8		9					23
1	2	3	4	9			7		10					6		11				8	5						24
1	2	3	4	9			7		10	11					6					8	5						25
1	2	3	4	9			7		10	11					6					8	5						26
1	2	3	4	9			7		10	11					6					8	5						27
1	2	3	4				7		10	11				6						8	5	9					28
1		3	4				8		10	11			2	6		7				9	5						29
1		3	4			11	8		10					6		7				9	5		2				30
1		3	4	9		11	7		10					6						8	5		2				31
1			4	9		11	7		10					6						8	5		3	2			32
1		3	4	8	6	7	9		11				2	5						10							33
1		3	4	8	6	7			10	11			2	5											9		34
1		3	4				9		8	11			2	6		7				10	5						35
1		3		4				9	7	11			2	6						10	5					8	36
1		3	4			11	8		10				2	6		7				9	5						37
1		3	4				8		10	11			2	6		7				9	5						38
18	27	24	33	27	6	13	32	5	37	18	18	20	21	22	21	20	9	1	1	22	14	3	3	1	1	1	
				9		2	11	2	16	5	1				2	1	1			6	1	1					

	2	3		4			8			11		1		5	6	7				10		9					R1
1	2	3		4			7		10	11					6					8	5	9					R2
1	2	3		4			7		10	11					6					8	5	9					rep
1	2	3		4			7		10	11					6					8	5	9					R3
3	4	4		4			4		3	4		1		1	4	1				4	3	4					
							2			1												4					

1910-11

Division Two

	P	W	D	L	F	A	Pts
West Bromwich Albion	38	22	9	7	67	41	53
Bolton Wanderers	38	21	9	8	69	40	51
Chelsea	38	20	9	9	71	35	49
Clapton Orient	38	19	7	12	44	35	45
Hull City	38	14	16	8	55	39	44
Derby County	38	17	8	13	73	52	42
Blackpool	38	16	10	12	49	38	42
Burnley	38	13	15	10	45	45	41
Wolverhampton W	38	15	8	15	51	52	38
Fulham	38	15	7	16	52	48	37
Leeds City	38	15	7	16	58	56	37
Bradford Park Avenue	38	14	9	15	53	55	37
Huddersfield Town	38	13	8	17	57	58	34
Glossop	38	13	8	17	48	62	34
Leicester Fosse	38	14	5	19	52	62	33
Birmingham	38	12	8	18	42	64	32
Stockport County	38	11	8	19	47	79	30
Gainsborough Trinity	38	9	11	18	37	55	29
Barnsley	38	7	14	17	52	62	28
Lincoln City	38	7	10	21	28	72	24

Secretary-manager: Fred Everiss

- Albion clinched the Second Division title by beating Huddersfield Town in their final game, Fred Buck's 30th minute penalty deciding the contest.
- Harry Wright returned to the club from Stourbridge; winger Claude Jephcott was signed from Brierley Hill Alliance, left-half Bobby McNeal arrived from Hobson Wanderers and full-back Joe Smith was secured from Cradley St Luke's. The latter two both went on to become England internationals.
- Among the outgoing players were Billy Garraty (to Lincoln City) and Jim Stringer (to Dudley Town).

Match No.	Date			Opponents	Result		Scorers	Attendance
1	Sep	3	A	Hull City	D	1-1	Buck	10,400
2		5	A	Bolton Wanderers	L	1-3	Buck	8,500
3		10	H	Fulham	W	2-1	Bowser 2	10,144
4		17	A	Bradford Park Avenue	D	3-3	Bowser, Pailor 2	9,500
5		24	H	Burnley	W	2-1	Waterhouse, Wollaston	15,280
6	Oct	1	A	Gainsborough Trinity	D	1-1	Bowser	3,600
7		8	H	Leeds City	W	2-0	Bowser, Pailor	13,149
8		15	A	Stockport County	W	1-0	Bowser	6,000
9		22	H	Derby County	D	1-1	Pailor	18,488
10		29	A	Barnsley	D	1-1	Lloyd	10,000
11	Nov	5	H	Leicester Fosse	W	5-1	Bowser, Lloyd 2, Wollaston, Buck (pen)	15,200
12		12	A	Wolverhampton Wanderers	W	3-2	Pailor 2 (1 pen), Bowser	18,500
13		19	H	Chelsea	L	1-3	Bowser	21,305
14		26	A	Clapton Orient	D	0-0		7,000
15	Dec	3	H	Blackpool	L	0-1		8,840
16		10	A	Glossop	W	2-0	Baddeley, Pailor	4,000
17		17	H	Lincoln City	W	3-0	Buck 2 (1 pen), Walker	3,577
18		24	A	Huddersfield Town	W	2-0	Waterhouse, Bowser	20,700
19		26	H	Bolton Wanderers	W	2-0	Bowser, Lloyd	20,301
20		27	A	Birmingham	D	1-1	Pailor	37,520
21		31	H	Hull City	L	0-2		11,790
22	Jan	7	A	Fulham	W	1-0	Lloyd	16,000
23		21	H	Bradford Park Avenue	W	3-0	Buck, Pailor, Lloyd	6,952
24		28	A	Burnley	L	0-2		8,300
25	Feb	11	A	Leeds City	L	1-3	Wright	10,700
26		18	H	Stockport County	W	4-2	Buck 2 (1 pen), Bowser 2	6,107
27	Mar	1	A	Derby County	W	3-1	Bowser, Pailor, Wright	21,640
28		4	H	Barnsley	D	3-3	Bowser, Wright, Pailor	7,770
29		11	A	Leicester Fosse	W	3-2	Bowser 2, Wright	10,547
30		18	H	Wolverhampton Wanderers	W	2-1	Buck (pen), Pailor	20,303
31		29	A	Chelsea	L	1-2	Wright	12,640
32	Apr	1	H	Clapton Orient	W	3-0	Waterhouse, McNeal, Wright	12,852
33		8	A	Blackpool	D	0-0		6,100
34		15	H	Glossop	W	3-1	Lloyd, Wright, Bowser	13,404
35		17	H	Birmingham	W	1-0	Bowser	27,042
36		18	H	Gainsborough Trinity	W	2-1	Bowser 2	23,788
37		22	A	Lincoln City	W	2-1	Lloyd, Bowser	8,000
38		29	H	Huddersfield Town	W	1-0	Buck (pen)	30,135

Appearances
Goals

FA Cup

R1	Jan	14	H	Fulham	W	4-1	Bowser 2, Wollaston, Lloyd	18,034
R2	Feb	4	A	Derby County	L	0-2		20,242

Appearances
Goals

Pearson HP	Betteley RH	Timmins S	Baddeley G	Waterhouse F	Manners JA	Wollaston W	Bowser S	Pailor R	Buck FR	Lloyd JA	Richards A	Smith J	Pennington J	Nevin J	McNeal R	Hibbert JW	Wright HF	Deacey C	Wheeler W	Moorwood L	Thompson W	Simpson G	
1	2	3	4	5	6	7	8	9	10	11													1
1		6	4	5		7	8	9	10	11	2	3											2
1	2	6	4	5		7	8	9	10	11			3										3
1	2		4	5	6	7	8	9	10	11			3										4
1	2		4	5	6	7	8	9	10	11			3										5
1	2		4	5		7	8	9	10	11			3	6									6
1	2	6	4	5		7	8	9		11			3		10								7
1	2	6	4	5		7	8	9		11			3		10								8
1	2	6	4	5		7	8	9		11			3		10								9
1			4	5		7	8	9		11		2	3		6	10							10
1			4	5		7	8	9	10	11		2	3		6								11
1			4	5			8	9	10	11		2	3		6		7						12
1			4	5			8	9	10	11		2	3		6		7						13
1			4	5			8		10	11		2	3		6		7	9					14
1			4	5			8		10	11		2	3		6		7	9					15
1			4	5		7	8	9	10	11		2	3		6								16
1			4	5		7	8		10	11		2	3		6				9				17
1			4	5		7	8	9	10	11		2	3		6								18
1			4	5		7	8	9	10	11		2	3		6								19
1			4	5		7	8	9	10	11		2	3		6								20
1			4	5		7	8	9	10	11		2	3		6								21
1			4	5		7	8	9	10	11		2	3		6								22
1			4	5		7	8	9	10	11		2	3		6								23
1			4	5			8	9	10	11		2	3		6		7						24
	2		4	5			10	9	11			3		6			8			1	7		25
			4	5			8	9	10	11		2	3		6					1	7		26
			4	5			8	9	11			2	3		6		10			1	7		27
	2	7	4	5	6		8	9	11			3					10			1			28
1			4	5	6		8	9	10	11		2	3				7						29
1			4	5			8	9	10	11		2	3		6		7						30
1			4	5			8		10	11		2	3		6		9				7		31
1	2		4	5	6		8		10	11		3			9		7						32
1			4	5	6		8		10	11		2	3		9		7						33
1				5	6		9		10	11		2	3		4		8				7		34
1				5	6		8	9	10	11		2	3		4		7						35
1				5	6		9		10	11		2	3		4		7				8		36
1				5	6		9		10	11		2	3		4		7				8		37
1				5	6		9		10	11		2	3		4		7				8		38
34	11	7	33	38	12	19	38	28	34	35	1	30	33	2	29	1	18	2	1	4	8		
			1	3		2	22	12	10	8					1		7		1				

Pearson HP	Betteley RH	Timmins S	Baddeley G	Waterhouse F	Manners JA	Wollaston W	Bowser S	Pailor R	Buck FR	Lloyd JA	Richards A	Smith J	Pennington J	Nevin J	McNeal R	Hibbert JW	Wright HF	Deacey C	Wheeler W	Moorwood L	Thompson W	Simpson G	
1			4	5		7	8	9	10	11		2	3		6								R1
1			4	5			8	9	10			2	3		6						7	11	R2
2			2	2		1	2	2	2	1		2	2		2						2	1	
						1	2			1													

1911-12

Division One

	P	W	D	L	F	A	Pts
Blackburn Rovers	38	20	9	9	60	43	49
Everton	38	20	6	12	46	42	46
Newcastle United	38	18	8	12	64	50	44
Bolton Wanderers	38	20	3	15	54	43	43
Sheffield Wednesday	38	16	9	13	69	49	41
Aston Villa	38	17	7	14	76	63	41
Middlesbrough	38	16	8	14	56	45	40
Sunderland	38	14	11	13	58	51	39
West Bromwich Albion	38	15	9	14	43	47	39
Woolwich Arsenal	38	15	8	15	55	59	38
Bradford City	38	15	8	15	46	50	38
Tottenham Hotspur	38	14	9	15	53	53	37
Manchester United	38	13	11	14	45	60	37
Sheffield United	38	13	10	15	63	56	36
Manchester City	38	13	9	16	56	58	35
Notts County	38	14	7	17	46	63	35
Liverpool	38	12	10	16	49	55	34
Oldham Athletic	38	12	10	16	46	54	34
Preston North End	38	13	7	18	40	57	33
Bury	38	6	9	23	32	59	21

Secretary-manager: Fred Everiss

- Jesse Pennington was appointed team captain but was bitterly disappointed when he allowed Harry Tufnell to race clear to score Barnsley's winning goal in the FA Cup Final with only a minute of extra-time remaining.
- Albion played 12 competitive games during the month of April – seven in the space of nine days. They won only one against Sunderland when new signing Fred Morris from Redditch scored on his debut.
- Hubert Pearson netted two penalties this term – thus becoming the first goalkeeper to score in League football for the club. Both games ended in wins.
- Arthur Cook from Wrexham, Howard Gregory from Birchfield Trinity and Ben Shearman from Bristol City were also signed, while full-back Dick Betteley moved into non-League football with Bilston United.

Match No.	Date			Opponents	Result		Scorers	Attendance
1	Sep	2	H	Notts County	W	2-1	Buck, Shearman	26,638
2		4	A	Aston Villa	W	3-0	Allan, Shearman, Bowser	31,884
3		9	A	Tottenham Hotspur	L	0-1		31,100
4		16	H	Manchester United	W	1-0	Allan	34,921
5		23	A	Liverpool	W	3-1	Shearman, Bowser, Allan	18,000
6		30	H	Aston Villa	D	2-2	Shearman 2	46,203
7	Oct	7	A	Newcastle United	D	0-0		28,000
8		14	H	Sheffield United	L	0-1		18,595
9		21	A	Oldham Athletic	L	1-3	Pailor	13,000
10		28	H	Bolton Wanderers	D	0-0		14,377
11	Nov	4	A	Bradford City	L	1-4	Allan	19,800
12		11	H	Woolwich Arsenal	D	1-1	Shearman	13,900
13		18	A	Manchester City	W	2-0	Bowser 2	12,000
14		25	H	Everton	W	1-0	Pailor	12,240
15	Dec	2	A	Preston North End	D	1-1	Bowser	19,000
16		9	A	Sunderland	L	2-3	Pailor 2	10,000
17		16	H	Blackburn Rovers	W	2-0	Bowser, Pailor	13,176
18		23	A	Sheffield Wednesday	L	1-4	Bowser	13,000
19		26	H	Bury	W	2-0	Wright, Pearson (pen)	10,133
20		30	A	Notts County	L	0-2		10,000
21	Jan	1	A	Bury	L	0-1		12,000
22		20	A	Manchester United	W	2-1	Wright 2	11,000
23		27	H	Liverpool	W	1-0	Wright	16,057
24	Feb	10	H	Newcastle United	W	3-1	Pailor 3	30,252
25		17	A	Sheffield United	D	1-1	Pailor	15,000
26	Mar	2	A	Bolton Wanderers	L	0-2		9,980
27		13	H	Tottenham Hotspur	W	2-0	Jephcott 2	17,406
28		16	A	Woolwich Arsenal	W	2-0	Bowser, Pailor	15,000
29		23	H	Manchester City	D	1-1	Shearman	12,331
30	Apr	5	A	Middlesbrough	L	0-1		12,000
31		8	H	Middlesbrough	W	3-1	Pearson (pen), Jephcott 2	25,027
32		9	H	Preston North End	L	0-2		8,240
33		13	H	Sunderland	W	1-0	Morris	20,117
34		22	A	Everton	L	0-3		7,000
35		25	A	Blackburn Rovers	L	1-4	Morris	12,000
36		26	H	Bradford City	D	0-0		10,663
37		27	H	Sheffield Wednesday	L	1-5	Morris	9,405
38		29	H	Oldham Athletic	D	0-0		3,122

Appearances
Goals

FA Cup

R1	Jan	13	H	Tottenham Hotspur	W	3-0	Bowser, Deacey, Wright	21,947
R2	Feb	3	A	Leeds City	W	1-0	Bowser	21,320
R3		24	A	Sunderland	W	2-1	Pailor 2	43,383
R4	Mar	9	H	Fulham	W	3-0	Bowser 2, Wright	41,880
SF		30	N	Blackburn Rovers	D	0-0		30,063
rep	Apr	3	N	Blackburn Rovers	W	1-0*	Pailor	20,050
F		20	N	Barnsley	D	0-0		55,213
rep		24	N	Barnsley	L	0-1*		38,555

SF at Anfield, Liverpool, replay at Hillsborough, Sheffield
Final at Crystal Palace, replay at Bramall Lane, Sheffield
* after extra-time

Appearances
Goals

Pearson HP	Smith J	Pennington J	Baddeley G	Waterhouse F	McNeal R	Wright HF	Bowser S	Allan SJ	Buck FR	Shearman B	Manners JA	Pailor R	Wollaston W	Jephcott AC	Cook A	Moorwood L	Deacey C	Lloyd JA	Hibbert JW	Morris F	Wood M	Gregory H	Betteley RH	
1	2	3	4	5	6	7	8	9	10	11														1
1	2	3	4		6	7	8	9	10	11	5													2
1	2	3	4		6	7	8	9	10	11	5													3
1	2	3	4		6	7	8	9	10	11	5													4
1	2	3	4		6	7	8	9	10	11	5													5
1	2	3	4		6	7	8	9	10	11	5													6
1	2	3	4		6	7	8	9	10	11	5													7
1	2	3	4	5	6	7	8	9	10	11														8
1	2	3	4	5	6	7	8	10	11			9												9
1	2	3	4	5	6	7	8	9	10	11														10
1	2	3	4		6	7		10	8	11	5	9												11
1	2	3	4		6	8			10	11	5	9	7											12
1	2	3	4		6	8	10			11	5	9	7											13
1	2	3	4		6	8	10			11	5	9	7											14
1	2	3	4		6	8	10			11	5	9	7											15
1	2	3	4		6	8	10			11	5	9		7										16
1	2	3			6	8	10		4	11	5	9		7										17
1	2	3			6	8	10		4	11	5	9		7										18
1	2	3		5	6	8	10		4	11		9		7										19
1		3		5	6	8	10	9	4	11				7	2									20
		3		5	6	7	10	8	4	11		9			2	1								21
1		3	4		6	8	10		5	11		9		7	2									22
1	2		4		6	8	10		5	11		9		7	3									23
1	2		4		6	8	10		5	11		9		7	3									24
1	2		4		6	8	10		5	11		9		7	3									25
1		3	4		6	8	10		5					7	2		9	11						26
1	2		4		6	8	10		5	11		9		7	3									27
1		3	4		6	8	10		5	11		9		7	2									28
1	2		4		6	8	10		5	11		9		7	3									29
1	2	3		4	6	8		10		11	5			7			9							30
1		3	4		6	8		10	5	11				7	2		9							31
1	2	3			6	8		10		11	5			7			9		4					32
1	2		4		6			8	5	11				7	3		9			10				33
	2			5							6		7			1	9	11	4	10	3	8		34
1	2	3		4	6	8			5	11		9		7						10				35
1	2	3	4		6			8	5	11		9		7						10				36
1	2		4		6	8			5	11				7						9	3	10		37
1	3			4	6			8			5		7					11		9		10	2	38
36	32	29	28	11	37	34	27	19	30	34	18	20	6	20	12	2	6	3	2	6	2	3	1	
2						4	8	4	1	7		10		4						3				

Pearson HP	Smith J	Pennington J	Baddeley G	Waterhouse F	McNeal R	Wright HF	Bowser S	Allan SJ	Buck FR	Shearman B	Manners JA	Pailor R	Wollaston W	Jephcott AC	Cook A	Moorwood L	Deacey C	Lloyd JA	Hibbert JW	Morris F	Wood M	Gregory H	Betteley RH	
1		3	4		6	8	10		5	11				7	2		9							R1
1		3	4		6	8	10		5	11		9		7	2									R2
1		3	4		6	8	10		5	11		9		7	2									R3
1		3	4		6	8	10		5	11		9		7	2									R4
1		3	4		6	8	10		5	11		9		7	2									SF
1		3	4		6	8		10	5	11		9		7	2									rep
1		3	4		6	8	10		5	11		9		7	2									F
1		3	4		6	8	10		5	11		9		7	2									rep
8		8	8		8	8	7	1	8	8		7		8	8		1							
						2	4					3					1							

1912-13

Division One

	P	W	D	L	F	A	Pts
Sunderland	38	25	4	9	86	43	54
Aston Villa	38	19	12	7	86	52	50
Sheffield Wednesday	38	21	7	10	75	55	49
Manchester United	38	19	8	11	69	43	46
Blackburn Rovers	38	16	13	9	79	43	45
Manchester City	38	18	8	12	53	37	44
Derby County	38	17	8	13	69	66	42
Bolton Wanderers	38	16	10	12	62	63	42
Oldham Athletic	38	14	14	10	50	55	42
West Bromwich Albion	38	13	12	13	57	50	38
Everton	38	15	7	16	48	54	37
Liverpool	38	16	5	17	61	71	37
Bradford City	38	12	11	15	50	60	35
Newcastle United	38	13	8	17	47	47	34
Sheffield United	38	14	6	18	56	70	34
Middlesbrough	38	11	10	17	55	69	32
Tottenham Hotspur	38	12	6	20	45	72	30
Chelsea	38	11	6	21	51	73	28
Notts County	38	7	9	22	28	56	23
Woolwich Arsenal	38	3	12	23	26	74	18

Secretary-manager: Fred Everiss

- In June 1913 Albion purchased the freehold of The Hawthorns for £5,350.
- Defender Fred Reed was signed from Lintz Colliery and wing-half Sammy Richardson arrived from Great Bridge Celtic, while Sid Bowser was transferred to the Irish club Belfast Distillery but would return to the club later.
- Wing-half Jack Manners left Albion for Hartlepools United after making over 200 senior appearances.

Match No.	Date			Opponents	Result		Scorers	Attendance
1	Sep	4	H	Middlesbrough	W	2-0	Buck (pen), Pailor	15,085
2		7	A	Notts County	D	1-1	Wright	13,000
3		14	H	Manchester United	L	1-2	Bowser	26,140
4		21	A	Aston Villa	W	4-2	Wright, Pailor 3	55,064
5		28	H	Liverpool	W	3-1	Pailor, Shearman, McNeal	21,908
6	Oct	5	A	Bolton Wanderers	L	1-2	Morris	24,000
7		12	H	Sheffield United	W	3-1	Morris 2, Wright	18,040
8		19	A	Newcastle United	D	1-1	Bowser	30,000
9		26	H	Oldham Athletic	L	2-3	Wright, Shearman	15,101
10	Nov	2	A	Chelsea	W	2-0	Jephcott, Pailor	35,100
11		9	H	Woolwich Arsenal	W	2-1	Morris 2	15,980
12		16	A	Bradford City	D	1-1	Torrance (og)	13,000
13		23	H	Manchester City	L	0-2		16,799
14		30	H	Sunderland	W	3-1	Morris, Pailor, Buck (pen)	13,529
15	Dec	7	A	Everton	W	3-1	Pailor 2, Jephcott	25,000
16		14	H	Sheffield Wednesday	D	1-1	Pailor	15,258
17		21	A	Blackburn Rovers	W	4-2	Pailor 3, Morris	22,000
18		25	A	Derby County	W	2-1	Buck, Shearman	21,000
19		26	H	Derby County	D	0-0		22,567
20		28	H	Notts County	W	2-0	Gregory, Morris	21,041
21	Jan	1	A	Middlesbrough	L	1-3	Buck	18,020
22		4	A	Manchester United	D	1-1	Bowser	15,000
23		18	H	Aston Villa	D	2-2	Morris, Gregory	40,589
24		25	A	Liverpool	L	1-2	Bowser	30,400
25	Feb	8	H	Bolton Wanderers	D	2-2	Waterhouse, Shearman	18,225
26		15	A	Sheffield United	L	0-1		12,000
27	Mar	1	A	Oldham Athletic	D	0-0		10,500
28		8	H	Chelsea	L	0-1		16,293
29		15	A	Woolwich Arsenal	L	0-1		6,800
30		21	A	Tottenham Hotspur	L	1-3	Sherman	31,500
31		22	H	Bradford City	D	1-1	Pailor	6,565
32		24	H	Tottenham Hotspur	W	4-1	Bowser, Shearman, Pailor 2	13,882
33		29	A	Manchester City	L	1-2	Bowser	21,500
34	Apr	5	A	Sunderland	L	1-3	Gregory	33,700
35		9	H	Newcastle United	W	1-0	Shearman	8,277
36		12	H	Everton	D	0-0		10,795
37		19	A	Sheffield Wednesday	L	2-3	Shearman, Gregory	11,400
38		26	H	Blackburn Rovers	D	1-1	Waterhouse	11,834
								Appearances
								Goals

FA Cup

R1	Jan	13	H	West Ham United	D	1-1	Wright	19,958
rep		16	A	West Ham United	D	2-2	Gregory, Bowser	14,762
rep2		22	N	West Ham United	L	0-3		26,689
Replay 2 at Stamford Bridge								Appearances
								Goals

Pearson HP	Cook AF	Pennington J	Baddeley G	Buck FR	McNeal R	Jephcott AC	Wright HF	Pailor R	Bowser S	Shearman BW	Waterhouse F	Smith J	Moorwood L	Gregory H	Morris F	Varty JW	Wood MC	Deacey C	Jackson WH	Lloyd JA	
1	2	3	4	5	6	7	8	9	10	11											1
1	2	3	4		6	7	8	9	10	11	5										2
1	2	3		5	6	7	8	9	10	11	4										3
1		3		5	6	7	10	9	8	11	4	2									4
1		3		5	6	7	10	9	8	11	4	2									5
		3		5	6	7	10			11	4	2	1	8	9						6
1		3		5	6	7	10	9		11	4	2			8						7
1		3		5	6	7	10		8	11	4	2			9						8
1		3		5	6	7	10	9	8	11	4	2									9
1		3		5	6	7	10	9	8	11	4	2									10
1		3		5		7	10		8	11	4	2			9	6					11
1		3		5		7	10		8	11	4	2			9	6					12
1		3		5		7	10		8	11	4	2			9	6					13
			4	5		7	10	9		11	6	2	1		8		3				14
		3	4	5		7	10	9		11	6	2	1		8						15
		3	4	5		7	10	9		11	6	2	1		8						16
		3		5	6	7		9	10	11	4	2	1		8						17
		3	4	5		7		9	10	11	6	2	1		8						18
		3	4	5	6	7	8		10	11		2	1		9						19
		3			6	7			10	11	4	2	1	8	9			5			20
				5	6	7		9	10	11	4	2	1		8		3				21
		3		5	6	7	8		10	11	4	2	1		9						22
	3		4	5	6	7			10	11		2	1	8	9						23
	3		4	5	6	7			10	11		2	1	8	9						24
1	3			5	6	7			10	11	4	2			8			9			25
1	3			5	6	7	8		10	11	4	2						9			26
1		3		5	6	7	8		10	11	4	2							9		27
1		3	4	8		7					6	2		10				5	9	11	28
1		3		5	6	7		9	10	11	4	2			8						29
1		3		5	6	7		9	10	11	4	2		8							30
1		3		5	6	7		9	10	11	4	2		8							31
		3		5	6	7		9	10	11	4	2	1	8							32
		3		5	6	7		9	10	11	4	2	1	8							33
	3			5	6	7		9	10	11	4	2	1	8							34
		3		5	6	7		9	10	11	4	2	1	8							35
		3		5	6	7		9	8	11	4	2	1						10		36
		3		5	6	7		9	10	11	4	2	1	8							37
		3		5	6	7		9	10	11	4	2	1	8							38
9	8	31	10	36	30	38	20	24	32	37	34	35	19	13	19	3	2	4	3	1	
				4	1	2	4	16	6	8	2			4	9						

One own-goal

	3			5	6	7	9		10	11	4	2	1		8						R1
	3			5	6	7			10	11	4	2	1	8	9						rep
	3			5	6	7			10	11	4	2	1	8	9						rep2
	3			3	3	3	1		3	3	3	3	3	2	3						
							1		1					1							

1913-14

Division One

	P	W	D	L	F	A	Pts
Blackburn Rovers	38	20	11	7	78	42	51
Aston Villa	38	19	6	13	65	50	44
Middlesbrough	38	19	5	14	77	60	43
Oldham Athletic	38	17	9	12	55	45	43
West Bromwich Albion	38	15	13	10	46	42	43
Bolton Wanderers	38	16	10	12	65	52	42
Sunderland	38	17	6	15	63	52	40
Chelsea	38	16	7	15	46	55	39
Bradford City	38	12	14	12	40	40	38
Sheffield United	38	16	5	17	63	60	37
Newcastle United	38	13	11	14	39	48	37
Burnley	38	12	12	14	61	53	36
anchester City	38	14	8	16	51	53	36
Manchester United	38	15	6	17	52	62	36
Everton	38	12	11	15	46	55	35
Liverpool	38	14	7	17	46	62	35
Tottenham Hotspur	38	12	10	16	50	62	34
Sheffield Wednesday	38	13	8	17	53	70	34
Preston North End	38	12	6	20	52	69	30
Derby County	38	8	11	19	55	71	27

Secretary-manager: Fred Everiss

- Defender George Baddeley became the oldest player ever to appear in a senior game for Albion when he lined up against Sheffield Wednesday on 18 April at the age of 39 years and 345 days.
- Alf Bentley, signed from Bolton Wanderers for £500, scored four goals on his Albion debut against Burnley in September.
- Amateur centre-forward Harold Bache was signed from Eastbourne, Alf Bentley from Bolton Wanderers and Sid Bowser returned from Ireland. And Bob Pailor was sold to Newcastle United after scoring 47 goals in 92 games for the club.
- Albion's left-back Jesse Pennington was involved in a bribery incident in November whereby a man approached him with cash to fix the result of the home game with Everton. A trap was set, the culprit (Pascoe Bioletti) was arrested and he was later sentenced at the Stafford Assize Court, to a term of imprisonment.

Match No.	Date			Opponents	Result		Scorers	Attendance
1	Sep	6	H	Burnley	W	4-1	Bentley 4	27,014
2		8	A	Chelsea	D	1-1	Morris	21,000
3		13	A	Preston North End	W	2-0	Lewis, Morris	15,000
4		20	H	Newcastle United	D	1-1	Newall	29,147
5		27	A	Liverpool	D	0-0		25,000
6	Oct	4	H	Aston Villa	W	1-0	Lewis	48,057
7		11	A	Middlesbrough	L	0-3		15,000
8		18	H	Sheffield United	W	2-1	Morris, Bentley	15,282
9		25	A	Derby County	W	2-1	Morris, Bentley	12,000
10	Nov	1	H	Manchester City	D	0-0		17,443
11		8	A	Bradford City	L	0-1		10,000
12		15	H	Blackburn Rovers	W	2-0	Shearman, Buck	32,524
13		22	A	Sunderland	D	0-0		39,700
14		29	H	Everton	D	1-1	Lewis	16,627
15	Dec	6	A	Tottenham Hotspur	L	0-3		26,000
16		13	A	Sheffield Wednesday	W	4-1	Edwards 2, Morris, Pailor	17,000
17		20	H	Bolton Wanderers	D	1-1	McNeal	21,311
18		25	A	Oldham Athletic	L	0-2		12,000
19		26	H	Oldham Athletic	D	2-2	Bentley 2 (2 pens)	30,294
20		27	A	Burnley	D	0-0		15,100
21	Jan	1	A	Manchester United	L	0-1		16,400
22		3	H	Preston North End	W	1-0	Buck (pen)	13,659
23		17	A	Newcastle United	D	3-3	Edwards, Shearman, Bentley	18,200
24		24	H	Liverpool	L	0-1		13,582
25	Feb	7	A	Aston Villa	L	0-2		48,000
26		14	H	Middlesbrough	W	2-1	McNeal, Bentley	15,692
27		28	H	Derby County	W	2-1	Bentley, Swift	14,746
28	Mar	7	A	Bolton Wanderers	L	0-1		14,649
29		14	H	Bradford City	W	2-1	Bentley 2	12,057
30		19	A	Sheffield United	D	1-1	Morris	10,120
31		21	A	Blackburn Rovers	L	0-2		22,126
32		25	A	Manchester City	W	3-2	Swift, Bentley, Gregory	16,700
33		28	H	Sunderland	W	2-1	Gregory 2	23,366
34	Apr	4	A	Everton	L	0-2		21,000
35		11	H	Tottenham Hotspur	D	1-1	Swift	13,627
36		13	H	Manchester United	W	2-1	Wright, Bentley	16,907
37		14	H	Chelsea	W	3-1	Jephcott 2, Swift	16,479
38		18	H	Sheffield Wednesday	D	1-1	Bentley	14,134
								Appearances
								Goals

FA Cup

R1	Jan	10	H	Grimsby Town	W	2-0	Edwards, Morris	13,976
R2		31	A	Leeds City	W	2-0	Bentley, Jephcott	29,733
R3	Feb	21	A	Aston Villa	L	1-2	Bowser	57,293
								Appearances
								Goals

Pearson HP	Smith J	Pennington J	Waterhouse F	Buck FR	McNeal R	Jephcott AC	Morris F	Bentley A	Lewis AE	Shearman BW	Newall JT	Gregory H	Baddeley G	Deacey C	Pailor R	Wright HF	Edwards EJ	Cook AF	Nicholls HJ	Swift A	Bowser S	Wood MC	Lloyd JA	Bache HG	
1	2	3	4	5	6	7	8	9	10	11															1
1	2	3	4	5	6	7	8	9	10	11															2
1	2	3	4	5	6	7	8	9	10	11															3
1	2	3	4	5	6	7	8		10	11	9														4
1	2	3	4	5	6	7	8		10	11	9														5
1	2	3	4	5	6	7	8	9	10	11															6
1	2	3	4	5	6	7	8	9		11		10													7
1	2	3	5		6	7	8	9	10	11			4												8
1	2	3	5		6	7	8	9	10	11			4												9
1	2	3	5		6	7	8		10	11	9		4												10
1	2	3	4		6	7	8		10	11				5	9										11
1	2	3	4	5	6	7	8	9	10	11															12
1	2	3	4	5	6	7	8	9	10	11															13
1	2	3	4	5	6	7		9	10	11						8									14
1	2	3	4	5	6	7			10	11	9	8													15
1	2	3	4	5	6	7	10			11					9		8								16
1	2	3	4	5	6	7	10	9		11							8								17
1	2	3	4	5	6	7	10	9		11							8								18
1		3	4		6	7	10	9		11				5			8	2							19
1		3	4		6	7	10	9						5			8	2	11						20
1		3	4		6	7	10	9						5			8	2	11						21
1	2		4	5	6	7	8		10	11								3		9					22
1	2	3	4		6	7	10	9		11				5			8								23
1	2	3	4		6	7	10	9		11	8			5											24
1	2	3	4	5	6	7	8	9		11											10				25
1	2		4	5	6	7		9	10	11											8	3			26
1	2	3	4		6	7		8	10											9	5		11		27
1	2	3	4		6	7		8	10											9	5		11		28
1	2	3	4		6	7	10	8												9	5		11		29
1	2		4	5	6	7	10	8												9		3	11		30
1	2		6	11				8				10	4			7				9	5	3			31
1	2		4		6	7		8				10							11	9	5	3			32
1	2	3	4		6	7		8				10							11	9	5				33
1	2		6			7	10	8		11			4							9	5	3			34
1	2	3	4		6	7		8		11						10				9	5				35
1	2	3	4		6	7		8		11						10				9	5				36
1	2	3	4		6	7		8			10									9	5		11		37
1	2	3			6	7		8			10		4							9	5		11		38
38	35	32	37	19	36	37	26	31	18	27	7	5	6	6	2	4	7	4	4	13	13	5	6		
				2	2	2	6	16	3	2	1	3			1	1	3			4					

Pearson HP	Smith J	Pennington J	Waterhouse F	Buck FR	McNeal R	Jephcott AC	Morris F	Bentley A	Lewis AE	Shearman BW	Newall JT	Gregory H	Baddeley G	Deacey C	Pailor R	Wright HF	Edwards EJ	Cook AF	Nicholls HJ	Swift A	Bowser S	Wood MC	Lloyd JA	Bache HG	
1	2	3	4	5	6	7	10	9		11							8								R1
1	2	3	4	5	6	7	8	9	10	11															R2
1	2	3	4	5	6	7		10		11											8			9	R3
3	3	3	3	3	3	3	2	3	1	3							1				1			1	
						1	1	1									1				1				

1914-15

Division One

	P	W	D	L	F	A	Pts
Everton	38	19	8	11	76	47	46
Oldham Athletic	38	17	11	10	70	56	45
Blackburn Rovers	38	18	7	13	83	61	43
Burnley	38	18	7	13	61	47	43
Manchester City	38	15	13	10	49	39	43
Sheffield United	38	15	13	10	49	41	43
Sheffield Wednesday	38	15	13	10	61	54	43
Sunderland	38	18	5	15	81	72	41
Bradford Park Avenue	38	17	7	14	69	65	41
West Bromwich Albion	38	15	10	13	49	43	40
Bradford City	38	13	14	11	55	49	40
Middlesbrough	38	13	12	13	62	74	38
Liverpool	38	14	9	15	65	75	37
Aston Villa	38	13	11	14	62	72	37
Newcastle United	38	11	10	17	46	48	32
Notts County	38	9	13	16	41	57	31
Bolton Wanderers	38	11	8	19	68	84	30
Manchester United	38	9	12	17	46	62	30
Chelsea	38	8	13	17	51	65	29
Tottenham Hotspur	38	8	12	18	57	90	28

Secretary-manager: Fred Everiss

- The first senior representative match took place at The Hawthorns when the Football League beat the Irish League 2–1 on 7 October before a crowd of 9,250.
- Albion gave senior debuts to seven players this season – former Bradford City winger Louis Bookman, Teddy Bowen (ex-Nuneaton Town), Jack Crisp from Ordnance FC and formerly with Leicester Fosse, local lad Jackie Mann, defender Fred Reed, Sammy Richardson from Great Bridge and Wednesbury-born Ted Shore.

Match No.	Date			Opponents	Result		Scorers	Attendance
1	Sep	2	A	Newcastle United	W	2-1	Bentley, Bookman	15,000
2		5	A	Middlesbrough	L	0-2		14,500
3		12	H	Sheffield United	D	1-1	Poulton	6,481
4		19	A	Aston Villa	L	1-2	Swift	29,000
5		26	H	Liverpool	W	4-0	Bentley 2, Morris 2	18,026
6		28	A	Tottenham Hotspur	L	0-2		22,000
7	Oct	3	A	Bradford Park Avenue	W	4-1	Bentley, Bache, Morris 2	19,000
8		10	H	Oldham Athletic	D	0-0		15,768
9		17	A	Manchester United	D	0-0		13,200
10		24	H	Bolton Wanderers	W	3-0	Bentley, Shearman, Bache	7,817
11		31	A	Blackburn Rovers	L	1-2	Morris	8,005
12	Nov	7	H	Notts County	W	4-1	Morris 2, Bentley, Bache	10,368
13		14	A	Sunderland	W	2-1	Jephcott, Bentley	15,000
14		21	H	Sheffield Wednesday	D	0-0		11,254
15		28	H	Manchester City	L	0-1		9,398
16	Dec	5	A	Everton	L	1-2	Crisp	22,000
17		12	H	Chelsea	W	2-0	Jephcott, Swift	6,421
18		19	A	Bradford City	L	0-5		5,300
19		25	A	Burnley	W	2-0	Morris, Swift	10,000
20		26	H	Burnley	W	3-0	Swift 2, Crisp	15,853
21	Jan	2	H	Middlesbrough	W	1-0	Bache	10,914
22		16	A	Sheffield United	L	0-2		7,800
23		23	H	Aston Villa	W	2-0	Swift, Morris	19,492
24	Feb	6	H	Bradford Park Avenue	W	1-0	Bowser (pen)	7,466
25		20	H	Manchester United	D	0-0		10,169
26		27	A	Bolton Wanderers	D	1-1	Crisp	8,900
27	Mar	6	H	Blackburn Rovers	D	0-0		15,168
28		9	A	Oldham Athletic	D	1-1	Crisp	11,400
29		13	A	Notts County	D	1-1	Morris	28,000
30		20	H	Sunderland	L	1-2	Morris	10,233
31		24	A	Liverpool	L	1-3	Newall	16,000
32		27	A	Sheffield Wednesday	D	0-0		9,000
33	Apr	3	A	Manchester City	L	0-4		8,400
34		5	H	Newcastle United	W	2-0	Bentley 2	11,858
35		6	H	Tottenham Hotspur	W	3-2	Gregory 3	5,813
36		10	H	Everton	L	1-2	Swift	8,748
37		17	A	Chelsea	L	1-4	McNeal	6,000
38		24	H	Bradford City	W	3-0	Gregory, Newall, McNeal	4,410
								Appearances
								Goals

FA Cup

R1	Jan	9	A	Hull City	L	0-1		12,142
								Appearances

	Pearson HP	Smith J	Pennington J	Waterhouse F	Bowser S	McNeal R	Wright HF	Bentley A	Poulton A	Bache HG	Bookman LO	Shearman BW	Moorwood L	Swift A	Morris F	Wood MC	Newall JT	Mann JF	Jephcott AC	Crisp J	Richardson S	Parkes HA	Shore EW	Bowen WE	Gregory H	Reed FWM
1	1	2	3	4	5	6	7	8	9	10	11															
2	1	2	3	4	5	6	7	8	9	10		11														
3	1	2	3	4	5	6	7	8	9	10	11															
4		2	3	4	5	6		8		10	11	7	1	9												
5	1	2	3	4	5	6		8		9	11	7			10											
6	1	2	3	4	5	6		8			11	7		9	10											
7	1		3	4	5	6		8		9	11	7			10	2										
8	1	2	3	4	5	6		8			11	7			10		9									
9	1	2	3	4	5	6			9		11	7			10			8								
10	1	2	3	4	5	6		8		9		11			10				7							
11	1	2		4	5	6		8		9		11			10	3			7							
12	1	2		4	5	6		8		9		11			10	3			7							
13	1	2	3	4	5	6		8		9		11			10				7							
14	1	2	3	4	5	6		8		9		11			10				7							
15	1	2	3	4	5	6		8	9		11				10				7							
16	1	2	3	4	5	6		8	9		11				10					7						
17	1	2	3	4	5	6					11			9	10				7	8						
18	1	2	3	4	5	6					11			9	10				7	8						
19	1	2	3	4	5	6					11			9	10				7	8						
20	1	2	3	4	5	6					11			9	10				7	8						
21	1	2	3	4	5	6				9	11				10				7	8						
22	1	2	3		5	6						11		9	10				7	8	4					
23	1	2	3	4	5	6						11		9	10				7	8						
24	1	2	3	4	5	6						11		9	10				7	8						
25	1	2	3	4	5	6						11		9	10				7	8						
26	1	2	3	4	5	6						11		9	10					8		7				
27	1	2	3	4	5	6		8				11		9	10							7				
28	1	2	3	4	5	6			9			11			10					8		7				
29	1	2	3	4	5	6			9			11			10					8		7				
30	1	2	3	4	5				9			11			10					8	6	7				
31	1		3	4		6						11					9	8				7	2	5	10	
32	1		3	5		6		9				11			8		4					7	2		10	
33	1			5		6		9				11			8	3	4			7			2		10	
34	1			5	3	6		9				11				2	4		7	8					10	
35					3	6	10					11	1	9		2	4		7						8	5
36	1			4	3	6	10					11		9		2			7	8						5
37	1				3	6	8					11		9			4					7	2		10	5
38	1			4	5	6	8				11					3	9			7			2		10	
	36	29	30	35	35	37	7	19	9	12	16	28	2	15	28	8	8	2	18	18	2	8	5	1	7	3
					1	2		9	1	4	1	1		7	11		2		2	4					4	

	Pearson HP	Smith J	Pennington J	Waterhouse F	Bowser S	McNeal R	Wright HF	Bentley A	Poulton A	Bache HG	Bookman LO	Shearman BW	Moorwood L	Swift A	Morris F	Wood MC	Newall JT	Mann JF	Jephcott AC	Crisp J	Richardson S	Parkes HA	Shore EW	Bowen WE	Gregory H	Reed FWM
R1	1	2	3	4	5	6				9		11			10				7	8						
	1	1	1	1	1	1				1		1			1				1	1						

1919-20

Division One

	P	W	D	L	F	A	Pts
West Bromwich Albion	42	28	4	10	104	47	60
Burnley	42	21	9	12	65	59	51
Chelsea	42	22	5	15	56	51	49
Liverpool	42	19	10	13	59	44	48
Sunderland	42	22	4	16	72	59	48
Bolton Wanderers	42	19	9	14	72	65	47
Manchester City	42	18	9	15	71	62	45
Newcastle United	42	17	9	16	44	39	43
Aston Villa	42	18	6	18	75	73	42
Arsenal	42	15	12	15	56	58	42
Bradford Park Avenue	42	15	12	15	60	63	42
Manchester United	42	13	14	15	54	50	40
Middlesbrough	42	15	10	17	61	65	40
Sheffield United	42	16	8	18	59	69	40
Bradford City	42	14	11	17	54	63	39
Everton	42	12	14	16	69	68	38
Oldham Athletic	42	15	8	19	49	52	38
Derby County	42	13	12	17	47	57	38
Preston North End	42	14	10	18	57	73	38
Blackburn Rovers	42	13	11	18	64	77	37
Notts County	42	12	12	18	56	74	36
Sheffield Wednesday	42	7	9	26	28	64	23

Secretary-manager: Fred Everiss

- Albion created several records when winning the League Championship for the first, and so far only, time in the club's history – most victories (28), fewest draws (4), most goals scored for (104) and most points gained (60). The total number of goals was also the most by a team in the First Division.
- Fred Morris became the first player to score over 30 goals in a season for the club, netting 37, all in the League. He was also the first Baggies player to net five in a League game (against Notts County, won 8–0).
- Sid Bowser became the first Albion defender to score a hat-trick in a competitive game when he netted three times in a 4–1 home League win over Bradford City in September. Two of his goals came from the penalty spot.
- Wartime signing Tommy Magee made his League debut against Oldham Athletic on the opening day of the season. Forwards George James and Andrew Smith were two other new recruits, secured from Bilston United and Birmingham respectively.
- Defender Frank Waterhouse moved to Derby County and winger Ben Shearman signed for Nottingham Forest.

Match No.	Date			Opponents	Result		Scorers	Attendance
1	Aug	30	H	Oldham Athletic	W	3-1	Morris 2, Gregory	19,058
2	Sep	3	A	Newcastle United	W	2-0	Magee, Gregory	50,000
3		6	A	Oldham Athletic	L	1-2	Bowser (pen)	16,000
4		8	H	Newcastle United	W	3-0	A. Smith, Bowser (pen), Morris	20,052
5		13	H	Everton	W	4-3	Magee, Morris, Gregory, Crisp	31,245
6		20	A	Everton	W	5-2	Jephcott, Crisp 2, A. Smith 2	25,000
7		27	H	Bradford City	W	4-1	Bowser 3 (2 pens), Morris	29,680
8	Oct	4	A	Bradford City	L	0-3		17,000
9		11	H	Bolton Wanderers	W	4-1	Magee, Bowser (pen), Crisp, A. Smith	35,227
10		18	A	Bolton Wanderers	W	2-1	Morris, Gregory	24,000
11		25	H	Notts County	W	8-0	Morris 5, Foster (og), Gregory, Magee	36,086
12	Nov	1	A	Notts County	L	0-2		12,050
13		10	H	Aston Villa	L	1-2	Gregory	43,121
14		15	A	Aston Villa	W	4-2	Gregory 2, Morris 2	58,273
15		22	H	Sheffield Wednesday	L	1-3	A. Smith	22,193
16		29	A	Sheffield Wednesday	W	3-0	Bowser (pen), Bentley, Morris	25,000
17	Dec	6	A	Manchester City	W	3-2	Bowser (pen), Morris 2	26,000
18		13	H	Manchester City	W	2-0	Morris 2	25,040
19		20	A	Derby County	W	4-0	Bentley, Morris 2, Gregory	21,000
20		26	H	Sunderland	W	4-0	Magee, Morris 2, Bentley	43,579
21		27	H	Derby County	W	3-0	Morris 2, Magee	34,167
22	Jan	1	A	Sunderland	L	1-4	Morris	32,500
23		3	A	Blackburn Rovers	W	5-1	Bentley 3, Morris, Gregory	18,000
24		17	H	Blackburn Rovers	W	5-2	Magee, Bentley, Morris, Crisp, Gregory	23,360
25		24	H	Manchester United	W	2-1	Bowser, Morris	30,192
26	Feb	7	H	Sheffield United	L	0-2		28,975
27		14	A	Sheffield United	L	0-1		39,850
28		21	H	Middlesbrough	W	4-1	Bentley 2, Morris 2	24,955
29		25	A	Manchester United	W	2-1	Bentley 2	21,000
30		28	A	Middlesbrough	D	0-0		16,500
31	Mar	6	A	Burnley	D	2-2	Jephcott, Crisp	30,200
32		13	H	Burnley	W	4-1	Bentley, Morris 2, Crisp	32,213
33		20	A	Preston North End	W	1-0	Crisp	20,000
34		27	H	Preston North End	W	4-1	Jephcott 2, Morris 2	24,188
35	Apr	3	A	Bradford Park Avenue	W	4-0	Bentley, Morris, McNeal (pen), A. Smith	9,000
36		5	A	Arsenal	L	0-1		38,000
37		6	H	Arsenal	W	1-0	Morris	39,397
38		10	H	Bradford Park Avenue	W	3-1	Jephcott, Bentley, Bowser (pen)	29,414
39		17	A	Liverpool	D	0-0		45,100
40		24	H	Liverpool	D	1-1	Morris	33,349
41		26	A	Chelsea	L	0-2		39,902
42	May	1	H	Chelsea	W	4-0	McNeal, Gregory, A. Smith, Bentley	35,668

Appearances

Goals

FA Cup

R1	Jan	10	H	Barnsley	L	0-1		32,327

Appearances

Pearson HP	Smith J	Pennington J	Richardson S	Bowser S	McNeal R	Crisp J	Magee TP	Smith AW	Morris F	Gregory H	Jephcott AC	Moorwood L	Cook AF	Reed FWM	Bentley A	Hatton SEO	Waterhouse F	
1	2	3	4	5	6	7	8	9	10	11								1
1	2	3	4	5	6	7	8	9	10	11								2
1	2	3	4	5	6	7	8	9	10	11								3
1	2	3	4	5	6	7	8	9	10	11								4
1	2	3	4	5	6	7	8	9	10	11								5
1	2	3	4	5	6	11	8	9	10		7							6
1	2	3	4	5	6	11	8	9	10		7							7
1	2	3	4	5	6	11	8	9	10		7							8
1	2	3	4	5	6	11	8	9	10		7							9
		3	4	5	6	11	8		9	10	7	1	2					10
		3	4		6	7	8	9	10	11		1	2	5				11
	2	3	4	5	6	7	8	9	10	11		1						12
1	2	3	4	5	6	7	8	9	10	11								13
1	2	3	4	5	6	8		9	10	11	7							14
1	2	3	4	5	6	8		9	10	11	7							15
1	2	3	4	5	6	11	8		10		7				9			16
1	2	3	4	5	6	11	8		10		7				9			17
1	2	3	4	5	6	7	8		10	11					9			18
1	2	3	4	5	6	7	8		10	11					9			19
1	2	3	4	5	6	7	8		10	11					9			20
1	2	3	4	5	6	7	8		10	11					9			21
1	2	3	4	5	6	7	8		10	11					9			22
1	2	3	4	5	6	7	8		10	11					9			23
1	2	3	4	5	6	7	8		10	11					9			24
1	2	3	4	5	6	7	8	9	10	11								25
1	2	3	4	5	6	7	8		10	11						9		26
1	2	3	4	5	6			8	10	11	7				9			27
1	2	3	4	5	6			8	10	11	7				9			28
1	2		4	5	6	11		8		10	7		3		9			29
1	2	3		5	6	11		8	10		7				9		4	30
1	2	3		5	6	8			10	11	7				9		4	31
1	2	3	4	5	6	8			10	11	7				9			32
1	2		4	5	6	11		8		10	7		3		9			33
1	2	3	4	5	6	11		8	10		7				9			34
1	2	3	4	5	6			8	10	11	7				9			35
1	2	3	4	5	6			8	10	11	7				9			36
1	2		4	5	6	8		9	10	11	7		3					37
1	2		4	5	6	11		8		10	7		3		9			38
1	2	3	4	5	6	7		8	10	11					9			39
1	2		4	5	6	7		8	10	11			3		9			40
1	2	3	4	5	6	7		8	10	11					9			41
1	2	3	4	5	6	7		8	10	11					9			42
39	40	37	40	41	42	38	24	29	39	34	21	3	7	1	24	1	2	
				10	2	8	7	7	37	12	5				15			

One own-goal

Pearson HP	Smith J	Pennington J	Richardson S	Bowser S	McNeal R	Crisp J	Magee TP	Smith AW	Morris F	Gregory H	Jephcott AC	Moorwood L	Cook AF	Reed FWM	Bentley A	Hatton SEO	Waterhouse F	
1	2	3	4	5	6	7	8		10	11					9			R1
1	1	1	1	1	1	1	1		1	1					1			

1920-21

Division One

	P	W	D	L	F	A	Pts
Burnley	42	23	13	6	79	36	59
Manchester City	42	24	6	12	70	50	54
Bolton Wanderers	42	19	14	9	77	53	52
Liverpool	42	18	15	9	63	35	51
Newcastle United	42	20	10	12	66	45	50
Tottenham Hotspur	42	19	9	14	70	48	47
Everton	42	17	13	12	66	55	47
Middlesbrough	42	17	12	13	53	53	46
Arsenal	42	15	14	13	59	63	44
Aston Villa	42	18	7	17	63	70	43
Blackburn Rovers	42	13	15	14	57	59	41
Sunderland	42	14	13	15	57	60	41
Manchester United	42	15	10	17	64	68	40
West Bromwich Albion	42	13	14	15	54	58	40
Bradford City	42	12	15	15	61	63	39
Preston North End	42	15	9	18	61	65	39
Huddersfield Town	42	15	9	18	42	49	39
Chelsea	42	13	13	16	48	58	39
Oldham Athletic	42	9	15	18	49	86	33
Sheffield United	42	6	18	18	42	68	30
Derby County	42	5	16	21	32	58	26
Bradford Park Avenue	42	8	8	26	43	76	24

Secretary-manager: Fred Everiss:

- Future England international George Ashmore conceded five goals on his League debut for Albion against Blackburn in October.
- Another debutant was centre-forward Bobby Blood, who had one leg shorter than the other. He was signed from Port Vale and netted a penalty against Spurs. Joe Carter also arrived at the club from Westbourne Celtic (Handsworth). He became an England international and remained at The Hawthorns until 1936. Out of the camp went goalkeeper Len Moorwood, sold to Burnley for £1,100.
- A record crowd of 66,094 witnessed Albion's 0–0 draw away to Aston Villa in November.

Match No.	Date			Opponents	Result		Scorers	Attendance
1	Aug	28	A	Newcastle United	D	1-1	Morris	61,080
2	Sep	1	H	Liverpool	D	1-1	Gregory	32,475
3		4	H	Newcastle United	D	0-0		29,202
4		6	A	Liverpool	D	0-0		27,550
5		11	A	Bolton Wanderers	L	0-3		41,584
6		18	H	Bolton Wanderers	W	2-1	Crisp, Bentley	34,865
7		25	A	Derby County	D	1-1	Morris	18,300
8	Oct	2	H	Derby County	W	3-0	McNeal, Morris, Bowser (pen)	26,893
9		9	A	Blackburn Rovers	L	1-5	Taylor	15,300
10		16	H	Blackburn Rovers	D	1-1	Morris	35,025
11		23	A	Huddersfield Town	L	1-5	Taylor	25,100
12		30	H	Huddersfield Town	W	3-0	Bowser (pen), A. Smith, Morris	44,049
13	Nov	6	A	Aston Villa	D	0-0		66,094
14		13	H	Aston Villa	W	2-1	A. Smith, Bowser (pen)	42,334
15		27	H	Bradford City	W	2-0	Morris, Gregory	22,068
16	Dec	4	H	Sunderland	W	4-1	Bentley, Gregory, Bowser 2 (1 pen)	23,726
17		11	A	Sunderland	L	0-3		20,000
18		18	H	Everton	L	1-2	Crisp	19,932
19		25	A	Manchester City	L	0-4		22,306
20		27	H	Manchester City	D	2-2	A. Smith, Morris	32,147
21	Jan	1	A	Everton	D	2-2	Morris, James	59,964
22		15	A	Manchester United	W	4-1	James 2, A. Smith, Morris	40,100
23		22	H	Manchester United	L	0-2		26,826
24		29	A	Middlesbrough	W	1-0	A. Smith	25,500
25	Feb	5	H	Middlesbrough	L	0-1		24,920
26		9	A	Bradford City	D	1-1	James	12,000
27		12	A	Chelsea	L	0-3		15,000
28		23	H	Tottenham Hotspur	W	3-1	Crisp, Bentley, Blood (pen)	31,753
29		26	A	Tottenham Hotspur	L	0-1		35,000
30	Mar	12	A	Oldham Athletic	W	3-0	Blood, Morris 2	13,000
31		14	H	Chelsea	D	1-1	Blood	28,140
32		19	H	Oldham Athletic	D	0-0		23,908
33		26	H	Preston North End	L	0-3		23,511
34		28	A	Arsenal	L	1-2	Crisp	20,152
35		29	H	Arsenal	L	3-4	A. Smith, Bowser (pen), Morris	23,650
36	Apr	2	A	Preston North End	L	1-2	Blood	18,052
37		9	H	Burnley	W	2-0	Crisp, Morris	17,242
38		16	A	Burnley	D	1-1	A. Smith	13,700
39		23	H	Sheffield United	D	1-1	Blood	23,697
40		30	A	Sheffield United	W	2-0	Morris, Blood	21,000
41	May	2	H	Bradford Park Avenue	L	0-1		17,472
42		7	A	Bradford Park Avenue	W	3-0	Morris 2 (1 pen), Blood	8,105
								Appearances
								Goals

FA Cup

R1	Jan	8	A	Notts County	L	0-3		32,995
								Appearances

Pearson HP	Smith J	Pennington J	Richardson S	Bowser S	McNeal R	Crisp J	Smith AW	Bentley A	Morris F	Gregory H	Jephcott AC	Magee TP	Cook AF	Taylor H	Adams W	James RW	Long WR	Ashmore GSA	Hatton SEO	Clark B	Newall JT	Reed FWM	Blood R	Bedford L	
1	2	3	4	5	6	7	8	9	10	11															1
1	2	3	4	5	6	11	9			10	7	8													2
1	2	3	4	5	6	11	9			10	7	8													3
1		3	4	5	6	11	9			10	7	8	2												4
1		3	4	5	6	11		9		10	7	8	2												5
1	2	3	4	5	6	7		8	10	11				9											6
1	2		4	5		7		8	10	11				9	3	6									7
1	2		4	5	6			8	10	11				9	3		7								8
	2		4	5				8	10					9	3		7	1	6	11					9
1	2		4	5				8	10	11	7			9	3				6						10
1	2		4	5			10	8		11	7			9	3				6						11
1	2	3	4	5	6		8		10	11	7			9											12
1	2	3	4	5	6		8		10	11	7			9											13
1	2	3	4	5	6		8		10	11	7			9											14
1	2	3	4	5	6		8	9	10	11	7														15
1	2	3	4	5	6		8	9	10	11	7														16
1	2	3	4	5	6		8	9	10	11	7														17
1	2	3	4	5	6	7	8	9	10	11															18
1	2	3	4	5	6	7	8	9	10	11															19
1	2	3	4	5	6	8	8		10	11	7														20
1	2		4	5	6	7		8	10	11			3			9									21
1	2	3		5	6		8		10	11	7					9					4				22
1	2	3		5	6		8		10	11	7					9					4				23
1	2	3		5	6		8		10	11	7					9					4				24
1	2	3		5	6		8		10	11	7					9					4				25
1	2		4	5	6	11		8	10		7		3			9									26
1	2	3	4		6	11	8		10		7					9						5			27
1	2	3	4	5	6	11		8	10		7												9		28
1	2	3	4	5		11		8	10		7								6				9		29
1	2	3	4	5	6	8			10	11	7												9		30
1	2	3	4	5	6	8			10	11	7												9		31
1	2		4	5	6	8			10	11	7				3								9		32
1	2	3	4	5	6	8			10	11	7												9		33
1	2		4	5	6	11	8		10		7				3								9		34
1	2	3	4	5	6	7	8		10														9	11	35
1	2	3	4	5	6	7	8		10														9	11	36
	2	3	4	5	6	11	8		10		7							1					9		37
	2	3	4	5	6	11	8		10		7							1					9		38
	2	3	4	5	6	11	8		10		7							1					9		39
	2	3	4	5	6	11	8		10		7							1					9		40
	2	3	4	5	6	11	8		10		7							1					9		41
	2	3	4		6		5	8	10	11		7						1					9		42
5	40	33	38	40	37	27	28	18	37	29	31	5	4	9	7	8	2	7	4	1	4	1	15	2	
				6	1	5	7	3	16	3				2		4							7		

1	2		4	5	6	7	9	8	10	11			3	R1
1	1		1	1	1	1	1	1	1	1			1	

1921-22

Division One

	P	W	D	L	F	A	Pts
Liverpool	42	22	13	7	63	36	57
Tottenham Hotspur	42	21	9	12	65	39	51
Burnley	42	22	5	15	72	54	49
Cardiff City	42	19	10	13	61	53	48
Aston Villa	42	22	3	17	74	55	47
Bolton Wanderers	42	20	7	15	68	59	47
Newcastle United	42	18	10	14	59	45	46
Middlesbrough	42	16	14	12	79	69	46
Chelsea	42	17	12	13	40	43	46
Manchester City	42	18	9	15	65	70	45
Sheffield United	42	15	10	17	59	54	40
Sunderland	42	16	8	18	60	62	40
West Bromwich Albion	42	15	10	17	51	63	40
Huddersfield Town	42	15	9	18	53	54	39
Blackburn Rovers	42	13	12	17	54	57	38
Preston North End	42	13	12	17	42	65	38
Arsenal	42	15	7	20	47	56	37
Birmingham	42	15	7	20	48	60	37
Oldham Athletic	42	13	11	18	38	50	37
Everton	42	12	12	18	57	55	36
Bradford City	42	11	10	21	48	72	32
Manchester United	42	8	12	22	41	73	28

Secretary-manager: Fred Everiss

- The legendary Jesse Pennington retired after serving Albion for 19 years. His last game was against Liverpool, the same club he made his debut against in 1903. He made 496 senior appearances but never scored a goal.
- New recruits included Welsh international Stan Davies from Everton, future FA Cup-winning captain Tommy Glidden from Sunderland West End (signed in April), Welshman Ivor Jones from Swansea Town, local lad Ernie Watson and inside-forward Charlie 'Tug' Wilson, recruited from the Sheffield club Hallam. Wilson was only 16 years and 73 days old when he made his senior debut at Oldham – Albion's youngest ever League player.
- One departure saw defender Matt Wood sold to Kidderminster Harriers.
- Albion's 1,000th League game was played against Tottenham Hotspur at White Hart Lane in January.

Match No.	Date			Opponents	Result		Scorers	Attendanc
1	Aug	27	H	Middlesbrough	D	0-0		24,880
2		29	A	Manchester United	W	3-2	Brett (og), Blood 2	20,000
3	Sep	3	A	Middlesbrough	L	2-3	Blood, A. Smith	15,000
4		7	H	Manchester United	D	0-0		20,557
5		10	H	Blackburn Rovers	L	0-2		20,160
6		17	A	Blackburn Rovers	W	3-2	Crisp, Bentley 2	13,000
7		24	H	Oldham Athletic	L	0-1		19,840
8	Oct	1	A	Oldham Athletic	L	0-1		10,107
9		8	H	Aston Villa	L	0-1		45,077
10		15	A	Aston Villa	W	1-0	Blood	55,000
11		22	H	Cardiff City	D	2-2	Gregory, A. Smith	20,969
12		29	A	Cardiff City	L	0-2		16,000
13	Nov	5	H	Bolton Wanderers	L	0-1		15,502
14		12	A	Bolton Wanderers	L	0-2		20,207
15		19	A	Manchester City	L	1-6	Bentley	18,000
16		26	H	Manchester City	W	2-0	Blagden, Morris	14,145
17	Dec	3	A	Everton	W	2-1	Morris, Reed	21,000
18		10	H	Everton	D	1-1	Morris	16,606
19		17	H	Sunderland	W	2-1	Morris, Davies	18,251
20		24	A	Sunderland	L	0-5		10,522
21		26	H	Birmingham	W	1-0	Davies	49,488
22		27	A	Birmingham	W	2-0	Magee, Morris	44,500
23		31	H	Huddersfield Town	W	3-2	Morris, Blagden, Gregory	25,036
24	Jan	14	A	Huddersfield Town	L	0-2		6,000
25		21	H	Tottenham Hotspur	W	3-0	Davies 2, Magee	21,498
26		30	A	Tottenham Hotspur	L	0-2		20,400
27	Feb	4	H	Bradford City	D	1-1	Crisp	15,170
28		25	A	Preston North End	W	3-0	Morris, A. Smith, Davies	16,000
29	Mar	4	H	Chelsea	D	2-2	Davies 2	11,026
30		8	A	Bradford City	D	1-1	A. Smith	10,400
31		11	A	Chelsea	D	1-1	Morris	20,000
32		18	A	Sheffield United	D	0-0		10,900
33		25	H	Sheffield United	W	3-0	A. Smith, Richardson, Davies	12,113
34		29	H	Preston North End	W	2-0	Morris, Davies	12,585
35	Apr	1	H	Burnley	W	2-0	Morris 2	13,304
36		8	A	Burnley	L	2-4	Davies 2	8,900
37		15	A	Newcastle United	L	0-3		28,000
38		17	H	Arsenal	L	0-3		23,997
39		18	A	Arsenal	D	2-2	Hutchins (og), Davies	23,663
40		22	H	Newcastle United	L	1-2	Davies	32,063
41		29	A	Liverpool	W	2-1	Gregory 2	20,551
42	May	6	H	Liverpool	L	1-4	Davies	23,247

Appearances

Goals

FA Cup

R1	Jan	7	A	Chelsea	W	4-2	Blagden 2, Davies, Crisp	36,365
R2		28	A	Liverpool	W	1-0	Davies	42,118
R3	Feb	18	H	Notts County	D	1-1	Davies (pen)	43,853
rep		22	A	Notts County	L	0-2		24,278

Appearances

Goals

Ashmore GS	Smith J	Adams W	Richardson S	Bowser S	McNeal R	Jephcott AC	Smith AW	Blood R	Morris F	Crisp J	Magee T	Bedford L	Cook AF	Bentley A	Gregory H	Pennington J	Newall JT	Wilson C	Blagden J	Savage G	Jones L	Pearson HP	Hatton S	Davies S	Reed FWM	James GC	Jones I	Watson E	
1	2	3	4	5	6	7	8	9	10	11																			1
1	2	3	4	5	6	7	8	9	10	11																			2
1	2	3	4	5	6	7	8	9	10	11																			3
1	2	3	4	5	6		8	9	10	11	7																		4
1	2	3	4	5	6		8	9	10		7	11																	5
1	2		4	5	6			9	10	7			3	8	11														6
1	2		4	5	6			9	10	7			3	8	11														7
1	2			5	6		8		10	7					11	3	4	9											8
1	2		4	5	6		9		10	7				8	11	3													9
1	2		4	5	6		8	9	10	7					11	3													10
1	2		4	5	6		8	9	10	7					11	3													11
1	2		4	5	6			9	10		7			8	11	3													12
1	2			5	6			9			7		3		11		4		8	10									13
1	2		4	5	6		8				7				11	3				10	9								14
	2			5	6			9			7			10	11	3			8			1	4						15
	2		4	5	6				10		7				11	3			8			1		9					16
	2		4		6				10		7				11	3			8			1		9	5				17
	2		4	5	6				10		7				11	3			8			1		9					18
	2		4	5	6				10		7				11	3			8			1		9					19
	2		4	5	6				10		7				11	3			8			1		9					20
	2		4		6				10		7				11	3			8			1		9	5				21
	2		4		6				10		7				11	3			8			1		9	5				22
	2		4		6				10		7				11	3			8			1		9	5				23
	2		4	10	6					11	7					3			8			1		9	5				24
	2		4		6				10	11	7					3			8			1		9	5				25
	2	3	4						10	11	7								8			1		9	5	6			26
	2		4		6			9	10	11	7					3			8			1			5				27
	2		4	5	6		8		10		7				11	3						1		9					28
	2		4	5	6		8		10		7				11	3						1		9					29
	2		4		6		8		10	11	7					3						1		9	5				30
	2		4		6		8		10	11	7					3						1		9	5				31
	2		4		6		8	9	10	11	7					3						1		8					32
	2		4		6		8		10	11	7					3						1		9	5				33
	2		4	5	6		8		10	11						3			7			1		9					34
	2		4	5	6				10		8				11	3			7		9	1							35
	2	3	4	5	6		8		10		7				11							1		9					36
	2	3	4	5	6				10		7				11							1		9			8		37
	2	3	4	5	6		8		10		7				11							1		9					38
	2	3	4		6				10		7				11			8				1		9	5				39
	2		4	5	6	7			10						11	3						1		9			8		40
	2		4	5	6				10		7				11	3		8				1		9					41
	2			5	6				10		7				11	3		8				1		9				4	42
14	42	10	38	30	41	4	19	14	38	19	31	1	3	5	28	29	2	4	16	2	2	28	1	25	12	1	2	1	
			1				5	4	11	2	2			3	4				2					14	1				

Two own-goals

Ashmore GS	Smith J	Adams W	Richardson S	Bowser S	McNeal R	Jephcott AC	Smith AW	Blood R	Morris F	Crisp J	Magee T	Bedford L	Cook AF	Bentley A	Gregory H	Pennington J	Newall JT	Wilson C	Blagden J	Savage G	Jones L	Pearson HP	Hatton S	Davies S	Reed FWM	James GC	Jones I	Watson E	
	2		4		6				10	11	7					3			8			1		9	5				R1
	2		4	6					10	11	7					3			8			1		9	5				R2
	2		4		6				10	11	7					3			8			1		9	5				R3
	2		4		6				10	11	7					3			8			1		9	5				rep
	4		4	1	3				4	4	4					4			4			4		4	4				
										1									2					3					

1922-23

Division One

	P	W	D	L	F	A	Pts
Liverpool	42	26	8	8	70	31	60
Sunderland	42	22	10	10	72	54	54
Huddersfield Town	42	21	11	10	60	32	53
Newcastle United	42	18	12	12	45	37	48
Everton	42	20	7	15	63	59	47
Aston Villa	42	18	10	14	64	51	46
West Bromwich Albion	42	17	11	14	58	49	45
Manchester City	42	17	11	14	50	49	45
Cardiff City	42	18	7	17	73	59	43
Sheffield United	42	16	10	16	68	64	42
Arsenal	42	16	10	16	61	62	42
Tottenham Hotspur	42	17	7	18	50	50	41
Bolton Wanderers	42	14	12	16	50	58	40
Blackburn Rovers	42	14	12	16	47	62	40
Burnley	42	16	6	20	58	59	38
Preston North End	42	13	11	18	60	64	37
Birmingham	42	13	11	18	41	57	37
Middlesbrough	42	13	10	19	57	63	36
Chelsea	42	9	18	15	45	53	36
Nottingham Forest	42	13	8	21	41	70	34
Stoke	42	10	10	22	47	67	30
Oldham Athletic	42	10	10	22	35	65	30

Secretary-manager: Fred Everiss

- 'Wee' Tommy Magee, who stood just over 5ft 2in tall, gained the first of his five England caps this season, against Wales at Cardiff in March.
- Unfortunately right-winger Claude Jephcott was forced to retire through injury, never recovering from a broken leg suffered against Aston Villa in September 1922. He became a director in 1934.
- Albion's reserve side won the Central League title for the first time, amassing 63 points from 26 wins and 11 draws. They scored 95 goals and conceded only 33 in their 42 matches.
- The first full international was staged at The Hawthorns when England beat Ireland 2–0 in October before a crowd of 20,173.
- Andrew Smith was transferred to Stoke.

Match No.	Date			Opponents	Result		Scorers	Attendance
1	Aug	26	A	Burnley	L	0-3		30,000
2		28	H	Preston North End	D	2-2	Davies, Morris	25,343
3	Sep	2	H	Burnley	W	2-1	Davies 2	23,561
4		4	A	Preston North End	D	0-0		22,067
5		9	A	Aston Villa	L	0-2		40,000
6		16	H	Aston Villa	W	3-0	Davies 2, Morris	39,576
7		23	A	Stoke	W	2-0	Davies, A. Smith	20,000
8		30	H	Stoke	L	0-1		20,385
9	Oct	7	A	Arsenal	L	1-3	Gregory	32,500
10		14	H	Arsenal	W	7-0	Morris 4, Crisp 2, Gregory	21,730
11		21	A	Tottenham Hotspur	L	1-3	Gregory	35,000
12		28	H	Tottenham Hotspur	W	5-1	Jones, Davies 2, Gregory, Crisp	21,150
13	Nov	4	H	Manchester City	W	2-0	Davies, Morris	17,124
14		11	A	Manchester City	D	1-1	Davies	25,000
15		18	H	Everton	D	0-0		18,539
16		25	A	Everton	W	1-0	Morris	35,000
17	Dec	2	H	Bolton Wanderers	D	1-1	Davies	16,527
18		9	A	Bolton Wanderers	L	0-3		21,625
19		16	A	Sunderland	L	2-3	Morris, Gregory	10,000
20		23	H	Sunderland	D	1-1	Morris	23,092
21		26	A	Cardiff City	L	0-3		39,000
22		27	H	Cardiff City	W	3-0	Davies (pen), Morris, Spencer	14,898
23		30	A	Blackburn Rovers	L	1-5	Morris (pen)	7,000
24	Jan	6	H	Blackburn Rovers	W	3-0	Gregory, Davies, Morris (pen)	17,024
25		20	A	Birmingham	W	2-0	Davies, Gregory	32,180
26		27	H	Birmingham	W	1-0	Morris	25,123
27	Feb	7	A	Liverpool	L	0-2		26,000
28		10	H	Liverpool	D	0-0		20,464
29		14	A	Newcastle United	L	0-2		10,000
30	Mar	3	A	Nottingham Forest	W	4-0	Bowser, Blood 3	17,134
31		10	H	Nottingham Forest	D	0-0		15,990
32		14	H	Newcastle United	W	2-1	Jones, Blood	5,520
33		17	H	Chelsea	D	0-0		12,242
34		31	H	Sheffield United	W	4-0	Carter, Davies 3	15,147
35	Apr	2	H	Huddersfield Town	L	0-2		24,291
36		3	A	Huddersfield Town	L	1-4	Carter	13,000
37		7	A	Sheffield United	L	1-3	Davies	10,000
38		14	H	Oldham Athletic	W	1-0	Carter	8,405
39		21	A	Oldham Athletic	D	0-0		4,700
40		25	A	Chelsea	D	2-2	Spencer, Jones	15,000
41		28	H	Middlesbrough	W	1-0	Davies	10,021
42	May	5	A	Middlesbrough	W	1-0	Davies	9,000

Appearances

Goals

FA Cup

R1	Jan	13	H	Stalybridge Celtic	D	0-0		24,008
rep		17	A	Stalybridge Celtic	W	2-0	Davies, Morris	9,753
R2	Feb	3	H	Sunderland	W	2-1	Morris, Jones	56,474
R3		24	A	Charlton Athletic	L	0-1		31,489

Appearances

Goals

Pearson HP	Smith J	Adams W	Magee TP	Bowser S	McNeal R	Jephcott AC	Jones I	Davies SC	Morris F	Gregory H	Crisp J	Smith AW	Chamberlain HG	Fitton GA	Glidden TW	Carter JH	Blood R	Ashmore GSA	Richardson S	Dutton HR	Spencer JL	Wilson C	Ford EF	
1	2	3	4	5	6	7	8	9	10	11														1
1	2	3	4	5	6	7	8	9	10	11														2
1	2	3	4	5	6	7	8	9	10	11														3
1	2	3	4	5	6	7	8	9	10		11													4
1	2	3	4	5	6	7	8	9	10		11													5
1	2	3	4	5	6			9	10	11	7	8												6
1	2	3	4	5	6			9	10	11	7	8												7
1	2	3	4	5	6			9	10	11	7	8												8
1	2	3	4	5	6		8	9	10	11	7													9
1	2	3	4	5	6		8	9	10	11	7													10
1		2	4	5	6		8	9	10	11	7		3											11
1	2	3	4	5	6		8	9	10	11	7													12
1	2	3	4	5	6		8	9	10	11	7													13
1	2	3	4	5	6		8	9	10		7			11										14
1	2	3	4	5	6		8	9	10		7			11										15
1	2	3	4	5	6		8	9	10					11	7									16
1	2		4	5	6		8	9	10				3	11	7									17
1	2		4	5	6			9	10	11			3		7	8								18
1	2	3	4	5	6			8	10	11					7		9							19
1	2	3	4	5	6			8	10	11					7		9							20
1	2	3	4	5	6			8	10	11					7		9							21
	2	3		5				8	10	11							9	1	4	6	7			22
1	2	3		5			8		10	11							9		4	6	7			23
1	2	3	4	5	6		8	9	10	11											7			24
1	2	3	4	5	6		8	9	10	11											7			25
1	2	3	4	5	6		8	9	10	11											7			26
1	2	3	4	5	6		8	9	10	11											7			27
1	2	3	4	5	6		8	9	10	11											7			28
1	2	3	4	5	6		8	9	10	11											7			29
1	2	3	4	5	6		8		10	11	7						9							30
1	2	3	4	5	6		8		10	11							9				7			31
1	2	3	4	5	6		8		10	11							9				7			32
1	2	3	4	5	6					11						8	9				7	10		33
1	2	3	4	5	6		10	9								8					7		11	34
1	2	3	4	5	6		10	9	11							8					7			35
1	2	3	4	5	6		10	9	11							8					7			36
1	2	3	4	5	6		10	9	11							8					7			37
1	2	3	4	5	6			9	10						11	8					7			38
1	2	3	4	5	6		8	9	10						11						7			39
	2	3	4	5	6		8	9	10						11			1			7			40
	2	3	4	5	6		8	9	10						11			1			7			41
	2	3	4	5	6			9	10						11	8		1			7			42
38	41	40	40	42	40	5	31	37	40	27	13	3	3	4	11	8	9	4	2	2	20	1	1	
				1			3	20	14	7	3	1				3	4				2			

1	2	3	4	5	6		8	9	10	11											7			R1
1	2	3	4	5	6		8	9	10	11											7			rep
1	2	3	4	5	6		8	9	10	11											7			R2
1	2	3	4	5	6		8	9	10	11											7			R3
4	4	4	4	4	4					4											4			
							1	1	2															

1923-24

Division One

	P	W	D	L	F	A	Pts
Huddersfield Town	42	23	11	8	60	33	57
Cardiff City	42	22	13	7	61	34	57
Sunderland	42	22	9	11	71	54	53
Bolton Wanderers	42	18	14	10	68	34	50
Sheffield United	42	19	12	11	69	49	50
Aston Villa	42	18	13	11	52	37	49
Everton	42	18	13	11	62	53	49
Blackburn Rovers	42	17	11	14	54	50	45
Newcastle United	42	17	10	15	60	54	44
Notts County	42	14	14	14	44	49	42
Manchester City	42	15	12	15	54	71	42
Liverpool	42	15	11	16	49	48	41
West Ham United	42	13	15	14	40	43	41
Birmingham	42	13	13	16	41	49	39
Tottenham Hotspur	42	12	14	16	50	56	38
West Bromwich Albion	42	12	14	16	51	62	38
Burnley	42	12	12	18	55	60	36
Preston North End	42	12	10	20	52	67	34
Arsenal	42	12	9	21	40	63	33
Nottingham Forest	42	10	12	20	42	64	32
Chelsea	42	9	14	19	31	53	32
Middlesbrough	42	7	8	27	37	60	22

Secretary-manager: Fred Everiss

- In the transfer market, Albion signed winger Jack Byers from Blackburn Rovers and sold Sid Bowser to Walsall and prolific goalscorer Fred Morris to Coventry City. Bowser scored 72 goals in 371 appearances in his two spells with the club, while Morris netted118 in 287 outings. Both players were capped by England and helped the Baggies win the League title in 1920.
- Albion's reserve team retained their Central League crown by scoring 103 goals in their 42 matches.
- Albion met West Ham United for the first time in the Football League.

Match No.	Date			Opponents	Result		Scorers	Attendance
1	Aug	25	H	Liverpool	W	2-0	Fitton, Davies	25,121
2		27	A	Nottingham Forest	D	1-1	Davies	21,000
3	Sep	1	A	Liverpool	D	0-0		40,000
4		3	H	Nottingham Forest	W	3-2	Davies 2, Jones	26,909
5		8	H	Arsenal	W	4-0	Jones, Davies 2 (2 pens), Fitton	35,233
6		15	A	Arsenal	L	0-1		36,004
7		22	H	Blackburn Rovers	D	3-3	Morris 2, Jones	21,238
8		29	A	Blackburn Rovers	L	0-4		20,209
9	Oct	6	H	Huddersfield Town	L	2-4	Davies, Carter	17,041
10		13	A	Huddersfield Town	D	0-0		19,000
11		20	H	Aston Villa	W	1-0	Morris	42,096
12		27	A	Aston Villa	L	0-4		52,550
13	Nov	3	A	Cardiff City	L	0-3		20,600
14		10	H	Cardiff City	L	2-4	Blood 2 (1 pen)	15,143
15		17	A	Everton	L	0-2		28,700
16		24	H	Everton	W	5-0	Blood 3, Morris, Gregory	14,387
17	Dec	1	A	Tottenham Hotspur	D	0-0		23,048
18		8	H	Tottenham Hotspur	W	4-1	Carter 4	15,048
19		15	H	Birmingham	D	0-0		24,786
20		22	A	Birmingham	D	0-0		32,000
21		25	A	Bolton Wanderers	L	0-2		20,000
22		26	H	Bolton Wanderers	L	0-5		12,148
23		29	A	Manchester City	D	3-3	Carter 2, Bowser	16,402
24	Jan	5	H	Manchester City	W	2-1	Bowser	11,991
25		19	H	Burnley	L	0-3		8,527
26		26	A	Burnley	L	0-4		12,000
27	Feb	9	A	Middlesbrough	W	1-0	Spencer	15,000
28		16	H	Preston North End	L	1-2	Carter	10,024
29	Mar	1	H	Chelsea	D	2-2	Byers, James	11,485
30		12	A	Chelsea	D	0-0		17,900
31		15	A	Newcastle United	D	1-1	Reed	20,000
32		19	A	Preston North End	W	2-1	Wilson, Dutton	12,100
33		22	H	Newcastle United	D	0-0		16,053
34		29	A	West Ham United	L	0-1		18,112
35	Apr	5	H	West Ham United	D	0-0		13,248
36		9	H	Middlesbrough	D	1-1	Blood	14,473
37		12	H	Notts County	W	5-0	Jones, James 2, Wilson 2 (1 pen)	8,003
38		18	A	Sunderland	L	0-2		13,000
39		19	A	Notts County	L	0-1		20,000
40		21	H	Sunderland	W	3-1	James, Wilson, Gregory	12,033
41		26	A	Sheffield United	L	0-2		10,500
42	May	3	H	Sheffield United	W	3-1	Blood 3 (1 pen)	10,023

Appearances

Goals

FA Cup

R1	Jan	12	A	Millwall	W	1-0	Carter	30,922
R2	Feb	2	H	Corinthians	W	5-0	Morris, Reed, Carter, Davies 2 (1 pen)	49,005
R3		23	H	Wolverhampton Wanderers	D	1-1	Wilson	53,649
rep		27	A	Wolverhampton Wanderers	W	2-0	Wilson, Gregory	40,083
R4	Mar	8	H	Aston Villa	L	0-2		43,743

Appearances

Goals

Ashmore GSA	Smith J	Adams W	Magee TP	Bowser S	McNeal R	Spencer JL	Jones I	Davies SC	Morris F	Fitton GA	Glidden TW	Richardson S	Carter JH	Pearson HP	Blood R	Smith H	Perry AA	Reed FWM	Gregory H	Chamberlain HG	Byers JE	Dutton HR	James GC	Wilson C	
1	2	3	4	5	6	7	8	9	10	11															1
1	2	3	4	5	6	7	8	9	10	11															2
1	2	3	4	5	6	7	8	9	10	11															3
1	2	3	4	5	6	7	8	9	10	11															4
1	2	3	4	5	6	7	8	9	10	11															5
1	2	3	4	5	6		8	9	10	11	7														6
1	2	3	4	5	6		8	9	10	11	7														7
1	2	3		5	6		8	9	10	11	7	4													8
1	2	3	4	5	6	7	10	9		11			8												9
1	2	3	4	5	6			9	10	11	7		8												10
1	2	3	4	5	6			9	10	11	7		8												11
1	2	3	4	5	6			9	10	11	7		8												12
1	2	3	4	5	6			9	10	11	7		8												13
	2	3	4	5	6	7			10				8	1	9	11									14
1	2	3	4	5	6	7			10				8		9	11									15
1	2		4		6	7			10				8		9		3	5	11						16
1	2		4		6	7			10				8		9		3	5	11						17
1	2		4		6	7			10				8		9		3	5	11						18
1	2		4		6	7			10				8		9		3	5	11						19
1	2		4		6	7		9	10				8				3	5	11						20
1	2		4		6	7			10				8		9		3	5	11						21
1	2		4		6	7		8	10						9		3	5	11						22
1	2		4	9	6			7	10				8					5	11	3					23
1	2		4	9	6			7	10				8				3	5	11						24
1	2		4		6		8	7	10	11			9				3	5							25
1	2				6	7		9	10			4	8				3	5			11				26
1	2				6	7		9	10			4	8				3	5			11				27
1	2				6	7		9	10			4	8				3	5	11						28
	2					7			8			4		1			3	5			11	6	9	10	29
	2		4						10		7			1			3	5			11	6	9	8	30
	2		4				8				7			1			3	5			11	6	9	10	31
	2		4				8				7			1			3	5			11	6	9	10	32
	2				6		8				7			1			3	5			11	4	9	10	33
	2		4				8				7			1			3	5			11	6	9	10	34
1	2		4			7	8								9		3	5			11	6		10	35
1	2		4			7	8								9		3	5			11	6		10	36
1	2		4			7	8										3	5	11			6	9	10	37
1	2		4			7	8										3	5	11			6	9	10	38
1	2		4			7	8										3	5			11	6	9	10	39
1	2	3	4			7												5	10		11	6	9	8	40
1	2		4			7	8										3	5			11	6	9	10	41
1	2		4			7	8		10						9		3	5	11			6			42
35	42	16	36	17	29	27	21	21	30	14	12	5	19	7	11	2	25	27	14	1	13	14	11	13	
				2		1	4	7	5	2			8		9			1	2		1	1	4	4	

Ashmore GSA	Smith J	Adams W	Magee TP	Bowser S	McNeal R	Spencer JL	Jones I	Davies SC	Morris F	Fitton GA	Glidden TW	Richardson S	Carter JH	Pearson HP	Blood R	Smith H	Perry AA	Reed FWM	Gregory H	Chamberlain HG	Byers JE	Dutton HR	James GC	Wilson C	
1	2		4	9	6				10	11	7		8				3	5							R1
1	2				6	7		9	10			4	8				3	5	11						R2
1	2				6	7						4	8				3	5	11				9	10	R3
1	2					7			8			4					3	5	11			6	9	10	rep
1	2		4		6			7	10								3	5	11				9	8	R4
5	5		2	1	4	3		2	4	1	1	3	3				5	5	4			1	3	3	
								2	1				2					1	1					2	

1924-25

Division One

	P	W	D	L	F	A	Pts
Huddersfield Town	42	21	16	5	69	28	58
West Bromwich Albion	42	23	10	9	58	34	56
Bolton Wanderers	42	22	11	9	76	34	55
Liverpool	42	20	10	12	63	55	50
Bury	42	17	15	10	54	51	49
Newcastle United	42	16	16	10	61	42	48
Sunderland	42	19	10	13	64	51	48
Birmingham	42	17	12	13	49	53	46
Notts County	42	16	13	13	42	31	45
Manchester City	42	17	9	16	76	68	43
Cardiff City	42	16	11	15	56	51	43
Tottenham Hotspur	42	15	12	15	52	43	42
West Ham United	42	15	12	15	62	60	42
Sheffield United	42	13	13	16	55	63	39
Aston Villa	42	13	13	16	58	71	39
Blackburn Rovers	42	11	13	18	53	66	35
Everton	42	12	11	19	40	60	35
Leeds United	42	11	12	19	46	59	34
Burnley	42	11	12	19	46	75	34
Arsenal	42	14	5	23	46	58	33
Preston North End	42	10	6	26	37	74	26
Nottingham Forest	42	6	12	24	29	65	24

Secretary-manager: Fred Everiss

- A then record Hawthorns crowd of 64,612 witnessed Albion's FA Cup draw with Aston Villa in February. This was to stand for 12 years.
- New signings included full-back Dickie Baugh from Wolves, goalkeeper Harold Pearson (son of Hubert) from Tamworth Castle and Bob Finch from Hednesford Town.
- Bobby Blood was transferred to Stockport County after netting 26 times in 53 games, and Bobby McNeal retired after making 403 senior appearances.
- Albion and Leeds United met for the first time in the Football League.
- George James scored the fastest goal ever recorded at The Hawthorns, after just five seconds of Albion's home League game against Nottingham Forest in December.

Match No.	Date			Opponents	Result		Scorers	Attendance
1	Aug	30	H	Notts County	L	1-2	Blood	21,572
2	Sep	1	A	Bolton Wanderers	D	1-1	Jones	25,000
3		6	A	Everton	L	0-1		24,700
4		8	H	Tottenham Hotspur	W	2-0	Blood, Wilson	20,880
5		13	H	Sunderland	W	2-1	Wilson, James	21,166
6		20	A	Cardiff City	W	1-0	Carter	21,000
7		22	A	Tottenham Hotspur	W	1-0	James	37,000
8		27	H	Preston North End	D	1-1	Wilson	30,183
9	Oct	4	A	Burnley	W	1-0	Carter	30,000
10		11	H	Leeds United	W	3-1	James 2, Carter	21,332
11		18	H	Birmingham	D	1-1	James	35,617
12		25	A	Aston Villa	L	0-1		48,126
13	Nov	1	H	Huddersfield Town	W	1-0	James	15,683
14		8	A	Blackburn Rovers	L	0-1		16,000
15		15	H	West Ham United	W	4-1	Carter, Wilson 3	23,959
16		22	A	Sheffield United	L	0-2		15,100
17		29	H	Newcastle United	W	2-0	Carter, Byers	13,141
18	Dec	6	A	Liverpool	D	1-1	James	18,000
19		13	H	Nottingham Forest	W	5-1	James 4, Carter	16,227
20		20	A	Bury	W	2-0	James 2	12,000
21		25	A	Manchester City	W	2-1	James, Carter	20,000
22		26	H	Manchester City	W	3-1	James 2, Carter	41,990
23		27	A	Notts County	W	2-0	James, Smith (og)	12,000
24	Jan	3	H	Everton	W	3-0	James 2, Wilson	21,773
25		17	A	Sunderland	L	0-3		33,000
26		24	H	Cardiff City	W	1-0	Wilson	22,508
27	Feb	7	H	Burnley	L	1-4	James	24,492
28		12	A	Preston North End	W	2-1	Carter, Wilson	16,000
29		14	A	Leeds United	W	1-0	Carter	18,505
30		28	H	Aston Villa	W	4-1	Davies, James 3	22,123
31	Mar	11	A	Huddersfield Town	D	1-1	Carter	21,000
32		14	H	Blackburn Rovers	D	1-1	James	21,858
33		16	A	Birmingham	D	0-0		30,000
34		21	A	West Ham United	L	1-2	Wilson	10,900
35		30	H	Sheffield United	W	2-1	Glidden, Davies	9,892
36	Apr	4	A	Newcastle United	W	1-0	Carter	25,402
37		11	H	Liverpool	D	0-0		13,157
38		13	H	Arsenal	W	2-0	Glidden, Wilson	23,285
39		14	A	Arsenal	L	0-2		21,000
40		18	A	Nottingham Forest	W	1-0	Carter	6,000
41		25	H	Bury	D	1-1	James	15,277
42	May	2	H	Bolton Wanderers	D	0-0		13,383

Appearances

Goals

FA Cup

R1	Jan	10	H	Luton Town	W	4-0	James 3, Wilson	30,287
R2		31	H	Preston North End	W	2-0	James, Wilson	39,752
R3	Feb	21	H	Aston Villa	D	1-1	Carter	64,612
rep		25	A	Aston Villa	W	2-1	Gregory, James	60,015
R4	Mar	7	A	Sheffield United	L	0-2		57,197

Appearances

Goals

Ashmore GS	Smith J	Perry AA	Magee TP	Reed FWM	Dutton HR	Spencer JL	Jones I	Bload R	Wilson C	Byers JE	McNeal R	Carter JH	James GC	Glidden TW	Richardson S	Fitton GA	Davies S	Rooke EJH	Baugh R	Gregory H	Pearson HP	Adams W	
1	2	3	4	5	6	7	8	9	10	11													1
1	2	3	4	5	6	7	8	9	10	11													2
1	2	3	4	5		7	8	9	10	11	6												3
1	2	3	4	5		7		9	10	11	6	8											4
1	2	3	4	5		7			10	11	6	8	9										5
1	2	3	4	5		7			10	11	6	8	9										6
1	2	3	4	5		7			10	11	6	8	9										7
1	2	3	4	5		7			10	11	6	8	9										8
1	2	3	4	5		7			10	11	6	8	9										9
1	2	3	4	5					10	11	6	8	9	7									10
1	2	3	4	5		7			10	11	6	8	9										11
1	2	3	4	5		7			10	11	6	8	9										12
1	2	3	4	5			7		10	11		8	9		6								13
1	2	3	4	5			7		10			8	9		6	11							14
1	2	3	4	5					10	11		8		7	6		9						15
1	2	3	4	5					10	11	6	8		7			9						16
1	2	3	4	5	6				10	11		8	9	7									17
1	2	3	4	5	6				10	11		8	9	7									18
1	2	3	4	5	6				10	11		8	9	7									19
1	2	3	4	5	6				10	11		8	9	7									20
1	2	3	4	5	6				10	11		8	9	7									21
1	2	3	4	5					10	11		8	9	7	6								22
1	2	3							10	11	6		9	7	4		8	5					23
1	2	3	4	5					10	11		8	9	7	6								24
1	2	3	4	5					10	11		8	9	7	6								25
1	2	3	4	5					10	11		8	9	7	6								26
1	2	3	4	5					10	11		8	9	7	6								27
1	2		4	5					10	11		8	9	7	6				3				28
1	2		4	5					10	11		8	9	7	6				3				29
1	2		4	5					10	11			9	7	6		8		3				30
1	2		4	5					10			8	9	7	6				3	11			31
1	2		4	5	6				10			8	9	7					3	11			32
1	2		4	5			10					8	9	7	6	11			3				33
	2		4	5					10			8	9	7	6	11			3		1		34
1	2		4									8	9	7	6	11	10	5	3				35
1	2			5	4				10	11		8	9	7	6				3				36
1	2		4	5					10	11		8	9	7	6				3				37
1	2		4	5					10	11		8	9	7	6				3				38
1	2		4	5					10			8	9	7	6	11			3				39
1	2		4	5					10			8	9	7	6	11						3	40
1	2		4	5					10	11		8	9	7	6				3				41
1	2		4	5					10	11		8	9	7	6				3				42
41	42	27	40	40	9	11	6	4	40	34	12	37	36	29	23	6	5	2	14	2	1	1	
							1	2	11	1		13	25	2			2						

One own-goal

Ashmore GS	Smith J	Perry AA	Magee TP	Reed FWM	Dutton HR	Spencer JL	Jones I	Bload R	Wilson C	Byers JE	McNeal R	Carter JH	James GC	Glidden TW	Richardson S	Fitton GA	Davies S	Rooke EJH	Baugh R	Gregory H	Pearson HP	Adams W	
1	2	3	4	5					10	11		8	9	7	6								R1
1	2	3	4	5					10	11		8	9	7	6								R2
1	2		4	5					10	11		8	9	7	6				3				R3
1	2		4	5						11		8	9	7	6				3	10			rep
1	2		4	5					10	11		8	9	7	6				3				R4
5	5	2	5	5					4	5		5	5	5	5				3	1			
								2			1	5							1				

1925-26

Division One

	P	W	D	L	F	A	Pts
Huddersfield Town	42	23	11	8	92	60	57
Arsenal	42	22	8	12	87	63	52
Sunderland	42	21	6	15	96	80	48
Bury	42	20	7	15	85	77	47
Sheffield United	42	19	8	15	102	82	46
Aston Villa	42	16	12	14	86	76	44
Liverpool	42	14	16	12	70	63	44
Bolton Wanderers	42	17	10	15	75	76	44
Manchester United	42	19	6	17	66	73	44
Newcastle United	42	16	10	16	84	75	42
Everton	42	12	18	12	72	70	42
Blackburn Rovers	42	15	11	16	91	80	41
West Bromwich Albion	42	16	8	18	79	78	40
Birmingham	42	16	8	18	66	81	40
Tottenham Hotspur	42	15	9	18	66	79	39
Cardiff City	42	16	7	19	61	76	39
Leicester City	42	14	10	18	70	80	38
West Ham United	42	15	7	20	63	76	37
Leeds United	42	14	8	20	64	76	36
Burnley	42	13	10	19	85	108	36
Manchester City	42	12	11	19	89	100	35
Notts County	42	13	7	22	54	74	33

Secretary-manager: Fred Everiss

- Joe Carter made his England debut against Belgium, scoring in a 5–3 win in Antwerp. He went on to win another two full caps.
- Welsh international Ivor Jones moved to Swansea Town, Joe Smith switched to nearby Birmingham (after 471 appearances for Albion) and Hubert Pearson announced his retirement, having played in 377 first-class games in 20 years.

Match No.	Date			Opponents	Result		Scorers	Attendance
1	Aug	29	A	Huddersfield Town	D	1-1	James	21,975
2	Sep	2	H	Everton	D	1-1	Wilson	29,856
3		5	H	Sunderland	L	2-5	Wilson, Jones	21,520
4		12	A	Blackburn Rovers	W	2-1	Dutton, Davies	24,199
5		16	A	Everton	L	0-4		20,355
6		23	H	Manchester City	W	4-1	Davies 2, Wilson 2	8,287
7		26	A	Birmingham	L	0-3		26,484
8	Oct	3	H	Aston Villa	D	1-1	Davies	52,332
9		10	H	Sheffield United	W	2-0	Wilson, Davies	15,973
10		17	A	Leicester City	L	0-3		24,479
11		24	H	West Ham United	W	7-1	Davies 3 (1 pen), Glidden, Wilson, Carter 2	20,851
12		31	A	Bolton Wanderers	D	2-2	Carter, James	17,063
13	Nov	7	H	Notts County	D	4-4	Carter 2, Davies, Wilson	17,186
14		9	H	Bury	W	4-0	Davies 2, Fitton, Carter	8,072
15		14	A	Liverpool	L	0-2		23,440
16		21	H	Burnley	W	5-3	Davies 2, Carter, Glidden, Wilson	15,133
17		28	A	Leeds United	W	1-0	Glidden	14,774
18	Dec	5	H	Newcastle United	W	4-0	Davies 2, Wilson, Fitton	15,633
19		12	A	Arsenal	L	0-1		34,178
20		19	H	Manchester United	W	5-1	Carter, Glidden, Davies 2, James	16,554
21		25	A	Cardiff City	L	2-3	Davies 2	13,683
22		26	H	Cardiff City	W	3-0	Cater 2, James	31,554
23	Jan	1	A	Manchester City	L	1-3	Carter	22,513
24		2	H	Huddersfield Town	D	2-2	Reed, Glidden (pen)	22,435
25		16	A	Sunderland	L	0-4		20,352
26		23	H	Blackburn Rovers	D	1-1	Byers	11,105
27	Feb	6	H	Birmingham	W	5-1	James 2, Wilson 3	23,104
28		13	A	Aston Villa	L	1-2	Byers	42,714
29		20	A	Sheffield United	L	2-3	Carter 2	21,383
30		24	A	Bury	L	0-2		8,569
31		27	H	Leicester City	W	3-1	Glidden (pen), James, Byers	19,532
32	Mar	6	A	West Ham United	L	0-3		23,030
33		13	H	Bolton Wanderers	L	0-3		14,388
34		20	A	Notts County	D	0-0		14,888
35		27	H	Liverpool	L	0-3		10,503
36	Apr	2	A	Tottenham Hotspur	L	2-3	James, Wilson	27,914
37		3	A	Burnley	W	4-3	James 2, Wilson, Reed	25,243
38		5	H	Tottenham Hotspur	W	1-0	Wilson (pen)	10,180
39		10	H	Leeds United	W	3-0	Hart (og), Carter, Wilson	13,065
40		17	A	Newcastle United	L	0-3		13,084
41		24	H	Arsenal	W	2-1	James, Wilson	16,802
42	May	1	A	Manchester United	L	2-3	James, Magee	11,198
								Appearances
								Goals

FA Cup

R3	Jan	9	H	Bristol City	W	4-1	Glidden 2 (1 pen), Carter, Byers	33,295
R4		30	H	Aston Villa	L	1-2	Carter	52,160
								Appearances
								Goals

Match	Ashmore GSA	Smith J	Baugh RH	Magee TP	Reed FWM	Richardson S	Glidden TW	Carter JH	James GC	Wilson C	Byers JE	Adams W	Dutton HR	Jones I	Davies SC	Rooke EJH	Perry AA	Fitton GA	Sproson T	Spencer JL	Finch EAR	Evans JT	Darnell L
1	1	2	3	4	5	6	7	8	9	10	11												
2	1	2	3	4	5	6	7	8	9	10	11												
3	1		3		5	4	7			10	11	2	6	8	9								
4	1	2	3			4	7		9		11		6	8	10	5							
5	1	2	3			4	7		9		11		6	8	10	5							
6	1	2			5	4	7		9	8			6		10		3	11					
7	1	2			5	4	7		9	8			6		10		3	11					
8	1	2	3		5	4	7	8		10			6		9			11					
9	1	2	3		5	4	7	8		10			6		9			11					
10	1	2	3		5	4	7	8		10			6		9			11					
11	1	2	3		5	4	7	8		10			6		9			11					
12		2	3		5	4	7	8	9	10			6					11	1				
13	1	2	3		5	4	7	8		10			6		9			11					
14	1	2	3		5	4	7	8		10			6		9			11					
15	1	2	3		5	4	7	8		10			6		9			11					
16	1	2	3		5	4	7	8		10			6		9			11					
17	1	2			5	4	7	8	9	10		3	6					11					
18	1	2			5	4	7	8		10		3	6		9			11					
19	1	2			5	4	7	8		10		3	6		9			11					
20	1	2			5	4	7	8	9			3	6		10			11					
21	1	2			5	4	7	8	9			3	6		10			11					
22	1	2			5	4	7	8	9			3	6		10			11					
23	1	2			5	4	7	8	9			3	6		10			11					
24	1	2			5	4	7	8	9			3	6		10			11					
25	1		2	4	5		7	8	9	10	11	3	6										
26	1		2	4	5			8		10	11	3	6		9					7			
27	1		2	7	5	4		8	9	10	11	3	6										
28	1	2	3	7	5	4		8	9	10	11		6										
29		2	3	7	5	4		8		10	11		6		9				1				
30	1	2	3	7	5	4		8		10	11		6		9								
31	1		3	4	5	6	7	8	9		11				10						2		
32	1		3	4		6	7	8	9		11				10						2	5	
33	1		3	4	5		7	8	9		11		6		10						2		
34	1		3	4	5		7	8	9		11					6					2		10
35	1		3	4	5		7	8	9		11					6					2		10
36	1		3	4	5		7	8	9	10	11					6	2						
37	1		3	4	5	6	7	8	9	10	11						2						
38	1		3	4	5	6	7	8	9	10	11						2						
39	1		3	4	5	6	7	8	9	10	11						2						
40	1		3	4	5	6	7	8	9	10	11						2						
41	1		3	4	5	6	7	8	9	10	11						2						
42	1		3	4	5	6	7	8	9	10	11						2						
	40	26	32	20	39	36	37	37	28	30	23	12	29	3	26	5	9	19	2	1	5	1	2
				1	2		6	14	12	17	3		1	1	19			2					

One own-goal

Round	Ashmore GSA	Smith J	Baugh RH	Magee TP	Reed FWM	Richardson S	Glidden TW	Carter JH	James GC	Wilson C	Byers JE	Adams W	Dutton HR	Jones I	Davies SC
R3	1	2		4	5		7	8	9		11	3	6		10
R4	1		2		5	4	7	8	9	10	11	3	6		
	2	1	1	1	2	1	2	2	2	1	2	2	2		1
							2	2			1				

1926-27

Division One

	P	W	D	L	F	A	Pts
Newcastle United	42	25	6	11	96	58	56
Huddersfield Town	42	17	17	8	76	60	51
Sunderland	42	21	7	14	98	70	49
Bolton Wanderers	42	19	10	13	84	62	48
Burnley	42	19	9	14	91	80	47
West Ham United	42	19	8	15	86	70	46
Leicester City	42	17	12	13	85	70	46
Sheffield United	42	17	10	15	74	86	44
Liverpool	42	18	7	17	69	61	43
Aston Villa	42	18	7	17	81	83	43
Arsenal	42	17	9	16	77	86	43
Derby County	42	17	7	18	86	73	41
Tottenham Hotspur	42	16	9	17	76	78	41
Cardiff City	42	16	9	17	55	65	41
Manchester United	42	13	14	15	52	64	40
Sheffield Wednesday	42	15	9	18	75	92	39
Birmingham	42	17	4	21	64	73	38
Blackburn Rovers	42	15	8	19	77	96	38
Bury	42	12	12	18	68	77	36
Everton	42	12	10	20	64	90	34
Leeds United	42	11	8	23	69	88	30
West Bromwich Albion	42	11	8	23	65	86	30

Secretary-manager: Fred Everiss

- Full-back George Shaw was signed from Huddersfield Town for a club-record fee of £4,100. Nelson Howarth (from Bolton Wanderers), Bill Ashurst (from Notts County) and Bill Richardson (from Great Bridge Celtic) were also new signings. Full-back Arthur Perry was among those who left the club, joining Crystal Palace. Centre-half Fred Reed retired after making 157 appearances to become the club's trainer.
- Albion's second XI won the Central League Championship for the third time in five years.

Match No.	Date			Opponents	Result		Scorers	Attendance
1	Aug	28	H	Sunderland	W	3-0	Davies, Carter, Byers	31,132
2		30	A	Huddersfield Town	L	1-4	Wilson	16,130
3	Sep	4	A	Cardiff City	D	1-1	Byers	19,213
4		6	H	Everton	W	3-2	Davies 2, Carter	12,048
5		11	A	Bury	L	3-7	Carter, James 2	14,667
6		15	A	Everton	D	0-0		15,310
7		18	H	Birmingham	L	1-2	Jones (og)	26,803
8		25	A	Tottenham Hotspur	L	0-3		31,236
9	Oct	2	H	West Ham United	L	1-3	Fitton	24,737
10		9	A	Sheffield Wednesday	L	1-2	Glidden	15,508
11		16	H	Bolton Wanderers	D	1-1	Glidden	24,246
12		23	A	Aston Villa	L	0-2		49,952
13		30	H	Burnley	W	4-2	Carter 2, Byers, Magee	20,957
14	Nov	6	A	Newcastle United	L	2-5	Glidden, Wilson	28,864
15		13	H	Leeds United	L	2-4	James 2	15,103
16		20	A	Liverpool	L	1-2	Wilson	20,763
17		27	H	Arsenal	L	1-3	Carter	16,351
18	Dec	4	A	Sheffield United	L	1-2	James	19,180
19		11	H	Derby County	W	3-1	Davies 2, Magee	19,557
20		18	A	Manchester United	L	0-2		18,585
21		25	A	Leicester City	L	0-5		26,150
22		27	H	Leicester City	L	0-1		31,286
23	Jan	1	H	Huddersfield Town	D	2-2	Short 2	30,998
24		15	A	Sunderland	L	1-4	Wilson	16,413
25		29	H	Bury	W	3-1	Davies 2, Carter	10,043
26	Feb	5	A	Birmingham	L	0-1		29,681
27		12	H	Tottenham Hotspur	W	5-0	Davies 2, Carter 2, Short	15,998
28		19	A	West Ham United	W	2-1	Rooke, Short	18,231
29		21	H	Cardiff City	L	1-2	Glidden	10,068
30		26	H	Sheffield Wednesday	D	2-2	Carter, Short	12,006
31	Mar	5	A	Bolton Wanderers	D	1-1	Carter	12,954
32		12	H	Aston Villa	W	6-2	Glidden 2, Carter, Davies 2, Short	50,392
33		19	A	Burnley	L	1-2	Davies	18,863
34		26	H	Newcastle United	W	4-2	Byers, Davies, Carter, Short (pen)	22,135
35	Apr	2	A	Leeds United	L	1-3	Carter	20,176
36		9	H	Liverpool	L	0-1		20,268
37		16	A	Arsenal	L	1-4	Davies	24,506
38		18	H	Blackburn Rovers	W	2-0	Byers, Ashurst	14,383
39		19	A	Blackburn Rovers	D	0-0		10,670
40		23	H	Sheffield United	W	1-0	James (pen)	13,104
41		30	A	Derby County	L	1-2	Carter	11,830
42	May	7	H	Manchester United	D	2-2	Magee, Davies	11,022
								Appearances
								Goals

FA Cup

R3	Jan	8	A	Hull City	L	1-2	Howarth	24,909
								Appearances
								Goals

Ashmore GSA	Perry AA	Baugh RH	Magee TP	Reed FWM	Howarth N	Glidden TW	Carter JH	Davies SC	Wilson C	Byers JE	James GC	Dutton HR	Short JS	Adams W	Fitton GA	Sproson T	Rooke EJH	Richardson S	Evans JT	Finch EAR	Corbett FJ	Ashurst W	Shaw GE	Poxton JH	
1	2	3	4	5	6	7	8	9	10	11															1
1	2	3	4	5	6	7	8	9	10	11															2
1	2	3	4	5	6	7	8	10		11	9														3
1	2	3	4	5	6	7	8	10		11	9														4
1	2	3	4	5	6	7	8	10		11	9														5
1	2	3	4	5	6	7		10	8	11	9														6
1	2	3	4	5		7		8	10	11		6	9												7
1	2		4	5	6	7		8	10	11	9			3											8
1	2		4	5	6	7	8		10		9			3	11										9
1		2	4	5	6	7	8	9	10					3	11										10
1		2	4	5	6	7	8	9	10	11				3											11
	3	2	4		6	9	8	7	10	11						1	5								12
	3	2	7		6	9	8		10	11						1		4	5						13
	3	2	7		6	9		8	10	11						1		4	5						14
	3	2	7		6	8			10	11	9					1		4	5						15
1			7		6	8			10	11	9	4							5	2	3				16
1			7		6	9	8		10	11		4							5		3	2			17
1			4	5	6	7	8	10			9				11							2	3		18
1			4	5		7	8	10			9				11		6					2	3		19
1			4	5			8	7	10		9				11		6					2	3		20
1			4	5		7	8	10					9		11		6					2	3		21
1			4		6	7	8	9					10	2	11		5						3		22
1			4		6	7	8	9					10	2	11		5						3		23
1			4		6	7	8	9	10						11		5					2	3		24
1			4		6	7	8	9	10						11		5					2	3		25
1			4		6	7	8	9	10						11		5					2	3		26
1			4			7	8	9		11			10				5	6				2	3		27
1			4			7	8	9		11			10				5	6				2	3		28
1			4			7	8	9		11			10				5	6				2	3		29
1			4			7	8	9					10		11		5	6				2	3		30
1			4		6	7	8	9		11			10				5					2	3		31
1			4		6	7	8	9		11			10				5					2	3		32
1			4		6	7	8	9		11			10				5					2	3		33
1			4		6	7	8	9		11			10				5					2	3		34
1			4		6	7	8			11	9		10				5					2	3		35
1			4		6	7	8	9		11			10				5					2	3		36
1			4		6	7	8	10		11	9						5					2	3		37
1			4		6	7	8	10		11	9						5					2	3		38
1			4		6	7	8			11	9		10				5				3		2		39
1			4		6	7	8			11	9		10				5				3		2		40
1			4		6	7	8			11	9		10				5					2	3		41
1			4		6	7	8	9					10				5					2	3	11	42
38	13	13	42	15	34	41	36	33	18	29	17	3	18	6	12	4	25	7	5	1	4	22	25	1	
			3			6	15	15	4	5	6		7		1		1					1			

One own-goal

1			4		6	7	8	10					9		11		5					2	3		R3
1			1		1	1	1	1					1		1		1					1	1		
					1																				

1927-28

Division Two

	P	W	D	L	F	A	Pts
Manchester City	42	25	9	8	100	59	59
Leeds United	42	25	7	10	98	49	57
Chelsea	42	23	8	11	75	45	54
Preston North End	42	22	9	11	100	66	53
Stoke City	42	22	8	12	78	59	52
Swansea Town	42	18	12	12	75	63	48
Oldham Athletic	42	19	8	15	75	51	46
West Bromwich Albion	42	17	12	13	90	70	46
Port Vale	42	18	8	16	68	57	44
Nottingham Forest	42	15	10	17	83	84	40
Grimsby Town	42	14	12	16	69	83	40
Bristol City	42	15	9	18	76	79	39
Barnsley	42	14	11	17	65	85	39
Hull City	42	12	15	15	41	54	39
Notts County	42	13	12	17	68	74	38
Wolverhampton W	42	13	10	19	63	91	36
Southampton	42	14	7	21	68	77	35
Reading	42	11	13	18	53	75	35
Blackpool	42	13	8	21	83	101	34
Clapton Orient	42	11	12	19	55	85	34
Fulham	42	13	7	22	68	89	33
South Shields	42	7	9	26	56	111	23

Secretary-manager: Fred Everiss

- Centre-forward Jimmy Cookson, a £2,500 bargain buy from Chesterfield, set a new club record (which still stands today) by scoring a double hat-trick in Albion's 6–3 home League win over Blackpool in September.
- Wing-half Sammy Richardson was transferred to Newport County after 212 appearances for the club, Charlie Wilson moved to Sheffield Wednesday, and Stan Davies joined Birmingham. The last two named, between them, scored 128 goals for Albion.
- Debutants included winger George Bytheway, veteran England international Harry Chambers (who arrived from Liverpool), Jimmy 'Iron' Edwards, half-back Reg Fryer, goalkeeper Harold Pearson, who made the first of his 303 appearances for the club, and competent half-back Jack Rix. Left-winger Stan Wood arrived from Winsford in April and would remain at the club until 1938, while future Welsh international Jimmy Murphy was signed from Mid-Rhondda in February.
- Albion played Southampton for the first time in the Football League.

Match No.	Date			Opponents	Result		Scorers	Attendance
1	Aug	27	A	Oldham Athletic	L	1-3	Cookson	13,035
2		31	H	Stoke City	L	2-4	Cookson, Byers	20,329
3	Sep	3	H	Grimsby Town	W	3-1	Carter 2, Wilson	16,615
4		5	A	Stoke City	D	1-1	Cookson	20,614
5		10	A	Reading	W	4-1	Cookson, Fitton, Glidden, Wilson	16,238
6		17	H	Blackpool	W	6-3	Cookson 6 (1 pen)	20,203
7		24	A	Chelsea	D	1-1	Carter	44,724
8	Oct	1	H	Clapton Orient	W	4-1	Fitton, Carter, Glidden, Cookson	21,324
9		8	A	Wolverhampton Wanderers	L	1-4	Evans	40,816
10		15	A	Bristol City	W	1-0	Glidden	24,442
11		22	H	Swansea Town	W	5-2	Fitton, Carter 2, Cookson, Wilson	22,779
12		29	A	Fulham	L	1-3	Cookson	20,577
13	Nov	5	H	Barnsley	D	1-1	Wilson	18,350
14		12	A	Preston North End	D	3-3	Cookson, Glidden 2	15,827
15		19	H	Hull City	D	1-1	Glidden	8,116
16		26	A	Leeds United	W	2-1	Carter 2	23,690
17	Dec	3	H	Nottingham Forest	L	2-3	Carter, Glidden	10,205
18		10	A	Manchester City	L	1-3	Glidden	29,747
19		17	H	South Shields	W	3-0	Glidden, Evans, Cookson	11,376
20		24	A	Port Vale	L	1-4	Cookson	8,216
21		26	H	Notts County	D	2-2	Cookson, Poxton	28,038
22		27	A	Notts County	L	0-3		17,755
23		31	H	Oldham Athletic	D	0-0		9,203
24	Jan	7	A	Grimsby Town	W	6-0	Cookson 4, Short, Bytheway	12,242
25		21	H	Reading	W	5-3	Inglis (og), Cookson 4	15,014
26		28	A	Blackpool	L	3-4	Cookson 2, Short	8,102
27	Feb	4	H	Chelsea	W	3-0	Short 2, Carter	25,865
28		11	A	Clapton Orient	D	0-0		11,443
29		18	H	Wolverhampton Wanderers	W	4-0	Cookson 2, Carter, Wilson	37,342
30		25	H	Bristol City	D	0-0		32,115
31	Mar	3	A	Swansea Town	L	2-3	Cookson 2	15,355
32		10	H	Fulham	W	4-0	Cookson, Chambers, Glidden 2	17,029
33		17	A	Barnsley	W	4-2	Carter, Cookson 2, Glidden	8,144
34		24	H	Preston North End	L	2-4	Carter, Cookson	28,055
35		31	A	Hull City	D	1-1	Bromage	7,964
36	Apr	7	H	Leeds United	L	0-1		25,180
37		9	A	Southampton	L	2-3	Glidden, Carter	18,000
38		10	H	Southampton	W	2-1	Cookson, Short	20,046
39		14	A	Nottingham Forest	W	2-0	Cookson, Carter	6,158
40		21	H	Manchester City	D	1-1	Chanbers	14,238
41		28	A	South Shields	W	3-2	Bromage, Dunn (og), Cookson	5,514
42	May	5	H	Port Vale	D	0-0		10,095
								Appearances
								Goals

FA Cup

R3	Jan	14	A	Arsenal	L	0-2		41,298
								Appearances

Sproson T	Baugh RH	Shaw GE	Magee TP	Evans JT	Howarth N	Glidden TW	Carter JH	Cookson J	Wilson C	Byers JE	Finch EAR	Fryer ER	Ashmore GSA	Fitton GA	James GC	Rooke EJH	Poxton JH	Bytheway GS	Pearson HF	Short JS	Chambers H	Bromage E	Corbett FJ	Edwards J	Rix J	Taylor GA	
1	2	3	4	5	6	7	8	9	10	11																	1
1	2	3	4	5	6	7	8	9	10	11																	2
1		3	4	5		7	8	9	10	11	2	6															3
		3	4	5		7	8	9	10		2	6	1	11													4
		3	4	5		7	8	9	10		2	6	1	11													5
		3	4	5		7	8	9	10		2	6	1	11													6
		3	4	5		7	8	9	10		2	6	1	11													7
		3	4	5		7	8	9	10		2	6	1	11													8
		3	4	5		7	8		10		2	6	1	11	9												9
		3	7	5		9	8		10		2	6	1	11		4											10
		3	4	5		7	8	9	10		2	6	1	11													11
		3	4	5		7	8	9	10		2	6	1	11													12
		3	4	5		7	8	9	10		2		1			6	11										13
		3	4	5		7	8	9	10		2		1			6	11										14
		3	4	5		7	8	9	10		2	6	1				11										15
		3	4	5		9	8		10		2	6	1				11	7									16
		3	4	5		9	8		10		2	6	1				11	7									17
		3	4	5		10	8	9			2	6	1				11	7									18
		3	4	5		10	8	9		11	2	6						7	1								19
		3	4	5		10	8	9		11	2	6						7	1								20
		3	4	5	6	10	8	9			2						11	7	1								21
		3		5	6	7	8	9	10		2	4					11		1								22
		3	4	5	6	10	8	9			2		1	11				7									23
		3	4	5	6	8		9			2		1	11				7		10							24
		3	4	5	6	8		9			2		1	11				7		10							25
		3	4	5	6	8		9			2		1	11				7		10							26
		3	4	5	6	7	8	9			2		1	11						10							27
		3	4	5	6	7	8	9			2		1	11						10							28
		3	4	5	6	7	8	9	10		2		1	11													29
		3	4	5	6	7	8	9			2			11					1	10							30
		3	4	5	6	7	8	9			2			11					1	10							31
		3	4	5	6	7	8	9			2		1	11							10						32
		3	4	5	6	7	8	9			2		1								10	11					33
		3	4	5	6	7	8	9			2		1							10		11					34
		2	4	5	6	7		9					1								10	11	3	8			35
		3	4	5	6	7	8	9			2		1								10	11					36
		3	4		6	7	8	9			2		1			5				10		11					37
		3	4		6	7	8	9			2					5			1	10		11					38
		3	4		6		8	9			2					5		7	1		10	11					39
		3	4		6	7	8	9			2					5			1		10	11					40
		3	4		6		8	9			2					5		7	1		10	11					41
		3	4				8	9			2					5		7	1		10	11			6		42
3	2	42	41	36	23	39	38	38	19	5	39	17	28	19	1	9	8	13	11	10	8	10	1	1	1		
				2		13	15	38	5	1				3			1	1		5	2	2					

Two own-goals

		3	4	5	6	8		9			2		1	11						10						7	R3
		11	1	1	1	1		1			1		1	1						1						1	

1928-29

Division Two

	P	W	D	L	F	A	Pts
Middlesbrough	42	22	11	9	92	57	55
Grimsby Town	42	24	5	13	82	61	53
Bradford Park Avenue	42	22	4	16	88	70	48
Southampton	42	17	14	11	74	60	48
Notts County	42	19	9	14	78	65	47
Stoke City	42	17	12	13	74	51	46
West Bromwich Albion	42	19	8	15	80	79	46
Blackpool	42	19	7	16	92	76	45
Chelsea	42	17	10	15	64	65	44
Tottenham Hotspur	42	17	9	16	75	81	43
Nottingham Forest	42	15	12	15	71	70	42
Hull City	42	13	14	15	58	63	40
Preston North End	42	15	9	18	78	79	39
Millwall	42	16	7	19	71	86	39
Reading	42	15	9	18	63	86	39
Barnsley	42	16	6	20	69	66	38
Wolverhampton W	42	15	7	20	77	81	37
Oldham Athletic	42	16	5	21	54	75	37
Swansea Town	42	13	10	19	62	75	36
Bristol City	42	13	10	19	58	72	36
Port Vale	42	15	4	23	71	86	34
Clapton Orient	42	12	8	22	45	72	32

Secretary-manager: Fred Everiss

- Albion's average home League attendance this season was just 13,220 – their lowest since 1909–10. In fact, the crowd dropped to below 7,000 at one point.
- Debutants this season included Len Darnell, Fred Leedham, ex-Birmingham defender Dicky Dale, centre-half Bill Richardson, goalkeeper Herbert Webster, who went on to live until well into his 90s, and Stan Wood. Also signed was Bert Trentham from Hereford.
- Players who left included George James to Reading after scoring 57 goals in 115 appearances.

Match No.	Date			Opponents	Result		Scorers	Attendance
1	Aug	25	H	Clapton Orient	W	3-1	Chambers, Glidden, Carter	19,756
2		27	A	Notts County	L	1-3	Howarth	10,395
3	Sep	1	A	Stoke City	L	1-4	Glidden	22,796
4		3	H	Notts County	L	1-3	Cookson	15,221
5		8	H	Grimsby Town	W	1-0	Glidden (pen)	15,132
6		15	A	Bradford Park Avenue	L	1-4	Glidden	20,487
7		22	H	Swansea Town	W	5-1	Carter 2, Short, James 2	12,333
8		29	A	Blackpool	W	2-0	Short, Wood	16,415
9	Oct	6	H	Chelsea	W	3-0	Bytheway, Short, Glidden	16,447
10		13	A	Barnsley	L	0-2		11,072
11		20	A	Millwall	D	2-2	Short, Glidden	20,938
12		27	H	Port Vale	W	3-1	James, Glidden, Short	12,725
13	Nov	3	A	Hull City	L	1-4	James	11,301
14		10	H	Wolverhampton Wanderers	L	0-2		24,902
15		17	A	Reading	L	3-5	Cookson 3	10,298
16		24	H	Preston North End	D	1-1	Glidden	8,048
17	Dec	1	A	Middlesbrough	D	1-1	Glidden	15,075
18		8	H	Oldham Athletic	W	1-0	Cookson	6,994
19		15	A	Southampton	D	1-1	Carter	13,329
20		22	H	Tottenham Hotspur	W	3-2	Shaw (pen), Cookson, Carter	11,565
21		25	H	Bristol City	D	1-1	Glidden	11,303
22		26	A	Bristol City	W	3-2	Wood 2, Cookson	21,070
23		29	A	Clapton Orient	W	2-0	Cookson, Glidden	10,209
24	Jan	5	H	Stoke City	L	2-3	Magee, Cookson	20,067
25		19	A	Grimsby Town	L	1-3	Cookson	9,276
26	Feb	2	A	Swansea Town	L	1-6	Carter	8,695
27		9	H	Blackpool	D	2-2	Carter 2	12,094
28		23	H	Barnsley	W	6-2	Saw (pen), Glidden 2, Carter, Cookson 2	13,810
29	Mar	9	A	Port Vale	L	1-8	James	11,538
30		11	H	Bradford Park Avenue	L	1-2	Cookson	9,952
31		16	H	Hull City	W	2-0	Cookson, Chambers	7,138
32		23	A	Wolverhampton Wanderers	W	1-0	Cookson	24,340
33		29	A	Nottingham Forest	W	2-1	Cookson 2	13,170
34		30	H	Reading	W	5-0	Cookson 2, Fitton, Edwards, Glidden	10,382
35	Apr	1	H	Nottingham Forest	W	3-0	Glidden, Cookson, Fitton	12,130
36		6	A	Preston North End	D	1-1	Edwards	10,609
37		10	H	Millwall	W	3-2	Edwards, Glidden, Carter	13,532
38		13	H	Middlesbrough	D	1-1	Glidden	14,068
39		17	A	Chelsea	W	5-2	Glidden 3, Carter, Evans	7,086
40		20	A	Oldham Athletic	L	0-3		13,106
41		27	H	Southampton	W	3-1	Cookson, Glidden, Carter	10,024
42	May	4	A	Tottenham Hotspur	L	0-2		15,787

Appearances

Goals

FA Cup

R3	Jan	12	A	Grimsby Town	D	1-1	Cookson	12,516
rep		16	H	Grimsby Town	W	2-0	Cookson, Chambers	20,381
R4		26	H	Middlesbrough	W	1-0	Cookson	33,446
R5	Feb	16	H	Bradford Park Avenue	W	6-0	Cookson 4, Glidden, Carter	30,307
R6	Mar	2	H	Huddersfield Town	D	1-1	Glidden	52,333
rep		6	A	Huddersfield Town	L	1-2	Wood	36,779

Appearances

Goals

	Pearson HF	Finch EAR	Shaw GE	Magee TP	Evans JT	Howarth N	Glidden TW	Carter JH	Cookson J	Chambers H	Fitton GA	Ashmore GSA	Wood S	Darnell L	James GC	Corbett FJ	Rix J	Fryer ER	Short JS	Bytheway GS	Leedham FA	Dale RA	Richardson W	Webster H	Edwards J
1	1	2	3	4	5	6	7	8	9	10	11														
2	1	2	3	4	5	6	7	8	9	10	11														
3		2	3	4	5	6	7	8	9	10	11	1													
4		2	3	4	5	6	7	8	9	10		1	11												
5		2	3	4	5		7	8		10		1	11	6	9										
6			2	4	5		7	8		10		1	11		9	3	6								
7		2	3	4			7	8		5		1	11		9			6	10						
8		2	3	4			7	8		5		1	11		9			6	10						
9		2	3	4			8			5		1	11		9			6	10	7					
10		2	3	4			8			5		1	11		9			6	10	7					
11		2	3	4			7	8		5		1	11	6	9				10						
12		2	3	4			7	8		5		1	11	6	9				10						
13		2	3	4			7	8		5		1	11	6	9				10						
14		2	3	4			7	8		5		1	11	6	9				10						
15		2	3	4			8		9	5		1	11	6					10		7				
16		2	3	4			7	8	9	5		1	11						10			6			
17		2	3	4			7	8	9	10		1	11									6	5		
18		2	3	4				8	9	10		1	11								7	6	5		
19		2	3	4				8	9	10		1	11								7	6	5		
20		2	3	4			7	8	9	10		1	11									6	5		
21		2	3	4			7	8	9	10		1	11	6									5		
22		2	3	4			7	8	9	10		1	11	6									5		
23		2	3	4			7	8	9	10		1	11	6									5		
24		2	3	4			7	8	9	10		1	11	6									5		
25		2	3	4			7	8	9	10		1	11									6	5		
26		2	3	4			7	8	9	10		1	11	6									5		
27		2	3	4			7	8	9	10		1	11	6									5		
28		2	3	4			7	8	9	10		1	11	6									5		
29		2	3	7			8			10		1	11	4	9							6	5		
30			3				7		9	8			11	6		2			10			4	5	1	
31	1		3		5		7		9	10	11			6		2							4		8
32	1	2	3		5		7	8	9	10				6							11		4		
33	1	2	3	4	5		7	8	9		11			6											10
34	1	2	3	4			7	8	9		11			6								5			10
35	1	2	3				7	8	9		11			6								5	4		10
36	1	2	3		5		7	8	9		11			6									4		10
37	1	2	3		5		7	8	9		11			6									4		10
38	1	2	3		5		7	8	9		11			6									4		10
39	1	2	3		5		7	8	9		11			6									4		10
40	1	2	3		5		7	8	9		11			6									4		10
41	1	2	3		5		7	8	9		11			6									4		10
42	1	2	3		5		7	8	9		11			6									4		10
	14	39	42	31	16	4	40	36	31	32	14	27	27	27	11	3	1	4	11	2	4	10	24	1	11
			2	1	1	1	21	12	21	2	2		3		5				5	1					3

	Pearson HF	Finch EAR	Shaw GE	Magee TP	Evans JT	Howarth N	Glidden TW	Carter JH	Cookson J	Chambers H	Fitton GA	Ashmore GSA	Wood S	Darnell L	James GC	Corbett FJ	Rix J	Fryer ER	Short JS	Bytheway GS	Leedham FA	Dale RA	Richardson W	Webster H	Edwards J
R3		2	3	4			7	8	9	10		1	11									6	5		
rep		2	3	4			7	8	9	10		1	11									6	5		
R4		2	3	4			7	8	9	10		1	11	6									5		
R5		2	3	4			7	8	9	10		1	11	6									5		
R6		2	3	4			7	8	9	10		1	11	6									5		
rep		2	3	4			7	8	9	10		1	11	6									5		
		6	6	6			6	6	6	6		6	6	4								2	6		
							2	1	7	1			1												

1929-30

Division Two

	P	W	D	L	F	A	Pts
Blackpool	42	27	4	11	98	67	58
Chelsea	42	22	11	9	74	46	55
Oldham Athletic	42	21	11	10	90	51	53
Bradford Park Avenue	42	19	12	11	91	70	50
Bury	42	22	5	15	78	67	49
West Bromwich Albion	42	21	5	16	105	73	47
Southampton	42	17	11	14	77	76	45
Cardiff City	42	18	8	16	61	59	44
Wolverhampton W	42	16	9	17	77	79	41
Nottingham Forest	42	13	15	14	55	69	41
Stoke City	42	16	8	18	74	72	40
Tottenham Hotspur	42	15	9	18	59	61	39
Charlton Athletic	42	14	11	17	59	63	39
Millwall	42	12	15	15	57	73	39
Swansea Town	42	14	9	19	57	61	37
Preston North End	42	13	11	18	65	80	37
Barnsley	42	14	8	20	56	71	36
Bradford City	42	12	12	18	60	77	36
Reading	42	12	11	19	54	67	35
Bristol City	42	13	9	20	61	83	35
Hull City	42	14	7	21	51	78	35
Notts County	42	9	15	18	54	70	33

Secretary-manager: Fred Everiss

- Albion's total of 105 goals was the highest total the team had ever scored in a season of League football. They netted 73 at home and 32 away.
- New signing 'W.G' Richardson from Hartlepools United scored on his debut against Millwall in December and ended the campaign with 50 goals for the second XI.
- Goalkeeper Jimmy Adams, raven-haired Teddy Sandford (from Smethwick Highfield) and winger Harry Boston (from Bolton Wanderers) were other major signings made by Albion. Inside-forward Frank Cresswell was transferred to Chester and Len Darnell to Reading.
- Albion's reserve team recorded their biggest ever Central League win – beating Derby County 12–2 at The Hawthorns.

Match No.	Date			Opponents	Result		Scorers	Attendance
1	Aug	31	A	Wolverhampton Wanderers	W	4-2	Cookson 2, Carter, Shaw	25,961
2	Sep	2	H	Oldham Athletic	L	0-3		25,221
3		7	H	Bradford Park Avenue	W	5-0	Cresswell, Cookson 3, Evans	22,997
4		9	A	Southampton	L	2-3	Cookson 2	8,519
5		14	A	Barnsley	D	2-2	Wood, Glidden	9,705
6		21	H	Blackpool	W	5-1	Carter 2, Cookson 2, Glidden	16,515
7		28	A	Bury	L	2-3	Cookson, Shaw (pen)	10,147
8	Oct	5	H	Chelsea	W	2-0	Cookson, Glidden	19,317
9		12	A	Nottingham Forest	W	2-0	Cookson, Glidden	11,958
10		19	A	Bradford City	D	2-2	Glidden 2	19,963
11		26	H	Swansea Town	W	6-2	Glidden 4, Cresswell, Carter	21,070
12	Nov	2	A	Cardiff City	L	2-3	Carter, Cresswell	11,916
13		9	H	Preston North End	W	2-0	Carter 2	18,869
14		16	A	Bristol City	L	1-2	Shaw (pen)	10,040
15		23	H	Notts County	W	4-2	Carter, Glidden, Evans, Cookson	15,118
16		30	A	Reading	D	2-2	Cooksn 2	9,208
17	Dec	7	H	Charlton Athletic	D	1-1	Cookson	10,886
18		14	A	Hull City	L	2-3	Cookson, Carter	4,935
19		21	H	Stoke City	L	2-3	Boston, Cookson	11,809
20		25	A	Millwall	L	1-2	Carter	19,388
21		26	H	Millwall	W	6-1	Carter 2, Glidden 2, Richardson (G), Wood	24,032
22		28	H	Wolverhampton Wanderers	W	7-3	Evans, Cresswell 2, Glidden, Carter 2, Shaw (og)	20,211
23	Jan	1	A	Oldham Athletic	L	0-5		12,546
24		4	A	Bradford Park Avenue	L	1-5	Carter	17,740
25		18	H	Barnsley	W	4-2	Shaw (pen), Richardson (G), Cresswell, Carter	8,138
26	Feb	1	H	Bury	W	5-1	Fitton, Evans, Glidden, Carter 2	10,445
27		8	A	Chelsea	L	0-2		23,146
28		22	H	Bradford City	W	4-2	Carter, Glidden, Cookson 2	11,770
29	Mar	1	A	Swansea Town	L	0-1		12,976
30		5	A	Blackpool	L	0-1		10,225
31		8	H	Cardiff City	L	0-2		15,310
32		15	A	Preston North End	D	2-2	Wood, Glidden	7,080
33		19	H	Nottingham Forest	L	1-3	Wood	1,495
34		22	H	Bristol City	W	2-0	Cookson, Evans	5,060
35		29	A	Notts County	L	1-2	Cookson	10,026
36	Apr	5	H	Reading	W	1-0	Edwards	8,020
37		12	A	Charlton Athletic	W	1-0	Wood	9,966
38		18	A	Tottenham Hotspur	W	2-0	Wood, Boston	25,228
39		19	H	Hull City	W	7-1	Glidden 2, Cookson 4, Boston	10,036
40		21	H	Tottenham Hotspur	W	4-3	Cookson, Wood, Reddish (og), Glidden	12,908
41		26	A	Stoke City	W	3-0	Cookson 2, Edwards	6,338
42	May	3	H	Southampton	W	5-1	Cookson 4, Edwards	14,685
								Appearances
								Goals

FA Cup

R3	Jan	11	A	Wrexham	L	0-1		16,750
								Appearances

Pearson HF	Finch EAR	Shaw GE	Richardson W	Evans JT	Darnell L	Glidden TW	Carter JH	Cookson J	Cresswell F	Wood S	Ashmore GSA	Magee TP	Edwards J	Adams J	Fitton GA	Boston HJ	Corbett FJ	Richardson W(G)	Trentham HF	Dale RA	Murphy JP	Rix J	
1	2	3	4	5	6	7	8	9	10	11													1
1	2	3	4	5	6	7	8	9	10	11													2
1	2	3	4	5	6	7	8	9	10	11													3
1	2	3	4	5	6	7	8	9	10	11													4
1	2	3	4	5	6	7	8	9	10	11													5
1	2	3	4	5	6	7	8	9	10	11													6
1	2	3	4	5	6	7	8	9	10	11													7
1	2	3	4	5	6	7	8	9	10	11													8
1	2	3	4	5	6	7	8	9	10	11													9
1	2	3	4	5	6	7	8	9	10	11													10
1	2	3	4	5	6	7	8	9	10	11													11
	2	3	4	5	6	7	8	9	10	11	1												12
	2	3	5		6	7	8	9	10	11	1	4											13
	2	3	4	5	6	7	8	9		11	1		10										14
	2	3	4	5	6	7	8	9	10	11				1									15
	2	3	4	5	6	7	8	9	10	11				1									16
	2	3	4	5	6	7	8	9	10	11				1									17
	2	3	4	5	6	7	8	9					10	1	11								18
	2	3	5		6	8		9		11		4	10	1		7							19
	2	3	5		6	7	8	9	10	11		4		1									20
		3	6	5		7	8		10	11		4		1			2	9					21
		3	6	5		7	8		10	11		4		1			2	9					22
		3	6	5		7	8		10	11		4		1			2	9					23
		3	6	5		7	8	9	10	11	1	4					2						24
	2	3	4	5	6	7	8		10		1				11			9					25
	2	3	4	5	6	7	8		10		1				11			9					26
	2	3	4	5	6	7	8		10		1				11			9					27
	2	3	4	5	6	7	8	9	10		1				11								28
	2	3	4	5	6	8		9	10		1				11	7							29
	2		6			7			10		1	4			11			9	3	5	8		30
	2	3	6			7			10	11	1	4						9		5	8		31
1	2	3	6	5	8	7		9	10	11										4			32
1	2	3	6	5	8	7		9	10	11										4			33
1	2	3	6	5	4	8		9		11			10			7							34
1	2	3	6			8		9		11		4	10			7				5			35
1	2	3	6			8		9		11		4	10			7				5			36
1	2	3	6			8		9		11		4	10			7				5			37
1	2	3	6			8		9		11		4	10			7				5			38
1	2	3	6			8		9		11		4	10			7				5			39
1	2	3	6	5		8		9		11		4	10			7							40
1	2	3	5			8		9		11		4	10			7						6	41
	2	3	5					9		11	1	4	10			7		8				6	42
21	38	41	42	30	28	41	27	34	30	35	12	17	12	9	7	11	4	9	1	9	2	2	
		4		5		20	19	33	6	7			3		1	3		2					

Two own-goals

	2	3	4	5	6	7	8	9	10	11	1	R3
	1	1	1	1	1	1	1	1	1	1	1	

1930-31

Division Two

	P	W	D	L	F	A	Pts
Everton	42	28	5	9	121	66	61
West Bromwich Albion	42	22	10	10	83	49	54
Tottenham Hotspur	42	22	7	13	88	55	51
Wolverhampton W	42	21	5	16	84	67	47
Port Vale	42	21	5	16	67	61	47
Bradford Park Avenue	42	18	10	14	97	66	46
Preston North End	42	17	11	14	83	64	45
Burnley	42	17	11	14	81	77	45
Southampton	42	19	6	17	74	62	44
Bradford City	42	17	10	15	61	63	44
Stoke City	42	17	10	15	64	71	44
Oldham Athletic	42	16	10	16	61	72	42
Bury	42	19	3	20	75	82	41
Millwall	42	16	7	19	71	80	39
Charlton Athletic	42	15	9	18	59	86	39
Bristol City	42	15	8	19	54	82	38
Nottingham Forest	42	14	9	19	80	85	37
Plymouth Argyle	42	14	8	20	76	84	36
Barnsley	42	13	9	20	59	79	35
Swansea Town	42	12	10	20	51	74	34
Reading	42	12	6	24	72	96	30
Cardiff City	42	8	9	25	47	87	25

Secretary-manager: Fred Everiss

- Albion completed the unique double – winning the FA Cup and gaining promotion from the Second Division in the same season – a feat never accomplished before or since.
- Fielding 11 English-born players, Albion beat Birmingham in the first all-Midland Cup Final since 1895.
- Goalkeeping cousins Harold Pearson (Albion) and Harry Hibbs (Birmingham) played against each other at Wembley.
- Players signed by Albion included Jack Sankey from Winsford United, Walter Boyes from Woodhouse FC (Sheffield) and Harry Raw from Huddersfield Town.
- An Albion home game was covered 'live' on radio for the first time – the sixth-round FA Cup game against Wolves in February.

Match No.	Date			Opponents	Result		Scorers	Attendance
1	Aug	30	H	Bristol City	W	3-0	Glidden 2, Edwards	11,037
2	Sep	1	A	Charlton Athletic	W	4-0	Cookson, Wood, Pitcairn (og), Boston	11,325
3		6	A	Cardiff City	W	6-3	Cookson 4, Carter, Boston	10,987
4		8	H	Bradford City	W	1-0	Shaw (pen)	18,126
5		13	H	Everton	L	1-2	Cookson	23,517
6		17	A	Bradford City	W	3-2	Glidden, Boston, Cookson	12,171
7		20	A	Bury	D	2-2	Carter 2	11,525
8		27	H	Plymouth Argyle	L	1-2	Cookson	19,938
9	Oct	4	A	Swansea Town	D	1-1	Carter	12,497
10		11	H	Wolverhampton Wanderers	W	2-1	Carter, Cookson	40,065
11		18	A	Southampton	D	1-1	Carter	16,614
12		25	H	Reading	W	1-0	Wood	19,112
13	Nov	1	A	Millwall	L	0-2		14,584
14		8	H	Oldham Athletic	W	2-0	Cookson, Carter	12,880
15		15	A	Preston North End	W	3-2	Wood, Cookson, Sandford	15,550
16		22	H	Tottenham Hotspur	L	0-2		18,078
17		29	A	Nottingham Forest	W	6-1	Wood 2, Richardson 2, Carter, Sandford	4,359
18	Dec	6	H	Burnley	W	2-0	Wood, Richardson	17,197
19		13	A	Bradford Park Avenue	L	1-3	Richardson	14,790
20		20	H	Stoke City	W	4-0	Richardson, Glidden 2, Magee	15,629
21		25	A	Barnsley	D	0-0		10,217
22		26	H	Barnsley	W	5-0	Richardson, Glidden 2, Wood, Shaw (pen)	22,981
23		27	A	Bristol City	D	1-1	Richardson	17,709
24	Jan	3	H	Cardiff City	W	3-2	Sandford, Carter, Richardson	24,028
25		17	A	Everton	L	1-2	Glidden	30,190
26		26	H	Bury	W	2-0	Glidden, Sandford	20,160
27		31	A	Plymouth Argyle	L	1-5	Wood	9,319
28	Feb	7	H	Swansea Town	D	0-0		15,977
29		18	A	Wolverhampton Wanderers	W	4-1	Wood 2, Richardson 2	36,054
30		21	H	Southampton	L	1-2	Richardson	20,682
31	Mar	7	H	Millwall	D	0-0		17,763
32		21	H	Preston North End	W	2-0	Glidden 2	26,558
33		23	A	Oldham Athletic	D	2-2	Raw, Glidden	6,245
34		28	A	Tottenham Hotspur	D	2-2	Sandford, Glidden	56,012
35	Apr	3	A	Port Vale	L	0-1		18,043
36		4	H	Nottingham Forest	W	2-1	Wood 2	19,054
37		6	H	Port Vale	W	4-1	Glidden, Richardson 2, Wood	23,806
38		11	A	Burnley	L	1-2	Richardson	12,109
39		15	A	Reading	W	3-0	Richardson 2, Sandford	10,026
40		18	H	Bradford Park Avenue	D	1-1	Shaw (pen)	21,176
41		30	A	Stoke City	W	1-0	Richardson	26,063
42	May	2	H	Charlton Athletic	W	3-2	Sandford, Richardson, Glidden	52,415

All Richardson goals are 'W.G.' ('Ginger') Richardson — Appearances

Goals

FA Cup

R3	Jan	10	H	Charlton Athletic	D	2-2	Wood, Sandford	27,249
rep		14	A	Charlton Athletic	D	1-1*	Carter	18,703
rep2		19	N	Charlton Athletic	W	3-1	Carter, Wood, 'W.G.' Richardson	27,764
R4		24	H	Tottenham Hotspur	W	1-0	Wood	40,850
R5	Feb	14	A	Portsmouth	W	1-0	'W.G.' Richardson	30,891
R6		28	H	Wolverhampton Wanderers	D	1-1	'W.G.' Richardson	52,285
rep	Mar	4	A	Wolverhampton Wanderers	W	2-1	Wood, 'W.G.' Richardson	46,860
SF		14	N	Everton	W	1-0	Glidden	69,241
F	Apr	25	N	Birmingham	W	2-1	'W.G.' Richardson 2	90,368

R3 replay 2 at Villa Park — Appearances

SF at Old Trafford — Goals

Final at Wembley Stadium

* after extra-time

Pearson HF	Finch EAR	Shaw GE	Magee TP	Richardson W	Rix J	Boston HJ	Glidden TW	Cookson J	Edwards J	Wood S	Trentham HF	Carter JH	Richardson W	Sandford EA	Fitton GA	Raw H	Murphy JP	Bytheway GS	Ashmore GSA	
1	2	3	4	5	6	7	8	9	10	11										1
1		2	4	5	6	7	8	9	10	11	3									2
1		2	4	5		7	8	9	6	11	3	10								3
1		2	4	5		7	8	9	6	11	3	10								4
1	2	3	4	5		7	8	9	6	11		10								5
1	2	3		5	4	7	8	9	6	11		10								6
1	2	3		5	4	7	8	9	6	11		10								7
1	2	3		5	4	7	8	9	6	11		10								8
1		2		5	4	7	8	9	6	11	3	10								9
1		2		5	4	7	8	9	6	11	3	10								10
1		2		5	4	7	8	9	6	11	3	10								11
1		2		5	4	7	8	9	6	11	3	10								12
1		2		5	4	7	8	9	6	11	3	10								13
1		2	4	5			7	9	6	11	3	10	8							14
1		2	4	5			7	9	6	11	3		8	10						15
1		2	4	5			7	9	6	11	3		8	10						16
1		2	4	5			7		6	11	3	8	9	10						17
1		2	4	5			7		6	11	3	8	9	10						18
1		2	4	5			7		6	11	3	8	9	10						19
1		2	4	5		7	8		6	11	3		9	10						20
1		2	4	5		7	8		6	11	3		9	10						21
1		2	4	5			7		6	11	3	8	9	10						22
1		2	4	5			7		6	11	3	8	9	10						23
1		2	4	5			7		6	11	3	8	9	10						24
1		2	4	5			7		6	11	3	8	9	10						25
1		2	4	5			7		6	11	3	8	9	10						26
1		2	4	5		7			6	11	3	8	9	10						27
1		2	4	5	6		7				3	8	9	10	11					28
1		2	4	5			7	9	6	11	3		8	10						29
1		2	4	5			7	9	6	11	3		8	10						30
1		2	4	5					6	11	3	8	9	10		7				31
1		2	4	5			7		6	11	3	8	9	10						32
1		2	4	5			7		6	11	3		9	10		8				33
1		2		5			7		6	11	3	8	9	10			4			34
1		2		5			7		6	11	3	8	9	10			4			35
1		2	4	5			7		6	11	3	8	9	10						36
1		2	4	5			7		6	11	3	8	9	10						37
1		2	4	5					6	11	3		9	10		8		7		38
1	2	3	4	5			7		6	11		8	9	10						39
1	2	3	4	5			7		6	11		8	9	10						40
1		2	4	5			7		6	11	3	8	9	10						41
1	2	3	4	5			7		6	11		8	9	10						42
42	8	42	32	42	11	16	39	18	41	41	34	32	29	28	1	3	2	1		
		3	1			3	15	11	1	13		9	18	7		1				

One own-goal

Pearson HF	Finch EAR	Shaw GE	Magee TP	Richardson W	Rix J	Boston HJ	Glidden TW	Cookson J	Edwards J	Wood S	Trentham HF	Carter JH	Richardson W	Sandford EA	Fitton GA	Raw H	Murphy JP	Bytheway GS	Ashmore GSA	
1		2	4	5			7		6	11	3	8	9	10						R3
1		2	4	5			7		6	11	3	8	9	10						rep
		2	4	5			7		6	11	3	8	9	10					1	rep2
1		2	4	5			7		6	11	3	8	9	10						R4
1		2	4	5			7	9	6	11	3		8	10						R5
1		2	4	5			7		6	11	3	8	9	10						R6
1		2	4	5			7		6	11	3	8	9	10						rep
1		2	4	5			7		6	11	3	8	9	10						SF
1		2	4	5			7		6	11	3	8	9	10						F
8		9	9	9			9	1	9	9	9	8	9	9					1	
							1			4		2	6	1						

1931-32

Division One

	P	W	D	L	F	A	Pts
Everton	42	26	4	12	116	64	56
Arsenal	42	22	10	10	90	48	54
Sheffield Wednesday	42	22	6	14	96	82	50
Huddersfield Town	42	19	10	13	80	63	48
Aston Villa	42	19	8	15	104	72	46
West Bromwich Albion	42	20	6	16	77	55	46
Sheffield United	42	20	6	16	80	75	46
Portsmouth	42	19	7	16	62	62	45
Birmingham	42	18	8	16	78	67	44
Liverpool	42	19	6	17	81	93	44
Newcastle United	42	18	6	18	80	87	42
Chelsea	42	16	8	18	69	73	40
Sunderland	42	15	10	17	67	73	40
Manchester City	42	13	12	17	83	73	38
Derby County	42	14	10	18	71	75	38
Blackburn Rovers	42	16	6	20	89	95	38
Bolton Wanderers	42	17	4	21	72	80	38
Middlesbrough	42	15	8	19	64	89	38
Leicester City	42	15	7	20	74	94	37
Blackpool	42	12	9	21	65	102	33
Grimsby Town	42	13	6	23	67	98	32
West Ham United	42	12	7	23	62	107	31

Secretary-manager: Fred Everiss

- Centre-forward 'W.G.' Richardson scored four goals between the fourth and ninth minutes of Albion's League game against West Ham in November to equal the record for rapid League marksmanship.
- Jimmy Cookson made his last senior appearance for Albion against Birmingham on Boxing Day. He would move south to Plymouth Argyle in August 1933.
- Joe Carter became the first Albion player to be sent off at The Hawthorns – dismissed during the League game against Blackburn Rovers in September.
- Welshman Walter Robbins, signed from Cardiff City, made an impressive debut at Chelsea while other debutants were fellow countryman Hugh Foulkes against Sunderland, Wally Boyes, in front of almost 60,000 fans at home to Aston Villa, schoolmaster Arthur Gale, a £1,000 signing from Chester, and goalkeeper Jimmy Adams.
- Albion and Portsmouth met at League level for the first time.

Match No.	Date			Opponents	Result		Scorers	Attendance
1	Aug	29	A	Arsenal	W	1-0	Wood	52,478
2	Sep	2	A	Sunderland	L	1-2	Richardson	16,981
3		5	H	Blackpool	W	4-0	Richardson 2, Longden (og), Glidden	18,506
4		7	H	Sunderland	W	1-0	Wood	24,950
5		12	A	Sheffield United	L	0-1		22,410
6		14	H	Manchester City	D	1-1	Richardson	19,042
7		19	H	Blackburn Rovers	W	4-1	Edwards, Sandford, Glidden 2	25,885
8		23	A	Manchester City	W	5-2	Richardson, Wood, Raw 2, Glidden	16,194
9		26	A	Portsmouth	W	1-0	Glidden (pen)	19,723
10	Oct	3	H	Derby County	W	4-0	Shaw (pen), Glidden, Sandford, Richardson	33,192
11		10	A	Huddersfield Town	D	2-2	Richardson 2	19,556
12		17	H	Liverpool	L	1-2	Glidden	30,065
13		24	A	Bolton Wanderers	L	0-1		19,695
14		31	H	Sheffield Wednesday	D	1-1	Richardson	31,334
15	Nov	7	A	West Ham United	W	5-1	Richardson 4, Sandford	20,685
16		14	H	Aston Villa	W	3-0	Glidden, Raw, Richardson	59,674
17		21	A	Newcastle United	L	1-5	Glidden	35,871
18		28	H	Middlesbrough	D	1-1	Sandford	17,824
19	Dec	5	A	Leicester City	W	3-2	Richardson, Glidden, Wood	15,267
20		12	H	Chelsea	W	4-0	Richardson 2, Boyes, Glidden	24,186
21		19	A	Grimsby Town	D	0-0		9,225
22		25	H	Birmingham	L	0-1		38,053
23		26	A	Birmingham	L	0-1		57,806
24	Jan	2	H	Arsenal	W	1-0	Glidden	25,790
25		16	A	Blackpool	W	2-1	Richardson, Sandford	12,269
26		25	H	Sheffield United	L	0-1		11,382
27		30	A	Blackburn Rovers	L	0-2		14,678
28	Feb	6	H	Portsmouth	W	3-0	Glidden 2, Richardson	21,065
29		17	A	Derby County	L	1-3	Glidden	8,584
30		20	H	Huddersfield Town	W	3-2	Richardson, Raw, Glidden	20,105
31	Mar	2	A	Liverpool	L	1-4	Richardson	13,029
32		5	H	Bolton Wanderers	W	3-0	Richardson, Glidden, Wood	16,050
33		12	A	Sheffield Wednesday	W	5-2	Carter, Glidden, Richardson, Sandford, Wood	15,110
34		19	H	West Ham United	W	3-1	Wood, Richardson, Carter	19,271
35		25	A	Everton	L	1-2	Richardson	51,783
36		26	A	Aston Villa	L	0-2		43,347
37		28	H	Everton	D	1-1	Carter	31,486
38	Apr	2	H	Newcastle United	W	2-1	Davidson (og), Glidden	18,614
39		9	A	Middlesbrough	L	0-1		7,551
40		16	H	Leicester City	L	1-2	Sandford	15,014
41		23	A	Chelsea	W	2-0	Carter, Richardson	23,873
42		30	H	Grimsby Town	L	5-6	Richardson, Sandford, Carter, Edwards (pen), Glidden	7,796

All Richardson goals are 'W.G.' ('Ginger') Richardson

Appearances

Goals

FA Cup

R3	Jan	9	H	Aston Villa	L	1-2	'W.G.' Richardson	49,232

Appearances

Goals

Pearson HF	Shaw GE	Trentham HF	Magee TP	Richardson W	Edwards J	Glidden TW	Carter JH	Richardson WG	Sandford EA	Wood S	Foulkes HE	Raw H	Murphy JP	Boyes WE	Cookson J	Rix J	Gale AR	Adams J	Finch EAR	Robbins WW	
1	2	3	4	5	6	7	8	9	10	11											1
1	2		4	5	6	7	8	9	10	11	3										2
1	2	3	4	5	6	7	8	9	10	11											3
1	2	3	4	5	6	7	8	9	10	11											4
1	2	3	4	5	6	7	8	9	10	11											5
1	2	3	4	5	6	7	8	9	10	11											6
1	2	3	4	5	6	7	8	9	10	11											7
1	2	3	4	5	6	7		9	10	11		8									8
1	2	3	4	5	6	7		9	10	11		8									9
1	2	3	4	5	6	7		9	10	11		8									10
1	2	3	4	5	6	7		9	10	11		8									11
1	2	3	4	5	6	7		9	10	11		8									12
1	2		4	5	6	7		9	10	11	3	8									13
1	2	3	4	5	6	7		9	10	11		8									14
1	2	3	4	5		7		9	10	11		8	6								15
1	2	3	4	5	6	7		9		11		8		10							16
1	2	3	4	5		7		9	10	11		8	6								17
1	2	3	4	5		7		9	10	11		8	6								18
1	2	3	4	5		7		9	10	11		8	6								19
1	2	3	4	5		7		9	10	11			6	8							20
1	2	3	4	5		7		9	10	11			6	8							21
1	2	3	4	5		7		9	10	11			6	8							22
1	2	3		5	6	7	8		10	11			4		9						23
1	2	3		5	6	7	8	9	10	11			4								24
1	2	3		5		7		9	10	11		8	4			6					25
1	2	3		5		7	8	9	10	11			4			6					26
1	2	3				7		9	5	11		8	4	10		6					27
1	2	3		5		7		9	6	11		8	4	10							28
1	2			5		7		9	6	11	3	8	4	10							29
1	2			5		7		9	6	11	3	8	4	10							30
1	2			5		7	10	9	3	11		8	4	6							31
1	2	3		5		7	8	9	10	11			4	6							32
1	2	3		5		7	8	9	10	11			4	6							33
1	2	3		5		7	8	9	10	11			4	6							34
1	2	3		5	6	7	8	9	10	11			4								35
1	2	3		5		7	8	9	10	11			4	6							36
1	2	3		5		7	8	9	10	11			4	6							37
1	2	3		5	6	7		9	10				4	11			8				38
		3		5	6	7		9		11			4	10			8	1	2		39
1	2	3		5		7	8		10	11			4	6			9				40
1	2	3		5	6	7	8	9	10				4							11	41
1	2	3		5	6	7	8	9	10	11			4								42
41	41	37	22	41	22	42	20	40	40	40	4	18	27	17	1	3	3	1	1	1	
	1				2	20	5	27	8	7		4		1							

Two own-goals

1	2	3		5	6	7	8	9	10	11			4								R3
1	1	1		1	1	1	1	1	1	1			1								
								1													

1932-33

Division One

	P	W	D	L	F	A	Pts
Arsenal	42	25	8	9	118	61	58
Aston Villa	42	23	8	11	92	67	54
Sheffield Wednesday	42	21	9	12	80	68	51
West Bromwich Albion	42	20	9	13	83	70	49
Newcastle United	42	22	5	15	71	63	49
Huddersfield Town	42	18	11	13	66	53	47
Derby County	42	15	14	13	76	69	44
Leeds United	42	15	14	13	59	62	44
Portsmouth	42	18	7	17	74	76	43
Sheffield United	42	17	9	16	74	80	43
Everton	42	16	9	17	81	74	41
Sunderland	42	15	10	17	63	80	40
Birmingham	42	14	11	17	57	57	39
Liverpool	42	14	11	17	79	84	39
Blackburn Rovers	42	14	10	18	76	102	38
Manchester City	42	16	5	21	68	71	37
Middlesbrough	42	14	9	19	63	73	37
Chelsea	42	14	7	21	63	73	35
Leicester City	42	11	13	18	75	89	35
Wolverhampton W	42	13	9	20	80	96	35
Bolton Wanderers	42	12	9	21	78	92	33
Blackpool	42	14	5	23	69	85	33

Secretary-manager: Fred Everiss

- 'W.G.' Richardson set a new club record by scoring in nine consecutive League games between 4 February and 1 April. He bagged 12 goals in total.
- Centre-half Alf Ridyard was signed from Barnsley as cover for Bill Richardson and made his debut at Derby; Harry 'Popeye' Jones was secured from Preston North End (May) and was to stay with the club for 10 years.
- Albion's second team won the Central League title for the fourth time, scoring 106 goals in the process.

Match No.	Date			Opponents	Result		Scorers	Attendance
1	Aug	27	H	Everton	W	3-1	Sandford, Carter, Richardson	31,922
2		31	A	Arsenal	W	2-1	Glidden, John (og)	37,748
3	Sep	3	A	Blackpool	W	4-2	Glidden 3, Richardson	20,646
4		10	H	Derby County	W	2-0	Richardson, Glidden	30,715
5		14	H	Arsenal	D	1-1	Carter	45,038
6		17	A	Blackburn Rovers	D	4-4	Carter 2, Glidden, Wood	21,081
7		24	H	Leeds United	L	0-1		26,497
8	Oct	1	A	Sheffield Wednesday	L	1-3	Robbins	10,775
9		8	H	Wolverhampton Wanderers	W	4-1	Richardson 2, Glidden, Sandfor	30,058
10		15	H	Birmingham	W	1-0	Sandford	29,145
11		22	A	Newcastle United	L	0-3		26,026
12		29	H	Aston Villa	W	3-1	Robbins, Carter, Richardson	42,093
13	Nov	5	A	Portsmouth	L	0-3		22,863
14		12	H	Chelsea	W	3-2	Wood, Robbins, Sandford	21,569
15		19	A	Huddersfield Town	L	1-2	Richardson	12,008
16		26	H	Sheffield United	L	0-1		16,882
17	Dec	3	A	Middlesbrough	L	1-3	Raw	8,276
18		10	H	Bolton Wanderers	W	4-0	Raw, Robbins 2, Richardson	12,662
19		17	A	Liverpool	L	0-2		18,631
20		24	H	Leicester City	W	4-3	Richardson 3, Sandford	15,905
21		26	H	Sunderland	W	5-1	Richardson 3, Carter, Robbins	26,113
22		31	A	Everton	W	2-1	Glidden, Robbins	30,234
23	Jan	2	A	Sunderland	D	2-2	Richardson, Wood	28,095
24		7	H	Blackpool	W	2-1	Richardson, Wood	17,280
25		21	A	Derby County	D	2-2	Glidden, Carter	15,447
26	Feb	4	A	Leeds United	D	1-1	Richardson	19,696
27		8	H	Blackburn Rovers	L	1-3	Richardson	10,775
28		11	H	Sheffield Wednesday	W	2-0	Richardson, Sandford	20,863
29		18	A	Wolverhampton Wanderers	D	3-3	Glidden, Richardson, Wood	34,534
30	Mar	4	H	Newcastle United	W	3-2	Richardson 2, Wood	21,847
31		11	A	Aston Villa	L	2-3	Richardson 2	50,600
32		18	H	Portsmouth	W	4-2	Richardson 2, Sandford 2	16,356
33		25	A	Chelsea	W	2-1	Gale, Richardson	33,377
34	Apr	1	H	Huddersfield Town	W	2-1	Richardson, Carter	17,610
35		8	A	Sheffield United	D	1-1	Robbins	11,003
36		14	A	Manchester City	L	0-1		42,086
37		15	H	Middlesbrough	L	0-1		17,530
38		17	H	Manchester City	W	4-0	Robbins, Carter 3	18,998
39		22	A	Bolton Wanderers	D	2-2	Robbins, Carter	11,647
40		26	A	Birmingham	D	1-1	Richardson	16,509
41		29	H	Liverpool	W	2-1	Carter, Richardson	8,933
42	May	6	A	Leicester City	L	2-6	Carter, Sandford	20,389

All Richardson goals are 'W.G.' ('Ginger') Richardson

Appearances

Goals

FA Cup

R3	Jan	14	H	Liverpool	W	2-0	Wood, 'W.G.' Richardson	29,329
R4		28	A	West Ham United	L	0-2		37,222

Appearances

Goals

Pearson HF	Shaw GE	Trentham HF	Magee TP	Richardson W	Edwards J	Glidden TW	Carter JH	Richardson WG	Sandford EA	Wood S	Finch EAR	Gale AR	Robbins WW	Murphy JP	Rix J	Raw H	Ridyard A	Match
1	2	3	4	5	6	7	8	9	10	11								1
1	2	3	4	5	6	7	8	9	10	11								2
1	2	3	4	5	6	7	8	9	10	11								3
1	2	3	4	5	6	7	8	9	10	11								4
1	2	3	4	5	6	7	8	9	10	11								5
1	2	3	4	5	6	7	8	9	10	11								6
1	2	3	4	5	6	7	8	9	10	11								7
1	3		4	5	6	7	8		10		2	9	11					8
1	2	3		5	6	7	8	9	10	11				4				9
1	2	3		5	6	7	8	9	10	11				4				10
1	2	3		5	6	7	8	9	10				11	4				11
1	2	3		5	6	7	8	9	10				11	4				12
1	2	3		5	6	7	8	9	10				11	4				13
1	2	3		5	6	7	8		10	11			9	4				14
1	2	3				7		9	5	11			10	4	6	8		15
1	2	3		5		7	8		10	11			9	4	6			16
1	2	3	4	5		7			10	11			9	6		8		17
1	2	3		5		7		9	6	11			10	4		8		18
1	2	3		5		7		9	6	11			10	4		8		19
1	2	3		5	6	7		9	8	11			10	4				20
1	2	3		5	6	7	8	9		11			10	4				21
1	2	3		5		7	8	9		11			10	4	6			22
1	2	3		5		7	8	9		11			10	4	6			23
1	2	3		5	6	7		9	8	11			10	4				24
1	2	3			6	7	8	9	10	11				4			5	25
1	2	3			6	7	8	9	10	11				4			5	26
1	2	3			6	7	8	9	10	11				4			5	27
1	2	3		5	6	7	8	9	10	11				4				28
1	2	3		5	6	7	8	9	10	11				4				29
1	2	3		5	6	7	8	9	10	11				4				30
1	3			5	6	7	8	9	10	11	2			4				31
1	2	3		5	6		8	9	10	11		7		4				32
1	2	3		5	6		8	9	10			7	11	4				33
1	2	3		5	6		8	9	10			7	11	4				34
1	2	3		5	6	7	8	9	10				11	4				35
1	2	3		5	6	7	8	9	10				11	4				36
1	2	3		5	6	7	8	9	10				11	4				37
1	2	3		5	6	7	8	9	10				11	4				38
1	2	3		5	6	7	8	9	10				11	4				39
1	2	3		5	6	7	8	9	10				11	4				40
1	2	3		5		7	8	9	10				11	4	6			41
1	2	3		5		7	8	9	10				11	4	6			42
42	42	40	9	38	33	39	36	38	39	28	2	4	25	34	6	4	3	
						10	14	30	9	6		1	10			2		

One own-goal

Pearson HF	Shaw GE	Trentham HF	Magee TP	Richardson W	Edwards J	Glidden TW	Carter JH	Richardson WG	Sandford EA	Wood S	Finch EAR	Gale AR	Robbins WW	Murphy JP	Rix J	Raw H	Ridyard A	Round
	2	3		5	6	7	8	9	10	11				4				R3
	2	3			6	7	8	9	10	11				4			5	R4
	2	2		1	2	2	2	2	2	2				2			1	
								1		1								

1933-34

Division One

	P	W	D	L	F	A	Pts
Arsenal	42	25	9	8	75	47	59
Huddersfield Town	42	23	10	9	90	61	56
Tottenham Hotspur	42	21	7	14	79	56	49
Derby County	42	17	11	14	68	54	45
Manchester City	42	17	11	14	65	72	45
Sunderland	42	16	12	14	81	56	44
West Bromwich Albion	42	17	10	15	78	70	44
Blackburn Rovers	42	18	7	17	74	81	43
Leeds United	42	17	8	17	75	66	42
Portsmouth	42	15	12	15	52	55	42
Sheffield Wednesday	42	16	9	17	62	67	41
Stoke City	42	15	11	16	58	71	41
Aston Villa	42	14	12	16	78	75	40
Everton	42	12	16	14	62	63	40
Wolverhampton W	42	14	12	16	74	86	40
Middlesbrough	42	16	7	19	68	80	39
Leicester City	42	14	11	17	59	74	39
Liverpool	42	14	10	18	79	87	38
Chelsea	42	14	8	20	67	69	36
Birmingham	42	12	12	18	54	56	36
Newcastle United	42	10	14	18	68	77	34
Sheffield United	42	12	7	23	58	101	31

Secretary-manager: Fred Everiss

- Tommy Magee left Albion after more than 15 years' service to become player-coach of Crystal Palace. He appeared in 434 first-class matches for the club and is the only player to gain both League Championship and FA Cup-winners' medals with Albion.
- A record crowd for a second team game at The Hawthorns – 22,372 – saw Albion entertain Aston Villa in March. The reserves retained their Central League title.
- Albion's 7–2 League win at Manchester City (the FA Cup winners this season) was their biggest away from home, in terms of goals scored, since December 1893. Frank Swift was in goal for City.
- Two players – Tommy Green and Bos Trevis – both made their League debuts this season. Trevis holds the record for having the longest name in the history of professional football. He was christened Arthur Stanley Sackville Redvers Trevor Boscawen Griffith Trevis.

Match No.	Date			Opponents	Result		Scorers	Attendance
1	Aug	26	A	Everton	L	0-1		32,212
2	Sep	2	H	Middlesbrough	W	3-0	Glidden, Richardson 2	21,152
3		6	A	Arsenal	L	1-3	Wood	34,688
4		9	A	Blackburn Rovers	L	0-4		12,883
5		13	H	Arsenal	W	1-0	Carter	29,398
6		16	H	Newcastle United	D	1-1	Glidden	24,481
7		23	A	Leeds United	L	0-3		17,364
8		30	H	Derby County	W	5-1	Richardson 4, Glidden	24,570
9	Oct	7	A	Wolverhampton Wanderers	D	0-0		37,308
10		14	A	Birmingham	W	1-0	Richardson	29,961
11		21	H	Stoke City	W	5-1	Beachill (og), Richardson, Sandford 2, Wood	22,771
12		28	A	Huddersfield Town	L	1-3	Richardson	11,592
13	Nov	4	H	Tottenham Hotspur	L	1-2	Wood	32,276
14		11	A	Sunderland	D	2-2	Glidden, Carter	18,013
15		18	H	Chelsea	W	3-1	Richardson, Sandford, Glidden	13,325
16		25	A	Liverpool	D	1-1	Carter	26,167
17	Dec	2	H	Sheffield United	W	3-0	Wood, Richardson, Sandford	10,493
18		9	A	Leicester City	W	1-0	Carter	17,220
19		16	H	Aston Villa	W	2-1	Richardson, Glidden	25,503
20		23	A	Portsmouth	D	2-2	Richardson, Wood	14,365
21		26	A	Sheffield Wednesday	L	1-3	Glidden	33,675
22		27	H	Sheffield Wednesday	D	1-1	Carter	32,660
23		30	H	Everton	D	3-3	Gale, Richardson, Sanford	18,876
24	Jan	1	A	Manchester City	W	7-2	Robbins 2, Richardson 3, Carter, Sandford	27,781
25		6	A	Middlesbrough	L	0-3		11,947
26		20	H	Blackburn Rovers	L	0-1		16,297
27		27	A	Newcastle United	W	2-1	Gale, Sandford	21,148
28	Feb	3	H	Leeds United	L	0-3		13,34
29		10	A	Derby County	D	1-1	Richardson	20,193
30		17	H	Wolverhampton Wanderers	W	2-0	Richardson, Sandford	24,89
31		24	H	Birmingham	L	1-2	Glidden	24,52
32	Mar	8	A	Stoke City	L	1-4	Carter	13,69
33		10	H	Huddersfield Town	L	2-3	Richardson, Sankey	16,28
34		17	A	Tottenham Hotspur	L	1-2	Boyes	26,39
35		24	H	Sunderland	W	6-5	Richardson, Boyes, Glidden 2, Carter, Sandford (pen)	11,88
36		31	A	Chelsea	L	2-3	Richardson, Boyes	36,59
37	Apr	2	H	Manchester City	W	4-0	Carter, Boyes, Richardson 2	22,19
38		7	H	Liverpool	D	2-2	Carter, Sandford (pen)	15,73
39		14	A	Sheffield United	W	1-0	Boyes	9,97
40		21	H	Leicester City	W	2-0	Richardson, Boyes	11,30
41		28	A	Aston Villa	D	4-4	Glidden 2, Green, Richardson	16,55
42	May	5	H	Portsmouth	W	2-1	Glidden, Green	10,67

All Richardson goals are 'W.G.' ('Ginger') Richardson

Appearance

Goal

FA Cup

R3	Jan	13	A	Chelsea	D	1-1	Robbins	51,45
rep		17	H	Chelsea	L	0-1*		20,06

* after extra-time

Appearance

Goa

Match	Pearson HF	Shaw GE	Trentham HF	Murphy JP	Richardson W	Edwards J	Glidden TW	Carter JH	Richardson WG	Sandford EA	Wood S	Ridyard A	Finch EAR	Robbins WW	Boyes WE	Gale AR	Crowe EW	Magee TP	Sankey J	Rix J	Green T	Foulkes HE	Trevis BG
1	1	2	3	4	5	6	7	8	9	10	11												
2	1	2	3	4	5	6	7	8	9	10	11												
3	1	2	3	4		6	7	8	9	10	11	5											
4	1		3	4		6	7	8	9	10	11	5	2										
5	1		3	4	5	6	7	8	9	10	11		2										
6	1		3	4		6	7	8	9	10	11	5	2										
7	1	2	3	4	5	6	7	8	9	10	11												
8	1	2	3	4	5	6	7	8	9	10				11									
9	1	2	3	4	5	6	7	8	9	10				11									
10	1	2	3	4	5	6	7	8	9	10				11									
11	1	2	3	4	5	6	7		9	10	11				8								
12	1	2	3	4	5	6	7		9	10	11				8								
13	1	2	3	4	5	6	7		9	10	11				8								
14	1	2	3	4	5	6	7	8	9	10	11												
15	1	2	3	4	5	6	7	8	9	10	11												
16	1	2	3	4	5	6	7	8	9	10	11												
17	1	2	3	4	5	6	7	8	9	10	11												
18	1	2	3	4	5	6	7	8	9	10	11												
19	1	2	3	4	5	6	7	8	9	10	11												
20	1	2	3	4	5	6	7	8	9	10	11												
21	1	2	3	4	5	6	7	8	9	10	11												
22	1	2	3		5	6	7	8	9	4	11			10									
23	1	2	3		5	6	7	8	9	4	11					10							
24	1	2	3	4	5	6	7	8	9	10				11									
25	1	2	3	4	5	6	7	8	9	10				11									
26			3		5		7	8	9	10	11		2				1	4	6				
27		2	3		5		7	8		10					11	9	1	4	6				
28		2	3	4	5		7			10					11	9	1			6	8		
29					5		7	8	9	10			2		11		1	4	6			3	
30				4	5		7	8	9	10			2		11		1		6			3	
31		2		4	5		7	8	9	10					11		1		6			3	
32		2		4	5		7	8	9	10					11		1		6			3	
33					5		7	8	9	10			2		11		1	4	6			3	
34			3	4			7	8	9	10		5	2		11		1		6				
35			3	4			7	8	9	10		5	2		11		1		6				
36			3	4	5		7	8	9	10			2		11		1		6				
37	1	2	3	4	5		7	8	9	10					11				6				
38	1	2	3		5		7	8	9	10					11				6				4
39	1	2	3	4	5		7	8	9	10					11				6				
40	1	2	3	4	5		7	8	9	10					11				6				
41	1	2	3	4	5		7		9	10					11				6		8		
42	1	2	3	4	5		7		9	10					11				6		8		
	31	32	37	35	37	25	42	36	40	42	21	5	10	6	19	3	11	4	16	1	3	5	1
							13	10	26	10	5			2	6	2			1		2		

One own-goal

Round	Pearson HF	Shaw GE	Trentham HF	Murphy JP	Richardson W	Edwards J	Glidden TW	Carter JH	Richardson WG	Sandford EA	Wood S	Ridyard A	Finch EAR	Robbins WW	Boyes WE	Gale AR	Crowe EW	Magee TP	Sankey J	Rix J	Green T	Foulkes HE	Trevis BG
R3	1	2	3	4	5		7	8	9	10				11					6				
rep	1	2	3	4	5		7	8	9	10				11					6				
	2	2	2	2	2		2	2	2	2				2					2				
														1									

1934-35

Division One

	P	W	D	L	F	A	Pts
Arsenal	42	23	12	7	115	46	58
Sunderland	42	19	16	7	90	51	54
Sheffield Wednesday	42	18	13	11	70	64	49
Manchester City	42	20	8	14	82	67	48
Grimsby Town	42	17	11	14	78	60	45
Derby County	42	18	9	15	81	66	45
Liverpool	42	19	7	16	85	88	45
Everton	42	16	12	14	89	88	44
West Bromwich Albion	42	17	10	15	83	83	44
Stoke City	42	18	6	18	71	70	42
Preston North End	42	15	12	15	62	67	42
Chelsea	42	16	9	17	73	82	41
Aston Villa	42	14	13	15	74	88	41
Portsmouth	42	15	10	17	71	72	40
Blackburn Rovers	42	14	11	17	66	78	39
Huddersfield Town	42	14	10	18	76	71	38
Wolverhampton W	42	15	8	19	88	94	38
Leeds United	42	13	12	17	75	92	38
Birmingham	42	13	10	19	63	81	36
Middlesbrough	42	10	14	18	70	90	34
Leicester City	42	12	9	21	61	86	33
Tottenham Hotspur	42	10	10	22	54	93	30

Secretary-manager: Fred Everiss

- Albion equalised twice against Sheffield Wednesday in the FA Cup Final but succumbed in the end to two late goals from Ronnie Starling.
- Arthur Gale scored in rounds three, four, five and six, played in the semi-final but was dropped in favour of previously injured skipper Tommy Glidden for the Final.
- Albion signed winger Sid Rawlings from Huddersfield Town and also gave League debuts to goalkeeper Ted Crowe, amateur Norman Whitehead and full-back Jack Screen.

Match No.	Date			Opponents	Result		Scorers	Attendance
1	Aug	25	H	Manchester City	D	1-1	Richardson	24,480
2		29	H	Birmingham	L	1-2	Richardson	22,025
3	Sep	1	A	Middlesbrough	D	0-0		16,761
4		3	A	Birmingham	W	2-1	Richardson 2	22,074
5		8	H	Blackburn Rovers	D	2-2	Richardson, Glidden	19,063
6		15	A	Arsenal	L	3-4	Richardson 2, Boyes	40,016
7		22	H	Portsmouth	W	4-2	Richardson 2, Glidden, Sandford	11,396
8		29	A	Liverpool	L	2-3	Sandford 2	20,888
9	Oct	6	H	Leeds United	W	6-3	Richardson 4, Boyes, Carter	15,843
10		13	A	Wolverhampton Wanderers	L	2-3	Sandford 2 (1 pen)	35,386
11		20	H	Huddersfield Town	W	4-1	Boyes 2, Glidden, Richardson	19,250
12		27	A	Everton	L	0-4		27,005
13	Nov	3	H	Aston Villa	D	2-2	Boyes 2	44,503
14		10	A	Chelsea	W	3-2	Boyes 2, Sandford	18,362
15		17	H	Tottenham Hotspur	W	4-0	Sandford, Boyes 2, Richardson	20,397
16		24	A	Sunderland	W	1-0	Carter	30,128
17	Dec	1	H	Leicester City	W	4-1	Boyes 2, Glidden 2	17,174
18		8	A	Derby County	L	3-9	Richardson, Sandford, Glidden	14,782
19		15	H	Grimsby Town	W	4-2	Boyes 2, Sandford 2	17,098
20		22	A	Preston North End	W	2-1	Richardson, Boyes	16,764
21		25	H	Stoke City	W	3-0	Carter 2, Richardson	38,531
22		26	A	Stoke City	L	0-3		38,319
23		29	A	Manchester City	L	2-3	Gale, Sandford	34,615
24	Jan	1	A	Sheffield Wednesday	L	1-2	Gale	29,653
25		5	H	Middlesbrough	W	6-3	Richardson, Boyes, Gale, Sandford 2, Carter	18,582
26		19	A	Blackburn Rovers	L	0-3		12,492
27		30	H	Arsenal	L	0-3		30,667
28	Feb	2	A	Portsmouth	W	2-0	Sandford, Richardson	11,009
29		9	H	Liverpool	D	1-1	Sandford	20,182
30		20	A	Leeds United	L	1-4	Sandford	7,408
31		23	H	Wolverhampton Wanderers	W	5-2	Sandford, Boyes 2, Richardson 2	31,494
32	Mar	6	A	Huddersfield Town	L	0-3		8,822
33		9	H	Everton	L	0-1		20,002
34		23	H	Chelsea	D	2-2	Sandford, Jones	13,721
35		30	A	Tottenham Hotspur	W	1-0	Richardson	29,161
36	Apr	3	A	Aston Villa	W	3-2	Gibson (og), Boyes, Richardson	19,549
37		6	H	Sunderland	D	1-1	Sandford (pen)	24,510
38		13	A	Leicester City	D	0-0		21,506
39		20	H	Derby County	W	4-3	Sandford, Richardson, Glidden, Jones	16,464
40		22	H	Sheffield Wednesday	D	1-1	Boyes	33,540
41	May	1	A	Grimsby Town	L	0-3		12,304
42		4	H	Preston North End	D	0-0		10,420

All Richardson goals are 'W.G.' ('Ginger') Richardson

Appearances

Goals

FA Cup

R3	Jan	12	H	Port Vale	W	2-1	Gale, 'W.G.' Richardson	18,989
R4		26	H	Sheffield United	W	7-1	'W.G.' Richardson 3, Sandford 2, Carter, Gale	34,908
R5	Feb	16	A	Stockport County	W	5-0	'W.G.' Richardson 2, Carter, Gale, Boyes	24,684
R6	Mar	2	H	Preston North End	W	1-0	Gale	56,227
SF		16	N	Bolton Wanderers	D	1-1	'W.G.' Richardson	49,605
rep		20	N	Bolton Wanderers	W	2-0	'W.G.' Richardson, Sandford (pen)	49,110
F	Apr	27	N	Sheffield Wednesday	L	2-4	Sandford, Boyes	93,204

SF at Elland Road, Leeds, replay at the Victoria Ground, Stoke

Final at Wembley Stadium

Appearances

Goals

Pearson HF	Shaw GE	Trentham HF	Murphy JP	Richardson W	Sankey J	Glidden TW	Carter JH	Richardson WG	Sandford EA	Robbins WW	Boyes WE	Edwards J	Wood S	Crowe EW	Ridyard A	Whitehead NJ	Gale AR	Jones HJ	Screen J	Finch EAR	Rawlings JSD	
1	2	3	4	5	6	7	8	9	10	11												1
1	2	3	4	5	6	7	8	9	10		11											2
1	2	3	4	5		7	8	9	10		11	6										3
1	2	3	4	5		7	8	9	6		10		11									4
1	2	3	4	5		7	8	9	10		11	6										5
	2	3	4	5		7	8	9	10		11	6		1								6
1	2	3	4	5		7	8	9	10		11	6										7
1	2	3		5	4	7	8	9	10		11	6										8
1	2	3	4	5	6	7	8	9	10		11											9
1	2	3	4	5	6	7	8	9	10		11											10
1	2	3	4	5	6	7	8	9	10		11											11
1	2	3	4	5	6	7	8	9	10		11											12
1	2	3	4	5	6	7	8	9	10		11											13
1	2	3	4	5	6	7	8	9	10		11											14
1	2	3	4	5	6	7	8	9	10		11											15
1	2	3	4	5	6	7	8	9	10		11											16
1	2	3	4	5	6	7	8	9	10		11											17
1	2	3	4	5	6	7	8	9	10		11											18
1	2	3	4			7	8	9	10		11	6			5							19
1	2	3	4			7	8	9	10		11	6			5							20
1	2	3	4	5		7	8	9	10		11	6										21
1	2	3	4	5			8	9	10		11	6				7						22
1	2	3	4	5			8	9	10		11	6					7					23
1	2	3	4	5			8	9			11	6					7	10				24
1		3	4	5	6		8	9	10		11						7		2			25
1	2	3	4	5	6		8	9	10		11						7					26
1	2	3	4	5	6		8	9	10		11						7					27
1	2	3	4	5			8	9	10		11	6					7					28
1	2	3	4	5			8	9	10		11	6					7					29
1	2	3	4	5	7		8	9	10		11	6										30
1	2	3	4	5			8	9	10		11	6					7					31
1		3	4	5	7		8	9			11	6						10		2		32
1	2	3	4	5	10		8	9			11	6					7					33
1	2	3	4	5				9	10		11	6						8			7	34
1	2	3	4	5				9	10		11	6						8			7	35
1		3	4	5				9	10		11	6						8		2	7	36
1		3	4	5				9	10		11	6						8		2	7	37
1	2	3	4	5				9	10		11	6						8			7	38
1	2	3	4			7		9	10		11	6			5			8				39
1	2	3	4		6			9		10	11				5		7	8				40
1	2	3	4	5		7		9	8	10	11	6										41
1	2	3	4	5		7		9	8	10	11	6										42
1	38	42	41	38	20	24	33	42	38	4	41	25	1	1	4	1	10	9	1	3	5	
						7	5	25	20		20						3	2				

One own-goal

Pearson HF	Shaw GE	Trentham HF	Murphy JP	Richardson W	Sankey J	Glidden TW	Carter JH	Richardson WG	Sandford EA	Robbins WW	Boyes WE	Edwards J	Wood S	Crowe EW	Ridyard A	Whitehead NJ	Gale AR	Jones HJ	Screen J	Finch EAR	Rawlings JSD	
1	2	3	4	5	6		8	9	10		11						7					R3
1	2	3	4	5	6		8	9	10		11						7					R4
1	2	3	4	5			8	9	10		11	6					7					R5
1	2	3	4	5			8	9	10		11	6					7					R6
1	2	3	4	5			8	9	10		11	6					7					SF
1	2	3	4	5			8	9	10		11	6					7					rep
1	2	3	4	5		7	8	9	10		11	6										F
7	7	7	7	7	2	1	7	7	7		7	5					6					
							2	8	4		2						4					

1935-36

Division One

	P	W	D	L	F	A	Pts
Sunderland	42	25	6	11	109	74	56
Derby County	42	18	12	12	61	52	48
Huddersfield Town	42	18	12	12	59	56	48
Stoke City	42	20	7	15	57	57	47
Brentford	42	17	12	13	81	60	46
Arsenal	42	15	15	12	78	48	45
Preston North End	42	18	8	16	67	64	44
Chelsea	42	15	13	14	65	72	43
Manchester City	42	17	8	17	68	60	42
Portsmouth	42	17	8	17	54	67	42
Leeds United	42	15	11	16	66	64	41
Birmingham	42	15	11	16	61	63	41
Bolton Wanderers	42	14	13	15	67	76	41
Middlesbrough	42	15	10	17	84	70	40
Wolverhampton W	42	15	10	17	77	76	40
Everton	42	13	13	16	89	89	39
Grimsby Town	42	17	5	20	65	73	39
West Bromwich Albion	42	16	6	20	89	88	38
Liverpool	42	13	12	17	60	64	38
Sheffield Wednesday	42	13	12	17	63	77	38
Aston Villa	42	13	9	20	81	110	35
Blackburn Rovers	42	12	9	21	55	96	33

Secretary-manager: Fred Everiss

- 'W.G.' Richardson scored a club record 40 goals this season, including four in a record 7–0 win over Aston Villa (away) in October. This was Albion's biggest away win in terms of goal difference since December 1893 when they beat Wolves 8–0.
- Gilbert Alsop from Walsall was recruited as cover for 'W.G.', goalkeeper Billy Light was signed from Southampton and winger Jack Mahon arrived from Leeds United.
- Inside-forward Joe Carter moved to Tranmere Rovers after scoring 155 goals in 451 first-class matches since 1921, Harry Raw switched to Lincoln City, and at the end of the season Tommy Glidden retired, having netted 140 goals in 479 games for the Baggies. He later became a director of the club. Teddy Sandford took over the captaincy.

Match No.	Date			Opponents	Result		Scorers	Attendance
1	Aug	31	A	Manchester City	L	0-1		41,777
2	Sep	4	H	Sunderland	L	1-3	Rawlings	24,385
3		7	H	Stoke City	W	2-0	Green, Richardson	24,060
4		11	A	Sunderland	L	1-6	Richardson	35,276
5		14	A	Blackburn Rovers	L	1-3	Boyes	13,625
6		18	H	Birmingham	D	0-0		18,083
7		21	H	Chelsea	L	1-2	Gale	17,183
8		28	A	Liverpool	L	0-5		30,625
9	Oct	5	H	Grimsby Town	W	4-1	Richardson, Mahon, Carter 2	20,787
10		12	A	Leeds United	D	1-1	Richardson	21,657
11		19	A	Aston Villa	W	7-0	Richardson 4, Wood, Mahon, Sankey	43,411
12		26	H	Wolverhampton Wanderers	W	2-1	Richardson, Sandford	42,402
13	Nov	2	A	Sheffield Wednesday	W	5-2	Wood 2, Sandford, Mahon, Richardson	22,597
14		9	H	Portsmouth	W	2-0	Richardson 2	23,055
15		16	A	Preston North End	L	0-3		19,070
16		23	H	Huddersfield Town	L	1-2	Richardson	24,324
17		30	A	Derby County	L	0-2		21,786
18	Dec	7	H	Everton	W	6-1	Richardson 2, Mahon 2, Sandford, Carter	17,151
19		14	A	Bolton Wanderers	L	1-3	Sandford	21,736
20		21	H	Brentford	W	1-0	Mahon	14,625
21		26	H	Middlesbrough	W	5-2	Shaw, Richardson 4	26,049
22		28	H	Manchester City	W	5-1	Mahon, Robbins, Glidden, Richardson 2	31,012
23	Jan	1	A	Middlesbrough	L	1-3	Richardson	22,379
24		4	A	Stoke City	L	2-3	Richardson , Mahon	20,296
25		18	H	Blackburn Rovers	W	8-1	Richardson 3, Mahon 3, Robbins, Sankey	16,464
26	Feb	1	H	Liverpool	W	6-1	Richardson 3, Mahon, Wood 2	23,080
27		8	A	Grimsby Town	L	2-4	Richardson 2	11,122
28		19	H	Leeds United	W	3-2	Sandford 2, Wood	7,893
29		29	A	Portsmouth	L	1-3	Richardson	12,916
30	Mar	7	H	Derby County	L	0-3		18,408
31		11	A	Chelsea	D	2-2	Mahon, Richardson	13,225
32		14	A	Wolverhampton Wanderers	L	0-2		34,790
33		21	H	Preston North End	L	2-4	Richardson, Mahon	19,665
34		28	A	Huddersfield Town	W	3-2	Richardson 2, Boyes	11,694
35	Apr	1	H	Aston Villa	L	0-3		28,821
36		4	H	Sheffield Wednesday	D	2-2	Jones 2	17,604
37		10	A	Arsenal	L	0-4		59,245
38		11	A	Everton	L	3-5	Jones, Mahon 2	24,793
39		13	H	Arsenal	W	1-0	Jones	42,286
40		18	H	Bolton Wanderers	D	2-2	Glidden, Richardson	27,398
41		25	A	Brentford	D	2-2	Richardson, Wood	24,527
42	May	2	A	Birmingham	W	3-1	Mahon, Richardson, Boyes	18,312

All Richardson goals are 'W.G.' ('Ginger') Richardson

Appearances

Goals

FA Cup

R3	Jan	11	H	Hull City	W	2-0	Wood, 'W.G.' Richardson	27,505
R4		29	A	Bradford Park Avenue	D	1-1	Robbins	14,958
rep	Feb	3	H	Bradford Park Avenue	D	1-1*	Sandford (pen)	27,503
rep2		10	A	Bradford Park Avenue	L	0-2		11,685

* after extra-time

Appearances

Goals

Pearson HF	Shaw GE	Trentham HF	Murphy JP	Richardson W	Edwards J	Glidden TW	Green T	Richardson WG	Sandford EA	Boyes WE	Rawlings JSD	Finch EAR	Robbins WW	Sankey J	Wood S	Gale AR	Rix J	Mahon J	Jones HJ	Carter JH	Crowe EW	Alsop GA	Ridyard A	Adams J	Light WH	Foulkes HE	
1	2	3	4	5	6	7	8	9	10	11																	1
1	2	3	4	5	6		8	9	10	11	7																2
1	2	3	4	5	6		8	9	10	11	7																3
1	2	3	4	5	6		8	9	10	11	7																4
1		3	4	5	6			9	8	11	7	2	10														5
1		3	4	5				9	10	8	7	2		6	11												6
1		3	4	5		7			10	8		2		6	11	9											7
1	2	3		5				9	10	11				4			6	7	8								8
1	2	3		5				9	10	11				4			6	7		8							9
1	2	3		5				9	10	11				4			6	7		8							10
1	2	3	4	5				9	10					6	11			7		8							11
1	2	3	4	5				9	10					6	11			7		8							12
1	2	3	4	5				9	10					6	11			7		8							13
1	2	3	4	5				9	10					6	11			7		8							14
1	2	3	4	5				9	10					6	11			7		8							15
	2	3	4	5				10		11				6				7		8	1	9					16
1	2	3		5				9		10				4	11		6	7		8							17
1	2	3		5				9	10					4	11		6	7		8							18
1	2	3		5				9	10					4	11		6	7		8							19
1	2	3		5				9	10					4	11		6	7		8							20
1	2	3	4	5				9					10		11		6	7		8							21
1	2	3				8		9					10	4	11		6	7					5				22
1	2	3				8		9					10	4	11		6	7					5				23
1	2	3						9					10	4	11		6	7		8			5				24
	2	3		5				9	8				10	4	11		6	7			1						25
		3		5				9	10			2		4	11		6	7		8	1						26
		3			10			9	8			2		4	11		6	7					5	1			27
		3						9	8			2	10	4	11		6	7					5	1			28
		3			6			9	8			2	10	4	11			7					5	1			29
	2	3		5			8	9					10	4	11		6	7						1			30
	2	3		6		8		9					10	4	11			7					5	1			31
	2	3	4			8		9					10	6	11			7					5		1		32
	2	3		5		8		9						4	11		6	7	10						1		33
				5				9		10		2		4	11		6	7		8					1	3	34
				5				9		10		2		4	11		6	7		8					1	3	35
	3			5				9		11		2		4			6	7	10	8					1		36
				5				9		10		2		4	11		6	7		8					1	3	37
	3		4	5	6			9		11		2		8				7	10						1		38
	2	3		5	6	7	8	9		11				4					10						1		39
	2	3		5	6	7	8	9		11				4					10						1		40
	2	3		5	6			9		10				4	11			7	8						1		41
	2	3		5				9		10				4	11		6	7	8						1		42
23	32	37	16	35	11	9	7	41	23	21	5	12	11	36	29	1	22	33	8	19	3	1	8	5	11	3	
	1					2	1	39	6	3	1		2	2	7	1	1	17	4	3							

1		3		5				9	8			2	10	4	11		6	7									R3
	2	3		5				9	8				10	4	11		6	7			1						R4
		3		5		8		9	10			2		4	11		6	7						1			rep
		3						9	8			2	10	4	11		6	7					5	1			rep2
1	1	4		3		1		4	4			3	3	4	4		4	4			1		1	2			
								1	1				1		1												

1936-37

Division One

	P	W	D	L	F	A	Pts
Manchester City	42	22	13	7	107	61	57
Charlton Athletic	42	21	12	9	58	49	54
Arsenal	42	18	16	8	80	49	52
Derby County	42	21	7	14	96	90	49
Wolverhampton W	42	21	5	16	84	67	47
Brentford	42	18	10	14	82	78	46
Middlesbrough	42	19	8	15	74	71	46
Sunderland	42	19	6	17	89	87	44
Portsmouth	42	17	10	15	62	66	44
Stoke City	42	15	12	15	72	57	42
Birmingham	42	13	15	14	64	60	41
Grimsby Town	42	17	7	18	86	81	41
Chelsea	42	14	13	15	52	55	41
Preston North End	42	14	13	15	56	67	41
Huddersfield Town	42	12	15	15	62	64	39
West Bromwich Albion	42	16	6	20	77	98	38
Everton	42	14	9	19	81	78	37
Liverpool	42	12	11	19	62	84	35
Leeds United	42	15	4	23	60	80	34
Bolton Wanderers	42	10	14	18	43	66	34
Manchester United	42	10	12	20	55	78	32
Sheffield Wednesday	42	9	12	21	53	69	30

Secretary-manager: Fred Everiss

- Albion suffered their heaviest League defeat in the club's history when going down 10–3 at Stoke in February. Goalkeeper Billy Light was injured early in the game and thereafter hobbled in pain on his line.
- Ex-bus driver 'W.G.' Richardson became the first player to score 200 goals for Albion in senior competitions when he netted against Darlington in the fourth round of the FA Cup.
- A record Hawthorns crowd of 64,815, with gate receipts totalling £3,913, saw Albion beat the holders and favourites Arsenal 3–1 in a fifth-round FA Cup tie on a snowbound pitch.
- Full-back Cecil Shaw joined his namesake George at The Hawthorns after making 183 senior appearances for Black Country neighbours Wolves. Having never missed a penalty during his time at Molineux, he fluffed his first spot-kick for Albion in a 3–2 FA Cup win at Coventry. Bill Brockhurst, Lol Coen, Sammy Heaselgrave, Jimmy Prew and Sid Swinden were other debutants this season.
- Albion played and lost their Cup semi-final at Highbury just a few days after learning of the death of chairman and ex-player Billy Bassett.
- Goalkeeper Harold Pearson moved to Millwall after 12 years and 303 games for Albion; Jimmy Edwards joined Norwich City after 202 games; Bill Richardson signed for Swindon Town, having played 352 times for the Baggies; Bert Trentham switched to Hereford United after 272 appearances; Gilbert Alsop returned to his former club Walsall after making just one senior outing for Albion; Arthur Gale rejoined Chester and Tommy Green went to West Ham.
- Sir Ernest J. Spencer's reign as Albion president ended after 33 years.

Match No.	Date			Opponents	Result		Scorers	Attendance
1	Aug	29	H	Derby County	L	1-3	'W.G.' Richardson	30,149
2	Sep	2	H	Birmingham	W	3-2	Jones, 'W.G.' Richardson, Wood	26,013
3		5	A	Manchester City	L	2-6	Boyes, 'W.G.' Richardson	33,063
4		9	A	Birmingham	D	1-1	Jones	23,813
5		12	H	Portsmouth	W	3-1	Wood, 'W.G.' Richardson, Sandford	12,224
6		19	A	Chelsea	L	0-3		41,112
7		26	H	Stoke City	D	2-2	'W.G.' Richardson, Mahon	27,806
8	Oct	3	A	Charlton Athletic	L	2-4	Jones, Sandford	37,435
9		10	H	Grimsby Town	W	4-2	'W.G.' Richardson 3 (1 pen), Sandford	24,445
10		17	H	Wolverhampton Wanderers	W	2-1	W. Richardson, Prew	33,962
11		24	A	Sunderland	L	0-1		24,503
12		31	H	Huddersfield Town	W	2-1	Jones, Wood	20,605
13	Nov	7	A	Everton	L	2-4	'W.G.' Richardson, Wood	20,901
14		14	H	Bolton Wanderers	L	0-2		20,125
15		21	A	Brentford	L	1-2	Jones	20,110
16		28	H	Arsenal	L	2-4	Gale, Wood	27,609
17	Dec	5	A	Preston North End	L	2-3	Mahon 2	12,000
18		19	A	Manchester United	D	2-2	Wood, Mahon	21,051
19		25	H	Liverpool	W	3-1	Jones 2, Wood	23,697
20		26	A	Derby County	L	0-1		29,935
21		28	A	Liverpool	W	2-1	Sandford, Robbins	12,395
22	Jan	1	A	Middlesbrough	L	1-4	Robbins	28,231
23		2	H	Manchester City	D	2-2	Wood, Mahon	18,004
24		9	A	Portsmouth	L	3-5	Jones, 'W.G.' Richardson 2	17,211
25		23	H	Chelsea	W	2-0	Jones, Sandford	9,642
26	Feb	4	A	Stoke City	L	3-10	'W.G.' Richardson, Boyes, Robbins	8,325
27		6	H	Charlton Athletic	L	1-2	Mahon	26,459
28		13	A	Grimsby Town	W	3-2	'W.G.' Richardson, Jones 2	9,898
29		27	H	Sunderland	W	6-4	'W.G.' Richardson, Boyes, Coen, C. Shaw (pen), Jones 2	25,267
30	Mar	10	A	Huddersfield Town	D	1-1	Boyes	4,179
31		13	H	Everton	W	2-1	C. Shaw (pen), 'W.G.' Richardson	26,283
32		20	A	Bolton Wanderers	L	1-4	Jones	20,268
33		22	H	Preston North End	D	0-0		9,068
34		27	H	Brentford	W	1-0	Coen	29,858
35		29	H	Leeds United	W	3-0	Jones, Mahon, 'W.G.' Richardson	31,251
36		30	A	Leeds United	L	1-3	Coen	16,016
37	Apr	3	A	Arsenal	L	0-2		38,773
38		14	A	Wolverhampton Wanderers	L	2-5	Robbins 2	28,486
39		17	A	Sheffield Wednesday	W	3-2	Robbins 2, Mahon	12,002
40		21	H	Sheffield Wednesday	L	2-3	Robbins 2	10,826
41		24	H	Manchester United	W	1-0	Jones	16,245
42	May	1	H	Middlesbrough	W	3-1	Coen, Jones, Mahon	7,022
								Appearances
								Goals

FA Cup

R3	Jan	16	H	Spennymoor United	W	7-1	Sandford 2, 'W.G.' Richardson 2, Wood, Jones, Mahon	23,746
R4		30	H	Darlington	W	3-2	'W.G.' Richardson 3	15,917
R5	Feb	20	A	Coventry City	W	3-2	Boyes, Mahon 2	44,492
R6	Mar	6	H	Arsenal	W	3-1	Mahon 2, 'W.G.' Richardson	64,815
SF	Apr	10	N	Preston North End	L	1-4	Robbins	42,636
								Appearances
								Goals

SF at Highbury

	Light WH	Shaw GE	Trentham HF	Murphy JP	Richardson W	Sankey J	Mahon J	Sandford EA	Richardson WG	Robbins WW	Wood S	Swinden SA	Jones HJ	Edwards J	Boyes WE	Finch EAR	Pearson HF	Prew JH	Brockhurst WJ	Green T	Ridyard A	Gale AR	Foulkes HE	Shaw CE	Adams J	Rix J	Coen RWL	Heaselgrave SE
1	1	2	3	4	5	6	7	8	9	10	11																	
2	1		3	4	5	6	7	10	9		11	2	8															
3	1		3		5	4	7	10	9			2	8	6	11													
4	1		3		5	4	7	10	9		11	2	8		6													
5	1		3		5	4	7	10	9		11	2	8		6													
6	1		3		5	4	7	10	9		11		8		6	2												
7	1		3		5	4	7	10	9		11		8		6	2												
8	1		3		5	4	7	10	9		11		8		6	2												
9			3		5	4		10	9		11		8		6	2	1	7										
10			3		5	4		10	9		11		8		6	2	1	7										
11			3		5	4		10	9		11		8		6	2	1	7										
12			3		5	4		10	9		11		8		6	2	1	7										
13			3		5	4		10	9		11		8		6	2	1	7										
14			3			4			9		11		10		6	2	1	7	5	8								
15			3			4	7			11			10		6	2	1			8	5	9						
16	1		3			4	7				11		10		6	2				8	5	9						
17			3			4	7	10	9		11		8		6	2	1				5							
18			3			4	7	10	9		11		8		6	2	1				5							
19						4	7	10	9		11		8		6	2	1				5		3					
20					5	4	7	10	8		11		9		6	2	1						3					
21					5	4	7	8	9	10	11				6	2	1							3				
22					5	4	7	8	9	10	11				6	2	1							3				
23				4	5		7	10	9		11		8		6		1						3	2				
24				4	5		7	10	9		11		8		6	2	1							3				
25	1			4	5	6		10	9	11			8			2		7						3				
26	1			4	5		7	10	9	11			8		6	2								3				
27					5		7	10	9				8		6	2								3	1	4	11	
28				4		6	7	5	9				8		10	2								3	1		11	
29				4		6	7	5	9				8		10	2								3	1		11	
30				4		6	7	5	9	11			8		10	2								3	1			
31				4		6	7	5	9	11			8		10	2								3	1			
32				4	5	6	7		9	11			8		10	2								3	1			
33		2		4		6	7		9	11			8		10						5			3	1			
34		2		4		6	7		9						10						5			3	1		11	8
35		2		4		6	7		9				8		10						5			3	1		11	
36		2		4		6	7		9						10						5			3	1		11	8
37				4			7		9	11					10	2					5			3	1	6		8
38				4		6	7		9	10	11				8	2					5			3	1			
39	1	2		4		6	7		9	10			8		11				5					3				
40	1	2		4		6	7		9	10			8		11				5					3				
41		2		4		6	7		9	10			8		11				5					3	1			
42		2		4		6	7			10			8		11				5					3	1		9	
	13	9	18	21	22	37	35	28	39	16	23	4	35	1	39	28	15	7	5	3	11	2	3	22	14	2	7	3
					1		9	5	16	9	8		17		4			1				1		2			4	

	Light WH	Shaw GE	Trentham HF	Murphy JP	Richardson W	Sankey J	Mahon J	Sandford EA	Richardson WG	Robbins WW	Wood S	Swinden SA	Jones HJ	Edwards J	Boyes WE	Finch EAR	Pearson HF	Prew JH	Brockhurst WJ	Green T	Ridyard A	Gale AR	Foulkes HE	Shaw CE	Adams J	Rix J	Coen RWL	Heaselgrave SE
R3	1			4	5		7	10	9		11		8		6	2								3				
R4	1			4	5	6	7	10	9				8		11	2								3				
R5				4			7	5	9				8	6	10	2								3	1		11	
R6				4		6	7	5	9				8		10	2								3	1		11	
SF				4		6	7		9	11			8		10	2					5			3	1			
	2			5	2	3	5	5	5		1		5	1	5	5					1			5	3		2	
							5	2	6	1	1		1		1													

1937-38

Division One

	P	W	D	L	F	A	Pts
Arsenal	42	21	10	11	77	44	52
Wolverhampton W	42	20	11	11	72	49	51
Preston North End	42	16	17	9	64	44	49
Charlton Athletic	42	16	14	12	65	51	46
Middlesbrough	42	19	8	15	72	65	46
Brentford	42	18	9	15	69	59	45
Bolton Wanderers	42	15	15	12	64	60	45
Sunderland	42	14	16	12	55	57	44
Leeds United	42	14	15	13	64	69	43
Chelsea	42	14	13	15	65	65	41
Liverpool	42	15	11	16	65	71	41
Blackpool	42	16	8	18	61	66	40
Derby County	42	15	10	17	66	87	40
Everton	42	16	7	19	79	75	39
Huddersfield Town	42	17	5	20	55	68	39
Leicester City	42	14	11	17	54	75	39
Stoke City	42	13	12	17	58	59	38
Birmingham	42	10	18	14	58	62	38
Portsmouth	42	13	12	17	62	68	38
Grimsby Town	42	13	12	17	51	68	38
Manchester City	42	14	8	20	80	77	36
West Bromwich Albion	42	14	8	20	74	91	36

Secretary-manager: Fred Everiss

- 'W.G.' Richardson topped Albion's scoring charts for the eighth successive season – a club record that still holds good today.
- Albion suffered the humiliation of losing 3–2 to Third Division North side York City in the fourth round of the FA Cup. This was the first time Albion had been ousted by opponents from this section since falling to Wrexham in 1930.
- Players signed this season included England international winger Joe Johnson from Stoke City, Scotland wing-half and 1937 FA Cup winner Sandy McNab from Sunderland and future Welsh star Doug Witcomb from Enfield. Johnson and McNab made their debuts for Albion, as did Black Country lad Ike Clarke, wing-half Harry Lowery, goalkeepers Bill Harris and Harry Baldwin, full-back Idris Bassett and centre-half Cyril Davies. Another new face was right-back Jim Pemberton.
- Out of The Hawthorns went 1931 FA Cup winners George Shaw, who joined Stalybridge Celtic after 425 appearances for the Baggies, and winger Stan Wood, who switched to Halifax Town, having played in 281 games for the club. Goalkeeper Billy Light also left for Colchester United.
- Following the death of Billy Bassett, Lou Nurse was appointed chairman of Albion at the club's AGM in August 1937.
- In October 1937 George Dudley signed for Albion from Vono Sports – the first Scottish-born player at the club for 30 years.

Match No.	Date			Opponents	Result		Scorers	Attendance
1	Aug	28	A	Portsmouth	W	3-2	Richardson, Mahon	27,137
2		30	H	Stoke City	L	0-1		22,113
3	Sep	4	H	Chelsea	W	4-0	Mahon, Robbins 2, Richardson	23,097
4		6	A	Stoke City	L	0-4		20,499
5		11	A	Charlton Athletic	L	1-3	Sankey	25,570
6		13	H	Middlesbrough	W	3-1	Richardson, Clarke, Jones	8,028
7		18	H	Preston North End	D	1-1	Mahon	23,469
8		25	A	Grimsby Town	W	4-1	Jones 2, Male, Clarke	9,410
9	Oct	2	H	Leeds United	W	2-1	Mahon, Robbins	25,619
10		9	A	Liverpool	W	1-0	Wood	22,463
11		16	A	Leicester City	L	1-4	Robbins	20,658
12		23	H	Sunderland	L	1-6	Wood (pen)	27,705
13		30	A	Derby County	L	3-5	Robbins, Mahon, Jones	13,654
14	Nov	6	H	Bolton Wanderers	L	2-4	Sankey, Jones	20,281
15		13	A	Arsenal	D	1-1	Mahon	34,324
16		20	H	Everton	W	3-1	Mahon 2, Boyes	20,800
17		27	A	Brentford	W	2-0	Richardson 2	16,702
18	Dec	11	A	Huddersfield Town	L	1-2	Richardson	6,938
19		18	H	Blackpool	L	1-2	Jones	18,077
20		27	H	Wolverhampton Wanderers	D	2-2	Clarke 2	55,444
21	Jan	1	H	Portsmouth	L	1-2	Clarke	19,442
22		15	A	Chelsea	D	2-2	Richardson, Johnson	20,378
23		26	H	Charlton Athletic	D	0-0		9,579
24		29	A	Preston North End	D	1-1	Smith (og)	16,299
25	Feb	5	H	Grimsby Town	W	2-1	Johnson, Mahon	19,648
26		12	A	Leeds United	L	0-1		21,819
27		19	H	Liverpool	W	5-1	Richardson 3, Clarke, Johnson	17,765
28		26	H	Leicester City	L	1-3	Johnson	21,563
29	Mar	9	A	Sunderland	L	0-3		15,011
30		12	H	Derby County	W	4-2	Richardson 2, Johnson, Heaselgrave	25,439
31		16	H	Manchester City	D	1-1	Shaw (pen)	10,792
32		19	A	Bolton Wanderers	L	0-3		23,098
33		26	H	Arsenal	D	0-0		33,944
34	Apr	2	A	Everton	L	3-5	Mahon, Shaw (pen), Jones	24,395
35		9	H	Brentford	W	4-3	Mahon, Heaselgrave, Johnson 2	23,462
36		15	A	Birmingham	L	1-2	Jones	34,631
37		16	A	Manchester City	L	1-7	Shaw (pen)	33,076
38		18	H	Birmingham	W	4-3	Richardson 2, Shaw (pen), Jones	34,406
39		23	H	Huddersfield Town	W	5 1	Heaselgrave 2, Jones 2, Richardson	27,530
40		30	A	Blackpool	L	1-3	Mahon	13,506
41	May	2	A	Wolverhampton Wanderers	L	1-2	Sandford	43,639
42		7	A	Middlesbrough	L	1-4	Heaselgrave	12,905
								Appearances
								Goals

FA Cup

R3	Jan	8	H	Newcastle United	W	1-0	Richardson	33,932
R4		22	A	York City	L	2-3	Richardson, Pinder (og)	18,795
								Appearances
								Goals

Adams J	Shaw GE	Shaw CE	Murphy JP	Sandford EA	Sankey J	Mahon J	Jones HJ	Richardson WG	Robbins WW	Boyes WE	Rix J	Clarke I	Wood S	Male NA	Finch EAR	Light WH	Johnson JA	Heaselgrave SE	Lowery H	McNab A	Harris W	Baldwin HJA	Bassett ICH	Davies C	
1	2	3	4	5	6	7	8	9	10	11															1
1	2	3	4	5	6	7	8	9	10	11															2
1	2	3	4	5	6	7	8	9	10	11															3
1	2	3	4	5		7	8	9	10	11	6														4
1	2	3	4	5	6	7		9	10			8	11												5
1	2	3	4	5		7	8	9			6	10	11												6
1	2	3	4	5	6	7	8	9				10	11												7
1		3	4	5		7	9		10		6	8	11	2											8
1		3	4	5		7	9		10		6	8	11		2										9
1		3	4	5		7	9		10		6	8	11		2										10
1		3	4	5		7	9		10		6	8	11		2										11
1		3	4	5		7	9		10		6	8	11		2										12
		3		5	4	7	9		10	6		8	11	2		1									13
		3	4	5	6	7	9			10		8	11	2		1									14
1		3	4	5		7	10	9		6		8	11		2										15
1		3	4	5	6	7	10	9		11		8			2										16
1		3	4	5	6	7	10	9		11		8			2										17
1		3	4	5		7	10	9		6		8			2		11								18
1		3	4	5		7	10	9		6		8			2		11								19
1		3	4	5		7	9		10	6		8			2		11								20
1		3	4	5		7	9		10	6		8			2		11								21
1		3	4	5	6	7		9		10		8			2		11								22
1		3	4	5			7	9			6	10			2		11	8							23
1		3		5			9	7			6	10			2		11	8	4						24
1		3		5		7	9				6	10			2		11	8	4						25
1		3		5		7		9			6	10			2		11	8	4						26
1		3		5		7		9			6	10			2		11	8	4						27
1		3		5		7		9			6	10			2		11	8	4						28
1		3		5		7		9	10		6	8			2		11		4						29
1		3		5		7	10	9							2		11	8	4	6					30
1		3		5		7		9				10			2		11	8	4	6					31
1		3		5		7		9			6	10			2		11	8	4						32
1		3		5		7	10	9	11						2			8	4	6					33
		3		5		7	10	9	11						2			8	4	6	1				34
		3		10		7	9		5						2		11	8	4	6	1				35
		3		5		7	9		10						2	1	11	8	4	6					36
		3	4	5	11	7	9								2	1		8	6	10					37
		3		5	6	11	9	7							2			8	4	10		1			38
		3		5	6	11	9	7							2			8	4	10		1			39
		3		5	6	7		9							2		11	8	4	10		1			40
		3		10	4	11	9	7										8		6		1	2	5	41
		3		10	4	11	9	7										8		6		1	2	5	42
31	7	42	23	42	16	40	33	29	18	14	15	27	11	3	30	4	18	19	17	12	2	5	2	2	
		4		1	2	13	11	15	5	1		6	2	1			7	5							

One own-goal

Adams J	Shaw GE	Shaw CE	Murphy JP	Sandford EA	Sankey J	Mahon J	Jones HJ	Richardson WG	Robbins WW	Boyes WE	Rix J	Clarke I	Wood S	Male NA	Finch EAR	Light WH	Johnson JA	Heaselgrave SE	Lowery H	McNab A	Harris W	Baldwin HJA	Bassett ICH	Davies C	
1		3	4	5	6	7		9		10		8			2		11								R3
1		3	4		6		7	9	5	10		8			2		11								R4
2		2	2	1	2	1	1	2	1	2		2			2		2								
								2																	

One own-goal

1938-39

Division Two

	P	W	D	L	F	A	Pts
Blackburn Rovers	42	25	5	12	94	60	55
Sheffield United	42	20	14	8	69	41	54
Sheffield Wednesday	42	21	11	10	88	59	53
Coventry City	42	21	8	13	62	45	50
Manchester City	42	21	7	14	96	72	49
Chesterfield	42	20	9	13	69	52	49
Luton Town	42	22	5	15	82	66	49
Tottenham Hotspur	42	19	9	14	67	62	47
Newcastle United	42	18	10	14	61	48	46
West Bromwich Albion	42	18	9	15	89	72	45
West Ham United	42	17	10	15	70	52	44
Fulham	42	17	10	15	61	55	44
Millwall	42	14	14	14	64	53	42
Burnley	42	15	9	18	50	56	39
Plymouth Argyle	42	15	8	19	49	55	38
Bury	42	12	13	17	65	74	37
Bradford Park Avenue	42	12	11	19	61	82	35
Southampton	42	13	9	20	56	82	35
Swansea Town	42	11	12	19	50	83	34
Nottingham Forest	42	10	11	21	49	82	31
Norwich City	42	13	5	24	50	91	31
Tranmere Rovers	42	6	5	31	39	99	17

Secretary-manager: Fred Everiss

- 'W.G.' Richardson became the first Albion player to score 200 League goals when he netted against Sheffield United at Bramall Lane in mid-January. 'W.G.' also played his last senior game for the club against Norwich City on 29 April, finishing with a record of 328 goals in 355 competitive games. He remained at the club during the war, eventually moving to Shrewsbury Town in 1945.
- Albion's lowest home League crowd since March 1930 – just 3,109 – witnessed that last game against Norwich when George Banks scored twice on his debut.
- Players who left the club included Teddy Sandford (to Sheffield United after scoring 75 goals in 317 games), Jack Rix (to Lincoln City after 12 years' service), Walter Robbins (to Newport County), Jimmy Murphy (to Swindon Town) and winger Jack Mahon (to Huddersfield Town). Billy Elliott was signed from Bournemouth to replace Mahon.
- Besides Banks and Elliott, nine other players made their Albion debuts, namely Stan Butler, George Dudley, Billy Gripton, Ernie Hoyland, Dick Pike, Wilf Saunders, Geoff Spencer, Bill Tudor and Harold White.
- Albion and Coventry City met at League level for the first time.

Match No.	Date			Opponents	Result		Scorers	Attendance
1	Aug	27	H	Luton Town	W	3-0	Jones 2, Burgin	24,377
2	Sep	1	A	Norwich City	W	3-2	Burgin 2, Jones	19,933
3		3	A	Plymouth Argyle	L	1-2	Jones	25,792
4		7	H	Newcastle United	W	5-2	Burgin, Heaselgrave 2, Jones 2	17,016
5		10	H	Sheffield United	L	3-4	Heaselgrave 3	25,866
6		14	A	Newcastle United	L	1-5	Jones	31,128
7		17	A	Burnley	W	3-0	Heaselgrave, Jones, Spencer	15,990
8		24	H	Tottenham Hotspur	W	4-3	Jones 3, Heaselgrave	25,041
9	Oct	1	A	Southampton	L	1-2	Clarke	16,423
10		8	H	Coventry City	W	3-1	Sandford, Johnson, McNab	30,943
11		15	H	Chesterfield	W	1-0	Johnson	23,702
12		22	A	Tranmere Rovers	L	1-3	Johnson	11,930
13		29	H	Manchester City	W	3-1	Clarke 2, Johnson	22,274
14	Nov	5	A	Bury	D	3-3	Dudley, Shaw (pen), Clarke	10,600
15		12	H	Sheffield Wednesday	W	5-1	Spencer, Burgin 2, Clarke, Witcomb	18,297
16		19	A	Fulham	L	0-3		22,664
17		26	H	Blackburn Rovers	W	2-0	Burgin, Richardson	22,127
18	Dec	3	A	Millwall	W	5-1	McNab, Clarke, Jones 2, Heaselgrave	35,369
19		10	H	West Ham United	W	3-2	Clarke 2, Jones	23,909
20		17	A	Bradford Park Avenue	D	4-4	Burgin 2, Clarke, Witcomb	8,637
21		24	A	Luton Town	L	1-3	Johnson	8,887
22		27	A	Swansea Town	L	2-3	Jones, Elliott	22,690
23		31	H	Plymouth Argyle	W	4-2	Heaselgrave, Shaw (pen), Jones, Clarke	19,833
24	Jan	14	A	Sheffield United	D	1-1	Richardson	27,343
25		28	A	Tottenham Hotspur	D	2-2	Johnson 2	38,190
26	Feb	1	H	Burnley	L	1-2	Jones	7,781
27		4	H	Southampton	W	2-0	Johnson, Elliott	21,757
28		11	A	Coventry City	D	1-1	Johnson	37,680
29		18	A	Chesterfield	L	1-3	Heaselgrave	14,836
30		25	H	Tranmere Rovers	W	2-0	Elliott, Shaw (pen)	17,193
31	Mar	4	A	Manchester City	D	3-3	Johnson 2, Clarke	28,810
32		11	H	Bury	W	6-0	Clarke, Heaselgrave, Johnson 4	17,062
33		18	A	Sheffield Wednesday	L	1-2	Shaw (pen)	31,061
34		25	H	Fulham	W	3-0	Jones, Clarke, Dudley	19,541
35	Apr	1	A	Blackburn Rovers	L	0-3		22,360
36		7	A	Nottingham Forest	L	0-2		21,712
37		8	H	Millwall	D	0-0		19,895
38		10	H	Nottingham Forest	D	0-0		16,058
39		15	A	West Ham United	L	1-2	Clarke	13,624
40		19	H	Swansea Town	D	0-0		5,162
41		22	H	Bradford Park Avenue	L	0-2		6,885
42		29	H	Norwich City	W	4-2	Banks 2, Richardson 2	3,109

Appearances
Goals

FA Cup

R3	Jan	7	H	Manchester United	D	0-0		23,899
rep		11	A	Manchester United	W	5-1	Jones 2, Witcomb, Clarke, Richardson	17,641
R4		21	A	Portsmouth	L	0-2		36,661

Appearances
Goals

Adams J	Bassett ICH	Shaw CE	Sankey J	Davies C	McNab A	Mahon J	Heaselgrave SE	Jones HJ	Burgin M	Johnson JA	White HA	Robbins WW	Tudor WH	Hoyland E	Sandford EA	Murphy JP	Witcomb DF	Spencer G	Clarke I	Dudley G	Richardson WG	Elliott WB	Saunders WW	Pike RSGA	Gripton EW	Butler S	Banks GE	Wilkes AG	
1	2	3	4	5	6	7	8	9	10	11																			1
1	2	3	4	5	6	7	8	9	10	11																			2
1	2	3	4	5	6	7	8	9	10	11																			3
1	2	3	4	5	6	7	8	9	10	11																			4
1		3	4	5	6	7	8		9	11	2	10																	5
1		3	4		6		8	9		11	2		5	7	10														6
1		3					8	9		11	2		5		10	4	6	7											7
1		3					8	9		11	2		5		10	4	6	7											8
1		3			10			9		11	2		5			4	6	7	8										9
1		3			6			9		11	2		5		10		4	7	8										10
1		3			6			9		11	2		5		10		4	7	8										11
1		3			6		8	9		11	2		5		10		4	7											12
1		3			6			9	8	11	2		5				4	7	10										13
1		3			6			9	8		2		5				4	7	10	11									14
1		3			6			9	8		2		5				4	7	10	11									15
1		3			6			9	8		2		5				4	7	10	11									16
1		3			6		7		8	11	2		5				4		10		9								17
1		3			6		7	9	8	11	2		5				4		10										18
1		3			6		7	9	8	11	2		5				4		10										19
1		3			6		7	9	8	11	2		5				4		10										20
1		3			6			9	8	11	2		5				4		10			7							21
		3			6		8	9		11	2		5				4		10			7	1						22
1		3			6		8	9		11	2		5				4		10			7							23
1		3			6		8			11	2		5				4		10		9	7							24
1		3			6		8	9		11	2		5				4		10			7							25
1		3	8		6			9		11	2		5				4		10			7							26
1		3			6			8		11	2		5				4		10		9	7							27
		3			6			8		11	2		5				4		10		9	7	1						28
1		3			6		10	8		11	2		5				4				9	7							29
1		3	4		6		8	9		11	2		5						10			7							30
1		3	4		6		8	9		11	2		5						10			7							31
1	2	3	4		6		8	9		11			5						10			7							32
1	2	3			6		8	9		11			5				4		10			7							33
1		3	4		6		8	9			2		5						10	11		7							34
1		3	4		6			9			2	11	5						10		8	7							35
1		3	4		6					11	2	10	5						8		7			9					36
1		3	4		10					11	2						6	7	8		9				5				37
1		3	4		10					11	2						6	7	8		9				5				38
1		3	4				8				2						6		10		9	7			5	11			39
1		3	4				8				2						6		10	11	9	7			5				40
1		3	4				8				2						6	7	10	11	9				5				41
1		3	4		6		7			11	2								10		9				5		8		42
40	6	42	19	5	37	5	27	32	14	34	36	3	31	1	6	3	29	13	32	6	13	17	2	1	6	1	1		
		4			2		11	18	9	15					1		2	2	14	2	4	3					2		

1		3			6		7	9		11	2		5				4		10									8	R3
1		3			6		8	9		11	2		5				4		10		7								rep
1		3			6		8	9		11	2		5				4		10		7								R4
3		3			3		3	3		3	3		3				3		3		2							1	
								2									1		1		1								

1939-40

Division One

Match No.	Date			Opponents	Result		Scorers	Attendance
1	Aug	26	A	Swansea Town	W	2-1	H. Jones 2	17,259
2		29	A	Coventry City	D	3-3	E. Jones, Banks, Connelly	18,554
3	Sep	2	H	Tottenham Hotspur	L	3-4	E. Jones 3	16,021
								Appearances
								Goals

Secretary-manager: Fred Everiss

1945-46

FA Cup

R3/1	Jan	5	A	Cardiff City	D	1-1	Connelly	28,928
R3/2		9	H	Cardiff City	W	4-0	Clarke 2, Newsome 2	18,025
R4/1		26	A	Derby County	L	0-1		31,440
R4/2		30	H	Derby County	L	1-3	Clarke	35,882
								Appearances
								Goals

Secretary-manager: Fred Everiss

- This is the only season when all FA Cup ties have been played over two legs up to the semi-final stage.

Adams J	White HA	Shaw CE	Sankey J	Gripton EW	McNab A	Jones E	Banks GE	Jones HJ	Connelly E	Johnson JA	
1	2	3	4	5	6	7	8	9	10	11	1
1	2	3	4	5	6	7	8	9	10	11	2
1	2	3	4	5	6	7	8	9	10	11	3
3	3	3	3	3	3	3	3	3	3	3	
						4	1	2	1		

Sanders JA	Shaw C	Kinsell HF	Witcomb DF	Tranter G	Millard L	Elliott WB	Clarke I	Newsome R	Connelly E	Saunders DG	Twigg L	Hodgetts F	Butler S	
1	2	3	4	5	6	7	8	9	10	11				R3/1
	2	3	4	5	6	7	8	9	10		1	11		R3/2
1	2	3	4	5	6	7	8	9	10				11	R4/1
1	2	3	4	5	6	7	8	9	10				11	R4/2
3	4	4	4	4	4	4	4	4	4	1	1	1	2	
							3	2	1					

1946-47

Division Two

	P	W	D	L	F	A	Pts
Manchester City	42	26	10	6	78	35	62
Burnley	42	22	14	6	65	29	58
Birmingham City	42	25	5	12	74	33	55
Chesterfield	42	18	14	10	58	44	50
Newcastle United	42	19	10	13	95	62	48
Tottenham Hotspur	42	17	14	11	65	53	48
West Bromwich Albion	42	20	8	14	88	75	48
Coventry City	42	16	13	13	66	59	45
Leicester City	42	18	7	17	69	64	43
Barnsley	42	17	8	17	84	86	42
Nottingham Forest	42	15	10	17	69	74	40
West Ham United	42	16	8	18	70	76	40
Luton Town	42	16	7	19	71	73	39
Southampton	42	15	9	18	69	76	39
Fulham	42	15	9	18	63	74	39
Bradford Park Avenue	42	14	11	17	65	77	39
Bury	42	12	12	18	80	78	36
Millwall	42	14	8	20	56	79	36
Plymouth Argyle	42	14	5	23	79	96	33
Sheffield Wednesday	42	12	8	22	67	88	32
Swansea Town	42	11	7	24	55	83	29
Newport County	42	10	3	29	61	133	23

Secretary-manager: Fred Everiss

- Irish international centre-forward Dave Walsh, signed from Linfield, scored in his first six Second Division games for Albion at the start of the season – an all-time Football League record.
- Fellow Irishman Jack Vernon, a centre-half, signed for a record fee of £9,500 from Belfast Celtic, and inside-forward George Drury from Arsenal also joined Albion. Vernon represented Great Britain against the Rest of Europe at Hampden Park in May 1947.
- Other players who broke into Albion's League side this season were Norman Aldridge, Ray Barlow, Jimmy Duggan, Cliff Edwards, Charlie Evans, Roy Finch, goalkeeper Tommy Grimley, Frank Hodgetts (who actually made his debut in 1940 at the age of 16 years and 26 days against Notts County – the club's youngest ever first-team player), Glynn Hood, Harry Kinsell, Billy Lunn, Len Millard (signed initially in 1937), Jim Pemberton, Geoff Richards, Arthur Rowley, Reg Ryan, John Tighe, and George Tranter.
- Defenders Cecil Shaw and George Tranter both signed for Hereford United, the former after making 251 senior appearances in 10 years, and Doug Witcomb moved to Sheffield Wednesday.

Match No.	Date			Opponents	Result		Scorers	Attendance
1	Aug	31	A	Swansea Town	W	3-2	Walsh 2, Hodgetts	24,629
2	Sep	2	A	Coventry City	L	2-3	Walsh 2	24,051
3		7	H	Tottenham Hotspur	W	3-2	Clarke, Walsh, Hodgetts	38,670
4		14	A	Burnley	W	2-0	Walsh, Clarke	22,252
5		18	H	Birmingham City	W	3-0	Walsh, Elliott 2	40,031
6		21	H	Barnsley	L	2-5	Duggan, Walsh	38,925
7		25	A	Birmingham City	L	0-1		50,535
8		28	A	Newport County	W	7-2	Southam (og), Barlow, Elliott, Clarke 4	17,614
9	Oct	5	H	Southampton	W	2-0	Clarke, Duggan	27,122
10		12	A	Nottingham Forest	D	1-1	Witcomb	25,449
11		19	A	Millwall	W	2-1	Duggan, Walsh	29,840
12		26	H	Bradford Park Avenue	D	1-1	Duggan	20,028
13	Nov	2	A	Manchester City	L	0-5		40,611
14		9	H	West Ham United	L	2-3	Walsh, Millard	23,284
15		16	A	Sheffield Wednesday	D	2-2	Walsh 2	24,175
16		23	H	Fulham	W	6-1	Clarke 2, Walsh, Barlow 2, Hodgetts	20,243
17		30	A	Bury	L	0-4		17,790
18	Dec	7	H	Luton Town	L	1-2	Richards	20,685
19		14	A	Plymouth Argyle	L	1-2	Walsh	26,293
20		21	H	Leicester City	W	4-2	Duggan 2, Millard, Walsh	18,820
21		25	A	Newcastle United	W	4-2	Walsh 2, Duggan, Elliott	44,722
22		26	H	Newcastle United	W	3-2	Walsh 2, Clarke	52,701
23		28	H	Swansea Town	W	2-1	Hodgetts, Elliott	34,933
24	Jan	4	A	Tottenham Hotspur	L	0-2		40,537
25		18	H	Burnley	D	1-1	Duggan	43,427
26	Feb	1	H	Newport County	D	2-2	Walsh 2	15,089
27		8	A	Southampton	W	1-0	Elliott	13,416
28	Mar	15	A	West Ham United	L	2-3	Hodgetts, Elliott	23,928
29		22	H	Sheffield Wednesday	W	2-1	Drury, Clarke	35,448
30		29	A	Fulham	W	1-0	Hodgetts	25,717
31	Apr	4	A	Chesterfield	D	1-1	Walsh	17,772
32		5	H	Bury	W	3-0	Clarke 3	27,745
33		7	H	Chesterfield	W	3-2	Walsh 2, Hodgetts	29,806
34		12	A	Luton Town	L	0-2		14,920
35		19	H	Plymouth Argyle	L	2-5	Walsh, Clarke	25,068
36		26	A	Leicester City	D	1-1	Clarke	17,363
37	May	3	H	Coventry City	D	1-1	Hodgetts	23,807
38		10	H	Millwall	L	2-4	Elliott, Clarke	11,381
39		17	H	Nottingham Forest	W	5-1	Lunn, Millard, Walsh, Elliott, Clarke	12,566
40		26	A	Barnsley	L	1-2	Edwards	16,426
41		27	A	Bradford Park Avenue	W	4-2	Walsh (pen), Lunn 2, Elliott	10,777
42		31	H	Manchester City	W	3-1	Walsh, Clarke, Williams (og)	21,281

Appearances

Goals

FA Cup

R3	Jan	11	H	Leeds United	W	2-1	Barlow, Walsh	31,007
R4		25	H	Charlton Athletic	L	1-2	Elliott	29,996

Appearances

Goals

	Sanders JA	Pemberton JHA	Kinsell TH	Witcomb DF	Tranter GH	Millard L	Elliott WB	Clarke I	Walsh DJ	Duggan J	Hodgetts F	Hood GO	Shaw CE	Edwards CL	Barlow RJ	Butler S	Evans CJ	Drury GB	Grimley TW	Richards GM	Gripton EW	Tighe J	Vernon J	Ryan RA	Lumn WJ	Aldridge NH	Finch AR	Rowley GA
1	1	2	3	4	5	6	7	8	9	10	11																	
2	1	2	3	4	5	6	7	8	9	10	11																	
3	1	2	3	4	5	6	7	8	9	10	11																	
4	1	2	3	4	5	6	7	8	9	10	11																	
5	1	2	3	4		6	7	10	9	8	11	5																
6	1	2		4		6	7	10	9	8	11	5	3															
7	1	2	3	4	5		7	10	9	8	11			6														
8	1	2	3	4	5	6	7	9		8					10	11												
9	1	2	3	4	5	6	7	9		8					10	11												
10	1	2	3	4	5	6	7	9		8						11	10											
11	1	2	3		5	6	7		9	8	11			4	10													
12	1	2	3	4	5	6	7		9	10	11							8										
13	1	2	3	4	5	6	7	10	9		11							8										
14	1	2	3	4	5	6	7		9		11				10			8										
15	1	2	3	4	5	6	7	8	9		11				10													
16		2		4	5	6	7	8	9		11		3		10				1									
17		2		4	5	6	7	8	9		11		3		10				1									
18		2	3	4	5	6		8	9		11				10				1	7								
19		2	3	4		6	7	8	9	10	11			5					1									
20	1	2	3	4		6	7	8	9	10	11			5														
21	1	2	3	4		6	7	8	9	10	11			5														
22	1	2	3	4		6	7	8	9	10	11			5														
23	1	2	3	4		6	7	8	9	10	11			5														
24	1	2	3	4		6	7	8	9	10	11			5														
25	1	2	3	4		6	7		9	8	11				10						5							
26		2	3	4		6	7		9	8	11			5	10							1						
27		2	3	4		6	7	8	9		11			5				10	1									
28		2	3			6	7	8	9		11			4				10	1				5					
29		2	3			6	7	8	9		11			4				10	1				5					
30		2	3			6	7	8	9	10	11			4					1				5					
31		2	3			6	7	8	9	10	11			4					1				5					
32		2	3			6	7	8	9	10	11			4					1				5					
33		2	3					8	9	10	7			4					1				5	6	11			
34		2				3	11	8	9	10	7			4					1				5	6				
35							7	8	9		11		3	4					1				5	6		2	10	
36		2	3			6	7	8	9		11			4					1				5				10	
37		2	3			6	7	8			11			4					1				5				10	9
38		2	3			6	7	8	9		11			4					1		5							10
39		2	3			6	7	8	9		11			4					1				5		10			
40		2	3			6	7	8	9		11			4					1				5		10			
41		2				3	7	8	9		11			4					1				5	6	10			
42		2				3	7	8	9		11			4					1				5	6	10			
	21	41	35	26	16	39	40	37	38	25	39	2	4	25	10	3	1	6	20	1	2	1	14	5	5	1	3	2
				1		3	10	19	28	8	8			1	3			1		1					3			

Two own-goals

	Sanders JA	Pemberton JHA	Kinsell TH	Witcomb DF	Tranter GH	Millard L	Elliott WB	Clarke I	Walsh DJ	Duggan J	Hodgetts F	Hood GO	Shaw CE	Edwards CL	Barlow RJ
R3	1	2	3	4		6	7		9	8	11			5	10
R4	1	2	3	4		6	7		9	8	11			5	10
	2	2	2	2		2	2		2	2	2			2	2
							1		1						1

1947-48

Division Two

	P	W	D	L	F	A	Pts
Birmingham City	42	22	15	5	55	24	59
Newcastle United	42	24	8	10	72	41	56
Southampton	42	21	10	11	71	53	52
Sheffield Wednesday	42	20	11	11	66	53	51
Cardiff City	42	18	11	13	61	58	47
West Ham United	42	16	14	12	55	53	46
West Bromwich Albion	42	18	9	15	63	58	45
Tottenham Hotspur	42	15	14	13	56	43	44
Leicester City	42	16	11	15	60	57	43
Coventry City	42	14	13	15	59	52	41
Fulham	42	15	10	17	47	46	40
Barnsley	42	15	10	17	62	64	40
Luton Town	42	14	12	16	56	59	40
Bradford Park Avenue	42	16	8	18	68	72	40
Brentford	42	13	14	15	44	61	40
Chesterfield	42	16	7	19	54	55	39
Plymouth Argyle	42	9	20	13	40	58	38
Leeds United	42	14	8	20	62	72	36
Nottingham Forest	42	12	11	19	54	60	35
Bury	42	9	16	17	58	68	34
Doncaster Rovers	42	9	11	22	40	66	29
Millwall	42	9	11	22	44	74	29

Secretary-manager: Fred Everiss

- Arthur Rowley scored the first of what was to be a record total of 434 career League goals when he netted for Albion against Leeds United at Elland Road in February.
- Albion handed League debuts to Dennis Gordon, Jack Haines, goalkeeper Norman Heath (who saved a penalty in his first game against Sheffield Wednesday), Danny Smith, Arthur 'Biff' Taylor and George Williams.
- Peter McKennan, signed from Partick Thistle, also made his League bow. He had guested for Albion during the war but before the season ended was exchanged for Jack Haines of Leicester City. Eddie 'Ginger' Wilcox and Bristol City's Cyril Williams (in exchange for Cliff Edwards) were also recruited, while Ike Clarke left The Hawthorns, joining Portsmouth, with whom he won two League Championship medals.
- Fred Everiss handed over his 'managerial' duties to the former Chelsea and Wolves player Jack Smith. Everiss had been 'in charge' since 1902. He became a director at The Hawthorns and was associated with Albion for 55 years (1896–1951).

Match No.	Date			Opponents	Result		Scorers	Attendance
1	Aug	23	H	Tottenham Hotspur	W	1-0	Walsh	32,521
2		27	H	Fulham	W	2-1	Walsh 2 (1 pen)	23,064
3		30	A	Barnsley	W	1-0	Walsh	23,796
4	Sep	3	A	Fulham	W	1-0	Drury	24,710
5		6	H	Plymouth Argyle	D	1-1	Drury	31,427
6		10	H	Coventry City	W	3-1	Walsh 2, Drury	21,421
7		13	A	Luton Town	D	1-1	Drury	21,019
8		15	A	Coventry City	L	0-1		19,213
9		20	H	Brentford	W	3-2	Drury 2, Walsh	29,445
10		27	A	Leicester City	D	1-1	Elliott	32,195
11	Oct	4	H	Leeds United	W	3-2	Lunn 2, Elliott	30,479
12		11	H	Millwall	W	2-1	Walsh 2	32,661
13		18	A	Chesterfield	W	2-0	Elliott, Walsh	15,502
14		25	H	West Ham United	L	1-2	Walsh	37,764
15	Nov	1	A	Bury	W	2-1	Walsh 2	24,179
16		8	H	Southampton	W	1-0	Smith	45,985
17		15	A	Doncaster Rovers	L	1-2	Walsh	19,609
18		22	H	Nottingham Forest	W	3-2	Elliott, Drury, McKennan	28,568
19		29	A	Bradford Park Avenue	L	1-3	McKennan	19,297
20	Dec	6	H	Cardiff City	L	2-3	Walsh, McKennan	38,914
21		13	A	Sheffield Wednesday	W	2-1	Walsh, Elliott	36,201
22		20	A	Tottenham Hotspur	D	1-1	Walsh	40,219
23		26	H	Newcastle United	L	0-1		48,322
24	Jan	1	A	Newcastle United	L	1-3	Walsh	60,909
25		3	H	Barnsley	L	0-2		25,045
26		17	A	Plymouth Argyle	L	1-2	Walsh	22,547
27		31	H	Luton Town	W	1-0	Walsh	26,979
28	Feb	7	A	Brentford	L	0-1		25,234
29		14	H	Leicester City	L	1-3	McKennan	29,322
30		21	A	Leeds United	L	1-3	Rowley	22,333
31		28	A	Millwall	D	1-1	Walsh	23,125
32	Mar	6	H	Chesterfield	W	1-0	Hodgetts	25,242
33		13	A	West Ham United	W	2-0	Haines, Elliott	25,170
34		20	H	Bury	D	3-3	Walsh, Hodgetts, Rowley	28,638
35		27	A	Southampton	D	1-1	Rowley	26,635
36		29	A	Birmingham City	L	0-4		47,074
37		30	H	Birmingham City	D	1-1	Elliott	51,945
38	Apr	3	H	Doncaster Rovers	L	1-3	Squires (og)	22,076
39		10	A	Nottingham Forest	L	1-3	Taylor	20,023
40		17	H	Bradford Park Avenue	W	6-0	Haines 3, Taylor 2, Finch	13,349
41		24	A	Cardiff City	W	5-0	Taylor 2, Haines 2 (1 pen), Rowley	26,179
42	May	1	H	Sheffield Wednesday	D	1-1	Elliott	24,818
								Appearances
								Goals

FA Cup

R3	Jan	10	H	Reading	W	2-0	Finch, Drury	30,241
R4		24	A	Tottenham Hotspur	L	1-3	Rowley	71,853
								Appearances
								Goals

Grimley TW	Pemberton JHA	Millard L	Edwards CL	Vernon J	Hood GO	Elliott WB	Clarke I	Walsh DJ	Drury GB	Hodgetts F	Sanders JA	Williams G	Lunn WJ	Kinsell TH	Ryan RA	Gripton EW	Evans AJ	Smith D	McKennan PS	Heath NH	Rowley GA	Finch AR	Gordon DW	Haines JTW	Richards GM	Taylor AS	
1	2	3	4	5	6	7	8	9	10	11																	1
1	2	3	4	5	6	7	8	9	10	11																	2
1	2	3	4	5	6	7	8	9	10	11																	3
1	2	3	4	5	6	7	8	9	10	11																	4
1	2	3	4	5	6	7	8	9	10	11																	5
	2	3	4	5	6	7	8	9	10	11	1																6
	2	3		5	6	7	8	9	10	11	1	4															7
	2	3		5	6	7	8	9	10	11	1	4															8
	2	3		5	6	7		9	8	11	1	4	10														9
	2	3		5	6	7		9	8	11	1	4	10														10
	2	6				7	9		8	11	1		10	3	4	5											11
	2	6		5		7	8	9		11	1		10	3	4												12
	2	6		5		7	8	9			1			3	4		10	11									13
	2	6		5		7	8	9			1			3	4		10	11									14
	2	3	4	5	6	7		9			1						10	11	8								15
	2	3	4	5	6	7		9			1						10	11	8								16
1	2	3	4		6	7		9								5	10	11	8								17
1	2	6	5		4	7		9	10					3				11	8								18
1	2	6	5		4	7		9	10					3				11	8								19
1	2	3	4	5		7		9	10	11					6				8								20
	2	3	4			7		9	8	11					6	5				1	10						21
	2	3	4			7		9	8	11					6	5				1	10						22
	2	3	4			7			8	11			9		6	5				1	10						23
	2	4		5		7		9	8	11				3	6					1	10						24
1	2	3		5	4	7		9	8	11					6						10						25
	2	3		5		7		9	8		1	4			6		11					10					26
	2	4		5		7		9			1			3			6		8		11	10					27
	2	4		5		7		9			1			3			6		8		11	10					28
	2	4		5				9			1			3			6		8		11	10	7				29
	2	4		5				9						3			6		8	1	11	10	7				30
	2	4		5				9	10	7				3			6		8	1	11						31
	2	4		5		7		9	10	8				3			6			1	11						32
	2	4		5		7		9		8				3			6			1	11			10			33
	2	4		5		7		9		8				3			6			1	11			10			34
	2	4		5		7		9		8				3			6			1	11			10			35
	2	4		5		7		9	8					3			6			1	11			10			36
	2	3		5		7		9				4					6			1	11			10	8		37
	2	3		5		7						4					6			1	9	8	11	10			38
	2	4		5	6	7					1			3							11			10	8	9	39
	2	3		5	6	7					1				4						10	11		8		9	40
	2	3		5	6	7					1				4						10	11		8		9	41
	2	3		5	6	7					1				4						10	11		8		9	42
10	42	42	15	35	20	39	12	35	23	23	19	7	5	18	14	5	18	7	11	13	21	9	3	10	2	4	
						8		22	7	2			2					1	4		4	1		6		5	

One own-goal

	2	3		5		11			9		1	4			6		10					8	7				R3
	2	3		5		7		9	10		1	4			6				8		11						R4
	2	2		2		2		1	2		2	2			2		1		1		1	1	1				
								1												1	1						

1948-49

Division Two

	P	W	D	L	F	A	Pts
Fulham	42	24	9	9	77	37	57
West Bromwich Albion	42	24	8	10	69	39	56
Southampton	42	23	9	10	69	36	55
Cardiff City	42	19	13	10	62	47	51
Tottenham Hotspur	42	17	16	9	72	44	50
Chesterfield	42	15	17	10	51	45	47
West Ham United	42	18	10	14	56	58	46
Sheffield Wednesday	42	15	13	14	63	56	43
Barnsley	42	14	12	16	62	61	40
Luton Town	42	14	12	16	55	57	40
Grimsby Town	42	15	10	17	72	76	40
Bury	42	17	6	19	67	76	40
Queen's Park Rangers	42	14	11	17	44	62	39
Blackburn Rovers	42	15	8	19	53	63	38
Leeds United	42	12	13	17	55	63	37
Coventry City	42	15	7	20	55	64	37
Bradford Park Avenue	42	13	11	18	65	78	37
Brentford	42	11	14	17	42	53	36
Leicester City	42	10	16	16	62	79	36
Plymouth Argyle	42	12	12	18	49	64	36
Nottingham Forest	42	14	7	21	50	54	35
Lincoln City	42	8	12	22	53	91	28

Manager: Jack Smith

- Albion clinched promotion by beating FA Cup finalists Leicester City 3–0 at Filbert Street in their penultimate game of the season... And the Baggies would have won the Second Division title if they had defeated Grimsby Town in their last match at Blundell Park.
- Young Bobby Barker, Sammy Cox (from Denaby United), Joe Kennedy (from Altrincham), Irishman Hugh Morrow, Cyril Williams (from Bristol City), Jack Boyd (from Sunderland), Ernie Shepherd (from Fulham), Arthur Smith (from Leicester City) and Eddie Wilcox (ex-Oxford City) were all League debutants. Left-winger Shepherd actually played for three promoted clubs this season – Albion, Fulham and Hull City, the latter of Division Three North.
- Arthur Rowley was transferred to Second Division champions-elect Fulham, Harry Kinsell joined Bolton Wanderers, Frank Hodgetts went to Millwall and Roy Finch switched to Lincoln City.
- Albion met Queen's Park Rangers at League level for the first time.

Match No.	Date			Opponents	Result		Scorers	Attendance
1	Aug	21	A	Nottingham Forest	W	1-0	Walsh	32,281
2		25	H	Chesterfield	D	0-0		29,041
3		28	H	Bury	L	2-3	Barlow, Walsh	31,904
4	Sep	1	A	Chesterfield	D	0-0		14,079
5		4	A	West Ham United	L	0-1		28,065
6		8	H	Lincoln City	W	5-0	Haines 2, Walsh 3	13,009
7		11	H	Tottenham Hotspur	D	2-2	Haines, Walsh	32,279
8		15	A	Lincoln City	W	3-0	Walsh, Barker, Ryan	14,902
9		18	A	Brentford	D	0-0		28,212
10		25	H	Leicester City	W	2-1	Williams, Walsh	32,517
11	Oct	2	A	Leeds United	W	3-1	Williams 2, Walsh	33,706
12		9	A	Fulham	W	2-1	Haines, Barker	31,636
13		16	H	Plymouth Argyle	W	3-0	Williams, Haines, Walsh	32,849
14		23	A	Blackburn Rovers	D	0-0		28,107
15		30	H	Cardiff City	W	2-0	Haines, Williams	46,036
16	Nov	6	A	Queen's Park Rangers	W	2-0	Walsh, Hodgetts	24,459
17		13	H	Luton Town	W	2-1	Williams, Elliott	32,589
18		20	A	Bradford Park Avenue	L	1-4	Haines	18,064
19		27	H	Southampton	W	2-0	Millard, Elliott	47,028
20	Dec	4	A	Barnsley	L	0-2		20,936
21		11	H	Grimsby Town	W	5-2	Williams 3, Haines (pen), Walsh	22,664
22		18	H	Nottingham Forest	W	2-1	Haines, Elliott	32,583
23		25	H	Sheffield Wednesday	W	1-0	Vernon	34,881
24		27	A	Sheffield Wednesday	L	1-2	Westlake (og)	59,857
25	Jan	1	A	Bury	L	0-4		16,861
26		15	H	West Ham United	W	2-1	Walsh 2	33,100
27		22	A	Tottenham Hotspur	L	0-2		62,566
28	Feb	5	H	Brentford	W	2-0	Walsh, Smith	39,482
29	Mar	5	H	Fulham	L	1-2	Elliott	27,595
30		12	A	Plymouth Argyle	W	2-1	Walsh, Elliott	25,422
31		19	H	Blackburn Rovers	W	2-1	Elliott, Haines	36,053
32		26	A	Cardiff City	D	2-2	Haines, Walsh	47,649
33	Apr	2	H	Queen's Park Rangers	D	1-1	Elliott	35,093
34		6	H	Leeds United	W	1-0	Barlow (pen)	28,562
35		9	A	Luton Town	W	1-0	Morrow	16,651
36		16	H	Bradford Park Avenue	W	7-1	Walsh 4 (1 pen), Haines 2, Morrow	39,241
37		18	H	Coventry City	W	1-0	Haines	42,488
38		19	A	Coventry City	L	0-1		39,488
39		23	A	Southampton	D	1-1	Smith	30,586
40		30	H	Barnsley	W	2-0	Barlow, Walsh	31,966
41	May	5	A	Leicester City	W	3-0	Walsh, Kennedy, Barlow	35,800
42		7	A	Grimsby Town	L	0-1		18,564

Appearances

Goals

FA Cup

R3	Jan	8	A	Lincoln City	W	1-0	Barlow	19,602
R4		29	A	Gateshead	W	3-1*	Walsh 2, Smith	16,885
R5	Feb	12	H	Chelsea	W	3-0	Walsh 3	57,843
R6		26	A	Wolverhampton Wanderers	L	0-1		55,684

* after extra-time

Appearances

Goals

Sanders JA	Pemberton JHA	Kinsell TH	Millard L	Vernon J	Hood GO	Elliott WB	Haines JTW	Walsh DJ	Barlow RJ	Smith AE	Hodgetts F	Williams CE	Finch AR	Ryan RA	Boyd J	Barker RC	Cox S	Rowley GA	Morrow HJE	Wilcox EE	Shepherd E	Kennedy JP	
1	2	3	4	5	6	7	8	9	10	11													1
1	2	3	4	5	6	7	8	9	10	11													2
1	2	3	4	5	6		8	9	10	11	7												3
1	2	3	4	5	6	7	10	9				8	11										4
1	2	3	4	5	6	7	10	9				8	11										5
1	2	3	6		5	7	10	9				8	11	4									6
1		3	6		5	7	10	9			11	8		4	2								7
1	2	3	6		5	7	10	9				8		4		11							8
1		3	2	5	6	7	10	9				8		4		11							9
1		3		5	6	7	10	9				8		4		11	2						10
1		3	4	5	6	7	10	9				8				11	2						11
1	2	3	6		5	7	10		4			8				11		9					12
1	2	3	4	5	6	7	10	9				8				11							13
1	2	3	4	5	6	7	10	9				8				11							14
1	2	3	4	5	6	7	10	9				8				11							15
1	2	3	4	5	6	7	10	9			11	8											16
1	2	3	4	5	6	7	10	9			11	8											17
1	2	3	4	5	6	7	10	9			11	8											18
1	2	3	4	5	6	7	10	9				8							11				19
1	2	3	4	5	6	7		9	10			8								11			20
1	2	3	4	5	6	7	10	9				8								11			21
1	2	3	4	5	6	7	10	9				8									11		22
1	2	3	4	5	6	7	10	9				8									11		23
1	2	3	4	5	6	7	10	9				8									11		24
1	2	3	4	5	6	7	10	9				8									11		25
1	2	3	4	5	6	7	11	9	10			8											26
1	2	3	4	5	6	7	11	9	10			8											27
1	2		3	5	6	7	10	9	4	11		8											28
1	2	11	3	5	6	7	10	9	4			8											29
1	2		3	5	6	7	10	9	4			8				11							30
1	2		3	5	6	7	10	9	4			8				11							31
1	2	3	6	5		7	10	9	4			8				11							32
1	2	3	6	5		7	10	9	4			8				11							33
1	2		3	5		7	10	9	4			8		6		11							34
1	2		3	5			10	9	8					6		11			7			4	35
1	2		3	5		7	10	9	8					6					11			4	36
1	2		3	5		7	10	9	8					6					11			4	37
1	2		3	5		7	10	9	8					6					11			4	38
1	2		3	5		7	8	9	10	11				6								4	39
1	2		3	5	6	7		9	10	11				4								8	40
1	2		3	5	6	7		9	10	11				4								8	41
1	2		3	5	6	7		9	10	11				4								8	42
42	38	30	41	38	34	40	38	41	22	8	5	31	3	14	1	14	2	1	5	2	4	8	
			1	1		7	14	23	4	2	1	9		1		2			2			1	

One own-goal

1	2	3	4	5	6	7	11	9	10			8				R3
1	2	3	4	5	6	7		9	10	11		8				R4
1	2		3	5	6	7	10	9	4	11		8				R5
1	2		3	5	6	7	10	9	4	11		8				R6
4	4	2	4	4	4	4	3	4	4	3		4			4	
								5	1	1						

1949-50

Division One

	P	W	D	L	F	A	Pts
Portsmouth	42	22	9	11	74	38	53
Wolverhampton W	42	20	13	9	76	49	53
Sunderland	42	21	10	11	83	62	52
Manchester United	42	18	14	10	69	44	50
Newcastle United	42	19	12	11	77	55	50
Arsenal	42	19	11	12	79	55	49
Blackpool	42	17	15	10	46	35	49
Liverpool	42	17	14	11	64	54	48
Middlesbrough	42	20	7	15	59	48	47
Burnley	42	16	13	13	40	40	45
Derby County	42	17	10	15	69	61	44
Aston Villa	42	15	12	15	61	61	42
Chelsea	42	12	16	14	58	65	40
West Bromwich Albion	42	14	12	16	47	53	40
Huddersfield Town	42	14	9	19	52	73	37
Bolton Wanderers	42	10	14	18	45	59	34
Fulham	42	10	14	18	41	54	34
Everton	42	10	14	18	42	66	34
Stoke City	42	11	12	19	45	75	34
Charlton Athletic	42	13	6	23	53	65	32
Manchester City	42	8	13	21	36	68	29
Birmingham City	42	7	14	21	31	67	28

Manager: Jack Smith

- A record League crowd at The Hawthorns of 60,945 saw ex-Port Vale winger Ronnie Allen score on his Albion debut against Wolves.
- Others making their debuts were winger George Lee, signed from Nottingham Forest, full-back Stan Rickaby, recruited from Middlesbrough, centre-half Les Horne, forwards Gordon Inwood and Mike Betteridge and wing-half Jimmy Dudley, whose elder brother George had been at The Hawthorns before the war.

Match No.	Date			Opponents	Result		Scorers	Attendance
1	Aug	20	H	Charlton Athletic	W	1-0	Williams	49,596
2		24	A	Birmingham City	L	0-2		46,945
3		27	A	Manchester United	D	1-1	Williams	46,407
4		31	H	Birmingham City	W	3-0	Haines 2, Walsh	50,299
5	Sep	3	H	Chelsea	D	1-1	Williams	45,337
6		7	H	Arsenal	L	1-2	Elliott	43,663
7		10	A	Stoke City	W	3-1	Haines, Williams 2	35,909
8		14	A	Arsenal	L	1-4	Walsh	40,755
9		17	H	Burnley	W	3-0	Elliott (pen), Walsh, Williams	37,091
10		24	A	Sunderland	L	1-2	Elliott	50,896
11	Oct	1	H	Liverpool	L	0-1		44,219
12		8	H	Aston Villa	D	1-1	Wilcox	53,690
13		15	A	Wolverhampton Wanderers	D	1-1	Elliott	56,661
14		22	H	Portsmouth	W	3-0	Walsh, Williams, Elliott	40,808
15		29	A	Huddersfield Town	D	1-1	Walsh	22,461
16	Nov	5	H	Everton	W	4-0	Walsh 2, Smith, Williams	29,309
17		12	A	Middlesbrough	L	0-3		28,408
18		26	A	Newcastle United	L	1-5	Walsh	32,415
19	Dec	3	H	Fulham	W	4-1	Walsh 2, Elliott, Barlow	30,883
20		10	A	Manchester City	D	1-1	Elliott	29,660
21		17	A	Charlton Athletic	W	2-1	Walsh 2	20,369
22		24	H	Manchester United	L	1-2	Walsh	44,885
23		26	A	Bolton Wanderers	L	0-3		38,764
24		27	H	Bolton Wanderers	W	2-1	Walsh, Barlow	41,746
25		31	A	Chelsea	L	1-2	Gordon	41,610
26	Jan	14	H	Stoke City	D	0-0		34,840
27		21	A	Burnley	D	0-0		26,129
28	Feb	4	H	Sunderland	L	0-2		36,101
29		18	A	Liverpool	L	1-2	Lee	46,634
30		25	A	Aston Villa	L	0-1		47,539
31	Mar	4	H	Wolverhampton Wanderers	D	1-1	Allen	60,945
32		11	A	Blackpool	L	0-3		23,104
33		18	H	Newcastle United	D	1-1	Walsh	33,469
34		29	A	Everton	W	2-1	Allen, Barlow	18,630
35	Apr	1	H	Middlesbrough	L	0-3		32,972
36		7	A	Derby County	L	1-3	Allen	25,198
37		8	A	Portsmouth	W	1-0	Ryan	33,494
38		10	H	Derby County	W	1-0	Lee	31,516
39		15	H	Huddersfield Town	D	0-0		28,240
40		22	A	Fulham	W	1-0	Allen	25,025
41		26	H	Blackpool	W	1-0	Allen	28,858
42		29	H	Manchester City	D	0-0		16,780

Appearances
Goals

FA Cup

R3	Jan	7	A	Cardiff City	D	2-2	Williams, Inwood	39,980
rep		11	H	Cardiff City	L	0-1		37,358

Appearances
Goals

Sanders JA	Pemberton JHA	Millard L	Kennedy JP	Vernon J	Barlow RJ	Elliott WB	Williams CE	Walsh DJ	Haines JTW	Lee GT	Hood GO	Ryan RA	Smith AE	Wilcox EE	Horne LH	Inwood GF	Dudley JG	Gordon DW	Betteridge RM	Allen R	Rickaby S	
1	2	3	4	5	6	7	8	9	10	11												1
1	2	3	4	5		7	8	9	10	11	6											2
1	2	3	4	5		7	8	9	10	11	6											3
1	2	3	4	5		7	8	9	10	11	6											4
1	2	3	4	5		7	8	9	10	11	6											5
1	2	3		5		7	8	9	10		6	4	11									6
1	2	3		5		7	8		10		6	4	11	9								7
1	2	3		5		7	8	9	10		6	4	11									8
1	2	3		5		7	8	9	10		6	4	11									9
1	2	3		5		7	8	9	10		6	4	11									10
1	2	3				7	8	9	10	11	6	4			5							11
1	2	3	4	5		7	8			11		6	10	9								12
1	2	3	4	5		7	8	9				6	10			11						13
1	2	3	4	5		7	8	9				6	10			11						14
1	2	3	4	5		7	8	9				6	10			11						15
1	2	3	4	5		7	8	9				6	10			11						16
1	2	3	4	5		7	8	9				6	10			11						17
1	2	3	4	5	10	7	8	9				6				11						18
1	2	3	4	5	10	7	8	9				6				11						19
1	2			5	10	7	8	9			3	6				11	4					20
1	2	3	4	5	10		8	9		11		6						7				21
1	2	3	4	5	10	7	8	9		11		6										22
1		2	4	5	10			9		11	3	6					8	7				23
1	2	3	4	5	10		8	9				6				11		7				24
1	2	3	4	5	10		8	9				6				11		7				25
1	2	3	8	5			10	9				6	11				4		7			26
1	2	3	8	5	10			9				6	11				4		7			27
1	2	3	8	5	10			9		11		6					4	7				28
1	2	3	4	5	6		8	9		11		10	7									29
1	2	3	4	5	6			9		11		10	7				8					30
1	2	3	4	5	10					11		6	8	9						7		31
1	2	3	4		10					11		6	8	9	5					7		32
1	2	3	4	5	10			9		11		6	8							7		33
1	2	3		5	10			9		11	4	6	8							7		34
1	2	3	4	5	10			9		11		6	8							7		35
1	2	3	4	5				9		11		6					10	7		8		36
1	2	3	4	5				9		11		6	8				10	7				37
1	2	3	4	5	10			9		11		6					8			7		38
1	2	3	4	5	10					11		6					8	9		7		39
1	2	3	4	5	6			9		11							10	8		7		40
1	2	3	4	5	6			9		11							10	8		7		41
1		3	4	5	6			9		11							10	8		7	2	42
42	40	41	34	40	23	21	26	37	11	25	13	34	21	4	2	10	13	11	2	11	1	
					3	7	8	15	3	2		1	1	1			1			5		

Sanders JA	Pemberton JHA	Millard L	Kennedy JP	Vernon J	Barlow RJ	Elliott WB	Williams CE	Walsh DJ	Haines JTW	Lee GT	Hood GO	Ryan RA	Smith AE	Wilcox EE	Horne LH	Inwood GF	Dudley JG	Gordon DW	Betteridge RM	Allen R	Rickaby S	
1	2	3	4	5	10		8	9				6				11		7				R3
1	2	3	4	5	10		8	9				6				11		7				rep
2	2	2	2	2	2		2	2				2				2		2				
							1									1						

1950-51

Division One

	P	W	D	L	F	A	Pts
Tottenham Hotspur	42	25	10	7	82	44	60
Manchester United	42	24	8	10	74	40	56
Blackpool	42	20	10	12	79	53	50
Newcastle United	42	18	13	11	62	53	49
Arsenal	42	19	9	14	73	56	47
Middlesbrough	42	18	11	13	76	65	47
Portsmouth	42	16	15	11	71	68	47
Bolton Wanderers	42	19	7	16	64	61	45
Liverpool	42	16	11	15	53	59	43
Burnley	42	14	14	14	48	43	42
Derby County	42	16	8	18	81	75	40
Sunderland	42	12	16	14	63	73	40
Stoke City	42	13	14	15	50	59	40
Wolverhampton W	42	15	8	19	74	61	38
Aston Villa	42	12	13	17	66	68	37
West Bromwich Albion	42	13	11	18	53	61	37
Charlton Athletic	42	14	9	19	63	80	37
Fulham	42	13	11	18	52	68	37
Huddersfield Town	42	15	6	21	64	92	36
Chelsea	42	12	8	22	53	65	32
Sheffield Wednesday	42	12	8	22	64	83	32
Everton	42	12	8	22	48	86	32

Manager: Jack Smith

- Ronnie Allen top scored for Albion in this the first of six successive seasons.
- Frank Griffin joined Albion from Shrewsbury Town, 1951 FA Cup finalist Andy McCall joined from Blackpool and centre-forward Fred Richardson joined from Barnsley.
- Winger Billy Elliott was transferred to Bilston United and Dave Walsh joined rivals Aston Villa (after scoring 100 goals for Albion), while wing-half Glyn Hood retired through injury. Jim Pemberton was forced to retire through injury after making 172 appearances. On the credit side, Albion recruited Welshman Stuart Williams from Wrexham.
- Albion lost 4–3 to the Austrian club SC Wacker and beat Floriana of Malta 2–0 in Festival of Britain matches at The Hawthorns.

Match No.	Date		Opponents		Result		Scorers	Attendance
1	Aug	19	A	Aston Villa	L	0-2		65,036
2		23	A	Newcastle United	D	1-1	Elliott	48,720
3		26	H	Stoke City	D	1-1	Elliott	33,215
4		30	H	Newcastle United	L	1-2	Walsh	29,377
5	Sep	2	A	Everton	W	3-0	Barlow, Allen, Smith	46,502
6		6	A	Middlesbrough	L	1-2	Walsh	28,829
7		9	H	Portsmouth	W	5-0	Walsh, Elliott, Williams, Smith 2	34,460
8		13	H	Middlesbrough	L	2-3	Elliott, Allen	31,530
9		16	A	Chelsea	D	1-1	Walsh	39,570
10		23	H	Burnley	W	2-1	Lee, Walsh	32,638
11		30	A	Arsenal	L	0-3		51,928
12	Oct	7	A	Derby County	D	1-1	Williams	27,098
13		14	H	Liverpool	D	1-1	Walsh	35,030
14		21	A	Blackpool	L	1-2	Allen	30,536
15		28	H	Tottenham Hotspur	L	1-2	Barlow	44,543
16	Nov	4	A	Fulham	W	1-0	Richardson	21,133
17		11	H	Bolton Wanderers	L	0-1		28,816
18		18	A	Charlton Athletic	W	3-2	Richardson, Allen, E. Croker (og)	21,876
19		25	H	Manchester United	L	0-1		28,146
20	Dec	2	A	Wolverhampton Wanderers	L	1-3	Ryan	45,087
21		9	H	Sunderland	W	3-1	Richardson 2, Wilcox	26,666
22		16	H	Aston Villa	W	2-0	Richardson, Wilcox	28,796
23		23	A	Stoke City	D	1-1	Allen	19,789
24		25	H	Sheffield Wednesday	L	1-3	Ryan	28,023
25		26	A	Sheffield Wednesday	L	0-3		44,863
26		30	H	Everton	L	0-1		17,912
27	Jan	13	A	Portsmouth	D	2-2	Richardson, Allen	23,559
28		20	H	Chelsea	D	1-1	Lee	30,985
29	Feb	3	A	Burnley	W	1-0	Allen	19,101
30		17	H	Arsenal	W	2-0	Richardson 2	35,999
31		24	H	Derby County	L	1-2	Dudley	33,702
32	Mar	3	A	Liverpool	D	1-1	McCall	36,654
33		17	A	Tottenham Hotspur	L	0-5		45,353
34		24	H	Fulham	D	0-0		23,803
35		26	H	Huddersfield Town	L	0-2		24,360
36		27	A	Huddersfield Town	W	2-1	Barlow 2	32,401
37		31	A	Bolton Wanderers	W	2-0	Barlow, Gordon	21,860
38	Apr	4	H	Blackpool	L	1-3	Barlow (pen)	39,591
39		7	H	Charlton Athletic	W	3-0	Allen, McCall, Ryan	26,083
40		14	A	Manchester United	L	0-3		26,523
41		21	H	Wolverhampton Wanderers	W	3-2	Barlow 2, Allen	39,066
42		28	A	Sunderland	D	1-1	Allen	17,727

Appearances
Goals

FA Cup

R3	Jan	6	A	Derby County	D	2-2	Lee, Barlow	24,807
rep		10	H	Derby County	L	0-1		33,223

Appearances
Goals

Sanders JA	Pemberton JHA	Millard L	Kennedy JP	Vernon J	Barlow RJ	Elliott WB	Williams CE	Walsh DJ	Allen R	Lee GT	Rickaby S	Richardson F	Smith AE	Gordon DW	Ryan RA	Betteridge RM	Heath NH	Dudley JG	Wilcox EE	Guy HG	Horne HL	McCall A	Griffin FA	
1	2	3	4	5	6	7	8	9	10	11														1
1		3	4	5	6	7	8	9	10	11	2													2
1		3	4	5	6	7	8	9	11		2	10												3
1		3	4	5	6	7	8	9	11		2	10												4
1		3	4	5	6	7	8	9	11		2		10											5
1		3	4	5	6		8	9	11		2		10	7										6
1		3	4	5	6	7	8	9	11		2		10											7
1		3	4	5	6	7	8	9	11		2		10											8
1		3	4	5	6	7	8	9	11		2			10										9
1		3	4	5	10		8	9	7	11	2				6									10
1		3	4	5	10	7		9	8	11	2				6									11
1		3	5		6		8	9	7	11	2		10		4									12
1		3	4	5	6		8	9	7	11	2					10								13
1		3	4	5	6		8		7	11	2	9				10								14
1		3	4	5	6	7	8		11		2	9				10								15
		3	4	5	6				7	11	2	9		8	10		1							16
		3	4	5	6				7	11	2	9		8	10		1							17
		3		5	6				7	11	2	9		8	10		1	4						18
		3		5	6				7	11	2	9		8	10		1	4						19
		3		5	6				7	11	2	9			8		1	4	10					20
		3	4	5	6				7	11	2	9			8		1		10					21
		3	4	5	6				11		2	9		7	10		1		8					22
		3	4	5	6				11		2	9		7	10		1		8					23
				5	6				7	11	2	9			10		1	4	8	3				24
				5	6			8	7	11	2	9			10		1	4			3			25
1		3		5	6				7	11	2	9			10			4	8					26
1		3	4	5	8				7	11	2	9			10			6						27
1		3	4	5	8				7	11	2	9			6							10		28
1		3	4	5	6				7	11	2	9						8				10		29
1		3	4	5	6				7	11	2	9						8				10		30
1		3	4	5	6				7	11	2	9						8				10		31
1		3		5	6				7	11	2	9			4			8				10		32
1		3	4	5	6				7	11	2	9						8				10		33
1		3	4	5	6				7	11	2	9						8				10		34
1		3	4	5	6				7	11	2	9						8				10		35
1		3	4	5	9				11		2		8	7	6							10		36
1		3	4	5	9					11	2			7	6			8				10		37
1		3	4	5	9					11	2			7	6			8				10		38
1		3	4	5	9	7			8	11	2				6							10		39
1		3	4	5	9	7			8	11	2				6							10		40
1		3	4	5	9	7			10	11	2				6							8		41
		3	4	5	9				10	11	2				6		1					8	7	42
31	1	40	35	41	42	13	14	14	40	31	41	24	6	11	24	3	11	16	6	1	1	15	1	
					8	4	2	6	10	2		8	3	1	3			1	2			2		

One own-goal

Sanders JA	Pemberton JHA	Millard L	Kennedy JP	Vernon J	Barlow RJ	Elliott WB	Williams CE	Walsh DJ	Allen R	Lee GT	Rickaby S	Richardson F	Smith AE	Gordon DW	Ryan RA	Betteridge RM	Heath NH	Dudley JG	Wilcox EE	Guy HG	Horne HL	McCall A	Griffin FA	
1		3	4	5	8				7	11	2	9			10			6						R3
1		3	4	5	8				7	11	2	9			10			6						rep
2		2	2	2	2				2	2	2	2			2			2						
					1					1														

1951-52

Division One

	P	W	D	L	F	A	Pts
Manchester United	42	23	11	8	95	52	57
Tottenham Hotspur	42	22	9	11	76	51	53
Arsenal	42	21	11	10	80	61	53
Portsmouth	42	20	8	14	68	58	48
Bolton Wanderers	42	19	10	13	65	61	48
Aston Villa	42	19	9	14	79	70	47
Preston North End	42	17	12	13	74	54	46
Newcastle United	42	18	9	15	98	73	45
Blackpool	42	18	9	15	64	64	45
Charlton Athletic	42	17	10	15	68	63	44
Liverpool	42	12	19	11	57	61	43
Sunderland	42	15	12	15	70	61	42
West Bromwich Albion	42	14	13	15	74	77	41
Burnley	42	15	10	17	56	63	40
Manchester City	42	13	13	16	58	61	39
Wolverhampton W	42	12	14	16	73	73	38
Derby County	42	15	7	20	63	80	37
Middlesbrough	42	15	6	21	64	88	36
Chelsea	42	14	8	20	52	72	36
Stoke City	42	12	7	23	49	88	31
Huddersfield Town	42	10	8	24	49	82	28
Fulham	42	8	11	23	58	77	27

Manager: Jack Smith

- Johnny Nicholls made his Albion debut in the fifth-round FA Cup tie at Blackburn, replacing the injured Ronnie Allen.
- Jack Vernon completed five years' service with Albion and returned to Ireland to sign for Crusaders. He made exactly 200 appearances for the club. Fred Richardson moved north to Chester, Cyril Williams to Chippenham Town (as manager) and Eddie Wilcox to Worcester City.
- Albion's 'A' team beat Bearwood Juniors 36–0 in a Handsworth League game. Centre-forward Kenny Knight scored 15 times, including a hat-trick in three minutes.

Match No.	Date			Opponents	Result		Scorers	Attendance
1	Aug	18	H	Manchester United	D	3-3	Allen, Smith 2	29,897
2		20	A	Stoke City	D	1-1	Smith	22,752
3		25	A	Tottenham Hotspur	L	1-3	Allen	51,544
4		29	H	Stoke City	W	1-0	Allen	18,903
5	Sep	1	H	Preston North End	D	1-1	Allen	27,645
6		5	H	Newcastle United	D	3-3	McMichael (og), McCall, Lee	29,311
7		8	A	Burnley	L	1-6	Smith	23,868
8		15	H	Charlton Athletic	D	1-1	Allen	23,197
9		22	A	Fulham	L	0-1		26,139
10		29	H	Middlesbrough	L	2-3	Smith, Allen	28,961
11	Oct	6	H	Huddersfield Town	D	0-0		24,236
12		13	A	Chelsea	W	3-1	Carter, Allen 2	34,917
13		20	H	Portsmouth	W	5-0	Griffin 2, Smith, Kennedy, Allen (pen)	26,736
14		27	A	Liverpool	W	5-2	Ryan, Lee, Griffin 2, Allen	34,891
15	Nov	3	H	Blackpool	D	1-1	Allen	43,214
16		10	A	Arsenal	L	3-6	Allen 2, Griffin	50,431
17		17	H	Manchester City	W	3-2	Lee, Griffin, Allen	32,126
18		24	A	Derby County	L	1-2	Lee	21,811
19	Dec	1	H	Aston Villa	L	1-2	Allen	47,782
20		8	A	Sunderland	D	3-3	Lee, Allen, Hall (og)	26,774
21		15	A	Manchester United	L	1-5	Allen	29,402
22		22	H	Tottenham Hotspur	W	3-1	Dudley 2, Allen	30,094
23		25	A	Bolton Wanderers	L	2-3	Dudley, Rickaby	32,562
24		26	H	Bolton Wanderers	W	3-2	Allen 3	37,822
25		29	A	Preston North End	L	0-1		32,814
26	Jan	5	H	Burnley	D	1-1	Lee	26,115
27		19	A	Charlton Athletic	D	3-3	Lee, Allen, Griffin	18,126
28		26	H	Fulham	L	0-2		24,375
29	Feb	9	A	Middlesbrough	W	1-0	Lee	21,604
30		16	A	Huddersfield Town	L	0-3		16,983
31	Mar	1	H	Chelsea	L	0-1		24,431
32		12	A	Portsmouth	D	1-1	Nicholls	21,721
33		15	H	Liverpool	D	3-3	Ryan, Allen 2	27,183
34		22	A	Blackpool	L	0-2		20,128
35	Apr	5	A	Manchester City	W	2-1	Nicholls, Allen	13,933
36		12	H	Derby County	W	1-0	Allen	27,733
37		14	H	Wolverhampton Wanderers	W	2-1	Griffin, Nicholls	33,429
38		15	A	Wolverhampton Wanderers	W	4-1	Allen 3, Nicholls	35,940
39		19	A	Aston Villa	L	0-2		50,137
40		21	H	Arsenal	W	3-1	Allen, Lee, Ryan	29,618
41		23	A	Newcastle United	W	4-1	Ryan, Nicholls, Allen, Lee	31,188
42		26	H	Sunderland	D	1-1	Allen (pen)	31,154
								Appearances
								Goals

FA Cup

R3	Jan	12	H	Bolton Wanderers	W	4-0	Lee 2, Allen, Griffin	38,428
R4	Feb	6	A	Gateshead	W	2-0	Allen 2	38,681
R5		23	A	Blackburn Rovers	L	0-1		51,177
								Appearances
								Goals

R4 played at St James' Park, Newcastle

Sanders JA	Rickaby S	Millard L	Dudley JG	Vernon J	Ryan RA	Allen R	Smith AE	Richardson F	McCall A	Lee GT	Gordon DW	Kennedy JP	Heath NH	Barlow RJ	Carter W	Griffin FA	Horne HL	Williams SG	Nicholls J	Cutler RV	Corbett G	
1	2	3	4	5	6	7	8	9	10	11												1
1	2	3	4	5	6	7	8	9	10	11												2
1	2	3	4	5	6	7	8	9	10	11												3
1	2	3	4	5	6	7	8		10	11	9											4
1	2	3	4	5	6	7	8		10	11	9											5
1	2	3	4		6	7	8	9	10	11		5										6
1	2	3	4		6	7	8	9	10	11		5										7
	2	3		5	6	7	8		10	11		4	1	9								8
	2	3		5	6	7			10	11		4	1	9	8							9
	2	3		5	10	9	8			11		4	1	6		7						10
	2	3			4	9	8		10	11		5	1	6		7						11
	2	3		5	10	9				11		4	1	6	8	7						12
	2	3		5	10	9	8			11		4	1	6		7						13
	2	3		5	10	9	8			11		4	1	6		7						14
	2	3		5	10	9	8			11		4	1	6		7						15
	2	3		5	10	9	8			11		4	1	6		7						16
1	2	3		5	10	9			8	11		4		6		7						17
1	2	3		5	10	9			8	11		4		6		7						18
1	2	3		5	10	9			8	11		4		6		7						19
1	2	3		5	10	9			8	11		4		6		7						20
1	2	3	6	5	10	9			8	11		4				7						21
1	2	3	8	5	10	9				11		4		6		7						22
1	2	3	8	5	10	9				11		4		6		7						23
1	2	3	8	5	10	9				11		4		6		7						24
	2	3	8		10	9				11		4	1	6		7	5					25
	2	3	8		10	9				11		4	1	6		7	5					26
	2	3	8		10	9				11		4	1	6		7	5					27
	2	3	8		10	9				11		4	1	6		7	5					28
	2	3	8		10	9				11		4	1	6		7	5					29
	2	3	4		10				8	11			1	6		7	5	9				30
	2		8	5	10					11		4	1			7	3	6	9			31
	2	3			10	9				11		4	1	6		7	5		8			32
	2	3			10	9				11		4	1	6		7	5		8			33
	2	3			10	9				11		4	1	6		7	5		8			34
	2	3	4		10	9				11		5	1	6		7			8			35
	2	3	4		10	9						5	1	6		7			8	11		36
	2	3	4		10	9						5	1	6		7			8	11		37
	2	3	4		10	9						5	1	6		7			8		11	38
	2	3	4		10	9				11		5	1	6		7			8			39
	2	3	4		10	9				11		5	1	6		7			8			40
	2	3	4		10	9				11		5	1	6		7			8			41
	2	3	4		10	9				11		5	1	6		7			8			42
15	42	41	26	22	42	40	14	5	16	39	2	36	27	33	2	33	10	2	12	2	1	
	1		3		4	32	6		1	10		1			1	8			5			

Two own-goals

	2	3	8		10	9				11		4	1	6		7	5					R3
	2	3	8		10	9				11		4	1	6		7	5					R4
	2	3	8		6				10	11		4	1			7	5		9			R5
	3	3	3		3	2			1	3		3	3	2		3	3		1			
						3				2						1						

1952-53

Division One

	P	W	D	L	F	A	Pts
Arsenal	42	21	12	9	97	64	54
Preston North End	42	21	12	9	85	60	54
Wolverhampton W	42	19	13	10	86	63	51
West Bromwich Albion	42	21	8	13	66	60	50
Charlton Athletic	42	19	11	12	77	63	49
Burnley	42	18	12	12	67	52	48
Blackpool	42	19	9	14	71	70	47
Manchester United	42	18	10	14	69	72	46
Sunderland	42	15	13	14	68	82	43
Tottenham Hotspur	42	15	11	16	78	69	41
Aston Villa	42	14	13	15	63	61	41
Cardiff City	42	14	12	16	54	46	40
Middlesbrough	42	14	11	17	70	77	39
Bolton Wanderers	42	15	9	18	61	69	39
Portsmouth	42	14	10	18	74	83	38
Newcastle United	42	14	9	19	59	70	37
Liverpool	42	14	8	20	61	82	36
Sheffield Wednesday	42	12	11	19	62	72	35
Chelsea	42	12	11	19	56	66	35
Manchester City	42	14	7	21	72	87	35
Stoke City	42	12	10	20	53	66	34
Derby County	42	11	10	21	59	74	32

Manager: Jesse Carver and then Vic Buckingham

- Albion had two managers this season – first Jesse Carver and then the former Spurs full-back Vic Buckingham, who took charge in February when Albion were in the throws of a long, drawn out FA Cup tie with Chelsea.
- Elfed Evans was signed from Cardiff City and Andy McCall joined from Leeds United.
- Albion lost 3–1 to Wolves in a Coronation Cup game at The Hawthorns.
- Albion played their 2,000th League game this season against Manchester United (h) in November.

Match No.	Date			Opponents	Result		Scorers	Attendance
1	Aug	23	A	Tottenham Hotspur	W	4-3	Clarke (og), Allen 2, Lee	56,552
2		27	H	Newcastle United	W	1-0	Lee	46,206
3		30	H	Burnley	L	1-2	Allen	31,543
4	Sep	6	A	Preston North End	L	0-1		34,109
5		10	H	Cardiff City	W	1-0	Barlow	23,494
6		13	H	Stoke City	W	3-2	Griffin, Ryan, Allen	27,409
7		17	A	Cardiff City	W	2-1	Dudley, Allen	40,338
8		20	A	Manchester City	W	1-0	Allen	33,143
9		27	H	Liverpool	W	3-0	Griffin 2, Allen	33,142
10	Oct	4	A	Middlesbrough	L	2-4	Allan, Evans	24,420
11		11	A	Sunderland	L	0-1		40,756
12		18	H	Wolverhampton Wanderers	D	1-1	Lee	54,480
13		25	A	Charlton Athletic	D	0-0		24,550
14	Nov	1	H	Arsenal	W	2-0	Lee, Ryan	43,041
15		8	A	Derby County	D	1-1	Lee	26,234
16		15	H	Blackpool	L	0-1		33,869
17		22	A	Chelsea	W	2-0	Allen, Nicholls	35,304
18		29	H	Manchester United	W	3-1	Allen, Lee, Griffin	23,617
19	Dec	6	A	Portsmouth	W	2-1	Griffin, Allen	27,365
20		13	H	Bolton Wanderers	L	0-1		16,250
21		20	H	Tottenham Hotspur	W	2-1	Ryan, Allen	18,816
22		26	A	Sheffield Wednesday	W	5-4	Curtis (og), Barlow, Gannon (og), Nicholls, Allen	59,398
23		27	H	Sheffield Wednesday	L	0-1		52,681
24	Jan	1	A	Newcastle United	W	5-3	Ryan, Lee, Nicholls, Griffin, Barlow	48,944
25		3	A	Burnley	L	0-5		35,780
26		17	H	Preston North End	W	2-1	Ryan, Nicholls	44,763
27		24	A	Stoke City	L	1-5	Nicholls	34,807
28	Feb	7	H	Manchester City	W	2-1	Allen, Barlow	27,932
29		14	A	Liverpool	L	0-3		25,313
30		21	H	Middlesbrough	W	3-0	Allen 2, Lee	24,433
31		28	H	Sunderland	D	1-1	Ryan	31,831
32	Mar	7	A	Wolverhampton Wanderers	L	0-2		48,275
33		14	H	Charlton Athletic	W	3-1	Evans, Griffin 2	26,944
34		21	A	Arsenal	D	2-2	Evans, Lee	49,078
35		28	H	Derby County	D	2-2	Ryan, Lee	17,686
36	Apr	4	A	Blackpool	L	0-2		30,592
37		6	H	Aston Villa	W	3-2	Allen 2 (1 pen), Griffin	34,310
38		7	A	Aston Villa	D	1-1	Allen	46,821
39		11	H	Chelsea	L	0-1		34,207
40		18	A	Manchester United	D	2-2	Hodgkisson, Ryan	33,161
41		22	A	Bolton Wanderers	W	1-0	Allen	17,189
42		25	H	Portsmouth	W	2-0	Hodgkisson 2	24,879
								Appearances
								Goals

FA Cup

R3	Jan	10	A	West Ham United	W	4-1	Lee, Ryan, Allen, Nicholls	35,150
R4		31	A	Chelsea	D	1-1	Nicholls	58,912
rep	Feb	4	H	Chelsea	D	0-0*		37,974
rep2		9	N	Chelsea	D	1-1*	Dudley	33,534
rep3		11	N	Chelsea	L	0-4		27,997
								Appearances
								Goals

Replay 2 at Villa Park, Birmingham, replay 3 at Highbury

* after extra-time

	Heath NH	Rickaby S	Millard L	Dudley JG	Kennedy JP	Barlow RJ	Griffin FA	Nicholls J	Allen R	Ryan RA	Lee GT	Evans EE	Williams SG	Cutler RV	Dugdale JR	Gallagher M	Mountford D	Sanders JA	Carter W	Hodgkisson WK
1	1	2	3	4	5	6	7	8	9	10	11									
2	1	2	3	4	5	6	7	8	9	10	11									
3	1	2	3	4	5	6	7	8	9	10	11									
4	1	2	3	4	5	6	7	8	9	10	11									
5	1	2	3	4	5	6	7		9	10	11	8								
6	1	2	3	4	5	6	7		9	10	11	8								
7	1	2	3	4	5	6	7		9	10	11	8								
8	1	2	3	4	5	6	7		9	10	11	8								
9	1	2	3	4	5	6	7		9	10	11	8								
10	1	2	3	4		6	7		9	10	11	8	5							
11	1	2	3	4	5	6	7		9	10	11	8								
12	1	2	3	4	5	6	7		9	10	11	8								
13	1	2	3	4	5	6	7	8	9	10	11									
14	1	2	3	4	5	6	7	8	9	10	11									
15	1	2	3	4	5	6	7	8	9	10	11									
16	1	2	3	4	5	6	7	8	9		11			10						
17	1	2	3	4	5	6	7	8	9	10	11									
18	1	2	3	4	5	6	7	8	9	10	11									
19	1	2	3	4	5	6	7	8	9	10	11									
20	1	2	3	4		6	7	8		10	11	9			5					
21	1	2	3	4	5	6	7	8	9	10	11									
22	1	2	3	4	5	6	7	8	9	10	11									
23	1	2	3	4	5	6	7	8	9	10	11									
24	1	2	3	4	5	6	7	8	9	10	11									
25	1	2	3	4	5		7	8	9	10			6			11				
26	1	2	3	4	5	6	7	8	9	10	11									
27	1	2	3	4	5	6	7	8	9	10	11									
28	1	2	3	4	5	6	7	8	9	10	11									
29	1	2		4		6			9	10	11	8	3		5		7			
30	1	2	3	4		6			9	10	11	8			5		7			
31	1	2	3	4		6			9	10	11	8			5		7			
32	1	2	3	4		6			9	10	11	8			5		7			
33	1	2	3	4		6	7		9	10	11	8			5					
34	1	2	3	4		6	7		9	10	11	8			5					
35	1	2	3	4		6	7		9	10	11	8			5					
36	1	2	3	4		6	7		9	10	11	8			5					
37		2	3	4		6	7		9	10	11				5			1	8	
38		2	3	4		6	7		9	8	11				5			1		10
39		2	3	4		6	7		9	8	11				5			1		10
40		2	3	4		6		7	9	10	11				5			1		8
41		2	3	4		6		7	9	10	11				5			1		8
42		2	3	4		6		7	9		11				5			1	8	10
	36	42	41	42	26	41	35	23	41	40	41	17	3	1	15	1	4	6	2	5
				1		4	9	5	20	8	10	3								3

Three own-goals

	Heath NH	Rickaby S	Millard L	Dudley JG	Kennedy JP	Barlow RJ	Griffin FA	Nicholls J	Allen R	Ryan RA	Lee GT	Evans EE	Williams SG	Cutler RV	Dugdale JR	Gallagher M	Mountford D	Sanders JA	Carter W	Hodgkisson WK
R3	1	2	3	4	5		7	8	9	10	11		6							
R4	1		3	4		6		8	9	10	11		2		5		7			
rep	1		3	4	5	6	7	8	9	10	11		2							
rep2	1	2	3	4		6	7	8	9	10	11				5					
rep3	1	2		4		6	7	8	9	10	11		3		5					
	5	3	4	5	2	4	4	5	5	5	5		4		3		1			
				1				2	1	1	1									

1953-54

Division One

	P	W	D	L	F	A	Pts
Wolverhampton W	42	25	7	10	96	56	57
West Bromwich Albion	42	22	9	11	86	63	53
Huddersfield Town	42	20	11	11	78	61	51
Manchester United	42	18	12	12	73	58	48
Bolton Wanderers	42	18	12	12	75	60	48
Blackpool	42	19	10	13	80	69	48
Burnley	42	21	4	17	78	67	46
Chelsea	42	16	12	14	74	68	44
Charlton Athletic	42	19	6	17	75	77	44
Cardiff City	42	18	8	16	51	71	44
Preston North End	42	19	5	18	87	58	43
Arsenal	42	15	13	14	75	73	43
Aston Villa	42	16	9	17	70	68	41
Portsmouth	42	14	11	17	81	89	39
Newcastle United	42	14	10	18	72	77	38
Tottenham Hotspur	42	16	5	21	65	76	37
Manchester City	42	14	9	19	62	77	37
Sunderland	42	14	8	20	81	89	36
Sheffield Wednesday	42	15	6	21	70	91	36
Sheffield United	42	11	11	20	69	90	33
Middlesbrough	42	10	10	22	60	91	30
Liverpool	42	9	10	23	68	97	28

Manager: Vic Buckingham

- Albion, so close to completing the double, scored late on through Frank Griffin to beat Preston in the FA Cup Final.
- The crowd of 99,852 at Wembley for that Final is the biggest any Albion team has ever played in front of.
- Albion goalkeeper Norman Heath was so badly injured in the League game at Sunderland in March that he never played football again.
- Derek Kevan was signed from Bradford Park Avenue and Freddie Cox was recruited from Arsenal, with whom he gained FA Cup-winners' medals in 1950 and 1952 and a League Championship medal in 1953.
- Albion were applauded off the pitch at St James' Park after whipping Newcastle United 7–3 in September – the finest performance displayed by an Albion side away from home since the mid-1930s.

Match No.	Date			Opponents	Result		Scorers	Attendance
1	Aug	19	H	Arsenal	W	2-0	Nicholls 2	41,812
2		22	H	Bolton Wanderers	D	1-1	Barlow	29,122
3		26	A	Manchester United	W	3-1	Dudley, Nicholls, Lee	33,652
4		29	A	Preston North End	W	2-0	Nicholls 2	30,462
5	Sep	2	H	Manchester United	W	2-0	Allen, Hodgkisson	29,036
6		5	H	Tottenham Hotspur	W	3-0	Allen, Nicholls, Ramsey (og)	43,168
7		9	H	Newcastle United	D	2-2	Ryan, Barlow	32,953
8		12	A	Burnley	W	4-1	Nicholls 2, Allen, Ryan	38,948
9		16	A	Newcastle United	W	7-3	Nicholls 3, Allen 2, Griffin, Ryan	58,075
10		19	H	Charlton Athletic	L	2-3	Barlow, Griffin	43,809
11		26	A	Sheffield Wednesday	W	3-2	Griffin, Nicholls, Lee	44,573
12	Oct	3	H	Middlesbrough	W	2-1	Nicholls, Lee	37,042
13		10	H	Huddersfield Town	W	4-0	Allen 3, Nicholls	47,043
14		17	A	Sheffield United	W	2-1	Allen, Nicholls	38,367
15		24	H	Chelsea	W	5-2	Allen 3, Nicholls, Lee	35,443
16		31	A	Blackpool	L	1-4	Allen	27,106
17	Nov	7	H	Sunderland	W	2-0	Barlow, Lee	37,704
18		14	A	Wolverhampton Wanderers	L	0-1		56,590
19		21	H	Cardiff City	W	6-1	Allen 4, Nicholls 2	39,618
20		28	A	Manchester City	W	3-2	Lee, Allen, Nicholls	40,753
21	Dec	5	H	Portsmouth	L	2-3	Nicholls, Allen	29,623
22		12	A	Arsenal	D	2-2	Nicholls 2	55,264
23		19	A	Bolton Wanderers	L	1-2	Ryan	32,246
24		25	H	Liverpool	W	5-2	Nicholls, Griffin 2, Barlow, Allen	30,390
25		26	A	Liverpool	D	0-0		51,167
26	Jan	2	H	Preston North End	W	3-2	Allen 2, Nicholls	20,306
27		16	A	Tottenham Hotspur	W	1-0	Allen	48,812
28		23	H	Burnley	D	0-0		42,650
29	Feb	6	A	Charlton Athletic	D	1-1	Allen	27,553
30		13	H	Sheffield Wednesday	W	4-2	Nicholls, Butler (og), Rickaby, Ryan	38,475
31		24	A	Middlesbrough	D	1-1	Allen	17,144
32		27	A	Huddersfield Town	W	2-0	Ryan, Nicholls	48,237
33	Mar	6	H	Sheffield United	D	2-2	Nicholls, Lee	37,650
34		17	A	Chelsea	L	0-5		46,089
35		20	H	Blackpool	W	2-1	Allen, Ryan	53,210
36		31	A	Sunderland	L	1-2	Cox	26,632
37	Apr	3	H	Wolverhampton Wanderers	L	0-1		49,884
38		10	A	Cardiff City	L	0-2		43,614
39		17	H	Manchester City	W	1-0	Allen (pen)	38,742
40		19	H	Aston Villa	D	1-1	Nicholls	45,972
41		20	A	Aston Villa	L	1-6	Griffin	57,899
42		24	A	Portsmouth	L	0-3		28,004

Appearances

Goals

FA Cup

R3	Jan	9	H	Chelsea	W	1-0	Greenwood (og)	35,294
R4		30	H	Rotherham United	W	4-0	Nicholls 2, Allen, Ryan	48,242
R5	Feb	20	H	Newcastle United	W	3-2	Allen 3	61,088
R6	Mar	13	H	Tottenham Hotspur	W	3-0	Barlow, Nicholls 2	51,049
SF		27	N	Port Vale	W	2-1	Dudley, Allen (pen)	68,221
F	May	1	N	Preston North End	W	3-2	Alllen 2 (1 pen), Griffin	99,852

SF at Villa Park, Final at Wembley Stadium

Appearances

Goals

	Heath NH	Rickaby S	Millard L	Dudley JG	Dugdale JR	Barlow RJ	Griffin FA	Hodgkisson WK	Allen R	Nicholls J	Lee GT	Ryan RA	Williams SG	Cox FJA	Brookes WA	Kennedy JP	Carter W	Sanders JA	Jones GA	Cutler RV	Davies RW
1	1	2	3	4	5	6	7	8	9	10	11										
2	1	2	3	4	5	6	7	8	9	10	11										
3	1	2	3	4	5	6	7	8	9	10	11										
4	1	2	3	4	5	6	7	8	9	10	11										
5	1	2	3	4	5	6	7	8	9	10	11										
6	1	2	3	4	5	6	7		9	10	11	8									
7	1	2	3	4	5	6	7		9	10	11	8									
8	1	2	3	4	5	6	7		9	10	11	8									
9	1	2	3	4	5	6	7		9	10	11	8									
10	1	2	3	4	5	6	7		9	10	11	8									
11	1	2		4	5	6	7		9	10	11	8	3								
12	1	2	3	4	5	6	7		9	10	11			8							
13	1	2	3	4	5		7		9	10	11	8			6						
14	1	2	3	4	5	6	7		9	10	11	8									
15	1	2	3	4	5	6	7		9	10	11	8									
16	1	2	3	4	5	6	7		9	10	11	8									
17	1	2	3	4		6	7		9	8	11	10				5					
18	1	2	3	4		6	7		9	8	11	10				5					
19	1		3	4		6	7		9	10	11	8	2			5					
20	1	2	3	4		6	7		9	10	11	8				5					
21	1	2	3	4		6	7		9	10	11	8				5					
22	1	2	3	4		6	7		9	10	11	8				5					
23	1	2	3	4		6	7		9	10	11	8				5					
24	1	2	3	4		6	7		9	10	11	8				5					
25	1	2	3	4		6	7		9	10	11	8				5					
26	1	2	3	4		6	7		9	10	11	8				5					
27	1	2	3	4	5	6	7		9		11	8					10				
28	1	2	3	4	5	6	7		9	10	11	8									
29	1	2	3	4	5	6	7		9		11	8					10				
30	1	2	3	4	5		7		9	10	11	8			6						
31	1	2	3	4	5	6	7		9	10	11	8									
32		2	3	4	5	6	7		9	10	11	8						1			
33		2	3	4	5	6	7		9	10	11	8						1			
34	1	2	3	4	5	6	7		9	10	11	8									
35	1		3	4	5	6	7		9	10	11	8	2								
36	1			4	5	6					11	8	3	9		2	10		7		
37			3	4	5	9						8	2	7		6	10	1		11	
38			3	4	5				9	10	11	8	2	7		6		1			
39			3	4	5	6	7		9	10	11	8	2					1			
40			3	4	5	6	7		9	10	11	8	2					1			
41			3	4	5	6	7		9	10	11	8	2					1			
42			3	4	5	6				10	11	8	2				9		7		1
	34	33	40	42	32	39	38	5	39	38	41	36	10	4	2	13	5	7	2	1	1
		1		1		5	6	1	27	28	7	7		1							

Two own-goals

	Heath NH	Rickaby S	Millard L	Dudley JG	Dugdale JR	Barlow RJ	Griffin FA	Hodgkisson WK	Allen R	Nicholls J	Lee GT	Ryan RA	Williams SG	Cox FJA	Brookes WA	Kennedy JP	Carter W	Sanders JA	Jones GA	Cutler RV	Davies RW
R3	1	2	3	4	5	6	7		9	10	11	8									
R4	1	2	3	4	5	6	7		9	10	11	8									
R5	1	2	3	4	5	6	7		9	10	11	8									
R6	1	2	3	4	5	6	7		9	10	11	8									
SF	1	2	3	4	5	6	7		9	10	11	8									
F			3	4	5	6	7		9	10	11	8				2		1			
	5	5	6	6	6	6	6		6	6	6	6				1		1			
				1		1	1		7	4		1									

One own-goal

1954-55

Division One

	P	W	D	L	F	A	Pts
Chelsea	42	20	12	10	81	57	52
Wolverhampton W	42	19	10	13	89	70	48
Portsmouth	42	18	12	12	74	62	48
Sunderland	42	15	18	9	64	54	48
Manchester United	42	20	7	15	84	74	47
Aston Villa	42	20	7	15	72	73	47
Manchester City	42	18	10	14	76	69	46
Newcastle United	42	17	9	16	89	77	43
Arsenal	42	17	9	16	69	63	43
Burnley	42	17	9	16	51	48	43
Everton	42	16	10	16	62	68	42
Huddersfield Town	42	14	13	15	63	68	41
Sheffield United	42	17	7	18	70	86	41
Preston North End	42	16	8	18	83	64	40
Charlton Athletic	42	15	10	17	76	75	40
Tottenham Hotspur	42	16	8	18	72	73	40
West Bromwich Albion	42	16	8	18	76	96	40
Bolton Wanderers	42	13	13	16	62	69	39
Blackpool	42	14	10	18	60	64	38
Cardiff City	42	13	11	18	62	76	37
Leicester City	42	12	11	19	74	86	35
Sheffield Wednesday	42	8	10	24	63	100	26

Manager: Vic Buckingham

- Albion drew 4–4 with Wolves in the annual FA Charity Shield game under the Molineux floodlights in September.
- In October Albion lost 5–3 to the crack Hungarian side Honved in a festival game in front of 55,000 fans in Brussels. Honved featured several internationals including Grosics, Bozsik, Puskas, Kocsis, Tichy and Czibor.
- Future FA Cup and League Cup-winning captain Graham Williams was signed from Rhyl Athletic, and Maurice Setters arrived from Exeter City for £3,000. Stan Rickaby left to join Poole Town after 205 games for the club, while Reg Ryan switched to Derby County after 272 appearances for Albion.
- Albion's youngsters lost to Manchester United (the Busby Babes) in the FA Youth Cup Final.

Match No.	Date			Opponents	Result		Scorers	Attendance
1	Aug	21	A	Sunderland	L	2-4	Ryan, Nicholls	56,827
2		25	A	Newcastle United	L	0-3		58,548
3		28	H	Arsenal	W	3-1	Allen, Ryan, Nicholls	46,247
4	Sep	1	H	Newcastle United	W	4-2	Nicholls 2, Allen, Ryan	36,414
5		4	A	Sheffield United	W	2-1	Carter, Allen	27,232
6		8	A	Everton	W	2-1	Griffin, Allen	55,147
7		11	H	Preston North End	W	2-0	Lee, Allen	41,125
8		15	H	Everton	D	3-3	Allen 2, Lee	32,442
9		18	A	Burnley	W	2-0	Allen 2,	29,727
10		25	H	Leicester City	W	6-4	Allen, Griffin, Nicholls 3, Lee	48,422
11	Oct	2	A	Chelsea	D	3-3	Allen, Lee, Millard	67,440
12		9	A	Tottenham Hotspur	L	1-3	Nicholls	45,547
13		16	H	Sheffield Wednesday	L	1-2	Lee	35,407
14		23	A	Wolverhampton Wanderers	L	0-4		55,374
15		30	H	Aston Villa	L	2-3	Allen, Lee	51,833
16	Nov	6	A	Charlton Athletic	W	3-1	Jackson, Allen 2	36,074
17		13	H	Bolton Wanderers	D	0-0		35,136
18		20	A	Huddersfield Town	D	3-3	Nicholls, Lee 2	28,372
19		27	H	Manchester United	W	2-0	Nicholls, Allen (pen)	33,267
20	Dec	4	A	Portsmouth	L	1-6	Allen	28,027
21		11	H	Blackpool	L	0-1		33,792
22		18	H	Sunderland	D	2-2	Williams, Nicholls	27,828
23		25	A	Cardiff City	L	2-3	Carter, Allen	22,845
24		27	H	Cardiff City	W	1-0	Millard	51,051
25	Jan	1	A	Arsenal	D	2-2	Allen, Nicholls	40,246
26		22	A	Preston North End	L	1-3	Williams	23,464
27	Feb	5	H	Burnley	D	2-2	Ryan, Allen	22,896
28		12	A	Leicester City	L	3-6	Carter 2, Lee	28,785
29	Mar	5	A	Blackpool	L	1-3	Carter	20,430
30		9	H	Chelsea	L	2-4	Allen 2	7,764
31		12	H	Sheffield United	D	3-3	Carter 2, Barlow	22,249
32		16	H	Wolverhampton Wanderers	W	1-0	Lee	28,573
33		19	A	Aston Villa	L	0-3		40,175
34		26	H	Charlton Athletic	W	2-1	Griffin, Lee	8,191
35	Apr	2	A	Bolton Wanderers	W	4-2	Allen 2, Lee, Carter	17,715
36		8	A	Manchester City	L	0-4		57,663
37		9	H	Portsmouth	W	3-1	Carter, Allen, Griffin	27,696
38		11	H	Manchester City	W	2-1	Griffin, Lee	30,303
39		16	A	Manchester United	L	0-3		26,568
40		23	H	Huddersfield Town	W	2-1	Allen 2	18,661
41		27	H	Tottenham Hotspur	L	1-2	Allen	16,743
42		30	A	Sheffield Wednesday	L	0-5		15,671
								Appearances
								Goals

FA Cup

R3	Jan	8	A	Bournemouth	W	1-0	Williams	22,794
R4		29	H	Charlton Athletic	L	2-4	Williams 2	36,264
								Appearances
								Goals

Sanders JA	Rickaby S	Millard L	Dudley JG	Dugdale JR	Barlow RJ	Griffin FA	Ryan RA	Allen R	Nicholls J	Lee GT	Kennedy JP	Carter W	Williams SG	Davies RW	Jackson A	Crowshaw AA	Barnsley GRT	Hodgkisson WK	Brookes WA	Cutler RV	Jones RG	
1	2	3	4	5	6	7	8	9	10	11												1
1	2	3	4		6	7	8	9	10	11	5											2
1	2	3	4		6	7	8	9	10	11	5											3
1	2	3	4		6	7	8	9	10	11	5											4
1	2	3	4		6	7	8	9		11	5	10										5
1	2	3	4		6	7	8	9		11	5	10										6
1	2	3	4		6	7	8	9		11	5	10										7
1	2	3	4		6	7	8	9		11	5	10										8
1	2	3	4		6	7	8	9		11	5	10										9
1	2	3	4		6	7	8	9	10	11	5											10
1	2	3	4	5		7	8	9		11	6		10									11
1	2	3	4	5		7	8	9	10	11	6											12
1	2	3	4			7	6	9	10	11	5	8										13
1	2	3	4		6	7	8	9	10	11	5											14
	2	3	4			7	8	9	10	11	5		6	1								15
1	2	3	4			7		9			5	8	6		10	11						16
1	2	3	4			7	8	9		11	5		6		10							17
1	2	3	4			7	8	9	10	11	5		6									18
1	2	3	4			7	8	9	10		5	11	6									19
1	2	3	4			7	8	9	10		5	11	6									20
1	2	3	4			7	8	9	10	11	5		6									21
1	2	3	4	5	6			9	10	11		7	8									22
1	2	3	4	5	6			9	10	11		7	8									23
1	2	3	4	5	6	7	10	9					8			11						24
1	2	3	4	5	6	7		9	10				8			11						25
	2	3	4	5	6	7		9	10	11			8				1					26
	2	3	4	5	6	7	10	9		11			8	1								27
		3	4	5	6	7	10	9		11	2	8		1								28
1	2	3	4	5	6	7		9		11		8						10				29
1	2	3	4	5	6	7		9		11		8						10				30
1	2	3	4	5	9			7		11		8						10	6			31
1		3	4		9		10	7		11	5	8	2						6			32
1		3	4		9		10	7		11	5	8	2						6			33
1		3	4		10	7		9		11	5	8	2						6			34
1		3	4		10	7		9		11	5	8	2						6			35
1		3	4		10	7		9		11	5	8	2						6			36
1		3	4		10	7		9		11	5	8	2						6			37
1		3	4		10	7		9		11	5	8	2						6			38
1		3	4		10	7		9		11	5	8	2						6			39
1		3	4		10	7		9		11	5	8	2						6			40
1		3	4		10	7		9		11	5	8	2						6			41
1		3	4		10			9		11	5	8	2						6	7		42
8	30	42	42	13	32	36	25	42	17	37	32	26	25	3	2	3	1	3	12	1		
		2			1	5	4	27	12	13		9	2		1							
[illegible]	2	3	4	5	6			9	10	11			8								7	R3
[illegible]	2	3	4	5	6	7		9	10	11			8									R4
2	2	2	2	2	2	1		2	2	2			2								1	
													3									

1955-56

Division One

	P	W	D	L	F	A	Pts
Manchester United	42	25	10	7	83	51	60
Blackpool	42	20	9	13	86	62	49
Wolverhampton W	42	20	9	13	89	65	49
Manchester City	42	18	10	14	82	69	46
Arsenal	42	18	10	14	60	61	46
Birmingham City	42	18	9	15	75	57	45
Burnley	42	18	8	16	64	54	44
Bolton Wanderers	42	18	7	17	71	58	43
Sunderland	42	17	9	16	80	95	43
Luton Town	42	17	8	17	66	64	42
Newcastle United	42	17	7	18	85	70	41
Portsmouth	42	16	9	17	78	85	41
West Bromwich Albion	42	18	5	19	58	70	41
Charlton Athletic	42	17	6	19	75	81	40
Everton	42	15	10	17	55	69	40
Chelsea	42	14	11	17	64	77	39
Cardiff City	42	15	9	18	55	69	39
Tottenham Hotspur	42	15	7	20	61	71	37
Preston North End	42	14	8	20	73	72	36
Aston Villa	42	11	13	18	52	69	35
Huddersfield Town	42	14	7	21	54	83	35
Sheffield United	42	12	9	21	63	77	33

Manager: Vic Buckingham

- Two future England World Cup players – Don Howe and Derek Kevan – made their League debuts in the home game against Everton in August, Kevan scoring both goals in the 2–2 draw.
- Bobby Robson was signed from Fulham and FA Cup winner Jimmy Dugdale was transferred to Aston Villa, with whom he would gain a second Cup medal in 1957. Forward Kenny Hodgkisson also left The Hawthorns, signing for Walsall. He later returned to the club as coach and scout.

Match No.	Date			Opponents	Result		Scorers	Attendanc
1	Aug	20	H	Wolverhampton Wanderers	D	1-1	Nicholls	45,306
2		24	H	Everton	W	2-0	Kevan 2	24,402
3		27	A	Manchester United	L	1-3	Kevan	32,267
4		31	A	Everton	L	0-2		38,449
5	Sep	3	H	Sheffield United	W	2-1	Kevan, Nicholls	20,061
6		7	H	Newcastle United	D	1-1	Jackson	20,555
7		10	A	Preston North End	W	1-0	Docherty (og)	28,203
8		17	H	Burnley	W	1-0	Nicholls	23,510
9		24	A	Luton Town	W	2-0	Griffin, Allen (pen)	24,440
10	Oct	1	H	Charlton Athletic	D	3-3	Allen 2 (1 pen), Kennedy	31,168
11		8	H	Aston Villa	W	1-0	Nicholls	37,395
12		15	A	Sunderland	L	1-2	Allen (pen)	47,094
13		22	H	Cardiff City	W	2-1	Allen 2	22,286
14		29	A	Manchester City	L	0-2		25,081
15	Nov	5	H	Bolton Wanderers	W	2-0	Allen 2	23,808
16		12	A	Chelsea	L	0-2		41,898
17		19	H	Blackpool	L	1-2	Allen	38,294
18		26	A	Huddersfield Town	L	0-1		18,731
19	Dec	3	H	Portsmouth	W	4-0	Setters 2, Griffin, Lee	22,949
20		10	A	Arsenal	L	0-2		33,227
21		17	A	Wolverhampton Wanderers	L	2-3	Allen, Carter	31,068
22		24	H	Manchester United	L	1-4	Lee	25,286
23		26	A	Tottenham Hotspur	L	1-4	Allen (pen)	32,430
24		27	H	Tottenham Hotspur	W	1-0	Lee	31,522
25		31	A	Sheffield United	D	2-2	Allen, Lee	23,764
26	Jan	2	A	Newcastle United	W	3-0	Allen 3 (1 pen)	50,768
27		14	H	Preston North End	W	3-2	Crowshaw 2, Lee	22,471
28		21	A	Burnley	W	2-1	Lee, Griffin	23,749
29	Feb	4	H	Luton Town	W	3-1	Griffin, Lee, Williams	25,310
30		11	A	Charlton Athletic	L	1-5	Nicholls	13,573
31		25	H	Sunderland	W	3-0	Barlow, Griffin, Lee	23,620
32	Mar	3	A	Blackpool	L	1-5	Allen (pen)	19,768
33		10	H	Manchester City	L	0-4		32,680
34		17	A	Bolton Wanderers	L	0-4		23,603
35		24	H	Chelsea	W	3-0	Nicholls 2, Griffin	20,219
36		31	A	Cardiff City	W	3-1	Allen, Robson, Nicholls	31,641
37	Apr	2	A	Birmingham City	L	0-2		38,891
38		3	H	Birmingham City	L	0-2		35,986
39		7	H	Huddersfield Town	L	1-2	Horobin	16,141
40		14	A	Portsmouth	D	1-1	Lee	15,675
41		21	H	Arsenal	W	2-1	Lee, Goring (og)	22,392
42		28	A	Aston Villa	L	0-3		42,876
								Appearances
								Goals

FA Cup

R3	Jan	7	A	Wolverhampton Wanderers	W	2-1	Griffin, Lee	55,564
R4		28	H	Portsmouth	W	2-0	Lee, Allen (pen)	59,448
R5	Feb	18	H	Birmingham City	L	0-1		57,213
								Appearances
								Goals

Sanders JA	Williams SG	Millard L	Dudley JG	Kennedy JP	Barlow RJ	Griffin FA	Carter W	Allen R	Nicholls J	Lee GT	Howe D	Kevan DT	Jackson A	Hodgkisson WK	Perkins E	Dugdale JR	Brown F	Brookes WA	Crowshaw AA	Williams GE	Setters ME	Summers GT	Robson RW	Horobin R	Whitehouse B	
1	2	3	4	5	6	7	8	9	10	11																1
1		3	4	5	6	7	8		10	11	2	9														2
1		3	4	5	6	7	8		10	11	2	9														3
1		3	4	5	6	7	8		10	11	2	9														4
1	2	3	4	5	6	7	8		10	11		9														5
1	2	3	4	5	6	7			8	11		9	10													6
1	2	3	4	5	6	7			8	11		9	10													7
1	2	3	4	5	6	7		9	8	11				10												8
1	2	3	4	5	6	7		9	8	11				10												9
1	2		4	5	6	7		9	8	11				10	3											10
1	2	3	4	5	6	7		9	8	11				10												11
1	2	3	4	5	6	7		9	8	11				10												12
1		3	4		6	7		9	8	11	2			10		5										13
	2	3	4	5		7		9	8	11				10			1	6								14
1	2	3	4	5		7		9	10	11				8				6								15
1	2	3	4	5		7	8	9	10	11								6								16
1	2	3	4	5	6	8		9	10										7	11						17
1	2	3	4	5	6	7		9	10											11	8					18
1	2	3	4	5	6	7	10	9		11											8					19
1	2	3	4	5	6	7	10	9		11											8					20
1	2	3	4	5	6	7	10	9		11											8					21
1	2	3	4	5	8		9	10		11									7			6				22
1		3	4	5	8		9	10		11	2								7			6				23
1		3	4		8		9	10		11	2					5			7			6				24
1		3	4		8		9	10		11	2					5			7			6				25
1		3	4	5	9	7		10		11	2										8	6				26
1			4	5	9			10		11	2				3				7		8	6				27
1		3	4	5	9	7		10		11	2										8	6				28
1	10	3	4	5	9	7				11	2										8	6				29
1		3	4	5	9	7		10	8	11	2											6				30
1		3	4	5	9	7		10		11	2										8	6				31
1		3	4	5	9			10		11	2								7		8	6				32
1		3		5				10		11	2	9						4	7			6	8			33
1		3	4	5	10	7		9		11	2											6	8			34
1		3	4		5	7		9	10	11	2											6	8			35
1		3	4		5			9	10	11	2											6	8	7		36
1		3	4		5			9	10	11	2											6	8	7		37
1		3	4		5	7		9	10	11	2										6		8			38
1	10	3	4		5				9	11	2											6	8	7		39
1		3	4		5			9		11	2											6	8	7	10	40
1		3	4		5	7		9		11	2											6	8		10	41
1		3	4		5	7		9		11	2											6	8		10	42
41	20	40	41	31	38	31	13	34	24	40	24	7	2	8	2	3	1	4	8	2	11	20	10	4	3	
	1			1	1	6	1	17	8	10		4	1						2		2		1	1		

Two own-goals

1		3	4	5	9	7		10		11	2										8	6				R3
1		3	4	5	9	7		10		11	2										8	6				R4
1		3	4	5	9	7		10		11	2										8	6				R5
3		3	3	3	3	3		3		3	3										3	3				
						1		1		2																

1956-57

Division One

	P	W	D	L	F	A	Pts
Manchester United	42	28	8	6	103	54	64
Tottenham Hotspur	42	22	12	8	104	56	56
Preston North End	42	23	10	9	84	56	56
Blackpool	42	22	9	11	93	65	53
Arsenal	42	21	8	13	85	69	50
Wolverhampton W	42	20	8	14	94	70	48
Burnley	42	18	10	14	56	50	46
Leeds United	42	15	14	13	72	63	44
Bolton Wanderers	42	16	12	14	65	65	44
Aston Villa	42	14	15	13	65	55	43
West Bromwich Albion	42	14	14	14	59	61	42
Chelsea	42	13	13	16	73	73	39
Birmingham City	42	15	9	18	69	69	39
Sheffield Wednesday	42	16	6	20	82	88	38
Everton	42	14	10	18	61	79	38
Luton Town	42	14	9	19	58	76	37
Newcastle United	42	14	8	20	67	87	36
Manchester City	42	13	9	20	78	88	35
Portsmouth	42	10	13	19	62	92	33
Sunderland	42	12	8	22	67	88	32
Cardiff City	42	10	9	23	53	88	29
Charlton Athletic	42	9	4	29	62	120	22

Manager: Vic Buckingham

- Derek Kevan scored on his international debut for England against Scotland at Wembley (won 2–1).
- Albion led Aston Villa twice in the FA Cup semi-final showdown at Molineux before Peter McParland scored a second late equaliser. Ronnie Allen was injured in the replay when Billy Myerscough's stooping header decided the contest in favour of Villa.
- Two Black Country-born forwards left the club – Johnny Nicholls joined Cardiff City and Wilf Carter signed for Plymouth Argyle.
- Albion toured Soviet Russia in the summer of 1957, becoming the first professional team to win behind the Iron Curtain when they defeated Dynamo Tiblisi 3–0. They also drew 1–1 with FC Zenit and beat the CDSA (Red Army side) 4–2.

Match No.	Date			Opponents	Result		Scorers	Attendance
1	Aug	18	A	Sheffield Wednesday	L	2-4	Lee, Allen	22,013
2		22	H	Aston Villa	W	2-0	Robson, Whitehouse	37,255
3		25	H	Manchester United	L	2-3	Allen, Lee	26,516
4		27	A	Aston Villa	D	0-0		31,785
5	Sep	1	A	Arsenal	L	1-4	Whitehouse	39,973
6		5	H	Portsmouth	W	2-1	Robson, Kevan	15,059
7		8	H	Burnley	D	2-2	Allen, Griffin	23,746
8		15	A	Preston North End	L	2-3	Robson 2	28,380
9		22	H	Chelsea	W	2-1	Griffin, Kevan	24,684
10		29	A	Cardiff City	D	0-0		22,362
11	Oct	6	H	Wolverhampton Wanderers	D	1-1	Allen	34,379
12		13	A	Bolton Wanderers	D	1-1	Griffin	24,969
13		20	H	Sunderland	W	2-0	Robson, Allen (pen)	33,075
14		27	A	Luton Town	W	1-0	Kevan	16,786
15	Nov	3	H	Everton	W	3-0	Robson, Allen 2	23,810
16		10	A	Blackpool	W	1-0	Robson	18,839
17		17	H	Manchester City	D	1-1	Griffin	26,082
18		24	A	Charlton Athletic	L	2-3	Barlow, Kevan	16,361
19	Dec	1	H	Leeds United	D	0-0		29,135
20		8	A	Tottenham Hotspur	D	2-2	Kevan 2	36,098
21		15	H	Sheffield Wednesday	L	1-4	Kevan	17,150
22		25	H	Newcastle United	W	1-0	Barlow	13,780
23		26	A	Newcastle United	L	2-5	Kevan, Williams	20,319
24		29	H	Arsenal	L	0-2		26,162
25	Jan	12	A	Burnley	L	0-1		24,299
26		19	H	Preston North End	D	0-0		24,304
27	Feb	2	A	Chelsea	W	4-2	Kevan 2, Allen (pen), Robson	29,362
28		9	H	Cardiff City	L	1-2	Kevan	23,662
29		23	H	Luton Town	W	4-0	Dudley, Whitehouse, Griffin, Kevan	21,934
30	Mar	9	H	Tottenham Hotspur	D	1-1	Whitehouse	30,739
31		13	A	Sunderland	W	4-1	Kevan 2, Whitehouse, Allen	26,336
32		16	A	Everton	W	1-0	Kevan	36,116
33		30	A	Manchester City	L	1-2	Robson	26,361
34	Apr	3	H	Blackpool	L	1-3	Whitehouse	6,397
35		6	H	Charlton Athletic	D	2-2	Setters, Carter (pen)	15,055
36		13	A	Leeds United	D	0-0		20,905
37		15	A	Wolverhampton Wanderers	L	2-5	Robson 2	27,942
38		20	H	Bolton Wanderers	W	3-2	Whitehouse, Kevan, Robson	18,465
39		22	H	Birmingham City	D	0-0		18,828
40		23	A	Birmingham City	L	0-2		30,332
41		27	A	Portsmouth	W	1-0	Allen,	23,831
42		29	A	Manchester United	D	1-1	Millard (pen)	20,976

Appearances

Goals

FA Cup

R3	Jan	5	A	Doncaster Rovers	D	1-1	Robson	25,627
rep		9	H	Doncaster Rovers	W	2-0	Allen 2	18,043
R4		26	H	Sunderland	W	4-2	Kevan 2, Horobin, Allen (pen)	42,406
R5	Feb	16	A	Blackpool	D	0-0		32,707
rep		20	H	Blackpool	W	2-1	Kevan, Allen	48,054
R6	Mar	2	H	Arsenal	D	2-2	Allen, Wills (og)	53,459
rep		5	A	Arsenal	W	2-1	Whitehouse, Kevan	58,757
SF		23	N	Aston Villa	D	2-2	Whitehouse 2	55,549
rep		27	N	Aston Villa	L	0-1		58,067

SF at Molineux, Wolverhampton

SF replay at St Andrew's, Birmingham

Appearances

Goals

	Sanders JA	Howe D	Williams SG	Dudley JG	Barlow RJ	Summers GT	Griffin FA	Robson RW	Allen R	Whitehouse B	Lee GT	Brookes WA	Kennedy JP	Millard L	Kevan DT	Setters ME	Nicholls J	Horobin R	Carter W	Lee MJ	Brown F	Jackson A
1	1	2	3	4	5	6	7	8	9	10	11											
2	1	2	3	4	6		7	8	9	10	11	5										
3	1	2	3	4	6		7	8	9	10	11		5									
4	1	2	3	4	6		7	8	9	10	11		5									
5	1	2	3	4	6		7	8	9	10	11		5									
6	1	2		4	6		7	8		10	11		5	3	9							
7	1	2		4	6		7	8	10		11		5	3	9							
8	1	2		4	6		7	8	10		11		5	3	9							
9	1	2			6		7	8	11				5	3	9	4	10					
10	1	2			6			8	11				5	3	9	4	10	7				
11	1	2			6		7	8	11				5	3	9	4	10					
12	1	2			6		7	10	11				5	3	9	4	8					
13	1	2			6		7	10	11				5		9	4	8		3			
14	1	2			6		7	10	11				5	3	9	4	8					
15	1	2			6		7	8	11				5	3	9	4	10					
16	1	2		4	6		7	8	11				5	3	9		10					
17	1	2		4	6		7	8	11				5	3	9		10					
18	1	2		4	6		7	8	11				5	3	9		10					
19	1	2		4	6		7	8	11				5	3	9		10					
20	1	2		4	6		7	8	11				5	3	9		10					
21	1	2		4	6		7	8					5	3	9		10			11		
22	1	2		4	6		7	10	11				5		9	8			3			
23	1	2	10	4	6		7		11				5		9	8			3			
24	1	2		4	6		7	10	11				5		9	8			3			
25	1	2		4	6		7	10	11				5		9	8			3			
26	1	2		4	6		7	10	8				5		9			11	3			
27	1	2		4	6		7	8	9				5		10			11	3			
28	1	2		4	6			8	9		11		5		10			7	3			
29		2		4	6		7		9	8			5	3	10			11			1	
30	1	2		4	5		7		9	8				3	10	6		11				
31	1		2		5		7	4	9	8				3	10	6		11				
32	1	2			5		7	4	9	8				3	10	6		11				
33	1	2		4	6		7	9		8			5	3	10			11				
34		2				6	7	9		8			5	3		4	10	11			1	
35	1	2	4					8					5	3		6	7	11	9			10
36	1	2			6			8	9				5	3	10	4	7	11				
37	1	2	3		6			8	9				5		10	4	7	11				
38		2			6			8	9	7			5	3	10	4		11			1	
39		2	4		6			8	9	7			5	3	10			11			1	
40		2	4		6			8	9	7			5	3	10			11			1	
41		2	4		5		7	8	9					3	10	6		11			1	
42	1	2	4		5		7	8	9					3	10	6		11				
	36	41	13	24	40	2	34	39	37	15	9	1	35	28	35	21	17	18	9	1	6	1
			1	1	2		5	12	10	7	2			1	16	1			1			

	Sanders JA	Howe D	Williams SG	Dudley JG	Barlow RJ	Summers GT	Griffin FA	Robson RW	Allen R	Whitehouse B	Lee GT	Brookes WA	Kennedy JP	Millard L	Kevan DT	Setters ME	Nicholls J	Horobin R	Carter W	Lee MJ	Brown F	Jackson A
R3	1	2		4	6		7	10	11				5		9	8			3			
rep	1	2		4	6		7	10	11				5		9	8			3			
R4	1	2		4	6		7		9		11		5		10			8	3			
R5	1	2		4	6		7		9	8	11		5	3	10							
rep	1	2		4	6		7		9	8			5	3	10			11				
R6	1	2		4	6		7		9	8			5	3	10			11				
rep	1	2		4	5		7		9	8				3	10	6		11				
SF	1	2		4	6		7		9	8			5	3	10			11				
rep	1	2		4	6		7		9	8			5	3	10			11				
	9	9		9	9		9	2	9	6	2		8	6	9	3		6	3			
								1	5	3					4			1				

One own-goal

1957-58

Division One

	P	W	D	L	F	A	Pts
Wolverhampton W	42	28	8	6	103	47	64
Preston North End	42	26	7	9	100	51	59
Tottenham Hotspur	42	21	9	12	93	77	51
West Bromwich Albion	42	18	14	10	92	70	50
Manchester City	42	22	5	15	104	100	49
Burnley	42	21	5	16	80	74	47
Blackpool	42	19	6	17	80	67	44
Luton Town	42	19	6	17	69	63	44
Manchester United	42	16	11	15	85	75	43
Nottingham Forest	42	16	10	16	69	63	42
Chelsea	42	15	12	15	83	79	42
Arsenal	42	16	7	19	73	85	39
Birmingham City	42	14	11	17	76	89	39
Aston Villa	42	16	7	19	73	86	39
Bolton Wanderers	42	14	10	18	65	87	38
Everton	42	13	11	18	65	75	37
Leeds United	42	14	9	19	51	63	37
Leicester City	42	14	5	23	91	112	33
Newcastle United	42	12	8	22	73	81	32
Portsmouth	42	12	8	22	73	88	32
Sunderland	42	10	12	20	54	97	32
Sheffield Wednesday	42	12	7	23	69	92	31

Manager: Vic Buckingham

- Albion recorded their biggest home League win since 1892 when they thrashed Manchester City 9–2 in September.
- In-form and England possible Frank Griffin broke his leg in an FA Cup replay with Sheffield United and was never the same player again.
- Albion won their fourth-round FA Cup replay 5–1 at Nottingham Forest with 10 men. The scores were level at 1–1 when Maurice Setters was carried off injured.
- Goalkeeper Clive Jackman was signed from Aldershot and winger Derek Hogg from Leicester City (April).
- FA Cup-winning captain Len Millard left The Hawthorns for Stafford Rangers after serving Albion for 21 years, during which time he appeared in 627 first-team matches, including 436 in the League. Goalkeeper Jimmy Sanders also departed, joining Coventry City after making almost 400 appearances for the Baggies, while left-winger George Lee switched to Lockheed Leamington, having played in nearly 300 senior matches.
- The floodlights were switched on at The Hawthorns for the first time when Albion entertained Chelsea in September. In a return friendly, the Russia Red Army team lost 6–5 in a game arranged to officially open the lights shortly afterwards.
- Albion's run of 17 League games without defeat came to an end on 7 December. This equalled a club record set in 1902.

Match No.	Date			Opponents	Result		Scorers	Attendance
1	Aug	24	H	Newcastle United	W	2-1	Robson, Allen	31,064
2		27	A	Arsenal	D	2-2	Allen 2 (1 pen)	45,988
3		31	A	Burnley	D	2-2	Setters, Lee	24,428
4	Sep	4	H	Arsenal	L	1-2	Allen	26,117
5		7	H	Preston North End	W	4-1	Allen, Kevan, Griffin, Horobin	29,903
6		11	A	Chelsea	D	2-2	Allen, Horobin	29,824
7		14	A	Sheffield Wednesday	W	2-1	McEvoy (og), Allen (pen)	26,395
8		18	H	Chelsea	D	1-1	Allen (pen)	36,835
9		21	H	Manchester City	W	9-2	Griffin 3, Howe 2 (1 pen), Robson, Horobin, Whitehouse, Kevan (pen)	26,222
10		28	A	Nottingham Forest	W	2-0	Robson 2	41,825
11	Oct	1	H	Birmingham City	D	0-0		39,909
12		5	H	Portsmouth	W	3-1	Allen 2, Robson	32,030
13		12	H	Bolton Wanderers	D	2-2	Kevan, Allen (pen)	31,522
14		19	A	Leeds United	D	1-1	Allen	24,614
15		26	H	Manchester United	W	4-3	Robson 2, Allen, Kevan	52,839
16	Nov	2	A	Everton	D	1-1	Griffin	53,579
17		9	H	Aston Villa	W	3-2	Robson, Allen (pen), Horobin	41,454
18		16	A	Wolverhampton Wanderers	D	1-1	Kevan	55,618
19		23	H	Sunderland	W	3-0	Kevan, Robson, Setters	32,682
20		30	A	Leicester City	D	3-3	Robson 2, Allen	33,755
21	Dec	7	H	Blackpool	D	1-1	Robson	28,236
22		14	A	Luton Town	L	1-5	Robson	15,365
23		21	A	Newcastle United	L	0-3		31,699
24		26	A	Birmingham City	W	5-3	Robson 2, Kevan 2, Allen	48,396
25		28	H	Burnley	W	5-1	Robson 4, Kevan	38,386
26	Jan	11	A	Preston North End	L	1-3	Kevan	25,262
27		18	H	Sheffield Wednesday	W	3-1	Griffin 2, Setters	28,963
28	Feb	1	A	Manchester City	L	1-4	Kevan	38,702
29		8	H	Nottingham Forest	W	3-2	Kevan 2, Robson	32,868
30		22	A	Bolton Wanderers	D	2-2	Kevan 2	19,132
31	Mar	8	A	Manchester United	W	4-0	Allen 2, Greaves (og), Kevan	63,479
32		12	H	Leeds United	W	1-0	Charlton (og)	16,518
33		15	H	Everton	W	4-0	Robson, Kevan 2, Allen (pen)	28,915
34		19	A	Portsmouth	D	2-2	Horobin, Allen	24,791
35		22	A	Sunderland	L	0-2		38,323
36		29	H	Wolverhampton Wanderers	L	0-3		56,904
37	Apr	4	A	Tottenham Hotspur	D	0-0		56,166
38		5	A	Aston Villa	L	1-2	Allen	32,010
39		7	H	Tottenham Hotspur	L	0-2		26,672
40		12	H	Leicester City	W	6-2	Robson 3, Whitehouse 2, Kevan	25,241
41		19	A	Blackpool	L	0-2		17,327
42		26	H	Luton Town	W	4-2	Lee 2, Howe, Allen (pen)	20,286
								Appearances
								Goals

FA Cup

R3	Jan	4	H	Manchester City	W	5-1	Allen 2, Griffin, Barlow, Ewing (og)	49,669
R4		25	H	Nottingham Forest	D	3-3	Allen, Kevan, Robson	58,163
rep		29	A	Nottingham Forest	W	5-1	Kevan, Whitehouse, Griffin, Robson, Howe (pen)	46,477
R5	Feb	15	A	Sheffield United	D	1-1	Allen	55,847
rep		19	H	Sheffield United	W	4-1	Kevan 2, Allen (pen), Robson	57,503
R6	Mar	1	H	Manchester United	D	2-2	Allen, Horobin	57,574
rep		5	A	Manchester United	L	0-1		60,523
								Appearances
								Goals

	Brown F	Howe D	Williams SG	Setters ME	Kennedy JP	Barlow RJ	Griffin FA	Robson RW	Allen R	Kevan DT	Lee GT	Horobin R	Jackson A	Whitehouse B	Sanders JA	Dudley JG	Millard L	Burnside DG	Drury CE	Jackman CEJ	Campbell JC	Williams GE	Robinson EM
1	1	2	3	4	5	6	7	8	9	10	11												
2	1	2	3	4	5	6	7	8	9	10		11											
3	1	2	3	4	5	6	7	8	9		11		10										
4	1	2	3	4	5	6	7	8	9			11		10									
5		2	3	4	5	6	7	8	9	10		11			1								
6		2	3	4	5	6	7	8	9	10		11			1								
7		2	3	4	5	6	7	8	9	10		11			1								
8		2	3	4	5	6	7	8	9	10		11			1								
9		2	3		5	6	7	9		10		11		8	1	4							
10		2	3	4	5	6	7	8	9	10		11			1								
11		2	3	6	5		7	8	9	10		11			1	4							
12		2	3	4	5	6	7	8	9	10		11			1								
13		2	3	4	5	6	7	8	9	10		11			1								
14				2	5		7	6	9			11		8	1	4	3	10					
15		2		3	5	6	7	8	9	10		11			1	4							
16		2	3	4	5	6	7	8	9	10		11			1								
17		2	3	4	5	6	7	8	9	10		11			1								
18		2	3	4	5	6	7	8	9	10		11			1								
19		2	3	4	5	6	7	8	9	10		11			1								
20		2	3	4	5	6	7	8	9	10		11			1								
21		2	3	4	5	6	7	8	9	10		11			1								
22		2	3	4	5	6	7	8	9	10		11			1								
23		2	3	4	5	6	7	8	9	10	11				1								
24		2	3	4	5	6	7	8	9	10	11				1								
25		2	3	4	5	6	7	8	9	10	11				1								
26		2	3	4	5	6	7	8	9	10		11			1								
27		2	3	4	5	6	7	8	9	10		11			1								
28		2	3		5	6	7	9		10		11		8	1	4							
29		2	3		5	6	7	9		10		11		8	1	4							
30		2	3			5		8	9	10		11		7	1	4			6				
31		2	3		5	6		8	9	10		11		7	1	4							
32		2	3			5		8	9	10		11		7	1	4			6				
33		2	3			5		8	9	10		11		7	1	4			6				
34		2	3		5	6		8	9	10		11				4				1	7		
35		2	3		5	6		8	9	10		11				4				1	7		
36		2	3		5	6		8	9	10		11				4				1	7		
37		2	3			5		8	11	9			10			4			6	1	7		
38		2				5		10	11	9		7		8		4			6	1		3	
39		2	3			5		9	11	10				8		4			6	1	7		
40			2			5		8	9	10	11			7		4			6	1		3	
41			2		5	6			9		11			7		4		10		1		3	8
42		2		6		5		8	9	10	11			7		4				1		3	
	4	39	38	27	34	40	29	41	39	38	8	32	2	14	29	19	1	2	7	9	5	4	1
		3		3			7	24	22	19	3	5		3									

Three own-goals

	Brown F	Howe D	Williams SG	Setters ME	Kennedy JP	Barlow RJ	Griffin FA	Robson RW	Allen R	Kevan DT	Lee GT	Horobin R	Jackson A	Whitehouse B	Sanders JA	Dudley JG
R3		2	3	4	5	6	7	8	9	10		11			1	
R4		2	3	4	5	6	7	8	9	10		11			1	
rep		2	3	4	5	6	7	9		10		11		8	1	
R5		2	3		5	6	7	8	9	10		11			1	4
rep		2	3		5	6	7	8	9	10		11			1	4
R6		2	3		5	6		8	9	10		11		7	1	4
rep		2	3		5	6		8	9	10		11		7	1	4
		7	7	3	7	7	5	7	6	7		7		3	7	4
		1				1	2	3	6	4		1		1		

One own-goal

1958-59

Division One

	P	W	D	L	F	A	Pts
Wolverhampton W	42	28	5	9	110	49	61
Manchester United	42	24	7	11	103	66	55
Arsenal	42	21	8	13	88	68	50
Bolton Wanderers	42	20	10	12	79	66	50
West Bromwich Albion	42	18	13	11	88	68	49
West Ham United	42	21	6	15	85	70	48
Burnley	42	19	10	13	81	70	48
Blackpool	42	18	11	13	66	49	47
Birmingham City	42	20	6	16	84	68	46
Blackburn Rovers	42	17	10	15	76	70	44
Newcastle United	42	17	7	18	80	80	41
Preston North End	42	17	7	18	70	77	41
Nottingham Forest	42	17	6	19	71	74	40
Chelsea	42	18	4	20	77	98	40
Leeds United	42	15	9	18	57	74	39
Everton	42	17	4	21	71	87	38
Luton Town	42	12	13	17	68	71	37
Tottenham Hotspur	42	13	10	19	85	95	36
Leicester City	42	11	10	21	67	98	32
Manchester City	42	11	9	22	64	95	31
Aston Villa	42	11	8	23	58	87	30
Portsmouth	42	6	9	27	64	112	21

Manager: Vic Buckingham

- In May/June 1959 Albion played nine games on tour in Canada and the US. They won seven, drew one and lost one, scoring 59 goals, including a 15–0 win over Alberta All Stars when Bobby Robson netted six times.
- Manager Vic Buckingham quit after six years in office.
- Goalkeeper Ray Potter was signed from Crystal Palace, while winger Frank Griffin moved to Northampton Town and fellow winger Roy Horobin went to Notts County.
- Goalkeeper Clive Jackman was injured in the League game at Villa Park and never played again.

Match No.	Date			Opponents	Result		Scorers	Attendance
1	Aug	23	A	Luton Town	D	1-1	Kevan	24,425
2		27	H	Birmingham City	D	2-2	Hogg, Allen (pen)	46,468
3		30	H	Bolton Wanderers	D	1-1	Allen	37,244
4	Sep	3	A	Birmingham City	W	6-0	Burnside 2, Campbell 2, Allen, Kevan	35,983
5		6	A	Burnley	W	3-1	Burnside 2, Campbell	23,589
6		10	H	Portsmouth	L	1-2	Campbell	34,445
7		13	H	Preston North End	D	1-1	Dudley	36,402
8		17	A	Portsmouth	W	6-2	Allen 2 (1 pen), Burnside 2, Kevan, Hayward (og)	32,952
9		20	A	Leicester City	D	2-2	Allen, Kevan	38,551
10		27	H	Everton	L	2-3	Campbell, Burnside	30,721
11	Oct	4	A	Arsenal	L	3-4	Kevan 3	58,570
12		11	A	Aston Villa	W	4-1	Burnside, Hogg, Robson, Howe (pen)	45,778
13		18	H	West Ham United	W	2-1	Campbell, Howe (pen)	36,991
14		25	A	Manchester United	W	2-1	Robson, Kevan	51,721
15	Nov	1	H	Wolverhampton Wanderers	W	2-1	Campbell, Kevan	48,898
16		8	A	Blackpool	D	1-1	Burnside	18,664
17		15	H	Blackburn Rovers	L	2-3	Burnside, Dudley	31,679
18		22	A	Newcastle United	W	2-1	Kevan, Robson	51,636
19		29	H	Tottenham Hotspur	W	4-3	Howe, Kevan, Forrester, Allen (pen)	21,861
20	Dec	6	A	Nottingham Forest	D	1-1	Allen (pen)	34,784
21		13	H	Chelsea	W	4-0	Forrester 2, Allen, Kevan	19,856
22		26	H	Leeds United	L	1-2	Gibson (og)	35,020
23		27	A	Leeds United	W	1-0	Kevan	44,929
24	Jan	3	A	Bolton Wanderers	L	1-2	Allen	27,847
25		31	A	Preston North End	W	4-2	Kevan 2, Griffin, O'Farrell (og)	23,138
26	Feb	7	H	Leicester City	D	2-2	Kevan, Allen	25,375
27		18	A	Everton	D	3-3	Setters, Kevan, Allen	32,629
28		21	H	Arsenal	D	1-1	Kevan	32,706
29	Mar	7	A	West Ham United	L	1-3	Robson	29,510
30		11	H	Burnley	L	2-4	Setters, Hogg	18,824
31		14	H	Manchester United	L	1-3	Kevan	35,608
32		21	A	Wolverhampton Wanderers	L	2-5	Kevan 2	44,240
33		28	H	Blackpool	W	3-1	Kevan 2, Allen	29,803
34		30	A	Manchester City	W	2-0	Kevan, Allen	25,551
35		31	H	Manchester City	W	3-0	Campbell, Allen (pen), Hogg	32,076
36	Apr	4	A	Blackburn Rovers	D	0-0		27,217
37		11	H	Newcastle United	D	2-2	Kevan 2	23,750
38		15	H	Luton Town	W	2-0	Burnside, Allen	19,293
39		18	A	Tottenham Hotspur	L	0-5		36,805
40		22	A	Chelsea	W	2-0	Burnside, Hogg	31,948
41		25	H	Nottingham Forest	W	2-0	Campbell, Allen	17,071
42		29	H	Aston Villa	D	1-1	Allen	48,281
								Appearances
								Goals

FA Cup

R3	Jan	19	A	Sheffield Wednesday	W	2-0	Jackson, Hogg	50,455
R4		24	H	Brentford	W	2-0	Kevan 2	41,948
R5	Feb	14	A	Blackpool	L	1-3	Robson	30,415
								Appearances
								Goals

Jackman CEJ	Howe D	Williams SG	Setters ME	Barlow RJ	Drury CE	Campbell JC	Robson RW	Allen R	Kevan DT	Hogg D	Dudley JG	Burnside DG	Whitehouse B	Williams GE	Potter RJ	Forrester AC	Jackson A	Kennedy JP	Griffin FA	
1	2	3	4	5	6	7	8	9	10	11										1
1	2	3	4	5	6	7	8	9	10	11										2
1	2	3	6	5		7	8	9	10	11	4									3
1	2	3	6	5		7		9	8	11	4	10								4
1	2	3	6	5		7		9	8	11	4	10								5
1	2	3	6	5		7		9	8	11	4	10								6
1	2	3	6	5				9	8	11	4	10	7							7
1	2	3	6	5		7		9	10	11	4	8								8
1	2	3	4	5		7		9	10	11	6	8								9
1	2	3	4	5		7		9	8	11	6	10								10
1		2	4	5			8	7	9	11	6	10		3						11
1	2	3	4	5		7	8		9	11	6	10								12
	2		4	5		7	8		9	11	6	10		3	1					13
	2	3	4	5		7	8		9	11	6	10			1					14
	2	3	4	5		7	8		9	11	6	10			1					15
	2	3	4	5		7	9		8	11	6	10			1					16
	2	3	4	5		7	9		10	11	6	8			1					17
	2	3	4	5		7	8	9	10	11	6				1					18
	2	3	4	5	6		8	9	10	11					1	7				19
	2	3	4	5	6		8	9	10	11					1	7				20
	2	3	4	5	6		8	9	10	11					1	7				21
	2	3	4	5	6		8	9	10	11					1	7				22
	2	3	4	5	6			9	10	11					1	7	8			23
	2	3	4	5	6		8	9		11					1	7	10			24
	2	3	4		6		9	11	10						1		8	5	7	25
	2	3	4	5	6			9	10	11					1		8		7	26
	2	3	4	5	6			11	9			10			1		8		7	27
	2	3	4	5	6			7	10	11		8			1		9			28
	2	3	4	5	6		9	7	10	11					1		8			29
	2	3	6	5			9	7	10	11					1		8	4		30
	2	3	4	5			8	7	9	11		10			1			6		31
	2	3	4	5			8	7	9	11		10			1			6		32
	2	3	4			7	6	9	10	11		8			1			5		33
	2	3	4			7	6	9	10	11		8			1			5		34
	2	3	4			7		9	10	11	6	8			1			5		35
	2	3	4			7		9	10	11	6	8			1			5		36
		2	4			7	6	9	10	11		8		3	1			5		37
	2	3	4	5		7	6	9	10	11		8			1					38
	2	3	4	5		7	6	9	10	11		8			1					39
	2		4	5		11	6	9	10	7		8		3	1					40
	2	3	4	5		11	6	9	10	7		8			1					41
	2	3		6		11	4	9	10	7					1		8	5		42
12	40	40	41	36	13	26	29	36	41	40	18	27	1	4	30	6	9	10	3	
	3		2			9	4	17	27	5	2	12				3			1	

Three own-goals

	2	3	4	5	6			9	10	11					1		8		7	R3
	2	3	4	5	6			9	10	11					1		8		7	R4
	2	3	4	5	6		8	9		11					1		10		7	R5
	3	3	3	3	3		1	3	2	3					3		3		3	
							1		2	1							1			

1959-60

Division One

	P	W	D	L	F	A	Pts
Burnley	42	24	7	11	85	61	55
Wolverhampton W	42	24	6	12	106	67	54
Tottenham Hotspur	42	21	11	10	86	50	53
West Bromwich Albion	42	19	11	12	83	57	49
Sheffield Wednesday	42	19	11	12	80	59	49
Bolton Wanderers	42	20	8	14	59	51	48
Manchester United	42	19	7	16	102	80	45
Newcastle United	42	18	8	16	82	78	44
Preston North End	42	16	12	14	79	76	44
Fulham	42	17	10	15	73	80	44
Blackpool	42	15	10	17	59	71	40
Leicester City	42	13	13	16	66	75	39
Arsenal	42	15	9	18	68	80	39
West Ham United	42	16	6	20	75	91	38
Everton	42	13	11	18	73	78	37
Manchester City	42	17	3	22	78	84	37
Blackburn Rovers	42	16	5	21	60	70	37
Chelsea	42	14	9	19	76	91	37
Birmingham City	42	13	10	19	63	80	36
Nottingham Forest	42	13	9	20	50	74	35
Leeds United	42	12	10	20	65	92	34
Luton Town	42	9	12	21	50	73	30

Manager: Gordon Clark

- Albion came back from 2–0 down to beat Everton 6–2 at The Hawthorns, and Derek Kevan netted five goals to set a new post-war individual scoring record.
- Albion made it 18 goals in three visits to St Andrew's when they thrashed Birmingham City 7–1, following earlier wins of 5–3 and 6–0.
- New manager Gordon Clark signed two Scotsmen, goalkeeper Jock Wallace and winger Andy Aitken from Airdrieonians and Hibernian respectively. He also bought Stan Jones and Peter Billingham from Walsall. Maurice Setters (to Manchester United for £30,000), captain Ray Barlow (to Birmingham City after 16 years' service), Jimmy Dudley (to Walsall) and Brian Whitehouse (to Norwich City) were among the players who found pastures new.

Match No.	Date			Opponents	Result		Scorers	Attendanc
1	Aug	22	H	Manchester United	W	3-2	Burnside 2, Foulkes (og)	40,733
2		26	A	Tottenham Hotspur	D	2-2	Robson, Kevan	54,114
3		29	A	Preston North End	D	1-1	Kevan	24,876
4	Sep	2	H	Tottenham Hotspur	L	1-2	Hogg	35,924
5		5	H	Leicester City	W	5-0	Dixon, Kevan, Jackson, Robson 2	27,259
6		9	H	Newcastle United	D	2-2	Hogg, Kevan	27,570
7		12	A	Burnley	L	1-2	Robson	23,907
8		16	A	Newcastle United	D	0-0		39,266
9		19	H	Leeds United	W	3-0	Robson, Allen 2	26,369
10		26	A	West Ham United	L	1-4	Burnside	29,957
11	Oct	3	H	Chelsea	L	1-3	Jackson	27,784
12		10	H	Fulham	L	2-4	Setters 2	20,395
13		17	A	Bolton Wanderers	D	0-0		22,581
14		24	H	Luton Town	W	4-0	Allen 2, Whitehouse, Kevan	22,445
15		31	A	Sheffield Wednesday	L	0-2		26,075
16	Nov	7	H	Blackpool	W	2-1	Whitehouse, Jackson	30,568
17		14	A	Blackburn Rovers	L	2-3	Burnside, Whitehouse	18,449
18		21	H	Manchester City	W	2-0	McTavish (og), Burnside	24,219
19		28	A	Arsenal	W	4-2	Allen 2 (1 pen), Robson, Kevan	41,011
20	Dec	5	H	Wolverhampton Wanderers	L	0-1		40,739
21		12	A	Everton	D	2-2	Kevan, Burnside	25,769
22		19	A	Manchester United	W	3-2	Hogg, Allen, Burnside	33,902
23		26	H	Nottingham Forest	L	2-3	Kevan 2	28,817
24		28	A	Nottingham Forest	W	2-1	Hogg, Jackson	34,755
25	Jan	2	H	Preston North End	W	4-0	Richardson (og), Jackson, Kevan, Allen	23,917
26		16	A	Leicester City	W	1-0	Jackson	23,802
27		23	H	Burnley	D	0-0		23,512
28	Feb	6	A	Leeds United	W	4-1	Burnside 2, Hogg, Kevan	23,729
29		24	A	Chelsea	D	2-2	Kevan, Allen	26,225
30		27	A	Wolverhampton Wanderers	L	1-3	Jackson	49,791
31	Mar	5	H	Bolton Wanderers	D	1-1	Kevan	23,857
32		9	H	West Ham United	W	3-2	Kevan 2, Allen (pen)	12,204
33		12	A	Luton Town	D	0-0		18,285
34		19	H	Everton	W	6-2	Kevan 5, Burnside	24,887
35		26	A	Blackpool	L	0-2		16,190
36	Apr	2	H	Blackburn Rovers	W	2-0	Kevan, Allen	24,180
37		9	A	Manchester City	W	1-0	Jackson	24,342
38		16	H	Sheffield Wednesday	W	3-1	Burnside, Kevan, Jackson	27,899
39		18	A	Birmingham City	W	7-1	Allen 3 (1 pen), Jackson, Kevan 3	28,685
40		19	H	Birmingham City	D	1-1	Kevan	37,937
41		23	A	Fulham	L	1-2	Allen	23,631
42		30	H	Arsenal	W	1-0	Jackson	26,380
								Appearances
								Goals

FA Cup

R3	Jan	9	H	Plymouth Argyle	W	3-2	Kevan 3	27,548
R4		30	H	Bolton Wanderers	W	2-0	Jackson, Burnside	36,411
R5	Feb	20	A	Leicester City	L	1-2	Kennedy	37,753
								Appearances
								Goals

Potter RJ	Howe D	Williams SG	Setters ME	Kennedy JP	Barlow RJ	Allen R	Burnside DG	Robson RW	Kevan DT	Dixon R	Hogg D	Dudley JG	Jackson A	Aitken AFS	Styles AJ	Wallace JMB	Cram R	Williams GE	Whitehouse B	Drury CE	Smith KW	Bannister J	Hope R	Carter G	
1	2	3	4	5	6	7	8	9	10	11															1
1	2	3	4	5	6	7	8	9	10		11														2
1	2	3	4	5	6		8	9	10	11	7														3
1	2	3		5	6			9	10	11	7	4	8												4
1	2	3	4	5	6			9	10	11	7		8												5
1	2	3	4	5		9		6	10	11	7		8												6
1	2	3	4	5		7	8	6	9		11		10												7
1	2	3	4	5	6	7	8	9	10					11											8
1	2	3	4	5		9		6	10		11		8	7											9
1	2	3	4	5		9	8	6	10	7	11														10
1	2	3	4	5			8	9	10		11	6	7												11
1	2	3	4	5		9		8	10		11		7		6										12
			4	5		9		6	10	11			7	8		1	2	3							13
	2	3	4	5		9		6	10				7	11		1			8						14
	2	3	4	5		9		6	10				7	11		1			8						15
	2	3	4		5		9	6	10				7	11		1			8						16
	2	3	4	5			9	6	10				7	11		1			8						17
	2	3	4	5		9	8	6	10		11			7		1									18
	2	3	4	5		9	8	6	10		11			7		1									19
	2	3	4	5		9	8	6	10		11			7		1									20
	2	3		5		9	8	6	10		11			7		1				4					21
	2	3		5		9	8	6	10		11			7		1				4					22
	2	3	4	5		9	8	6	10		11			7		1									23
	2			5		9	8	6	10		11		7			1		3		4					24
	2			5		9	8	6	10		11		7			1		3		4					25
	2			5		9	8	6	10		11		7			1		3		4					26
	2			5		9	8	6	10		11		7			1		3		4					27
	2			5		9	8	6	10		11		7			1		3		4					28
	2			5		9	8	6	10		11		7			1		3		4					29
	2	4		5		9	8	6	10		11		7			1		3							30
	2			5		9	8	6	10				7	11		1		3		4					31
	2			5		9	8	6	10				7	11		1		3		4					32
	2			5		9	8	6	10				7	11		1		3		4					33
	2			5		9	8	6	10		11		7			1		3		4					34
	2			5		9	8	6	10		11		7			1		3		4					35
	2			5		9		6	10		11		7			1		3		4	8				36
	2			5		9			10		11		7			1		3		4	8	6			37
	2			5		9	8	6	10		11		7			1		3		4					38
	2			5		9	8	6	10		11		7			1		3		4					39
	2			5		9	8	6	10		11		7			1		3		4					40
	2			5		9	8	6	10		11		7			1		3		4					41
	2			5		9		6	8				7			1		3		4			10	11	42
12	41	23	20	41	7	36	31	41	42	7	31	2	31	16	1	30	1	20	4	20	2	1	1	1	
			2			15	11	6	26	1	5		11						3						

Three own-goals

Potter RJ	Howe D	Williams SG	Setters ME	Kennedy JP	Barlow RJ	Allen R	Burnside DG	Robson RW	Kevan DT	Dixon R	Hogg D	Dudley JG	Jackson A	Aitken AFS	Styles AJ	Wallace JMB	Cram R	Williams GE	Whitehouse B	Drury CE	Smith KW	Bannister J	Hope R	Carter G	
	2			5		9	8	6	10		11		7			1		3		4					R3
	2			5		9	8	6	10		11		7			1		3		4					R4
	2			5		9	8	6	10		11		7			1		3		4					R5
	3			3		3	3	3	3		3		3			3		3		3					
				1			1		3				1												

1960-61

Division One

	P	W	D	L	F	A	Pts
Tottenham Hotspur	42	31	4	7	115	55	66
Sheffield Wednesday	42	23	12	7	78	47	58
Wolverhampton W	42	25	7	10	103	75	57
Burnley	42	22	7	13	102	77	51
Everton	42	22	6	14	87	69	50
Leicester City	42	18	9	15	87	70	45
Manchester United	42	18	9	15	88	76	45
Blackburn Rovers	42	15	13	14	77	76	43
Aston Villa	42	17	9	16	78	77	43
West Bromwich Albion	42	18	5	19	67	71	41
Arsenal	42	15	11	16	77	85	41
Chelsea	42	15	7	20	98	100	37
Manchester City	42	13	11	18	79	90	37
Nottingham Forest	42	14	9	19	62	78	37
Cardiff City	42	13	11	18	60	85	37
West Ham United	42	13	10	19	77	88	36
Fulham	42	14	8	20	72	95	36
Bolton Wanderers	42	12	11	19	58	73	35
Birmingham City	42	14	6	22	62	84	34
Blackpool	42	12	9	21	68	73	33
Newcastle United	42	11	10	21	86	109	32
Preston North End	42	10	10	22	43	71	30

Manager: Gordon Clark

- Albion paid a record fee of £20,000 for left-winger Clive Clark from Queen's Park Rangers.
- Stan Steele was signed from Port Vale. Steele, in fact, stayed at the club for just three months, making one League appearance against Blackburn Rovers.
- Ronnie Allen left The Hawthorns after scoring a club record 234 goals in 415 games; he joined Crystal Palace. Joe Kennedy also left for Chester (after making almost 400 senior appearances) and Derek Hogg for Cardiff City.
- Jimmy Greaves scored five of Chelsea's goals in their 7–1 win over Albion in December.
- Alan Everiss took over as Albion secretary from Eph Smith – a position he would retain for 20 years.

Match No.	Date			Opponents	Result		Scorers	Attendance
1	Aug	20	A	Sheffield Wednesday	L	0-1		34,177
2		24	H	Birmingham City	L	1-2	Jackson	32,102
3		27	H	Fulham	L	2-4	Jackson, Burnside	20,609
4		31	A	Birmingham City	L	1-3	Kevan	37,811
5	Sep	3	A	Preston North End	L	1-2	Hogg	18,476
6		5	H	Newcastle United	W	6-0	Jackson 3, Robson, Kevan, Burnside	22,548
7		10	H	Burnley	L	0-2		26,407
8		14	A	Newcastle United	L	2-3	Smith, Burnside	16,107
9		17	A	Nottingham Forest	W	2-1	Allen, Kevan	22,906
10		24	H	Manchester City	W	6-3	Allen 3, Kevan 2, Burnside	25,163
11	Oct	1	A	Arsenal	L	0-1		27,105
12		8	A	Bolton Wanderers	W	1-0	Allen	18,672
13		15	H	West Ham United	W	1-0	Robson	22,009
14		22	A	Leicester City	D	2-2	Burnside, Allen	20,770
15		29	H	Aston Villa	L	0-2		41,903
16	Nov	5	A	Everton	D	1-1	Jackson	40,705
17		12	H	Blackburn Rovers	L	1-2	Burnside	18,701
18		19	A	Manchester United	L	0-3		32,834
19		26	H	Tottenham Hotspur	L	1-3	Howe	39,017
20	Dec	3	A	Chelsea	L	1-7	Jackson	19,568
21		10	H	Blackpool	W	3-1	Kevan 2, Jackson	15,099
22		17	H	Sheffield Wednesday	D	2-2	Aitken, Burnside	17,862
23		26	A	Cardiff City	L	1-3	Macready	25,214
24		27	H	Cardiff City	D	1-1	Kevan	30,131
25		31	A	Fulham	W	2-1	Kevan, Burnside	18,080
26	Jan	14	H	Preston North End	W	3-1	Jackson 2, Howe (pen)	19,639
27		21	A	Burnley	W	1-0	Kevan	15,005
28		28	A	Wolverhampton Wanderers	L	2-4	Kevan, Burnside	31,385
29	Feb	4	H	Nottingham Forest	L	1-2	Burnside	24,927
30		11	A	Manchester City	L	0-3		21,382
31		18	H	Arsenal	L	2-3	Jackson, Robson	21,962
32		25	H	Bolton Wanderers	W	3-2	Allen, Hope, Burnside	15,171
33	Mar	4	A	West Ham United	W	2-1	Lovatt, Hope	21,607
34		11	H	Leicester City	W	1-0	Clark	25,168
35		25	H	Everton	W	3-0	Kevan 2, Jackson	20,590
36		28	A	Aston Villa	W	1-0	Lovatt	41,033
37	Apr	1	A	Blackpool	W	1-0	Lovatt	20,809
38		3	H	Wolverhampton Wanderers	W	2-1	Kevan, Burnside	34,108
39		8	H	Manchester United	D	1-1	Howe	28,033
40		15	A	Blackburn Rovers	L	1-2	Kevan	14,669
41		22	H	Chelsea	W	3-0	Kevan 2, Robson	17,691
42		29	A	Tottenham Hotspur	W	2-1	Kevan, Robson	52,054

Appearances
Goals

FA Cup

R3	Jan	7	A	Lincoln City	L	1-3	Burnside	14,025

Appearances
Goals

Wallace JMB	Howe D	Williams GE	Drury CE	Kennedy JP	Robson RW	Jackson A	Burnside DG	Allen R	Kevan DT	Hope R	Billingham PA	Jones SG	Hogg D	Potter RJ	Williams SG	Smith KW	Bannister J	Aitken AFS	Carter G	Cram R	Macready BL	Clark C	Lovatt J	Steele SF	
1	2	3	4	5	6	7	8	9	10	11															1
1	2	3	4	5	6	7	10	9	8	11															2
1	2	3	4	5	6	7	10	9	8	11															3
1	2	3			6	7	8		9	10	4	5	11												4
	2	3	6		9	7	8		10		4	5	11	1											5
	2		4	5	6	7	8		9	10			11	1	3										6
	2		4	5	6	7	8		9	10			11	1	3										7
	2		4	5	6	7	8	9					11	1	3	10									8
	2	3	4	5	6	7	8	9	10				11	1											9
	2	3	4	5	6	7	8	9	10				11	1											10
	2	3	4	5	6	7	8	9	10				11	1											11
	2	3		5		10	8	9			4		11	1		7	6								12
	2	3		5	6	10	8	9			4		11	1		7									13
	2			5	6		8	9	10		4			1	3			7	11						14
	2	3	4	5	6	7	8	9	10					1					11						15
	2	3	4	5	8	7	10	9						1			6		11						16
	2	3	6	5	8	7	10	9			4			1				11							17
1	2	3	4	5	6	7	8	9		10									11						18
1	8	11	4	5	6	7		9	10						3					2					19
1	8	11	4	5	6	7		9	10						3					2					20
1	2	3	6	5	4	8	10		9									11			7				21
1	2	3	6	5	4	8	10		9									11			7				22
1	2	3	6	5	4	8	10		9									11			7				23
	2	3		5	4	10		11	9					1		8	6				7				24
	2	3	6	5	4	11	8	9	10					1							7				25
	2	3	6	5	4	9	8		10					1							7	11			26
	2	3	6	5	4	9	8		10					1							7	11			27
	2	3	6	5	4	9	8		10					1							7	11			28
1	2	3	6	5	4	9	8		10									7				11			29
	2	3	6	5	4	9	8							1		10					7	11			30
	8	3	6	5	4	7		9	10					1						2		11			31
1	2		6		4	7	8	9		10		5			3							11			32
1	2		6		4	7	8			10		5			3							11	9		33
1	2		6		4	7	8			10		5			3							11	9		34
1	2	3	6		4	7	8		10			5										11	9		35
1	2	3	6		4	7	8		10			5										11	9		36
1	2		6		4	7	8		10			5			3				11				9		37
1	2		6		4	7	8		10			5			3				11				9		38
1	2	3	6		4	7	8		10			5										11	9		39
1	2	3	6			7			10		4	5										11	9	8	40
1	2		6		4	7			10	8		5			3							11	9		41
1	2		6		4	7			10	8		5			3							11	9		42
22	42	31	37	29	40	41	35	20	32	12	7	13	10	20	13	5	3	6	6	3	9	15	10	1	
	3				5	12	12	6	18	2			1			1		2			1	1	3		
	2	3	6	5	4	11	8	9	10					1							7				R3
	1	1	1	1	1	1	1	1	1					1							1				
							1																		

1961-62

Division One

	P	W	D	L	F	A	Pts
Ipswich Town	42	24	8	10	93	67	56
Burnley	42	21	11	10	101	67	53
Tottenham Hotspur	42	21	10	11	88	69	52
Everton	42	20	11	11	88	54	51
Sheffield United	42	19	9	14	61	69	47
Sheffield Wednesday	42	20	6	16	72	58	46
Aston Villa	42	18	8	16	65	56	44
West Ham United	42	17	10	15	76	82	44
West Bromwich Albion	42	15	13	14	83	67	43
Arsenal	42	16	11	15	71	72	43
Bolton Wanderers	42	16	10	16	62	66	42
Manchester City	42	17	7	18	78	81	41
Blackpool	42	15	11	16	70	75	41
Leicester City	42	17	6	19	72	71	40
Manchester United	42	15	9	18	72	75	39
Blackburn Rovers	42	14	11	17	50	58	39
Birmingham City	42	14	10	18	65	81	38
Wolverhampton W	42	13	10	19	73	86	36
Nottingham Forest	42	13	10	19	63	79	36
Fulham	42	13	7	22	66	74	33
Cardiff City	42	9	14	19	50	81	32
Chelsea	42	9	10	23	63	94	28

Manager: Gordon Clark then Archie Macaulay

- The last ever 50,000 plus crowd at The Hawthorns (54,992) saw Albion beaten by the reigning double winners Tottenham Hotspur 4–2 in a fifth-round FA Cup tie in February.
- Gordon Clark was replaced as Albion manager by the former Arsenal player and Scottish international Archie Macaulay.
- Goalkeeper Jock Wallace joined non-League Bedford Town.
- Albion's right-back Don Howe was voted Midlands Footballer of the Year.

Match No.	Date			Opponents	Result		Scorers	Attendance
1	Aug	19	H	Sheffield Wednesday	L	0-2		25,464
2		23	H	Everton	W	2-0	Robson, Kevan	21,594
3		26	A	Leicester City	L	0-1		20,899
4		30	A	Everton	L	1-3	Robson	36,569
5	Sep	2	H	Ipswich Town	L	1-3	Jackson	19,016
6		6	H	Birmingham City	D	0-0		20,541
7		9	A	Burnley	L	1-3	Burnside	22,001
8		16	H	Arsenal	W	4-0	Clark, Jackson, Burnside, Kevan	20,298
9		20	A	Birmingham City	W	2-1	Burnside, Kevan	23,931
10		23	A	Bolton Wanderers	L	2-3	Kevan, Hope	14,155
11		30	H	Manchester City	D	2-2	Kevan 2	20,820
12	Oct	7	H	Manchester United	D	1-1	Kevan,	25,645
13		18	A	Cardiff City	D	2-2	Williams, Smith	16,819
14		21	H	Aston Villa	D	1-1	Jackson	39,071
15		28	A	Nottingham Forest	D	4-4	Howe (pen), Clark, Kevan, Smith	20,424
16	Nov	4	H	Blackburn Rovers	W	4-0	Kevan, Jackson, Smith 2	17,298
17		11	A	West Ham United	D	3-3	Jackson, Howe (pen), Kevan	18,213
18		18	H	Sheffield United	W	3-1	Kevan 3	19,392
19		25	A	Chelsea	L	1-4	Smith	25,025
20	Dec	2	H	Tottenham Hotspur	L	2-4	Kevan, Smith	28,701
21		9	A	Blackpool	D	2-2	Burnside, Kevan	13,076
22		16	A	Sheffield Wednesday	L	1-2	Smith	22,168
23		23	H	Leicester City	W	2-0	Kevan, Smith	14,286
24		26	H	Wolverhampton Wanderers	D	1-1	Kevan	24,778
25	Jan	13	A	Ipswich Town	L	0-3		18,378
26		20	H	Burnley	D	1-1	Smith	22,141
27	Feb	3	A	Arsenal	W	1-0	Clark	29,607
28		10	H	Bolton Wanderers	W	6-2	Smith 2, Hope, Williams, Kevan 2	20,226
29		21	A	Manchester City	L	1-3	Kevan	17,225
30		24	A	Manchester United	L	1-4	Jackson	32,456
31	Mar	3	H	Cardiff City	W	5-1	Kevan 2, Clark, Smith, Howe (pen)	13,894
32		14	A	Aston Villa	L	0-1		34,969
33		17	H	Nottingham Forest	D	2-2	Smith 2	16,974
34		24	A	Blackburn Rovers	D	1-1	Jackson	11,644
35		28	A	Wolverhampton Wanderers	W	5-1	Robson, Drury, Smith, Kevan, Thomson (og)	20,558
36		31	H	West Ham United	L	0-1		16,937
37	Apr	7	A	Sheffield United	D	1-1	Smith	18,697
38		14	H	Chelsea	W	4-0	Kevan 2, Smith, Howe	14,573
39		21	A	Tottenham Hotspur	W	2-1	Kevan 2,	53,512
40		23	A	Fulham	W	2-1	Lovatt, Jackson	29,332
41		24	H	Fulham	W	2-0	Kevan 2	22,022
42		28	H	Blackpool	W	7-1	Kevan 4, Lovett, Robson, Howe (pen)	17,463

Appearances

Goals

FA Cup

R3	Jan	6	A	Blackpool	D	0-0		19,560
rep		10	H	Blackpool	W	2-1	Burnside, Smith	27,781
R4		27	A	Wolverhampton Wanderers	W	2-1	Clark 2	46,411
R5	Feb	17	H	Tottenham Hotspur	L	2-4	Kevan, Smith	54,992

Appearances

Goals

Match	Wallace JMB	Howe D	Williams SG	Robson RW	Jones SG	Drury C	Jackson A	Burnside DG	Lovatt J	Kevan DT	Clark C	Hope R	Smith KW	Potter RJ	Millington AH	Carter G	Cram R	Bannister J	Williams GE
1	1	2	3	4	5	6	7	8	9	10	11								
2	1	2	3	4	5	6	7	8	9	10	11								
3	1	2	3	4	5	6	7	8	9	10	11								
4	1	2	3	4	5	6	7		9	10	11	8							
5	1	2	3	4	5	6	7			10	11	8	9						
6	1	2	3	4	5	6	7			10	11	8	9						
7		2	3	4	5	6	7	9		10	11	8		1					
8	1	2	3	4	5	6	7	9		10	11	8							
9	1	2	3	4	5	6	7	9		10	11	8							
10	1	2	3	4	5	6	7	9		10	11	8							
11		2	3	4	5	6	7	9		10	11	8			1				
12		2	3	4	5	6	7	9		10	11	8			1				
13		2	3	4	5	6	7	8		10	11		9		1				
14		2	3	4	5	6	7	8		10	11		9		1				
15		2	3	4	5	6	7	8		10	11		9		1				
16		2	3	4	5	6	7	8		10	11		9		1				
17		2	3	4	5	6	7	8		10	11		9		1				
18		2	3	4	5	6	7	8		10			9		1	11			
19		2	3	4	5	6	7	8		10	11		9		1				
20		2	3	4	5	6	7	8		10	11		9		1				
21		2	3	4	5	6	7	8		10	11		9		1				
22		2	3	4	5	6	7	8		10	11		9		1				
23		2	3	4	5	6	7	8		10	11		9		1				
24	1	2	3	4	5	6	7	8		10	11		9						
25	1	2	3	4	5	6	7	8		10	11		9						
26	1	2	3	4	5	6	7	8		10	11		9						
27	1	2	3	4	5	6	7	8		10	11		9						
28	1	2	3	4	5	6	7	8		10		11	9						
29	1	4	3	6	5		7	8		10		11	9				2		
30		4	3		5	6	7	8		10	11		9		1		2		
31		4	3		5		7	8		10	11		9		1		2	6	
32	1	2	3	4	5	6	7	8		10	11		9						
33	1	2	3	4	5	6	7	8		10	11		9						
34		4	3		5	6	7			10	11	8	9		1		2		
35		2		4	5	6	7			10	11	8	9		1				3
36		2		4	5	6	7			10	11	8	9		1				3
37		2		4	5	6	7			10	11	8	9		1				3
38		2		4	5	6	7			10	11	8	9		1				3
39		2		4	5	6	7			10	11	8	9		1				3
40		2		4	5	6	7		9	10	11	8			1				3
41		2		4	5	6	7		9	10	11	8			1				3
42		2		4	5	6	7		9	10	11	8			1				3
	17	42	34	39	42	40	42	30	7	42	39	20	29	1	24	1	4	1	8
		5	2	4		1	8	4	2	33	4	2	17						

One own-goal

Round	Wallace JMB	Howe D	Williams SG	Robson RW	Jones SG	Drury C	Jackson A	Burnside DG	Lovatt J	Kevan DT	Clark C	Hope R	Smith KW	Potter RJ	Millington AH	Carter G	Cram R	Bannister J	Williams GE
R3	1	2	3	4	5	6	7	8		10	11		9						
rep	1	2	3	4	5	6	7	8		10	11		9						
R4	1	2	3	4	5	6	7	8		10	11		9						
R5	1	2	3	4	5	6	7	8		10	11		9						
	4	4	4	4	4	4	4	4		4	4		4						
									1		1	2		2					

1962-63

Division One

	P	W	D	L	F	A	Pts
Everton	42	25	11	6	84	42	61
Tottenham Hotspur	42	23	9	10	111	62	55
Burnley	42	22	10	10	78	57	54
Leicester City	42	20	12	10	79	53	52
Wolverhampton W	42	20	10	12	93	65	50
Sheffield Wednesday	42	19	10	13	77	63	48
Arsenal	42	18	10	14	86	77	46
Liverpool	42	17	10	15	71	59	44
Nottingham Forest	42	17	10	15	67	69	44
Sheffield United	42	16	12	14	58	60	44
Blackburn Rovers	42	15	12	15	79	71	42
West Ham United	42	14	12	16	73	69	40
Blackpool	42	13	14	15	58	64	40
West Bromwich Albion	42	16	7	19	71	79	39
Aston Villa	42	15	8	19	62	68	38
Fulham	42	14	10	18	50	71	38
Ipswich Town	42	12	11	19	59	78	35
Bolton Wanderers	42	15	5	22	55	75	35
Manchester United	42	12	10	20	67	81	34
Birmingham City	42	10	13	19	63	90	33
Manchester City	42	10	11	21	58	102	31
Leyton Orient	42	6	9	27	37	81	21

Manager: Archie Macaulay then Jimmy Hagan

- Derek Kevan scored a hat-trick in his last game for Albion before his £50,000 move to Chelsea - in a 6–1 home win over Ipswich Town. He netted 173 goals in 291 games for the club in 10 years.
- John Kaye was signed from Scunthorpe United for £44,750 (May), Ronnie Fenton arrived from Burnley and Terry Simpson from Peterborough United (in exchange for Keith Smith). In reverse, Bobby Robson returned to Fulham (after scoring 61 goals in 257 games) and both Davey Burnside and Stuart Williams teamed up with Southampton.
- Manager Macaulay was replaced in the hot-seat by the former England, Derby County and Sheffield United forward Jimmy Hagan.

Match No.	Date			Opponents	Result		Scorers	Attendance
1	Aug	18	A	Manchester United	D	2-2	Kevan, Smith	51,896
2		22	H	Leyton Orient	W	2-1	Smith, Kevan	22,409
3		25	H	Burnley	L	1-2	Smith	24,040
4		29	A	Leyton Orient	W	3-2	Lewis (og), Jackson, Clark	16,709
5	Sep	1	A	Sheffield Wednesday	L	1-3	Jackson	21,042
6		8	H	Fulham	W	6-1	Kevan 4, Smith 2	19,304
7		12	H	Birmingham City	W	1-0	Jackson	25,499
8		15	A	Leicester City	L	0-1		21,517
9		19	A	Birmingham City	D	0-0		28,660
10		22	H	Bolton Wanderers	W	5-4	Kevan 3, Foggo, Howe,(pen)	18,670
11		29	A	Everton	L	2-4	Harris (og), Jackson	45,471
12	Oct	6	A	Aston Villa	L	0-2		43,583
13		13	H	Tottenham Hotspur	L	1-2	Jackson	32,450
14		20	A	Ipswich Town	D	1-1	Kevan	19,141
15		27	H	Liverpool	W	1-0	Kevan	17,852
16	Nov	3	A	Blackpool	W	2-0	Jackson, Hope	15,526
17		10	H	Blackburn Rovers	L	2-5	Carter, Hope	14,103
18		17	A	Sheffield United	L	0-1		17,821
19		24	H	Nottingham Forest	L	1-4	Jackson	18,670
20	Dec	1	A	West Ham United	D	2-2	Smith 2	20,769
21		8	H	Manchester City	W	2-1	Smith 2	12,402
22		15	H	Manchester United	W	3-0	Cram, Smith, Jackson	17,595
23	Jan	12	H	Sheffield Wednesday	L	0-3		15,712
24	Mar	2	A	Tottenham Hotspur	L	1-2	Fenton	41,193
25		9	H	Ipswich Town	W	6-1	Kevan 3, Jackson, Clark, Smith	10,759
26		16	A	Wolverhampton Wanderers	L	0-7		22,618
27		20	A	Liverpool	D	2-2	Fenton, Smith	43,977
28		23	H	Blackpool	L	1-2	Jones	15,202
29		25	A	Bolton Wanderers	W	2-1	Cram, Hope	14,997
30	Apr	3	H	Wolverhampton Wanderers	D	2-2	Cram, Hope	15,517
31		6	H	Sheffield United	L	1-2	Cram	12,497
32		12	A	Arsenal	L	2-3	Hope, Jackson	28,219
33		13	A	Blackburn Rovers	L	1-3	Hope,	11,451
34		15	H	Arsenal	L	1-2	Fenton	16,597
35		20	H	West Ham United	W	1-0	Jackson	11,192
36		27	A	Manchester City	W	5-1	Fenton, Foggo 2, Clark, Jackson	14,995
37		30	A	Burnley	L	1-2	Fenton	15,981
38	May	4	H	Leicester City	W	2-1	Fenton, Howe (pen)	20,564
39		7	H	Everton	L	0-4		24,730
40		11	H	Aston Villa	W	1-0	Jackson	25,617
41		14	A	Nottingham Forest	D	2-2	Clark 2	13,068
42		18	A	Fulham	W	2-1	Jackson, Fenton	17,481

Appearances

Goals

FA Cup

R3	Jan	5	A	Plymouth Argyle	W	5-1	Kevan 2, Smith, Cram, Newman (og)	21,915
R4	Mar	6	H	Nottingham Forest	D	0-0		21,511
rep		11	A	Nottingham Forest	L	1-2*	Smith	21,540

* after extra-time

Appearances

Goals

Millington AH	Howe D	Williams GE	Williams SG	Jones SG	Drury CE	Jackson A	Burnside DG	Smith KW	Kevan DT	Clark C	Potter RJ	Hope R	Cram R	Foggo KT	Carter G	Bannister J	Lovatt J	Murray M	Fenton R	Bradley RJ	Macready BL	Fairfax RJ	
1	2	3	4	5	6	7	8	9	10	11													1
1	2	3	4	5	6	7	8	9	10	11													2
	2	3	4	5	6	7		9	10	11	1	8											3
	2	3	4	5	6	7		9	10	11	1	8											4
	2	3	4	5	6	7		9	10	11	1	8											5
1	2	3		5	6	7		9	10	11			4	8									6
1	2	3		5	6	7		9	10	11			4	8									7
1	2	3		5	6	7		9	10	11			4	8									8
1	2	3		5	6	7		9	10				4	8	11								9
1	2	3		5	6	7		9	10				4	8	11								10
1	2	3		5	6	7		9	10	11			4	8									11
1	2	3			5	7			10	11		8	4			6	9						12
1	2	3			5	10			9			8	4	7	11	6							13
	2	3		5	6	9			10		1	8	4	7	11								14
1	2	3		5	6	7		9	10	11		8	4										15
1	2	3		5	6	7		9	10	11		8	4										16
1	2	3		5	6	7		9	10			8	4		11								17
1	2	3		5	6	7		9	10	11		8	4										18
1	2	3		5	6	7			10	11		8	4					9					19
	2	3		5	6	7		9	10	11	1		4						8				20
	2	3		5		7		9	10	11	1		4						8	6			21
	2	3		5	6	7		9	10	11	1		4						8				22
	2	3		5	6	7		9	10	11	1		4						8				23
	2	3		5	6				10	11	1		4					9	8		7		24
	2	3		5	6	7		9	10	11	1		4						8				25
1	2	3		5				9		11		10	4	7					8	6			26
	2			5				9		11	1	10	4	7					8	6		3	27
	2	3		5				9		11	1	10	4	7					8	6			28
		3		5				9		11	1	10	4	7					8	6		2	29
	2			5				9		11	1	10	4	7					8	6		3	30
		3		5				9		11	1	10	4	7					8	6		2	31
	2	3		5		8				11	1	10	4	7		6		9					32
		3		5		8		9		11	1	10	4	7		6						2	33
		3		5		8				11	1	10	4	7					9	6		2	34
	2	3		5		8					1	10	4	7	11				9	6			35
	2	3		5		8				11	1	10	4	7					9	6			36
	2	3		5		8				11	1	10	4	7					9	6			37
	2	3		5		8				11	1	10	4	7					9	6			38
	2	3		5		8				11	1	10	4	7					9	6			39
	2	3		5	6	8				11	1	10	4	7					9				40
	2	3		5	6	8				11	1	10	4	7					9				41
	4	3		5	6	8				11	1	10		7					9			2	42
16	38	40	5	40	27	35	2	27	25	36	26	28	36	25	6	4	1	3	21	13	1	7	
	2			1		14		12	14	5		6	4	3	1				7				

Two own-goals

	2	3		5	6	7		9	10	11	1		4						8				R3
	2	3		5	6	7		9	10	11	1		4						8				R4
	2	3		5	6	7		9	10	11	1		4						8				rep
	3	3		3	3	3		3	3	3	3		3						3				
								2	2				1										

One own-goal

1963-64

Division One

	P	W	D	L	F	A	Pts
Liverpool	42	26	5	11	92	45	57
Manchester United	42	23	7	12	90	62	53
Everton	42	21	10	11	84	64	52
Tottenham Hotspur	42	22	7	13	97	81	51
Chelsea	42	20	10	12	72	56	50
Sheffield Wednesday	42	19	11	12	84	67	49
Blackburn Rovers	42	18	10	14	89	65	46
Arsenal	42	17	11	14	90	82	45
Burnley	42	17	10	15	71	64	44
West Bromwich Albion	42	16	11	15	70	61	43
Leicester City	42	16	11	15	61	58	43
Sheffield United	42	16	11	15	61	64	43
Nottingham Forest	42	16	9	17	64	68	41
West Ham United	42	14	12	16	69	74	40
Fulham	42	13	13	16	58	65	39
Wolverhampton W	42	12	15	15	70	80	39
Stoke City	42	14	10	18	77	78	38
Blackpool	42	13	9	20	52	73	35
Aston Villa	42	11	12	19	62	71	34
Birmingham City	42	11	7	24	54	92	29
Bolton Wanderers	42	10	8	24	48	80	28
Ipswich Town	42	9	7	26	56	121	25

Manager: Jimmy Hagan

- Tony Brown scored on his League debut in a 2–1 win at Ipswich – the first of a record 279 senior goals the 'Bomber' would net for the Baggies.
- Clive Clark, with 17 goals, was the first direct winger to top Albion's scoring charts since Ronnie Allen in 1949–50.
- Among the new faces at The Hawthorns were Terry Simpson from Peterborough United, Doug Fraser from Aberdeen and John Kaye from Scunthorpe United.
- Among those who departed were full-back Don Howe (to Arsenal, after 379 appearances) and winger Alec Jackson (to Birmingham City after 208 outings).
- In December 1963, 11 Albion players went on strike after a row with manager Jimmy Hagan over training rules. A further eight players joined the strike later before chairman Jim Gaunt stepped in to sort things out.

Match No.	Date			Opponents	Result		Scorers	Attendance
1	Aug	24	H	Leicester City	D	1-1	Fenton	23,078
2		27	A	Arsenal	L	2-3	Clark, Kaye	31,267
3		31	A	Bolton Wanderers	W	2-1	Williams, Fenton	14,398
4	Sep	4	H	Arsenal	W	4-0	Foggo 2, Kaye, Clark	20,258
5		7	H	Fulham	W	3-0	Jackson, Clark, Foggo	17,995
6		11	A	Birmingham City	W	1-0	Foggo	34,666
7		14	A	Manchester United	L	0-1		51,624
8		18	H	Birmingham City	W	3-1	Foggo, Clark, Jackson	29,662
9		21	H	Burnley	D	0-0		24,591
10		28	A	Ipswich Town	W	2-1	Brown, Clark	13,859
11	Oct	2	A	Wolverhampton Wanderers	D	0-0		36,338
12		5	H	Sheffield Wednesday	L	1-3	Clark	21,145
13		12	H	Aston Villa	W	4-3	Cram, Jackson, Brown, Foggo	28,602
14		19	A	Liverpool	L	0-1		43,099
15		26	H	Stoke City	L	2-3	Williams, Foggo	23,973
16	Nov	2	A	West Ham United	L	2-4	Foggo, Cram	22,882
17		9	H	Chelsea	D	1-1	Simpson	16,267
18		16	A	Blackpool	L	0-1		11,047
19		23	H	Blackburn Rovers	L	1-3	Fenton	16,441
20		30	A	Nottingham Forest	W	3-0	Fenton, Clark, Carter	18,931
21	Dec	7	H	Sheffield United	W	2-0	Kaye, Clark	14,149
22		14	A	Leicester City	W	2-0	Fraser, Foggo	17,480
23		21	H	Bolton Wanderers	D	1-1	Kaye	10,715
24		26	H	Tottenham Hotspur	D	4-4	Kaye, Clark, Fudge, Howe	37,189
25		28	A	Tottenham Hotspur	W	2-0	Fenton, Foggo	47,863
26	Jan	11	A	Fulham	D	1-1	Clark	16,398
27		18	H	Manchester United	L	1-4	Simpson	25,624
28	Feb	1	A	Burnley	L	2-3	Brown, Clark	15,840
29		8	H	Ipswich Town	W	2-1	Kaye, Fenton	13,476
30		15	A	Sheffield Wednesday	D	2-2	Clark, Williams	19,084
31		22	A	Aston Villa	L	0-1		27,723
32		29	H	Wolverhampton Wanderers	W	3-1	Kaye, Clark, Fenton	19,829
33	Mar	7	A	Stoke City	D	1-1	Kaye	24,893
34		13	H	Blackpool	W	2-1	Kaye, Clark,	13,694
35		21	A	Chelsea	L	1-3	Kaye	19,434
36		27	A	Everton	D	1-1	Simpson	61,187
37		28	H	West Ham United	L	0-1		15,444
38		31	H	Everton	W	4-2	Williams, Fudge 3	27,194
39	Apr	4	A	Blackburn Rovers	W	2-0	Fenton, Clark	12,052
40		11	H	Nottingham Forest	L	2-3	Brown, Foggo	14,442
41		18	A	Sheffield United	L	1-2	Brown	16,607
42		25	H	Liverpool	D	2-2	Kaye, Clark,	17,833
								Appearances
								Goals

FA Cup

R3	Jan	4	H	Blackpool	D	2-2	Clark, Howe (pen)	22,459
rep		8	A	Blackpool	W	1-0	Fenton	21,241
R4		25	H	Arsenal	D	3-3	Fenton, Kaye, Jones	39,703
rep		29	A	Arsenal	L	0-2		57,698
								Appearances
								Goals

Potter RJ	Howe D	Williams GE	Cram R	Jones SG	Simpson TJN	Foggo KT	Fenton R	Kaye J	Hope R	Clark C	Jackson A	Readfern TE	Crawford CHR	Fraser DM	Brown T	Fairfax RJ	Drury CE	Macready BL	Carter G	Fudge MH	Howshall GT	
1	2	3	4	5	6	7	8	9	10	11												1
1	2	3	4	5	6	7	10	9		11	8											2
1	2	3	4	5	6	7	10	9		11	8											3
1	2	3	4	5	6	7	10	9		11	8											4
1	2	3	4	5	6	7	10	9		11	8											5
1	2	3	4	5	6	7	10			11	8	9										6
1	4	3	8	5	6	7	10			11		9	2									7
1	2	3		5	6	7	10			11	8	9		4								8
1	2	3		5	6	7	10			11	8	9		4								9
1	2	3		5	6	7	9			11	10			4	8							10
1	2	3		5	6	7	10	9		11	8			4								11
1		3		5	6	7	10	9		11	8		2	4								12
1			9	5	6	7				11	10		2	4	8	3						13
1		3	9	5	6	7				11	10			4	8		2					14
1		3	9	5	6	7				11	10			4	8		2					15
1	2	3	9	5	6	7				11	10			4				8				16
1		3	9	5	6	7	8			11	10		2	4								17
1	2	3		5	6	7	8	9	10	11				4								18
1	2	3		5	6		8	9	10	7				4					11			19
1	2	3		5	6		8	9	10	7				4					11			20
1	2	3		5	6		8	9		7				4					11	10		21
1	2	3		5	6	7	8	9		11				4						10		22
1	2	3		5	6	7	8	9		11				4						10		23
1	2	3		5	6	7	8	9		11				4						10		24
1	2	3		5	6	7	8	9		11				4						10		25
1	2	3		5	6	7	8	9		11				4						10		26
1	2	3		5	6		8	9		7				4					11	10		27
1	2	3		5	6	7		9		11	10			4	8							28
1	2	3		5	6		10	9		11	8			4				7				29
1	2	3		5	6	7				11	10			4	9			8				30
1	2	3		5	6	7		9		11					10			8			4	31
1	2	3		5	6	7	8	9		11	10										4	32
1	2	3		5	6	7		9		11	10			4	8							33
1	2	3		5	6	7		9		11	10			4	8							34
1	2	3		5	6	7		9		11	10			4	8							35
1	2	3		5	6	7	8	9		11	10			4								36
1	2	3		5	6	7	8	9		11	10			4								37
1	2	3		5	6	7	9			11	8			4						10		38
1	2	3		5	6	7	9			11	8			4						10		39
1	2	3		5	6	7	9			11	8			4	10							40
1		3	2	5	6	7	9			11				4	8					10		41
1		3	2	5	6	7		9		11				4	8					10		42
42	35	41	14	42	42	37	31	27	4	42	27	4	4	33	13	1	2	4	4	11	2	
	1	4	2		3	11	8	11		16	3			1	5				1	4		

Potter RJ	Howe D	Williams GE	Cram R	Jones SG	Simpson TJN	Foggo KT	Fenton R	Kaye J	Hope R	Clark C	Jackson A	Readfern TE	Crawford CHR	Fraser DM	Brown T	Fairfax RJ	Drury CE	Macready BL	Carter G	Fudge MH	Howshall GT	
1	2	3		5	6	7	8			11		9		4						10		R3
1	2	3		5	6	7	8	9		11				4						10		rep
1	2	3		5	6	7	8	9		11	10			4								R4
1	2	3	8	5	6	7		9		11	10			4								rep
4	4	4	1	4	4	4	3	3		4	2	1		4						2		
	1			1			2	1		1												

1964-65

Division One

	P	W	D	L	F	A	Pts
Manchester United	42	26	9	7	89	39	61
Leeds United	42	26	9	7	83	52	61
Chelsea	42	24	8	10	89	54	56
Everton	42	17	15	10	69	60	49
Nottingham Forest	42	17	13	12	71	67	47
Tottenham Hotspur	42	19	7	16	87	71	45
Liverpool	42	17	10	15	67	73	44
Sheffield Wednesday	42	16	11	15	57	55	43
West Ham United	42	19	4	19	82	71	42
Blackburn Rovers	42	16	10	16	83	79	42
Stoke City	42	16	10	16	67	66	42
Burnley	42	16	10	16	70	70	42
Arsenal	42	17	7	18	69	75	41
West Bromwich Albion	42	13	13	16	70	65	39
Sunderland	42	14	9	19	64	74	37
Aston Villa	42	16	5	21	57	82	37
Blackpool	42	12	11	19	67	78	35
Leicester City	42	11	13	18	69	85	35
Sheffield United	42	12	11	19	50	64	35
Fulham	42	11	12	19	60	78	34
Wolverhampton W	42	13	4	25	59	89	30
Birmingham City	42	8	11	23	64	96	27

Manager: Jimmy Hagan

- Bobby Cram's hat-trick against Stoke City in September was the first by an Albion defender for 45 years, since Sid Bowser's treble against Bradford City in 1919.
- Manager Hagan paid £25,000 for centre-forward Jeff Astle from Notts County. He scored twice on his home debut in a 5–1 win over Wolves.
- Another striker, ex-England star Ray Crawford, was also recruited from Wolves.
- Out of The Hawthorns went Welsh international goalkeeper Tony Millington, sold to Crystal Palace for £7,000, and Ronnie Fenton transferred to Birmingham City.

Match No.	Date			Opponents	Result		Scorers	Attendance
1	Aug	22	A	Manchester United	D	2-2	Brown, Foulkes (og)	52,268
2		26	H	Sunderland	W	4-1	Brown 3, Clark	26,139
3		29	H	Fulham	D	2-2	Williams, Clark	18,702
4	Sep	2	A	Sunderland	D	2-2	Brown, Clark	52,177
5		5	A	Nottingham Forest	D	0-0		28,334
6		9	A	Birmingham City	D	1-1	Foggo	26,568
7		12	H	Stoke City	W	5-3	Foggo, Cram 3 (2 pens), Brown	24,505
8		16	H	Birmingham City	L	0-2		26,013
9		19	A	Tottenham Hotspur	L	0-1		36,993
10		26	H	Burnley	L	1-2	Cram (pen)	15,009
11		30	A	Leicester City	L	2-4	Cram (pen), Williams	17,218
12	Oct	3	A	Sheffield United	D	1-1	Carter	17,592
13		10	H	Wolverhampton Wanderers	W	5-1	Astle 2, Kaye 2, Cram (pen)	23,006
14		17	A	Aston Villa	W	1-0	Howshall	26,091
15		24	H	Liverpool	W	3-0	Clark 2, Astle	22,045
16		31	A	Sheffield Wednesday	D	1-1	Clark	18,434
17	Nov	7	H	Blackpool	L	1-3	Kaye	17,504
18		14	A	Blackburn Rovers	L	2-4	Foggo, Brown	13,828
19		21	H	Arsenal	D	0-0		18,489
20		28	A	Leeds United	L	0-1		29,553
21	Dec	5	H	Chelsea	L	0-2		15,518
22		12	H	Manchester United	D	1-1	Kaye	28,504
23		19	A	Fulham	L	1-3	Jones	10,390
24		26	A	Everton	L	2-3	Fenton, Clark	46,719
25	Jan	2	H	Nottingham Forest	D	2-2	Fudge, Clark	16,040
26		16	A	Stoke City	L	0-2		25,628
27		23	H	Tottenham Hotspur	W	2-0	Cram, Clark	24,233
28	Feb	6	A	Burnley	W	1-0	Foggo	12,902
29		13	H	Sheffield United	L	0-1		10,511
30		27	H	Aston Villa	W	3-1	Astle, Cram (pen), Hope	24,040
31	Mar	13	H	Leicester City	W	6-0	Astle 2, Howshall, Clark, Foggo, Williams	15,162
32		15	A	Wolverhampton Wanderers	L	2-3	Foggo, Harris (og)	26,722
33		20	A	Blackpool	L	0-3		11,168
34		23	H	Everton	W	4-0	Astle 2, Foggo, Cram (pen)	13,013
35		26	H	Blackburn Rovers	D	0-0		17,045
36	Apr	3	A	Arsenal	D	1-1	Hope	18,824
37		6	A	Liverpool	W	3-0	Kaye, Hope, Clark	34,152
38		12	H	Leeds United	L	1-2	Foggo	22,010
39		16	A	West Ham United	L	1-6	Astle	27,710
40		17	A	Chelsea	D	2-2	Crawford, Howshall	30,792
41		19	H	West Ham United	W	4-2	Foggo, Astle, Brown 2	14,018
42		24	H	Sheffield Wednesday	W	1-0	Crawford	16,002
								Appearances
								Goals

FA Cup

R3	Jan	9	H	Liverpool	L	1-2	Astle	29,851
								Appearances
								Goals

Potter RJ	Cram R	Williams GE	Fraser DM	Jones SG	Simpson TJN	Foggo KT	Brown T	Kaye J	Hope R	Clark C	Collard I	Howshall GT	Astle J	Fairfax RJ	Fenton R	Carter G	Lovett GJ	Krzywicki RL	Fudge MH	Williams WT	Crawford R	
1	2	3	4	5	6	7	8	9	10	11												1
1	2	3	4	5	6	7	8	9	10	11												2
1	2	3	4	5	6	7	8	9	10	11												3
1	2	3	4	5	6	7	8	9	10	11												4
1	2	3	4	5	6	7	8	9	10	11												5
1	2	3	4	5	6	7	8	9	10	11												6
1	2	3	4	5	6	7	8	9	10	11												7
1	2	3	4	5	6	7	8	9	10	11												8
1	2	3	4	5	6	7	8	9	10	11												9
1	2	3	4	5	6	7	9		10	11	8											10
1	2	3		5	6	7	8	9		11		4	10									11
1	2			5	6	7	8					4	9	3	10	11						12
1	2	3		5	6			8	10	7		4	9			11						13
1	2	3		5	6			8	10	7		4	9			11						14
1	2	3		5	6			8	10	7		4	9			11						15
1	2	3		5	6			8	10	7		4	9			11						16
1	2			5	6			8	10	7		4	9	3		11						17
1	2	3		5	6	7	8			11		4	9		10							18
1	2	3		5	6		8		11	7		4	9		10							19
1	2	3	4	5	6	7			10	11			9		8							20
1		3	4	5		7			10	11			9	2	8		6					21
1		3	4	5	6	7		8	10	11			9	2								22
1		3	4	5			10	8		11			9	2			6	7				23
1	2	3	4	5	6				10	11			9		7				8			24
1	2	3	4		6				10	11			9		7				8	5		25
1	2	3	4	5	6	7			10	11		8	9									26
1	2	3	4	5	6	7			10	11		8	9									27
1		3	4	5	6	7			10	11		8	9	2								28
1	2	3	4	5	6	7			10	11		8	9									29
1	2	3	6	5		7			10	11		4	8								9	30
1	2	3	6	5		7			10	11		4	8								9	31
1	2	3	6	5		7		9	10	11		4	8									32
1	2	3	6	5	4	7		9		11		8	10									33
1	2	3	6	5		7		9	10	11		4	8									34
1	2	3	6	5		7		9	10	11		4	8									35
1	2	3	6	5		7		9	10	11		4	8									36
1	2	3	6	5		7		9	10	11		4	8									37
1	2	3	6	5		7		9	10	11		4	8									38
1	2	3	6	5		7		9	10	11		4	8									39
1	2	3	6	5		7			10			4	8			11					9	40
1	2	3	6	5		7	11		10			4	8								9	41
1	2	3	6	5		7	11		10			4	8								9	42
42	38	40	33	41	28	33	17	25	37	38	1	26	32	6	7	7	2	1	2	1	5	
	9	3		1		9	9	5	3	11		3	10		1	1			1		2	

Two own-goals

1	2	3	4	5	6				10	11			9		7				8			R3
1	1	1	1	1	1				1	1			1		1				1			
													1									

1965-66

Division One

	P	W	D	L	F	A	Pts
Liverpool	42	26	9	7	79	34	61
Leeds United	42	23	9	10	79	38	55
Burnley	42	24	7	11	79	47	55
Manchester United	42	18	15	9	84	59	51
Chelsea	42	22	7	13	65	53	51
West Bromwich Albion	42	19	12	11	91	69	50
Leicester City	42	21	7	14	80	65	49
Tottenham Hotspur	42	16	12	14	75	66	44
Sheffield United	42	16	11	15	56	59	43
Stoke City	42	15	12	15	65	64	42
Everton	42	15	11	16	56	62	41
West Ham United	42	15	9	18	70	83	39
Blackpool	42	14	9	19	55	65	37
Arsenal	42	12	13	17	62	75	37
Newcastle United	42	14	9	19	50	63	37
Aston Villa	42	15	6	21	69	80	36
Sheffield Wednesday	42	14	8	20	56	66	36
Nottingham Forest	42	14	8	20	56	72	36
Sunderland	42	14	8	20	51	72	36
Fulham	42	14	7	21	67	85	35
Northampton Town	42	10	13	19	55	92	33
Blackburn Rovers	42	8	4	30	57	88	20

Manager: Jimmy Hagan

- Albion gained their first major trophy success in 12 years by winning the League Cup in the first season of entry, and the game against West Ham United was the last of the two-leg Finals.
- By virtue of their League Cup victory, Albion qualified for a place in a European competition for the first time – the Fairs Cup.
- Tony Brown became the first player to score in every round of the League Cup.
- Substitutes were allowed in League games for the first time this season, and Graham Lovett was the first to enter the play for Albion, replacing Kenny Foggo in the 4–3 win at Northampton in September.
- Ray Crawford left The Hawthorns and returned to his former club, Ipswich Town.
- John Kaye was voted Midlands Footballer of the Year. He would win the award again in 1969–70.

Match No.	Date			Opponents	Result		Scorers	Attendance
1	Aug	21	H	West Ham United	W	3-0	Clark 2, Astle	19,956
2		25	A	Newcastle United	W	1-0	Kaye	43,901
3		28	A	Nottingham Forest	L	2-3	Astle, Foggo	27,366
4	Sep	1	H	Newcastle United	L	1-2	Kaye	22,043
5		4	H	Sheffield Wednesday	W	4-2	Astle 3, Kaye	15,229
6		7	A	Everton	W	3-2	Brown, Kaye, Astle	43,468
7		10	A	Northampton Town	W	4-3	Hope, Astle 3	18,528
8		15	H	Everton	D	1-1	Astle	25,513
9		18	H	Stoke City	W	6-2	Setters (og), Kaye 3, Cram (pen), Brown	24,374
10		25	A	Burnley	L	0-2		20,487
11	Oct	2	H	Chelsea	L	1-2	Fraser	23,049
12		9	H	Sunderland	W	4-1	Kaye, Cram (pen), Brown 2	19,617
13		16	A	Aston Villa	D	1-1	Astle	41,455
14		23	H	Liverpool	W	3-0	Brown, Kaye, Clark	29,669
15		30	A	Tottenham Hotspur	L	1-2	Crawford	43,658
16	Nov	6	H	Fulham	W	6-2	Wilson, Brown 2, Lovatt 2, Clark	19,858
17		13	A	Blackpool	D	1-1	Brown	12,642
18		20	H	Blackburn Rovers	W	2-1	Cram (pen), Brown	17,189
19		27	A	Leicester City	L	1-2	Crawford	21,214
20	Dec	4	H	Sheffield United	D	1-1	Brown	15,607
21		11	A	Leeds United	L	0-4		33,140
22		27	A	Manchester United	D	1-1	Crawford	54,370
23	Jan	1	A	Sunderland	W	5-1	Kaye, Hope, Brown 2, Crawford	34,938
24		8	H	Leeds United	L	1-2	Wilson	24,900
25		15	A	Liverpool	D	2-2	Brown, Kaye	46,687
26		29	A	West Ham United	L	0-4		25,518
27	Feb	5	H	Nottingham Forest	W	5-3	Clark, Kaye, Cram (pen), Brown, Hope	14,054
28		11	H	Aston Villa	D	2-2	Kaye, Brown	17,089
29		19	A	Sheffield Wednesday	W	2-1	Clark, Mobley (og)	17,703
30		26	H	Northampton Town	D	1-1	Clark	18,923
31	Mar	12	A	Stoke City	D	1-1	Clark	23,667
32		19	H	Burnley	L	1-2	Brown	18,747
33	Apr	2	A	Fulham	L	1-2	Astle	20,426
34		5	A	Arsenal	D	1-1	Cram (pen)	8,738
35		9	H	Blackpool	W	2-1	Brown, Foggo	13,079
36		11	H	Arsenal	D	4-4	Cram 2 (2 pens), Astle, Lovett	16,094
37		16	A	Blackburn Rovers	W	1-0	Astle	7,637
38		22	H	Leicester City	W	5-1	Kaye 2, Sjoberg 2 (2 ogs), Astle	15,229
39		25	A	Chelsea	W	3-2	Clark, Astle 2	22,804
40		30	A	Sheffield United	W	2-0	Kaye 2	16,022
41	May	4	H	Manchester United	D	3-3	Clark, Lovett, Kaye	22,609
42		7	H	Tottenham Hotspur	W	2-1	Hope, Astle	22,586

Appearances
Sub appearances
Goals

FA Cup

R3	Jan	22	A	Bolton Wanderers	L	0-3		24,425

Appearances

League Cup

R2	Sep	22	H	Walsall	W	3-1	Brown 2, Bennett (og)	41,188
R3	Oct	13	A	Leeds United	W	4-2	Brown, Kaye, Clark, Astle	13,455
R4	Nov	3	A	Coventry City	D	1-1	Kaye	38,476
rep		10	H	Coventry City	W	6-1	Astle 3, Fraser 2, Brown	31,956
R5		17	H	Aston Villa	W	3-1	Kaye 2, Brown	40,694
SF1	Dec	1	H	Peterborough United	W	2-1	Brown, Astle	20,933
SF2		15	A	Peterborough United	W	4-2	Brown 3, Crawford	18,288
F1	Mar	9	A	West Ham United	L	1-2	Astle	28,588
F2		23	H	West Ham United	W	4-1	Kaye, Brown, Clark, Williams	32,013

Final won 5-3 on aggregate

Appearances
Goals

Potter RJ	Cram R	Williams GE	Lovett GJ	Jones SG	Fraser DM	Foggo KT	Astle J	Kaye J	Hope R	Clark C	Fairfax RJ	Howshall GT	Brown T	Wilson RT	Sheppard RJ	Crawford R	Collard I	Crawford CHR	Krzywicki RL	Campbell D	
1	2	3	4	5	6	7	8	9	10	11											1
1		3	4	5	6	7	8	9	10	11	2										2
1		3	4	5	6	7	8	9	10	11	2										3
1		3	4	5	6	7	8	9	10	11	2										4
1	2	3		5	6	7	8	9	10	11		4									5
1	2	3		5	6	7	8	9	10			4	11								6
1	2	3	12	5	6	**7**	8	9	10			4	11								7
1	2	3	10	5	6		8	9	11			4	7								8
1	2	3	4	5	6		8	9	10	11			7								9
1	2		4	5	6		8	9	10	11	3		7								10
1	2		4	5	6		8	9	10		3		7	11							11
	2	3	4	5	6		8	9	10	11			7		1						12
	2		4	5	6		8	9	10	11	3		7		1						13
	2		4	5	6			9	10	11	3		7		1	8					14
	2		4	5	6			9	10	11	3		7		1	8					15
	2		4	5	6			9	10	7	3		8	11	1						16
	2		4	5	6		8	9	10	11	3		7		1						17
	2		4	5	6		8	9	10	11	3		7		1						18
	2		4	5	6			9	10	11	3		7		**1**	8	12				19
	2		4	5	6		8	9	10	11	3		7		1						20
	2		4	5	6	7		9	10	11	3				1	8					21
1	2		4	5	6	7		9	10	11	3					8					22
1	2		4	5	**6**	12		9	10	11	3		7			8					23
1	2		4	5	6			9	10		3		7	11		8					24
1	2		4	5	6			9	10	11	3		7			8					25
1		3	4	5	6			9	10	11			8					2	7		26
1	2		4	5	6	7		**9**	10	11	3	12	8								27
1	2		4	5	**6**	7		9	10	11	3	12	8								28
1		3	4	5	6			9	10	11	2	8	7								29
1		3	4	5	6			9		11	2	**8**	7			10	12				30
1	2	6	10		4		8	9		11	3		7							5	31
1	2	6	10		4		8	9		11	3		7							5	32
1	2		4		6		8	9	10	11	3		7							5	33
1	2		4		6		8	9	10	11	3		7							5	34
1	2		4	5	6	7		9	**10**	11	3		8				12				35
1	2	4	10	5	6		8	9		11	3		7								36
1	2	4	10	5	6		8	9		11	3		7								37
1	2	4		5	6		8	9	10	11	3		7								38
1	2	4	12	5	**6**		8	9	10	11	3		7								39
1		3	4	5	6		8	9	10	11	2		7								40
1		3	4	5	6		8	9	10	11	2		7								41
1	2	4		5	6		8	9	10	11	3		7								42
32	34	22	36	38	42	12	27	42	37	37	34	6	35	3	10	9		1	1	4	
			2			1						2					3				
	7		4		1	2	18	18	4	10			17	2		4					

Four own-goals

1	2		4	5	6			9	10	11	3		7			8					R3
1	1		1	1	1			1	1	1	1		1			1					

1	2		4	5	6		8	9	10	11	3		7								R2
	2		4	5	6		8	9	10	11	3		7		1						R3
	2		4	5	6			9	10	11	3		7		1	8					R4
	2		4	5	6		8	9	10	11	3		7		1						rep
	2		4	5	6		8	9	10	11	3		7		1						R5
	2		4	5	6		8	9	10	11	3		7		1						SF1
1	2		4	5	6			9	10	11	3		7			8					SF2
1	2	6	10		4		8	9		11	3		7							5	F1
1	2	6			4		8	9	10	11	3		7							**5**	F2
4	9	2	8	7	9		7	9	8	9	9		9		5	2				2	
		1			2		6	5		2			10			1					

One own-goal

1966-67

Division One

	P	W	D	L	F	A	Pts
Manchester United	42	24	12	6	84	45	60
Nottingham Forest	42	23	10	9	64	41	56
Tottenham Hotspur	42	24	8	10	71	48	56
Leeds United	42	22	11	9	62	42	55
Liverpool	42	19	13	10	64	47	51
Everton	42	19	10	13	65	46	48
Arsenal	42	16	14	12	58	47	46
Leicester City	42	18	8	16	78	71	44
Chelsea	42	15	14	13	67	62	44
Sheffield United	42	16	10	16	52	59	42
Sheffield Wednesday	42	14	13	15	56	47	41
Stoke City	42	17	7	18	63	58	41
West Bromwich Albion	42	16	7	19	77	73	39
Burnley	42	15	9	18	66	76	39
Manchester City	42	12	15	15	43	52	39
West Ham United	42	14	8	20	80	84	36
Sunderland	42	14	8	20	58	72	36
Fulham	42	11	12	19	71	83	34
Southampton	42	14	6	22	74	92	34
Newcastle United	42	12	9	21	39	81	33
Aston Villa	42	11	7	24	54	85	29
Blackpool	42	6	9	27	41	76	21

Manager: Jimmy Hagan

- Albion lost the first League Cup Final to be staged at Wembley, going down 3–2 to the Third Division champions-elect Queen's Park Rangers, having been 2–0 up at half-time. And Baggies winger Clive Clark, who struck both goals in the Final against his former club, became the first player to score in every game of a League Cup competition.
- Bobby Hope had the pleasure of scoring Albion's first ever goal in a European competition – earning a draw in Holland against DOS Utrecht.
- Clive Clark, with 29 goals, was the first out-and-out winger to top Albion's scoring charts three times (the previous two were in 1963–64 and 1964–65).
- Transfers included goalkeeper John Osborne (from Chesterfield), defender John Talbot (from Burnley) and Eddie Colquhoun (from Bury), while out went goalkeeper Ray Potter, sold to Portsmouth, having made 238 appearances.
- Manager Jimmy Hagan was dismissed at the end of the season.
- Albion reached the milestone of 100 League games against both Burnley and Everton this season.

Match No.	Date			Opponents	Result		Scorers	Attendance
1	Aug	20	A	Manchester United	L	3-5	Hope, Clark 2	41,543
2		24	A	Leeds United	L	1-2	Astle	35,102
3		27	H	Burnley	L	1-2	Lovett	21,732
4		31	H	Leeds United	W	2-0	Clark, Brown	22,072
5	Sep	3	A	Nottingham Forest	L	1-2	Brown	21,871
6		7	A	Newcastle United	W	3-1	Clark 2, Kaye	24,748
7		10	H	Fulham	W	5-1	Clark 2, Hope 2, Astle	17,160
8		17	A	Everton	L	4-5	Astle, Fraser, Cram (pen), Kaye	45,165
9		24	H	Stoke City	L	0-1		24,865
10	Oct	1	A	Sheffield United	L	3-4	Astle, Fraser, Clark	15,313
11		8	A	Sunderland	D	2-2	Treacy, Clark	26,632
12		15	H	Aston Villa	W	2-1	Astle, Krzywicki	31,128
13		22	A	Arsenal	W	3-2	Hope 2, Clark	31,636
14		29	H	Sheffield Wednesday	L	1-2	Astle	19,335
15	Nov	5	A	Aston Villa	L	2-3	Kaye, Lovett	23,984
16		12	H	Chelsea	L	0-1		28,151
17		19	A	Leicester City	L	1-2	Foggo	25,003
18		26	H	Liverpool	W	2-1	Brown, Clark	25,931
19	Dec	3	A	West Ham United	L	0-3		22,961
20		10	H	Manchester City	L	0-3		17,299
21		17	H	Manchester United	L	3-4	Astle 2, Kaye	32,080
22		26	H	Tottenham Hotspur	W	3-0	Brown 3 (1 pen)	37,969
23		27	A	Tottenham Hotspur	D	0-0		39,129
24		31	A	Burnley	L	1-5	Astle	18,508
25	Jan	7	H	Nottingham Forest	L	1-2	Clark	21,795
26		14	A	Fulham	D	2-2	Collard, Cram	20,680
27		21	H	Everton	W	1-0	Clark	26,104
28	Feb	4	A	Stoke City	D	1-1	Astle	26,280
29		11	H	Sheffield United	L	1-2	Cram	20,354
30		25	H	Sunderland	D	2-2	Fraser, Astle	22,296
31	Mar	18	H	Arsenal	L	0-1		16,832
32		25	A	Manchester City	D	2-2	Kaye, Fraser	22,780
33		27	H	Southampton	W	3-2	Brown, Clark, Astle	19,732
34		29	A	Southampton	D	2-2	Astle, Clark	28,878
35	Apr	1	H	Blackpool	W	3-1	Clark, Williams, Brown	19,441
36		10	A	Chelsea	W	2-0	Clark, Foggo	18,448
37		15	H	Leicester City	W	1-0	Clark	22,872
38		19	A	Sheffield Wednesday	L	0-1		23,156
39		22	A	Liverpool	W	1-0	Astle	39,883
40		28	H	West Ham United	W	3-1	Brown 2 (2 pens), Astle	23,210
41	May	6	A	Blackpool	W	3-1	Astle, Williams, Brown (pen)	9,986
42		13	H	Newcastle United	W	6-1	Foggo, Brown 3, Williams, Clark	20,036
								Appearances
								Sub appearances
								Goals

FA Cup

R3	Jan	28	A	Northampton Town	W	3-1	Astle, Clark, Brown	16,899
R4	Feb	18	A	Leeds United	L	0-5		41,329
								Appearances
								Goals

League Cup

R2	Sep	14	H	Aston Villa	W	6-1	Hope 3, Fraser 2, Clark	25,039
R3	Oct	5	H	Manchester City	W	4-2	Stephens, Krzywicki, Astle, Clark	19,016
R4		25	A	Swindon Town	W	2-0	Astle, Clark	16,254
R5	Dec	7	A	Northampton Town	W	3-1	Brown, Simpson, Clark	14,706
SF1	Jan	18	H	West Ham United	W	4-0	Astle 3, Clark	30,193
SF2	Feb	8	A	West Ham United	D	2-2	Hope, Clark	35,790
F	Mar	4	N	Queen's Park Rangers	L	2-3	Clark 2	97,952
Final at Wembley Stadium								Appearances
								Sub appearances
								Goals

Potter RJ	Cram R	Fairfax RJ	Williams GE	Jones SG	Fraser DM	Brown T	Astle J	Kaye J	Hope R	Clark C	Sheppard RJ	Collard I	Lovett GJ	Foggo KT	Campbell D	Crawford CHR	Krzywicki RL	Stephens KJ	Treacy RCP	Simpson TJN	Howshall GT	Clarke D	Talbut J	Osborne J	Colquhoun EPS	
1	2	3	4	5	6	7	8	9	10	11																1
1	2	3	4	5	6	7	8	9	10	11																2
		2		5	6	7	8	9	10	11	1	3	4													3
		2		5	6	7	8	9	10	11	1	3	4													4
		2		5	6	7	8	9	10	11	1	3	4													5
	2			5	6	7	8	9	10	11	1	3	4													6
	2			5	6	7	8	9	10	11	1	3	4													7
	2			5	6		8	9	10	11	1	3	4	7												8
		2		5	6		8	9	10	11	1	3	4	7												9
		2	4		6		8	9	10	11	1	3	7		5											10
1			4						10	11		3	6		5	2	7	8	9							11
1			4	5	6		8	9	**10**	11		3	12			2	7									12
1				5	6		8	9	10	11		3	4			2	7									13
1			7	5	6		8	9	10	11		3	4			2										14
1		3	7	5	6		8	9	10	11			4			2										15
1		2	4	5	6	7	8	9	10	11		3														16
		2	4	5	**6**	10	8	9		11	1	3		7						12						17
	2	3		5	6	8		9	10	11	1		4	7												18
	2	3		5	6	8		9	10	11	1		4	7												19
			3	5	6	7	8	9	10	11	1		4							2						20
1		2	12	5	6	7	8	9	10	11		**3**									4					21
1			3		6	7	8	9	10	11											4	2	5			22
1			3	5	6	7	8	9	10	11											4	2				23
1			3		6	9	8		10	11								7			4	2	5			24
			3		6	7	8	9	10	11											4	2	5	1		25
	2		3		6	7	8	9	10	11		4											5	1		26
	2		3		6		8	9	10	11		4						7					5	1		27
	2		3		6	7	8	9	10	11		4										12	**5**	1		28
	2	12	3	5	6	8		**9**	10	11		4		7										1		29
				5	6	7	8	9	10	11		3		4								12		1	**2**	30
		2	3	5	6		8	9		11	1	10		7											4	31
		2	3		4		8	9	10	11				7								6		1	5	32
		2	3		6	4	8	9	10	11				7										1	5	33
		2	3		6	4	8	9	10	11	1			7											5	34
		2	3			4	8	9	10	11		6		7										1	5	35
		2	3			4	8	9	10	11		6		7										1	5	36
		2	3			10	8	9		11		6		7									4	1	5	37
		2	3			10	8	9		11		6		7									4	1	5	38
		2	3			10	8	9		11		6		7									4	1	5	39
		2	3			6	8	9	10	11				7									4	1	5	40
		2	3		12	6	8	**9**	10	11				7									4	1	5	41
		2	3		6	10	8	9		11				7							4		5	1		42
12	11	25	30	23	34	31	38	40	36	42	14	26	15	19	2	5	3	3	1	1	6	5	12	16	12	
		1	1		1								1							1		2				
	3		3		4	14	16	5	5	19		1	2	3			1		1							

Potter RJ	Cram R	Fairfax RJ	Williams GE	Jones SG	Fraser DM	Brown T	Astle J	Kaye J	Hope R	Clark C	Sheppard RJ	Collard I	Lovett GJ	Foggo KT	Campbell D	Crawford CHR	Krzywicki RL	Stephens KJ	Treacy RCP	Simpson TJN	Howshall GT	Clarke D	Talbut J	Osborne J	Colquhoun EPS	
	2		3		6	7	8	9	10	11	1	4											5			R3
	2		3	5	6	8	9		10	11	1	4		7												R4
	2		2	1	2	2	2	1	2	2	2	2		1									1			
						1	1			1																

Potter RJ	Cram R	Fairfax RJ	Williams GE	Jones SG	Fraser DM	Brown T	Astle J	Kaye J	Hope R	Clark C	Sheppard RJ	Collard I	Lovett GJ	Foggo KT	Campbell D	Crawford CHR	Krzywicki RL	Stephens KJ	Treacy RCP	Simpson TJN	Howshall GT	Clarke D	Talbut J	Osborne J	Colquhoun EPS	
	2			5	6		8	9	10	11	1	3	4	7												R2
1			4		**6**		9		10	11		3	8		5	2	12	7								R3
1			7	5	6		8	9	10	11		3	4			2										R4
			3	5	6	7	8	9	10	11	1		4							2						R5
	2		3	5	6	7	8	9	10	11	1	4														SF1
	2		3	5	6	8		9	10	11	1	4		7												SF2
	2		3		6	7	8	**9**	10	11	1	4										5				F
2	4		6	5	7	4	6	6	7	7	5	6	4	2	1	2		1		1		1				
																	1									
					2	1	5		4	8							1	1		1						

1967-68

Division One

	P	W	D	L	F	A	Pts
Manchester City	42	26	6	10	86	43	58
Manchester United	42	24	8	10	89	55	56
Liverpool	42	22	11	9	71	40	55
Leeds United	42	22	9	11	71	41	53
Everton	42	23	6	13	67	40	52
Chelsea	42	18	12	12	62	68	48
Tottenham Hotspur	42	19	9	14	70	59	47
West Bromwich Albion	42	17	12	13	75	62	46
Arsenal	42	17	10	15	60	56	44
Newcastle United	42	13	15	14	54	67	41
Nottingham Forest	42	14	11	17	52	64	39
West Ham United	42	14	10	18	73	69	38
Leicester City	42	13	12	17	64	69	38
Burnley	42	14	10	18	64	71	38
Sunderland	42	13	11	18	51	61	37
Southampton	42	13	11	18	66	83	37
Wolverhampton W	42	14	8	20	66	75	36
Stoke City	42	14	7	21	50	73	35
Sheffield Wednesday	42	11	12	19	51	63	34
Coventry City	42	9	15	18	51	71	33
Sheffield United	42	11	10	21	49	70	32
Fulham	42	10	7	25	56	98	27

Manager: Alan Ashman

- Alan Ashman was named as Albion's new manager.
- Jeff Astle scored in every round of the FA Cup. He also netted two hat-tricks in the space of three days in home League games against Manchester United and West Ham United in April/May. Astle was also named Midlands Footballer of the Year.
- Albion's Dennis Clarke became the first substitute used in an FA Cup Final, replacing the injured John Kaye at the end of normal time.
- Eddie Colquhoun was injured in the League game at Newcastle in April and missed the FA Cup Final.
- Albion's 8–1 home win over Burnley was their biggest in the League since 1957.
- Welsh international Ronnie Rees was signed from Coventry City and forward Dennis Martin from Carlisle United, the manager's previous club.
- Bobby Cram left to join Bromsgrove Rovers, winger Kenny Foggo signed for Portsmouth, Mickey Fudge joined Exeter City, Gerry Howshall moved to Norwich City and Stan Jones returned to his former club Walsall after making 267 appearances at the heart of Albion's defence.

Match No.	Date			Opponents	Result		Scorers	Attendance
1	Aug	19	H	Chelsea	L	0-1		33,283
2		23	A	Wolverhampton Wanderers	D	3-3	Foggo, Kaye, Brown	52,438
3		26	A	Southampton	L	0-4		22,714
4		30	H	Wolverhampton Wanderers	W	4-1	Astle, Clark, Stephens, Kaye	38,373
5	Sep	2	H	Liverpool	L	0-2		32,159
6		6	H	Arsenal	L	1-3	Clark	20,153
7		9	A	Stoke City	D	0-0		20,892
8		16	H	Nottingham Forest	W	2-1	Hope, Stephens	21,136
9		23	A	Coventry City	L	2-4	Astle, Clark	31,258
10		30	H	Sheffield United	W	4-1	Astle 3, Brown	15,186
11	Oct	7	A	Fulham	W	2-1	Astle, Brown	17,316
12		14	H	Leeds United	W	2-0	Astle 2	21,024
13		24	A	Everton	L	1-2	Kaye	44,092
14		28	H	Leicester City	D	0-0		20,961
15	Nov	11	H	Burnley	W	8-1	Hope 2, Clark, 2, Brown, Colquhoun, Kaye, Astle	18,952
16		18	A	Sheffield Wednesday	D	2-2	Clark, Astle	27,659
17		25	H	Tottenham Hotspur	W	2-0	Clark, Hope	29,033
18	Dec	2	A	Manchester United	L	1-2	Kaye	52,897
19		11	A	West Ham United	W	3-2	Kryzwicki, Astle, Hope (pen)	19,018
20		16	A	Chelsea	W	3-0	Clark, Astle, Kryzwicki	27,739
21		23	H	Southampton	D	0-0		24,082
22		26	H	Manchester City	W	3-2	Astle 2, Brown	44,897
23		30	A	Manchester City	W	2-0	Kryzwicki, Brown	45,754
24	Jan	6	A	Liverpool	L	1-4	Brown (pen)	51,092
25		20	A	Nottingham Forest	L	2-3	Clark 2	34,298
26	Feb	3	H	Coventry City	L	0-1		28,231
27		10	A	Sheffield United	D	1-1	Astle	19,261
28		24	H	Fulham	W	2-1	Astle, Brown (pen)	17,969
29	Mar	1	A	Tottenham Hotspur	D	0-0		31,318
30		13	H	Stoke City	W	3-0	Astle 2 (1 pen), Collard	20,621
31		16	H	Everton	L	2-6	Collard 2	26,285
32		23	A	Leicester City	W	3-2	Clark 2, Astle	23,097
33	Apr	2	H	Sunderland	D	0-0		15,490
34		6	A	Burnley	D	0-0		11,918
35		12	A	Newcastle United	D	2-2	Rees 2	40,308
36		13	H	Sheffield Wednesday	D	1-1	Astle	20,677
37		15	H	Newcastle United	W	2-0	Brown 2	22,194
38		20	A	Leeds United	L	1-3	Lovett	38,334
39		29	H	Manchester United	W	6-3	Astle 3, Rees, Brown (pen), Hartford	45,992
40	May	1	H	West Ham United	W	3-1	Astle 3	25,686
41		4	A	Sunderland	D	0-0		31,892
42		11	A	Arsenal	L	1-2	Fraser	24,896

Appearances
Sub appearances
Goals

FA Cup

R3	Jan	27	A	Colchester United	D	1-1	Brown (pen)	15,981
rep		31	H	Colchester United	W	4-0	Astle 2, Kaye, Clark	38,448
R4	Feb	17	H	Southampton	D	1-1	Brown (pen)	29,957
rep		21	A	Southampton	W	3-2	Astle 2, Brown	26,036
R5	Mar	9	A	Portsmouth	W	2-1	Astle, Clark	42,642
R6		30	H	Liverpool	D	0-0		43,503
rep	Apr	8	A	Liverpool	D	1-1*	Astle	54,273
rep2		18	N	Liverpool	W	2-1	Astle, Clark	56,139
SF		27	N	Birmingham City	W	2-0	Astle, Brown	60,831
F	May	18	N	Everton	W	1-0*	Astle	99,665

R6 replay 2 at Maine Road, SF at Villa Park, Final at Wembley Stadium

* after extra-time

Appearances
Sub appearances
Goals

League Cup

R2	Sep	13	A	Reading	L	1-3	Collard	18,910

Appearances
Goals

Osborne J	Fraser DM	Williams GE	Howshall GT	Colquhoun EPS	Talbut J	Foggo KT	Astle J	Kaye J	Brown T	Clark C	Collard I	Clarke D	Hope R	Fairfax RJ	Stephens KJ	Sheppard RJ	Campbell D	Treacy RCP	Krzywicki RL	Lovett GJ	Hartford RA	Martin DW	Rees RR	
1	2	3	4	5	**6**	7	8	9	10	11	12													1
1	2	3	4	5	6	7	8	9	10	11														2
1	6	3	4		5		8	9	7	11		2	10											3
1	4	3		**5**	6		9	12	8	11			10	2	7									4
	4	3		5	6		9	12	**8**	11			10	2	7	1								5
1	4	3		5	6		9	8		11			10	2	7									6
1	2	3		5	6		12	9	8	11	4		10		**7**									7
1	2			3	5		9			11	4		10		7		6	8						8
1		3		2	5		9	8		11	**4**		10		7		6	12						9
1	6	3		2	5		9	8	4	11			10		7									10
1	6	3		2	5		9	8	4	11			10		7									11
1	6	3		2	5		9	8	4	11			10		**7**				12					12
1	6			2	5		**9**	8	4		3		10		11			12	7					13
1	6	3		2	5		9	8	4	11			10					12	**7**					14
1	6	3		2	5		9	8	4	11			10		7									15
1	6	3		2	5		9	8	4	11			10		7									16
1	6	3		2	5		9	8	4	11			10		7									17
1	6	3		2	5		9	8	4	11			10						7					18
1	6	3		2	5		9	8	4	11			10						7					19
1	6	3		2	5		9	8	4	11			10						7					20
1	6	3		2	5		9	8	4	11			10						7					21
1	6	3		2	5		9	8	4	**11**			10						7	12				22
1	6	3		2	5		9	8	4	11			10						7					23
1	6	3		2	5		9	8	4	11			10						7					24
1	6	3		2	5		9	8	4	11			10						7					25
	6	3		2	5		9	8	4	11			10		12	1				**7**				26
	6	3		2	5		9	8	4	11			10			1					7			27
1	6	3			5		9	8	7	**11**	4	2	10							12				28
1	6	3		2	5		9	8	7	11	4		10											29
1	6	3		2	5		9	8			4				7					10	12	**11**		30
1	6	3		2	5		9	8			4				**7**					10	12		11	31
	6	3		**2**	5		9	8	4	11	12		10			1							**7**	32
1	3			6	5		9	8	4	11	10	2											7	33
1	3			6	5		9	8	4	11	10	2											7	34
1	3			**6**	5		9	8	4	11	10	2		12									7	35
1	4	3			5		9	6	8		10	2			7								11	36
1	4	3			5		9	6	8		12	2	10		7								**11**	37
1	6	3			5				4		10			2	7				9	8			11	38
1	6	3			5		9		4		8	2	10							12	11		**7**	39
1					5		9	6			8	2	10	3						4	11		7	40
1	4				5		9	6		11	10	2		3					12	8	**7**			41
	2	3			5		9	6	4	11	8		10			1				7				42
37	40	35	3	33	42	2	40	37	35	34	17	10	32	6	18	5	2	1	11	7	4	1	10	
							1	2			3			1	1			3	2	3	2			
	1			1		1	26	5	11	12	3		5		2				3	1	1		3	

Osborne J	Fraser DM	Williams GE	Howshall GT	Colquhoun EPS	Talbut J	Foggo KT	Astle J	Kaye J	Brown T	Clark C	Collard I	Clarke D	Hope R	Fairfax RJ	Stephens KJ	Sheppard RJ	Campbell D	Treacy RCP	Krzywicki RL	Lovett GJ	Hartford RA	Martin DW	Rees RR	
1	6	3		2	5		9	8	4	11			10						**7**	12				R3
	6	3		2	5		9	8	4	11			10			1				7				rep
	6	3			5		9	8	4	11		2	10			1			7					R4
1	6	3			5		9	8	7	11	4	2	10							12				rep
1	6	3		2	5		9	8	7	11	4		10											R5
1	6	3		2	5		9	8	4	11	10								7					R6
1	4	3		6	5		9	7	8	11	**10**	2			12									rep
1	4	3			5		9	6	7	11	8	**2**	10		12									rep2
1	2	3			5		9	6	4	11	8		10		7									SF
1	2	3			5		9	**6**	4	11	8	12	10							7				F
8	10	10		5	10		10	10	10	10	7	4	8		1	2			3	2				
												1			2					2				
							9	1	4	3														

Osborne J	Fraser DM	Williams GE	Howshall GT	Colquhoun EPS	Talbut J	Foggo KT	Astle J	Kaye J	Brown T	Clark C	Collard I	Clarke D	Hope R	Fairfax RJ	Stephens KJ	Sheppard RJ	Campbell D	Treacy RCP	Krzywicki RL	Lovett GJ	Hartford RA	Martin DW	Rees RR	
1	2	3		5	6		8	9	7	11	4		10											R2
1	1	1		1	1		1	1	1	1	1		1											
											1													

1968-69

Division One

	P	W	D	L	F	A	Pts
Leeds United	42	27	13	2	66	26	67
Liverpool	42	25	11	6	63	24	61
Everton	42	21	15	6	77	36	57
Arsenal	42	22	12	8	56	27	56
Chelsea	42	20	10	12	73	53	50
Tottenham Hotspur	42	14	17	11	61	51	45
Southampton	42	16	13	13	57	48	45
West Ham United	42	13	18	11	66	50	44
Newcastle United	42	15	14	13	61	55	44
West Bromwich Albion	42	16	11	15	64	67	43
Manchester United	42	15	12	15	57	53	42
Ipswich Town	42	15	11	16	59	60	41
Manchester City	42	15	10	17	64	55	40
Burnley	42	15	9	18	55	82	39
Sheffield Wednesday	42	10	16	16	41	54	36
Wolverhampton W	42	10	15	17	41	58	35
Sunderland	42	11	12	19	43	67	34
Nottingham Forest	42	10	13	19	45	57	33
Stoke City	42	9	15	18	40	63	33
Coventry City	42	10	11	21	46	64	31
Leicester City	42	9	12	21	39	68	30
Queen's Park Rangers	42	4	10	28	39	95	18

Manager: Alan Ashman

- Allan Clarke, who supported Albion as a youngster, scored the winning goal for Leicester City in the FA Cup semi-final with just three minutes remaining.
- Albion's 6–1 defeat by Manchester City was the heaviest by any team in the FA Charity Shield since 1925.
- Ronnie Rees, who was the first Albion player to be sent off in a European game against Bucharest (a), left The Hawthorns for Nottingham Forest, while Danny Hegan arrived from Ipswich Town, Ian Collard going to Portman Road in exchange. Goalkeeper Dick Sheppard was transferred to Bristol Rovers and winger Clive Clark returned to Queen's Park Rangers in exchange for Allan Glover.
- Tony Brown was voted Midlands Footballer of the Year for the first time. He would win the honour again in 1970–71 and 1978–79.
- Albion's teenagers were defeated by Sunderland in the Final of the FA Youth Cup.

Match No.	Date			Opponents	Result		Scorers	Attendance
1	Aug	10	H	Sheffield Wednesday	D	0-0		25,031
2		14	H	Manchester United	W	3-1	Astle 2, Brown	38,299
3		17	A	Chelsea	L	1-3	Brown	33,766
4		21	A	Tottenham Hotspur	D	1-1	Astle	35,746
5		24	H	Burnley	W	3-2	Astle 2, Collard	21,882
6		27	A	Coventry City	L	2-4	Rees, Brown	36,678
7		31	A	West Ham United	L	0-4		29,908
8	Sep	7	H	Nottingham Forest	L	2-5	Astle, Brown	23,377
9		14	A	Newcastle United	W	3-2	Hartford, Astle 2	35,128
10		21	H	Wolverhampton Wanderers	D	0-0		35,175
11		28	A	Everton	L	0-4		47,792
12	Oct	5	H	Queen's Park Rangers	W	3-1	Rees, Hartford, Astle	22,944
13		9	H	Coventry City	W	6-1	Astle 2, Tudor (og), Brown (pen), Hartford, Rees	29,255
14		12	A	Leicester City	W	2-0	Astle, Hartford	26,348
15		19	H	Arsenal	W	1-0	Brown	29,324
16		26	A	Leeds United	D	0-0		33,926
17	Nov	2	H	Liverpool	D	0-0		34,805
18		9	A	Southampton	L	0-2		19,885
19		16	H	Stoke City	W	2-1	Fraser, Hartford	21,026
20		23	A	Manchester City	L	1-5	Brown	24,667
21		30	H	Sunderland	W	3-0	Brown, Rees, Hartford	19,411
22	Dec	7	A	Ipswich Town	L	1-4	Rees	19,725
23		14	H	Leicester City	D	1-1	Brown (pen)	16,483
24		21	A	Arsenal	L	0-2		30,765
25		26	A	Queen's Park Rangers	W	4-0	Collard 2, Martin, Rees	18,649
26	Jan	11	A	Liverpool	L	0-1		47,587
27		18	H	Southampton	L	1-2	Brown (pen)	22,856
28	Feb	1	A	Stoke City	D	1-1	Astle	21,309
29	Mar	5	A	Sheffield Wednesday	L	0-1		18,346
30		8	H	Chelsea	L	0-3		25,137
31		10	A	Sunderland	W	1-0	Brown	15,769
32		15	A	Burnley	D	2-2	Brown 2	12,218
33		22	A	Nottingham Forest	L	0-3		20,546
34	Apr	2	A	Manchester United	L	1-2	Astle	38,846
35		5	H	Everton	D	1-1	Astle	23,156
36		7	H	Tottenham Hotspur	W	4-3	Hope, Astle 2, Brown	24,173
37		9	H	Leeds United	D	1-1	Kryzwicki	28,186
38		12	A	Wolverhampton Wanderers	W	1-0	Clark	37,920
39		14	H	West Ham United	W	3-1	Astle 2, Brown	19,780
40		16	H	Manchester City	W	2-0	Kryzwicki, Book (og)	22,717
41		19	H	Newcastle United	W	5-1	Kaye, Hartford, Brown (pen), Clark, Astle	22,481
42		23	H	Ipswich Town	D	2-2	Astle, Brown	21,426

Appearances
Sub appearances
Goals

FA Cup

R3	Jan	4	H	Norwich City	W	3-0	Rees, Astle (pen), Forbes (og)	30,004
R4		25	A	Fulham	W	2-1	Hartford, Rees	31,204
R5	Feb	12	H	Arsenal	W	1-0	Brown	45,354
R6	Mar	1	A	Chelsea	W	2-1	Brown, Astle	52,285
SF		29	N	Leicester City	L	0-1		53,207

SF at Hillsborough, Sheffield

Appearances
Sub appearances
Goals

League Cup

R2	Sep	3	A	Nottingham Forest	W	3-2	Astle 2, Rees	23,900
R3		25	A	Peterborough United	L	1-2	Brown (pen)	16,510

R2 played at Meadow Lane, Nottingham

Appearances
Goals

Sheppard RJ	Fraser DM	Williams GE	Brown T	Talbut J	Kaye J	Krzywicki RL	Hartford RA	Astle J	Hope R	Rees RR	Collard I	Wilson RT	Clarke D	Osborne J	Lovett GJ	Clark C	Colquhoun EPS	Merrick AR	Potter RC	Hughes LJ	Martin DW	Reed HD	Cantello L	
1	2	3	4	5	6	7	8	9	10	11														1
1	2	3	4	5	6	7		9	10	11	8													2
1	2	**3**	4	5	6	7		9	10	11	8	12												3
1		3	4	5	6	7		9	10	11	8		2											4
		3	4	5	6	7		9	10	11	**8**	12	2	1										5
1	4	3	8	5	6	7		9		11			2		10									6
1		3	8	5	6			9	10	7			2		4	11								7
1	2	3	4	5	8			9	10	7						11	6							8
1	2	3	4	5	6		8	9	10	7						11								9
	2	3	4	5	6	**9**	10			7				1	8	11		12						10
	2	3	4	5	6			9	**10**	7				1	8	11			12					11
	2	3	4	5			8	9	10	7	6			1		**11**				12				12
	2		4	5	6		11	9	10	7	8	3		1										13
	2		4	5	6		11	9	10	7	8	3		1										14
	2	12	4	5	6		11	**9**	10	7		3		1						8				15
	2		4	5	6		11		10	7	8	3		1							9			16
	2		4	5	6		11	9	10	7	8	3		1										17
	2		4	5	6		11	9	10	7	8	**3**		1						12				18
	2		4	5	6		11	9	10	12	8	3		1								**7**		19
1	2	12	4	5	6		11	9	10	7	**8**	3												20
	2	12	4	5			10	9		7		3		1	8	11				6				21
	2		**4**	5	6		11	9		7	10	3		1	8								12	22
	2		4	5	6		11	9	10	7	8	3		1										23
	2		4	5	6			9	10		8	3		1	7						11			24
	2		4	5	6			9		11	10	3		1	8						7			25
	2		4	5	6		11	9	7		10	3		1	8									26
	2		4	5			12	9	7	11	**10**	3		1	8					6				27
			4	6		8	11	9	7			3		1	10				5	2				28
1	2		4	5	**6**	12		9	10			3			8	11					7			29
			4	5	6	8	11	9	10			3		1						2	7			30
		2	8	4					10			3		1		11		6	5		9		7	31
		2	4	5			10				**6**			1	8	11		3			9	12	7	32
		2	4	5				9	10			3		1	8	11		6			7			33
	2		4	5	6	7		9	10			3		1	8	11								34
	2		4	5	6	7	12	9	**10**			3		1	8	11								35
	2		4	5	6	7	11	9	10			3		1	8									36
	2		4	5	6	7	11	9	10			3		1	8									37
	2		4	5	6	7	**11**		10			3		1	8	12					9			38
	2	3	4	5	6			9	10					1	8	11					7			39
	2	3	4	5		7	12	9	**10**					1	8	11		6						40
	2		4	5	6	7	10	9				3		1	8	11								41
	2		4	5	6	7		9	10			3		1	8	11								42
10	34	17	42	42	34	17	23	37	35	24	19	27	4	32	23	17	1	4	2	5	10	1	2	
		3				1	3			1		2				1		1	1	2		1	1	
	1		17		1	2	7	21	1	6	3					2					1			

Two own-goals

Sheppard RJ	Fraser DM	Williams GE	Brown T	Talbut J	Kaye J	Krzywicki RL	Hartford RA	Astle J	Hope R	Rees RR	Collard I	Wilson RT	Clarke D	Osborne J	Lovett GJ	Clark C	Colquhoun EPS	Merrick AR	Potter RC	Hughes LJ	Martin DW	Reed HD	Cantello L	
	2			5	6			9	7	11	10	3		1	8					4				R3
	2	3	**4**	5	6		11	9	7	12	10			1	8									R4
	2		4	5	6		11	9			8	3		1	10						7			R5
	2		4	5	6	12	**11**	9	10			3		1	8						7			R6
	2		**4**	5	6		11	9	10			3		1	8	12					**7**			SF
	5	1	4	5	5		4	5	4	1	3	4		5	5					1	3			
						1				1						1								
			2				1	2		2														

One own-goal

Sheppard RJ	Fraser DM	Williams GE	Brown T	Talbut J	Kaye J	Krzywicki RL	Hartford RA	Astle J	Hope R	Rees RR	Collard I	Wilson RT	Clarke D	Osborne J	Lovett GJ	Clark C	Colquhoun EPS	Merrick AR	Potter RC	Hughes LJ	Martin DW	Reed HD	Cantello L	
1	2	3	4	5	8			9	10	7						11	6							R2
	2	3	4	5	10			9		7				1	8	11		6						R3
1	2	2	2	2	2			2	1	2				1	1	2	1	1						
			1					2		1														

1969-70

Division One

	P	W	D	L	F	A	Pts
Everton	42	29	8	5	72	34	66
Leeds United	42	21	15	6	84	49	57
Chelsea	42	21	13	8	70	50	55
Derby County	42	22	9	11	64	37	53
Liverpool	42	20	11	11	65	42	51
Coventry City	42	19	11	12	58	48	49
Newcastle United	42	17	13	12	57	35	47
Manchester United	42	14	17	11	66	61	45
Stoke City	42	15	15	12	56	52	45
Manchester City	42	16	11	15	55	48	43
Tottenham Hotspur	42	17	9	16	54	55	43
Arsenal	42	12	18	12	51	49	42
Wolverhampton W	42	12	16	14	55	57	40
Burnley	42	12	15	15	56	61	39
Nottingham Forest	42	10	18	14	50	71	38
West Bromwich Albion	42	14	9	19	58	66	37
West Ham United	42	12	12	18	51	60	36
Ipswich Town	42	10	11	21	40	63	31
Southampton	42	6	17	19	46	67	29
Crystal Palace	42	6	15	21	34	68	27
Sunderland	42	6	14	22	30	68	26
Sheffield Wednesday	42	8	9	25	40	71	25

Manager: Alan Ashman

- Jeff Astle created a record by becoming the first player to score in both the FA Cup and League Cup Finals at Wembley when he headed Albion into an early lead against Manchester City in the latter competition.
- Albion's first £100,000 footballer – Colin Suggett – arrived from Sunderland (July), and goalkeeper Jim Cumbes was signed from Tranmere Rovers to put pressure on John Osborne. Danny Hegan left to join Wolves and winger Dick Krzywicki signed for Huddersfield Town for a record fee of £45,000.
- Centre-half John Talbot scored his only goal for Albion in a 4–0 Anglo-Italian Cup win over AS Roma.

Match No.	Date			Opponents	Result		Scorers	Attendance
1	Aug	9	A	Southampton	W	2-0	Suggett 2	22,093
2		12	A	Coventry City	L	1-3	Kryzwicki	37,025
3		16	H	Arsenal	L	0-1		32,215
4		20	H	Coventry City	L	0-1		33,933
5		23	A	West Ham United	W	3-1	Suggett, Brown, Kryzwicki	29,156
6		26	A	Nottingham Forest	L	0-1		22,924
7		30	H	Derby County	L	0-2		34,173
8	Sep	6	A	Sunderland	D	2-2	Suggett, Brown	14,410
9		13	H	Ipswich Town	D	2-2	Astle 2	21,173
10		17	H	Stoke City	L	1-3	Astle	24,482
11		20	A	Crystal Palace	W	3-1	Hegan, Hope, Astle	27,684
12		27	H	Liverpool	D	2-2	Astle, Hegan	34,295
13	Oct	4	A	Manchester City	L	1-2	Pardoe (og)	34,329
14		7	A	Arsenal	D	1-1	Astle	21,165
15		11	H	Leeds United	D	1-1	Astle	33,037
16		18	A	Chelsea	L	0-2		34,810
17		25	H	Manchester United	W	2-1	Brown, Hope	45,120
18	Nov	1	A	Wolverhampton Wanderers	L	0-1		39,832
19		8	H	Everton	W	2-0	Astle, Kryzwicki	34,298
20		15	A	Tottenham Hotspur	L	0-2		28,340
21		22	H	Sheffield Wednesday	W	3-0	Hope, Suggett, Astle	20,382
22	Dec	6	H	Burnley	L	0-1		18,512
23		13	A	Ipswich Town	W	1-0	Astle	18,379
24		26	H	West Ham United	W	3-1	Suggett 2, Astle	32,246
25		27	A	Derby County	L	0-2		35,581
26	Jan	10	H	Crystal Palace	W	3-2	Astle 3	19,234
27		17	A	Liverpool	D	1-1	Brown	43,526
28		27	H	Sunderland	W	3-1	Astle 2, Brown	19,024
29		31	H	Manchester City	W	3-0	Suggett, Astle, Hartford	30,341
30	Feb	6	A	Newcastle United	L	0-1		32,054
31		10	A	Leeds United	L	1-5	Astle	31,515
32		20	H	Southampton	W	1-0	Suggett	19,453
33		28	H	Wolverhampton Wanderers	D	3-3	Astle, Suggett 2	37,391
34	Mar	10	A	Sheffield Wednesday	L	0-2		21,990
35		14	H	Newcastle United	D	2-2	Astle 2	19,322
36		21	A	Burnley	L	1-2	Brown	12,821
37		28	H	Tottenham Hotspur	D	1-1	Astle	24,890
38		30	H	Chelsea	W	3-1	Brown 2, Astle	31,207
39	Apr	1	A	Everton	L	0-2		58,523
40		4	H	Nottingham Forest	W	4-0	Brown 2, Astle, Glover	20,691
41		8	A	Manchester United	L	0-7		29,396
42		15	A	Stoke City	L	2-3	Astle, Suggett	11,804

Appearances
Sub appearances
Goals

FA Cup

R3	Jan	3	A	Sheffield Wednesday	L	1-2	Brown	29,174

Appearances
Goals

League Cup

R2	Sep	3	A	Aston Villa	W	2-1	Suggett, Astle	40,202
R3		24	A	Ipswich Town	D	1-1	Suggett	19,261
rep		30	H	Ipswich Town	W	2-0	Hope, Astle	24,631
R4	Oct	14	H	Bradford City	W	4-0	Cantello, Hope, Brown, Kryzwicki	25,343
R5		29	A	Leicester City	D	0-0		35,121
rep	Nov	5	H	Leicester City	W	2-1	Astle 2	26,981
SF1		19	A	Carlisle United	L	0-1		20,322
SF2	Dec	3	H	Carlisle United	W	4-1	Hope, Suggett, Brown, Martin	34,835
F	Mar	7	N	Manchester City	L	1-2*	Astle	97,963

Final at Wembley Stadium
* after extra-time

Appearances
Sub appearances
Goals

Osborne J	Williams GE	Wilson RT	Brown T	Talbut J	Kaye J	Hegan D	Suggett C	Krzywicki RL	Hope R	Freeman RPP	Nisbet GJM	Astle J	Fraser DM	Cumbes J	Hartford RA	Merrick AR	Hughes LJ	Potter RC	Cantello L	Robertson A	Martin DW	Glover AR	Lovett GJ	
1	2	3	4	5	6	7	8	9	10	11														1
	2	**3**	4	5	6	7	8	11	10		1	9	12											2
	3		4	5	6	7	8	11	10	9			2	1										3
	3		4	5	6	7	8	9	10				2	1	11									4
	3		4	5		7	8	9					2	1	11	6	10							5
	3		4	5	6	**7**	8	9					2	1	11	12	10							6
			4	5	6		7	9	10				2	1	11	3	8							7
			4	5	6	**7**	9	12	10				2	1	11	3	8							8
	2	3	4		6	**10**	8	7	11			9		1	12			5						9
		3	4		6		8	7	11			9	2	1	10			5						10
		3	7	5	6	10	8		11			9	2	1			4							11
		3	7	5	6	10	8		11			9	2	1			4							12
1	12		7	5	6		8	2	11			9	3		10		**4**							13
1		3		5	6		8	7	11			9	2		10				4					14
1	3			5	6	12	8	7	11			9	2		10				**4**					15
	3		7	5	6		8		11			9	2	1	10				4					16
1	3		4	5		7	8	12	11			9	2		**10**					6				17
1	3		4	5	6	7	8		11			**9**	2		10		12							18
1	3		4	5	6		8	7	11			9	2		10									19
1	3		4	5	6		8	7	11			**9**	2		10		12							20
		3	4	5	6		8	7	11			9	2	1	10				12					21
1		3	4				8	**7**	11			9	2		10			5	12	6				22
1	12	3	4		6		8		11			**9**			10		2	5			7			23
1		3	4		6		8		**11**			9	2		10		12	5			7			24
1	2	3	4			7	8	12				9			10		6	5			**11**			25
1		3	4	5	6		8	7	11			9	2		10									26
1		3	4	5	6		8	9	**11**				2		10		7				12			27
1			4	5	6		8		11			9	2		10	3	7							28
1		3	4	5	6		8		11			9	2		10				7					29
		3	4	5	6		8		11			9	2	1	10				7					30
		3	4	5			8		11			9	2	1	10		6		7					31
1		3	4	5	6		8		**11**			9	2		10				7		12			32
		3	4	5	6		8		11			9	2	1	10				**7**			12		33
1		3	4	5			8		11			9			10		2		7	6				34
1		3	4	5			8		11			9	**2**		10				7	6			12	35
1		3	**4**				8		11			9			12	6	2		10	5			7	36
1		3	4				8		11			9			12	6	2		**10**	5			7	37
1		3	4				8		11			9			10	6	2		7	5				38
1		3	10				8		11			9	4			6	2		7	5				39
1		3	10				8			12		9	4			6	2		**11**	5		7		40
1		3	10				8		11			9	4		7	6	2			5				41
1		3	10	5			8		11			9	4		7	6	2							42
26	14	28	40	30	28	13	42	18	38	2	1	34	33	15	32	11	20	6	15	10	3	1	2	
	2					1		3		1			1		3	1	3		2		2	1	1	
			10			2	12	3	3			25			1							1		

One own-goal

Osborne J	Williams GE	Wilson RT	Brown T	Talbut J	Kaye J	Hegan D	Suggett C	Krzywicki RL	Hope R	Freeman RPP	Nisbet GJM	Astle J	Fraser DM	Cumbes J	Hartford RA	Merrick AR	Hughes LJ	Potter RC	Cantello L	Robertson A	Martin DW	Glover AR	Lovett GJ	
1		3	4	5	6		9	7					2		10		8				11			R3
1		1	1	1	1		1	1					1		1		1				1			
			1																					

Osborne J	Williams GE	Wilson RT	Brown T	Talbut J	Kaye J	Hegan D	Suggett C	Krzywicki RL	Hope R	Freeman RPP	Nisbet GJM	Astle J	Fraser DM	Cumbes J	Hartford RA	Merrick AR	Hughes LJ	Potter RC	Cantello L	Robertson A	Martin DW	Glover AR	Lovett GJ	
1			4	5	6		7		10			9	2		11	3	8							R2
1		3	7	5	**6**	8	10	12	11			9	2				4							R3
1		**3**	12	5	6	10	8	7	11			9	2				4							rep
1	3		8	5	6			7	11			9	2		10				4					R4
1	3		4	5	6	7	8		11			9	2		10									R5
1	3		4	5	6	7	8		11			9	2		10									rep
1	3		4	5	6		8	7	11			9	2		10									SF1
1	3		4	**5**	6		8	7	11			9	2		10						12			SF2
1	3		4	5	6		8	12	11			9	2		**10**				7					F
9	6	2	8	9	9	4	8	4	9			9	9		7	1	3		2					
			1					2													1			
			2				3	1	3			5							1		1			

1970-71

Division One

	P	W	D	L	F	A	Pts
Arsenal	42	29	7	6	71	29	65
Leeds United	42	27	10	5	72	30	64
Tottenham Hotspur	42	19	14	9	54	33	52
Wolverhampton W	42	22	8	12	64	54	52
Liverpool	42	17	17	8	42	24	51
Chelsea	42	18	15	9	52	42	51
Southampton	42	17	12	13	56	44	46
Manchester United	42	16	11	15	65	66	43
Derby County	42	16	10	16	56	54	42
Coventry City	42	16	10	16	37	38	42
Manchester City	42	12	17	13	47	42	41
Newcastle United	42	14	13	15	44	46	41
Stoke City	42	12	13	17	44	48	37
Everton	42	12	13	17	54	60	37
Huddersfield Town	42	11	14	17	40	49	36
Nottingham Forest	42	14	8	20	42	61	36
West Bromwich Albion	42	10	15	17	58	75	35
Crystal Palace	42	12	11	19	39	57	35
Ipswich Town	42	12	10	20	42	48	34
West Ham United	42	10	14	18	47	60	34
Burnley	42	7	13	22	29	63	27
Blackpool	42	4	15	23	34	66	23

Manager: Alan Ashman

- Tony Brown won his only England cap this season, playing inside-left alongside Geoff Hurst in the 0–0 draw with Wales at Wembley.
- Wingers George McVitie and Dennis Martin changed clubs for unusual fees – McVitie joined Albion from Carlisle United for £33,333, while Dennis Martin moved to the Cumbrian club for £22,222. Centre-half John Wile was also signed from Peterborough United and John Talbot (who was replaced by Wile) was transferred to KV Mechelen in Belgium. Long-serving defender Graham Williams was appointed to the club's coaching staff.
- The Centenary League game between Albion and Wolves took place at The Hawthorns in March.

Match No.	Date			Opponents	Result		Scorers	Attendance
1	Aug	15	H	Crystal Palace	D	0-0		25,127
2		18	A	Nottingham Forest	D	3-3	Brown 2, Astle	24,423
3		22	A	Blackpool	L	1-3	Astle	22,162
4		26	H	Stoke City	W	5-2	Reed, Brown 2, Astle 2	22,015
5		29	H	Liverpool	D	1-1	Astle	31,474
6	Sep	2	H	Newcastle United	L	1-2	Astle	25,112
7		5	A	Manchester City	L	1-4	Hope	30,549
8		12	H	West Ham United	W	2-1	Suggett 2	24,606
9		19	A	Arsenal	L	2-6	Reed, Brown	33,303
10		26	H	Derby County	W	2-1	McVitie, Brown	31,216
11	Oct	3	A	Ipswich Town	D	2-2	Brown, Astle	17,578
12		10	H	Leeds United	D	2-2	Suggett, McVitie	37,124
13		17	A	Crystal Palace	L	0-3		28,330
14		24	A	Manchester United	L	1-2	Brown	42,504
15		31	H	Everton	W	3-0	Brown, Astle, McVitie	29,628
16	Nov	7	A	Wolverhampton Wanderers	L	1-2	Lovett	39,300
17		14	H	Southampton	W	1-0	Hartford	17,824
18		21	A	Huddersfield Town	L	1-2	Brown	18,209
19		28	H	Chelsea	D	2-2	Astle, Suggett	29,374
20	Dec	5	A	Burnley	D	1-1	Brown	12,477
21		12	H	Tottenham Hotspur	W	3-1	Brown 3 (1 pen)	26,584
22		19	H	Blackpool	D	1-1	Suggett	17,909
23		26	A	Coventry City	D	1-1	Brown (pen)	27,527
24	Jan	9	H	Nottingham Forest	L	0-1		20,015
25		16	A	Stoke City	L	0-2		20,882
26		30	A	Chelsea	L	1-4	Astle	26,874
27	Feb	6	H	Burnley	W	1-0	Brown	16,982
28		17	A	Tottenham Hotspur	D	2-2	Brown 2	22,695
29		20	H	Huddersfield Town	W	2-1	Brown 2	18,254
30		27	A	Everton	D	3-3	Brown, Astle, Wile	35,940
31	Mar	6	H	Manchester United	W	4-3	Brown 3, Wile	41,134
32		13	A	Southampton	L	0-1		19,008
33		20	H	Wolverhampton Wanderers	L	2-4	McVitie, Brown	36,754
34		27	H	Manchester City	D	0-0		20,363
35	Apr	2	A	Liverpool	D	1-1	Brown	43,630
36		9	A	West Ham United	L	1-2	Astle	34,981
37		10	H	Coventry City	D	0-0		18,726
38		12	H	Ipswich Town	L	0-1		12,684
39		17	A	Leeds United	W	2-1	Brown, Astle	36,812
40		24	H	Arsenal	D	2-2	Hartford, Brown	36,621
41		28	A	Newcastle United	L	0-3		18,444
42	May	1	A	Derby County	L	0-2		33,661

Appearances
Sub appearances
Goals

FA Cup

R3	Jan	2	H	Scunthorpe United	D	0-0		22,844
rep		11	A	Scunthorpe United	W	3-1	Brown 2, Astle	15,926
R4		23	H	Ipswich Town	D	1-1	Suggett	27,178
rep		26	A	Ipswich Town	L	0-3		27,015

Appearances
Sub appearances
Goals

League Cup

R2	Sep	8	H	Charlton Athletic	W	3-1	Kaye, Astle, Suggett	16,124
R3	Oct	6	A	Preston North End	W	1-0	Hartford	18,222
R4		28	A	Tottenham Hotspur	L	0-5		31,598

Appearances
Sub appearances
Goals

	Osborne J	Hughes LJ	Wilson RT	Merrick AR	Talbut J	Johnson LG	Reed HD	Brown T	Astle J	Suggett C	Hope R	Cantello L	Robertson A	Kaye J	Cumbes J	McVitie GJ	Hartford RA	Minton RC	Fraser DM	Lovett GJ	Wile JD	Glover AR
1	1	2	3	4	5	6	7	8	9	10	11											
2	1	2	3	4	5	6	7	8	9	10	11											
3	**1**	2		3	5		7	8	9	10	11	4	6	12								
4		2	3	4	5		12	8	9	10	11	**7**	6		1							
5		2	3	4	5		12	8	9	10	11	**7**	6		1							
6		2	3	4	5	6		8	9	10	11				1	7						
7		2	3		5	6		**8**	9	10	11	4	12		1	7						
8		2		3	5	6		4	9	8	10	11			1	7						
9		2		3	5		7	4	9	8		6			1	11	10					
10			3	2	5	6		4	9	8	10				1	7	11					
11				3	5	6		4	9	8	10				1	7	11	2				
12				3	5	6		4	9	8	10				1	7	11	2				
13				3	5	6		4	9	8	10				1	7	11	2				
14				3	5	6		4	9		**10**	8			1	7	11	12	2			
15					5	6		8	9	10		3			1	7	11		2	4		
16					5	6		10	9	8		3			1	7	11		2	4		
17					**5**	6		8	9	12	10	3			1	7	11		2	4		
18				6		5		8	9	12	10	3			1	7	11		**2**	4		
19				6		5		4	9	8	10	3			1	7	11		**2**	12		
20				6	12	5		4	9	8	11	**3**			1	7	10			2		
21				6		5		4	9	8	10	3			1	7	11			2		
22				3		6		4	9	8		10			1	7	11			2	5	
23			3	6				4	9	8		10			1	7	11			2	5	
24			3			6		4	9	8	10				1	7	11			2	5	
25			3			6		4	9	8	10				1	7	11			2	5	
26			3			6		4	9	8	10				1	7	11			2	5	
27		2	3			6		8	9		10				1	7	11			4	5	
28			3	6		2		8	9		10				1	7	11			4	5	
29			3	6		2		8	9		10					7	11			4	5	
30			3	6		2		8	9		10				1	7	11			4	5	
31			3	6		2		8	9		10				1	7	11			4	5	
32			3	6		2		8	9		10	7			1		11			4	5	
33			3	6		2		8	9		10				1	7	11			4	5	
34		2		3		6		8		9	10	4			1	7	11				5	
35		2		3		6		8	9		10	4			1	7	11				5	
36		2		3		6		8	9	12	10	4			1	**7**	11				5	
37		2		3		6		10	9	8		4			1	7	11				5	
38		2		3		6		8	9	10		4			1	7	11				5	
39		2		3		6		8	9	7	10				1		11			4	5	
40		2		3		6		8	9	7	10				1		11			4	5	
41		2		3		6		8	9	7	**10**	12			1		11			4	5	
42			2	3		6		8	9	7		4			1	11	10				5	
Apps		18	19	34	17	37	4	42	41	30	34	23	3		38	33	34	3	6	21	21	
Sub					1		2			3		1	1	1				1		1		
Goals							2	28	13	5	1					4	2			1	2	

	Osborne J	Hughes LJ	Wilson RT	Merrick AR	Talbut J	Johnson LG	Reed HD	Brown T	Astle J	Suggett C	Hope R	Cantello L	Robertson A	Kaye J	Cumbes J	McVitie GJ	Hartford RA	Minton RC	Fraser DM	Lovett GJ	Wile JD	Glover AR
R3			3		5	6		4	9	8		10			1	7	11			2		
rep			3		5	6		4	9	8	10				1	7	11			2		
R4			3	12	5	6		4	9	8	**10**				1	7	11			2		
rep				3	5	6		4	9	8	10				1	7	11			2		
Apps			3	1	4	4		4	4	4	3	1			4	4	4			4		
Sub				1																		
Goals								2	1	1												

	Osborne J	Hughes LJ	Wilson RT	Merrick AR	Talbut J	Johnson LG	Reed HD	Brown T	Astle J	Suggett C	Hope R	Cantello L	Robertson A	Kaye J	Cumbes J	McVitie GJ	Hartford RA	Minton RC	Fraser DM	Lovett GJ	Wile JD	Glover AR
R2		2		3	5		7		9	8	10	11	**4**	6	1							12
R3				3	5			4	9	8	10			6	1	7	11	2				
R4				3	5			10	9	8		**4**		6	1	7	11		2	12		
Apps		1		3	3		1	2	3	3	2	2	1	3	3	2	2	1	1			
Sub																				1		1
Goals									1	1				1			1					

1971-72

Division One

	P	W	D	L	F	A	Pts
Derby County	42	24	10	8	69	33	58
Leeds United	42	24	9	9	73	31	57
Liverpool	42	24	9	9	64	30	57
Manchester City	42	23	11	8	77	45	57
Arsenal	42	22	8	12	58	40	52
Tottenham Hotspur	42	19	13	10	63	42	51
Chelsea	42	18	12	12	58	49	48
Manchester United	42	19	10	13	69	61	48
Wolverhampton W	42	18	11	13	65	57	47
Sheffield United	42	17	12	13	61	60	46
Newcastle United	42	15	11	16	49	52	41
Leicester City	42	13	13	16	41	46	39
Ipswich Town	42	11	16	15	39	53	38
West Ham United	42	12	12	18	47	51	36
Everton	42	9	18	15	37	48	36
West Bromwich Albion	42	12	11	19	42	54	35
Stoke City	42	10	15	17	39	56	35
Coventry City	42	9	15	18	44	67	33
Southampton	42	12	7	23	52	80	31
Crystal Palace	42	8	13	21	39	65	29
Nottingham Forest	42	8	9	25	47	81	25
Huddersfield Town	42	6	13	23	27	59	25

Manager: Don Howe

- Don Howe replaced Alan Ashman and became the first former player to return to the club as manager.
- Forwards Bobby Gould (from Wolves) and Ally Brown (from Leicester City) and goalkeeper Graham Smith (from Colchester United) were among the new signings. Brown scored on his debut.
- Several players left The Hawthorns, including Jim Cumbes (to Aston Villa), Bobby Hope (to Birmingham City, after 403 senior appearances), Graham Lovett (to Worcester City), John Kaye (to Hull City after 361 games and 54 goals) and FA Cup and League Cup-winning captain Graham Williams to Weymouth as player-manager (after 360 games).

Match No.	Date			Opponents	Result		Scorers	Attendance
1	Aug	14	A	West Ham United	W	1-0	T. Brown	27,420
2		18	H	Everton	W	2-0	Wile, T. Brown	29,055
3		21	H	Coventry City	D	1-1	T. Brown	24,692
4		23	A	Manchester United	L	1-3	T. Brown	23,146
5		28	A	Sheffield United	D	0-0		32,768
6	Sep	1	A	Chelsea	L	0-1		29,931
7		4	H	Arsenal	L	0-1		29,809
8		11	A	Huddersfield Town	L	0-1		9,938
9		18	H	Ipswich Town	L	1-2	T. Brown	18,885
10		25	A	Derby County	D	0-0		30,628
11	Oct	2	H	Manchester City	L	0-2		25,834
12		9	A	Crystal Palace	W	2-0	T. Brown, Gould	22,399
13		16	H	West Ham United	D	0-0		20,620
14		23	H	Leicester City	L	0-1		23,088
15		30	A	Southampton	D	1-1	Hartford	16,972
16	Nov	6	H	Stoke City	L	0-1		19,204
17		13	A	Nottingham Forest	L	1-4	Astle	20,024
18		20	A	Tottenham Hotspur	L	2-3	Gould, T. Brown	31,895
19		27	H	Wolverhampton Wanderers	L	2-3	T. Brown (pen), Gould	37,696
20	Dec	4	A	Leeds United	L	0-3		32,521
21		11	H	Newcastle United	L	0-3		18,142
22		18	A	Arsenal	L	0-2		28,177
23		27	H	Liverpool	W	1-0	T. Brown	43,785
24	Jan	1	A	Ipswich Town	W	3-2	T. Brown, Gould, McVitie	16,883
25		8	H	Sheffield United	D	2-2	T. Brown 2	21,255
26		22	A	Everton	L	1-2	Gould	36,412
27		29	H	Manchester United	W	2-1	Gould, Astle	46,992
28	Feb	12	A	Leicester City	W	1-0	T. Brown	24,255
29		19	H	Southampton	W	3-2	Gould, Cantello, T. Brown	17,875
30	Mar	1	A	Manchester City	L	1-2	T. Brown (pen)	25,672
31		4	H	Nottingham Forest	W	1-0	Wile	16,702
32		11	H	Crystal Palace	D	1-1	A. Brown	17,105
33		17	A	Coventry City	W	2-0	Wile, A. Brown	22,887
34		25	H	Huddersfield Town	D	1-1	Gould	18,373
35	Apr	1	A	Liverpool	L	0-2		46,564
36		5	H	Derby County	D	0-0		32,439
37		8	H	Tottenham Hotspur	D	1-1	Hope (pen)	20,862
38		15	A	Wolverhampton Wanderers	W	1-0	T. Brown	30,419
39		22	H	Leeds United	L	0-1		40,675
40		27	H	Chelsea	W	4-0	T. Brown, Gould, A. Brown, Cantello	18,41[illegible]
41	May	3	A	Newcastle United	L	2-4	Gould 2	18,92[illegible]
42		5	A	Stoke City	D	1-1	Gould	16,205

Appearances
Sub appearances
Goals

FA Cup

R3	Jan	15	H	Coventry City	L	1-2	T. Brown	26,31[illegible]

Appearances
Goals

League Cup

R2	Sep	8	H	Tottenham Hotspur	L	0-1		26,18[illegible]

Appearances

Cumbes J	Hughes LJ	Wilson RT	Cantello L	Wile JD	Kaye J	Hope R	Suggett C	Astle J	Brown T	Merrick AR	Hartford RA	Minton RC	MacLean H	Gould RA	McVitie GJ	Osborne J	Robertson A	Johnson LG	Glover AR	Smith GWC	Nisbet GJM	Brown A	
1	2	3	4	5	6	7	8	9	10	11													1
1	2	3	4	5	6	10	7	9	8		11												2
1	2	3	4	5	6	10	7	9	8		11												3
1	2	3	4	5	6	10	7	9	8		11												4
1	2	3	4	5	6	10	8		9	7	11												5
1	2	3	4	5	6	10	7		8	9	11												6
1	2	3	4	5	6	10	**7**	9	8	12	11												7
1	2		4	5	6	12	7		8	11	10	3	**9**										8
1	2	3	4	5	6		7		8		10			9	11								9
1	2	3	4	5	6	10			8		11			9	7								10
1	2	3	4	5	6	**10**	12		8		11			9	7								11
	2	3	4	5		12		10	8		11			9	**7**	1	6						12
	2	3	4	5		12		9	8		11		**7**	10		1	6						13
		3	4	5		**7**		9	8		11	2		10		1	6	12					14
		3	4	5					11		8	2		9		1	6	10	7				15
		3	4	5		11			7			2		10		1	6	9	8				16
		3	4	5				10	7		11	2		9		1	6		8				17
		3	4	5	12			**9**	11		8	2		10		1	6		7				18
		3	4	5				9	8		11	2		10		1	6		7				19
		3	4	5				9	7	8	11	2		10			6			1			20
		3	4	5		12		10	8		11	2		9			6		**7**	1			21
		3	4	5			10	9	8		11				7		6			1	2		22
		3	4	5			10		8		11			9	7		6			1	2		23
		3	4	5			10		8		11			9	7		6			1	2		24
		3	4	5			8		10		11			9	7		6			1	2		25
		3	4	5			10		8		11			9	**7**	1	6		12		2		26
		3	4	5			10	9	8		11			7		1	6				2		27
		3	4	5			10	9	8		11			7		1	6				2		28
		3	4	5			10	9	8		11			7		1	6				2		29
		3	4	5			10	9	8		11			7		1	6				2		30
		3	4	5			10	9	8		11			7		1	6				2		31
		3	4	5			10	9	8		11					1	6				2	7	32
		3	4	5			9		8		11			7		1	6				2	10	33
		3	4	5			9		8		11			7		1	6				2	10	34
		3	**4**	5			9		8		11			7		1	6		12		2	10	35
		3		5		7	4	9	8		11					1	6				2	10	36
		3		5		7	4	9			11			8		1	6				2	10	37
		3		5		10	4		8		11			7		1	6				2	9	38
		3		5		10	4		8		11			7		1	6				2	10	39
			11	5		7	4		9	3				8		1	6				2	10	40
		3	4	5		12	7		**9**		11			8		1	6				2	10	41
	12	3	**4**	5		7	9				11			8		1	6				2	10	42
11	13	40	38	42	11	17	30	22	40	6	39	9	2	31	9	25	31	2	6	6	21	11	
	1				1	5	1			1								1	2				
			2	3		1		2	17		1			12	1							3	

		3	4	5			10		8		11			9	7	1	6				2		R3
		1	1	1			1		1		1			1	1	1	1				1		
									1														

1	2		4	5	6	10	7		8		11	3	9										R2
1	1		1	1	1	1	1		1		1	1	1										

1972-73

Division One

	P	W	D	L	F	A	Pts
Liverpool	42	25	10	7	72	42	60
Arsenal	42	23	11	8	57	43	57
Leeds United	42	21	11	10	71	45	53
Ipswich Town	42	17	14	11	55	45	48
Wolverhampton W	42	18	11	13	66	54	47
West Ham United	42	17	12	13	67	53	46
Derby County	42	19	8	15	56	54	46
Tottenham Hotspur	42	16	13	13	58	48	45
Newcastle United	42	16	13	13	60	51	45
Birmingham City	42	15	12	15	53	54	42
Manchester City	42	15	11	16	57	60	41
Chelsea	42	13	14	15	49	51	40
Southampton	42	11	18	13	47	52	40
Sheffield United	42	15	10	17	51	59	40
Stoke City	42	14	10	18	61	56	38
Leicester City	42	10	17	15	40	46	37
Everton	42	13	11	18	41	49	37
Manchester United	42	12	13	17	44	60	37
Coventry City	42	13	9	20	40	55	35
Norwich City	42	11	10	21	36	63	32
Crystal Palace	42	9	12	21	41	58	30
West Bromwich Albion	42	9	10	23	38	62	28

Manager: Don Howe

- Albion were relegated to the Second Division for the first time since 1949.
- John Wile was named team captain.
- Scottish-born left-winger Willie Johnston was signed for a club record fee of £138,000 from Glasgow Rangers, inside-forward David Shaw arrived from Oldham Athletic and striker Joe Mayo from Walsall.
- Bobby Gould left to join Bristol City, George McVitie signed for Oldham Athletic and Colin Suggett moved to Norwich City for £70,000.
- Albion had an FA Cup tie abandoned for the first time in their history – fog ending the clash with Nottingham Forest at The City Ground in January.

Match No.	Date			Opponents	Result		Scorers	Attendance
1	Aug	12	H	West Ham United	D	0-0		22,234
2		16	H	Tottenham Hotspur	L	0-1		19,175
3		19	A	Leeds United	L	0-2		36,555
4		23	A	Newcastle United	D	1-1	A. Brown	29,695
5		26	H	Sheffield United	L	0-2		15,559
6		30	H	Birmingham City	D	2-2	Gould, Suggett	37,108
7	Sep	2	A	Everton	L	0-1		36,269
8		9	H	Derby County	W	2-1	Gould, T. Brown	17,262
9		16	A	Crystal Palace	W	2-0	Gould, Robertson	17,858
10		23	H	Coventry City	W	1-0	Suggett	15,373
11		30	A	Manchester City	L	1-2	T. Brown	27,332
12	Oct	7	H	Manchester United	D	2-2	A. Brown 2	39,209
13		14	A	Chelsea	L	1-3	T. Brown (pen)	28,998
14		21	H	Wolverhampton Wanderers	W	1-0	Gould	30,121
15		28	A	Southampton	L	1-2	Hartford	15,810
16	Nov	4	H	Newcastle United	L	2-3	Suggett, Gould	14,668
17		11	A	Tottenham Hotspur	D	1-1	T. Brown	25,875
18		18	A	Norwich City	L	0-2		21,607
19		25	H	Stoke City	W	2-1	T. Brown 2 (1 pen)	13,332
20	Dec	2	A	Leicester City	L	1-3	Gould	15,307
21		9	H	Liverpool	D	1-1	T. Brown	27,171
22		16	A	Arsenal	L	1-2	T. Brown	27,199
23		23	H	Ipswich Town	W	2-0	Glover, Hartford	12,147
24		26	A	Coventry City	D	0-0		31,545
25	Jan	6	A	Sheffield United	L	0-3		16,231
26		27	A	Derby County	L	0-2		28,833
27	Feb	10	H	Crystal Palace	L	0-4		15,173
28		17	A	West Ham United	L	1-2	T. Brown	26,079
29		28	H	Arsenal	W	1-0	T. Brown	23,308
30	Mar	3	A	Manchester United	L	1-2	Astle	46,735
31		10	H	Chelsea	D	1-1	T. Brown	21,466
32		17	A	Ipswich Town	L	0-2		17,614
33		20	A	Wolverhampton Wanderers	L	0-2		33,520
34		24	H	Southampton	D	1-1	T. Brown	12,599
35		28	H	Leeds United	D	1-1	Shaw	32,804
36		31	A	Stoke City	L	0-2		21,299
37	Apr	7	H	Leicester City	W	1-0	Astle	15,235
38		11	H	Everton	W	4-1	Astle, Hartford, Shaw 2	21,281
39		14	A	Liverpool	L	0-1		43,853
40		21	H	Norwich City	L	0-1		23,263
41		25	H	Manchester City	L	1-2	Astle	21,480
42		28	A	Birmingham City	L	2-3	Astle, Wile	36,784

Appearances
Sub appearances
Goals

FA Cup

R3	Jan	13	H	Nottingham Forest	D	1-1	Winfield (og)	15,743
rep		22	A	Nottingham Forest	D	0-0*		17,069
rep2		29	N	Nottingham Forest	W	3-1	Cantello, Hartford, Suggett	12,606
R4	Feb	3	H	Swindon Town	W	2-0	T. Brown, Suggett	20,795
R5		24	A	Leeds United	L	0-2		39,229

R3 replay 2 at Filbert Street, Leicester
* after extra-time

Appearances
Sub appearances
Goals

League Cup

R2	Sep	6	H	Queen's Park Rangers	W	2-1	Evans (og), T. Brown (pen)	10,494
R3	Oct	3	H	Liverpool	D	1-1	Hartford	17,661
rep		10	A	Liverpool	L	1-2*	Robertson	26,461

* after extra-time

Appearances
Sub appearances
Goals

Smith GWC	Nisbet GJM	Wilson RT	Cantello L	Wile JD	Robertson A	Brown T	Brown A	Gould RA	Suggett C	Hartford RA	Latchford PW	MacLean H	Merrick AR	Hughes LJ	Woolgar JS	Johnston WM	Glover AR	Astle J	Shaw DG	Osborne J	Minton RC	
1	2	3	4	5	6	7	8	9	10	11												1
1	2	3	4	5	6	7	8	9	10	11												2
1	2	3	4	5	6	7	8	9	10	11												3
1	2	3	4	5	6	7	8	9	10	11												4
	2	3	4	5	6	7	8	**9**	10	11	1	12										5
	2	3		5	6		8	9	10	11	1		4	7								6
	2	3		5	6		10	9	7	11	1		8	4								7
	2	3	4	5	6	8	10	9	7	11	1											8
	2	3	4	5	6	8	10	9	7	11	1											9
	2		4	5	6	8	10	9	7	11	1		3									10
	2	3	4	5	6	8	10	9	7	11	1											11
	2	3	**4**	5	6	8	10	9	7	11	1				12							12
	2	3	4	5	6	8	10	9	7	11	1											13
	2		**4**	5	6	8	10	9	7	11	1		3		12							14
	2			5	6	8	10	9	7	11	1		3		4							15
	2	3		5	6	8	10	9	7	11	1		4									16
	2	3		5	6	8	10	9	7	11	1		4									17
	2	3	4		5	8	10	9	7	11	1		6									18
	2	3	4		5	8	7	9		10	1	11	6									19
	2	3	**4**	5	6	8	10	9		11	1	12	7									20
	2	3	4	5	6	8	7	9	12	10	1					11						21
	2	3	4	5		8	**9**		7	10	1		6			11	12					22
	2	3	4	5		8	7			10	1		6			11	9					23
	2	3	4	5	6	8	9			10	1		7			11						24
	2		4	5	3	8	9			10	1		6			11	7					25
	2	3	4	5		8	9		7	10	1		6			11						26
	2	3	4	5	9	8	12		**7**	10	1		6			11						27
	2	3	4	5	9	8				10	1		6		7	**11**	12					28
	2	3	4	5	6	8	12			10	1		7			11		**9**				29
	2	3	4	5	6	8				10	1		7			**11**		9	12			30
	2	3	4	5	6	8				10			**7**			11		9	12	1		31
	2	3	4	5	6	8						**7**	12			11		9	10	1		32
	2	3	4	5	6	8				10			7			11		9		1		33
		3	2	5	6	8				10			**7**			11		9	4	1		34
		3	2	5	6	4				10			7			11		9	8	1		35
		3	2	5	6	**4**				10			7			11	12	9	8	1		36
		3	4	5		7				10			6			11		9	8	1	2	37
		3	4	5		7				10			6			11		9	8	1	2	38
		3	4	5		7				10			6			11		9	8	1	2	39
		3	4	5	12	7				10			6			11		9	8	1	**2**	40
		3	4	5	7		12			10			6			**11**		9	8	1	2	41
		3	4	5	7	12				10			6			11		9	8	1	**2**	42
4	33	38	37	40	35	38	26	21	21	41	26	2	30	2	2	22	2	14	10	12	6	
					1	1	3		1			2	1		2		3		2			
				1	1	12	3	6	3	3							1	5	3			

	2	3	4	5		8	9		7	10	1		6			11						R3
	2	3	4	5	12	8	**9**		7	10	1		6			11						rep
	2	3	4	5		8	9		7	10	1		6			11						rep2
	2	3	4	5	12	8	**9**		7	10	1		6			11						R4
	2	3	4	5	6	8	12			10	1		7			11		9				R5
	5	5	5	5	1	5	4		4	5	5		5			5		1				
					2		1															
			1			1			2	1												

One own-goal

	2	3		5	6	8	10	9	7	11	1			4								R2
	2	3	4	5	6	8	10	9	7	11	1											R3
	2	3	**4**	5	6	8	10	9	7	11	1				12							rep
	3	3	2	3	3	3	3	3	3	3	3			1								
															1							
					1	1				1												

One own-goal

1973-74

Division Two

	P	W	D	L	F	A	Pts
Middlesbrough	42	27	11	4	77	30	65
Luton Town	42	19	12	11	64	51	50
Carlisle United	42	20	9	13	61	48	49
Orient	42	15	18	9	55	42	48
Blackpool	42	17	13	12	57	40	47
Sunderland	42	19	9	14	58	44	47
Nottingham Forest	42	15	15	12	57	43	45
West Bromwich Albion	42	14	16	12	48	45	44
Hull City	42	13	17	12	46	47	43
Notts County	42	15	13	14	55	60	43
Bolton Wanderers	42	15	12	15	44	40	42
Millwall	42	14	14	14	51	51	42
Fulham	42	16	10	16	39	43	42
Aston Villa	42	13	15	14	48	45	41
Portsmouth	42	14	12	16	45	62	40
Bristol City	42	14	10	18	47	54	38
Cardiff City	42	10	16	16	49	62	36
Oxford United	42	10	16	16	35	46	36
Sheffield Wednesday	42	12	11	19	51	63	35
Crystal Palace	42	11	12	19	43	56	34
Preston North End	42	9	14	19	40	62	31
Swindon Town	42	7	11	24	36	72	25

Manager: Don Howe

- Tony Brown scored seven goals against Nottingham clubs in seven days – a hat-trick against County in the FA Cup and a four-timer against Forest in the League.
- Jeff Astle, the scorer of 174 goals in 361 appearances, left The Hawthorns after 10 years, joining the South African side Hellenic.
- Albion played their first ever Sunday game this season against Everton in a third-round FA Cup tie at Goodison Park in January. Their first Sunday League game followed soon afterwards at Portsmouth.
- Willie Johnston became the first Albion player to be sent off in an FA Cup tie (the fourth-round replay against Everton).

Match No.	Date			Opponents	Result		Scorers	Attendance
1	Aug	25	A	Blackpool	W	3-2	T. Brown 2, Glover	14,238
2	Sep	1	H	Crystal Palace	W	1-0	Glover	17,828
3		8	A	Swindon Town	L	0-1		11,761
4		12	A	Sheffield Wednesday	L	1-3	T. Brown	15,527
5		15	H	Nottingham Forest	D	3-3	A. Brown, Minton, T. Brown	14,779
6		18	H	Preston North End	L	0-2		11,722
7		22	A	Hull City	D	0-0		7,089
8		29	H	Sunderland	D	1-1	A. Brown	16,940
9	Oct	1	A	Preston North End	L	1-3	T. Brown	15,419
10		6	A	Bristol City	D	1-1	T. Brown	14,325
11		13	H	Carlisle United	D	1-1	T. Brown	12,556
12		20	A	Middlesbrough	D	0-0		18,997
13		24	H	Sheffield Wednesday	W	2-0	Shaw 2	12,667
14		27	H	Bolton Wanderers	D	0-0		16,148
15	Nov	3	A	Cardiff City	W	1-0	T. Brown	10,432
16		10	H	Notts County	W	2-1	T. Brown, Shaw	15,564
17		17	A	Orient	L	0-2		11,581
18		24	H	Fulham	W	2-0	Glover, Hartford	12,606
19	Dec	1	A	Luton Town	W	2-0	Shaw, Hartford	10,192
20		8	H	Oxford United	W	1-0	Shaw	12,277
21		15	H	Portsmouth	L	1-2	Cantello	11,498
22		22	A	Sunderland	D	1-1	Shaw	18,389
23		26	H	Aston Villa	W	2-0	T. Brown 2	43,029
24		29	H	Swindon Town	W	2-0	Merrick, Johnston	14,969
25	Jan	1	A	Crystal Palace	L	0-1		23,823
26		12	A	Nottingham Forest	W	4-1	T. Brown 4	15,301
27		19	H	Blackpool	D	1-1	Wile	17,808
28	Feb	3	A	Portsmouth	D	1-1	Glover	19,767
29		23	H	Bristol City	D	2-2	Wile, Astle	18,928
30		25	A	Carlisle United	W	1-0	Johnston	6,407
31	Mar	2	A	Aston Villa	W	3-1	Wile, T. Brown 2 (1 pen)	37,323
32		9	A	Bolton Wanderers	D	1-1	T. Brown	18,061
33		16	H	Middlesbrough	L	0-4		24,178
34		19	H	Hull City	L	2-3	Shaw, A. Brown	13,712
35		23	A	Notts County	L	0-1		9,672
36		30	H	Cardiff City	D	2-2	Murray (og), Shaw	11,528
37	Apr	6	A	Fulham	D	0-0		9,494
38		12	A	Millwall	L	0-1		8,723
39		13	H	Orient	W	1-0	Hartford	11,546
40		17	H	Millwall	D	1-1	Glover	12,346
41		20	A	Oxford United	L	0-1		9,492
42		27	H	Luton Town	D	1-1	T. Brown (pen)	13,164
								Appearances
								Sub appearances
								Goals

FA Cup

R3	Jan	5	H	Notts County	W	4-0	T. Brown 3, Johnston	13,123
R4		27	A	Everton	D	0-0		53,509
rep		30	H	Everton	W	1-0	T. Brown	27,556
R5	Feb	16	H	Newcastle United	L	0-3		42,747
								Appearances
								Sub appearances
								Goals

League Cup

R2	Oct	8	H	Sheffield United	W	2-1	Shaw, Cantello	10,482
R3		31	H	Exeter City	L	1-3	Johnston	10,719
								Appearances
								Sub appearances
								Goals

	Latchford PW	Minton RC	Merrick AR	Hughes LJ	Wile JD	Robertson A	Cantello L	Shaw DG	Glover AR	Brown T	Johnston WM	Hartford RA	Brown A	Donaghy B	Nisbet GJM	Mayo J	Wilson RT	Thompson JT	Astle J
1	1	2	3	4	5	6	7	8	9	10	11								
2	1	2	3	4	5	6	7	8	9	10	11								
3	1	**2**	3		5	6	4	8	7	10	11	9	12						
4	1	2	3	9	5	6	4	10	7	8	**11**		12						
5	1	2	3	4	5	6	7		12	10		8	9	11					
6	1	2	3	8	5	6		12	7	10		4	9	11					
7	1		3	**4**	5	6		11	7	10		8	9		2	12			
8	1		3		5	6		9	7	10		4	8	11	2				
9	1		3		5	6		11	4	9	7	8	10		2				
10	1		3		5	6	4	10		8	11	7	9		2				
11	1		3		5	6	4	11		9	7	10	8		2				
12	1		3		5	6	4	10		8	11	7	9		2				
13	1		3		5	6	4	11		9	7	10	8		2				
14	1		3		5	6	4	11		9	7	10	8		2				
15	1				5	6	4		11	8	7	10			2	9	3		
16	1				5	6	4	12	11	**8**	7	10			2	9	3		
17	1				5	6	4	12	**11**	8	7	10			2	9	3		
18	1				5	6	4	12	11	8	7	10			2	**9**	3		
19	1				5	6	4	12	11	8	7	10			2	**9**	3		
20	1				5	6	4	12	11	8	7	10			2	**9**	3		
21	1				5	6	4	9	11	8	7	10			2		3		
22	1		12		5	6	4	9	**11**	8	7	10			2		3		
23	1		10		5	6	4	9	11	8	7				2		3		
24	1		10		5	6	4	9	11	8	7				2		3		
25	1		12		5	6	4	9	11	8	7	10			2		**3**		
26	1				5	6	4	9	11	8	7	10			2		3		
27	1				5	6	4	9	11	8	7	10			2		3		
28	1				5	6	4	9	11	8	7	10			2		3		
29	1				5	6	4		11	8	7	10			2			3	9
30	1				5	6	4		11	8	7	**10**		12	2			3	9
31	1		10		5	6	4	12	11	8	7				2		3		**9**
32	1		10		5	6	4	12	11	8	7				2		3		**9**
33	1				5	6	4	12	11	8	7	10			**2**		3		9
34	1		10		5	6	4	7	11	8			9		2		3		
35	1		10		5	6	4	7	8			11	9		2		3		
36	1				5	6	4	7	10	**9**		8		11	2		3		12
37	1		6		5		4	8	7	9	11	10			2			3	
38	1			6	5		4	8	9	7	11	10			2			3	
39	1				5	6	**4**	9	11	8	7	10			2	12		3	
40	1				5	6		8	11	4	7	10			2	9		3	
41	1				5	6		9	11	8	7	10				4	3	2	
42	1			4	5	6			11	8	7		10			9	3	2	
	42	6	21	8	42	40	35	28	36	41	35	33	13	4	34	9	22	8	5
			2					9	1				2	1		2			1
		1	1		3		1	8	5	19	2	3	3						1

One own-goal

R3	1				5	6	4	9	11	8	7	10			2		3		
R4	1				5	6	4	9	11	8	7	10			2		3		
rep	1				5	6	4	9	11	8	7	10			2		3		
R5	1		12		5	6	**4**	9	11	8	7	10			2		3		
	4				4	4	4	4	4	4	4	4			4		4		
			1																
										4	1								

R2	1		3		5	6	**4**	11	12	9	7	10	8		2				
R3	1		3		5	6	4	11		9	7	10	8		2				
	2		2		2	2	2	2		2	2	2	2		2				
									1										
							1	1			1								

1974-75

Division Two

	P	W	D	L	F	A	Pts
Manchester United	42	26	9	7	66	30	61
Aston Villa	42	25	8	9	79	32	58
Norwich City	42	20	13	9	58	37	53
Sunderland	42	19	13	10	65	35	51
Bristol City	42	21	8	13	47	33	50
West Bromwich Albion	42	18	9	15	54	42	45
Blackpool	42	14	17	11	38	33	45
Hull City	42	15	14	13	40	53	44
Fulham	42	13	16	13	44	39	42
Bolton Wanderers	42	15	12	15	45	41	42
Oxford United	42	15	12	15	41	51	42
Orient	42	11	20	11	28	39	42
Southampton	42	15	11	16	53	54	41
Notts County	42	12	16	14	49	59	40
York City	42	14	10	18	51	55	38
Nottingham Forest	42	12	14	16	43	55	38
Portsmouth	42	12	13	17	44	54	37
Oldham Athletic	42	10	15	17	40	48	35
Bristol Rovers	42	12	11	19	42	64	35
Millwall	42	10	12	20	44	56	32
Cardiff City	42	9	14	19	36	62	32
Sheffield Wednesday	42	5	11	26	29	64	21

Manager: Don Howe

- Asa Hartford joined Manchester City for £225,000 – three years after a move to Leeds United had fallen through when the Scottish midfielder was diagnosed with a heart problem.
- Goalkeeper Peter Latchford joined Celtic and Lyndon Hughes moved to Peterborough United.
- For the first time in Albion's history, the admission price for a seat rose to £1.
- Mr F.A. 'Bert' Millichip was appointed Albion chairman, a position he retained until 1983.

Match No.	Date			Opponents	Result		Scorers	Attendance
1	Aug	17	H	Fulham	L	0-1		11,425
2		24	A	Hull City	L	0-1		7,864
3		31	H	Sunderland	W	1-0	Glover	12,501
4	Sep	7	A	Portsmouth	W	3-1	Johnston, Shaw, Merrick	9,158
5		14	H	Manchester United	D	1-1	Merrick	23,666
6		18	H	Hull City	D	2-2	Shaw 2	9,973
7		21	A	Notts County	D	0-0		10,004
8		25	A	Sheffield Wednesday	D	0-0		12,478
9		28	H	Oxford United	W	3-0	T. Brown, Merrick, Cantello	9,590
10	Oct	5	H	York City	W	2-0	Johnston, Merrick	11,770
11		12	A	Cardiff City	W	2-0	Mayo, Donaghy	6,737
12		19	H	Nottingham Forest	L	0-1		13,868
13		22	A	Bristol Rovers	L	1-2	Shaw	12,101
14		26	A	Millwall	D	2-2	Hughes, Kitchener (og)	8,057
15	Nov	2	H	Norwich City	D	1-1	Shaw	12,064
16		6	H	Bristol Rovers	D	2-2	T. Brown, Glover	8,849
17		9	A	Southampton	L	0-1		15,638
18		16	H	Bristol City	W	1-0	Mayo	11,936
19		23	A	Orient	W	2-0	Hughes, Johnston	6,766
20		30	H	Oldham Athletic	W	1-0	T. Brown	11,311
21	Dec	7	A	Bolton Wanderers	W	1-0	Mayo	12,633
22		14	A	Fulham	L	0-1		6,730
23		21	H	Aston Villa	W	2-0	Johnston, Mayo	29,614
24		26	A	Manchester United	L	1-2	Cantello	51,104
25		28	H	Blackpool	W	2-0	Johnston, Mayo	14,839
26	Jan	18	A	Oldham Athletic	D	0-0		11,343
27	Feb	1	H	Southampton	L	0-3		15,763
28		8	A	Norwich City	L	2-3	Mayo, Hughes	34,160
29		15	H	Orient	W	1-0	Johnston	9,388
30		22	A	Bristol City	L	1-2	Shaw	14,180
31	Mar	1	A	Sunderland	L	0-3		28,867
32		8	H	Sheffield Wednesday	W	4-0	T. Brown 2 (1 pen), Wile, Edwards	10,330
33		15	A	Oxford United	D	1-1	T. Brown	7,404
34		22	H	Portsmouth	W	2-1	T. Brown, Wilson	10,048
35		29	A	Aston Villa	L	1-3	T. Brown	47,574
36		31	A	Blackpool	L	0-2		11,611
37	Apr	2	H	Notts County	W	4-1	Edwards, T. Brown 2 (1 pen), Cantello	7,812
38		5	H	Millwall	W	2-1	T. Brown 2	8,130
39		8	H	Bolton Wanderers	L	0-1		7,957
40		12	A	York City	W	3-1	Johston, Mayo 2	8,181
41		19	H	Cardiff City	W	2-0	Robson, Robertson	10,071
42		26	A	Nottingham Forest	L	1-2	Robson	11,721

Appearances
Sub appearances
Goals

FA Cup

R3	Jan	4	A	Bolton Wanderers	D	0-0		17,305
rep		8	H	Bolton Wanderers	W	4-0	Cantello, Wile, Shaw, Mayo	21,210
R4		25	A	Carlisle United	L	2-3	T. Brown (pen), Nisbet	14,843

Appearances
Goals

League Cup

R2	Sep	10	H	Millwall	W	1-0	Cantello	8,294
R3	Oct	9	H	Norwich City	D	1-1	Stringer (og)	11,625
rep		16	A	Norwich City	L	0-2*		18,235

* after extra-time

Appearances
Sub appearances
Goals

Latchford PW	Nisbet GJM	Wilson RT	Cantello L	Robertson A	Merrick AR	Glover AR	Brown T	Shaw DG	Hughes LJ	Johnston WM	Wile JD	Mayo J	Donaghy B	Osborne J	Rushbury DG	Trewick J	Thompson JT	Ward RA	Edwards RI	Minton R	Brown A	Robson B	
1	2	3	4	5	6	7	8	9	10	11													1
1	2	3	4	5	6	7	8	9	10	11													2
1	2	3	4	5		7	8	9	10	11	6												3
1	2	3	4	5	10	7	8	9		11	6												4
1	2	3	4	6	10	7	8	9		11	5												5
1	2	3	4	6	10	7	8	9		11	5												6
1	2	3	4	6	10	7	8	9		11	5												7
1	2	3	4	6	10	7	8	**9**	12	11	5												8
1	2	3	4	6	**10**	7	8		12	11	5	9											9
1	2	3	4	6	10	7	8			11	5	9											10
1	2	3	4	6	**10**	7	8			11	5	9	12										11
1	2	3	4	6	**10**	7	8	12		11	5	9											12
1	2	3	4	6	10	7	8	9		11	5												13
	2	3	4		10	7	8	**9**	11		5	12		1	6								14
	2	3			10	7	8	**9**	4	11	5	12		1	6								15
	2	3	4		10	7	8	9		11	5			1	6								16
	2	3	**4**		10	7	8	9	12	11	5			1	6								17
	2	3				7		9	10	11	5	8		1	6	4							18
	2	3	4			7		9	10	11	5	8		1	6								19
	2	3	4			7	11	9	10		5	8		1	6								20
	2	3	4		12	7	**11**	8	10		5	9		1	6								21
	2	3	4		12	7	11	9	10		5	**8**		1	6								22
	2		4			7		8	10	11	5	9		1	6		3						23
	2	3	4			7		8	10	11	5	9		1	6								24
	2	3	4			**7**	12	8	10	11	5	9		1	6								25
	2	3	4				7	8	10	11	5	9		1	6								26
	2	3	4			12	7	**8**	10	11	5	9		1	6								27
	2		4			7	8	12	10	11	5	9		1	6		3						28
	2		4			**7**	8	12	10	11	5	9		1	6		3						29
		3	4	5			8	7	10	11		**9**		1	6	12	2						30
	2		4	5		7	12	8	10	11		9		**1**	6		3						31
	2	3	4			7	8		10	11	5				6			1	9				32
	2	3	4			7	8	12	10	11	5			1	6				**9**				33
	2	3	4			7	8	12		11	5				6	**10**		1	9				34
	2		4		10	7	8			11	5			1	6		3		9				35
	2				4	7	8	10		11	5			1	6		**3**			12	9		36
	2		4	6	7		8		10	11	5			1	3				9				37
	2		4	6	7		8	12	**10**	11	5				3			1	9				38
	2	3	4	6	7			8		11	5				10			1	9				39
	2	3	4	6	7					11	5	9						1			8	10	40
	2	3		6	7	4				11	5	9						1			8	10	41
	2	3		6	7	4				11	5	9						1			8	10	42
13	41	34	37	21	24	35	32	27	23	38	38	21		22	26	2	7	7	7		4	3	
					2	1	2	6	3			2	1			1				1			
		1	3	1	4	2	12	6	3	7	1	8							2			2	

	2	3	4				7	8	10	11	5	9		1	6								R3
	2	3	4				7	8	10	11	5	9		1	6								rep
	2	3	4				7	8	10	11	5	9		1	6								R4
	3	3	3				3	3	3	3	3	3		3	3								
	1		1				1	1			1	1											

1	2	3	4	6	10	7	8	9		11	5												R2
1	2	3	4	6	10	7	8			11	5	9											R3
1	2	3	4	6		7		8	10	11	5	**9**	12										rep
3	3	3	3	3	2	3	2	2	1	3	3	2											
													1										
			1																				

One own-goal

1975-76

Division Two

	P	W	D	L	F	A	Pts
Sunderland	42	24	8	10	67	36	56
Bristol City	42	19	15	8	59	35	53
West Bromwich Albion	42	20	13	9	50	33	53
Bolton Wanderers	42	20	12	10	64	38	52
Notts County	42	19	11	12	60	41	49
Southampton	42	21	7	14	66	50	49
Luton Town	42	19	10	13	61	51	48
Nottingham Forest	42	17	12	13	55	40	46
Charlton Athletic	42	15	12	15	61	72	42
Blackpool	42	14	14	14	40	49	42
Chelsea	42	12	16	14	53	54	40
Fulham	42	13	14	15	45	47	40
Orient	42	13	14	15	37	39	40
Hull City	42	14	11	17	45	49	39
Blackburn Rovers	42	12	14	16	45	50	38
Plymouth Argyle	42	13	12	17	48	54	38
Oldham Athletic	42	13	12	17	57	68	38
Bristol Rovers	42	11	16	15	38	50	38
Carlisle United	42	12	13	17	45	59	37
Oxford United	42	11	11	20	39	59	33
York City	42	10	8	24	39	71	28
Portsmouth	42	9	7	26	32	61	25

Player-manager: Johnny Giles

- Republic of Ireland international Johnny Giles was appointed as Albion's first ever player-manager, signed for £48,000 from Leeds United.
- Albion gained promotion from the Second Division after beating Oldham Athletic on the last day of the season, courtesy of Tony Brown's 12th goal of the campaign.
- World Cup winner Geoff Hurst was signed from Stoke City but left for Seattle Sounders at the end of the season, and two more Irish internationals were recruited, Mick Martin from Manchester United and Paddy Mulligan from Crystal Palace, along with goalkeeper Tony Godden from Ashford Town. Goalkeeper Peter Latchford also left the club, joining Celtic for £35,000, while David Shaw returned to Oldham and Alan Merrick switched to Kidderminster Harriers.
- Albion's youngsters won the FA Youth Cup, beating near neighbours Wolves 5–0 on aggregate over two legs.

Match No.	Date			Opponents	Result		Scorers	Attendance
1	Aug	16	A	Southampton	L	0-3		15,246
2		20	H	Chelsea	D	0-0		17,962
3		23	H	Luton Town	W	1-0	Trewick	14,062
4		30	A	Fulham	L	0-4		9,910
5	Sep	6	H	York City	D	2-2	T. Brown, Hurst	10,904
6		13	A	Sunderland	L	0-2		25,159
7		20	H	Charlton Athletic	D	1-1	Hurst	10,424
8		27	A	Carlisle United	D	1-1	A. Brown	6,625
9	Oct	4	H	Oldham Athletic	D	1-1	Johnston	10,606
10		11	A	Blackburn Rovers	D	0-0		9,973
11		18	H	Plymouth Argyle	W	1-0	A. Brown	10,892
12		25	A	Bristol City	W	2-0	A. Brown, T. Brown	19,133
13	Nov	1	H	Notts County	D	0-0		12,610
14		4	A	Bristol Rovers	D	1-1	Edwards	13,116
15		8	A	Blackpool	W	1-0	Johnston	8,271
16		12	A	Oxford United	W	1-0	Mayo	5,909
17		15	H	Hull City	W	2-0	Martin, T. Brown	14,398
18		22	A	Plymouth Argyle	L	1-2	Giles	17,380
19		29	A	Bolton Wanderers	W	2-1	Mayo, Robson	19,401
20	Dec	6	H	Portsmouth	W	3-1	A. Brown 2, T. Brown	15,275
21		13	A	Luton Town	L	1-2	Martin	10,203
22		19	H	Southampton	L	0-2		16,780
23		26	A	Nottingham Forest	W	2-0	Giles, Johnston	19,393
24		27	H	Orient	D	1-1	Mayo	20,601
25	Jan	10	H	Sunderland	D	0-0		24,287
26		17	A	York City	W	1-0	A. Brown	6,224
27		31	A	Chelsea	W	2-1	Martin, T. Brown	15,896
28	Feb	7	H	Bristol Rovers	W	3-0	Cantello, Mayo, A. Brown	16,732
29		21	A	Hull City	L	1-2	Johnston	6,496
30		25	H	Oxford United	W	2-0	T. Brown, Robertson	14,338
31	Mar	6	A	Notts County	W	2-0	Mayo, Johnston	20,032
32		13	H	Blackburn Rovers	D	2-2	Mayo, Wile	17,746
33		17	H	Bristol City	L	0-1		26,278
34		20	H	Bolton Wanderers	W	2-0	Mayo, Wile	25,650
35		27	A	Portsmouth	W	1-0	Cantello	10,617
36		31	H	Blackpool	D	0-0		20,257
37	Apr	3	H	Carlisle United	W	3-0	A. Brown, Martin, Mayo	17,133
38		9	A	Charlton Athletic	L	1-2	T. Brown (pen)	14,252
39		14	H	Fulham	W	3-1	A. Brown 2, Cantello	18,237
40		17	H	Nottingham Forest	W	2-0	Martin, Johnston	26,580
41		20	A	Orient	D	0-0		10,857
42		24	A	Oldham Athletic	W	1-0	T. Brown	22,356
								Appearances
								Sub appearances
								Goals

FA Cup

R3	Jan	3	H	Carlisle United	W	3-1	T. Brown 2 (1 pen), A. Brown	16,159
R4		24	H	Lincoln City	W	3-2	T. Brown, Martin, Robson	26,878
R5	Feb	14	H	Southampton	D	1-1	T. Brown	36,645
rep		17	A	Southampton	L	0-4		27,614
								Appearances
								Sub appearances
								Goals

League Cup

R2	Sep	9	H	Fulham	D	1-1	Johnston	10,912
rep		24	A	Fulham	L	0-1		10,785
								Appearances
								Goals

Osborne J	Nisbet GJM	Wilson RT	Cantello L	Wile JD	Robertson A	Trewick J	Brown A	Mayo J	Merrick AR	Johnston WM	Brown T	Hurst GC	Giles MJ	Robson B	Thompson JT	Rushbury DG	Glover AR	Martin MP	Mulligan PM	Edwards RI	
1	2	3	4	5	6	7	8	**9**	10	11	12										1
1	2	3	4	5	6	7				11	8	9	10								2
1	2	3		5	6	7				11	8	9	10	4							3
1	2	3	4	5	6	7				11	**8**	9	10	12							4
1	2		4	5	6	7				11	8	9	10		3						5
1	2		4	5	6	7				**11**	8	9	10	12	3						6
1		3	4		5		12			11	**8**	9	10		2	6	7				7
1		3	4	5	6		8			11	12	**9**	10		2		7				8
1		3	4	5	6		8			11	12	**9**			2		7	10			9
1		3	4	5	6		8			11		9	10					7	2		10
1		3	4	5	6		8			11		9	10					7	2		11
1		3	4	5	6		9			11	8		10					7	2		12
1		3	4	5	6		9			11	8		10					**7**	2	12	13
1		3	4	5	6		9			11	8		**10**					7	2	12	14
1		3	**4**	5	6	12		9		11	8		10					7	2		15
1		3		5	6	4		9			8		10					7	2	11	16
1		3		5	6	4		9			8		10					7	2	11	17
1		3		5	6	**4**	9	11			8		10					7	2	12	18
1		3		5	6		8	9		11	7			10				4	2		19
1		3			6		8	9		11	4		10	5				7	2		20
1		3			6		8	9		11	4		10	5				7	2		21
1			4		6	10	9			11	8			5		3		7	2		22
1			4	5	6		9	3		11	8		10					7	2		23
1			4	5	6		9	3		11	7		10					8	2		24
1			4	5	6		9	3		11	7		10					8	2		25
1			4	5	6		9	3		11	7		10					8	2		26
1				5	6		9	3		11	7		10	4				8	2		27
1			8	5	6		9	3		11	4		10					7	2		28
1			**8**	5	6		12	9		11	4		10	3				7	2		29
1			3		6		8	9		11	4		10	5				7	2		30
1			8	5	6			9		11	4		10	3				7	2		31
1			8	5	6			9		11	4		10	3				7	2		32
1			**8**	5	6		12	9		11	4		10	3				7	2		33
1			8	5	6		12	9		11	4		**10**	3				7	2		34
1			8	5	6			9		11	4		10	3				7	2		35
1			8	5	6		12	9		11	4		10	**3**				7	2		36
1			3	5	6		8	9		11	4		10					7	2		37
1			3	5	6		8	9		11	4		10					7	2		38
1			3	5	6		8	9		11	4		10					7	2		39
1			3	5	6		8	9		11	4		10					7	2		40
1			3	5	6		8	9		11	4		10					7	2		41
1			3	5	6		8	9		11	4		10					7	2		42
42	6	19	34	37	42	10	26	28	1	39	37	10	38	14	5	2	3	34	33	2	
						1	5				3			2						3	
			3	2	1	1	10	8		6	8	2	2	1				5		1	

Osborne J	Nisbet GJM	Wilson RT	Cantello L	Wile JD	Robertson A	Trewick J	Brown A	Mayo J	Merrick AR	Johnston WM	Brown T	Hurst GC	Giles MJ	Robson B	Thompson JT	Rushbury DG	Glover AR	Martin MP	Mulligan PM	Edwards RI	
1			4	5	6		9	3		11	7		10					8	2		R3
1				5	6		9	3		11	7		10	4				8	2		R4
1			8	5	6		9	3		11	4		10					7	2		R5
1			8	5	6		**9**	3		11	4		10	12				7	2		rep
4			3	4	4		4	4		4	4		4	1				4		4	
														1							
							1				4			1				1			

Osborne J	Nisbet GJM	Wilson RT	Cantello L	Wile JD	Robertson A	Trewick J	Brown A	Mayo J	Merrick AR	Johnston WM	Brown T	Hurst GC	Giles MJ	Robson B	Thompson JT	Rushbury DG	Glover AR	Martin MP	Mulligan PM	Edwards RI	
1			4	5	6	7				11	8	9	10		3				2		R2
1		3	4	5	6		8			11		9	10		2		7				rep
2		1	2	2	2	1	1			2	1	2	2		2		1		1		
										1											

1976-77

Division One

	P	W	D	L	F	A	Pts
Liverpool	42	23	11	8	62	33	57
Manchester City	42	21	14	7	60	34	56
Ipswich Town	42	22	8	12	66	39	52
Aston Villa	42	22	7	13	76	50	51
Newcastle United	42	18	13	11	64	49	49
Manchester United	42	18	11	13	71	62	47
West Bromwich Albion	42	16	13	13	62	56	45
Arsenal	42	16	11	15	64	59	43
Everton	42	14	14	14	62	64	42
Leeds United	42	15	12	15	48	51	42
Leicester City	42	12	18	12	47	60	42
Middlesbrough	42	14	13	15	40	45	41
Birmingham City	42	13	12	17	63	61	38
Queen's Park Rangers	42	13	12	17	47	52	38
Derby County	42	9	19	14	50	55	37
Norwich City	42	14	9	19	47	64	37
West Ham United	42	11	14	17	46	65	36
Bristol City	42	11	13	18	38	48	35
Coventry City	42	10	15	17	48	59	35
Sunderland	42	11	12	19	46	54	34
Stoke City	42	10	14	18	28	51	34
Tottenham Hotspur	42	12	9	21	48	72	33

Manager: Johnny Giles

- Albion signed two black players – Laurie Cunningham from Leyton Orient for £110,000 in March and Cyrille Regis from Hayes for £5,000 in May. Strikers David Cross (from Coventry City) and Ray Treacy (from Preston North End) also arrived, the latter for a second spell.
- Those who left included Joe Mayo (to Orient in a deal involving Cunningham), Ian Edwards (to Chester), Gordon Nisbet (to Hull City) and Johnny Giles to Shamrock Rovers (as player-manager), while full-back Ray Wilson was forced to retire through injury after making 284 first-team appearances.
- Albion played their 3,000th League game this season (against Manchester United in October, won 4–0).
- Willie Johnston became the first Albion player to be sent off in a League Cup tie, dismissed against Brighton for aiming a kick at the referee.
- Derek Statham made his League debut at Stoke, scoring a fine goal past England 'keeper Gordon Banks.
- Bryan Robson fractured his leg three times during this season, twice playing for Albion's first team and once for the reserves.

Match No.	Date			Opponents	Result		Scorers	Attendance
1	Aug	21	A	Leeds United	D	2-2	A. Brown, T. Brown	40,248
2		25	H	Liverpool	L	0-1		29,735
3		28	H	Norwich City	W	2-0	A. Brown, T. Brown (pen)	16,434
4	Sep	4	A	Queen's Park Rangers	L	0-1		18,876
5		11	A	Birmingham City	W	1-0	T. Brown	39,450
6		17	H	Coventry City	D	1-1	Wile	24,474
7		25	A	Derby County	D	2-2	Treacy 2	24,378
8	Oct	2	H	Tottenham Hotspur	W	4-2	T. Brown (pen), Martin 2, Treacy	23,461
9		6	A	Newcastle United	L	0-2		28,746
10		16	H	Manchester United	W	4-0	Giles, A. Brown, Cantello, Treacy	36,615
11		23	A	Middlesbrough	L	0-1		22,643
12		30	H	West Ham United	W	3-0	Martin, A. Brown 2	20,396
13	Nov	6	A	Ipswich Town	L	0-7		25,373
14		10	H	Aston Villa	D	1-1	Wile	41,867
15		20	A	Manchester City	L	0-1		36,656
16		27	H	Everton	W	3-0	T. Brown, Cross, Treacy	21,078
17	Dec	11	H	Leicester City	D	2-2	Treacy, Cross	19,049
18		18	A	Stoke City	W	2-0	Statham, Trewick	16,006
19		27	H	Bristol City	D	1-1	Cross	30,497
20	Jan	3	A	West Ham United	D	0-0		25,236
21		15	A	Liverpool	D	1-1	Cross	39,195
22		22	H	Leeds United	L	1-2	T. Brown (pen)	25,989
23	Feb	5	A	Norwich City	L	0-1		19,094
24		12	H	Queen's Park Rangers	D	1-1	Wile	18,342
25		22	A	Sunderland	L	1-6	Robson	30,317
26		28	H	Birmingham City	W	2-1	Robson, A. Brown	28,639
27	Mar	5	H	Derby County	W	1-0	Robson	19,280
28		8	A	Arsenal	W	2-1	Cross 2	19,517
29		12	A	Tottenham Hotspur	W	2-0	Robson, Cross	28,834
30		16	H	Ipswich Town	W	4-0	Robson 3, Cunningham	23,054
31		19	H	Newcastle United	D	1-1	Cunningham	23,843
32		23	A	Manchester United	D	2-2	Cross, Robson	51,053
33	Apr	2	H	Middlesbrough	W	2-1	Cunningham, Johnston	18,519
34		5	A	Bristol City	W	2-1	Hunter (og), Cross	23,474
35		9	H	Arsenal	L	0-2		24,242
36		16	H	Manchester City	L	0-2		24,889
37		19	A	Coventry City	D	1-1	Wile	19,136
38		30	H	Sunderland	L	2-3	Cunningham, Cross	21,859
39	May	7	A	Leicester City	W	5-0	Martin 2, Cross, Cunningham, T. Brown	18,139
40		14	H	Stoke City	W	3-1	Martin, Cunningham, Cross	22,754
41		16	A	Everton	D	1-1	T. Brown	20,102
42		23	A	Aston Villa	L	0-4		42,532

Appearances
Sub appearances
Goals

FA Cup

R3	Jan	8	A	Manchester City	D	1-1	Johnston	38,195
rep		11	H	Manchester City	L	0-1		27,218

Appearances
Sub appearances
Goals

League Cup

R2	Aug	31	A	Liverpool	D	1-1	Giles	22,984
rep	Sep	6	H	Liverpool	W	1-0	Martin	22,662
R3		22	H	Brighton & Hove Albion	L	0-2		18,728

Appearances
Sub appearances
Goals

Osborne J	Mulligan PM	Cantello L	Brown T	Wile JD	Robertson A	Martin MP	Brown A	Mayo J	Giles MJ	Johnston WM	Robson B	Edwards RI	Treacy RCP	Trewick J	Ward RA	Cross D	Statham DJ	Glover AR	Godden AL	Cunningham LP	Hughes W	
1	2	3	4	5	6	7	8	9	10	11												1
1	2	3	4	5	6	7	8	9	10	11												2
1	2	3	4	5	6	7	8	9	10	11												3
1	2	3	4	5	6	7	8	9	**10**	11	12											4
1	2	**3**	4	5	6	7		9	12	11	8	10										5
1	2		4	5	6	7		9	10	11	3	8										6
1	2		4	5	6	7	11	9	10		3		8									7
1	2	9	4	5	6	7		12	10	11	**3**		8									8
1	2	3	4	5	6	7	12	**9**	10	11			8									9
1	2	3	4	5	6	7	9		10	11			8									10
1	2	3	4	5	6	7	9		10			11	8									11
1	2	3	4	5	6	7	9		10			**11**	8	12								12
1	2	3	4	5	6	7	9		10				8	11								13
	2	3	4	5	6	7	11	9	10				8		1							14
1	2	3	4	5	6	7	11		10				8			9						15
1	2	3	4	5	6	7	12		**10**	11			8			9						16
1	2	3	4	5	6	7	10			11			8			9						17
	2		4	5	6	7				11			8	10	1	9	3					18
1	2		4	5	6	7	12			11	3		8	10		**9**						19
1	2		4	5	6	7				11	3		8	10		9						20
1	**2**	3	4	5	6	7				11	12		8	10		9						21
1		2	4	5	6	7			10	11	3		8			9						22
1	2	7	4	5	6				10	**11**	3		8	12		9						23
1	2	3	4	5	6				10		7		8			9		11				24
1	2	3	4	5	6				10	11	7		8			9						25
1	2		4	5	6		8		10	11	7					9	3					26
1	2	3	4	5	6		8		10	11	7					9						27
1	2		4	5	6		8		10	11	**7**			12		9	3					28
	2		4	5	6				10	11	7					9	3		1	8		29
	2		**4**	5	6		12		10	11	7					9	3		1	8		30
	2			5	6	4			10	11	7					9	3		1	8		31
	2			5	6	4			10	11	7					9	3		1	8		32
	2			5	6	4			10	11	7					9	3		1	8		33
	2			5	6	4			10	11	7					9	3		1	8		34
1	2			5	6	4			10	11	7					9	3			8		35
1	2		12	5	6	4			10	11	**7**					9	3			8		36
1	2		7	5	6	4	9		10	11							3			8		37
1	2		7	5	6	4			10	11						9	3			8		38
1	2		7	**5**	6	4	11		10				12			9	3			8		39
1	2		7	5	6	4			10	11						9	3			8		40
1			7	5	6	2	4		10	11						9	3			8		41
1	2		7	5	**6**	3	4		10	11			8			9					12	42
34	40	21	36	42	42	34	19	9	36	34	21	4	20	5	2	27	16	1	6	13		
			1				4	1	1		2		1	3							1	
		1	8	4		6	6		1	1	8		6	1		12	1			6		

One own-goal

1	2	3	4	5	6	7				11			8	10		9						R3
1	2	**3**	4	5	6	7				11	12		8	10		9						rep
	2	2	2	2	2	2	2				2			2	2		2					
												1										
										1												

1	2	3	4	5	6	7	8	9	10	11												R2
1	2	3	4	5	6	7		9		11	8	10										rep
1	2	3	4	5	6	7		9	10	11	12	**8**										R3
3	3	3	3	3	3	3	1	3	2	3	1	2										
											1											
						1			10													

1977-78

Division One

	P	W	D	L	F	A	Pts
Nottingham Forest	42	25	14	3	69	24	64
Liverpool	42	24	9	9	65	34	57
Everton	42	22	11	9	76	45	55
Manchester City	42	20	12	10	74	51	52
Arsenal	42	21	10	11	60	37	52
West Bromwich Albion	42	18	14	10	62	53	50
Coventry City	42	18	12	12	75	62	48
Aston Villa	42	18	10	14	57	42	46
Leeds United	42	18	10	14	63	53	46
Manchester United	42	16	10	16	67	63	42
Birmingham City	42	16	9	17	55	60	41
Derby County	42	14	13	15	54	59	41
Norwich City	42	11	18	13	52	66	40
Middlesbrough	42	12	15	15	42	54	39
Wolverhampton W	42	12	12	18	51	64	36
Chelsea	42	11	14	17	46	69	36
Bristol City	42	11	13	18	49	53	35
Ipswich Town	42	11	13	18	47	61	35
Queen's Park Rangers	42	9	15	18	47	64	33
West Ham United	42	12	8	22	52	69	32
Newcastle United	42	6	10	26	42	78	22
Leicester City	42	5	12	25	26	70	22

Manager: Ronnie Allen then Ron Atkinson

- Former player Ronnie Allen took over as team manager in June, but was replaced in the hot seat by Ron Atkinson in January.
- Full-back Brendon Batson was signed from Cambridge United, while David Cross and Mick Martin were sold to West Ham United and Newcastle United respectively.
- Cyrille Regis scored on his League, FA Cup, League Cup, and reserve-team debuts for Albion.
- John Wile, who led Albion on an historic end-of-season tour to the Far East (China and Hong Kong), was voted Midlands Footballer of the Year.
- A cricket match was staged at The Hawthorns for the first time when India played Pakistan before a crowd of 2,641.

Match No.	Date			Opponents	Result		Scorers	Attendance
1	Aug	20	H	Chelsea	W	3-0	T. Brown 2 (1 pen), Cross	20,146
2		24	A	Leeds United	D	2-2	Cunningham, Cross	21,846
3		27	A	Liverpool	L	0-3		48,525
4	Sep	3	H	Middlesbrough	W	2-1	Robson, Regis	19,044
5		10	A	Newcastle United	W	3-0	Regis, Cunningham, Robson	22,705
6		17	H	Wolverhampton Wanderers	D	2-2	T. Brown (pen), Cross	30,359
7		24	H	Birmingham City	W	3-1	T. Brown 2 (1 pen), Regis	29,115
8	Oct	1	A	Coventry City	W	2-1	T. Brown 2	25,707
9		4	A	Everton	L	1-3	T. Brown (pen)	34,582
10		8	H	Ipswich Town	W	1-0	Robson	22,881
11		15	A	Derby County	D	1-1	Regis	28,397
12		22	H	Manchester United	W	4-0	Cross 2, Wile, Cunningham	27,526
13		29	A	Queen's Park Rangers	L	1-2	Johnston	18,800
14	Nov	5	H	Leicester City	W	2-0	T. Brown, Cross	20,082
15		12	A	West Ham United	D	3-3	Wile 2, Cunningham	23,601
16		19	H	Manchester City	D	0-0		26,953
17		26	A	Nottingham Forest	D	0-0		31,908
18	Dec	3	H	Norwich City	D	0-0		18,137
19		10	A	Aston Villa	L	0-3		43,196
20		17	H	West Ham United	W	1-0	A. Brown	18,896
21		26	A	Bristol City	L	1-3	T. Brown	29,292
22		27	H	Arsenal	L	1-3	Cunningham	27,786
23		31	H	Leeds United	W	1-0	T. Brown (pen)	24,206
24	Jan	2	A	Chelsea	D	2-2	A. Brown, T. Brown	29,540
25		14	H	Liverpool	L	0-1		36,067
26		21	A	Middlesbrough	L	0-1		19,172
27	Feb	25	H	Coventry City	D	3-3	Trewick 2, Wile	25,269
28		28	A	Birmingham City	W	2-1	T. Brown, A. Brown	26,633
29	Mar	4	A	Ipswich Town	D	2-2	T. Brown 2 (1 pen)	20,130
30		14	A	Wolverhampton Wanderers	D	1-1	Trewick	29,757
31		18	A	Manchester United	D	1-1	Robertson	46,329
32		22	H	Queen's Park Rangers	W	2-0	A. Brown, Regis	19,536
33		25	A	Arsenal	L	0-4		36,763
34		27	H	Bristol City	W	2-1	Johnston, T. Brown	23,741
35	Apr	1	A	Leicester City	W	1-0	T. Brown	14,637
36		12	H	Newcastle United	W	2-0	Regis, Mulligan	17,053
37		15	A	Manchester City	W	3-1	Regis, Cunningham, A. Brown	36,521
38		18	H	Derby County	W	1-0	T. Brown (pen)	20,961
39		22	H	Aston Villa	L	0-3		35,112
40		25	H	Everton	W	3-1	Regis 2, Hughes	20,247
41		29	A	Norwich City	D	1-1	Regis	17,302
42	May	2	H	Nottingham Forest	D	2-2	T. Brown, Hughes	23,523

Appearances
Sub appearances
Goals

FA Cup

R3	Jan	7	H	Blackpool	W	4-1	Johnston 2, Regis, T. Brown (pen)	21,379
R4		28	A	Manchester United	D	1-1	Johnston	57,056
rep	Feb	1	H	Manchester United	W	3-2*	Regis 2, T. Brown	37,792
R5		22	A	Derby County	W	3-2	Regis 2, Johnston	32,689
R6	Mar	11	H	Nottingham Forest	W	2-0	Martin, Regis	36,506
SF	Apr	8	N	Ipswich Town	L	1-3	T. Brown (pen)	50,922

SF at Highbury
* after extra-time

Appearances
Sub appearances
Goals

League Cup

R2	Aug	31	H	Rotherham United	W	4-0	Regis 2 (1 pen), Wile, Martin	15,005
R3	Oct	25	H	Watford	W	1-0	T. Brown	21,985
R4	Nov	29	A	Bury	L	0-1		13,898

Appearances
Sub appearances
Goals

Godden AL	Mulligan PM	Statham DJ	Brown AJ	Wile JD	Robertson A	Cantello L	Cunningham LP	Cross D	Robson B	Johnston WMcC	Trewick J	Regis C	Martin MP	Hughes BW	Brown A	Batson BM	
1	2	3	4	5	6	7	8	9	10	11							1
1	2	3	4	5	6	7	8	9	10	11							2
1	2	3	4	5	6	7	8	**9**	10	11			12				3
1	2	3		5	6	7	8		10	11	**4**	9		12			4
1	2	3	4	5	6	7	**8**		10	11		9	12				5
1	2	3	4	5	6	7		8	10	11		9					6
1	2	3	4	5	6	7			10	11		9			8		7
1	2	3	4	5	6	**7**			10	11		9	12		8		8
1	2	3	4	5	6	7	8		10	11		9					9
1	2	3	4	5	6	7	8		10	11		9					10
1	2	3	4	5	6	7	8		10	11		9					11
1	2	3	4	5	6	7	8	9	10	11							12
1	2	3	4	5	6	**7**	8	9	10	11		12					13
1	2	3	4	5	6	7	8	9	10	11							14
1	2	3	4	5	6	7	8	9	10	11							15
1	2	3	4	5	6		8	9	10	11			7				16
1	2	3	4	5	6		8	9	10	11			7				17
1	2	3	4	5	6		11	9	10			8	7				18
1	2	3	4	5	6	7	**11**		10			8	12		9		19
1	2	3	4	5	6				10	11		8	7		9		20
1	2	3	4	5	6		12		10	11		**9**	7		8		21
1	2	3	4	5	6		12		**10**	11		9	7		8		22
1	2		4	5	6				3	11	10	8	7		9		23
1	**2**		4	5	6				3	11	10	8	7	12	9		24
1	2	3	4	5	6		9			11	10	**8**	7		12		25
1	2	3	4	5	6		8			11	10	9	7				26
1		3	4	5	6		12		**2**	11	10	9	7		8		27
1		3	4	5	6					11	10	9	7		8	2	28
1		3	4	5	6		12			11	10	9	**7**		8	2	29
1	2	3	4	5	6		8			11	10	9	7				30
1	2	3	4	5	6		8		7	11	10	9					31
1	2	3	4	5	6				7	11	10	9			8		32
1	2	3	4	5	6		11		7		10	9			8		33
1	2	3	4	5	6		8			11	10	9	7				34
1	2	3	4	5	6					11	10	9	7		8		35
1	2	3	4		6	7	11		5		10	9			8		36
1	2	3	4		6	7	11		5		10	9			8		37
1	2	3	4		6	7	11		5		10	**9**			8		38
1	**2**	3	4	12	6	7	11		5		10	9			8		39
1		3	4	5	6	7	11		8			9		10		2	40
1		3	4	5	6	7	11		8			9		10		2	41
1		3	4	5	6	7	11		8			9		10		2	42
42	36	40	41	38	42	23	29	11	35	32	18	33	16	3	18	5	
				1			4					1	4	2	1		
	1		19	4	1		6	6	3	2	3	10		2	5		

1		3	4	5	6		9			11	10	8	2		7		R3
1	2	3	4	5					6	11	10	8	7		9		R4
1	2	3	4	**5**					6	11	10	8	7	12	9		rep
1	**2**	3	4	5	6		12			11	10	8	7		9		R5
1	2	3	4	5	6		12			11	10	8	7		**9**		R6
1	2	3	4	**5**	6		12			11	10	9	7		8		SF
6	5	6	6	6	4		1		2	6	6	6	6		6		
							3							1			
			3							4		6	1				

1	**2**	3		5	6	7	8		10	11	12	9	4				R2
1	2	3	4	5	6	7	8	9	10	11							R3
1	2	3	**4**	5	6		8	9	10	11		12	7				R4
3	3	3	2	3	3	2	3	2	3	3		1	2				
										1	1						
			1	1								2	1				

1978-79

Division One

	P	W	D	L	F	A	Pts
Liverpool	42	30	8	4	85	16	68
Nottingham Forest	42	21	18	3	61	26	60
West Bromwich Albion	42	24	11	7	72	35	59
Everton	42	17	17	8	52	40	51
Leeds United	42	18	14	10	70	52	50
Ipswich Town	42	20	9	13	63	49	49
Arsenal	42	17	14	11	61	48	48
Aston Villa	42	15	16	11	59	49	46
Manchester United	42	15	15	12	60	63	45
Coventry City	42	14	16	12	58	68	44
Tottenham Hotspur	42	13	15	14	48	61	41
Middlesbrough	42	15	10	17	57	50	40
Bristol City	42	15	10	17	47	51	40
Southampton	42	12	16	14	47	53	40
Manchester City	42	13	13	16	58	56	39
Norwich City	42	7	23	12	51	57	37
Bolton Wanderers	42	12	11	19	54	75	35
Wolverhampton W	42	13	8	21	44	68	34
Derby County	42	10	11	21	44	71	31
Queen's Park Rangers	42	6	13	23	45	73	25
Birmingham City	42	6	10	26	37	64	22
Chelsea	42	5	10	27	44	92	20

Manager: Ron Atkinson

- Tony Brown broke Ronnie Allen's Albion League scoring record with his 209th goal against Leeds United in October.
- The biggest crowd to watch an Albion game for nine years – 95,300 – witnessed the UEFA Cup clash against Red Star Belgrade in Yugoslavia in March.
- John Wile played in 75 of Albion's 76 games this season – a club record.
- Having been sent home from the World Cup in Argentina by his country, Scotland, for drug abuse, fiery winger Willie Johnston joined Vancouver Whitecaps for £100,000. Midfielder Gary Owen, the recipient of a record 22 England Under–21 caps, was signed from Manchester City for £465,000 before Albion's manager Ron Atkinson splashed out a new British record fee of £516,000 for the Middlesbrough midfielder David Mills (January).

Match No.	Date			Opponents	Result		Scorers	Attendance
1	Aug	19	H	Ipswich Town	W	2-1	A. Brown, T. Brown	23,674
2		22	A	Queen's Park Rangers	W	1-0	Howe (og)	15,481
3		26	H	Bolton Wanderers	W	4-0	A. Brown 2, Cunningham, Regis	23,095
4	Sep	2	A	Nottingham Forest	D	0-0		28,239
5		9	H	Norwich City	D	2-2	Cunningham, Robson	21,893
6		16	A	Derby County	L	2-3	Regis, Cunningham	23,772
7		23	H	Liverpool	D	1-1	Cunningham	33,772
8		30	A	Chelsea	W	3-1	Regis, Wile, T. Brown	21,022
9	Oct	7	H	Tottenham Hotspur	L	0-1		33,068
10		14	A	Leeds United	W	3-1	T. Brown, Regis 2	25,931
11		21	H	Coventry City	W	7-1	Cantello, Cunningham 2, Regis 2, T. Brown, Statham	27,409
12		28	A	Manchester City	D	2-2	Regis, Robson	40,521
13	Nov	4	H	Birmingham City	W	1-0	Trewick	32,130
14		11	A	Ipswich Town	W	1-0	A. Brown	21,980
15		18	A	Bolton Wanderers	W	1-0	A. Brown	22,278
16		25	H	Aston Villa	D	1-1	T. Brown (pen)	35,166
17	Dec	9	H	Middlesbrough	W	2-0	Regis, Cantello	19,865
18		16	A	Wolverhampton Wanderers	W	3-0	A. Brown 2, T. Brown	29,117
19		26	A	Arsenal	W	2-1	Robson, A. Brown	40,055
20		30	A	Manchester United	W	5-3	T. Brown 2, Cantello, Cunningham, Regis	45,091
21	Jan	1	H	Bristol City	W	3-1	A. Brown 2, Wile	31,738
22		13	A	Norwich City	D	1-1	Regis	20,081
23	Feb	3	A	Liverpool	L	1-2	A. Brown	52,211
24		24	H	Leeds United	L	1-2	T. Brown	27,846
25	Mar	3	A	Coventry City	W	3-1	Robson, A. Brown, Mills	25,676
26		14	H	Chelsea	W	1-0	A. Brown	20,472
27		24	H	Queen's Park Rangers	W	2-1	A. Brown, Cunningham	21,063
28		26	H	Derby County	W	2-1	Cunningham, A. Brown	19,801
29	Apr	4	H	Manchester City	W	4-0	Trewick, Power (og), Mills, Summerfield	21,940
30		7	H	Everton	W	1-0	A. Brown	29,593
31		13	A	Southampton	D	1-1	Regis	22,063
32		14	H	Arsenal	D	1-1	T. Brown	28,539
33		17	A	Bristol City	L	0-1		30,191
34		21	H	Wolverhampton Wanderers	D	1-1	Robson	32,131
35		24	A	Birmingham City	D	1-1	Robson	19,897
36		28	A	Middlesbrough	D	1-1	A. Brown	18,063
37	May	1	A	Everton	W	2-0	Mills, Robson	30,083
38		5	H	Manchester United	W	1-0	Regis	27,960
39		8	H	Southampton	W	1-0	A. Brown	17,499
40		11	A	Aston Villa	W	1-0	Trewick	35,991
41		14	A	Tottenham Hotspur	L	0-1		24,789
42		18	H	Nottingham Forest	L	0-1		28,210

Appearances
Sub appearances
Goals

FA Cup

R3	Jan	9	A	Coventry City	D	2-2	Cunningham, A. Brown	38046
rep		15	H	Coventry City	W	4-0	Batson, T. Brown 2, A. Brown	36175
R4	Feb	26	H	Leeds United	D	3-3	Cunningham, A. Brown, Regis	32424
rep	Mar	1	H	Leeds United	W	2-0*	Wile, A. Brown	31143
R5		10	H	Southampton	D	1-1	A. Brown	30789
rep		12	A	Southampton	L	1-2*	Cunningham	25755

* after extra-time

Appearances
Sub appearances
Goals

League Cup

R2	Aug	29	H	Leeds United	D	0-0		25,188
rep	Sep	6	A	Leeds United	D	0-0*		29,316
rep2	Oct	2	N	Leeds United	L	0-1		8,164

Replay 2 at Maine Road, Manchester

* after extra-time

Appearances
Sub appearances

	Godden AL	Batson BM	Statham DJ	Brown T	Wile JD	Robertson A	Robson B	Brown A	Regis C	Cantello L	Cunningham LP	Johnston WM	Trewick J	Martin MP	Mills DJ	Summerfield K	Bennett M
1	1	2	3	4	5	6	7	8	9	10	11						
2	1	2	3	4	5	6	7	8	9	10	11						
3	1	2	3	4	5	6	7	8	9	10	**11**	12					
4	1	2	3		5	6	7	8	9	4	10	11					
5	1	2	3		5	6	7	8	9	10	4	11					
6	1	2	3		5	6	7	8	9		4	11	10				
7	1	2	3		5	6	7	8	9	10	4		11				
8	1	2	3	**11**	5	6	7	8	9	10	4		12				
9	1	2	3	11	5	6	7	8	9		4		10				
10	1	2	**3**	11	5	6	7	8	9	10	4	12					
11	1	2	3	11	5	6	7	8	9	**10**	4	12					
12	1	2	3	11	5	6	7	8	9	10	4						
13	1	2		4	5	6	7	8	9	10	11		3				
14	1	2		4	5	6	7	8	9	10	11		3				
15	1	2		4	5	6	7	8		10	11		3	9			
16	1	2	3	4	5	6	7	8	9	10	11						
17	1	2	3	4	5	6	7	8	9	10	11						
18	1	2	3	4	5	6	7	8	9	10	11						
19	1	2	3	4	5	6	7	8	9	10	11						
20	1	2	3	4	5	6	7	8	9	10	11						
21	1	2	3	4	5	6	7	8	9	10	11						
22	1	2	3	4	5	6	7	8	9		11		10				
23	1	2	3	4	5	6	7	8	9	**10**	11				12		
24	1	2	3	4	5	6	7	**8**	9	10	11				12		
25	1	2	3		5	6	7	8	9		11		4		10		
26	1	2	3	4	5	6		8	**9**		11	12	7		10		
27	1	2	3	**4**	5	6	7	8		10	11		12		9		
28	1	2	3		5	6	7	**8**		10	11		4		9	12	
29	1	**2**	3		5	6	7		9	10	11		4		8	12	
30	1		3		5	6	7	8	9		11		4		10		2
31	1	2	3	12	5	6	7	8	9		11		4		**10**		
32	1	2	3	10	5	6	7	8	9		11		4				
33	1	2	3		5	6	7	8	9	10	11				4		
34	1	2	3	4	5	6	7	8	9	10	11						
35	1	2	3	4	5	6	7	**8**	9	10	11				12		
36	1	2	3	4	5	6	7	8	12	10	**11**				9		
37	1	2	3	4	5	6	7	8	9	10					11		
38	1	2	3	**4**	5	6	7	8	9		12		10		11		
39	1	2	3	12	5	6	7	8	9		4		**10**		11		
40	1	2	3		5		7	8	9	6	4		10		11		
41	1	2	3		5		7	8	9	10	11		4		6		
42	1	2	3	4	5		7	8	9	10			11		6		
	42	41	39	29	42	39	41	41	38	32	39	3	19	1	15		1
				2					1		1	4	2		3	2	
			1	10	2		7	18	13	3	9		3		3	1	

Two own-goals

	Godden AL	Batson BM	Statham DJ	Brown T	Wile JD	Robertson A	Robson B	Brown A	Regis C	Cantello L	Cunningham LP	Johnston WM	Trewick J	Martin MP	Mills DJ	Summerfield K	Bennett M
R3	1	2	3	4	5	6	7	8	9		11		10				
rep	1	2	3	4	5	6	7	8	9	10	11						
R4	1	2	3	4	5	6	7	**8**	9	10	11				12		
rep	1	2	3	**4**	5	6	7	8	9	10	11				12		
R5	1	2	3	4	5	6	7	8	9		11				10		
rep	1	2	3	10	5	6		8	**9**		11	12	4		7		
	6	6	6	6	6	6	5	6	6	3	6		3		2		
												1			2		
		1		2	1			5	1		3						

	Godden AL	Batson BM	Statham DJ	Brown T	Wile JD	Robertson A	Robson B	Brown A	Regis C	Cantello L	Cunningham LP	Johnston WM	Trewick J	Martin MP	Mills DJ	Summerfield K	Bennett M
R2	1	2	3		5	6	7	**8**	9		10	11	4	12			
rep	1	2	3		5	6	7	8	9	10	4	11					
rep2	1	2	3	11	5	6	7	8	9	10	4						
	3	3	3	1	3	3	3	3	3	2	3	2	1				
														1			

1979-80

Division One

	P	W	D	L	F	A	Pts
Liverpool	42	25	10	7	81	30	60
Manchester United	42	24	10	8	65	35	58
Ipswich Town	42	22	9	11	68	39	53
Arsenal	42	18	16	8	52	36	52
Nottingham Forest	42	20	8	14	63	43	48
Wolverhampton W	42	19	9	14	58	47	47
Aston Villa	42	16	14	12	51	50	46
Southampton	42	18	9	15	65	53	45
Middlesbrough	42	16	12	14	50	44	44
West Bromwich Albion	42	11	19	12	54	50	41
Leeds United	42	13	14	15	46	50	40
Norwich City	42	13	14	15	58	66	40
Crystal Palace	42	12	16	14	41	50	40
Tottenham Hotspur	42	15	10	17	52	62	40
Coventry City	42	16	7	19	56	66	39
Brighton & Hove Albion	42	11	15	16	47	57	37
Manchester City	42	12	13	17	43	66	37
Stoke City	42	13	10	19	44	58	36
Everton	42	9	17	16	43	51	35
Bristol City	42	9	13	20	37	66	31
Derby County	42	11	8	23	47	67	30
Bolton Wanderers	42	5	15	22	38	73	25

Manager: Ron Atkinson

- Winger Peter Barnes joined Albion for a club record outgoing fee of £748,000 from Manchester City. He replaced Laurie Cunningham who was sold to Real Madrid for a record incoming fee of £995,000.
- John Deehan was also signed for £424,000 from Aston Villa – the first player to join Albion direct from that club since George Harris in 1909, and defender Garry Pendrey arrived from Birmingham City, directly after his testimonial match against Albion.
- Bryan Robson was voted Midlands Footballer of the Year, and Albion beat Ajax of Amsterdam 1–0 in the club's 'late' Centenary game at The Hawthorns.
- Tony Brown scored his last goal for Albion, against West Ham in the FA Cup.

Match No.	Date			Opponents	Result		Scorers	Attendance
1	Aug	18	H	Derby County	D	0-0		24,643
2		22	A	Manchester United	L	0-2		53,377
3		25	A	Liverpool	L	1-3	Barnes	48,021
4	Sep	1	H	Nottingham Forest	L	1-5	Owen	26,315
5		8	A	Bolton Wanderers	D	0-0		17,033
6		15	H	Manchester City	W	4-0	Robson, A. Brown, Owen, Summerfield	22,183
7		22	A	Tottenham Hotspur	D	1-1	A. Brown	29,914
8		29	H	Brighton & Hove Albion	D	2-2	Robson, A. Brown	21,225
9	Oct	6	A	Middlesbrough	L	1-2	Owen	16,312
10		10	H	Manchester United	W	2-0	Robson, Deehan	27,713
11		13	A	Aston Villa	D	0-0		36,007
12		20	H	Southampton	W	4-0	Robson, A. Brown, Owen, Deehan	22,671
13		27	H	Coventry City	W	4-1	A. Brown 2, T. Brown 2 (1 pen)	22,656
14	Nov	3	A	Derby County	L	1-2	Robson	21,408
15		10	H	Norwich City	W	2-1	Wile, Robson	19,308
16		17	A	Leeds United	L	0-1		17,481
17		24	A	Wolverhampton Wanderers	D	0-0		32,564
18	Dec	1	H	Everton	D	1-1	Regis	21,237
19		8	A	Stoke City	L	2-3	Barnes (pen), Regis	18,865
20		15	H	Arsenal	D	2-2	Trewick, Robson	18,081
21		26	H	Bristol City	W	3-0	Owen, Barnes 2	19,490
22		29	H	Liverpool	L	0-2		34,993
23	Jan	1	A	Ipswich Town	L	0-4		22,511
24		12	A	Nottingham Forest	L	1-3	Regis	27,724
25		26	A	Crystal Palace	D	2-2	Robertson, Regis	23,869
26	Feb	2	A	Manchester City	W	3-1	Barnes 2, Regis	32,904
27		9	H	Tottenham Hotspur	W	2-1	Regis 2	26,319
28		16	A	Brighton & Hove Albion	D	0-0		22,598
29		23	H	Aston Villa	L	1-2	Robson	33,618
30	Mar	1	A	Southampton	D	1-1	Regis	22,138
31		8	A	Coventry City	W	2-0	Barnes 2 (1 pen)	23,251
32		14	H	Middlesbrough	D	0-0		15,875
33		18	H	Bolton Wanderers	D	4-4	Barnes 3 (2 pens), Moses	11,655
34		22	A	Norwich City	D	1-1	Bond (og)	14,303
35		29	H	Leeds United	W	2-1	Barnes (pen), Deehan	19,108
36	Apr	1	H	Crystal Palace	W	3-0	Trewick, Barnes 2	15,643
37		5	A	Bristol City	D	0-0		16,873
38		7	H	Ipswich Town	D	0-0		19,814
39		19	H	Wolverhampton Wanderers	D	0-0		29,843
40		26	A	Arsenal	D	1-1	Barnes	30,203
41		28	A	Everton	D	0-0		20,356
42	May	3	H	Stoke City	L	0-1		18,396

Appearances
Sub appearances
Goals

FA Cup

R3	Jan	5	H	West Ham United	D	1-1	Regis	21,321
rep		8	A	West Ham United	L	1-2	T. Brown	30,869

Appearances
Sub appearances
Goals

League Cup

R2	Aug	29	H	Fulham	D	1-1	Robson	14,617
rep	Sep	5	A	Fulham	W	1-0	Robson	11,542
R3		26	H	Coventry City	W	2-1	Wile, T. Brown (pen)	18,058
R4	Oct	31	H	Norwich City	D	0-0		24,251
rep	Nov	7	A	Norwich City	L	0-3		19,677

Appearances
Sub appearances
Goals

	Godden AL	Batson BM	Statham DJ	Trewick J	Wile JD	Robertson A	Robson B	Brown A	Brown T	Owen GA	Barnes PS	Mills DJ	Summerfield K	Deehan JM	Pendrey GJS	Regis C	Bennett M	Moses RM	Monaghan DJ	Cowdrill BJ
1	1	2	3	4	5	6	7	8	9	10	11									
2	1	2	3		5	6	7	8	4	10	11	9								
3	1	2	3		5	6	7	8	4	10	11	**9**	12							
4	1	2	3	12	5	6	7		4	10	11	**9**	8							
5	1	2	3	4	5	6	7	8	9	10	11									
6	1	2	3	4	5	6	7	8	9	10	**11**		12							
7	1	2	3	4	5	6	7	8	12	**10**	11			9						
8	1	2	3	4	5	6	7	8		10	11			9						
9	1	2	3		5	6	7	8	12	**10**	11	4		9						
10	1	2	3		5	6	7	8		**10**	11	4		9						
11	1	2	3		5	**6**	7	8	12	10	11	4		9						
12	1	2	3	12	5		7	8	11	**10**		4		9	6					
13	1	2	3		5	6	7	8	11	10		4		9						
14	1	2	3		5	6	7	8	**11**	10		4		9		12				
15	1			2	5	6	7	8		10	11	4		9	3					
16	1	2			5	6	7	8	10		11	4		9	3					
17	1	2			5	6	7	8		10		4		9	3	11				
18	1	2			5	6	7	8	4	10	11				3	9				
19	1	2		7	5	6		8		**10**	11	4		12	3	9				
20	1	2		10	5		7	8			11	4			3	9	6			
21	1	2		4	5	6	7			10	11			8	3	9				
22	1	2		4	5	6	7	12		**10**	11			8	3	9				
23	1	2		4	5	6	7	8	10		11			9	3	12				
24	1	2	3	4	5	6			12	10	**11**	7		8		9				
25	1	2	**3**		5	6	7	12		10	11			8		9		4		
26	1	2			5	6	7	8		10	11				3	9		4		
27	1	2			5		7	8		10	11				3	9	6	4		
28	1	**2**			5		7	10			11	12		8	3	9	6	4		
29	1	2			5	6	7	8			11			10	3	9		4		
30	1	2			5	6	7			11	12			10	3	9		4	8	
31	1	2			5	6	7			10	11			8	3	9		4		
32	1	2			5	6	7			10	11			8	3	9		4		
33	1				5	6	7			10	11	12		8	3	**9**	2	4		
34	1	2			5	6	7	8		10	11			9				4		3
35	1	2			5	6	7			10	11			8		9		4	12	3
36	1	2		7	5	6				10	11			8		9		4		3
37	1	2		7	5	6				10	11			8		9		4		3
38	1	2		12	5	6	7			10	11			**8**		9		4		3
39	1	2			5	6	7	8		10	11					9		4		3
40	1	2		7	5	6		8		10	11					9		4		3
41	1	2		7	5	6				10	11					9		4	8	3
42	1	2		7	5	6				10	11					9		4	8	3
	42	40	16	17	42	38	35	27	12	37	37	15	1	27	18	24	4	18	3	9
				3				2	4		1	2	2	1		2			1	
				2	1	1	8	6	2	5	15		1	3		8		1		

One own-goal

R3	1	2	3	4	5	6		8		10	11			7		9				
rep	1	2	3	4	5	6		8	12	**10**	11			7		9				
	2	2	2	2	2	2		2		2	2			2		2				
									1											
									1							1				

R2	1	2	3		5	6	7	8	4	10	11	9								
rep	1	2	3	4	5	6	7		9	10	11	8								
R3	1	2	3	4	5	6	7		8	10	11	9								
R4	1	2	3		5	6	7	8	11	10		4				9				
rep	1		3	2	5	6	7	8	11	**10**	12	4				9				
	5	4	5	3	5	5	5	3	5	5	3	5				2				
											1									
					1		2		1											

1980-81

Division One

	P	W	D	L	F	A	Pts
Aston Villa	42	26	8	8	72	40	60
Ipswich Town	42	23	10	9	77	43	56
Arsenal	42	19	15	8	61	45	53
West Bromwich Albion	42	20	12	10	60	42	52
Liverpool	42	17	17	8	62	42	51
Southampton	42	20	10	12	76	56	50
Nottingham Forest	42	19	12	11	62	44	50
Manchester United	42	15	18	9	51	36	48
Leeds United	42	17	10	15	39	47	44
Tottenham Hotspur	42	14	15	13	70	68	43
Stoke City	42	12	18	12	51	60	42
Manchester City	42	14	11	17	56	59	39
Birmingham City	42	13	12	17	50	61	38
Middlesbrough	42	16	5	21	53	61	37
Everton	42	13	10	19	55	58	36
Coventry City	42	13	10	19	48	68	36
Sunderland	42	14	7	21	52	53	35
Wolverhampton W	42	13	9	20	43	55	35
Brighton & Hove Albion	42	14	7	21	54	67	35
Norwich City	42	13	7	22	49	73	33
Leicester City	42	13	6	23	40	67	32
Crystal Palace	42	6	7	29	47	83	19

Manager: Ron Atkinson

- Albion came from 2–0 down to beat Spurs 4–2 in their last home League game, and Brendon Batson's weak back pass let in Peter Withe to score Villa's late winner in April as they strove on towards the title.
- Peter Barnes moved to Leeds United for £930,000 in July, midfielder John Trewick signed for Newcastle United for £234,000 in December and right-back Paddy Mulligan returned 'home' to sign for Shamrock Rovers.
- Into The Hawthorns came Ian Benjamin from Sheffield United.

Match No.	Date			Opponents	Result		Scorers	Attendance
01	Aug	16	H	Arsenal	L	0-1		22,161
2		20	A	Stoke City	D	0-0		14,086
3		23	H	Wolverhampton Wanderers	D	1-1	Regis	25,324
4		30	A	Brighton & Hove Albion	W	2-1	Regis, Owen	18,112
5	Sep	6	H	Norwich City	W	3-0	Owen, Barnes (pen), Brown	15,292
6		13	A	Liverpool	L	0-4		36,792
7		20	A	Birmingham City	D	1-1	Brown	22,016
8		27	H	Southampton	W	2-1	Brown 2	20,659
9	Oct	4	A	Crystal Palace	W	1-0	Regis	16,436
10		8	H	Coventry City	W	1-0	Barnes	16,300
11		11	H	Manchester City	W	3-1	Trewick, Robson, Regis	19,382
12		18	A	Nottingham Forest	L	1-2	Moses	25,096
13		21	A	Everton	D	1-1	Wile	24,046
14		25	H	Middlesbrough	W	3-0	Regis 2, Brown	15,907
15	Nov	1	A	Ipswich Town	D	0-0		23,041
16		8	H	Aston Villa	D	0-0		34,195
17		15	A	Arsenal	D	2-2	Owen (pen), Barnes	25,858
18		22	H	Leicester City	W	3-1	Moses, Robson, Owen (pen)	17,751
19		25	H	Stoke City	D	0-0		15,804
20		29	A	Tottenham Hotspur	W	3-2	Robson, Barnes, Brown	27,372
21	Dec	6	H	Leeds United	L	1-2	Moses	17,791
22		13	A	Coventry City	L	0-3		16,034
23		26	A	Sunderland	D	0-0		28,296
24		27	H	Manchester United	W	3-1	Regis, Owen (pen), Barnes	30,326
25	Jan	10	A	Leicester City	W	2-0	Deehan, Bennett	17,778
26		17	H	Brighton & Hove Albion	W	2-0	Regis, Barnes	15,414
27		31	A	Wolverhampton Wanderers	L	0-2		19,764
28	Feb	7	H	Liverpool	W	2-0	Robson, Regis	27,932
29		14	A	Norwich City	W	2-0	Regis, Owen (pen)	14,590
30		21	A	Southampton	D	2-2	Robson, Regis	21,910
31		28	H	Birmingham City	D	2-2	Moses, Brown	24,848
32	Mar	7	H	Crystal Palace	W	1-0	Robson	15,056
33		14	A	Manchester City	L	1-2	Robson	36,581
34		21	H	Nottingham Forest	W	2-1	Gunn (og), Deehan	19,532
35		28	A	Middlesbrough	L	1-2	Robson	13,228
36		31	H	Everton	W	2-0	Robson, Brown	14,861
37	Apr	4	H	Ipswich Town	W	3-1	Barnes, Batson, Brown	22,566
38		8	A	Aston Villa	L	0-1		47,998
39		18	A	Manchester United	L	1-2	Regis	44,442
40		20	H	Sunderland	W	2-1	Regis 2	15,304
41	May	2	H	Tottenham Hotspur	W	4-2	Robson, Barnes, Brown, Cross	20,549
42		6	A	Leeds United	D	0-0		17,218

Appearances
Sub appearances
Goals

FA Cup

R3	Jan	3	H	Grimsby Town	W	3-0	Robson, Barnes, Cowdrill	22,477
R4		24	A	Middlesbrough	L	0-1		28,285

Appearances
Sub appearances
Goals

League Cup

R2/1	Aug	26	H	Leicester City	W	1-0	Barnes	13,810
R2/2	Sep	3	A	Leicester City	W	1-0	Regis	17,081
R3		24	A	Everton	W	2-1	Moses, Robertson	23,436
R4	Oct	29	H	Preston North End	D	0-0		17,579
rep	Nov	4	A	Preston North End	D	1-1*	Brown	14,420
rep2		12	H	Preston North End	W	2-1*	Regis 2	15,218
R5	Dec	3	A	Manchester City	L	1-2	Booth (og)	35,611

* after extra-time

Appearances
Sub appearances
Goals

Godden AL	Trewick J	Statham DJ	Moses RM	Wile JD	Robertson AP	Robson B	Deehan JM	Regis C	Owen GA	Barnes PS	Batson BM	Brown A	Monaghan DJ	Mills DJ	Benjamin IT	Cowdrill BJ	Bennett M	Cross NJR	
1	2	3	4	5	6	7	8	9	10	11									1
1	2	3	4	5	6	7	8	9	10	11									2
1		3	4	5	6	7	8	9	10	11	2	12							3
1	2	3	4	5	6	7		9	10	11		8							4
1	2	3	4	5	6	**7**	12	9	10	11		8							5
1	12	3	4	5	6	7		9	**10**	11	2	8							6
1	10	3	4	5	6	7		9		11	2	8							7
1	7	3	4	5	6			9	10	11	2	8							8
1	7	3	4	5	6			9	10	11	2	8							9
1	12	3	**4**	5	6	7			10	11	2	8	9						10
1	4	3		5	6	7		9	10	11	2	8							11
1	12	3	4	5	6	7		9	10	**11**	2	8							12
1	10	3	4	5	6	7		9			2	8	11						13
1	10	3	4	5	6	7		9			2	8	**11**	12					14
1	2	**3**	4	5	6	7		9				8	11	10	12				15
1			4	5	6	7		9	10	11	2	8				3			16
1			4	5	6	7		9	10	**11**	2	8		12		3			17
1			4	5	6	7		9	10	11	2	8				3			18
1			4	5	6	7		9	10	11	2	8				3			19
1	3		4	5		7		9	10	11	2	8					6		20
1			4	5		7		9	10	11	2	**8**		12		3	6		21
1			4	5	6	7	12	9	10	**11**	2	8				3			22
1			4	5		7		9	10	11	2	8				3	6		23
1			4	5		7		9	10	11	2	8				3	6		24
1			4	5		7	9		10	11	2	8				3	6		25
1			4	5	2	7		9	10	11		8				3	6		26
1		3	4	5		7		9	10	11	2			8			6		27
1		3	4	5		**7**	8	9	10	11	2	12					6		28
1		3	4	5		7	8	9	10	11	2						6		29
1		3	4	5		7	8	9	10	11	2						6		30
1		3	4	5		7	8	**9**	10	11	2	12					6		31
1		3	4	5		7	9		10	11	**2**	8		12			6		32
1		3	4	5	6	7	9		**10**	11		8		12			2		33
1		3	4	5		7	8	9		11	2			10			6		34
1		3	4	5		7	**10**	9		11	2	12		8			6		35
1		3	4	5		7	8	9		11	2	12		10			**6**		36
1		3	4	5	6	7		9	10	11	2	8							37
1		3	4	5	6	7		9	10	11	2	8							38
1		3	4	5	6	7		9	10	11	2	**8**						12	39
1		3	4	5	6	7		9	10	11	2	8							40
1		3	4	5	6	7		9	**10**	11	2	8						12	41
1		3	4	5	6	7		9		11	2	8			10				42
42	12	31	41	42	28	40	13	38	34	39	35	31	4	5	1	10	16		
	3						2					5		5	1			2	
	1		4	1		10	2	14	6	8	1	10					1	1	

One own-goal

1			4	5		7		9	10	11	2	**8**		12		3	6		R3
1			4	5	6	7		9	10	11		**8**		12		3	2		R4
2			2	2	1	2		2	2	2	1	2				2	2		
														2					
						1				1						1			

1	2	3	4	5	6	7		9	10	11		8							R2/1
1	2	3	4	5	6			9	10	11		8					7		R2/2
1	7	3	4	5	6			9	10	**11**	2	8	12						R3
1	10	3	4	5	6	7		9		**11**	2	8		12					R4
1	12		4	5	6	7		9	**10**		2	8		11		3			rep
1			4	5	6	7		9	10	**11**	2	8		12		3			rep2
1	3		4	5		7		9	10	11	2	8					6		R5
7	5	4	7	7	6	5	0	7	6	6	5	7		1		2	2		
	1												1	2					
			1		1			3		1		1							

One own-goal

1981-82

Division One

	P	W	D	L	F	A	Pts
Liverpool	42	26	9	7	80	32	87
Ipswich Town	42	26	5	11	75	53	83
Manchester United	42	22	12	8	59	29	78
Tottenham Hotspur	42	20	11	11	67	48	71
Arsenal	42	20	11	11	48	37	71
Swansea City	42	21	6	15	58	51	69
Southampton	42	19	9	14	72	67	66
Everton	42	17	13	12	56	50	64
West Ham United	42	14	16	12	66	57	58
Manchester City	42	15	13	14	49	50	58
Aston Villa	42	15	12	15	55	53	57
Nottingham Forest	42	15	12	15	42	48	57
Brighton & Hove Albion	42	13	13	16	43	52	52
Coventry City	42	13	11	18	56	62	50
Notts County	42	13	8	21	61	69	47
Birmingham City	42	10	14	18	53	61	44
West Bromwich Albion	42	11	11	20	46	57	44
Stoke City	42	12	8	22	44	63	44
Sunderland	42	11	11	20	38	58	44
Leeds United	42	10	12	20	39	61	42
Wolverhampton W	42	10	10	22	32	63	40
Middlesbrough	42	8	15	19	34	52	39

Manager: Ronnie Allen

- Ronnie Allen returned to the club for his second spell as manager.
- Bryan Robson and Remi Moses both joined their former boss Ron Atkinson at Manchester United, for fees of £1.5m and £500,000 respectively. Steve Mackenzie was signed from Manchester City for £650,000, two Dutchmen, Maarten Jol and Romeo Zondervan, arrived from FC Twente Enschede and Andy King was secured from Everton, only to return to Goodison Park in a player-exchange deal involving Peter Eastoe at the end of the season. The versatile Clive Whitehead was also recruited from Bristol City.
- Albion lost two Cup semi-finals in the space of seven weeks – both 1–0.
- Tony Brown left the club after scoring a record 279 goals in 720 first-class matches. He joined Torquay United.
- John Wile was an ever-present for a record seventh time this season, and Tony Godden's club record 228 consecutive appearances came to an end (October).

Match No.	Date			Opponents	Result		Scorers	Attendance
1	Aug	29	A	Manchester City	L	1-2	Mills (pen)	36,187
2	Sep	2	H	Arsenal	L	0-2		17,060
3		5	H	Swansea City	W	4-1	Regis 3, Mackenzie	18,087
4		12	A	Nottingham Forest	D	0-0		22,618
5		19	H	West Ham United	D	0-0		19,459
6		22	A	Ipswich Town	L	0-1		20,658
7		26	A	Everton	L	0-1		23,881
8	Oct	3	H	Middlesbrough	W	2-0	Regis, Summerfield	12,977
9		10	H	Brighton & Hove Albion	D	0-0		13,893
10		17	A	Leeds United	L	1-3	Mills	19,164
11		24	H	Southampton	D	1-1	Brown	15,772
12		31	A	Birmingham City	D	3-3	Regis 3	21,601
13	Nov	7	A	Tottenham Hotspur	W	2-1	Hughton (og), Jol	32,436
14		14	H	Stoke City	L	1-2	Smith (og)	15,705
15		21	H	Liverpool	D	1-1	Regis	20,706
16		28	A	Sunderland	W	2-1	Regis, Brown	15,867
17	Dec	5	H	Wolverhampton Wanderers	W	3-0	Regis 2, Whitehead	23,329
18		26	A	Coventry City	W	2-0	Owen, Regis	15,215
19	Jan	30	A	West Ham United	L	1-3	King	24,423
20	Feb	6	H	Nottingham Forest	W	2-1	Bennett, Summerfield	14,975
21		20	H	Everton	D	0-0		14,809
22		27	A	Brighton & Hove Albion	D	2-2	Bennett, Cross	14,539
23	Mar	9	A	Middlesbrough	L	0-1		9,403
24		13	A	Southampton	D	0-0		21,376
25		16	A	Arsenal	D	2-2	Cross, King	15,779
26		20	H	Birmingham City	D	1-1	Robertson	20,936
27		24	H	Notts County	L	2-4	Regis, King	12,637
28		27	H	Tottenham Hotspur	W	1-0	Regis	20,151
29		30	A	Aston Villa	L	1-2	King	28,440
30	Apr	6	A	Swansea City	L	1-3	Mackenzie	15,744
31		10	H	Coventry City	L	1-2	Mackenzie	12,443
32		12	A	Manchester United	L	0-1		38,717
33		17	A	Liverpool	L	0-1		34,286
34		21	H	Manchester City	L	0-1		11,632
35		24	H	Sunderland	L	2-3	Owen (pen), Brown	13,092
36	May	1	A	Wolverhampton Wanderers	W	2-1	Regis, Monaghan	19,813
37		5	H	Ipswich Town	L	1-2	Owen	12,532
38		8	H	Aston Villa	L	0-1		19,556
39		12	H	Manchester United	L	0-3		19,772
40		15	A	Notts County	W	2-1	Mackenzie, Regis	8,734
41		18	H	Leeds United	W	2-0	Mackenzie, Regis	23,041
42		20	A	Stoke City	L	0-3		19,695

Appearances
Sub appearances
Goals

FA Cup

R3	Jan	2	H	Blackburn Rovers	W	3-2	Mackenzie, King (pen), Whitehead	17,892
R4		23	A	Gillingham	W	1-0	Statham	16,038
R5	Feb	13	H	Norwich City	W	1-0	Regis	18,897
R6	Mar	6	H	Coventry City	W	2-0	Owen, Regis	28,045
SF	Apr	3	N	Queen's Park Rangers	L	0-1		45,015

SF at Highbury

Appearances
Sub appearances
Goals

League Cup

R2/1	Oct	6	A	Shrewsbury Town	D	3-3	Mackenzie, Cross, Regis	9,291
R2/2		28	H	Shrewsbury Town	W	2-1	Owen, Brown	12,598
R3	Nov	10	A	West Ham United	D	2-2	Regis, King	24,168
rep		24	H	West Ham United	D	1-1*	Regis	15,985
rep2	Dec	1	A	West Ham United	W	1-0	Regis	24,502
R4		15	A	Crystal Palace	W	3-1	Regis 2, Monaghan	10,311
R5	Jan	19	A	Aston Villa	W	1-0	Statham	35,197
SF1	Feb	3	H	Tottenham Hotspur	D	0-0		32,166
SF2		10	A	Tottenham Hotspur	L	0-1		47,241

* after extra-time

Appearances
Sub appearances
Goals

Godden AL	Batson BM	Statham DJ	Moses RM	Wile JD	Bennett M	Robson B	Mills DJ	Deehan JM	Lowery AW	Mackenzie S	Cross NJR	Robertson AP	Owen GA	Regis C	Brown A	Arthur DR	King AE	Summerfield K	Jol MC	Grew MS	Whitehead CR	Monaghan DJ	Lewis M	Childs GPC	Webb AR	Zondervan R	Cowdrill BJ	
1	2	3	4	5	6	7	8	9	**10**	11	12																	1
1	2	3	**4**	5		7	8	9		11	12	6	10															2
1	2	3	4	5		7	8			11		6	10	9														3
1	2	3	4	5		7	8			11		6	10	9														4
1	2	3		5			8	7		11	12	6	10	9	**4**													5
1	2	3		5			8	7		11	10	**6**		9	4	12												6
1	2	3		5		7	8			11	6		10	9			4											7
1	2	3		5						11	7	6	10	9			4	8										8
1	2	3		5			12			11	**7**	6	10	9			4	8										9
1	2	3		5			7			11		6	10	9	8		4											10
1	2	3		5			12			11		6	10	9	8		**4**		7									11
1	2	3		5			4			11		6	10	9	8				**7**									12
	2	3		5						11		6	10	9	8		12		7	1	4							13
	2	3		5						11		6	10	9	8		12		7	1	4							14
	2	3		5						11		6	10	9	**8**		12		7	1	4							15
	2	3		5						11		6	10	9	8				7	1	4							16
	2	3		5						11		6	10	9	8		12		**7**	1	4							17
	2			5	3					11		6	**10**	9			4			1	7	8	12					18
	2	3		5						11	12	6	10	9			4		7	1	**8**							19
	2			5	6					11			10	9		3		8		1	7		4					20
		3		5	2					11	12	6	10	9			**8**			1			4	7				21
		3		5	6					11	12		10	9			8			1			**4**	7	2			22
	2	3		5	4					11		6	**10**	9	7		8			1						12		23
	2			5	4					11		6	10	9	7		8			1						3		24
	2	3		5	4						12	6	10		7		8			1		9				11		25
	2	3		5	4						7	6	10	9			8			1						11		26
	2	**3**		5	4						7	6	10	9	12		8			1						11		27
	2			5	4						7	6	10	9			8			1					3	11		28
	2			5	4					11	7	6	10		9		8			1					3			29
		3		5	**4**					11	8	6	10	9	12	2				1						7		30
	2	3		5	4					11	**8**	6	10	9	12					1						7		31
	2	3		5						11	12	6	10	9	8		4			1						**7**		32
	2	3		5	7					11	12	**6**		9	8		10			1							4	33
	2	3		5						11		6	**10**	9			8	4		1						7	12	34
	2	3		5	6					**11**			10	9	4		8			1		12				7		35
1	2			5	4					11		6	10	9	8							12				**7**	3	36
1	2			5	4					**11**		6	10	9	8							12				7	3	37
1	2	3		5	4							6	10	9	8							11				7		38
1	2	3		5	4					7	12		10	9			**8**					11					6	39
1	2	3		5	4					7	12		10	9								**11**			6		8	40
1	2	3		5	4					11			10	9	8										6		7	41
1	2	3		5	4					7	9		10		11				8						**6**		12	42
19	39	35	4	42	23	5	9	4	1	37	11	33	39	37	22	2	21	4	9	23	8	5	3	2	6	13	6	
							2			11					3	1	4					3	1			1	2	
					2		2			5	2	1	3	17	3		4	2	1		1	1						Two own-goals
	2	3		5						11		6		9			10		7	1	4	8						R3
	2	3		5						11		6	10	9	4				7	1	8							R4
		3		5	2					11	7	6	10	9			8			1			4					R5
	2	3		5	4					11		6	10	9	7		8			1								R6
	2	3		5	7					11	10	6	12	9			**8**			1						4		SF
	4	5		5	3					5	2	5	3	5	2		4		2	5	3	1	1			1		
													1															
		1								1			1	2			1				1							
1	2	3		5						11	7	6	10	9			4	8										R2/1
1	2	3		5						11		6	10	9	8		4		7									R2/2
		3		5						11		**6**	10	9	8	2	4		**7**	1								R3
	2	3		5						11		6	10	9	8		4		7	1								rep
	2	3		5						11		6	10	9	8		4		**7**	1								rep2
	2			5	3					11		**6**	10	9		7	4			1		8	12					R4
	2	3		5						11		6	10	9	4		8		**7**	1								R5
	2	3		5	6					11	12		10	9			4		7	1		**8**						SF1
		3		5	6					11		4	**10**	9		2	12	8	7	1								SF2
2	7	8		9	3					9	1	8	9	9	5	3	8	2	7	7		2						
											1						1						1					
		1								1	1		1	6	1		1					1						

1982-83

Division One

	P	W	D	L	F	A	Pts
Liverpool	42	24	10	8	87	37	82
Watford	42	22	5	15	74	57	71
Manchester United	42	19	13	10	56	38	70
Tottenham Hotspur	42	20	9	13	65	50	69
Nottingham Forest	42	20	9	13	62	50	69
Aston Villa	42	21	5	16	62	50	68
Everton	42	18	10	14	66	48	64
West Ham United	42	20	4	18	68	62	64
Ipswich Town	42	15	13	14	64	50	58
Arsenal	42	16	10	16	58	56	58
West Bromwich Albion	42	15	12	15	51	49	57
Southampton	42	15	12	15	54	58	57
Stoke City	42	16	9	17	53	64	57
Norwich City	42	14	12	16	52	58	54
Notts County	42	15	7	20	55	71	52
Sunderland	42	12	14	16	48	61	50
Birmingham City	42	12	14	16	40	55	50
Luton Town	42	12	13	17	65	84	49
Coventry City	42	13	9	20	48	59	48
Manchester City	42	13	8	21	47	70	47
Swansea City	42	10	11	21	51	69	41
Brighton & Hove Albion	42	9	13	20	38	68	40

Manager: Ron Wylie

- The former Notts County, Aston Villa and Birmingham City player Ron Wylie replaced Ronnie Allen as Albion's manager.
- Albion's average home League attendance of 15,260 was the lowest at The Hawthorns since 1914–15.
- Peter Eastoe (from Everton), Paul Barron (from Crystal Palace) and Garry Thompson (from Coventry City) were among the players signed.
- Those transferred out of The Hawthorns included David Mills to Sheffield Wednesday for a cut-down price of £30,000, Mark Grew to Leicester City, Ally Brown to Crystal Palace, Andy King to Everton and John Wile to his former club Peterborough United as player-manager, this after he had made 619 appearances for Albion in 13 years.
- When beating the Army 5–0 in a friendly match at Aldershot in May, Albion used a record 21 players.
- Albion's second team won the Central League title for the first time since 1935.

Match No.	Date			Opponents	Result		Scorers	Attendance
1	Aug	28	A	Liverpool	L	0-2		35,652
2	Sep	1	H	Brighton & Hove Albion	W	5-0	Jol, Brown 2, Eastoe, Cross	11,370
3		4	H	Manchester United	W	3-1	Bennett, Brown, Eastoe	24,928
4		8	A	Stoke City	W	3-0	Brown, Eastoe, Regis	17,447
5		11	A	Watford	L	0-3		17,639
6		18	H	West Ham United	L	1-2	Eastoe	15,204
7		25	A	Norwich City	W	3-1	Regis 3	14,404
8	Oct	2	H	Aston Villa	W	1-0	Cross	25,165
9		9	H	Nottingham Forest	W	2-1	Owen, Regis	13,657
10		16	A	Arsenal	L	0-2		21,666
11		23	H	Luton Town	W	1-0	Whitehead	16,488
12		30	A	Ipswich Town	L	1-6	Regis	18,884
13	Nov	6	A	Birmingham City	L	1-2	Eastoe	18,520
14		13	H	Swansea City	D	3-3	Jol, Eastoe, Cross	12,369
15		20	A	Everton	D	0-0		16,001
16		27	H	Coventry City	W	2-0	Robertson, Regis	12,082
17	Dec	4	A	Tottenham Hotspur	D	1-1	Mills	26,608
18		11	H	Sunderland	W	3-0	Zondervan, Robertson, Owen	11,072
19		18	A	Southampton	L	1-4	Regis	16,896
20		27	H	Notts County	D	2-2	Eastoe, Owen	17,756
21		28	A	Manchester City	L	1-2	Brown	25,172
22	Jan	1	H	Everton	D	2-2	Zondervan, Owen	15,135
23		3	A	Manchester United	D	0-0		39,123
24		15	H	Liverpool	L	0-1		24,401
25		22	A	West Ham United	W	1-0	Eastoe	19,887
26	Feb	5	H	Stoke City	D	1-1	Cross	11,462
27		12	A	Brighton & Hove Albion	D	0-0		9,892
28		19	A	Nottingham Forest	D	0-0		14,507
29		26	H	Arsenal	D	0-0		16,923
30	Mar	5	A	Luton Town	D	0-0		10,852
31		12	H	Ipswich Town	W	4-1	Gernon (og), Statham, Thompson 2	12,792
32		19	H	Birmingham City	W	2-0	Regis, Thompson	20,682
33		26	A	Swansea City	L	1-2	Thompson	11,222
34	Apr	2	H	Manchester City	L	0-2		13,764
35		4	A	Notts County	L	1-2	Thompson	8,696
36		9	H	Watford	L	1-3	Jol	11,845
37		19	A	Aston Villa	L	0-1		26,921
38		23	H	Tottenham Hotspur	L	0-1		14,879
39		30	A	Coventry City	W	1-0	Perry	9,457
40	May	2	H	Norwich City	W	1-0	Thompson	9,189
41		7	H	Southampton	W	1-0	Statham	11,130
42		14	A	Sunderland	D	1-1	Thompson	16,375

Appearances
Sub appearances
Goals

FA Cup

R3	Jan	8	H	Queen's Park Rangers	W	3-2	Owen 2 (1 pen), Eastoe	16,528
R4		29	A	Tottenham Hotspur	L	1-2	Whitehead	38,208

Appearances
Sub appearances
Goals

League Cup

R2/1	Oct	6	A	Nottm Forest	L	1-6	Regis	11,969
R2/2		27	H	Nottm Forest	W	3-1	Regis, Cross, Whitehead	6,536

Appearances
Sub appearances
Goals

Grew MS	Batson BM	Cowdrill BJ	Zondervan R	Bennett M	Robertson AP	Jol MC	Brown A	Eastoe PR	Mackenzie S	Whitehead CR	Webb AR	Owen GA	Cross NJR	Regis C	Statham DJ	Godden AL	Wile JD	Mills DJ	Barron PG	Lewis M	Thompson GL	Perry MA	Luke NE	Robson B	
1	2	3	4	5	**6**	7	8	9	10	11	12														1
1	2		4	5	6	7	8	9		3		10	11												2
1	2		4	5	6	7	8	11		3		10		9											3
1	2		4	5	6	7	8	11		3		10		9											4
1	2		4	5	6	7	8	11		3		10		9											5
1	2		4	5	6	7	**8**	11		3		10	12	9											6
1	2		4	5	6	7	8	11		3		10		9											7
1	2		4	5	6	7	8	11		3		10	9												8
1	2		4	5	6	7	8	**11**		3		10	12	9											9
1	2		4	5	6	7	8			3		10	**11**	9	12										10
	2		4	5	6	7	8			11		10		9	3	1									11
	2		4		6	7	8			11		10	12	9	3	1	5								12
			2	**4**	6	7		8		11		10	12	9	3	1	5								13
			4		6	7		11		2		10	8	9	3	1	5								14
			4		6	7		11		2		10	8	9	3	1	5								15
			4		6	7		11		2		10	8	9	3	1	5								16
			4		6	7		**11**		2		10	8	9	3	1	5	12							17
			4		6	7		11		2		10	**8**	9	3	1	5	12							18
			4		6	7		11		2		10	8	9	3	1	5								19
			4		6	7		11		2		10	8	9	3	1	5								20
			4	12	6	7	8	11		2		10		9	3	1	5								21
			4		6	7		11		2		10	**8**	9	3	1	5	12							22
			4	8	6	7		11		2		10		9	3		5		1						23
			4	8	6	7		11		2		10		9	3		5		1						24
			4	8	6	7		11		2		10	12	**9**	3		5		1						25
			4	2	6	7	8	11				10	9		3		5		1						26
			4	6		7	8	11			2		9		3		5		1	10					27
			4	6		7	8	11			2		9		3		5		1	10					28
			4	**2**	6	7		11		12		10	8		3		5		1		9				29
			4	2	6	7		11				10	8		3		5		1		9				30
			4	6				12		7	2	10	11	**9**	3		5		1		8				31
			4	6						7	2	10	11	9	3		5		1		8				32
			4		6	7				**11**	2	10	12	9	3		5		1		8				33
			4		6	7		11		2		**10**	9		3		5		1	12	8				34
			12		6	**7**		9		4	2		11		3		5		1	10	8				35
		3	4		6	7		9		2		10	11				5		1			8			36
			4		6	7				2	9	10	11		3		5		1			8			37
			4		6	7				**11**	2	10		9	3		5		1		8	12			38
					6	7				4	2	10	11		3		5		1		8	9			39
			4		6						2	10	11		3		5		1	**7**	9	8	12		40
			4		6	7					2	10	11		3		5		1		9	8		12	41
			4			7				2	6	10	11		3		5		1		9	**8**		12	42
10	12	2	40	22	37	39	16	30	1	35	12	38	26	26	31	12	31		20	4	12	6			
			1	1				1		1	1		6		1			3		1		1	1	2	
			2	1	2	3	5	8		1		4	4	9	2			1			7	1			

One own-goal

			4	8	6	7		11		2		10		9	3		5		1						R3
			4	8	6	7	12	11		**2**		10	9		3		5		1						R4
			2	2	2	2		2		2		2	1	1	2		2		2						
							1																		
								1		1		2													

1	2		4	5	6	7	8	11		3		10		9											R2/1
	2	12	4		6	7	8			11			10	**9**	3	1	5								R2/2
1	2		2	1	2	2	2	1		2		1	1	2	1	1	1								
		1																							
										1			1	2											

1983-84

Division One

	P	W	D	L	F	A	Pts
Liverpool	42	22	14	6	73	32	80
Southampton	42	22	11	9	66	38	77
Nottingham Forest	42	22	8	12	76	45	74
Manchester United	42	20	14	8	71	41	74
Queen's Park Rangers	42	22	7	13	67	37	73
Arsenal	42	18	9	15	74	60	63
Everton	42	16	14	12	44	42	62
Tottenham Hotspur	42	17	10	15	64	65	61
West Ham United	42	17	9	16	60	55	60
Aston Villa	42	17	9	16	59	61	60
Watford	42	16	9	17	68	77	57
Ipswich Town	42	15	8	19	55	57	53
Sunderland	42	13	13	16	42	53	52
Norwich City	42	12	15	15	48	49	51
Leicester City	42	13	12	17	65	68	51
Luton Town	42	14	9	19	53	66	51
West Bromwich Albion	42	14	9	19	48	62	51
Stoke City	42	13	11	18	44	63	50
Coventry City	42	13	11	18	57	77	50
Birmingham City	42	12	12	18	39	50	48
Notts County	42	10	11	21	50	72	41
Wolverhampton W	42	6	11	25	27	80	29

Manager: Ron Wylie then Johnny Giles

- European Cup winners Ken McNaught and Tony Morley joined Albion from Aston Villa; also signed were Steve Hunt (from Coventry City) and Tony Grealish (from Brighton & Hove Albion). Hunt played for England against Scotland – the last home international match staged between the two countries.
- Dutch internationals Romeo Zondervan and Maarten Jol joined Ipswich Town and Coventry City respectively, while Derek Monaghan and Alan Webb both signed for Port Vale.
- Johnny Giles returned for a second spell as manager, replacing Wylie in mid-February.
- Former Birmingham Road supporter Sid Lucas commenced a five-year spell as Albion's chairman.

Match No.	Date			Opponents	Result		Scorers	Attendance
1	Aug	27	A	Aston Villa	L	3-4	Zondervan, Thompson, Regis	30,590
2		29	A	Stoke City	L	1-3	Cross	16,139
3	Sep	3	H	Leicester City	W	1-0	Whitehead	11,976
4		7	H	Tottenham Hotspur	D	1-1	Regis	14,830
5		10	A	Everton	D	0-0		15,556
6		17	H	West Ham United	W	1-0	Thompson	15,113
7		24	A	Ipswich Town	W	4-3	Zondervan, Thompson (pen), Regis, Perry	16,661
8	Oct	1	H	Watford	W	2-0	Thompson, Regis	14,398
9		15	A	Manchester United	L	0-3		42,221
10		22	A	Coventry City	W	2-1	Regis, Perry	13,321
11		29	H	Birmingham City	L	1-2	Perry	20,109
12	Nov	5	H	Notts County	W	2-0	McNaught, Luke	10,760
13		12	A	Southampton	L	0-1		16,450
14		19	A	Norwich City	L	0-2		13,045
15		26	H	Wolverhampton Wanderers	L	1-3	Thompson	17,914
16	Dec	3	A	Arsenal	W	1-0	Monaghan	22,272
17		10	H	Queen's Park Rangers	L	1-2	Morley	11,643
18		18	A	Luton Town	L	0-2		11,566
19		26	H	Liverpool	L	1-2	Morley	25,094
20		27	A	Sunderland	L	0-3		17,968
21		31	A	Leicester City	D	1-1	Thompson	15,128
22	Jan	2	H	Ipswich Town	W	2-1	Thompson, Owen	11,330
23		14	H	Aston Villa	W	3-1	Thompson 2, Regis	20,359
24		21	A	West Ham United	L	0-1		17,213
25	Feb	4	A	Watford	L	1-3	Zondervan	14,469
26		8	H	Nottingham Forest	L	0-5		11,066
27		11	H	Everton	D	1-1	Perry	10,261
28		25	H	Coventry City	D	1-1	Cross	10,906
29		28	A	Birmingham City	L	1-2	Mackenzie	16,780
30	Mar	3	A	Notts County	D	1-1	Cross	7,373
31		17	A	Tottenham Hotspur	W	1-0	Regis	22,385
32		24	H	Stoke City	W	3-0	Mackenzie, Morley, Hunt	13,642
33		31	H	Manchester United	W	2-0	Regis, Mackenzie	28,104
34	Apr	7	A	Nottingham Forest	L	1-3	Thompson	15,245
35		14	H	Norwich City	D	0-0		11,469
36		21	A	Liverpool	L	0-3		35,320
37		23	H	Sunderland	W	3-1	Thompson, Regis, Hunt	11,199
38		28	A	Wolverhampton Wanderers	D	0-0		13,208
39	May	5	H	Arsenal	L	1-3	Thompson	13,454
40		7	A	Queen's Park Rangers	D	1-1	Thompson	14,418
41		12	H	Luton Town	W	3-0	Regis, Mackenzie, Morley	12,004
42		14	H	Southampton	L	0-2		10,308

Appearances
Sub appearances
Goals

FA Cup

R3	Jan	7	A	Rotherham United	D	0-0		8,142
rep		11	H	Rotherham United	W	3-0	Thompson, Morley 2	12,107
R4	Feb	1	H	Scunthorpe United	W	1-0	Forsyth	18,235
R5		18	H	Plymouth Argyle	L	0-1		23,795

Appearances
Sub appearances
Goals

League Cup

R2/1	Oct	4	A	Millwall	L	0-3		10,721
R2/2		25	H	Millwall	W	5-1	Thompson 2, Regis 2, Owen (pen)	13,311
R3	Nov	9	A	Chelsea	W	1-0	Thompson	22,932
R4		30	H	Aston Villa	L	1-2	Regis	31,114

Appearances
Sub appearances
Goals

	Barron PG	Webb AR	Whitehead CR	Zondervan R	McNaught K	Bennett M	Jol MC	Thompson GL	Regis C	Owen GA	Cross NJR	Robson G	Robertson AP	Cowdrill BJ	Perry MA	Lewis M	Childs GPC	Luke NE	Monaghan DJ	Forsyth ME	Mackenzie S	Morley WA	Ebanks MWA	Statham DJ	Kent KJ	Hunt SK	Grealish AP	Smith J
1	1	2	3	**4**	5	6	7	8	9	10	11	12																
2	1		3		5	6	7	8	9	10	11	4	2															
3	1		3	2	5	6	7	8	9	10	11	4																
4	1		2	4	5	6	**7**	8	9	10	11			3	12													
5	1		2	4	5	6		8	9	10	12	**7**		3	11													
6	1		2	4	5	6		8	9	10	**11**			3	12	7												
7	1		2	4	5	6		8	9		11	**10**		3	12	7												
8	1	10	2	4	5	6		8	9		**11**			3		7	12											
9	1		2	4	5	6		8	9	10	11			3		7												
10	1		2	4	5	6		8	**9**	10		12		3	11	7												
11	1		2	4	5	**6**		8	9	10	12			3	11	7												
12	1		2	4	5			8		10			6	3	9	7		11										
13	1		2	**4**	5			8		10	12	7	6	3	9			11										
14	1		2	4	5		7	8		10	12		6	3	**9**			11										
15	1		2	4	5		7	8		10			6	3	9			11	12									
16	1	2		4	5			8		11				3				7	9	6	10							
17	1	2		4	5	6		8		10				3	12				9		**11**	7						
18	1			2	5		7		9		10			3		8		4		6		11						
19	1	2		4	5		7		9		**10**			3	12	8				6		11						
20	1			4	5			8	9	10	12			3		7				6		11	**2**					
21	1		2	4	5	6	7	8	9	10				3								11						
22	1		2	**4**	5	6		8	9	10	12			3		7						11						
23	1		2	7	5	6		8	9	10				3				4				11						
24	1		2	**7**	5		12	8	9	10			6	3				4				11						
25	1		2	4	5		7	8	9					3		10				6		11						
26	1		2	4	5		7	8	**9**							10				6	12	11		3				
27	1		2	4	5		7				12				9					**6**	10	11		3	8			
28	1			4	5	6	7	8			9										10	11	2	3				
29	1			4	5	6	7	8			9										10	11	2	3				
30	1		2	4	5	6	7	8			9										10	11		3				
31	1		2		5	6		8	9												10	11		3		4	7	
32	1		2		5	**6**		8	9												10	11	12	3		4	7	
33	1		2		5	6		8	9												10	11		3		4	7	
34	1		2		5	6		8	9												10	11		3		4	7	
35	1				5	6		8			9										10	11	2	3		4	7	
36	1		2		5	6		8	9												10	11		3		4	7	
37	1		2		5	6		8	9		12										10	11		**3**		4	7	
38	1		2		5	6		8	9												10	11		3		4	7	
39	1		2		5	6		8	9		12										10	11		3		4	**7**	
40	1		2		5			8	9											6	10	11	7	3		4		
41	1		2		5	6			9		8										10	11		3		4	7	
42	1		2		5	6					8				9						10	11	**3**		12	4	7	
	42	5	34	29	42	29	15	37	30	20	16	5	6	22	8	14		8	2	8	18	26	6	16	1	12	11	
							1				9	2			5		1		1		1		1		1			
			1	3	1			13	10	1	3				4			1	1		4	4				2		

	Barron PG	Webb AR	Whitehead CR	Zondervan R	McNaught K	Bennett M	Jol MC	Thompson GL	Regis C	Owen GA	Cross NJR	Robson G	Robertson AP	Cowdrill BJ	Perry MA	Lewis M	Childs GPC	Luke NE	Monaghan DJ	Forsyth ME	Mackenzie S	Morley WA	Ebanks MWA	Statham DJ	Kent KJ	Hunt SK	Grealish AP	Smith J
R3	1		2		5	6		8	9	**10**	4			3		7		12				11						
rep	1		2		5	6		8	9	10				3		7		4				11						
R4	1		2	7	5			8	9					3		10		4		6		11						
R5	1		2	4	5	6	7	8							**9**			12			10	11		3				
	4		4	2	4	3	1	4	3	2	1			3	1	3		2		1	1	4		1				
																		2										
								1												1		2						

	Barron PG	Webb AR	Whitehead CR	Zondervan R	McNaught K	Bennett M	Jol MC	Thompson GL	Regis C	Owen GA	Cross NJR	Robson G	Robertson AP	Cowdrill BJ	Perry MA	Lewis M	Childs GPC	Luke NE	Monaghan DJ	Forsyth ME	Mackenzie S	Morley WA	Ebanks MWA	Statham DJ	Kent KJ	Hunt SK	Grealish AP	Smith J
R2/1	1		2	4	5			8	9		11	10		3		7					12							6
R2/2	1		2	4	5	6		8	9	10	12			3	11	7												
R3	1		2	4	5			8		10			6	3	9	7		11										
R4	1		2	4	5		7	8	9	10	11		6	3							12							
	4		4	4	4	1	1	4	3	3	2	1	2	4	2	3		1										1
											1										2							
								3	3	1																		

1984-85

Division One

	P	W	D	L	F	A	Pts
Everton	42	28	6	8	88	43	90
Liverpool	42	22	11	9	68	35	77
Tottenham Hotspur	42	23	8	11	78	51	77
Manchester United	42	22	10	10	77	47	76
Southampton	42	19	11	12	56	47	68
Chelsea	42	18	12	12	63	48	66
Arsenal	42	19	9	14	61	49	66
Sheffield Wednesday	42	17	14	11	58	45	65
Nottingham Forest	42	19	7	16	56	48	64
Aston Villa	42	15	11	16	60	60	56
Watford	42	14	13	15	81	71	55
West Bromwich Albion	42	16	7	19	58	62	55
Luton Town	42	15	9	18	57	61	54
Newcastle United	42	13	13	16	55	70	52
Leicester City	42	15	6	21	65	73	51
West Ham United	42	13	12	17	51	68	51
Ipswich Town	42	13	11	18	46	57	50
Coventry City	42	15	5	22	47	64	50
Queen's Park Rangers	42	13	11	18	53	72	50
Norwich City	42	13	10	19	46	64	49
Sunderland	42	10	10	22	40	62	40
Stoke City	42	3	8	31	24	91	17

Manager: Johnny Giles

- Three players joined Albion from Canada: forwards David Cross and Carl Valentine arrived from the manager's former club, Vancouver Whitecaps, and right-back Jimmy Nicholl was recruited from Toronto Blizzard.
- Cross moved to Bolton Wanderers at the end of the season, while Cyrille Regis was transferred to Coventry City, Paul Barron to Queen's Park Rangers and Ken McNaught to Sheffield United.
- The crowd of 7,423 for the Albion against Sunderland League game in April was the lowest at The Hawthorns for 28 years.

Match No.	Date			Opponents	Result		Scorers	Attendance
1	Aug	25	A	Queen's Park Rangers	L	1-3	Mackenzie	12,683
2		27	H	Everton	W	2-1	Hunt, Thompson	14,062
3	Sep	1	H	Luton Town	W	4-0	Hunt, Thompson, Regis, N. Cross	11,653
4		5	A	Norwich City	L	1-2	Grealish	13,070
5		8	A	Sunderland	D	1-1	Thompson	18,206
6		15	H	Sheffield Wednesday	D	2-2	Thompson 2	16,428
7		22	A	Leicester City	L	1-2	N. Cross	11,960
8		29	H	Manchester United	L	1-2	Thompson (pen)	26,292
9	Oct	6	A	Liverpool	D	0-0		29,346
10		13	H	Nottingham Forest	W	4-1	Thompson 3, Mackenzie	12,991
11		20	A	Ipswich Town	L	0-2		14,325
12		27	H	Southampton	D	0-0		12,461
13	Nov	3	A	Tottenham Hotspur	W	3-2	Statham (pen), Mackenzie, D. Cross	24,494
14		10	H	Stoke City	W	2-0	Hunt, Mackenzie	12,173
15		17	A	Chelsea	L	1-3	Thompson	17,573
16		24	H	Coventry City	W	5-2	Statham, Grealish, Thompson, Mackenzie, Valentine	12,618
17	Dec	1	A	West Ham United	W	2-0	Hunt, Thompson	15,572
18		8	H	Watford	W	2-1	Thompson, D. Cross	13,513
19		15	A	Arsenal	L	0-4		23,728
20		18	A	Luton Town	W	2-1	Statham (pen), Thompson	7,286
21		26	H	Newcastle United	W	2-1	Hunt, Thompson	20,303
22		29	H	Norwich City	L	0-1		13,754
23	Jan	1	A	Aston Villa	L	1-3	Statham (pen)	31,710
24		12	A	Sheffield Wednesday	L	0-2		24,345
25		26	H	Queen's Park Rangers	D	0-0		9,194
26	Feb	2	A	Manchester United	L	0-2		36,681
27		23	H	Tottenham Hotspur	L	0-1		16,159
28	Mar	2	A	Southampton	L	3-4	Thompson 2, Valentine	15,842
29		12	A	Stoke City	D	0-0		6,942
30		16	A	Nottingham Forest	W	2-1	N. Cross, Owen	12,663
31		23	H	Liverpool	L	0-5		20,319
32		30	H	Leicester City	W	2-0	Hunt 2	9,323
33	Apr	3	H	Ipswich Town	L	1-2	Hunt	8,036
34		6	A	Newcastle United	L	0-1		22,694
35		8	H	Aston Villa	W	1-0	Valentine	20,936
36		16	A	Everton	L	1-4	Grealish	29,671
37		20	H	Chelsea	L	0-1		11,079
38		24	H	Sunderland	W	1-0	N. Cross	7,423
39		27	A	Coventry City	L	1-2	Mackenzie	10,329
40	May	4	H	West Ham United	W	5-1	Hunt, Grealish, Mackenzie 2, N. Cross	8,834
41		7	A	Watford	W	2-0	Thompson, Owen	14,074
42		11	H	Arsenal	D	2-2	Thompson, Valentine	13,326

Appearances
Sub appearances
Goals

FA Cup

R3	Jan	5	A	Orient	L	1-2	N. Cross	7,061

Appearances
Sub appearances
Goals

League Cup

R2/1	Sep	25	A	Wigan Athletic	D	0-0		6,209
R2/2	Oct	10	H	Wigan Athletic	W	3-1	Hunt, Thompson, N. Cross	8,133
R3		30	A	Birmingham City	D	0-0		17,616
rep	Nov	7	H	Birmingham City	W	3-1	Robertson, Thompson, D. Cross	16,717
R4		20	A	Watford	L	1-4	D Cross	16,378

Appearances
Sub appearances
Goals

Godden AL	Whitehead CR	Statham DJ	Hunt SK	Robertson AP	Bennett M	Grealish AP	Thompson GL	Regis C	Mackenzie S	Cross NJR	Morley WA	Robson G	Forsyth ME	Valentine CH	Cross D	Lewis M	Nicholl JM	Barron PG	Owen GA	Cowdrill BJ	
1	2	3	4	5	6	7	8	9	10	11											1
1	2	3	4	6	5	**7**	8	9	10	12	11										2
1	2	3	4	6	5	7	8	**9**	10	12	11										3
1	2	3	4	6	5	7	8	9	10		11										4
1	2	3	4	5	6	7	8	9	10		11										5
1	2	3	4	6	5	7	8	9	10		11										6
1	2	3	4	6	5	7	8		10	9	11										7
1	2	3	4	**6**	5	7	8	9	10	12	11										8
1	2	3	4	6	5	7	8		10	9		**11**	12								9
1	2	3	4	6	5	7	8		10	9		11									10
1	2	3	4	6	5	7	8		10	9		12		**11**							11
1	2	**3**	4	6	5	7	8		10	12					9	11					12
1	2	3	4	6	5	7	8		9			12		**11**	10						13
1	12	3	4	6	5	**7**	8		9			11			10		2				14
1	11	3	4	6	5	7	8		9	12					10		2				15
1		3	4	6	5	7	8		9	12				11	**10**		2				16
1		3	4	6	5	7	8		9					11	10		2				17
1		3	4	6		7	8		9				5	11	10		2				18
1	4	3		6	5	7	8		9	12				11	**10**		2				19
1	4	3		6	5	7	8		9	10				11			2				20
1		3	4	6	5	7	8		9					11	10		2				21
1	12	3	4	6	5	7	8		9					11	10		2				22
1	7	3	4	**6**	5		8		9	12				11	10		2				23
1	12	3	4	6	5	7	8		9					11	10		2				24
1	4	3			5	7	8		9				6	11	10		2				25
	10	3	4		5	7	8		**9**				6	11			2	1	12		26
1	10		4	6	5		8		9				3	11			2		7		27
1	12	3	4	6	5		8		**9**					11	10		2		7		28
1	**3**		4		5	12	8		9				6	11	10		2		7		29
1	3		4		5	12	8		9	**10**			6	11			2		7		30
1	12	3	4	6	5	7	8		**9**	10				11			2				31
1	2	3	4	6		12	8			10		**9**	5	11					7		32
1	2	3	4	6		12	8			**10**		9	5	11					7		33
1			4	6	5	12	8					9		11	10		2		7	3	34
1			4	6	5	10	8			12		**9**		11			2		7	3	35
1	12		4	**6**	5	10	8		7			9		11			2			3	36
1			4		5	10	8		12			**9**	6	11			2		7	3	37
1	12			6	5	**10**	8		4	9				11			2		7	3	38
1	**9**			6	5	12	8		4	10				11			2		7	3	39
1			4	6	5	12	8		9	10				11			2		7	3	40
1			4	6	5	12	8		9	**10**				11			2		7	3	41
1			4	6	5		8		9	10				11			2		7	3	42
41	25	30	37	37	39	30	42	7	37	15	7	9	9	29	16	1	27	1	14	9	
	7					8			1	9		2	1						1		
		4	9			4	19	1	8	5				4	2				2		

Godden AL	Whitehead CR	Statham DJ	Hunt SK	Robertson AP	Bennett M	Grealish AP	Thompson GL	Regis C	Mackenzie S	Cross NJR	Morley WA	Robson G	Forsyth ME	Valentine CH	Cross D	Lewis M	Nicholl JM	Barron PG	Owen GA	Cowdrill BJ	
1	11	**3**	4		5	7	8		9	10		12	6				2				R3
1	1	1	1		1	1	1		1	1			1				1				
												1									
										1											

Godden AL	Whitehead CR	Statham DJ	Hunt SK	Robertson AP	Bennett M	Grealish AP	Thompson GL	Regis C	Mackenzie S	Cross NJR	Morley WA	Robson G	Forsyth ME	Valentine CH	Cross D	Lewis M	Nicholl JM	Barron PG	Owen GA	Cowdrill BJ	
1	2	3	4	6	5	7	8		10	9	11										R2/1
1	2	3	4		5	7	8		10	9		11	6								R2/2
1	2		4	6	5		8		9			11			10	7				3	R3
1	2	3	4	6	5	7	8		9			12		**11**	10						rep
1		3	4	6	5	7	8		9					11	10		2				R4
5	4	4	5	4	5	4	5		5	2	1	2	1	2	3	1	1			1	
												1									
			1	1			2			1					2						

1985-86

Division One

	P	W	D	L	F	A	Pts
Liverpool	42	26	10	6	89	37	88
Everton	42	26	8	8	87	41	86
West Ham United	42	26	6	10	74	40	84
Manchester United	42	22	10	10	70	36	76
Sheffield Wednesday	42	21	10	11	63	54	73
Chelsea	42	20	11	11	57	56	71
Arsenal	42	20	9	13	49	47	69
Nottingham Forest	42	19	11	12	69	53	68
Luton Town	42	18	12	12	61	44	66
Tottenham Hotspur	42	19	8	15	74	52	65
Newcastle United	42	17	12	13	67	72	63
Watford	42	16	11	15	69	62	59
Queen's Park Rangers	42	15	7	20	53	64	52
Southampton	42	12	10	20	51	62	46
Manchester City	42	11	12	19	43	57	45
Aston Villa	42	10	14	18	51	67	44
Coventry City	42	11	10	21	48	71	43
Oxford United	42	10	12	20	62	80	42
Leicester City	42	10	12	20	54	76	42
Ipswich Town	42	11	8	23	32	55	41
Birmingham City	42	8	5	29	30	73	29
West Bromwich Albion	42	4	12	26	35	89	24

Manager: Johnny Giles then Ron Saunders

- This was Albion's worst ever season of League football. Their record included fewest wins (four, three at home, one away), most defeats (26, 10 at home), nine games lost on the trot, lowest number of points (24, only seven away) and just 21 home goals. Bottom of the Division from the third game onwards, in the end Albion were 18 points from safety, having used a total of 33 players.
- Transfers included Albion's first £100,000 goalkeeper Stuart Naylor from Lincoln City, strikers George Reilly from Newcastle United, Garth Crooks from Tottenham Hotspur, Imre Varadi from Sheffield Wednesday and Craig Madden from Bury. Midfielder Mickey Thomas arrived from Chelsea, while Garry Thompson moved to Hillsborough to replace Varadi and Gary Owen signed for the Greek club Panionios after 229 appearances for Albion. Madden was, in fact, the 100th player signed by Ron Saunders during his managerial career.
- The former Manchester City, Norwich City, Aston Villa and Birmingham City manager Ron Saunders replaced Johnny Giles in The Hawthorns hot seat.
- Albion played their first Sunday game at The Hawthorns, beating Watford 3–1 in December.

Match No.	Date			Opponents	Result		Scorers	Attendance
1	Aug	17	H	Oxford United	D	1-1	Varadi	14,571
2		20	A	Everton	L	0-2		26,791
3		24	A	Watford	L	1-5	Varadi	13,599
4		26	H	Manchester City	L	2-3	Mackenzie 2	12,088
5		31	A	Chelsea	L	0-3		15,376
6	Sep	4	H	Aston Villa	L	0-3		17,267
7		7	H	Ipswich Town	L	1-2	Crooks	7,720
8		14	A	Newcastle United	L	1-4	Mackenzie	21,902
9		21	H	Manchester United	L	1-5	Crooks	24,962
10		28	A	Coventry City	L	0-3		10,270
11	Oct	5	H	Tottenham Hotspur	D	1-1	Valentine	12,130
12		12	A	Leicester City	D	2-2	Crooks 2	7,237
13		19	H	Birmingham City	W	2-1	Varadi, Valentine	13,553
14		26	A	Sheffield Wednesday	L	0-1		19,873
15	Nov	3	A	Nottingham Forest	L	1-2	Hunt	19,610
16		9	H	Queen's Park Rangers	L	0-1		9,016
17		16	A	Liverpool	L	1-4	Crooks	28,407
18		23	H	Arsenal	D	0-0		9,165
19		30	A	West Ham United	L	0-4		16,325
20	Dec	7	H	Everton	L	0-3		12,406
21		14	A	Oxford United	D	2-2	Varadi, Hunt	9,020
22		22	H	Watford	W	3-1	Varadi, Hunt (pen), Dennison	11,092
23		26	H	Luton Town	L	1-2	Varadi	12,508
24		28	A	Aston Villa	D	1-1	Hunt	18,796
25	Jan	1	A	Southampton	L	1-3	Varadi	13,154
26		11	H	Newcastle United	D	1-1	Varadi	9,100
27		18	H	Chelsea	L	0-3		11,213
28	Feb	1	A	Manchester City	L	1-2	Grealish	20,540
29		8	A	Birmingham City	W	1-0	Bennett	11,514
30		22	A	Manchester United	L	0-3		45,193
31	Mar	8	A	Tottenham Hotspur	L	0-5		10,841
32		15	H	Leicester City	D	2-2	Varadi, Mackenzie	8,626
33		19	H	Coventry City	D	0-0		8,831
34		22	A	Ipswich Town	L	0-1		12,386
35		29	H	Southampton	W	1-0	Thompson	7,325
36	Apr	1	A	Luton Town	L	0-3		9,226
37		5	H	Nottingham Forest	D	1-1	Bennett	7,901
38		12	A	Queen's Park Rangers	L	0-1		11,866
39		19	H	Liverpool	L	1-2	Madden	22,010
40		22	H	Sheffield Wednesday	D	1-1	Reilly	6,201
41		26	A	Arsenal	D	2-2	Reilly 2	14,821
42	May	3	H	West Ham United	L	2-3	Reilly (pen), Madden	17,751

Appearances
Sub appearances
Goals

FA Cup

R3	Jan	13	A	Sheffield Wednesday	D	2-2	Reilly, Statham	17,042
rep		16	H	Sheffield Wednesday	L	2-3	Hunt, Thomas	11,152

Appearances
Sub appearances
Goals

League Cup

R2/1	Sep	24	H	Port Vale	W	1-0	Armstrong	6,268
R2/2	Oct	7	A	Port Vale	D	2-2	Varadi 2	7,895
R3		29	A	Coventry City	D	0-0		9,804
rep	Nov	6	H	Coventry City	W	4-3	Varadi 2, Crooks, Hunt	8,987
R4		19	A	Aston Villa	D	2-2	Bennett, Crooks	20,204
rep		26	H	Aston Villa	L	1-2	Hunt	18,868

Appearances
Sub appearances
Goals

Godden AL	Nicholl JM	Statham DJ	Whitehead CR	Bennett M	Robertson AP	Grealish AP	Varadi I	Mackenzie S	Valentine CH	Crooks GA	Cowdrill BJ	Hunt SK	Forsyth ME	Anderson CR	Robson G	Armstrong GJ	Dennison RS	Palmer CL	Thomas MR	Bradshaw PW	Thompson AR	Reilly GG	Owen GA	Grew MS	Naylor SW	Dickinson MJ	Dyson PI	Bradley DM	Madden CA	Bull SG	Burrows D	Robinson MJ	
1	2	3	4	5	6	7	8	9	10	**11**	12																						1
1	2	10	7	5			8	9	11		**3**	4	6	12																			2
1	2	10	12	5	**6**		8	9	11					3	4	7																	3
1	2	10		5			8	9	11				6	3	4	7																	4
1	5	10	2				8	9	11				6	3	4	7																	5
1	2	3			**5**	10	8	9	11				6	12	4	7																	6
1	2	3				10	8	9	11	7			6	12	**4**	5																	7
1	2	3	5					9		11			6	7	4	8	**10**	12															8
1	2	3			5			9	10	11		4	6		8	7																	9
1	2	3		5	6	12	8	**9**	7	11		4							10														10
	2	**3**	12	5	6	4	9		7	11		8							10	1													11
	2	3	4	5	6	8	9		7	11									10	1													12
		3	4	5	6	8	9		7	11								2	10	1													13
	2	3	**8**	5	6		9		7	11		4						12	10	1													14
	2	3		5	6	8	9		7	11		4							10	1													15
	6	3	2	5		8	9		7	11		4						12	**10**	1													16
1	2	3		**5**	6		9			11		4			7	12			10		8												17
		3	8	5	6		9			11		4			12		7	2	10	1													18
	2		**8**	5	6	7	9	12		11	3	4							10	1													19
1	2			5	**6**		8	7		11	3	4						12	10			9											20
1	2	3		5	6	11	8	7				4							10			9											21
1	2	3		5	6	**11**	8	7				4					12		10			9											22
1	2	3		5	6	**7**	8	11				4					12		10			9											23
1	2	3		5	6		8	7				4					12		10		11	9											24
1	2	3		5	6		8	7				**4**					12		10		11	9											25
1	2	3		5	6		8	**7**									11		10		12	9	4										26
	2	3					**8**			11		4	6				9	5	10		7		12	1									27
1	2	3		6		7	**8**			12		4						5	10			9	11										28
1	2	3		6		7	12			**8**		4						5	10			9	11										29
	2	3		6			12	9		11			4		7		**10**	5				8			1								30
1	2	3	8				**7**	10			4		5	11							12	9				6							31
		3	2				8	10					4								7	9			1	6	5	11					32
		3	2				8	10										4			7	9			1	6	5	11					33
		3	2					10							12			4			7	9			1	6	5	**11**	8				34
		3	2					10										4			11	9			1	6	5	7	8				35
		3	2			12	**9**	10										4			7				1	6	5	11	8				36
		3	2	6				10									12	4			**7**	9			1		5	11	8				37
			2					10			6			3			9	4			**7**				1		5	11	8	12			38
		3	2					9			4			12			11	7				8			1		5	**6**	10				39
			2					9			4				12			7			6	8			1		5		10		3	**11**	40
			2					8			4			3	12			6			**7**	9			1		5	11	10				41
		3	2					**8**			4				12			6				9			1	7	5	11	10				42
21	29	37	22	25	20	14	30	30	15	18	9	19	11	7	9	7	7	16	20	8	13	20	3	1	12	7	11	10	9		1	1	
			2			2	2	1		1	1			4	5	1	5	4			2		1							1			
				2		1	9	4	2	5		4					1				1	4							2				

Godden AL	Nicholl JM	Statham DJ	Whitehead CR	Bennett M	Robertson AP	Grealish AP	Varadi I	Mackenzie S	Valentine CH	Crooks GA	Cowdrill BJ	Hunt SK	Forsyth ME	Anderson CR	Robson G	Armstrong GJ	Dennison RS	Palmer CL	Thomas MR	Bradshaw PW	Thompson AR	Reilly GG	Owen GA	
1	2	3		5	6		8										11		10		7	9	4	R3
1	2	3		**5**	6		8					4					11		10		7	9	12	rep
2	2	2		2	2		2					1					2		2		2	2	1	
																							1	
		1										1							1			1		

Godden AL	Nicholl JM	Statham DJ	Whitehead CR	Bennett M	Robertson AP	Grealish AP	Varadi I	Mackenzie S	Valentine CH	Crooks GA	Cowdrill BJ	Hunt SK	Forsyth ME	Anderson CR	Robson G	Armstrong GJ	Dennison RS	Palmer CL	Thomas MR	Bradshaw PW	
1	2	3			5			**9**	10	11	6	4		12	8	7					R2/1
	2	3	12	5	6	4	9		**7**	11		8							10	1	R2/2
	2	3		5	6	8	9		7	11		4							10	1	R3
	2	3	12	5	**6**	8	9		7	11		4							10	1	rep
	2	3	8	5	6		9			11		4				**7**		12	10	1	R4
		3	8	5	6	12	9			11		4					**7**	2	10	1	rep
1	5	6	2	5	6	3	5	1	4	6	1	6			1	2	1	1	5	5	
			2			1								1				1			
				1			4			2		2				1					

1986-87

Division Two

	P	W	D	L	F	A	Pts
Derby County	42	25	9	8	64	38	84
Portsmouth	42	23	9	10	53	28	78
Oldham Athletic	42	22	9	11	65	44	75
Leeds United	42	19	11	12	58	44	68
Ipswich Town	42	17	13	12	59	43	64
Crystal Palace	42	19	5	18	51	53	62
Plymouth Argyle	42	16	13	13	62	57	61
Stoke City	42	16	10	16	63	53	58
Sheffield United	42	15	13	14	50	49	58
Bradford City	42	15	10	17	62	62	55
Barnsley	42	14	13	15	49	52	55
Blackburn Rovers	42	15	10	17	45	55	55
Reading	42	14	11	17	52	59	53
Hull City	42	13	14	15	41	55	53
West Bromwich Albion	42	13	12	17	51	49	51
Millwall	42	14	9	19	39	45	51
Huddersfield Town	42	13	12	17	54	61	51
Shrewsbury Town	42	15	6	21	41	53	51
Birmingham City	42	11	17	14	47	59	50
Sunderland	42	12	12	18	49	59	48
Grimsby Town	42	10	14	18	39	59	44
Brighton & Hove Albion	42	9	12	21	37	54	39

Manager: Ron Saunders

- For the first time since 1910, Albion's average home League attendance dropped below the 10,000 mark to 9,280. And only 957 hardy supporters witnessed the Full Members Cup defeat at Millwall.
- Bobby Williamson (from Glasgow Rangers), Don Goodman (from Bradford City), Steve Lynex (for a second spell) and Robert Hopkins (from Manchester City) were four new recruits, while among those who left The Hawthorns were Tony Grealish and Imre Varadi to Manchester City, Mickey Thomas to Wichita Wings, Jimmy Nicholls to Glasgow Rangers, Garth Crooks and Steve MacKenzie to Charlton Athletic, Craig Madden to Blackpool, Steve Bull, Ally Robertson, Robbie Dennison and Andy Thompson all to Wolves. And the Baggies supporters have never forgiven manager Saunders for selling 'Bully.' Robertson left after making 729 first-team appearances for Albion (626 at senior level).

Match No.	Date			Opponents	Result		Scorers	Attendance
1	Aug	23	A	Hull City	L	0-2		8,656
2		25	H	Sheffield United	W	1-0	Evans	9,002
3		30	H	Huddersfield Town	W	1-0	Bennett	9,250
4	Sep	2	A	Stoke City	D	1-1	Palmer	8,668
5		6	A	Reading	D	1-1	Madden	7,757
6		13	H	Ipswich Town	L	3-4	Williamson, Bull 2	9,031
7		20	A	Brighton & Hove Albion	L	0-2		8,767
8		27	H	Derby County	W	2-0	Mackenzie 2	10,847
9	Oct	4	H	Oldham Athletic	W	2-0	Whitehead, Crooks	9,351
10		11	A	Blackburn Rovers	W	1-0	Dyson	5,701
11		18	H	Grimsby Town	D	1-1	Hopkins	8,618
12		25	A	Portsmouth	L	1-2	Crooks	11,698
13	Nov	1	H	Birmingham City	W	3-2	Williamson 2, Crooks	15,029
14		8	A	Sunderland	W	3-0	Dickinson, Williamson, Crooks	16,162
15		15	A	Plymouth Argyle	L	0-1		14,697
16		22	H	Millwall	L	0-1		8,005
17		29	A	Barnsley	D	2-2	Williamson, Crooks	5,750
18	Dec	6	H	Leeds United	W	3-0	Whitehead 2, Crooks	9,853
19		12	A	Bradford City	W	3-1	Abbott (og), Williamson, Hopkins	4,580
20		19	H	Reading	L	1-2	Crooks	7,558
21		26	A	Shrewsbury Town	L	0-1		9,261
22		27	H	Plymouth Argyle	D	0-0		12,678
23	Jan	1	H	Crystal Palace	L	1-2	Hopkins	8,420
24		3	A	Sheffield United	D	1-1	Crooks	9,240
25		24	H	Hull City	D	1-1	Reilly	6,707
26	Feb	7	A	Huddersfield Town	L	1-2	Reilly	5,218
27		14	H	Stoke City	W	4-1	Crooks 2, Reilly 2 (1 pen)	12,366
28		21	A	Derby County	D	1-1	Anderson	16,237
29		28	H	Brighton & Hove Albion	D	0-0		8,359
30	Mar	3	A	Ipswich Town	L	0-1		9,843
31		14	A	Grimsby Town	L	1-3	Crooks	5,024
32		21	H	Blackburn Rovers	L	0-1		8,565
33		28	A	Oldham Athletic	L	1-2	Bradley	6,954
34	Apr	4	H	Sunderland	D	2-2	Bennett, Lynex	6,123
35		12	A	Birmingham City	W	1-0	Reilly	11,158
36		18	A	Crystal Palace	D	1-1	Goodman	7,127
37		20	H	Shrewsbury Town	L	1-2	Williamson	7,307
38		25	A	Millwall	W	1-0	Williamson	3,158
39		29	H	Portsmouth	W	1-0	Hopkins	10,007
40	May	2	H	Barnsley	L	0-1		6,361
41		4	A	Leeds United	L	2-3	Burrows, Dyson	24,685
42		9	H	Bradford City	D	2-2	Robson, Goodman	8,367

Appearances
Sub appearances
Goals

FA Cup

R3	Jan	10	A	Swansea City	L	2-3	Lewis (og), Anderson	8,792

Appearances
Sub appearances
Goals

League Cup

R2/1	Sep	24	A	Derby County	L	1-4	Bull	11,304
R2/2	Oct	7	H	Derby County	L	0-1		6,765

Appearances
Sub appearances
Goals

	Naylor SW	Whitehead CR	Burrows D	Bennett M	Dyson PI	Dickinson MJ	Palmer CL	Evans SJ	Mackenzie S	Williamson R	Madden CA	Thompson AR	Dennison RS	Dobbins LW	Bull SG	Cowdrill BJ	Anderson CR	Robinson MJ	Crooks GA	Hopkins RA	Singleton MD	Statham DJ	Bradley DM	Reilly GG	Steggles KP	Robson G	Lynex SC	Goodman DR
1	1	2	3	4	5	6	7	8	9	10	**11**	12																
2	1		3	4	5	6	7	8	9	10		2	**11**	12														
3	1	2	3	4	5	6	7	8	9	**10**		11		12														
4	1	2	3	4	5	6	7	8	9	10		11																
5	1	2	3	4	5	6	7			10	12	**11**		9	8													
6	1	2	3	4	5	6	7		9	10	12				8	**11**												
7	1	2	3	4	5	6	7	8	9	10				**11**	12													
8	1	2			5	6	4	8	9	10		12				7	3	**11**										
9	1	2			5	6	4	8	9	10						7	3		11									
10	1	2			5		4	8	9	10		12		6		7	**3**		11									
11	1	2			5		4	8	9	10		6				3			11	7								
12	1	2	**9**		5	6	4	12		10			8			3			11	**7**								
13	1	2			5	6	4		9	10						3	8		11	7								
14	1	2			5	6	4		9	10		12				3	**8**		11	**7**								
15	1	2			5	6	4		9	10						3	8		11	7								
16	1	2			5	6	4		**9**	10			12			3	8		11	**7**								
17	1	2			5	6	4		9	10			12			3	8		11	7								
18	1	2			5	6	4		9	10						3	8		11	**7**								
19	1	2	12		5	**6**	4		9	10						3	8		11	7								
20	1	2			5	12	4		9	10						3	8		11	7	6							
21	1	2			5	6		10	9	12						3	8		**11**	7	4							
22	1	2			5	4			9	**10**				12		3	8		11	7	6							
23	1	2			5	**6**	4	10	9							3	8		11	7	12							
24	1	2	6		5		4		9	10						3			11	7		8						
25	1	2			5		4	8	10	**7**						3	11				12		6	9				
26	1	12			5	4	2	**8**	10								11			7		3	6	9				
27	1	4			5		2		10								11		8	7		3	6	9				
28	1	2			5					7						10	8		11			3	6	9	4			
29	1	2			5	8				**7**						12	10		11			3	6	9	4			
30	1	2			5	8	12									**10**			11	7		3	6		4	9		
31	1		3		5	8	2										10		11	7			6	9	4			
32	1	3	12		5	8	2			11							10			7			6		4	**9**		
33	1			4	5		2			11						3				7			6		10	12	8	**9**
34	1			4	5		2									3	11			7				9	6		10	8
35	1			4	5		2		11							3				7			6	9			10	8
36	1				5		2		11							3				7			6	9	4		10	8
37	1				5		**2**		11	9						3	12			7			6		4		10	8
38	1	2		4	5					9						3	6				11				7		10	8
39	1	2		4	5		3		9								11			7			6				10	8
40	1	2	12	4	5		3		**9**	7							11						6				10	8
41	1		3	4	5	2	7										11				6					9	10	8
42	1	2	3	4	5		7									6	11									9	10	8
	2	33	12	15	42	26	36	13	30	30	1	5	2	3	2	28	27	1	21	25	5	6	14	9	10	4	10	10
		1	3			1	1	1		1	2	4	2	3	1	1	1				2					1		
		3	1	2	2	1	1	1	2	8	1				2		1		11	4			1	5		1	1	2

One own-goal

	Naylor SW	Whitehead CR	Burrows D	Bennett M	Dyson PI	Dickinson MJ	Palmer CL	Evans SJ	Mackenzie S	Williamson R	Madden CA	Thompson AR	Dennison RS	Dobbins LW	Bull SG	Cowdrill BJ	Anderson CR	Robinson MJ	Crooks GA	Hopkins RA	Singleton MD	Statham DJ	Bradley DM	Reilly GG	Steggles KP	Robson G	Lynex SC	Goodman DR
R3	1	2	6		**5**		4		9	10							3		11	7	12	8						
	1	1	1		1		1		1	1							1		1	1		1						
																					1							
																	1											

One own-goal

	Naylor SW	Whitehead CR	Burrows D	Bennett M	Dyson PI	Dickinson MJ	Palmer CL	Evans SJ	Mackenzie S	Williamson R	Madden CA	Thompson AR	Dennison RS	Dobbins LW	Bull SG	Cowdrill BJ	Anderson CR	Robinson MJ	Crooks GA	Hopkins RA	Singleton MD	Statham DJ	Bradley DM	Reilly GG	Steggles KP	Robson G	Lynex SC	Goodman DR
R2/1	1	2	12	**4**	5	6	7	8		10				11	9		3	13										
R2/2	1	2			5	6	4	8	9	10		12			**11**	7	3											
	2	2		1	2	2	2	2	1	2				1	2	1	2											
			1									1						1										
															1													

1987-88

Division Two

	P	W	D	L	F	A	Pts
Millwall	44	25	7	12	72	52	82
Aston Villa	44	22	12	10	68	41	78
Middlesbrough	44	22	12	10	63	36	78
Bradford City	44	22	11	11	74	54	77
Blackburn Rovers	44	21	14	9	68	52	77
Crystal Palace	44	22	9	13	86	59	75
Leeds United	44	19	12	13	61	51	69
Ipswich Town	44	19	9	16	61	52	66
Manchester City	44	19	8	17	80	60	65
Oldham Athletic	44	18	11	15	72	64	65
Stoke City	44	17	11	16	50	57	62
Swindon Town	44	16	11	17	73	60	59
Leicester City	44	16	11	17	62	61	59
Barnsley	44	15	12	17	61	62	57
Hull City	44	14	15	15	54	60	57
Plymouth Argyle	44	16	8	20	65	67	56
Bournemouth	44	13	10	21	56	68	49
Shrewsbury Town	44	11	16	17	42	54	49
Birmingham City	44	11	15	18	41	66	48
West Bromwich Albion	44	12	11	21	50	69	47
Sheffield United	44	13	7	24	45	74	46
Reading	44	10	12	22	44	70	42
Huddersfield Town	44	6	10	28	41	100	28

Manager: Ron Saunders then Ron Saunders

- Albion finished in their lowest ever League position (20th in the Division), avoiding relegation to the Third Division by just a single point.
- Ron Atkinson returned to The Hawthorns for a second spell as manager, replacing Saunders in early September.
- Players signed included Andy Gray from Aston Villa, Tony Morley (for the second time) from FC Den Haag in Holland, former England international Brian Talbot and Tony 'Zico' Kelly both from Stoke City, the South African John Paskin from KV Kortrikj in Belgium and Stacey North from Luton Town.
- Out of The Hawthorns camp went Martin Dickinson (to Sheffield United), Bobby Williamson (to Rotherham United), Derek Statham (to Southampton after 378 appearances), Clive Whitehead to Portsmouth (after 196 appearances), George 'Mother' Reilly (to Cambridge United) and Barry Cowdrill (to Bolton Wanderers).

Match No.	Date			Opponents	Result		Scorers	Attendanc
1	Aug	15	H	Oldham Athletic	D	0-0		8,873
2		22	A	Blackburn Rovers	L	1-3	Sulley (og)	5,619
3		29	H	Swindon Town	L	1-2	Bennett	7,503
4		31	A	Leeds United	L	0-1		19,847
5	Sep	5	H	Shrewsbury Town	W	2-1	Pearson (og), Goodman	8,560
6		8	A	Crystal Palace	L	1-4	Williamson	8,554
7		12	A	Plymouth Argyle	D	3-3	Palmer, Gray 2	10,578
8		16	H	Aston Villa	L	0-2		22,072
9		19	H	Bournemouth	W	3-0	Morley 2, Palmer	7,749
10		26	A	Millwall	L	0-2		6,564
11		30	H	Birmingham City	W	3-1	Palmer, Singleton, Gray	15,399
12	Oct	3	A	Reading	W	2-1	Williamson, Gray	5,763
13		10	H	Bradford City	L	0-1		12,241
14		17	A	Middlesbrough	L	1-2	Kelly (pen)	10,491
15		21	A	Leicester City	L	0-3		9,262
16		24	H	Huddersfield Town	W	3-2	Morley 3	8,450
17	Nov	4	H	Sheffield United	W	4-0	Goodman, Williamson, Morley, Gray	8,068
18		7	A	Stoke City	L	0-3		9,992
19		14	H	Ipswich Town	D	2-2	Goodman, Gray	8,457
20		21	A	Hull City	L	0-1		7,654
21		28	H	Manchester City	D	1-1	Goodman	15,425
22	Dec	5	A	Barnsley	L	1-3	Futcher (og)	5,395
23		12	H	Blackburn Rovers	L	0-1		7,413
24		18	A	Aston Villa	D	0-0		24,437
25		26	H	Millwall	L	1-4	Morley (pen)	9,291
26		28	A	Bournemouth	L	2-3	Goodman, Gray	8,969
27	Jan	1	A	Swindon Town	L	0-2		12,155
28		2	H	Plymouth Argyle	W	1-0	Goodman	8,445
29		16	A	Oldham Athletic	L	1-2	Robson	5,559
30		30	H	Leeds United	L	1-4	Dickinson	9,005
31	Feb	6	A	Shrewsbury Town	W	1-0	Anderson	6,360
32		13	H	Crystal Palace	W	1-0	Goodman	8,944
33		27	H	Reading	L	0-1		8,509
34	Mar	5	H	Middlesbrough	D	0-0		8,742
35		8	A	Birmingham City	W	1-0	Hopkins	12,331
36		12	A	Bradford City	L	1-4	Talbot (pen)	12,502
37		26	A	Huddersfield Town	W	3-1	Gray 2, Swain	4,503
38	Apr	2	H	Stoke City	W	2-0	Gray, Talbot (pen)	12,144
39		4	A	Ipswich Town	D	1-1	Phillips	10,732
40		9	H	Leicester City	D	1-1	Lynex	11,013
41		23	A	Sheffield United	D	0-0		12,091
42		30	H	Hull City	D	1-1	Dyson	8,004
43	May	2	A	Manchester City	L	2-4	Lynex, Dyson	16,490
44		7	H	Barnsley	D	2-2	Hopkins, Phillips	8,473

Appearances

Sub appearances

Goals

FA Cup

R3	Jan	9	A	Wimbledon	L	1-4	Thorn (og)	7,252

Appearances

League Cup

R1/1	Aug	19	H	Walsall	L	2-3	Forbes (og), Bradley	9,605
R1/2		25	A	Walsall	D	0-0		8,965

Appearances

Sub appearances

Goals

	Naylor SW	Robson G	Statham DJ	Bennett M	Dickinson MJ	Kelly AG	Hopkins RA	Goodman DR	Williamson R	Bradley DM	Morley WA	Palmer CL	Burrows D	Reilly GG	Dobbins LW	Singleton MD	Steggles KP	Cowdrill BJ	Gray AM	Anderson CR	Lynex SC	Hogg GJ	Powell DR	North SS	Hucker IP	Talbot BE	Swain KM	Phillips SG	Dyson PI	Hodson SP
1	1	**2**	3	4	5	6	7	8	9	10	11	12	13																	
2	1	10		4	5	6	7	**8**		2	11	12	3	9	13															
3	1	9		4	5	6		8	13	12	**11**	7	3		2	10														
4	1	9			5	6		8	12	2	11	**7**	3			10	4													
5	1	7			5	6		8	9	12	11	2				10	**4**	3												
6	1	7			5	6	13	8	9	12	11	2				10	**4**	3												
7	1			**4**	13		7	8	12	6	11	2		5		10		3	9											
8	1			4			7	**8**	12	6	11	2		5		10		3	9											
9	1			4	12	**6**	7	8		10	11	2		5		13		3	9											
10	1				4	6	7	8	13	10		2		5		12		3	**9**	11										
11	1					6	7	8	12	2		4	5			10		3	**9**	11										
12	1					6	7	8	12	2	11	4	5			10		3	**9**											
13	1					6	7	8	12	2	11	4	5			**10**		3	9											
14	1					6	7	8	11	2		4	5		12	10		3	**9**											
15	1	10				6		13	8	2	11	4	5		12			**3**	9		7									
16	1	**10**				6			8	2	11	4	3	5					9	12	7									
17	1					6		**8**	13	10	11	2	3	5					9	12	7	4								
18	1	12				6			**8**	10	11	2	3	5					9	13	7	4								
19	1					6		8			11	5	3				2		9	10	7	4								
20	1	12				6		8			11	2	3	5					9	10	**7**	4								
21	1				5		7	8			11	2	3		10				9		6	4								
22	1	10			5		7	8			12	2		13	11				9	3	**6**	4								
23	1	13				5	7	8	12		11	2	3	9	10						**6**	4								
24	1	12				5	7	8			11	4	2	9				3		**10**	6									
25	1	13			7	5		8			11	4	2	**9**				3	12	10	6									
26	1	10			2	6		8	13		11	4	12	**5**				3	9		7									
27		10			2	6	7	8	11			4						3	9				1	5						
28		**10**			2	6	7	8	13		11	4						3	9		12		1	5						
29	1	10				6	2	12	8		**11**	4						3	9		7			5						
30		7			12	**10**	2	8			11	6						3	9					5	1	4				
31		10					7	8				6						3	9	11				5	1	4	2			
32		10					7	8				6						3	9	11				5	1	4	2			
33		10						8	9		**11**	6	13		12			3			7			5	1	4	2			
34		10						8				6			7			3		11				5	1	4	2	9		
35		**10**					7	8				6	12					3		11				5	1	4	2	9		
36		**10**					7	8				6						3	12	11				5	1	4	2	9		
37	1						7	**8**			11				12			3	9	10				5		4	2		6	
38	1	12					7					10						3	**9**	11				5		4		8	6	2
39	1						7	12				**10**						3	9	11				5		4		8	6	2
40	1	10						12										3	9	11	**7**			5		4		8	6	2
41	1	**10**						12										3	9	11	7			5		4		8	6	2
42	1	10					7	12										3	**9**	11				5		4		8	6	2
43	1	10					7	9		12								3		**11**	13			5		4		8	6	2
44	1	10					7											3	9	**11**	12			5		4		8	6	2
	35	25	1	6	13	26	28	34	10	15	27	36	17	13	5	10	4	32	30	20	16	7	2	18	7	15	7	10	8	7
		6			3		1	6	12	4	1	2	4	1	5	2			2	3	3									
		1		1	1	1	2	7	3		7	3				1			10	1	2					2	1	2	2	

Three own-goals

R3					2	6	7	8	11			4	10	9				3					1	5						
					1	1	1	1	1			1	1	1				1					1	1						

One own-goal

R1/1	1			4		6	7	8		10	11	9	3		2		**5**				12									
R1/2	1	9		4	5	6		8			11	**7**	3		2	10					12									
	2	1		2	1	2	1	2		1	2	2	2		2	1	1													
																					2									
										1																				

One own-goal

1988-89

Division Two

	P	W	D	L	F	A	Pts
Chelsea	46	29	12	5	96	50	99
Manchester City	46	23	13	10	77	53	82
Crystal Palace	46	23	12	11	71	49	81
Watford	46	22	12	12	74	48	78
Blackburn Rovers	46	22	11	13	74	59	77
Swindon Town	46	20	16	10	68	53	76
Barnsley	46	20	14	12	66	58	74
Ipswich Town	46	22	7	17	71	61	73
West Bromwich Albion	46	18	18	10	65	41	72
Leeds United	46	17	16	13	59	50	67
Sunderland	46	16	15	15	60	60	63
Bournemouth	46	18	8	20	53	62	62
Stoke City	46	15	14	17	57	72	59
Bradford City	46	13	17	16	52	59	56
Leicester City	46	13	16	17	56	63	55
Oldham Athletic	46	11	21	14	75	72	54
Oxford United	46	14	12	20	62	70	54
Plymouth Argyle	46	14	12	20	55	66	54
Brighton & Hove Albion	46	14	9	23	57	66	51
Portsmouth	46	13	12	21	53	62	51
Hull City	46	11	14	21	52	68	47
Shrewsbury Town	46	8	18	20	40	67	42
Birmingham City	46	8	11	27	31	76	35
Walsall	46	5	16	25	41	80	31

Manager: Ron Atkinson then Brian Talbot

- Manager Ron Atkinson quit his position as manager in October, taking his assistant Colin Addison with him to the Spanish club Atletico Madrid.
- The former Arsenal defender Chris Whyte was signed from Los Angeles Aztecs and Paul Raven arrived from Doncaster Rovers, while those who left the club included David Burrows to Liverpool, Carlton Palmer to Sheffield Wednesday (in exchange for Striker Colin West) and Andy Gray to Glasgow Rangers.
- Albion topped the Second Division table halfway through the season but fell away after their FA Cup replay defeat at Everton and eventually finished in ninth position.
- Albion played Walsall for the first time in the League this season, and John Silk took over as club chairman from Sid Lucas.

Match No.	Date			Opponents	Result		Scorers	Attendance
1	Aug	27	A	Leicester City	D	1-1	Paskin	13,082
2		29	H	Watford	L	0-1		10,242
3	Sep	3	H	Swindon Town	W	3-1	Dyson, Goodman, Paskin	7,518
4		10	A	Shrewsbury Town	D	1-1	Robson	5,848
5		17	H	Walsall	D	0-0		13,977
6		21	A	Brighton & Hove Albion	W	1-0	Goodman	7,395
7		24	A	Plymouth Argyle	D	1-1	Phillips	8,539
8	Oct	1	H	Ipswich Town	L	1-2	Whyte	9,357
9		5	H	Bournemouth	D	0-0		7,248
10		8	A	Barnsley	L	1-2	Talbot	5,674
11		15	A	Birmingham City	W	4-1	Hopkins 2, Robson, Phillips	10,453
12		22	H	Bradford City	W	1-0	Talbot	8,989
13		26	H	Manchester City	W	1-0	Durnin	14,258
14		29	A	Blackburn Rovers	W	2-1	Anderson, Whyte	9,503
15	Nov	5	H	Oxford United	W	3-2	Hopkins, Goodman, Anderson	11,643
16		12	A	Leeds United	L	1-2	Durnin	20,449
17		19	A	Sunderland	D	1-1	Robson	18,141
18		26	H	Crystal Palace	W	5-3	Hopkins, Goodman 3, Paskin	11,054
19	Dec	3	A	Portsmouth	D	0-0		12,764
20		10	H	Hull City	W	2-0	Goodman 2	10,094
21		18	H	Stoke City	W	6-0	Goodman 2, Paskin 2, Robson 2	17,634
22		26	A	Oldham Athletic	W	3-1	Hopkins, Goodman, Robson	9,832
23		31	A	Chelsea	D	1-1	Anderson	25,816
24	Jan	2	H	Shrewsbury Town	W	4-0	Moyes (og), Albiston, Goodman, Robson	18,411
25		14	A	Watford	L	0-2		15,168
26		21	H	Leicester City	D	1-1	Robson	15,792
27	Feb	4	A	Bournemouth	L	1-2	Albiston	11,571
28		11	H	Barnsley	D	1-1	Goodman	12,650
29		18	A	Bradford City	L	0-2		11,047
30		25	H	Birmingham City	D	0-0		16,148
31	Mar	1	A	Manchester City	D	1-1	Whyte	25,109
32		5	H	Leeds United	W	2-1	Goodman 2	15,914
33		11	A	Oxford United	D	1-1	West	7,581
34		15	H	Blackburn Rovers	W	2-0	West 2	12,821
35		18	H	Brighton & Hove Albion	W	1-0	Bartlett	11,586
36		25	A	Swindon Town	D	0-0		12,240
37		27	H	Oldham Athletic	W	3-1	Anderson (pen), Bartlett, West	13,812
38	Apr	1	A	Walsall	D	0-0		9,520
39		4	A	Stoke City	D	0-0		11,151
40		8	H	Chelsea	L	2-3	Anderson, Ford	22,858
41		15	H	Plymouth Argyle	D	2-2	Brown (og), West	11,358
42		22	A	Ipswich Town	L	1-2	West	12,184
43		29	A	Crystal Palace	L	0-1		13,728
44	May	1	H	Portsmouth	W	3-0	Anderson (pen), West 2	9,586
45		6	H	Sunderland	D	0-0		10,451
46		13	A	Hull City	W	1-0	Bartlett	5,217

Appearances
Sub appearances
Goals

FA Cup

R3	Jan	7	H	Everton	D	1-1	Anderson	31,186
R3		11	A	Everton	L	0-1		31,697

Appearances
Sub appearances
Goals

League Cup

R1/1	Aug	31	H	Peterborough Utd	L	0-3		4,264
R1/2	Sep	7	A	Peterborough Utd	W	2-0	Gray, Palmer	4,216

Appearances
Sub appearances
Goals

Naylor SW	Bradley DM	Albiston AR	Talbot BE	Dyson PI	North SS	Hopkins RA	Goodman DR	Paskin WJ	Palmer CL	Anderson CR	Gray AM	Hodson SP	Burrows D	Robson G	Whyte CA	Cork D	Phillips SG	Durnin JP	Dobbins LW	Bradshaw PW	Rice B	Cartwright NA	Bartlett KF	West C	Walford SJ	Ford T	Banks IF	Raven PD	Robinson R	Easter G	
1	2	3	4	5	6	7	8	9	10	11																					1
1	2	3	4	5	6	7		9	10	11	8																				2
1	4	3		5	6	7	8	**9**	10	11	12	2	14																		3
1	12	3			6	7	8		10	11	**9**	2	13	4	5																4
1			4		6	7	8	9	10	11		**2**	3	12	5	13															5
1		2	4		6	7	8	**9**	10	11			3		5	12															6
1		2	4		6	7	8		**10**	11			3		5	12	9														7
1		2	4		6	7	8		10	11			3		5		9														8
1		2	4		6	7	8		10	11			3		5		9														9
1	12	2	4		6	**7**			10	11			3	13	5	8	9														10
1	12	2	4		6	**7**			10	11			3	8	5		9														11
1	2	3	4		6	7			10	11				8	5			9													12
1		3	4		6	7			10	11				8	5			9	2												13
1		3	4		6	7	12		10	11				8	5			**9**	2												14
1		3	4		6	7	12		10	11				8	5			**9**	2												15
1	2	3	4		6	**7**	11	12	10					**8**	5			9													16
1	2	3	4		6	7	8	12	10	11				**9**	5																17
1	2	3	**4**		6	7	8	12	10	11				9	5																18
1	7	3	4		6		8	12	10	11		2		**9**	5																19
1	**7**	3	4		6		8	12	10	11		2		9	**5**																20
1		3	4		6		8	10		11		2		9	5				7												21
1		3			6	7	8	10		11		2		9	5				4												22
1		3	4		6	7	8	10		11		2		9	5																23
		3	4		6	7	8	12	10	11		2		**9**	5				13	1											24
	11	3	4		6	7		8	10					9	5				**2**	1	12										25
1	2	3	4		6	7		**8**	10					9	5				13		11	12									26
1		3	4		6	7		8	10					9	5				2		11										27
1		3	**4**		6	7	8	12	10	11				9	5				2												28
1		3	4		6	7	8		10	11				2	5								9								29
1	2	3	4		6	7	**8**			11				10	5								12	9							30
1	2	**3**			6	7	8			11				4	5				12				10	9							31
1	7	**3**			6		8	12		11				4	5				2				10	9	13						32
1	7				6		8			11				4	5				2				10	9	3						33
1	2	3	4		6		8			11				7	5								10	9							34
1	2	3	4		6	12	8			11				**7**	5								10	9							35
1	2	3	4		6		**8**			11				10									12	9	5	7					36
1	2	3	4		6		**8**			11				10	5								12	9		7	13				37
1	2	3	4		6					11				10									8	9	5	7					38
1	2	3	4		6			12		11				10	**5**								8	9		7	13				39
1	6	3	4		5		**8**			11									2				12	9		7	10				40
1	**2**	3	4		6		8			11				10	5								12	9		7					41
1		3			6		**8**	13		11				10	5				12				7	9		2	4				42
1		3	4		6		12	8		**11**				10	5				2					9		7					43
1		3	4		6		13	8		11				10	5								12	**9**		7		2			44
1		3	4		6		13	**8**		11				10	5								12	9		7		2			45
1			4		6		13	12		11				10	5								**8**	9		7		2	3		46
44	23	43	39	3	46	28	30	14	26	42	2	9	7	36	40	1	5	5	12	2	2		10	17	3	11	2	3	1		
	3					1	6	11			1		2	2		3			4		1	1	7		1		2				
		2	2	1		5	15	5		6				8	3		2	2					3	8		1					

Two own-goals

Naylor SW	Bradley DM	Albiston AR	Talbot BE	Dyson PI	North SS	Hopkins RA	Goodman DR	Paskin WJ	Palmer CL	Anderson CR	Gray AM	Hodson SP	Burrows D	Robson G	Whyte CA	Cork D	Phillips SG	Durnin JP	Dobbins LW	Bradshaw PW	Rice B	Cartwright NA	Bartlett KF	West C	Walford SJ	Ford T	Banks IF	Raven PD	Robinson R	Easter G	
		3	4		6	7	8	12	10	**11**				9	5				2	1											R3
	11	3	4		6	7	**8**	12	10					9	5				2	1											R3
	1	2	2		2	2	2		2	1				2	2				2	2											
								2																							
										1																					

Naylor SW	Bradley DM	Albiston AR	Talbot BE	Dyson PI	North SS	Hopkins RA	Goodman DR	Paskin WJ	Palmer CL	Anderson CR	Gray AM	Hodson SP	Burrows D	Robson G	Whyte CA	Cork D	Phillips SG	Durnin JP	Dobbins LW	Bradshaw PW	Rice B	Cartwright NA	Bartlett KF	West C	Walford SJ	Ford T	Banks IF	Raven PD	Robinson R	Easter G	
1	2	3		5	6	7	**8**	9	10	11	4			12																	R1/1
1					6	7	8		10	11	**9**	2	3	4	5															12	R1/2
2	1	1		1	2	2	2	1	2	2	2	1	1	1	1																
														1																1	
									1		1																				

1989-90

Division Two

	P	W	D	L	F	A	Pts
Leeds United	46	24	13	9	79	52	85
Sheffield United	46	24	13	9	78	58	85
Newcastle United	46	22	14	10	80	55	80
Swindon Town	46	20	14	12	79	59	74
Blackburn Rovers	46	19	17	10	74	59	74
Sunderland	46	20	14	12	70	64	74
West Ham United	46	20	12	14	80	57	72
Oldham Athletic	46	19	14	13	70	57	71
Ipswich Town	46	19	12	15	67	66	69
Wolverhampton W	46	18	13	15	67	60	67
Port Vale	46	15	16	15	62	57	61
Portsmouth	46	15	16	15	62	65	61
Leicester City	46	15	14	17	67	79	59
Hull City	46	14	16	16	58	65	58
Watford	46	14	15	17	58	60	57
Plymouth Argyle	46	14	13	19	58	63	55
Oxford United	46	15	9	22	57	66	54
Brighton & Hove Albion	46	15	9	22	56	72	54
Barnsley	46	13	15	18	49	71	54
West Bromwich Albion	46	12	15	19	67	71	51
Middlesbrough	46	13	11	22	52	63	50
Bournemouth	46	12	12	22	57	76	48
Bradford City	46	9	14	23	44	68	41
Stoke City	46	6	19	21	35	63	37

Manager: Brian Talbot

- Albion trailed Bradford City 3–1 after the first leg of their League Cup tie, but stormed back to win the return game 5–3 and went through on the away-goals rule after a 6–6 aggregate score.
- During the course of the season, new manager Brian Talbot used four different goalkeepers: Paul Bradshaw, Andy Marriott, Stuart Naylor and Gavin Ward.
- Striker Don Goodman became the first Albion player since 1970–71 to score over 20 League goals in a season.
- Gary Bannister was signed from Coventry City, Steve Parkin from Stoke City, Craig Shakespeare for £275,000 from Sheffield Wednesday and Bernard McNally from Shrewsbury Town. Chris Whyte joined Leeds United for £450,000 and fellow defender Martyn Bennett moved to Worcester City after 13 years and 218 senior appearances for Albion, his last in the 7–0 home win over Barnsley.

Match No.	Date			Opponents	Result		Scorers	Attendance
1	Aug	19	H	Sheffield United	L	0-3		14,907
2		22	A	Bournemouth	D	1-1	Goodman	8,226
3		26	A	Port Vale	L	1-2	Whyte	7,695
4	Sep	2	H	Sunderland	D	1-1	Goodman	10,885
5		9	A	Leicester City	W	3-1	Whyte, Goodman, West	10,700
6		16	H	Oxford United	W	3-2	Greenall (og), Bradley, Robson	9,628
7		23	A	Oldham Athletic	L	1-2	West	6,907
8		27	H	Blackburn Rovers	D	2-2	Ford, Goodman	9,269
9		30	A	West Ham United	W	3-2	Ford, McNally 2 (1 pen)	19,842
10	Oct	7	A	Watford	W	2-0	Whyte, Thomas	10,444
11		15	H	Wolverhampton Wanderers	L	1-2	Talbot	21,316
12		17	A	Stoke City	L	1-2	Bartlett	11,991
13		21	H	Hull City	D	1-1	Parkin	9,228
14		28	A	Middlesbrough	D	0-0		14,076
15	Nov	1	H	Newcastle United	L	1-5	Goodman	12,339
16		4	A	Ipswich Town	L	1-3	Goodman	11,887
17		11	H	Barnsley	W	7-0	Ford, Goodman 3, McNally (pen), Bartlett 2	9,317
18		18	A	Portsmouth	D	1-1	McNally (pen)	9,069
19		25	H	Leeds United	W	2-1	Goodman, Bartlett	15,116
20	Dec	2	A	Sheffield United	L	1-3	Robson	14,094
21		9	H	Bournemouth	D	2-2	Goodman, Bartlett	8,568
22		17	H	Swindon Town	L	1-2	Goodman (pen)	9,884
23		26	A	Plymouth Argyle	D	2-2	Goodman 2	9,782
24		30	A	Bradford City	L	0-2		8,560
25	Jan	1	H	Brighton & Hove Albion	W	3-0	West, Robson, Bartlett	9,407
26		13	H	Port Vale	L	2-3	Ford, Goodman	13,575
27		20	A	Sunderland	D	1-1	Robson	15,569
28	Feb	3	H	Oldham Athletic	D	2-2	West, Robson	12,237
29		10	A	Oxford United	W	1-0	Shakespeare	6,750
30		21	H	Leicester City	L	0-1		10,902
31		24	A	Leeds United	D	2-2	Goodman, Bartlett	30,531
32	Mar	3	H	Portsmouth	D	0-0		10,502
33		10	A	Blackburn Rovers	L	1-2	Ford	8,148
34		14	H	Bradford City	W	2-0	Ford, McNally	8,017
35		17	H	Watford	W	2-0	Whyte, Hackett	9,915
36		20	A	Wolverhampton Wanderers	L	1-2	Foster	24,475
37		24	H	Stoke City	D	1-1	Ford	12,771
38		31	A	Hull City	W	2-0	Goodman, Hackett	5,418
39	Apr	4	H	West Ham United	L	1-3	Goodman	11,556
40		7	H	Middlesbrough	D	0-0		9,458
41		11	A	Newcastle United	L	1-2	Goodman	19,471
42		14	A	Brighton & Hove Albion	W	3-0	Ford, Goodman, Bannister	8,371
43		16	H	Plymouth Argyle	L	0-3		9,728
44		21	A	Swindon Town	L	1-2	Goodman	8,495
45		28	A	Barnsley	D	2-2	Tiler (og), Bradley	10,334
46	May	5	H	Ipswich Town	L	1-3	Bannister	11,567

Appearances
Sub appearances
Goals

FA Cup

R3	Jan	6	H	Wimbledon	W	2-0	Robson, Bartlett	12,986
R4		27	H	Charlton Athletic	W	1-0	Ford	18,172
R5	Feb	17	H	Aston Villa	L	0-2		26,585

Appearances
Sub appearances
Goals

League Cup

R2/1	Sep	20	H	Bradford City	L	1-3	McNally	7,771
R2/2	Oct	4	A	Bradford City	W	5-3*	Talbot, Whyte, Thomas 3	5,731
R3		25	A	Newcastle United	W	1-0	Whyte	22,639
R4	Nov	22	A	Derby County	L	0-2		21,313

R2 won on away-goals rule after extra-time in second leg

Appearances
Sub appearances
Goals

	Bradshaw PW	Bradley DM	Parkin SJ	Talbot BE	Whyte CA	North SS	Ford T	Goodman DR	West C	McNally BA	Anderson CR	Robson G	Thomas JW	Burgess D	Marriott A	Naylor SW	Barham MF	Bartlett KF	Hodson SP	Allardyce S	Harbey GK	Bennett M	Raven PD	Andersen V	Dobbins LW	Cartwright NA	Foster AM	Shakespeare CR	Hackett GS	Bannister G	Ward G
1	1	2	3	**4**	5	6	7	8	9	10	11	12	13																		
2	1	2	3		5	6	7	8	**9**	10	11	4	12																		
3	1	6	3	12	5		7	8	9	**10**	11	4	13	2																	
4	1	6	3	12	5		7	**8**	9	10	11	4	13	2																	
5		6	3	12	5		7	8	9	10	11	**4**		2	1																
6		6	3		5	12	7	8	9	10	11	4	13	**2**	1																
7		2			5	6	7	8	9	10	**11**	4	12	3	1																
8		2		12	5	6	7	8	**9**	10	11	4	13	3		1															
9		2		12	5	6	7	8		10	11	**4**	9	3		1															
10		2		4	5	6	11			10			9	3		1	7	8													
11		**2**		4	5	6	11	8		10		12	9	3		1	7														
12			2	12	5	6	7	8		10		**4**	9	3		1	11	13													
13			2	12	5	6	7	8		10		4	9	3		1		**11**													
14			2	4	5	6	7	8		10		11	9			1			3												
15			2	4	5	6	7	8		10		**11**	9			1		12	3	13											
16				4	5	6	11	8		10			12	2		1	**7**	9	3												
17			11	4	6		7	8		10			13	12		1		9	2		3	**5**									
18			11	4	6		7	8		10						1		9	2		3		5								
19			11	**4**	6		7	8		10		12		2		1		9			3		5								
20			11	**4**	6		7	8		10		12	13	2		1		9			3		5								
21					6		7	8	12	10	11	4		2		1		**9**			3		5	13							
22					6	12	7	8	9	10	11	4		2		1		13			3		**5**								
23					6	5	7	8	9	10	11	**4**				1		13			3				2	12					
24					6	5	7	8		**10**	11	4	9			1		13			3				2	12					
25					6	5	7	8	9	10		4				1		11			3				2						
26					6		7	8	9	10		4				1		11			3		5		2						
27				13	6		7	8	9	10		4		12		1		11			3		5		**2**						
28					6	5	**7**		9	10		4		2		1		11			3					12	8				
29					6	5			9	10		4		2		1		11			3						8	7			
30		13		4	6	5		8	**9**	10				2		1					3					11	12	7			
31		4				5		8	12	10				6		1		11	2		3						**9**	7			
32		4				5		**8**	9	10				6		1		11	2		3							**7**	12		
33					13	5	7		**9**	10				6		1			2		3						12	4	11	8	
34		12			6	5	7			**10**				2		1					3						9	4	11	8	
35		10			6	5	7							2		1					3						9	4	11	8	
36		10			6	5	7		12					2		1					3					13	**8**	4	11	9	
37		10			6	5	7	8						2		1					3							4	11	9	
38		10			6	5	7	8						**2**		1					3					12		4	11	9	
39		2			6	5	7	8								1					3					10	12	4	**11**	9	
40		2			6	5	7	8		10						1					3							4	11	9	
41		2			6	5	7	8		10				13		1					3						12	4	11	**9**	
42		11			6	5	7	8		10				2		1					3						12	4		**9**	
43		11			6	5	7	8		10				**2**		1					3						13	4	12	9	
44		11			6	5	7	8		10						1			2		3						9	**4**	12		
45		11			6		7	8		10				5		1			2		3							4	12	9	
46		**2**		4	6		7	8		10				5		1					3						13	11	12	9	
	4	25	14	12	43	32	42	39	18	41	13	21	8	31	3	39	4	15	10		30	1	7		5	2	7	18	9	13	
		2		8	1	2			3			4	10	3				5		1				1		5	7		5		
		2	1	1	4		8	21	4	5		5	1					7									1	1	2	2	

Two own-goals

	Bradshaw PW	Bradley DM	Parkin SJ	Talbot BE	Whyte CA	North SS	Ford T	Goodman DR	West C	McNally BA	Anderson CR	Robson G	Thomas JW	Burgess D	Marriott A	Naylor SW	Barham MF	Bartlett KF	Hodson SP	Allardyce S	Harbey GK	Bennett M	Raven PD	Andersen V	Dobbins LW	Cartwright NA	Foster AM	Shakespeare CR	Hackett GS	Bannister G	Ward G
R3					6	5	7	8	9	10		4				1		11			3				2						
R4				12	6	5	7	8	9	10		**4**		2		1		11			3						13				
R5				12	6	5		8	9	10		**4**		2		1		11			3						13	7			
					3	3	2	3	3	3		3		2		3		3			3				1			1			
				2																							2				
							1					1						1													

	Bradshaw PW	Bradley DM	Parkin SJ	Talbot BE	Whyte CA	North SS	Ford T	Goodman DR	West C	McNally BA	Anderson CR	Robson G	Thomas JW	Burgess D	Marriott A	Naylor SW	Barham MF	Bartlett KF	Hodson SP	Allardyce S	Harbey GK	Bennett M	Raven PD	Andersen V	Dobbins LW	Cartwright NA	Foster AM	Shakespeare CR	Hackett GS	Bannister G	Ward G
R2/1		2	**3**		5	6	7	8	9	10	11	4		12																	1
R2/2		2		4	5	6		**8**		10			9	3		1	7	11									12				
R3			2	4	5	6	7	8		10	12	**11**	9			1			3												
R4			11	4	6		7	8		10				12		1		9	**2**		3		5								
		2	3	3	4	3	3	4	1	4	1	2	2	1		3	1	2	2		1		1								1
											1			2													1				
				1	2					1			3																		

1990-91

Division Two

	P	W	D	L	F	A	Pts
Oldham Athletic	46	25	13	8	83	53	88
West Ham United	46	24	15	7	60	34	87
Sheffield Wednesday	46	22	16	8	80	51	82
Notts County	46	23	11	12	76	55	80
Millwall	46	20	13	13	70	51	73
Brighton & Hove Albion	46	21	7	18	63	69	70
Middlesbrough	46	20	9	17	66	47	69
Barnsley	46	19	12	15	63	48	69
Bristol City	46	20	7	19	68	71	67
Oxford United	46	14	19	13	69	66	61
Newcastle United	46	14	17	15	49	56	59
Wolverhampton W	46	13	19	14	63	63	58
Bristol Rovers	46	15	13	18	56	59	58
Ipswich Town	46	13	18	15	60	68	57
Port Vale	46	15	12	19	56	64	57
Charlton Athletic	46	13	17	16	57	61	56
Portsmouth	46	14	11	21	58	70	53
Plymouth Argyle	46	12	17	17	54	68	53
Blackburn Rovers	46	14	10	22	51	66	52
Watford	46	12	15	19	45	59	51
Swindon Town	46	12	14	20	65	73	50
Leicester City	46	14	8	24	60	83	50
West Bromwich Albion	46	10	18	18	52	61	48
Hull City	46	10	15	21	57	85	45

Manager: Brian Talbot the Bobby Gould

- Albion crashed through the trapdoor and into the Third Division for the first time in the club's history after drawing seven of their last eight League games. A win on the final day at Bristol Rovers would have saved them from the drop. This season surpassed the horrible 1985–86 campaign as non-League Woking dumped the Baggies out of the FA Cup in the third round, which led to the dismissal of manager Brian Talbot, who was replaced by ex-player Bobby Gould.
- Graham Roberts from Tottenham Hotspur and Garry Strodder from West Ham United were two players signed by Talbot before his departure. Stacey North joined Fulham and was forced to retire, injured, in 1993 at the age of 28.
- Albion's reserve side won the Pontins League Division Two Championship.

Match No.	Date			Opponents	Result		Scorers	Attendance
1	Aug	25	A	Portsmouth	D	1-1	Ford	12,008
2	Sep	1	H	Ipswich Town	L	1-2	Bannister	10,311
3		8	A	Oxford United	W	3-1	Bannister, West 2	5,294
4		15	H	Bristol City	W	2-1	Harbey, Bannister	12,081
5		22	A	Hull City	D	1-1	McNally	5,953
6		29	H	Oldham Athletic	D	0-0		13,782
7	Oct	2	A	Plymouth Argyle	L	0-2		5,617
8		6	A	Millwall	L	1-4	West	10,781
9		13	H	Brighton & Hove Albion	D	1-1	Gatting (og)	9,833
10		20	H	Barnsley	D	1-1	West (pen)	9,577
11		22	A	Port Vale	W	2-1	Bannister, West (pen)	8,824
12		27	A	Newcastle United	D	1-1	Anderson	14,944
13	Nov	3	H	Bristol Rovers	W	3-1	West 2, Anderson	10,997
14		6	H	Middlesbrough	L	0-1		10,512
15		10	A	Notts County	L	3-4	Bannister 2, Bradley	8,162
16		17	H	Blackburn Rovers	W	2-0	Bannister, West	10,985
17		24	H	Sheffield Wednesday	L	1-2	Robson	16,546
18	Dec	1	A	West Ham United	L	1-3	Ford	24,755
19		5	H	Watford	D	1-1	Roberts (pen)	7,657
20		15	H	Portsmouth	D	0-0		7,856
21		22	A	Swindon Town	L	1-2	Roberts (pen)	8,256
22		26	H	Charlton Athletic	W	1-0	Goodman	9,305
23		29	H	Wolverhampton Wanderers	D	1-1	Bannister	28,310
24	Jan	1	A	Leicester City	L	1-2	Ford	12,210
25		12	A	Ipswich Town	L	0-1		10,882
26		19	H	Oxford United	W	2-0	Bannister, Shakespeare	8,017
27	Feb	2	A	Bristol City	L	0-2		11,492
28		16	A	Blackburn Rovers	W	3-0	Robson, Goodman 2	7,695
29		19	A	Middlesbrough	L	2-3	Bannister 2	15,273
30		23	H	Notts County	D	2-2	Bannister 2	11,068
31	Mar	2	H	West Ham United	D	0-0		16,089
32		9	A	Sheffield Wednesday	L	0-1		26,934
33		13	H	Plymouth Argyle	L	1-2	Palmer	8,673
34		16	A	Oldham Athletic	L	1-2	Ford	12,584
35		20	A	Brighton & Hove Albion	L	0-2		6,676
36		23	H	Millwall	L	0-1		9,116
37		30	A	Charlton Athletic	L	0-2		5,606
38	Apr	1	H	Swindon Town	W	2-1	Roberts (pen), Parkin	10,415
39		6	A	Wolverhampton Wanderers	D	2-2	Ford, Goodman	22,982
40		10	H	Hull City	D	1-1	Roberts	10,356
41		13	H	Leicester City	W	2-1	Goodman, White	13,991
42		20	A	Barnsley	D	1-1	Strodder	9,594
43		23	A	Watford	D	1-1	Goodman	15,054
44		27	H	Port Vale	D	1-1	Goodman	13,650
45	May	4	H	Newcastle United	D	1-1	Goodman	16,706
46		11	A	Bristol Rovers	D	1-1	Ampadu	7,595

Appearances
Sub appearances
Goals

FA Cup

R3	Jan	5	H	Woking	L	2-4	Bradley, West	14,516

Appearances
Sub appearances
Goals

League Cup

R1/1	Aug	29	H	Bristol City	D	2-2	Bannister, Hackett	8,721
R1/2	Sep	5	A	Bristol City	L	0-1*		9,851

* after extra-time

Appearances
Sub appearances
Goals

Naylor SW	Hodson SP	Harbey GK	Robson G	Burgess D	Strodder GJ	Ford T	Goodman DR	Bannister G	Bradley DM	Shakespeare CR	Hackett GS	West C	McNally BA	Hawker PN	Raven PD	Ehiogu U	Anderson CR	Foster AM	Dobbins LW	Palmer LJ	Roberts GP	Parkin SJ	Rees MJ	Rogers DJ	Williams PA	White EW	Ampadu PK	
1	2	3	**4**	5	6	7	8	9	10	11	12																	1
1	2	3	4	5	6	7		9	10	**11**	12	8																2
1	2	3	4	**5**	6	7		9	10	11		8	12															3
1	2	3	**4**		6	7	12	9	5	11		8	10															4
1	2		4			7	12	9	5	11		**8**	10	3	6	13												5
1	2	3	4		6	7		9	5	11		8	10															6
1	2	3	4		6	7		9	5	**11**	12	8	10															7
1		3	4		6	**7**		9	5	11	12	8	10		2		13											8
1		3	4	2	6	7		**9**	5			8	10				11	12	13									9
1		3	4	2	6	7		9	5			8	10				11											10
1		3	4	2	6	7		9	5			8	10				11											11
1		3	4	2	6	7		9	5			8	10				**11**		12									12
1		3	4	2	6	7		9	**5**	13		8	10				11		12									13
1	12		**4**	2	6	7		9	5	11		8	10						3									14
1	12		4	2	6	7		9	5			8	10				11		**3**	13								15
1		3	2		6	7	12	**9**	5			8	10				11				4							16
1		3	2	13	6	7	12	**9**	5			8	10				11				4							17
1		3	2		6	7	12	9	5			8					**11**				4	10						18
1		3	2	6		7	**8**	9	5	13		12					11				4	10						19
1	13	3	2			7	**8**	12	5			9	10		6		11				4							20
1	2	3	9			7	**8**	12	5				10		6		11				4	13						21
1		3	11		6	7	**8**	9	5	2		12	10								4	13						22
1		3	11		6	7		9	5	2		8	10								4							23
1		3	11		6	7		9	5	2		**8**	10							12	4	13						24
	13				6	7		9		2		12	10		5		3			**11**	4	8	1					25
	2				5	7		10		11		9			6		3				4	8	1					26
	2				5	7	8	9		11					6		3				4	10	1					27
	2		**10**	5	13	7	8	9	6	11			12								4	3	1					28
	2		10	5		7	**8**	9	6	11			12								4	3	1					29
	2		10	5	13	7		9	6	3			12				11				4	**8**	1					30
	2		10	6		7		9	5	3							11				4	8	1					31
	2			5	13	7		9		**3**		10	12				11		6		4	8	1					32
	2		3	5		7		9		13					12		11		6	**10**	4	8	1					33
	2		13	5		7		9	11	3								12	6	**10**	4	8	1					34
	2			5	10	7		9	6	3	12							**8**		11	4		1	13				35
	2				5	7		9	6	10		8			4	13		12		**11**			1	3				36
					5	7	10		6	3					4							8	1	2	9	**11**	12	37
				5		7	10	8	2	11					12		3				4	6	1		9			38
	2			5		7	10	**8**	13	11							3				4	6	1		9	12		39
	2			5		7	**10**	8		11		12					3				4	6	1		9			40
	2			5		7	12	**8**	3	11											4	6	1		9	10	13	41
	2				13	7	**8**	12	3	11											4	6	1		9	10	5	42
1	2				5	7	8			11					3						4	6			9	**10**	12	43
1	2		**10**		5	7	8	12	3	14											4	6			9		11	44
1	2			4	5	7	8	12	3	10												6			9	13	**11**	45
1					5	7		12	3	11		**10**			2			8				6		4	9		13	46
28	26	21	30	24	30	46	16	38	38	32		24	20	1	11		22	2	5	5	27	22	18	3	10	4	3	
	4		1	1	4		6	6	1	4	5	4	5		2	2	1	3	3	2		3		1		2	4	
		1	2		1	5	8	13	1	1		8	1				2			1	4	1				1	1	

One own-goal

Naylor SW	Hodson SP	Harbey GK	Robson G	Burgess D	Strodder GJ	Ford T	Goodman DR	Bannister G	Bradley DM	Shakespeare CR	Hackett GS	West C	McNally BA	Hawker PN	Raven PD	Ehiogu U	Anderson CR	Foster AM	Dobbins LW	Palmer LJ	Roberts GP	Parkin SJ	Rees MJ	Rogers DJ	Williams PA	White EW	Ampadu PK	
		3	11		6	7		9	5	2		8	10							12	4		1					R3
		1	1		1	1		1	1	1		1	1								1		1					
																				1								
									1			1																

Naylor SW	Hodson SP	Harbey GK	Robson G	Burgess D	Strodder GJ	Ford T	Goodman DR	Bannister G	Bradley DM	Shakespeare CR	Hackett GS	West C	McNally BA	Hawker PN	Raven PD	Ehiogu U	Anderson CR	Foster AM	Dobbins LW	Palmer LJ	Roberts GP	Parkin SJ	Rees MJ	Rogers DJ	Williams PA	White EW	Ampadu PK	
	12		**10**	11				9		8	6	2	3				7	5	1				4					R1/1
	12		10	11		13		9			6	2	3				7	5	1				**4**		8			R1/2
			2	2				2		1	2	2	2				2	2	2				2		1			
	2					1																						
								1			1																	

1991-92

Division Three

	P	W	D	L	F	A	Pts
Brentford	46	25	7	14	81	55	82
Birmingham City	46	23	12	11	69	52	81
Huddersfield Town	46	22	12	12	59	38	78
Stoke City	46	21	14	11	69	49	77
Stockport County	46	22	10	14	75	51	76
Peterborough United	46	20	14	12	65	58	74
West Bromwich Albion	46	19	14	13	64	49	71
Bournemouth	46	20	11	15	52	48	71
Fulham	46	19	13	14	57	53	70
Leyton Orient	46	18	11	17	62	52	65
Hartlepool United	46	18	11	17	57	57	65
Reading	46	16	13	17	59	62	61
Bolton Wanderers	46	14	17	15	57	56	59
Hull City	46	16	11	19	54	54	59
Wigan Athletic	46	15	14	17	58	64	59
Bradford City	46	13	19	14	62	61	58
Preston North End	46	15	12	19	61	72	57
Chester City	46	14	14	18	56	59	56
Swansea City	46	14	14	18	55	65	56
Exeter City	46	14	11	21	57	80	53
Bury	46	13	12	21	55	74	51
Shrewsbury Town	46	12	11	23	53	68	47
Torquay United	46	13	8	25	42	68	47
Darlington	46	10	7	29	56	90	37

Manager: Bobby Gould

- Albion beat Exeter City 6–3 in their first ever game in Division Three, and by finishing seventh in the final table the Baggies claimed their lowest ever League placing.
- Bobby Gould made his best signing as manager, recruiting striker Bob Taylor from Bristol City. Taylor, replacing Don Goodman who was sold to Sunderland, scored on his debut against Brentford, the first of 131 goals he would net for the club overall.
- Graham Roberts left The Hawthorns to become player-manager of Enfield, and Steve Parkin joined Mansfield Town.

Match No.	Date			Opponents	Result		Scorers	Attendance
1	Aug	17	H	Exeter City	W	6-3	Goodman 2, Foster, Shakespeare 2 (2 pens), Williams	12,892
2		24	A	Darlington	W	1-0	Goodman	5,658
3		31	H	Wigan Athletic	D	1-1	McNally	12,053
4	Sep	3	A	Fulham	D	0-0		4,523
5		7	A	Bolton Wanderers	L	0-3		7,980
6		14	H	Stockport County	W	1-0	Williams	11,845
7		17	H	Peterborough United	W	4-0	Williams, Robson 2, Bowen	10,037
8		21	A	Chester City	W	2-1	Burgess, Robson	3,895
9		28	H	Hull City	W	1-0	Burgess	11,932
10	Oct	1	A	Preston North End	L	0-2		5,292
11		12	H	Shrewsbury Town	W	2-0	Goodman, West	12,437
12		19	A	Brentford	W	2-1	Goodman, Ampadu	8,575
13		26	H	Birmingham City	L	0-1		26,168
14	Nov	2	H	Bury	D	1-1	Robson	8,439
15		5	A	Hartlepool United	D	0-0		2,970
16		9	A	Reading	W	2-1	Goodman, Robson	5,826
17		23	H	Huddersfield Town	W	2-1	Harbey, Robson	14,029
18		30	H	Stoke City	D	2-2	Goodman, Shakespeare	17,207
19	Dec	14	A	Bradford City	D	1-1	Bradley	7,195
20		22	H	Darlington	W	3-1	Strodder, Sinclair, Fereday	13,261
21		26	A	Wigan Athletic	W	1-0	Shakespeare (pen)	5,068
22		28	A	Exeter City	D	1-1	Shakespeare (pen)	5,830
23	Jan	1	H	Fulham	L	2-3	Shakespeare (pen), Robson	16,442
24		4	A	Torquay United	L	0-1		4,159
25		11	H	Bournemouth	W	4-0	Bannister 2, Williams, Robson	10,932
26		18	A	Leyton Orient	D	1-1	Bradley	6,328
27		25	H	Swansea City	L	2-3	Roberts 2 (1 pen)	10,395
28	Feb	1	H	Brentford	W	2-0	Fereday, Taylor	15,984
29		8	A	Birmingham City	W	3-0	Robson, Taylor 2	27,508
30		12	A	Stoke City	L	0-1		23,626
31		15	H	Bradford City	D	1-1	Shakespeare	12,607
32		22	A	Bournemouth	L	1-2	Taylor	7,721
33		29	H	Torquay United	W	1-0	Hunter	11,669
34	Mar	3	H	Leyton Orient	L	1-3	Bannister	11,276
35		6	A	Swansea City	D	0-0		5,629
36		11	H	Hartlepool United	L	1-2	Williams	10,307
37		14	A	Bury	D	1-1	Taylor	3,810
38		21	H	Reading	W	2-0	Strodder, Raven	10,707
39		28	A	Huddersfield Town	L	0-3		7,428
40		31	A	Stockport County	L	0-3		6,090
41	Apr	4	H	Bolton Wanderers	D	2-2	Ampadu, Taylor	10,287
42		11	A	Peterborough United	D	0-0		9,040
43		18	H	Chester City	D	1-1	Rogers	10,137
44		20	A	Hull City	L	0-1		4,815
45		25	H	Preston North End	W	3-0	Ampadu, West, Taylor	11,318
46	May	2	A	Shrewsbury Town	W	3-1	Strodder, Shakespeare, Taylor	7,442
								Appearances
								Sub appearances
								Goals

FA Cup

R1	Nov	16	H	Marlow	W	6-0	Shakespeare 2 (1 pen), Strodder, McNally, Goodman, Robson	11,082
R2	Dec	9	A	Leyton Orient	L	1-2	Williams	6,189
								Appearances
								Sub appearances
								Goals

League Cup

R1/1	Aug	20	A	Swindon Town	L	0-2		6,611
R1/2		28	H	Swindon Town	D	2-2	Goodman, Shakespeare	8,522
								Appearances
								Sub appearances
								Goals

Miller AJ	Bradley DM	Harbey GK	Ford T	Strodder GJ	Burgess D	Bannister G	Goodman DR	Foster AM	Shakespeare CR	Ampadu PK	Williams PA	McNally BA	Piggott GD	Hodson SP	Naylor SW	Parkin SJ	Robson G	Bowen SA	Pritchard DM	Palmer L	Hackett GS	West C	White EW	Rogers DJ	Sinclair FM	Fereday W	Roberts GP	Taylor R	Dibble AG	Raven PD	Hunter RI	Cartwright NA	Heggs CS	
1	2	3	4	5	6	7	8	9	10	11	12	13																						1
1	2	3	4	5	6		8		10	11	12	7	9																					2
1	2	3	4	5		8		12	10	11	9	7		6																				3
	2	3	4	5	6	8		11	10	12	9	7			1	13																		4
		3	4	5	6			9	10	11	12	7	8		1	2																		5
		3	4	5	6	7			10		12			2	1	8	9	11	13															6
		3	4	5	6				10		7			2	1	8	9	11		12	13													7
	13	3	4	5	6				10		7		12	2	1	8	9	11																8
		3	4	5	6		7		10		12			2	1	8	9	11	13															9
		3	4	5	6				10		8			2	1	7	9	11	12															10
		3	4	5	6		8		10		13			2	1	7		11	12			9												11
	7	3	4	5	6		8		10	11		12		2	1							9												12
	6	3	4	5			8		10	11	12	7		2	1							9												13
	13	3	4	5	6		8		10					2	1		12	11	7			9												14
	7	3	4	5	6	12	8		10	11				2	1		9																	15
	4	3		5	6	12	8		10			7		2	1		9				13		11											16
	4	3		5	6		8		10		12	7		2	1		9						11											17
	4	3		5	6		8		10		12	7			1	2	9						11	13										18
	4	3		5					10	12	8	7		6	1		9								2	11								19
	4	3		5	6	12			10		8	7			1		9								2	11								20
	4	3		5	6			13	10	12	8	7			1		9								2	11								21
	4	3		5				9	10	12	8	7		6	1								11	13	2									22
	4	3		5					10	12	8	7			1		9						11	6	2	13								23
	4	3				9			10	12	8	7		11	1									6	2	13	5							24
	4	3		5	6	8			10	11	12			2	1		9						13			7								25
	4	3		5	6	8								2	1		9				11					7	10							26
	4	3		5	6	8			12		13			2	1		9				11					7	10							27
	4	3			6				5		13	12		2	1		9				11					7	10	8						28
	4	3			6				5			12		2	1		9				11					7	10	8						29
	4	3			6	12			5					2	1		9				11					7	10	8						30
	4	3			6			12	5					2	1		9				11			13		7	10	8						31
	4	3			6			12	5					2	1		9	11						13		7	10	8						32
	4	3			6				5		12						9						11			7	10	8	1	2	13			33
	4	3			6	9			5		12	11														7	10	8	1	2	13			34
	4	3			6	9			5			11					7										10	8	1	2				35
	4	3		5	6	9			13		12	11					7									2	10	8	1					36
		3		4	6				5		9												10					8	1	2		7	11	37
	4	3		5	6				10		12												7					8	1	2	13	9	11	38
	4	3		5	6				10		12						13						7					8	1	2		9	11	39
		3		5	6				10	11	12			2			9				7							8	1	13	4			40
	4	3		5	6				10	11	9										7					12		8	1		2			41
	4	3		5	6				10	11	9				1		12				7					2		8						42
	4	3		5					10	11	9				1		6				7	12		13		2		8						43
	4	3		5					10	11	9				1		6				7	12		13		2		8						44
	4	3		5						11			12		1		10				7	9		6		2		8			13			45
		3		5					4	11			9		1		10				7			6		2		8						46
3	35	46	15	37	36	11	11	4	42	15	16	17	3	25	34	8	29	8	1		13	5	9	4	6	19	12	19	9	6	2	3	3	
	2					4		4	2	6	18	4	2			1	3		4	1	2	2	1	6		3				1	4			
	2	1		3	2	3	7	1	8	3	5	1					9	1				2		1	1	2	2	8		1	1			

	4	3	2	5	6		8		10		12	7			1		9						11	13										R1
	4	3		5	6	12			10		8	7		2	1		9						11											R2
	2	2	1	2	2		1		2		1	2		1	2		2						2											
						1					1													1										
				1			1		2		1	1					1																	

	2	3	4	5	6	7	8	9	10	11	13	12			1																			R1/1
	2	3	4	5	6	13	8	12	10	11	9	7			1																			R1/2
	2	2	2	2	2	1	2	1	2	2	1	1			2																			
						1		1			1	1																						
							1		1																									

1992-93

Division Two

	P	W	D	L	F	A	Pts
Stoke City	46	27	12	7	73	34	93
Bolton Wanderers	46	27	9	10	80	41	90
Port Vale	46	26	11	9	79	44	89
West Bromwich Albion	46	25	10	11	88	54	85
Swansea City	46	20	13	13	65	47	73
Stockport County	46	19	15	12	81	57	72
Leyton Orient	46	21	9	16	69	53	72
Reading	46	18	15	13	66	51	69
Brighton & Hove Albion	46	20	9	17	63	59	69
Bradford City	46	18	14	14	69	67	68
Rotherham United	46	17	14	15	60	60	65
Fulham	46	16	17	13	57	55	65
Burnley	46	15	16	15	57	59	61
Plymouth Argyle	46	16	12	18	59	64	60
Huddersfield Town	46	17	9	20	54	61	60
Hartlepool United	46	14	12	20	42	60	54
Bournemouth	46	12	17	17	45	52	53
Blackpool	46	12	15	19	63	75	51
Exeter City	46	11	17	18	54	69	50
Hull City	46	13	11	22	46	69	50
Preston North End	46	13	8	25	65	94	47
Mansfield Town	46	11	11	24	52	80	44
Wigan Athletic	46	10	11	25	43	72	41
Chester City	46	8	5	33	49	102	29

Manager: Ossies Ardiles

- The Argentinian World Cup winner Ossie Ardiles was named Albion's new manager in May 1992, and in his first season he guided the Baggies to promotion via the Play-off Final at Wembley against Port Vale when, backed by the biggest ever away following, over 42,000 saw Albion win 3–0.
- Kevin Donovan (signed from Huddersfield Town) became the first Albion player to score a hat-trick in an FA Cup tie since January 1974 – his treble helping the team beat Aylesbury United 8–0 – their biggest win, in League or Cup, for 36 years.
- Taylor also became the first Albion player since Tony Brown in 1970–71 to score 30 goals in a season.
- Ian Hamilton was signed from Scunthorpe United and Andy Hunt from Newcastle United. The latter scored on his home debut against Brighton & Hove Albion and also in the Play-off Final at Wembley. Gary Robson joined Bradford City after scoring 35 goals in 282 appearances for Albion, and Colin West switched his allegiance to Swansea City (he was sent off in the Play-off semi-final game at The Hawthorns).
- Local businessman Trevor Summers became Albion's chairman. He held office for two seasons.

Match No.	Date			Opponents	Result		Scorers	Attendance
1	Aug	15	H	Blackpool	W	3-1	Taylor 2, McNally	16,527
2		22	A	Huddersfield Town	W	1-0	Garner	7,947
3		29	H	Bournemouth	W	2-1	Shakespeare (pen), Taylor	12,563
4	Sep	2	H	Stockport County	W	3-0	Garner 2, Hamilton	12,305
5		5	A	Fulham	D	1-1	Taylor	9,143
6		9	H	Reading	W	3-0	Shakespeare, Garner, Taylor	13,164
7		15	A	Bolton Wanderers	W	2-0	Taylor 2	8,531
8		19	A	Stoke City	L	3-4	Garner, Taylor 2	18,756
9		26	H	Exeter City	W	2-0	Hamilton, McNally	14,676
10	Oct	3	A	Burnley	L	1-2	Garner	14,816
11		10	H	Port Vale	L	0-1		17,512
12		17	A	Wigan Athletic	L	0-1		4,308
13		24	H	Rotherham United	D	2-2	Taylor, Donovan	13,170
14		31	A	Hull City	W	2-1	Garner, Bradley	5,443
15	Nov	3	H	Hartlepool United	W	3-1	Taylor, Robson, Blissett	13,046
16		7	A	Leyton Orient	L	0-2		8,633
17		21	H	Bradford City	D	1-1	Raven	15,416
18		28	A	Preston North End	D	1-1	Robson	6,306
19	Dec	12	A	Swansea City	D	0-0		5,763
20		20	H	Mansfield Town	W	2-0	McNally, Dickens	13,134
21		26	H	Chester City	W	2-0	Raven 2	15,209
22		28	A	Plymouth Argyle	D	0-0		11,370
23	Jan	9	H	Bolton Wanderers	W	3-1	Strodder, Hamilton, Taylor	14,581
24		16	A	Exeter City	W	3-2	Hamilton (pen), Hackett, Heggs	5,437
25		23	H	Stoke City	L	1-2	Taylor	29,341
26		26	A	Bournemouth	W	1-0	Speedie	5,687
27		30	H	Huddersfield Town	D	2-2	Donovan, Speedie	13,667
28	Feb	6	A	Blackpool	L	1-2	Taylor	9,386
29		13	H	Fulham	W	4-0	Fereday, Hamilton, Taylor (pen), Mellon	12,859
30		20	A	Stockport County	L	1-5	Taylor	7,181
31		27	A	Port Vale	L	1-2	Hamilton	13,291
32	Mar	6	H	Burnley	W	2-0	Garner, Taylor	15,722
33		10	A	Brighton & Hove Albion	L	1-3	Taylor (pen)	7,440
34		13	H	Leyton Orient	W	2-0	Donovan, Burgess	15,023
35		20	A	Hartlepool United	D	2-2	Hamilton, Raven	3,697
36		24	H	Preston North End	W	3-2	Taylor 2, Mellon	13,270
37		28	A	Bradford City	D	2-2	Taylor (pen), Hunt	6,627
38	Apr	3	H	Brighton & Hove Albion	W	3-1	Hunt 3	13,002
39		7	H	Swansea City	W	3-0	Taylor 2, Hunt	13,401
40		10	A	Chester City	W	3-1	Raven, Donovan, Hunt	4,812
41		12	H	Plymouth Argyle	L	2-5	Taylor, Donovan	16,130
42		17	A	Mansfield Town	W	3-0	Taylor, Heggs, Hunt	6,659
43		21	A	Reading	D	1-1	Taylor	8,026
44		24	H	Wigan Athletic	W	5-1	Taylor 2, Raven, Donovan, Mellon	14,867
45	May	1	A	Rotherham United	W	2-0	Taylor, Raven	8,059
46		8	H	Hull City	W	3-1	Taylor, Hunt 2	20,122

Appearances
Sub appearances
Goals

FA Cup

R1	Nov	14	H	Aylesbury United	W	8-0	Donovan 3, Hamilton, Taylor, McNally, Robson, Raven	12,337
R2	Dec	6	A	Wycombe Wanderers	D	2-2	Taylor, Bradley	6,904
rep		15	H	Wycombe Wanderers	W	1-0	Taylor	17,640
R3	Jan	2	H	West Ham United	L	0-2		25,896

Appearances
Sub appearances
Goals

League Cup

R1/1	Aug	19	H	Plymouth Argyle	W	1-0	Taylor	8,264
R1/2		25	A	Plymouth Argyle	L	0-2		7,880

Appearances
Sub appearances
Goals

	Naylor SW	Fereday W	Lilwall S	Hunter RI	Strodder GJ	Shakespeare CR	Garner S	Hamilton IR	Taylor R	McNally BA	Robson G	Hodson SP	Bradley DM	Ampadu PK	Hackett GS	Raven PD	Coldicott S	Heggs CS	Donovan K	Blissett LL	Burgess D	Reid NS	Dickens AW	Speedie DR	Lange AS	Mellon MJ	Hunt A	Darton SR	Williams PA
1	1	**2**	3	4	5	6	7	8	9	10	11	12																	
2	1		3		5	6	**7**	8	9	10	11	2	4	12															
3	1	2	3		5	6	10	8	9		11		4	12	**7**	13													
4	1		3		5		7	8	9	10	11		4			6	2												
5	1		3		5	12	7	8	9	10	**11**		4			6	2												
6	1		3		5	6	7	8	9		11		4			10	2												
7	1		3		**5**	6	7	8	9	10	11		4		13	2	12												
8	1	13	3			6	7	8	9	10	11		4		12	5	**2**												
9	1	**2**	3			6	7	8	9	10	11		4			5	12	13											
10	1	**2**	3			6	7	8	9	10	11		4			5	12	13											
11	1	**2**	3		6		7	8	9	10	11		4			5	12		13										
12	1		3		6			8	9	10	11		4	12		5	2		**7**										
13	1		3		12	**6**		8	9	10			4	13		5	2		7	11									
14	1	12	3		6		7	8	9	10	13		4	**11**		5	2												
15	1	2	3		6	**7**		8	9	10	12		4			5				11	13								
16	1		3		6			8	9	10	7		4			5				11	2								
17	1		3		6		7	8	9	10			4			5			11		2								
18	1	12	3		6		7	8	9	10	13		4			5	**2**		11										
19	1		3		6		**7**	8	9	10	12		4			5						2	11						
20	1		3		6			8	9	10			4			5			7			2	11						
21	1		3		6	12	13	8	9	10			**4**			5			7			2	11						
22	1		3		6	4	13	8	9	10	11				12	5			7			**2**							
23	1	2	3		6			8	9	10	12		4		**7**	5		13	11										
24	1	2	3			6		8	9	10	12		4		7	**5**		13	11										
25	1	2	3		6			8	9	10			4		12	5		13	**11**					7					
26	1	2	3		6			8	9	10			4		**11**	5			12					7					
27		2	3		6			8	9	10			4		13	5		12	11					**7**	1				
28	1	2	3		6			8	9	**10**			4		12	5			11					7					
29	1	2	3		6			8	9	10			4			5		13	**11**					7		12			
30	1		3		6			8	9	10	2		4	12		5			11					**7**					
31	1		3		6			8	9		**2**		4	12		5		13	11					7		10			
32	1		3				**7**	8	9	4						5	2	12	11		6					10			
33	1		3				7	8	9	4			12			5	2	13	11		6					**10**			
34			3		12		**7**	8	9				4			5			11		6	2			1	10			
35			3		12		7	8	9				4	13		5			11		6	**2**			1	10			
36			3				**7**	8	9				4	13		5		12	11		6	2			1	10			
37			3				**7**	8	9	10			4			5			11		6	2			1	12	13		
38							12	8	9	13			4			5			11		6	2			1	**10**	7	3	
39							12	8	**9**	2			4			5			11		6	13			1	10	7	3	
40			3					8	9	2			4			5		12	11		6	13			1	10	**7**		
41			3					8	9	2			4			5		12	11		6	13			1	**10**	7		
42			3					**8**	9	4				12		5		13	11		6	2			1	10	7		
43			3					8	9	2			4			5		12	11		6	13			1	10	**7**		
44			3					8	9	2			4			5		12	11		6				1	10	**7**		
45			3					8	9	2			4			5		12	11		6	13			1	10	**7**		
46			3					8	9	2			4			5			11		6				1	10	7		
	32	13	44	1	26	12	21	46	46	39	16	1	41	1	4	43	10		30	3	17	10	3	7	14	15	9	2	
		3			3	2	4			1	6	1	1	9	6	1	4	17	2		1	5				2	1		
		1			1	2	8	7	30	3	2		1		1	7		2	6	1	1			2		3	9	1	

	Naylor SW	Fereday W	Lilwall S	Hunter RI	Strodder GJ	Shakespeare CR	Garner S	Hamilton IR	Taylor R	McNally BA	Robson G	Hodson SP	Bradley DM	Ampadu PK	Hackett GS	Raven PD	Coldicott S	Heggs CS	Donovan K	Blissett LL	Burgess D	Reid NS	Dickens AW	Speedie DR	Lange AS	Mellon MJ	Hunt A	Darton SR	Williams PA
R1	1		3		6		7	8	9	10	13		4			5	12		11		**2**								
R2	1		3		6		7	8	9	10	11		**4**			5			12			2							13
rep	1		3		6			8	9	10	**11**		4			5		12	7			2							
R3	1	12	3		6	**2**	7	8	9	10			4			5	13		11										
	4		4		4	1	3	4	4	4	2		4			4			3		1	2							
		1									1					1	2	1	1										1
								1	3	1	1		1			1			3										

	Naylor SW	Fereday W	Lilwall S	Hunter RI	Strodder GJ	Shakespeare CR	Garner S	Hamilton IR	Taylor R	McNally BA	Robson G	Hodson SP	Bradley DM	Ampadu PK	Hackett GS	Raven PD	Coldicott S	Heggs CS	Donovan K	Blissett LL	Burgess D	Reid NS	Dickens AW	Speedie DR	Lange AS	Mellon MJ	Hunt A	Darton SR	Williams PA
R1/1	1		3		5	6	7	8	**9**	10	11	2	4	12															
R1/2	1		3		5	6	7	8	9		11	**2**	4			10	12												
	2		2		2	2	2	2	2	1	2	2	2			1													
														1			1												
									1																				

1993-94

Division One

	P	W	D	L	F	A	Pts
Crystal Palace	46	27	9	10	73	46	90
Nottingham Forest	46	23	14	9	74	49	83
Millwall	46	19	17	10	58	49	74
Leicester City	46	19	16	11	72	59	73
Tranmere Rovers	46	21	9	16	69	53	72
Derby County	46	20	11	15	73	68	71
Notts County	46	20	8	18	65	69	68
Wolverhampton W	46	17	17	12	60	47	68
Middlesbrough	46	18	13	15	66	54	67
Stoke City	46	18	13	15	57	59	67
Charlton Athletic	46	19	8	19	61	58	65
Sunderland	46	19	8	19	54	57	65
Bristol City	46	16	16	14	47	50	64
Bolton Wanderers	46	15	14	17	63	64	59
Southend United	46	17	8	21	63	67	59
Grimsby Town	46	13	20	13	52	47	59
Portsmouth	46	15	13	18	52	58	58
Barnsley	46	16	7	23	55	67	55
Watford	46	15	9	22	66	80	54
Luton Town	46	14	11	21	56	60	53
West Bromwich Albion	46	13	12	21	60	69	51
Birmingham City	46	13	12	21	52	69	51
Oxford United	46	13	10	23	54	75	49
Peterborough United	46	8	13	25	48	76	37

Manager: Keith Burkinshaw

- Ardiles quit as manager, handing over his duties to his assistant Keith Burkinshaw, whose signings included winger Lee Ashcroft from Preston North End, defender Neil Parsley from Huddersfield Town, Paul Mardon and winger David Smith from Birmingham City and left-back Paul Edwards from Wolves.
- Moving to pastures new were Wayne Fereday to Cardiff City, veteran striker Simon Garner and Nicky Reid both to Wycombe Wanderers, Craig Shakespeare to Grimsby Town and midfielder Kwame Ampadu to Swansea City.
- Albion avoided relegation back to the Second Division thanks to a last-match win at Portsmouth, Ashcroft's header deciding the contest.

Match No.	Date			Opponents	Result		Scorers	Attendance
1	Aug	14	A	Barnsley	D	1-1	Donovan	12,940
2		21	H	Oxford United	W	3-1	Hunt, O'Regan, Donovan	17,227
3		28	A	Stoke City	L	0-1		17,924
4	Sep	1	H	Southend United	D	2-2	Taylor 2	14,482
5		5	H	Wolverhampton Wanderers	W	3-2	Bradley, Raven, Donovan	25,615
6		11	A	Notts County	L	0-1		9,870
7		18	H	Crystal Palace	L	1-4	Taylor	17,873
8		25	H	Middlesbrough	D	1-1	Taylor	15,766
9	Oct	3	A	Derby County	L	3-5	Hunt 2, Taylor	13,370
10		9	A	Millwall	L	1-2	Bradley	11,004
11		16	H	Peterborough United	W	3-0	Taylor 2, Strodder	15,134
12		23	A	Sunderland	L	0-1		19,363
13		30	H	Watford	W	4-1	Hunt 2, Hamilton, Taylor	15,299
14	Nov	2	A	Tranmere Rovers	L	0-3		7,882
15		6	H	Bolton Wanderers	D	2-2	Hunt, Taylor (pen)	15,709
16		21	H	Nottingham Forest	L	0-2		15,581
17		27	H	Portsmouth	W	4-1	Hunt 2, Taylor, O'Regan	13,867
18	Dec	7	A	Bolton Wanderers	D	1-1	Hunt	9,277
19		11	A	Southend United	W	3-0	Hunt, Hamilton, Taylor	6,809
20		19	H	Barnsley	D	1-1	Ashcroft	16,062
21		27	H	Bristol City	L	0-1		22,888
22		28	A	Birmingham City	L	0-2		28,228
23	Jan	1	H	Luton Town	D	1-1	Mellon	16,138
24		3	A	Charlton Athletic	L	1-2	Hamilton	8,272
25		12	A	Leicester City	L	2-4	Strodder, Mellon	15,640
26		15	A	Peterborough United	L	0-2		7,757
27		22	H	Millwall	D	0-0		15,172
28	Feb	1	A	Grimsby Town	D	2-2	Taylor, Fenton	4,740
29		5	H	Sunderland	W	2-1	Donovan, Fenton	17,089
30		12	A	Watford	W	1-0	Burgess	10,087
31		19	H	Leicester City	L	1-2	Fenton	18,153
32		26	A	Wolverhampton Wanderers	W	2-1	Taylor, Mardon	28,039
33	Mar	5	H	Stoke City	D	0-0		16,129
34		12	A	Crystal Palace	L	0-1		17,106
35		16	H	Notts County	W	3-0	Hunt, Taylor 2	14,594
36		19	A	Middlesbrough	L	0-3		10,516
37		26	H	Derby County	L	1-2	Donovan	17,437
38		30	H	Charlton Athletic	W	2-0	Hunt, Donovan	14,091
39	Apr	2	A	Bristol City	D	0-0		8,624
40		12	A	Oxford United	D	1-1	Taylor	9,032
41		16	H	Tranmere Rovers	L	1-3	Nixon (og)	15,835
42		24	A	Nottingham Forest	L	1-2	Taylor	24,018
43		27	H	Birmingham City	L	2-4	Burgess, Donovan	20,316
44		30	H	Grimsby Town	W	1-0	Donovan	16,870
45	May	3	A	Luton Town	L	2-3	Taylor, Ashcroft	10,053
46		8	A	Portsmouth	W	1-0	Ashcroft	17,629

Appearances
Sub appearances
Goals

FA Cup

R1	Nov	14	A	Halifax Town	L	1-2	Hunt	4,250

Appearances
Sub appearances
Goals

League Cup

R1/1	Aug	18	A	Bristol Rovers	W	4-1	Burgess, Hunt, Donovan 2	4,562
R1/2		25	H	Bristol Rovers	D	0-0		9,123
R2/1	Sep	22	H	Chelsea	D	1-1	Donovan	14,919
R2/2	Oct	6	A	Chelsea	L	1-2	Taylor	11,959

Appearances
Sub appearances
Goals

Lange AS	Coldicott S	Darton SR	Bradley DM	Raven PD	Burgess D	Hunt A	Hamilton IR	Taylor R	O'Regan KM	Donovan K	Strodder GJ	Garner S	Fereday W	Lilwall S	Ampadu PK	Parsley NR	Ashcroft L	Mellon MJ	McNally BA	Reid NS	Naylor SW	Williams PRC	Mardon PJ	Hunter RI	Heggs CS	Fenton GA	Edwards PR	Smith D	McCue J	
1	2	3	4	5	6	7	8	**9**	10	11	12	13																		1
1			4	5	6	7	8	9	10	11	12	13	2	**3**																2
1			4	5	6	7	8	9	10	11			2	3																3
1			4	5		7	8	9	10	11	6		2	3																4
1			4	5	6	7	8		10	11	12	9	**2**	3	13															5
1			4	5	6	7	8		10	11	12	9	**2**	3	13															6
1			4	5	6	7	8	9	10	**11**			2	3	12															7
1			4	5	6	7		9	10	11				**3**	8	2	12													8
1			4	5	6	7	8	9	10						3	2		11												9
1			4	5	6	7	**8**	9	2	11					3			10	12											10
1			4		6	**7**	8	9	11	12	5				3	2	13	10												11
1			4		6	7	8	9	11		5				3	2	12	**10**												12
1					6	7	8	9	4	11	5			3		2	10													13
1					6	7	8	9	4	11	5	13		3		**2**	10			12										14
			4		6	7	8	9	5	11			2		3		**10**			12	1									15
1				5		7		9	8	11	**6**	12						10		2		3	4	13						16
1				5	2	7	11	9	8								**6**	10				3	4		12					17
1				5	2	7	**11**	9	8								6	10				**3**	4	12						18
1				5	2	7	11	9	8								6	10				3	4							19
1				5	2	**7**	8	9	11								6	10				3	4		12					20
1	13			5	2		11	9	8	12				3			6	10					4		**7**					21
1	11			5	2		8	9	7	12		**10**		3			6						4							22
1	8			5	2		11	9				7	12	3			**6**	10					4							23
1	**7**			5	2		11	9	8		13		12	3			6	10					4							24
1				5	2		11				8				6			10		3			4		7	9				25
1				5	2		11			13	4				8		6	10		3	12				7	9				26
			4	5	6		8	9		11						2		**10**	12		1					7	3			27
			4		6		8	9		10						2					1		5			7	3	11		28
			4		6		8	9		10	13					2			12		1		**5**			7	3	11		29
12			4		6		8	9		10						2					**1**		5			7	**3**	11		30
1			4		6	7		9		10						2							5			8	3	11		31
			4	6	2	**7**		9		10			13			12			8		1		5				3	**11**		32
			4	6	2	7	12	9		10									**8**		1		5				3	11		33
			4	6	2	**7**	8	9		10											1		5		12		**3**	**11**		34
			4	6	2	7	8	9		10											1		5				3	11		35
			4	6	2	7	8	9		10							12				1		5				3	**11**		36
			4	6	2	7	8	9		10								12			1		5				3	**11**		37
				6	2	7	8	9		10						5		4			1						3	11		38
				6	2	**7**	8	9	4	10	12					5					1						3	11		39
				5	6	7	8	9	12	10	13					2		**4**			1						3	11		40
				5	6	7	8	9		10	12					2		4			1						**3**	11		41
		3		5	6	7	8	9		10							4				1		2					11		42
		3			6	7	8	9		10	12					5	4				1		2					**11**		43
		3			6	7	8	9		10	2					5	**4**		12		1							11		44
12		3			6		8	9		10	5					2	4	13	7		**1**							11		45
1		3		6		7	8	9		10	2					5	**4**	12	11											46
27	4	6	24	34	43	35	41	42	24	33	11	4	7	13	8	19	17	18	4	3	19	5	22		3	7	15	18		
2	1						1		1	4	10	4	3		3	1	4	3	4	2	1			2	3					
			2	1	2	12	3	18	2	8	2						3	2					1			3				

One own-goal

Lange AS	Coldicott S	Darton SR	Bradley DM	Raven PD	Burgess D	Hunt A	Hamilton IR	Taylor R	O'Regan KM	Donovan K	Strodder GJ	Garner S	Fereday W	Lilwall S	Ampadu PK	Parsley NR	Ashcroft L	Mellon MJ	McNally BA	Reid NS	Naylor SW	Williams PRC	Mardon PJ	Hunter RI	Heggs CS	Fenton GA	Edwards PR	Smith D	McCue J	
1	2				6	7	8	9	5	11					**3**		10	13	4	12										R1
1	1				1	1	1	1	1	1					1		1		1											
																		1		1										
						1																								

Lange AS	Coldicott S	Darton SR	Bradley DM	Raven PD	Burgess D	Hunt A	Hamilton IR	Taylor R	O'Regan KM	Donovan K	Strodder GJ	Garner S	Fereday W	Lilwall S	Ampadu PK	Parsley NR	Ashcroft L	Mellon MJ	McNally BA	Reid NS	Naylor SW	Williams PRC	Mardon PJ	Hunter RI	Heggs CS	Fenton GA	Edwards PR	Smith D	McCue J	
1	2		**4**	5	6	7	8	9	10	11	12				3															R1/1
				5				9	13		6	**8**	2	3	10		7	11	4		1								12	R1/2
1			**4**	5	6	7	8	9	10	11					3	2	13	12												R2/1
1			4	5	6	7	8	9	2	11					3			10												R2/2
3	1		3	4	3	3	3	4	3	3	1	1	1	1	4	1	1	2	1		1									
									1		1						1	1											1	
					1	1		1		3																				

1994-95

Division One

	P	W	D	L	F	A	Pts
Middlesbrough	46	23	13	10	67	40	82
Reading	46	23	10	13	58	44	79
Bolton Wanderers	46	21	14	11	67	45	77
Wolverhampton W	46	21	13	12	77	61	76
Tranmere Rovers	46	22	10	14	67	58	76
Barnsley	46	20	12	14	63	52	72
Watford	46	19	13	14	52	46	70
Sheffield United	46	17	17	12	74	55	68
Derby County	46	18	12	16	66	51	66
Grimsby Town	46	17	14	15	62	56	65
Stoke City	46	16	15	15	50	53	63
Millwall	46	16	14	16	60	60	62
Southend United	46	18	8	20	54	73	62
Oldham Athletic	46	16	13	17	60	60	61
Charlton Athletic	46	16	11	19	58	66	59
Luton Town	46	15	13	18	61	64	58
Port Vale	46	15	13	18	58	64	58
Portsmouth	46	15	13	18	53	63	58
West Bromwich Albion	46	16	10	20	51	57	58
Sunderland	46	12	18	16	41	45	54
Swindon Town	46	12	12	22	54	73	48
Burnley	46	11	13	22	49	74	46
Bristol City	46	11	12	23	42	63	45
Notts County	46	9	13	24	45	66	40

Manager: Keith Burkinshaw then Alan Buckley

- The new redeveloped and redesigned Hawthorns was officially opened for the home League game against Bristol City on Boxing Day.
- Alan Buckley took over from Burkinshaw to become Albion's 16th managerial change in a little over 30 years.
- Players signed included Mike Phelan from Manchester United and Paul Agnew and Tony Rees from Buckley's former club Grimsby Town.
- Those who left included Tony Lange (to Fulham), Roy Hunter (to Northampton Town), Bernard McNally (to Hednesford Town, after 189 appearances), former captain Darren Bradley (to Walsall after 288 outings), Neil Parsley (to Exeter City), Micky Mellon (to Blackpool), Carl Heggs (to Swansea City) and Gary Strodder (to Notts County).
- Tony Hale (now a Life Member) replaced Trevor Summers as club chairman.

Match No.	Date			Opponents	Result		Scorers	Attendance
1	Aug	13	A	Luton Town	D	1-1	Taylor	8,640
2		28	A	Wolverhampton Wanderers	L	0-2		27,764
3		31	A	Swindon Town	D	0-0		10,964
4	Sep	10	A	Millwall	D	2-2	Taylor 2	8,407
5		14	A	Middlesbrough	L	1-2	Ashcroft	14,878
6		17	H	Grimsby Town	D	1-1	Ashcroft	14,496
7		24	H	Burnley	W	1-0	Taylor	13,539
8		28	H	Portsmouth	L	0-2		13,545
9	Oct	2	A	Stoke City	L	1-4	Taylor	14,183
10		8	H	Sunderland	L	1-3	Ashcroft	13,717
11		15	A	Tranmere Rovers	L	1-3	Hunt	7,397
12		18	H	Sheffield United	W	1-0	Mellon	12,713
13		22	A	Barnsley	L	0-2		5,082
14		29	H	Reading	W	2-0	Ashcroft, Hunt	14,313
15	Nov	2	H	Port Vale	D	0-0		14,513
16		5	A	Watford	L	0-1		8,419
17		13	A	Charlton Athletic	D	1-1	Taylor	10,921
18		19	H	Oldham Athletic	W	3-1	Ashcroft, Taylor, Donovan	14,616
19		26	A	Notts County	L	0-2		10,088
20	Dec	3	H	Barnsley	W	2-1	Hamilton, Heggs	13,921
21		10	A	Sheffield United	L	0-2		13,891
22		18	H	Luton Town	W	1-0	Donovan	14,392
23		26	H	Bristol City	W	1-0	Munro (og)	21,071
24		27	A	Southend United	L	1-2	Ashcroft	6,847
25		31	H	Bolton Wanderers	W	1-0	Hunt	18,134
26	Jan	2	A	Derby County	D	1-1	Hamilton	16,035
27		14	A	Reading	W	2-0	Donovan, Hunt	9,390
28	Feb	1	H	Watford	L	0-1		15,455
29		5	H	Charlton Athletic	L	0-1		12,084
30		11	A	Port Vale	L	0-1		10,751
31		18	H	Notts County	W	3-2	Mardon, Hunt 2	13,748
32		21	A	Oldham Athletic	L	0-1		7,750
33		25	H	Stoke City	L	1-3	Hamilton	16,591
34	Mar	4	A	Burnley	D	1-1	Hunt	11,885
35		8	A	Portsmouth	W	2-1	Taylor 2	7,160
36		15	H	Wolverhampton Wanderers	W	2-0	Ashcroft, Taylor	20,661
37		19	H	Swindon Town	L	2-5	Hunt, Rees	12,960
38		22	H	Millwall	W	3-0	Hunt 3 (1 pen)	11,782
39		25	A	Grimsby Town	W	2-0	Donovan, Hunt	7,393
40	Apr	1	H	Middlesbrough	L	1-3	Rees	20,256
41		8	A	Bolton Wanderers	L	0-1		16,207
42		15	H	Southend United	W	2-0	Hamilton, Strodder	14,635
43		17	A	Bristol City	L	0-1		8,777
44		22	H	Derby County	D	0-0		15,365
45		30	H	Tranmere Rovers	W	5-1	Ashcroft 3 (1 pen), Taylor, Donovan	17,484
46	May	7	A	Sunderland	D	2-2	Hunt, Agnew	18,232

Appearances
Sub appearances
Goals

FA Cup

R3	Jan	7	A	Coventry City	D	1-1	Ashcroft (pen)	16,555
rep		18	H	Coventry City	L	1-2	Raven	23,230

Appearances
Sub appearances
Goals

League Cup

R1/1	Aug	16	A	Hereford United	D	0-0		5,425
R1/2	Sep	7	H	Hereford United	L	0-1		10,604

Appearances
Sub appearances

Naylor SW	Parsley NR	Edwards PR	Phelan MC	Herbert CJ	Burgess D	Ashcroft L	Hamilton IR	Taylor R	Heggs CS	McNally BA	Donovan K	Darton SR	Mellon MJ	Strodder GJ	Lilwall S	Boere JWJ	Smith D	Coldicott S	Mardon PJ	Hunt A	O'Regan KM	Raven PD	Bradley DM	Rees AA	Agnew P	Lange AS	
1	2	3	4	5	6	**7**	8	9	10	11	12																1
1	2		4	5	6	12	8	9	**10**	11	7	3	13														2
1	2		4		6		8	9	10		7	3	11	5													3
1			4	6	2	8		9		12		3		5	7	10	**11**	13									4
1				6	**2**	8		9				3		5	7	10	11	4	12								5
1	12			6		**8**		9				3		5	7	10	11	4	2	13							6
1	2		4	6		8		9		12	11	3		5	13	10				**7**							7
1	2		4	6		8		9		12	11	3		5	13	10				**7**							8
1	2		4	6		8		9		**10**				5	3		11	12		7							9
1	2		4			8		9	12				11	5	3		**10**	6		7							10
1	2	6				8		9	12				11	5	3		**10**		4	7							11
1	2	6				8		9					11		3		10	4	**5**	7	12						12
1	2	6	12			**8**		9	13				10	5	3		11	4		7							13
1	2	3	4			8	11	9		7									5	10		6					14
1	2	3	4			**8**	11	9		7			12						5	10		6					15
1	2	3	4			8	11	9	12	7									5	**10**		6	13				16
1	2	3	4			8	11	9	12	7									5	**10**	13	6					17
1		3				8	11	9	**10**	7	4								5	12	2	6					18
1	12	3				8	11	9	13	**7**	4								5		2	6		10			19
1		3				8	11	9	**10**	7	4								5	12	2	6	14				20
1						8	11	9	10	**7**	4				3				5	13	2	6	12				21
1	13					8	11	**9**	12		7				3				5	10	2	6	4				22
1		6				8	11	12	**9**		7				3				5	10	2		4				23
1	13	6				8	11	9			7				3		12		5	10	**2**		4				24
1	2	3				**8**	11	9			7						12		5	10		6	4				25
1	2	3				8	11	**9**			7						13		5	10		6	4	12			26
1	2	3				8	11				7						13		5	10	12	6	**4**	9			27
1	**2**	3	13				11	9		12	7						8		5	10	4	6					28
1						13	11	14			7				3		8		5	**10**	2	6	4	9		12	29
		3	11		**2**	8		9			7								5	10		6	4	12		1	30
		3	12		2	8	11	9			**7**								5	10		6	4			1	31
		3	4		2	8	11	9			12						7		5	10		6		13		1	32
	2				5	8	11	9			7									10	12	6	4	13	3	1	33
1			4		2		11							5			8			10	7	6		9	3		34
1			4		2		11	9		12	**8**								5	10	7	6			3		35
1			**4**		2	8	11	9			7								5	10	12	6			3		36
1					2	8	11	9		4	7								**5**	10	12	6		13	3		37
1					2	8	11			4	7								5	10		6		9	3		38
1					2		11			4	7			8					**5**	10	12	6		9	3		39
1					2	8	11	13		**4**	7			5						10	12	6		9	3		40
1					2		11	13		**4**	7			5	8		12			10		6		9	3		41
1					2		11	9			7			5			8			10		6	4		3		42
1					2		11	9			7			5			12	4		10	8	**6**		13	3		43
1					2	8	11	9			7			5			10	4				6			3		44
1					2	8	11	9			**7**			5			10	4		13		6	12		3		45
1					2	8	11	9			7			5			10	**4**		13		6	12		3		46
42	19	20	17	8	22	36	35	38	7	16	31	7	5	19	14	5	16	9	27	33	12	31	11	8	14	4	
	4		3			2		4	7	5	2		2		2		6	2	1	6	8		5	6		1	
						10	4	11	1		5		1	1					1	13				2	1		

One own-goal

Naylor SW	Parsley NR	Edwards PR	Phelan MC	Herbert CJ	Burgess D	Ashcroft L	Hamilton IR	Taylor R	Heggs CS	McNally BA	Donovan K	Darton SR	Mellon MJ	Strodder GJ	Lilwall S	Boere JWJ	Smith D	Coldicott S	Mardon PJ	Hunt A	O'Regan KM	Raven PD	Bradley DM	Rees AA	Agnew P	Lange AS	
1	2	3				8	11				7						12		5	9		6	4	**10**			R3
1		3				8	11	13			7						12		5	10	2	**6**	4	9			rep
2	1	2				2	2				2								2	2	1	2	2	2			
								1						2			2										
						1																1					

Naylor SW	Parsley NR	Edwards PR	Phelan MC	Herbert CJ	Burgess D	Ashcroft L	Hamilton IR	Taylor R	Heggs CS	McNally BA	Donovan K	Darton SR	Mellon MJ	Strodder GJ	Lilwall S	Boere JWJ	Smith D	Coldicott S	Mardon PJ	Hunt A	O'Regan KM	Raven PD	Bradley DM	Rees AA	Agnew P	Lange AS	
1	2	3	4	5	6		8	9	10	**11**	7		12														R1/1
1			4	6	2	8			9		10	3	7	5			11										R1/2
2	1	1	2	2	2	1	1	1	2	2	2	1	1	1			1										
													1														

1995-96

Division One

	P	W	D	L	F	A	Pts
Sunderland	46	22	17	7	59	33	83
Derby County	46	21	16	9	71	51	79
Crystal Palace	46	20	15	11	67	48	75
Stoke City	46	20	13	13	60	49	73
Leicester City	46	19	14	13	66	60	71
Charlton Athletic	46	17	20	9	57	45	71
Ipswich Town	46	19	12	15	79	69	69
Huddersfield Town	46	17	12	17	61	58	63
Sheffield United	46	16	14	16	57	54	62
Barnsley	46	14	18	14	60	66	60
West Bromwich Albion	46	16	12	18	60	68	60
Port Vale	46	15	15	16	59	66	60
Tranmere Rovers	46	14	17	15	64	60	59
Southend United	46	15	14	17	52	61	59
Birmingham City	46	15	13	18	61	64	58
Norwich City	46	14	15	17	59	55	57
Grimsby Town	46	14	14	18	55	69	56
Oldham Athletic	46	14	14	18	54	50	56
Reading	46	13	17	16	54	63	56
Wolverhampton W	46	13	16	17	56	62	55
Portsmouth	46	13	13	20	61	69	52
Millwall	46	13	13	20	43	63	52
Watford	46	10	18	18	62	70	48
Luton Town	46	11	12	23	40	64	45

Manager: Alan Buckley

- Another former Grimsby Town player joined Albion: midfielder Dave Gilbert. Also recruited were ex-Birmingham City full-back Paul Holmes from Everton and Dutchman Richard Sneekes from Bolton Wanderers. Sneekes's 10 goals at the end of the season swept Albion clear of the relegation zone. Neil Parsley left to join Exeter City and Stuart Naylor joined Bristol City after making the most appearances for Albion by a goalkeeper (468, including 390 at senior level).
- A total of 14 players/personnel based at The Hawthorns this season had previously been associated with Grimsby Town.
- West Bromwich Albion football club became a public liability company (11 April).

Match No.	Date			Opponents	Result		Scorers	Attendance
1	Aug	12	H	Charlton Athletic	W	1-0	Gilbert	14,586
2		20	A	Wolverhampton Wanderers	D	1-1	Taylor	26,329
3		26	H	Ipswich Town	D	0-0		14,123
4		29	A	Southend United	L	1-2	Raven	4,622
5	Sep	2	H	Sheffield United	W	3-1	Burgess, Hunt, Hamilton	14,101
6		9	A	Oldham Athletic	W	2-1	Gilbert, Taylor	8,397
7		12	A	Tranmere Rovers	D	2-2	Hunt, Ashcroft (pen)	7,196
8		17	H	Birmingham City	W	1-0	Hunt	17,854
9		24	A	Stoke City	L	1-2	Hunt (pen)	9,609
10		30	H	Huddersfield Town	L	1-2	Taylor	16,045
11	Oct	7	H	Reading	W	2-0	Gilbert, Taylor	12,907
12		14	A	Luton Town	W	2-1	Hunt, Ashcroft	8,042
13		21	H	Portsmouth	W	2-1	Hunt, Ashcroft	16,255
14		28	A	Millwall	L	1-2	Hunt	9,907
15	Nov	5	H	Leicester City	L	2-3	Raven, Hamilton	16,001
16		11	A	Derby County	L	0-3		13,765
17		18	A	Grimsby Town	L	0-1		8,155
18		21	H	Norwich City	L	1-4	Hunt	13,550
19		25	H	Sunderland	L	0-1		15,920
20	Dec	2	A	Reading	L	1-3	Ashcroft	7,910
21		9	H	Stoke City	L	0-1		14,772
22		16	A	Huddersfield Town	L	1-4	Hamilton	12,664
23		23	H	Crystal Palace	L	2-3	Hunt, Darby	13,098
24		26	A	Port Vale	L	1-3	Gilbert	10,807
25	Jan	13	H	Wolverhampton Wanderers	D	0-0		21,658
26		20	A	Charlton Athletic	L	1-4	Hunt (pen)	11,876
27	Feb	3	A	Ipswich Town	L	1-2	Taylor	10,845
28		10	H	Southend United	W	3-1	Taylor 2, Hunt	12,764
29		17	H	Tranmere Rovers	D	1-1	Hunt (pen)	14,992
30		20	A	Sheffield United	W	2-1	Burgess, Hunt	10,943
31		27	H	Oldham Athletic	W	1-0	Taylor	10,956
32	Mar	2	H	Port Vale	D	1-1	Taylor	13,689
33		9	A	Crystal Palace	L	0-1		19,254
34		12	H	Watford	D	4-4	Taylor 3, Sneekes	11,764
35		16	H	Barnsley	W	2-1	Raven, Sneekes	12,645
36		20	A	Birmingham City	D	1-1	Sneekes	19,147
37		23	A	Watford	D	1-1	Taylor	10,334
38		30	A	Portsmouth	W	2-0	Sneekes 2	8,126
39	Apr	2	H	Luton Town	L	0-2		15,130
40		6	H	Millwall	W	1-0	Sneekes	13,708
41		9	A	Leicester City	W	2-1	Raven, Sneekes	17,889
42		13	H	Grimsby Town	W	3-1	Taylor 2, Sneekes	16,073
43		20	A	Norwich City	D	2-2	Taylor, Sneekes	14,667
44		27	A	Sunderland	D	0-0		22,027
45		30	A	Barnsley	D	1-1	Gilbert	6,979
46	May	5	H	Derby County	W	3-2	Taylor, Hunt, Sneekes	23,858

Appearances
Sub appearances
Goals

FA Cup

R3	Jan	6	A	Crewe Alexandra	L	3-4	Mardon, Hunt, Coldicott	5,750

Appearances
Sub appearances
Goals

League Cup

R1/1	Aug	15	H	Northampton Town	D	1-1	Taylor	6,489
R1/2		22	A	Northampton Town	W	4-2	Donovan, Taylor 2, Hunt	7,083
R2/1	Sep	20	A	Reading	D	1-1	Burgess	6,948
R2/2	Oct	3	H	Reading	L	2-4	Burgess, Donovan	8,163

Appearances
Sub appearances
Goals

Match	Naylor SW	Burgess D	Edwards PR	Cunnington SG	Mardon PJ	Raven PD	Donovan K	Gilbert DJ	Taylor R	Hunt A	Coldicott S	Smith D	Hamilton IR	Ashcroft L	Rees AA	Brien AJ	Agnew P	King PG	Reece PJ	Fettis AW	Darby JT	Hargreaves C	Phelan MC	Holmes P	Spink NP	Nicholson SM	Sneekes R	Butler PJF	Angel M	Comyn AJ
1	1	2	3	4	5	6	7	8	9	10	11	12																		
2	1	2	3		5	6	7	8	9	10	4		11																	
3	1	2	3		5	6	7	8	9	10	4		11	12																
4	1	2	3		5	6	7	8	9	10	4		11	12	13															
5	1	2	3		5	6	7	8	9	10	4		11	12																
6	1	2	3		5		7	8	9	10	4		11			6														
7	1	2			5	6	7		9	10	4	8	11	12	13	3														
8	1	2	3		5	6	7	8	9	10	4		11																	
9	1	2	3		5	6	7	8	9	10	4		11	12	13															
10	1	2		4	5	6	7	8	9	10	13		11	12			3													
11	1	2		11	5	6	7	8	9		4			10			3													
12	1	2		11	5	6	7	8	9	13	4	12		10			3													
13	1	2	3	11	5	6	7	12	9	10	4		13	8																
14	1	2	3		5	6		8	9	10	4	12	11	7	13															
15	1	2		12	5	6		8	9	10	4		11	7				3												
16	1	2		4	5	6	7	8	9	10	13		11	12				3												
17		2	12	4	5	6	7	8	14	10			11	13	9			3	1											
18		2	12		5	6	7	8	9	10	4	13	11	14				3		1										
19		2			5	6	7	8		10	12	3	11	9						1	4	13								
20		2	3			6	7	8		10	5	12	11	9						1	4									
21	1	2	5			6	12	8	9	10	13	3	7	11							4									
22	1	2	3		5	6	7	8	9	10		12	11	13							4									
23	1	2	13		5	6	12	8	14	10		3	11	9							4		7							
24	1	2			5	6	7	8	9	10		3	11		12						4									
25	1	2			5	6	7		9	10	4	3									11			8						
26	1	2			5	6	7	13	9	10	4	3	12	14							11			8						
27		5		4		6	7	8	14	10	12	3		13	9						11			2	1					
28		5				6	7	8	9	10			11								4			2	1	3				
29		5			13	6	7	8	9	10	12		11	14							4			2	1	3				
30		5				6	7	8	9	10	12		11								4			2	1	3				
31		5			13	6		8	9	10	12		11	7							4			2	1	3				
32		5				6			9	10	12	8	11	7	13						4			2	1	3				
33		5			12	6	7	8	9	10	14	13	11								4			2	1	3				
34		5			13	6	7	8	9	10			11								12			2	1	3	4			
35		5			8	6			9	10	12		11								7			2	1	3	4			
36		5			8	6			9	10	12		11	13							7			2	1	3	4			
37		5			8	6			9	10	7		11	13							12			2	1	3	4			
38		5			8	6		13	9	10			11								12			2	1	3	4	7		
39	1	5			8	6	14	13	9	10			11								2					3	4	7	12	
40					5		12	8	9	10	2		11												1	3	4	7		6
41		2			5	6		12	9	10	8		11												1	3	4	7		
42		2			5	6		8	9	10			11												1	3	4	7		
43		2			5		12	6	9	10			11											8	1	3	4	7	13	
44		2						8		10			11		5						3			9	1		4	7	12	6
45		2			5		12	8		10			11											9	1	3	4	7		6
46		6			5			8	9	10			11											2	1	3	4	7		
	23	45	13	8	35	40	28	35	39	44	21	9	39	11	3	2	3	4	1	3	19		1	18	19	18	13	9		3
		3	1	4		6	5	3	1	12	7	2	15	6							3	1							3	
		2				4		5	17	14			3	4							1						10			

Round	Naylor SW	Burgess D	Edwards PR	Cunnington SG	Mardon PJ	Raven PD	Donovan K	Gilbert DJ	Taylor R	Hunt A	Coldicott S	Smith D	Hamilton IR	Ashcroft L	Rees AA	Brien AJ	Agnew P	King PG	Reece PJ	Fettis AW	Darby JT
R3	1	2	3		5	6	7	8	9	10	4	12	14	13							11
	1	1	1		1	1	1	1	1	1	1										1
												1	1	1							
					1					1	1										

Round	Naylor SW	Burgess D	Edwards PR	Cunnington SG	Mardon PJ	Raven PD	Donovan K	Gilbert DJ	Taylor R	Hunt A	Coldicott S	Smith D	Hamilton IR	Ashcroft L	Rees AA	Brien AJ	Agnew P
R1/1	1	2	3		5	6	7	8	9	10	11	12			13	4	
R1/2	1	2	3		5	6	7	8	9	10	4		11		12		
R2/1	1	2	3		5	6	7	8	9	10	4		11				
R2/2	1	2		11	5	6	7	8	9	10	4	12		13			3
	4	4	3	1	4	4	4	4	4	4	4		2			1	1
												2		1	2		
		2					2		3	1							

1996-97

Division One

	P	W	D	L	F	A	Pts
Bolton Wanderers	46	28	14	4	100	53	98
Barnsley	46	22	14	10	76	55	80
Wolverhampton W	46	22	10	14	68	51	76
Ipswich Town	46	20	14	12	68	50	74
Sheffield United	46	20	13	13	75	52	73
Crystal Palace	46	19	14	13	78	48	71
Portsmouth	46	20	8	18	59	53	68
Port Vale	46	17	16	13	58	55	67
Queen's Park Rangers	46	18	12	16	64	60	66
Birmingham City	46	17	15	14	52	48	66
Tranmere Rovers	46	17	14	15	63	56	65
Stoke City	46	18	10	18	51	57	64
Norwich City	46	17	12	17	63	68	63
Manchester City	46	17	10	19	59	60	61
Charlton Athletic	46	16	11	19	52	66	59
West Bromwich Albion	46	14	15	17	68	72	57
Oxford United	46	16	9	21	64	68	57
Reading	46	15	12	19	58	67	57
Swindon Town	46	15	9	22	52	71	54
Huddersfield Town	46	13	15	18	48	61	54
Bradford City	46	12	12	22	47	72	48
Grimsby Town	46	11	13	22	60	81	46
Oldham Athletic	46	10	13	23	51	66	43
Southend United	46	8	15	23	42	86	39

Manager: Alan Buckley then Ray Harford

- Ray Harford took over from Buckley as team manager (February) and immediately appointed former Hawthorns favourite Cyrille Regis as coach.
- Midfielder Graham Potter (from Southampton), Canadian international Paul Peschisolido (from Birmingham City), goalkeeper Alan Miller (from Middlesbrough) and defender Shaun Murphy (from Notts County) were among the new faces at the club.
- Departures included Lee Ashcroft and Julian Darby to Preston North End, Sean Cunnington to Notts County and Kevin Donovan to Grimsby Town.
- Albion were Stoke City's opponents for the last ever League game at The Victoria Ground. Some 109 years earlier, Albion had been the first to visit there in September 1888.

Match No.	Date			Opponents	Result		Scorers	Attendance
1	Aug	17	H	Barnsley	L	1-2	Hunt (pen)	18,627
2		24	A	Charlton Athletic	D	1-1	Taylor	9,631
3		27	A	Crystal Palace	D	0-0		14,328
4	Sep	7	A	Queen's Park Rangers	W	2-0	Taylor, Peschisolido	12,886
5		10	H	Reading	W	3-2	Hunt 3	13,114
6		15	H	Wolverhampton Wanderers	L	2-4	Hamilton, Taylor	21,179
7		21	A	Tranmere Rovers	W	3-2	Groves, Gilbert, Peschisolido	7,848
8		28	H	Ipswich Town	D	0-0		15,648
9	Oct	1	A	Oldham Athletic	D	1-1	Groves	5,817
10		12	H	Huddersfield Town	D	1-1	Hunt	14,938
11		16	H	Stoke City	L	0-2		15,536
12		19	A	Grimsby Town	D	1-1	Sneekes	7,187
13		26	H	Bradford City	D	0-0		14,172
14		30	A	Swindon Town	W	3-2	Holmes, Sneekes, Peschisolido	9,704
15	Nov	2	A	Portsmouth	L	0-4		7,354
16		9	H	Port Vale	D	1-1	Taylor	13,827
17		13	H	Sheffield United	L	1-2	Coldicott	12,219
18		16	A	Southend United	W	3-2	Hunt, Peschisolido, Smith	5,046
19		27	A	Manchester City	L	2-3	Hamilton, Peschisolido	24,200
20		30	A	Bradford City	D	1-1	Groves	12,003
21	Dec	8	H	Bolton Wanderers	D	2-2	Taylor (pen), Peschisolido	12,946
22		18	H	Norwich City	W	5-1	Hamilton 2, Hunt 2, Peschisolido	12,585
23		21	H	Oxford United	D	3-3	Sneekes, Taylor, Hunt (pen)	13,693
24		26	A	Reading	D	2-2	Groves, Peschisolido	10,583
25		28	H	Queen's Park Rangers	W	4-1	Sneekes, Hunt, Peschisolido, Smith	18,866
26	Jan	1	H	Tranmere Rovers	L	1-2	Burgess	14,861
27		12	A	Wolverhampton Wanderers	L	0-2		27,336
28		18	H	Oldham Athletic	D	1-1	Taylor	11,919
29		25	A	Ipswich Town	L	0-5		9,460
30	Feb	1	A	Port Vale	D	2-2	Peschisolido 2	8,093
31		4	A	Birmingham City	W	3-2	Sneekes, Taylor 2	21,600
32		8	H	Swindon Town	L	1-2	Hunt (pen)	16,219
33		15	A	Norwich City	W	4-2	Sneekes, Peschisolido 3	14,845
34		22	H	Portsmouth	L	0-2		15,800
35	Mar	2	A	Bolton Wanderers	L	0-1		13,258
36		5	H	Southend United	W	4-0	Sneekes, Raven, Hunt, Murphy	11,792
37		8	A	Oxford United	L	0-1		8,502
38		16	H	Birmingham City	W	2-0	Sneekes, Hamilton	15,972
39		22	H	Charlton Athletic	L	1-2	Hunt	14,168
40		28	A	Barnsley	L	0-2		12,042
41	Apr	5	A	Sheffield United	W	2-1	Taylor, Coldicott	15,004
42		9	H	Crystal Palace	W	1-0	Peschisolido	12,906
43		12	H	Manchester City	L	1-3	Murphy	20,087
44		19	A	Huddersfield Town	D	0-0		12,748
45		26	H	Grimsby Town	W	2-0	Hunt, Coldicott	15,572
46	May	4	A	Stoke City	L	1-2	Hunt (pen)	21,735

Appearances
Sub appearances
Goals

FA Cup

R3	Jan	4	A	Chelsea	L	0-3		27,446

Appearances
Sub appearances

League Cup

R1/1	Aug	20	A	Colchester United	W	3-2	Hamilton, Hunt, Donovan	3,521
R1/2	Sep	3	H	Colchester United	L	1-3	Groves	9,809

Appearances
Sub appearances
Goals

Spink NP	Holmes P	Nicholson SM	Sneekes R	Burgess D	Raven PD	Hamilton IR	Mardon PJ	Taylor R	Hunt A	Groves P	Gilbert DJ	Cunnington SG	Donovan K	Peschisolido PP	Smith D	Crichton PA	Darby JT	Ashcroft L	Agnew P	Coldicott S	Butler PJF	Murphy SP	Potter GS	Miller AJ	Rodosthenous M	Joseph RA	McDermott A	Bennett D	
1	2	3	4	5	6	7	**8**	9	10	11	12	13																	1
1	2	3	4	5	6	7		9	10	11	**8**	12	13																2
1	2	3	4	5	**6**	7	12	9	10	11	8	13																	3
1	2	3	4	**5**	6	7	8	13	10	11				9	12														4
	2	3	4		**6**	7	5	14	*10*	11	13		12	9	8	1													5
	2	3	4	6		7	**5**	14	10	11	13		12	9	*8*	1													6
	2	3	4	6		7	5		10	11	8		12	**9**		1													7
	2	3	4	6		7	5		10	11	**8**			9		1	12												8
	2	3	4	5	**6**	7	8		10	11	12		13	9		1													9
	2	3	4	6		7	5		10	11	**8**					1	12	9											10
	2	3	4	6		7	5	12	10	11	8			13		1		9											11
	2	3	**4**	5	6	7	8	14	*10*	11	13		12	9		1													12
	2	3	4	5	6				10	11	**8**		7			1	9	12											13
	2	3	4	5	6				10	11				**9**		1	7	12	8										14
	2	3	4	5	6			14	*10*	11			12	9		1	7	13	8										15
	12	3	4	2	6			*9*	14	11	8		7	10		1			**5**	13									16
	2		13	5	6	4		*9*	14	11	**8**		7	10		1			3	12									17
	2				6	11			10	5	**8**		7	9	12	1			3	4									18
	2		13	5		11		14	*10*	**6**	12		7	9		1	8		3	4									19
	2		12	5		**11**			10	7				9	8	1	6		3	4									20
	2		**4**	5		11		13	10	7				9	8	1	6		3	12									21
	2		**4**	5		11			10	7				9	8	1	6		3		12								22
	2		4	5		11		13	10	7			12	9	8	1	6		**3**										23
	2		4	5		11		12	**10**	7				9	8	1	6		3										24
	2		4	5	6	11			10	**7**			12	9	8	1	3												25
	2		4	**5**	6	11		12	*10*	13			14	9	8	1	3				7								26
	2		4	5	**6**	11		13	10	7	12			9		1			3			8							27
			4	2	**6**	11		9	*10*	13	8		7	14		1	3		12			5							28
	2		8	5	6	11		9	10				12	13		1	3			7		4							29
	2		8	5	6	11		13	10				12	9		1			3	**7**	4								30
	2		8	5	6	11		9	10				13			1	12		**3**	7	4								31
	2		8	5	6	11		9	10			12	7	13		1				**3**	4								32
	2		4	**5**	6	11			*9*				7	10	8	1			3		13	12	14						33
	2		4		**6**	11			9				7	10	8	1	13		**3**	14		5	12						34
	2		4		6	11		9					7		8				**3**		10	5	12	1	13				35
	2		4		6	11		9	14				7	**10**					3		13	5	8	1		12			36
	2		4		6	11		13	9				7	10	12						8	5	**3**	1					37
	2		4	6		11		9	10				7		8				**3**	12	13	5		1					38
	2		4	6		11		12	10				7	9	8				**3**			5		1		13			39
			4		6	11	5	14	10				*7*	9	8				**3**	12	13	2		1					40
			4		6	11		9	10						3					7	8	5		1			2		41
			4		6	11	13	*9*	10				12	14	3					7	8	5		1			2		42
			4		**6**		13	9	10				11	14	3					7	8	5	*12*	1			2		43
			4		6	11		**9**	10					12	3					7	8	5		1			2		44
		13	4		6				10				**11**	9	3					7	8	5		1			2	12	45
		12	4		6				10	11			13	9	3					7	**8**	5		1			2		46
4	37	16	42	33	33	39	11	16	42	27	11		17	30	21	30	13	2	21	13	12	16	2	12			6		
	1	2	3				3	16	3	2	7	4	15	7	3		4	3	1	6	5	1	4		1	2		1	
10	15	15				1				5	4		1		8						3		1	2	2			1	
	2		4	5	**6**	11		12	10	7				9	*8*	1			14		13	3							R3
	1		1	1	1	1			1	1				1	1	1						1							
								1											1		1								
1	2	3	4		6	7	5	9	**10**	11	8	13	12																R1/1
1	2	**3**	4	6		7	5	9		11	*8*	13	12	10				14											R1/2
2	2	2	2	1	1	2	2	2	1	2	2			1															
												2	2					1											
						1			1	1			1																

1997-98

Division One

	P	W	D	L	F	A	Pts
Nottingham Forest	46	28	10	8	82	42	94
Middlesbrough	46	27	10	9	77	41	91
Sunderland	46	26	12	8	86	50	90
Charlton Athletic	46	26	10	10	80	49	88
Ipswich Town	46	23	14	9	77	43	83
Sheffield United	46	19	17	10	69	54	74
Birmingham City	46	19	17	10	60	35	74
Stockport County	46	19	8	19	71	69	65
Wolverhampton W	46	18	11	17	57	53	65
West Bromwich Albion	46	16	13	17	50	56	61
Crewe Alexandra	46	18	5	23	58	65	59
Oxford United	46	16	10	20	60	64	58
Bradford City	46	14	15	17	46	59	57
Tranmere Rovers	46	14	14	18	54	57	56
Norwich City	46	14	13	19	52	69	55
Huddersfield Town	46	14	11	21	50	72	53
Bury	46	11	19	16	42	58	52
Swindon Town	46	14	10	22	42	73	52
Port Vale	46	13	10	23	56	66	49
Portsmouth	46	13	10	23	51	63	49
Queen's Park Rangers	46	10	19	17	51	63	49
Manchester City	46	12	12	22	56	57	48
Stoke City	46	11	13	22	44	74	46
Reading	46	11	9	26	39	78	42

Manager: Ray Harford then Denis Smith

- Denis Smith became Albion's 12th manager in 15 years when he replaced Harford in December.
- Players signed this season included striker Lee Hughes from Kidderminster Harriers, Matt Carbon and Sean Flynn from Derby County, James Quinn from Blackpool, winger Kevin Kilbane from Preston North End and defender Jason Van Blerk from Manchester City.
- Out of The Hawthorns went Paul Agnew to Swansea City, Andy Hunt to Charlton Athletic, Bob Taylor to Bolton Wanderers – later to return, Ian Hamilton to Sheffield United, Paul Peschisolido to Fulham, ageing goalkeeper Nigel Spink to Millwall and Stacey Coldicott and Dave Smith to Grimsby Town, signed by ex-boss Alan Buckley.
- The first women's international was staged at The Hawthorns – England losing 2–1 to Italy. Also the first 'B' international took place when England lost 2–1 to Chile in front of almost 14,000 spectators.

Match No.	Date			Opponents	Result		Scorers	Attendance
1	Aug	9	H	Tranmere Rovers	W	2-1	Hunt, Kilbane	16,727
2		16	A	Crewe Alexandra	W	3-2	Hunt (pen), Hughes 2	5,234
3		24	H	Wolverhampton Wanderers	W	1-0	Curle (og)	21,511
4		30	A	Ipswich Town	D	1-1	Sneekes	13,512
5	Sep	3	A	Stoke City	D	0-0		17,439
6		7	H	Reading	W	1-0	Hunt	15,966
7		13	A	Queen's Park Rangers	L	0-2		14,399
8		20	H	Swindon Town	D	0-0		16,237
9		27	A	Bury	W	3-1	Peschisolido 3	6,439
10	Oct	4	H	Oxford United	L	1-2	Hunt	15,887
11		18	A	Portsmouth	W	3-2	Mardon, Hunt 2	9,158
12		21	A	Nottingham Forest	L	0-1		19,243
13		25	H	Sheffield United	W	2-0	Hunt, Hughes	17,311
14	Nov	1	A	Bradford City	D	0-0		16,212
15		4	H	Norwich City	W	1-0	Hughes	13,949
16		8	H	Charlton Athletic	W	1-0	Hunt	16,124
17		15	A	Port Vale	W	2-1	Hunt, Hamilton	11,124
18		23	H	Birmingham City	W	1-0	Sneekes	18,444
19		29	A	Middlesbrough	L	0-1		30,164
20	Dec	2	H	Manchester City	L	0-1		17,904
21		6	H	Stockport County	W	3-2	Sneekes, Hunt, Hughes	14,074
22		13	A	Sunderland	L	0-2		28,879
23		20	H	Huddersfield Town	L	0-2		14,619
24		26	A	Reading	L	1-2	Kilbane	10,154
25		28	H	Stoke City	D	1-1	Hunt	17,690
26	Jan	9	A	Tranmere Rovers	D	0-0		8,058
27		17	H	Crewe Alexandra	L	0-1		15,257
28		27	H	Ipswich Town	L	2-3	Murphy, Flynn	12,402
29		31	A	Wolverhampton Wanderers	W	1-0	Hunt	28,244
30	Feb	7	A	Swindon Town	W	2-0	Evans, Carbon	10,304
31		14	H	Queen's Park Rangers	D	1-1	Hughes	19,143
32		17	A	Oxford United	L	1-2	Taylor	9,412
33		21	H	Bury	D	1-1	Hughes	15,879
34		24	H	Portsmouth	L	0-3		12,757
35		28	A	Manchester City	L	0-1		28,460
36	Mar	3	A	Charlton Athletic	L	0-5		10,923
37		7	H	Bradford City	D	1-1	Burgess	13,281
38		14	A	Norwich City	D	1-1	Hughes	19,069
39		21	H	Port Vale	D	2-2	Flynn, Taylor	14,242
40		28	A	Birmingham City	L	0-1		23,260
41	Apr	4	H	Middlesbrough	W	2-1	Quinn 2 (1 pen)	20,620
42		11	A	Stockport County	L	1-2	Hughes	7,943
43		13	H	Sunderland	D	3-3	Kilbane, Hughes 2	20,181
44		18	A	Huddersfield Town	L	0-1		11,704
45		25	A	Sheffield United	W	4-2	Hunt, Kilbane, Hughes 2	21,248
46	May	3	H	Nottingham Forest	D	1-1	Hughes (pen)	23,012
								Appearances
								Sub appearances
								Goals

FA Cup

R3	Jan	13	H	Stoke City	W	3-1	Sneekes 2, Kilbane	17,598
R4		24	A	Aston Villa	L	0-4		39,372
								Appearances
								Sub appearances
								Goals

League Cup

R1/1	Aug	12	A	Cambridge United	D	1-1	Peschisolido	3,520
R1/2		27	H	Cambridge United	W	2-1	Sneekes (pen), Hunt	10,264
R2/1	Sep	16	A	Luton Town	D	1-1	Taylor	3,437
R2/2		23	H	Luton Town	W	4-2	McDermott, Peschisolido 2, Raven	7,227
R3	Oct	15	H	Liverpool	L	0-2		21,986
								Appearances
								Sub appearances
								Goals

Miller AJ	McDermott A	Nicholson SM	Sneekes R	Mardon PJ	Murphy SP	Flynn SM	Butler PJF	Peschisolido PP	Hunt A	Kilbane KD	Hamilton IR	Hughes L	Coldicott S	Holmes P	Smith D	Raven PD	Taylor R	Burgess D	Thomas JA	Dobson AJ	Evans MJ	Carbon MP	Carr FA	Quinn SJ	Potter GS	Quailey BS	Gilbert DJ	Van Blerk J	Beesley P	Nicol S	Adamson C	Crichton PA	Spink NP	
1	2	3	**4**	5	6	7	8	9	10	*11*	12	13	14																					1
1		3	**4**	5	6	7	8	9	10	11	12	13		2	14																			2
1		3	4	5		7	8	9	10	**11**	12	13		2		6																		3
1		3	4	5		7	8		**10**	*11*	12		13	2	14	6	9																	4
1		3	4			7	8		**10**		12			2	11	6	9	5	13															5
1		3	**4**			7	8		10		12			2	11	6	9	5	13															6
1		3	4			**7**	*8*		10	13	12			2	11	6		5	9	14														7
1	2		4			7		12	10	11	8		13		3	6	**9**	5																8
1	2		4			7		**9**	10	11	8	12			3	6		5																9
1	**2**		4			7		9	10	11	8	13	12		3	6		5																10
1			4	6		**7**	12	9	10	11	8	13		2	3			5																11
1			4	6			9	12	10	*11*	**8**	13	7	2	3			5		14														12
1			**4**	6		7	9		10	11	8	13	12	2	3			5																13
1			4	6		**7**	9		10	11	8	13	12	2	3			5		14														14
1			4	6		**7**	9		10	11	8	13	12	2	3					5														15
1			4	6		**7**	9		10	11	8	13	12	2	3			5																16
1			4	**6**		7	9		10		8		11	2	3			5		12														17
1			4	6		**7**	9		10	11	8	12		2	3			5																18
1			4	6			9		10	11	8	12	7	**2**	3			5			13													19
1			4	6			9		10	11	8	12	7	2	3			5			13													20
1			**4**	6		12	7		10	*11*	8	13		2	14			5		3	9													21
1		3	**4**	6		9	7		10	11	8	13					12	2		5														22
1	2		4	6			7		10	**11**	8	13			12		9	5		*3*	14													23
1	2		4	6		**7**	*9*		10	11	8	12			3			5		13	14													24
1	2		4		6		7		10	11	**8**	9	12		3			5			13													25
1		3	4		5	12	7		10	**11**	8	9		2						6	13													26
1		3	4		5	12	9		10	11	**8**	13		2						6	7													27
1		3	4		5	**7**	12		10	11	8	9		2								6												28
1		3	**4**		5		7		10	11	8	9	12	2							13	6												29
1		3	4		5		7		**10**	11	8	9		2							12	6												30
1		3	4		5		7		10	11		9		2			12					6	**8**											31
1		3	4		5		**7**		10	11		9	12	2			8					6	13											32
1		3	4		5		**7**			11	8	9	13	2			10					6		12										33
1					5		7			11	10	**9**	12	2			8	6					13	4	3									34
1						12	7			11	*10*		**8**	2			9	5				6		4	3	13	14							35
1						12	*7*			11	10		8	2			9	5				6	13	**4**	3		14							36
1						7				11	8	10	**4**	2			9	5				6			3	12	13							37
1			4			7				11	12	9		**2**			13	5						10				3	6	8				38
1			4			7	12			*11*	**2**	9					13					6		10			14	3	5	8				39
1			4		3	**7**			9	11			12					2				6		10		13			5	8				40
1	2		12			4			**9**	11		10	13									6		7				3	5	8				41
	2		12			4			**9**	11		10										6		7				3	5	8	1			42
	2		12		13	4			**9**	11		10										6		7				3	5	8	1			43
	2		12		13	4			9	11		10										6		7				3	5	**8**	1			44
	2		12		5	4			9	11		*10*						6						**7**	13	14		3		8		1		45
	2		9		12	4				11		10										6		7		13		3	**5**	8		1		46
41	13	16	37	18	14	30	31	6	38	42	29	18	7	30	18	8	11	27	1	6	2	16	1	12	4			8	8	9	3	2		
			5		3	5	3	2		1	8	19	15		4		4		2	5	8		3	1	1	5	4							
			3	1	1	2		3	13	4	1	14					2	1			1	1		2										

One own-goal

1		3	4		5		12		10	11	8	9		2						6	**7**													R3
1		3	4		5	14	**7**		10	11	8	*9*	13	2						6	12													R4
2		2	2		2		1		2	2	2	2		2						2	1													
						1	1						1								1													
			2							1																								

1	2	3	4	5	6	7	**8**	9	10	11	12																							R1/1
		3	4	5		7	8	9	10	11	13	*12*		**2**		6				14													1	R1/2
1			4						10	11	8		7	2	3	6	9	5																R2/1
1	2		4			7		12	10	11	8				3	6	**9**	5																R2/2
1			4			7	13	10		11	8	14		2	3	**6**	*9*	5		12														R3
4	2	2	5	2	1	4	2	3	4	5	3		1	3	3	4	3	3															1	
							1	1			2	2								2														
	1		1					3	1							1	1																	

1998-99

Division One

	P	W	D	L	F	A	Pts
Sunderland	46	31	12	3	91	28	105
Bradford City	46	26	9	11	82	47	87
Ipswich Town	46	26	8	12	69	32	86
Birmingham City	46	23	12	11	66	37	81
Watford	46	21	14	11	65	56	77
Bolton Wanderers	46	20	16	10	78	59	76
Wolverhampton W	46	19	16	11	64	43	73
Sheffield United	46	18	13	15	71	66	67
Norwich City	46	15	17	14	62	61	62
Huddersfield Town	46	15	16	15	62	71	61
Grimsby Town	46	17	10	19	40	52	61
West Bromwich Albion	46	16	11	19	69	76	59
Barnsley	46	14	17	15	59	56	59
Crystal Palace	46	14	16	16	58	71	58
Tranmere Rovers	46	12	20	14	63	61	56
Stockport County	46	12	17	17	49	60	53
Swindon Town	46	13	11	22	59	81	50
Crewe Alexandra	46	12	12	22	54	78	48
Portsmouth	46	11	14	21	57	73	47
Queen's Park Rangers	46	12	11	23	52	61	47
Port Vale	46	13	8	25	45	75	47
Bury	46	10	17	19	35	60	47
Oxford United	46	10	14	22	48	71	44
Bristol City	46	9	15	22	57	80	42

Manager: Denis Smith

- This was Albion's 100th season of League football.
- On the transfer front, midfielders Mario Bortolazzi (from Genoa) and Enzo Maresca (from Cagliari) became the first Italians to sign for the club. Forward Fabien de Freitas (from Osasuna) and goalkeeper Phil Whitehead (from Oxford United) were also signed, while out of The Hawthorns went two centre-halves, Garry Strodder, sold to Hartlepool United, and Shaun Murphy, transferred to Sheffield United.
- Brothers Adam and James Chambers became the first set of twins to represent England when they starred in the Youth World Cup Finals in Nigeria. And goalkeeper Phil Whitehead, at 15st 4lb, was declared to be the heaviest player ever to represent Albion.

Match No.	Date			Opponents	Result		Scorers	Attendance
1	Aug	8	A	Barnsley	D	2-2	Quinn, Sneekes	18,114
2		15	H	Sheffield United	W	4-1	Carbon, Hughes 2, Kilbane	16,901
3		22	A	Port Vale	W	3-0	Hughes 3	8,146
4		29	H	Norwich City	W	2-0	De Freitas 2	17,401
5		31	A	Grimsby Town	L	1-5	Sneekes	7,931
6	Sep	8	H	Bolton Wanderers	L	2-3	Flynn, Kilbane	16,121
7		13	A	Bristol City	W	3-1	Quinn, Hughes 2	13,761
8		20	H	Bradford City	L	0-2		12,426
9		26	A	Stockport County	D	2-2	Hughes 2	8,804
10		29	A	Oxford United	L	0-3		7,437
11	Oct	4	H	Watford	W	4-1	Hughes 2, Kilbane, De Freitas	11,840
12		18	H	Sunderland	L	2-3	Hughes 2	20,370
13		21	H	Queen's Park Rangers	W	2-0	Murphy, Evans	11,842
14		24	A	Swindon Town	D	2-2	Flynn, Hughes	8,967
15		31	A	Ipswich Town	L	0-2		15,568
16	Nov	3	H	Crystal Palace	W	3-2	Hughes 3 (1 pen)	11,606
17		7	H	Birmingham City	L	1-3	Carbon	19,472
18		14	H	Huddersfield Town	W	3-1	Hughes 3 (2 pens)	13,626
19		21	A	Portsmouth	L	1-2	Hughes	11,144
20		29	H	Wolverhampton Wanderers	W	2-0	Murphy, Kilbane	22,682
21	Dec	5	A	Bury	L	0-2		5,007
22		8	A	Crewe Alexandra	D	1-1	Hughes (pen)	5,007
23		12	A	Huddersfield Town	W	3-0	Quinn 2, Hughes	11,947
24		19	H	Tranmere Rovers	L	0-2		13,966
25		26	H	Port Vale	W	3-2	Murphy, Hughes (pen), Bortolazzi	14,929
26		28	A	Crystal Palace	D	1-1	Hughes	19,137
27	Jan	9	H	Barnsley	W	2-0	Murphy, Hughes	15,029
28		16	A	Norwich City	D	1-1	Bortolazzi	15,411
29		23	A	Watford	W	2-0	Sneekes, Angel	11,664
30		30	H	Grimsby Town	D	1-1	Hughes	17,843
31	Feb	6	A	Sheffield United	L	0-3		16,566
32		13	A	Bolton Wanderers	L	1-2	De Freitas	20,657
33		20	H	Bristol City	D	2-2	Hughes 2	16,343
34		27	A	Bradford City	L	0-1		14,278
35	Mar	2	H	Stockport County	W	3-1	Hughes, Kilbane, De Freitas	11,801
36		6	H	Oxford United	W	2-0	Quinn, Maresca	13,853
37		13	A	Birmingham City	L	0-4		29,060
38		20	H	Ipswich Town	L	0-1		15,552
39	Apr	3	A	Sunderland	L	0-3		41,135
40		5	H	Crewe Alexandra	L	1-5	Sneekes	12,305
41		10	A	Queen's Park Rangers	L	1-2	Kilbane	11,158
42		13	H	Swindon Town	D	1-1	Hughes	9,741
43		17	H	Portsmouth	D	2-2	Quinn, Maresca	12,750
44		25	A	Wolverhampton Wanderers	D	1-1	Evans	27,038
45	May	1	H	Bury	W	1-0	De Freitas	12,891
46		9	A	Tranmere Rovers	L	1-3	De Freitas	10,540

Appearances
Sub appearances
Goals

FA Cup

R3	Jan	2	A	Bournemouth	L	0-1		10,881

Appearances
Sub appearances

League Cup

R1/1	Aug	11	H	Brentford	W	2-1	Evans, Hughes	8,460
R1/2		18	A	Brentford	L	0-3		4,664

Appearances
Sub appearances
Goals

	Miller AJ	Mardon PJ	Van Blerk J	Flynn SM	Murphy SP	Carbon MP	Quinn SJ	Sneekes R	Evans MJ	Hughes L	Kilbane KD	Bortolazzi M	De Freitas F	Burgess D	Angel M	Raven PD	McDermott A	Maresca E	Potter GS	Holmes P	Whitehead PM	Gabbidon DL	Richards J	Quailey BS	Oliver A	
	1	2	3	4	5	6	7	8	9	10	11															1
	1	2	3	**4**	5	6	7	8	9	10	11	12														2
	1	2	3	4	5	6	7	8		**10**	11	9	12													3
	1	2	3	4	*5*	6	**7**	8	9	10	11	12	13	14												4
	1	2	3	*4*	5	6	7	8	**9**	10		12	13	14	11											5
	1	2	3	4		6	7	8	**9**	10	11		12			5										6
	1	12	3	4		6	7	8		**10**	11	13	9			5	2									7
	1	12	3	*4*		**6**	7	8		10	11		9		13	5	2	14								8
	1	6	3	4	12		**7**	8		10	11	13	9			5	2									9
	1	*6*			12	3	7	8		10	11	4	9			**5**	2	13	14							10
	1		3	4	5	6	7			10	11	8	**9**		12		2	13								11
	1	12	3	4	5	6	7	13		10	11	8	**9**				2									12
	1		3	4	5	6	7		12	10	11	8	**9**				2									13
	1		3	4	5	6	7		**9**	10	11	8			12		2									14
	1		3	4	5	6	7		**9**	10	11	8	12				2	13								15
	1	12	3	*4*	5	6	7		9	10	11	8	13				**2**	14								16
	1	12	3	4	5	6	*7*		9	10	11	8	13				**2**	14								17
	1		3	4	5	6	7	12		10	11	8	**9**		13					2						18
	1		3	4	5	6	*7*	12		10	**11**	8	9	14	13					2						19
	1		3	4	5	6	**7**	12	9	10	11	8	13							2						20
		12		4	5	6	7	13	**9**		11	*8*	10		14				3	2	1					21
			3	4	5	6	**7**	9		10	11	8	12					13		2	1					22
		6		4	5		12	8		10	11		**9**		13			7	3	2	1					23
		6		4	5	12		8	13	10	**11**		*9*		14			7	3	2	1					24
					5	6	**9**	8		10	11	4	12					7	3	2	1					25
		2		12	5	6	9	8		10	11	4						**7**	3		1					26
				12	5	6	9	8		10	*11*	**4**	13	14				7	3	2	1					27
				11	5	6	7	8		10		**4**	9		12			13	3	2	1					28
				12		6	7	8		10	11	4	**9**	5	13				3	2	1					29
				12	13	6	7	8	*9*	10	11	**4**		5	14				3	2	1					30
					12	6	7	8		10	11	4	9	**5**	13				3	2	1					31
				4	5	*6*	7	8		10	**11**	12	9	14	13				3	2	1					32
			3	12	5		7	8		10	11	4	**9**		13	6				2	1					33
			3		5		**9**	8		10	11	4	12	6	7	13				2	1					34
				4		6	**7**	8		10	11		9	5	12		2	13	3		1					35
				4		6	7	8		**10**	11	13	9	5			2	12	3		1					36
				4	12	6	*7*	8			11	13	9	5	14		2	10	**3**		1					37
				4	12	6	*7*	8			11		9	5	10			13	**3**		1	2	14			38
			4		5	6	7	**8**		10	11	9	12		13				3		1	2				39
			3		12	6		8		**10**	11	*4*		5	9			7	13	2	1			14		40
			3		4	*6*	7	8	12		11		**9**	5			2	13	14		1			10		41
			6		4		**7**	8	9	10	11			5	12		2		3		1					42
			6	7	4		12	8	**9**	10	11			5			2	13	3		1					43
			4	7		6	12	8	**9**	10	11			5			2		3		1					44
			3	7		6	12	8	*9*	10	**11**	13	14	5			2	4			1					45
		6	3	**7**				8	9	10	11	12	13	5			2	*4*			1				14	46
	20	12	30	33	30	38	39	35	17	42	44	25	22	15	4	6	20	9	19	17	26	2		1		
		6		5	7	1	4	5	3			10	15	5	18	1		13	3				1	1	1	
				2	4	2	6	4	2	31	6	2	7		1			2								

	Miller AJ	Mardon PJ	Van Blerk J	Flynn SM	Murphy SP	Carbon MP	Quinn SJ	Sneekes R	Evans MJ	Hughes L	Kilbane KD	Bortolazzi M	De Freitas F	Burgess D	Angel M	Raven PD	McDermott A	Maresca E	Potter GS	Holmes P	Whitehead PM	Gabbidon DL	Richards J	Quailey BS	Oliver A	
				14	5	6	*9*	8		10	11	**4**	13		12			7	3	2	1					R3
					1	1	1	1		1	1	1						1	1	1	1					
				1									1		1											

	Miller AJ	Mardon PJ	Van Blerk J	Flynn SM	Murphy SP	Carbon MP	Quinn SJ	Sneekes R	Evans MJ	Hughes L	Kilbane KD	Bortolazzi M	De Freitas F	Burgess D	Angel M	Raven PD	McDermott A	Maresca E	Potter GS	Holmes P	Whitehead PM	Gabbidon DL	Richards J	Quailey BS	Oliver A	
	1	**2**	3	4	5	6	7	8	9	10	*11*			12	13										14	R1/1
	1	2	3	4	5	6	7	8	**9**	10	11								13					12		R1/2
	2	2	2	2	2	2	2	2	2	2	2															
														1	1				1					1	1	
									1	1																

1999-2000

Division One

	P	W	D	L	F	A	Pts
Charlton Athletic	46	27	10	9	79	45	91
Manchester City	46	26	11	9	78	40	89
Ipswich Town	46	25	12	9	71	42	87
Barnsley	46	24	10	12	88	67	82
Birmingham City	46	22	11	13	65	44	77
Bolton Wanderers	46	21	13	12	69	50	76
Wolverhampton W	46	21	11	14	64	48	74
Huddersfield Town	46	21	11	14	62	49	74
Fulham	46	17	16	13	49	41	67
Queen's Park Rangers	46	16	18	12	62	53	66
Blackburn Rovers	46	15	17	14	55	51	62
Norwich City	46	14	15	17	45	50	57
Tranmere Rovers	46	15	12	19	57	68	57
Nottingham Forest	46	14	14	18	53	55	56
Crystal Palace	46	13	15	18	57	67	54
Sheffield United	46	13	15	18	59	71	54
Stockport County	46	13	15	18	55	67	54
Portsmouth	46	13	12	21	55	66	51
Crewe Alexandra	46	14	9	23	46	67	51
Grimsby Town	46	13	12	21	41	67	51
West Bromwich Albion	46	10	19	17	43	60	49
Walsall	46	11	13	22	52	77	46
Port Vale	46	7	15	24	48	69	36
Swindon Town	46	8	12	26	38	77	36

Manager: Denis Smith, Brian Little then Gary Megson

- Albion had three different managers this season: Denis Smith (briefly during June and July 1999), Brian Little (August 1999 to February 2000) and Gary Megson (from March 2000).
- Albion transferred Enzo Maresca to Juventus for a club record fee of £4.5 million in January 2000, beating the previous record of £2.5 million received from Sunderland for Kevin Kilbane who moved to The Stadium of Light in December 1999.
- Players signed included defender Larus Sigurdsson from Stoke City for £325,000, full-backs Neil Clement from Chelsea and Des Lyttle from Watford, and goalkeeper Brian 'The Beast' Jensen from AZ Alkmaar (Holland). Paul Raven moved to Grimsby Town after 10 years with the club and 'keeper Alan Miller signed for Blackburn Rovers.
- Albion gained seven points from the last three games to retain their First Division status – and the 4–4 home draw with Bolton Wanderers was the first such scoreline at The Hawthorns since March 1996.
- Paul Thompson moved in as club chairman, taking over from Tony Hale.

Match No.	Date			Opponents	Result		Scorers	Attendance
1	Aug	7	H	Norwich City	D	1-1	Raven	16,196
2		14	A	Port Vale	W	2-1	Hughes, Kilbane	7,891
3		20	H	Nottingham Forest	D	1-1	Hughes	13,202
4		28	A	Swindon Town	W	2-1	Evans, Kilbane	6,565
5		30	H	Fulham	D	0-0		13,194
6	Sep	11	A	Birmingham City	D	1-1	Hughes	25,495
7		18	H	Blackburn Rovers	D	2-2	Kilbane 2	16,912
8		25	H	Crystal Palace	D	0-0		13,161
9	Oct	3	A	Wolverhampton Wanderers	D	1-1	Carbon	25,500
10		16	H	Walsall	L	0-1		19,582
11		19	H	Queen's Park Rangers	L	0-1		9,643
12		23	A	Charlton Athletic	D	0-0		19,345
13		26	A	Crystal Palace	W	2-0	Flynn, Maresca	12,203
14		31	H	Wolverhampton Wanderers	D	1-1	McDermott	21,097
15	Nov	6	A	Tranmere Rovers	L	0-3		6,623
16		14	H	Portsmouth	W	3-2	Maresca, Evans, Van Blerk	11,483
17		20	A	Huddersfield Town	L	0-1		14,244
18		23	H	Stockport County	W	2-0	Hughes 2	9,104
19		27	H	Sheffield United	D	2-2	Maresca, Evans	12,140
20	Dec	4	A	Norwich City	L	1-2	Kilbane	15,183
21		7	A	Crewe Alexandra	L	0-2		5,419
22		14	A	Grimsby Town	D	1-1	Hughes	4,759
23		18	A	Ipswich Town	L	1-3	De Freitas	14,713
24		26	H	Manchester City	L	0-2		19,481
25		28	A	Bolton Wanderers	D	1-1	Burgess	16,269
26	Jan	3	H	Barnsley	L	0-2		13,354
27		15	H	Port Vale	D	0-0		10,696
28		22	A	Nottingham Forest	D	0-0		19,863
29		29	H	Swindon Town	D	1-1	Hughes (pen)	11,856
30	Feb	5	A	Fulham	L	0-1		12,044
31		12	H	Crewe Alexandra	W	1-0	Hughes	12,406
32		19	A	Sheffield United	L	0-6		14,519
33		26	A	Blackburn Rovers	L	1-2	Carbon	18,184
34	Mar	4	H	Birmingham City	L	0-3		17,029
35		7	H	Tranmere Rovers	W	2-0	Flynn, Hughes	11,819
36		11	A	Stockport County	W	1-0	Hughes	8,238
37		18	H	Huddersfield Town	L	0-1		15,484
38		21	A	Portsmouth	L	0-2		14,760
39		25	A	Manchester City	L	1-2	Hughes	30,072
40	Apr	4	H	Ipswich Town	D	1-1	Hughes	12,498
41		8	A	Barnsley	D	2-2	Sneekes (pen), Taylor	16,329
42		15	H	Bolton Wanderers	D	4-4	Flynn, Sneekes (pen), Oliver, Taylor	12,802
43		22	A	Walsall	L	1-2	Flynn	9,161
44		24	H	Grimsby Town	W	2-1	Taylor 2	15,291
45		29	A	Queen's Park Rangers	D	0-0		15,244
46	May	7	H	Charlton Athletic	W	2-0	Sneekes, Taylor	22,101

Appearances
Sub appearances
Goals

FA Cup

R3	Dec	11	H	Blackburn Rovers	D	2-2	Evans, Hughes	10,609
rep		22	A	Blackburn Rovers	L	0-2*		11,766

* after extra-time

Appearances
Sub appearances
Goals

League Cup

R1/1	Aug	10	A	Halifax Town	D	0-0		2,451
R1/2		24	H	Halifax Town	W	5-1	Evans, Hughes, Kilbane 2, De Freitas	8,316
R2/1	Sep	14	H	Wycombe Wanderers	D	1-1	Flynn	9,383
R2/2		21	A	Wycombe Wanderers	W	4-3*	Hughes, Raven, Quinn, De Freitas	5,047
R3	Oct	12	H	Fulham	L	1-2	Hughes	10,556

* after extra-time

Appearances
Sub appearances
Goals

Miller AJ	Gabbidon DL	Potter GS	Flynn SM	Burgess D	Carbon MP	Maresca E	Sneekes R	Evans MJ	Hughes L	Kilbane KD	Raven PD	Quinn SJ	De Freitas F	Van Blerk J	Oliver A	Sigurdsson LO	Townsend AD	McDermott A	Angel M	Adamson C	Chambers JA	Hall PA	Fredgaard C	Jensen B	Lyttle D	Clement N	Butler PA	Taylor R	Santos G	Richards J	
1	**2**	3	4	5	6	7	8	*9*	10	11	12	13	14																		1
1	2		4	5		12	8		10	11	6	**7**	9	3																	2
1	2		4	5	12	**7**	8		10	11	6		9	3																	3
1	2		7	5	6	12	8	9	10	11	4			**3**																	4
1	2		7	5	6	11	8	12	10		4		**9**	3	13																5
1	2	13	4		6	*7*	8	12	10	11	5		**9**	3	14																6
1	2		4		5		**8**		10	11		12	9	3		6	7														7
1	2		4		5	12	8		10	11	3	13	9			6	**7**														8
1	2		7		5	12	8		10	11	6	13	9	**3**		4															9
1	2		*4*	13		14	8		**10**	11	5	9	12	3		6	7														10
1			4		5	10	8	12		11	3	9				6	**7**	2													11
1			4		5	7	8	12	10	11	**3**	9				6		2													12
1			4		5	7	8		10	11	3	9				6		2													13
1			4		5	7	8		10	11	3	9				6		2													14
1			4		5	**7**		12	10	11	3	9		8		6		2													15
1			4	5		7	8	12	10		3	9		11		6		**2**													16
1			4	2		**7**	8	12	10	11	5	9	13	3		6															17
1			4	2		7	8		10	11	5	9		3		6															18
1			4	**2**		7	8	12		11	5	9	*10*	3	14	6		13													19
1				2	5	7	8	*9*	10	11	3		12	13		6	**4**	14													20
1	**2**			5	6	12	8	13	10	11	3	9		7		4															21
1	2			5	6		8	9	10		3	7		11		4															22
1	2				5	11	8	9	**10**		6	*7*	12	3		4		13	14												23
1	**2**			5		7	8	9	10		6	11	12	3		4															24
1				2		7	8	**9**	10		5	11	12	3		6	4		13												25
	5	3		6		7	8	9				11	10				4	2		1											26
	2	3		5	6	7	*8*	13	10			9		12	14		11			1	4										27
	2	3		5	6		8	12	10			9		11			7			1	4										28
		12	7	2	5		8	13	10			9		3		6	11			1	**4**										29
		3	7		5		8	12	10		13	9		2	**11**	6			14	1	4										30
			2		5		*8*	**9**	10		3	12			14	6	13			1	4	7	11								31
			2		5		8	9	**10**		3					6	12			1	4	7	11								32
			2		**5**		8	9	10		12			3		6				1	4	7	11								33
			2		5			9				10	12	3		6	11			1	4	**7**	8								34
		12	4		5			9	10			7	13	3	14	6	*11*	2					**8**	1							35
		3			5			**9**	10		13	7	12	11	14	6	8	*2*			4			1							36
			7	12	5		8	9	10		*6*		13	3	14		11	**2**			4			1							37
	2		4	5	6		8	9	10		12	7		3	13		**11**							1	14						38
			4		5		8		10			**7**					12				13			1	2	3	6	9	11		39
			4				8		**10**			7	12	11										1	2	3	6	9	5		40
			4	12			8				**5**	13	10	11	14									1	2	3	6	9	7		41
		12	7	4	5		8					13	*10*		14									1	2	**3**	6	9	11		42
			7	**4**	5		8	12					10	*3*	13									1	2	14	6	9	11		43
			7	5			8	12				**10**		11										1	2	3	6	9	4		44
			7	5	6		8	12				10		**11**	13						14			1	*2*	3		9	4		45
			7		5		8	12				**10**		11	13									1	2	3	6	9	4		46
25	18	6	36	23	33	19	42	16	36	19	27	30	12	33	1	27	15	10		9	10	4	5	12	8	7	7	8	8		
		4		3	1	6		17			5	7	12	2	14		3	3	3		2				1	1					
			4	1	2	3	3	3	12	5	1		1	1	1			1										5			

	2			5	6	7	8	12	10	11	3	9				4				1											R3
1	2				5		8	9	10		6		**7**	3	4			12	11											13	rep
1	2			1	2	1	2	1	2	1	2	1	1	1	1	1			1	1											
								1										1												1	
								1	1																						

1	12		4	5	**6**		8	13	10	11	2	7	9	3																	R1/1
1	2	13	**4**	5	12	7	8	14	10	11	6		*9*	3																	R1/2
1	5	12	4		6	13	**8**	9	10	11			7	3				2													R2/1
1	**2**		4	5	6	13	8	14	10	11	3	12	*9*				7														R2/2
1	**2**		4		5	12	8		10	11	6	14	*9*	13			7	3													R3
5	4		5	3	4	1	5	1	5	5	4	1	5	3			2	2													
	1	2			1	3		3				2		1																	
			1					1	3	2	1	1	2																		

2000-01

Division One

	P	W	D	L	F	A	Pts
Fulham	46	30	11	5	90	32	101
Blackburn Rovers	46	26	13	7	76	39	91
Bolton Wanderers	46	24	15	7	76	45	87
Preston North End	46	23	9	14	64	52	78
Birmingham City	46	23	9	14	59	48	78
West Bromwich Albion	46	21	11	14	60	52	74
Burnley	46	21	9	16	50	54	72
Wimbledon	46	17	18	11	71	50	69
Watford	46	20	9	17	76	67	69
Sheffield United	46	19	11	16	52	49	68
Nottingham Forest	46	20	8	18	55	53	68
Wolverhampton W	46	14	13	19	45	48	55
Gillingham	46	13	16	17	61	66	55
Crewe Alexandra	46	15	10	21	47	62	55
Norwich City	46	14	12	20	46	58	54
Barnsley	46	15	9	22	49	62	54
Sheffield Wednesday	46	15	8	23	52	71	53
Grimsby Town	46	14	10	22	43	62	52
Stockport County	46	11	18	17	58	65	51
Portsmouth	46	10	19	17	47	59	49
Crystal Palace	46	12	13	21	57	70	49
Huddersfield Town	46	11	15	20	48	57	48
Queen's Park Rangers	46	7	19	20	45	75	40
Tranmere Rovers	46	9	11	26	46	77	38

Manager: Gary Megson

- Striker Jason Roberts signed from Bristol Rovers (the club's first £2m player), midfielder Derek McInnes from Glasgow Rangers, Jordao from Sporting Braga (Portugal), Ruel Fox from Tottenham Hotspur, Igor Balis from Slovan Bratislava and Russell Hoult from Portsmouth.
- Players who left The Hawthorns included long-serving defender Daryl Burgess (to Northampton Town after 375 first-team appearances), Matthew Carbon (to Walsall) and Richard Sneekes (to Stockport County), while Paul Mardon was forced to retire through injury.
- Albion held a 2–0 first-leg lead over Bolton Wanderers in their Play-off semi-final but were pegged back and eventually beaten 5–2 on aggregate.

Match No.	Date			Opponents	Result		Scorers	Attendance
1	Aug	12	A	Nottingham Forest	L	0-1		21,209
2		19	H	Bolton Wanderers	L	0-2		17,316
3		26	A	Barnsley	L	1-4	Hughes	14,324
4		28	H	Queen's Park Rangers	W	2-1	Hughes, Van Blerk	15,135
5	Sep	3	H	Crystal Palace	W	1-0	McInnes	13,980
6		9	A	Stockport County	D	0-0		6,632
7		12	A	Crewe Alexandra	W	1-0	Hughes	6,222
8		17	H	Birmingham City	D	1-1	Taylor	19,858
9		23	A	Portsmouth	W	1-0	Roberts	11,937
10		30	H	Blackburn Rovers	W	1-0	Hughes	16,794
11	Oct	8	A	Sheffield Wednesday	W	2-1	Roberts 2	15,338
12		14	H	Norwich City	L	2-3	Clement, Hughes (pen)	16,511
13		17	H	Wolverhampton Wanderers	W	1-0	Hughes (pen)	21,492
14		21	A	Tranmere Rovers	D	2-2	Roberts, Hughes	8,931
15		24	H	Wimbledon	W	3-1	Sneekes, Roberts, Van Blerk	15,570
16		29	A	Grimsby Town	L	0-2		5,429
17	Nov	4	H	Burnley	D	1-1	Roberts	17,828
18		11	A	Huddersfield Town	W	2-0	Hughes, Batista	11,801
19		18	H	Gillingham	W	3-1	Hughes 3	16,410
20		25	H	Preston North End	W	3-1	Hughes 3	20,043
21	Dec	2	A	Wimbledon	W	1-0	Williams (og)	8,608
22		9	H	Fulham	L	1-3	Lyttle	22,301
23		16	A	Watford	D	3-3	Sneekes, Roberts, Hughes	14,601
24		23	H	Nottingham Forest	W	3-0	Olsen (og), Roberts 2	20,350
25		26	A	Sheffield United	L	0-2		22,281
26		30	A	Bolton Wanderers	W	1-0	Roberts	18,985
27	Jan	1	H	Barnsley	W	1-0	Morgan (og)	19,423
28		13	A	Queen's Park Rangers	L	0-2		11,881
29		20	H	Sheffield United	W	2-1	Hughes, Fox	16,778
30	Feb	3	A	Crystal Palace	D	2-2	Sneekes, Hughes	16,692
31		10	H	Stockport County	D	1-1	Roberts	16,385
32		17	A	Birmingham City	L	1-2	Butler	25,025
33		20	H	Crewe Alexandra	D	2-2	Roberts, Taylor	16,177
34		24	H	Portsmouth	W	2-0	Roberts, A. Chambers	17,645
35	Mar	3	A	Blackburn Rovers	L	0-1		23,926
36		6	A	Norwich City	W	1-0	Hughes (pen)	16,372
37		10	H	Sheffield Wednesday	L	1-2	Hughes	18,662
38		18	A	Wolverhampton Wanderers	L	1-3	Clement	25,069
39		25	H	Tranmere Rovers	W	2-1	Taylor 2	17,151
40		31	H	Watford	W	3-0	Clement, Quinn, Hughes	17,261
41	Apr	7	A	Fulham	D	0-0		16,190
42		14	A	Burnley	D	1-1	Taylor	17,132
43		16	H	Grimsby Town	L	0-1		16,493
44		21	A	Gillingham	W	2-1	Clement, Hughes	9,920
45		28	H	Huddersfield Town	D	1-1	Roberts	17,522
46	May	6	A	Preston North End	L	1-2	Clement	16,226

Appearances
Sub appearances
Goals

FA Cup

R3	Jan	6	A	Derby County	L	2-3	Hughes, Taylor	19,232

Appearances
Sub appearances
Goals

League Cup

R1/1	Aug	22	A	Swansea City	D	0-0		4,758
R1/2	Sep	6	H	Swansea City	W	2-1	Roberts 2	7,328
R2/1		19	A	Derby County	W	2-1	Clement, Sneekes	12,183
R2/2		26	H	Derby County	L	2-4	Clement, Batista	19,112

Appearances
Sub appearances
Goals

	Jensen B	Lyttle D	Clement N	McInnes DJ	Carbon MP	Butler PA	Quinn SJ	Sneekes R	Roberts JAD	Hughes L	Van Blerk J	Oliver A	Taylor R	Chambers JA	Batista AJM	Fox RA	Chambers AC	Burgess D	Grant AJ	Balis I	Sigurdsson LO	Appleton MA	Derveld F	Hoult R	Gilchrist PA	Cummings W	Adamson C
1	1	2	3	4	5	6	7	8	9	10	11	12	13	14													
2	1	2	3	4	5	6	7	8	9	10	11	13	12														
3	1	2	3	7	5	6	12	8		10		4	9	13	11	14											
4	1	2	3	4		6		12		10	8	13	9	5	11	7											
5	1	2	3	4	12	6		13	14	10	8		9	5	11	7											
6	1	2	3		5	6		8	13	10	7	12	9	4	11		14										
7	1	2	3	4		6		8	12	10	7		9	5	11												
8	1	2	3	4		6		8	12	10	7		9	5	11	13											
9	1	2	3	4		6		12	9	10	8		13	5	11	7											
10	1	2	3	4		6		12	9	10	8		13	5	11	7		14									
11	1	2	3	4		6		8	9	10	11			5		7											
12	1	2	3	4	12	6		8	9	10	11		13	5	14	7											
13	1		3	4	5	6		12	9	10	8		13	2	11	7											
14	1		3	4	5	6			9	10	8		12	2	11	7											
15	1		3	4	5	6		12	9	10	8			2	11	7											
16	1	12	4		5	6		8	9	10	3		13	2	11	7		14									
17	1	2	4			6	12	8	10		3		9	5	11	7	13										
18	1	2	4			6	12	8	9	10	3	13		5	11	7											
19	1	2	3		5	6	9	8		10		12		4	11	7											
20	1	2	4		12	6		8	9	10	3		13	5	11	7											
21	1	2	4			6		8	9	10	3		12	5	11	7											
22	1	2	4			6	12	8	9	10	3		13	5	11	7			14								
23	1	2	4		12	6		8	9	10	3		13	5	11	7			14								
24	1	2	4			6		8	9	10	3			5	12	7			11	13							
25	1	2	4		12	6		8	9	10	3		13	5		7			11	14							
26	1	2	3		5	6		8	9	10			12	4	11				7		13						
27	1	2	3		5	6		8	9	10			12	4	11	7				13							
28	1	2	3		5	6		8	9	10			12	4	11	7				13							
29	1	2	3		5	6		8	9	10			12	4		7				14	13	11					
30	1	2	4					8	9	10	3		12	5	13	7		6				11					
31	1	2	4		5	6		8	9	10	3		12			7						11	13				
32	1	2	4		5	6		8	9	10	12		13		14	7						11	3				
33	1		4		5	6		8	10		3		9		11	7	2				12						
34			3		5	6	12	8	10				9			7	2				4	11		1			
35		12			5	6		8	13		3		9	14	10	7	2				4	11		1			
36		2	4			6		8	9	10	3		13		12	7					5	11		1			
37		2	4			6		8	9	10	3		12		13	7	14				5	11		1			
38		2	4		5	6		8	9	10	3				12	7				14	13	11		1			
39		2	4			6		8	12	10	3		9		11	7								1	5	13	
40		2	4			6	12	8	13	10			9		11							7		1	5	3	
41		2	4			6		8	12	10	3		9		11		13					7		1	5		
42		2	4			6	13	8	12	10	3		9			7					14	11		1	5		
43		2	4			6	12	8	13	10	3		9			7	14					11		1	5		
44		2	3			6	14	8	12	10			9			7	13				4	11		1	5		
45		2	3			6	12	8	9	10			13			7	14				4	11		1	5		
46			4				13	8	10		3		9	12	11		7			2	6			1	5	14	
	33	38	45	14	19	44	3	39	32	41	35	1	17	27	28	36	4	1	3	1	7	15	1	13	8	1	
		2			5		11	6	11		1	6	23	4	7	2	7	2	2	6	5		1			2	
		1	5	1		1	1	2	14	21	2		5		1	1	1										

Three own-goals

	Jensen B	Lyttle D	Clement N	McInnes DJ	Carbon MP	Butler PA	Quinn SJ	Sneekes R	Roberts JAD	Hughes L	Van Blerk J	Oliver A	Taylor R	Chambers JA	Batista AJM	Fox RA	Chambers AC	Burgess D	Grant AJ	Balis I	Sigurdsson LO	Appleton MA	Derveld F	Hoult R	Gilchrist PA	Cummings W	Adamson C
R3		2	3		5	6		8	9	10			12	4	11	7				13							1
		1	1		1	1		1	1	1				1	1	1											1
													1							1							
										1			1														

	Jensen B	Lyttle D	Clement N	McInnes DJ	Carbon MP	Butler PA	Quinn SJ	Sneekes R	Roberts JAD	Hughes L	Van Blerk J	Oliver A	Taylor R	Chambers JA	Batista AJM	Fox RA	Chambers AC	Burgess D	Grant AJ	Balis I	Sigurdsson LO	Appleton MA	Derveld F	Hoult R	Gilchrist PA	Cummings W	Adamson C
R1/1	1	2	3	7	5	6		12	11	10		8	9	4													
R1/2	1	2	3	4	13	6			12	10	8	14	9	5	11	7											
R2/1	1	2	3	8		6		12	9	13	10			4	11	7	5										
R2/2	1	2	3	4		6		12	9	10	8		13	5	11	7	14										
	4	4	4	4	1	4			3	3	3	1	2	4	3	3	1										
					1			3	1	1		1	1				1										
			2					1	2						1												

2001-02

Division One

	P	W	D	L	F	A	Pts
Manchester City	46	31	6	9	108	52	99
West Bromwich Albion	46	27	8	11	61	29	89
Wolverhampton W	46	25	11	10	76	43	86
Millwall	46	22	11	13	69	48	77
Birmingham City	46	21	13	12	70	49	76
Norwich City	46	22	9	15	60	51	75
Burnley	46	21	12	13	70	62	75
Preston North End	46	20	12	14	71	59	72
Wimbledon	46	18	13	15	63	57	67
Crystal Palace	46	20	6	20	70	62	66
Coventry City	46	20	6	20	59	53	66
Gillingham	46	18	10	18	64	67	64
Sheffield United	46	15	15	16	53	54	60
Watford	46	16	11	19	62	56	59
Bradford City	46	15	10	21	69	76	55
Nottingham Forest	46	12	18	16	50	51	54
Portsmouth	46	13	14	19	60	72	53
Walsall	46	13	12	21	51	71	51
Grimsby Town	46	12	14	20	50	72	50
Sheffield Wednesday	46	12	14	20	49	71	50
Rotherham United	46	10	19	17	52	66	49
Crewe Alexandra	46	12	13	21	47	76	49
Barnsley	46	11	15	20	59	86	48
Stockport County	46	6	8	32	42	102	26

Manager: Gary Megson

- By beating Crystal Palace 2–0 at The Hawthorns in the final game of the season, Albion gained automatic promotion to the Premiership.
- The Albion against Sheffield United League game at Bramall Lane in March was abandoned after 83 minutes because the Blades had only six players on the pitch – three had been sent off and two more had walked off injured. The result (3–0 to Albion) was allowed to stand.
- Russell Hoult kept a club record 27 clean sheets this season (24 in the League) and Albion also gained a record 17 1–0 wins, 15 in the League.
- Players signed were strikers Danny Dichio (from Sunderland) and Scott Dobie (from Carlisle United, who was Albion's top scorer), Andy Johnson (from Nottingham Forest) and defender Darren Moore (from Portsmouth).
- The Chambers, Adam and James, played in the same League game together for the first time against Gillingham in August.
- Boss Gary Megson was named as the First Division's Manager of the Year.
- Record gate receipts of £375,272 were banked from Albion's home FA Cup tie with Cheltenham Town.

Match No.	Date			Opponents	Result		Scorers	Attendance
1	Aug	11	A	Walsall	L	1-2	Clement	9,181
2		18	H	Grimsby Town	L	0-1		17,971
3		25	A	Sheffield Wednesday	D	1-1	Dobie	18,844
4		27	H	Gillingham	W	1-0	Dichio	18,180
5	Sep	8	H	Manchester City	W	4-0	Clement 2 (1 pen), McInnes, Dobie	23,524
6		15	A	Watford	W	2-1	Dobie 2	15,726
7		18	H	Preston North End	W	2-0	Dobie 2	18,289
8		22	H	Wimbledon	L	0-1		19,122
9		25	A	Portsmouth	W	2-1	Clement, Dobie	17,287
10		29	H	Burnley	W	1-0	Dobie	21,422
11	Oct	11	H	Millwall	L	0-2		17,335
12		16	A	Stockport County	W	2-1	Taylor 2	6,052
13		19	A	Norwich City	L	0-2		20,465
14		25	H	Wolverhampton Wanderers	D	1-1	Clement	26,143
15		28	A	Barnsley	L	2-3	Clement, Johnson	12,490
16		31	A	Crystal Palace	W	1-0	Taylor	17,273
17	Nov	4	H	Nottingham Forest	W	1-0	Rosler	18,281
18		7	A	Birmingham City	W	1-0	Johnson	23,554
19		17	A	Rotherham United	L	1-2	Moore	8,509
20		24	H	Bradford City	W	1-0	McInnes	18,910
21	Dec	2	A	Wolverhampton Wanderers	W	1-0	Batista	27,515
22		8	H	Sheffield United	L	0-1		19,462
23		12	H	Coventry City	W	1-0	Konjic (og)	22,543
24		15	A	Crewe Alexandra	D	1-1	Batista	8,154
25		22	H	Sheffield Wednesday	D	1-1	Fox	20,340
26		26	A	Manchester City	D	0-0		34,407
27		29	A	Gillingham	L	1-2	Johnson	9,912
28	Jan	1	H	Stockport County	W	4-0	Dichio 2, Roberts, Johnson	20,541
29		12	A	Grimsby Town	D	0-0		6,011
30		20	H	Walsall	W	1-0	Roberts	20,290
31		29	H	Birmingham City	W	1-0	Roberts	25,266
32	Feb	3	A	Burnley	W	2-0	Roberts 2	15,846
33		10	H	Norwich City	W	1-0	Dichio	19,115
34		19	A	Millwall	L	0-1		13,716
35		23	H	Portsmouth	W	5-0	Balis, Sigurdsson, Dobie, Roberts 2	21,028
36		26	A	Preston North End	L	0-1		14,487
37	Mar	2	A	Wimbledon	W	1-0	Dichio	8,363
38		5	H	Watford	D	1-1	Dichio	19,580
39		16	A	Sheffield United	W	3-0	McInnes, Dobie 2	17,653
40		22	A	Nottingham Forest	W	1-0	Taylor	24,788
41		26	H	Crewe Alexandra	W	4-1	Batista 2, Dichio, Wright (og)	21,303
42		30	H	Barnsley	W	3-1	Dobie, Batista, Dichio	23,167
43	Apr	1	A	Coventry City	W	1-0	Taylor	21,513
44		7	H	Rotherham United	D	1-1	Taylor	22,376
45		13	A	Bradford City	W	1-0	Balis (pen)	20,209
46		21	H	Crystal Palace	W	2-0	Taylor, Moore	26,712
								Appearances
								Sub appearances
								Goals

FA Cup

R3	Jan	5	A	Sunderland	W	2-1	Clement (pen), Johnson	29,133
R4		26	H	Leicester City	W	1-0	Clement (pen)	26,820
R5	Feb	16	H	Cheltenham Town	W	1-0	Dichio	27,179
R6	Mar	10	H	Fulham	L	0-1		24,811
								Appearances
								Sub appearances
								Goals

League Cup

R1	Aug	22	A	Cambridge United	D	1-1*	Dobie	3,363
R2	Sep	11	H	Swindon Town	W	2-0*	Dobie, Batista	14,540
R3	Oct	9	H	Charlton Athletic	L	0-1		17,734
								Appearances
								Sub appearances
								Goals

R1 won on 4-3 on penalties

* after extra-time

Hoult R	Bailis I	Clement N	Sigurdsson LO	Gilchrist PA	Butler PA	Appleton MA	McInnes DJ	Taylor R	Dobie RS	Batista AJM	Cummings W	Quinn SJ	Fox RA	Lyttle D	Dichio DSE	Chambers AC	Chambers JA	Roberts JAD	Moore DM	Johnson AJ	Jensen B	Rosler U	Varga S	Benjamin T	
1	2	3	4	5	6	7	8	9	10	11	12	13	14												1
1	6	3	4	5		11	8	9	10	12	2	13	7												2
1		6	4	5	12	7	8	13	10	11	3			2	9	14									3
1	2	3	4	5	6	7	8	10	11	12					9	13	14								4
1		3	4	5	6	11	8	12	13					2	9	7	14	10							5
1			4	5	6	11	8	9	10		3	12		2		7	13		14						6
1		3	4	5	6	11	8	9	10		12		13	2		7									7
1		3	4	5	6	11	8	9	10			12	13	2		7				14					8
1		6	4		5	11	8	9	10		3			2		12				7					9
1		3	4	5		11	8	9	10			12		2					6	7					10
		3	4	5		11	8	12	10		13		7	2		14			6	9	1				11
1		3	4	5		11	8	9	10					2					6	7					12
1		3	4	5		11	8	9	10		12		14			13	2		6	7					13
1		3	4	5		11	8	9	10			13	12	2					6	7					14
1	12	3	4	5	13	11	8	9				10	14	2					6	7					15
1		3	4	5		11	8	9			12			2					6	7		10			16
1	2	3	4	5		11	8	9	10										6	12		7			17
1	2	3	4	5	6	11	8	12	10								13			7		9			18
1	2	3	4	5	12		8		10	11			14	13					6	7		9			19
1	2	3	4	5			8		10	11	13			12		7			6			9			20
1	2	3	4	5			8		10	11					9	7			6						21
1	2	3	4	5			8	12	10	11	13		14		9	7			6						22
1	2	3	4	5			8	12	10	11					9	7			6	13					23
1	2	3	4	5			8	10		11					9	7		12	6	13					24
1	2	3	4	5			8		10	11			13		9			12	6	7					25
1	2	3	4		12		8		13	11	5		14		9			10	6	7					26
1	2	3			6		8		12	11	4		13	14	9			10	5	7					27
1	2	3	4	5			8	12	11						9	13		10	6	7					28
1	2	3	4	5			8		12					13	9	7		10	6	11					29
1	2	3	4	5			8	13	12	11					9	14		10	6	7					30
1	2	3	4	5			8		12				13	14	9	7		10	6	11					31
1	2	3	4	5			8		12					13	9	7		10	6	11					32
1	2	3	4	5			8		12					13	9	7		10	6	11					33
1	12	3	4	5	6		8		9	11			14	2	13			10		7					34
1	2	3	4	5	6		8	12	9	13	14					7		10		11					35
1	2	3	4	5	6		8	13	9				14	12		7		10		11					36
1	2	3	4	5	6			12	10	8					9	7				11					37
1	2	3	4	5	6		8	14	10	12			13		9	7				11					38
1	2	3	4	5	12		8	14	10	13					9	7			6	11					39
1	2	3	4	5			8	12	10	11					9	7			6						40
1	2	3	4	5			8	12	10	11			13		9	7			6				14		41
1	2	3		5			8		10	11			13	12	9	7			6				4	14	42
1	2	3		5			8	10	12	11				13	9	7			6				4	14	43
1	2	3	12	5			8	10	13	11					9	14			6	7			4		44
1	2	3	4	5			8	12	10						9	7			6	11				13	45
1	2	3	4	5			8	10	12	13			14		9	7			6	11					46
45	32	45	42	43	14	18	45	18	32	19	6	1	2	13	26	24	1	12	31	28	1	5	3		
	2		1		5			16	11	6	8	6	18	10	1	8	4	2	1	4			1	3	
	2	6	1				3	7	10	5			1		9			7	2	4		1			

Two own-goals

1		3	4	5			8		12					2	9	7		10	6	11					R3
1	2	3	4	5			8		14				13	12	9	7		10	6	11					R4
1	2	3	4	5	12		8		13						9	7		10	6	11					R5
1	2	3	4	5			8	12	10				13		9	7			6	11					R6
4	3	4	4	4			4		1					1	4	4		3	4	4					
					1			1	3				2	1											
		2													1					1					

1	12	3	4	5	6	11	8	9	10			13		2		7									R1
1		3	4	5	6	11	8	9	10	14	13	12		2		7									R2
1		3	4	5	6	11	8	9	10		14		13	2		7	12								R3
3		3	3	3	3	3	3	3	3					3		3									
	1									1	2	2	1				1								
									2	1															

2002-03

Premiership

	P	W	D	L	F	A	Pts
Manchester United	38	25	8	5	74	34	83
Arsenal	38	23	9	6	85	42	78
Newcastle United	38	21	6	11	63	48	69
Chelsea	38	19	10	9	68	38	67
Liverpool	38	18	10	10	61	41	64
Blackburn Rovers	38	16	12	10	52	43	60
Everton	38	17	8	13	48	49	59
Southampton	38	13	13	12	43	46	52
Manchester City	38	15	6	17	47	54	51
Tottenham Hotspur	38	14	8	16	51	62	50
Middlesbrough	38	13	10	15	48	44	49
Charlton Athletic	38	14	7	17	45	56	49
Birmingham City	38	13	9	16	41	49	48
Fulham	38	13	9	16	41	50	48
Leeds United	38	14	5	19	58	57	47
Aston Villa	38	12	9	17	42	47	45
Bolton Wanderers	38	10	14	14	41	51	44
West Ham United	38	10	12	16	42	59	42
West Bromwich Albion	38	6	8	24	29	65	26
Sunderland	38	4	7	27	21	65	19

Manager: Gary Megson

- The biggest League crowd ever to watch Albion in action – 67,645 – saw the opening-day defeat against Manchester United at Old Trafford when Derek McInnes was harshly sent off with the scores level.
- Bob Taylor played his 377th and final game for Albion against Newcastle United on the last day of the season. Over 16,000 fans attended his testimonial match 48 hours later.
- The Chambers brothers became the first set of twins to appear in the same Premiership match – for Albion against Arsenal in December.
- Fresh faces at The Hawthorns included Lee Hughes (a record buy from Coventry City, who rejoined the club), Scott Marshall (from Leicester City), Lloyd Dyer (a former Aston Villa junior), Sean Gregan (from Preston North End), Jason Koumas (from Tranmere Rovers for a record £2.25 million), Joe Murphy (from Tranmere Rovers), Nigerian international Ifeanyi Udeze (from PAOL Salonika) and Ronnie Wallwork (from Manchester United).
- Jordao and Des Lyttle were among those who departed.
- Jeremy Peace was named as the club's new chairman, replacing Paul Thompson.

Match No.	Date			Opponents	Result		Scorers	Attendance
1	Aug	17	A	Manchester United	L	0-1		67,645
2		24	H	Leeds United	L	1-3	Marshall	26,618
3		27	A	Arsenal	L	2-5	Roberts, Dobie	37,920
4		31	H	Fulham	W	1-0	Moore	25,461
5	Sep	11	A	West Ham United	W	1-0	Roberts	34,957
6		14	H	Southampton	W	1-0	Gregan	26,383
7		21	A	Liverpool	L	0-2		43,830
8		30	H	Blackburn Rovers	L	0-2		25,170
9	Oct	5	A	Newcastle United	L	1-2	Balis	52,142
10		19	H	Birmingham City	D	1-1	Roberts	27,021
11		26	A	Chelsea	L	0-2		40,893
12	Nov	2	H	Manchester City	L	1-2	Clement	27,044
13		9	A	Bolton Wanderers	D	1-1	Dobie	23,630
14		16	H	Aston Villa	D	0-0		27,091
15		23	A	Everton	L	0-1		40,113
16		30	H	Middlesbrough	W	1-0	Dichio	27,029
17	Dec	8	A	Tottenham Hotspur	L	1-3	Dobie	35,958
18		14	A	Aston Villa	L	1-2	Koumas	40,391
19		21	H	Sunderland	D	2-2	Dichio, Koumas	26,703
20		26	H	Arsenal	L	1-2	Dichio	27,025
21		28	A	Charlton Athletic	L	0-1		26,196
22	Jan	11	H	Manchester United	L	1-3	Koumas	27,129
23		18	A	Leeds United	D	0-0		39,708
24		29	H	Charlton Athletic	L	0-1		26,113
25	Feb	1	A	Manchester City	W	2-1	Clement, Moore	34,765
26		8	H	Bolton Wanderers	D	1-1	Johnson	26,933
27		19	A	Fulham	L	0-3		15,799
28		23	H	West Ham United	L	1-2	Dichio	27,042
29	Mar	1	A	Southampton	L	0-1		31,915
30		16	H	Chelsea	L	0-2		27,024
31		22	A	Birmingham City	L	0-1		29,449
32	Apr	5	A	Middlesbrough	L	0-3		30,187
33		12	H	Everton	L	1-2	Balis (pen)	27,039
34		19	A	Sunderland	W	2-1	McInnes 2	36,025
35		21	H	Tottenham Hotspur	L	2-3	Clement, Dichio	26,899
36		26	H	Liverpool	L	0-6		27,128
37	May	3	A	Blackburn Rovers	D	1-1	Koumas	27,470
38		11	H	Newcastle United	D	2-2	Dobie 2	27,036
								Appearances
								Sub appearances
								Goals

FA Cup

R3	Jan	4	H	Bradford City	W	3-1	Dichio 3	19,909
R4		25	A	Watford	L	0-1		16,975
								Appearances
								Sub appearances
								Goals

League Cup

R2	Oct	2	A	Wigan Athletic	L	1-3	Hughes	6,558
								Appearances
								Sub appearances
								Goals

Hoult R	Balis I	Clement N	Sigurdsson LO	Gilchrist PA	Moore DM	Johnson AJ	McInnes DJ	Dichio DSE	Roberts JAD	Gregan SM	Taylor R	Dobie RS	Marshall LK	Wallwork R	Hughes L	Koumas J	Chambers JA	Murphy J	Chambers AC	Udeze I	Batista AJM	Lyttle D	Dyer LR	
1	2	3	4	5	6	7	8	9	*10*	**11**	12	13	14											1
1	2	3	4	5	**6**	*7*	*8*	12	10	11		9	13	14										2
1	2	3	4	5	6	7	**8**		10	11		9	12											3
1	2	3		5	6	7			*9*	4	12		8	11	**10**	13	14							4
1	2	3	12	5	6	7			*9*	4		13		11	10	**8**	14							5
1	2	3	12	5	**6**	7		13	9	4		14		**11**	*10*	8								6
1	2	3	4	5	6	7		12	10	8		*9*	13			**11**		14						7
1	2	3	*4*	5	6	7			10	8	**9**	12	13	14		11								8
	2	3		5	6	7	8		10	4		9	**11**		13	12		1						9
1	2	3		5	6	7			9	4		12	8	11	**10**									10
1	2	3	12	5	6	7	8		10	**4**		9	11		13									11
1	2	3		5	6	7	8		10	4		**9**			12	13			11					12
1	2	3	5		6	7	8		10	4		**9**				12			11					13
1	2	3	4	**5**	6	7	8	13	10	11		*9*			14				12					14
1	2	3	5		6	7	8		10	4		**9**		11	12	13								15
1	2	3	5		*6*	7	8	12	9	4		13			**10**	11	14							16
1	2	3	5			7	8	12	**9**	4		13		6	10	11			14					17
1	2	3	5		6	7	8	12	9	4		13			**10**	11								18
1	2	3	5		6	7	8	9	**10**	4		12				11			13					19
1		3	5		6	7		9	10	4		12		11		8	13		**2**					20
1		3	5		6	7		9	10	4		12		11	13	8			**2**					21
1	12	3	4	5	6	7		9	10			13		11		8			**2**					22
1	*2*	3	12	5	6	7	8	9		4		10		14	13	**11**								23
1				5	**6**	7	12	9	10	4		13		11		8			2	3				24
1		3	12	5	6		8	13	9	4				11	10	**7**			2					25
1		3		*5*	6	12	**8**	9	10	4				11	13	7			2	14				26
1		3		5	6		8	*9*		4		12		11	**10**	7			2	13	14			27
1			12	5	6		8	9		4		13		**11**	10	7			2	3				28
1		12	4	5	6		*8*	9		11		13		2	10	7				**3**	14			29
1	2	5	4		*6*		8	12	9	11				13	10	7	14			**3**				30
1	2	6	4				8	9	10	5				11	12	**7**				3				31
1	*2*	3	4	5		13	8	9	**10**	6		12		11		7						14		32
1	2	3	4			7	**8**	9		5		12		6	10	11				13				33
1	2	3	4			7	8	9	12	5				6	**10**	11								34
1	2	12	4			7	8	9	10	5		13		6		11				**3**				35
1	2	6				7	8	9	10	5				**4**		11	12			*3*	13	14		36
1		3				7	8	**9**	10	4		12		6		11	5					2		37
1		3	4			7	8	9			**10**	12		6		11	5			13		2		38
37	27	34	23	22	29	30	28	19	31	36	2	10	4	23	14	27	2	1	10	7		2		
	1	2	6			2	1	9	1		2	21	5	4	9	5	6	1	3	4	3	2		
	2	3			2	1	2	5	3	1		5	1			4								

1	14	3	5	12	6	7		9	10	**4**		13		11		8			2					R3
1		3	13	5	**6**	7	8	9	*10*	4		14		2		11			12					R4
2		2	1	1	2	2	2	2	2	2				2		2			1					
	1		1	1								2							1					
								3																

		12	4					9				13	7	6	10	8	**5**	1			11	2	3	R2
			1					1					1	1	1	1	1	1			1	1	1	
		1										1												
														1										

2003-04

Division One

	P	W	D	L	F	A	Pts
Norwich City	46	28	10	8	79	39	94
West Bromwich Albion	46	25	11	10	64	42	86
Sunderland	46	22	13	11	62	45	79
West Ham United	46	19	17	10	67	45	74
Ipswich Town	46	21	10	15	84	72	73
Crystal Palace	46	21	10	15	72	61	73
Wigan Athletic	46	18	17	11	60	45	71
Sheffield United	46	20	11	15	65	56	71
Reading	46	20	10	16	55	57	70
Millwall	46	18	15	13	55	48	69
Stoke City	46	18	12	16	58	55	66
Coventry City	46	17	14	15	67	54	65
Cardiff City	46	17	14	15	68	58	65
Nottingham Forest	46	15	15	16	61	58	60
Preston North End	46	15	14	17	69	71	59
Watford	46	15	12	19	54	68	57
Rotherham United	46	13	15	18	53	61	54
Crewe Alexandra	46	14	11	21	57	66	53
Burnley	46	13	14	19	60	77	53
Derby County	46	13	13	20	53	67	52
Gillingham	46	14	9	23	48	67	51
Walsall	46	13	12	21	45	65	51
Bradford City	46	10	6	30	38	69	36
Wimbledon	46	8	5	33	41	89	29

Manager: Gary Megson

- New faces at The Hawthorns this season included Thomas Gaardsoe (from Ipswich Town), Swiss international Bernt Haas (from Sunderland), Watford defender Paul Robinson, striker Rob Hulse (from Crewe Alexandra), midfielder James O'Connor (from Stoke City), Geoff Horsfield (from Wigan Athletic), Mark Kinsella (from Aston Villa), Joost Volmer (from Fortuna Sittard), the Macedonian midfielder Artim Sakiri (from CSKA Sofia), Delroy Facey (from Bolton Wanderers), Sekou Berthe (from French club Troyes), Alassane N'Dour (on loan from St Etienne) and Morten Skoubo (on loan from the German side Borussia Mönchengladbach).
- Albion recorded their first League win at Derby for 84 years and their first at Ipswich since 1983. They also came back from 3–0 down (after 22 minutes) to beat West Ham United 4–3 at Upton Park.
- The Baggies clinched promotion – and a return to the Premiership – with a 2–0 home win over Bradford City with three games remaining, all of which were lost!
- Manager Gary Megson became the first manager to lead Albion to promotion twice and the first to take the club back up into the top flight at the first attempt. He also took over the mantle as the club's longest-serving boss since Vic Buckingham in the 1950s.

Match No.	Date			Opponents	Result		Scorers	Attendance
1	Aug	9	A	Walsall	L	1-4	Koumas	11,030
2		16	H	Burnley	W	4-1	Hulse, Sakiri, Hughes 2	22,489
3		23	A	Watford	W	1-0	Hughes	15,023
4		25	H	Preston North End	W	1-0	Hughes (pen)	24,402
5		30	A	Derby County	W	1-0	Hulse	21,499
6	Sep	13	H	Ipswich Town	W	4-1	Diallo (og), Hulse 2, Gaardsoe	24,954
7		16	A	Wigan Athletic	L	0-1		12,874
8		20	A	Crystal Palace	D	2-2	Koumas, Hulse	17,477
9		27	H	Stoke City	W	1-0	Dobie	24,297
10		30	H	Millwall	W	2-1	Koumas, Dobie	22,909
11	Oct	4	A	Gillingham	W	2-0	Clement, Dobie	8,883
12		14	H	Sheffield United	L	0-2		27,195
13		18	H	Norwich City	W	1-0	Koumas	24,966
14		21	H	Wimbledon	L	0-1		22,048
15		25	A	Rotherham United	W	3-0	Barker (og), Hulse 2	7,815
16	Nov	1	H	Sunderland	D	0-0		26,135
17		8	A	West Ham United	W	4-3	Deane (og), Hulse 2, Hughes	30,359
18		22	H	Reading	D	0-0		22,839
19		25	A	Cardiff City	D	1-1	Koumas	17,678
20		29	A	Nottingham Forest	W	3-0	Louis-Jean (og), Koumas 2	27,331
21	Dec	6	H	West Ham United	D	1-1	Mullins (og)	26,194
22		9	A	Bradford City	W	1-0	Dobie	11,198
23		13	H	Crewe Alexandra	D	2-2	Haas, Gregan	22,825
24		20	A	Coventry City	L	0-1		17,616
25		26	H	Derby County	D	1-1	Gaardsoe	26,412
26		30	A	Wimbledon	D	0-0		6,376
27	Jan	9	H	Walsall	W	2-0	O'Connor, Horsfield	24,558
28		17	A	Burnley	D	1-1	Horsfield	13,106
29		31	H	Watford	W	3-1	Hughes, Horsfield 2	23,958
30	Feb	7	A	Preston North End	L	0-3		16,569
31		14	H	Cardiff City	W	2-1	Clement, Hughes	25,196
32		21	A	Sheffield United	W	2-1	Gaardsoe, Moore	24,805
33		28	H	Rotherham United	L	0-1		24,104
34	Mar	2	A	Norwich City	D	0-0		23,223
35		6	H	Coventry City	W	3-0	Hulse, Horsfield, Kinsella	25,414
36		13	A	Crewe Alexandra	W	2-1	Johnson, Hughes	8,335
37		16	H	Wigan Athletic	W	2-1	Gaardsoe, Hughes (pen)	26,215
38		27	H	Crystal Palace	W	2-0	Moore, Dyer	24,990
39	Apr	4	A	Ipswich Town	W	3-2	Koumas, Horsfield, Dyer	24,608
40		10	H	Gillingham	W	1-0	Hughes	24,524
41		12	A	Millwall	D	1-1	Johnson	13,304
42		18	A	Sunderland	W	1-0	Koumas	32,201
43		24	H	Bradford City	W	2-0	Hughes, Horsfield	26,143
44	May	1	A	Reading	L	0-1		20,619
45		4	A	Stoke City	L	1-4	Dobie	18,352
46		9	H	Nottingham Forest	L	0-2		26,821

Appearances
Sub appearances
Goals

FA Cup

R3	Jan	3	A	Nottingham Forest	L	0-1		30,617

Appearances
Sub appearances

League Cup

R1	Aug	12	H	Brentford	W	4-0	Haas, Hulse 2, Dobie	10,440
R2	Sep	23	A	Hartlepool United	W	2-1	Clement, Hulse	5,265
R3	Oct	29	A	Newcastle United	W	2-1*	Ameobi (og), Hughes	46,932
R4	Dec	3	H	Manchester United	W	2-0	Haas, Dobie	25,282
R5		16	H	Arsenal	L	0-2		20,369

* after extra-time

Appearances
Sub appearances
Goals

Hoult R	Haas B	Clement N	Gregan SM	Sigurdsson LO	Volmer JGB	Johnson AJ	Koumas J	Dichio DSE	Hulse RW	O'Connor JK	Wallwork R	Sakiri A	Dobie RS	Gaardsoe T	Hughes L	Chambers JA	Gilchrist PA	N'Dour A	Berthe S	Robinson PP	Moore DM	Horsfield GM	Dyer LR	Kinsella MA	Facey DM	Skoubo M	Murphy J	Chambers A	
1	2	3	4	**5**	6	7	8	*9*	10	11	12	13	14																1
1	2	3			6	12	*8*		10	11		**7**	9	5	13	4	14												2
1	2	3	8		6	7	13	12	**9**	11			14	5	*10*	4													3
1	2	3	4		6	14	8	**9**	12	11		*7*	13	5	10														4
1	2	3	8	4	6	13	7		9	**11**		12	14	5	*10*														5
1	2	3	8	4	6	12	7		9	**11**		13	14	5	*10*														6
1	2	3	8	4	**6**	12	7	13	9	11		*10*		5	14														7
1	2		8	**4**		7	11	13	9	12			14	5	*10*		6	3											8
1	2	3	**4**			7	8		9	11		12	10	5			6												9
1	2	3	4			7	8	12	9	11			**10**	5			6		13										10
1	2	3	8		12	7			9	11			10	5	13		**6**		4										11
1	2	3	8				7	12	*9*	11		13	10	5	14		6		**4**										12
1	2		4		12		7		*9*	11	**8**	13	10	5	14		6			3									13
1	2	12	4				7		9	11	8	13	*10*	5	14		6			**3**									14
1	2	12	4			7	8		9	**11**		12	13	5	*10*		6			3									15
1	2	12	4			7	8		**9**	*11*		14	13	5	10		6			3									16
1	2	12	4			7	8		9	11		13	*10*	5	14		6			**3**									17
1	2	12	4			7	8	*9*	10	11		13		5	14		6			**3**									18
1	2		4			7	8	13	9	11		12	**10**	5			6			3									19
1	**2**		4			7	8	9	10	11				5		12	6			3	13								20
1	2	3	4			7	*8*	9	10	11		14	13	5			**6**			12									21
1	2				12	7	8		*9*	11		13	10	5	14		6			3	**4**								22
1	2		4		6	7	8		9	**11**		12	10	5	13					3									23
1	2		4		6		7		**10**	11	8		12	5						3	13	9							24
1	2		4			7	8		12	**11**		14	13	5	*10*		6			3		9							25
1		3			6	**7**	8		10	12	11		13	5		2					4	9							26
1	2	3	8				**7**		13	12		*11*	10	5						6	4	9	14						27
1	**2**	11	8			7			10					5		6				3	4	9	12	13					28
1	2	3	8			**7**								5	*10*	12				6	4	9	13	11	14				29
1	2	**3**	8			7	12							5	*10*					6	4	9	13	11		14			30
	2	3	12			7	**8**							5	10	13				6	4	9	14	*11*			1		31
	2	3	12		13	7	8							5	*10*			**6**			4	9		11	14		1		32
1	2	3	13		12	7	8							5	*10*					**6**	4	9		11	14				33
1	2	12	4			7	8						13	5		6				3		9		**11**	10				34
1			4			7	**8**		*10*					5		2				3	6	9	12	11	14	13			35
1	2	12	4			7	**8**		10					5	13					3	6	9	14	*11*					36
1	2	3	8			7	**11**							5	10					6	4	*9*	13	12	14				37
1			4			7	12		*9*			**11**		5	10	2				3	6		13	8	14				38
1			4			7	12					**11**		5	10	2				3	6	9	13	8			14		39
1		12	4			**7**	**8**							5	10	2				3	6	9	13	11					40
1		3	4			7	8			**11**			12	5		2					6	9	14	13	*10*				41
1		11	4			7	12		13				*10*	5		2				3	**6**	9	14	8					42
1		3	4			7	8						12	5	10	2				6		**9**	13	*11*	14				43
1		12	4							7		14	13	5	*10*	2				**3**	6	9	11	8					44
1	2	12	4				7					13	9	5	10					3	6		11	**8**					45
1		11	4				7		**9**	8		13	12	5	10	2				*3*	6		14						46
44	36	25	40	5	10	33	37	5	29	27	4	6	14	45	21	14	16	2	2	30	20	20	2	15	2		2		
		10	3		5	5	5	6	4	3	1	19	17			3	1		1	1	2		15	3	7	2	1		
	1	2	1			2	10		10			1	5	4	11						2	7	2	1					

Five own-goals

Hoult R	Haas B	Clement N	Gregan SM	Sigurdsson LO	Volmer JGB	Johnson AJ	Koumas J	Dichio DSE	Hulse RW	O'Connor JK	Wallwork R	Sakiri A	Dobie RS	Gaardsoe T	Hughes L	Chambers JA	Gilchrist PA	N'Dour A	Berthe S	Robinson PP	Moore DM	Horsfield GM	Dyer LR	Kinsella MA	Facey DM	Skoubo M	Murphy J	Chambers A	
1	2	3					8		10	11		**7**	13	5						6	4	9	12						R3
1	1	1					1		1	1		1		1						1	1	1							
													1										1						

Hoult R	Haas B	Clement N	Gregan SM	Sigurdsson LO	Volmer JGB	Johnson AJ	Koumas J	Dichio DSE	Hulse RW	O'Connor JK	Wallwork R	Sakiri A	Dobie RS	Gaardsoe T	Hughes L	Chambers JA	Gilchrist PA	N'Dour A	Berthe S	Robinson PP	Moore DM	Horsfield GM	Dyer LR	Kinsella MA	Facey DM	Skoubo M	Murphy J	Chambers A	
1	2	3	4		6	14	8	**9**	10	*11*		7	13	5	12														R1
1	2	12				7	8	14	9	11			*13*	5	10		6	**3**	4										R2
1	2	3	4		12	7			*9*	11	13	8	10	5	14		**6**												R3
1	2	3	4			7	8	**9**	*10*	11		13	**14**	**5**			6											12	R4
1	2	3	4		**6**	7			9	*11*	8	14	10	5	13		12												R5
5	5	4	4		2	4	3	2	5	5	1	2	2	5	1		3	1	1										
		1			1	1		1			1	2	3		3		1											1	
	2	1							3				2		1														

One own-goal

2004-05

Premiership

	P	W	D	L	F	A	Pts
Chelsea	38	29	8	1	72	15	95
Arsenal	38	25	8	5	87	36	83
Manchester United	38	22	11	5	58	26	77
Everton	38	18	7	13	45	46	61
Liverpool	38	17	7	14	52	41	58
Bolton Wanderers	38	16	10	12	49	44	58
Middlesbrough	38	14	13	11	53	46	55
Manchester City	38	13	13	12	47	39	52
Tottenham Hotspur	38	14	10	14	47	41	52
Aston Villa	38	12	11	15	45	52	47
Charlton Athletic	38	12	10	16	42	58	46
Birmingham City	38	11	12	15	40	46	45
Fulham	38	12	8	18	52	60	44
Newcastle United	38	10	14	14	47	57	44
Blackburn Rovers	38	9	15	14	32	43	42
Portsmouth	38	10	9	19	43	59	39
West Bromwich Albion	38	6	16	16	36	61	34
Crystal Palace	38	7	12	19	41	62	33
Norwich City	38	7	12	19	42	77	33
Southampton	38	6	14	18	45	66	32

Manager: Gary Megson then Bryan Robson

- This was the season of the 'Great Escape' when Albion became the first club to be bottom of the Premiership at Christmas and then avoid relegation at the death.
- The Baggies had to win their last game of the season at home to Portsmouth to stay in the top flight – and they did so in front of a record crowd for The 'new' Hawthorns of 27,751.
- Former player Bryan Robson returned to the club as manager in place of Gary Megson, who was sacked after bad defeats by Crystal Palace and Chelsea in October.
- Among the new faces at the club this season were the Hungarian captain Zoltan Gera, signed from Ferencvaros for £1.5m, Polish goalkeeper Tomasz Kuszczak from Hertha Berlin, Jonathan Greening from the manager's former club Middlesbrough, Nigerian international Kanu from Arsenal, strikers Rob Earnshaw from Cardiff City for £3.6m and Kevin Campbell from Everton, and defenders Darren Purse from Birmingham City and Martin Albrechtsen from FC Copenhagen. The Japanese World Cup star Junichi Inamoto and Kieran Richardson also arrived on loan from Gamba Osaka and Old Trafford respectively.
- Swiss international Bernt Haas had his contract cancelled and in February joined the Corsican club, Bastia. Sean Gregan also left for Leeds United.

Match No.	Date			Opponents	Result		Scorers	Attendance
1	Aug	14	A	Blackburn Rovers	D	1-1	Clement	23,475
2		22	H	Aston Villa	D	1-1	Clement	26,601
3		25	H	Tottenham Hotspur	D	1-1	Gera	27,191
4		28	A	Everton	L	1-2	Dobie	34,510
5	Sep	11	A	Liverpool	L	0-3		42,947
6		18	H	Fulham	D	1-1	Kanu	24,128
7		25	A	Newcastle United	L	1-3	Horsfield	52,308
8	Oct	2	H	Bolton Wanderers	W	2-1	Kanu, Gera	23,849
9		16	H	Norwich City	D	0-0		26,257
10		23	A	Crystal Palace	L	0-3		22,922
11		30	H	Chelsea	L	1-4	Gera	27,399
12	Nov	6	A	Southampton	D	2-2	Earnshaw 2	31,057
13		14	H	Middlesbrough	L	1-2	Earnshaw	24,008
14		20	A	Arsenal	D	1-1	Earnshaw	38,109
15		27	H	Manchester United	L	0-3		27,709
16	Dec	4	A	Portsmouth	L	2-3	Stefanovic (og), Earnshaw	20,110
17		11	H	Charlton Athletic	L	0-1		24,697
18		18	A	Birmingham City	L	0-4		28,880
19		26	H	Liverpool	L	0-5		27,533
20		28	A	Manchester City	D	1-1	Dunne (og)	47,177
21	Jan	1	A	Bolton Wanderers	D	1-1	Gera	25,205
22		3	H	Newcastle United	D	0-0		25,259
23		16	A	Fulham	L	0-1		16,180
24		22	H	Manchester City	W	2-0	Wallwork, Campbell	25,348
25	Feb	1	H	Crystal Palace	D	2-2	Earnshaw, Campbell	25,092
26		5	A	Norwich City	L	2-3	Earnshaw, Richardson	24,292
27		22	H	Southampton	D	0-0		25,865
28	Mar	6	H	Birmingham City	W	2-0	Clement, Campbell	25,749
29		15	A	Chelsea	L	0-1		41,713
30		19	A	Charlton Athletic	W	4-1	Earnshaw 3 (1 pen), Horsfield	27,104
31	Apr	3	H	Everton	W	1-0	Gera	26,805
32		10	A	Aston Villa	D	1-1	Robinson	39,402
33		20	A	Tottenham Hotspur	D	1-1	Gera	35,885
34		23	A	Middlesbrough	L	0-4		32,951
35		26	H	Blackburn Rovers	D	1-1	Richardson	25,154
36	May	2	H	Arsenal	L	0-2		27,351
37		7	A	Manchester United	D	1-1	Earnshaw (pen)	67,827
38		15	H	Portsmouth	W	2-0	Horsfield, Richardson	27,751

Appearances
Sub appearances
Goals

FA Cup

R3	Jan	8	A	Preston North End	W	2-0	Earnshaw 2	13,005
R4		29	H	Tottenham Hotspur	D	1-1	Earnshaw	22,441
R4r	Feb	12	A	Tottenham Hotspur	L	1-3	Kanu	27,860

Appearances
Sub appearances
Goals

League Cup

R2	Sep	21	A	Colchester United	L	1-2*	Horsfield	4,591

* after extra-time

Appearances
Sub appearances
Goals

Hoult R	Haas B	Robinson PP	Scimeca R	Purse DJ	Gaardsoe T	Greening J	Johnson AJ	Kanu N	Horsfield GM	Clement N	Gera Z	Moore DM	Dobie RS	Dyer LR	Albrechtsen M	Koumas J	Earnshaw R	Kuszczak T	Contra CM	Hulse RW	Sakiri A	Wallwork R	Campbell KJ	Richardson KE	Chaplow RD	Inamoto J	O'Connor JK	
1	2	3	4	5	6	7	**8**	9	*10*	11	12	13	14															1
1	**2**	3	4	5	6	7	8	9	10	11	12		13															2
1		2	4	5	6	7	*8*	9	**10**	3	11	13	12	14														3
1	12	2	4	5	*6*	7	8	9		3	**11**	13	10		14													4
1	**2**	3	4	5		7		9	10	11	12				6	8	13											5
		2	4	5	6	7	**11**	9		3	14			12	*13*	8	10	1										6
1			2	5	6	7	11	9	12	3	13				4	8	**10**											7
1	2		4		6	7	8	9	10		11	5		12	**3**													8
1	2	12	4		6	*7*	8	*9*	10		**11**	5			3	14	13											9
1	2	11	4		6	12	8	9			7	5			**3**		10											10
1		3	2		6	*7*	8	9		11	4	5	12	14		13	**10**											11
1		3	2	5		7	8	**9**	12	11	4	6				13	10											12
1			2	5		7	8	9	12	3	**11**	6					10		4	13								13
1			2	5	12	7	8	9	13	3	11	6					14		*4*		**10**							14
1		14	2	5	12	7	8		13	3	11	**6**					9		*4*		10							15
1	**2**		4	5	12	7	8	9		3	*11*	6					10			13	14							16
1	2		6	5		7	8	9	12	3	**11**					13	10		4									17
1	2		4	5	6	7	11	9		3	**10**					8	12					13						18
1			2	5	6	7	**11**		9	3	12					8	10		4	13								19
1		3	2	5	6	*7*	8		9	11	**10**				13		14			12		4						20
1		3	2	5		*7*	8	*10*	**9**	6	11				13		14			12		4						21
1		3	7	5			8	**10**	9	6	12				2		11					4						22
1		3	12	5		7	**8**			6	11				2		10					4	9					23
1		3	8	5	12	7			13	6	11				2		10					4	**9**					24
1		3	8	5		7			**9**	6	11				2		12					4	10	13				25
1		3	2	5		**7**			12	6	11						10					4	9	8				26
1		3	12		5	7				6	**11**				2	13	10					4	9	8				27
1		3	12		5	7		13	9	6	11				2							4	10	**8**				28
1		3			5	12		10	9	6	11				2		13					4	7	**8**				29
1		3			5	7			9	6	*11*	13			2		12					4	10	**8**	14			30
1		3	12		5	7			9	6	11	13			**2**							4	10	8				31
1		3	12		5	7		13	*9*	6	11				**2**		14					4	10	8				32
1		3	2		5			**9**		6	7	13					12					4	10	*8*	11	14		33
1		3	8		5			12	13	6	7				*2*		10					4	**9**		11	14		34
1		3	12		5			13	*9*	6	7				2		14					4	**10**	8	11			35
1		3			5	7		12	13	6	**11**	4			*2*		14					10	9	8				36
1		3			5	7		12	**9**	6	11				2		10	14				4	8			13		37
		3			5	**7**		13	12	6	11				2		10	1				4	9	8				38
36	9	28	27	22	25	32	22	21	18	35	31	10	1		20	5	18	2	5		2	19	16	11	3			
	1	2	6		4	2		7	11		7	6	4	4	4	5	13	1		5	1	1		1	1	3		
		1						2	3	3	6		1				11					1	3	3				

Two own-goals

1		3		5		**7**	8		9	6	11				2	12	10			13		4						R3
1		3	8	5		7		**9**	12	6	11				2		10					4	13					R4
1		3	8		5			*9*		6	7				2	11	14	12				4	10				13	R4
3		3	2	2	1	2	1	2	1	3	3				3	1	2						1					
									1							1	1	1		1		3	1				1	
								1									3											

			2		6	13			9		7	5	*10*	11	4	8		1	**3**	14							12	R2
			1		1	1			1		1	1	1	1	1	1		1	1									
																				1							1	
									1																			

2005-06

Premiership

	P	W	D	L	F	A	Pts
Chelsea	38	29	4	5	72	22	91
Manchester United	38	25	8	5	72	34	83
Liverpool	38	25	7	6	57	25	82
Arsenal	38	20	7	11	68	31	67
Tottenham Hotspur	38	18	11	9	53	38	65
Blackburn Rovers	38	19	6	13	51	42	63
Newcastle United	38	17	7	14	47	42	58
Bolton Wanderers	38	15	11	12	49	41	56
West Ham United	38	16	7	15	52	55	55
Wigan Athletic	38	15	6	17	45	52	51
Everton	38	14	8	16	34	49	50
Fulham	38	14	6	18	48	58	48
Charlton Athletic	38	13	8	17	41	55	47
Middlesbrough	38	12	9	17	48	58	45
Manchester City	38	13	4	21	43	48	43
Aston Villa	38	10	12	16	42	55	42
Portsmouth	38	10	8	20	37	62	38
Birmingham City	38	8	10	20	28	50	34
West Bromwich Albion	38	7	9	22	31	58	30
Sunderland	38	3	6	29	26	69	15

Manager: Bryan Robson

- Albion suffered relegation for the ninth time in the club's history.
- Curtis Davies (from Luton Town), Steve Watson (from Everton), Diomansy Kamara (from Portsmouth), Nathan Ellington (from Wigan Athletic), Darren Carter (from Birmingham City), Nigel Quashie (from Southampton) and Chris Kirkland (on loan from Liverpool) were among the players who made their Albion debuts this season.
- Those who left The Hawthorns included Darren Purse and Riccy Scimeca (both to Cardiff City), Jason Koumas (also to Cardiff, on a season loan), midfielder Cosmin Contra went back to Atletico Madrid, Macedonian skipper Artim Sakiri was released, Robert Earnshaw joined Norwich City and James O'Connor signed for Burnley.
- Darren Carter scored a brilliant winning goal against Arsenal – his first for Albion in what was the Baggies first home victory over the Gunners since 1973.
- Inamoto also scored a spectacular goal from 35 yards, which proved to be the winner in a 3–2 League Cup triumph at Fulham.
- Goalkeeper Tomasz Kuszczak pulled off the 'Save of the Season' to thwart former Albion striker Jason Roberts in a 1–0 victory at Wigan with 10 men, following Darren Moore's dismissal.

Match No.	Date			Opponents	Result		Scorers	Attendance
1	Aug	13	A	Manchester City	D	0-0		42,983
2		20	H	Portsmouth	W	2-1	Horsfield 2	24,404
3		24	A	Chelsea	L	0-4		41,201
4		27	H	Birmingham City	L	2-3	Horsfield 2	23,993
5	Sep	10	H	Wigan Athletic	L	1-2	Greening	25,617
6		17	A	Sunderland	D	1-1	Gera	31,657
7		24	H	Charlton Athletic	L	1-2	Davies	23,909
8	Oct	1	A	Blackburn Rovers	L	0-2		20,721
9		15	H	Arsenal	W	2-1	Kanu, Carter	26,604
10		23	A	Bolton Wanderers	L	0-2		24,151
11		30	H	Newcastle United	L	0-3		26,216
12	Nov	5	A	West Ham United	L	0-1		34,325
13		19	H	Everton	W	4-0	Ellington 2 (1 pen), Clement, Earnshaw	24,784
14		27	A	Middlesbrough	D	2-2	Ellington, Kanu	27,041
15	Dec	3	H	Fulham	D	0-0		23,144
16		10	H	Manchester City	W	2-0	Kamara, Campbell	25,472
17		17	A	Portsmouth	L	0-1		20,052
18		26	A	Manchester United	L	0-3		67,972
19		28	H	Tottenham Hotspur	W	2-0	Kanu 2	27,510
20		31	A	Liverpool	L	0-1		44,192
21	Jan	2	H	Aston Villa	L	1-2	Watson	27,073
22		15	A	Wigan Athletic	W	1-0	Albrechtsen	17,421
23		21	H	Sunderland	L	0-1		26,464
24		31	A	Charlton Athletic	D	0-0		25,921
25	Feb	4	H	Blackburn Rovers	W	2-0	Campbell, Greening	23,993
26		11	A	Fulham	L	1-6	Campbell	21,508
27		26	H	Middlesbrough	L	0-2		24,061
28	Mar	4	H	Chelsea	L	1-2	Kanu	26,581
29		11	A	Birmingham City	D	1-1	Ellington	28,041
30		18	H	Manchester United	L	1-2	Ellington	27,623
31		27	A	Tottenham Hotspur	L	1-2	Davies	36,152
32	Apr	1	H	Liverpool	L	0-2		27,576
33		9	A	Aston Villa	D	0-0		33,303
34		15	A	Arsenal	L	1-3	Quashie	38,167
35		17	H	Bolton Wanderers	D	0-0		23,181
36		22	A	Newcastle United	L	0-3		52,272
37	May	1	H	West Ham United	L	0-1		24,462
38		7	A	Everton	D	2-2	Gera, Martinez	39,671

Appearances
Sub appearances
Goals

FA Cup

R3	Jan	7	H	Reading	D	1-1	Gera (pen)	19,197
rep		17	A	Reading	L	2-3*	Chaplow 2	16,737

*after extra-time

Appearances
Sub appearances
Goals

League Cup

R2	Sep	20	H	Bradford City	W	4-1	Kamara, Earnshaw, Ellington 2	10,792
R3	Oct	25	A	Fulham	W	3-2*	Inamoto, Kanu, Earnshaw	7,373
R4	Nov	30	A	Manchester United	L	1-3	Ellington	48,924

*after extra-time

Appearances
Sub appearances
Goals

Kirkland CE	Albrechtsen M	Robinson PP	Wallwork R	Gaardsoe T	Clement N	Greening J	Inamoto J	Kanu N	Campbell KJ	Gera Z	Chaplow RD	Watson SC	Kamara DM	Johnson AJ	Horsfield GM	Earnshaw R	Scimeca R	Ellington NLF	Carter DA	Davies CE	Kuszczak T	Moore DM	Hoult R	Hodgkiss J	Nicholson SI	Quashie NF	Kozak J	Martinez WG	Dyer L	Davies R	
1	2	3	**4**	5	6	7	8	*9*	10	11	12	13	14																		1
1	13	3	4	5	6	7			10	11		**2**		8	9	12															2
1	2	3		5	6	**7**	13	9			11		10	8			4	12													3
1	12	3	4	5	6	7			*10*	11		**2**			9	13		14	8												4
1	2	3	**4**	5	6	7			12		14	8			9	13		10	*11*												5
1		3	4		6	7			9	11		2	12	8		**10**		13		5											6
1		3	4		6	7			**9**	11		2	12	8	13	*10*		14		5											7
1	2	3	4		6	7			**9**	11	8		10		13			12		5											8
1	2	3	**4**		6	11		*10*				7	8		9			13	12	5		14									9
1	2	11			**3**	7		13				8	10		9	12			4	5		6									10
					3	**7**	8	9				4			12	10	2	13	11	5	1	6									11
	6		4		3	11	8	**9**	12			2	7		13	10				5	**1**										12
	6		4		3	11	8	13				2	7		**9**	14		*10*	12	5	1										13
	12	3	4		6	11	8	9				**2**	7					10	13	5	1										14
		3	4		6	*11*	8	9				2	**7**		13	14		10	12	5	1										15
	12	3	4		6	11	8	9	14			**2**	7					*10*	13	5	1										16
	2	3	4		6	11	8	9	13				**7**			12		10		5	1										17
	2	**3**	4	6		7			14	13	11	10	12					*9*	8	5	1										18
	6		4		3	11		9	13			2	**7**		14			*10*	8	5	1	12									19
	2	3	4		6	14			**10**		11	7	12		9			13	8	5	1										20
	2	3			**6**	11		9	13			4	7		12			10	8	5	1										21
	12	3	4			7	8		9			2				13		**10**	11	5	1	6									22
	6	3	**4**			7	8		9		12	2			13			*10*	11	5	1				14						23
	2	3			6	7	8		**10**					4	9			12	11	5	1										24
	2	3	4		6	7	8		10						**9**			13	14	5	1					*11*	12				25
	2		4	6	3	7	8		10						*9*			14		5	**1**		12			11		13			26
	2	3	4		6	11	12	9	*10*				7					13		5	1					8	14				27
	2	3	4		6	11	8	14	*9*			12	10					13		5	1						7				28
	2	**3**	4		12	11	8	13	*9*			6	10					14		5	1						7				29
	2	3	4			11	8	13	9			6	*10*					14	12	5	1						**7**				30
	2	3	4			11	12	9	13	14		6		8				*10*		5	1						**7**				31
	2	3	4		12	11		*9*	14	13		**6**	7	8				10		5	1										32
		3	**4**		6	7	12	13	9	11		2	*10*							5	1				14	8					33
	2	3	**4**		6	7	14	9	13	*11*			10						12	5	1					8					34
		3			6	7		12	**9**	11		2	10	4						5	1				13	8					35
	2	3			6	7	12	13	9	11		**4**	*10*					14		5	1					8					36
	2	3	4			7		9		11		6						10		5	1					8					37
		3	4			7		9		*11*		**2**						10	14	5	1			12	13	8		6			38
10	26	33	31	7	29	37	16	17	19	12	4	28	21	8	10	4	2	15	11	33	28	3				9	4	1			
	5				2	1	6	8	10	3	3	2	5		8	8		16	9			2	1	1	4		2	1			
	1				1	2		5	3	2		1	1		4	1		5	1	2						1		1			

Kirkland CE	Albrechtsen M	Robinson PP	Wallwork R	Gaardsoe T	Clement N	Greening J	Inamoto J	Kanu N	Campbell KJ	Gera Z	Chaplow RD	Watson SC	Kamara DM	Johnson AJ	Horsfield GM	Earnshaw R	Scimeca R	Ellington NLF	Carter DA	Davies CE	Kuszczak T	Moore DM	Hoult R	Hodgkiss J	Nicholson SI	Quashie NF	Kozak J	Martinez WG	Dyer L	Davies R	
1	2	3	4			**7**	8	9	14	12					13			*10*	11	**5**		6									R3
1	6		**4**			7	*8*				11					10		9	3	5				2	12				13	14	rep
2	2	1	2			2	2	1			1					1		2	2	2		1		1							
									1	1					1										1				1	1	
										1	2																				

Kirkland CE	Albrechtsen M	Robinson PP	Wallwork R	Gaardsoe T	Clement N	Greening J	Inamoto J	Kanu N	Campbell KJ	Gera Z	Chaplow RD	Watson SC	Kamara DM	Johnson AJ	Horsfield GM	Earnshaw R	Scimeca R	Ellington NLF	Carter DA	Davies CE	Kuszczak T	Moore DM	Hoult R	Hodgkiss J	Nicholson SI	Quashie NF	Kozak J	Martinez WG	Dyer L	Davies R	
	6				3	**7**		12			11	2	8			10	13	9	4		1	5									R2
		3	4	13	6		8	9	12		14		**7**			10	2		*11*		**1**	5									R3
	2	3	4	12	6		8				14		7		*9*	13		10	11			**5**	1								R4
	2	2	2		3	1	2	1			1	1	3		1	2	1	2	3		2	3	1								
				2				1	1		2					1	1														
							1	1					1			2		3													

2006-07

Championship

	P	W	D	L	F	A	Pts
Chelsea	38	29	4	5	72	22	91
Sunderland	46	27	7	12	76	47	88
Birmingham City	46	26	8	12	67	42	86
Derby County	46	25	9	12	62	46	84
West Bromwich Albion	46	22	10	14	81	55	76
Wolverhampton W	46	22	10	14	59	56	76
Southampton	46	21	12	13	77	53	75
Preston North End	46	22	8	16	64	53	74
Stoke City	46	19	16	11	62	41	73
Sheffield Wednesday	46	20	11	15	70	66	71
Colchester United	46	20	9	17	70	56	69
Plymouth Argyle	46	17	16	13	63	62	67
Crystal Palace	46	18	11	17	59	51	65
Cardiff City	46	17	13	16	57	53	64
Ipswich Town	46	18	8	20	64	59	62
Burnley	46	15	12	19	52	49	57
Norwich City	46	16	9	21	56	71	57
Coventry City	46	16	8	22	47	62	56
Queen's Park Rangers	46	14	11	21	54	68	53
Leicester City	46	13	14	19	49	64	53
Barnsley	46	15	5	26	53	85	50
Hull City	46	13	10	23	51	67	49
Southend United	46	10	12	24	47	80	42
Luton Town	46	10	10	26	53	81	40
Leeds United	46	13	7	26	46	72	36

Manager: Bryan Robson then Tony Mowbray

- Bryan Robson was dismissed as manager in September and replaced by Tony Mowbray, who took over his duties in October (after Nigel Pearson had acted as caretaker manager).
- New signings this term included goalkeepers Pascal Zuberbühler (on loan from FC Basel) and Dean Kiely (Portsmouth), Sam Sodje (on loan from Reading), Paul McShane (Manchester United), Chris Perry (Charlton Athletic), Robert Koren (Lillestrøm), Kevin Phillips (Aston Villa) and John Hartson (Celtic), while Jason Koumas returned after his loan spell with Cardiff City.
- Out of the camp went Kevin Campbell, Geoff Horsfield, Russell Hoult, Junichi Inamoto, Darren Moore, Nigel Quashie and Tomasz Kuszczak.
- Albion beat Leeds United in September with only 10 men; Paul McShane was sent off with the score level at 0–0.
- The Wolves Play-off semi-final second leg realised record gate receipts for a game at The Hawthorns of £560,100.

Match No.	Date			Opponents	Result		Scorers	Attendance
1	Aug	5	H	Hull City	W	2-0	Hartson 2	20,682
2		8	A	Cardiff City	D	1-1	Gera	18,506
3		12	A	Southampton	D	0-0		24,233
4		19	H	Colchester United	W	2-1	Ellington (pen), Wallwork	17,509
5		28	A	Sunderland	L	0-2		24,242
6	Sep	9	H	Leicester City	W	2-0	Kenton (og), Phillips (pen)	19,322
7		12	A	Preston North End	L	0-1		12,119
8		16	H	Southend United	D	1-1	Ellington	19,576
9		23	A	Luton Town	D	2-2	Carter, Gera	9,332
10		30	H	Leeds United	W	4-2	Albrechtsen, Kamara 2, Phillips	21,435
11	Oct	14	A	Ipswich Town	W	5-1	Kamara 2, Phillips 3	22,581
12		17	A	Crystal Palace	W	2-0	Gera, Kamara	16,105
13		22	H	Wolverhampton Wanderers	W	3-0	Greening, Kamara, Hartson (pen)	26,606
14		28	A	Birmingham City	L	0-2		21,009
15		31	H	Queen's Park Rangers	D	3-3	Ellington, Kamara 2	17,417
16	Nov	4	A	Derby County	L	1-2	Chaplow	25,342
17		11	H	Norwich City	L	0-1		18,718
18		18	H	Burnley	W	3-0	Koumas, Ellington, Carter	18,707
19		25	A	Stoke City	L	0-1		18,282
20		28	A	Sheffield Wednesday	L	1-3	Koumas	21,695
21	Dec	2	H	Derby County	W	1-0	Hartson	20,494
22		10	A	Barnsley	D	1-1	Koumas	9,512
23		16	H	Coventry City	W	5-0	Kamara 2 (1 pen), Koumas, Phillips, Robinson	20,370
24		23	A	Plymouth Argyle	D	2-2	Phillips 2	15,172
25		26	H	Preston North End	W	4-2	Koumas, Kamara, Ellington 2	22,905
26		30	H	Ipswich Town	W	2-0	Kamara, Koumas	20,328
27	Jan	1	A	Southend United	L	1-3	Hartson	9,907
28		12	H	Luton Town	W	3-2	Koumas, Phillips 2	19,927
29		20	A	Leeds United	W	3-2	Greening, Kamara 2	20,019
30		31	H	Plymouth Argyle	W	2-1	Kamara 2 (1 pen)	19,894
31	Feb	3	A	Hull City	W	1-0	Kamara	18,005
32		10	H	Southampton	D	1-1	Phillips	21,138
33		13	A	Colchester United	W	2-1	McShane, Kamara	5,611
34		20	H	Cardiff City	W	1-0	Ellington	18,802
35		24	A	Leicester City	D	1-1	Kamara (pen)	25,581
36	Mar	3	H	Sunderland	L	1-2	Carter	23,252
37		11	A	Wolverhampton Wanderers	L	0-1		28,016
38		14	H	Crystal Palace	L	2-3	Clement, Phillips	17,960
39		18	H	Birmingham City	D	1-1	McShane	21,434
40		31	A	Queen's Park Rangers	W	2-1	Phillips, Gera	14,784
41	Apr	7	H	Stoke City	L	1-3	Koumas	20,386
42		9	A	Norwich City	W	2-1	Sodje, Kamara	25,422
43		13	H	Sheffield Wednesday	L	0-1		20,415
44		23	A	Burnley	L	2-3	Koumas, Ellington	12,500
45		28	A	Coventry City	W	1-0	Robinson	26,343
46	May	6	H	Barnsley	W	7-0	Phillips 3, Ellington 2 (1 pen), Koren, Gera	23,568

Appearances
Sub appearances
Goals

FA Cup

R3	Jan	6	H	Leeds United	W	3-1	McShane, Hartson, Phillips	16,957
R4		28	A	Wolverhampton Wanderers	W	3-0	Kamara, Phillips, Gera	28,107
R5	Feb	17	A	Middlesbrough	D	2-2	Kamara, Phillips	31,491
rep		27	H	Middlesbrough	D	1-1	Carter	24,925

R5 replay lost 4-5 on penalties after extra-time

Appearances
Sub appearances
Goals

League Cup

R1	Aug	24	A	Leyton Orient	W	3-0	Nicholson, Carter, Greening	3,058
R2	Sep	19	H	Cheltenham Town	W	3-1	Wallwork, Ellington (pen), Nicholson (pen)	10,974
R3	Oct	24	H	Arsenal	L	0-2		21,566

Appearances
Sub appearances
Goals

	Zuberbühler P	Watson SC	Robinson PP	Perry C	Wallwork R	Davies CE	Quashie NF	Greening J	Ellington NLF	Hartson J	Gera Z	Carter DA	Inamoto J	Albrechtsen M	Chaplow RD	Phillips K	McShane P	Koumas J	Nicholson SI	Kamara DM	Hoult R	Hodgkiss J	Clement N	Koren R	Kiely D	MacDonald S	Sodje S
1	1	2	3	4	5	6	7	*8*	9	10	**11**	12	13	14													
2	1	2	3	4	*5*	6	7	8	**9**	10	11	12	14		13												
3	1	2	3	4	*5*	6	7	8	**9**	10	11	12	13		14												
4	1	2	3	4	*5*	6	7	8	9	10	**11**	12		14	13												
5	1	2	3	4	13	6	5	*8*	**9**	10	11	14			7	12											
6	1		3	4	5		*7*	**8**	13	10		11		2	14	9	6	12									
7	1		3	4	5		8		12	**10**	11	7		2		9	6	13									
8	1		3	4	5		8	12	9		11	7		**2**		10	6	13									
9	1	**2**	3	4	5		8	13	*9*		12	7				10	6	11	14								
10	1		3	4				8		**10**	11	7		2	13	9	6	5		12							
11	1		3	4		6	12	8	13		11	7		2		10		**5**		9							
12	1		3	4		6	12	8	**9**		11	7		2				5		10							
13	1	14	3	4		6	7	8	**9**	12	*11*			2	13			5		10							
14	1		3	4		6	**7**	8	9	12	11			2				5		10							
15	1	2		4	7	6		8	**9**	13	11			3		12		5		10							
16		2		4		6		8	**9**	13	11			3	7	12		5		10	1						
17		**2**		4		6		8	12			11		3		10	7	5		9	1	13					
18			3	4		6	7		**9**			11		2	12	10		5		8	1						
19			3	4		6	7	8	13		12	11		**2**		10		5		9	1						
20			3	**4**		6	7	8			13	11		2		10	12	5		9	1						
21			3			6	7	8		12	11			2		10	4	5		**9**	1		13				
22			3			6	7	8	13	*10*	11	14		2		9	**4**	5			1		12				
23			3			6	7	8	12	**10**	13			2		11	4	*5*		9	1		14				
24			3			6		8	14	*10*	13	7		**2**		11	4	5		9	1		12				
25			3			6	12	8	13	**10**		7		2	14	*11*	4	5		9	1						
26		13				6		8			**11**	7		2	12	3	4	9		10	1		5				
27			3			6		8	13	14	11	7		**2**		*5*	4	9		10	1		12				
28		2	3			**6**		8		*10*	14				7	11		9		4	1	12	5	13			
29			3			6		8			11				7	4	2		12	**10**	1		5	**9**			
30			3			6		8			12	14			7	*11*	2	**9**		10			5	4	1	**13**	
31			3			6		8	13		12	14			7	10	2	**9**		*11*			5	4	1		
32			3			6			12		*11*	14			7	**4**	2	9		10			5	8	1	13	
33			3			6				**10**	11	8			7		2			4			5	9	1	12	
34			3					8	12	13		14		2	7	**11**	4	*6*		10			5	9	1		
35			3			6		8	12		13				7	**11**	2	9		10			5	4	1		
36			3			6		8			14	13			7	**11**	2	4		10			5	*9*	1	12	
37			3			6		8			11	13		14	7	**9**	*2*	4		10			5		1	12	
38			3			**6**		8			11			12	7	9	2	4		10			5	13	1		
39			3					8	9		**11**	13					2	6		10			5	7	1	12	4
40			3					8	12		13	**7**			14	11	2	9		*10*			5	6	1		4
41			3					8	9			13		2	7	*11*	5	10				12		6	1	14	**4**
42			3					8	9		*11*	**7**		2	13		5	12		10		14		6	1		4
43			3					**8**	9		*11*	7		2		14	5	12		10			13	6	1		4
44			3	4				8	**9**		11			2	12	13	5	7		10				6	1		
45			3	4				8			11			12	*7*	6	2	9		10				14	1	13	**5**
46			3	4				8	*9*		13				7	11	**2**	10				12		6	1	14	5
	15	10	42	23	9	32	17	40	19	14	28	19		26	16	31	31	34		33	14		14	15	17		7
		2			1		3	2	15	7	12	14	3	5	12	5	1	5	2	1		5	6	3		9	
			2		1			2	10	5	5	3		1	1	16	2	9		20			1	1			1

One own-goal

R3			5			3		7		10		12			**8**	11	2	9		6	1		4	13			
R4	1		5			3		7			12	13			8	11	2	6		10			4	**9**			
R5			5			4		7	12		13			14	8	**10**	2	9		*11*			3	6	1		
rep			5			4		7	11		*6*	9			**8**		2	10		13			3	12	1	14	
	1		4			4		4	1	1	1	1			4	3	4	4		3	1		4	2	2		
									1		2	2		1						1				2		1	
										1	1	1				3	1			2							

R1	1		3		4	5		7		12		8		2	11	**10**	6		9								
R2	1		3	5	**4**			12	10		13	*8*			11		6	7	9	14		2					
R3		2	3			5	*8*	7	10	9	14	**4**		13	11		6			12	1						
	2	1	3	1	2	2	1	2	2	1		3		1	3	1	3	1	2		1	1					
								1		1	2			1						2							
					1			1	1			1							2								

West Bromwich Albion in the FA Cup, pre-League days – 1883 to 1888

1883–84

Round One
10 November v Wednesbury Town (h) 0–2
Roberts, H. Bell, Stanton, E. Horton, Bunn, Swallow, Whitehouse, Aston, Bisseker, Timmins, G. Bell
Att. 5,129

1884–85

Round One
25 October v Junction Street School, Derby (a) 7–1
Bayliss 2, G. Bell 2, Aston 2, Loach
Roberts, H. Bell, H. Green, E. Horton, Bunn, Stanton, Woodhall, Aston, Bayliss, Loach, G. Bell
Att. 4,000
Round Two
6 December v Wednesbury Old Athletic (h) 4–2
Aston 2, Woodhall, Taylor (og)
Roberts, J. Horton, H. Green, E. Horton, Bunn, Stanton, Woodhall, Aston, Bayliss, Loach, G. Bell
Att. 4,497
Round Three
3 January v Aston Villa (a) 0–0
Roberts, H. Bell, H. Green, E. Horton, Bunn, Stanton, Woodhall, Aston, Bayliss, Loach, G. Bell
Att. 22,088
Round Three replay
10 January v Aston Villa (h) 3–0
Loach 2, Bayliss
Roberts, H. Bell, H. Green, E. Horton, Bunn, Stanton, Woodhall, Aston, Bayliss, Loach, G. Bell
Att. 10,021
Round Four
24 January v Druids (h) 1–0
Loach
Roberts, H. Bell, H. Green, E. Horton, Bunn, Stanton, Woodhall, Aston, Bayliss, Loach, G. Bell
Att. 5,537
Round Five
Albion received a bye
Round Six
21 February v Blackburn Rovers (h) 0–2
Matthews, H. Bell, H. Green, E. Horton, Bunn, Timmins, Woodhall, Aston, Bayliss, Loach, G. Bell
Att. 16,393

1885–86

Round One
31 October v Aston Unity (h) 4–1
T. Green 2, Woodhall 2
Roberts, H. Bell, H. Green, E. Horton, Bunn, Timmins, Woodhall, T. Green, Bayliss, Loach, G. Bell
Att. 4,027
Round Two
21 November v Wednesbury Old Athletic (h) 3–2
Loach 2, G. Bell
Roberts, H. Bell, H. Green, E. Horton, Bushell, Timmins, Woodhall, T. Green, Bayliss, Loach, G. Bell
Att. 3,578
Round Three
Albion received a bye
Round Four
2 January v Wolverhampton Wanderers (h) 3–1
G. Bell, T. Green, Loach
Roberts, H. Bell, H. Green, E. Horton, Bunn, Timmins, Woodhall, T. Green, Bayliss, Loach, G. Bell
Att. 5,196

Round Five
23 January v Old Carthusians (h) 1–0
T. Green
Roberts, H. Bell, H. Green, E. Horton, Bunn, Timmins, Woodhall, Bayliss, T. Green, Loach, G. Bell
Att. 8,137

Round Six
13 February v Old Westminsters (h) 6–0
Bayliss 3, G. Bell 2, Woodhall
Roberts, H. Bell, H. Green, E. Horton, Bunn, Timmins, Woodhall, T. Green, Bayliss, Loach, G. Bell
Att. 5,884

Semi-final
6 March v Small Heath (at Aston) 4–0
Loach 2, Woodhall 2
Roberts, H. Bell, H. Green, E. Horton, Bunn, Timmins, Woodhall, T. Green, Bayliss, Loach, G. Bell
Att. 4,100

Final
3 April v Blackburn Rovers (The Oval) 0–0
Roberts, H. Bell, H. Green, E. Horton, C. Perry, Timmins, Woodhall, T. Green, Bayliss, Loach, G. Bell
Att. 15,156

Final replay
10 April v Blackburn Rovers (at Derby) 0–2
Roberts, H. Bell, H. Green, E. Horton, C. Perry, Timmins, Woodhall, T. Green, Bayliss, Loach, G. Bell
Att. 16,144

1886–87

Round One
30 October v Burton Wanderers (h) 6–0
T. Green 2, Bayliss 2, Holden, Paddock
Roberts, Aldridge, H. Green, E. Horton, C. Perry, Timmins, Woodhall, T. Green, Bayliss, Holden, W. Paddock
Att. 5,107

Round Two
20 November v Derby Junction (a) 2–1
*G. Bell, Roberts**
Roberts, Aldridge, Walker, E. Horton, J. Horton, Bayliss, Woodhall, Holden, T. Green, W. Paddock, G. Bell
Att. 2,100
* Roberts credited with the goal after his long punt downfield bounced between the posts via a scrimmage.

Round Three
Albion received a bye

Round Four
15 January v Mitchell's St George (at Aston) 1–0
T. Green
Roberts, H. Green, Aldridge, E. Horton, C. Perry, Timmins, Woodhall, Holden, Bayliss, T. Green, W. Paddock
Att. 4,061

Round Five
29 January v Lockwood Brothers, Sheffield (a) 1–0*
Woodhall
Roberts, H. Green, Aldridge, E. Horton, C. Perry, Timmins, Woodhall, T. Green, Bayliss, Holden, W. Paddock
Att. 6,029
* Following a protest over the goal, the FA ordered the tie to be replayed.

Round Five replay
12 February v Lockwood Brothers, Sheffield (at Derby) 2–1
T. Green, Paddock
Roberts, Aldridge, H. Green, E. Horton, C. Perry, Timmins, Woodhall, Holden, Bayliss, T. Green, W. Paddock
Att. 2,120

Round Six
19 February v Notts County (a) 4–1
Bayliss 2, T. Green, Woodhall
Roberts, Aldridge, H. Green, E. Horton, C. Perry, Timmins, Woodhall, T. Green, Bayliss, Pearson, W. Paddock
Att. 16,067

Semi-final
5 March v Preston North End (at Nottingham) 3–1
Pearson 2, Paddock
Roberts, Aldridge, H. Green, E. Horton, C. Perry, Timmins, Woodhall, T. Green, Bayliss, Pearson, W. Paddock
Att. 16,068

Final
2 April v Aston Villa (at The Oval) 0–1
Roberts, Aldridge, H. Green, E. Horton, C. Perry, Timmins, Woodhall, T. Green, Bayliss, Pearson, W. Paddock
Att. 15,534

1887–88

Round One
15 October v Wednesbury Old Athletic (h) 7–1
Bayliss 3, Wilson 2, Pearson, Horton
Roberts, Aldridge, H. Green, E. Horton, C. Perry, Timmins, Woodhall, Bassett, Bayliss, Wilson, Pearson
Att. 2,484

Round Two
5 November v Mitchell's St George (a) 1–0
Bayliss
Roberts, Aldridge, H. Green, E. Horton, C. Perry, Timmins, Woodhall, Bassett, Bayliss, Pearson, Wilson
Att. 7,800

Round Three
26 November v Wolverhampton Wanderers (h) 2–0
Bassett, Wilson
Roberts, Aldridge, H. Green, E. Horton, C. Perry, Timmins, Bassett, Woodhall, Bayliss, Askin, Wilson
Att. 7,429

Round Four
Albion received a bye

Round Five
7 January v Stoke (h) 4–1
Bayliss 4
Roberts, Aldridge, H. Green, E. Horton, C. Perry, Timmins, Woodhall, Bassett, Bayliss, Pearson, Wilson
Att. 9,093

Round Six
28 January v Old Carthusians (h) 4–2
Pearson 2, Wilson 2
Roberts, Aldridge, H. Green, E. Horton, C. Perry, Timmins, Bassett, Woodhall, Bayliss, Pearson, Wilson
Att. 8,818

Semi-final
18 February v Derby Junction (at Stoke) 3–0
Bayliss, Wilson, Woodhall
Roberts, Aldridge, H. Green, E. Horton, C. Perry, Timmins, Bassett, Woodhall, Bayliss, Pearson, Wilson
Att. 5,996

Final
24 March v Preston North End (at The Oval) 2–1
Bayliss, Woodhall
Roberts, Aldridge, H. Green, E. Horton, C. Perry, Timmins, Woodhall, Bassett, Bayliss, Pearson, Wilson
Att. 18,904

Albion's record in other senior competitions

Full Members Cup

1985–86

Group Eight
2 October v Brighton & Hove Albion (a) won 2–1
Crooks (2)
Bradshaw, Nicholl, Statham, Hunt, Bennett, Robertson, Valentine, Grealish, Varadi, Thomas, Crooks
Att. 4,469

Group Eight
23 October v Crystal Palace (h) won 2–1
Hunt, Nicholl
Powell, Nicholl, Palmer, Hunt, Bennett, Forsyth, Valentine, Grealish, Armstrong (Robson), Whitehead, Crooks (Bull)
Att. 3,914

Semi-final Southern Section
13 November v Chelsea (h) 2–2 (aet): lost 4–5 on penalties
Valentine, Crooks: penalties scored by Bull, Hunt, Varadi, Thompson
Godden, C. Palmer (Anderson), Statham, Hunt, Bennett, Robertson, Valentine (Bull), Robson, Varadi, Thompson, Crooks
Att. 4,070

1986–87

Round One
21 October v Millwall (a) lost 0–2
Naylor, Whitehead, Cowdrill, C. Palmer, Dyson, Hayward, Dennison, Evans, Bull (Thompson), Williamson, Crooks
Att. 967

Simod Cup

1987–88

Round One
10 November v Oldham Athletic (a) won 3–0
Williamson, Lynex, Morley
Naylor, Steggles, Anderson, C. Palmer, Burrows, Kelly, Lynex, Dobbins, Reilly (Williamson), Robson, Morley
Att. 1,841

Round Two
1 December v Ipswich Town (a) lost 1–2
Lynex (pen)
Naylor, C. Palmer, Anderson, Dickinson, Hogg, Lynex, Hopkins, Goodman, Reilly Dobbins, Morley (Robson)
Att. 5,308

1988–89

Round One
9 November v West Ham United (a) lost 2–5
Goodman, Robson
Naylor, Dobbins (Phillips), Albiston, Talbot, Whyte, North, Hopkins, Goodman, Robson (Goodall), C. Palmer, Bradley
Att. 5,960

Zenith Data Systems Cup

1989–90

Round One
29 November v Derby County (h) lost 0–5
Naylor, Burgess (Robson), Harbey, Talbot, Raven, Whyte, Ford, Goodman, Bartlett (Thomas) McNally, Parkin
Att. 4,880

1990–91

Round One
21 November v Barnsley (h) lost 3–5
Bradley, Banister, Robson
Naylor, Dobbins, Harbey (Parkin), Roberts, Bradley, Strodder, Goodman, West, Bannister, McNally, Robson (Ford)
Att. 4,452

Autoglass Trophy

1991–92

Preliminary round
22 October v Shrewsbury Town (h) won 4–0
Shakespeare, West, Ampadu, Rogers
Naylor, Hodson, Harbey, Ford, Rogers, Bradley, McNally, Goodman (Robson), West, Shakespeare (Williams) Ampadu
Att. 6,992

Preliminary round
4 December v Lincoln City (a) won 2–1
Williams, Robson
Naylor, Hodson, Harbey, Bradley, Strodder, Burgess, McNally, Williams, Robson, Shakespeare, White (Banister)
Att. 1,861

Round One
14 January v Exeter City (h) lost 0–1
Naylor, Hodson, Harbey, Bradley, Strodder, Burgess, White, Bannister, Robson, Parkin (Williams), Hackett (Cartwright)
Att. 6,034

1992–93

Preliminary round
5 January v Walsall (h) won 4–0
Donovan, Taylor, Hamilton, Heggs
Lange, Fereday, Darton, Bradley, Raven, Shakespeare (Hamilton), Hackett, Donovan, Taylor, Dickens (Heggs), Robson
Att. 6,702

Preliminary round
12 January v Mansfield Town (a) won 1–0
Taylor
Lange, Coldicott (Hamilton), Darton, Sinfield, Raven, Shakespeare, Hackett, Hunter, Taylor (McCue), Heggs, Donovan
Att. 2,356

Round Two
9 February v Torquay United (h) won 2–1
Donovan 2
Lange, Fereday, Darton, Hackett (Heggs), Hunter (Coldicott), Strodder, Speedie, Hamilton, Taylor, McNally, Donovan
Att. 5,219

Round Three
16 February v Stoke City (a) lost 1–2
Taylor
Naylor, Fereday (Robson), Lilwall, Bradley, Raven, Strodder, Speedie, Hamilton, Taylor, Shakespeare, Donovan
Att. 17,568

FA Charity Shield

1920

15 May v Tottenham Hotspur (a) won 2–0
A. Smith 2
Pearson, J. Smith, Pennington, S. Richardson, Bowser, McNeal, Crisp, A. Smith, Bentley, Morris, Gregory
Att. 38,168

1931

7 October v Arsenal (Villa Park) lost 0–1
Pearson, Shaw, Trentham, Magee, W. Richardson, Edwards, Glidden, Raw, 'W.G.' Richardson, Sandford, Wood
Att. 21,276

1954

29 September v Wolverhampton Wanderers (a) drew 4–4
Allen 3, Ryan
Sanders, Rickaby, Millard, Dudley, Kennedy (Dugdale), Brookes, Griffin, Ryan (Hodgkisson), Allen, Carter, Lee
Att. 45,035
(Each club held the shield for six months)

1968

3 August v Manchester City (a) lost 1–6
Krzywicki
Osborne (Merrick), Fraser, Williams, Lovett, Talbot, Kaye, Stephens, T. Brown, Krzywicki, Collard, Hartford
Att. 35,510
(Osborne went off injured, Williams took over in goal)

Anglo-Italian Tournament

1969–70

Group Two
May 2 v Lanerossi Vicenza (h) drew 0–0
Osborne, Hughes, Fraser, Lovett (Reed), Talbot, Merrick, T. Brown, Hartford, Suggett, Cantello, Hope
Att. 17,655

8 May v AS Roma (h) won 4–0
T. Brown 2, Hope, Talbot
Osborne, Hughes, Fraser, Lovett (Glover), Talbot, Merrick, T. Brown, Hartford, Suggett (Martin), Cantello, Hope
Att. 11,833

16 May v Lanerossi Vicenza (a) drew 1–1
Osborne, Hughes, Fraser, Lovett, Talbot, Merrick, T. Brown, Hartford, Suggett (Martin), Cantello (Glover), Hope
Att. 12,000
(Game abandoned after 76 minutes due to fighting on and off the field)

23 May v AS Roma (a) drew 1–1
Suggett
Osborne, Hughes, Fraser, T. Brown, Talbot, Merrick, Suggett, Kaye, Martin (Lovett), Hartford, Hope
Att. 16,000
(Albion failed to qualify for next stage)

1970–71

Group Two
26 May v Internationale (h) drew 1–1
Wile
Cumbes, Hughes, Wilson, Cantello, Wile, Kaye, Suggett, T. Brown, Astle, Hope, Hartford
Att. 17,645

29 May v Cagliari (h) lost 1–2
Astle
Cumbes, Hughes, Wilson, Cantello, Wile, Kaye, Suggett, T. Brown, Astle, Hope, Hartford
Att. 17,620

1 June v Internationale (a) lost 0–1
Osborne, Hughes, Wilson, Lovett, Wile, Kaye, Suggett, T. Brown, Astle, Hope (MacLean), Hartford
Att. 15,000

1993–94

Preliminary round
8 September v Leicester City (a) drew 0–0
Naylor, Coldicott, Lilwall, McNally, Burgess, Strodder, Ashcroft, Mellon, Garner, Heggs, Ampadu
Att. 3,058

15 September v Peterborough United (h) won 3–1
McNally, Mellon, Darton
Naylor, Parsley, Darton, McNally, Raven, Strodder, Ashcroft, Garner, Heggs (Taylor), Mellon, Ampadu
Att. 4,168

Group B
12 October v Pescara (h) lost 1–2
Taylor
Naylor, McNally, Ampadu, O'Regan, Strodder, Burgess, Garner (Ashcroft), Hamilton, Taylor, Mellon, Donovan
Att. 5,458

9 November v Padova (h) lost 3–4
Hamilton, Ottoni (og), Garner
Naylor, Fereday, Ampadu, McNally, Hunter, O'Regan, Garner, Hamilton, Taylor, Ashcroft (Donovan). Heggs
Att. 2,745

16 November v Fiorentina (a) lost 0–2
Naylor, Reid Ampadu, Hunter, Coldicott, Burgess, Heggs, Hamilton, Taylor, Ashcroft (McNally), Donovan
Att. 7,808

22 December v Cosenza (a) lost 1–2
Taylor
Lange, Burgess (Hunter), Lilwall, Bradley, Raven, O'Regan, Ashcroft (Garner), Mellon, Taylor, Heggs, Hamilton
Att. 139

1995–96

Group
5 September v Salernitana (a) drew 0–0
Naylor, Smith, Edwards, Coldicott, Mardon, Brien, Donovan, Gilbert, Taylor, Hunt (Ashcroft), Hamilton
Att. 2,220

11 October v Foggia (h) lost 1–2
Herbert
Naylor, Burgess, Smith, Coldicott, Herbert (Hunt), Raven, Donovan, Gilbert, Taylor, Ashcroft (Rees), Cunnington
Att. 8,155

8 November v Reggiana (h) won 2–1
Hunt, Taylor
Naylor, Burgess, King, Coldicott, Mardon, Raven, Donovan (Taylor), Gilbert, Ashcroft, Hunt, Hamilton
Att. 6,009

13 December v Brescia (a) won 1–0
Taylor
Naylor, Burgess, Smith, Darby, Edwards, Raven, Donovan (Coldicott), Gilbert, Taylor, Rees (Hargreaves), Hamilton
Att. 196

Semi-final
30 January v Birmingham City (a) drew 2–2
Rees, Raven. Penalties: Ashcroft, Hunt, Taylor, Smith
Naylor, Holmes, Smith, Cunnington (Coldicott), Burgess, Raven, Donovan, Gilbert (Taylor), Rees (Ashcroft), Hunt, Darby.
(Albion won 4–1 on penalties)
Att. 9,113

Area final, first leg
24 February v Port Vale (h) drew 0–0
Spink, Holmes, Nicholson, Darby, Burgess, Raven, Donovan (Ashcroft), Gilbert, Taylor, Hunt (Rees), Hamilton
Att. 10,862

Area final, second leg
5 March v Port Vale (a) lost 1–2 (1–2 on aggregate)
Taylor
Spink, Holmes, Nicholson, Darby (Smith), Burgess, Raven, Ashcroft, Gilbert, Taylor, Hunt, Hamilton
Att. 7,640

Texaco Cup

1970–71

Round One, first leg
14 September v Morton (a) lost 1–2
Rankin (og)
Cumbes, Hughes, Wilson, T. Brown, Kaye, Merrick (Lovett), McVitie, Suggett, Astle, Hartford, Cantello
Att. 7.943

Round One, second leg
30 September v Morton (h) lost 0–1 (1–3 on aggregate)
Cumbes, Minton, Merrick, T. Brown, Talbot, Kaye, McVitie, Suggett, Astle, Hope, Hartford
Att. 16,168

1972–73

Round One, first leg
19 September v Sheffield United (a) drew 1–1
A. Brown
Latchford, Nisbet, Wilson, Cantello, Wile, Robertson, Suggett, T. Brown, Gould, A. Brown, Hartford
Att. 13,381

Round One, second leg
26 September v Sheffield United (h) won 1–0 (aggregate 2–1)
Gould
Latchford, Nisbet, Wilson, Cantello, Wile, Robertson, Suggett, T. Brown, Gould, A. Brown, Hartford
Att. 8,340

Round Two, first leg
25 October v Newcastle United (h) won 2–1
T. Brown 2 (1 pen)
Latchford, Nisbet, Wilson, Woolgar, Wile, Robertson, Suggett, T. Brown, Gould, A. Brown, Hartford
Att. 8,425

Round Two, second leg
8 November v Newcastle United (a) lost 1–3 (3–4 on aggregate)
Hartford
Latchford, Nisbet, Wilson, Merrick, Wile, Robertson, Suggett, T. Brown, Gould, A. Brown, Hartford
Att. 20,420

1974–75

Group 1
3 August v Birmingham City (h) drew 0–0
Osborne, Nisbet, Wilson, Cantello, Wile, Robertson, Hughes, T. Brown, A. Brown (Shaw), Hartford, Johnston
Att. 18,317

6 August v Norwich City (h) won 5–1
T. Brown, Shaw, A. Brown, Hughes, Johnston
Latchford, Nisbet, Wilson, Glover, Wile, Robertson, Hughes, T. Brown (A. Brown), Shaw, Hartford, Johnston
Att. 5,393

10 August v Peterborough United (a) lost 1–2
Shaw
Latchford, Nisbet, Wilson, Glover, Wile, Robertson, Hughes, T. Brown, Shaw (A. Brown), Hartford, Johnston
Att. 8,803

Watney Cup

1971–72

Round One
31 July v Wrexham (a) won 2–1
T. Brown 2 (1 pen)
Cumbes, Hughes, Wilson, Cantello (Merrick), Wile, Robertson, Suggett, T. Brown, Astle, Hope, Hartford
Att. 11,218

Semi-final
4 August v Halifax Town (a) won 2–0
Suggett 2
Cumbes, Hughes, Wilson, Cantello, Wile, Kaye, McVitie (Merrick), T. Brown, Astle, Suggett, Hartford
Att. 12,069

Final
7 August v Colchester United (h) drew 4–4*
Astle 2, Cantello, Suggett. Penalties: Astle, T. Brown, Hope
Cumbes, Hughes, Wilson, Cantello, Wile, Kaye, Suggett, T. Brown, Astle, Hope, Hartford
Att. 19,009
(Colchester won 4–3 on penalties)

Anglo-Scottish Cup

1975–76

Group Two
2 August v Mansfield Town (h) drew 1–1
Cantello
Osborne, Nisbet, Wilson, Cantello (Mayo), Wile, Robertson, Robson, T. Brown, A. Brown, Giles, Johnston
Att. 5,704

6 August v Hull City (a) won 2–1
A. Brown 2
Osborne, Nisbet, Wilson, Cantello, Robson, Robertson, Trewick, A Brown, Mayo, Giles, Johnston
Att. 3,094

9 August v Leicester City (a) lost 1–2
Giles
Osborne, Nisbet, Wilson, Cantello, Wile, Robertson, Robson, A. Brown, Mayo, Giles (Trewick), Johnston
Att. 8,219

1976–77

Midland Group
7 August v Bristol City (a) lost 0–1
Osborne, Mulligan, Cantello, T. Brown, Wile, Robertson, Martin, A. Brown, Mayo, Giles, Johnston
Att. 4,941

10 August v Nottingham Forest (a) lost 2–3
Mulligan, Mayo
Ward, Mulligan, Cantello, T. Brown, Wile, Robson, Martin, Edwards, Mayo, Trewick, Johnston
Att. 7,018

14 August v Notts County (h) lost 0–1
Osborne, Mulligan, Robson, T. Brown, Wile, Robertson, Martin, Edwards, Mayo, Giles, Johnston
Att. 6,936

Tennent Caledonian Cup

(All games played at Ibrox Park)

1977–78

Semi-final
6 August v St Mirren, won 4–3
T. Brown 2 (1 pen), D. Cross, Robson
Osborne, Mulligan, Statham, T. Brown, Wile, Robertson, Robson, Cunningham, D. Cross, Cantello, Johnston
Att. 40,404

Final
7 August v Glasgow Rangers, won 2–0
Cunningham 2
Godden, Mulligan, Statham, Martin, Wile, Robertson, Robson, Cunningham, A. Brown (D. Cross), Trewick, Johnston
Att. 35,066

1978–79

Semi-final
5 August v Southampton, drew 1–1
Regis, penalty: T. Brown
Godden, Batson, Statham, T. Brown, Wile, Robertson, Robson, A. Brown (Johnston), Regis, Trewick, Cunningham
Att. 25,563
(Southampton won 3–1 on penalties)

Third place Play-off
6 August v Heart of Midlothian, lost 0–2
Godden, Batson, Statham, T. Brown, Wile, Robertson, Martin, Robson, Regis (Hughes), Trewick, Cunningham (A. Brown)
Att. 18,823

United Counties League

1893–94

(Group A, played on League basis)
24 February v Small Heath (a) won 5–4
Pearson 2, McLeod 2, Geddes
Reader, Nicholson, Crone, T. Perry, C. Perry, Taggart, Bassett, McLeod, Bostock, Pearson, Geddes
Att. 3,000

26 February v Small Heath (h) won 3–1
Pearson, McLeod 2
Reader, J. Horton, Crone, T. Perry, B. Hadley, Taggart, Norman, McLeod, Bostock, Pearson, Geddes
Att. 2,700

10 March v Stoke (h) won 5–0
Bostock, McLeod 2, Bassett, Geddes
Reader, Nicholson, Crone, T. Perry, C. Perry, Taggart, Bassett, McLeod, Bastock, Pearson, Geddes
Att. 3,000

19 March v Stoke (a) lost 2–5
C. Perry, Geddes
Reader, Nicholson, Crone, T. Perry, C. Perry, Taggart, Bassett, McLeod, Bastock, Pearson, Geddes
Att. 3,000

2 April v Wolverhampton Wanderers (a) lost 2–4
Geddes, Pearson
Reader, J. Horton, Crone, T. Perry, C. Perry, Taggart, Bassett, McLeod, O. Williams, Pearson, Geddes
Att. 4,000

9 April v Wolverhampton Wanderers (h) won 3–1
McLeod, Bassett, Taggart
Reader, J. Horton, Crone, T. Perry, C. Perry, Taggart, Bassett, McLeod, O. Williams, Bostock, Geddes
Att. 5,853
(Albion won the group with eight points)

Final
30 April v Derby County (a) 1–1 aet
Geddes
Reader, J. Horton, Crone, T. Perry, C. Perry, Taggart, Bassett, McLeod, Bostock, Pearson, Geddes
Att. 9,000

Replay, also at Derby (held over until 1894–95 season)
6 October v Derby County (a) lost 1–2
McLeod
Reader, W Williams, Crone, T. Perry, C. Perry, Taggart, Bassett, McLeod, Hutchinson, O. Williams, Newall
Att. 6,000

Championship of the World

1887–88

19 May v Renton (at Hampden Park) lost 1–4
Pearson
Roberts, C. Mason, H. Green, E. Horton, C. Perry, Timmins, Woodhall, Bassett, Bayliss, Pearson, Wilson
Att. 6,000

Bass Charity Vase

1892–93

Final
27 February v Stoke (h) drew 3–3
Geddes, Boyd, Reynolds (pen)
Reader, Nicholson, McCulloch, Reynolds, C. Perry, Groves, Bassett, McLeod, Boyd, Fellows, Geddes
Att. 5,150

Replay
9 March v Stoke (a) drew 1–1
Bassett
Reader, Sheldon, McCulloch, Reynolds, T. Perry, Groves, McLeod, Bassett, Boyd, Fellows, Geddes
Att. 6,000
(Each club held trophy for six months)

1893–94

Round
21 March v Burton Swifts (a) won 4–1
Bassett 2, Bostock, Geddes
Reader, J. Horton, Crone, T. Perry, C. Perry, Taggart, Bassett, Bostock, Pearson, McLeod, Geddes
Att. 2,000

Semi-final
11 April v Aston Villa (a) lost 2–5
O. Williams 2
Reader, J. Horton, Crone, T. Perry, Banks, Taggart, Norman, McLeod, Bostock, O. Williams, Geddes
Att. 5,800

1987–88

Semi-final
22 July v Burton Albion (n) won 3–1
Bradley 2, Hopkins
Naylor, Robson, Cowdrill, Bennett, Steggles, Kelly, Hopkins, Goodman, Reilly, C. Palmer, Bradley
Att. 1,057

Final
31 July v Derby County (n) lost 0–1
Naylor, Robson, Statham, Bennett, Steggles, Kelly, Hopkins, Goodman, Reilly, Bradley, Morley
Att. 2,500

Le Soir International Festival

1954–55

13 October v Honved (Heysel Stadium) lost 3–5
Allen, Nicholls 2
Sanders, Rickaby, Millard, Dudley, Kennedy, Barlow, Griffin, Ryan, Allen, Nicholls, Lee
Att. 55,000

Festival of Britain

1950–51

12 May v SC Wacker, Austria (h) lost 3–4
Allen 2, Barlow
Sanders, Rickaby, Millard, Kennedy, Horne, Dudley, Griffin, McCall, Barlow, Allen, Lee
Att. 16,074

15 May v FC Floriana, Malta (h) won 2–0
Smith, Barlow
Sanders, Rickaby, Millard, Kennedy, Vernon, S. Williams, Griffin, A. Smith, Barlow, Allen, Lee
Att. 15,133

Overseas tournaments

International Tournament (New York, US)

(Section 2)
July 1966
Results:

v Kilmarnock	lost 0–2, won 2–0
v Ferencvaros	drew 1–1, lost 1–2
v Polonia Byton	drew 2–2, lost 0–6

Palo Alto International Tournament (US)

May 1969
Results:

v Dukla Prague	won 2–1
v California Clippers	drew 2–2
v Vitoria Setubal	lost 0–1
v Edmonton All Stars	won 12–0

Orenduscupen Tournament (Sweden)

July/August 1972
Results:

v Kamar FF	won 3–0
v Helsingborgs IF	won 3–1
v Landskrona Bols	drew 1–1

Trofeo Costa Blanca Tournament (Alicante, Spain)

August 1977
Results

v Dinamo Tbilisi	won 1–0
v Heracles CF	lost 1–5

Trofeo Teresa Tournament (La Coruna, Spain)

August 1979
Results

v Sporting Gijon	lost 0–1
v Honved	lost 0–1

Trofej Marjan Tournament (Yugoslavia)

August 1980
Results

v Hajduk Split	lost 1–5
v FC Zurich	drew 0–0

X Trofeo Futbol Ciudad de Sevilla Tournament (Spain)

August 1981
Results

v Real Betis	won 4–1
v FC Sevilla	won 2–0

Spanish IX Trofeo Futbol Ciudad de Barcelona Tournament (Spain)

August 1982
Results

v RCD Espanyol	lost 2–3
v CA Osasuna	lost 1–2

San Jose Cup (USA)

May 1990
Results

v Real Madrid	lost 1–6
v Vasco da Gama	lost 2–4

N.B.
Albion's first team competed (sometimes regularly) in the following local competitions:

* Birmingham Charity Cup 1883–84 to1932–33
* Birmingham Senior Cup 1881–82 to 1905–06
* Liverpool Charity Cup 1895–96
* Coventry Charity Cup 1929–30
* Staffordshire Cup 1882–83 to 1905–06
* West Bromwich Charity Cup 1887–88 to 1897–98
* Walsall Cup 1886–87 and 1887–88
* Wednesbury Charity Cup 1882–83 and 1883–84

International Baggies

Players capped at various levels while with Albion.

Full International

Australia
J. Van Blerk (4)
Canada
P.P. Peschisolido (9, 3 goals), C.H. Valentine (1)
Denmark
T. Gaardsoe (2), M. Albrechten (1)
England
A.A. Aldridge (1), R. Allen (5, 2 goals), G.S. Ashmore (1), J. Astle (5), R.J. Barlow (1), P.S. Barnes (6), W.I. Bassett (16, 7 goals), A.J.E.M. Bayliss (1), S. Bowser (1), W.E. Boyes (2), A. Brown (1), J.H. Carter (3, 4 goals), L.P. Cunningham (3), W.B. Elliott (2), B. Garfield (1), H. Hadley (1), J.T.W. Haines (1, 2 goals), D. Howe (23), S.K. Hunt (2), D.T. Kevan (14, 8 goals), T.H. Kinsell (2), R. McNeal (2), T.P. Magee (5), F. Morris (2, 1 goal), J. Nicholls (2, 1 goal), H.F. Pearson (1), J. Pennington (25), C. Perry (3), T. Perry (1), J. Reader (1), C. Regis (4), J. Reynolds (3, 2 goals), K. Richardson (3, 2 goals), 'W.G.' Richardson (1), S. Rickaby (1), R. Roberts (3), B. Robson (13, 1 goal), R.W. Robson (20, 4 goals), E.A. Sandford (1), G.E. Shaw (1), J. Smith (3), D.J. Statham (3), W. Williams (6), G. Woodhall (2, 1 goal)
Hungary
Z. Gera (20, 7 goals)
Iceland
L. Sigurdsson (12)
Japan
J. Inamoto (14)
Macedonia
A. Sakiri (14, 1 goal)
Nigeria
N. Kanu (13, 2 goals), I. Udezi (1)
Northern Ireland
G.J. Armstrong (4), D. Hegan (1), J.M. Nicholl (11), S.J. Quinn (15, 2 goals), R.A. Ryan (1), J. Vernon (15), D.J. Walsh (9, 5 goals), P.A. Williams (1)
Poland
T. Kuszczak (2)
Republic of Ireland
M.J. Giles (7), A. Grealish (10, 1 goal), K. Kilbane (10), M.A. Kinsella (4), M.P. Martin (10), P.M. Mulligan (15), J. Murphy (1), R.A. Ryan (15, 3 goals), R.C. Treacy (6), D.J. Walsh (14, 7 goals)
Scotland
S. Dobie (6, 1 goal), D.M. Fraser (2), R.A. Hartford (6), R. Hope (2), W.M. Johnston (13),

D. McInnes (2), A. McNab (1), N. Quashie (1)
Senegal
D. Kamara (15, 2 goals)
Slovakia
I. Balis (3)
Slovenia
R. Koren (3)
Switzerland
B. Haas (8)
Wales
S. Davies (11, 1 goal), W.C. Davies (2), R. Earnshaw (11, 3 goals), H.E. Foulkes (1), A.J. Johnson (8), I. Jones (4), J. Koumas (20), P. Mardon (1), A.H. Millington (3), J.P. Murphy (15), S. Powell (4), R.R. Rees (2), W.W. Robbins (6, 3 goals), M.R. Thomas (2), G.E. Williams (26, 1 goal), S.G. Williams (33), D.F. Witcomb (9, 1 goal)

B International

England
R. Allen (2), J. Astle (2, 4 goals), R.J. Barlow (2), P.S. Barnes (1), B.M. Batson (3), L.P. Cunningham (1), J.R. Dugdale (3) A. Ford (2), D. Howe (1), J.P. Kennedy (3), S. Naylor (3), J. Nicholls (1), C. Regis (3), B. Robson (2), D.J. Statham (2, 2 goals)
Scotland
J.G. Dudley (1)
Wales
P.J. Mardon (1)

Under-19 & 20 International

England
A. Chambers (2), J. Chambers (2), R. Chaplow (2), L. Daniels (1), S. Nicholson (1), A. Oliver (4)

Under-21 international

England
D. Burrows (1), L.P. Cunningham (6, 2 goals),C. Davies (2), S.W. Mackenzie (3), R. Moses (7), G.A. Owen (12, 4 goals), C. Regis (6, 3 goals), K. Richardson (3), B. Robson (7, 1 goal), D.J. Statham (6)
Netherlands
S. McDonald (1)
Northern Ireland
E. Morris (1)
Republic of Ireland
K. Ampadu (1), J. Anderson (5), K.D. Kilbane (7, 1 goal), J. Murphy (3)

Scotland
W. Cummings (4*), G. Germaine (1)
Wales
R. Davies (3), D. Gabbidon (9), B.W. Hughes (3)

Under-23 international
Australia
A. McDermott (3)
England
D.G. Burnside (1), L. Cantello (8), C. Clark (1), D. Howe (6), D.T. Kevan (4), P.W. Latchford (2), J. Nicholls (1), G.J.M. Nisbet (1), M.E. Setters (11)
Republic of Ireland
R.C.P. Treacy (1)
Scotland
E.P. Colquhoun (1), R.A. Hartford (5), R. Hope (1), R.T. Wilson (1)
St Kitts + Nevis
B. Quailey (2, 1 goal)
Wales
R.L. Krzywicki (3), A.H. Millington (4), G.E. Williams (2)

Amateur Internationals
England
R. Banks (1), L.F. Cooling (1), W.C. Jordan (2, 8 goals)

Inter League
Football League
R. Allen (1, 1 goal), J. Astle (2, 4 goals), H.G. Bache (1), R.J. Barlow (5), W.I. Bassett (3, 2 goals), W.E. Boyes (1, 1 goal), A. Brown (2, 1 goal), F.R. Buck (2), J.H. Carter (1), J. Crisp (1), J.R. Dugdale (1), J. Edwards (1), W. Groves (1), T. Higgins (2), D. Howe (6), A. Jackson (1), A.C. Jephcott (2), J. Kaye (2, 2 goals), D.T. Kevan (1, 3 goals), R. McNeal (5), F. Morris (1, 2 goals), D.G. Nurse (1), H.F. Pearson (2), J. Pennington (9), C. Perry (1), T. Perry (3), J. Reader (3), J. Reynolds (2), S. Richardson (1), S. Rickaby (1), R.W. Robson (5), G.E. Shaw (1), B.W. Shearman (2), J.L. Spencer (1), H.F. Trentham (1), W. Williams (5), S.W. Wood (1, 1 goal)

Junior International
England
W. Adams, W. Bowser, E. Bradley, T. Broad, H. Chamberlain, L. Cowen, R. Corbett, J. Crisp, E. Crowe, L. Darnell, C. Davies, T. Green, W.E. Harper, S.E. Heaselgrave, J.W. Hudson, A.C. Jephcott, H. Kinsell, W.A. Lambert, J. Law, N. Male, J.F. Mann, F. Morris, A. Parry, E. Perkins, A.A. Perry, H.F. Pearson, H.P. Pearson, T. Picken, A. Randle, J. Rix, W. Rotton, J. Screen, S. Short, J. Smith, A.J. Timmins, S.G.B. Trevis, J.T. Turner, F. Waterhouse
Wales
H. Foulkes

Miscellaneous Representative Honours

All British XI

D.F. Witcomb

England XI

J. Astle, W.I. Bassett, D. Howe, D.T. Kevan, C. Perry, C. Regis, R.W. Robson

FA XI

W. Adams, R. Allen, G.S. Ashmore, R.J. Barlow, W.I. Bassett, D.G. Burnside, J.H. Carter, J. Cookson, J.R. Dugdale, W.B. Elliott, D. Howe, C.E. Jackman, J.P. Kennedy, D.T. Kevan, T.H. Kinsell, G.J. McVitie, T.P. Magee, F. Morris, H.F. Pearson, S. Richardson, S. Rickaby, R.W. Robson, M.E. Setters, G.E. Shaw

FA Amateur XI

N.J. Whitehead

Football League XI

W.I. Bassett, A. McNab, R. McNeal, H.F. Pearson, J. Pennington, T. Perry, J. Reader, G. Robson

Great Britain XI

J. Vernon

Jamaica XI

D.M. Moore (1)

Republic of Ireland XI

A. Grealish, M.P. Martin, P.M. Mulligan

Rest of the United Kingdom

J. Vernon

Scotland XI

E.P. Colquhoun, J.G. Dudley, D.M. Fraser, R. Hope

Wales XI

A. Evans, S. Powell

Young England

A. Brown, M.E. Setters

International trials

England

W.I. Bassett, A.J.E.M. Bayliss, J.H. Carter, J. Crisp, E.A.R. Finch, T.W. Glidden, T. Green jnr, G.C. James, A.C. Jephcott, T.P. Magee, F. Morris, H.F. Pearson, J. Pennington, C. Perry, J. Reynolds, S. Richardson, W. Richardson, R.J. Roberts, E.A. Sandford, G.E. Shaw, C. Simmons, J. Smith, J.L. Spencer, W. Williams

Scotland

J. Stevenson

Wales

L. Davies, H. Foulkes

Youth international

England

I. Benjamin, R. Bradley, A. Brown, P. Bunch, D.G. Burnside, L. Cantello, A. Chambers, J. Chambers, G. Childs, B. Cooke, J. Crosby, N. Cutler, L.L. Daniels, B. Donaghy, C. Drury, M. Forsyth, P. Frain, M. Gibson, L. Hughes, A. Jones, G. Jones, M. Lewis, A. Littlejohn, A.R. Merrick, D. Monaghan, A. Oliver, B. Robson, J. Rumjahn, M.E. Setters, D.J. Statham, K. Summerfield, J. Trewick, A. Wileman

Italy

M. Iezzi, Maresco

Northern Ireland

G. McDonald, J. McGovern, B. McMenamin, E.W. Morris, D. Patterson

Republic of Ireland

J. Anderson, A. Bruce, R.P. Treacy

Scotland

M. Brown, G. Germaine, R.A. Hartford, M. McCartney, S. McLaren, H. Reed, A.P. Robertson

Wales

D. Bowman, D. Gabbidon, W. Hughes, A. James, M. Lee, M. Trenter

* Honoured as a loan player

International Facts

* In September 2004 Albion had 15 full internationals on their books.
* Bob Roberts (England) was Albion's first full international versus Scotland in March 1887.
* Albion's most capped player is Stuart Williams (Wales) with 33 caps between 1954 and 1962.
* Jimmy Cookson scored 24 goals in 11 matches on the FA tour of Canada in 1931.

Albion Career Records

The following is a list of the players who have played for Albion since they joined the League. Included under 'Other' matches are Test matches, Play-off games, the Fairs Cup, European Cup-winners' Cup, Anglo-Italian and Anglo-Scottish tournaments and the FA Charity Shield.

									League			FA Cup			FL Cup			Other			Total		
Name		Date of Birth	Birthplace	Died	Year with Club	Loan	Previous Club	Next Club	A	S	G	A	S	G	A	S	G	A	S	G	A	S	G
Adams A	Amos	10/06/1878	West Bromwich	1941	1897-1910		Springfields	Retired	209	0	3	15	0	0	0	0	0	0	0	0	224	0	3
Adams J	Jimmy	04/01/1908	Cannock	1983	1929-1945		Cannock Town	Retired	103	0	0	0	0	0	0	0	0	0	0	0	103	0	0
Adams W	Billy	12/08/1892	Blackheath, Worcestershire	1945	1919-1928		Rowley Victoria	Barrow	92	0	0	6	0	0	0	0	0	0	0	0	98	0	0
Adamson C	Chris	04/11/1978	Ashington		1995-2002		School	St Patrick's Athletic	12	0	0	2	0	0	0	0	0	0	0	0	14	0	0
Agnew P	Paul	15/08/1965	Lisburn		1995-1997		Grimsby Town	Ilkeston Town	38	1	1	0	1	0	1	0	0	0	0	0	39	2	1
Aitken AFS	Andy	21/08/1934	Craigmillar	2005	1959-1961		Hibernian	Falkirk	22	0	2	0	0	0	0	0	0	0	0	0	22	0	2
Albiston AR	Arthur	14/07/1957	Edinburgh		1988-1989		Manchester United	Dundee	43	0	2	2	0	0	1	0	0	1	0	0	47	0	2
Albrechtsen M	Martin	30/03/1980	Copenhagen, Denmark		2004		FC Copenhagen		72	14	2	5	1	0	4	1	0	0	0	0	81	16	2
Aldridge AJ	Albert	18/04/1864	Walsall	1891	1886-1888		Walsall Swifts	Walsall Town Swifts	0	0	0	15	0	0	0	0	0	0	0	0	15	0	0
Aldridge NH	Norman	23/02/1921	Coventry		1945-1948		Foxford FC	Northampton Town	1	0	0	0	0	0	0	0	0	0	0	0	1	0	0
Allan SJE	Stan	28/12/1886	Wallsend-on-Tyne	1919	1911-1912		Newcastle United	Nottingham Forest	19	0	4	1	0	0	0	0	0	0	0	0	20	0	4
Allardyce S	Sam	19/10/1954	Dudley		1989-1992		Preston NE	Preston NE	0	1	0	0	0	0	0	0	0	0	0	0	0	1	0
Allen R	Ronnie	15/01/1929	Fenton	2001	1950-1961		Port Vale	Crystal Palace	415	0	208	42	0	23	0	0	0	1	0	3	458	0	234
Alsop GA	Gilbert	10/09/1908	Frampton Cotterell	1992	1935-1937		Walsall	Ipswich Town	1	0	0	0	0	0	0	0	0	0	0	0	1	0	0
Ampadu PK	Kwame	20/12/1970	Bradford		1991-1994		Arsenal	Swansea City	27	22	4	1	0	0	6	1	0	5	0	1	39	23	5
Anderson CR	Colin	26/04/1962	Newcastle		1985-1991		Torquay United	Walsall	131	9	10	2	0	2	5	2	0	2	1	0	140	12	12
Andersen VG	Vetle	20/04/1964	Kristiansand, Norway		1989-1990		Lyngby United	Lyngby United	0	1	0	0	0	0	0	0	0	0	0	0	0	1	0
Angel M	Mark	23/08/1975	Newcastle		1998-2000		Oxford United	Darlington	4	21	1	1	1	0	0	1	0	0	0	0	5	23	1
Angell BAM	Brett	20/08/1968	Marlborough		1996	L	Sunderland (L)	Sunderland	0	3	0	0	0	0	0	0	0	0	0	0	0	3	0
Appleby B	Ben	09/09/1878	Burton-on-Trent	1961	1901-1903		Burton Swifts	Bristol Rovers	1	0	0	0	0	0	0	0	0	0	0	0	1	0	0
Appleton MA	Michael	04/12/1975	Salford		2001-2003		Preston NE	Retired	33	0	0	0	0	0	2	0	0	3	0	0	38	0	0
Armstrong GJ	Gerry	23/05/1954	Belfast		1985-1986		Real Mallorca	Carlisle United	7	1	0	0	0	0	2	0	1	1	0	0	10	1	1
Arthur DR	David	09/03/1960	Bushbury		1976-1982		School	Walsall	2	1	0	0	0	0	3	0	0	0	0	0	5	1	0
Ashcroft L	Lee	07/09/1972	Preston		1993-1996		Preston NE	Preston NE	66	24	17	3	1	1	2	3	0	8	3	0	79	31	18
Ashmore GSA	George	05/05/1898	Plymouth	1973	1919-1931		Nineveh Wesley	Chesterfield	246	0	0	22	0	0	0	0	0	0	0	0	268	0	0
Ashurst W	Bill	04/05/1894	Willington	1947	1926-1928		Notts County	Newark Town	22	0	1	1	0	0	0	0	0	0	0	0	23	0	1
Askin GW	George	15/07/1861	West Bromwich	1925	1882-1889		Elwells	Hednesford Town	0	0	0	1	0	0	0	0	0	0	0	0	1	0	0
Astle J	Jeff	13/05/1942	Eastwood	2002	1964-1974		Notts County	Hellenic	290	2	137	23	0	14	28	0	19	18	0	4	359	2	174
Aston HM	Harry	10/10/1855	Bloxwich	1914	1879-1885		George Salter Works	Wolverhampton Wanderers	0	0	0	7	0	3	0	0	0	0	0	0	7	0	3
Aston HJ	Harold	02/02/1881	Redditch	1938	1904-1905		Army	Walsall	25	0	9	1	0	1	0	0	0	0	0	0	26	0	10
Bache HG	Harold	20/08/1889	Churchill	1916	1914-1916	A	Eastbourne	Killed at war	12	0	4	2	0	0	0	0	0	0	0	0	14	0	4
Baddeley G	George	08/05/1874	Fegg Hayes	1952	1908-1914		Stoke City	Retired	145	0	1	12	0	0	0	0	0	0	0	0	157	0	1
Baldwin HJA	Harry	17/07/1920	Erdington		1937-1939		Sutton Town	Brighton & Hove Albion	5	0	0	0	0	0	0	0	0	0	0	0	5	0	0
Balis I	Igor	05/01/1970	Zalozinik, Slovakia		2000-2003		Spartak Trnava	Retired	60	9	4	3	2	0	0	1	0	0	0	0	63	12	4
Bamford JAE	John	12/12/1880	Weedon	1941	1905-1906		Wellingborough	Wellingborough	3	0	0	0	0	0	0	0	0	0	0	0	3	0	0
Banks GE	George	28/03/1919	Wednesbury	1991	1933-1947		Brownhills Albion	Mansfield Town	4	0	3	0	0	0	0	0	0	0	0	0	4	0	3
Banks IF	Ian	09/01/1961	Mexborough		1989		Bradford City	Barnsley	2	2	0	0	0	0	0	0	0	0	0	0	2	2	0
Banks J	Jack	14/05/1874	West Bromwich	1947	1893-1901		Oldbury Town	Newton Heath	119	0	5	12	0	1	0	0	0	3	0	0	134	0	6

									League			FA Cup			FL Cup			Other			Total		
Name		Date of Birth	Birthplace	Died	Year with Club	Loan	Previous Club	Next Club	A	S	G	A	S	G	A	S	G	A	S	G	A	S	G
Bannister G	Gary	22/07/1960	Warrington		1990-1992		Coventry City	Nottingham Forest	62	10	18	1	1	0	3	1	1	3	0	1	69	12	20
Bannister J	Jack	26/01/1942	Chesterfield		1958-1964		School	Scunthorpe United	9	0	0	0	0	0	0	0	0	0	0	0	9	0	0
Barham MF	Mark	12/07/1972	Folkestone		1989		Middlesbrough	Brighton & Hove Albion	4	0	0	0	0	0	1	0	0	0	0	0	5	0	0
Barker RC	Bobby	01/12/1927	Kinglassie		1945-1950		Kelty Rovers	Shrewsbury Town	14	0	2	0	0	0	0	0	0	0	0	0	14	0	2
Barlow RJ	Ray	17/08/1926	Swindon		1944-1960		Garrards FC	Birmingham City	403	0	31	46	0	5	0	0	0	0	0	0	449	0	36
Barnes PS	Peter	10/06/1957	Manchester		1979-81		Manchester City	Leeds United	76	1	23	4	0	1	9	1	1	0	0	0	89	2	25
Barnsley GRT	Geoff	09/11/1935	Bilston		1951-1957		Erdington Albion	Plymouth Argyle	1	0	0	0	0	0	0	0	0	0	0	0	1	0	0
Barron PG	Paul	16/09/1953	Woolwich		1982-1985		Crystal Palace	QPR	63	0	0	6	0	0	4	0	0	0	0	0	73	0	0
Bartlett KF	Kevin	12//10/1962	Portsmouth		1989-1990		Cardiff City	Notts County	25	12	10	3	0	1	2	0	0	1	0	0	31	12	11
Bassett ICH	Idris	12/03/1915	Brithdir	1979	1936-1944		Sutton Town	Retired	8	0	0	0	0	0	0	0	0	0	0	0	8	0	0
Bassett WI	Billy	27/01/1869	West Bromwich	1937	1886-1899		West Bromwich Strollers	Retired	261	0	61	40	0	11	0	0	0	10	0	5	311	0	77
Bastock AME	Archie	07/04/1869	Brecon	1954	1892-1893		Shrewsbury Town	Burton Swifts	26	0	11	8	0	2	0	0	0	0	0	0	34	0	13
Batista AJM	Jordao	30/08/1971	Malange, Angola		2000-2004		Sporting Braga	Estrela Amadora	47	16	6	1	0	0	4	1	2	0	2	0	52	19	8
Batson BM	Brendan	06/02/1953	St George's, Grenada		1978-1984		Cambridge United	Retired	172	0	1	13	0	1	21	0	0	14	0	0	220	0	2
Baugh RH	Dicky	06/03/1896	Wolverhampton	1972	1924-1929		Wolverhampton Wanderers	Exeter City	61	0	0	4	0	0	0	0	0	0	0	0	65	0	0
Bayliss AEJM	Jem	14/01/1863	Tipton	1933	1884-1892		Wednesbury Old Athletic	Retired	56	0	12	39	0	24	0	0	0	0	0	0	95	0	36
Bedford L	Lewis	26/03/1904	Erdington	1975	1920-1922		School	Walsall	3	0	0	0	0	0	0	0	0	0	0	0	3	0	0
Beesley P	Paul	21/07/1965	Liverpool		1998	L	Port Vale (L)	Port Vale	8	0	0	0	0	0	0	0	0	0	0	0	8	0	0
Bell G	George	04/03/1861	West Bromwich	1959	1878-1888		George Salter Works	Kidderminster Harriers	0	0	0	16	0	7	0	0	0	0	0	0	16	0	7
Bell H	Harry	18/04/1862	West Bromwich	1948	1879-87		George Salter Works	Retired	0	0	0	15	0	0	0	0	0	0	0	0	15	0	0
Bell SLT	Laurie	05/05/1875	Langbank	1933	1904-1905		Brentford	Hibernian	16	0	6	1	0	0	0	0	0	0	0	0	17	0	6
Benjamin IT	Ian	11/12/1961	Nottingham		1979-1982		Sheffield United	Notts County	1	1	0	0	0	0	0	0	0	0	0	0	1	1	0
Benjamin TJ	Trevor	08/02/1979	Kettering		2002	L	Leicester City (L)	Leicester City	0	3	1	0	0	0	0	0	0	0	0	0	0	3	1
Bennett DA	Dean	13/12/1977	Wolverhampton		1996-1998		Aston Villa (Jnrs)	Bromsgrove Rovers	0	1	0	0	0	0	0	0	0	0	0	0	0	1	0
Bennett M	Martyn	04/08/1961	Birmingham		1977-1990		Streetly FC	Worcester City	180	1	9	13	0	0	20	0	1	3	0	0	216	1	10
Bentley A	Alf	15/09/1887	Alfreton	1940	1913-1922		Bolton Wanderers	Burton Albion	97	0	46	5	0	1	0	0	0	3	1	0	105	1	47
Berthe S	Sekou	07/10/1977	Bamoko, Mali		2003-2005		Troyes	Panionious	2	1	0	0	0	0	1	0	0	0	0	0	3	1	0
Betteley RH	Dick	14/07/1880	Bradley, Staffordshire	1942	1906-1912		Wolverhampton Wanderers	Bilston United	85	0	0	4	0	0	0	0	0	0	0	0	89	0	0
Betteridge RM	Mick	11/08/1924	Redditch	1999	1948-1951		Warslow Celtic	Swindon Town	5	0	0	0	0	0	0	0	0	0	0	0	5	0	0
Billingham PA	Peter	08/10/1938	Pensnett		1960-1962		Walsall	Worcester City	7	0	0	0	0	0	0	0	0	0	0	0	7	0	0
Bisseker WM	Billy	11/11/1863	West Bromwich	1902	1878-1884		George Salter Works	Retired	0	0	0	1	0	0	0	0	0	0	0	0	1	0	0
Blagden J	Jonathan	12/04/1900	Sheffield	1964	1921-1923		Cresswell Colliery	Worksop Town	16	0	2	4	0	2	0	0	0	0	0	0	20	0	4
Blissett LL	Luther	01/02/1958	Falmouth, Jamaica		1992-1993	L	Watford (L)	Bury	3	0	1	0	0	0	0	0	0	0	0	0	3	0	1
Blood R	Bobby	18/03/1894	Harpur Hill	1988	1921-1924		Port Vale	Stockport County	53	0	26	0	0	0	0	0	0	0	0	0	53	0	26
Boere JWJ	Jeroen	18/11/1967	Arnhem, Holland		1994	L	West Ham United (L)	West Ham United	5	0	0	0	0	0	0	0	0	0	0	0	5	0	0
Bookman LJAO	Louis	08/11/1890	Zagaren, Lithuania	1943	1914-1919		Bradford City	Luton Town	16	0	1	0	0	0	0	0	0	0	0	0	16	0	1
Bortolazzi M	Mario	10/01/1968	Verona, Italy		1998-1999		Genoa	Livomo	25	10	2	1	0	0	0	0	0	0	0	0	26	10	2
Boston HJ	Harry	20/10/1899	Nantwich	1973	1929-1931		Bolton Wanderers	Swansea City	27	0	6	0	0	0	0	0	0	0	0	0	27	0	6
Bourne RA	Dickie	12/01/1881	Roundle	1944	1907-1908		Clapton Orient	Walsall	9	0	1	0	0	0	0	0	0	0	0	0	9	0	1
Bowden JW	James	15/08/1882	Wolverhampton	1951	1904-1906		Handsworth Rovers	Southampton	8	0	0	0	0	0	0	0	0	0	0	0	8	0	0
Bowen SA	Stewart	12/12/1972	West Bromwich		1989-1992		School	Coventry City	8	0	1	0	0	0	0	0	0	0	0	0	8	0	1
Bowen WE	Walter 'Tod'	03/09/1891	Hednesford	1944	1914-1915		Nuneaton Town	Hednesford Town	1	0	0	0	0	0	0	0	0	0	0	0	1	0	0
Bowser S	Sid	06/04/1891	Birmingham	1961	1908-1913,1914-1924		Willenhall Town	Walsall	341	0	64	28	0	8	0	0	0	0	0	0	369	0	72

Name		Date of Birth	Birthplace	Died	Year with Club	Loan	Previous Club	Next Club	League A	League S	League G	FA Cup A	FA Cup S	FA Cup G	FL Cup A	FL Cup S	FL Cup G	Other A	Other S	Other G	Total A	Total S	Total G
Bowser W	William	12/11/1886	Birmingham	1975	1907-1909		Dudley Town	Walsall	1	0	0	0	0	0	0	0	0	0	0	0	1	0	0
Boyd H	Henry	06/05/1868	Pollokshaws	1935	1892-1894		Burnley	Royal Arsenal	7	0	1	1	0	0	0	0	0	2	0	1	10	0	2
Boyd J	Jack	10/04/1925	Consett		1948-1949		Sunderland	Consett Town	1	0	0	0	0	0	0	0	0	0	0	0	1	0	0
Boyes WE	Wally	05/01/1913	Killamarsh	1960	1931-1938		Woodhouse Mills United	Everton	151	0	35	14	0	3	0	0	0	0	0	0	165	0	38
Bradley CH	Charles	19/01/1882	Smethwick	1949	1905		Invention Street Boys	Dudley Town	3	0	0	0	0	0	0	0	0	0	0	0	3	0	0
Bradley DM	Darren	24/11/1965	Birmingham		1986-1995		Aston Villa	Walsall	236	18	9	10	0	2	13	0	1	11	0	1	270	18	13
Bradley EJ	Eli	24/12/1882	Dudley	1962	1905-1908		Bilston Town	Luton Town	25	0	6	2	0	0	0	0	0	0	0	0	27	0	6
Bradley RJ	Ron	24/04/1939	Bilston		1954-1964		Bilston Boys	Norwich City	13	0	0	0	0	0	0	0	0	0	0	0	13	0	0
Bradshaw PW	Paul	28/04/1956	Altrincham		1985-1986,1988-1990		Vancouver Whitecaps	Peterborough United	14	0	0	2	0	0	5	0	0	1	0	0	22	0	0
Brett RS	Ralph	22/06/1878	Chester	1940	1898-1899		Army	Wellingborough	12	0	3	0	0	0	0	0	0	0	0	0	12	0	3
Brett SS	Sammy	25/12/1879	St Asaph	1939	1898-1902		Southport Central	Wellingborough	8	0	2	2	0	1	0	0	0	0	0	0	10	0	3
Brien AJ	Tony	10/02/1969	Dublin		1995-1996		Rotherham United	Hull City	2	0	0	0	0	0	1	0	0	1	0	0	4	0	0
Brittain JW	John	16/01/1880	Wednesbury	1960	1902-1906		Wednesbury Old Athletic	Willenhall Swifts	9	0	0	1	0	0	0	0	0	0	0	0	10	0	0
Broad TH	Tommy	31/07/1887	Stalybridge	1966	1905-1908		Openshaw Lads Club	Chesterfield	11	0	0	4	0	1	0	0	0	0	0	0	15	0	1
Brockhurst WJ	Bill	25/11/1913	Brownhills	1995	1935-1938		Cannock Chase Colliery	Hednesford Town	5	0	0	0	0	0	0	0	0	0	0	0	5	0	0
Bromage E	Enos	22/10/1898	Mickleover	1978	1928-1929		Gillingham	Nottingham Forest	10	0	2	0	0	0	0	0	0	0	0	0	10	0	2
Brookes WA	Billy	19/04/1931	Dudley		1947-1958		Erdington Albion	Allen's Cross	19	0	0	0	0	0	0	0	0	1	0	0	20	0	0
Brooks J	Joe	11/11/1886	Stairfoot	1955	1907-1908		Barnsley	Barnsley	21	0	1	1	0	0	0	0	0	0	0	0	22	0	1
Brown A	Ally	12/04/1951	Musselburgh		1972-1983		Leicester City	Crystal Palace	254	25	72	26	2	6	27	0	2	24	1	5	331	28	85
Brown AJ	Tony	03/10/1945	Oldham		1961-1981		School	Torquay United	561	13	218	53	1	27	46	1	17	44	1	17	704	16	279
Brown F	Fred	06/12/1931	Stratford		1955-1958		Aldershot	Portsmouth	11	0	0	0	0	0	0	0	0	0	0	0	11	0	0
Brown H	Harry	15/11/1883	Northampton	1934	1903-1905		Northampton Town	Southampton	35	0	5	1	0	0	0	0	0	0	0	0	36	0	5
Brown JF	Freddie	23/02/1886	Brierley Hill	1939	1908-1910		Stoke City	Kidderminster Harriers	8	0	1	0	0	0	0	0	0	0	0	0	8	0	1
Buck FR	Fred	12/07/1880	Newcastle-under-Lyme	1952	1900-1903,1906-1914		Stafford Rangers	Swansea Town	287	0	90	32	0	4	0	0	0	0	0	0	319	0	94
Bull SG	Steve	28/03/1965	Tipton		1984-1986		Tipton Town	Wolverhampton Wanderers	2	2	2	0	0	0	2	0	1	1	2	0	5	4	3
Bunn ATF	Fred	07/02/1861	West Bromwich	1921	1879-1885		George Salter Works	Crosswell's Brewery	0	0	0	12	0	1	0	0	0	0	0	0	12	0	1
Burgess D	Daryl	24/11/1971	Marston Green		1987-2001		School	Northampton Town	317	15	10	9	0	0	19	3	3	14	0	0	359	18	13
Burgin M	Meynell	29/11/1911	Sheffield	1994	1938-1943		Nottingham Forest	Retired	14	0	9	0	0	0	0	0	0	0	0	0	14	0	9
Burns JA	Alf	20/06/1865	Liverpool	1957	1889-1892		London Caledonians	Notts County	15	0	5	2	0	0	0	0	0	0	0	0	17	0	5
Burns JA	Jack	10/06/1871	Walsall	1933	1892-1894		Fairfield Villa	Stafford Rangers	1	0	0	0	0	0	0	0	0	0	0	0	1	0	0
Burnside DG	Davey	10/12/1939	Kingswood		1955-1962		Bristol City	Southampton	127	0	39	8	0	3	0	0	0	0	0	0	135	0	42
Burrows D	David	25/10/1968	Dudley		1985-1988		School	Liverpool	37	9	1	2	0	0	3	1	0	1	0	0	43	10	1
Burton EC	Edward	23/06/1881	Birmingham	1963	1905		Walsall	Walsall	1	0	0	0	0	0	0	0	0	0	0	0	1	0	0
Burton HA	Harry	17/01/1882	West Bromwich	1923	1909-1911		Sheffield Wednesday	Scunthorpe United	32	0	4	4	0	0	0	0	0	0	0	0	36	0	4
Bushell GP	George	20/03/1864	Wednesbury	1945	1883-1889		West Bromwich FC	Wednesbury Old Athletic	0	0	0	1	0	0	0	0	0	0	0	0	1	0	0
Butler PJF	Peter	27/08/1966	Halifax		1996-1998		Notts County	Halifax Town	52	8	0	2	1	0	1	2	0	0	0	0	55	11	0
Butler PA	Tony	28/09/1972	Stockport		2000-2001		Port Vale	Bristol City	65	5	1	1	1	0	7	0	0	2	0	0	75	6	1
Butler S	Stan	07/01/1919	Stillington	1969	1938-1947		Scunthorpe United	Southport	4	0	0	2	0	0	0	0	0	0	0	0	6	0	0
Byers JE	Jack	12/08/1897	Selby	1931	1924-1928		Blackburn Rovers	Worcester City	104	0	11	7	0	1	0	0	0	0	0	0	111	0	12
Bytheway GS	George	23/03/1908	Shuttlewood	1979	1927-1933		Staveley Town	Coventry City	16	0	2	0	0	0	0	0	0	0	0	0	16	0	2
Cameron JR	Jack	14/08/1875	Currie	1944	1896-1897		Everton	Blackburn Rovers	13	0	2	2	0	0	0	0	0	0	0	0	15	0	2
Campbell D	Danny	03/02/1944	Manchester		1961-1968		Droysden	Los Angeles Wolves	8	0	0	0	0	0	3	0	0	0	0	0	11	0	0
Campbell JC	Jimmy	11/04/1937	St Pancras	1994	1954-1959		Maidenhead United	Portsmouth	31	0	9	0	0	0	0	0	0	0	0	0	31	0	9

Name		Date of Birth	Birthplace	Died	Year with Club	Loan	Previous Club	Next Club	League			FA Cup			FL Cup			Other			Total		
									A	S	G	A	S	G	A	S	G	A	S	G	A	S	G
Campbell KJ	Kevin	04/02/1970	Lambeth		2005-2006		Everton	Cardiff City	35	10	6	1	2	0	0	1	0	0	0	0	36	13	6
Cantello L	Len	11/09/1951	Newton Heath		1967-1979		School	Bolton Wanderers	297	4	13	22	0	3	21	0	3	25	0	2	365	4	21
Carbon MP	Matt	08/06/1975	Nottingham		1998-2001		Derby County	Walsall	106	7	5	4	0	0	7	2	0	0	0	0	117	9	5
Carr FA	Franz	24/09/1966	Preston		1998		Bolton Wanderers	Grimsby Town	1	3	0	0	0	0	0	0	0	0	0	0	1	3	0
Carter DA	Darren	18/12/1983	Solihull		2005		Birmingham City		30	23	4	3	2	1	6	0	1	0	2	0	39	27	6
Carter G	Geoff	14/02/1943	Moulton		1954-1966		Moulton FC	Bury	25	0	3	0	0	0	0	0	0	0	0	0	25	0	3
Carter JH	Joe	27/07/1899	Aston	1977	1921-1936		Westbourne FC	Tranmere Rovers	414	0	145	37	0	10	0	0	0	0	0	0	451	0	155
Carter W	Wilf	04/10/1933	Wednesbury		1949-1957		School	Plymouth Argyle	57	0	12	3	0	0	0	0	0	1	0	0	61	0	12
Cartwright NA	Neil	20/02/1971	Stourbridge		1987-1993		Wollaston Hales	Kidderminster Harriers	5	6	0	0	0	0	0	0	0	0	1	0	5	7	0
Castle J	Jack	20/02/1871	Birmingham	1929	1891-1892		Birmingham St Geroge	Brierley Hill Alliance	4	0	0	0	0	0	0	0	0	0	0	0	4	0	0
Cave GH	George	15/06/1874	Great Bridge	1904	1895-1901		Great Bridge Unity	Retired	77	0	0	6	0	0	0	0	0	0	0	0	83	0	0
Chadburn JL	John	12/02/1873	Mansfield	1923	1900-1903		Wolverhampton Wanderers	Liverpool	43	0	3	5	0	1	0	0	0	0	0	0	48	0	4
Chamberlain HG	Bert	10/11/1899	Langley	1975	1922-1926		Cradley Heath	Brighton & Hove Albion	4	0	0	0	0	0	0	0	0	0	0	0	4	0	0
Chambers AC	Adam	20/11/1980	West Bromwich		1997-2005		Grove Vale FC	Kidderminster Harriers	38	18	1	5	1	0	4	2	0	0	1	0	47	22	1
Chambers H	Harry	17/11/1896	Willington Quay	1949	1928-1929		Liverpool	Oakengates	40	0	4	6	0	1	0	0	0	0	0	0	46	0	5
Chambers JA	James	20/11/1980	West Bromwich		1997-2004		Grove Vale FC	Watford	54	19	0	1	0	0	5	1	0	0	0	0	60	20	0
Chaplow RD	Richard	02/02/1985	Accrington		2005		Burnley		23	16	1	5	0	2	4	2	0	1	0	0	33	18	3
Charsley CC	Chris	07/11/1864	Leicester	1945	1891		Small Heath	Small Heath	1	0	0	0	0	0	0	0	0	0	0	0	1	0	0
Childs GPC	Gary	19/04/1964	Birmingham		1980-1983		School	Walsall	2	1	0	0	0	0	0	0	0	0	0	0	2	1	0
Clark B	Benjamin	13/01/1900	Wednesbury	1970	1919-1920		Wednesbury Old Athletic	Blakenhall	1	0	0	0	0	0	0	0	0	0	0	0	1	0	0
Clark C	Clive	19/09/1940	Leeds		1961-1969		QPR	QPR	300	1	80	25	1	7	19	0	10	7	0	1	351	2	98
Clarke D	Dennis	18/01/1984	Stockton		1963-1969		Birmingham City	Huddersfield Town	19	0	0	4	1	0	1	0	0	1	0	0	25	1	0
Clarke I	Ike	09/01/1915	Tipton	2002	1937-1947		Toll End Wesley	Portsmouth	108	0	39	9	0	4	0	0	0	0	0	0	117	0	43
Clement N	Neil	03/10/1978	Reading		2000		Chelsea		234	21	21	15	0	2	14	2	3	2	1	0	265	24	26
Clements HW	Harry	22/07/1883	Worcester	1939	1903-1904		Worcester City	Worcester City	10	0	0	0	0	0	0	0	0	0	0	0	10	0	0
Coen RWL	Laurie	04/12/1914	Lowestoft	1972	1932-1938		Milford Haven	Coventry City	7	0	4	2	0	0	0	0	0	0	0	0	9	0	4
Coldicott S	Stacy	29/04/1974	Redditch		1990-1998		School	Grimsby Town	64	40	3	2	21	0	8	1	0	7	3	0	81	65	3
Cole HJS	John	23/02/1885	West Bromwich	1933	1902-1904		Bloxwich Strollers	Wellingborough	9	0	3	0	0	0	0	0	0	0	0	0	9	0	3
Collard I	Ian	31/08/1947	South Hetton		1962-1969		Durham Boys	Ipswich Town	63	6	7	12	0	0	7	0	1	8	1	0	90	7	8
Colquhoun EPS	Eddie	29/03/1945	Prestonpans		1967-1968		Bury	Sheffield United	46	0	1	5	0	0	2	0	0	1	0	0	54	0	1
Comyn AJ	Andy	02/08/1968	Wakefield		1996	N	Plymouth Argyle	Hednesford Town	3	0	0	0	0	0	0	0	0	0	0	0	3	0	0
Connelly EJ	Eddie	09/12/1916	Dumbarton	1990	1939-1946		Luton Town	Luton Town	3	0	1	4	0	1	0	0	0	0	0	0	7	0	2
Connor MJJ	Joe	14/07/1880	Lochee	1934	1898-1899		Queen's Gordon Highlanders	Walsall	10	0	0	0	0	0	0	0	0	0	0	0	10	0	0
Contra CM	Cosmin	15/12/1975	Timisoara, Romania		2004-2005	L	Atletico Madrid	Atletico Madrid	5	0	0	0	0	0	1	0	0	0	0	0	6	0	0
Cook AF	Arthur	14/09/1890	Stafford	1930	1911-1921		Wrexham	Luton Town	38	0	0	12	0	0	0	0	0	0	0	0	50	0	0
Cook CFW	Fred	12/11/1880	Rugby	1934	1903-1905		Northampton Town	Portsmouth	28	0	0	1	0	0	0	0	0	0	0	0	29	0	0
Cookson J	Jimmy	06/12/1904	Manchester	1970	1927-1933		Chesterfield	Plymouth Argyle	122	0	110	9	0	7	0	0	0	0	0	0	131	0	117
Corbett FJ	Frank	02/08/1903	Willenhall	1970	1926-1931		Hednesford Town	Coventry City	12	0	0	0	0	0	0	0	0	0	0	0	12	0	0
Corbett G	George	11/05/1925	North Warbottle	1999	1951-1953		Sheffield Wednesday	Workington	1	0	0	0	0	0	0	0	0	0	0	0	1	0	0
Corbett R	Richard	30/03/1887	Wolverhampton	1933	1909-1911		Willenhall Swifts	Walsall	3	0	0	0	0	0	0	0	0	0	0	0	3	0	0
Corfield S	Sidney	24/06/1883	Tipton	1941	1902-1904		Toll End Wesley	Wolverhampton Wanderers	8	0	0	0	0	0	0	0	0	0	0	0	8	0	0
Cork D	David	28/10/1962	Doncaster		1988	L	Huddersfield Town	Huddersfield Town	1	3	0	0	0	0	0	0	0	0	0	0	1	3	0
Cowdrill BJ	Barry	03/01/1957	Castle Bromwich		1979-1988		Sutton Coldfield Town	Bolton Wanderers	127	4	0	6	0	1	9	1	0	1	0	0	143	5	1

Name		Date of Birth	Birthplace	Died	Year with Club	Loan	Previous Club	Next Club	League A	League S	League G	FA Cup A	FA Cup S	FA Cup G	FL Cup A	FL Cup S	FL Cup G	Other A	Other S	Other G	Total A	Total S	Total G
Cox FJA	Freddie	01/11/1920	Reading	1973	1953-1954		Tottenham Hotspur	Retired	4	0	1	0	0	0	0	0	0	0	0	0	4	0	1
Cox S	Sam	30/10/1920	Mexborough	1985	1948-1951		Denaby United	Accrington Stanley	2	0	0	0	0	0	0	0	0	0	0	0	2	0	0
Crabtree FW	Frederick	06/01/1865	West Bromwich	1939	1887-1889		Christ Church	Old Stephen's FC	1	0	1	0	0	0	0	0	0	0	0	0	1	0	1
Cram R	Bobby	19/11/1939	Hetton-le-Hole	2007	1955-1967		School	Bromsgrove Rovers	141	0	25	8	0	1	13	0	0	1	0	0	163	0	26
Crawford CHR	Campbell	01/12/1943	Alexandria		1959-1967		School	Exeter City	10	0	0	0	0	0	2	0	0	2	0	0	14	0	0
Crawford R	Ray	13/07/1936	Portsmouth		1965-1966		Wolverhampton Wanderers	Ipswich Town	14	0	6	1	0	0	2	0	1	0	0	0	17	0	7
Cresswell F	Frank	05/09/1908	South Shields	1979	1929-1930		Sunderland	Chester City	30	0	6	1	0	0	0	0	0	0	0	0	31	0	6
Crichton PA	Paul	03/10/1968	Pontefract		1996-1998		Grimsby Town	Burnley	32	0	0	1	0	0	1	0	0	0	0	0	34	0	0
Crisp J	Jack	27/11/1896	Hamstead	1939	1914-1923		Ordnance FC	Blackburn Rovers	115	0	22	7	0	1	0	0	0	0	0	0	122	0	23
Crone R	Bob	04/01/1897	Belfast	1943	1893-1895		Middlesbrough	Notts County	40	0	0	1	0	0	0	0	0	10	0	0	51	0	0
Crooks GA	Garth	10/03/1958	Stoke-on-Trent		1988-1987		Tottenham Hotspur	Charlton Athletic	39	0	16	1	0	0	6	0	2	4	0	3	50	0	21
Cross D	David	08/12/1950	Heywood		1976-1977, 1984-1985		Coventry City	Bolton Wanderers	54	0	20	2	0	0	5	0	2	0	1	1	61	1	23
Cross NJR	Nicky	07/02/1961	Birmingham		1977-1985		Woodbank Albion	Walsall	68	37	15	5	0	1	6	2	3	0	1	0	79	40	19
Crowe EW	Ted	27/11/1911	Stourport	1982	1930-1936		Stourport Swifts	Swansea City	15	0	0	1	0	0	0	0	0	0	0	0	16	0	0
Crowshaw AA	Allan	12/12/1932	Bloxwich		1946-1956		Bloxwich Strollers	Derby County	11	0	2	0	0	0	0	0	0	0	0	0	11	0	2
Crump A	Arthur	22/08/1886	Smethwick	1960	1909-1910		Reading	Dudley Town	1	0	0	0	0	0	0	0	0	0	0	0	1	0	0
Cumbes J	Jim	04/05/1944	Didsbury		1969-1971		Tranmere Rovers	Aston Villa	64	0	0	4	0	0	4	0	0	7	0	0	79	0	0
Cummings W	Warren	15/10/1980	Aberdeen		2001-2002	L	Chelsea	Chelsea	7	10	0	0	0	0	0	2	0	0	0	0	7	12	0
Cunningham LP	Laurie	08/03/1956	Archway	1989	1977-1979		Leyton Orient	Real Madrid	81	5	21	7	3	3	6	0	0	12	0	6	106	8	30
Cunnington SG	Shaun	04/01/1966	Bourne		1995-1997		Sunderland	Notts County	8	5	0	0	0	0	1	2	0	2	0	0	11	7	0
Cutler RV	Reg	17/02/1938	Blackheath, Worcesters		1950-1956		School	Bournemouth	5	0	0	0	0	0	0	0	0	0	0	0	5	0	0
Dale RA	Dickie	21/03/1896	Willington	1970	1928-1931		Birmingham City	Tranmere Rovers	19	0	0	2	0	0	0	0	0	0	0	0	21	0	0
Darby JT	Julian	03/10/1967	Farnworth		1995-1997		Coventry City	Preston NE	32	7	1	1	0	0	1	0	0	4	0	0	38	7	1
Darnell L	Len	14/09/1905	Irchester	1968	1924-1930		Rushden Town	Reading	57	0	0	5	0	0	0	0	0	0	0	0	62	0	0
Darton SR	Scott	27/03/1975	Ipswich		1991-1995		School	Blackpool	15	0	0	0	0	0	1	0	0	5	0	1	21	0	1
Davies A	Arthur	10/01/1880	Bodhovel	1949	1904-1905		Druids	Middlesbrough	12	0	1	0	0	0	0	0	0	0	0	0	12	0	1
Davies CE	Curtis	15/03/1985	Waltham Forest		2005		Luton Town		65	0	2	6	0	0	2	0	0	0	0	0	73	0	2
Davies C	Cyril	13/05/1917	West Bromwich	1975	1935-1947		Kidderminster Harriers	Stourbridge	7	0	0	0	0	0	0	0	0	0	0	0	7	0	0
Davies LC	Llew	29/07/1881	Wrexham	1961	1904-1905		Wrexham	Wrexham	3	0	0	0	0	0	0	0	0	0	0	0	3	0	0
Davies RJ	Rob	24/03/1987	Tywyn		2005		School		0	0	0	0	1	0	0	0	0	0	0	0	0	1	0
Davies RW	Reg	10/10/1933	Tipton		1949-1955		Palethorpe's	Walsall	4	0	0	0	0	0	0	0	0	0	0	0	4	0	0
Davies SC	Stan	24/04/1898	Chirk	1972	1921-1927		Everton	Birmingham City	147	0	77	12	0	6	0	0	0	0	0	0	159	0	83
Davies WC	Billy	16/04/1883	Forden	1960	1908-1910		Crystal Palace	Crystal Palace	53	0	4	3	0	0	0	0	0	0	0	0	56	0	4
Dawes J	Jack	05/06/1891	Smethwick	1933	1903-1905		Smethwick Centaur	Smethwick Centaur	2	0	0	0	0	0	0	0	0	0	0	0	2	0	0
Deacey C	Charlie	06/10/1889	Wednesbury	1952	1910-1914		Wednesbury Old Athletic	Hull City	18	0	0	1	0	1	0	0	0	0	0	0	19	0	1
Dean A	Alf	02/01/1877	West Bromwich	1959	1896-1898		Walsall	Walsall	7	0	3	1	0	0	0	0	0	0	0	0	8	0	3
Deehan JM	John	06/08/1957	Solihull		1979-1981		Aston Villa	Norwich City	44	3	5	2	0	0	0	0	0	1	0	0	47	3	5
De Freitas F	Fabian	28/07/1972	Paramaribo, Surinam		1998-2000		Osasuna	SC Cambuur	34	27	8	1	1	0	5	0	2	0	0	0	40	28	10
Dennison RS	Robbie	30/04/1963	Banbridge		1985-1987		Glenavon	Wolverhampton Wanderers	9	7	1	2	0	0	1	0	0	1	0	0	13	7	1
Derveld F	Fernando	13/05/1976	Vlissingen, Holland		2001	L	Norwich City	Norwich City	1	1	0	0	0	0	0	0	0	0	0	0	1	1	0
Dibble AG	Andy	08/05/1965	Cwmbran		1992	L	Manchester City	Manchester City	9	0	0	0	0	0	0	0	0	0	0	0	9	0	0
Dichio DSE	Danny	19/10/1974	Hammersmith		2001-2004		Sunderland	Preston NE	50	16	14	6	0	4	3	1	0	0	0	0	59	17	18
Dicken HJ	Harold	19/11/1890	Wednesbury	1965	1909-1910		Bilston United	Bilston United	1	0	0	0	0	0	0	0	0	0	0	0	1	0	0

									League			FA Cup			FL Cup			Other			Total		
Name		Date of Birth	Birthplace	Died	Year with Club	Loan	Previous Club	Next Club	A	S	G	A	S	G	A	S	G	A	S	G	A	S	G
Dickens AW	Alan	03/09/1964	Plaistow		1992-1993	L	Chelsea	Chelsea	3	0	1	0	0	0	0	0	0	1	0	0	4	0	1
Dickinson MJ	Martin	14/03/1963	Leeds		1986-1988		Leeds United	Sheffield United	46	4	2	1	0	0	3	0	0	1	0	0	51	4	2
Dilly T	Tommy	12/11/1882	Arbroath	1960	1906-1907		Everton	Derby County	30	0	9	7	0	0	0	0	0	0	0	0	37	0	9
Dixon R	Bobby	11/01/1936	Felling		1959-1960		Workington	Hereford United	7	0	1	0	0	0	0	0	0	0	0	0	7	0	1
Dobbins LW	Wayne	30/08/1968	Bromsgrove		1984-1991		Burlish Olympic	Torquay United	30	5	0	3	0	0	3	0	0	4	0	0	40	5	0
Dobie RS	Scott	10/10/1978	Workington		2001-2004		Carlisle United	Millwall	57	53	21	1	6	0	6	4	4	0	0	0	64	63	25
Dobson AJ	Tony	05/02/1969	Coventry		1997-1998		Swindon Town	Northampton Town	6	5	0	2	0	0	0	2	0	0	0	0	8	7	0
Donaghy B	Barry	21/03/1956	Consett		1971-1975		School	Workington	4	2	1	0	0	0	0	0	0	0	0	0	4	2	1
Donnachie C	Charles	18/04/1869	Invergowrie	1923	1889-1890		Dundee	Cambuslang Rangers	2	0	0	0	0	0	0	0	0	0	0	0	2	0	0
Donovan K	Kevin	17/12/1971	Halifax		1992-1997		Huddersfield Town	Grimsby Town	139	29	19	7	1	3	9	2	6	15	1	4	170	33	32
Dorsett G	George	09/08/1881	Brownhills	1943	1901-1904		Birmingham City	Manchester City	95	0	22	5	0	0	0	0	0	0	0	0	100	0	22
Dorsett JAH	Joe	19/04/1888	Brownhills	1951	1907-1910		Brownhills Albion	Manchester City	18	0	3	0	0	0	0	0	0	0	0	0	18	0	3
Drury CE	Chuck	04/07/1937	Darlaston		1954-1964		FH Lloyds	Bristol City	146	0	1	14	0	0	0	0	0	0	0	0	160	0	1
Drury GB	George	22/01/1914	Hucknall	1972	1946-1948		Arsenal	Watford	29	0	8	2	0	1	0	0	0	0	0	0	31	0	9
Dudley G	George	12/02/1916	Gartcosh	1979	1937-1946		Vono Sports	Banbury Spencer	6	0	2	0	0	0	0	0	0	0	0	0	6	0	2
Dudley JG	Jimmy	24/08/1928	Gartcosh	2006	1944-1959		Albright Youth Club	Walsall	285	0	9	34	0	2	0	0	0	1	0	0	320	0	11
Dugdale JR	Jimmy	15/01/1932	Liverpool		1950-1956		Harrowby	Aston Villa	63	0	0	11	0	0	0	0	0	0	1	0	74	1	0
Duggan J	Jim	17/11/1920	Droitwich	1982	1935-1947		Droitwich Old Boys	Hereford United	25	0	8	2	0	0	0	0	0	0	0	0	27	0	8
Dunn A	Archie	14/12/1876	Bridgeton	1943	1898-1901		Queen's 2nd Gordon Highlanders	Grimsby Town	71	0	2	10	0	1	0	0	0	0	0	0	81	0	3
Durnin JP	John	18/08/1965	Bootle		1988	L	Liverpool	Liverpool	5	0	2	0	0	0	0	0	0	0	0	0	5	0	2
Dutton HR	Harry	16/01/1898	Edmonton	1972	1922-1927		Tufnell Park	Bury	57	0	2	3	0	0	0	0	0	0	0	0	60	0	2
Dyer F	Frank	05/08/1870	Bishopbriggs	1940	1890-1892		Warwick County	Woolwich Arsenal	41	0	2	5	0	1	0	0	0	0	0	0	46	0	3
Dyer LR	Lloyd	13/09/1982	Birmingham		2001		Aston Villa	Millwall	2	19	2	0	2	0	2	0	0	0	0	0	4	21	2
Dyson PI	Paul	27/12/1959	Birmingham		1986-1989		Stoke City	Darlington	64	0	5	1	0	0	3	0	0	1	0	0	69	0	5
Earnshaw R	Rob	06/04/1981	Mulfulira, Zambia		2004-2006		Cardiff City	Norwich City	22	21	12	3	1	3	2	1	2	0	0	0	27	23	17
Easter GP	Graham	26/09/1969	Epsom		1986-1989		School	Huddersfield Town	0	0	0	0	0	0	0	1	0	0	0	0	0	1	0
Eastoe PR	Peter	02/08/1953	Tamworth		1982-1983		Everton	Sporting Farense	30	1	8	2	0	1	1	0	0	0	0	0	33	1	9
Ebanks MWA	Wayne	02/10/1964	Longbridge		1981-1984		School	Port Vale	6	1	0	0	0	0	0	0	0	0	0	0	6	1	0
Edwards CI	Cliff	08/03/1921	Chase Terrace	1989	1938-1948		Cannock Town	Bristol City	40	0	1	2	0	0	0	0	0	0	0	0	42	0	1
Edwards EJ	Ernie	28/03/1892	Dudley Port	1962	1913-1920		Old Hill Unity	Walsall	7	0	3	1	0	1	0	0	0	0	0	0	8	0	4
Edwards J	Jimmy	11/12/1905	Tipton	1982	1926-1937		Stourbridge	Norwich City	182	0	9	19	0	0	0	0	0	1	0	0	202	0	9
Edwards PR	Paul	25/12/1963	Birkenhead		1994-1997		Wolverhampton Wanderers	Hednesford Town	48	3	0	3	0	0	4	0	0	2	0	0	57	3	0
Edwards RI	Ian	30/01/1955	Rossett		1973-1976		Rhyl	Chester City	15	3	3	0	0	0	2	0	0	2	0	0	19	3	3
Edwards SH	Sam	05/06/1885	Wolverhampton	1938	1901-1905		Brades Park	Stafford Rangers	1	0	0	0	0	0	0	0	0	0	0	0	1	0	0
Ehiogu U	Ugo	03/11/1972	Hackney		1988-1991		School	Aston Villa	0	2	0	0	0	0	0	0	0	0	0	0	0	2	0
Ellington NLF	Nathan	02/07/1981	Bradford		2005		Wigan Athletic		34	31	15	3	1	0	4	0	4	0	3	0	41	35	19
Elliott WB	Billy	06/08/1919	Harrington	1966	1938-1951		Bournemouth	Bilston United	170	0	39	12	0	1	0	0	0	0	0	0	182	0	40
Elmore GV	George	27/09/1884	Wednesbury	1952	1902-1903		Broadheath FC	Bristol Rovers	3	0	1	1	0	0	0	0	0	0	0	0	4	0	1
Evans AJ	Albert	12/03/1874	Barnard Castle	1966	1907-1909		Aston Villa	Retired	37	0	0	3	0	0	0	0	0	0	0	0	40	0	0
Evans AJ	Alun	01/12/1922	Penrycadery		1941-1948		Wilden FC	Retired	18	0	0	1	0	0	0	0	0	0	0	0	19	0	0
Evans CJ	Charlie	04/02/1923	West Bromwich	1998	1937-1950		Cordley Vics	Stafford Rangers	1	0	0	0	0	0	0	0	0	0	0	0	1	0	0
Evans EE	Elfed	28/08/1926	Ferndale	1988	1952-1955		Cardiff City	Wrexham	17	0	3	0	0	0	0	0	0	0	0	0	17	0	3
Evans G	George	18/12/1865	Sutton-in-Ashfield	1930	1889-1890		Derby County	Brierley Hill Alliance	13	0	8	2	0	0	0	0	0	0	0	0	15	0	8

Name		Date of Birth	Birthplace	Died	Year with Club	Loan	Previous Club	Next Club	League			FA Cup			FL Cup			Other			Total		
									A	S	G	A	S	G	A	S	G	A	S	G	A	S	G
Evans JT	Joseph	12/02/1906	Darlaston	1971	1922-1931		Darlaston	Retired	88	0	8	2	0	0	0	0	0	0	0	0	90	0	8
Evans MJ	Mickey	01/01/1973	Plymouth		1997-2000		Southampton	Bristol Rovers	35	28	6	2	2	1	3	3	2	0	0	0	40	33	9
Evans SJ	Stewart	15/11/1960	Maltby		1986-1987		Wimbledon	Plymouth Argyle	13	1	1	0	0	0	2	0	0	1	0	0	16	1	1
Evans TJ	Thomas	12/09/1872	Wolverhampton	1950	1896-1897		Fairfield FC	Wellington Town	21	0	0	1	0	0	0	0	0	0	0	0	22	0	0
Evenson I	Ike	20/11/1882	Manchester	1936	1907-1908		Clapton Orient	Plymouth Argyle	8	0	1	0	0	0	0	0	0	0	0	0	8	0	1
Facey DM	Delroy	22/04/1980	Huddersfield		2004		Bolton Wanderers	Hull City	2	7	0	0	0	0	0	0	0	0	0	0	2	7	0
Fairfax RJ	Ray	13/11/1941	Smethwick		1959-1968		School	Northampton Town	79	2	0	1	0	0	9	0	0	1	0	1	90	2	1
Farrington GS	George	11/07/1884	Burslem	1946	1903-1904		Hanley Swifts	Castleford Town	1	0	1	0	0	0	0	0	0	0	0	0	1	0	1
Fellows JE	Ernest	12/02/1870	West Bromwich	1933	1892-1897, 1899		Cooper's Hill Meths	Studley Rovers	12	0	0	0	0	0	0	0	0	2	0	0	14	0	0
Fenton F	Freddie	02/11/1878	Gainsborough	1944	1903-1904		Preston NE	Bristol City	6	0	1	0	0	0	0	0	0	0	0	0	6	0	1
Fenton GA	Graham	22/05/1974	Wallsend		1994	L	Aston Villa	Aston Villa	7	3	0	0	0	0	0	0	0	0	0	0	7	3	0
Fenton R	Ronnie	02/09/1940	South Shields		1962-1965		Burnley	Birmingham City	59	0	16	7	0	2	0	0	0	0	0	0	66	0	18
Fereday W	Wayne	16/06/1963	Warley		1991-1994		Bournemouth	Cardiff City	39	9	3	0	1	0	1	0	0	3	0	0	43	10	3
Fettis AW	Alan	01/02/1973	Newtownards		1995	L	Hull City	Hull City	3	0	0	0	0	0	0	0	0	0	0	0	3	0	0
Fielding AR	Ross	07/01/1880	Trentham	1952	1908-1909		Stoke City	Stoke City	10	0	1	0	0	0	0	0	0	0	0	0	10	0	1
Finch EAR	Bob	31/08/1908	Hednesford	2000	1925-1939		Hednesford Town	Swansea City	216	0	0	18	0	0	0	0	0	0	0	0	234	0	0
Finch AR	Roy	07/04/1922	Barry Island		1944-1949		Swansea City	Lincoln City	15	0	1	1	0	1	0	0	0	0	0	0	16	0	2
Fitton GA	Arthur	03/05/1902	Melton Mowbray	1984	1922-1932		Kidderminster Harriers	Manchester United	96	0	11	3	0	0	0	0	0	0	0	0	99	0	11
Flavell AE	Arthur	15/06/1875	West Bromwich	1939	1896-1898		West Bromwich Baptist	Bournbrook FC	2	0	0	0	0	0	0	0	0	0	0	0	2	0	0
Fletcher F	Frank	02/04/1874	Caversham	1936	1892-1896		Reading	Grimsby Town	1	0	0	0	0	0	0	0	0	0	0	0	1	0	0
Flewitt AW	Albert	10/02/1872	Beeston	1943	1896-1899		Everton	Bedminster	65	0	18	7	0	3	0	0	0	4	0	2	76	0	23
Flynn SM	Sean	13/03/1968	Birmingham		1997-2000		Derby County	Tranmere Rovers	99	10	8	0	2	0	11	0	1	0	0	0	110	12	9
Foggo KT	Ken	07/11/1943	Perth		1959-1967		Peebles YMCA	Norwich City	128	1	29	5	0	0	2	0	0	0	0	0	135	1	29
Folks WT	William	09/09/1886	Tottenham	1944	1904		Clapton FC	Clapton FC	1	0	0	0	0	0	0	0	0	0	0	0	1	0	0
Ford EF	Ernest	09/01/1896	Chingford	1960	1922-1923		Ilford	Retired	1	0	0	0	0	0	0	0	0	0	0	0	1	0	0
Ford T	Tony	14/05/1959	Grimsby		1989-1991		Stoke City	Grimsby Town	114	0	14	4	0	1	7	0	0	2	1	0	127	1	15
Ford WG	Bill	07/05/1876	Dundee	1948	1896		Dundee	Hereford Thistle	12	0	1	0	0	0	0	0	0	0	0	0	12	0	1
Forrester AC	Tony	14/01/1940	Parkstone		1955-1959		School	Southend United	6	0	3	0	0	0	0	0	0	0	0	0	6	0	3
Forsyth ME	Mike	20/03/1966	Liverpool		1982-1986		Earlswood Juniors	Derby County	28	1	0	2	0	1	1	0	0	0	0	0	31	1	1
Foster AM	Adrian	19/03/1971	Kidderminster		1987-1992		School	Torquay United	13	14	2	0	2	0	1	3	0	0	0	0	14	19	2
Foster J	Jabez	19/11/1877	Rawmarsh	1946	1898-1901		Worcester City	Blackpool	1	0	0	0	0	0	0	0	0	0	0	0	1	0	0
Foulkes HE	Hugh	13/04/1909	Llandudno	1981	1930-1937		Llandudno Town	Guildford City	15	0	0	0	0	0	0	0	0	0	0	0	15	0	0
Fox RA	Ruel	14/01/1968	Ipswich		2000-2002		Tottenham Hotspur	Southend United	38	20	2	1	2	0	3	1	0	2	0	0	44	23	2
Fraser DM	Doug	08/12/1941	Busby		1963-1971		Aberdeen	Nottingham Forest	255	2	8	24	0	0	29	0	4	15	0	0	323	2	12
Fredgaard C	Carsten	20/05/1976	Hillesod, Denmark		2000	L	Sunderland	Sunderland	5	0	0	0	0	0	0	0	0	0	0	0	5	0	0
Freeman RPP	Percy	04/07/1975	Newark		1968-1970		Stourbridge	Lincoln City	2	1	0	0	0	0	0	0	0	0	0	0	2	1	0
Fryer ER	Edward	12/08/1904	South Yardley	1987	1923-1930		Harbourne Lynwood	Shrewsbury Town	21	0	0	0	0	0	0	0	0	0	0	0	21	0	0
Fudge MH	Micky	05/12/1945	Bristol		1961-1967		Bristol Rovers	Exeter City	13	0	5	0	0	0	0	0	0	0	0	0	13	0	5
Gaardsoe T	Thomas	23/11/1979	Randers, Denmark		2003		Ipswich Town		77	4	4	2	0	0	6	2	0	0	0	0	85	6	4
Gabbidon DL	Danny	08/08/1979	Cwmbran		1996-2000		School	Cardiff City	20	0	0	2	0	0	4	1	0	0	0	0	26	1	0
Gale AR	Arthur	16/11/1904	Salford	1976	1931-1936		Chester City	Chester City	23	0	8	6	0	4	0	0	0	0	0	0	29	0	12
Gallagher M	Mike	16/01/1932	Cambuslang	1975	1952-1953		Bolton Wanderers	Selkirk	1	0	0	0	0	0	0	0	0	0	0	0	1	0	0
Garfield BW	Ben	18/08/1872	Higham Ferrers	1942	1896-1902		Burton Wanderers	Brighton & Hove Albion	109	0	34	8	0	4	0	0	0	0	0	0	117	0	38

Name		Date of Birth	Birthplace	Died	Year with Club	Loan	Previous Club	Next Club	League A	League S	League G	FA Cup A	FA Cup S	FA Cup G	FL Cup A	FL Cup S	FL Cup G	Other A	Other S	Other G	Total A	Total S	Total G
Garner S	Simon	23/11/1959	Boston		1992-1994		Blackburn Rovers	Wycombe Wanderers	25	8	8	3	0	0	3	0	0	4	2	1	35	10	9
Garratt GT	George	05/04/1882	Byker	1960	1908-1910		Plymouth Argyle	Crystal Palace	29	0	3	1	0	0	0	0	0	0	0	0	30	0	3
Garraty W	Billy	06/10/1878	Saltley	1931	1908-1910		Leicester Fosse	Lincoln City	53	0	20	6	0	2	0	0	0	0	0	0	59	0	22
Geddes AJ	Alf 'Jasper'	14/04/1871	West Bromwich	1927	1891-1894, 1895		Causeway Green Villa	Bedminster	73	0	25	9	0	6	0	0	0	11	0	7	93	0	38
Gera Z	Zoltan	22/04/1979	Pecs, Hungary		2004		Ferencvaros		71	22	13	4	3	2	1	2	0	2	1	0	78	28	15
Gilbert DJ	David	22/06/1963	Lincoln		1995-1998		Grimsby Town	Grimsby Town	46	16	6	1	0	0	6	0	0	7	0	0	60	16	6
Gilchrist PA	Phil	25/08/1973	Stockton		2001-2004		Leicester City	Rotherham United	51	0	0	4	0	0	3	0	0	2	0	0	60	0	0
Giles MJ	Johnny	06/11/1940	Cabra		1975-1977		Leeds United	Shamrock Rovers	74	1	3	4	0	0	4	0	1	5	0	1	87	1	5
Glidden TW	Tommy	20/07/1902	Coxlodge	1974	1922-1936		Sunderland West End	Retired	445	0	135	33	0	5	0	0	0	1	0	0	479	0	140
Glover AR	Allan	21/10/1950	Laleham		1969-1977		QPR	Leyton Orient	84	8	9	4	0	0	4	2	0	0	3	1	92	13	10
Godden AL	Tony	02/08/1955	Gillingham		1975-1986		Ashford Town	Chelsea	267	0	0	19	0	0	27	0	0	16	0	0	329	0	0
Gollings P	Platt	11/10/1878	Winson Green	1935	1899-1904		Hereford Thistle	Brierley Hill Alliance	5	0	0	0	0	0	0	0	0	0	0	0	5	0	0
Goodman D	Darren	09/04/1971	Oldbury		1987-1989		Stourbridge Falcons	Walsall	0	0	0	0	0	0	0	0	0	0	1	0	0	1	0
Goodman DR	Don	09/05/1966	Leeds		1987-1991		Bradford City	Sunderland	140	18	60	7	0	1	11	0	1	5	0	1	163	18	63
Gordon DW	Denis	07/06/1924	Bilston	1998	1947-1952		Oxford City	Brighton & Hove Albion	27	0	10	3	0	0	0	0	0	0	0	0	30	0	10
Gould RA	Bobby	12/06/1946	Coventry		1971-1972		Wolverhampton Wanderers	Bristol City	52	0	18	1	0	0	4	0	0	3	0	1	60	0	19
Grant AJ	Tony	14/11/1974	Liverpool		2000-2001	L	Manchester City	Manchester City	3	2	0	0	0	0	0	0	0	0	0	0	3	2	0
Gray AM	Andy	30/11/1955	Glasgow		1987-1988		Notts County	Glasgow Rangers	32	3	10	0	0	0	2	0	1	0	0	0	34	3	11
Grealish AP	Tony	21/09/1956	Paddington		1984-1986		Brighton & Hove Albion	Manchester City	55	10	5	1	0	0	7	1	0	0	0	0	63	11	5
Green H	Harry	19/01/1860	West Bromwich	1900	1881-1891		George Salter Works	Old Hill Wanderers	33	0	0	32	0	0	0	0	0	0	0	0	65	0	0
Green T	Thomas	14/07/1873	King's Heath	1921	1894-1896		Coles Farm Unity	Small Heath	8	0	2	0	0	0	0	0	0	0	0	0	8	0	2
Green T	Tommy	07/08/1863	Droitwich	1931	1885-1887		Church FC	Kidderminster Harriers	0	0	0	16	0	8	0	0	0	0	0	0	16	0	8
Greening J	Jonathan	07/01/1979	Scarborough		2004-		Middlesbrough		109	5	4	8	0	0	3	2	1	3	0	0	123	7	5
Gregan SM	Sean	29/03/1974	Guisborough		2002-2004		Preston NE	Leeds United	76	3	2	2	0	0	4	0	0	0	0	0	82	3	2
Gregory H	Howard	06/04/1893	Aston Manor	1954	1911-1926		Birchfield Trinity	Retired	162	0	39	13	0	3	0	0	0	1	0	0	176	0	42
Grew MS	Mark	15/02/1958	Bilston		1974-1983, 1986		School	Ipswich	34	0	0	5	0	0	8	0	0	1	0	0	48	0	0
Griffin FA	Frank	28/03/1938	Pendlebury	2007	1951-1959		Shrewsbury Town	Northampton Town	240	0	47	34	0	5	0	0	0	1	0	0	275	0	52
Grimley TW	Tom	01/11/1920	Dinnington	1976	1938-1948		Swallownest FC	New Brighton	30	0	0	0	0	0	0	0	0	0	0	0	30	0	0
Gripton EW	Billy	02/07/1920	Tipton	1981	1935-1948		Bush Rangers	Luton Town	16	0	0	0	0	0	0	0	0	0	0	0	16	0	0
Groves P	Paul	28/02/1966	Derby		1996-1997		Grimsby Town	Grimsby Town	27	2	4	1	0	0	2	0	1	0	0	0	30	2	5
Groves W	Willie	09/11/1869	Leith	1908	1890-1893		Celtic	Aston Villa	58	0	7	9	0	3	0	0	0	2	0	0	69	0	10
Guy HG	Harold	01/01/1932	Wolverhampton		1948-1956		Springfield Old Boys	Peterborough United	1	0	0	0	0	0	0	0	0	0	0	0	1	0	0
Haas B	Bernt	08/04/1978	Vienna, Austria		2003-2005		FC Basel	Bastia	45	1	1	1	0	0	5	0	2	0	0	0	51	1	3
Hackett GS	Gary	11/10/1962	Stourbridge		1990-1993		Stoke City	Peterborough United	26	18	3	0	1	0	0	2	1	4	0	0	30	21	4
Hadley B	Ben	12/03/1871	West Bromwich	1931	1892-1896		Hereford Thistle	Hereford Town	7	0	1	0	0	0	0	0	0	1	0	0	8	0	1
Hadley H	Harry	26/10/1877	Barrow	1942	1897-1905		Halesowen	Aston Villa	167	0	2	14	0	0	0	0	0	0	0	0	181	0	2
Haines JTW	Jack	24/04/1920	Wickhamford	1987	1948-1949		Leicester City	Bradford Park Avenue	59	0	23	3	0	0	0	0	0	0	0	0	62	0	23
Hall PA	Paul	03/07/1972	Manchester		2000	L	Coventry City	Coventry City	4	0	0	0	0	0	0	0	0	0	0	0	4	0	0
Hamilton IR	Ian	14/12/1967	Stevenage		1992-1998		Scunthorpe United	Sheffield United	229	11	23	10	1	1	13	2	1	14	2	3	266	16	28
Hancock HB	Harry	07/07/1874	Tranmere	1924	1909-1910		Manchester City	Brierley Hill Alliance	2	0	0	0	0	0	0	0	0	0	0	0	2	0	0
Harbey GK	Graham	29/08/1964	Chesterfield		1989-1992		Ipswich Town	Stoke City	97	0	2	6	0	0	5	0	0	5	0	0	113	0	2
Hargreaves C	Chris	12/05/1972	Cleethorpes		1995-1996		Hull City	Hereford United	0	1	0	0	0	0	0	0	0	0	1	0	0	2	0
Harper WE	Billy	19/11/1876	Nechells	1944	1899-1903		Smethwick Weslyon Rovers	Leicester Fosse	8	0	1	0	0	0	0	0	0	0	0	0	8	0	1

Name		Date of Birth	Birthplace	Died	Year with Club	Loan	Previous Club	Next Club	League A	League S	League G	FA Cup A	FA Cup S	FA Cup G	FL Cup A	FL Cup S	FL Cup G	Other A	Other S	Other G	Total A	Total S	Total G
Harris GA	George	04/01/1878	Halesowen	1923	1909-1910		Aston Villa	Coventry City	19	0	0	2	0	1	0	0	0	0	0	0	21	0	1
Harris W	Bill	01/12/1918	Dudley	1996	1936-1946		Whiteheath	Oldham Athletic	2	0	0	0	0	0	0	0	0	0	0	0	2	0	0
Hartford RA	Asa	24/10/1950	Clydebank		1966-1971		Drumchapel Amateurs	Manchester City	206	8	18	19	0	2	15	0	2	26	0	4	266	8	26
Hartson J	John	05/04/1975	Swansea		2006-2007		Celtic	Released	14	7	5	1	0	1	1	1	0	0	0	0	16	8	6
Hatton SEO	Sid	08/04/1891	West Bromwich	1961	1912-1922		West Bromwich Baptist	Shrewsbury Town	6	0	0	0	0	0	0	0	0	0	0	0	6	0	0
Hawker PN	Phil	07/12/1962	Solihull		1990		Walsall	Walsall	1	0	0	0	0	0	0	0	0	0	0	0	1	0	0
Haycock FJ	Fred	10/08/1886	Smethwick	1955	1904-1907		Coombs Wood FC	Crewe Alexandra	15	0	8	0	0	0	0	0	0	0	0	0	15	0	8
Haynes GH	George	11/11/1865	West Bromwich	1937	1887-1892		West Bromwich Sandwell	Coles Farm Unity	11	0	1	0	0	0	0	0	0	0	0	0	11	0	1
Haywood A	Adam	23/03/1875	Horninglow	1932	1905-1907		Wolverhampton Wanderers	Blackpool	62	0	25	5	0	2	0	0	0	0	0	0	67	0	27
Haywood A	Archie	28/07/1878	Oldham	1972	1896		Blackburn Rovers	Chorley	3	0	0	0	0	0	0	0	0	0	0	0	3	0	0
Haywood S	Sean	21/07/1968	Bloxwich		1985-1987		School	Derby County	0	0	0	0	0	0	0	0	0	1	0	0	1	0	0
Haywood T	Tom	22/03/1877	Walsall	1947	1905-1908		Aston Villa	Crewe Alexandra	15	0	0	0	0	0	0	0	0	0	0	0	15	0	0
Heaselgrave SE	Sammy	01/10/1916	Smethwick	1975	1934-1945		Smethwick Highfield	Northampton Town	49	0	16	3	0	0	0	0	0	0	0	0	52	0	16
Heath NH	Norman	31/01/1924	Wolverhampton	1983	1942-1955		Henry Meadows FC	Retired	121	0	0	13	0	0	0	0	0	0	0	0	134	0	0
Hegan D	Danny	14/06/1943	Coatbridge		1969-1970		Ipswich Town	Wolverhampton Wanderers	13	1	2	0	0	0	4	0	0	0	0	0	17	1	2
Heggs CS	Carl	11/10/1970	Leicester		1991-1998		Leicester United	Swansea City	13	27	3	0	1	0	2	0	0	6	3	1	21	31	4
Hendry WH	Billy	16/06/1864	Newport-on-Tay	1901	1888-1889		Dundee Wanderers	Stoke City	18	0	4	0	0	0	0	0	0	0	0	0	18	0	4
Herbert CJ	Craig	09/11/1975	Coventry		1994-1997		Torquay United	Shrewsbury Town	8	0	0	0	0	0	0	0	0	0	0	0	8	0	0
Hewitt CW	Charlie	10/04/1884	Greatham	1966	1908-1910		Liverpool	Spennymoor United	60	0	26	4	0	2	0	0	0	0	0	0	64	0	28
Hibbert JW	James	05/01/1890	Heworth Colliery	1955	1910-1912		Pelaw FC	Hartlepools United	3	0	0	0	0	0	0	0	0	0	0	0	3	0	0
Higgins JT	Tom	08/09/1874	Halesowen	1916	1894-1898		Stourbridge	Retired	78	0	4	12	0	0	0	0	0	4	0	1	94	0	5
Hobson AF	Fred	26/11/1878	Tipton	1944	1899-1905		Wednesbury Town	Crewe Alexandra	13	0	4	2	0	0	0	0	0	0	0	0	15	0	4
Hodgetts F	Frank	30/09/1924	Dudley		1939-1949		Accles & Pollocks Works	Millwall	67	0	11	3	0	0	0	0	0	0	0	0	70	0	11
Hodgkiss J	Jared	15/11/1986	Stafford		2004		School		0	6	0	1	0	0	1	0	0	0	0	0	2	6	0
Hodgkisson WK	Ken	13/03/1933	West Bromwich		1949-1955		Church Army Social	Walsall	21	0	4	0	0	0	0	0	0	0	0	0	21	0	4
Hodson SP	Simeon	05/03/1966	Lincoln		1988-1992		Newport County	Doncaster Rovers	78	5	0	1	0	0	7	0	0	3	0	0	89	5	0
Hogg D	Derek	04/11/1930	Stockton Heath		1958-1960		Leicester City	Cardiff City	81	0	11	6	0	1	0	0	0	0	0	0	87	0	12
Hogg GJ	Graeme	17/06/1964	Aberdeen		1987	L	Manchester United	Manchester United	7	0	0	0	0	0	0	0	0	1	0	0	8	0	0
Holden GH	George	06/10/1858	West Bromwich	1922	1886-1887		Wednesbury Old Athletic	Wednesbury Old Athletic	0	0	0	4	0	1	0	0	0	0	0	0	4	0	1
Holmes P	Paul	18/02/1968	Stocksbridge		1996-1999		Everton	Torquay United	102	1	1	4	0	0	5	0	0	3	0	0	114	1	1
Hood OG	Glyn	12/03/1925	Pentwyn	2004	1943-1951		Nuffield FC	Retired	69	0	0	4	0	0	0	0	0	0	0	0	73	0	0
Hope R	Bobby	28/09/1943	Bridge of Allan		1959-1972		Drumchapel Amateurs	Birmingham City	331	5	33	19	0	0	28	0	7	19	0	2	397	5	42
Hopkins RA	Robert	25/10/1961	Hall Green		1986-1989		Manchester City	Birmingham City	81	2	11	4	0	0	3	0	0	4	0	1	92	2	12
Horne HL	Les	02/05/1925	Dudley	1986	1944-1952		Herman Smith's FC	Plymouth Argyle	13	0	0	3	0	0	0	0	0	0	0	0	16	0	0
Horobin R	Roy	10/03/1935	Brownhills		1950-1958		Walsall Wood	Notts County	54	0	6	13	0	2	0	0	0	0	0	0	67	0	8
Horsfield GM	Geoff	11/11/1973	Barnsley		2003-2006		Wigan Athletic	Sheffield United	48	19	14	2	2	0	2	0	1	0	0	0	52	21	15
Horton E	Ezra	20/08/1861	West Bromwich	1939	1882-1891		West Bromwich FC	Retired	47	0	0	36	0	1	0	0	0	0	0	0	83	0	1
Horton JH	Jack	21/02/1866	West Bromwich	1946	1882-1899		Wednesbury Old Athletic	Retired	129	0	0	13	0	0	0	0	0	10	0	0	152	0	0
Hoult R	Russell	22/11/1972	Ashby-de-la-Zouch		2001-2007		Portsmouth	Stoke City	189	1	0	11	0	0	10	0	0	2	0	0	212	1	0
Howarth N	Nelson	15/04/1905	Irlams o' th' Height	1970	1926-1929		Bolton Wanderers	Retired	61	0	1	2	0	1	0	0	0	0	0	0	63	0	2
Howe D	Don	12/10/1935	Wolverhampton		1950-1964		Wolverhampton Wanderers	Arsenal	342	0	17	37	0	2	0	0	0	0	0	0	379	0	19
Howshall GT	Gerry	27/10/1944	Stoke-on-Trent		1960-1967		Plymouth Argyle	Norwich City	43	2	3	0	0	0	0	0	0	0	0	0	43	2	3
Hoyland E	Ernie	17/01/1914	Thurnscoe	1988	1938-1939		Blackpool	Lincoln City	1	0	0	0	0	0	0	0	0	0	0	0	1	0	0

Name		Date of Birth	Birthplace	Died	Year with Club	Loan	Previous Club	Next Club	League A	League S	League G	FA Cup A	FA Cup S	FA Cup G	FL Cup A	FL Cup S	FL Cup G	Other A	Other S	Other G	Total A	Total S	Total G
Hucker IP	Peter	28/10/1959	Hampstead		1988	L	Oxford United	Oxford United	7	0	0	0	0	0	0	0	0	0	0	0	7	0	0
Hughes BW	Wayne		Port Talbot		1974-1979		Brinton Ferry	Cardiff City	3	3	2	0	1	0	0	0	0	0	1	0	3	5	2
Hughes L	Lee	22/05/1976	Smethwick		1997-2001, 2002-2004		Kidderminster Harriers	Prison (Featherstone)	172	39	89	6	0	2	12	6	6	2	0	1	192	45	98
Hughes LJ	Lyndon	16/09/1950	Smethwick		1964-1975		School	Peterborough United	91	9	3	5	0	0	7	0	0	15	0	1	118	9	4
Hulse RW	Rob	25/10/1979	Crewe		2003-2005		Crewe Alexandra	Leeds United	29	9	10	1	1	0	5	1	3	0	0	0	35	11	13
Humpage WLF	William	12/02/1870	Birmingham		1893-1896		Wednesbury Old Athletic	Hereford Thistle	4	0	0	0	0	0	0	0	0	0	0	0	4	0	0
Hunt A	Andy	09/06/1970	Thurrock	1936	1993-1998		Newcastle United	Charlton Athletic	201	11	76	7	0	2	12	0	4	8	1	3	228	12	85
Hunt SK	Steve	04/08/1956	Birmingham		1984-1986		Coventry City	Aston Villa	68	0	15	2	0	1	11	0	2	3	0	1	84	0	19
Hunter RI	Roy	29/10/1973	Saltburn		1990-1995		School	Northampton Town	3	6	1	0	0	0	0	0	0	4	1	0	7	7	1
Hurst GC	Geoff	08/12/1941	Ashton-under-Lyne		1975-1976		Stoke City	Seattle Sounders	10	0	2	0	0	0	2	0	0	0	0	0	12	0	2
Hutchinson T	Tom	20/06/1872	Glasgow	1933	1894-1896		Nelson	Stockport County	45	0	19	10	0	2	0	0	0	3	0	0	58	0	21
Inamoto J	Junichi	18/09/1979	Kagoshima, Japan		2004-2006		Gamba Oskaka	Galatasaray	16	12	0	2	0	0	2	0	1	0	0	0	20	12	1
Inwood GF	Gordon	18/06/1928	Kislingbury		1946-1950		Rushden Town	Hull City	10	0	0	2	0	1	0	0	0	0	0	0	12	0	1
Jack WR	Walter	17/11/1874	Grangemouth	1936	1904-1905		Bristol Rovers	Clyde	25	0	13	1	0	0	0	0	0	0	0	0	26	0	13
Jackman CEJ	Clive	21/03/1936	Farnborough		1957-1960		Aldershot	Retired	21	0	0	0	0	0	0	0	0	0	0	0	21	0	0
Jackson A	Alec	29/05/1937	Tipton		1954-1964		WG Allen's FC	Birmingham City	192	0	50	16	0	2	0	0	0	0	0	0	208	0	52
Jackson WH	Bill	11/07/1894	Oldbury	1917	1912-1917		Langley St Michael's	Killed at War	3	0	0	0	0	0	0	0	0	0	0	0	3	0	0
James GC	George	02/02/1899	Oldbury	1976	1920-1929		Bilston United	Reading	106	0	52	10	0	5	0	0	0	0	0	0	116	0	57
James RW	Roly	09/05/1897	Smethwick	1979	1919-1922		Smethwick Highfield	Brentford	9	0	4	0	0	0	0	0	0	0	0	0	9	0	4
Jensen B	Brian	08/06/1975	Copenhagen, Denmark		2000-2003		AZ Aalkmaar	Burnley	46	0	0	0	0	0	4	0	0	0	0	0	50	0	0
Jephcott AC	Claude	30/10/1891	Smethwick	1950	1911-1923		Brierley Hill Alliance	Retired	174	0	15	15	0	1	0	0	0	1	0	0	190	0	16
Johnson AJ	Andy	02/05/1974	Bristol		2001-2006		Nottingham Forest	Leicester City	121	11	7	7	0	1	4	1	0	0	0	0	132	12	8
Johnson G	George	11/11/1871	West Bromwich	1934	1895-1896		Wrockwardine Wood	Walsall	1	0	0	1	0	0	0	0	0	1	0	1	3	0	1
Johnson JA	Joe	04/04/1911	Grimsby	1983	1937-1946		Stoke City	Hereford United	52	0	22	5	0	0	0	0	0	0	0	0	57	0	22
Johnson LG	Glenn	22/04/1951	Vancouver, Canada		1969-1972		Vancouver Spartans	Vancouver Royals	2	0	0	0	0	0	0	0	0	0	0	0	2	0	0
Johnston WM	Willie	19/12/1956	Glasgow		1972-1979		Rangers	Vancouver Whitecaps	203	4	18	24	2	6	15	0	2	12	1	2	254	7	28
Johnstone WR	William	18/05/1867	Kirriemuir	1933	1889-1890		Dundee Harps	Ayr United	3	0	0	0	0	0	0	0	0	0	0	0	3	0	0
Jol MC	Martin	16/01/1956	Den Haag, Holland		1981-1984		FC Twente	Coventry City	63	1	4	5	0	0	10	0	0	0	0	0	78	1	4
Jones A	Abraham	20/02/1875	Tipton	1942	1896-1901		Cameron Highlanders	Middlesbrough	104	0	6	13	0	4	0	0	0	0	0	0	117	0	10
Jones GA	Grenville	23/11/1932	Nuneaton	1991	1947-1955		Erdington Albion	Wrexham	2	0	0	1	0	0	0	0	0	0	0	0	3	0	0
Jones H	Harry	10/07/1881	West Bromwich	1948	1902-1904, 1905-1907		Brierley Hill Alliance	Shrewsbury Town	2	0	0	0	0	0	0	0	0	0	0	0	2	0	0
Jones HJ	Harry	26/10/1911	Haydock	1957	1933-1943		Preston NE	Retired	117	0	52	9	0	3	0	0	0	0	0	0	126	0	55
Jones I	Ivor	31/07/1899	Merthyr Tydfil	1974	1922-1926		Swansea Town	Swansea Town	63	0	9	4	0	1	0	0	0	0	0	0	67	0	10
Jones SG	Stan	16/11/1938	Highley		1960-1968		Walsall	Walsall	239	0	2	14	0	1	12	0	0	2	0	0	267	0	3
Jordan WC	Willie	09/12/1885	Langley	1949	1904-1909		Langley St Michael's	Everton	31	0	13	4	0	4	0	0	0	0	0	0	35	0	17
Joseph RA	Roger	24/12/1965	Paddington		1997	N	Leyton Orient	Leyton Orient	0	2	0	0	0	0	0	0	0	0	0	0	0	2	0
Kamara DM	Diomansy	08/11/1980	Paris, France		2005		Modena		54	6	21	3	1	2	3	2	2	3	0	1	63	9	26
Kanu N	Nwankwo	01/08/1976	Owerri, Nigeria		2004-2006		Arsenal	Portsmouth	38	15	7	3	0	1	1	1	1	0	0	0	42	16	9
Kaye J	John	03/03/1940	Goole		1963-1971		Scunthorpe United	Hull City	281	3	45	25	0	2	31	0	6	21	0	1	358	3	54
Kelly AG	Tony	01/10/1964	Huyton		1987-1989		Stoke City	Shrewsbury Town	26	0	1	1	0	0	2	0	0	1	0	0	30	0	1
Kelsey AG	Arthur	12/05/1871	Wallingford	1955	1895-1896		Worcester Regiment	Brierley Hill Alliance	11	0	0	0	0	0	0	0	0	0	0	0	11	0	0
Kennedy JP	Joe	15/11/1925	Cleator Moor	1986	1948-1961		Altrincham	Chester City	364	0	3	32	0	1	0	0	0	1	0	0	397	0	4
Kent KJ	Kevin	19/03/1965	Stoke-on-Trent		1981-1984		Newcastle Town	Newport County	1	1	0	0	0	0	0	0	0	0	0	0	1	1	0

Name		Date of Birth	Birthplace	Died	Year with Club	Loan	Previous Club	Next Club	League A	League S	League G	FA Cup A	FA Cup S	FA Cup G	FL Cup A	FL Cup S	FL Cup G	Other A	Other S	Other G	Total A	Total S	Total G
Kevan DT	Derek	06/03/1935	Ripon		1953-63		Bradford	Chelsea	262	0	157	29	0	16	0	0	0	0	0	0	291	0	173
Kiely D	Dean	10/10/1970	Salford		2007-		Portsmouth		17	0	0	2	0	0	0	0	0	3	0	0	22	0	0
Kifford J	Jackie	12/08/1878	Paisley	1955	1901-1905		Portsmouth	Millwall	96	0	8	3	0	0	0	0	0	0	0	0	99	0	8
Kilbane KD	Kevin	01/02/1977	Preston		1997-1999		Preston NE	Sunderland	105	1	15	4	0	1	12	0	2	0	0	0	121	1	18
King AE	Andy	14/08/1956	Luton		1981-1982		QPR	Everton	21	4	4	4	0	1	8	1	1	0	0	0	33	5	6
King PG	Phil	28/12/1967	Bristol		1995	L	Aston Villa	Aston Villa	4	0	0	0	0	0	0	0	0	1	0	0	5	0	0
Kinsell TH	Harry	03/05/1921	Cannock	2000	1935-1949		Chadsmoor	Bolton Wanderers	83	0	0	8	0	0	0	0	0	0	0	0	91	0	0
Kinsella MA	Mark	12/08/1972	Dublin		2004		Aston Villa	Walsall	15	3	1	0	0	0	0	0	0	0	0	0	15	3	1
Kirkland CE	Chris	02/05/1981	Barwell		2005-2006	L	Liverpool	Liverpool	10	0	0	2	0	0	0	0	0	0	0	0	12	0	0
Knowles JW	John	17/07/1879	Wednesbury	1937	1897-1898, 1900-1901		School	Dudley Town	3	0	0	0	0	0	0	0	0	0	0	0	3	0	0
Koren R	Robert	20/09/1980	Slovenia		2007		Lillestrøm		15	3	1	2	2	0	0	0	0	3	0	0	20	5	1
Koumas J	Jason	25/09/1979	Wrexham		2002		Tranmere Rovers		103	20	23	8	1	0	6	0	0	3	0	1	120	21	24
Kozak J	Jan	22/04/1980	Kosice, Slovakia		2006	L	Artmeda Bratislava	Artmeda Bratislava	4	2	0	0	0	0	0	0	0	0	0	0	4	2	0
Krzywicki RL	Dick	02/02/1947	Penley		1962-1970		Leek Youth Club	Huddersfield Town	51	0	9	4	1	0	4	3	2	1	0	1	60	4	12
Kuszczak T	Tomasz	23/03/1962	Krosno Odrzanskie, Poland		2004-2006		Hertha Berlin	Manchester United	30	1	0	0	1	0	3	0	0	0	0	0	33	2	0
Lange AS	Tony	10/12/1964	West Ham		1992-1995		Wolverhampton Wanderers	Fulham	45	3	0	1	0	0	3	0	0	7	0	0	56	3	0
Latchford PW	Peter	27/09/1952	Birmingham		1969-1975		Sutton Coldfield Town	Celtic	81	0	0	9	0	0	8	0	0	6	0	0	104	0	0
Law A	Abraham	07/02/1874	Wealdstone	1932	1896-1897		Millwall Athletic	Stafford Rangers	1	0	0	0	0	0	0	0	0	0	0	0	1	0	0
Law WD	Billy	05/03/1882	Pleck	1952	1905-1906		Doncaster Rovers	Watford	10	0	0	1	0	0	0	0	0	0	0	0	11	0	0
Lee GT	George	04/06/1919	York	1991	1949-1958		Nottingham Forest	Lockheed Leamington	271	0	59	23	0	6	0	0	0	1	0	0	295	0	65
Lee MJ	Mike	27/06/1938	Mold		1956-1958		Saltney Juniors	Crewe Alexandra	1	0	0	0	0	0	0	0	0	0	0	0	1	0	0
Lee W	Billy	12/08/1878	West Bromwich	1934	1901-1903		Bournville Athletic	Portsmouth	71	0	25	5	0	0	0	0	0	0	0	0	76	0	25
Leedham FA	Fred	18/02/1909	Lye	1996	1926-1929		Kidderminster Harriers	Kidderminster Harriers	4	0	0	0	0	0	0	0	0	0	0	0	4	0	0
Legge SG	Samuel	08/06/1881	Willenhall	1973	1906-1907, 1908-1909		Willenhall Swifts	Coventry City	9	0	3	0	0	0	0	0	0	0	0	0	9	0	3
Lewis AE	Albert	03/09/1884	Wolverhampton	1923	1902-1906, 1913-1914		Stafford Rangers	South Shields	47	0	9	1	0	0	0	0	0	0	0	0	48	0	9
Lewis M	Mickey	15/02/1965	Birmingham		1981-1984		Olton Rovers	Derby County	22	2	0	4	0	0	4	1	0	0	0	0	30	3	0
Light WH	Billy	11/06/1913	Woolston	1993	1936-1938		Southampton	Colchester United	28	0	0	2	0	0	0	0	0	0	0	0	30	0	0
Lilwall S	Steve	05/02/1970	Solihull		1992-1995		Kidderminster Harriers	Kidderminster Harriers	71	2	0	4	0	0	3	0	0	6	0	0	84	2	0
Lloyd JA	Amos	19/05/1889	Pelsall	1943	1910-1914		Hednesford Town	Swansea Town	45	0	8	1	0	1	0	0	0	0	0	0	46	0	9
Loach AA	Arthur	08/01/1863	West Bromwich	1958	1882-1886		George Salter Works	Aston Villa	0	0	0	14	0	9	0	0	0	0	0	0	14	0	9
Long WR	Billy	19/04/1899	Tividale	1960	1919-1921		Hednesford Town	Hednesford Town	2	0	0	0	0	0	0	0	0	0	0	0	2	0	0
Lovatt J	Jack	23/08/1941	Burton-on-Trent		1956-1963		Erdington Albion	Nuneaton Borough	18	0	5	0	0	0	0	0	0	0	0	0	18	0	5
Lovett GJ	Graham	05/08/1947	Sheldon		1964-1972		School	Worcester City	106	8	8	12	2	0	13	1	0	10	5	1	141	16	9
Lowe JA	Joseph	15/07/1876	West Bromwich	1931	1899-1903		Coombs Wood FC	Willenhall Pickwick	4	0	0	0	0	0	0	0	0	0	0	0	4	0	0
Lowery AW	Tony	06/07/1961	Wallsend		1981-1983		Ashington	Mansfield Town	1	0	0	0	0	0	0	0	0	0	0	0	1	0	0
Lowery H	Harry	26/02/1918	Moor Row	2004	1934-1945		Cleator Moor Celtic	Northampton Town	17	0	0	0	0	0	0	0	0	0	0	0	17	0	0
Luke NE	Noel	28/12/1964	Birmingham		1981-1984		Olton Ravens	Mansfield Town	8	1	1	2	2	0	1	0	0	0	0	0	11	3	1
Lunn WJ	Billy	08/05/1923	Lurgan	2000	1946-1948		Glenavon	Bournemouth	10	0	5	0	0	0	0	0	0	0	0	0	10	0	5
Lynex SC	Steve	23/01/1958	West Bromwich		1974-1977, 1987-1988		Sandwell Rangers	Cardiff City	26	3	3	0	0	0	0	2	0	2	0	2	28	5	5
Lyttle D	Des	24/09/1971	Wolverhampton		2000-2003		Watford	Northampton Town	61	15	1	2	1	0	8	0	0	2	0	0	73	16	1
McCall A	Andy	15/03/1925	Hamilton		1951-1952		Blackpool	Leeds United	31	0	3	1	0	0	0	0	0	0	0	0	32	0	3
McCue J	James	29/06/1975	Glasgow		1991-1996		West Park United	Partick Thistle	0	0	0	0	0	0	0	0	0	0	1	0	0	1	0
McCulloch T	Thomas	12/12/1868	Strathblane	1940	1891-1893		Glasgow United	Stirling	46	0	0	9	0	0	2	0	0	0	0	0	57	0	0

Name		Date of Birth	Birthplace	Died	Year with Club	Loan	Previous Club	Next Club	League			FA Cup			FL Cup			Other			Total		
									A	S	G	A	S	G	A	S	G	A	S	G	A	S	G
McCullum WD	William	14/06/1870	Paisley	1935	1891		Celtic	Dumbarton	3	0	0	0	0	0	0	0	0	0	0	0	3	0	0
McDermott A	Andy	24/03/1977	Sydney, Australia		1997-2000		QPR	Notts County	49	3	1	0	1	0	4	1	0	0	0	0	53	5	1
MacDonald S	Sherjill	20/11/1984	Netherlands		2007	L	AGOVV Apeldoorn		0	9	0	0	1	0	0	0	0	0	2	0	0	12	0
McInnes DJ	Derek	05/07/1971	Paisley		2000-2003		Toulouse	Dundee United	87	1	6	5	0	0	7	0	0	0	0	0	99	1	6
McKennan PS	Peter	16/07/1918	Airdrie	1991	1947-1948		Partick Thistle	Leicester City	11	0	4	1	0	0	0	0	0	0	0	0	12	0	4
McKenzie AD	Alex	28/03/1875	Greenock	1950	1897-1899		Millwall Athletic	Dumbarton	51	0	9	4	0	0	0	0	0	0	0	0	55	0	9
Mackenzie S	Steve	23/11/1961	Romford		1981-1987		Manchester City	Charlton Athletic	153	3	23	8	0	1	16	2	1	2	0	0	179	5	25
MacLean H	Hugh	20/01/1952	Stornoway		1967-1974		Tantallon Youth Club	Swindon Town	4	0	0	0	0	0	1	0	0	1	2	0	6	2	0
McLean JC	Jimmy	15/11/1877	Stoke-on-Trent	1914	1901-1903		Walsall	Preston NE	57	0	10	3	0	0	0	0	0	0	0	0	60	0	10
McLeod R	Roddie	12/02/1872	Kilsyth	1931	1891-1897		Partick Thistle	Leicester Fosse	149	0	50	20	0	7	0	0	0	16	0	8	185	0	65
McManus PT	Peter	18/04/1873	Winchburgh	1936	1896-1898		St Bernard's	Warmley	28	0	1	0	0	0	0	0	0	0	0	0	28	0	1
McNab A	Sandy	27/12/1911	Glasgow	1962	1938-1946		Sunderland	Newport County	52	0	2	3	0	0	0	0	0	0	0	0	55	0	2
McNally BA	Bernard	17/02/1963	Shrewsbury		1989-1995		Shrewsbury Town	Hednesford Town	137	19	10	11	2	0	8	1	1	12	1	1	168	23	12
McNaught K	Ken	17/01/1955	Kirkcaldy		1983-1985		Aston Villa	Sheffield United	42	0	1	4	0	0	4	0	0	0	0	0	50	0	1
McNeal R	Bobby	19/01/1891	Hobson Village	1956	1910-1925		Hobson Wanderers	Retired	370	0	9	30	0	0	0	0	0	3	0	1	403	0	10
Macready BL	Brian	25/03/1942	Leicester		1959-1964		Hull City	Mansfield Town	14	0	1	1	0	0	0	0	0	0	0	0	15	0	1
McShane PD	Paul	06/01/1986	Wicklow		2006		Manchester United		31	1	2	4	0	1	3	0	0	3	0	0	41	1	3
McVitie GJ	George	07/09/1948	Carlisle		1970-1972		Carlisle United	Oldham Athletic	42	0	5	5	0	0	2	0	0	3	0	0	52	0	5
Madden CA	Craig	25/09/1958	Manchester		1986-1987		Bury	Blackpool	10	2	3	0	0	0	0	0	0	0	0	0	10	2	3
Magee TP	Tommy	06/05/1899	Widnes	1974	1919-1934		Widnes Athletic	Crystal Palace	394	0	15	34	0	0	0	0	0	6	0	3	434	0	18
Mahon J	Jack	08/12/1911	Gillingham	1988	1935-1938		Leeds United	Huddersfield Town	113	0	39	10	0	5	0	0	0	0	0	0	123	0	44
Male NA	Norman	27/05/1917	West Bromwich	1992	1933-1938		Bush Rangers	Walsall	3	0	1	0	0	0	0	0	0	0	0	0	3	0	1
Mann JF	Jack	03/03/1891	West Bromwich	1969	1912-1919		Bilston United	Newport County	2	0	0	0	0	0	0	0	0	0	0	0	2	0	0
Manners JA	Jack	12/03/1878	Morpeth	1946	1904-1913		Morpeth Harriers	Hartlepools United	193	0	7	16	0	0	0	0	0	0	0	0	209	0	7
Matthews J	Joe	17/05/1860	West Bromwich	1928	1883-1885		Aston Unity	Crosswells Brewery	0	0	0	1	0	0	0	0	0	0	0	0	1	0	0
Mardon PJ	Paul	14/09/1969	Bristol		1993-2001		Birmingham City	Retired	125	14	3	3	0	0	10	0	0	2	0	0	140	14	3
Maresca E	Enzo	10/02/1980	Pontecagnano, Italy		1998-2000		Cagliari	Juventus	28	19	5	2	0	0	1	3	0	0	0	0	31	22	5
Marriott A	Andy	11/10/1970	Sutton-in-Ashfield		1989	L	Nottingham Forest	Nottingham Forest	3	0	0	0	0	0	0	0	0	0	0	0	3	0	0
Marshall LK	Lee	21/01/1979	Islington		2002-2005		Leicester City	Retired	4	5	1	0	0	0	1	0	0	0	0	0	5	5	1
Martin DW	Dennis	27/10/1947	Edinburgh		1967-1970		Carlisle United	Newcastle United	14	2	1	4	0	0	0	1	1	2	2	0	20	5	2
Martin MP	Mick	09/07/1951	Dublin		1975-1978		Manchester United	Newcastle United	85	4	11	12	0	2	5	1	2	6	2	0	108	7	15
Martinez WG	Williams	18/12/1982	Montevideo, Uruguay		2006	L	Defensor	Defensor	1	1	1	0	0	0	0	0	0	0	0	0	1	1	1
Mayo J	Joe	25/05/1951	Tipton		1973-1977		Walsall	Leyton Orient	67	5	16	7	0	1	5	0	0	5	1	3	84	6	20
Mellon MJ	Mickey	18/03/1972	Paisley		1993-1994		Bristol City	Blackpool	38	7	6	0	1	0	3	2	0	6	1	0	47	11	6
Merrick AR	Alan	20/06/1950	Birmingham		1966-1976		School	Kidderminster Harriers	131	8	5	6	2	0	9	0	0	10	3	0	156	13	5
Millar J	Jimmy	02/03/1870	Annbank	1907	1904-1905		Sunderland	Chelsea	1	0	0	0	0	0	0	0	0	0	0	0	1	0	0
Millard AR	Albert	18/09/1868	West Bromwich	1930	1888-1892		West Bromwich V	Halesowen	5	0	0	0	0	0	0	0	0	0	0	0	5	0	0
Millard L	Len	07/03/1919	Coseley	1997	1937-1958		Sunbeam FC	Stafford Rangers	436	0	7	40	0	0	0	0	0	1	0	0	477	0	7
Miller AJ	Alan	29/03/1970	Epping		1991, 1997-2000		Arsenal	Blackburn Rovers	101	0	0	3	0	0	9	0	0	0	0	0	113	0	0
Millington AH	Tony	05/06/1943	Hawarden		1959-1964		Sutton Town	Crystal Palace	40	0	0	0	0	0	0	0	0	0	0	0	40	0	0
Mills DJ	David	06/12/1951	Robin Hood's Bay		1979-1983		Middlesbrough	Sheffield Wednesday	44	15	6	2	3	0	6	2	0	3	1	0	55	21	6
Minton RC	Roger	04/06/1951	Birmingham		1966-1975		School	Dunstable Town	24	2	1	0	0	0	2	0	0	1	0	0	27	2	1
Monaghan DJ	Derek	20/01/1959	Bromsgrove		1976-1984		Astwood Bank	Port Vale	14	5	2	1	0	0	2	1	1	0	1	0	17	7	3

Name		Date of Birth	Birthplace	Died	Year with Club	Loan	Previous Club	Next Club	League			FA Cup			FL Cup			Other			Total		
									A	S	G	A	S	G	A	S	G	A	S	G	A	S	G
Moore DM	Darren	22/04/1974	Birmingham		2001-2006		Portsmouth	Derby County	93	11	6	8	0	0	4	0	0	0	0	0	105	11	6
Moorwood TL	Len	06/09/1888	Wednesbury	1976	1909-1920		Bilston	Burnley	30	0	0	3	0	0	0	0	0	0	0	0	33	0	0
Morley WA	Tony	26/08/1954	Ormskirk		1983-1985, 1987-1989		Aston Villa	Tampa Bay Rowdies	60	1	11	4	0	2	3	0	0	2	0	1	69	1	14
Morris F	Fred	27/08/1893	Tipton	1962	1911-1924		Redditch	Coventry City	263	0	112	20	0	4	0	0	0	4	0	2	287	0	118
Morrow HJE	Hughie	09/07/1930	Larne		1945-1950		Wolverhampton Wanderers	Nuneaton Borough	5	0	2	0	0	0	0	0	0	0	0	0	5	0	2
Moses RM	Remi	14/11/1960	Manchester		1977-1981		Corpus Christi Boys Club	Manchester United	63	0	5	2	0	0	7	0	1	1	0	0	73	0	6
Mountford D	David	09/01/1931	Hanley	1985	1951-1953		Crewe Alexandra	Crewe Alexandra	4	0	0	1	0	0	0	0	0	0	0	0	5	0	0
Mulligan PM	Paddy	17/03/1945	Dublin		1975-1979		Crystal Palace	Shamrock Rovers	109	0	1	11	0	0	7	0	0	5	0	1	132	0	2
Murphy J	Joe	21/08/1981	Dublin		2002-2005		Tranmere Rovers	Sunderland	3	2	0	0	0	0	1	0	0	0	0	0	4	2	0
Murphy JP	Jimmy	27/10/1910	Ton Pentre	1989	1928-1939		Mid-Rhondda Boys	Swindon Town	209	0	0	19	0	0	0	0	0	0	0	0	228	0	0
Murphy SP	Shaun	05/11/1970	Sydney, Australia		1996-1999		Notts County	Sheffield United	60	11	7	4	0	0	3	0	0	0	0	0	67	11	7
Murray M	Max	07/11/1935	Falkirk		1962-1963		Glasgow Rangers	Third Lanark	3	0	0	0	0	0	0	0	0	0	0	0	3	0	0
Naylor SW	Stuart	06/12/1962	Wetherby		1986-1996		Lincoln City	Bristol City	354	1	0	13	0	0	22	0	0	20	0	0	409	1	0
N'Dour A	Alassane	12/12/1981	Dakar, Senegal		2003-2004	L	St Etienne	St Etienne	2	0	0	0	0	0	1	0	0	0	0	0	3	0	0
Neale WS	William	17/01/1872	West Bromwich	1932	1893-1894		Grove Hall Saints	Brierley Hill Alliance	6	0	3	1	0	0	0	0	0	0	0	0	7	0	3
Nevin JW	John	20/02/1887	Lintz	1951	1910-1912		Hobson Wanderers	Bristol Rovers	2	0	0	0	0	0	0	0	0	0	0	0	2	0	0
Newall JT	Tommy	16/09/1890	West Bromwich	1957	1912-1922		Great Bridge Celtic	Retired	21	0	3	0	0	0	0	0	0	0	0	0	21	0	3
Newall WT	William	07/03/1869	Lye	1954	1894-1895		Stourbridge	Worcester City	14	0	2	0	0	0	0	0	0	1	0	0	15	0	2
Newsome R	Robbie	25/09/1919	Hebden Bridge	2000	1939-1947		Congleton Town	Coventry City	0	0	0	4	0	2	0	0	0	0	0	0	4	0	2
Nicholl JM	Jimmy	28/12/1956	Hamilton, Canada		1984-1986		Toronto Blizzard	Glasgow Rangers	56	0	0	3	0	0	6	0	0	2	0	1	67	0	1
Nicholls F	Frederick	05/11/1884	Handsworth	1956	1904-1906		Handsworth Rovers	Goldenhill Wanderers	7	0	0	0	0	0	0	0	0	0	0	0	7	0	0
Nicholls HJ	Jack	18/06/1891	Walsall Wood	1921	1913-1914		Hednesford Town	Cannock Town	4	0	0	0	0	0	0	0	0	0	0	0	4	0	0
Nicholls J	James	16/09/1867	West Bromwich	1934	1889-1891		St John's United	Kidderminster O	4	0	0	2	0	0	0	0	0	0	0	0	6	0	0
Nicholls J	Johnny	03/04/1931	Wolverhampton	1995	1950-1957		Heath Town United	Cardiff City	131	0	58	14	0	6	0	0	0	0	0	0	145	0	64
Nicholls S	Sammy	12/01/1871	West Bromwich	1912	1890-1892, 1893-1894		West Bromwich Victoria	Retired	41	0	14	9	0	3	0	0	0	0	0	0	50	0	17
Nicholson MD	Mark	06/03/1871	Oakengates	1941	1891-1894		Oswestry Town	Luton Town	56	0	0	8	0	0	0	0	0	4	0	0	68	0	0
Nicholson SI	Stuart	03/02/1987	Newcastle		2004		School		0	6	0	0	1	0	2	0	2	0	0	0	2	7	2
Nicholson SM	Shane	03/06/1970	Newark		1996-1998		Derby County	Chesterfield	50	2	0	2	0	0	2	0	0	4	0	0	58	2	0
Nicol S	Steve	11/12/1961	Irvine		1998	L	Sheffield Wednesday	Sheffield Wednesday	9	0	0	0	0	0	0	0	0	0	0	0	9	0	0
Nisbet GJM	Gordon	18/09/1951	Wallsend		1968-1976		Willington BC	Hull City	136	0	0	13	0	1	8	0	0	10	0	0	167	0	1
Nock JF	John	22/10/1875	West Bromwich	1933	1897-1900		Halesowen Town	Langley Richmond	15	0	6	0	0	0	0	0	0	0	0	0	15	0	6
Norman AEO	Oliver	15/08/1866	West Bromwich	1943	1893-1896		Wednesbury Old Athletic	Hereford Town	18	0	4	0	0	0	0	0	0	2	0	0	20	0	4
North SS	Stacey	25/11/1964	Luton		1987-1990		Luton Town	Fulham	96	2	0	6	0	0	5	0	0	1	0	0	108	2	0
Nurse DG	Dan	23/06/1873	Princes End	1959	1901-1905		Wolverhampton Wanderers	Retired	85	0	4	3	0	0	0	0	0	0	0	0	88	0	4
O'Connor JK	James	01/09/1979	Dublin		2003-2005		Stoke City	Burnley	27	3	0	1	1	0	5	1	0	0	0	0	33	5	0
Oliver A	Adam	25/10/1980	West Bromwich		1997-2002		School	Retired	2	21	1	1	0	0	1	2	0	0	0	0	4	23	1
Oliver HSM	Harold	07/02/1863	Birmingham	1935	1888-1889		Small Heath All	Small Heath All	1	0	0	0	0	0	0	0	0	0	0	0	1	0	0
O'Regan KM	Kieran	09/11/1963	Cork		1993-1995		Huddersfield T	Halifax Town	36	9	2	2	0	0	3	1	0	3	0	0	44	10	2
Osborne J	John	01/12/1948	Barlborough	1998	1967-1978		Chesterfield	Preston NE	250	0	0	24	0	0	16	0	0	22	0	0	312	0	0
Owen AG	Alfred	21/03/1880	Coalbrookdale	1944	1903-1905		Ironbridge	Walsall	7	0	1	0	0	0	0	0	0	0	0	0	7	0	1
Owen GA	Gary	07/07/1958	St Helens		1979-1986		Manchester City	Panionos	185	2	21	12	2	3	24	0	2	4	0	0	225	4	26
Owers EH	Ernest	11/02/1889	Bromley	1951	1907-1909		Leyton FC	Chesterfield	4	0	0	0	0	0	0	0	0	0	0	0	4	0	0
Paddock JW	Jack	11/07/1877	West Bromwich	1928	1894-1896, 1899-1900		School	Halesowen	20	0	5	0	0	0	0	0	0	0	0	0	20	0	5

									League			FA Cup			FL Cup			Other			Total		
Name		Date of Birth	Birthplace	Died	Year with Club	Loan	Previous Club	Next Club	A	S	G	A	S	G	A	S	G	A	S	G	A	S	G
Paddock W	Billy	06/02/1862	West Bromwich	1938	1886-1888		West Bromwich Unity	Retired	0	0	0	8	0	3	0	0	0	0	0	0	8	0	3
Pailor R	Bob	07/07/1887	Stockton	1976	1908-1914		West Hartlepool	Newcastle United	79	0	40	13	0	7	0	0	0	0	0	0	92	0	47
Palmer CL	Carlton	05/12/1965	Rowley Regis		1983-1989		Dudley Town	Sheffield Wednesday	114	7	4	4	0	0	7	1	1	6	0	0	131	8	5
Palmer LJ	Les	05/09/1971	Birmingham		1988-1992		School	Kidderminster Harriers	5	3	1	0	1	0	0	0	0	0	0	0	5	4	1
Parkes HA	Harry	09/09/1888	Halesowen	1947	1906-1908, 1914-1919		Halesowen	Newport County	27	0	4	4	0	0	0	0	0	0	0	0	31	0	4
Parkin SJ	Steve	07/11/1965	Mansfield		1989-1992		Stoke City	Mansfield Town	44	4	2	0	0	0	3	0	0	2	1	0	49	5	2
Parry J	John	04/02/1871	Glanmule	1936	1895		Newton	Aberystwyth	1	0	0	0	0	0	0	0	0	0	0	0	1	0	0
Parsley NR	Neil	25/04/1966	Liverpool		1993-1995		Huddersfield Town	Exeter City	38	5	0	1	0	0	3	0	0	1	0	0	43	5	0
Paskin WJ	John	01/02/1962	Cape Town, South Africa		1988-1989		KV Kortrijk	Wolverhampton Wanderers	14	11	5	0	2	0	1	0	0	0	0	0	15	13	5
Pearson HF	Harold	07/05/1908	Tamworth	1994	1925-1937		Tamworth Castle	Millwall	281	0	0	21	0	0	0	0	0	1	0	0	303	0	0
Pearson HP	Hubert	15/05/1886	Kettlebrook	1955	1906-1926		Tamworth Althetic	Retired	341	0	2	29	0	0	0	0	0	1	0	0	371	0	2
Pearson T	Tom	20/05/1866	West Bromwich	1918	1886-1894		West Bromwich Sandwell	Retired	138	0	72	26	0	12	0	0	0	7	0	4	171	0	88
Pemberton JHA	Jim	30/04/1916	Wolverhampton	1996	1937-1951		Brownhills Albion	Retired	162	0	0	10	0	0	0	0	0	0	0	0	172	0	0
Pendrey GJS	Garry	09/02/1949	Birmingham		1979-1981		Birmingham City	Torquay United	18	0	0	0	0	0	0	0	0	0	0	0	18	0	0
Pennington J	Jesse	23/08/1883	West Bromwich	1970	1902-1922		Dudley Town	Retired	455	0	0	39	0	0	0	0	0	1	0	0	495	0	0
Perkins E	Ernie	12/12/1883	Astwood Bank	1941	1904-1907		Worcester City	Worcester City	33	0	1	1	0	0	0	0	0	0	0	0	34	0	1
Perkins E	Eric	19/08/1934	West Bromwich		1951-1956		Hill Top Foundry	Walsall	2	0	0	0	0	0	0	0	0	0	0	0	2	0	0
Perry AA	Arthur	25/07/1897	West Bromwich	1977	1921-1927		West Bromwich Baptist	Crystal Palace	74	0	0	7	0	0	0	0	0	0	0	0	81	0	0
Perry C	Charlie	03/01/1866	West Bromwich	1977	1884-1896		West Bromwich Strollers	Retired	171	0	12	39	0	3	0	0	0	9	0	1	219	0	16
Perry CJ	Chris	26/04/1973	Carshalton		2006		Charlton Athletic		23	0	0	0	0	0	1	0	0	3	0	0	27	0	0
Perry MA	Micky	04/04/1964	Wimbledon		1980-1985		School	Torquay United	14	6	5	1	0	0	2	0	0	0	0	0	17	6	5
Perry T	Tom	05/08/1871	West Bromwich	1927	1890-1901		Stourbridge	Aston Villa	248	0	14	29	0	0	0	0	0	14	0	1	291	0	15
Perry W	Walter	11/10/1868	West Bromwich	1928	1886-1889, 1894-1895		West Bromwich Excelsior	Burton Swifts	11	0	4	4	0	3	0	0	0	0	0	0	15	0	7
Peschisolido PP	Paul	25/05/1971	Scarborough, Canada		1996-1997		Stoke City	Fulham	36	9	18	1	0	0	4	1	3	0	0	0	41	10	21
Peters S	Sam	20/10/1886	West Bromwich	1957	1904-1907		Churchfields	Crewe Alexandra	6	0	1	0	0	0	0	0	0	0	0	0	6	0	1
Pheasant E	Ted	15/02/1877	Darlaston	1910	1904-1910		Wolverhampton Wanderers	Leicester Fosse	140	0	20	12	0	2	0	0	0	0	0	0	152	0	22
Phelan MC	Mike	24/09/1962	Nelson		1994-1996		Manchester United	Norwich City	18	3	0	0	0	0	2	0	0	0	0	0	20	3	0
Phillips KM	Kevin	25/07/1973	Hitchin		2006		Aston Villa		31	5	16	3	0	3	1	0	0	3	0	3	38	5	22
Phillips SG	Stewart	30/12/1961	Halifax		1988-89		Hereford United	Swansea City	15	0	4	0	0	0	0	0	0	0	1	0	15	1	4
Picken T	Tom	30/05/1883	Hednesford	1960	1905-1910		Shrewsbury Town	Road End FC	2	0	0	0	0	0	0	0	0	0	0	0	2	0	0
Pickering TG	Thomas	21/02/1879	Wednesbury	1934	1900-1901		Brierley Hill Alliance	Kettering Town	10	0	2	0	0	0	0	0	0	0	0	0	10	0	2
Piggott GD	Gary	01/04/1969	Warley		1991-1993		Dudley Town	Shrewsbury Town	3	2	0	0	0	0	0	0	0	0	0	0	3	2	0
Pike RSGA	Richard	15/03/1917	Finchley	1988	1937-1946		Banbury Spencer	Banbury Spencer	1	0	0	0	0	0	0	0	0	0	0	0	1	0	0
Pittaway J	James	07/11/1867	West Bromwich	1937	1889-1890		West Bromwich Wednesday	Stourbridge	2	0	1	0	0	0	0	0	0	0	0	0	2	0	1
Potter GS	Graham	20/05/1975	Solihull		1997-2000		Southampton	York City	31	12	0	1	0	0	0	3	0	0	0	0	32	15	0
Potter RC	Ron	05/12/1948	Wolverhampton		1964-1970		School	Swindon Town	8	0	0	0	0	0	0	0	0	0	0	0	8	0	0
Potter RJ	Ray	07/05/1936	Beckenham	2006	1958-1967		Crystal Palace	Portsmouth	217	0	0	13	0	0	6	0	0	2	0	0	238	0	0
Poulton A	Alonzo	28/03/1890	Wolverhampton	1966	1913-1919		Priestfield Albion	Merthyr Town	9	0	1	0	0	0	0	0	0	0	0	0	9	0	1
Powell DR	David	24/09/1967	Cannock		1984-1988		Cherry Valley	Retired	2	0	0	1	0	0	0	0	0	0	0	0	3	0	0
Powell S	Seth	06/08/1862	Cerney	1945	1889-1892		Oswestry Town	Burton Swifts	30	0	0	5	0	0	0	0	0	0	0	0	35	0	0
Poxton JH	Jimmy	02/02/1904	Staveley	1971	1924-1927		Staveley Town	Gillingham	9	0	1	0	0	0	0	0	0	0	0	0	9	0	1
Poynton W	William	07/06/1883	Hill Top	1958	1902-1907		Britannia Victoria	Retired	2	0	2	0	0	0	0	0	0	0	0	0	2	0	2
Prew JH	Jimmy	23/02/1914	Coventry	1986	1936-1938		Hinckley United	Walsall	7	0	1	0	0	0	0	0	0	0	0	0	7	0	1

Name		Date of Birth	Birthplace	Died	Year with Club	Loan	Previous Club	Next Club	League			FA Cup			FL Cup			Other			Total		
									A	S	G	A	S	G	A	S	G	A	S	G	A	S	G
Price GW	Gilbert	22/10/1888	Wolverhampton	1955	1910-1911		Chillingham Rangers	Cradley St Luke's	1	0	0	0	0	0	0	0	0	0	0	0	1	0	0
Pritchard DM	David	27/05/1972	Wolverhampton		1988-1992		School	Telford United	1	4	0	0	0	0	0	0	0	0	0	0	1	4	0
Purse DJ	Darren	14/02/1977	Stepney		2004-2005		Birmingham City	Cardiff City	22	0	0	2	0	0	0	0	0	0	0	0	24	0	0
Quailey BS	Brian	24/03/1978	Leicester		1997-2000		Nuneaton Borough	Scunthorpe United	1	0	6	0	0	0	0	1	0	0	0	0	1	1	6
Quashie NF	Nigel	20/07/1978	Nunhead		2006-2007		Southampton	West Ham United	26	3	1	0	0	0	1	0	0	0	0	0	27	3	1
Quinn SJ	James	14/12/1974	Coventry		1998-2002		Blackpool	William II	85	29	9	2	0	0	3	4	1	0	0	0	90	33	10
Ramsey AR	Alexander	24/03/1867	Collington	1935	1888-1890		Kidderminster Harriers	Kidderminster Harriers	1	0	0	0	0	0	0	0	0	0	0	0	1	0	0
Randle AJ	Arthur	03/12/1880	West Bromwich	1913	1901-1908		Darlaston	Leicester Fosse	132	0	1	11	0	1	0	0	0	0	0	0	143	0	2
Rankin B	Bruce	02/07/1880	Glasgow	1946	1906-1907		Everton	Manchester City	29	0	5	2	0	1	0	0	0	0	0	0	31	0	6
Raven PD	Paul	28/07/1970	Salisbury		1989-2000		Doncaster Rovers	Grimsby Town	249	10	15	10	0	3	20	0	2	15	0	1	294	10	21
Raw H	Harry	06/07/1903	Tow Law	1965	1931-1936		Huddersfield Town	Lincoln City	25	0	7	1	0	0	0	0	0	1	0	0	27	0	7
Rawlings JSD	Syd	05/05/1913	Wombwell	1956	1935-1936		Huddersfield Town	Northampton Town	10	0	1	0	0	0	0	0	0	0	0	0	10	0	1
Rea JC	John	13/02/1868	Lledrod	1944	1894-1895, 1896-1898		Aberystwyth Town	Retired	1	0	0	0	0	0	0	0	0	0	0	0	1	0	0
Reader J	Joe	27/02/1866	West Bromwich	1954	1885-1901		School	Retired	315	0	0	39	0	0	0	0	0	16	0	0	370	0	0
Readfern TE	Eddie	09/07/1944	Crook		1960-1964		Langley Park Juniors	Kidderminster Harriers	4	0	0	1	0	0	0	0	0	0	0	0	5	0	0
Reece PJ	Paul	17/07/1968	Nottingham		1995-1996		Notts County	Ilkeston Town	1	0	0	0	0	0	0	0	0	0	0	0	1	0	0
Reed FWM	Fred	10/03/1894	Scotswood	1967	1913-1927		Lintz Institute	Retired	138	0	4	16	0	1	0	0	0	3	0	0	157	0	5
Reed HD	Hugh	23/08/1950	Dumbarton	1992	1966-1971		Drumchapel Amateurs	Plymouth Argyle	5	3	2	0	0	0	0	0	0	0	1	0	5	4	2
Rees AA	Tony	01/08/1964	Merthyr Tydfil		1994-1996		Grimsby Town	Merthyr Tydfil	11	12	2	2	0	0	0	2	0	2	1	1	15	15	3
Rees MJ	Mel	25/01/1967	Cardiff	1993	1990-1992		Watford	Sheffield United	18	0	0	1	0	0	0	0	0	0	0	0	19	0	0
Rees RR	Ronnie	04/04/1944	Ystradgynlais		1968-1969		Coventry City	Nottingham Forest	34	0	9	1	1	2	2	0	1	3	0	0	40	1	12
Regis C	Cyrille	09/02/1958	Maripiasoula, French Guyana		1977-1984		Hayes	Coventry City	233	4	82	25	0	10	27	1	16	12	0	4	297	5	112
Reid GA	George	03/02/1872	Handsworth, Yorkshire	1934	1897-1898		Sheffield Wednesday	Warmley	11	0	3	2	0	0	0	0	0	0	0	0	13	0	3
Reid NS	Nicky	30/10/1960	Urmston		1992-1994		Blackburn Rovers	Wycombe Wanderers	13	7	0	2	1	0	0	0	0	2	1	1	17	9	1
Reilly GG	George	14/09/1957	Bellshill		1985-1988		Newcastle United	Cambridge United	42	1	9	3	0	1	0	0	0	2	0	0	47	1	10
Reynolds J	Jack 'Baldy'	21/02/1869	Blackburn	1917	1891-1892		Ulster	Aston Villa	37	0	3	7	0	3	0	0	0	2	0	1	46	0	7
Rice B	Brian	11/10/1963	Bellshill		1989	L	Nottingham Forest	Nottingham Forest	2	1	0	0	0	0	0	0	0	0	0	0	2	1	0
Richards AJ	Arthur	07/07/1888	Knighton	1949	1910-1911		New Invention	Kilnhurst	1	0	0	0	0	0	0	0	0	0	0	0	1	0	0
Richards GM	Geoff	24/04/1929	Bilston		1943-1952		Albion Works	Stafford Rangers	3	0	1	0	0	0	0	0	0	0	0	0	3	0	1
Richards J	John	15/11/1893	Martley	1934	1895-1896		City Ramblers	Loughborough Town	14	0	0	2	0	1	0	0	0	4	0	1	20	0	2
Richards J	Justin	16/10/1980	West Bromwich		1997-2000		Bustleholme Boys	Bristol Rovers	0	1	0	0	1	0	0	0	0	0	0	0	0	2	0
Richards W	William	06/10/1874	West Bromwich	1926	1894-19010		West Bromwich Standard	Newton Heath	123	0	35	21	0	6	0	0	0	4	0	1	148	0	42
Richardson F	Fred	18/08/1925	Spennymoor		1950-1952		Barnsley	Chester City	29	0	8	2	0	0	0	0	0	0	0	0	31	0	8
Richardson KE	Kieran	21/10/1984	Greenwich		2005	L	Manchester United	Manchester United	11	1	3	0	0	0	0	0	0	0	0	0	11	1	3
Richardson S	Sammy	11/08/1894	Great Bridge	1989	1913-1927		Great Bridge Celtic	Newport County	191	0	1	15	0	0	0	0	0	6	0	0	212	0	1
Richardson W	Bill	14/02/1908	Great Bridge	1985	1926-1937		Great Bridge Celtic	Swindon Town	319	0	1	32	0	0	0	0	0	1	0	0	352	0	1
Richardson W	Billy 'Ginger'	29/05/1909	Framwellgate Moor	1959	1929-1949		Hartlepool United	Shrewsbury Town	320	0	202	34	0	26	0	0	0	1	0	0	355	0	228
Rickaby S	Stan	12/03/1924	Stockton		1950-1955		Middlesbrough	Poole Town	189	0	2	15	0	0	0	0	0	1	0	0	205	0	2
Ridyard A	Alf	05/03/1908	Cudworth	1981	1932-1938		Barnsley	QPR	31	0	0	3	0	0	0	0	0	0	0	0	34	0	0
Riley JH	James	09/09/1869	West Bromwich	1932	1889-1902		Wednesbury Old Athletic	Walsall Town	3	0	1	0	0	0	0	0	0	0	0	0	3	0	1
Rix J	Jack	12/07/1908	Lintz	1979	1927-1939		Lintz Collery	Lincoln City	64	0	0	4	0	0	0	0	0	0	0	0	68	0	0
Robbins WW	Walter	24/11/1910	Cardiff	1979	1932-1939		Cardiff City	Newport County	84	0	28	7	0	3	0	0	0	0	0	0	91	0	31
Roberts GP	Graham	03/07/1959	Southampton		1990-1992		Chelsea	Enfield	39	0	6	1	0	0	0	0	0	1	0	0	41	0	6

Name		Date of Birth	Birthplace	Died	Year with Club	Loan	Previous Club	Next Club	League			FA Cup			FL Cup			Other			Total		
									A	S	G	A	S	G	A	S	G	A	S	G	A	S	G
Roberts JAD	Jason	25/01/1978	Park Royal		2000-2004		Bristol Rovers	Wigan Athletic	75	14	24	6	0	0	3	1	2	2	0	1	86	15	27
Roberts RHC	Robert	07/09/1870	Marchweil	1935	1890-1891		Wrexham	Corwen	1	0	0	0	0	0	0	0	0	0	0	0	1	0	0
Roberts RJ	Bob	09/04/1859	West Bromwich	1929	1879-1890, 1891-1892		George Salter Works	Aston Villa	49	0	0	35	0	0	0	0	0	0	0	0	84	0	0
Roberts RJ	Richard	22/01/1878	Bromsgrove	1931	1899-1901		Redditch Excelsior	Newcastle United	43	0	8	9	0	2	0	0	0	0	0	0	52	0	10
Roberts TF	Frederick	13/03/1898	Smethwick	1928	1890-1891		School	Birmingham St Green's	2	0	0	0	0	0	0	0	0	0	0	0	2	0	0
Robertson AP	Ally	09/09/1952	Philpstoun		1968-1986		Uphill Saints	Wolverhampton Wanderers	504	2	8	34	2	0	53	0	3	31	0	1	622	4	12
Robinson EM	Eric	06/07/1858	Manchester	1934	1889-, 1891-		Bolton Wanderers	Hyde United	0	0	0	4	0	0	0	0	0	0	0	0	4	0	0
Robinson EM	Eric	01/07/1935	Manchester		1957-1959		Altrincham	Rotherham United	1	0	0	0	0	0	0	0	0	1	0	0	2	0	0
Robinson MJ	Mark	21/11/1968	Rochdale		1983-1987		School	Barnsley	2	0	0	0	0	0	0	1	0	0	0	0	2	1	0
Robinson PP	Paul	14/12/1978	Watford		2003		Watford		133	3	3	9	0	0	5	0	0	3	0	0	150	3	3
Robinson R	Ronnie	22/10/1966	Sunderland		1989		Doncaster Rovers	Rotherham United	1	0	0	0	0	0	0	0	0	0	0	0	1	0	0
Robson B	Bryan	11/01/1957	Chester-le-Street		1972-1981		Chester-le-Street Cubs	Manchester United	194	4	39	10	2	2	17	1	2	31	0	3	252	7	46
Robson G	Gary	06/07/1965	Pelaw		1981-1993		Chester-le-Street Boys	Bradford City	184	34	28	10	2	3	12	2	0	7	5	3	213	43	34
Robson RW	Bobby	18/02/1933	Sacriston		1956-62		Fulham	Fulham	239	0	56	18	0	5	0	0	0	0	0	0	257	0	61
Rodosthenous M	Michael	25/08/1976	Islington		1993-1997		Tottenham Hotspur	Cambridge United	0	1	0	0	0	0	0	0	0	0	0	0	0	1	0
Rogers DJ	Darren	09/04/1970	Birmingham		1986-1992		School	Birmingham City	7	7	1	0	1	0	0	0	0	1	1	0	8	9	1
Rooke EJH	Edward	18/11/1899	Hockley	1974	1921-1929		Brierley Hill Alliance	Nuneaton Borough	41	0	1	1	0	0	0	0	0	0	0	0	42	0	1
Rosler U	Uwe	15/11/1968	Attenburg, Germany		2001	L	Southampton	Southampton	5	0	1	0	0	0	0	0	0	0	0	0	5	0	1
Rouse FW	Fred	28/01/1882	Cranford	1953	1909-1910		Chelsea	Croydon Common	5	0	2	0	0	0	0	0	0	0	0	0	5	0	2
Rowley GA	Arthur	21/04/1925	Wolverhampton	2002	1944-1948		Wolverhampton Wanderers	Fulham	24	0	4	1	0	1	0	0	0	0	0	0	25	0	5
Rushbury DG	David	20/02/1956	Wolverhampton		1972-1977		School	Sheffield Wednesday	28	0	0	3	0	0	0	0	0	0	0	0	31	0	0
Ryan RA	Reg	30/10/1925	Dublin	1997	1945-1955		Coventry City	Derby County	234	0	28	20	0	2	0	0	0	0	0	0	254	0	30
Sakiri A	Artim	23/09/1973	Struga, Macedonia		2003-2005		CSKA Sofia	Inter Turku	8	20	1	1	0	0	2	2	0	0	0	0	11	22	1
Sanders JA	Jim	05/07/1920	Holborn	2003	1945-1958		Charlton Athletic	Coventry City	327	0	0	36	0	0	0	0	0	1	0	0	364	0	0
Sandford EA	Teddy	22/10/1910	Handsworth	1995	1929-1939		Smethwick Highfield	Sheffield United	286	0	67	30	0	8	0	0	0	1	0	0	317	0	75
Sankey J	Jack	19/03/1912	Winsford	1985	1930-1945		Winsford United	Northampton Town	147	0	5	13	0	0	0	0	0	0	0	0	160	0	5
Santos G	Georges	15/08/1970	Marseille, France		2000		Tranmere Rovers	Sheffield United	8	0	0	0	0	0	0	0	0	0	0	0	8	0	0
Saunders DG	Doug	22/04/1927	Birmingham	2000	1942-1948		West Bromwich Hawthorne	Banbury Spencer	0	0	0	1	0	0	0	0	0	0	0	0	1	0	0
Saunders S	Sidney	01/06/1872	West Bromwich	1939	1895-1896		Unity Gas	Birmingham Centinels	2	0	0	0	0	0	0	0	0	0	0	0	2	0	0
Saunders WW	Wilf	20/04/1916	Banbury	1981	1938-1946		Banbury Spencer	Banbury Spencer	2	0	0	0	0	0	0	0	0	0	0	0	2	0	0
Savage G	George	12/08/1903	Aston	1968	1921-1922		Willenhall	Wrexham	2	0	0	0	0	0	0	0	0	0	0	0	2	0	0
Scimeca R	Riccy	13/06/1975	Leamington Spa		2004-2006		Leicester City	Cardiff City	29	6	0	2	0	0	2	1	0	0	0	0	33	7	0
Screen J	Jack	03/01/1915	Oldbury	1968	1933-1939		Smethwick Highfield	Wrexham	1	0	0	0	0	0	0	0	0	0	0	0	1	0	0
Setters ME	Maurice	16/12/1936	Honiton		1955-1960		Exeter City	Manchester United	120	0	10	12	0	0	0	0	0	0	0	0	132	0	10
Shakespeare CR	Craig	26/10/1963	Birmingham		1990-1993		Sheffield Wednesday	Grimsby Town	104	8	12	5	0	2	6	0	1	5	0	1	120	8	16
Shaw CE	Cecil	22/06/1911	Mansfield	1977	1936-1947		Wolverhampton Wanderers	Hereford United	113	0	10	14	0	0	0	0	0	0	0	0	127	0	10
Shaw CR	Charlie	18/11/1862	Willenhall	1931	1888		Walsall Town Swifts	Walsall Town Swifts	1	0	1	0	0	0	0	0	0	0	0	0	1	0	1
Shaw GD	David	11/10/1948	Huddersfield		1973-1975		Oldham Athletic	Oldham Athletic	65	17	17	7	0	1	4	0	1	2	1	1	78	18	20
Shaw GE	George	13/10/1899	Swinton	1973	1926-1938		Huddersfield Town	Stalybridge Celtic	393	0	11	31	0	0	0	0	0	1	0	0	425	0	11
Shearman BW	Ben	12/12/1884	Lincoln	1958	1911-1919		Bristol City	Nottingham Forest	126	0	18	15	0	0	0	0	0	0	0	0	141	0	18
Shepherd E	Ernie	14/08/1919	Wombwell	2001	1948-1949		Fulham	Hull City	4	0	0	0	0	0	0	0	0	0	0	0	4	0	0
Sheppard RJ	Dick	14/02/1945	Bristol	1998	1960-1969		School	Bristol Rovers	39	0	0	4	0	0	11	0	0	0	0	0	54	0	0
Shinton F	Fred	07/03/1883	Wednesbury	1923	1905-1907		Hednesford Town	Leicester Fosse	64	0	46	4	0	0	0	0	0	0	0	0	68	0	46

Name		Date of Birth	Birthplace	Died	Year with Club	Loan	Previous Club	Next Club	League A	League S	League G	FA Cup A	FA Cup S	FA Cup G	FL Cup A	FL Cup S	FL Cup G	Other A	Other S	Other G	Total A	Total S	Total G
Shore EW	Ernie	12/10/1891	Wednesbury	1960	1913-1919		Willenhall Swifts	Stourbridge	5	0	0	0	0	0	0	0	0	0	0	0	5	0	0
Short JS	Sammy	10/05/1903	Norbrigg	1955	1923-1931		Seamore FC	Retired	39	0	17	2	0	0	0	0	0	0	0	0	41	0	17
Sigurdsson LO	Larus	04/06/1973	Akureyri, Iceland		1999-2004		Stoke City	Retired	104	12	1	6	1	0	4	0	0	0	1	0	114	14	1
Simmons C	Charlie 'Chippy'	09/09/1878	West Bromwich	1937	1898-1904, 1905-1907		Worcester City	Chesterfield	178	0	75	15	0	6	0	0	0	0	0	0	193	0	81
Simpson G	George	11/08/1883	Jarrow	1958	1909-1910		Sheffield Wednesday	North Shields	19	0	5	5	0	1	0	0	0	0	0	0	24	0	6
Simpson TJN	Terry	08/10/1938	Southampton		1963-1967		Peterborough United	Walsall	71	0	3	5	0	0	1	0	1	0	0	0	77	0	4
Sinclair FM	Frank	03/12/1971	Lambeth		1991-1992	L	Chelsea	Chelsea	6	0	1	0	0	0	0	0	0	0	0	0	6	0	1
Sinfield MR	Marc	24/03/1974	Cheshunt		1990-1993		Cheshunt	Enfield	0	0	0	0	0	0	0	0	0	1	0	0	1	0	0
Singleton MD	Martin	02/08/1963	Banbury		1986-1987		Bradford City	Northampton Town	15	4	1	0	1	0	1	0	0	0	0	0	16	5	1
Skoubo M	Morten	30/06/1980	Struer, Denmark		2003-2004	L	Borussia Mönchengladbach	Borussia Mönchengladbach	0	2	0	0	0	0	0	0	0	0	0	0	0	2	0
Smith A	Arthur	21/09/1878	West Bromwich	1953	1898-1901		West Bromwich Baptist	Retired	6	0	1	0	0	0	0	0	0	0	0	0	6	0	1
Smith A	Archibald	11/07/1880	West Bromwich	1943	1903-1904		Worcester City	Brierley Hill Alliance	8	0	1	2	0	1	0	0	0	0	0	0	10	0	2
Smith AE	Arthur	05/09/1921	Whetstone, Leicestershire		1948-1952		Leicester City	Plymouth Argyle	49	0	12	3	0	1	0	0	0	0	0	0	52	0	13
Smith AW	Andrew	15/05/1879	Slamannan	1960	1900-1903		Stoke City	Newton Heath	23	0	8	2	0	0	0	0	0	0	0	0	25	0	8
Smith AW	Andy	04/04/1890	Birmingham	1968	1919-1923		Birmingham City	Stoke City	79	0	20	1	0	0	0	0	0	1	0	2	81	0	22
Smith D	Danny	07/09/1921	Armadale	1998	1939-1945		Coltness United	Chesterfield	7	0	1	0	0	0	0	0	0	0	0	0	7	0	1
Smith D	David	29/03/1968	Stonehouse, Gloucester		1994-1998		Birmingham City	Grimsby Town	82	20	2	1	3	0	4	2	0	4	1	0	91	26	2
Smith E	Ted	12/09/1880	Old Hill	1954	1899-1900, 1901-1904		Old Hill Wanderers	Dudley Town	10	0	4	0	0	0	0	0	0	0	0	0	10	0	4
Smith GWC	Graham	02/11/1947	Liverpool		1971-1973		Colchester United	Cambridge United	10	0	0	0	0	0	0	0	0	0	0	0	10	0	0
Smith H	Horace	21/08/1903	Netherton	1954	1922-1927		Hingley's FC	Blackpool	2	0	0	0	0	0	0	0	0	0	0	0	2	0	0
Smith J	John	15/06/1964	Birmingham		1980-1984		School	Telford United	0	0	0	0	0	0	0	1	0	0	0	0	0	1	0
Smith J	Joe	10/04/1890	Darby End	1956	1910-1926		Cradley St Luke's	Birmingham City	434	0	0	30	0	0	0	0	0	7	0	0	471	0	0
Smith KW	Keith	15/09/1940	Woodville		1957-1963		Coalville Boys	Peterborough United	63	0	30	7	0	4	0	0	0	0	0	0	70	0	34
Smith WA	Billy	22/11/1882	Bedworth	1916	1902-1905		Worcester City	Birmingham City	21	0	3	1	0	0	0	0	0	0	0	0	22	0	3
Sneekes R	Richard	30/10/1968	Amsterdam, Holland		1996-2001		Bolton Wanderers	Stockport County	208	19	30	7	2	0	14	3	2	2	0	0	231	24	32
Sodje SA	Sam	29/05/1979	Greenwich		2007	L	Reading		7	0	1	0	0	0	0	0	0	3	0	0	10	0	1
Speedie DR	David	20/02/1960	Glenrothes		1993	L	Southampton	Southampton	7	0	2	0	0	0	0	0	0	0	0	0	7	0	2
Spencer G	Geoff	09/11/1913	Shavington	1991	1933-1939		Nantwich Victoria	Brighton & Hove Albion	13	0	2	0	0	0	0	0	0	0	0	0	13	0	2
Spencer JL	James	20/01/1900	Mosborough	1979	1922-1927		Beighton YC	Aston Villa	59	0	3	7	0	0	0	0	0	0	0	0	66	0	3
Spink NP	Nigel	08/08/1958	Chelmsford		1996-1997		Aston Villa	Millwall	19	0	0	0	0	0	3	0	0	2	0	0	24	0	0
Spooner J	James	11/11/1871	Hednesford	1950	1895-1896		Hednesford Town	Chadsmoor Swifts	2	0	0	0	0	0	0	0	0	0	0	0	2	0	0
Sproson T	Thomas	09/12/1903	Stoke-on-Trent	1976	1922-1928		Audley FC	Port Vale	9	0	0	0	0	0	0	0	0	0	0	0	9	0	0
Stanton J	Jim	18/11/1860	West Bromwich	1932	1878-1885		George Salter Works	Newton Heath	0	0	0	5	0	0	0	0	0	0	0	0	5	0	0
Statham DJ	Derek	24/03/1959	Wolverhampton		1975-1987		School	Southampton	298	1	8	26	0	2	34	0	1	4	0	0	362	1	11
Steele SF	Stan	05/01/1937	Fenton	2005	1961		Port Vale	Port Vale	1	0	0	0	0	0	0	0	0	0	0	0	1	0	0
Steggles KP	Kevin	19/03/1961	Ditchingham		1987		Ipswich Town	Port Vale	14	0	0	0	0	0	1	0	0	1	0	0	16	0	0
Stephens KJ	Kenny	14/11/1946	Bristol		1962-1968		Phildown Rovers	Walsall	21	1	2	1	2	0	1	0	0	1	0	0	24	3	2
Stevenson J	Jim	02/08/1875	Bonhill	1925	1900-1904		Preston NE	Dunbarton	120	0	9	9	0	0	0	0	0	0	0	0	129	0	9
Stringer J	Jimmy	12/05/1878	Netherton	1933	1905-1910		Wolverhampton Wanderers	Dudley Town	160	0	0	12	0	0	0	0	0	0	0	0	172	0	0
Strodder GJ	Gary	11/04/1965	Cleckheaton		1990-1995		West Ham United	Notts County	123	17	8	7	0	1	8	1	0	10	0	0	148	18	9
Styles AJ	Archie	29/10/1939	Smethwick		1956-1960		School	Wrexham	1	0	0	0	0	0	0	0	0	0	0	0	1	0	0
Suggett C	Colin	30/12/1948	Chester-le-Street		1969-1973		Sunderland	Norwich City	123	5	20	10	0	2	15	0	4	17	0	4	165	5	30
Summerfield K	Kevin	07/01/1959	Walsall		1975-1982		Walsall Town Boys	Birmingham City	5	4	4	0	0	0	2	0	0	0	0	0	7	4	4

Name		Date of Birth	Birthplace	Died	Year with Club	Loan	Previous Club	Next Club	League A	League S	League G	FA Cup A	FA Cup S	FA Cup G	FL Cup A	FL Cup S	FL Cup G	Other A	Other S	Other G	Total A	Total S	Total G
Summers GTF	Gerry	04/10/1933	Birmingham		1950-1957		Erdington Albion	Sheffield United	22	0	0	3	0	0	0	0	0	0	0	0	25	0	0
Swain KM	Kenny	28/11/1952	Birkenhead		1978, 1988	L	Chelsea	Portsmouth	7	0	1	0	0	0	0	0	0	0	0	0	7	0	1
Swallow J	John	22/02/1860	Sheffield	1917	1883-1884		Oldbury Town	Wednesbury Town	0	0	0	1	0	0	0	0	0	0	0	0	1	0	0
Swift A	Arthur	15/07/1892	Seaton Carew	1962	1913-1920		Hartlepool United	Crystal Palace	28	0	11	0	0	0	0	0	0	0	0	0	28	0	11
Swinden SA	Sidney	20/08/1913	Smethwick	1990	1931-1937		Smethwick Highfield	Swindon Town	4	0	0	0	0	0	0	0	0	0	0	0	4	0	0
Taggart J	Jack 'Mit'	03/01/1872	Belfast	1927	1893-1896		Middlesbrough	Walsall	68	0	4	11	0	0	0	0	0	14	0	0	93	0	4
Talbot BE	Brian	21/07/1953	Ipswich		1988-1991		Stoke City	Fulham	66	8	5	2	2	0	3	0	1	2	0	0	73	10	6
Talbut J	John	20/10/1940	Headington		1966-1971		Burnley	KV Mechelen	143	1	0	21	0	0	15	0	0	13	0	1	192	1	1
Taylor AS	Arthur	14/03/1925	Birmingham		1941-1950		Gower Old Boys	Retired	4	0	5	0	0	0	0	0	0	0	0	0	4	0	5
Taylor GA	Griff	23/12/1905	Pontypridd	1978	1927-1929		Trehafod FC	Leamington Town	0	0	0	1	0	0	0	0	0	0	0	0	1	0	0
Taylor H	Harold	15/09/1893	Dudley	1974	1920-1921		Dudley Bean	Barrow	9	0	2	0	0	0	0	0	0	0	0	0	9	0	2
Taylor O	Oliver	02/02/1880	Wednesfield	1938	1901-1903		Bilston United	Coventry City	5	0	0	0	0	0	0	0	0	0	0	0	5	0	0
Taylor R	Bob	03/02/1967	Horden		1992-1998, 2000-2003		Bristol City	Cheltenham Town	256	68	113	6	4	4	21	1	6	16	5	8	299	78	131
Thomas JA	James	16/01/1979	Swansea		1997	L	Blackburn Rovers	Blackpool	1	2	0	0	0	0	0	0	0	0	0	0	1	2	0
Thomas JW	John	05/08/1958	Wednesbury		1989-1990		Bolton Wanderers	Preston NE	8	10	1	0	0	0	2	0	3	0	1	0	10	11	4
Thomas MR	Mickey	07/07/1954	Mochdre		1985-1986		Chelsea	Wichita Wings	20	0	0	2	0	1	5	0	0	1	0	0	28	0	1
Thompson AR	Andy	09/11/1967	Featherstone		1984-1986		Featherstone FC	Wolverhampton Wanderers	18	6	1	2	0	0	0	1	0	1	1	0	21	8	1
Thompson GL	Garry	07/10/1959	Birmingham		1983-1985		Coventry City	Sheffield Wednesday	91	0	39	5	0	1	9	0	5	0	0	0	105	0	45
Thompson JT	Trevor	21/05/1955	North Shields		1970-1978		School	Newport County	20	0	0	0	0	0	2	0	0	0	0	0	22	0	0
Thompson WT	Billy	14/08/1886	Morpeth	1933	1908-1911		Morpeth Harriers	Sunderland	54	0	6	3	0	0	0	0	0	0	0	0	57	0	6
Tighe J	John	13/03/1923	Aghamore		1945-1948		Larkhill Thistle	Hednesford Town	1	0	0	0	0	0	0	0	0	0	0	0	1	0	0
Timmins G	George	06/02/1858	West Bromwich	1926	1879-1891		George Salter Works	Old Hill Wanderers	35	0	0	28	0	1	0	0	0	0	0	0	63	0	1
Timmins S	Sammy	27/06/1879	West Bromwich	1956	1906-1911		Nottingham Forest	Retired	111	0	3	5	0	0	0	0	0	0	0	0	116	0	3
Townsend AD	Andy	23/07/1963	Maidstone		1999-2000		Middlesbrough	Retired	15	3	0	0	0	0	2	0	0	0	0	0	17	3	0
Tranter GH	George	11/09/1915	Birmingham	1998	1934-1947		Rover Works FC	Hereford United	16	0	0	4	0	0	0	0	0	0	0	0	20	0	0
Treacy RCP	Ray	18/06/1946	Dublin		1961-1968, 1976-1977		Home Farm	Shamrock Rovers	22	4	7	2	0	0	0	0	0	0	0	0	24	4	7
Trentham HF	Bert	22/04/1908	Chirbury	1979	1929-1937		Hereford United	Hereford United	246	0	0	25	0	0	0	0	0	0	0	0	271	0	0
Trevis ASSRT	Bos	23/12/1910	Blackheath, Worcestershire	1984	1929-1937		Leamington Town	Chester City	1	0	0	0	0	0	0	0	0	0	0	0	1	0	0
Trewick J	John	03/06/1957	Bedlington		1972-1980		School	Newcastle United	83	13	11	12	0	0	10	2	0	11	3	0	116	18	11
Tudor WH	Billy	14/02/1918	Shotton	1955	1934-1946		Lavender FC	Wrexham	31	0	0	3	0	0	0	0	0	0	0	0	34	0	0
Turner I	Ike	08/07/1876	Netherton	1936	1898-1899		Dudley St James	Stourbridge	1	0	0	0	0	0	0	0	0	0	0	0	1	0	0
Turner SI	Isaiah	07/08/1882	Langley, Worcestershire	1964	1904-1905		Darlaston	Brierley Hill Alliance	1	0	0	0	0	0	0	0	0	0	0	0	1	0	0
Twigg L	Lew	05/08/1921	Buxton		1945-1947		Buxton FC	Retired	0	0	0	2	0	0	0	0	0	0	0	0	2	0	0
Udeze I	Iffy	21/07/1980	Nigeria		2003	L	POAK Salonika	PAOK Salonika	7	4	0	0	0	0	0	0	0	0	0	0	7	4	0
Valentine CH	Carl	04/07/1958	Clayton		1984-1986		Oldham Athletic	Wichita Wings	44	0	6	0	0	0	5	0	0	3	0	1	52	0	7
Van Blerk J	Jason	16/03/1968	Sydney, Australia		1998-2001		Manchester City	Stockport County	106	3	3	1	0	0	8	1	0	2	0	0	117	4	3
Varadi I	Imre	08/07/1959	Paddington		1985-1986		Sheffield Wednesday	Manchester City	30	2	9	2	0	0	5	0	4	2	0	0	39	2	13
Varga S	Stanislav	08/10/1972	Lipany, Slovakia		2002	L	Sunderland	Sunderland	3	1	0	0	0	0	0	0	0	0	0	0	3	1	0
Varney H	Herbert	12/02/1885	Belper	1952	1905-1907		Belper Town	Belper Town	5	0	0	0	0	0	0	0	0	0	0	0	5	0	0
Varty JW	James	02/12/1890	Scotswood	1958	1911-1913		Scotswood Rovers	Hartlepools United	3	0	0	0	0	0	0	0	0	0	0	0	3	0	0
Vernon JJ	Jack	26/09/1919	Belfast	1981	1947-1952		Belfast Celtic	Crusaders	190	0	1	10	0	0	0	0	0	0	0	0	200	0	1
Vigrow S	Scott	20/03/1878	Muirhead	1945	1896-1897		Dundee	Aidrieonians	1	0	0	0	0	0	0	0	0	0	0	0	1	0	0
Volmer JGB	Joost	07/03/1974	Enschede, Holland		2003-2004		Fortuna Sittard	FC Den Bosch	10	5	0	0	0	0	2	1	0	0	0	0	12	6	0

Name		Date of Birth	Birthplace	Died	Year with Club	Loan	Previous Club	Next Club	League A	League S	League G	FA Cup A	FA Cup S	FA Cup G	FL Cup A	FL Cup S	FL Cup G	Other A	Other S	Other G	Total A	Total S	Total G
Walford SJ	Steve	05/01/1958	Highgate		1989	L	West Ham United	West Ham United	3	1	0	0	0	0	0	0	0	0	0	0	3	1	0
Walker D	Davie	02/07/1894	Oakdene	1935	1907-1908		Bristol Rovers	Leicester Fosse	36	0	15	3	0	0	0	0	0	0	0	0	39	0	15
Walker L	Luther	06/04/1860	West Bromwich	1903	1883-1892		West Bromwich Royal	Retired	18	0	0	1	0	0	0	0	0	0	0	0	19	0	0
Walker W	William	21/02/1888	Walsall	1968	1910-1911		Halesowen	Willenhall Swifts	1	0	1	0	0	0	0	0	0	0	0	0	1	0	1
Walker WW	Billy	12/12/1879	Horseley Heath	1944	1898-1903		Toll End Wesley	Brierley Hill Alliance	32	0	5	2	0	0	0	0	0	0	0	0	34	0	5
Wallace JMB	Jock	06/09/1935	Wallyford	1996	1959-1962		Aidrieonians	Bedford Town	69	0	0	7	0	0	0	0	0	0	0	0	76	0	0
Wallwork R	Ronnie	10/09/1977	Manchester		2002		Manchester United		86	7	2	7	0	0	6	1	1	0	0	0	99	8	3
Walsh DJ	Dave	28/04/1923	Waterford		1946-1950		Linfield	Aston Villa	165	0	94	9	0	6	0	0	0	0	0	0	174	0	100
Ward GJ	Gavin	30/06/1970	Sutton Coldfield		1989		Shrewsbury Town	Cardiff City	0	0	0	0	0	0	1	0	0	0	0	0	1	0	0
Ward RA	Bob	04/08/1953	West Bromwich		1972-1977		Imperial Star	Blackpool	9	0	0	0	0	0	0	0	0	1	0	0	10	0	0
Waterhouse F	Frank	23/07/1889	Langley Green	1967	1908-1913		Wednesbury Old Athletic	Kidderminster Harriers	171	0	6	12	0	0	0	0	0	4	0	0	187	0	6
Watson AEC	Arthur	04/07/1868	Hucknall Torkard	1937	1896-1898		Mansfield Town	Lincoln City	28	0	2	2	0	1	0	0	0	0	0	0	30	0	3
Watson E	Ernest	06/12/1901	West Bromwich	1980	1922-1923		Tanfield FC	Hereford United	1	0	0	0	0	0	0	0	0	0	0	0	1	0	0
Watson SC	Steve	01/04/1974	North Shields		2005		Everton		38	4	1	0	0	0	2	0	0	0	0	0	40	4	1
Webb AR	Alan	01/01/1963	Wrockwardine Wood		1978-1984		Oakengates	Port Vale	23	1	0	0	0	0	0	0	0	0	0	0	23	1	0
Webb I	Ike	01/10/1874	Worcester	1950	1901-1904		Small Heath	Sunderland	96	0	0	5	0	0	0	0	0	0	0	0	101	0	0
Webster H	Herbert	05/10/1910	Walsall	2003	1928-1929		Burntwood Villa	Swindon Town	1	0	0	0	0	0	0	0	0	0	0	0	1	0	0
West C	Colin	13/11/1962	Wallsend		1989-1992		Sheffield Wednesday	Swansea City	64	9	22	4	0	1	2	0	0	2	0	0	72	9	23
Wheldon GF	Fred	01/11/1869	Langley Green	1924	1900-1901		Aston Villa	QPR	26	0	3	3	0	0	0	0	0	0	0	0	29	0	3
Wheldon S	Samuel	08/02/1865	Smethwick	1930	1891-1892		Langley Victoria	Walsall	1	0	0	0	0	0	0	0	0	0	0	0	1	0	0
White EW	Winston	26/10/1958	Leicester		1991-1992		Burnley	Bury	13	3	1	2	0	0	0	0	0	1	1	0	16	4	1
White HA	Harold	16/06/1916	Wednesbury	1981	1937-1946		Darlaston	Worcester City	39	0	0	3	0	0	0	0	0	0	0	0	42	0	0
Whitehead CR	Clive	24/11/1955	Birmingham		1981-1987		Bristol City	Portsmouth	157	11	6	10	0	2	14	2	1	2	0	0	183	13	9
Whitehead NJ	Norman	27/07/1914	Tamworth	1987	1932-1935		Birmingham Uni	Birmingham City	1	0	0	0	0	0	0	0	0	0	0	0	1	0	0
Whitehead PM	Phil	17/12/1969	Halifax		1998-1999		Oxford United	Reading	26	0	0	1	0	0	1	1	0	0	0	0	28	1	0
Whitehouse B	Brian	08/09/1935	West Bromwich		1950-1960		Vono Sports	Norwich City	37	0	13	9	0	4	0	0	0	0	0	0	46	0	17
Whitehouse JW	Jank	12/08/1861	West Bromwich	1933	1880-1884		West Bromwich Rovers	Retired	0	0	0	1	0	0	0	0	0	0	0	0	1	0	0
Whyte CA	Chris	02/09/1961	Islington		1988-1990		Los Angeles Lazers	Leeds United	83	1	7	5	0	0	5	0	2	2	0	0	95	1	9
Wilcox EE	Edward	24/03/1927	Blaengarw		1947-1951		Oxford United	Worcester City	12	0	3	0	0	0	0	0	0	0	0	0	12	0	3
Wilcox HM	Harold	07/01/1878	Dalston	1937	1907-1908		Leicester Fosse	Plymouth Argyle	17	0	5	3	0	2	0	0	0	0	0	0	20	0	7
Wile JD	John	09/03/1947	Sherburn		1970-1983		Peterborough United	Rotterdam United	499	1	24	42	0	2	42	0	2	35	0	1	618	1	29
Wilkes AG	Graham	03/09/1918	Hagley	1985	1938-1946		Dudley Training College	Blackheath	0	0	0	1	0	0	0	0	0	0	0	0	1	0	0
Williams CE	Cyril	17/11/1921	Bristol	1980	1948-1951		Bristol City	Bristol City	71	0	19	6	0	1	0	0	0	0	0	0	77	0	20
Williams G	Gilbert	12/01/1925	West Bromwich	1993	1943-1949		Hawthorn Juniors	Banbury Spencer	7	0	0	2	0	0	0	0	0	0	0	0	9	0	0
Williams GE	Graham	02/04/1938	Hellan		1954-1972		Rhyl Athletic	Weymouth	308	6	10	25	0	0	15	0	1	6	0	0	354	6	11
Williams GO	George	10/09/1879	Birmingham	1916	1900-1902		Wednesbury Old Athletic	Brierley Hill Alliance	16	6	0	2	0	0	0	0	0	0	0	0	18	6	0
Williams J	Jimmy	10/08/1882	Brownhills	1936	1905-1909		Aston Villa	Brownhills Albion	31	0	1	4	0	0	0	0	0	0	0	0	35	0	1
Williams O	Owen	22/11/1874	Smethwick	1944	1893-1895		Oldbury Town	Oldbury Town	14	0	7	1	0	0	0	0	0	4	0	2	19	0	9
Williams PA	Paul	08/09/1963	Sheffield		1991-1993		Stockport County	Stockport County	26	18	5	1	1	1	1	1	0	1	2	1	29	22	7
Williams PRC	Paul	11/09/1969	Leicester		1993	L	Coventry City	Coventry City	5	0	0	0	0	0	0	0	0	0	0	0	5	0	0
Williams SG	Stuart	09/07/1930	Wrexham		1950-1962		Wrexham	Southampton	226	0	6	20	0	3	0	0	0	0	0	0	246	0	9
Williams W	Billy	20/01/1876	West Smethwick	1929	1894-1901		Old Hill Wanderers	Retired	180	0	8	23	0	2	0	0	0	5	0	2	208	0	12
Williams WT	Bill	23/08/1942	Esher		1963-1966		QPR	Mansfield Town	1	0	0	0	0	0	0	0	0	0	0	0	1	0	0

									League			FA Cup			FL Cup			Other			Total		
Name		Date of Birth	Birthplace	Died	Year with Club	Loan	Previous Club	Next Club	A	S	G	A	S	G	A	S	G	A	S	G	A	S	G
Williamson R	Bobby	13/08/1961	Glasgow		1986-1988		Glasgow Rangers	Rotherham United	40	13	11	2	0	0	2	0	0	1	1	1	45	14	12
Wilson C	Charlie	20/07/1905	Heeley	1985	1920-1928		Halam FC	Sheffield Wednesday	125	0	41	8	0	4	0	0	0	0	0	0	133	0	45
Wilson JJ	Joe	08/01/1861	Handsworth	1952	1887-1890		Walsall Town	Kidderminster Harriers	40	0	8	13	0	12	0	0	0	0	0	0	53	0	20
Wilson RT	Ray	08/04/1947	Grangemouth		1963-1977		Woodburn Athletic	Retired	230	2	3	21	0	0	11	0	0	20	0	0	282	2	3
Witcomb DF	Doug	18/04/1918	Cwm	1997	1937-1947		Enfield	Sheffield Wednesday	55	0	3	9	0	1	0	0	0	0	0	0	64	0	4
Wollaston W	William	31/12/1889	Willenhall	1933	1910-1913		Willenhall Pickwick	Darlston	25	0	2	1	0	1	0	0	0	0	0	0	26	0	3
Wood HF	Harold	03/10/1870	West Bromwich	1951	1890-1893		Oldham Town	Walsall Victoria	1	0	1	0	0	0	0	0	0	0	0	0	1	0	1
Wood MC	Matt	19/02/1890	Hobson Village	1923	1911-1922		Hobson Wanderers	Kidderminster Harriers	17	0	0	0	0	0	0	0	0	0	0	0	17	0	0
Wood S	Stan	01/07/1905	Winsford	1967	1928-1938		Winsford United	Halifax Town	256	0	58	24	0	8	0	0	0	1	0	0	281	0	66
Woodhall G	George 'Spry'	05/09/1863	West Bromwich	1924	1883-1892		Churchfield Foresters	Wolverhampton Wanderers	44	0	10	30	0	10	0	0	0	0	0	0	74	0	20
Woolgar JS	Stewart	27/09/1952	Chesterfield		1968-1974		School	Doncaster Rovers	2	2	0	0	0	0	0	1	0	1	0	0	3	3	0
Worton T	Tommy	04/02/1878	Wolverhampton	1940	1901-1905		Wolverhampton Wanderers	Retired	72	0	23	3	0	0	0	0	0	0	0	0	75	0	23
Wright F	Franklin	22/12/1872	Wednesbury	1940	1895-1896		Wednesbury Old Athletic	Rowley Star	2	0	0	0	0	0	0	0	0	0	0	0	2	0	0
Wright HF	Harry	12/10/1888	West Bromwich	1950	1906-1909, 1910-1919		West Bromwich St Marks	Newport County	89	0	17	10	0	3	0	0	0	6	0	0	105	0	20
Young G	George	16/04/1880	Kirkintilloch	1938	1905-1906		Portsmouth	West Bromwich Strollers	16	0	0	0	0	0	0	0	0	0	0	0	16	0	0
Young WC	William	12/09/1884	Chadsmoor	1917	1907-1910		Hednesford Town	Hednesford Town	19	0	2	3	0	0	0	0	0	0	0	0	22	0	2
Zondervan R	Romeo	04/03/1959	Surinam		1982-1984		FC Twente	Ipswich Town	82	2	5	5	0	0	6	0	0	0	0	0	93	2	5
Zuberbuhler P	Pascal	08/01/1971	Frauenfeld, Switzerland		2006-2007	L	FC Basel	FC Basel	15	0	0	1	0	0	2	0	0	0	0	0	18	0	0

Roll of Honour

Stephen Straw
Christopher Nickless
Leigh Raybould
John Joseph Homer
Paul John Davies-Abingdon
Neil Griffin
Robert L. Mills
Dave Langran
Neil Reynolds
Charlie Reynolds
Thomas Bagley
Keith Godfrey
Roger Graham Morris
Julie Ann Morris
Ian Hoult
Julian Rowe
Clive Blake
Paul Harrison
Darren Partridge
Chris Cadman
Michael Thomas
Michael Igoe
Matthew Patrick
David Coulson
Robert S. Bradley
Keith Young (Artic Air)
Bill Gibbons
Kevan Whitehouse
Karen Wright
Ian Hoverd
Bob Colley
Karl Brealey
Keith Brealey
Norman W. Munslow
Reginald Lockley
Robert Callaghan

Martyn Ridout
Keith Saunders
Roger Leeson
Adam Walters
Ron Johnson
David Grant
Ray Parkes
Craig Biffen
Colin Jerromes
Dean Barry Fanthom
Anthony Pitt
Adrian Woodcock
Ben Woodcock
Tom Woodcock
Norman Beard
Michael Roberts
Gary Howen
John Thomas Jarvis
Colin Edward Jones
George William Lunn
Sally Benton
Michael Phipps
Mick Bryan
John David Russell
Mr. Eric Norton
Bajinder Mahandru
Richard Butler
Peter Baxendale
Graham Millard
Scott Millard
Barry Norris
Jack Heaven
Hazel Hughes
Dean Anthony Gritton
Andrew Detheridge
Richard Detheridge

Mr. Carl Jones
Bernard O'Connor
Richard Waplington
Sarah Turner
Paul Robottom
Graham Woodall
William Grove
Dominic Slim
Matthew Slim
Alan Nock
Mark Griffiths
Harry Clift
Harry Morgan
Allister Collings
Jonathan Collins
Stephen Tongue
Paul M. Deighton
Alan Davis
Mason Sean Woodfield
Neil Hipkiss
Dean Walton
Ken Bissell
John Edmunds
Michael Hadley
Samantha Lunn
Joe MacKay
Jeff Badland
Andrew Saunders
Alex Griffiths
George Doughty
Graham Doughty
Paul Morris
David Johnson
John Tuzzio
Mitchel Jeffery
Nigel Anthony Powell

Michael Baxter
Robert Hawkins
Gwen Mullins
Phil Knowles
Peter Caldicott
Jerry Tromans
Patrick Cluxton
John Barlow
Robert Higgins
Christopher Rogers
Dr. Richard Murrin
Brian Sambrooks
Roderick John Ross
John Cole
Nigel Stockton
Peter Shufflebotham
Angela Haddow
Alan Turley
Dave Sefton
Lee Sefton
Stuart Sefton
Mick McConkey
Archie Ryan
Sam Staniland
Mark Wilkins
Mike Browning
Gavin Paul
Roy Jackson
George Mitchell
Janis Lea
Bernard J. Taylor
John Beardsmore
Paula Beardsmore
Stephen Burrows
Ray Priest
Dave Tilt
Mike Tilt
Colin Tromans 1936-2004
Christopher Scott

Garry Evenden
Laura Anne Taylor
Mark Bennett
Denis Grainger
Darren Parker
Peter J. Gregory
Daragh Guest
Christine Martin
Stan Bratt
Richard Hadley
Marc Jackson
Thomas W. Blundell
Paul Michael Hadley
John Higgitt
Derek Tudor
The Corfield Family
Mark Darby
Richard Wilmot
James French
Graeme Brown
Happy Birthday Kieren
Paul Welch
John Guy
Olly Ridge
Julie L. Stevens
Wayne McLeod
Mark Hamer
Richard Bennett
Robert Harrison
Michael Tomkinson
Robert Tomkinson
Mike Hammett
Mike M. Mihailovic
Mitchell Sprigg
Jason Sherwood
James Moyes
Helen Moore
Ivan Bratt
Kevin Bratt

Tyrone Bratt
Damian Barratt
Adam Cotton
Robert Wood
Ian Moore
Jonathan Moore
Jonathan Weeks
Juergen Billenstein
Peter Thursfield
Shane Harper
Stephen Tudor
Kirk Guest
Clive Evans
Matt Bevan
Ciaran Bromley
Derick Bromley
Elliot Bromley
Michael J. Mills
Abigail Bromley-Smith
Terry Owens
Amanda Hayden
Callum Newman
Roger Bullock
Leanne Batsford
Kenneth Anthony Salt
Peter Walker
Luke Willetts
Mark Walker
Chris Scrine
Mike Jackman
Cyril Abbotts
Graham Cartwright
Sharon Cartwright
Terence Tumelty
John Frederick Langley
Neil Goldsmith
Peter Black
Roy Cooksley
Daniel Noakes

Owen Noakes
Mike Vass
Paul Beaman
Ian Blackham
David Derricott
Peter Amass
Glenn Jones
Steven Edmunds
David Payne - Australia
Gary Steptoe
Edward Arthur Field
Olle Kannö
Paul Adams
Martin Dunn
Michael Joyce
Graham Cartwright
Andrew Edwards
Ray Hyde
Daniel Rose
Joseph Rose
Adam Round
David Round
Lew Clews Warwick
Matthew Round
Robert Willis
Dave Knott

Antony Atkinson
Alistair Hickman
Billy Smith
Ashley Bourne
Sid Francis
Aaron Hilliard
Dave Tickle
Linda Davis
Richard Brooks
Ian Edmunds
Graham Filmer
A. P. Davies
Stephen Caron
James Caron
Matthew Caron
Daniel Caron
Barbara Hayden
In memory of Stephen Hayden
Roy Hayden
David John Metcalfe
Darren Underwood
Nigel Underwood
Stuart Rudge
Callan Luke
Chris Hatton

Jonathan Clive Round
Michelle Bennett
Steve Winstanley
Terence Checketts
Colin Emms
David J. Hill
Gary Philip Bates
Martin Grange
Phil Allan-Smith
David Dresch
Adam P. Bates
Laura L. Bates
Ian Atkins
Anthony "Hoppo" Hopkins
Malcolm Rose
Chris Foxall
Dale Walker
Alan Smith
Scott J. Harper (Mr.)
Steven Handley (Mr.)
Mike Buckland
John Kenna, Ireland
Ray Wimbury
Mel Guest
Paul Simper